A TEXTBOOK OF ENGINEERING MATHEMATICS

A TEXTBOOK OF

ENGINEERING MATHEMATICS

For

B.TECH. I Year (*II Semester*)
MAHAMAYA TECHNICAL UNIVERSITY (M.T.U.), NOIDA
(*Strictly According to the Latest Revised Syllabus*)

By

N.P. BALI
Former Principal
S.B. College, Gurgaon
Haryana

Dr. MANISH GOYAL
M.Sc. (Mathematics), Ph.D., CSIR–NET
Associate Professor
Department of Mathematics
Institute of Applied Sc. and Humanities
G.L.A. University, Mathura
U.P.

UNIVERSITY SCIENCE PRESS

(An Imprint of Laxmi Publications Pvt. Ltd.)

BANGALORE • CHENNAI • COCHIN • GUWAHATI • HYDERABAD
JALANDHAR • KOLKATA • LUCKNOW • MUMBAI • RANCHI
NEW DELHI • BOSTON, USA

Published by :
UNIVERSITY SCIENCE PRESS
(*An Imprint of Laxmi Publications Pvt. Ltd.*)
113, Golden House, Daryaganj,
New Delhi-110002
Phone : 011-43 53 25 00
Fax : 011-43 53 25 28
www.laxmipublications.com
info@laxmipublications.com

First Edition : 2002 ; Second Edition : 2003 ;Third Revised Edition : 2004 ; Fourth Revised Edition : 2005 ;Fifth Revised Edition : 2006 ; Sixth Edition : 2009 ; Seventh Revised Edition : 2011 ; Eighth Edition : 2012 ; Ninth Edition : 2013 ; Tenth Edition : 2014

OFFICES

✆ **Bangalore**	080-26 75 69 30	✆ **Jalandhar**	0181-222 12 72
✆ **Chennai**	044-24 34 47 26	✆ **Kolkata**	033-22 27 43 84
✆ **Cochin**	0484-237 70 04, 405 13 03	✆ **Lucknow**	0522-220 99 16
✆ **Guwahati**	0361-254 36 69, 251 38 81	✆ **Mumbai**	022-24 91 54 15, 24 92 78 69
✆ **Hyderabad**	040-24 65 23 33	✆ **Ranchi**	0651-221 47 64

UEM-9682-425-ENGG MATH II (MTU)–BAL C—
Typeset at : Goswami Associates, Delhi. *Printed at* : Repro Knowledgecast Limited, Thane

CONTENTS

PREFACE TO THE TENTH EDITION

श्रद्धावाँल्लभते ज्ञानं तत्परः संयतेन्द्रियः।

ज्ञानं लब्ध्वा परां शान्तिमचिरेणाधिगच्छति।।

The book has been revised and updated according to the latest revised syllabus of M.T.U., Noida. Questions from latest university question papers have been included and incorporated at proper places. Misprints have been eradicated and all the answers are rechecked. Suggestions with a view to enhance the utility of the text are most welcome.

We wish all the readers success in life.

—AUTHORS

PREFACE TO THE FIRST EDITION

The basic object of this book is to furnish the reader with the thorough understanding of Mathematics Topics included in the syllabus of Mathematics for **I Year—II Semester** engineering students.

★ The book broadly covers the syllabus of degree students of II semester of I year.

★ The book is presented with an approach to explain the concepts in lucid and communicable language.

★ The subject is exposed systematically and students are better prepared to solve the problems.

★ All fundamentals of the included topics have been explained with a micro-analysis.

★ Sufficient number of solved examples have been given to let the readers understand the various skills necessary to solve the problems. These examples are well graded.

★ Unsolved exercises of multi-varieties have been given in a well-graded style. To attempt these will enable a student to create independence and confidence in him/her regarding the understanding of the subject.

★ Daily life problems and practical problems have been incorporated in the body of the text.

★ A large number of attractive and accurate figures have been drawn which enable a student to grasp the subject in an easier way.

★ All questions of previous year papers of various Technical Universities have been marked and included at proper places.

The author **Dr. Manish Goyal** is thankful and obliged to his father, **Dr. Hari Kishan,** Associate Professor and Head, Department of Mathematics, K.R.(P.G.) College, Mathura and an eminent author for his guidance and necessary instructions in the preparation of the book.

—AUTHORS

SYLLABUS

(M.T.U., NOIDA)

ENGINEERING MATHEMATICS-II

AS-201

L	T	P	Credit
3	1	0	4

Unit-I : Ordinary Differential Equations

First order exact differential equations, Linear differential equations of nth order with constant coefficients, complementary functions and particular integrals. Cauchy-Euler differential equations. Solution of second order differential equations using the method of reduction, change of independent variable and variation of parameters. Simultaneous differential equations. Applications to mechanical vibrations and electric circuits. **[9 Hours]**

Unit-II : Series Solution of Ordinary Differential Equations and Special Functions

Power series solution of ordinary differential equations of second order with variable coefficients (Frobenius Method), Legendre and Bessel differential equations and their series solutions, Rodrigue's formula. Recurrence relations and orthogonality of Legendre polynomials and Bessel functions. **[9 Hours]**

Unit-III : Laplace Transform

Definition, existence theorem (statement only). Laplace transform of derivatives, integrals and periodic functions. Units step (Heaviside) and impulse (Dirac-delta) functions. Inverse Laplace transform. Convolution theorem, Application to solution of simple linear and simultaneous differential equations. **[9 Hours]**

Unit-IV : Fourier Series and Partial Differential Equations

Periodic functions, Fourier series of period 2π, Euler's formulae. Fourier series of arbitrary period. Fourier series of even and odd functions. Half range sine and cosine series, Harmonic analysis.

Formation of partial differential equations, types of solutions, solution of Lagrange's linear partial differential equations of first order Non-linear different equations of first order and its solution by Charpit's method (without proof), simple problems. Homogeneous and non-homogeneous partial differential equations with constant coefficients. **[9 Hours]**

Unit-V : Classification and Applications of Partial Differential Equations

Classification of partial differential equations of second order into parabolic, hyperbolic and elliptic with illustrative examples.

Method of separation of variables. One dimensional wave and heat equations and problems, Laplace equation in two-dimensions. Wave and heat in two-dimensions illustrative examples, Equations of transmission lines. **[9 Hours]**

New Study and Evaluation Scheme

Year I, Semester-II

S. No.	Code	Subjects	Periods			Evaluation Scheme						Total	Credits
						Sessional				End Semester			
			L	T	P	CT	TA	TOT	P	Th	P		
1.	AS201	Engineering Mathematics-II	3	1	0	30	20	50		100	—	150	4
2.	AS202#	Engineering Physics-II /(E/M/C)	3	0	2	15	10	25	15	80	30	150	4
3.	ME201/ CS201	Engineering Mechanics/ Computer Programming	3	1	2	20	10	30	15	100	30	175	5
4.	EC201/ EE201	Electronics Engineering/ Electrical Engineering	3	1	2	20	10	30	15	100	30	175	5
5.	ME202/ AS203	Manufacturing Practices/ Engineering Chemistry	3	0	2	15	10	25	15	80	30	150	4
6.	CE201/*	Energy, Environment and Ecology/ Branch Elective	3	0	0	10	10	20	—	80	—	100	3
7.	CE202/ AS205	Computer Aided Engineering Graphics/ Professional Communication	0	1	2	—	—	—	20		30	50	2
8.	GP201	General Proficiency							50	—	—	50	—
			18	4	10							1000	27

Engineering Physics II paper will have two parts; first three units shall be common for all branches and fourth and fifth units will be branch specific.

Engineering Physics II (E)-for EE/EC etc.

Engineering Physics II (M)-for ME/AU/MT/CH/CE/EV/TE/TT/FT/TC etc.

Engineering Physics II (C)-CS/IT etc.

TA = 10 (5 for teachers assessment plus 5 for attendance),

TA = 20 (10 for teachers assessment plus 10 for attendance)

P = 15 (4 for Practical Exams plus 4 for viva, 4 marks for lab record & 3 marks for quiz)

P = 30 (10 for Practical Exams plus 10 for viva, 5 marks for lab record & 5 marks for quiz)

Note: *Grouping of batches will be done in a way that groups select either all subjects given in numerator or denominator, choice of mix of numerator and denominator is not permitted.*

IMPORTANT NOTE

The format of the question paper will be as follows:

Section A will (20% marks)	:	Consist of short answer questions of 2 marks each from all the units and not having more than 10 questions. This section will have no choice. The answers are expected to be in 50–75 words.
Section B will (30% marks)	:	Consist of medium answer questions with answer in 100–200 words. This section can also have numerical questions. This section will have 5 questions from all the units and student will have to attempt 3 out of 5 for a total marks of 30.
Section C will (50% marks)	:	Consist of 5 questions from all the units with internal choice. The student has to answer all the questions and the answers are to be up to 300–500 words such that it tests the knowledge application and the learning in this subject. This section can also have numerical questions. Generally it shall include design, addition and synthesis of multiple concept integration from the same course.

STANDARD RESULTS

1. $\frac{d}{dx}(x^n) = nx^{n-1}$

2. $\frac{d}{dx}(a^x) = a^x \log_e a$

3. $\frac{d}{dx}(e^x) = e^x$

4. $\frac{d}{dx}(\log_e x) = \frac{1}{x}$

5. $\frac{d}{dx}(\log_{10} x) = \frac{1}{x}\log_{10} e$

6. $\frac{d}{dx}(\sin x) = \cos x$

7. $\frac{d}{dx}(\cos x) = -\sin x$

8. $\frac{d}{dx}(\tan x) = \sec^2 x$

9. $\frac{d}{dx}(\text{cosec } x) = -\text{cosec } x \cot x$

10. $\frac{d}{dx}(\cot x) = -\text{cosec}^2 x$

11. $\frac{d}{dx}(\sec x) = \sec x \tan x$

12. $\frac{d}{dx}(\sin^{-1} x) = \frac{1}{\sqrt{1-x^2}}$

13. $\frac{d}{dx}(\cos^{-1} x) = \frac{-1}{\sqrt{1-x^2}}$

14. $\frac{d}{dx}(\tan^{-1} x) = \frac{1}{1+x^2}$

15. $\frac{d}{dx}(\sec^{-1} x) = \frac{1}{x\sqrt{x^2-1}}$

16. $\frac{d}{dx}(\cot^{-1} x) = \frac{-1}{1+x^2}$

17. $\frac{d}{dx}(\text{cosec}^{-1} x) = -\frac{1}{x\sqrt{x^2-1}}$

18. $\sinh x = \frac{e^x - e^{-x}}{2}$

19. $\cosh x = \frac{e^x + e^{-x}}{2}$

20. $\tanh x = \frac{e^x - e^{-x}}{e^x + e^{-x}}$

21. $\cosh^2 x - \sinh^2 x = 1$, $\text{sech}^2 x + \tanh^2 x = 1$, $\coth^2 x = 1 + \text{cosech}^2 x$

22. $\cosh^2 x + \sinh^2 x = \cosh 2x$

23. $\sinh^{-1} x = \log(x + \sqrt{x^2+1})$

    $\cosh^{-1} x = \log(x + \sqrt{x^2-1})$

24. $\frac{d}{dx}(\sinh x) = \cosh x$

25. $\frac{d}{dx}(\cosh x) = \sinh x$

26. $\frac{d}{dx}(\tanh x) = \text{sech}^2 x$

27. $\frac{d}{dx}(\coth x) = -\text{cosech}^2 x$

28. $\frac{d}{dx}(\text{sech } x) = -\text{sech } x \tanh x$

29. $\frac{d}{dx}(\text{cosech } x) = -\text{cosech } x \coth x$

30. Product rule : $\frac{d}{dx}(uv) = u\frac{dv}{dx} + v\frac{du}{dx}$

31. Quotient rule : $\frac{d}{dx}\left(\frac{u}{v}\right) = \frac{v\frac{du}{dx} - u\frac{dv}{dx}}{v^2}$

32. $\frac{dy}{dx} = \frac{dy}{dt} \cdot \frac{dt}{dx}$ if $y = f_1(t)$ and $x = f_2(t)$

33. $\sin^{-1} x + \cos^{-1} x = \frac{\pi}{2}$, $\tan^{-1} x + \cot^{-1} x = \frac{\pi}{2}$, $\sec^{-1} x + \text{cosec}^{-1} x = \frac{\pi}{2}$

34. $\tan^{-1}\left(\frac{a-b}{1+ab}\right) = \tan^{-1} a - \tan^{-1} b$, $\tan^{-1}\left(\frac{a+b}{1-ab}\right) = \tan^{-1} a + \tan^{-1} b$

35. $\tan^{-1}\left(\frac{2x}{1-x^2}\right) = \sin^{-1}\left(\frac{2x}{1+x^2}\right) = 2\tan^{-1} x$

36. $\sin 3x = 3\sin x - 4\sin^3 x$, $\cos 3x = 4\cos^3 x - 3\cos x$, $\tan 3x = \frac{3\tan x - \tan^3 x}{1 - 3\tan^2 x}$

$\sin 2x = 2\sin x \cos x$, $\tan 2x = \frac{2\tan x}{1-\tan^2 x}$,

$\cos 2x = 2\cos^2 x - 1 = 1 - 2\sin^2 x = \cos^2 x - \sin^2 x = \frac{1-\tan^2 x}{1+\tan^2 x}$

37. $\sin x = x - \frac{x^3}{3!} + \frac{x^5}{5!} - \frac{x^7}{7!} + \ldots$

$\cos x = 1 - \frac{x^2}{2!} + \frac{x^4}{4!} - \frac{x^6}{6!} + \ldots$

$e^x = 1 + x + \frac{x^2}{2!} + \frac{x^3}{3!} + \ldots$

$(1-x)^{-1} = 1 + x + x^2 + x^3 + \ldots\ ;\ |x| < 1$

$(1+x)^{-1} = 1 - x + x^2 - x^3 + \ldots$

$(1-x)^{-2} = 1 + 2x + 3x^2 + 4x^3 + \ldots$

$(1+x)^{-2} = 1 - 2x + 3x^2 - 4x^3 + \ldots$

38. $\sin C + \sin D = 2\sin\frac{C+D}{2}\cos\frac{C-D}{2}$, $\sin C - \sin D = 2\cos\frac{C+D}{2}\sin\frac{C-D}{2}$

$\cos C + \cos D = 2\cos\frac{C+D}{2}\cos\frac{C-D}{2}$, $\cos C - \cos D = 2\sin\frac{C+D}{2}\sin\frac{D-C}{2}$

39. $2\cos A\cos B = \cos(A+B) + \cos(A-B)$, $2\sin A\sin B = \cos(A-B) - \cos(A+B)$

$2\sin A\cos B = \sin(A+B) + \sin(A-B)$, $2\cos A\sin B = \sin(A+B) - \sin(A-B)$

40. $\sin(A+B) = \sin A\cos B + \cos A\sin B$, $\sin(A-B) = \sin A\cos B - \cos A\sin B$

$\cos(A+B) = \cos A\cos B - \sin A\sin B$, $\cos(A-B) = \cos A\cos B + \sin A\sin B$

41. $\frac{d}{dx}(\sinh^{-1} x) = \frac{1}{\sqrt{1+x^2}}$, $\frac{d}{dx}(\cosh^{-1} x) = \frac{1}{\sqrt{x^2-1}}$

$$\frac{d}{dx}(\tanh^{-1} x) = \frac{1}{1-x^2}, \text{ where } |x| < 1$$

$$\frac{d}{dx}(\coth^{-1} x) = \frac{1}{x^2-1}, \text{ where } |x| > 1$$

$$\frac{d}{dx}(\text{sech}^{-1} x) = -\frac{1}{x\sqrt{1-x^2}}, \quad \frac{d}{dx}(\text{cosech}^{-1} x) = -\frac{1}{x\sqrt{x^2+1}}$$

42. $(\cos\theta + i\sin\theta)^n = \cos n\theta + i\sin n\theta$, $(\cos\theta + i\sin\theta)^{-n} = \cos n\theta - i\sin n\theta$

43. $\sin^2\theta + \cos^2\theta = 1$, $\sec^2\theta - \tan^2\theta = 1$, $1 + \cot^2\theta = \text{cosec}^2\theta$

44.

θ	0°	30°	45°	60°	90°	180°	270°	360°
$\sin\theta$	0	1/2	$1/\sqrt{2}$	$\sqrt{3}/2$	1	0	– 1	0
$\cos\theta$	1	$\sqrt{3}/2$	$1/\sqrt{2}$	1/2	0	– 1	0	1
$\tan\theta$	0	$1/\sqrt{3}$	1	$\sqrt{3}$	∞	0	∞	0

45.

θ	$90° - \theta$	$90° + \theta$	$\pi - \theta$	$\pi + \theta$
$\sin\theta$	$\cos\theta$	$\cos\theta$	$\sin\theta$	$-\sin\theta$
$\cos\theta$	$\sin\theta$	$-\sin\theta$	$-\cos\theta$	$-\cos\theta$
$\tan\theta$	$\cot\theta$	$-\cot\theta$	$-\tan\theta$	$\tan\theta$

46. sine formula : $\frac{a}{\sin A} = \frac{b}{\sin B} = \frac{c}{\sin C}$

cosine formula : $\cos A = \frac{b^2 + c^2 - a^2}{2bc}$

47. Area of triangle $= \sqrt{s(s-a)(s-b)(s-c)}$ where $s = \frac{a+b+c}{2}$ and a, b, c are sides of triangle

48. ${}^nC_r = \frac{n!}{r!\,\underline{n-r}!}$

49. $\int x^n\, dx = \frac{x^{n+1}}{n+1} + c \,;\, n \neq -1$

$$\int \frac{1}{x}\,dx = \log_e x + c \,;\, \int e^x\,dx = e^x + c \,;\, \int a^x\,dx = \frac{a^x}{\log_e a} + c$$

$$\int \sin x\,dx = -\cos x + c \,;\, \int \cos x\,dx = \sin x + c$$

$$\int \tan x\,dx = \log \sec x + c \,;\, \int \cot x\,dx = \log \sin x + c$$

$$\int \sec x\, dx = \log(\sec x + \tan x) + c = \log\tan\left(\frac{\pi}{4} + \frac{x}{2}\right) + c$$

$$\int \operatorname{cosec} x\, dx = \log(\operatorname{cosec} x - \cot x) + c = \log\tan\frac{x}{2} + c$$

$$\int \sec x \tan x\, dx = \sec x + c\ ;\ \int \operatorname{cosec} x \cot x\, dx = -\operatorname{cosec} x + c$$

50. $$\int \frac{dx}{\sqrt{a^2 - x^2}} = \sin^{-1}\left(\frac{x}{a}\right) + c\ ;\ \int \frac{-dx}{\sqrt{a^2 - x^2}} = \cos^{-1}\left(\frac{x}{a}\right) + c$$

$$\int \frac{dx}{a^2 + x^2} = \frac{1}{a}\tan^{-1}\left(\frac{x}{a}\right) + c\ ;\ \int \frac{-dx}{a^2 + x^2} = \frac{1}{a}\cot^{-1}\left(\frac{x}{a}\right) + c$$

$$\int \frac{dx}{a^2 - x^2} = \frac{1}{2a}\log\left(\frac{a + x}{a - x}\right) + c\ ;\ \int \frac{dx}{x^2 - a^2} = \frac{1}{2a}\log\left(\frac{x - a}{x + a}\right) + c$$

$$\int \frac{dx}{x\sqrt{x^2 - a^2}} = \frac{1}{a}\sec^{-1}\left(\frac{x}{a}\right) + c\ ;\ \int \frac{-dx}{x\sqrt{x^2 - a^2}} = \frac{1}{a}\operatorname{cosec}^{-1}\left(\frac{x}{a}\right) + c$$

51. $$\int \operatorname{sech}^2 x\, dx = \tanh x + c,\ \int \operatorname{cosech}^2 x\, dx = -\coth x + c$$

$$\int \sinh x\, dx = \cosh x + c,\ \int \cosh x\, dx = \sinh x + c$$

$$\int \operatorname{sech} x \tanh x\, dx = -\operatorname{sech} x + c,\ \int \operatorname{cosech} x \coth x\, dx = -\operatorname{cosech} x + c$$

52. $$\int \sqrt{a^2 - x^2}\, dx = \frac{1}{2}x\sqrt{a^2 - x^2} + \frac{1}{2}a^2\sin^{-1}\frac{x}{a} + c$$

$$\int \sqrt{a^2 + x^2}\, dx = \frac{1}{2}x\sqrt{a^2 + x^2} + \frac{1}{2}a^2\log\left(x + \sqrt{a^2 + x^2}\right) + c$$

$$\int \sqrt{x^2 - a^2}\, dx = \frac{1}{2}x\sqrt{x^2 - a^2} - \frac{1}{2}a^2\log\left(x + \sqrt{x^2 - a^2}\right) + c$$

$$\int \frac{dx}{\sqrt{a^2 + x^2}} = \sinh^{-1}\left(\frac{x}{a}\right) + c\ ;\ \int \frac{dx}{\sqrt{x^2 - a^2}} = \cosh^{-1}\left(\frac{x}{a}\right) + c$$

53. $$\int_a^b f(x)\, dx = \int_a^b f(y)\, dy\ ;\ \int_a^b f(x)\, dx = -\int_b^a f(x)\, dx\ ;\ \int_0^a f(x)\, dx = \int_0^a f(a - x)\, dx$$

$$\int_{-a}^{a} f(x)\, dx = \begin{cases} 2\int_0^a f(x)\, dx, & \text{if } f(x) \text{ is even function} \\ 0, & \text{if } f(x) \text{ is odd function} \end{cases}$$

$$\int_0^{2a} f(x)\, dx = \begin{cases} 2\int_0^a f(x)\, dx, & \text{if } f(2a - x) = f(x) \\ 0, & \text{if } f(2a - x) = -f(x) \end{cases}$$

54. Leibnitz rule for differentiation under the integral sign

$$\frac{d}{dx}\int_{\phi(\alpha)}^{\psi(\alpha)} f(x,\alpha)\,dx = \int_{\phi(\alpha)}^{\psi(\alpha)} \frac{\partial}{\partial\alpha}\{f(x,\alpha)\}\,dx + f\{\psi(\alpha),\alpha\}\frac{d\psi(\alpha)}{d\alpha} - f\{\phi(\alpha),\alpha\}\frac{d\phi(\alpha)}{d\alpha}$$

55. If $\vec{r} = x\hat{i} + y\hat{j} + z\hat{k}$ then $|\vec{r}| = \sqrt{x^2+y^2+z^2}$ and $\hat{r} = \dfrac{\vec{r}}{|\vec{r}|} = \dfrac{x\hat{i}+y\hat{j}+z\hat{k}}{\sqrt{x^2+y^2+z^2}}$

56. $\overrightarrow{AB}$ = position vector of B–position vector of A = $\overrightarrow{OB} - \overrightarrow{OA}$

57. $\vec{a}\,.\,\vec{b} = |\vec{a}|\,|\vec{b}|\cos\theta$; work done $= \int_C \vec{F}\,.\,d\vec{r}$

58. $\vec{a}\times\vec{b} = |\vec{a}|\,|\vec{b}|\sin\theta\,\hat{n}$

59. Area of parallelogram = $\vec{a}\times\vec{b}$, Moment of force = $\vec{r}\times\vec{F}$

60. $\vec{a}\cdot(\vec{b}\times\vec{c}) = [\vec{a}\,\vec{b}\,\vec{c}\,] = \begin{vmatrix} a_1 & a_2 & a_3 \\ b_1 & b_2 & b_3 \\ c_1 & c_2 & c_3 \end{vmatrix} = (\vec{a}\times\vec{b})\cdot\vec{c}$

where $\vec{a} = \Sigma\, a_1\hat{i}$, $\vec{b} = \Sigma\, b_1\hat{i}$ and $\vec{c} = \Sigma c_1\hat{i}$

If $\vec{a}\,.\,(\vec{b}\times\vec{c}) = 0$, then $\vec{a}, \vec{b}, \vec{c}$ are coplanar.

61. $\vec{a}\times(\vec{b}\times\vec{c}) = (\vec{a}\,.\,\vec{c})\,\vec{b} - (\vec{a}\,.\,\vec{b})\,\vec{c}$

62. $(\vec{a}\times\vec{b})\,.\,(\vec{c}\times\vec{d}) = \begin{vmatrix} \vec{a}\,.\,\vec{c} & \vec{a}\,.\,\vec{d} \\ \vec{b}\,.\,\vec{c} & \vec{b}\,.\,\vec{d} \end{vmatrix}$

63. $(\vec{a}\times\vec{b})\times(\vec{c}\times\vec{d}) = [\vec{a}\,\vec{b}\,\vec{d}\,]\,\vec{c} - [\vec{a}\,\vec{b}\,\vec{c}\,]\,\vec{d}$

64. A (Adj. A) = | A | I

65. $AA^{-1} = I = A^{-1}A$

66. AI = A = IA

67. $(ABC)' = C'B'A'$

68. (AB)C = A(BC) ; A(B + C) = AB + AC

69. A + B = B + A ; A + (B + C) = (A + B) + C

70. $(AB)^{-1} = B^{-1}A^{-1}$

71. Walli's formula

$$\int_0^{\pi/2} \sin^n \theta \, d\theta = \int_0^{\pi/2} \cos^n \theta \, d\theta = \begin{cases} \dfrac{n-1}{n} \cdot \dfrac{n-3}{n-2} \cdot \dfrac{n-5}{n-4} \cdots\cdots \dfrac{3}{4} \cdot \dfrac{1}{2} \cdot \dfrac{\pi}{2} & \text{if } n \text{ is even} \\ \dfrac{n-1}{n} \cdot \dfrac{n-3}{n-2} \cdot \dfrac{n-5}{n-4} \cdots\cdots \dfrac{4}{5} \cdot \dfrac{2}{3} & \text{if } n \text{ is odd} \end{cases}$$

72. $\displaystyle\int e^{ax} \sin bx \, dx = \frac{e^{ax}}{a^2 + b^2} (a \sin bx - b \cos bx) + c$

$$\int e^{ax} \cos bx \, dx = \frac{e^{ax}}{a^2 + b^2} (a \cos bx + b \sin bx) + c$$

73. $\Gamma(1/2) = \sqrt{\pi}$, $\Gamma(-1/2) = -2\sqrt{\pi}$

74. $\log (1 + x) = x - \dfrac{x^2}{2} + \dfrac{x^3}{3} - \dfrac{x^4}{4} + \dfrac{x^5}{5} - \dfrac{x^6}{6} + \cdots\cdots$

$$\log (1 - x) = -x - \frac{x^2}{2} - \frac{x^3}{3} - \frac{x^4}{4} - \frac{x^5}{5} - \frac{x^6}{6} - \cdots\cdots$$

75. $\sin n\pi = 0$; $\cos n\pi = (-1)^n$, $\sin \left(n + \dfrac{1}{2}\right) \pi = (-1)^n$; $\cos \left(n + \dfrac{1}{2}\right) \pi = 0$, where $n \in \text{I}$.

UNIT 1

Ordinary Differential Equations

1.1. DEFINITIONS

1.1.1. Differential Equation

A **differential equation** is an equation involving differentials or differential coefficients.

Or

An equation involving the dependent variable, independent variable and the differential coefficient (or coefficients) of the dependent variable with respect to the independent variable (or variables) is known as a differential equation. For example :

$$\frac{dy}{dx} = \cot x \quad \ldots(1) \qquad \frac{d^2y}{dx^2} + y = 0 \quad \ldots(2)$$

$$y = x\frac{dy}{dx} + \left(\frac{dy}{dx}\right)^3 \quad \ldots(3) \qquad x\frac{\partial z}{\partial x} + y\frac{\partial z}{\partial y} = z \quad \ldots(4)$$

$$\frac{d^2y}{dx^2} + \sqrt{1 + \left(\frac{dy}{dx}\right)^3} = 0 \quad \ldots(5) \qquad \rho = \frac{\left\{1 + \left(\frac{dy}{dx}\right)^2\right\}^{3/2}}{\frac{d^2y}{dx^2}} \quad \ldots(6)$$

are all differential equations.

1.1.2. Ordinary Differential Equation

A differential equation which involves only one independent variable is called an ordinary differential equation *e.g.,* All equations excluding (4) given above are ordinary differential equations.

1.1.3. Partial Differential Equation

A differential equation which involves two or more independent variables and partial derivatives with respect to them is called partial differential equation.
e.g., Equation (4) given above is a partial differential equation.

1.1.4. Order of a Differential Equation

The **order** of a differential equation is the order of the highest ordered derivative occurring in the differential equation. *e.g.,* Eqns. (1), (2) and (5) are of orders 1, 2 and 2 respectively.

1.1.5. Degree of a Differential Equation

The **degree** of a differential equation is the degree of the highest ordered derivative present in the differential equation when it is made free from radical signs and fractional powers. *e.g.,* Degree of equation (1) is 1.

Now consider equation (5)

$$\frac{d^2y}{dx^2} + \sqrt{1 + \left(\frac{dy}{dx}\right)^3} = 0$$

It involves radical sign. So to find the degree, we shall remove the radical sign. To achieve the purpose, squaring, we get

$$\left(\frac{d^2y}{dx^2}\right)^2 = 1 + \left(\frac{dy}{dx}\right)^3$$

Clearly its degree is 2.

Again, consider equation (6)

$$\rho = \frac{\left\{1 + \left(\frac{dy}{dx}\right)^2\right\}^{3/2}}{\frac{d^2y}{dx^2}}.$$

It involves fractional powers. So to find the degree, we shall remove the fractional power. To achieve the purpose, squaring, we get

$$\rho^2 = \frac{\left\{1 + \left(\frac{dy}{dx}\right)^2\right\}^3}{\left(\frac{d^2y}{dx^2}\right)^2}$$

Clearly its degree is 2.

Note. Equations of degree higher than one are called non-linear equations.

1.1.6. Solution of a Differential Equation

The solution is one which satisfies. A solution (or integral) of a differential equation is a relation, free from derivatives, between the variables which satisfies the given equation. It is also called **primitive** because the differential equation can be regarded as a relation derived from it.

Thus if $y = f(x)$ is the solution, then by replacing y and its derivatives with respect to x, the given differential equation will reduce to an identity.

e.g., $y = c_1 \cos x + c_2 \sin x$ is the solution of the differential equation $\frac{d^2y}{dx^2} + y = 0$.

1.1.7. General Solution

The **general** (or **complete**) **solution** of a differential equation is the solution in which the number of arbitrary constants is equal to the order of the differential equation.

Thus, $y = c_1 \cos x + c_2 \sin x$ (involving two arbitrary constants c_1, c_2) is the general solution of the differential equation $\frac{d^2y}{dx^2} + y = 0$ of second order.

1.1.8. Particular Solution

A **particular solution** of a differential equation is the solution which is obtained from its general solution by giving particular values to the arbitrary constants.

For example, $y = c_1e^x + c_2e^{-x}$ is the general solution of the differential equation $\frac{d^2y}{dx^2} - y = 0$, whereas $y = e^x - e^{-x}$ or $y = e^x$ are its particular solutions.

The solution of a differential equation of nth order is its particular solution if it contains less than n arbitrary constants.

1.2. ARBITRARY CONSTANTS

In order to find out the number of arbitrary constants in the most general solution of a differential equation, we shall study how a differential equation is formed if the solution is given.

Let the solution be $f(x, y, a) = 0$ ...(1)

where 'a' is an arbitrary constant.

Differentiating equation (1) w.r.t. x, we get

$$\phi\left(x, y, \frac{dy}{dx}, a\right) = 0 \qquad ...(2)$$

Eliminating 'a' between eqns. (1) and (2), we get

$$\psi\left(x, y, \frac{dy}{dx}\right) = 0 \qquad ...(3)$$

which is a differential equation of I order.

Thus, the general solution of a differential equation of I order contains one arbitrary constant.

Again, Let the solution be

$$f(x, y, a, b) = 0 \qquad ...(1)$$

where 'a' and 'b' are two arbitrary constants.

Differentiating equation (1) w.r.t. x, we get

$$\phi_1\left(x, y, \frac{dy}{dx}, a, b\right) = 0 \qquad ...(2)$$

Again, Differentiation w.r.t. x yields

$$\phi_2\left(x, y, \frac{dy}{dx}, \frac{d^2y}{dx^2}, a, b\right) = 0 \qquad ...(3)$$

Eliminating a and b from eqns. (1), (2) and (3), we get

$$\psi\left(x, y, \frac{dy}{dx}, \frac{d^2y}{dx^2}\right) = 0 \qquad ...(4)$$

which is a differential equation of II order.

Thus, the general solution of a differential equation of II order contains two arbitrary constants and so on.

Therefore, it is concluded that the number of arbitrary constants in the general solution of an ordinary differential equation is equal to the order of the differential equation.

1.3. FORMATION OF A DIFFERENTIAL EQUATION

Differential equations are formed by elimination of arbitrary constants. To eliminate two arbitrary constants, we require two more equations besides the given relation, leading us to second order derivatives and hence a differential equation of the second order. Elimination of n arbitrary constants leads us to n^{th} order derivatives and hence a differential equation of the nth order.

Example. *Eliminate the arbitrary constants A and B from the equation* $y = e^x(A\cos x + B\sin x)$ *and obtain the differential equation.*

Sol. We have the relation.

$$y = e^x(\text{A}\cos x + \text{B}\sin x) \quad \text{...(1)}$$

Differentiating equation (1) w.r.t. x, we have

$$\frac{dy}{dx} = e^x(\text{A}\cos x + \text{B}\sin x) + e^x(-\text{A}\sin x + \text{B}\cos x)$$

$$= y + e^x(-\text{A}\sin x + \text{B}\cos x) \quad \text{...(2)}$$

Differentiating again w.r.t. x, we have

$$\frac{d^2y}{dx^2} = \frac{dy}{dx} + e^x(-\text{A}\sin x + \text{B}\cos x) + e^x(-\text{A}\cos x - \text{B}\sin x)$$

$$= \frac{dy}{dx} + \left(\frac{dy}{dx} - y\right) - y \quad \text{[Using (1) and (2)]}$$

or

$$\frac{d^2y}{dx^2} - 2\frac{dy}{dx} + 2y = 0$$

which is the required differential equation.

1.4. LINEARLY DEPENDENT AND INDEPENDENT SOLUTIONS

Consider a second order differential equation

$$a_0(x)\frac{d^2y}{dx^2} + a_1(x)\frac{dy}{dx} + a_2(x)\,y = 0 \quad \text{...(1)}$$

where $a_0(x)$, $a_1(x)$ and $a_2(x)$ are continuous on an interval (a, b) and $a_0(x) \neq 0 \ \forall \ x \in (a, b)$. Then two solutions $y_1(x)$ and $y_2(x)$ of equation (1) are said to be linearly dependent if $\exists$ two constants c_1 and c_2, not both zero, such that

$$c_1y_1 + c_2y_2 = 0 \quad \forall \quad x \in (a, b)$$

Two solutions $y_1(x)$ and $y_2(x)$ are said to be linearly independent if they are not linearly dependent.

In other words, two solutions $y_1(x)$ and $y_2(x)$ are said to be linearly independent if

$$c_1y_1 + c_2y_2 = 0$$

$$\Rightarrow \quad c_1 = 0 \quad \text{and} \quad c_2 = 0 \,;\, x \in (a, b).$$

1.5. THE WRONSKIAN OR WRONSKI DETERMINANT

I.M. Hone (1778–1853) was a Polish mathematician who changed his name to Wronski. Let $y_1(x)$ and $y_2(x)$ be two solutions of the second order differential equation

$$a_0(x)\frac{d^2y}{dx^2} + a_1(x)\frac{dy}{dx} + a_2(x)\,y = 0.$$

Then the Wronskian of $y_1(x)$ and $y_2(x)$ is given by

$$W(y_1, y_2) \quad \text{or} \quad W(x) = \begin{vmatrix} y_1(x) & y_2(x) \\ y_1'(x) & y_2'(x) \end{vmatrix}$$

Again, Let $y_1(x), y_2(x), \ldots\ldots, y_n(x)$ be n solutions of

$$\frac{d^ny}{dx^n} + P_1\frac{d^{n-1}y}{dx^{n-1}} + \ldots\ldots + P_ny = 0$$

Then, Wronskian of $y_1(x), y_2(x), \ldots\ldots, y_n(x)$ is denoted by $W(y_1, y_2, \ldots\ldots, y_n)$ or $W(x)$ and defined by the determinant

$$W(x) = \begin{vmatrix} y_1 & y_2 & \ldots\ldots & y_n \\ y_1' & y_2' & \ldots\ldots & y_n' \\ y_1'' & y_2'' & \ldots\ldots & y_n'' \\ \vdots & \vdots & \vdots & \vdots \\ y_1^{(n-1)} & y_2^{(n-1)} & \ldots\ldots & y_n^{(n-1)} \end{vmatrix}.$$

1.6. SOME IMPORTANT THEOREMS

(*i*) If $y_1(x)$ and $y_2(x)$ are any two solutions of $a_0(x)\frac{d^2y}{dx^2} + a_1(x)\frac{dy}{dx} + a_2(x)\,y = 0$, then the linear combination $c_1y_1(x) + c_2y_2(x)$, where c_1 and c_2 are constants is also a solution of the given equation.

(*ii*) Two solutions $y_1(x)$ and $y_2(x)$ of the equation

$$a_0(x)\frac{d^2y}{dx^2} + a_1(x)\frac{dy}{dx} + a_2(x)\,y = 0\ ;\ a_0(x) \neq 0,\ x \in (a, b)$$

are linearly dependent iff their Wronskian is identically zero.

Corollary. Solutions are linearly independent iff their Wronskian is not zero at some point $x_0 \in (a, b)$.

ILLUSTRATIVE EXAMPLES

Example 1. *Show that $y_1(x) = \sin x$ and $y_2(x) = \sin x - \cos x$ are linearly independent solutions of $y'' + y = 0$. Determine the constants c_1 and c_2 so that*

$$\sin x + 3\cos x \equiv c_1y_1(x) + c_2y_2(x).$$

Sol. Given equation is $\quad y'' + y = 0 \qquad \ldots(1)$

Here, $\quad y_1(x) = \sin x$

$\therefore \quad y_1'(x) = \cos x \quad$ and $\quad y_1''(x) = -\sin x$

Since, $y_1''(x) + y_1(x) = -\sin x + \sin x = 0$ hence $y_1(x)$ is a solution of (1).

Similarly, we can show that $y_2(x)$ is also a solution of (1).

Now, the Wronskian of $y_1(x)$ and $y_2(x)$ is given by

$$W(x) = \begin{vmatrix} y_1(x) & y_2(x) \\ y_1'(x) & y_2'(x) \end{vmatrix} = \begin{vmatrix} \sin x & \sin x - \cos x \\ \cos x & \cos x + \sin x \end{vmatrix}$$

$$= \sin x (\cos x + \sin x) - \cos x(\sin x - \cos x) = 1 \neq 0$$

which shows that $y_1(x)$ and $y_2(x)$ are linearly independent solutions of (1).

Given that $\sin x + 3 \cos x \equiv c_1 y_1(x) + c_2 y_2(x)$

$$\equiv c_1 \sin x + c_2 (\sin x - \cos x)$$

Comparing the coefficients of $\sin x$ and $\cos x$ on both sides, we get

$$c_1 + c_2 = 1 \quad \text{and} \quad -c_2 = 3$$

so that, $c_1 = 4, \; c_2 = -3.$

Example 2. *Prove that the functions 1, x, x^2 are linearly independent. Hence form the differential equation whose roots are 1, x, x^2.*

Sol. Let $y_1(x) = 1, \; y_2(x) = x$ and $y_3(x) = x^2$.

Then the Wronskian $W(x)$ of y_1, y_2, y_3 is given by

$$W(x) = \begin{vmatrix} y_1 & y_2 & y_3 \\ y_1' & y_2' & y_3' \\ y_1'' & y_2'' & y_3'' \end{vmatrix} = \begin{vmatrix} 1 & x & x^2 \\ 0 & 1 & 2x \\ 0 & 0 & 2 \end{vmatrix}$$

or $W(x) = 2 \neq 0 \quad \forall \, x \in (-\infty, \infty)$

$\therefore$ y_1, y_2 and y_3 are linearly independent.

The general solution of the required differential equation may be written as

$$y = c_1 y_1 + c_2 y_2 + c_3 y_3 = c_1 + c_2 x + c_3 x^2 \qquad ...(1)$$

where c_1, c_2, c_3 are arbitrary constants.

Differentiating (1), we get $y' = c_2 + 2c_3 x$ ...(2)

Differentiating again, we get $y'' = 2c_3$ ...(3)

Differentiating (3), we get $y''' = 0$ or $\dfrac{d^3y}{dx^3} = 0$ ...(4)

Since equation (4) is free from arbitrary constants c_1, c_2 and c_3, hence equation (4) is the required differential equation.

Example 3. *Determine the differential equation whose set of independent solutions is $\{e^x, xe^x, x^2e^x\}$.*

Sol. Let the general solution of the required differential equation be

$$y = c_1 e^x + c_2 xe^x + c_3 x^2 e^x \qquad ...(1)$$

Differentiating (1) w.r.t. x, we get

$$y' = c_1 e^x + c_2 (x + 1)e^x + c_3 (x^2 + 2x)e^x \qquad ...(2)$$

From (1) and (2), we get

$$y = y' - c_2 e^x - 2c_3 xe^x \qquad ...(3)$$

Differentiating (3) w.r.t. x, we get

$$y' = y'' - c_2 e^x - 2c_3 (x + 1)e^x \qquad ...(4)$$

From (3) and (4), we get

$$y = y' + y' - y'' + 2c_3 e^x = 2y' - y'' + 2c_3 e^x \qquad ...(5)$$

Differentiating (5) w.r.t. x, we get

$$y' = 2y'' - y''' + 2c_3e^x \qquad ...(6)$$

From (5) and (6), we get $\quad y = 2y' - y'' + y' - 2y'' + y'''$

$\Rightarrow \qquad y''' - 3y'' + 3y' - y = 0$

1.7. DIFFERENTIAL EQUATIONS OF THE FIRST ORDER AND FIRST DEGREE

A differential equation of the form $\frac{dy}{dx} = f(x, y)$ or $Mdx + Ndy = 0$, where M, N are functions of x and y, is called a differential equation of the first order and first degree.

1.7.1. Geometrical Interpretation

Let
$$f\left(x, y, \frac{dy}{dx}\right) = 0 \qquad ...(1)$$
be a differential equation of the first order and first degree.

We know that the direction of a curve at a particular point is determined by drawing a tangent line at that point, *i.e.,* its slope is given by $\frac{dy}{dx}$ at that particular point.

Let $A_0(x_0, y_0)$ be any point in the plane. Let $m_0 = \frac{dy_0}{dx_0}$ be the slope of the curve at A_0 derived from (1). Take a neighbouring point $A_1(x_1, y_1)$ such that the slope of A_0A_1 is m_0. Let $m_1 = \frac{dy_1}{dx_1}$ be the slope of the curve at A_1 derived from (1). Take a neighbouring point A_2 (x_2, y_2) such that the slope of A_1A_2 is m_1. Continuing like this, we get a succession of points. If the points are taken sufficiently close to each other, they approximate a smooth curve $C : y = \phi(x)$ which is a solution of (1) corresponding to the initial point $A_0(x_0, y_0)$. Any point on C and the slope of the tangent at that point satisfy (1). If the moving point starts at any other point, not on C and moves as before, it will describe another curve. The equation of each such curve is a *particular solution* of the differential equation (1). The equation of the system of all such curves is the general solution of equation (1).

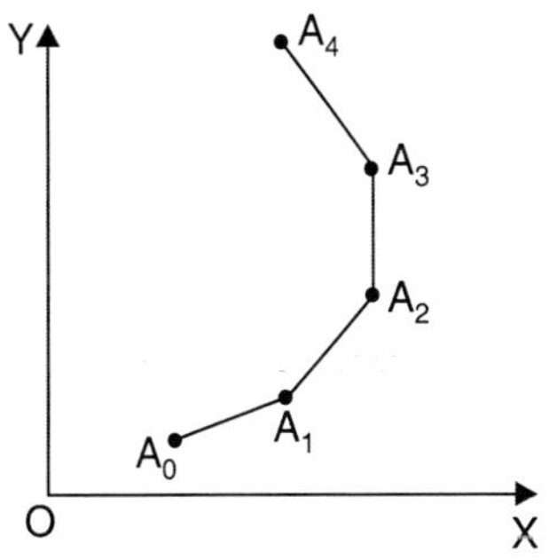

1.8. SOLUTION OF DIFFERENTIAL EQUATIONS OF FIRST ORDER AND FIRST DEGREE

As we cannot integrate every function so it is not possible to solve every differential equation. Even the differential equation of first order and first degree cannot be solved in every case. They can be solved, however, if they belong to some standard forms.

1.9. VARIABLES SEPARABLE FORM

If it is possible to write a differential equation of first order and first degree in the form

$$f_1(x)\,dx = f_2(y)\,dy$$

we say that the variables are separable. Such equations can be solved immediately by integration and the solution is given by

$$\int f_1(x)\,dx = \int f_2(y)\,dy + c$$

where c is an arbitrary constant of integration.

1.9.1. Steps for Solution

1. Separate the variables as $f_1(x)\,dx = f_2(y)\,dy$.
2. Integrate both sides as $\int f_1(x)\,dx = \int f_2(y)\,dy$.
3. Add an arbitrary constant to any of the sides.

1.9.2. Differential Equations of the Form $\dfrac{dy}{dx} = f(ax + by + c)$ ...(1)

can be reduced to a form in which the variables are separable by the substitution $ax + by + c = t$

so that $$a + b\frac{dy}{dx} = \frac{dt}{dx} \quad \text{or} \quad \frac{dy}{dx} = \frac{1}{b}\left(\frac{dt}{dx} - a\right)$$

$\therefore$ Equation (1) becomes $$\frac{1}{b}\left(\frac{dt}{dx} - a\right) = f(t) \quad \text{or} \quad \frac{dt}{dx} = a + bf(t)$$

or $$\frac{dt}{a + bf(t)} = dx$$

After integrating both sides, t is to be replaced by its value.

ILLUSTRATIVE EXAMPLES

Example 1. *Solve :* $\dfrac{dy}{dx} = \dfrac{1 + y^2}{1 + x^2}$.

Sol. Separating the variables, we get

$$\frac{dy}{1 + y^2} = \frac{dx}{1 + x^2}$$

Integrating both sides, we get

$$\tan^{-1} y = \tan^{-1} x + \tan^{-1} c$$

$$\Rightarrow \quad \tan^{-1} y - \tan^{-1} x = \tan^{-1} c$$

$$\Rightarrow \quad \tan^{-1}\left(\frac{y - x}{1 + xy}\right) = \tan^{-1} c$$

$$\Rightarrow \quad \frac{y - x}{1 + xy} = c.$$

where c is an arbitrary constant.

Example 2. *Solve :* $\sec^2 x \tan y\, dx + \sec^2 y \tan x\, dy = 0.$

[U.P.T.U.(B.Pharm.) SUM 2009]

Sol. Separating the variables, we get

$$\frac{\sec^2 x}{\tan x}\,dx + \frac{\sec^2 y}{\tan y}\,dy = 0$$

Integration yields

$$\log \tan x + \log \tan y = \log c$$

$$\Rightarrow \quad \log \tan x \tan y = \log c$$

$$\Rightarrow \quad \tan x \tan y = c.$$

where c is an arbitrary constant.

Example 3. *Solve :* $\dfrac{dy}{dx} = e^{x-y} + x^2 e^{-y}.$

Sol. We have $\dfrac{dy}{dx} = e^{x-y} + x^2 e^{-y}$

Multiplying both sides by e^y, we get

$$e^y \frac{dy}{dx} = e^x + x^2 \Rightarrow e^y\, dy = (e^x + x^2)\, dx$$

Integration gives

$$e^y = e^x + \frac{x^3}{3} + c,$$ where c is an arbitrary constant of integration.

Example 4. *Solve :* $x\,y\,y' = \left(\dfrac{1+y^2}{1+x^2}\right)(1+x+x^2).$

Sol. We have, $xy\,\dfrac{dy}{dx} = \dfrac{1+y^2}{1+x^2}\,(1+x+x^2)$

Separating the variables,

$$\frac{y\,dy}{1+y^2} = \frac{(1+x+x^2)\,dx}{x(1+x^2)} = \left(\frac{1}{x} + \frac{1}{1+x^2}\right) dx$$

Integrating both sides,

$$\frac{1}{2}\int \frac{2y}{1+y^2}\,dy = \int \left(\frac{1}{x} + \frac{1}{1+x^2}\right) dx$$

$$\Rightarrow \quad \frac{1}{2}\log(1+y^2) = \log x + \tan^{-1} x + c$$

where c is an arbitrary constant of integration.

Example 5. *Solve :* $3e^x \tan y\, dx + (1 + e^x) \sec^2 y\, dy = 0;\ y(0) = \frac{\pi}{4}$.

Sol. The given equation is

$$\frac{3e^x}{1+e^x}dx + \frac{\sec^2 y}{\tan y}dy = 0$$

Integrating, we have

$$3 \log (1 + e^x) + \log \tan y = \log c$$

$$\Rightarrow \quad \log (1 + e^x)^3 \tan y = \log c$$

$$\Rightarrow \quad (1 + e^x)^3 \tan y = c \qquad \text{...(1)}$$

which is the general solution of the given equation.

Since $y = \frac{\pi}{4}$ when $x = 0$, we have from equation (1),

$$(1 + 1)^3 \times 1 = c \quad \Rightarrow \quad c = 8$$

$\therefore$ The required particular solution is

$$(1 + e^x)^3 \tan y = 8.$$

Example 6. *Solve :* $\frac{dy}{dx} = \cos(x + y) + \sin (x + y)$.

Sol. Let $x + y = v$, then

$$1 + \frac{dy}{dx} = \frac{dv}{dx} \quad \Rightarrow \quad \frac{dy}{dx} = \frac{dv}{dx} - 1$$

$\therefore$ From the given equation

$$\frac{dv}{dx} - 1 = \cos v + \sin v$$

$$\Rightarrow \quad \frac{dv}{1 + \cos v + \sin v} = dx \qquad \text{| Separating the variables}$$

Integration yields

$$\int \frac{dv}{1 + \cos v + \sin v} = \int dx + c$$

$$\Rightarrow \quad \int \frac{dv}{1 + \frac{1 - \tan^2 v/2}{1 + \tan^2 v/2} + \frac{2 \tan v/2}{1 + \tan^2 v/2}} = x + c$$

$$\Rightarrow \quad \int \frac{\sec^2 v/2}{2(1 + \tan v/2)} dv = x + c$$

$$\Rightarrow \quad \log (1 + \tan v/2) = x + c$$

$$\Rightarrow \quad \log \left\{1 + \tan\left(\frac{x + y}{2}\right)\right\} = x + c$$

where c is an arbitrary constant of integration.

TEST YOUR KNOWLEDGE

Solve the following differential equations :

1. $y\,dx - x\,dy = 0$

2. $\dfrac{dy}{dx} = e^{2x+3y}$

3. $x\cos^2 y\,dx = y\cos^2 x\,dy$

4. $(1 - x)\,dy + (1 - y)\,dx = 0$

5. $(1 + x)y\,dx + (1 - y)x\,dy = 0$

6. $(1 - x^2)(1 - y)\,dx = xy(1 + y)\,dy$

7. $(e^x + 1)y\,dy = (y + 1)e^x\,dx$

8. $xy\dfrac{dy}{dx} = 1 + x + y + xy$

9. $(x + y)(dx - dy) = dx + dy$

10. $\sqrt{a + x}\dfrac{dy}{dx} + x = 0$

11. $y\sqrt{1 - x^2}\,dy + x\sqrt{1 - y^2}\,dx = 0$

12. $(e^y + 1)\cos x\,dx + e^y\sin x\,dy = 0$

13. $(xy^2 + x)\,dx + (yx^2 + y)\,dy = 0$

14. $e^y(1 + x^2)\dfrac{dy}{dx} - 2x(1 + e^y) = 0$

15. $\dfrac{y}{x}\dfrac{dy}{dx} = \sqrt{1 + x^2 + y^2 + x^2y^2}$

16. $x\dfrac{dy}{dx} + \cot y = 0$ if $y = \dfrac{\pi}{4}$ when $x = \sqrt{2}$

17. $a(x\,dy + y\,dx) = xy\,dy$

18. $y\,dx + (1 + x^2)\tan^{-1}x\,dy = 0$

19. $(y^2 - yx^2)\,dy + (y^2 + xy^2)\,dx = 0$

20. $e^{2x-3y}\,dx + e^{2y-3x}\,dy = 0$

21. $dr = e(r\sin\theta\,d\theta - \cos\theta\,dr)$

22. $(1 + x^3)\,dy - x^2y\,dx = 0$ if $y = 2$ when $x = 1$

23. $\dfrac{dy}{dx} = (4x + y + 1)^2$

24. $(x + y)^2\dfrac{dy}{dx} = a^2$

25. $\sin(x + y)\,dy = dx$

26. $\cos^{-1}\left(\dfrac{dy}{dx}\right) = x + y$

27. $\tan y\dfrac{dy}{dx} = \sin(x + y) + \sin(x - y)$

28. $\dfrac{dy}{dx} - x\tan(y - x) = 1$

29. (*i*) $e^{(dy/dx)} = x + 1$; $y(0) = 5$ (*ii*) $\dfrac{dy}{dx} = \cot^2(x + y)$

30. $\dfrac{(x + y - a)}{(x + y - b)}\dfrac{dy}{dx} = \dfrac{x + y + a}{x + y + b}$.

Answers

1. $x = cy$

2. $3e^{2x} + 2e^{-3y} = c$

3. $y\tan y + \log\cos y = x\tan x + \log\cos x + c$

4. $(1 - x)(1 - y) = c$

5. $xy = c\,e^{y-x}$

6. $\log\{x(1 - y)^2\} = c + \dfrac{1}{2}x^2 - \dfrac{1}{2}y^2 - 2y$

7. $(1 + y)(1 + e^x) = ce^y$

8. $y = x + \log\{x(1 + y)\} + c$

9. $x + y = ce^{x-y}$

10. $y + \dfrac{2}{3}(x - 2a)\sqrt{a + x} = c$

11. $\sqrt{1 - x^2} + \sqrt{1 - y^2} = c$

12. $(e^y + 1)\sin x = c$

13. $(1 + x^2)(1 + y^2) = c$

14. $1 + e^y = c(1 + x^2)$

15. $\sqrt{1 + y^2} = \dfrac{2}{3}(1 + x^2)^{3/2} + c$

16. $x\sec y = 2$

17. $y = a\log(xy) + c$

18. $y\tan^{-1}x = c$

19. $\log\left(\dfrac{x}{y}\right) = c + \dfrac{1}{y} + \dfrac{1}{x}$

20. $e^{5x} + e^{5y} = c$

21. $r(1 + e\cos\theta) = c$

22. $y^3 = 4(x^3 + 1)$ **23.** $4x + y + 1 = 2\tan(2x + c)$ **24.** $x + y = a\tan\left(\frac{y-c}{a}\right)$

25. $\tan(x + y) - \sec(x + y) = y + c$ **26.** $x + c = \tan\left(\frac{x+y}{2}\right)$ **27.** $2\cos x + \sec y = c$

28. $\log\sin(y - x) = \frac{x^2}{2} + c$ **29.** (*i*) $y = (x + 1)\log(x + 1) - x$ (*ii*) $2y - 2x - \sin 2(x + y) = c_1$

30. $\frac{y-x}{2} + \frac{b-a}{4}\log[(x + y)^2 - ab] = c.$

1.10. A TEST FOR HOMOGENEITY OF A FUNCTION OF *x* AND *y*

Let $f(x, y)$ be any function of x and y. Then $f(x, y)$ is said to be a homogeneous function of x and y of degree n, if

$$f(tx, ty) = t^n f(x, y)$$

1.11. HOMOGENEOUS DIFFERENTIAL EQUATIONS

A differential equation of the form

$$\frac{dy}{dx} = \frac{f_1(x, y)}{f_2(x, y)} \quad \text{...(1)}$$

where f_1 and f_2 are homogeneous functions of x and y of the same degree, is called a **homogeneous differential equation.**

For example : $\frac{dy}{dx} = \frac{y^3 + 3x^2y}{x^3 + 3xy^2}$

1.11.1. Steps for Solution

Step I. Put $y = vx$ so that $\frac{dy}{dx} = v + x\frac{dv}{dx}$

Step II. Separate the variables and solve the given equation in v and x.

Step III. In the last, put $v = \frac{y}{x}$ and simplify.

ILLUSTRATIVE EXAMPLES

Example 1. *Solve* : $y - x\frac{dy}{dx} = y\frac{dy}{dx} + x.$

Sol. We have $$y - x\frac{dy}{dx} = y\frac{dy}{dx} + x$$

$$\Rightarrow \quad \frac{dy}{dx}(y + x) = y - x \quad \Rightarrow \quad \frac{dy}{dx} = \frac{y-x}{y+x} \quad \text{...(1)}$$

which is a homogeneous differential equation.

Put $y = vx$ ...(2)

so that $$\frac{dy}{dx} = v + x\frac{dv}{dx} \quad \text{...(3)}$$

Then (1) becomes

$$v + x\frac{dv}{dx} = \frac{vx - x}{vx + x} = \frac{v-1}{v+1}$$

$$\Rightarrow \qquad x\frac{dv}{dx} = \frac{v-1}{v+1} - v = \frac{v - 1 - v^2 - v}{v+1} = -\frac{v^2+1}{v+1}$$

Separating the variables, $\frac{v+1}{v^2+1}dv = -\frac{dx}{x}$

$$\Rightarrow \qquad \frac{v}{v^2+1}dv + \frac{1}{v^2+1}dv + \frac{dx}{x} = 0$$

Integration yields

$$\frac{1}{2}\int \frac{2v}{v^2+1}dv + \int \frac{dv}{v^2+1} + \int \frac{dx}{x} = c \qquad | \; c \text{ is an arbitrary constant}$$

$$\Rightarrow \qquad \frac{1}{2}\log(v^2+1) + \tan^{-1} v + \log x = c$$

Putting the value of v, we get

$$\frac{1}{2}\log\left(\frac{y^2}{x^2}+1\right) + \tan^{-1}\left(\frac{y}{x}\right) + \log x = c$$

$$\Rightarrow \qquad \frac{1}{2}\log(y^2+x^2) - \log x + \tan^{-1}\left(\frac{y}{x}\right) + \log x = c$$

$$\Rightarrow \qquad \frac{1}{2}\log(y^2+x^2) + \tan^{-1}\left(\frac{y}{x}\right) = c$$

This gives the complete solution.

Example 2. *Solve :* $x(x-y)\,dy + y^2\,dx = 0.$

Sol. Here, $$\frac{dy}{dx} = -\frac{y^2}{x(x-y)} \qquad ...(1)$$

which is a homogeneous differential equation.

Put $y = vx$ ...(2)

so that $$\frac{dy}{dx} = v + x\frac{dv}{dx} \qquad ...(3)$$

Then (1) becomes

$$v + x\frac{dv}{dx} = -\frac{v^2x^2}{x(x-vx)} = -\frac{v^2}{1-v}$$

$$\Rightarrow \qquad x\frac{dv}{dx} = -\left[\frac{v^2}{1-v} + v\right] = -\left[\frac{v^2+v-v^2}{1-v}\right] = -\frac{v}{1-v}$$

Separating the variables

$$\frac{1-v}{v}dv = -\frac{dx}{x} \quad \Rightarrow \quad \left(\frac{1}{v} - 1\right)dv = -\frac{dx}{x}.$$

Integrating both sides, we get

$$\log v - v = -\log x + \log c$$

where $\log c$ is an arbitrary constant of integration.

$$\Rightarrow \quad \log v + \log x - \log c = v$$

$$\Rightarrow \quad \log\left(\frac{vx}{c}\right) = v$$

$$\Rightarrow \quad vx = c\, e^{v}$$

$$\Rightarrow \quad y = c\, e^{\frac{y}{x}} \qquad \left|\because\; v = \frac{y}{x}\right.$$

Example 3. *Solve :* $x \,.\, \cos\frac{y}{x} \,.\, (ydx + xdy) = y \,.\, \sin\frac{y}{x} \,.\, (xdy - ydx)$.

Sol. We have $\quad x \cos\frac{y}{x} \,.\, (ydx + xdy) = y \,.\, \sin\frac{y}{x} \,.\, (xdy - ydx)$

$$\Rightarrow \quad x \,.\, \cos\frac{y}{x}\left(y + x\frac{dy}{dx}\right) = y \sin\frac{y}{x}\left(x\frac{dy}{dx} - y\right)$$

$$\Rightarrow \quad x\frac{dy}{dx}\left(y\sin\frac{y}{x} - x\cos\frac{y}{x}\right) = y\left(y\sin\frac{y}{x} + x\cos\frac{y}{x}\right)$$

$$\Rightarrow \quad \frac{dy}{dx} = \frac{y\left(y\sin\frac{y}{x} + x\cos\frac{y}{x}\right)}{x\left(y\sin\frac{y}{x} - x\cos\frac{y}{x}\right)} \qquad ...(1)$$

which is a homogeneous differential equation.

Put $y = vx$ $\qquad ...(2)$

so that $\quad \dfrac{dy}{dx} = v + x\dfrac{dv}{dx}$ $\qquad ...(3)$

Then (1) becomes

$$v + x\frac{dv}{dx} = \frac{vx\,(vx\sin v + x\cos v)}{x\,(vx\sin v - x\cos v)} = \frac{v\,(v\sin v + \cos v)}{v\sin v - \cos v}$$

$$\Rightarrow x\frac{dv}{dx} = \frac{v\,(v\sin v + \cos v)}{v\sin v - \cos v} - v = \frac{v^2\sin v + v\cos v - v^2\sin v + v\cos v}{v\sin v - \cos v} = \frac{2v\cos v}{v\sin v - \cos v}$$

Separating the variables, we get $\dfrac{v\sin v - \cos v}{v\cos v}\,dv = 2\dfrac{dx}{x}$

$$\Rightarrow \quad \left(\tan v - \frac{1}{v}\right)dv = 2\frac{dx}{x}$$

Integrating both sides, we get $\quad \log\sec v - \log v = 2\log x + \log c$

where $\log c$ is an arbitrary constant of integration.

$$\Rightarrow \quad \log\left(\frac{\sec v}{v}\right) = \log\,(cx^2) \quad \Rightarrow \quad \frac{\sec v}{v} = cx^2$$

Putting the value of v, we get

$$\sec\left(\frac{y}{x}\right) = (cx^2)\left(\frac{y}{x}\right) = cxy$$

$$\Rightarrow \quad cxy\cos\left(\frac{y}{x}\right) = 1$$

TEST YOUR KNOWLEDGE

Solve the following differential equations :

1. $x + y\dfrac{dy}{dx} = 2y$
2. $x^2\,dy + y(x+y)\,dx = 0$
3. $y^2\,dx + x(y+x)\,dy = 0$
4. $x^2\dfrac{dy}{dx} = \dfrac{y(x+y)}{2}$
5. $\dfrac{dy}{dx} + \dfrac{x^2+3y^2}{3x^2+y^2} = 0$
6. $(x^2+y^2)\,dx - 2xy\,dy = 0$
7. $(x^2-y^2)\,dx + 2xy\,dy = 0$
8. $x(x-y)\dfrac{dy}{dx} = y(x+y)$
9. $x^2y\,dx - (x^3+y^3)\,dy = 0$
10. $(x^3-3xy^2)\,dx = (y^3-3x^2y)\,dy$
11. $(x^2+2xy)\,dy + (2xy+y^2+3x^2)\,dx = 0$
12. $\dfrac{dy}{dx} = \dfrac{y^3+3x^2y}{x^3+3xy^2}$
13. $(x^3+y^3)\,dx - 3xy^2\,dy = 0$
14. $x\,dy - y\,dx = 2\sqrt{y^2-x^2}\,dx$
15. $(x^2+2xy-y^2)\,dx + (y^2+2xy-x^2)\,dy = 0.$
16. $x\,dy - y\,dx = \sqrt{x^2+y^2}\,dx.$

Answers

1. $\log(y-x) = c + \dfrac{x}{y-x}$
2. $x^2y = c^2(y+2x)$
3. $xy^2 = c(2y+x)$
4. $(y-x)^2 = cxy^2$
5. $\dfrac{2xy}{(x+y)^2} + \log(x+y) = c$
6. $y^2 = x(x+c)$
7. $x^2+y^2 = cx$
8. $\dfrac{x}{y} + \log(xy) = c$
9. $y^3 = ce^{(x^3/y^3)}$
10. $y^2 - x^2 = c(x^2+y^2)^2$
11. $x(x^2+y^2+xy) = c$
12. $xy = c^2(x^2-y^2)^2$
13. $2y^3 - x^3 = cx$
14. $y + \sqrt{y^2-x^2} = cx^3$
15. $x^2+y^2 = c(x+y)$
16. $y + \sqrt{x^2+y^2} = cx^2.$

1.12. EQUATIONS REDUCIBLE TO HOMOGENEOUS FORM

Equations of the form

$$\frac{dy}{dx} = \frac{ax+by+c}{Ax+By+C} \qquad \text{...(1)}$$

are known as differential equations reducible to homogeneous form.

While solving such equations, two cases arise.

Case I. When $\dfrac{a}{A} \neq \dfrac{b}{B}$

In this case, equation (1) can be reduced to homogeneous form by introducing two new variables X and Y, related to x and y, by the equations

and $$\left.\begin{aligned} x &= X + h \\ y &= Y + k \end{aligned}\right\} \qquad \text{...(2)}$$

where h and k the constants which are yet to be chosen.

From (2), $dx = d\text{X}$ and $dy = d\text{Y}$

$\therefore$ $$\frac{dy}{dx} = \frac{d\text{Y}}{d\text{X}}$$

Hence equation (1) becomes

$$\frac{d\text{Y}}{d\text{X}} = \frac{a(\text{X}+h)+b(\text{Y}+k)+c}{\text{A}(\text{X}+h)+\text{B}(\text{Y}+k)+\text{C}} = \frac{(a\text{X}+b\text{Y})+(ah+bk+c)}{(\text{AX}+\text{BY})+(\text{A}h+\text{B}k+\text{C})} \quad ...(3)$$

Now choose h and k such that

$$ah + bk + c = 0 \quad ...(4)$$

and $$\text{A}h + \text{B}k + \text{C} = 0 \quad ...(5)$$

Then (3) becomes

$$\frac{d\text{Y}}{d\text{X}} = \frac{a\text{X}+b\text{Y}}{(\text{AX}+\text{BY})} \quad ...(6)$$

which is clearly a homogeneous equation in X and Y.

Solving (4) and (5) for h and k by cross-multiplication method, we get

$\Rightarrow$ $$\frac{h}{b\text{C}-\text{B}c} = \frac{k}{\text{A}c-a\text{C}} = \frac{1}{a\text{B}-\text{A}b}$$

$\Rightarrow$ $$h = \frac{b\text{C}-\text{B}c}{a\text{B}-\text{A}b}$$

and $$k = \frac{\text{A}c-a\text{C}}{a\text{B}-\text{A}b} \quad ...(7)$$

To solve (6), put $\text{Y} = v\text{X}$ so that $\dfrac{d\text{Y}}{d\text{X}} = v + \text{X}\dfrac{dv}{d\text{X}}$

We solve eqn. (6) in v and X. Then put $\dfrac{\text{Y}}{\text{X}}$ for v.

In the last, we shall put $x - h$ and $y - k$ for X and Y respectively (where h and k have the values given by (7)) to get the required general solution of the given differential equation.

Case II. When $\dfrac{a}{\text{A}} = \dfrac{b}{\text{B}}$ *i.e.,* $a\text{B} - \text{A}b = 0$

$\therefore$ h and k both become infinite | From (7)

Hence the method followed in case I fails.

so let $$\frac{a}{\text{A}} = \frac{b}{\text{B}} = \frac{1}{m} \quad \text{| say}$$

$\therefore$ $\text{A} = ma$, $\text{B} = mb$

$\therefore$ The given equation assumes the form

$$\boxed{\frac{dy}{dx} = \frac{ax+by+c}{m(ax+by)+\text{C}}} \quad ...(8)$$

To solve such equations, we put $ax + by = z$ so that $\dfrac{dy}{dx} = \dfrac{1}{b}\left(\dfrac{dz}{dx} - a\right)$

We solve eqn. (8) by separating the variables. In the last, we put $ax + by$ for z.

ILLUSTRATIVE EXAMPLES

Example 1. *Solve :* $\frac{dy}{dx}=\frac{x+2y-3}{2x+y-3}$.

Sol. We have $$\frac{dy}{dx}=\frac{x+2y-3}{2x+y-3} \quad ...(1)$$

Put $x = X + h$ and $y = Y + k$ so that $\frac{dy}{dx}=\frac{dY}{dX}$

Then (1) becomes

$$\frac{dY}{dX}=\frac{X+h+2(Y+k)-3}{2(X+h)+Y+k-3}$$

$$\Rightarrow \quad \frac{dY}{dX}=\frac{X+2Y+(h+2k-3)}{2X+Y+(2h+k-3)} \quad ...(2)$$

Choose h and k such that

$$h + 2k - 3 = 0 \quad ...(3)$$

and $$2h + k - 3 = 0 \quad ...(4)$$

Solving (3) and (4) for h and k, we get

$$\frac{h}{-6+3}=\frac{k}{-6+3}=\frac{1}{1-4} \Rightarrow h = 1, \quad k = 1$$

$$\therefore \quad x = X + 1, y = Y + 1$$

$$\Rightarrow \quad X = x - 1, Y = y - 1$$

Now (2) reduces to $$\frac{dY}{dX}=\frac{X+2Y}{2X+Y} \quad ...(5)$$

This is a homogeneous equation in X and Y.

Put $Y = vX$ so that $\frac{dY}{dX}=v+X\frac{dv}{dX}$

Then (5) becomes

$$v+X\frac{dv}{dX}=\frac{X+2vX}{2X+vX}=\frac{1+2v}{2+v}$$

$$\Rightarrow \quad X\frac{dv}{dX}=\frac{1+2v}{2+v}-v=\frac{1+2v-2v-v^2}{2+v}=\frac{1-v^2}{2+v}$$

Separating the variables, we get

$$\frac{2+v}{1-v^2}dv=\frac{dX}{X}$$

$$\Rightarrow \quad \frac{1}{2}\left(\frac{3}{1-v}+\frac{1}{1+v}\right)dv=\frac{dX}{X} \quad | \text{ Partial Fractions}$$

Integrating, we get

$$\frac{1}{2}[-3\log(1-v)+\log(1+v)]=\log X+\log c$$

where log c is an arbitrary constant of integration.

$$\Rightarrow \quad \log\left\{\frac{1+v}{(1-v)^3}\right\}=2\log(cX)=\log c^2X^2$$

$$\Rightarrow \quad \frac{1+v}{(1-v)^3}=c^2X^2$$

Putting the value of v, we get

$$\frac{1+\frac{Y}{X}}{\left(1-\frac{Y}{X}\right)^3}=c^2X^2 \quad \Rightarrow \quad \frac{X+Y}{(X-Y)^3}=c^2$$

$$\Rightarrow \quad X+Y=c^2(X-Y)^3$$

Putting the values of X and Y, we get

$$(x-1+y-1)=c^2\{(x-1)-(y-1)\}^3$$

$$\Rightarrow \quad x+y-2=c^2(x-y)^3.$$

Example 2. *Solve :* $\left(\frac{4x+6y+5}{3y+2x+4}\right)\frac{dy}{dx}=1.$

Sol. We have

$$\frac{dy}{dx}=\frac{2x+3y+4}{4x+6y+5}=\frac{2x+3y+4}{2(2x+3y)+5} \quad \text{...(1)}$$

Put $\quad 2x+3y=z$

$$\therefore \quad 2+3\frac{dy}{dx}=\frac{dz}{dx} \quad \Rightarrow \quad \frac{dy}{dx}=\frac{1}{3}\left(\frac{dz}{dx}-2\right)$$

Then (1) becomes

$$\frac{1}{3}\left(\frac{dz}{dx}-2\right)=\frac{z+4}{2z+5}$$

$$\Rightarrow \quad \frac{dz}{dx}=\frac{3z+12}{2z+5}+2=\frac{7z+22}{2z+5}$$

Separating the variables, we get

$$\frac{2z+5}{7z+22}dz=dx \quad \Rightarrow \quad \left(\frac{2}{7}-\frac{9}{7}\cdot\frac{1}{7z+22}\right)dz=dx$$

Integrating both sides, we get

$$\frac{2}{7}z-\frac{9}{7}\frac{\log(7z+22)}{7}=x+\frac{c}{49}$$

where $\frac{c}{49}$ is an arbitrary constant of integration.

$$\Rightarrow \quad 14z-9\log(7z+22)=49x+c$$

Putting the value of z, we get

$$14(2x+3y)-9\log\{7(2x+3y)+22]=49x+c$$

$$\Rightarrow \quad 42y-21x-9\log(14x+21y+22)=c$$

TEST YOUR KNOWLEDGE

Solve the following differential equations :

1. $(x - y - 2)\, dx + (x - 2y - 3)\, dy = 0$

2. $\dfrac{dy}{dx} = \dfrac{y - x + 1}{y + x + 5}$

3. $(x - y)\, dy = (x + y + 1)\, dx$

4. $(6x + 2y - 10) \dfrac{dy}{dx} - 2x - 9y + 20 = 0$

5. $(2x + 3y - 5) \dfrac{dy}{dx} + 3x + 2y - 5 = 0$

6. $(x - y - 2)\, dx - (2x - 2y - 3)\, dy = 0$

7. $\dfrac{dy}{dx} = \dfrac{x - y - 3}{2x - 2y + 5}$

8. $\dfrac{dy}{dx} = \dfrac{x + y + 1}{2x + 2y + 3}$

9. $(2x + y + 1)\, dx + (4x + 2y - 1)\, dy = 0$

10. $(2x + 4y + 3) \dfrac{dy}{dx} = 2y + x + 1.$

Answers

1. $\log \xi + C = -\dfrac{1}{2} \log (2v^2 - 1) + \dfrac{1}{2\sqrt{2}} \log \dfrac{\sqrt{2}\, v - 1}{\sqrt{2}\, v + 1}$, where $\xi = x - 1$ and $v = \dfrac{y + 1}{x - 1}$

2. $\tan^{-1} \dfrac{y + 3}{x + 2} - \log \{c \sqrt{(y + 3)^2 + (x + 2)^2}\} = 0$

3. $\tan^{-1} \dfrac{2y + 1}{2x + 1} = \log \{c \sqrt{x^2 + y^2 + x + y + \tfrac{1}{2}}\}$

4. $x + 2y - 5 = c(2x - y)^2$

5. $\dfrac{3}{2}(x^2 + y^2) + 2xy - 5(x + y) = c$

6. $\log (x - y - 1) = x - 2y + c$

7. $x - 2y + \log (x - y + 2) = c$

8. $x + y + \dfrac{4}{3} = c\, e^{3(x - 2y)}$

9. $\log (2x + y - 1) + x + 2y = c$

10. $4x + 8y + 5 = ce^{4(x - 2y)}$.

1.13. LINEAR DIFFERENTIAL EQUATION

A differential equation is said to be linear if the dependent variable and its derivative occur only in the first degree and are not multiplied together.

The general form of a linear differential equation of the first order is $\dfrac{dy}{dx} + \text{P}y = \text{Q}$ ...(1)

where P and Q are functions of x only or constants.

Equation (1) is also known as *Leibnitz's linear equation**.

To solve it, we multiply both sides by $e^{\int \text{P}dx}$ and get

$$\frac{dy}{dx} e^{\int \text{P}dx} + y(e^{\int \text{P}dx}\, \text{P}) = \text{Q}e^{\int \text{P}dx}$$

*Gottfried wilhelm Leibnitz (1646–1716) was a German mathematician.

or $$\frac{d}{dx}(ye^{\int Pdx}) = Qe^{\int Pdx}$$

Integrating both sides, we get

$$ye^{\int Pdx} = \int Qe^{\int Pdx}\, dx + c$$

Note 1. In the general form of a linear differential equation, the coefficient of $\frac{dy}{dx}$ is unity.

Note 2. The factor $e^{\int Pdx}$ on multiplying by which the L.H.S. of (1) becomes the differential coefficient of a single function is called the integrating factor (briefly written as I.F.) of (1).

Thus I.F. = $e^{\int Pdx}$ and the solution is

$$\boxed{y\,(\text{I.F.}) = \int Q\,(\text{I.F.})\, dx + c.}$$

Note 3. Sometimes a differential equation takes linear form if we regard x as dependent variable and y as independent variable. The equation can then be put as $\frac{dx}{dy} + Px = Q$, where P, Q are functions of y only or constants. The integrating factor in this case is $e^{\int Pdy}$ and the solution is

$$\boxed{x\,(\text{I.F.}) = \int Q\,(\text{I.F.})\, dy + c.}$$

ILLUSTRATIVE EXAMPLES

Example 1. *Solve :* $\frac{dy}{dx} + \frac{3x^2}{1+x^3}\, y = \frac{\sin^2 x}{1+x^3}$.

Sol. Comparing with $\frac{dy}{dx} + Py = Q$, we get

$$P = \frac{3x^2}{1+x^3}, \quad Q = \frac{\sin^2 x}{1+x^3}$$

$$\text{I.F.} = e^{\int Pdx} = e^{\int \frac{3x^2}{1+x^3}dx} = e^{\log(1+x^3)} = 1+x^3$$

Hence, solution is given by

$$y(1+x^3) = \int \frac{\sin^2 x}{1+x^3}(1+x^3)\, dx + c$$

$$= \frac{1}{2}\int (1-\cos 2x)\, dx + c = \frac{1}{2}\left(x - \frac{\sin 2x}{2}\right) + c$$

$$\Rightarrow \quad y(1+x^3) = \frac{x}{2} - \frac{\sin 2x}{4} + c$$

where c is an arbitrary constant of integration.

Example 2. *Solve :* $\dfrac{dy}{dx}+\dfrac{3y}{x}=\dfrac{1}{x^4}$. [U.P.T.U. (C.O.) 2009]

Sol. Comparing with $\dfrac{dy}{dx}$ + Py = Q, we get P = $\dfrac{3}{x}$ and Q = $\dfrac{1}{x^4}$

$$\text{I.F.} = e^{\int P\,dx} = e^{3\int \frac{1}{x}dx} = e^{3\log x} = x^3$$

∴ The solution is

$$y(\text{I.F.}) = \int Q(\text{I.F.})\,dx + c$$

$$\Rightarrow \quad yx^3 = \int \frac{1}{x^4}(x^3)\,dx + c$$

$$\Rightarrow \quad yx^3 = \log x + c$$

where c is an arbitrary constant of integration.

Example 3. *Solve :* $\cos^2 x\,\dfrac{dy}{dx}+y=\tan x.$

Sol. Dividing throughout by $\cos^2 x$, we get

$$\frac{dy}{dx} + \sec^2 x \,.\, y = \tan x \sec^2 x$$

Comparing with $\dfrac{dy}{dx}$ + Py = Q, we get P = $\sec^2 x$, Q = $\tan x \sec^2 x$

$$\therefore \quad \text{I.F.} = e^{\int P dx} = e^{\int \sec^2 x\,dx} = e^{\tan x}$$

Hence the solution is given by

$$y\,.\,e^{\tan x} = \int e^{\tan x}\,.\,\tan x \sec^2 x\,dx + c \qquad | \; c \text{ is an arbitrary constant}$$

$$= \int e^t\,.\,t\;dt + c = t\,e^t - e^t + c \qquad \left|\begin{array}{l}\text{Put } \tan x = t\\ \therefore\ \sec^2 x\,dx = dt\end{array}\right.$$

$$= \tan x\,.\,e^{\tan x} - e^{\tan x} + c$$

$$\Rightarrow \quad y = \tan x - 1 + c\,e^{-\tan x}.$$

Example 4. *Solve the equation* $x\dfrac{dy}{dx}-\dfrac{1}{2}y = x+1$ *and prove that the only solution for which x and y can attain the value unity is given by* $y = 2x+\sqrt{x}-2$. [G.B.T.U. (C.O.) 2011]

Sol. We have,

$$\frac{dy}{dx}-\frac{1}{2x}y = 1+\frac{1}{x} \qquad \text{...(1)}$$

$$\text{I.F.} = e^{-\int \frac{1}{2x}dx} = e^{-\frac{1}{2}\log x} = \frac{1}{\sqrt{x}}$$

Solution to equation (1) is

$$y\left(\frac{1}{\sqrt{x}}\right) = \int \left(1+\frac{1}{x}\right)\frac{1}{\sqrt{x}}\,dx + c = 2\sqrt{x} - \frac{2}{\sqrt{x}} + c$$

$$\Rightarrow \qquad y = 2x - 2 + c\sqrt{x} \qquad \text{...(2)}$$

Applying the condition $y = 1$ when $x = 1$ in equation (2),

$$1 = 2 - 2 + c$$

$$\Rightarrow \qquad c = 1$$

$\therefore$ From (2), we get

$$y = 2x + \sqrt{x} - 2$$

Example 5. *Solve : $(1 + y^2)\,dx = (\tan^{-1} y - x)\,dy$.* (U.K.T.U. 2012)

Sol. The given equation can be written as

$$\frac{dx}{dy} + \frac{x}{1+y^2} = \frac{\tan^{-1} y}{1+y^2}$$

which is of the form $\frac{dx}{dy} + \text{P}x = \text{Q}$

Here $$\text{P} = \frac{1}{1+y^2}, \text{Q} = \frac{\tan^{-1} y}{1+y^2}$$

$$\text{I.F.} = e^{\int \text{P}dy} = e^{\int \frac{1}{1+y^2}dy} = e^{\tan^{-1} y}$$

$\therefore$ The solution is

$$x\,(\text{I.F.}) = \int \text{Q}\,(\text{I.F.})\,dy + c$$

or $$xe^{\tan^{-1} y} = \int \frac{\tan^{-1} y}{1+y^2} e^{\tan^{-1} y}\,dy + c = \int te^t\,dt + c, \text{ where } t = \tan^{-1} y$$

$$= te^t - e^t + c = (\tan^{-1} y - 1)\,e^{\tan^{-1} y} + c$$

or $$x = \tan^{-1} y - 1 + ce^{-\tan^{-1} y}.$$

Example 6. *Solve the equation :*

$(y \log y)\,dx + (x - \log y)\,dy = 0$. [U.P.T.U. (B. Pharm.) 2009]

Sol. We have

$$(y \log y)\,dx + (x - \log y)\,dy = 0 \qquad \text{...(1)}$$

$$\Rightarrow \qquad \frac{dx}{dy} + \frac{x}{y\log y} = \frac{1}{y} \qquad \text{...(2)}$$

This is a linear differential equation of the form $\frac{dx}{dy} + Px = Q$

Here, $$P = \frac{1}{y \log y}, \quad Q = \frac{1}{y}$$

$$\text{I.F.} = e^{\int P dy} = e^{\int \frac{1}{y \log y} dy} = e^{\log (\log y)} = \log y$$

Solution to equation (2) is

$$x \cdot \log y = \int \frac{1}{y} \cdot \log y \, dy + c$$

$$\Rightarrow \qquad x \log y = \frac{1}{2} (\log y)^2 + c$$

where c is an arbitrary constant of integration.

TEST YOUR KNOWLEDGE

Solve the following differential equations :

1. $\frac{dy}{dx} + \frac{y}{x} = x^3 - 3$
2. $x \log x \frac{dy}{dx} + y = 2 \log x$
3. $(x + 1) \frac{dy}{dx} - y = e^x (x + 1)^2$
4. $(x^2 + 1) \frac{dy}{dx} + 2xy = x^2$
5. $x \frac{dy}{dx} + y = x^2 + 3x + 2$
6. $(1 + x^3) \frac{dy}{dx} + 6x^2 y = 1 + x^2$
7. $\frac{dy}{dx} + y \cot x = \cos x$
8. $(1 + x^2) \frac{dy}{dx} + y = e^{\tan^{-1} x}$
9. (*i*) $\frac{dy}{dx} + y \cot x = 4x \operatorname{cosec} x$, if $y = 0$ when $x = \frac{\pi}{2}$

   (*ii*) $\frac{dy}{dx} + y \cot x = 5e^{\cos x}$, if $y = -4$ when $x = \frac{\pi}{2}$

   (*iii*) $\frac{dy}{dx} - y \tan x = 3e^{-\sin x}$, if $y = 4$ when $x = 0$
10. $x (1 - x^2) \frac{dy}{dx} + (2x^2 - 1) y = x^3$
11. $x (x - 1) \frac{dy}{dx} - (x - 2) y = x^3 (2x - 1)$
12. $(1 - x^2) \frac{dy}{dx} + 2xy = x\sqrt{1 - x^2}$
13. $x \frac{dy}{dx} + y = e^x - xy$
14. $(1 + y^2) + (x - e^{-\tan^{-1} y}) \frac{dy}{dx} = 0$
15. $e^{-y} \sec^2 y \, dy = dx + x \, dy$
16. $(x + 2y^3) \frac{dy}{dx} = y$
17. $ye^y \, dx = (y^2 + 2xe^y) \, dy$
18. $\frac{dy}{dx} = \frac{y}{2y \log y + y - x}$
19. $x^2 \frac{dy}{dx} = 3x^2 - 2xy + 1$
20. $\sqrt{1 - y^2} \, dx = (\sin^{-1} y - x) \, dy$
21. $\frac{dy}{dx} = mx + ny + q$
22. $\frac{dy}{dx} + \frac{2}{x} y = \sin x$

23. $\dfrac{dy}{dx}+\dfrac{2x}{1+x^2}y=\dfrac{1}{(x^2+1)^2}$; if $y = 0$ when $x = 1$

24. $\dfrac{dy}{dx}+y\tan x-\sec x=0$

25. $\sec x\dfrac{dy}{dx}=y+\sin x$

26. $\dfrac{dy}{dx}=y\tan x-2\sin x$

27. $\sin 2x\dfrac{dy}{dx}=y+\tan x$

28. $(x+a)\dfrac{dy}{dx}-3y=(x+a)^5$

29. $(1+y+x^2y)\,dx+(x+x^3)\,dy=0$

30. (*i*) $(x+y+1)\dfrac{dy}{dx}=1$ (*ii*) $\cos x\,dy=(\sin x-y)\,dx.$

Answers

1. $10xy=2x^5-15x^2+c$

2. $y\log x=(\log x)^2+c$

3. $y=(x+1)(e^x+c)$

4. $y(x^2+1)=\dfrac{x^3}{3}+c$

5. $xy=\dfrac{1}{3}x^3+\dfrac{3}{2}x^2+2x+c$

6. $y(1+x^3)^2=y+\dfrac{x^3}{3}+\dfrac{x^4}{4}+\dfrac{x^6}{6}+c$

7. $y\sin x=\dfrac{1}{2}\sin^2 x+c$

8. $2y\,e^{\tan^{-1}x}=e^{2\tan^{-1}x}+c$

9. (*i*) $y\sin x=2x^2-\dfrac{\pi^2}{2}$ (*ii*) $y\sin x=5e^{\cos x}-9$ (*iii*) $y\cos x=7-3e^{-\sin x}$

10. $y=x+cx\sqrt{1-x^2}$

11. $y(x-1)=x^2(x^2-x+c)$

12. $y=\sqrt{1-x^2}+c(1-x^2)$

13. $xy=\frac{1}{2}e^x+ce^{-x}$

14. $x=e^{-\tan^{-1}y}(\tan^{-1}y+c)$

15. $xe^y=\tan y+c$

16. $x=y^3+cy$

17. $x=y^2(c-e^{-y})$

18. $x=\dfrac{c}{y}+y\log y$

19. $y=x+x^{-1}+cx^{-2}$

20. $x=\sin^{-1}y-1+ce^{-\sin^{-1}y}$

21. $y=ce^{nx}-\dfrac{m(nx+1)}{n^2}-\dfrac{q}{n}$

22. $yx^2=c+(2-x^2)\cos x+2x\sin x$

23. $y(1+x^2)=\tan^{-1}x-\dfrac{\pi}{4}$

24. $y=\sin x+c\cos x$

25. $y=ce^{\sin x}-(1+\sin x)$

26. $y=\cos x+c\sec x$

27. $y=\tan x+c\sqrt{\tan x}$

28. $y=c(x+a)^3+\frac{1}{2}(x+a)^5$

29. $xy=c-\tan^{-1}x$

30. (*i*) $x=ce^y-y-2$ (*ii*) $y(\sec x+\tan x)=\sec x+\tan x-x+c.$

1.14. EQUATIONS REDUCIBLE TO LINEAR FORM (BERNOULLI'S EQUATION)

(*i*) An equation of the form $\dfrac{dy}{dx}+Py=Qy^n$ ...(1)

where P and Q are functions of x only or constants is known as *Bernoulli's* equation. Though not linear, it can be made linear.

Dividing both sides of (1) by y^n, we have $y^{-n}\dfrac{dy}{dx}+Py^{1-n}=Q$ ...(2)

Putting $\quad y^{1-n} = z$ so that $(1-n)y^{-n}\dfrac{dy}{dx} = \dfrac{dz}{dx}$

or $\quad y^{-n}\dfrac{dy}{dx} = \dfrac{1}{1-n}\dfrac{dz}{dx}$

Equation (2) becomes $\dfrac{1}{1-n}\dfrac{dz}{dx} + \text{P}z = \text{Q}$ or $\dfrac{dz}{dx} + (1-n)\,\text{P}z = (1-n)\text{Q}$

which is a linear differential equation with z as the dependent variable.

(*ii*) General equation reducible to linear form is $f'(y)\dfrac{dy}{dx} + \text{P}f(y) = \text{Q}$ ...(1)

where P and Q are functions of x only or constants.

Putting $\quad f(y) = z$ so that $f'(y)\dfrac{dy}{dx} = \dfrac{dz}{dx}$

Equation (1) becomes $\dfrac{dz}{dx} + \text{P}z = \text{Q}$ which is linear.

ILLUSTRATIVE EXAMPLES

Example 1. *Solve :* $x\dfrac{dy}{dx} + y = x^3 y^6$.

Sol. We have $\quad x\dfrac{dy}{dx} + y = x^3 y^6$ ...(1)

Divide throughout by x, we get

$$\frac{dy}{dx} + \frac{y}{x} = x^2 y^6 \quad \text{...(2)}$$

Divide throughout by y^6, we get

$$\frac{1}{y^6}\frac{dy}{dx} + \frac{1}{xy^5} = x^2 \quad \text{...(3)}$$

Put $\quad \dfrac{1}{y^5} = v$ so that $\dfrac{1}{y^6}\dfrac{dy}{dx} = -\dfrac{1}{5}\dfrac{dv}{dx}$

then (3) reduces to $\quad -\dfrac{1}{5}\dfrac{dv}{dx} + \dfrac{v}{x} = x^2$

$\Rightarrow \quad \dfrac{dv}{dx} - \dfrac{5v}{x} = -5x^2$ which is linear in v and x.

Here, $\quad \text{P} = -5/x, \quad \text{Q} = -5x^2$

$$\text{I.F.} = e^{-5\int \frac{1}{x}dx} = e^{-5\log x} = \frac{1}{x^5}$$

Solution is $$v \cdot \frac{1}{x^5} = -5\int x^2 \cdot \frac{1}{x^5}\, dx + c$$

$$\Rightarrow \quad \frac{v}{x^5} = \frac{5}{2x^2} + c \qquad (c \text{ is arbitrary constant})$$

$$\Rightarrow \quad \frac{1}{y^5 x^5} = \frac{5}{2x^2} + c \qquad (v = y^{-5})$$

Example 2. *Solve :* $\dfrac{dy}{dx} + x \sin 2y = x^3 \cos^2 y.$

Sol. Dividing by $\cos^2 y$, we have $\sec^2 y \dfrac{dy}{dx} + x \dfrac{2 \sin y \cos y}{\cos^2 y} = x^3$

or $$\sec^2 y \frac{dy}{dx} + 2x \tan y = x^3 \qquad \ldots(1)$$

Putting $\tan y = z$ so that $\sec^2 y \dfrac{dy}{dx} = \dfrac{dz}{dx}$

Equation (1) becomes $\dfrac{dz}{dx} + 2xz = x^3$ which is linear in z and x.

$$\text{I.F.} = e^{\int 2x\, dx} = e^{x^2}$$

∴ The solution is

$$z \cdot e^{x^2} = \int x^3 \cdot e^{x^2}\, dx + c = \int x^2\, e^{x^2} \cdot x\, dx + c$$

$$= \frac{1}{2}\int t\, e^t\, dt + c, \quad \text{where } t = x^2$$

$$= \frac{1}{2}(t-1)\, e^t + c = \frac{1}{2}(x^2 - 1)\, e^{x^2} + c$$

or $$z = \frac{1}{2}(x^2 - 1) + c\, e^{-x^2}$$

or $$\tan y = \frac{1}{2}(x^2 - 1) + c\, e^{-x^2} \qquad (\because \ z = \tan y)$$

where c is an arbitrary constant of integration.

Example 3. *Solve :* $\dfrac{dy}{dx} + xy = y^2 e^{x^2/2} \sin x.$

Sol. Dividing throughout by y^2, we get

$$\frac{1}{y^2}\frac{dy}{dx} + \frac{x}{y} = e^{x^2/2} \sin x \qquad \ldots(1)$$

Put $\dfrac{1}{y} = v$ so that $\dfrac{1}{y^2}\dfrac{dy}{dx} = -\dfrac{dv}{dx}$

∴ From (1), $$-\frac{dv}{dx} + vx = e^{x^2/2} \sin x$$

$$\Rightarrow \quad \frac{dv}{dx} - vx = -e^{x^2/2} \sin x \qquad \ldots(2)$$

which is a linear equation in v and x.

Here $$P = -x, \quad Q = -e^{x^2/2} \sin x$$

$$\text{I.F.} = e^{\int P\, dx} = e^{-\int x\, dx} = e^{-x^2/2}$$

Solution to (2) is $ve^{-x^2/2} = \int (-e^{x^2/2} \sin x) e^{-x^2/2} dx + c = \cos x + c$

$\Rightarrow \quad \frac{1}{y} e^{-x^2/2} = \cos x + c \qquad \left(\because \; v = \frac{1}{y}\right)$

$\Rightarrow \quad e^{-x^2/2} = y(\cos x + c)$ | c is an arbitrary constant

Example 4. *Solve :* $6y^2 \, dx - x(2x^3 + y) \, dy = 0$.

Sol. We have $\frac{dx}{dy} = \frac{2x^4}{6y^2} + \frac{xy}{6y^2} \Rightarrow \frac{dx}{dy} - \frac{x}{6y} = \frac{x^4}{3y^2}$ ...(1)

$\Rightarrow \quad \frac{1}{x^4}\frac{dx}{dy} - \frac{1}{6x^3 y} = \frac{1}{3y^2}$ ...(2) | Dividing by x^4

Put $\frac{1}{x^3} = v \Rightarrow \frac{1}{x^4}\frac{dx}{dy} = -\frac{1}{3}\frac{dv}{dy}$

$\therefore$ From (2), $-\frac{1}{3}\frac{dv}{dy} - \frac{v}{6y} = \frac{1}{3y^2} \Rightarrow \frac{dv}{dy} + \frac{v}{2y} = -\frac{1}{y^2}$

which is linear in v and y.

Here, $P = \frac{1}{2y}, \quad Q = -\frac{1}{y^2}$

$$\text{I.F.} = e^{\int P dy} = e^{\int \frac{1}{2y} dy} = e^{\frac{1}{2}\log y} = \sqrt{y}$$

Hence the solution is given by

$$vy^{1/2} = -\int \frac{1}{y^{3/2}} dy + c = \frac{2}{\sqrt{y}} + c$$

$\Rightarrow \quad \frac{1}{x^3}\sqrt{y} = \frac{2}{\sqrt{y}} + c \qquad \left(\because \; v = \frac{1}{x^3}\right)$

where c is an arbitrary constant of integration.

TEST YOUR KNOWLEDGE

Solve the following differential equations :

1. $(x+1)\frac{dy}{dx} + 1 = 2e^{-y}$

2. $2\frac{dy}{dx} = \frac{y}{x} + \frac{y^2}{x^2}$

3. $\frac{dy}{dx} - x^2 y = y^2 e^{-\frac{1}{2}x^3}$

4. (*i*) $(x^3y^2 + xy)\, dx = dy$ (*ii*) $xy(1 + xy^2)\, dy = dx$

5. (*i*) $e^y\left(\frac{dy}{dx} + 1\right) = e^x$ (*ii*) $\frac{dy}{dx} + \frac{x}{1-x^2} y = x\sqrt{y}$

6. $\frac{dy}{dx} - \frac{\tan y}{1+x} = (1+x) e^x \sec y$

7. $(xy^2 - e^{\frac{1}{x^3}})\, dx - x^2 y \, dy = 0$

8. $\frac{dy}{dx} + y \tan x = y^3 \cos x$

9. $\frac{dy}{dx} + \frac{y \log y}{x} = \frac{y(\log y)^2}{x^2}$ *(U.K.T.U. 2011)*

10. $y - \cos x \dfrac{dy}{dx} = y^2 (1 - \sin x) \cos x$, given that $y = 2$ when $x = 0$

11. $y (2xy + e^x)\, dx = e^x\, dy$

12. $\tan y \dfrac{dy}{dx} + \tan x = \cos y \cos^2 x$.

Answers

1. $(x + 1)\, e^y = 2x + c$

2. $\dfrac{x}{y} = 1 + c\sqrt{x}$

3. $y(c - x) = e^{\frac{1}{3}x^3}$

4. (*i*) $\dfrac{1}{y} = x^2 - 2 + ce^{-\frac{1}{2}x^2}$ (*ii*) $\dfrac{1}{x} = 2 - y^2 + ce^{-(y^2/2)}$

5. (*i*) $e^{x+y} = \frac{1}{2} e^{2x} + c$ (*ii*) $\sqrt{y} = -\left(\dfrac{1 - x^2}{3}\right) + c\,(1 - x^2)^{1/4}$

6. $\sin y = (1 + x)(e^x + c)$

7. $3y^2 = \frac{1}{2}(x^2 - 1) + ce^{-x^2}$

8. $\cos^2 x = y^2\, (c + 2 \sin x)$

9. $\dfrac{1}{x \log y} = \dfrac{1}{2x^2} + c$

10. $2(\tan x + \sec x) = y(2 \sin x + 1)$

11. $e^x = y\, (c - x^2)$

12. $\sec y = (c + \sin x) \cos x$.

1.15. EXACT DIFFERENTIAL EQUATIONS

A differential equation is said to be exact if it can be obtained from its primitive directly by differentiation without any further operation of elimination or reduction. For example, the equation $xdx + ydy = 0$ is an exact differential equation, as it can be obtained from its primitive

$$x^2 + y^2 = c^2$$

directly by differentiation.

1.16. CONDITION THAT AN EQUATION OF FIRST ORDER AND FIRST DEGREE BE EXACT

The necessary and sufficient condition for a differential equation $\mathrm{M}dx + \mathrm{N}dy = 0$ of first order and first degree where M and N are functions of x and y, to be exact is

$$\frac{\partial \mathrm{M}}{\partial y} = \frac{\partial \mathrm{N}}{\partial x}$$

1.17. SOLUTION OF AN EXACT DIFFERENTIAL EQUATION

Step 1. Integrate M w.r.t. x keeping y constant.

Step 2. Write it as u.

Step 3. Integrate w.r.t. y, only those terms of N which donot contain x.

Step 4. Write it as F(y)

Step 5. Solution is given by

$$\boxed{u + \mathrm{F}(y) = c}$$

where $u = \displaystyle\int_{y \text{ constant}} \mathrm{M}\, dx$

and $\mathrm{F}(y) = \displaystyle\int$ (terms of N not containing x) dy.

ILLUSTRATIVE EXAMPLES

Example 1. *Solve :* $(x^2 - ay)\,dx = (ax - y^2)\,dy.$

Sol. We have $(x^2 - ay)\,dx + (y^2 - ax)\,dy = 0$ ...(1)

Comparing with M dx + N dy = 0, we get

$$M = x^2 - ay, \quad N = y^2 - ax$$

$$\therefore \quad \frac{\partial M}{\partial y} = -a, \quad \frac{\partial N}{\partial x} = -a$$

$$\because \quad \frac{\partial M}{\partial y} = \frac{\partial N}{\partial x}$$

∴ Equation (1) is exact.

Now, $$u = \int_{y\text{ constant}} M\,dx = \int_{y\text{ constant}} (x^2 - ay)\,dx = \frac{x^3}{3} - axy$$

$$F(y) = \int (\text{terms of N not containing } x)\,dy = \int y^2\,dy = \frac{y^3}{3}$$

Hence the solution is

$$u + F(y) = c \qquad | \; c \text{ is an arbitrary constant}$$

$$\Rightarrow \quad \frac{x^3}{3} - axy + \frac{y^3}{3} = c$$

$$\Rightarrow \quad x^3 - 3axy + y^3 = c_1, \quad \text{where } c_1 = 3c.$$

Example 2. *Solve :* $(1 + 4xy + 2y^2)\,dx + (1 + 4\,xy + 2x^2)\,dy = 0.$

Sol. We have $(1 + 4xy + 2y^2)\,dx + (1 + 4xy + 2x^2)\,dy = 0$ ...(1)

Comparing with M dx + Ndy = 0, we get

$$M = 1 + 4xy + 2y^2, \quad N = 1 + 4xy + 2x^2$$

$$\therefore \quad \frac{\partial M}{\partial y} = 4x + 4y, \quad \frac{\partial N}{\partial x} = 4y + 4x$$

$$\because \quad \frac{\partial M}{\partial y} = \frac{\partial N}{\partial x}$$

∴ Equation (1) is exact.

Now, $$u = \int_{y\text{ constant}} M\,dx = \int_{y\text{ constant}} (1 + 4xy + 2y^2)\,dx = x + 2x^2y + 2y^2x$$

$$F(y) = \int (\text{terms of N not containing } x)\,dy = \int (1)\,dy = y$$

Hence the solution is

$$u + F(y) = c \qquad | \; c \text{ is an arbitrary constant}$$

$$\Rightarrow \quad x + 2x^2y + 2y^2\;x + y = c$$

$$\Rightarrow \quad x + y + 2xy\,(x + y) = c$$

$$\Rightarrow \quad (x + y)\,(1 + 2xy) = c.$$

Example 3. *Solve :* $(1 + e^{x/y})\,dx + e^{x/y}\left(1 - \frac{x}{y}\right) dy = 0.$

Sol. We have $(1 + e^{x/y})\,dx + e^{x/y}\left(1 - \frac{x}{y}\right) dy = 0$ ...(1)

Comparing with Mdx + Ndy = 0, we get

$$\text{M} = 1 + e^{x/y},\ \text{N} = e^{x/y}\left(1 - \frac{x}{y}\right)$$

$$\therefore \quad \frac{\partial \text{M}}{\partial y} = e^{x/y} \cdot \left(-\frac{x}{y^2}\right),$$

$$\frac{\partial \text{N}}{\partial x} = e^{x/y}\left(-\frac{1}{y}\right) + \left(1 - \frac{x}{y}\right) \cdot e^{x/y} \cdot \frac{1}{y} = -\frac{x}{y^2}\, e^{x/y}$$

$$\because \quad \frac{\partial \text{M}}{\partial y} = \frac{\partial \text{N}}{\partial x}$$

$\therefore$ Equation (1) is exact.

Now, $u = \int_{y \text{ constant}} \text{M}\, dx = \int_{y \text{ constant}} (1 + e^{x/y})\, dx = x + \frac{e^{x/y}}{(1/y)} = x + y\, e^{x/y}$

Since there is no term in N containing function of y only,
Hence the solution is

$$u = c \qquad | \ c \text{ is an arbitrary constant}$$

$$\Rightarrow \quad x + y\, e^{x/y} = c$$

Example 4. *Solve :*

(*a*) $x\,dx + y\,dy + \frac{x\,dy - y\,dx}{x^2 + y^2} = 0$ (*b*) $x \cos \frac{y}{x}(y\,dx + x\,dy) = y \sin \frac{y}{x}(x\,dy - y\,dx).$

Sol. (*a*) We have $x\,dx + y\,dy + \frac{x\,dy - y\,dx}{x^2 + y^2} = 0$ ...(1)

Eqn. (1) can be rewritten as

$$\frac{1}{2}(2x\,dx + 2y\,dy) + \frac{\left(\frac{x\,dy - y\,dx}{x^2}\right)}{1 + \left(\frac{y}{x}\right)^2} = 0$$

$$\Rightarrow \quad d\left(\frac{x^2 + y^2}{2}\right) + \frac{d\left(\frac{y}{x}\right)}{1 + \left(\frac{y}{x}\right)^2} = 0 \Rightarrow d\left(\frac{x^2 + y^2}{2}\right) + d\left(\tan^{-1}\frac{y}{x}\right) = 0$$

Each term of this equation is an exact differential. Hence integrating each term separately, the required solution is

$$\frac{x^2 + y^2}{2} + \tan^{-1}\left(\frac{y}{x}\right) = c$$

where c is an arbitrary constant of integration.

(*b*) We have $x \cos \frac{y}{x} (y\,dx + x\,dy) = y \sin \frac{y}{x} (x\,dy - y\,dx)$ ...(1)

Eqn. (1) can be rewritten as

$$\frac{x\,dy + y\,dx}{xy} = \tan \frac{y}{x} \left(\frac{x\,dy - y\,dx}{x^2} \right)$$

$$\Rightarrow \qquad d\,(\log xy) = \tan \frac{y}{x}\, d\left(\frac{y}{x}\right) = d\left(\log \sec \frac{y}{x}\right)$$

Integration yields $\log xy = \log \sec\left(\frac{y}{x}\right) - \log c \quad \Rightarrow \quad c\,xy = \sec\left(\frac{y}{x}\right)$

where c is an arbitrary constant of integration.

Example 5. *Solve :* $(y^2 e^{xy^2} + 4x^3)\,dx + (2xy\,e^{xy^2} - 3y^2)\,dy = 0$. (U.K.T.U. 2012)

Sol. Comparing with M dx + N dy = 0, we get

$$M = y^2 e^{xy^2} + 4x^3, \; N = 2xy\,e^{xy^2} - 3y^2$$

$$\therefore \qquad \frac{\partial M}{\partial y} = y^2 e^{xy^2} . 2xy + e^{xy^2} . 2y = 2y\,e^{xy^2} (1 + xy^2)$$

and $$\frac{\partial N}{\partial x} = 2y\,(xe^{xy^2} . y^2 + e^{xy^2}) = 2ye^{xy^2}(1 + xy^2)$$

Since $$\frac{\partial M}{\partial y} = \frac{\partial N}{\partial x}$$

$\therefore$ The given equation is exact.

Now, $$u = \int_{y \text{ constant}} M\,dx = \int_{y \text{ constant}} (y^2 e^{xy^2} + 4x^3)\,dx$$

$$= y^2 . \frac{e^{xy^2}}{y^2} + x^4 = e^{xy^2} + x^4$$

$$F(y) = \int (\text{terms in N not containing } x)\,dy = \int (-3y^2)\,dy = -y^3$$

Hence the solution is

$$u + F(y) = c$$

$\Rightarrow \qquad e^{xy^2} + x^4 - y^3 = c$ where c is an arbitrary constant.

Example 6. *Find the value of* λ *for which the differential equation* $(xy^2 + \lambda\,x^2y)\,dx + (x + y)\,x^2dy = 0$ *is exact. Hence solve.*

Sol. We have,

$$(xy^2 + \lambda\,x^2y)\,dx + (x + y)\,x^2\,dy = 0 \qquad \text{...(1)}$$

Comparing (1) with M dx + N$d\,y$ = 0, we get

$$M = xy^2 + \lambda\,x^2y \quad \text{and} \quad N = (x + y)\,x^2$$

$$\Rightarrow \qquad \frac{\partial M}{\partial y} = 2xy + \lambda\,x^2 \quad \text{and} \quad \frac{\partial N}{\partial x} = 3x^2 + 2xy$$

Condition for eqn. (1) to be exact is

$$\frac{\partial M}{\partial y} = \frac{\partial N}{\partial x}$$

which is satisfied for $\lambda = 3$. when $\lambda = 3$,

$$M = xy^2 + 3x^2y \quad \text{and} \quad N = (x + y)\, x^2$$

Now,
$$u = \int_{y\ \text{constant}} M\, dx = \int_{y\ \text{constant}} (xy^2 + 3x^2y)\, dx = \frac{x^2}{2}y^2 + x^3y$$

Since there is no term in N containing function of y only hence the solution is

$$u = c$$

$$\Rightarrow \quad \frac{x^2}{2}y^2 + x^3y = c, \quad \text{where } c \text{ is an arbitrary constant.}$$

Example 7. *Solve the equation*

$$(2x^2 + 3y^2 - 7)\, x\, dx - (3x^2 + 2y^2 - 8)\, y\, dy = 0.$$

Sol. We have, $(2x^2 + 3y^2 - 7)\, x\, dx - (3x^2 + 2y^2 - 8)\, y\, dy = 0$ ...(1)

Eqn. (1) can be rewritten as

$$\frac{x\, dx}{y\, dy} = \frac{3x^2 + 2y^2 - 8}{2x^2 + 3y^2 - 7}$$

Applying Componendo and Dividendo rule,

$$\frac{x\, dx + y\, dy}{x\, dx - y\, dy} = \frac{5x^2 + 5y^2 - 15}{x^2 - y^2 - 1} \quad \Rightarrow \quad \frac{x\, dx + y\, dy}{x^2 + y^2 - 3} = 5\left(\frac{x\, dx - y\, dy}{x^2 - y^2 - 1}\right)$$

$$\Rightarrow \quad \frac{1}{2}\left(\frac{2x\, dx + 2y\, dy}{x^2 + y^2 - 3}\right) = \frac{5}{2}\left(\frac{2x\, dx - 2y\, dy}{x^2 - y^2 - 1}\right)$$

$$\Rightarrow \quad \frac{1}{2} d\,\{\log (x^2 + y^2 - 3)\} = \frac{5}{2} d\,\{\log (x^2 - y^2 - 1)\}$$

$$\Rightarrow \quad d\,\{\log (x^2 + y^2 - 3)\} = d\{5 \log (x^2 - y^2 - 1)\}$$

Integration yields,

$$\log (x^2 + y^2 - 3) = 5 \log(x^2 - y^2 - 1) + \log c \quad \Rightarrow \quad x^2 + y^2 - 3 = c(x^2 - y^2 - 1)^5$$

where c is an arbitrary constant of integration.

TEST YOUR KNOWLEDGE

Solve the following differential equations :

1. $(x^2 + y^2)\, dx + 2xy\, dy = 0$

2. $(a^2 - 2xy - y^2)\, dx - (x + y)^2\, dy = 0$

3. $(2ax + by)y\, dx + (ax + 2by)x\, dy = 0$

4. $(e^y + 1) \cos x\, dx + e^y \sin x\, dy = 0$

5. $e^y\, dx + (xe^y + y^2)\, dy = 0$

6. $y \sin 2x\, dx - (1 + y^2 + \cos^2 x)\, dy = 0$

7. $x\,(x^2 + 3y^2)\, dx + y\,(y^2 + 3x^2)\, dy = 0$

8. $\dfrac{dy}{dx} + \dfrac{ax + hy + g}{hx + by + f} = 0$

9. $(x + y - 10)\, dx + (x - y - 2)\, dy = 0$

10. $(5x^4 + 3x^2y^2 - 2xy^3)\, dx + (2x^3y - 3x^2y^2 - 5y^4)\, dy = 0$

11. $(2x - y)\, dx = (x - y)\, dy$

12. $(3x^2 + 6xy^2)\, dx + (6x^2y + 4y^3)\, dy = 0$

13. $(y^2 - x^2)\, dx + 2xy\, dy = 0$

14. $(y \sec^2 x + \sec x \tan x)\, dx + (\tan x + 2y)\, dy = 0$

15. $(1 + 3e^{x/y})\, dx + 3e^{x/y}\left(1 - \dfrac{x}{y}\right) dy = 0$

16. $(x^2 + 2y\, e^{2x})\, dy + (2xy + 2y^2 e^{2x})\, dx = 0$

17. $\left\{y\left(1 + \dfrac{1}{x}\right) + \cos y\right\} dx + (x + \log x - x \sin y)\, dy = 0$

18. $(e^y + 2) \sin x\, dx - e^y \cos x\, dy = 0$

19. $(2xy + e^y) + (x^2 + x\, e^y)\, \dfrac{dy}{dx} = 0$

20. $(y^2 - 3x^2)\, y\, dy + x(x^2 - 3y^2)\, dx = 0$; $y(0) = 1$

21. $(x^4 - 2xy^2 + y^4)\, dx - (2x^2y - 4xy^3 + \sin y)\, dy = 0$

22. $(2y^2 + x + x^8)\, dx + (y^8 - y + 4xy)\, dy = 0$

23. $x\, dx + y\, dy = \dfrac{a^2\,(x\, dy - y\, dx)}{x^2 + y^2}$ (*U.K.T.U. 2011*)

24. $\left[(\cos x) \log_e (2y - 8) + \dfrac{3}{x}\right] + \left(\dfrac{\sin x}{y - 4}\right) \dfrac{dy}{dx} = 0$; $y(1) = 9/2$

25. (*i*) $\cosh x\, dy + (y + \cosh x) \sinh x\, dx = 0$

(*ii*) $3x^2y^2 + \cos (xy) - xy \sin (xy) + \dfrac{dy}{dx}\{2x^3y - x^2 \sin (xy)\} = 0$.

Answers

1. $\dfrac{1}{3}\, x^3 + y^2x = c$

2. $a^2x - x^2y - xy^2 - \dfrac{1}{3} y^3 = c$

3. $xy\,(ax + by) = c$

4. $(e^y + 1) \sin x = c$

5. $e^y\, x + \dfrac{1}{3}\, y^3 = c$

6. $-\dfrac{1}{2}\, y \cos 2x - \dfrac{3}{2}\, y - \dfrac{1}{3} y^3 = c$

7. $x^4 + y^4 + 6\, x^2y^2 = c$

8. $ax^2 + 2h\, xy + by^2 + 2gx + 2\, fy + c = 0$

9. $\dfrac{x^2}{2} + xy - 10x - \dfrac{y^2}{2} - 2y = c$

10. $x^5 + x^3y^2 - x^2y^3 - y^5 = c$

11. $x^2 - xy + \dfrac{y^2}{2} = c$

12. $x^3 + 3x^2y^2 + y^4 = c$

13. $y^2x - \dfrac{x^3}{3} = c$

14. $y \tan x + \sec x + y^2 = c$

15. $x + 3y\, e^{x/y} = c$

16. $x^2y + y^2\, e^{2x} = c$

17. $y(x + \log x) + x \log y = c$

18. $(e^y + 2) \cos x = c$

19. $x^2y + x\, e^y = c$

20. $x^4 - 6x^2y^2 + y^4 = 1$

21. $\dfrac{x^5}{5} - x^2y^2 + xy^4 + \cos y = c$

22. $2xy^2 + \dfrac{x^2}{2} + \dfrac{x^9}{9} + \dfrac{y^9}{9} - \dfrac{y^2}{2} = c$

23. $x^2 + y^2 + 2a^2 \tan^{-1} \dfrac{x}{y} = c$

24. $\sin x \log_e (2y - 8) + 3 \log x = 0$

25. (*i*) $y \cosh x + \dfrac{1}{4} \cosh 2x = c$ (*ii*) $x(x^2y^2 + \cos xy) = c$.

1.18. INTEGRATING FACTOR

Some of the equations which are not exact can sometimes be made exact after multiplying them by some suitable function of x or y or x and y. Such a function is called an *integrating factor.*

Thus an integrating factor of a non-exact differential equation is a factor by multiplying which, the resulting equation becomes exact.

e.g., consider equation $x\, dy - y\, dx = 0$ ...(1)

This equation is not exact. But if we multiply it by $\dfrac{1}{xy}$, it becomes $\dfrac{dy}{y} - \dfrac{dx}{x} = 0$ ...(2)

which is an exact differential equation and its solution is $\log y - \log x = \log c$ or $y = cx$

Again if we multiply (1) by $\frac{1}{x^2}$, it becomes

$$\frac{x\,dy - y\,dx}{x^2} = 0 \Rightarrow d\left(\frac{y}{x}\right) = 0$$

which is an exact differential equation and its solution is

$$\frac{y}{x} = c \qquad \text{(on integration)}$$

$$\Rightarrow \qquad y = cx$$

Similarly $\frac{1}{y^2}$ is also an integrating factor of eqn. (1).

1.19. INTEGRATING FACTOR BY INSPECTION

Sometimes an integrating factor can be obtained by inspection. This method is illustrated in the following example.

Example. *Solve :* $(x^3 e^x - my^2)\, dx + mxy\, dy = 0.$

Sol. We have $(x^3 e^x - my^2)\, dx + mxy\, dy = 0$ ...(1)

The integrating factor by inspection is $\frac{1}{x^3}$. So multiplying (1) by $\frac{1}{x^3}$, we get

$$\left(e^x - \frac{my^2}{x^3}\right) dx + \frac{my}{x^2}\, dy = 0$$

$$\Rightarrow \qquad e^x - m\left\{\frac{y^2 - xy\frac{dy}{dx}}{x^3}\right\} = 0 \Rightarrow e^x + \frac{1}{2} m \left\{\frac{-2y^2x + 2x^2y\frac{dy}{dx}}{x^4}\right\} = 0$$

$$\Rightarrow \qquad e^x + \frac{1}{2} m \frac{d}{dx}\left(\frac{y^2}{x^2}\right) = 0$$

Integrating w.r.t. x, we get

$$e^x + \frac{1}{2} m \frac{y^2}{x^2} = c \qquad ...(2)$$

where c is an arbitrary constant of integration. (2) gives the required solution.

TEST YOUR KNOWLEDGE

Solve the following differential equations :

1. $y\, dx - x\, dy + \log x\, dx = 0$
2. $x\, dy - y\, dx = \log y\, dy$
3. $y\,(axy + e^x)\, dx - e^x\, dy = 0$
4. $a\,(x\, dy + 2y\, dx) = xy\, dy$
5. $a\,(2x^2y + e^x)\, dx - (e^x + y^3)\, dy = 0$
6. $y\, dx - x\, dy + (1 + x^2)\, dx + x^2 \sin y\, dy = 0.$

Answers

1. $\frac{y}{x} + \frac{1}{x}(1 + \log x) = c$
2. $x = -\log y - 1 + cy$
3. $ax^2y - cy + 2e^x = 0$
4. $2a \log x + a \log y - y = c$
5. $\frac{e^x}{y} + \frac{2}{3}x^3 - \frac{1}{2}\, y^2 = c$
6. $\frac{y}{x} + \frac{1}{x} - x + \cos y = c.$

1.20. RULES FOR FINDING OUT INTEGRATING FACTORS

1.20.1. Rule 1. When $Mx + Ny \neq 0$ and the equation $Mdx + Ndy = 0$ is homogeneous, then an integrating factor of this differential equation is $\dfrac{1}{Mx+Ny}$.

ILLUSTRATIVE EXAMPLES

Example 1. *Solve :* $x^2y\,dx - (x^3 + y^3)dy = 0.$

Sol. The given equation is $x^2y\,dx - (x^3 + y^3)\,dy = 0$ ...(1)

Comparing it with $Mdx + Ndy = 0,$

we get $M = x^2y, \quad N = -(x^3 + y^3)$

$$\therefore \quad \frac{\partial M}{\partial y} = x^2, \quad \frac{\partial N}{\partial x} = -3x^2$$

$$\because \quad \frac{\partial M}{\partial y} \neq \frac{\partial N}{\partial x}$$

$\therefore$ Equation (1) is not exact.

But (1) is homogeneous in x and y.

Moreover, $Mx + Ny = (x^2y)\,.\,x + \{-(x^3 + y^3)\}\,y = x^3y - x^3y - y^4 = -y^4 \neq 0$

$$\therefore \quad \text{I.F.} = \frac{1}{Mx+Ny} = -\frac{1}{y^4}$$

Multiplying (1) by $-\dfrac{1}{y^4}$, it becomes $-\dfrac{x^2}{y^3}dx + \left(\dfrac{x^3}{y^4} + \dfrac{1}{y}\right)dy = 0$ ...(2)

Comparing with $Mdx + Ndy = 0$, we get

$$M = -\frac{x^2}{y^3}, \quad N = \frac{x^3}{y^4} + \frac{1}{y}$$

$$\therefore \quad \frac{\partial M}{\partial y} = \frac{3x^2}{y^4}, \quad \frac{\partial N}{\partial x} = \frac{3x^2}{y^4}$$

$$\because \quad \frac{\partial M}{\partial y} = \frac{\partial N}{\partial x}$$

$\therefore$ Equation (2) is exact.

Now,
$$u = \int_{y \text{ constant}} M\,dx = \int_{y \text{ constant}} \left(-\frac{x^2}{y^3}\right) dx = -\frac{x^3}{3y^3}$$

$$F(y) = \int (\text{terms in N not containing } x)\,dy = \int \frac{1}{y}dy = \log y$$

Hence the solution is

$$u + F(y) = c \quad \Rightarrow \quad -\frac{x^3}{3y^3} + \log y - c.$$

where c is an arbitrary constant.

Example 2. *Solve the differential equation :*

$$y(y^2 - 2x^2)\,dx + x(2y^2 - x^2)\,dy = 0.$$

Sol. We have, $(y^3 - 2x^2y)\,dx + (2xy^2 - x^3)\,dy = 0$ ...(1)

Comparing it with $Mdx + Ndy = 0$, we get

$$M = y^3 - 2x^2y, \quad N = 2xy^2 - x^3$$

$$\therefore \quad \frac{\partial M}{\partial y} = 3y^2 - 2x^2, \quad \frac{\partial N}{\partial x} = 2y^2 - 3x^2$$

$$\because \quad \frac{\partial M}{\partial y} \neq \frac{\partial N}{\partial x}$$

$\therefore$ Eqn. (1) is not exact.

But eqn. (1) is homogeneous in x and y.

Moreover, $Mx + Ny = x(y^3 - 2x^2y) + y(2xy^2 - x^3) = 3xy\,(y^2 - x^2)$

$$\therefore \quad \text{I.F.} = \frac{1}{Mx + Ny} = \frac{1}{3xy\,(y^2 - x^2)}$$

Multiplying (1) by I.F., we get

$$\frac{y(y^2 - 2x^2)}{3xy(y^2 - x^2)}\,dx + \frac{x(2y^2 - x^2)}{3xy(y^2 - x^2)}\,dy = 0$$

$$\Rightarrow \quad \frac{(y^2 - 2x^2)}{x(y^2 - x^2)}\,dx + \frac{2y^2 - x^2}{y(y^2 - x^2)}\,dy = 0$$

$$\Rightarrow \quad \frac{1}{x}dx - \frac{x}{y^2 - x^2}\,dx + \frac{1}{y}\,dy + \frac{y\,dy}{y^2 - x^2} = 0$$

$$\Rightarrow \quad \frac{1}{x}\,dx + \frac{1}{y}\,dy + \frac{1}{2}\left(\frac{2y\,dy - 2x\,dx}{y^2 - x^2}\right) = 0$$

$$\Rightarrow \quad d(\log x) + d(\log y) + \frac{1}{2}\,d\{\log\,(y^2 - x^2)\} = 0$$

$$\Rightarrow \quad d(\log x) + d(\log y) + d(\log \sqrt{y^2 - x^2}) = d\,(\log c)$$

Integration yields, $\log x + \log y + \log \sqrt{y^2 - x^2} = \log c \;\Rightarrow\; xy\sqrt{y^2 - x^2} = c$

where c is an arbitrary constant of integration.

TEST YOUR KNOWLEDGE

Solve the following differential equations :

1. $(x^2y - 2xy^2)\,dx - (x^3 - 3x^2y)\,dy = 0$

2. $(3xy^2 - y^3)\,dx - (2x^2y - xy^2)\,dy = 0$

3. $(y^3 - 2y\,x^2)\,dx + (2xy^2 - x^3)\,dy = 0$

4. $xy^2dy - (x^3 + y^3)\,dx = 0.$

Answers

1. $\dfrac{x}{y} - 2\log x + 3\log y = c$

2. $3\log x + \dfrac{y}{x} - 2\log y = c$

3. $x^2y^4 - x^4y^2 = c$

4. $\log x - \dfrac{y^3}{3x^3} = c.$

1.20.2. Rule 2. If the equation Mdx + Ndy = 0 is of the form $f_1(xy)\, y dx + f_2(xy)\, x dy = 0$, then $\frac{1}{Mx - Ny}$ is an integrating factor, provided $Mx - Ny \neq 0$.

Example. *Solve :* $(y - xy^2)\, dx - (x + x^2y) dy = 0.$

Sol. The given equation is $(y - xy^2)\, dx - (x + x^2y)\, dy = 0$ ...(1)

Comparing with Mdx + Ndy = 0, we get

$$M = y - xy^2, \qquad N = -(x + x^2y)$$

$$\therefore \quad \frac{\partial M}{\partial y} = 1 - 2xy, \quad \frac{\partial N}{\partial x} = -1 - 2xy$$

$$\because \quad \frac{\partial M}{\partial y} \neq \frac{\partial N}{\partial x}$$

∴ Equation (1) is not exact.

But $M = y - xy^2 = y\,(1 - xy) = y\, f_1(xy)$

and $N = -(x + x^2y) = -x(1 + xy) = x\, f_2(xy)$

Moreover, $Mx - Ny = (y - xy^2)x + (x + x^2y)\, y = 2xy \neq 0$

$$\therefore \quad \text{I.F.} = \frac{1}{Mx - Ny} = \frac{1}{2xy}$$

Multiplying (1) by $\frac{1}{2xy}$, it becomes

$$\frac{y - xy^2}{2xy} dx - \frac{x + x^2y}{2xy} dy = 0$$

$$\Rightarrow \quad \frac{1}{2}\left(\frac{1}{x} - y\right) dx - \frac{1}{2}\left(\frac{1}{y} + x\right) dy = 0 \qquad ...(2)$$

Comparing with Mdx + Ndy = 0, we get

$$M = \frac{1}{2}\left(\frac{1}{x} - y\right), \quad N = -\frac{1}{2}\left(\frac{1}{y} + x\right)$$

$$\therefore \quad \frac{\partial M}{\partial y} = -\frac{1}{2}, \qquad \frac{\partial N}{\partial x} = -\frac{1}{2}$$

$$\because \quad \frac{\partial M}{\partial y} = \frac{\partial N}{\partial x}$$

∴ Equation (2) is exact.

Now, $$u = \int_{y \text{ constant}} M\, dx = \int_{y \text{ constant}} \frac{1}{2}\left(\frac{1}{x} - y\right) dx = \frac{1}{2}(\log x - yx)$$

$$F(y) = \int (\text{terms in N not containing } x)\, dy = \int -\frac{1}{2y} dy = -\frac{1}{2}\log y$$

Hence the solution is

$$u + F(y) = c \qquad | \; c \text{ is an arbitrary constant of integration}$$

$$\Rightarrow \quad \frac{1}{2}(\log x - yx) - \frac{1}{2}\log y = c \;\Rightarrow\; \log x - xy - \log y = 2c$$

$$\Rightarrow \quad \log\left(\frac{x}{y}\right) - xy = A, \text{ where } A = 2c.$$

TEST YOUR KNOWLEDGE

Solve the following differential equations :

1. $(x^2y^2 + xy + 1)y\,dx + (x^2y^2 - xy + 1)\,xdy = 0$
2. $(xy + 2x^2y^2)\,y\,dx + (xy - x^2y^2)\,x\,dy = 0$
3. $(x^4y^4 + x^2y^2 + xy)y\,dx + (x^4y^4 - x^2y^2 + xy)x\,dy = 0$
4. $(1 + xy)\,y\,dx + (1 - xy)x\,dy = 0$
5. $(xy \sin xy + \cos xy)\,y\,dx + (xy \sin xy - \cos xy)\,x\,dy = 0$
6. $(xy^2 + 2x^2y^3)\,dx + (x^2y - x^3y^2)\,dy = 0.$

Answers

1. $xy - \dfrac{1}{xy} + \log \dfrac{x}{y} = c$ 2. $-\dfrac{1}{xy} + 2 \log x - \log y = c$ 3. $\dfrac{x^2y^2}{2} - \dfrac{1}{xy} + \log \dfrac{x}{y} = c$

4. $-\dfrac{1}{xy} + \log \dfrac{x}{y} = c$ 5. $x \sec xy = cy$ 6. $\dfrac{-1}{xy} + 2 \log x - \log y = c$.

1.20.3. Rule 3. If in the equation Mdx + Ndy = 0, $\dfrac{1}{N}\left(\dfrac{\partial M}{\partial y} - \dfrac{\partial N}{\partial x}\right)$ is a function of x alone, say $f(x)$, then $e^{\int f(x)\,dx}$ is an integrating factor of the equation Mdx + Ndy = 0.

1.20.4. Rule 4. If in the equation Mdx + Ndy = 0, $\dfrac{1}{M}\left(\dfrac{\partial N}{\partial x} - \dfrac{\partial M}{\partial y}\right)$ is a function of y alone, say $f(y)$, then $e^{\int f(y)\,dy}$ is an integrating factor of the equation Mdx + Ndy = 0.

ILLUSTRATIVE EXAMPLES

Example 1. *Solve the equation :*

$$(y \log y)\,dx + (x - \log y)\,dy = 0.$$

Sol. The given equation is

$$(y \log y)\,dx + (x - \log y)\,dy = 0 \qquad ...(1)$$

Comparing with M dx + N dy = 0, we get

$$M = y \log y, \quad N = x - \log y$$

$$\therefore \quad \frac{\partial M}{\partial y} = y \cdot \frac{1}{y} + \log y = 1 + \log y \quad \text{and} \quad \frac{\partial N}{\partial x} = 1$$

$$\because \quad \frac{\partial M}{\partial y} \neq \frac{\partial N}{\partial x}$$

$\therefore$ Eqn. (1) is not exact.

$$\text{Now,} \quad \frac{1}{M}\left(\frac{\partial N}{\partial x} - \frac{\partial M}{\partial y}\right) = \frac{1}{y \log y}(1 - 1 - \log y) = -\frac{1}{y} = f(y)$$

$$\therefore \quad \text{I.F.} = e^{\int f(y)\,dy} = e^{-\int \frac{1}{y} dy} = e^{-\log y} = \frac{1}{y}$$

Multiplying eqn. (1) by $\frac{1}{y}$, we get

$$(\log y)\,dx + \left(\frac{x - \log y}{y}\right)dy = 0 \qquad ...(2)$$

Again comparing (2) with M dx + N dy = 0, we get

$$M = \log y,\ N = \frac{x}{y} - \frac{\log y}{y}$$

$$\therefore \qquad \frac{\partial M}{\partial y} = \frac{1}{y} \quad \text{and} \quad \frac{\partial N}{\partial x} = \frac{1}{y}$$

$$\therefore \qquad \frac{\partial M}{\partial y} = \frac{\partial N}{\partial x}$$

Hence eqn. (2) is exact.

Now, $$u = \int_{y\ \text{constant}} M\,dx = \int_{y\ \text{constant}} \log y\,dx = x \log y$$

$$F(y) = \int (\text{terms in N not containing } x)\,dy$$

$$= \int \left(-\frac{\log y}{y}\right)dy = -\frac{1}{2}(\log y)^2$$

Hence the solution is

$$u + F(y) = c \quad \Rightarrow \quad x \log y - \frac{1}{2}(\log y)^2 = c$$

where c is an arbitrary constant.

Example 2. *Solve :* $\left(y + \frac{1}{3}y^3 + \frac{1}{2}x^2\right)dx + \frac{1}{4}(1 + y^2)\,x\,dy = 0.$

Sol. The given equation is $\left(y + \frac{1}{3}y^3 + \frac{1}{2}x^2\right)dx + \frac{1}{4}(1 + y^2)\,x\,dy = 0$ ...(1)

Comparing with Mdx + Ndy = 0, we get

$$M = y + \frac{1}{3}y^3 + \frac{1}{2}x^2, \quad N = \frac{1}{4}(1 + y^2)\,x$$

$$\therefore \qquad \frac{\partial M}{\partial y} = 1 + y^2, \qquad \frac{\partial N}{\partial x} = \frac{1}{4}(1 + y^2).$$

$$\because \qquad \frac{\partial M}{\partial y} \neq \frac{\partial N}{\partial x}$$

$\therefore$ Equation (1) is not exact.

Now, $$\frac{1}{N}\left(\frac{\partial M}{\partial y} - \frac{\partial N}{\partial x}\right) = \frac{(1+y^2) - \frac{1}{4}(1+y^2)}{\frac{1}{4}(1+y^2)x} = \frac{3}{x} = f(x)$$

$$\therefore \qquad \text{I.F.} = e^{\int f(x)\,dx} = e^{\int \frac{3}{x}dx} = e^{3 \log x} = x^3$$

Multiplying (1) by x^3, we get

$$\left(y\,x^3 + \frac{1}{3}y^3x^3 + \frac{1}{2}x^5\right)dx + \frac{1}{4}(1 + y^2)\,x^4\,dy = 0 \qquad ...(2)$$

Comparing with $Mdx + Ndy = 0$, we get

$$M = yx^3 + \frac{1}{3}y^3x^3 + \frac{1}{2}x^5,\ N = \frac{1}{4}(1 + y^2)\,x^4$$

$$\therefore \qquad \frac{\partial M}{\partial y} = x^3 + y^2x^3 = x^3(1 + y^2)$$

$$\frac{\partial N}{\partial x} = \frac{1}{4}\,.\,(1 + y^2)\,.\,4x^3 = x^3(1 + y^2)$$

$$\because \qquad \frac{\partial M}{\partial y} = \frac{\partial N}{\partial x}$$

$\therefore$ Equation (2) is exact.

Now,
$$u = \int_{y\text{ constant}} M\,dx = \int_{y\text{ constant}} \left(yx^3 + \frac{1}{3}y^3x^3 + \frac{1}{2}x^5\right)dx$$

$$= \frac{yx^4}{4} + \frac{y^3x^4}{12} + \frac{x^6}{12}$$

Since there is no term in N containing function of y only, hence the solution is

$$u = c \ \Rightarrow\ \frac{yx^4}{4} + \frac{y^3x^4}{12} + \frac{x^6}{12} = c$$

where c is an arbitrary constant.

Example 3. *Solve :* $(xy^3 + y)\,dx + 2\,(x^2y^2 + x + y^4)dy = 0.$

Sol. The given equation is $(xy^3 + y)\,dx + 2\,(x^2y^2 + x + y^4)\,dx = 0$ ...(1)

Comparing with $M\,dx + N\,dy = 0$, we get

$$M = xy^3 + y, \qquad N = 2\,(x^2y^2 + x + y^4)$$

$$\therefore \qquad \frac{\partial M}{\partial y} = 3xy^2 + 1, \qquad \frac{\partial N}{\partial x} = 2(2xy^2 + 1)$$

$$\because \qquad \frac{\partial M}{\partial y} \neq \frac{\partial N}{\partial x}$$

$\therefore$ Equation (1) is not exact.

Now,
$$\frac{1}{M}\left(\frac{\partial N}{\partial x} - \frac{\partial M}{\partial y}\right) = \frac{2\,.\,(2xy^2 + 1) - (3xy^2 + 1)}{xy^3 + y} = \frac{xy^2 + 1}{y\,(xy^2 + 1)} = \frac{1}{y} = f(y)$$

$$\therefore \qquad \text{I.F.} = e^{\int f(y)\,dy} = e^{\int \frac{1}{y}dy} = e^{\log y} = y$$

Multiplying (1) by y, we get $(xy^4 + y^2)dx + 2(x^2y^3 + xy + y^5)\,dy = 0$ ...(2)

Comparing with $Mdx + Ndy = 0$, we get

$$M = xy^4 + y^2, \quad N = 2\,(x^2y^3 + xy + y^5)$$

$$\therefore \qquad \frac{\partial M}{\partial y} = 4xy^3 + 2y, \qquad \frac{\partial N}{\partial x} = 4xy^3 + 2y$$

$$\because \qquad \frac{\partial M}{\partial y} = \frac{\partial N}{\partial x}$$

$\therefore$ Equation (2) is exact.

Now, $$u = \int_{y\text{ constant}} \mathrm{M}\,dx = \int_{y\text{ constant}} (xy^4 + y^2)\,dx = \frac{x^2y^4}{2} + xy^2$$

$$\mathrm{F}(y) = \int (\text{terms in N not containing } x)\,dy = \int 2y^5\,dy = \frac{y^6}{3}$$

Hence the solution is

$$u + \mathrm{F}(y) = c \quad \Rightarrow \quad \frac{x^2y^4}{2} + xy^2 + \frac{y^6}{3} = c$$

where c is an arbitrary constant.

Example 4. *Solve the differential equation :*

$$2y\,dx + x\,(2\log x - y)\,dy = 0.$$

Sol. The given equation is

$$2y\,dx + x\,(2\log x - y)\,dy = 0 \quad \text{...(1)}$$

Here, $$\mathrm{M} = 2y,\ \mathrm{N} = x(2\log x - y)$$

$$\frac{\partial \mathrm{M}}{\partial y} = 2,\ \frac{\partial \mathrm{N}}{\partial x} = 2\left(x \cdot \frac{1}{x} + \log x\right) - y = 2(1 + \log x) - y$$

$\because$ $$\frac{\partial \mathrm{M}}{\partial y} \neq \frac{\partial \mathrm{N}}{\partial x}$$

$\therefore$ Eqn. (1) is not exact.

Now, $$\frac{1}{\mathrm{N}}\left(\frac{\partial \mathrm{M}}{\partial y} - \frac{\partial \mathrm{N}}{\partial x}\right) = \frac{1}{x\,(2\log x - y)}(2 - 2 - 2\log x + y) = -\frac{1}{x} = f(x)$$

$\therefore$ $$\text{I.F.} = e^{\int f(x)\,dx} = e^{-\int \frac{dx}{x}} = e^{-\log x} = \frac{1}{x}$$

Multiplying (1) by $\frac{1}{x}$, we get

$$\frac{2y}{x}\,dx + (2\log x - y)\,dy = 0 \quad \text{...(2)}$$

Again, $$\mathrm{M} = \frac{2y}{x}, \qquad \mathrm{N} = 2\log x - y$$

$$\frac{\partial \mathrm{M}}{\partial y} = \frac{2}{x}, \qquad \frac{\partial \mathrm{N}}{\partial x} = \frac{2}{x}$$

$\because$ $$\frac{\partial \mathrm{M}}{\partial y} = \frac{\partial \mathrm{N}}{\partial x}$$

$\therefore$ Eqn. (2) is exact.

Now, $$u = \int_{y\text{ constant}} \mathrm{M}\,dx = \int_{y\text{ constant}} \frac{2y}{x}\,dx = 2y\log x$$

$$\mathrm{F}(y) = \int (\text{terms in N not containing } x)\,dy = \int (-y)\,dy = -\frac{y^2}{2}$$

Hence the solution is

$$u + \mathrm{F}(y) = c \quad \Rightarrow \quad 2y\log x - \frac{y^2}{2} = c$$

where c is an arbitrary constant.

TEST YOUR KNOWLEDGE

Solve the following differential equations :

1. $(x^2 + y^2 + 2x)\,dx + 2y\,dy = 0$
2. $(y^4 + 2y)\,dx + (xy^3 + 2y^4 - 4x)\,dy = 0$
3. $(3x^2y^4 + 2xy)dx + (2x^3y^3 - x^2)\,dy = 0$
4. $(7x^4y + 2xy^2 - x^3)\,dx + (x^4 + xy)\,x\,dy = 0$
5. $(xy^2 - x^2)\,dx + (3x^2y^2 + x^2y - 2x^3 + y^2)\,dy = 0$
6. $(x \sec^2 y - x^2 \cos y)\,dy = (\tan y - 3x^4)\,dx.$

Answers

1. $e^x (x^2 + y^2) = c$
2. $\left(y + \dfrac{2}{y^2}\right) x + y^2 = c$
3. $x^3y^3 + x^2 = cy$
4. $6x^7y + 3x^4y^2 - x^6 = c$
5. $e^{6y} \left\{\dfrac{1}{2}x^2y^2 - \dfrac{1}{3}x^3 + \dfrac{1}{6}y^2 - \dfrac{1}{18}y + \dfrac{1}{108}\right\} = c$
6. $-\dfrac{1}{x}\tan y - x^3 + \sin y = c.$

1.20.5. Rule 5. An integrating factor for an equation of the form $x^ay^b(my\,dx + nx\,dy) + x^r y^s (py\,dx + qx\,dy) = 0$, where a, b, m, n, r, s, p, q are constants, is $\boldsymbol{x^hy^k}$, where h, k can be obtained by applying the condition that after multiplication by x^hy^k, the equation must become exact.

Multiplying by x^hy^k, the given equation becomes

$$(mx^{a+h}\,y^{b+k+1} + px^{r+h}\,y^{s+k+1})dx + (nx^{a+h+1}\,y^{b+k} + qx^{r+h+1}\,y^{s+k})\,dy = 0$$

Since this equation must be exact

$$\therefore \quad \frac{\partial M}{\partial y} \text{ must be equal to } \frac{\partial N}{\partial x}.$$

i.e., $m(b + k + 1)\,x^{a+h}\,y^{b+k} + p(s + k + 1)\,x^{r+h}\,y^{s+k} = n(a + h + 1)\,x^{a+h}\,y^{b+k} + q(r + h + 1)\,x^{r+h}\,y^{s+k}.$

This will be satisfied if

$$m(b + k + 1) = n(a + h + 1)$$

and $\quad p(s + k + 1) = q\,(r + h + 1) \quad$ | Equating coeff. of like powers from both sides

There two equations when solved will give the value of h and k.

Thus the integrating factor will be known.

Example. *Solve :* $\quad (2y\,dx + 3x\,dy) + 2xy\,(3y\,dx + 4x\,dy) = 0.$

Sol. We have, $\quad (2y\,dx + 3x\,dy) + 2xy\,(3y\,dx + 4x\,dy) = 0 \quad$ ...(1)

$\Rightarrow \quad (2y + 6xy^2)\,dx + (3x + 8x^2y)\,dy = 0 \quad$ ...(2)

Comparing (2) with $Mdx + Ndy = 0$, we get

$$M = 2y + 6xy^2,\ N = 3x + 8x^2y$$

$$\frac{\partial M}{\partial y} = 2 + 12xy,\ \frac{\partial N}{\partial x} = 3 + 16xy$$

Since $\quad \dfrac{\partial M}{\partial y} \neq \dfrac{\partial N}{\partial x}$

$\therefore$ Eqn. (2) is not exact.

Eqn. (1) is of the form $\quad x^ay^b\,(my\,dx + nx\,dy) + x^ry^s\,(py\,dx + qx\,dy) = 0$

$\therefore$ x^hy^k is an integrating factor of eqn. (1).

Multiplying (2) by x^hy^k, it becomes

$$(2x^hy^{k+1} + 6x^{h+1}\,y^{k+2})\,dx + (3x^{h+1}\,y^k + 8x^{h+2}\,y^{k+1})\,dy = 0 \quad ...(3)$$

Comparing (3) with $Mdx + Ndy = 0$, we get

$$M = 2x^hy^{k+1} + 6x^{h+1}\,y^{k+2}$$

$$N = 3x^{h+1}y^k + 8x^{h+2}\,y^{k+1}$$

Now (3) must be exact, the condition for which is

$$\frac{\partial M}{\partial y} = \frac{\partial N}{\partial x}$$

$$2(k+1)\,x^h y^k + 6(k+2)\,x^{h+1}y^{k+1} = 3(h+1)\,x^h y^k + 8(h+2)\,x^{h+1}\,y^{k+1}$$

Equating the coefficients of $x^h y^k$ and $x^{h+1}y^{k+1}$ from both sides, we get

$$2(k+1) = 3(h+1) \;\Rightarrow\; 3h - 2k + 1 = 0 \qquad ...(4)$$

and $$6(k+2) = 8(h+2) \;\Rightarrow\; 4h - 3k + 2 = 0 \qquad ...(5)$$

Solving (4) and (5), we get $h = 1$, $k = 2$

Hence xy^2 is an integrating factor.

Multiplying (2) by xy^2, we get

$$(2xy^3 + 6x^2y^4)\,dx + (3x^2y^2 + 8x^3y^3)\,dy = 0 \qquad ...(6)$$

Comparing (6) with $Mdx + Ndy = 0$, we get

$$M = 2xy^3 + 6x^2y^4$$
$$N = 3x^2y^2 + 8x^3y^3$$

$$\therefore \qquad \frac{\partial M}{\partial y} = 6xy^2 + 24x^2y^3, \quad \frac{\partial N}{\partial x} = 6xy^2 + 24x^2y^3$$

$$\because \qquad \frac{\partial M}{\partial y} = \frac{\partial N}{\partial x}$$

$\therefore$ Eqn. (6) is exact.

Now, $$u = \int_{y\ \text{constant}} M\,dx = \int_{y\ \text{constant}} (2xy^3 + 6x^2y^4)\,dx = x^2y^3 + 2x^3y^4$$

Since there is no term in N, containing function of y only, hence the solution is

$$u = c$$

$$\Rightarrow \qquad x^2y^3 + 2x^3y^4 = c$$

where c is an arbitrary constant.

TEST YOUR KNOWLEDGE

Solve :

1. $(y^2 + 2x^2y)\,dx + (2x^3 - xy)\,dy = 0$
2. $(3x + 2y^2)\,y\,dx + 2x\,(2x + 3y^2)\,dy = 0$
3. $(2x^2y - 3y^4)\,dx + (3x^3 + 2xy^3)\,dy = 0$
4. $(2x^2y^2 + y)\,dx - (x^3y - 3x)\,dy = 0$
5. $x(3y\,dx + 2x\,dy) + 8y^4\,(y\,dx + 3x\,dy) = 0.$

Answers

1. $4\,x^{1/2}\,y^{1/2} - \dfrac{2}{3}\,x^{-3/2}\,y^{3/2} = c$
2. $x^2y^4\,(x + y^2) = c$
3. $5x^{-36/13}\,y^{24/13} - 12x^{-10/13}\,y^{-15/13} = c$
4. $\dfrac{7}{5}\,x^{\frac{10}{7}}\,y^{-\frac{5}{7}} - \dfrac{7}{4}\,x^{-\frac{4}{7}}\,y^{-\frac{12}{7}} = c$
5. $x^3y^2 + 4x^2\,y^6 = c.$

1.21. CHANGE OF VARIABLES

Sometimes we come across the differential equations which do not directly come under any of the forms discussed so far. However, by suitable substitutions, some of them assume one of these forms and thus become integrable. This device is known as change of variable (dependent or independent as the case may be). The following examples will illustrate the device.

Note. There is no fixed rule for substitution. It depends upon the individual.

ILLUSTRATIVE EXAMPLES

Example 1. *Solve :* $\dfrac{dy}{dx} = e^{x-y}(e^x - e^y)$.

Sol. Multiplying both sides by e^y, we get

$$e^y \frac{dy}{dx} = e^{2x} - e^x e^y$$

$$\Rightarrow \qquad e^y \frac{dy}{dx} + e^x e^y = e^{2x} \qquad ...(1)$$

Put $e^y = v \quad \Rightarrow \quad e^y \dfrac{dy}{dx} = \dfrac{dv}{dx}$

$\therefore$ From (1), $\dfrac{dv}{dx} + ve^x = e^{2x}$ which is linear in v and x.

Here, $\qquad \mathrm{P} = e^x,\ \mathrm{Q} = e^{2x}$

$$\therefore \qquad \text{I.F.} = e^{\int \mathrm{P}\,dx} = e^{\int e^x\,dx} = e^{e^x}$$

Hence solution to (2) is $\quad ve^{e^x} = \displaystyle\int e^{2x} . e^{e^x}\ dx + c \qquad$ (c is arbitrary constant)

$$= \int t\, e^t\ dt + c \qquad \text{(where } e^x = t)$$

$$= (t - 1)\, e^t + c = (e^x - 1)\, e^{e^x} + c$$

$$\Rightarrow \qquad v = e^x - 1 + c\, e^{-e^x}$$

$$\Rightarrow \qquad e^y = e^x - 1 + ce^{-e^x}. \qquad (\because \quad v = e^y)$$

Example 2. *Solve :*

$$\frac{x\,dx + y\,dy}{x\,dy - y\,dx} = \sqrt{\frac{a^2 - x^2 - y^2}{x^2 + y^2}}.$$

Sol. Put $\qquad x = r\cos\theta,\ y = r\sin\theta$

$\therefore \qquad x^2 + y^2 = r^2$ and $\dfrac{y}{x} = \tan\theta$

Differentiating $\quad x^2 + y^2 = r^2$, we get

$$x\,dx + y\,dy = r\,dr \qquad ...(1)$$

Differentiating $\dfrac{y}{x} = \tan\theta$, we get

$$\frac{x\,dy - y\,dx}{x^2} = \sec^2\theta\, d\theta$$

$$\Rightarrow \qquad x\,dy - y\,dx = r^2\cos^2\theta\, .\, \sec^2\theta\, d\theta = r^2\, d\theta \qquad ...(2)$$

$\therefore$ The given equation becomes,

$$\frac{r\,dr}{r^2\,d\theta} = \sqrt{\frac{a^2 - r^2}{r^2}}$$

$$\Rightarrow \qquad \frac{dr}{\sqrt{a^2 - r^2}} = d\theta$$

Integration yields, $\quad \sin^{-1}\frac{r}{a} = \theta + c \qquad$ (c is arbitrary constant)

$$\Rightarrow \qquad r = a \sin(\theta + c)$$

$$\Rightarrow \qquad \sqrt{x^2 + y^2} = a \sin\left(\tan^{-1}\frac{y}{x} + c\right).$$

Example 3. *If $(x + y)^n$ is an integrating factor of*

$$(4x^2 + 2xy + 6y)dx + (2x^2 + 9y + 3x)dy = 0.$$

Find n and then solve the equation. (M.T.U., 2012)

Sol. By definition of integrating factor, if we multiply the given equation by $(x + y)^n$, it becomes exact.

Therefore, Let

$$M = (4x^2 + 2xy + 6y)(x + y)^n$$
$$N = (2x^2 + 9y + 3x)(x + y)^n$$

Now, The condition for the given equation to be exact is

$$\frac{\partial M}{\partial y} = \frac{\partial N}{\partial x}$$

$$\therefore \quad (4x^2 + 2xy + 6y)n(x + y)^{n-1} + (x + y)^n (2x + 6)$$
$$= (2x^2 + 9y + 3x).n(x + y)^{n-1} + (x + y)^n.(4x + 3)$$

$$\Rightarrow \quad n(4x^2 + 2xy + 6y) + (2x + 6)(x + y)$$
$$= n(2x^2 + 9y + 3x) + (4x + 3)(x + y)$$

$$\Rightarrow \quad (4n + 2)x^2 + (2n + 2)xy + (6n + 6)y + 6x$$
$$= (2n + 4)x^2 + 4xy + (9n + 3)y + (3n + 3)x$$

Comparing the coefficients,

$$\left.\begin{aligned} 4n + 2 &= 2n + 4 \\ 2n + 2 &= 4 \\ 6n + 6 &= 9n + 3 \\ 6 &= 3n + 3 \end{aligned}\right\} \Rightarrow \quad n = 1$$

Hence,

$$M = (4x^2 + 2xy + 6y)(x + y) \quad \text{and} \quad N = (2x^2 + 9y + 3x)(x + y)$$

Now,
$$u = \int_{y \text{ constant}} M\,dx = \int_{y \text{ constant}} (4x^3 + 6x^2y + 2xy^2 + 6xy + 6y^2)\,dx$$

$$= x^4 + 2x^3y + x^2y^2 + 3yx^2 + 6y^2x$$

$$F(y) = \int (\text{terms of N not containing } x)\,dy$$

$$= \int 9y^2\,dy = 3y^3$$

Hence, the solution is

$$u + F(y) = c$$

$$\Rightarrow \quad x^4 + 2x^3y + x^2y^2 + 3yx^2 + 6xy^2 + 3y^3 = c$$

where c is an arbitrary constant.

TEST YOUR KNOWLEDGE

Solve the following differential equations :

1. $\dfrac{dy}{dx} + 2(x+y)^2 = 1$
2. $(x - y^2)\,dx + 2xy\,dy = 0$
3. $(x^3 + y^2 + 2)\,dx + 2y\,dy = 0$
4. $x\dfrac{dy}{dx} + y\log y = xye^x$
5. $\sin y\,\dfrac{dy}{dx} = \cos y\,(1 - x\cos y)$
6. $\dfrac{dy}{dx} = \dfrac{e^y}{x^2} - \dfrac{1}{x}$
7. $x\,dx + y\,dy = m(x\,dy - y\,dx)$.

Answers

1. $1 + x + y = ce^{4x}(1 - x - y)$
2. $y^2 + x\log cx = 0$
3. $y^2 = 3x^2 - 6x - x^3 + ce^{-x} + 4$
4. $x\log y = e^x(x - 1) + c$
5. $\sec y = x + 1 + ce^x$
6. $cx^2 + 2x\,e^{-y} = 1$
7. $m\tan^{-1}\dfrac{y}{x} - \dfrac{1}{2}\log(x^2 + y^2) = c$.

1.22. LINEAR DIFFERENTIAL EQUATIONS WITH CONSTANT COEFFICIENTS

An equation of the form

$$a_0\frac{d^n y}{dx^n} + a_1\frac{d^{n-1}y}{dx^{n-1}} + a_2\frac{d^{n-2}y}{dx^{n-2}} + \ldots\ldots + a_n y = Q \qquad \ldots(1)$$

where $a_0, a_1, a_2, \ldots\ldots, a_n$ are all constants and Q is a function of x alone is called a linear differential equation of nth order with constant coefficients.

1.23. THE OPERATOR D

The part $\dfrac{d}{dx}$ of the symbol $\dfrac{dy}{dx}$ may be regarded as an operator such that when it operates on y, the result is the derivative of y. Similarly, $\dfrac{d^2}{dx^2}, \dfrac{d^3}{dx^3}, \ldots\ldots, \dfrac{d^n}{dx^n}$ may be regarded as operators.

For brevity, we write $\dfrac{d}{dx} \equiv D, \dfrac{d^2}{dx^2} \equiv D^2, \ldots\ldots, \dfrac{d^n}{dx^n} \equiv D^n$

Thus, the symbol D is a **differential operator** or simply an **operator.**

Written in symbolic form, equation (1) becomes

$$(a_0D^n + a_1D^{n-1} + a_2D^{n-2} + \ldots\ldots + a_{n-1}D + a_n)y = Q$$

or

$$\boxed{f(D)y = Q}$$

The operator D can be treated as an algebraic quantity. Thus,

$$D(u + v) = Du + Dv, \quad D(\lambda u) = \lambda\, Du \quad \text{and} \quad D^pD^q\, u = D^qD^p\, u = D^{p+q}\, u$$

The polynomial $f(D)$ can be factorised by ordinary rules of algebra and the factors may be written in any order.

1.24. THEOREMS

Theorem 1. *If $y = y_1, y = y_2, \ldots\ldots, y = y_n$ are n linearly independent solutions of the differential equation*

$$(D^n + a_1D^{n-1} + a_2D^{n-2} + \ldots + a_n)y = 0$$

then $u = c_1y_1 + c_2y_2 + \ldots + c_ny_n$ is also its solution, where $c_1, c_2, \ldots\ldots, c_n$ are arbitrary constants.

Theorem 2. *If $y = u$ is the complete solution of the equation $f(D)y = 0$ and $y = v$ is a particular solution (containing no arbitrary constants) of the equation $f(D)y = Q$, then the complete solution of the equation*

$$f(D)y = Q \text{ is } y = u + v.$$

Note 1. The part $y = u$ is called the **complementary function (C.F.)** and the part $y = v$ is called the **particular integral (P.I.)** of the equation $f(D)\, y = Q$.

Note 2. The complete solution is **y = C.F. + P.I.**

Thus in order to solve the equation $f(D)\ y = Q$, we first find the C.F. i.e., the complete solution of equation $f(D)\ y = 0$ and then the P.I. i.e., a particular integral (solution) of equation $f(D)\ y = Q$.

1.25. COMPLEMENTARY FUNCTION (C.F.)

Consider the differential equation

$$f(D)y = Q \qquad \ldots(1)$$

Complementary function is actually the solution of the given differential equation (1) when its right hand side member *i.e.*, Q is replaced by zero. To find C.F., we first find auxiliary equation.

1.26. AUXILIARY EQUATION (A.E.)

Consider the differential equation $(D^n + a_1D^{n-1} + a_2D^{n-2} + \ldots\ldots + a_n)y = 0$ ...(1)

Let $y = e^{mx}$ be a solution of (*i*), then

$$Dy = me^{mx},\ D^2y = m^2e^{mx},\ \ldots\ldots,\ D^{n-2}y = m^{n-2}e^{mx},\ D^{n-1}y = m^{n-1}e^{mx},\ D^ny = m^ne^{mx}$$

Substituting the values of y, Dy, D^2y, ..., D^ny in (1), we get

$$(m^n + a_1m^{n-1} + a_2m^{n-2} + \ldots\ldots + a_n)\, e^{mx} = 0$$

or
$$m^n + a_1m^{n-1} + a_2m^{n-2} + \ldots\ldots + a_n = 0, \text{ since } e^{mx} \neq 0 \qquad \ldots(2)$$

Thus $y = e^{mx}$ will be a solution of equation (1) if m satisfies equation (2).

Equation (2) is called the auxiliary equation for the differential equation (1).

1.26.1. Definition

The equation obtained by equating to zero the symbolic coefficient of y is called the **auxiliary equation,** briefly written as **A.E.**

1.26.2. Steps for Finding Auxiliary Equation

Step 1. Replace y by 1

Step 2. Replace $\frac{dy}{dx}$ by m

Step 3. Replace $\frac{d^2y}{dx^2}$ by m^2 and so on replace $\frac{d^ny}{dx^n}$ by m^n

Step 4. By doing so, we get an algebraic equation in m of degree n called auxiliary equation.

1.27. RULES FOR FINDING THE COMPLEMENTARY FUNCTION

Consider the equation $(D^n + a_1 D^{n-1} + a_2 D^{n-2} + \ldots\ldots + a_n)y = 0$ ...(1)

where all the a_i's are constant.

Its auxiliary equation is $m^n + a_1 m^{n-1} + a_2 m^{n-2} + \ldots\ldots + a_n = 0$ ...(2)

It is an algebraic equation in m of degree n. So it will give n values of m on solving.

Let $m = m_1, m_2, m_3, \ldots\ldots, m_n$ be the roots of the A.E. The C.F. of equation (1) depends upon the nature of roots of the A.E. The following cases arise.

Case I. When the roots of auxiliary equation are real and distinct

Equation (1) is equivalent to

$$(D - m_1)(D - m_2) \ldots\ldots (D - m_n)y = 0 \quad \ldots(3)$$

Equation (3) will be satisfied by the solutions of the equations

$$(D - m_1)y = 0, (D - m_2)y = 0, \ldots\ldots, (D - m_n)y = 0$$

Now, consider the equation $(D - m_1)y = 0$, *i.e.*, $\frac{dy}{dx} - m_1 y = 0$

It is a linear equation and $\text{I.F.} = e^{\int - m_1\, dx} = e^{-m_1 x}$

$\therefore$ Its solution is $y \,.\, e^{-m_1 x} = \int 0 \,.\, e^{-m_1 x}\, dx + c_1$ or $y = c_1 e^{m_1 x}$

Similarly, the solution of $(D - m_2)y = 0$ is $y = c_2 e^{m_2 x}$

....

the solution of $(D - m_n)y = 0$ is $y = c_n e^{m_n x}$

$$\therefore \quad \boxed{\text{C.F.} = c_1 e^{m_1 x} + c_2 e^{m_2 x} + \ldots\ldots + c_n e^{m_n x}} \quad \ldots(4)$$

Case II. When the roots of auxiliary equation are equal

(*a*) When two roots of auxiliary equation are equal

Let $m_1 = m_2$

Solution of eqn. (3) is (as in case I)

$$\begin{aligned} y &= \text{C.F.} + \text{P.I.} \\ &= c_1 e^{m_1 x} + c_2 e^{m_2 x} + \ldots\ldots + c_n e^{m_n x} + 0 && | \because \text{P.I.} = 0 \text{ as } Q = 0 \\ &= (c_1 + c_2) e^{m_1 x} + c_3 e^{m_3 x} + \ldots\ldots + c_n e^{m_n x} && | \text{ Here } m_1 = m_2 \\ &= c e^{m_1 x} + c_3 e^{m_3 x} + \ldots\ldots + c_n e^{m_n x} \end{aligned}$$

It contains $(n - 1)$ arbitrary constants and is, therefore, not the complete solution of equation (1).

The part of C.F. corresponding to the repeated root is the complete solution of

$$(\mathrm{D} - m_1)(\mathrm{D} - m_1)y = 0$$

$$\Rightarrow \quad (\mathrm{D} - m_1)v = 0 \qquad \mid \text{Putting } (\mathrm{D} - m_1)y = v$$

$$\Rightarrow \quad \frac{dv}{dx} - m_1 v = 0$$

Its solution is $\quad v = c_2 e^{m_1 x}$

$$\therefore \quad (\mathrm{D} - m_1)y = c_2 e^{m_1 x}$$

$$\Rightarrow \quad \frac{dy}{dx} - m_1 y = c_2 e^{m_1 x}, \quad \text{which is a linear equation}$$

$$\therefore \quad \text{I.F.} = e^{-m_1 x}$$

Its solution is

$$y e^{-m_1 x} = \int c_2 e^{m_1 x} . e^{-m_1 x}\, dx + c_1 = c_2 x + c_1$$

$$\Rightarrow \quad y = (c_2 x + c_1)\, e^{m_1 x}$$

$\therefore$ Part of C.F. $= (c_1 + c_2 x)\, e^{m_1 x}$

Hence, $\boxed{\text{complete C.F.} = (c_1 + c_2 x) e^{m_1 x} + c_3\, e^{m_3 x} + \ldots\ldots + c_n\, e^{m_n x}}$

(*b*) If however, three roots of the auxiliary equation are equal say $m_1 = m_2 = m_3$, then proceeding as above,

$$\boxed{\text{C.F.} = (c_1 + c_2 x + c_3 x^2) e^{m_1 x} + c_4\, e^{m_4 x} + \ldots\ldots + c_n\, e^{m_n x}}$$

Case III. When two roots of auxiliary equation are imaginary

Let $\quad m_1 = \alpha + i\beta \quad$ and $\quad m_2 = \alpha - i\beta$, then from (4),

$$\begin{aligned}
\text{C.F.} &= c_1 e^{(\alpha + i\beta)x} + c_2\, e^{(\alpha - i\beta)x} + c_3\, e^{m_3 x} + \ldots\ldots + c_n\, e^{m_n x} \\
&= e^{\alpha x}\, (c_1 e^{i\beta x} + c_2 e^{-i\beta x}) + c_3 e^{m_3 x} + \ldots\ldots + c_n e^{m_n x} \\
&= e^{\alpha x} [c_1 (\cos \beta x + i \sin \beta x) + c_2 (\cos \beta x - i \sin \beta x)] + c_3 e^{m_3 x} + \ldots\ldots + c_n e^{m_n x} \\
&= e^{\alpha x} [(c_1 + c_2) \cos \beta x + i\, (c_1 - c_2) \sin \beta x] + c_3 e^{m_3 x} + \ldots\ldots + c_n e^{m_n x}
\end{aligned}$$

$$\text{C.F.} = e^{\alpha x} (\mathrm{C}_1 \cos \beta x + \mathrm{C}_2 \sin \beta x) + c_3 e^{m_3 x} + \ldots\ldots + c_n e^{m_n x}$$

[taking $c_1 + c_2 = \mathrm{C}_1$, $i(c_1 - c_2) = \mathrm{C}_2$]

Case IV. When roots of auxiliary equation are repeated imaginary

Let $\quad m_1 = m_2 = \alpha + i\beta \quad$ and $\quad m_3 = m_4 = \alpha - i\beta$ then by case II,

$$\text{C.F.} = e^{\alpha x} [(c_1 + c_2 x) \cos \beta x + (c_3 + c_4\, x) \sin \beta x] + c_5\, e^{m_5 x} + \ldots\ldots + c_n\, e^{m_n x}$$

Case V. When roots of auxiliary equation are irrational

Let $m_1 = \alpha + \sqrt{\beta}$ and $m_2 = \alpha - \sqrt{\beta}$ then

C.F. of eqn. (1) is given by

$$\text{C.F.} = e^{\alpha x}\,(c_1 \cosh \sqrt{\beta}x + c_2 \sinh \sqrt{\beta}x) + c_3 e^{m_3 x} + \ldots\ldots + c_n e^{m_n x}$$

Case VI. When roots of auxiliary equation are repeated irrational

Let $m_1 = m_2 = \alpha + \sqrt{\beta}$ and $m_3 = m_4 = \alpha - \sqrt{\beta}$ then by case II,

$$\text{C.F.} = e^{\alpha x}\,[(c_1 + c_2 x) \cosh \sqrt{\beta}x + (c_3 + c_4 x) \sinh \sqrt{\beta}x\,] + c_5 e^{m_5 x} + c_6 e^{m_6 x} + \ldots\ldots + c_n e^{m_n x}$$

ILLUSTRATIVE EXAMPLES

Example 1. *Solve :* $\dfrac{d^3y}{dx^3} - 7\dfrac{dy}{dx} - 6y = 0.$

Sol. The auxiliary equation is

$$m^3 - 7m - 6 = 0$$

$$\Rightarrow \quad (m + 1)(m + 2)(m - 3) = 0 \quad \Rightarrow \quad m = -1, -2, 3$$

The roots are real and distinct

$\therefore$ Complementary Function (C.F.) $= c_1e^{-x} + c_2e^{-2x} + c_3e^{3x}$

Particular Integral (P.I.) = 0

Hence the complete solution is

$$y = \text{C.F.} + \text{P.I.} = c_1e^{-x} + c_2e^{-2x} + c_3e^{3x}$$

where c_1, c_2 and c_3 are arbitrary constants of integration.

Example 2. *Solve :* $(D^3 - 3D^2 + 4)\,y = 0$, *where* $D \equiv \dfrac{d}{dx}$.

Sol. The auxiliary equation is

$$m^3 - 3m^2 + 4 = 0$$

$$\Rightarrow \quad (m + 1)(m - 2)^2 = 0 \quad \Rightarrow \quad m = -1, 2, 2$$

$$\therefore \quad \text{C.F.} = c_1e^{-x} + (c_2 + c_3x)\,e^{2x}$$

$$\text{P.I.} = 0$$

$\therefore$ The complete solution is

$$y = \text{C.F.} + \text{P.I.} = c_1e^{-x} + (c_2 + c_3x)\,e^{2x}$$

where c_1, c_2 and c_3 are arbitrary constants of integration.

Example 3. *Solve :* $(D^4 - n^4)y = 0$, *where* $D \equiv \dfrac{d}{dx}$.

Sol. The auxiliary equation is

$$m^4 - n^4 = 0$$

$$\Rightarrow \quad (m^2 - n^2)(m^2 + n^2) = 0$$

$$\Rightarrow \quad m = \pm\, n, \pm\, ni$$

$$\therefore \quad \text{C.F.} = c_1e^{nx} + c_2e^{-nx} + e^{0x}\,(c_3 \cos nx + c_4 \sin nx)$$

$$= c_1e^{nx} + c_2e^{-nx} + c_3 \cos nx + c_4 \sin nx$$

$$\text{P.I.} = 0$$

Hence the complete solution is

$$y = \text{C.F.} + \text{P.I.} = c_1 e^{nx} + c_2 e^{-nx} + c_3 \cos nx + c_4 \sin nx$$

where c_1, c_2, c_3 and c_4 are arbitrary constants of integration.

Example 4. *Solve :* $\dfrac{d^4y}{dx^4} + 13\dfrac{d^2y}{dx^2} + 36y = 0.$

Sol. The auxiliary equation is

$$m^4 + 13m^2 + 36 = 0$$

$\Rightarrow$ $(m^2 + 9)(m^2 + 4) = 0 \Rightarrow m = \pm 3i, \pm 2i$

$\therefore$ $\text{C.F.} = e^{0x}(c_1 \cos 3x + c_2 \sin 3x) + e^{0x}(c_3 \cos 2x + c_4 \sin 2x)$

$$= c_1 \cos 3x + c_2 \sin 3x + c_3 \cos 2x + c_4 \sin 2x$$

$$\text{P.I.} = 0$$

Hence the complete solution is

$$y = \text{C.F.} + \text{P.I.} = c_1 \cos 3x + c_2 \sin 3x + c_3 \cos 2x + c_4 \sin 2x$$

where c_1, c_2, c_3 and c_4 are arbitrary constants of integration.

Example 5. *Solve :* $(D^2 - 2D + 4)^2 y = 0 ; D \equiv \dfrac{d}{dx}.$

Sol. The auxiliary equation is

$$(m^2 - 2m + 4)^2 = 0$$

$$m = \frac{2 \pm \sqrt{4 - 16}}{2} \text{ (twice)} = 1 \pm \sqrt{3}\,i,\ 1 \pm \sqrt{3}\,i$$

The roots are repeated imaginary

$\therefore$ $\text{C.F.} = e^x[(c_1 + c_2x)\cos\sqrt{3}\,x + (c_3 + c_4x)\sin\sqrt{3}\,x]$

$$\text{P.I.} = 0$$

Hence the complete solution is

$$y = \text{C.F.} + \text{P.I.} = e^x[(c_1 + c_2x)\cos\sqrt{3}\,x + (c_3 + c_4x)\sin\sqrt{3}\,x]$$

where c_1, c_2, c_3 and c_4 are arbitrary constants of integration.

Example 6. *Solve :* $\dfrac{d^4y}{dx^4} - 4\dfrac{d^3y}{dx^3} + 8\dfrac{d^2y}{dx^2} - 8\dfrac{dy}{dx} + 4y = 0.$

Sol. The auxiliary equation is

$$m^4 - 4m^3 + 8m^2 - 8m + 4 = 0$$

$\Rightarrow$ $(m^2 - 2m + 2)^2 = 0$

$\Rightarrow$ $m = \dfrac{2 \pm \sqrt{4 - 8}}{2} \text{ (twice)} = \dfrac{2 \pm 2i}{2} \text{ (twice)} = 1 \pm i,\ 1 \pm i$

$\therefore$ $\text{C.F.} = e^x[(c_1 + c_2x)\cos x + (c_3 + c_4x)\sin x]$

$$\text{P.I.} = 0$$

The complete solution is

$$y = \text{C.F.} + \text{P.I.}$$

$\Rightarrow$ $y = e^x[(c_1 + c_2x)\cos x + (c_3 + c_4x)\sin x]$

where c_1, c_2, c_3 and c_4 are arbitrary constants of integration.

Example 7. *Solve :* $\dfrac{d^4y}{dx^4} + m^4 y = 0.$

Sol. The auxiliary equation is

$$M^4 + m^4 = 0$$

$$\Rightarrow \quad M^4 + m^4 + 2M^2m^2 = 2\, M^2m^2$$

$$\Rightarrow \quad (M^2 + m^2)^2 = 2\, M^2m^2$$

$$\Rightarrow \quad M^2 + m^2 = \pm \sqrt{2}\; M\, m.$$

Case I. Taking (+)ve sign :

$$M^2 + m^2 - \sqrt{2}\; M\, m = 0$$

$$\therefore \quad M = \frac{\sqrt{2}m \pm \sqrt{2m^2 - 4m^2}}{2} = \frac{\sqrt{2}m \pm i\,\sqrt{2}m}{2} = \frac{m}{\sqrt{2}} \pm i\,\frac{m}{\sqrt{2}}.$$

Case II. Taking (–)ve sign :

$$M^2 + m^2 + \sqrt{2}\; Mm = 0$$

$$\therefore \quad M = \frac{-\sqrt{2}m \pm \sqrt{2m^2 - 4m^2}}{2} = \frac{-\sqrt{2}m \pm i\,\sqrt{2}m}{2} = -\frac{m}{\sqrt{2}} \pm i\,\frac{m}{\sqrt{2}}$$

$$\therefore \quad M = \frac{m}{\sqrt{2}} \pm i\,\frac{m}{\sqrt{2}}\,; -\frac{m}{\sqrt{2}} \pm i\,\frac{m}{\sqrt{2}}$$

$$\text{C.F.} = e^{\frac{m}{\sqrt{2}}x}\left(c_1 \cos\frac{m}{\sqrt{2}}x + c_2 \sin\frac{m}{\sqrt{2}}x\right) + e^{-\frac{m}{\sqrt{2}}x}\left(c_3 \cos\frac{m}{\sqrt{2}}x + c_4 \sin\frac{m}{\sqrt{2}}x\right)$$

$$\text{P.I.} = 0$$

$\therefore$ Complete solution is

$$y = \text{C.F.} + \text{P.I.}$$

$$= e^{\frac{m}{\sqrt{2}}x}\left(c_1 \cos\frac{m}{\sqrt{2}}x + c_2 \sin\frac{m}{\sqrt{2}}x\right) + e^{-\frac{m}{\sqrt{2}}x}\left(c_3 \cos\frac{m}{\sqrt{2}}x + c_4 \sin\frac{m}{\sqrt{2}}x\right).$$

where c_1, c_2, c_3, c_4 are arbitrary constants of integration.

Example 8. *Solve the differential equation :* $(D^2 + 1)^3\,(D^2 + D + 1)^2\, y = 0,\ D \equiv \dfrac{d}{dx}.$

Sol. Auxiliary equation is

$$(m^2 + 1)^3\,(m^2 + m + 1)^2 = 0$$

$$\Rightarrow \quad (m^2 + 1)^3 = 0 \text{ gives } m = \pm\, i, \pm\, i, \pm\, i$$

and $\quad (m^2 + m + 1)^2 = 0$ gives $\quad m = \dfrac{-1 \pm \sqrt{3}i}{2}, \dfrac{-1 \pm \sqrt{3}i}{2}$

Hence,

$$\text{C.F.} = e^{0x}[(c_1 + c_2x + c_3x^2) \cos x + (c_4 + c_5x + c_6x^2) \sin x]$$

$$+ e^{-x/2}\left[(c_7 + c_8x) \cos\frac{\sqrt{3}}{2}x + (c_9 + c_{10}x) \sin\frac{\sqrt{3}}{2}x\right]$$

$$\text{P.I.} = 0$$

Therefore the complete solution is

$$y = \text{C.F.} + \text{P.I.}$$
$$= (c_1 + c_2x + c_3x^2) \cos x + (c_4 + c_5 x + c_6x^2) \sin x$$
$$+ e^{-x/2} \left\{(c_7 + c_8x) \cos \frac{\sqrt{3}}{2} x + (c_9 + c_{10}x) \sin \frac{\sqrt{3}}{2} x\right\}$$

where $c_1, c_2, c_3, c_4, c_5, c_6, c_7, c_8, c_9$ and c_{10} are arbitrary constants of integration.

Example 9. *Solve the differential equation* $\frac{d^2i}{dt^2} + \frac{R}{L}\frac{di}{dt} + \frac{i}{LC} = 0,$ *where* $R^2C = 4L$ *and R, C, L are constants.* [G.B.T.U. (SUM) 2010]

Sol. The given equation is

$$\left(D^2 + \frac{R}{L}D + \frac{1}{LC}\right) i = 0, \quad \text{where } D \equiv \frac{d}{dt}$$

Auxiliary equation is

$$m^2 + \frac{R}{L} m + \frac{1}{LC} = 0$$

$$\Rightarrow \qquad m = \frac{-\frac{R}{L} \pm \sqrt{\frac{R^2}{L^2} - \frac{4}{LC}}}{2}$$

$$= -\frac{R}{2L} \pm \frac{1}{2}\sqrt{\frac{4}{LC} - \frac{4}{LC}} \qquad \left|\because R^2 = \frac{4L}{C}\right.$$

$$= -\frac{R}{2L}, -\frac{R}{2L}$$

Hence, $\qquad \text{C.F.} = (c_1 + c_2t)\, e^{-\frac{R}{2L}t}$

$$\text{P.I.} = 0$$

$\therefore$ The complete solution is

$$i = \text{C.F.} + \text{P.I.} = (c_1 + c_2t)\, e^{-\frac{R}{2L}t}$$

where c_1 and c_2 are arbitrary constants of integration.

Example 10. *Solve the differential equation :*

$$\frac{d^2y}{dx^2} + y = 0 \text{ ; given that } y(0) = 2 \text{ and } y\left(\frac{\pi}{2}\right) = -2. \qquad \text{(U.P.T.U. 2008)}$$

Sol. The auxiliary equation is

$$m^2 + 1 = 0 \quad \Rightarrow \quad m = \pm i$$

$$\therefore \qquad \text{C.F.} = c_1 \cos x + c_2 \sin x$$

$$\text{P.I.} = 0$$

Hence the general solution is

$$y = \text{C.F.} + \text{P.I.} = c_1 \cos x + c_2 \sin x \qquad ...(1)$$

Applying the condition $y(0) = 2$, we get $\quad 2 = c_1$

Applying the condition $y\left(\frac{\pi}{2}\right) = -2$, we get $\quad -2 = c_2$

Hence from (1), the particular solution is

$$y = 2(\cos x - \sin x)$$

TEST YOUR KNOWLEDGE

Solve the differential equations :

1. $\frac{d^2y}{dx^2} - 7\frac{dy}{dx} + 12y = 0$

2. $\frac{d^2y}{dx^2} + (a+b)\frac{dy}{dx} + aby = 0$

3. $\frac{d^3y}{dx^3} + 6\frac{d^2y}{dx^2} + 11\frac{dy}{dx} + 6y = 0$

4. $\frac{d^2x}{dt^2} + 6\frac{dx}{dt} + 9x = 0$

5. $\frac{d^3y}{dx^3} - 3\frac{d^2y}{dx^2} + 3\frac{dy}{dx} - y = 0$

6. $\frac{d^3y}{dx^3} - \frac{d^2y}{dx^2} - \frac{dy}{dx} + y = 0$

7. $(D^4 - D^3 - 9D^2 - 11D - 4)y = 0$

8. $\frac{d^4y}{dx^4} + 8\frac{d^2y}{dx^2} + 16y = 0$

9. $\frac{d^5y}{dx^5} - \frac{d^3y}{dx^3} = 0$ *(U.P.T.U. 2009)*

10. $\frac{d^3y}{dx^3} - 2\frac{d^2y}{dx^2} + 4\frac{dy}{dx} - 8y = 0$

11. $(D^2 + 1)^2 (D - 1)\, y = 0$

12. $\frac{d^2y}{dx^2} - 4\frac{dy}{dx} + y = 0$

13. $(D^6 - 1)\, y = 0$

14. $(D^6 + 1)\, y = 0$

15. $\frac{d^2x}{dt^2} - 3\frac{dx}{dt} + 2x = 0$, given that when $t = 0$, $x = 0$ and $\frac{dx}{dt} = 0$

16. $\frac{d^3y}{dx^3} + 6\frac{d^2y}{dx^2} + 12\frac{dy}{dx} + 8y = 0$ under the conditions $y(0) = 0$, $y'(0) = 0$ and $y''(0) = 2$

[G.B.T.U.(AG) SUM 2010]

Answers

1. $y = c_1e^{3x} + c_2e^{4x}$

2. $y = c_1e^{-ax} + c_2e^{-bx}$

3. $y = c_1e^{-x} + c_2e^{-2x} + c_3e^{-3x}$

4. $x = (c_1 + c_2t)e^{-3t}$

5. $y = (c_1 + c_2x + c_3x^2)e^x$

6. $y = (c_1 + c_2x)\, e^x + c_3\, e^{-x}$

7. $y = e^{-x}(c_1 + c_2x + c_3x^2) + c_4e^{4x}$

8. $y = (c_1 + c_2x)\cos 2x + (c_3 + c_4x)\sin 2x$

9. $y = c_1 + c_2x + c_3x^2 + c_4e^{-x} + c_5e^x$

10. $y = c_1e^{2x} + c_2\cos 2x + c_3\sin 2x$

11. $y = (c_1 + c_2x)\cos x + (c_3 + c_4x)\sin x + c_5e^x$

12. $y = e^{2x}(c_1\cosh\sqrt{3}\,x + c_2\sinh\sqrt{3}\,x)$

13. $y = c_1e^x + c_2e^{-x} + e^{x/2}\left(c_3 \cos \frac{\sqrt{3}}{2}x + c_4 \sin \frac{\sqrt{3}}{2}x\right) + e^{-x/2}\left(c_5 \cos \frac{\sqrt{3}}{2}x + c_6 \sin \frac{\sqrt{3}}{2}x\right)$

14. $y = c_1 \cos x + c_2 \sin x + e^{\sqrt{3}x/2}\left(c_3 \cos \frac{x}{2} + c_4 \sin \frac{x}{2}\right) + e^{-\sqrt{3}x/2}\left(c_5 \cos \frac{x}{2} + c_6 \sin \frac{x}{2}\right).$

15. $x = 0$ **16.** $y = x^2e^{-2x}$.

1.28. THE INVERSE OPERATOR $\frac{1}{f(D)}$

$\frac{1}{f(\text{D})}$ Q is that function of x, *free from arbitrary constants,* which when operated upon by f(D) gives Q.

Thus $$f(\text{D}) \left\{\frac{1}{f(\text{D})} \text{Q}\right\} = \text{Q}$$

$\therefore$ f(D) and $\frac{1}{f(\text{D})}$ are inverse operators.

Note 1. $\frac{1}{\text{D}} Q = \int Q\, dx.$

Note 2. $\frac{1}{\text{D} - a} Q = e^{ax} \int Qe^{-ax}\, dx.$

1.29. RULES FOR FINDING THE PARTICULAR INTEGRAL (P.I.)

Consider the differential equation, $(\text{D}^n + a_1\text{D}^{n-1} + a_2\text{D}^{n-2} + \ldots\ldots + a_{n-1}\text{D} + a_n)y = \text{Q}$

It can be written as $f(\text{D})y = \text{Q}$

$$\therefore \qquad \text{P.I.} = \frac{1}{f(\text{D})} \text{Q}.$$

1.29.1. Case I. When Q = e^{ax} (or e^{ax+b})

Since
$$\text{D}\, e^{ax} = a\, e^{ax}$$
$$\text{D}^2 e^{ax} = a^2 e^{ax}$$
$$\ldots\ldots\ldots\ldots\ldots\ldots$$
$$\ldots\ldots\ldots\ldots\ldots\ldots$$
$$\text{D}^{n-1} e^{ax} = a^{n-1} e^{ax}$$
$$\text{D}^n e^{ax} = a^n e^{ax}$$

$$\therefore \quad (\text{D}^n + a_1\text{D}^{n-1} + \ldots\ldots + a_{n-1}\text{D} + a_n)e^{ax} = (a^n + a_1a^{n-1} + \ldots\ldots + a_{n-1}\, a + a_n)e^{ax}$$

or
$$f(\text{D})\, e^{ax} = f(a)\, e^{ax}$$

Operating on both sides by $\frac{1}{f(\text{D})}$;

$$\frac{1}{f(\text{D})} [f(\text{D})\, e^{ax}] = \frac{1}{f(\text{D})} [f(a)\, e^{ax}]$$

or
$$e^{ax} = f(a) \frac{1}{f(D)} e^{ax}$$

Dividing both sides by $f(a)$, $\frac{1}{f(a)} e^{ax} = \frac{1}{f(D)} e^{ax}$, provided $f(a) \neq 0$

Hence
$$\boxed{\frac{1}{f(D)} e^{ax} = \frac{1}{f(a)} e^{ax}, \text{ provided } f(a) \neq 0.}$$

Case of failure : If $f(a) = 0$, the above method fails.

Since $f(a) = 0$, $D = a$ is a root of $f(D) = 0$

$\therefore$ $D - a$ is a factor of $f(D)$.

Let
$$f(D) = (D - a)\,\phi(D), \text{ where } \phi(a) \neq 0 \qquad ...(1)$$

Then
$$\frac{1}{f(D)} e^{ax} = \frac{1}{(D-a)\,\phi(D)} e^{ax} = \frac{1}{D-a} \cdot \frac{1}{\phi(a)} e^{ax}$$
$$= \frac{1}{\phi(a)} \cdot \frac{1}{D-a} e^{ax} = \frac{1}{\phi(a)} e^{ax} \int e^{ax} \, . \, e^{-ax}\, dx \qquad \text{[by Note 2]}$$
$$= \frac{1}{\phi(a)} e^{ax} \int 1\, dx = x \, . \, \frac{1}{\phi(a)} e^{ax} \qquad ...(2)$$

Differentiating both sides of (1) w.r.t. D, we get
$$f'(D) = (D - a)\,\phi'(D) + \phi(D)$$
$$\Rightarrow \qquad f'(a) = \phi(a)$$

$\therefore$ From (2), we have $\boldsymbol{\frac{1}{f(D)} e^{ax} = x \, . \, \frac{1}{f'(a)} e^{ax}}$ **provided** $\boldsymbol{f'(a) \neq 0}$

Another case of failure :

If $f'(a) = 0$, then $\frac{1}{f(D)} e^{ax} = x^2 \, . \, \frac{1}{f''(a)} e^{ax}$, provided $f''(a) \neq 0$ and so on.

ILLUSTRATIVE EXAMPLES

Example 1. *Find the P.I. of* $(4D^2 + 4D - 3)y = e^{2x}$.

Sol.
$$\text{P.I.} = \frac{1}{4D^2 + 4D - 3} e^{2x} = \frac{1}{4(2)^2 + 4(2) - 3} e^{2x} \qquad \text{(Replacing D by 2)}$$
$$= \frac{1}{21} e^{2x}.$$

Example 2. *Find the P.I. of* $(D^3 - 3D^2 + 4)y = e^{2x}$.

Sol.
$$\text{P.I.} = \frac{1}{D^3 - 3D^2 + 4} e^{2x}.$$

Here the denominator vanishes when D is replaced by 2. It is a case of failure. We multiply the numerator by x and differentiate the denominator w.r.t. D.

$$\therefore \qquad \text{P.I.} = x \, . \, \frac{1}{3D^2 - 6D} e^{2x}$$

It is again a case of failure. We multiply the numerator by x and differentiate the denominator w.r.t. D.

$$\therefore \qquad \text{P.I.} = x^2 \cdot \frac{1}{6D-6}\, e^{2x} = x^2 \cdot \frac{1}{6(2)-6}\, e^{2x} = \frac{x^2}{6}\, e^{2x}.$$

Example 3. *Find the P.I. of* $(D+1)^3 y = e^{-x}$.

Sol.
$$\text{P.I.} = \frac{1}{(D+1)^3}\, e^{-x} = x \cdot \frac{1}{3(D+1)^2}\, e^{-x} \qquad \text{| Case of failure}$$

$$= x^2 \cdot \frac{1}{3 \cdot 2\,(D+1)}\, e^{-x} \qquad \text{| Again case of failure}$$

$$= x^3 \cdot \frac{1}{3 \cdot 2 \cdot 1}\, e^{-x} = \frac{x^3}{6}\, e^{-x}.$$

Example 4. *Solve :*

(*i*) $(D^3 - 2D^2 + 4D - 8)\, y = 8$ [U.P.T.U. (B.Pharm.) SUM 2009]

(*ii*) $(D-2)^3\, y = 17\, e^{2x}$. (M.T.U. 2011)

Sol. (*i*) Auxiliary equation is

$$m^3 - 2m^2 + 4m - 8 = 0$$

$$\Rightarrow \qquad (m^2 + 4)(m - 2) = 0$$

$$\Rightarrow \qquad m = 2, \pm 2i$$

$$\therefore \qquad \text{C.F.} = c_1 e^{2x} + c_2 \cos 2x + c_3 \sin 2x$$

$$\text{P.I.} = \frac{1}{D^3 - 2D^2 + 4D - 8}\,(8\, e^{0x}) \qquad |\because \; e^{0x} = 1$$

$$= \frac{1}{(0)^3 - 2(0)^2 + 4(0) - 8}\,(8e^{0x}) = -1$$

Hence the complete solution is

$$y = \text{C.F.} + \text{P.I.} = c_1 e^{2x} + c_2 \cos 2x + c_3 \sin 2x - 1$$

where c_1, c_2 and c_3 are arbitrary constants of integration.

(*ii*) Auxiliary equation is

$$(m-2)^3 = 0$$

$$\Rightarrow \qquad m = 2, 2, 2$$

$$\therefore \qquad \text{C.F.} = (c_1 + c_2 x + c_3 x^2)\, e^{2x}$$

$$\text{P.I.} = \frac{1}{(D-2)^3}\, 17e^{2x} \qquad \text{| Case of failure}$$

$$= 17x \cdot \left[\frac{1}{3(D-2)^2}\, e^{2x}\right] \qquad \text{| Again case of failure}$$

$$= \frac{17}{3} x^2 \cdot \left[\frac{1}{2(D-2)}\, e^{2x}\right] \qquad \text{| Again a case of failure}$$

$$= \frac{17}{6} x^3\, e^{2x}$$

Hence the complete solution is

$$y = \text{C.F.} + \text{P.I.} = (c_1 + c_2x + c_3x^2)\, e^{2x} + \frac{17}{6}x^3e^{2x}$$

where c_1, c_2 and c_3 are arbitrary constants of integration.

Example 5. *Solve :* $2\dfrac{d^3y}{dx^3} - \dfrac{d^2y}{dx^2} + 4\dfrac{dy}{dx} - 2y = e^x$. (U.P.T.U. 2007)

Sol. The auxiliary equation is

$$2m^3 - m^2 + 4m - 2 = 0$$

$$\Rightarrow \quad (2m-1)(m^2+2) = 0$$

$$\Rightarrow \quad m = \frac{1}{2}, \pm \sqrt{2}\, i$$

$$\therefore \quad \text{C.F.} = c_1 e^{x/2} + c_2 \cos \sqrt{2}\, x + c_3 \sin \sqrt{2}\, x$$

$$\text{P.I.} = \frac{1}{2\text{D}^3 - \text{D}^2 + 4\text{D} - 2}\, e^x = \frac{1}{2(1)^3 - (1)^2 + 4(1) - 2}\, e^x = \frac{1}{3}\, e^x$$

Hence the complete solution is

$$y = \text{C.F.} + \text{P.I.} = c_1e^{x/2} + c_2 \cos \sqrt{2}\, x + c_3 \sin \sqrt{2}\, x + \frac{1}{3}\, e^x$$

where c_1, c_2 and c_3 are arbitrary constants of integration.

Example 6. *Solve* $(D^3 - 6D^2 + 11D - 6)y = e^{-2x} + e^{-3x}$.

Sol. Auxiliary equation is

$$m^3 - 6m^2 + 11m - 6 = 0$$

or $$(m-1)(m-2)(m-3) = 0$$

whence $$m = 1, 2, 3$$

$$\therefore \quad \text{C.F.} = c_1e^x + c_2e^{2x} + c_3e^{3x}$$

$$\text{P.I.} = \frac{1}{\text{D}^3 - 6\text{D}^2 + 11\text{D} - 6}\,(e^{-2x} + e^{-3x})$$

$$= \frac{1}{\text{D}^3 - 6\text{D}^2 + 11\text{D} - 6}\, e^{-2x} + \frac{1}{\text{D}^3 - 6\text{D}^2 + 11\text{D} - 6}\, e^{-3x}$$

$$= \frac{1}{(-2)^3 - 6(-2)^2 + 11(-2) - 6}\, e^{-2x} + \frac{1}{(-3)^3 - 6(-3)^2 + 11(-3) - 6}\, e^{-3x}$$

$$= -\frac{1}{60}\, e^{-2x} - \frac{1}{120}\, e^{-3x} = -\frac{1}{120}\,(2e^{-2x} + e^{-3x})$$

Hence the complete solution is

$$y = \text{C.F.} + \text{P.I.} = c_1e^x + c_2e^{2x} + c_3e^{3x} - \frac{1}{120}\,(2e^{-2x} + e^{-3x})$$

where c_1, c_2 and c_3 are arbitrary constants of integration.

Example 7. *Solve :* $(D^2 - a^2)y = e^{ax} - e^{-ax}$.

Sol. Auxiliary equation is

$$m^2 - a^2 = 0$$

$\Rightarrow \qquad m = \pm a$

$\therefore \qquad \text{C.F.} = c_1e^{ax} + c_2e^{-ax}$

$$\text{P.I.} = \frac{1}{D^2 - a^2}(e^{ax} - e^{-ax}) = \frac{1}{D^2 - a^2}(e^{ax}) - \frac{1}{D^2 - a^2}(e^{-ax})$$

$$= x \cdot \frac{1}{2D}(e^{ax}) - x \cdot \frac{1}{2D}(e^{-ax}) = \frac{x}{2}\frac{e^{ax}}{a} - \frac{x}{2}\left(\frac{e^{-ax}}{-a}\right)$$

$$= \frac{x}{2}\left(\frac{e^{ax} + e^{-ax}}{a}\right) = \frac{x}{a}\cosh ax$$

The complete solution is

$$y = \text{C.F.} + \text{P.I.} = c_1e^{ax} + c_2e^{-ax} + \frac{x}{a}\cosh ax$$

where c_1 and c_2 are arbitrary constants of integration.

Example 8. *Solve :* $(D^2 + D + 1)\, y = (1 + e^x)^2$.

Sol. Auxiliary equation is

$$m^2 + m + 1 = 0$$

$$\Rightarrow \qquad m = \frac{-1 \pm \sqrt{1-4}}{2} = -\frac{1}{2} \pm \frac{\sqrt{3}}{2}\, i$$

$$\text{C.F.} = e^{-\frac{1}{2}x}\left(c_1 \cos\frac{\sqrt{3}}{2}x + c_2 \sin\frac{\sqrt{3}}{2}x\right)$$

$$\text{P.I.} = \frac{1}{D^2 + D + 1}(1 + e^x)^2 = \frac{1}{D^2 + D + 1}(1 + e^{2x} + 2e^x)$$

$$= \frac{1}{D^2 + D + 1}(e^{0x}) + \frac{1}{D^2 + D + 1}(e^{2x}) + \frac{1}{D^2 + D + 1}(2e^x)$$

$$= \frac{1}{(0)^2 + (0) + 1}e^{0x} + \frac{1}{(2)^2 + (2) + 1}e^{2x} + \frac{2}{(1)^2 + (1) + 1}e^x = 1 + \frac{1}{7}e^{2x} + \frac{2}{3}e^x$$

Hence complete solution is

$$y = \text{C.F.} + \text{P.I.} = e^{-\frac{x}{2}}\left(c_1 \cos\frac{\sqrt{3}}{2}x + c_2 \sin\frac{\sqrt{3}}{2}x\right) + 1 + \frac{1}{7}e^{2x} + \frac{2}{3}e^x$$

where c_1 and c_2 are arbitrary constants of integration.

Example 9. *Solve :* $(D + 2)(D - 1)^2\, y = e^{-2x} + 2 \sinh x$.

Sol. Auxiliary equation is

$$(m + 2)(m - 1)^2 = 0 \quad \Rightarrow \quad m = -2, 1, 1$$

$\therefore \qquad \text{C.F.} = c_1e^{-2x} + (c_2 + c_3x)\, e^x$

$$\text{P.I.} = \frac{1}{(D+2)(D-1)^2}(e^{-2x} + 2\sinh x)$$

$$= \frac{1}{(D+2)(D-1)^2}(e^{-2x} + e^x - e^{-x}) \qquad \left[\because \sinh x = \frac{e^x - e^{-x}}{2}\right]$$

Now, $\frac{1}{(D+2)(D-1)^2} e^{-2x} = \frac{1}{D+2}\left[\frac{1}{(D-1)^2} e^{-2x}\right] = \frac{1}{D+2}\left[\frac{1}{(-2-1)^2} e^{-2x}\right]$

$$= \frac{1}{9} \cdot \frac{1}{D+2} e^{-2x} \qquad \text{| Case of failure}$$

$$= \frac{x}{9} e^{-2x}$$

$$\frac{1}{(D+2)(D-1)^2} e^{x} = \frac{1}{(D-1)^2}\left[\frac{1}{D+2} e^{x}\right] = \frac{1}{(D-1)^2}\left[\frac{1}{1+2} e^{x}\right]$$

$$= \frac{1}{3} \cdot \frac{1}{(D-1)^2} e^{x} \qquad \text{| Case of failure}$$

$$= \frac{1}{3} \cdot x \frac{1}{2(D-1)} e^{x} \qquad \text{| Case of failure}$$

$$= \frac{1}{3} \cdot x^2 \cdot \frac{1}{2} e^{x} = \frac{1}{6} x^2 e^{x}$$

$$\frac{1}{(D+2)(D-1)^2} e^{-x} = \frac{1}{(-1+2)(-1-1)^2} e^{-x} = \frac{1}{4} e^{-x}$$

$\therefore$ $$\text{P.I.} = \frac{x}{9} e^{-2x} + \frac{x^2}{6} e^{x} + \frac{1}{4} e^{-x}$$

Hence the complete solution is

$$y = \text{C.F.} + \text{P.I.} = c_1 e^{-2x} + (c_2 + c_3 x)e^{x} + \frac{x}{9} e^{-2x} + \frac{x^2}{6} e^{x} + \frac{1}{4} e^{-x}.$$

where c_1, c_2 and c_3 are arbitrary constants of integration.

Example 10. *Solve the differential equation*

$$\frac{d^3y}{dx^3} - 3\frac{d^2y}{dx^2} + 3\frac{dy}{dx} - y = e^x + 2.$$

Sol. The given equation is

$$(D^3 - 3D^2 + 3D - 1)y = e^x + 2$$

or $$(D-1)^3 y = e^x + 2$$

Auxiliary equation is

$$(m-1)^3 = 0 \quad \Rightarrow \quad m = 1, 1, 1$$

$\therefore$ $$\text{C.F.} = (c_1 + c_2 x + c_3 x^2)e^x$$

$$\text{P.I.} = \frac{1}{(D-1)^3}(e^x + 2) = \frac{1}{(D-1)^3} e^x + \frac{1}{(D-1)^3}(2e^{0x})$$

$$= x \cdot \frac{1}{3(D-1)^2} e^x + \frac{1}{(0-1)^3}(2e^{0x}) = x^2 \cdot \frac{1}{3.2\,(D-1)}(e^x) - 2$$

$$= x^3 \cdot \frac{1}{3.2.1}(e^x) - 2 = \frac{x^3}{6} e^x - 2$$

$\therefore$ The complete solution is

$$y = \text{C.F.} + \text{P.I.} = (c_1 + c_2 x + c_3 x^2)e^x + \frac{x^3}{6} e^x - 2$$

where c_1, c_2 and c_3 are arbitrary constants of integration.

TEST YOUR KNOWLEDGE

Solve the following differential equations :

1. $\frac{d^3y}{dx^3} + y = 3 + 5e^x$
2. $\frac{d^2y}{dx^2} - 4y = (1 + e^x)^2$
3. $\frac{d^2y}{dx^2} + 4\frac{dy}{dx} + 5y = -2\cosh x$
4. $(2D + 1)^2 y = 4e^{-x/2}$
5. $(D^2 - 2kD + k^2)\, y = e^{kx}$
6. $\frac{d^3y}{dx^3} + 3\frac{d^2y}{dx^2} + 3\frac{dy}{dx} + y = e^{-x}$
7. $(D + 2)(D - 1)^3 y = e^x$
8. $\frac{d^2y}{dx^2} + 31\frac{dy}{dx} + 240y = 272\, e^{-x}$
9. $\frac{d^2y}{dx^2} + 2p\frac{dy}{dx} + (p^2 + q^2)\, y = e^{2x}$
10. $(D^4 + D^3 + D^2 - D - 2)\, y = e^x$
11. $\frac{d^3y}{dx^3} + y = 3 + e^{-x} + 5e^{2x}$
12. $y'' + 4y' + 13y = 18e^{-2x};\ y(0) = 0,\ y'(0) = 9.$

Answers

1. $y = c_1 e^{-x} + e^{\frac{1}{2}x}\left(c_2 \cos\frac{\sqrt{3}}{2}x + c_3 \sin\frac{\sqrt{3}}{2}x\right) + 3 + \frac{5}{2}e^x$
2. $y = c_1 e^{2x} + c_2 e^{-2x} - \frac{1}{4} - \frac{2}{3}e^x + \frac{1}{4}xe^{2x}$
3. $y = e^{-2x}(c_1 \cos x + c_2 \sin x) - \frac{1}{10}e^x - \frac{1}{2}e^{-x}$
4. $y = \left(c_1 + c_2 x + \frac{x^2}{2}\right)e^{-x/2}$
5. $y = (c_1 + c_2 x)\, e^{kx} + \frac{x^2}{2}e^{kx}$
6. $y = (c_1 + c_2 x + c_3 x^2)\, e^{-x} + e^{-x} \cdot \frac{x^3}{6}$
7. $y = (c_1 + c_2 x + c_3 x^2)\, e^x + c_4\, e^{-2x} + \frac{x^3 e^x}{18}$
8. $y = c_1 e^{-15x} + c_2 e^{-16x} + \frac{136}{105}e^{-x}$
9. $y = e^{-px}(c_1 \cos qx + c_2 \sin qx) + \frac{e^{2x}}{(2 + p)^2 + q^2}$
10. $y = c_1\, e^x + c_2 e^{-x} + e^{-x/2}\left[c_3 \cos\frac{\sqrt{7}}{2}x + c_4 \sin\frac{\sqrt{7}}{2}x\right] + \frac{1}{8}xe^x$
11. $y = c_1\, e^{-x} + e^{x/2}\left(c_2 \cos\frac{\sqrt{3}}{2}x + c_3 \sin\frac{\sqrt{3}}{2}x\right) + 3 + \frac{5}{9}e^{2x} + \frac{1}{3}xe^{-x}$
12. $y = e^{-2x}(-2\cos 3x + 3\sin 3x + 2).$

1.29.2. Case II. When Q = sin (ax + b) or cos (ax + b)

$$D \sin(ax + b) = a\cos(ax + b)$$

$$\mathbf{D^2 \sin(ax + b) = (-a^2)\sin(ax + b)}$$

$$D^3 \sin(ax + b) = -a^3 \cos(ax + b)$$

$$D^4 \sin(ax + b) = a^4 \sin(ax + b)$$

or $$\mathbf{(D^2)^2 \sin (ax + b) = (- a^2)^2 \sin (ax + b)}$$

....

....

In general, $(D^2)^n \sin (ax + b) = (- a^2)^n \sin (ax + b)$

$\therefore$ $f(D^2) \sin (ax + b) = f(- a^2) \sin (ax + b)$

Operating on both sides by $\dfrac{1}{f(D^2)}$,

$$\frac{1}{f(D^2)} \{f(D^2) \sin (ax + b)\} = \frac{1}{f(D^2)} \{f(- a^2) \sin (ax + b)\}$$

or $$\sin (ax + b) = f(- a^2) \frac{1}{f(D^2)} \sin (ax + b).$$

Dividing both sides by $f(- a^2)$,

$$\mathbf{\frac{1}{f(D^2)} \sin (ax + b) = \frac{1}{f(- a^2)} \sin (ax + b), \text{ provided } f(- a^2) \neq 0}$$

Similarly, $$\mathbf{\frac{1}{f(D^2)} \cos (ax + b) = \frac{1}{f(- a^2)} \cos (ax + b), \text{ provided } f(- a^2) \neq 0}$$

Steps : When $Q = \sin (ax + b)$ or $\cos (ax + b)$,

1. Replace D^2 by $- a^2$,

D^4 by a^4,

D^6 by $- a^6$,

D^8 by a^8 and so on.

2. By doing so, following possibilities arise :

(*a*) If denominator reduces to a constant, it will be final step in finding P.I.

(*b*) If denominator reduces into D only, we are then only to integrate the given function Q once.

(*c*) If denominator reduces to a factor of the form $\alpha D + \beta$ then we operate by its conjugate $\alpha D - \beta$ on both numerator and denominator from left hand side such as

$$\frac{\alpha D - \beta}{\alpha D - \beta} \cdot \left[\frac{1}{(\alpha D + \beta)} \sin (ax + b)\right]$$

By doing so, denominator will become $\alpha^2 D^2 - \beta^2$ which in turn reduces to a constant by replacing D^2 by $- a^2$.

Now, we operate $\sin (ax + b)$ by $(\alpha D - \beta)$ and consequently, find the required particular integral.

Case of failure : If $f(- a^2) = 0$, the above method fails. Then we proceed as follows :

$$\mathbf{\frac{1}{f(D^2)} \cos (ax + b) = x \cdot \frac{1}{f'(D^2)} \cos (ax + b), \text{ provided } f'(- a^2) \neq 0}$$

$$\frac{1}{f(D^2)} \sin(ax+b) = x \cdot \frac{1}{f'(D^2)} \sin(ax+b), \text{ provided } f'(-a^2) \neq 0$$

If $f'(-a^2) = 0$, then

$$\frac{1}{f(D^2)} \sin(ax+b) = x^2 \cdot \frac{1}{f''(D^2)} \sin(ax+b), \text{ provided } f''(-a^2) \neq 0$$

$$\frac{1}{f(D^2)} \cos(ax+b) = x^2 \cdot \frac{1}{f''(D^2)} \cos(ax+b), \text{ provided } f''(-a^2) \neq 0$$

and so on.

Steps :

1. When $f(-a^2) = 0$, we differentiate the denominator w.r.t. D and multiply the expression by x simultaneously in the same step.
2. When $f'(-a^2) = 0$ (*i.e.*, step 1 fails) we again differentiate the reduced denominator in D w.r.t. D and again multiply the remaining expression by x simultaneously.
3. If there is another case of failure, above process is to be repeated again and again until we reach a constant in the denominator or any other possibility(ies) which we have discussed before in the same article.

ILLUSTRATIVE EXAMPLES

Example 1. *Solve the following differential equation:*

$(D^2 + 4)y = \sin 3x + \cos 2x.$ [U.P.T.U. (SUM) 2008]

Sol. Auxiliary equation is

$$m^2 + 4 = 0$$

$$\Rightarrow \quad m = \pm 2i$$

$$\therefore \quad \text{C.F.} = c_1 \cos 2x + c_2 \sin 2x$$

$$\text{P.I.} = \frac{1}{D^2+4}(\sin 3x) + \frac{1}{D^2+4}(\cos 2x)$$

$$= \frac{1}{-(3)^2+4} \sin 3x + x \cdot \frac{1}{2D}(\cos 2x)$$

$$= -\frac{1}{5}\sin 3x + \frac{x}{2}\left(\frac{\sin 2x}{2}\right) = -\frac{1}{5}\sin 3x + \frac{x}{4}\sin 2x$$

Hence the complete solution is

$$y = \text{C.F.} + \text{P.I.} = c_1 \cos 2x + c_2 \sin 2x - \frac{1}{5}\sin 3x + \frac{x}{4}\sin 2x$$

where c_1 and c_2 are arbitrary constants of integration.

Example 2. *Find the P.I. of $(D^3 + 1)y = \sin(2x + 1)$.*

Sol. $$\text{P.I.} = \frac{1}{D^3+1}\sin(2x+1) = \frac{1}{D(-2^2)+1}\sin(2x+1) \qquad [\text{Putting } D^2 = -2^2]$$

$$= \frac{1}{1-4D}\sin(2x+1)$$

Operating N^r and D^r by $(1 + 4D)$

$$= \frac{1+4D}{(1+4D)(1-4D)}\sin(2x+1) = \frac{1+4D}{1-16D^2}\sin(2x+1)$$

$$= \frac{1+4D}{1-16(-2^2)}\sin(2x+1) \qquad [\text{Putting } D^2 = -2^2]$$

$$= \frac{1}{65}[\sin(2x+1) + 4D\sin(2x+1)]$$

$$= \frac{1}{65}[\sin(2x+1) + 8\cos(2x+1)] \qquad \left[\because D \equiv \frac{d}{dx}\right]$$

Example 3. *Solve the following differential equations:*

(i) $\dfrac{d^2y}{dx^2} + a^2y = \sin ax$ (U.P.T.U. 2008)

(ii) $(D^2 + 4)y = \cos^2 x$. [M.T.U. (B. Pharm.) 2011]

Sol. (*i*) The auxiliary equation is

$$m^2 + a^2 = 0 \Rightarrow m = \pm ai$$

$$\therefore \quad \text{C.F.} = c_1\cos ax + c_2\sin ax$$

$$\text{P.I.} = \frac{1}{D^2+a^2}(\sin ax) = x \cdot \frac{1}{2D}\sin ax$$

$$= \frac{x}{2}\left[\frac{-\cos ax}{a}\right] = -\frac{x}{2a}\cos ax$$

Hence the complete solution is

$$y = \text{C.F.} + \text{P.I.} = c_1\cos ax + c_2\sin ax - \frac{x}{2a}\cos ax$$

where c_1 and c_2 are arbitrary constants of integration.

(*ii*) The auxiliary equation is

$$m^2 + 4 = 0 \Rightarrow m = \pm 2i$$

$$\therefore \quad \text{C.F.} = c_1\cos 2x + c_2\sin 2x$$

$$\text{P.I.} = \frac{1}{D^2+4}\cos^2 x = \frac{1}{2}\left[\frac{1}{D^2+4}(1+\cos 2x)\right]$$

$$= \frac{1}{2}\left[\frac{1}{D^2+4}(e^{ox}) + \frac{1}{D^2+4}(\cos 2x)\right]$$

$$= \frac{1}{2}\left[\frac{1}{4} + x \cdot \frac{1}{2D}(\cos 2x)\right]$$

$$= \frac{1}{2}\left[\frac{1}{4} + \frac{x}{4}\sin 2x\right] = \frac{1}{8}(1 + x\sin 2x)$$

Hence the complete solution is

$$y = \text{C.F.} + \text{P.I.} = c_1 \cos 2x + c_2 \sin 2x + \frac{1}{8}(1 + x\sin 2x)$$

where c_1 and c_2 are arbitrary constants of integration.

Example 4. *Solve* : $\dfrac{d^4y}{dx^4} - m^4y = \cos mx.$

Sol. Auxiliary equation is

$$M^4 - m^4 = 0$$

$$(M^2 - m^2)(M^2 + m^2) = 0$$

$$M = \pm m, \pm mi$$

$\therefore$
$$\text{C.F.} = c_1e^{mx} + c_2e^{-mx} + c_3 \cos mx + c_4 \sin mx$$

$$\text{P.I.} = \frac{1}{D^4 - m^4}(\cos mx) = x \cdot \frac{1}{4D^3}\cos mx$$

$$= \frac{x}{4} \cdot \frac{1}{D^2}\left(\frac{\sin mx}{m}\right) = -\frac{x}{4m^2}\left(\frac{\sin mx}{m}\right) = -\frac{x}{4m^3}\sin mx$$

Hence the complete solution is

$$y = \text{C.F.} + \text{P.I.} = c_1e^{mx} + c_2e^{-mx} + c_3 \cos mx + c_4 \sin mx - \frac{x}{4m^3}\sin mx$$

where c_1, c_2, c_3 and c_4 are arbitrary constants of integration.

Example 5. *Solve* : $\dfrac{d^3y}{dx^3} - 3\dfrac{d^2y}{dx^2} + 4\dfrac{dy}{dx} - 2y = e^x + \cos x.$ (U.P.T.U. 2006)

Sol. Auxiliary equation is

$$m^3 - 3m^2 + 4m - 2 = 0$$

$\Rightarrow$
$$(m^2 - 2m + 2)(m - 1) = 0 \quad \Rightarrow \quad m = 1, 1 \pm i$$

$\therefore$
$$\text{C.F.} = c_1e^x + e^x(c_2 \cos x + c_3 \sin x)$$

$$\text{P.I.} = \frac{1}{(D^3 - 3D^2 + 4D - 2)}e^x + \frac{1}{(D^3 - 3D^2 + 4D - 2)}\cos x$$

$$= x \cdot \frac{1}{3D^2 - 6D + 4}(e^x) + \frac{1}{(-D + 3 + 4D - 2)}(\cos x)$$

$$= x \cdot \frac{1}{(7-6)} e^x + \frac{1}{3D+1} (\cos x) = x e^x + \frac{3D-1}{9D^2-1} (\cos x)$$

$$= xe^x - \frac{1}{10} (-3 \sin x - \cos x)$$

$\therefore$ Complete solution is

$$y = \text{C.F.} + \text{P.I.} = c_1 e^x + e^x (c_2 \cos x + c_3 \sin x) + xe^x + \frac{1}{10} (3 \sin x + \cos x)$$

where c_1, c_2, c_3 are arbitrary constants of integration.

Example 6. *Solve:* $(D^2 - 4D + 1)y = \cos x \cos 2x + \sin^2 x$.

Sol. Auxiliary equation is

$$m^2 - 4m + 1 = 0$$

$$\Rightarrow \quad m = \frac{4 \pm \sqrt{16-4}}{2} = 2 \pm \sqrt{3}$$

$$\therefore \quad \text{C.F.} = e^{2x} (c_1 \cosh \sqrt{3}\, x + c_2 \sinh \sqrt{3}\, x)$$

$$\text{P.I.} = \frac{1}{D^2 - 4D + 1} (\cos x \cos 2x) + \frac{1}{D^2 - 4D + 1} (\sin^2 x)$$

$$= \frac{1}{2}\left[\frac{1}{D^2 - 4D + 1} (\cos 3x) + \frac{1}{D^2 - 4D + 1} (\cos x)\right] + \frac{1}{D^2 - 4D + 1}\left(\frac{1 - \cos 2x}{2}\right)$$

$$= \frac{1}{2} (P_1 + P_2) + P_3 \qquad \ldots(1)$$

where, $$P_1 = \frac{1}{D^2 - 4D + 1} (\cos 3x)$$

$$= \frac{1}{-9 - 4D + 1} (\cos 3x) = -\frac{1}{4(D+2)} \cos 3x$$

$$= -\frac{1}{4} \frac{D-2}{(D^2-4)} \cos 3x = -\frac{1}{4} \frac{(D-2)}{(-9-4)} \cos 3x = \frac{1}{52} (-3 \sin 3x - 2 \cos 3x)$$

$$P_2 = \frac{1}{D^2 - 4D + 1} (\cos x) = \frac{1}{-1 - 4D + 1} \cos x = -\frac{1}{4} \sin x$$

$$P_3 = \frac{1}{2}\left[\frac{1}{D^2 - 4D + 1} (1) - \frac{1}{D^2 - 4D + 1} (\cos 2x)\right]$$

$$= \frac{1}{2}\left[\frac{1}{D^2 - 4D + 1} (e^{0x}) - \frac{1}{-4 - 4D + 1} (\cos 2x)\right]$$

$$= \frac{1}{2}\left[\frac{1}{(0)^2 - 4(0) + 1} (e^{0x}) + \frac{1}{4D+3} (\cos 2x)\right]$$

$$= \frac{1}{2}\left[1 + \frac{4D - 3}{16D^2 - 9}(\cos 2x)\right] = \frac{1}{2}\left[1 + \frac{4D - 3}{(-64 - 9)}(\cos 2x)\right]$$

$$= \frac{1}{2}\left[1 - \frac{1}{73}(-8\sin 2x - 3\cos 2x)\right] = \frac{1}{2}\left[1 + \frac{1}{73}(8\sin 2x + 3\cos 2x)\right]$$

$\therefore$ From (1),

$$\text{P.I.} = -\frac{1}{104}(3\sin 3x + 2\cos 3x) - \frac{1}{8}\sin x + \frac{1}{2} + \frac{1}{146}(8\sin 2x + 3\cos 2x)$$

Hence the complete solution is

$$y = \text{C.F.} + \text{P.I.}$$

$$= e^{2x}(c_1 \cosh \sqrt{3}\, x + c_2 \sinh \sqrt{3}\, x) + \frac{1}{2} - \frac{1}{8}\sin x$$

$$- \frac{1}{104}(3\sin 3x + 2\cos 3x) + \frac{1}{146}(8\sin 2x + 3\cos 2x)$$

where c_1 and c_2 are arbitrary constants of integration.

Example 7. *Solve :* $\frac{d^2y}{dx^2} + 2\frac{dy}{dx} + 10y + 37\sin 3x = 0$ *and find the value of y when* $x = \frac{\pi}{2}$ *being given that* $y = 3$, $\frac{dy}{dx} = 0$ *when* $x = 0$. (G.B.T.U. 2011)

Sol. We have,

$$(D^2 + 2D + 10)\,y = -37\sin 3x$$

Auxiliary equation is

$$m^2 + 2m + 10 = 0$$

$$\Rightarrow \quad m = -1 \pm 3i$$

$$\therefore \quad \text{C.F.} = e^{-x}(c_1\cos 3x + c_2 \sin 3x)$$

$$\text{P.I.} = \frac{1}{D^2 + 2D + 10}(-37\sin 3x)$$

$$= (-37)\frac{1}{2D + 1}(\sin 3x) \qquad | \text{ Replacing } D^2 \text{ by } -9$$

$$= (-37)\frac{2D - 1}{4D^2 - 1}(\sin 3x) \qquad | \text{ Operating by } 2D - 1$$

$$= (-37)\frac{(2D - 1)}{(-37)}(\sin 3x) \qquad | \; D^2 = -9$$

$$= 6\cos 3x - \sin 3x$$

Hence the general solution is

$$y = \text{C.F.} + \text{P.I.} = e^{-x}(c_1\cos 3x + c_2\sin 3x) + 6\cos 3x - \sin 3x \qquad ...(1)$$

Applying the condition $y(0) = 3$ in (1),

$$3 = c_1 + 6 \Rightarrow c_1 = -3$$

From (1), $$\frac{dy}{dx} = e^{-x}(-3c_1 \sin 3x + 3c_2 \cos 3x) - e^{-x}(c_1 \cos 3x + c_2 \sin 3x) - 18 \sin 3x - 3 \cos 3x \quad ...(2)$$

Applying the condition $\frac{dy}{dx} = 0$ when $x = 0$ in (2),

$$0 = 3c_2 - c_1 - 3$$

$\Rightarrow$ $$0 = 3c_2 \qquad (\because c_1 = -3)$$

$\Rightarrow$ $$c_2 = 0$$

Substituting the values of c_1 and c_2 in equation (1), we get

$$y = (6 - 3e^{-x}) \cos 3x - \sin 3x$$

when $x = \frac{\pi}{2}$, $$y = -\sin\frac{3\pi}{2} = 1$$

TEST YOUR KNOWLEDGE

Solve the following differential equations :

1. $\frac{d^3y}{dx^3} + a^2 \frac{dy}{dx} = \sin ax$
2. $(D^2 - 4D + 3)y = \sin 3x \cos 2x$
3. $\frac{d^2y}{dx^2} + 4y = e^x + \sin 2x$ *[U.P.T.U. (B. Pharm.) 2009, 2010]*
4. (*i*) $(D^2 + 9)\, y = \cos 2x + \sin 2x$ (*ii*) $(D^2 + 5D - 6)\, y = \sin 3x + \cos 2x$ *[G.B.T.U. 2010; G.B.T.U. (C.O.) 2011]*
5. $\frac{d^2y}{dx^2} + 2k \frac{dy}{dx} + k^2y = a \cos px$
6. $(D^2 - 8D + 9)\, y = 40 \sin 5x$
7. $(D^2 - 4D + 4)y = e^{-4x} + 5 \cos 3x$
8. $(D^4 + 2D^3 - 3D^2)y = 3e^{2x} + 4 \sin x$
9. $(D^2 - 4D - 5)y = e^{2x} + 3 \cos (4x + 3)$ *(U.P.T.U. 2008)*
10. $(D^2 + 5D - 6)y = \sin 4x \sin x$ *[U.P.T.U. (SUM) 2009]*
11. $(D^2 + 4)y = \cos x \cos 3x$
12. $(D^4 + 2D^2n^2 + n^4)y = \cos mx \,;\, m \neq n.$

Answers

1. $y = c_1 + c_2 \cos ax + c_3 \sin ax - \frac{x}{2a^2} \sin ax$
2. $y = c_1e^x + c_2e^{3x} + \frac{1}{884}(10 \cos 5x - 11 \sin 5x) + \frac{1}{20}(\sin x + 2 \cos x)$
3. $y = c_1 \cos 2x + c_2 \sin 2x + \frac{1}{5}e^x - \frac{x}{4} \cos 2x$
4. (*i*) $y = c_1 \cos 3x + c_2 \sin 3x + \frac{1}{5}(\cos 2x + \sin 2x)$

   (*ii*) $y = c_1e^x + c_2e^{-6x} - \frac{1}{30}(\cos 3x + \sin 3x) + \frac{1}{20}(\sin 2x - \cos 2x)$

5. $y = (c_1 + c_2x)\, e^{-kx} + \dfrac{a\,\{(k^2 - p^2)\cos px + 2kp \sin px\}}{(k^2 + p^2)^2}$

6. $y = e^{4x}\,(c_1 \cosh \sqrt{7}\, x + c_2 \sinh \sqrt{7}\, x) + \dfrac{25}{29} \cos 5x - \dfrac{10}{29} \sin 5x$

7. $y = (c_1 + c_2x)\, e^{2x} + \dfrac{1}{36} e^{-4x} - \dfrac{5}{169}\,(12 \sin 3x + 5 \cos 3x)$

8. $y = c_1 + c_2x + c_3e^x + c_4\, e^{-3x} + \dfrac{3}{20}\, e^{2x} + \dfrac{2}{5}\,(\cos x + 2 \sin x)$

9. $y = c_1\, e^{-x} + c_2e^{5x} - \dfrac{1}{9} e^{2x} - \dfrac{3}{697}[16 \sin (4x + 3) + 21 \cos (4x + 3)]$

10. $y = c_1e^x + c_2e^{-6x} + \dfrac{1}{2}\left[\dfrac{\sin 3x - \cos 3x}{30} + \dfrac{31 \cos 5x - 25 \sin 5x}{1586}\right]$

11. $y = c_1 \cos 2x + c_2 \sin 2x + \dfrac{x}{8} \sin 2x - \dfrac{1}{24} \cos 4x.$

12. $y = (c_1 + c_2\, x)\,(c_3 \cos nx + c_4 \sin nx) + \dfrac{1}{(n^2 - m^2)^2} \cos mx.$

1.29.3. Case III. When $Q = x^m$, m being a positive integer.

Here $\qquad \text{P.I.} = \dfrac{1}{f(D)}\, x^m$

Steps :

1. Take out the lowest degree term from $f(D)$ to make the first term unity (so that Binomial Theorem for a negative index is applicable). The remaining factor will be of the form $1 + \phi(D)$ or $1 - \phi(D)$.
2. Take this factor in the numerator. It takes the form $[1 + \phi(D)]^{-1}$ or $[1 - \phi(D)]^{-1}$.
3. Expand it in ascending powers of D as far as the term containing D^m, since $D^{m+1}(x^m) = 0$, $D^{m+2}(x^m) = 0$ and so on.
4. Operate on x^m term by term.

ILLUSTRATIVE EXAMPLES

Example 1. *Find the P.I. of* $(D^2 + 5D + 4)y = x^2 + 7x + 9.$

Sol. $\text{P.I.} = \dfrac{1}{D^2 + 5D + 4}\,(x^2 + 7x + 9) = \dfrac{1}{4\left(1 + \dfrac{5D}{4} + \dfrac{D^2}{4}\right)}\,(x^2 + 7x + 9)$

$$= \frac{1}{4}\left[1 + \left(\frac{5D}{4} + \frac{D^2}{4}\right)\right]^{-1} (x^2 + 7x + 9)$$

$$= \frac{1}{4}\left[1 - \left(\frac{5D}{4} + \frac{D^2}{4}\right) + \left(\frac{5D}{4} + \frac{D^2}{4}\right)^2 - \ldots\ldots\right](x^2 + 7x + 9)$$

$$= \frac{1}{4}\left(1 - \frac{5D}{4} - \frac{D^2}{4} + \frac{25D^2}{16} + \ldots\ldots\right)(x^2 + 7x + 9)$$

$$= \frac{1}{4}\left(1 - \frac{5D}{4} + \frac{21D^2}{16}\right)(x^2 + 7x + 9) \qquad | \text{ Leaving higher powers of D}$$

$$= \frac{1}{4}\left[(x^2 + 7x + 9) - \frac{5}{4}D(x^2 + 7x + 9) + \frac{21}{16}D^2(x^2 + 7x + 9)\right]$$

$$= \frac{1}{4}\left[(x^2 + 7x + 9) - \frac{5}{4}(2x + 7) + \frac{21}{16}(2)\right] = \frac{1}{4}\left(x^2 + \frac{9}{2}x + \frac{23}{8}\right).$$

Example 2. *Find the P.I. of $y'' - 6y' + 9y = 2x^2 - x + 3$.*

Sol. $\text{P.I.} = \dfrac{1}{D^2 - 6D + 9}(2x^2 - x + 3) = \dfrac{1}{(D-3)^2}(2x^2 - x + 3)$

$$= \frac{1}{9}\left(1 - \frac{D}{3}\right)^{-2}(2x^2 - x + 3) = \frac{1}{9}\left(1 + \frac{2D}{3} + \frac{3D^2}{9} + \ldots\ldots\right)(2x^2 - x + 3)$$

$$= \frac{1}{9}\left(1 + \frac{2D}{3} + \frac{D^2}{3}\right)(2x^2 - x + 3) \qquad | \text{ Leaving higher powers of D}$$

$$= \frac{1}{9}\left[2x^2 - x + 3 + \frac{2}{3}(4x - 1) + \frac{1}{3}(4)\right] = \frac{1}{9}\left[2x^2 + \frac{5}{3}x + \frac{11}{3}\right].$$

Example 3. *Solve : $(D^3 - D^2 - 6D)\,y = 1 + x^2$.*

Sol. Auxiliary equation is

$$m^3 - m^2 - 6m = 0$$

$$\Rightarrow \quad m(m - 3)(m + 2) = 0 \quad \Rightarrow \quad m = 0, -2, 3$$

$\therefore \quad \text{C.F.} = c_1 + c_2e^{-2x} + c_3e^{3x}$

$$\text{P.I.} = \frac{1}{D^3 - D^2 - 6D}(1 + x^2) = \frac{1}{-6D - D^2 + D^3}(1 + x^2)$$

$$= -\frac{1}{6D\left\{1 + \left(\frac{D - D^2}{6}\right)\right\}}(1 + x^2) = -\frac{1}{6D}\left[1 + \left(\frac{D - D^2}{6}\right)\right]^{-1}(1 + x^2)$$

$$= -\frac{1}{6D}\left[1 - \left(\frac{D - D^2}{6}\right) + \left(\frac{D - D^2}{6}\right)^2 - \ldots\ldots\right](1 + x^2)$$

$$= -\frac{1}{6D}\left[1 - \frac{D}{6} + \frac{D^2}{6} + \frac{D^2}{36}\right](1 + x^2) = -\frac{1}{6D}\left[1 + x^2 - \frac{1}{6}(2x) + \frac{7}{36}(2)\right]$$

$$= -\frac{1}{6D}\left(1 + x^2 - \frac{x}{3} + \frac{7}{18}\right) = -\frac{1}{6D}\left(x^2 - \frac{x}{3} + \frac{25}{18}\right)$$

$$= -\frac{1}{6}\left(\frac{x^3}{3} - \frac{x^2}{6} + \frac{25}{18}x\right) = -\frac{x}{18}\left(x^2 - \frac{x}{2} + \frac{25}{6}\right)$$

Hence the complete solution is

$$y = \text{C.F.} + \text{P.I.} = c_1 + c_2e^{-2x} + c_3e^{3x} - \frac{x}{18}\left(x^2 - \frac{x}{2} + \frac{25}{6}\right)$$

where c_1, c_2 and c_3 are arbitrary constants of integration.

Example 4. *Solve* $(D - 2)^2y = 8(e^{2x} + \sin 2x + x^2)$.

Sol. Auxiliary equation is

$$(m - 2)^2 = 0 \quad \Rightarrow \quad m = 2, 2$$

$$\therefore \qquad \text{C.F.} = (c_1 + c_2x)\, e^{2x}$$

$$\text{P.I.} = \frac{1}{(D-2)^2}\,[8(e^{2x} + \sin 2x + x^2)]$$

$$= 8\left[\frac{1}{(D-2)^2}e^{2x} + \frac{1}{(D-2)^2}\sin 2x + \frac{1}{(D-2)^2}x^2\right]$$

Now, $\frac{1}{(D-2)^2}e^{2x} = x \cdot \frac{1}{2(D-2)}e^{2x}$ | Case of failure

$$= x^2 \cdot \frac{1}{2}e^{2x}$$ | Case of failure

$$\frac{1}{(D-2)^2}\sin 2x = \frac{1}{D^2 - 4D + 4}\sin 2x = \frac{1}{-2^2 - 4D + 4}\sin 2x$$ [Putting $D^2 = -2^2$]

$$= -\frac{1}{4D}\sin 2x = -\frac{1}{4}\int \sin 2x\, dx = -\frac{1}{4}\left(-\frac{\cos 2x}{2}\right) = \frac{1}{8}\cos 2x$$

$$\frac{1}{(D-2)^2}x^2 = \frac{1}{(2-D)^2}x^2 = \frac{1}{4\left(1 - \frac{D}{2}\right)^2}x^2 = \frac{1}{4}\left(1 - \frac{D}{2}\right)^{-2}x^2$$

$$= \frac{1}{4}\left[1 + D + \frac{3}{4}D^2 + \ldots\ldots\right]x^2 = \frac{1}{4}\left(x^2 + 2x + \frac{3}{2}\right)$$

$$\therefore \qquad \text{P.I.} = 8\left[\frac{x^2}{2}e^{2x} + \frac{1}{8}\cos 2x + \frac{1}{4}\left(x^2 + 2x + \frac{3}{2}\right)\right]$$

$$= 4x^2e^{2x} + \cos 2x + 2x^2 + 4x + 3$$

Hence the complete solution is

$$y = \text{C.F.} + \text{P.I.} = (c_1 + c_2x)e^{2x} + 4x^2e^{2x} + \cos 2x + 2x^2 + 4x + 3$$

where c_1 and c_2 are arbitrary constants of integration.

Example 5. *If* $\frac{d^2x}{dt^2}+\frac{g}{b}(x-a)=0$ *; a, b and g are positive numbers and* $x=a'$, $\frac{dx}{dt}=0$ *when* $t=0$, *show that* $x=a+(a'-a)\cos\sqrt{\frac{g}{b}}\,t$. [U.P.T.U. (SUM) 2007]

Sol. We have $\frac{d^2x}{dt^2}+\frac{g}{b}x=\frac{ag}{b}$

Auxiliary equation is $m^2+\frac{g}{b}=0 \Rightarrow m=\pm\sqrt{\frac{g}{b}}\,i$

$$\therefore \quad \text{C.F.} = c_1\cos\sqrt{\frac{g}{b}}\,t + c_2\sin\sqrt{\frac{g}{b}}\,t$$

$$\text{P.I.} = \frac{1}{D^2+\frac{g}{b}}\left(\frac{ag}{b}\right) = \frac{ag}{b}\cdot\frac{1}{\frac{g}{b}\left(1+\frac{bD^2}{g}\right)}(1) = a\left(1+\frac{bD^2}{g}\right)^{-1}(1) = a$$

$\therefore$ General solution is

$$x = \text{C.F.} + \text{P.I.}$$

$$\Rightarrow \quad x = c_1\cos\sqrt{\frac{g}{b}}\,t + c_2\sin\sqrt{\frac{g}{b}}\,t + a \qquad \ldots(1)$$

At $t=0$, $x=a'$

$\therefore$ From (1), $a' = c_1 + a$

$$\Rightarrow \quad c_1 = a' - a \qquad \ldots(2)$$

Now,
$$\frac{dx}{dt} = \sqrt{\frac{g}{b}}\left(-c_1\sin\sqrt{\frac{g}{b}}\,t + c_2\cos\sqrt{\frac{g}{b}}\,t\right) \qquad \ldots(3)$$

At $t=0,\ \frac{dx}{dt}=0$

$\therefore$ From (3), $0=\sqrt{\frac{g}{b}}\cdot c_2$

$$\Rightarrow \quad c_2 = 0 \qquad \ldots(4)$$

$\therefore$ From (1), (2) and (4), the complete solution is

$$x = (a'-a)\cos\sqrt{\frac{g}{b}}\,t + a$$

which is the required solution.

Example 6. *Find the solution of the equation* $(D^2-1)y=1$ *which vanishes when* $x=0$ *and tends to a finite limit as* $x\to-\infty$ *and D stands for* $\frac{d}{dx}$.

Sol. We have $(D^2-1)y=1$

Auxiliary equation is

$$m^2-1=0 \Rightarrow m=\pm 1$$

$\therefore$ $$\text{C.F.} = c_1e^x + c_2e^{-x}$$

$$\text{P.I.} = \frac{1}{D^2 - 1}(1)$$

$$= -(1 - D^2)^{-1}(1) = -(1 + D^2 + ...)(1) = -1$$

$\therefore$ General solution is

$$y = c_1e^x + c_2e^{-x} - 1 \qquad ...(1)$$

when $x = 0, y = 0$

$\therefore$ From (1), $0 = c_1 + c_2 - 1 \Rightarrow c_1 + c_2 = 1$ ...(2)

Also, y tends to a finite limit as $x \to -\infty$

This condition will be satisfied only when $c_2 = 0$

$\therefore$ From (2), $c_1 = 1$

Hence from (1), Particular solution is $y = e^x - 1$.

TEST YOUR KNOWLEDGE

Solve the following differential equations :

1. $\dfrac{d^2y}{dx^2} - 4y = x^2$
2. $\dfrac{d^2y}{dx^2} - 2\dfrac{dy}{dx} + 3y = \cos x + x^2$
3. $\dfrac{d^2y}{dx^2} + \dfrac{dy}{dx} - 2y = x + \sin x$
4. $\dfrac{d^3y}{dx^3} + 2\dfrac{d^2y}{dx^2} + \dfrac{dy}{dx} = e^{2x} + x^2 + x$
5. $(D^5 - D)y = 12e^x + 8 \sin x - 2x$
6. $\dfrac{d^2y}{dx^2} + y = e^{2x} + \cosh 2x + x^3$
7. $(D^3 + 8)y = x^4 + 2x + 1$
8. $(D^2 + 2D + 1)\, y = 2x + x^2$
9. $(D^2 + D - 6)y = x$
10. $(D^3 + 3D^2 + 2D)\, y = x^2$
11. $(D^6 - D^4)\, y = x^2$
12. $(D^2 - 1)\, y = 2x^4 - 3x + 1$
13. $(D^2 - 4D + 4)\, y = x^2 + e^x + \cos 2x$ *[U.P.T.U. (B.Pharm.) SUM 2009]*
14. $\dfrac{d^2y}{dx^2} - \dfrac{dy}{dx} + 4y = x^2 + e^x.$ *[U.P.T.U. (B.Pharm.) SUM 2010]*

Answers

1. $y = c_1\, e^{2x} + c_2\, e^{-2x} - \dfrac{1}{4}\left(x^2 + \dfrac{1}{2}\right)$
2. $y = e^x\,(c_1 \cos\sqrt{2}\,x + c_2 \sin\sqrt{2}\,x) + \dfrac{1}{4}(\cos x - \sin x) + \dfrac{1}{27}(9x^2 + 12x + 2)$
3. $y = c_1\, e^x + c_2e^{-2x} - \dfrac{1}{10}(\cos x + 3 \sin x) - \dfrac{1}{4}(2x + 1)$
4. $y = c_1 + (c_2 + c_3x)\, e^{-x} + \dfrac{1}{3}x^3 - \dfrac{3}{2}x^2 + 4x + \dfrac{1}{18}e^{2x}$
5. $y = c_1 + (c_2 + 3x)\, e^x + c_3\, e^{-x} + c_4 \cos x + c_5 \sin x + x^2 + 2x \sin x$
6. $y = c_1 \cos x + c_2 \sin x + \dfrac{1}{5}e^{2x} + \dfrac{1}{5}\cosh 2x + x^3 - 6x$

7. $y = c_1 e^{-2x} + e^x (c_2 \cos\sqrt{3}\, x + c_3 \sin\sqrt{3}\, x) + \frac{1}{8} (x^4 - x + 1)$

8. $y = (c_1 + c_2x) e^{-x} + x^2 - 2x + 2$

9. $y = c_1e^{-3x} + c_2e^{2x} - \frac{1}{6}\left(x + \frac{1}{6}\right)$

10. $y = c_1 + c_2 e^{-x} + c_3 e^{-2x} + \frac{x}{12} (2x^2 - 9x + 21)$

11. $y = c_1 + c_2x + c_3x^2 + c_4x^3 + c_5e^x + c_6e^{-x} - \frac{x^4}{12} - \frac{x^6}{360}$

12. $y = c_1e^x + c_2e^{-x} - 2x^4 - 24x^2 + 3x - 49$

13. $y = (c_1 + c_2x) e^{2x} + \frac{1}{8} (2x^2 + 4x + 3) - \frac{1}{8} \sin 2x + e^x$

14. $y = e^{x/2}\left(c_1 \cos \frac{\sqrt{15}}{2} x + c_2 \sin \frac{\sqrt{15}}{2} x\right) + \frac{1}{4}\left(e^x + x^2 + \frac{x}{2} - \frac{3}{8}\right).$

1.29.4. Case IV. When $Q = e^{ax} V$, where V is a function of x

Let u be a function of x, then by successive differentiation, we have

$$D(e^{ax} u) = e^{ax} Du + a\, e^{ax} u = e^{ax} (D + a)u$$

$$D^2 (e^{ax} u) = D[e^{ax} (D + a) u] = e^{ax} (D^2 + aD) u + ae^{ax} (D + a)u$$

$$= e^{ax} (D^2 + 2aD + a^2) u = e^{ax} (D + a)^2 u$$

Similarly, $D^3 (e^{ax} u) = e^{ax} (D + a)^3 u$

In general, $D^n (e^{ax} u) = e^{ax} (D + a)^n u$

$\therefore$ $f(D) (e^{ax} u) = e^{ax} f(D + a)u$

Operating on both sides by $\frac{1}{f(D)}$,

$$\frac{1}{f(D)} [f(D) (e^{ax} u)] = \frac{1}{f(D)} [e^{ax} f(D + a)u]$$

$$\Rightarrow \quad e^{ax} u = \frac{1}{f(D)} [(e^{ax} f(D + a) u] \quad ...(1)$$

Now let $f(D + a) u = V$, *i.e.*, $u = \frac{1}{f(D+a)} V$

$\therefore$ From (1) we have $e^{ax} \frac{1}{f(D+a)} V = \frac{1}{f(D)} (e^{ax} V)$

or

$$\boxed{\frac{1}{f(D)} (e^{ax} V) = e^{ax} \frac{1}{f(D+a)} V}$$

Thus e^{ax} which is on the right of $\frac{1}{f(D)}$ may be taken out to the left provided D is replaced by D + a.

ILLUSTRATIVE EXAMPLES

Example 1. *Obtain the general solution of the differential equation*

$$\frac{d^2y}{dx^2} + 4\frac{dy}{dx} - 12y = (x-1)\,e^{2x}.$$

Sol. The given equation is

$$(D^2 + 4D - 12)\, y = (x-1)\, e^{2x} \qquad ...(1)$$

Auxiliary equation is

$$m^2 + 4m - 12 = 0$$

$$\Rightarrow \quad (m-2)(m+6) = 0$$

$$\Rightarrow \quad m = 2, -6$$

$$\therefore \quad \text{C.F.} = c_1 e^{2x} + c_2 e^{-6x}$$

$$\text{P.I.} = \frac{1}{D^2 + 4D - 12}(x-1)\, e^{2x}$$

$$= e^{2x} \cdot \frac{1}{\{(D+2)^2 + 4(D+2) - 12\}}(x-1)$$

$$= e^{2x} \cdot \frac{1}{D^2 + 8D}(x-1) = e^{2x} \cdot \frac{1}{8D}\left(1 + \frac{D}{8}\right)^{-1}(x-1)$$

$$= e^{2x} \cdot \frac{1}{8D}\left(1 - \frac{D}{8}\right)(x-1) \qquad \text{| Leaving higher power terms}$$

$$= e^{2x} \cdot \frac{1}{8D}\left(x - 1 - \frac{1}{8}\right) = e^{2x} \cdot \frac{1}{8D}\left(x - \frac{9}{8}\right) = \frac{e^{2x}}{8}\left(\frac{x^2}{2} - \frac{9x}{8}\right)$$

Hence the complete solution is

$$y = \text{C.F.} + \text{P.I.} = c_1 e^{2x} + c_2 e^{-6x} + e^{2x}\left(\frac{x^2}{16} - \frac{9x}{64}\right)$$

where c_1 and c_2 are arbitrary constants of integration.

Example 2. *Find the complete solution of*

$$\frac{d^2y}{dx^2} - 3\frac{dy}{dx} + 2y = xe^{3x} + \sin 2x. \qquad \text{[G.B.T.U. (SUM) 2010]}$$

Sol. Auxiliary equation is

$$m^2 - 3m + 2 = 0$$

$$\Rightarrow \quad (m-1)(m-2) = 0 \quad \Rightarrow \quad m = 1, 2$$

$$\therefore \quad \text{C.F.} = c_1 e^{x} + c_2 e^{2x}$$

$$\text{P.I.} = \frac{1}{D^2 - 3D + 2}(x\, e^{3x} + \sin 2x)$$

$$= \frac{1}{D^2 - 3D + 2}(e^{3x} \,.\, x) + \frac{1}{D^2 - 3D + 2}(\sin 2x)$$

$$= e^{3x} \cdot \frac{1}{\{(D+3)^2 - 3(D+3) + 2\}}(x) + \frac{1}{-4 - 3D + 2}(\sin 2x)$$

$$= e^{3x} \cdot \frac{1}{D^2 + 3D + 2}(x) + \frac{1}{-3D - 2}(\sin 2x)$$

$$= e^{3x} \cdot \frac{1}{2\left[1 + \left(\frac{3D + D^2}{2}\right)\right]}(x) - \frac{(3D - 2)}{9D^2 - 4}(\sin 2x)$$

$$= \frac{e^{3x}}{2} \cdot \left[1 + \left(\frac{3D + D^2}{2}\right)\right]^{-1}(x) - \frac{(3D - 2)}{(-40)}\sin 2x$$

$$= \frac{e^{3x}}{2}\left(1 - \frac{3D}{2}\right)(x) + \frac{1}{40}(6\cos 2x - 2\sin 2x)$$

$$= \frac{e^{3x}}{2}\left(x - \frac{3}{2}\right) + \frac{1}{20}(3\cos 2x - \sin 2x)$$

Hence the complete solution is

$$y = \text{C.F.} + \text{P.I.} = c_1 e^x + c_2 e^{2x} + \frac{e^{3x}}{2}\left(x - \frac{3}{2}\right) + \frac{1}{20}(3\cos 2x - \sin 2x)$$

where c_1 and c_2 are arbitrary constants of integration.

Example 3. *Find the P.I. of* $(D^2 - 3D + 2)y = 2e^x \cos \frac{x}{2}$.

Sol. $\text{P.I.} = \frac{1}{D^2 - 3D + 2}\left(2e^x \cos\frac{x}{2}\right)$

$$= 2e^x \cdot \frac{1}{\{(D+1)^2 - 3(D+1) + 2\}}\cos\frac{x}{2} = 2e^x \cdot \frac{1}{D^2 - D}\cos\frac{x}{2}$$

$$= 2e^x \cdot \frac{1}{-\frac{1}{4} - D}\cos\frac{x}{2} = -2e^x\left[\frac{\left(\frac{1}{4} - D\right)}{\left(\frac{1}{4} - D\right)\left(\frac{1}{4} + D\right)}\cos\frac{x}{2}\right]$$

$$= -2e^x \frac{\left(\frac{1}{4} - D\right)}{\frac{1}{16} - D^2}\cos\frac{x}{2} = -2e^x \cdot \frac{\frac{1}{4} - D}{\left(\frac{1}{16} + \frac{1}{4}\right)}\cos\frac{x}{2}$$

$$= -\frac{32}{5}e^x\left(\frac{1}{4}\cos\frac{x}{2} + \frac{1}{2}\sin\frac{x}{2}\right) = -\frac{16}{5}e^x\left(\sin\frac{x}{2} + \frac{1}{2}\cos\frac{x}{2}\right).$$

Example 4. *Obtain the general solution of the differential equation*

$$y'' - 2y' + 2y = x + e^x \cos x.$$

Sol. The given equation is

$$(D^2 - 2D + 2)y = x + e^x \cos x.$$

Auxiliary equation is,

$$m^2 - 2m + 2 = 0$$

$$m = \frac{2 \pm \sqrt{4 - 8}}{2} = 1 \pm i$$

$\therefore \qquad \text{C.F.} = e^x (c_1 \cos x + c_2 \sin x)$

$$\text{P.I.} = \frac{1}{D^2 - 2D + 2}(x) + \frac{1}{D^2 - 2D + 2}(e^x \cos x)$$

$$= \frac{1}{2 - 2D + D^2}(x) + e^x \cdot \frac{1}{(D+1)^2 - 2(D+1) + 2}(\cos x)$$

$$= \frac{1}{2}\left[1 - \left(\frac{2D - D^2}{2}\right)\right]^{-1}(x) + e^x \cdot \frac{1}{D^2 + 1}\cos x$$

$$= \frac{1}{2}\left[1 + \left(\frac{2D - D^2}{2}\right)\right](x) + e^x \cdot x \cdot \frac{1}{2D}\cos x \qquad | \text{ Case of failure}$$

$$= \frac{1}{2}[1 + D](x) + e^x \cdot \frac{x}{2}\sin x \qquad | \text{ Leaving higher powers}$$

$$= \frac{1}{2}(x + 1) + \frac{xe^x}{2}\sin x$$

Hence the complete solution is

$$y = \text{C.F.} + \text{P.I.} = e^x (c_1 \cos x + c_2 \sin x) + \frac{1}{2}(x+1) + \frac{xe^x}{2}\sin x$$

where c_1 and c_2 are arbitrary constants of integration.

Example 5. *Solve :* $\frac{d^2y}{dx^2} - 4y = x \sinh x.$

Sol. Given equation is

$$(D^2 - 4)y = x \sinh x$$

Auxiliary equation is

$$m^2 - 4 = 0 \text{ so that } m = \pm 2$$

$\therefore \qquad \text{C.F.} = c_1 e^{2x} + c_2 e^{-2x}$

$$\text{P.I.} = \frac{1}{D^2 - 4} x \sinh x = \frac{1}{D^2 - 4} x \left(\frac{e^x - e^{-x}}{2}\right)$$

$$= \frac{1}{2}\left[\frac{1}{D^2 - 4} e^x \cdot x - \frac{1}{D^2 - 4} e^{-x} \cdot x\right] = \frac{1}{2}\left[e^x \frac{1}{(D+1)^2 - 4} x - e^{-x} \frac{1}{(D-1)^2 - 4} x\right]$$

$$= \frac{1}{2}\left[e^x \frac{1}{D^2 + 2D - 3} x - e^{-x} \frac{1}{D^2 - 2D - 3} x\right]$$

$$= \frac{1}{2}\left[e^x \frac{1}{-3\left(1 - \frac{2D}{3} - \frac{D^2}{3}\right)} x - e^{-x} \frac{1}{-3\left(1 + \frac{2D}{3} - \frac{D^2}{3}\right)} x\right]$$

$$= -\frac{1}{6}\left[e^x \left\{1 - \left(\frac{2D}{3} + \frac{D^2}{3}\right)\right\}^{-1} x - e^{-x}\left\{1 + \left(\frac{2D}{3} - \frac{D^2}{3}\right)\right\}^{-1} x\right]$$

$$= -\frac{1}{6}\left[e^x\left(1+\frac{2D}{3}......\right)x - e^{-x}\left(1-\frac{2D}{3}......\right)x\right] = -\frac{1}{6}\left[e^x\left(x+\frac{2}{3}\right) - e^{-x}\left(x-\frac{2}{3}\right)\right]$$

$$= -\frac{x}{3}\left(\frac{e^x - e^{-x}}{2}\right) - \frac{2}{9}\left(\frac{e^x + e^{-x}}{2}\right) = -\frac{x}{3}\sinh x - \frac{2}{9}\cosh x$$

Hence the complete solution is

$$y = \text{C.F.} + \text{P.I.} = c_1 e^{2x} + c_2 e^{-2x} - \frac{x}{3}\sinh x - \frac{2}{9}\cosh x$$

where c_1 and c_2 are arbitrary constants of integration.

Example 6. *Solve :* $\frac{d^4y}{dx^4} - y = \cos x \cosh x.$

Sol. Given equation is $(D^4 - 1)y = \cos x \cosh x$.

Auxiliary equation is

$$m^4 - 1 = 0 \quad \text{or} \quad (m^2 - 1)(m^2 + 1) = 0 \quad \text{so that } m = \pm 1, \pm i$$

$$\therefore \quad \text{C.F.} = c_1 e^x + c_2 e^{-x} + e^{0x}(c_3 \cos x + c_4 \sin x)$$

$$= c_1 e^x + c_2 e^{-x} + c_3 \cos x + c_4 \sin x$$

$$\text{P.I.} = \frac{1}{D^4 - 1}\cos x \cosh x = \frac{1}{D^4 - 1}\cos x\left(\frac{e^x + e^{-x}}{2}\right)$$

$$= \frac{1}{2}\left[\frac{1}{D^4 - 1}e^x \cos x + \frac{1}{D^4 - 1}e^{-x}\cos x\right]$$

$$= \frac{1}{2}\left[e^x \frac{1}{(D+1)^4 - 1}\cos x + e^{-x}\frac{1}{(D-1)^4 - 1}\cos x\right]$$

$$= \frac{1}{2}\left[e^x \frac{1}{D^4 + 4D^3 + 6D^2 + 4D}\cos x + e^{-x}\frac{1}{D^4 - 4D^3 + 6D^2 - 4D}\cos x\right]$$

$$= \frac{1}{2}\left[e^x \frac{1}{(-1^2)^2 + 4D(-1^2) + 6(-1^2) + 4D}\cos x \right.$$

$$\left. + e^{-x}\frac{1}{(-1^2)^2 - 4D(-1^2) + 6(-1^2) - 4D}\cos x\right]$$

$$= \frac{1}{2}\left[e^x \frac{1}{(-5)}\cos x + e^{-x}\frac{1}{(-5)}\cos x\right] = -\frac{1}{5}\left(\frac{e^x + e^{-x}}{2}\right)\cos x = -\frac{1}{5}\cosh x \cos x$$

Hence complete solution is

$$y = \text{C.F.} + \text{P.I.} = c_1 e^x + c_2 e^{-x} + c_3 \cos x + c_4 \sin x - \frac{1}{5}\cos x \cosh x$$

where c_1, c_2, c_3 and c_4 are arbitrary constants of integration.

Example 7. (*i*) *Solve:* $(D^2 - 2D + 1)y = x e^x \sin x$ [M.T.U. (B. Pharm.) 2011]

(*ii*) *Solve:* $\frac{d^2y}{dx^2} - 2\frac{dy}{dx} + y = xe^x \cos x.$ (U.P.T.U. 2009)

Sol. (*i*) Auxiliary equation is

$$m^2 - 2m + 1 = 0$$

$$\Rightarrow \quad m = 1, 1$$

$$\therefore \quad \text{C.F.} = (c_1 + c_2x)e^x$$

$$\text{P.I.} = \frac{1}{D^2 - 2D + 1}(x\,e^x \sin x) = \frac{1}{(D-1)^2}(x\,e^x \sin x)$$

$$= e^x \cdot \frac{1}{(D+1-1)^2}(x \sin x) = e^x \cdot \frac{1}{D^2}(x \sin x)$$

$$= e^x \cdot \frac{1}{D}(-x \cos x + \sin x) = -e^x (x \sin x + 2 \cos x)$$

Hence the complete solution is

$$y = \text{C.F.} + \text{P.I.} = (c_1 + c_2x)\,e^x - e^x (x \sin x + 2 \cos x)$$

where c_1 and c_2 are arbitrary constants of integration.

(*ii*) Auxiliary equation is

$$m^2 - 2m + 1 = 0 \qquad \Rightarrow \quad m = 1, 1$$

$$\therefore \quad \text{C.F.} = (c_1 + c_2\,x)e^x$$

$$\text{P.I.} = \frac{1}{D^2 - 2D + 1}(x\,e^x \cos x) = \frac{1}{(D-1)^2}(x\,e^x \cos x)$$

$$= e^x \cdot \frac{1}{(D+1-1)^2}(x \cos x) = e^x \cdot \frac{1}{D^2}(x \cos x)$$

$$= e^x \cdot \frac{1}{D}(x \sin x + \cos x) = e^x (-x \cos x + 2 \sin x)$$

Hence the complete solution is

$$y = \text{C.F.} + \text{P.I.} = (c_1 + c_2\,x)\,e^x + e^x (-x \cos x + 2 \sin x)$$

where c_1 and c_2 are arbitrary constants of integration.

Example 8. *Solve:* $(D^4 + 6D^3 + 11D^2 + 6D)y = 20\,e^{-2x} \sin x.$

Sol. Auxiliary equation is

$$m^4 + 6m^3 + 11m^2 + 6m = 0$$

$$\Rightarrow \quad m(m^3 + 6m^2 + 11m + 6) = 0$$

$$\Rightarrow \quad m = 0, -1, -2, -3$$

$$\therefore \quad \text{C.F.} = c_1 + c_2e^{-x} + c_3e^{-2x} + c_4\,e^{-3x}$$

$$\text{P.I.} = \frac{1}{D^4 + 6D^3 + 11D^2 + 6D}(20\,e^{-2x} \sin x)$$

$$= \frac{1}{D(D+1)(D+2)(D+3)}(20\,e^{-2x} \sin x)$$

$$= 20\,e^{-2x} \cdot \frac{1}{(D-2)(D-1)\,D(D+1)}(\sin x)$$

$$= 20\,e^{-2x} \cdot \frac{1}{D^4 - 2D^3 - D^2 + 2D}(\sin x)$$

$$= 20\, e^{-2x} \cdot \frac{1}{2+4D} \sin x = 10\, e^{-2x} \frac{1-2D}{1-4D^2} \sin x$$

$$= 2\, e^{-2x} (\sin x - 2 \cos x)$$

Hence the complete solution is

$$y = \text{C.F.} + \text{P.I.} = c_1 + c_2\, e^{-x} + c_3 e^{-2x} + c_4 e^{-3x} + 2e^{-2x}(\sin x - 2 \cos x)$$

where c_1, c_2, c_3 and c_4 are arbitrary constants of integration.

Example 9. *Solve the differential equation*

$$\frac{d^2y}{dx^2} + 2\frac{dy}{dx} + y = \frac{e^{-x}}{x+2}.$$

Sol. Auxiliary equation is

$$m^2 + 2m + 1 = 0$$

$$\Rightarrow \quad (m+1)^2 = 0 \quad \Rightarrow \quad m = -1, -1$$

$$\therefore \quad \text{C.F.} = (c_1 + c_2 x)\, e^{-x}$$

$$\text{P.I.} = \frac{1}{(D+1)^2}\left(\frac{e^{-x}}{x+2}\right) = e^{-x} \cdot \frac{1}{(D-1+1)^2}\left(\frac{1}{x+2}\right)$$

$$= e^{-x} \frac{1}{D^2}\left(\frac{1}{x+2}\right) = e^{-x} \cdot \frac{1}{D} \log(x+2)$$

$$= e^{-x}\left[\log(x+2) \cdot x - \int \frac{1}{x+2} \cdot x\, dx\right] = e^{-x}\left[x \log(x+2) - \int \left(1 - \frac{2}{x+2}\right) dx\right]$$

$$= e^{-x}\, [x \log(x+2) - x + 2 \log(x+2)] = e^{-x}\, [(x+2) \log(x+2) - x]$$

Hence the complete solution is

$$y = \text{C.F.} + \text{P.I.} = (c_1 + c_2 x)e^{-x} + e^{-x} \{(x+2) \log(x+2) - x\}$$

where c_1 and c_2 are arbitrary constants of integration.

Example 10. *Solve : $(D^2 + 2D + 1)y = x \cos x$.*

Sol. Auxiliary equation is

$$m^2 + 2m + 1 = 0$$

$$\Rightarrow \quad m = -1, -1$$

$$\text{C.F.} = (c_1 + c_2 x)\, e^{-x}$$

$$\text{P.I.} = \frac{1}{D^2 + 2D + 1}(x \cos x) = \text{Real part of } \frac{1}{D^2 + 2D + 1}(xe^{ix})$$

$$= \text{R.P. of } e^{ix} \cdot \frac{1}{(D+i)^2 + 2(D+i) + 1}(x) = \text{R.P. of } e^{ix} \cdot \frac{1}{D^2 + 2D(1+i) + 2i}(x)$$

$$= \text{R.P. of } \frac{e^{ix}}{2i}\left[1 + \frac{1+i}{i} D + \frac{D^2}{2i}\right]^{-1}(x)$$

$$= \text{R.P. of } \frac{e^{ix}}{2i}\left(1 - \frac{1+i}{i} D\right) x \qquad \text{| Leaving higher powers}$$

$$= \text{R.P. of } \frac{e^{ix}}{2i}\left(x - \frac{1+i}{i}\right)$$

$$= \text{R.P. of } \frac{1}{2}(\cos x + i \sin x)(-ix + 1 + i) = \frac{1}{2}\cos x + \frac{1}{2}(x-1)\sin x$$

∴ The complete solution is given by

$$y = \text{C.F.} + \text{P.I.} = (c_1 + c_2x)\, e^{-x} + \frac{1}{2} \cos x + \frac{1}{2} (x - 1) \sin x$$

where c_1 and c_2 are the arbitrary constants of integration.

Example 11. *Solve the following differential equation :*

$$(D^2 - 4D + 4)\, y = 8x^2 e^{2x} \sin 2x.$$ [U.P.T.U. (B. Pharm.) 2009]

Sol. The auxiliary equation is

$$m^2 - 4m + 4 = 0 \;\Rightarrow\; m = 2, 2$$

$$\therefore \quad \text{C.F.} = (c_1 + c_2x)\, e^{2x}$$

$$\text{P.I.} = \frac{1}{(D-2)^2} (8x^2 e^{2x} \sin 2x) = 8\, e^{2x} \cdot \frac{1}{(D+2-2)^2} (x^2 \sin 2x)$$

$$= 8\, e^{2x} \cdot \frac{1}{D^2} (x^2 \sin 2x) = 8\, e^{2x} \cdot \frac{1}{D} \int x^2 \sin 2x \, dx$$

$$= 8\, e^{2x} \cdot \frac{1}{D} \left[x^2 \cdot \left(-\frac{\cos 2x}{2} \right) - \int 2x \cdot \left(\frac{-\cos 2x}{2} \right) dx \right]$$

$$= 8\, e^{2x} \cdot \frac{1}{D} \left[\frac{-x^2}{2} \cos 2x + x \cdot \frac{\sin 2x}{2} - \int 1 \cdot \frac{\sin 2x}{2} dx \right]$$

$$= 8\, e^{2x} \cdot \frac{1}{D} \left[\frac{-x^2}{2} \cos 2x + \frac{x \sin 2x}{2} + \frac{\cos 2x}{4} \right]$$

$$= 8\, e^{2x} \cdot \left[\left(\frac{-x^2}{2} \right) \frac{\sin 2x}{2} - \int (-x) \frac{\sin 2x}{2} dx + \int x \frac{\sin 2x}{2} dx + \frac{\sin 2x}{8} \right]$$

$$= 8\, e^{2x} \left[\frac{-x^2}{4} \sin 2x + \frac{\sin 2x}{8} + \int x \sin 2x \, dx \right]$$

$$= 8\, e^{2x} \left[\left(\frac{1}{8} - \frac{x^2}{4} \right) \sin 2x + x \cdot \left(\frac{-\cos 2x}{2} \right) - \int 1 \cdot \left(\frac{-\cos 2x}{2} \right) dx \right]$$

$$= 8\, e^{2x} \left[\left(\frac{1}{8} - \frac{x^2}{4} \right) \sin 2x - \frac{x}{2} \cos 2x + \frac{\sin 2x}{4} \right]$$

$$= 8\, e^{2x} \left[\left(\frac{3}{8} - \frac{x^2}{4} \right) \sin 2x - \frac{x}{2} \cos 2x \right]$$

$$= e^{2x} \left[(3 - 2x^2) \sin 2x - 4x \cos 2x \right]$$

Hence the complete solution is

$$y = \text{C.F.} + \text{P.I.} = (c_1 + c_2x)\, e^{2x} + e^{2x} [(3 - 2x^2) \sin 2x - 4x \cos 2x]$$

where c_1 and c_2 are arbitrary constants of integration.

Example 12. *A body executes damped forced vibrations given by the equation*

$$\frac{d^2x}{dt^2} + 2k\frac{dx}{dt} + b^2x = e^{-kt} \sin \omega t.$$

Solve the equation for both the cases, when $\omega^2 \neq b^2 - k^2$ and $\omega^2 = b^2 - k^2$.

Sol. Auxiliary equation is

$$m^2 + 2km + b^2 = 0 \quad \Rightarrow \quad m = -k \pm \sqrt{k^2 - b^2}$$

For damped force vibrations, $k^2 < b^2$

$$\therefore \qquad m = -k \pm i\sqrt{b^2 - k^2}$$

Case I. When $\omega^2 \neq b^2 - k^2$

$$\therefore \qquad \text{C.F.} = e^{-kt}\{c_1 \cos \sqrt{b^2 - k^2}\, t + c_2 \sin \sqrt{b^2 - k^2}\, t\}$$

$$\text{P.I.} = \frac{1}{D^2 + 2kD + b^2}(e^{-kt} \sin \omega t)$$

$$= e^{-kt} \cdot \frac{1}{(D-k)^2 + 2k(D-k) + b^2} \sin \omega t$$

$$= e^{-kt} \cdot \frac{1}{D^2 + (b^2 - k^2)} \sin \omega t = e^{-kt} \cdot \frac{1}{-\omega^2 + b^2 - k^2} \sin \omega t$$

$$= \frac{e^{-kt}}{b^2 - k^2 - \omega^2} \sin \omega t$$

Hence complete solution is

$$x = e^{-kt}\{c_1 \cos \sqrt{b^2 - k^2}\, t + c_2 \sin \sqrt{b^2 - k^2}\, t\} + \frac{e^{-kt}}{b^2 - k^2 - \omega^2} \sin \omega t$$

where c_1 and c_2 are arbitrary constants of integration.

Case II. When $\omega^2 = b^2 - k^2$

$$\text{C.F.} = e^{-kt}(c_1 \cos \omega t + c_2 \sin \omega t)$$

$$\text{P.I.} = \frac{1}{D^2 + 2kD + b^2}(e^{-kt} \sin \omega t)$$

$$= e^{-kt} \cdot \frac{1}{(D-k)^2 + 2k(D-k) + b^2} \sin \omega t$$

$$= e^{-kt} \cdot \frac{1}{D^2 + b^2 - k^2} \sin \omega t$$

$$= e^{-kt} \cdot t \cdot \frac{1}{2D} \sin \omega t \qquad \text{| Case of failure}$$

$$= \frac{te^{-kt}}{2}\left(\frac{-\cos \omega t}{\omega}\right) = -\frac{t}{2\omega} e^{-kt} \cos \omega t$$

Hence complete solution is

$$x = \text{C.F.} + \text{P.I.} = e^{-kt}(c_1 \cos \omega t + c_2 \sin \omega t) - \frac{t}{2\omega} e^{-kt} \cos \omega t$$

where c_1 and c_2 are arbitrary constants of integration.

TEST YOUR KNOWLEDGE

Solve the following differential equations :

1. $(D-a)^2 y = e^{ax} f''(x)$

2. $(D^2 - 2D)y = e^x \sin x$

3. $(D^2 - 4D + 4)y = e^x \cos x$ [*G.B.T.U. (C.O.) 2010*]

4. $\frac{d^2y}{dx^2} - 2\frac{dy}{dx} + 4y = e^{2x} \cos x$ [*M.T.U. (B. Pharm.) 2011*]

5. $(D^2 - 2D + 5)y = e^{2x} \sin x$ [*M.T.U. (AG) 2011*]

6. $\frac{d^2y}{dx^2} + y = e^{-x} + \cos x + x^3 + e^x \sin x$

7. (*i*) $(D^2 - 3D + 2)\, y = xe^x + \sin 2x$ (*U.P.T.U. 2008*)

(*ii*) $(D^2 - 1)\, y = xe^x + \cos^2 x$ [*U.P.T.U. (SUM) 2007*]

8. $(D-1)^2 (D^2+1)^2\, y = \sin^2 \frac{x}{2} + e^x + x$

9. $(D^2 - 6D + 13)y = 8e^{3x} \sin 4x + 2^x$

10. $(D^2 + 4)y = e^x \sin^2 x$

11. $(D^3 + 2D^2 + D)y = x^2e^{2x} + \sin^2 x$

12. $(D^2 - 4D + 3)y = e^x \cos 2x + \cos 3x$

13. $(D^2 + 4D + 8)y = 12e^{-2x} \sin x \sin 3x$

14. $\frac{d^2y}{dx^2} + 2y = x^2e^{3x} + e^x \cos 2x$

15. $(D-1)^2\, y = e^x \sec^2 x \tan x$

16. $(D^3 - 7D - 6)y = (x+1)\, e^{2x}$

17. $(D^2 - 1)\, y = x^2 \cos x$

18. $(D^2 - 1)\, y = x \sin x + x^2e^x$ [*U.P.T.U. (SUM) 2009*]

19. $(D^2 - 2D + 1)\, y = x \sin x$ (*U.K.T.U. 2012*)

20. $\frac{d^2y}{dx^2} + 2\frac{dy}{dx} + y = x^2 e^{-x} \cos x$ (*G.B.T.U. 2012*)

Answers

1. $y = e^{ax} [c_1 + c_2 x + f(x)]$

2. $y = c_1 + c_2e^{2x} - \frac{1}{2} e^x \sin x$

3. $y = (c_1 + c_2x)\, e^{2x} - \frac{e^x}{2} \sin x$

4. $y = e^x(c_1 \cos \sqrt{3}\, x + c_2 \sin \sqrt{3}\, x) + \frac{1}{13} e^{2x} (2 \sin x + 3 \cos x)$

5. $y = e^x (c_1 \cos 2x + c_2 \sin 2x) + \frac{e^{2x}}{10} (2 \sin x - \cos x)$

6. $y = c_1 \cos x + c_2 \sin x + \frac{1}{2} e^{-x} + \frac{1}{2} x \sin x + x^3 - 6x - \frac{1}{5} e^x (2 \cos x - \sin x)$

7. (*i*) $y = c_1e^x + c_2 e^{2x} - e^x \left(\frac{x^2}{2} + x\right) + \frac{1}{20} (3 \cos 2x - \sin 2x)$

(*ii*) $y = c_1 e^x + c_2e^{-x} + \frac{1}{4} e^x (x^2 - x) - \frac{1}{2} - \frac{1}{10} \cos 2x$

8. $y = (c_1 + c_2x)e^x + (c_3 + c_4x) \cos x + (c_5 + c_6x) \sin x + \frac{1}{2} - \frac{x^2}{32} \sin x + \frac{x^2}{8} e^x + x + 2$

9. $y = e^{3x}(c_1 \cos 2x + c_2 \sin 2x) - \frac{2}{3} e^{3x} \sin 4x + \frac{2^x}{(\log 2)^2 - 6 \log 2 + 13}$

10. $y = c_1 \cos 2x + c_2 \sin 2x + \frac{e^x}{10} - \frac{e^x}{34}(4 \sin 2x + \cos 2x)$

11. $y = c_1 + (c_2 + c_3 x)e^{-x} + \frac{e^{2x}}{18}\left(x^2 - \frac{7}{3}x + \frac{11}{6}\right) + \frac{1}{100}(3 \sin 2x + 4 \cos 2x) + \frac{x}{2}$

12. $y = c_1 e^x + c_2 e^{3x} - \frac{1}{8} e^x (\sin 2x + \cos 2x) - \frac{1}{30}(2 \sin 3x + \cos 3x)$

13. $y = e^{-2x}(c_1 \cos 2x + c_2 \sin 2x) + \frac{1}{2} e^{-2x}(3x \sin 2x + \cos 4x)$

14. $y = c_1 \cos \sqrt{2}\, x + c_2 \sin \sqrt{2}\, x + \frac{e^{3x}}{11}\left(x^2 - \frac{12}{11}x + \frac{50}{121}\right) + \frac{e^x}{17}(4 \sin 2x - \cos 2x)$

15. $y = e^x\left(c_1 + c_2 x + \frac{1}{2}\tan x\right)$

16. $y = c_1 e^{-x} + c_2 e^{-2x} + c_3 e^{3x} - \frac{e^{2x}}{144}(12x + 17)$

17. $y = c_1 e^x + c_2 e^{-x} + x \sin x + \left(\frac{1 - x^2}{2}\right)\cos x.$

18. $y = c_1 e^x + c_2 e^{-x} - \frac{1}{2}(x \sin x + \cos x) + \frac{x e^x}{12}(2x^2 - 3x + 3)$

19. $y = (c_1 + c_2 x)\, e^x + \frac{1}{2}\,[(x + 1) \cos x - \sin x]$

20. $y = (c_1 + c_2 x)\, e^{-x} + e^{-x}(-x^2 \cos x + 4x \sin x + 6 \cos x).$

1.29.5. Case V. When Q is any other function of x

Resolve $f(\mathrm{D})$ into linear factors.

Let $f(\mathrm{D}) \equiv (\mathrm{D} - m_1)(\mathrm{D} - m_2) \ldots\ldots (\mathrm{D} - m_n)$

Then P.I. $= \frac{1}{f(\mathrm{D})}\mathrm{Q} = \frac{1}{(\mathrm{D} - m_1)(\mathrm{D} - m_2)\ldots\ldots(\mathrm{D} - m_n)}\mathrm{Q}$

$$= \left(\frac{\mathrm{A}_1}{\mathrm{D} - m_1} + \frac{\mathrm{A}_2}{\mathrm{D} - m_2} + \ldots\ldots + \frac{\mathrm{A}_n}{\mathrm{D} - m_n}\right)\mathrm{Q} \qquad \text{(Partial Fractions)}$$

$$= \mathrm{A}_1 \frac{1}{\mathrm{D} - m_1}\mathrm{Q} + \mathrm{A}_2 \frac{1}{\mathrm{D} - m_2}\mathrm{Q} + \ldots\ldots + \mathrm{A}_n \frac{1}{\mathrm{D} - m_n}\mathrm{Q}$$

$$= \mathrm{A}_1 e^{m_1 x}\int \mathrm{Q} e^{-m_1 x}\,dx + \mathrm{A}_2 e^{m_2 x}\int \mathrm{Q} e^{-m_2 x}\,dx + \ldots\ldots + \mathrm{A}_n e^{m_n x}\int \mathrm{Q} e^{-m_n x}\,dx.$$

Remark. Remember the following formulae:

(*i*) $\frac{1}{\mathrm{D} - \alpha}\mathrm{Q} = e^{\alpha x}\int e^{-\alpha x}\mathrm{Q}\,dx$

(*ii*) $\frac{1}{\mathrm{D} + \alpha}\mathrm{Q} = e^{-\alpha x}\int e^{\alpha x}\mathrm{Q}\,dx$

ILLUSTRATIVE EXAMPLES

Example 1. *Find the complete solution of* $(D^2 + a^2)y = \sec ax$.

[M.T.U. (B. Pharm.) 2011, U.K.T.U. 2011]

Sol. Auxiliary equation is

$$m^2 + a^2 = 0 \quad \Rightarrow \quad m = \pm\, ai$$

$$\therefore \quad \text{C.F.} = c_1 \cos ax + c_2 \sin ax$$

$$\text{P.I.} = \frac{1}{D^2 + a^2} \sec ax$$

$$= \frac{1}{(D - ia)(D + ia)} \sec ax = \frac{1}{2ia}\left[\frac{1}{D - ia} - \frac{1}{D + ia}\right] \sec ax$$

$$= \frac{1}{2ia}\left[\frac{1}{D - ia}(\sec ax) - \frac{1}{D + ia}(\sec ax)\right] = \frac{1}{2ia}(P_1 - P_2)$$

where $$P_1 = \frac{1}{D - ia}(\sec ax)$$

$$= e^{iax}\int e^{-iax} \sec ax\, dx = e^{iax}\int (\cos ax - i \sin ax) \sec ax\, dx$$

$$= e^{iax}\int (1 - i \tan ax)\, dx = e^{iax}\left\{x + i\left(\frac{\log \cos ax}{a}\right)\right\}$$

$$P_2 = \frac{1}{D + ia}(\sec ax) = e^{-iax}\left\{x - i\left(\frac{\log \cos ax}{a}\right)\right\}$$ | Replacing i by $-i$

$$\therefore \quad \text{P.I.} = \frac{1}{2ia}\left[e^{iax}\left\{x + i\left(\frac{\log \cos ax}{a}\right)\right\} - e^{-iax}\left\{x - i\left(\frac{\log \cos ax}{a}\right)\right\}\right]$$

$$= \frac{1}{2ia}\left[x(e^{iax} - e^{-iax}) + i\left(\frac{\log \cos ax}{a}\right)(e^{iax} + e^{-iax})\right]$$

$$= \frac{1}{2ia}\left[2ix \sin ax + \frac{i}{a}(\log \cos ax)(2 \cos ax)\right] = \frac{1}{a}\left[x \sin ax + \frac{1}{a} \cos ax \log \cos ax)\right]$$

Hence the complete solution is

$$y = \text{C.F.} + \text{P.I.} = c_1 \cos ax + c_2 \sin ax + \frac{1}{a}\left(x \sin ax + \frac{1}{a} \cos ax \log \cos ax\right)$$

where c_1 and c_2 are arbitrary constants of integration.

Example 2. *Find the general solution of the differential equation*

$$\frac{d^2y}{dx^2} + 3\frac{dy}{dx} + 2y = e^{e^x}.$$

Sol. Auxiliary equation is

$$m^2 + 3m + 2 = 0$$

$$\rightarrow \quad (m + 1)(m + 2) = 0 \quad \Rightarrow \quad m = -1, -2$$

$$\therefore \quad \text{C.F.} = c_1 e^{-x} + c_2 e^{-2x}$$

$$\text{P.I.} = \frac{1}{(D + 1)(D + 2)} e^{e^x} = \left(\frac{1}{D + 1} - \frac{1}{D + 2}\right) e^{e^x}$$

$$= \frac{1}{D+1}(e^{e^x}) - \frac{1}{D+2}(e^{e^x}) = P_1 - P_2$$

where $P_1 = \frac{1}{D+1}(e^{e^x}) = e^{-x}\int e^x e^{e^x}\,dx = e^{-x}\int e^z\,dz$ | Put $e^x = z$ $\therefore$ $e^x\,dx = dz$

$$= e^{-x} e^{e^x}$$

$P_2 = \frac{1}{D+2}(e^{e^x}) = e^{-2x}\int e^{2x} e^{e^x}\,dx = e^{-2x}\int z e^z\,dz,$ where $e^x = z$ $\therefore$ $e^x\,dx = dz$

$$= e^{-2x}(z-1)e^z = e^{-2x}(e^x - 1)e^{e^x} = (e^{-x} - e^{-2x})e^{e^x}$$

$\therefore$ $\text{P.I.} = e^{-x}e^{e^x} - (e^{-x} - e^{-2x})e^{e^x} = e^{-2x}e^{e^x}$

Hence the complete solution is

$$y = \text{C.F.} + \text{P.I.} = c_1 e^{-x} + c_2 e^{-2x} + e^{-2x}e^{e^x}$$

where c_1 and c_2 are arbitrary constants of integration.

Example 3. *Solve :* $\frac{d^2y}{dx^2} + y = \operatorname{cosec} x.$

Sol. Auxiliary equation is

$$m^2 + 1 = 0 \Rightarrow m = \pm i$$

$\therefore$ $\text{C.F.} = c_1 \cos x + c_2 \sin x$

$$\text{P.I.} = \frac{1}{D^2+1}\operatorname{cosec} x = \frac{1}{(D+i)(D-i)}\operatorname{cosec} x$$

$$= \frac{1}{2i}\left(\frac{1}{D-i} - \frac{1}{D+i}\right)\operatorname{cosec} x \qquad \text{(Partial Fractions)}$$

$$= \frac{1}{2i}\left(\frac{1}{D-i}\operatorname{cosec} x - \frac{1}{D+i}\operatorname{cosec} x\right)$$

Now $\frac{1}{D-i}\operatorname{cosec} x = e^{ix}\int \operatorname{cosec} x\, e^{-ix}\,dx$

$$= e^{ix}\int \operatorname{cosec} x(\cos x - i\sin x)\,dx = e^{ix}\int(\cot x - i)\,dx$$

$$= e^{ix}(\log\sin x - ix)$$

Changing i to $-i$, we have $\frac{1}{D+i}\operatorname{cosec} x = e^{-ix}(\log\sin x + ix)$

$\therefore$ $\text{P.I.} = \frac{1}{2i}[e^{ix}(\log\sin x - ix) - e^{-ix}(\log\sin x + ix)]$

$$= \log\sin x\left(\frac{e^{ix} - e^{-ix}}{2i}\right) - x\left(\frac{e^{ix} + e^{-ix}}{2}\right)$$

$$= (\log\sin x) \,.\, \sin x - x\cos x$$

Hence the complete solution is

$$y = \text{C.F.} + \text{P.I.} = c_1\cos x + c_2\sin x + \sin x\log\sin x - x\cos x$$

where c_1 and c_2 are arbitrary constants of integration.

Example 4. *Solve* : $\dfrac{d^2y}{dx^2} + a^2y = \tan ax.$

Sol. Auxiliary equation is $m^2 + a^2 = 0 \;\Rightarrow\; m = \pm\, ia$

$$\therefore \qquad \text{C.F.} = c_1 \cos ax + c_2 \sin ax$$

$$\text{P.I.} = \frac{1}{D^2 + a^2} \tan ax = \frac{1}{(D + ia)(D - ia)} \tan ax$$

$$= \frac{1}{2ia}\left[\frac{1}{D - ia} - \frac{1}{D + ia}\right] \tan ax \qquad \text{(Partial Fractions)}$$

$$= \frac{1}{2ia}\left[\frac{1}{D - ia} \tan ax - \frac{1}{D + ia} \tan ax\right]$$

Now, $\dfrac{1}{D - ia} \tan ax = e^{iax} \displaystyle\int \tan ax \,.\, e^{-iax}\, dx$

$$= e^{iax} \int \tan ax\,(\cos ax - i \sin ax) = e^{iax} \int \left(\sin ax - i\,\frac{\sin^2 ax}{\cos ax}\right) dx$$

$$= e^{iax} \int \left(\sin ax - i\,\frac{1 - \cos^2 ax}{\cos ax}\right) dx = e^{iax} \int [\sin ax - i(\sec ax - \cos ax)]\, dx$$

$$= e^{iax}\left[-\frac{\cos ax}{a} - \frac{i}{a} \log(\sec ax + \tan ax) + i\,\frac{\sin ax}{a}\right]$$

$$= -\frac{1}{a}\, e^{iax}\, [(\cos ax - i \sin ax) + i \log(\sec ax + \tan ax)]$$

$$= -\frac{1}{a}\, e^{iax}\, [e^{-iax} + i \log(\sec ax + \tan ax)] = -\frac{1}{a}\, [1 + ie^{iax} \log(\sec ax + \tan ax)]$$

Changing i to $-\,i$, we have $\dfrac{1}{D + ia} \tan ax = -\dfrac{1}{a}[1 - ie^{-iax} \log(\sec ax + \tan ax)]$

$$\therefore \quad \text{P.I.} = \frac{1}{2ia}\left[-\frac{1}{a}\{1 + ie^{iax} \log(\sec ax + \tan ax)\} + \frac{1}{a}\{1 - ie^{-iax} \log(\sec ax + \tan ax)\}\right]$$

$$= -\frac{1}{a^2} \log(\sec ax + \tan ax)\left(\frac{e^{iax} + e^{-iax}}{2}\right) = -\frac{1}{a^2} \log(\sec ax + \tan ax) \,.\, \cos ax$$

Hence the complete solution is

$$y = \text{C.F.} + \text{P.I.} = c_1 \cos ax + c_2 \sin ax - \frac{1}{a^2} \cos ax \log(\sec ax + \tan ax)$$

where c_1 and c_2 are arbitrary constants of integration.

Example 5. *Solve the differential equation* : $\dfrac{d^2y}{dx^2} + y = x - \cot x.$

Sol. Auxiliary equation is

$$m^2 + 1 = 0 \qquad \Rightarrow \qquad m = \pm\, i$$

$$\therefore \qquad \text{C.F.} = c_1 \cos x + c_2 \sin x$$

$$\text{P.I.} = \frac{1}{D^2+1}(x - \cot x) = \frac{1}{D^2+1}(x) - \frac{1}{(D-i)(D+i)}\cot x$$

$$= (1+D^2)^{-1}(x) - \frac{1}{2i}\left[\frac{1}{D-i} - \frac{1}{D+i}\right]\cot x$$

$$= (1-D^2)(x) - \frac{1}{2i}\left[\frac{1}{D-i}(\cot x) - \frac{1}{D+i}(\cot x)\right]$$

$$= x - \frac{1}{2i}(P_1 - P_2) \qquad ...(1)$$

Now,

$$P_1 = \frac{1}{D-i}\cot x = e^{ix}\int e^{-ix}\cot x\, dx$$

$$= e^{ix}\int(\cos x - i\sin x)\cot x\, dx = e^{ix}\int\left(\frac{\cos^2 x}{\sin x} - i\cos x\right)dx$$

$$= e^{ix}\int(\text{cosec}\, x - \sin x - i\cos x)\, dx$$

$$= e^{ix}[\log(\text{cosec}\, x - \cot x) + \cos x - i\sin x]$$

$$= e^{ix}[\log(\text{cosec}\, x - \cot x) + e^{-ix}]$$

$$P_2 = \frac{1}{D+i}\cot x = e^{-ix}[\log(\text{cosec}\, x - \cot x) + e^{ix}]$$

∴ From (1),

$$\text{P.I.} = x - \frac{1}{2i}[e^{ix}\{\log(\text{cosec}\, x - \cot x) + e^{-ix}\} - e^{-ix}\{\log(\text{cosec}\, x - \cot x) + e^{ix}\}]$$

$$= x - \frac{1}{2i}[(e^{ix} - e^{-ix})\log(\text{cosec}\, x - \cot x)]$$

$$= x - \sin x\log(\text{cosec}\, x - \cot x)$$

Hence the complete solution is

$$y = \text{C.F.} + \text{P.I.} = c_1\cos x + c_2\sin x + x - \sin x\log(\text{cosec}\, x - \cot x)$$

where c_1 and c_2 are arbitrary constants of integration.

TEST YOUR KNOWLEDGE

Solve the following differential equations :

1. $(D^2 + 4)y = \tan 2x$ **2.** $(D^2 + 1)y = \sec x$ **3.** $(D^2 + a^2)y = \text{cosec}\, ax$

4. $(D^2 + 2D + 2)y = e^{-x}\sec^3 x$ **5.** $(D^2 - 2D + 2)y = e^x \tan x.$

Answers

1. $y = c_1\cos 2x + c_2\sin 2x - \frac{1}{4}\cos 2x\log(\sec 2x + \tan 2x)$

2. $y = c_1\cos x + c_2\sin x + x\sin x + \cos x\log\cos x$

3. $y = c_1 \cos ax + c_2 \sin ax + \dfrac{1}{a^2} \sin ax \log \sin ax - \dfrac{x}{a} \cos ax$

4. $y = e^{-x}\left(c_1 \cos x + c_2 \sin x + \dfrac{\sin x \tan x}{2}\right)$

5. $y = e^x (c_1 \cos x + c_2 \sin x) - e^x \cos x \log (\sec x + \tan x)$.

1.30. HOMOGENEOUS LINEAR DIFFERENTIAL EQUATIONS (EULER-CAUCHY EQUATIONS)

An equation of the form

$$x^n \frac{d^n y}{dx^n} + a_1 x^{n-1} \frac{d^{n-1} y}{dx^{n-1}} + a_2 x^{n-2} \frac{d^{n-2} y}{dx^{n-2}} + \ldots\ldots + a_{n-1} x \frac{dy}{dx} + a_n y = Q \quad \ldots(1)$$

where a_i's are constants and Q is a function of x, is called Cauchy's homogeneous linear equation.

Such equations can be reduced to linear differential equations with constant coefficients by the substitution

$$x = e^z \quad \text{or} \quad z = \log x$$

so that

$$\frac{dy}{dx} = \frac{dy}{dz} \cdot \frac{dz}{dx} = \frac{dy}{dz} \cdot \frac{1}{x} \quad \text{or} \quad x \frac{dy}{dx} = \frac{dy}{dz} = Dy, \text{ where } D \equiv \frac{d}{dz}$$

$$\frac{d^2 y}{dx^2} = \frac{d}{dx}\left(\frac{1}{x}\frac{dy}{dz}\right) = -\frac{1}{x^2}\frac{dy}{dz} + \frac{1}{x} \cdot \frac{d^2 y}{dz^2} \cdot \frac{dz}{dx}$$

$$= -\frac{1}{x^2}\frac{dy}{dz} + \frac{1}{x^2}\frac{d^2 y}{dz^2} \qquad \left(\because \frac{dz}{dx} = \frac{1}{x}\right)$$

or

$$x^2 \frac{d^2 y}{dx^2} = \frac{d^2 y}{dz^2} - \frac{dy}{dz} = D^2 y - Dy = D(D-1)y$$

Similarly, $x^3 \dfrac{d^3 y}{dx^3} = D(D-1)(D-2)y$ and so on.

Substituting these values is equation (1), we get a linear differential equation with constant coefficients, which can be solved by the methods already discussed.

1.30.1. Steps for Solution

1. Put $x = e^z$ so that $z = \log x$ and Let $D \equiv \dfrac{d}{dz}$

2. Replace $x \dfrac{d}{dx}$ by D,

   $x^2 \dfrac{d^2}{dx^2}$ by D(D – 1)

   $x^3 \dfrac{d^3}{dx^3}$ by D(D – 1) (D – 2) and so on.

3. By doing so, this type of equation reduces to linear differential equation with constant coefficients which is then solved as before.

1.31. LEGENDRE'S LINEAR DIFFERENTIAL EQUATION

An equation of the form

$$(a + bx)^n \frac{d^n y}{dx^n} + a_1(a + bx)^{n-1} \frac{d^{n-1}y}{dx^{n-1}} + \ldots\ldots + a_{n-1} (a + bx) \frac{dy}{dx} + a_n y = Q \qquad \ldots(1)$$

where a_i's are constants and Q is a function of x, is called Legendre's linear differential equation.

Such equations can be reduced to linear differential equations with constant co-efficients by the substitution

$$a + bx = e^z \text{ i.e. } z = \log (a + bx) \text{ so that } \frac{dy}{dx} = \frac{dy}{dz} \cdot \frac{dz}{dx} = \frac{b}{a+bx} \frac{dy}{dz}$$

or $$(a + bx) \frac{dy}{dx} = b \frac{dy}{dz} = b \text{ D}y, \text{ where D} \equiv \frac{d}{dz}$$

$$\frac{d^2y}{dx^2} = \frac{d}{dx} \left(\frac{b}{a+bx} \frac{dy}{dz} \right) = - \frac{b^2}{(a+bx)^2} \frac{dy}{dz} + \frac{b}{a+bx} \frac{d^2y}{dz^2} \cdot \frac{dy}{dx}$$

$$= - \frac{b^2}{(a+bx)^2} \frac{dy}{dz} + \frac{b}{a+bx} \frac{d^2y}{dz^2} \cdot \frac{b}{a+bx} = \frac{b^2}{(a+bx)^2} \left(\frac{d^2y}{dz^2} - \frac{dy}{dz} \right)$$

or $$(a + bx)^2 \frac{d^2y}{dx^2} = b^2 (\text{D}^2y - \text{D}y) = b^2 \text{ D(D} - 1)y$$

Similarly, $(a + bx)^3 \dfrac{d^3y}{dx^3} = b^3 \text{ D(D} - 1)(\text{D} - 2)y.$

Substituting these values in equation (*i*), we get a linear differential equation with constant coefficients, which can be solved by the methods already discussed.

ILLUSTRATIVE EXAMPLES

Example 1. *Solve :* $x^3 \dfrac{d^3y}{dx^3} + 2x^2 \dfrac{d^2y}{dx^2} + 2y = 10 \left(x + \dfrac{1}{x} \right)$. [U.P.T.U. (C.O.) 2009]

Sol. Put $x = e^z$ so that $z = \log x$ and let $\text{D} \equiv \dfrac{d}{dz}$ then the given differential equation reduces to

$$[\text{D(D} - 1)(\text{D} - 2) + 2\text{D(D} - 1) + 2]y = 10(e^z + e^{-z})$$

or $$(\text{D}^3 - \text{D}^2 + 2)y = 10 (e^z + e^{-z})$$

which is a linear equation with constant coefficients.

Its Auxiliary equation is

$$m^3 - m^2 + 2 = 0 \quad \text{or} \quad (m + 1)(m^2 - 2m + 2) = 0$$

$$\therefore \quad m = - 1, \frac{2 \pm \sqrt{4-8}}{2} = - 1, 1 \pm i$$

$$\therefore \quad \text{C.F.} = c_1e^{-z} + e^z (c_1 \cos z + c_3 \sin z) = \frac{c_1}{x} + x [c_2 \cos (\log x) + c_3 \sin (\log x)]$$

$$\text{P.I.} = 10\,\frac{1}{D^3 - D^2 + 2}\,(e^z + e^{-z}) = 10\left(\frac{1}{D^3 - D^2 + 2}\,e^z + \frac{1}{D^3 - D^2 + 2}\,e^{-z}\right)$$

$$= 10\left(\frac{1}{1^3 - 1^2 + 2}\,e^z + z\,.\,\frac{1}{3D^2 - 2D}\,e^{-z}\right) = 10\left(\frac{1}{2}\,e^z + z\,.\,\frac{1}{3(-1)^2 - 2(-1)}\,e^{-z}\right)$$

$$= 5e^z + 2ze^{-z} = 5x + \frac{2}{x}\log x$$

Hence the complete solution is

$$y = \text{C.F.} + \text{P.I.} = \frac{c_1}{x} + x\,[c_2 \cos(\log x) + c_3 \sin(\log x)] + 5x + \frac{2}{x}\log x$$

where c_1, c_2 and c_3 are arbitrary constants of integration.

Example 2. *Solve :* $x^3\,\dfrac{d^3y}{dx^3} + 3x^2\,\dfrac{d^2y}{dx^2} + x\,\dfrac{dy}{dx} + y = x + \log x.$

Sol. Put $x = e^z$ so that $z = \log x$ and let $D \equiv \dfrac{d}{dz}$ then the given differential equation reduces to

$$[D(D-1)(D-2) + 3D(D-1) + D + 1]\,y = e^z + z$$

$$\Rightarrow \qquad (D^3 + 1)y = e^z + z$$

Auxiliary equation is

$$m^3 + 1 = 0$$

$$\Rightarrow \qquad (m+1)(m^2 - m + 1) = 0 \qquad \Rightarrow \qquad m = -1,\ \frac{1 \pm \sqrt{3}i}{2}$$

$$\therefore \qquad \text{C.F.} = c_1 e^{-z} + e^{z/2}\left(c_2 \cos\frac{\sqrt{3}}{2}z + c_3 \sin\frac{\sqrt{3}}{2}z\right)$$

$$\text{P.I.} = \frac{1}{D^3 + 1}\,(e^z + z) = \frac{1}{D^3 + 1}\,(e^z) + \frac{1}{1 + D^3}\,(z)$$

$$= \frac{e^z}{2} + (1 + D^3)^{-1}\,(z) = \frac{e^z}{2} + (1 - D^3)\,(z) \qquad \text{| Leaving higher terms}$$

$$= \frac{e^z}{2} + z$$

$\therefore$ The complete solution is

$$y = c_1\,e^{-z} + e^{z/2}\left(c_2 \cos\frac{\sqrt{3}}{2}z + c_3 \sin\frac{\sqrt{3}}{2}z\right) + \frac{e^z}{2} + z$$

$$\therefore \qquad y = \frac{c_1}{x} + \sqrt{x}\left[c_2 \cos\frac{\sqrt{3}}{2}(\log x) + c_3 \sin\frac{\sqrt{3}}{2}(\log x)\right] + \frac{x}{2} + \log x$$

where c_1, c_2 and c_3 are the arbitrary constants of integration.

Example 3. *Solve:* $x^2\,\dfrac{d^2y}{dx^2} + x\,\dfrac{dy}{dx} - \lambda^2 y = 0.$ (U.P.T.U. 2007)

Sol. Put $x = e^z$ so that $z = \log x$ and let $D \equiv \dfrac{d}{dz}$ then the given differential equation reduces to

$$[D(D-1) + D - \lambda^2]y = 0$$

$$\Rightarrow \qquad (D^2 - \lambda^2)y = 0$$

Auxiliary equation is

$$m^2 - \lambda^2 = 0$$

$$\Rightarrow \qquad m = \pm \lambda$$

$$\therefore \qquad \text{C.F.} = c_1 e^{\lambda z} + c_2 e^{-\lambda z}$$

$$\text{P.I.} = 0$$

Hence, the complete solution is

$$y = \text{C.F.} + \text{P.I.} = c_1 e^{\lambda z} + c_2 e^{-\lambda z} = c_1 x^{\lambda} + c_2 x^{-\lambda}$$

where c_1 and c_2 are arbitrary constants of integration.

Example 4. *Solve:* $x^2 \dfrac{d^2y}{dx^2} + 4x \dfrac{dy}{dx} + 2y = e^x$.

Sol. Put $x = e^z$ so that $z = \log x$ and let $D \equiv \dfrac{d}{dz}$ then the given differential equation reduces to

$$\{D(D-1) + 4D + 2\}y = e^{e^z}$$

$$(D^2 + 3D + 2)y = e^{e^z}$$

Auxiliary equation is

$$m^2 + 3m + 2 = 0$$

$$\Rightarrow \qquad (m+1)(m+2) = 0 \quad \Rightarrow \quad m = -1, -2$$

$$\therefore \quad \text{C.F.} = c_1 e^{-z} + c_2\, e^{-2z}$$

$$\text{P.I.} = \frac{1}{D^2 + 3D + 2}\,(e^{e^z}) = \left(\frac{1}{D+1} - \frac{1}{D+2}\right) e^{e^z}$$

$$= \frac{1}{D+1}\,(e^{e^z}) - \frac{1}{D+2}\, e^{e^z} = e^{-z} \int e^z \,.\, e^{e^z}\, dz - e^{-2z} \int e^{2z}\, e^{e^z}\, dz$$

$$= e^{-z}\, e^{e^z} - e^{-2z}\,(e^z - 1)\, e^{e^z} = e^{-2z}\, e^{e^z}$$

Hence the complete solution is

$$y = \text{C.F.} + \text{P.I.} = c_1 e^{-z} + c_2 e^{-2z} + e^{-2z}\; e^{e^z} = \frac{c_1}{x} + \frac{c_2}{x^2} + \frac{1}{x^2}\, e^x$$

where c_1 and c_2 are arbitrary constants of integration.

Example 5. *Solve:* $(3x+2)^2 \dfrac{d^2y}{dx^2} + 3(3x+2)\dfrac{dy}{dx} - 36y = 3x^2 + 4x + 1.$

Sol. Given equation is a Legendre's linear differential equation.

Put $\qquad 3x + 2 = e^z$ *i.e.,* $z = \log(3x+2)$ so that $(3x+2)\dfrac{dy}{dx} = 3Dy.$

$$(3x+2)^2\frac{d^2y}{dx^2}=3^2\,D(D-1)y,\quad \text{where } D\equiv\frac{d}{dz}.$$

Substituting these values in the given equation, it reduces to

$$[3^2\,D(D-1)+3.3D-36]y=3\left(\frac{e^z-2}{3}\right)^2+4\left(\frac{e^z-2}{3}\right)+1$$

or $$9(D^2-4)y=\frac{1}{3}e^{2z}-\frac{1}{3}$$

or $$(D^2-4)y=\frac{1}{27}(e^{2z}-1)$$

which is a linear equation with constant co-efficients.

Its Auxiliary equation is $m^2-4=0 \quad \therefore \quad m=\pm 2$

$$\text{C.F.}=c_1e^{2z}+c_2\,e^{-2z}=c_1\,(3x+2)^2+c_2(3x+2)^{-2}$$

$$\text{P.I.}=\frac{1}{27}\cdot\frac{1}{D^2-4}(e^{2z}-1)=\frac{1}{27}\left[\frac{1}{D^2-4}e^{2z}-\frac{1}{D^2-4}e^{0z}\right]$$

$$=\frac{1}{27}\left[z\cdot\frac{1}{2D}e^{2z}-\frac{1}{0-4}e^{0z}\right]=\frac{1}{27}\left[\frac{z}{2}\int e^{2z}\,dz+\frac{1}{4}\right]$$

$$=\frac{1}{27}\left[\frac{z}{4}e^{2z}+\frac{1}{4}\right]=\frac{1}{108}(ze^{2z}+1)=\frac{1}{108}[(3x+2)^2\log(3x+2)+1]$$

Hence the complete solution is

$$y=\text{C.F.}+\text{P.I.}=c_1(3x+2)^2+c_2(3x+2)^{-2}+\frac{1}{108}[(3x+2)^2\log(3x+2)+1].$$

where c_1 and c_2 are arbitrary constants of integration.

Example 6. *By reducing to homogeneous, solve the differential equation*

$$(1+x)^2\frac{d^2y}{dx^2}+(1+x)\frac{dy}{dx}+y=4\cos\{\log(1+x)\}.$$

Sol. Put $1+x=e^z$ so that $z=\log(1+x)$ and let $D\equiv\frac{d}{dz}$ then the given differential equation reduces to

$$\{D(D-1)+D+1\}y=4\cos z$$

$$\Rightarrow \quad (D^2+1)y=4\cos z$$

Auxiliary equation is

$$m^2+1=0 \quad\Rightarrow\quad m=\pm i$$

$$\therefore \quad \text{C.F.}=c_1\cos z+c_2\sin z$$

$$\text{P.I.}=\frac{1}{D^2+1}(4\cos z)=4z\cdot\frac{1}{2D}\cos z=2z\sin z$$

Hence the complete solution is

$$y=c_1\cos z+c_2\sin z+2z\sin z$$

$$=c_1\cos\{\log(1+x)\}+c_2\sin\{\log(1+x)\}+2\log(1+x)\sin\{\log(1+x)\}$$

where c_1 and c_2 are arbitrary constants of integration.

Example 7. *Solve the differential equation:*

$$(3x+2)^2 \frac{d^2y}{dx^2} - (3x+2)\frac{dy}{dx} - 12y = 6x. \qquad \text{(G.B.T.U. 2011)}$$

Sol. Put $3x + 2 = e^z$ so that $z = \log(3x + 2)$ and let $D \equiv \frac{d}{dz}$ then the given differential equation reduces to

$$[3^2D(D-1) - 3D - 12]y = 6\left(\frac{e^z - 2}{3}\right)$$

$$(9D^2 - 12D - 12)y = 2e^z - 4 \qquad \text{...(1)}$$

Auxiliary equation is

$$9m^2 - 12m - 12 = 0$$

$$\Rightarrow \quad (9m+6)(m-2) = 0$$

$$\Rightarrow \quad m = 2, -\frac{2}{3}$$

$$\therefore \quad \text{C.F.} = c_1 e^{2z} + c_2 e^{-\frac{2}{3}z}$$

$$\text{P.I.} = \frac{1}{9D^2 - 12D - 12} 2e^z - \frac{1}{9D^2 - 12D - 12} 4e^{0z} = -\frac{2}{15}e^z + \frac{1}{3}$$

Hence complete solution is

$$y = c_1 e^{2z} + c_2 e^{-\frac{2}{3}z} - \frac{2}{15}e^z + \frac{1}{3}$$

$$= c_1(3x+2)^2 + c_2(3x+2)^{-2/3} - \frac{2}{15}(3x+2) + \frac{1}{3}$$

where c_1 and c_2 are arbitrary constants of integration.

Example 8. *Solve:* $(x+1)^2 \frac{d^2y}{dx^2} + (x+1)\frac{dy}{dx} = (2x+3)(2x+4).$

[M.T.U. (SUM) 2011; G.B.T.U. (C.O.) 2011]

Sol. Put $x + 1 = e^z$ so that $z = \log(x + 1)$ and let $D \equiv \frac{d}{dz}$ then the given differential equation reduces to

$$[D(D-1) + D]y = (2e^z + 1)(2e^z + 2)$$

$$D^2y = 4e^{2z} + 6e^z + 2$$

Auxiliary equation is

$$m^2 = 0 \Rightarrow m = 0, 0$$

$$\therefore \quad \text{C.F.} = c_1 + c_2 z$$

$$\text{P.I.} = \frac{1}{D^2}(4e^{2z} + 6e^z + 2) = e^{2z} + 6e^z + z^2$$

Hence complete solution is

$$y = \text{C.F.} + \text{P.I.} = c_1 + c_2 z + e^{2z} + 6e^z + z^2$$

$$= c_1 + c_2 \log(x+1) + (x+1)^2 + 6(x+1) + [\log(x+1)]^2$$

where c_1 and c_2 are arbitrary constants of integration.

TEST YOUR KNOWLEDGE

Solve:

1. $\dfrac{d^3y}{dx^3} - \dfrac{4}{x}\dfrac{d^2y}{dx^2} + \dfrac{5}{x^2}\dfrac{dy}{dx} - \dfrac{2y}{x^3} = 1$

2. $x^2 \dfrac{d^2y}{dx^2} - 2y = x^2 + \dfrac{1}{x}$

3. $x^2 \dfrac{d^2y}{dx^2} + 2x \dfrac{dy}{dx} - 20y = (x+1)^2$

4. $x^2 \dfrac{d^3y}{dx^3} - 4x \dfrac{d^2y}{dx^2} + 6 \dfrac{dy}{dx} = 4$

5. (*i*) $x^4 \dfrac{d^3y}{dx^3} + 2x^3 \dfrac{d^2y}{dx^2} - x^2 \dfrac{dy}{dx} + xy = 1$ (*ii*) $x^2 \dfrac{d^2y}{dx^2} - 4x \dfrac{dy}{dx} + 6y = x^2$

6. (*i*) $x^2 \dfrac{d^2y}{dx^2} - x \dfrac{dy}{dx} + y = 2 \log x$ (*ii*) $x^2 \dfrac{d^2y}{dx^2} - 4x \dfrac{dy}{dx} + 6y = x$

7. (*i*) $x^2 \dfrac{d^2y}{dx^2} - x \dfrac{dy}{dx} - 3y = x^2 \log x$ (*ii*) $x^2 \dfrac{d^2y}{dx^2} - x \dfrac{dy}{dx} + 2y = x \log x$

8. (*i*) $x^2y'' + xy' - y = x^3 e^x$. (*ii*) $\left(\dfrac{d}{dx} + \dfrac{1}{x}\right)^2 y = x^{-4}$. (M.T.U. 2012)

9. $x^2 \dfrac{d^2y}{dx^2} + 2x \dfrac{dy}{dx} - 12y = x^3 \log x$

10. $(x^2D^2 - xD + 4)y = \cos(\log x) + x \sin(\log x)$

11. (*i*) $x^2 \dfrac{d^2y}{dx^2} - 3x \dfrac{dy}{dx} + 5y = \sin(\log x)$ (*ii*) $x^2 \dfrac{d^2y}{dx^2} + 5x \dfrac{dy}{dx} + 4y = x \log x$

12. (*i*) $x^2 \dfrac{d^2y}{dx^2} - 2x \dfrac{dy}{dx} + 2y = x^{-1}$ (*ii*) $x^3 y''' + xy' - y = 3x^4$

13. (*i*) $x^3 \dfrac{d^3y}{dx^3} + 2x^2 \dfrac{d^2y}{dx^2} + 3x \dfrac{dy}{dx} - 3y = x + x^2$ (*ii*) $x^2 \dfrac{d^2y}{dx^2} + x \dfrac{dy}{dx} - y = x^m$

14. (*i*) $x^4 \dfrac{d^4y}{dx^4} + 6x^3 \dfrac{d^3y}{dx^3} + 9x^2 \dfrac{d^2y}{dx^2} + 3x \dfrac{dy}{dx} + y = (1 + \log x)^2$

    (*ii*) $[x^2D^2 - (2m-1)xD + (m^2 + n^2)]y = n^2x^m \log x$

15. $\dfrac{d^2y}{dx^2} + \dfrac{1}{x} \cdot \dfrac{dy}{dx} = \dfrac{12 \log x}{x^2}$

16. $(x+a)^2 \dfrac{d^2y}{dx^2} - 4(x+a) \dfrac{dy}{dx} + 6y = x$

17. $(1+2x)^2 \dfrac{d^2y}{dx^2} - 6(1+2x) \dfrac{dy}{dx} + 16y = 8(1+2x)^2$

18. $(2x+3)^2 \dfrac{d^2y}{dx^2} - 2(2x+3) \dfrac{dy}{dx} - 12y = 6x$

19. $x^2 \dfrac{d^2y}{dx^2} + 3x \dfrac{dy}{dx} + y = \dfrac{1}{(1-x)^2}$

20. $x^2 \dfrac{d^2y}{dx^2} - 3x \dfrac{dy}{dx} + y = \dfrac{(\log x)\sin(\log x) + 1}{x}$.

Answers

1. $y = c_1x^2 + x^{5/2}\,(c_2x^{\sqrt{21}/2} + c_3x^{-\sqrt{21}/2}) - \frac{1}{5}x^3$ **2.** $y = c_1x^2 + \frac{c_2}{x} + \frac{1}{3}\left(x^2 + \frac{1}{x}\right)\log x$

3. $y = c_1x^{-5} + c_2x^{-4} - \frac{x^2}{14} - \frac{x}{9} - \frac{1}{20}$ **4.** $y = c_1 + c_2x^3 + c_3x^4 + \frac{2}{3}x$

5. (*i*) $y = (c_1 + c_2 \log x)x + c_2x^{-1} + \frac{1}{4x}\log x$ (*ii*) $y = c_1x^2 + c_2x^3 - x^2 \log x$

6. (*i*) $y = x\,(c_1 + c_2 \log x) + 2 \log x + 4$ (*ii*) $y = c_1x^2 + c_2x^3 + \frac{x}{2}$

7. (*i*) $y = c_1x^3 + \frac{c_2}{x} - \frac{x^2}{3}\left(\log x + \frac{2}{3}\right)$ (*ii*) $y = x\,[c_1 \cos(\log x) + c_2 \sin(\log x)] + x \log x$

8. (*i*) $y = c_1x + c_2 . \frac{1}{x} + \left(x - 3 + \frac{3}{x}\right)e^x$ (*ii*) $y = x^{-1/2}\left[c_1 \cos\frac{\sqrt{3}}{2}(\log x) + c_2 \sin\frac{\sqrt{3}}{2}(\log x)\right] + \frac{1}{3}x^{-2}$

9. $y = c_1x^3 + c_2x^{-4} + \frac{x^3}{98}\log x\,(7 \log x - 2)$

10. $y = x\,[c_1 \cos(\sqrt{3}\log x) + c_2 \sin(\sqrt{3}\log x)] + \frac{3}{13}\cos(\log x) - \frac{2}{13}\sin(\log x) + \frac{1}{2}x \sin(\log x)$

11. (*i*) $y = x^2\,[c_1 \cos(\log x) + c_2 \sin(\log x)] + \frac{1}{8}[\sin(\log x) + \cos(\log x)]$

(*ii*) $y = \left(\frac{c_1 + c_2 \log x}{x^2}\right) + \frac{x}{9}\left(\log x - \frac{2}{3}\right)$

12. (*i*) $y = c_1x + c_2x^2 + \frac{1}{6x}$ (*ii*) $y = x[c_1 + c_2 \log x + c_3(\log x)^2] + \frac{1}{9}x^4$

13. (*i*) $y = c_1x + c_2 \cos(\sqrt{3}\log x) + c_3 \sin(\sqrt{3}\log x) + \frac{1}{7}x^2 + \frac{1}{4}x \log x$

(*ii*) $y = c_1x + \frac{c_2}{x} + \frac{x^m}{m^2 - 1}$

14. (*i*) $y = (c_1 + c_2 \log x)\cos(\log x) + (c_3 + c_4 \log x)\sin(\log x) + (\log x)^2 + 2 \log x - 3$
(*ii*) $y = x^m\,[c_1 \cos(n \log x) + c_2 \sin(n \log x)] + x^m \log x$

15. $y = c_1 \log x + c_2 + 2(\log x)^3$ **16.** $y = c_1(x + a)^2 + c_2(x + a)^3 + \frac{1}{2}(x + a) - \frac{1}{6}a$

17. $y = (1 + 2x)^2\,[c_1 + c_2 \log(1 + 2x) + \{\log(1 + 2x)\}^2]$

18. $y = c_1(2x + 3)^{-1} + c_2(2x + 3)^3 - \frac{3}{4}(2x + 3) + 3$

19. $y = \frac{1}{x}(c_1 + c_2 \log x) + \frac{1}{x}\log\left(\frac{x}{1 - x}\right)$

20. $y = x^2\,[c_1 \cosh(\sqrt{3}\log x) + c_2 \sinh(\sqrt{3}\log x)] + \frac{1}{61x}[\log x\,\{5 \sin(\log x) + 6 \cos(\log x)\}$

$+ \frac{2}{61}\{27 \sin(\log x) + 191 \cos(\log x)\}] + \frac{1}{6x}$.

1.32. SIMULTANEOUS LINEAR DIFFERENTIAL EQUATIONS

Now we discuss differential equations in which there is one independent variable and two or more than two dependent variables. Such equations are called *simultaneous linear equations*. To solve such equations completely, we must have as many simultaneous equations as the number of dependent variables.

Let x, y be the two dependent variables and t be the independent variable. Consider the simultaneous equations

$$f_1(D)x + f_2(D)y = T_1 \qquad ...(1)$$

and
$$\phi_1(D)x + \phi_2(D)y = T_2 \qquad ...(2)$$

where $D \equiv \frac{d}{dt}$ and T_1, T_2 are functions of t.

To eliminate y, operating on both sides of (1) by $\phi_2(D)$ and on both sides of (2) by $f_2(D)$ and subtracting,

we get
$$[f_1(D)\,\phi_2(D) - \phi_1(D)\,f_2(D)]x = \phi_2(D)T_1 - f_2(D)T_2 \quad \text{or} \quad f(D)x = T$$

which is a linear equation in x and t and can be solved by the methods already discussed. Substituting the value of x in either (1) or (2), we get the value of y.

Note. We can also eliminate x to get a linear equation in y and t.

ILLUSTRATIVE EXAMPLES

Example 1. *Solve the following simultaneous differential equations*

$$\frac{dx}{dt} = 3x + 2y, \ \frac{dy}{dt} = 5x + 3y.$$ [M.T.U. (B. Pharm.) 2011; U.P.T.U. (SUM) 2008]

Sol. Let $\frac{d}{dt} \equiv D$ then the given system of equations become

$$(D - 3)x - 2y = 0 \qquad ...(1)$$

$$-5x + (D - 3)y = 0 \qquad ...(2)$$

Operating eqn. (1) by (D – 3) and multiplying eqn. (2) by 2 then adding, we get

$$[(D - 3)^2 - 10]\,x = 0$$

$$(D^2 - 6D - 1)\,x = 0$$

Auxiliary equation is

$$m^2 - 6m - 1 = 0$$

$$\Rightarrow \qquad m = \frac{6 \pm \sqrt{36 + 4}}{2} = 3 \pm \sqrt{10}$$

$$\text{C.F.} = e^{3t}(c_1 \cosh \sqrt{10}\,t + c_2 \sinh \sqrt{10}\,t)$$

$$\text{P.I.} = 0$$

$$\therefore \qquad x = e^{3t}\,(c_1 \cosh \sqrt{10}\,t + c_2 \sinh \sqrt{10}\,t) \qquad ...(3)$$

From (1),
$$2y = \frac{dx}{dt} - 3x$$

$$= e^{3t}\sqrt{10}\,(c_1 \sinh \sqrt{10}\,t + c_2 \cosh \sqrt{10}\,t)$$

$$+ 3e^{3t}\,(c_1 \cosh \sqrt{10}\,t + c_2 \sinh \sqrt{10}\,t)$$

$$- 3e^{3t}\,(c_1 \cosh \sqrt{10}\,t + c_2 \sinh \sqrt{10}\,t)$$

$$\Rightarrow \qquad y = \frac{\sqrt{10}}{2} e^{3t}\,(c_1 \sinh \sqrt{10}\,t + c_2 \cosh \sqrt{10}\,t) \qquad ...(4)$$

Equations (3) and (4), when taken together, give the complete solution. c_1 and c_2 are arbitrary constants of integration.

Example 2. *Solve the following simultaneous differential equations*

$$\frac{dx}{dt} = -wy, \quad \frac{dy}{dt} = wx.$$

Also show that the point (x, y) lies on a circle. [U.P.T.U. (SUM) 2007; U.P.T.U. 2009]

Sol. Let $\frac{d}{dt} \equiv D$ then the given system of equations becomes

$$Dx + wy = 0 \qquad ...(1)$$

$$-wx + Dy = 0 \qquad ...(2)$$

Operating eqn. (1) by D and multiplying eqn. (2) by w then subtracting (2) from (1), we get,

$$(D^2 + w^2)\,x = 0$$

Auxiliary equation is

$$m^2 + w^2 = 0$$

$$\Rightarrow \qquad m = \pm\, wi$$

$$\therefore \qquad \text{C.F.} = c_1 \cos wt + c_2 \sin wt$$

$$\text{P.I.} = 0$$

$$\therefore \qquad x = \text{C.F.} + \text{P.I.} = c_1 \cos wt + c_2 \sin wt \qquad ...(3)$$

From (3), $$\frac{dx}{dt} = -wc_1 \sin wt + wc_2 \cos wt$$

From (1), $$wy = -Dx = w\,(c_1 \sin wt - c_2 \cos wt)$$

$$\therefore \qquad y = c_1 \sin wt - c_2 \cos wt \qquad ...(4)$$

Eliminating w between eqns. (3) and (4), we get

$$x^2 + y^2 = c_1^2 + c_2^2 \qquad ...(5)$$

which is a circle with centre (0, 0) and radius $\sqrt{c_1^2 + c_2^2}$.

Eqn. (5) shows that the point (x, y) lies on a circle.

Example 3. *Solve the following simultaneous differential equations:*

$$\frac{dx}{dt} + 5x - 2y = t, \quad \frac{dy}{dt} + 2x + y = 0$$

given that $x = y = 0$ when $t = 0$. (U.P.T.U. 2008)

Sol. Let $\frac{d}{dt} \equiv D$ then the given system of equations becomes

$$(D + 5)\, x - 2y = t \quad \text{...(1)}$$

$$2x + (D + 1)\, y = 0 \quad \text{...(2)}$$

Operating (1) by (D + 1), we get

$$(D^2 + 6D + 5)\, x - 2\,(D + 1)\, y = 1 + t \quad \text{...(3)}$$

Multiplying (2) by 2, we get

$$4x + 2\,(D + 1)\, y = 0 \quad \text{...(4)}$$

Adding (3) and (4), we get

$$(D^2 + 6D + 9)\, x = 1 + t$$

Auxiliary equation is

$$m^2 + 6m + 9 = 0 \quad \Rightarrow \quad m = -3, -3$$

$$\therefore \quad \text{C.F.} = (c_1 + c_2 t)\, e^{-3t}$$

$$\text{P.I.} = \frac{1}{(D+3)^2}(1+t) = \frac{1}{9}\left(1+\frac{D}{3}\right)^{-2}(1+t)$$

$$= \frac{1}{9}\left(1-\frac{2D}{3}\right)(1+t) = \frac{1}{9}\left(1+t-\frac{2}{3}\right) = \frac{1}{9}\left(t+\frac{1}{3}\right)$$

$$\therefore \quad x = \text{C.F.} + \text{P.I.} = (c_1 + c_2 t)\, e^{-3t} + \frac{1}{9}\left(t+\frac{1}{3}\right) \quad \text{...(5)}$$

From (5),
$$\frac{dx}{dt} = -3\,(c_1 + c_2 t)\, e^{-3t} + c_2 e^{-3t} + \frac{1}{9}$$

From (1),
$$2y = \frac{dx}{dt} + 5x - t$$

$$= -3\,(c_1 + c_2 t)\, e^{-3t} + c_2 e^{-3t} + \frac{1}{9} + 5\,(c_1 + c_2 t)\, e^{-3t} + \frac{5}{9}\left(t+\frac{1}{3}\right) - t$$

$$= 2\,(c_1 + c_2 t)\, e^{-3t} + c_2 e^{-3t} - \frac{4}{9}t + \frac{8}{27}$$

$$y = (c_1 + c_2 t)\, e^{-3t} + \frac{c_2}{2} e^{-3t} - \frac{2}{9}t + \frac{4}{27} \quad \text{...(6)}$$

Eqns. (5) and (6), when taken together, give the general solution.

Applying condition $x(0) = 0$ in (5), we get

$$0 = c_1 + \frac{1}{27} \quad \Rightarrow \quad c_1 = -\frac{1}{27}$$

Applying condition $y(0) = 0$ in (6), we get

$$0 = c_1 + \frac{c_2}{2} + \frac{4}{27} = \frac{c_2}{2} + \frac{1}{9}$$

$$\Rightarrow \quad c_2 = -\frac{2}{9}$$

Hence the required particular solution is given by

$$x = -\frac{1}{27}(1+6t)\,e^{-3t} + \frac{1}{9}\left(t + \frac{1}{3}\right)$$

and $$y = -\frac{2}{27}(2+3t)\,e^{-3t} - \frac{2}{9}t + \frac{4}{27}$$

Example 4. *Solve :* $\dfrac{d^2x}{dt^2} + y = \sin t,\ \dfrac{d^2y}{dt^2} + x = \cos t.$

Sol. Let $\dfrac{d}{dt} \equiv \text{D}$ then the given system of equations become

$$\text{D}^2x + y = \sin t \quad \text{...(1)}$$

$$x + \text{D}^2y = \cos t \quad \text{...(2)}$$

Operating eqn. (1) by D^2, we get

$$\text{D}^4x + \text{D}^2y = -\sin t \quad \text{...(3)}$$

Subtracting (2) from (3), we get

$$(\text{D}^4 - 1)\,x = -\sin t - \cos t$$

Auxiliary equation is

$$m^4 - 1 = 0$$

$$(m^2 - 1)(m^2 + 1) = 0$$

$$\Rightarrow \quad m = 1, -1, \pm i$$

$$\therefore \quad \text{C.F.} = c_1e^t + c_2e^{-t} + c_3\cos t + c_4\sin t$$

$$\text{P.I.} = \frac{1}{\text{D}^4 - 1}(-\sin t - \cos t)$$

$$= -t.\frac{1}{4\text{D}^3}(\sin t + \cos t) = \frac{t}{4}(-\cos t + \sin t)$$

$$\therefore \quad x = c_1e^t + c_2e^{-t} + c_3\cos t + c_4\sin t + \frac{t}{4}(\sin t - \cos t) \quad \text{...(4)}$$

$$\text{D}x = c_1e^t - c_2e^{-t} - c_3\sin t + c_4\cos t + \frac{t}{4}(\cos t + \sin t) + \frac{1}{4}(\sin t - \cos t)$$

$$\text{D}^2x = c_1e^t + c_2e^{-t} - c_3\cos t - c_4\sin t + \frac{t}{4}(-\sin t + \cos t) + \frac{1}{4}(\cos t + \sin t) + \frac{1}{4}(\cos t + \sin t)$$

From (1), $$y = \sin t - \frac{d^2x}{dt^2}$$

$$y = -c_1e^t - c_2e^{-t} + c_3\cos t + c_4\sin t + \frac{t}{4}(\sin t - \cos t) + \frac{1}{2}(\sin t - \cos t) \quad \text{...(5)}$$

Equations (4) and (5), when taken together, give the complete solution of the given system of equations.

Example 5. *Solve :* $\dfrac{dx}{dt} + 4x + 3y = t,\ \dfrac{dy}{dt} + 2x + 5y = e^t.$ (U.P.T.U. 2006)

Sol. Writing D for $\dfrac{d}{dt}$, the given equations become

$$(D + 4)x + 3y = t \quad ...(1)$$

and $$2x + (D + 5)y = e^t \quad ...(2)$$

To eliminate y, operating (1) by $(D + 5)$ and multiplying (2) by 3 then subtracting, we get

$$[(D + 4)(D + 5) - 6]x = (D + 5)t - 3e^t$$

or $$(D^2 + 9D + 14)x = 1 + 5t - 3e^t$$

Auxiliary equation is

$$m^2 + 9m + 14 = 0 \quad \Rightarrow \quad m = -2, -7$$

$$\therefore \quad \text{C.F.} = c_1e^{-2t} + c_2e^{-7t}$$

$$\text{P.I.} = \frac{1}{D^2 + 9D + 14}(1 + 5t - 3e^t)$$

$$= \frac{1}{D^2 + 9D + 14}e^{0t} + 5\frac{1}{D^2 + 9D + 14}t - 3\frac{1}{D^2 + 9D + 14}e^t$$

$$= \frac{1}{0^2 + 9(0) + 14}e^{0t} + 5 \cdot \frac{1}{14\left(1 + \frac{9D}{14} + \frac{D^2}{14}\right)}t - 3\frac{1}{1^2 + 9(1) + 14}e^t$$

$$= \frac{1}{14} + \frac{5}{14}\left[1 + \left(\frac{9D}{14} + \frac{D^2}{14}\right)\right]^{-1}t - \frac{1}{8}e^t = \frac{1}{14} + \frac{5}{14}\left[1 - \left(\frac{9D}{14} + \frac{D^2}{14}\right) + ...\right]t - \frac{1}{8}e^t$$

$$= \frac{1}{14} + \frac{5}{14}\left(t - \frac{9}{14}\right) - \frac{1}{8}e^t = \frac{5}{14}t - \frac{31}{196} - \frac{1}{8}e^t$$

$$\therefore \quad x = c_1e^{-2t} + c_2e^{-7t} + \frac{5}{14}t - \frac{31}{196} - \frac{1}{8}e^t$$

Now, $\dfrac{dx}{dt} = -2c_1e^{-2t} - 7c_2e^{-7t} + \dfrac{5}{14} - \dfrac{1}{8}e^t$

Substituting the values of x and $\dfrac{dx}{dt}$ in (1), we have

$$3y = t - \frac{dx}{dt} - 4x$$

$$\Rightarrow \quad 3y = t + 2c_1e^{-2t} + 7c_2e^{-7t} - \frac{5}{14} + \frac{1}{8}e^t - 4c_1e^{-2t} - 4c_2e^{-7t} - \frac{10}{7}t + \frac{31}{49} + \frac{1}{2}e^t$$

$$\therefore \quad y = \frac{1}{3}\left[-2c_1e^{-2t} + 3c_2e^{-7t} - \frac{3}{7}t + \frac{27}{98} + \frac{5}{8}e^t\right]$$

Hence $$x = c_1e^{-2t} + c_2e^{-7t} + \frac{5}{14}t - \frac{31}{196} - \frac{1}{8}e^t$$

$$y = -\frac{2}{3}c_1e^{-2t} + c_2e^{-7t} - \frac{1}{7}t + \frac{9}{98} + \frac{5}{24}e^t.$$

Example 6. *Solve the simultaneous differential equations*

$$\frac{dx}{dt} + \frac{dy}{dt} + 3x = \sin t \quad \text{and} \quad \frac{dx}{dt} + y - x = \cos t.$$

Sol. Let $\frac{d}{dt} \equiv D$ then the given system of equations reduces to

$$(D + 3)x + Dy = \sin t \qquad ...(1)$$

$$(D - 1)x + y = \cos t \qquad ...(2)$$

Operating (2) by D and then subtracting from (1), we get

$$[(D + 3) - D(D - 1)]x = \sin t + \sin t = 2 \sin t$$

$$\Rightarrow \quad (D^2 - 2D - 3)x = -2 \sin t$$

Auxiliary equation is

$$m^2 - 2m - 3 = 0 \quad \Rightarrow \quad m = -1, 3$$

$$\therefore \quad \text{C.F.} = c_1e^{-t} + c_2e^{3t}$$

$$\text{P.I.} = \frac{1}{D^2 - 2D - 3}(-2 \sin t) = \frac{-2}{-2D - 4} \sin t$$

$$= \frac{1}{D+2} \sin t = \frac{D-2}{D^2 - 4} \sin t = -\frac{1}{5}(\cos t - 2 \sin t)$$

$$\therefore \quad x = c_1e^{-t} + c_2e^{3t} - \frac{1}{5}(\cos t - 2 \sin t) \qquad ...(3)$$

But $$y = x + \cos t - \frac{dx}{dt} = c_1e^{-t} + c_2e^{3t} - \frac{1}{5}(\cos t - 2 \sin t)$$

$$+ \cos t - \left[-c_1e^{-t} + 3c_2e^{3t} + \frac{1}{5}\sin t + \frac{2}{5}\cos t\right]$$

$$= 2\, c_1e^{-t} - 2\, c_2e^{3t} + \frac{2}{5}\cos t + \frac{1}{5}\sin t \qquad ...(4)$$

Eqns. (3) and (4) when taken together give the complete solution.

Example 7. *Solve the simultaneous differential equations*

$$\frac{d^2x}{dt^2} - 4\frac{dx}{dt} + 4x = y$$

and $$\frac{d^2y}{dt^2} + 4\frac{dy}{dt} + 4y = 25x + 16e^t.$$

Sol. Let $\frac{d}{dt} \equiv D$ then the given system of equations is

$$(D^2 - 4D + 4)\, x - y = 0 \qquad ...(1)$$

$$-25x + (D^2 + 4D + 4)y = 16e^t \qquad ...(2)$$

Operating (1) by $D^2 + 4D + 4$ and adding to (2), we get

$$(D^2 - 4D + 4)(D^2 + 4D + 4)x - 25x = 16\, e^t$$

$$\Rightarrow \quad (D^4 - 8D^2 - 9)x = 16\, e^t$$

Auxiliary equation is

$$m^4 - 8m^2 - 9 = 0$$

$$\Rightarrow \quad (m^2 - 9)(m^2 + 1) = 0 \quad \Rightarrow \quad m = \pm i, \pm 3$$

$\therefore$ $$\text{C.F.} = c_1e^{3t} + c_2e^{-3t} + c_3 \cos t + c_4 \sin t$$

$$\text{P.I.} = \frac{1}{D^4 - 8D^2 + 9} (16\, e^t) = 8\, e^t$$

$\therefore$ $$x = c_1e^{3t} + c_2e^{-3t} + c_3 \cos t + c_4 \sin t + 8e^t \qquad ...(3)$$

$$\frac{dx}{dt} = 3c_1e^{3t} - 3\, c_2e^{-3t} + c_3\,(-\sin t) + c_4 \cos t + 8e^t$$

$$\frac{d^2x}{dt^2} = 9c_1e^{3t} + 9c_2e^{-3t} - c_3 \cos t - c_4 \sin t + 8\, e^t$$

From (1), $$y = \frac{d^2x}{dt^2} - 4\frac{dx}{dt} + 4x$$

$$= 9c_1e^{3t} + 9c_2e^{-3t} - c_3 \cos t - c_4 \sin t + 8\, e^t$$
$$- 4\,(3c_1e^{3t} - 3c_2e^{-3t} - c_3 \sin t + c_4 \cos t + 8e^t)$$
$$+ 4\,(c_1e^{3t} + c_2e^{-3t} - c_3 \cos t + c_4 \sin t + 8\, e^t)$$

$\Rightarrow$ $$y = c_1e^{3t} + 25c_2e^{-3t} + (3c_3 - 4c_4) \cos t + (4c_3 + 3c_4) \sin t + 8\, e^t \quad ...(4)$$

Eqns. (3) and (4) when taken together give the complete solution.

Example 8. *Solve :* $\dfrac{d^2x}{dt^2} + 4x + 5y = t^2;\ \dfrac{d^2y}{dt^2} + 5x + 4y = t + 1.$

Sol. Writing D for $\dfrac{d}{dt}$, the given equations become

$$(D^2 + 4)x + 5y = t^2 \qquad ...(1)$$

and $$5x + (D^2 + 4)y = t + 1 \qquad ...(2)$$

To eliminate y, operating (1) by $(D^2 + 4)$ and multiplying (2) by 5 then subtracting, we get

$$[(D^2 + 4)^2 - 25]x = (D^2 + 4)t^2 - 5(t + 1)$$

or $$(D^4 + 8D^2 - 9)x = 2 + 4t^2 - 5t - 5 = 4t^2 - 5t - 3$$

Auxiliary equation is

$$m^4 + 8m^2 - 9 = 0$$

or $$(m^2 + 9)(m^2 - 1) = 0 \quad \therefore \quad m = \pm 1, \pm 3i$$

$\therefore$ $$\text{C.F.} = c_1e^t + c_2e^{-t} + c_3 \cos 3t + c_4 \sin 3t$$

$$\text{P.I.} = \frac{1}{D^4 + 8D^2 - 9}(4t^2 - 5t - 3) = \frac{1}{-9\left(1 - \frac{8D^2}{9} - \frac{D^4}{9}\right)}(4t^2 - 5t - 3)$$

$$= -\frac{1}{9}\left[1 - \left(\frac{8D^2}{9} + \frac{D^4}{9}\right)\right]^{-1}(4t^2 - 5t - 3)$$

$$= -\frac{1}{9}\left[1 + \left(\frac{8D^2}{9} + \frac{D^4}{9}\right) + \ldots\ldots\right](4t^2 - 5t - 3)$$

$$= -\frac{1}{9}\left[4t^2 - 5t - 3 + \frac{8}{9}(8)\right] = -\frac{1}{9}\left(4t^2 - 5t + \frac{37}{9}\right)$$

$$\therefore \quad x = c_1e^t + c_2e^{-t} + c_3 \cos 3t + c_4 \sin 3t - \frac{4}{9}t^2 + \frac{5}{9}t - \frac{37}{81}$$

Now $\dfrac{dx}{dt} = c_1e^t - c_2e^{-t} - 3c_3 \sin 3t + 3c_4 \cos 3t - \dfrac{8}{9}t + \dfrac{5}{9}$

$$\frac{d^2x}{dt^2} = c_1e^t + c_2e^{-t} - 9c_3 \cos 3t - 9c_4 \sin 3t - \frac{8}{9}$$

Substituting the values of x and $\dfrac{d^2x}{dt^2}$ in (1), we have

$$5y = t^2 - 4x - \frac{d^2x}{dt^2}$$

$$= t^2 - 4c_1e^t - 4c_2e^{-t} - 4c_3 \cos 3t - 4c_4 \sin 3t$$

$$+ \frac{16}{9}t^2 - \frac{20}{9}t + \frac{148}{81} - c_1e^t - c_2e^{-t} + 9c_3 \cos 3t + 9c_4 \sin 3t + \frac{8}{9}$$

$$\therefore \quad y = \frac{1}{5}\left[-5c_1e^t - 5c_2e^{-t} + 5c_3 \cos 3t + 5c_4 \sin 3t + \frac{25}{9}t^2 - \frac{20}{9}t + \frac{220}{81}\right]$$

Hence $x = c_1e^t + c_2e^{-t} + c_3 \cos 3t + c_4 \sin 3t - \dfrac{1}{9}\left(4t^2 - 5t + \dfrac{37}{9}\right)$

$$y = -c_1e^t - c_2e^{-t} + c_3 \cos 3t + c_4 \sin 3t + \frac{1}{9}\left(5t^2 - 4t + \frac{44}{9}\right).$$

Example 9. *Solve :* $\dfrac{d^2x}{dt^2} + \dfrac{dy}{dt} + 3x = e^{-t}$

$$\frac{d^2y}{dt^2} - 4\frac{dx}{dt} + 3y = \sin 2t.$$ [U.P.T.U. 2007 ; M.T.U. (SUM) 2011]

Sol. Let $D \equiv \dfrac{d}{dt}$ then we have

$$(D^2 + 3)\, x + Dy = e^{-t} \quad \text{...(1)}$$

$$-4Dx + (D^2 + 3)\, y = \sin 2t \quad \text{...(2)}$$

Operating (1) by $(D^2 + 3)$ and (2) by D then subtracting, we get

$$[(D^2 + 3)^2 + 4D^2]\, x = 4e^{-t} - 2 \cos 2t$$

$$(D^4 + 10D^2 + 9)\, x = 4e^{-t} - 2 \cos 2t$$

Auxiliary equation is

$$m^4 + 10m^2 + 9 = 0 \Rightarrow m = \pm i, \pm 3i$$

$$\text{C.F.} = c_1 \cos t + c_2 \sin t + c_3 \cos 3t + c_4 \sin 3t$$

$$\text{P.I.} = \frac{1}{D^4 + 10D^2 + 9}(4e^{-t}) - \frac{1}{D^4 + 10D^2 + 9}(2 \cos 2t)$$

$$= \frac{1}{1+10+9}(4e^{-t}) - \frac{1}{16-40+9}(2\cos 2t)$$

$$= \frac{1}{5}e^{-t} + \frac{2}{15}\cos 2t$$

$\therefore$ $$x = c_1 \cos t + c_2 \sin t + c_3 \cos 3t + c_4 \sin 3t + \frac{1}{5}e^{-t} + \frac{2}{15}\cos 2t \quad ...(3)$$

Again operating (1) by 4D and (2) by ($D^2 + 3$) then adding, we get

$$[(D^2+3)^2 + 4D^2]\, y = -4e^{-t} - \sin 2t$$

$$(D^4 + 10D^2 + 9)\, y = -4e^{-t} - \sin 2t$$

Auxiliary equation is

$$m^4 + 10m^2 + 9 = 0 \Rightarrow m = \pm i, \pm 3i$$

$$\text{C.F.} = c_5 \cos t + c_6 \sin t + c_7 \cos 3t + c_8 \sin 3t$$

$$\text{P.I.} = \frac{1}{D^4 + 10D^2 + 9}(-4e^{-t}) - \frac{1}{D^4 + 10D^2 + 9}(\sin 2t)$$

$$= -\frac{1}{5}e^{-t} + \frac{1}{15}\sin 2t$$

$\therefore$ $$y = c_5 \cos t + c_6 \sin t + c_7 \cos 3t + c_8 \sin 3t - \frac{1}{5}e^{-t} + \frac{1}{15}\sin 2t \quad ...(4)$$

Equations (3) and (4), when taken together, give the complete solution.

Example 10. *Solve the simultaneous equations :*

$$\frac{dx}{dt} + \frac{dy}{dt} - 2y = 2\cos t - 7\sin t$$

$$\frac{dx}{dt} - \frac{dy}{dt} + 2x = 4\cos t - 3\sin t. \quad \text{(U.K.T.U. 2011)}$$

Sol. The given equations may be written as

$$Dx + (D-2)y = 2\cos t - 7\sin t \quad ...(1)$$

$$(D+2)x - Dy = 4\cos t - 3\sin t \quad ...(2)$$

Operating (1) by D and (2) by ($D - 2$), we get

$$D^2x + D(D-2)y = -2\sin t - 7\cos t$$

$$(D^2 - 4)x - D(D-2)y = -4\sin t - 8\cos t - 3\cos t + 6\sin t$$

Adding, we get

$$(2D^2 - 4)x = -18\cos t$$

$$\Rightarrow \quad (D^2 - 2)x = -9\cos t$$

Auxiliary equation is

$$m^2 - 2 = 0 \Rightarrow m = \pm\sqrt{2}$$

$$\text{C.F.} = c_1 \cosh\sqrt{2}\,t + c_2 \sinh\sqrt{2}\,t$$

$$\text{P.I.} = \frac{1}{D^2 - 2}(-9\cos t) = 3\cos t$$

$\therefore$ $$x = \text{C.F.} + \text{P.I.} = c_1 \cosh\sqrt{2}\,t + c_2 \sinh\sqrt{2}\,t + 3\cos t \quad ...(3)$$

Again, operating (1) by (D + 2) and (2) by D, we get

$$(D + 2)\,Dx + (D^2 - 4)\,y = -\,2\sin t - 7\cos t + 4\cos t - 14\sin t$$

$$D\,(D + 2)\,x - D^2y = -\,4\sin t - 3\cos t$$

Subtracting, we get

$$(2D^2 - 4)\,y = -\,12\sin t$$

$$(D^2 - 2)\,y = -\,6\sin t$$

$$\text{C.F.} = c_3\cosh\sqrt{2}\,t + c_4\sinh\sqrt{2}\,t$$

$$\text{P.I.} = \frac{1}{D^2 - 2}\,(-\,6\sin t) = 2\sin t$$

$$\therefore \qquad y = \text{C.F.} + \text{P.I.} = c_3\cosh\sqrt{2}\,t + c_4\sinh\sqrt{2}\,t + 2\sin t \qquad ...(4)$$

Eqns. (3) and (4), when taken together, give the complete solution.

TEST YOUR KNOWLEDGE

Solve the following systems of simultaneous differential equations :

1. $\dfrac{dx}{dt} + 7x - y = 0,\ \dfrac{dy}{dt} + 2x + 5y = 0$ [*G.B.T.U. (AG) SUM 2010*]
2. $\dfrac{dx}{dt} + x - 2y = 0,\ \dfrac{dy}{dt} + x + 4y = 0\ ;\ x(0) = y(0) = 1$ (*M.T.U. 2011*)
3. $\dfrac{dx}{dt} - 7x + y = 0,\ \dfrac{dy}{dt} - 2x - 5y = 0$ [*U.P.T.U. (B. Pharm.) 2009*]
4. $\dfrac{dx}{dt} = 3x + 8y,\ \dfrac{dy}{dt} = -\,x - 3y;\ x(0) = 6,\ y(0) = -\,2$ (*G.B.T.U. 2010*)
5. $\dfrac{dx}{dt} - y = t,\ \dfrac{dy}{dt} + x = 1$
6. $\dfrac{dx}{dt} = y + 1,\ \dfrac{dy}{dt} = x + 1.$ [*U.P.T.U. (SUM) 2009*]
7. $\dfrac{dx}{dt} + y = \sin t,\ \dfrac{dx}{dt} + x = \cos t$; given that $x = 2$ and $y = 0$ when $t = 0$.
8. $\dfrac{dx}{dt} - y = e^t,\ \dfrac{dy}{dt} + x = \sin t;\ x(0) = 1,\ y(0) = 0$ [*G.B.T.U. (SUM) 2010 ; G.B.T.U. (C.O.) 2011*]
9. $\dfrac{dx}{dt} + 5x + y = e^t,\ \dfrac{dy}{dt} + x + 5y = e^{5t}.$ [*U.P.T.U. (C.O.) 2009*]
10. $\dfrac{dx}{dt} + 2x - 3y = t,\ \dfrac{dy}{dt} - 3x + 2y = e^{2t}$ [*U.K.T.U. 2012*]
11. $\dfrac{d^2x}{dt^2} + m^2y = 0,\ \dfrac{d^2y}{dt^2} - m^2x = 0$
12. $\dfrac{d^2x}{dt^2} - 3x - 4y = 0,\ \dfrac{d^2y}{dt^2} + x + y = 0$
13. $\dfrac{d^2x}{dt^2} + 16x - 6\dfrac{dy}{dt} = 0,\ 6\dfrac{dx}{dt} + \dfrac{d^2y}{dt^2} + 16y = 0$
14. $(D - 1)x + Dy = 2t + 1,\ (2D + 1)x + 2Dy = t$
15. $(D^2 - 1)x + 8Dy = 16e^t$ and $Dx + 3(D^2 + 1)y = 0$
16. $\dfrac{dx}{dt} + \dfrac{dy}{dt} + 2x + y = 0,\ \dfrac{dy}{dt} + 5x + 3y = 0$ [*G.B.T.U. (C.O.) 2011*]

17. $\frac{dx}{dt} = -4(x+y), \frac{dx}{dt} + 4\frac{dy}{dt} = -4y$ with conditions $x(0) = 1, y(0) = 0.$ *(G.B.T.U. 2011)*

18. $\frac{dx}{dt} + \frac{2}{t}(x-y) = 1, \quad \frac{dy}{dt} + \frac{1}{t}(x+5y) = t.$

Answers

1. $x = e^{-6t}(\text{A} \cos t + \text{B} \sin t), y = e^{-6t}[(\text{A}+\text{B})\cos t - (\text{A}-\text{B})\sin t]$
2. $x = 4e^{-2t} - 3e^{-3t}, y = -2e^{-2t} + 3e^{-3t}$
3. $x = e^{6t}(c_1 \cos t + c_2 \sin t), y = e^{6t}[(c_1+c_2)\sin t + (c_1 - c_2)\cos t]$
4. $x = 4e^t + 2e^{-t}, y = -e^t - e^{-t}$
5. $x = c_1 \cos t + c_2 \sin t + 2, y = -c_1 \sin t + c_2 \cos t - t$
6. $x = c_1 e^t + c_2 e^{-t} - 1, y = c_1 e^t - c_2 e^{-t} - 1$
7. $x = e^t + e^{-t}, y = e^{-t} - e^t + \sin t$
8. $x = 2\sin t + \frac{3}{2}\cos t + \frac{t}{2}\cos t - \frac{1}{2}e^t, y = \frac{1}{2}\cos t - \frac{3}{2}\sin t + \frac{t}{2}\sin t - \frac{1}{2}e^t$
9. $x = c_1 e^{-6t} + c_2 e^{-4t} + \frac{6e^t}{35} - \frac{e^{5t}}{99}, y = c_1 e^{-6t} - c_2 e^{-4t} - \frac{1}{35}e^t + \frac{10}{99}e^{5t}.$
10. $x = c_1 e^{-5t} + c_2 e^t + \frac{3}{7}e^{2t} - \frac{2}{5}t - \frac{13}{25}, y = c_1 e^{-5t} + c_2 e^t + \frac{4}{7}e^{2t} - \frac{3}{5}t - \frac{12}{25}$
11. $x = e^{mt/\sqrt{2}}\left(c_1 \cos\frac{mt}{\sqrt{2}} + c_2 \sin\frac{mt}{\sqrt{2}}\right) + e^{-mt/\sqrt{2}}\left(c_3 \cos\frac{mt}{\sqrt{2}} + c_4 \sin\frac{mt}{\sqrt{2}}\right);$

    $y = e^{mt/\sqrt{2}}\left(c_1 \sin\frac{mt}{\sqrt{2}} - c_2 \cos\frac{mt}{\sqrt{2}}\right) + e^{-mt/\sqrt{2}}\left(c_4 \cos\frac{mt}{\sqrt{2}} - c_3 \sin\frac{mt}{\sqrt{2}}\right)$
12. $x = (c_1 + c_2 t)e^{-t} + (c_3 + c_4 t)e^t, y = -\frac{1}{2}[c_1 + c_2(1+t)]e^{-t} + \frac{1}{2}[c_4(1-t) - c_3]e^t$
13. $x = c_1 \cos 2t + c_2 \sin 2t - c_3 \cos 8t + c_4 \sin 8t, \; y = c_1 \sin 2t + c_2 \cos 2t - c_3 \sin 8t + c_4 \cos 8t$
14. $x = -t - \frac{2}{3}, y = \frac{1}{2}t^2 + \frac{4}{3}t + c$
15. $y = c_1 \cos\frac{t}{\sqrt{3}} + c_2 \sin\frac{t}{\sqrt{3}} + c_3 \cosh\sqrt{3}\,t + c_4 \sinh\sqrt{3}\,t + 2e^t$

    $x = \sqrt{3}\,c_1 \sin\frac{t}{\sqrt{3}} - \sqrt{3}\,c_2 \cos\frac{t}{\sqrt{3}} - 3\sqrt{3}\,c_3 \sinh\sqrt{3}\,t - 3\sqrt{3}\,c_4 \cosh\sqrt{3}\,t - 6e^t - 3t.$
16. $x = \left(\frac{c_1 - 3c_2}{5}\right)\sin t - \left(\frac{c_2 + 3c_1}{5}\right)\cos t, y = c_1 \cos t + c_2 \sin t$
17. $x = (1 - 2t)e^{-2t}, y = te^{-2t}$
18. $x = \text{A}t^{-4} + \text{B}t^{-3} + \frac{t^2}{15} + \frac{3t}{10}; \; y = -\text{A}t^{-4} - \frac{1}{2}\text{B}t^{-3} + \frac{2t^2}{15} - \frac{t}{20}.$

1.33. LINEAR DIFFERENTIAL EQUATIONS OF SECOND ORDER

A differential equation of the form $\frac{d^2y}{dx^2} + \text{P}\frac{dy}{dx} + \text{Q}y = \text{R}$ is known as linear differential equation of second order, where P, Q and R are functions of x alone.

Note. Coefficient of $\frac{d^2y}{dx^2}$ must always be 1.

A linear differential equation of second order can be solved by changing dependent and independent variables as well as by the method of variation of parameters.

Above methods are illustrated below with some suitable and important examples.

1.33.1. Method 1. To Find the Complete Solution of $y'' + Py' + Qy = R$ when Part of Complementary Function is Known (*Method of reduction of order*)

Let $y = u$ be a part of the complementary function of the given differential equation

$$\frac{d^2y}{dx^2} + P\frac{dy}{dx} + Qy = R \qquad ...(1)$$

where u is a function of x. Then, we have

$$\frac{d^2u}{dx^2} + P\frac{du}{dx} + Qu = 0 \qquad ...(2)$$

Let $y = uv$ be the complete solution of equation (1), where v is a function of x.

Differentiating y w.r.t. x,

$$\frac{dy}{dx} = u\frac{dv}{dx} + \frac{du}{dx} \cdot v$$

Again,
$$\frac{d^2y}{dx^2} = u\frac{d^2v}{dx^2} + 2\frac{du}{dx} \cdot \frac{dv}{dx} + v\frac{d^2u}{dx^2}$$

Substituting the values of y, $\frac{dy}{dx}$ and $\frac{d^2y}{dx^2}$ in equation (1), we get

$$u\frac{d^2v}{dx^2} + 2\frac{du}{dx}\frac{dv}{dx} + v\frac{d^2u}{dx^2} + P\left(u\frac{dv}{dx} + v\frac{du}{dx}\right) + Q(uv) = R$$

$$\Rightarrow \quad u\frac{d^2v}{dx^2} + \left(2\frac{du}{dx} + Pu\right)\frac{dv}{dx} + \left(\frac{d^2u}{dx^2} + P\frac{du}{dx} + Qu\right)v = R$$

$$\Rightarrow \quad u\frac{d^2v}{dx^2} + \left(2\frac{du}{dx} + Pu\right)\frac{dv}{dx} = R$$

| Using (2)

$$\Rightarrow \quad \frac{d^2v}{dx^2} + \left(\frac{2}{u}\frac{du}{dx} + P\right)\frac{dv}{dx} = \frac{R}{u} \qquad ...(3)$$

Put $\frac{dv}{dx} = p$ then, $\frac{d^2v}{dx^2} = \frac{dp}{dx}$

Now (3) becomes, $\frac{dp}{dx} + \left(\frac{2}{u}\frac{du}{dx} + P\right)p = \frac{R}{u}$ ...(4)

Equation (4) is a linear differential equation of I order in p and x.

$$\text{I.F.} = e^{\int\left(\frac{2}{u}\frac{du}{dx} + P\right)dx} = e^{\left(\int \frac{2}{u}du + \int P\,dx\right)} = u^2 e^{\int P\,dx}$$

Solution of (4) is given by

$$pu^2 e^{\int P\,dx} = \int \frac{R}{u} u^2 e^{\int P\,dx}\,dx + c_1$$

where c_1 is an arbitrary constant of integration.

$$\Rightarrow \qquad p = \frac{1}{u^2} e^{-\int P\,dx} \left[\int Ru\, e^{\int P\,dx}\, dx + c_1\right]$$

$$\therefore \qquad \frac{dv}{dx} = \frac{1}{u^2} e^{-\int P\,dx} \left[\int Ru\, e^{\int P\,dx}\, dx + c_1\right]$$

Integration yields, $v = \int \frac{1}{u^2} e^{-\int P\,dx} \left[\int Ru\, e^{\int P\,dx}\, dx + c_1\right] dx + c_2$

where c_2 is an arbitrary constant of integration.

Hence the complete solution of (1) is given by,

$$y = uv$$

$$\Rightarrow \qquad y = u \int \frac{1}{u^2} e^{-\int P\,dx} \left[\int Ru\, e^{\int P\,dx}\, dx + c_1\right] dx + c_2 u$$

To find out the part of C.F. of the linear differential equation of II order given by

$$\frac{d^2y}{dx^2} + P\frac{dy}{dx} + Qy = R.$$

Remember :

Condition	*Part of C.F.*
(*i*) $1 + \frac{P}{a} + \frac{Q}{a^2} = 0$	e^{ax}
(*ii*) $1 + P + Q = 0$	e^x
(*iii*) $1 - P + Q = 0$	e^{-x}
(*iv*) $m(m-1) + P\,mx + Qx^2 = 0$	x^m
(*v*) $P + Qx = 0$	x
(*vi*) $2 + 2Px + Qx^2 = 0$	x^2

Proof. (*i*) Let $y = e^{ax}$ be a part of C.F. of the equation $\frac{d^2y}{dx^2} + P\frac{dy}{dx} + Qy = R.$

Then, $\qquad a^2e^{ax} + P\,ae^{ax} + Qe^{ax} = 0$

$$\Rightarrow \qquad a^2 + Pa + Q = 0$$

$$\Rightarrow \qquad 1 + \frac{P}{a} + \frac{Q}{a^2} = 0.$$

(*iv*) Let $y = x^m$ be a part of C.F. of the equation $\frac{d^2y}{dx^2} + P\frac{dy}{dx} + Qy = R$ then,

$$m(m-1)\,x^{m-2} + P\,mx^{m-1} + Qx^m = 0$$

$$\Rightarrow \qquad m(m-1) + P\,mx + Qx^2 = 0$$

Rest all the parts are the deductions from proofs (*i*) and (*iv*).

Steps for solution :

1. Make the coefficient of $\frac{d^2y}{dx^2}$ as 1 if it is not so.
2. Compare the given differential equation with the standard form $\frac{d^2y}{dx^2} + P\frac{dy}{dx} + Qy = R$ and hence find P, Q and R which are functions of x only.

3. Apply the mentioned conditions on P and Q. If any one of the conditions is satisfied, write down the corresponding part of C.F. as u.
4. Let $y = uv$ be the complete solution of the given differential equation, where v is, another function of x, to be determined.
5. Find y' and y'' from y and substitute the required values in the given equation.
6. Arrange the expression in decreasing order of the derivatives of v w.r.t. x.
7. Check whether the coefficient of v is zero ? If not, we are somewhere wrong. It is the time to recheck.
8. Put $\frac{dv}{dx} = p$ so that $\frac{d^2v}{dx^2} = \frac{dp}{dx}$. Then we get a I order differential equation in p and x, which we solve by the methods discussed before.
9. Integrating $\frac{dv}{dx}$ w.r.t. x, we get v in terms of x.
10. At last $y = uv$ will be the complete solution of the given differential equation having two arbitrary constants.

ILLUSTRATIVE EXAMPLES

Example 1. *Solve : $\sin^2 x \frac{d^2y}{dx^2} = 2y$, given that $y = \cot x$ is a solution of it.*

Sol.
$$\frac{d^2y}{dx^2} - 2(\text{cosec}^2 x)y = 0 \qquad \text{...(1)}$$

Here, a part of C.F. = $\cot x$

Let $y = v \cot x$ be the complete solution of (1)

$$\therefore \quad \frac{dy}{dx} = v(-\text{cosec}^2 x) + \cot x \frac{dv}{dx}$$

$$\frac{d^2y}{dx^2} = v(2\,\text{cosec}^2 x \cot x) - 2\,\text{cosec}^2 x \frac{dv}{dx} + \cot x \frac{d^2v}{dx^2}$$

Substituting the values of y, $\frac{d^2y}{dx^2}$, we get

$$\cot x \frac{d^2v}{dx^2} - 2\,\text{cosec}^2 x \frac{dv}{dx} = 0$$

$$\Rightarrow \quad \cot x \frac{dp}{dx} - 2\,\text{cosec}^2 x \,.\, p = 0, \qquad \text{where } p = \frac{dv}{dx}$$

$$\Rightarrow \quad \frac{dp}{p} = 2\frac{\text{cosec}^2 x}{\cot x}\,dx$$

Integration yields,

$$\log p = -2 \log \cot x + \log c_1 \qquad | \; c_1 \text{ is arbitrary constant}$$

$$\Rightarrow \quad \log p + \log \cot^2 x = \log c_1$$

$$\Rightarrow \qquad p = c_1 \tan^2 x$$

$$\therefore \qquad \frac{dv}{dx} = c_1 (\sec^2 x - 1)$$

Integrating with respect to x, we get

$$v = c_1 (\tan x - x) + c_2$$

where c_2 is an arbitrary constant of integration.

Hence the complete solution is given by

$$y = v \cot x = [c_1 (\tan x - x) + c_2] \cot x$$

$$y = c_1(1 - x \cot x) + c_2 \cot x.$$

Example 2. *Solve :* $\dfrac{d^2y}{dx^2} - \cot x \dfrac{dy}{dx} - (1 - \cot x)y = e^x \sin x.$

Sol. Comparing with the standard form, we get

$$P = -\cot x,\ Q = -(1 - \cot x),\ R = e^x \sin x$$

$$1 + P + Q = 1 - 1 + \cot x - \cot x = 0$$

$$\therefore \qquad \text{A part of C.F.} = e^x$$

Let $y = v e^x$ be the complete solution of given equation, then

$$\frac{dy}{dx} = v e^x + e^x \frac{dv}{dx}$$

$$\frac{d^2y}{dx^2} = v e^x + 2e^x \frac{dv}{dx} + e^x \frac{d^2v}{dx^2}$$

Substituting for y, $\dfrac{dy}{dx}$ and $\dfrac{d^2y}{dx^2}$ in given equation, we get

$$\frac{d^2v}{dx^2} + (2 - \cot x) \frac{dv}{dx} = \sin x$$

$$\Rightarrow \qquad \frac{dp}{dx} + (2 - \cot x)p = \sin x \qquad \text{...(1)} \quad \text{where } p = \frac{dv}{dx}.$$

This is a linear differential equation of I order in p and x.

$$\text{I.F.} = e^{\int (2 - \cot x)\, dx} = \frac{e^{2x}}{\sin x}$$

Solution of (1) is, $\qquad p \dfrac{e^{2x}}{\sin x} = \displaystyle\int \sin x \cdot \frac{e^{2x}}{\sin x}\, dx + c_1 = \frac{e^{2x}}{2} + c_1$

where c_1 is an arbitrary constant of integration.

$$p = \frac{1}{2} \sin x + c_1 e^{-2x} \sin x$$

$$\frac{dv}{dx} = \frac{1}{2} \sin x + c_1 e^{-2x} \sin x$$

Integrating, we get $\qquad v = -\dfrac{1}{2} \cos x - \dfrac{1}{5} c_1 e^{-2x} (\cos x + 2 \sin x) + c_2$

Hence the complete solution is given by,

$$y = v\,e^x = \left[-\frac{1}{2}\cos x - \frac{1}{5} c_1 e^{-2x} (\cos x + 2\sin x) + c_2 \right] e^x.$$

Example 3. *Solve :* $(1 - x^2)\dfrac{d^2y}{dx^2} + x\dfrac{dy}{dx} - y = x(1 - x^2)^{3/2}$.

Sol. Comparing with $\dfrac{d^2y}{dx^2} + P\dfrac{dy}{dx} + Qy = R$, we get

$$P = \frac{x}{1-x^2},\; Q = -\frac{1}{1-x^2},\; R = x\sqrt{1-x^2}$$

$\because$ $\quad P + Qx = 0$

$\therefore$ $\quad$ A part of C.F. $= x$

Let $y = vx$ be the complete solution of the given differential equation

$$\therefore \quad \frac{dy}{dx} = v + x\frac{dv}{dx} \quad \text{and} \quad \frac{d^2y}{dx^2} = x\frac{d^2v}{dx^2} + 2\frac{dv}{dx}$$

Substituting the values, we get

$$\frac{d^2v}{dx^2} + \frac{2-x^2}{x(1-x^2)}\frac{dv}{dx} = (1-x^2)^{1/2}$$

$$\Rightarrow \quad \frac{dp}{dx} + \frac{(2-x^2)}{x(1-x^2)}\,p = (1-x^2)^{1/2} \qquad \text{...(1)} \qquad \text{where } p = \frac{dv}{dx}.$$

$$\text{I.F.} = e^{\int \frac{(2-x^2)}{x(1-x^2)}dx} = e^{\int \left(\frac{2}{x} + \frac{x}{1-x^2}\right)dx} = \frac{x^2}{\sqrt{1-x^2}}$$

Solution of (1) is,

$$p.\frac{x^2}{\sqrt{1-x^2}} = \int \sqrt{1-x^2}\,.\,\frac{x^2}{\sqrt{1-x^2}}\,dx + c_1$$

$$\Rightarrow \quad p\frac{x^2}{\sqrt{1-x^2}} = \frac{x^3}{3} + c_1 \qquad | \; c_1 \text{ is arbitrary constant}$$

$$\Rightarrow \quad p = \frac{x}{3}\sqrt{1-x^2} + c_1\frac{\sqrt{1-x^2}}{x^2}$$

$$\frac{dv}{dx} = \frac{x}{3}\sqrt{1-x^2} + c_1\frac{\sqrt{1-x^2}}{x^2}$$

Integrating, we get

$$v = \frac{1}{3}\int x\sqrt{1-x^2}\,dx + c_1\int \frac{\sqrt{1-x^2}}{x^2}\,dx + c_2$$

$$= -\frac{1}{9}(1-x^2)^{3/2} + c_1\left[\frac{-\sqrt{1-x^2}}{x} - \sin^{-1}x\right] + c_2$$

where c_2 is also an arbitrary constant of integration.

Hence the complete solution is given by,

$$y = vx$$

$$\Rightarrow \quad y = \frac{-x(1-x^2)^{3/2}}{9} - c_1\left[\sqrt{1-x^2} + x\sin^{-1}x\right] + c_2 x.$$

Example 4. *Solve : (x sin x + cos x)* $\frac{d^2y}{dx^2}$ *– x cos x* $\frac{dy}{dx}$ *+ y cos x = 0 of which y = x is a solution.*

Sol.

$$\frac{d^2y}{dx^2} - \left(\frac{x\cos x}{x\sin x + \cos x}\right)\frac{dy}{dx} + \left(\frac{\cos x}{x\sin x + \cos x}\right)y = 0 \qquad \text{...(1)}$$

Here a part of C.F. $= x$ | Given

Let $y = vx$ be the complete solution of equation (1)

$$\therefore \quad \frac{dy}{dx} = v + x\frac{dv}{dx}$$

$$\frac{d^2y}{dx^2} = x\frac{d^2v}{dx^2} + 2\frac{dv}{dx}$$

Substituting the values of y, $\frac{dy}{dx}$, $\frac{d^2y}{dx^2}$ in (1), we get

$$\frac{d^2v}{dx^2} + \left(\frac{2}{x} - \frac{x\cos x}{x\sin x + \cos x}\right)\frac{dv}{dx} = 0$$

$$\Rightarrow \quad \frac{dp}{dx} + \left(\frac{2}{x} - \frac{x\cos x}{x\sin x + \cos x}\right)p = 0, \qquad \text{where } p = \frac{dv}{dx}$$

$$\Rightarrow \quad \frac{dp}{p} + \left(\frac{2}{x} - \frac{x\cos x}{x\sin x + \cos x}\right)dx = 0$$

Integration yields, $px^2 = c_1\,(x\sin x + \cos x)$

or

$$\frac{dv}{dx} = c_1\left(\frac{\sin x}{x} + \frac{\cos x}{x^2}\right)$$

Again integration yields,

$$v = -c_1\frac{\cos x}{x} + c_2$$

Hence the complete solution is given by

$$y = vx$$

$$\Rightarrow \quad y = -c_1\cos x + c_2 x$$

where c_1 and c_2 are the arbitrary constants of integration.

TEST YOUR KNOWLEDGE

Solve the following differential equations :

1. $x\frac{d^2y}{dx^2} - (2x-1)\frac{dy}{dx} + (x-1)y = 0$

2. $x\frac{d^2y}{dx^2} - (3+x)\frac{dy}{dx} + 3y = 0$

3. $x^2\frac{d^2y}{dx^2} - (x^2+2x)\frac{dy}{dx} + (x+2)y = x^3e^x$ of which $y = x$ is a solution.

4. $(x + 2)\dfrac{d^2y}{dx^2} - (2x + 5)\dfrac{dy}{dx} + 2y = (x + 1)\, e^x$

5. $y'' - 4xy' + (4x^2 - 2)\, y = 0$ given that $y = e^{x^2}$ is a solution.

6. Solve : $x^2 \dfrac{d^2y}{dx^2} + x\dfrac{dy}{dx} - y = 0$, given that $x + \dfrac{1}{x}$ is one integral.

Answers

1. $y = (c_1 \log x + c_2)\, e^x$
2. $y = - c_1(x^3 + 3x^2 + 6x + 6) + c_2 e^x$
3. $y = x\,(x - 1)e^x + c_1 x e^x + c_2 x$
4. $y = - e^x - \dfrac{1}{4}\, c_1\,(2x + 5) + c_2\, e^{2x}$
5. $y = e^{x^2}\,(c_1 x + c_2)$
6. $y = \dfrac{A}{x} + c_2\left(x + \dfrac{1}{x}\right)$.

1.33.2. Method 2. To Find the Complete Solution of $y'' + Py' + Qy = R$ when it is Reduced to Normal Form (*Removal of first derivative*)

When the part of C.F. can not be determined by the previous method, we reduce the given differential equation in **normal form** by eliminating the term in which there exists first derivative of the dependent variable.

$$\frac{d^2y}{dx^2} + P\frac{dy}{dx} + Qy = R \qquad ...(1)$$

Let $y = uv$ be the complete solution of eqn. (1), where u and v are the functions of x.

$$\therefore \qquad \frac{dy}{dx} = v\,\frac{du}{dx} + u\,\frac{dv}{dx}$$

and
$$\frac{d^2y}{dx^2} = v\,\frac{d^2u}{dx^2} + 2\,\frac{du}{dx}\frac{dv}{dx} + u\,\frac{d^2v}{dx^2}$$

Substituting the values of $y, \dfrac{dy}{dx}, \dfrac{d^2y}{dx^2}$ in eqn. (1), we get

$$\frac{d^2v}{dx^2} + \left(\frac{2}{u}\frac{du}{dx} + P\right)\frac{dv}{dx} + v\left(\frac{1}{u}\frac{d^2u}{dx^2} + \frac{P}{u}\frac{du}{dx} + Q\right) = \frac{R}{u} \qquad ...(2)$$

Let us choose u such that $\dfrac{2}{u}\dfrac{du}{dx} + P = 0$ ...(3)

which on solving gives,

$$u = e^{-\int \frac{P}{2} dx} \qquad ...(4)$$

From (3), $$\frac{du}{dx} = -\frac{Pu}{2}$$

Differentiating, we get $$\frac{d^2u}{dx^2} = -\frac{1}{2}\left[P\left(\frac{du}{dx}\right) + \frac{dP}{dx}(u)\right]$$

$$= -\frac{1}{2}\left[P\left(\frac{-Pu}{2}\right) + u\frac{dP}{dx}\right] = \frac{P^2u}{4} - \frac{u}{2}\frac{dP}{dx}$$

$$\text{Coefficient of } v = \frac{1}{u}\frac{d^2u}{dx^2} + \frac{P}{u}\frac{du}{dx} + Q = \frac{1}{u}\left[\frac{P^2u}{4} - \frac{u}{2}\frac{dP}{dx}\right] + \frac{P}{u}\left(\frac{-Pu}{2}\right) + Q$$

$$= Q - \frac{1}{2}\frac{dP}{dx} - \frac{P^2}{4} = I \text{ (say)}$$

$$\text{R.H.S} = \frac{R}{u} = Re^{\frac{1}{2}\int P\,dx} = S \text{ (say)}$$

Then (2) becomes, $\dfrac{d^2v}{dx^2} + Iv = S$ ...(5)

This is known as the normal form of equation (1).

Solving (5), we get v in terms of x. Ultimately, $y = uv$ is the complete solution.

Steps for solution :

1. Make the coefficient of $\dfrac{d^2y}{dx^2}$ as 1 if it is not so.
2. Compare with standard form $y'' + Py' + Qy = R$ to get P, Q and R.
3. Let $y = uv$ be the complete solution of the given equation.
4. Find $u = e^{-\frac{1}{2}\int P\,dx}$, $I = Q - \dfrac{1}{2}\dfrac{dP}{dx} - \dfrac{P^2}{4}$ and $S = \dfrac{R}{u}$.
5. Check whether I is a constant or $\dfrac{\text{constant}}{x^2}$? If I is not any one of them, the method is not applicable.
6. If I is a constant, we get a linear differential equation of II order with constant coefficients while if I is $\dfrac{\text{constant}}{x^2}$, we get a homogeneous linear differential equation with variable coefficients.
7. Normal form is given by $\dfrac{d^2v}{dx^2} + Iv = S$ which we solve for v.
8. $y = uv$ will be the complete solution of the given differential equation.

ILLUSTRATIVE EXAMPLES

Example 1. *Solve :* $\dfrac{d^2y}{dx^2} - 4x\dfrac{dy}{dx} + (4x^2 - 1)y = -3e^{x^2}\sin 2x.$

Sol. Here, $P = -4x$, $Q = 4x^2 - 1$, $R = -3e^{x^2}\sin 2x$

Let $y = uv$ be the complete solution.

Now, $$u = e^{-\frac{1}{2}\int(-4x)\,dx} = e^{x^2}$$

$$I = Q - \frac{1}{2}\frac{dP}{dx} - \frac{P^2}{4} = 4x^2 - 1 - \frac{1}{2}(-4) - \frac{1}{4}(16x^2) = 1.$$

Also, $$S = \frac{R}{u} = \frac{-3\,e^{x^2}\sin 2x}{e^{x^2}} = -3\sin 2x$$

Hence normal form is,

$$\frac{d^2v}{dx^2} + v = -3\sin 2x$$

Auxiliary equation is

$$m^2 + 1 = 0 \quad \Rightarrow \quad m = \pm i$$

$$\text{C.F.} = c_1 \cos x + c_2 \sin x$$

where c_1 and c_2 are arbitrary constants of integration.

$$\text{P.I.} = \frac{1}{D^2+1}(-3\sin 2x) = \frac{-3}{(-4+1)}\sin 2x = \sin 2x$$

$\therefore$ Solution is, $$v = c_1\cos x + c_2 \sin x + \sin 2x$$

Hence the complete solution of given differential equation is

$$y = uv = e^{x^2}(c_1 \cos x + c_2 \sin x + \sin 2x).$$

Example 2. *Solve :* $\dfrac{d^2y}{dx^2} + \dfrac{1}{x^{1/3}}\dfrac{dy}{dx} + \left(\dfrac{1}{4x^{2/3}} - \dfrac{1}{6x^{4/3}} - \dfrac{6}{x^2}\right)y = 0.$

Sol. Comparing with the standard form, we get

$$P = x^{-1/3},\ Q = \frac{1}{4}x^{-2/3} - \frac{1}{6}x^{-4/3} - 6x^{-2},\ R = 0$$

Let $y = uv$ be the complete solution of given equation.

Now, $$u = e^{-\frac{1}{2}\int P\,dx} = e^{-\frac{1}{2}\int x^{-1/3}\,dx} = e^{-\frac{3}{4}x^{2/3}}$$

$$I = Q - \frac{1}{2}\frac{dP}{dx} - \frac{P^2}{4}$$

$$= \frac{1}{4x^{2/3}} - \frac{1}{6x^{4/3}} - \frac{6}{x^2} - \frac{1}{2}\left(-\frac{1}{3}x^{-4/3}\right) - \frac{1}{4}\cdot\frac{1}{x^{2/3}}$$

$$\Rightarrow \quad I = -\frac{6}{x^2}$$

Also, $$S = \frac{R}{u} = 0$$

$\therefore$ Normal form is,

$$\frac{d^2v}{dx^2} - \frac{6}{x^2}v = 0$$

$$\Rightarrow \quad x^2\frac{d^2v}{dx^2} - 6v = 0 \qquad \ldots(1)$$

Put $x = e^z$ so that $z = \log x$ and let $D \equiv \frac{d}{dz}$ then eqn. (1) becomes,

$$[D(D-1)-6]\, v = 0$$

$$\Rightarrow \qquad (D^2 - D - 6)\, v = 0 \qquad ...(2)$$

Solution of eqn. (2) is, $\qquad v = c_1 e^{3z} + c_2\, e^{-2z} = c_1\, x^3 + c_2\, x^{-2}$

where c_1 and c_2 are arbitrary constants of integration.

$\therefore$ Complete solution of given differential equation is

$$y = e^{-\frac{3}{4}x^{2/3}}\left(c_1\, x^3 + \frac{c_2}{x^2}\right).$$

TEST YOUR KNOWLEDGE

Solve the following differential equations :

1. $x\frac{d}{dx}\left(x\frac{dy}{dx} - y\right) - 2x\frac{dy}{dx} + 2y + x^2y = 0$

2. $\frac{d}{dx}\left(\cos^2 x\frac{dy}{dx}\right) + y\cos^2 x = 0$

3. $\frac{d^2y}{dx^2} + \frac{2}{x}\frac{dy}{dx} = n^2y$

4. $\frac{d^2y}{dx^2} - 2\tan x\frac{dy}{dx} + 5y = e^x \sec x$

5. $\left(\frac{d^2y}{dx^2} + y\right)\cot x + 2\left(\frac{dy}{dx} + y\tan x\right) = \sec x$

6. $\frac{d^2y}{dx^2} - 4x\frac{dy}{dx} + (4x^2 - 3)y = e^{x^2}$

7. $\frac{d^2y}{dx^2} - 2x\frac{dy}{dx} + (x^2 + 2)y = e^{\frac{1}{2}(x^2 + 2x)}$ *[G.B.T.U. (C.O.) 2011]*

8. $\frac{d^2y}{dx^2} + 2x\frac{dy}{dx} + (x^2 - 8)\,y = x^2\, e^{-x^2/2}$. *[G.B.T.U. 2012]*

Answers

1. $y = x(c_1 \cos x + c_2 \sin x)$

2. $y = \sec x\,(c_1 \cos \sqrt{2}\,x + c_2 \sin \sqrt{2}\,x)$

3. $y = \frac{1}{x}\,(c_1\, e^{nx} + c_2\, e^{-nx})$

4. $y = \sec x\left[c_1 \cos\sqrt{6}x + c_2 \sin\sqrt{6}x + \frac{e^x}{7}\right]$

5. $y = \frac{1}{2}\,(\sin x - x\cos x) + c_1\, x\cos x + c_2 \cos x$

6. $y = e^{x^2}\,(c_1\, e^x + c_2\, e^{-x} - 1)$

7. $y = e^{x^2/2}\,(c_1 \cos\sqrt{3}\,x + c_2 \sin\sqrt{3}\,x) + \frac{1}{4}e^{\frac{1}{2}(x^2 + 2x)}$

8. $y = e^{-\frac{x^2}{2}}\left[c_1\, e^{3x} + c_2\, e^{-3x} - \frac{1}{9}\left(x^2 + \frac{2}{9}\right)\right]$.

1.33.3. Method 3. To Find the Complete Solution of $y'' + Py' + Qy = R$ by Changing the Independent Variable

$$\frac{d^2y}{dx^2} + P\frac{dy}{dx} + Qy = R \qquad ...(1)$$

Let us relate x and z by the relation,

$$z = f(x) \qquad ...(2)$$

$$\therefore \quad \frac{dy}{dx} = \frac{dy}{dz} \cdot \frac{dz}{dx} \qquad ...(3)$$

$$\frac{d^2y}{dx^2} = \frac{d}{dx}\left(\frac{dy}{dx}\right) = \frac{d}{dx}\left(\frac{dy}{dz} \cdot \frac{dz}{dx}\right)$$

$$= \frac{dy}{dz} \cdot \frac{d^2z}{dx^2} + \frac{dz}{dx} \cdot \frac{d}{dz}\left(\frac{dy}{dz}\right) \cdot \frac{dz}{dx} = \frac{dy}{dz} \cdot \frac{d^2z}{dx^2} + \left(\frac{dz}{dx}\right)^2 \frac{d^2y}{dz^2} \qquad ...(4)$$

Substituting in (1), we get

$$\frac{dy}{dz} \cdot \frac{d^2z}{dx^2} + \left(\frac{dz}{dx}\right)^2 \frac{d^2y}{dz^2} + P\frac{dy}{dz} \cdot \frac{dz}{dx} + Qy = R$$

$$\Rightarrow \quad \frac{d^2y}{dz^2} + P_1\frac{dy}{dz} + Q_1 y = R_1 \qquad ...(5)$$

where $$P_1 = \frac{\dfrac{d^2z}{dx^2} + P\dfrac{dz}{dx}}{\left(\dfrac{dz}{dx}\right)^2}, \quad Q_1 = \frac{Q}{\left(\dfrac{dz}{dx}\right)^2}, \quad R_1 = \frac{R}{\left(\dfrac{dz}{dx}\right)^2}$$

Here P_1, Q_1, R_1 are functions of x which can be transformed into functions of z using the relation $z = f(x)$.

Choose z such that Q_1 = constant = a^2 (say)

$$\Rightarrow \quad \frac{Q}{\left(\dfrac{dz}{dx}\right)^2} = a^2 \quad \Rightarrow \quad a\frac{dz}{dx} = \sqrt{Q}$$

$$\Rightarrow \quad dz = \frac{\sqrt{Q}}{a}\, dx$$

Integration yields, $$z = \int \frac{\sqrt{Q}}{a}\, dx$$

If this value of z makes P_1 as constant then equation (5) can be solved.

Steps for solution :

1. Make the coefficient of $\dfrac{d^2y}{dx^2}$ as 1 if it is not so.
2. Compare the equation with standard form $y'' + Py' + Qy = R$ and get P, Q and R.

3. Choose z such that $\left(\frac{dz}{dx}\right)^2 = Q$

Here Q is taken in such a way that it remains the whole square of a function without surd and its negative sign is ignored.

4. Find $\frac{dz}{dx}$ hence obtain z (on integration) and $\frac{d^2z}{dx^2}$ (on differentiation).

5. Find P_1, Q_1 and R_1 by the formulae

$$P_1 = \frac{\frac{d^2z}{dx^2} + P\frac{dz}{dx}}{\left(\frac{dz}{dx}\right)^2}, \quad Q_1 = \frac{Q}{\left(\frac{dz}{dx}\right)^2}, \quad R_1 = \frac{R}{\left(\frac{dz}{dx}\right)^2}.$$

6. Reduced equation is $\frac{d^2y}{dz^2} + P_1\frac{dy}{dz} + Q_1 y = R_1$ which we solve for y in terms of z.

7. We write the complete solution as y in terms of x by replacing the value of z in terms of x.

ILLUSTRATIVE EXAMPLES

Example 1. *By changing the independent variable, solve the differential equation*

$$\frac{d^2y}{dx^2} - \frac{1}{x}\frac{dy}{dx} + 4x^2y = x^4.$$

Sol.
$$\frac{d^2y}{dx^2} - \frac{1}{x}\frac{dy}{dx} + 4x^2y = x^4 \quad ...(1)$$

Here,
$$P = -\frac{1}{x},\ Q = 4x^2,\ R = x^4$$

Choose z such that
$$\left(\frac{dz}{dx}\right)^2 = 4x^2$$

$$\Rightarrow \quad \frac{dz}{dx} = 2x \quad ...(2)$$

$$z = x^2 \text{ (on integrating)} \quad ...(3)$$

From (2),
$$\frac{d^2z}{dx^2} = 2 \qquad | \text{ Differentiating (2) w.r.t. } x$$

$$\therefore \quad P_1 = \frac{\frac{d^2z}{dx^2} + P\frac{dz}{dx}}{\left(\frac{dz}{dx}\right)^2} = \frac{2 - \frac{1}{x}(2x)}{4x^2} = 0$$

$$Q_1 = \frac{Q}{\left(\frac{dz}{dx}\right)^2} = \frac{4x^2}{4x^2} = 1$$

$$R_1 = \frac{R}{\left(\frac{dz}{dx}\right)^2} = \frac{x^4}{4x^2} = \frac{x^2}{4}$$

Reduced equation is,

$$\frac{d^2y}{dz^2} + y = \frac{z}{4} \qquad \mid \because \ z = x^2 \text{ from (3)}$$

Auxiliary equation is,

$$m^2 + 1 = 0 \quad \Rightarrow \quad m = \pm i$$

$$\text{C.F.} = c_1 \cos z + c_2 \sin z$$

$$\text{P.I.} = \frac{1}{D^2+1}\left(\frac{z}{4}\right) = (1 + D^2)^{-1}\left(\frac{z}{4}\right)$$

$$= (1 - D^2 + ...)\left(\frac{z}{4}\right) = \frac{z}{4} \qquad \mid \text{Leaving higher powers}$$

$\therefore$ Solution is $\quad y = c_1 \cos z + c_2 \sin z + \frac{z}{4}$

Complete solution is given by

$$y = c_1 \cos (x^2) + c_2 \sin (x^2) + \frac{x^2}{4}.$$

Example 2. *Solve :* $(1 + x)^2 \frac{d^2y}{dx^2} + (1 + x) \frac{dy}{dx} + y = 4 \cos \log (1 + x)$.

Sol. $$\frac{d^2y}{dx^2} + \frac{1}{1+x}\frac{dy}{dx} + \frac{y}{(1+x)^2} = \frac{4}{(1+x)^2} \cos \log (1 + x) \qquad ...(1)$$

Choose z such that,

$$\left(\frac{dz}{dx}\right)^2 = \frac{1}{(1+x)^2}$$

$$\Rightarrow \qquad \frac{dz}{dx} = \frac{1}{1+x} \qquad ...(2)$$

Integration yields, $\quad z = \log (1 + x) \qquad ...(3)$

From (2), $$\frac{d^2z}{dx^2} = -\frac{1}{(1+x)^2}$$

$$\therefore \qquad P_1 = \frac{-\frac{1}{(1+x)^2} + \frac{1}{1+x}\cdot\frac{1}{1+x}}{\frac{1}{(1+x)^2}} = 0$$

$$Q_1 = \frac{Q}{\left(\frac{dz}{dx}\right)^2} = 1$$

$$R_1 = \frac{R}{\left(\frac{dz}{dx}\right)^2} = 4 \cos \log (1 + x) = 4 \cos z \qquad | \text{ From (3)}$$

Reduced equation is

$$\frac{d^2y}{dz^2} + y = 4 \cos z$$

Auxiliary equation is $m^2 + 1 = 0 \quad \Rightarrow \quad m = \pm i$

$$\text{C.F.} = c_1 \cos z + c_2 \sin z$$

$$\text{P.I.} = \frac{1}{D^2 + 1} (4 \cos z) = 4 \cdot \frac{z}{2} \sin z = 2z \sin z$$

Complete solution is

$$y = c_1 \cos z + c_2 \sin z + 2z \sin z$$

$$y = c_1 \cos \log (1 + x) + c_2 \sin \log (1 + x) + 2 \log (1 + x) \sin \log (1 + x).$$

Example 3. *Solve by changing the independent variable :*

$$\frac{d^2y}{dx^2} + (3 \sin x - \cot x) \frac{dy}{dx} + 2y \sin^2 x = e^{-\cos x} \sin^2 x.$$

Sol. Choose z such that

$$\left(\frac{dz}{dx}\right)^2 = \sin^2 x \Rightarrow \frac{dz}{dx} = \sin x \qquad ...(1)$$

Integration yields, $z = -\cos x \qquad ...(2)$

From (1), $$\frac{d^2z}{dx^2} = \cos x$$

$\therefore$ $$P_1 = \frac{\cos x + (3 \sin x - \cot x) \sin x}{\sin^2 x} = 3$$

$$Q_1 = \frac{2 \sin^2 x}{\sin^2 x} = 2$$

$$R_1 = \frac{e^{-\cos x} \cdot \sin^2 x}{\sin^2 x} = e^{-\cos x} = e^z$$

Reduced equation is, $$\frac{d^2y}{dz^2} + 3 \frac{dy}{dz} + 2y = e^z$$

Auxiliary equation is $m^2 + 3m + 2 = 0 \quad \Rightarrow \quad m = -1, -2$

$\therefore$ $$\text{C.F.} = c_1 e^{-z} + c_2 e^{-2z}$$

$$\text{P.I.} = \frac{1}{D^2 + 3D + 2} (e^z) = \frac{e^z}{6}$$

Complete solution is, $y = c_1 e^{-z} + c_2 e^{-2z} + \dfrac{e^z}{6}$

$\Rightarrow$ $$y = c_1 e^{\cos x} + c_2 e^{2 \cos x} + \frac{e^{-\cos x}}{6}$$

where c_1 and c_2 are arbitrary constants of integration.

Example 4. *Solve by changing the independent variable*

$$(1 + x^2)^2 \frac{d^2y}{dx^2} + 2x\,(1 + x^2) \frac{dy}{dx} + 4y = 0.$$

Sol. The given equation is

$$\frac{d^2y}{dx^2} + \frac{2x}{1+x^2}\frac{dy}{dx} + \frac{4}{(1+x^2)^2}\,y = 0 \qquad ...(1)$$

Here, $\quad P = \dfrac{2x}{1+x^2}, \quad Q = \dfrac{4}{(1+x^2)^2}, \quad R = 0$

Choose z such that

$$\left(\frac{dz}{dx}\right)^2 = \frac{4}{(1+x^2)^2}$$

$$\Rightarrow \qquad \frac{dz}{dx} = \frac{2}{1+x^2} \qquad ...(2)$$

Integration yields, $\quad z = 2\tan^{-1} x$

From (2), $\quad \dfrac{d^2z}{dx^2} = \dfrac{-4x}{(1+x^2)^2}$

$$\therefore \qquad P_1 = \frac{\dfrac{-4x}{(1+x^2)^2} + \dfrac{2x}{1+x^2}\cdot\dfrac{2}{1+x^2}}{\dfrac{4}{(1+x^2)^2}} = 0$$

$$Q_1 = \frac{\dfrac{4}{(1+x^2)^2}}{\dfrac{4}{(1+x^2)^2}} = 1, \quad R_1 = \frac{0}{\left\{4/(1+x^2)^2\right\}} = 0$$

Reduced equation is $\quad \dfrac{d^2y}{dz^2} + y = 0$

Auxiliary equation is $\quad m^2 + 1 = 0 \quad \Rightarrow \quad m = \pm i$

$$\text{C.F.} = c_1 \cos z + c_2 \sin z$$

$$\text{P.I.} = 0$$

$$\therefore \qquad y = c_1 \cos z + c_2 \sin z$$

Complete solution is $\quad y = c_1 \cos(2\tan^{-1} x) + c_2 \sin(2\tan^{-1} x)$

where c_1 and c_2 are arbitrary constants of integration.

Example 5. *Solve by changing the independent variable*

$$\cos x \frac{d^2y}{dx^2} + \sin x \frac{dy}{dx} - 2y\cos^3 x = 2\cos^5 x.$$

Sol. The given equation is

$$\frac{d^2y}{dx^2} + \tan x \frac{dy}{dx} - 2y\cos^2 x = 2\cos^4 x$$

Choose z such that

$$\left(\frac{dz}{dx}\right)^2 = \cos^2 x \Rightarrow \qquad \frac{dz}{dx} = \cos x \qquad ...(1)$$

Integration yields, $z = \sin x$ ...(2)

From (1), $\dfrac{d^2z}{dx^2} = -\sin x$

$\therefore$ $P_1 = \dfrac{-\sin x + \tan x \cos x}{\cos^2 x} = 0$

$Q_1 = \dfrac{-2\cos^2 x}{\cos^2 x} = -2$

$R_1 = \dfrac{2\cos^4 x}{\cos^2 x} = 2\cos^2 x = 2(1 - z^2)$

Reduced equation is

$$\frac{d^2y}{dz^2} - 2y = 2(1 - z^2)$$

Auxiliary equation is

$$m^2 - 2 = 0 \Rightarrow m = \pm\sqrt{2}$$

$\therefore$ $\text{C.F.} = c_1 \cosh\sqrt{2}\,z + c_2 \sinh\sqrt{2}\,z$

$$\text{P.I.} = \frac{1}{D^2 - 2}[2(1 - z^2)] = \frac{2}{-2 + D^2}(1 - z^2) = -\left(1 - \frac{D^2}{2}\right)^{-1}(1 - z^2)$$

$$= -\left(1 + \frac{D^2}{2}\right)(1 - z^2) = -\left[1 - z^2 + \frac{1}{2}(-2)\right] = -[1 - z^2 - 1] = z^2$$

$\therefore$ $y = c_1 \cosh\sqrt{2}\,z + c_2 \sinh\sqrt{2}\,z + z^2$

Complete solution is

$$y = c_1 \cosh\sqrt{2}\,(\sin x) + c_2 \sinh\sqrt{2}\,(\sin x) + \sin^2 x$$

where c_1 and c_2 are arbitrary constants of integration.

TEST YOUR KNOWLEDGE

Solve the following differential equations by changing the independent variable :

1. $\dfrac{d^2y}{dx^2} + \cot x \dfrac{dy}{dx} + 4y \operatorname{cosec}^2 x = 0$ *(U.K.T.U. 2012)*
2. $x\dfrac{d^2y}{dx^2} - \dfrac{dy}{dx} - 4x^3 y = 8x^3 \sin x^2$
3. $x\dfrac{d^2y}{dx^2} + (4x^2 - 1)\dfrac{dy}{dx} + 4x^3 y = 2x^3$ *(U.P.T.U. 2006)*
4. $x^6 \dfrac{d^2y}{dx^2} + 3x^5 \dfrac{dy}{dx} + a^2 y = \dfrac{1}{x^2}$
5. $\dfrac{d^2y}{dx^2} - \cot x \dfrac{dy}{dx} - y \sin^2 x = 0$
6. $x^4 \dfrac{d^2y}{dx^2} + 2x^3 \dfrac{dy}{dx} + n^2 y = 0$ *(U.K.T.U. 2011)*
7. $\dfrac{d^2y}{dx^2} + \tan x \dfrac{dy}{dx} + y \cos^2 x = 0$
8. $\dfrac{d^2y}{dx^2} - \cot x \dfrac{dy}{dx} - y \sin^2 x = \cos x - \cos^3 x$. *(G.B.T.U. 2011)*

Answers

1. $y = c_1 \cos\left(2 \log \tan \frac{x}{2}\right) + c_2 \sin\left(2 \log \tan \frac{x}{2}\right)$

2. $y = c_1 e^{x^2} + c_2 e^{-x^2} - \sin x^2$

3. $y = (c_1 + c_2 x^2) e^{-x^2} + \frac{1}{2}$

4. $y = c_1 \cos\left(\frac{a}{2x^2}\right) + c_2 \sin\left(\frac{a}{2x^2}\right) + \frac{1}{a^2x^2}$

5. $y = c_1 e^{-\cos x} + c_2 e^{\cos x}$

6. $y = c_1 \cos\left(-\frac{n}{x}\right) + c_2 \sin\left(-\frac{n}{x}\right)$

7. $y = c_1 \sin(\sin x) + c_2 \cos(\sin x)$

8. $y = c_1 e^{-\cos x} + c_2 e^{\cos x} - \cos x.$

1.33.4. Method 4. To Find the Complete Solution of y″ + Py′ + Qy = R by the Method of Variation of Parameters

$$\frac{d^2y}{dx^2} + P\frac{dy}{dx} + Qy = R \qquad ...(1)$$

Let the complementary function of (1) be

$$y = Au + Bv \qquad ...(2)$$

where u and v are the functions of x and A, B are constants.

$\because$ u and v are parts of C.F.

$$\therefore \quad \frac{d^2u}{dx^2} + P\frac{du}{dx} + Qu = 0 \qquad ...(3)$$

and

$$\frac{d^2v}{dx^2} + P\frac{dv}{dx} + Qv = 0 \qquad ...(4)$$

Let the complete solution of (1) be

$$y = Au + Bv \qquad ...(5)$$

where A and B are not constants but suitable functions of x to be so chosen that (5) satisfies (1). Now,

$$y_1 = Au_1 + Bv_1 + A_1u + B_1v$$

$$\Rightarrow \quad y_1 = Au_1 + Bv_1 + (A_1u + B_1v) \qquad ...(6)$$

Let us choose A and B such that

$$A_1u + B_1v = 0 \qquad ...(7)$$

Now (6) becomes, $\quad y_1 = Au_1 + Bv_1 \qquad ...(8)$

$$\therefore \quad y_2 = A_1u_1 + Au_2 + B_1v_1 + Bv_2 \qquad ...(9)$$

Substituting the values of y, y_1, y_2 from (5), (8) and (9) in (1) respectively, we get

$$(A_1u_1 + Au_2 + B_1v_1 + Bv_2) + P(Au_1 + Bv_1) + Q(Au + Bv) = R$$

$$\Rightarrow \quad A_1u_1 + B_1v_1 + A(u_2 + Pu_2 + Qu) + B(v_2 + Pv_1 + Qv) = R$$

$$\Rightarrow \quad A_1u_1 + B_1v_1 = R \qquad ...(10)$$

| Using (3) and (4)

Solving (7) and (10) for A_1 and B_1, we get

$$A_1u + B_1v = 0$$

$$A_1u_1 + B_1v_1 - R = 0$$

$$\Rightarrow \qquad \frac{A_1}{-Rv} = \frac{B_1}{Ru} = \frac{1}{uv_1 - u_1v}$$

$$\Rightarrow \qquad A_1 = \frac{-Rv}{uv_1 - u_1v} = \phi(x) \qquad | \text{ say} \qquad \text{...(11)}$$

$$B_1 = \frac{Ru}{uv_1 - u_1v} = \psi(x) \qquad | \text{ say} \qquad \text{...(12)}$$

Integrating (11), we get $A = \int \phi(x)\, dx + a$ ...(13)

where a is an arbitrary constant of integration.

Integrating (12), we get $B = \int \psi(x)\, dx + b$ ...(14)

where b is also an arbitrary constant of integration.

Putting the above values in (5), we get

$$y = \left[\int \phi(x)\, dx + a\right] u + \left[\int \psi(x)\, dx + b\right] v$$

$$\Rightarrow \qquad y = u \int \phi(x)\, dx + v \int \psi(x)\, dx + au + bv$$

This gives the complete solution of (1).

Steps for solution :

1. Find out the parts of C.F.
2. Let them be u and v.
3. Consider $y = Au + Bv$ as the complete solution of equation given.
4. A and B are determined by the formulae

$$A = \int \frac{-Rv}{uv_1 - u_1v}\, dx + c_1 \quad \text{and} \quad B = \int \frac{Ru}{uv_1 - u_1v}\, dx + c_2$$

where c_1 and c_2 are the arbitrary constants of integration.

5. Write $y = Au + Bv$ as the complete solution.

Note. A and B can also be obtained by the following formulae

$$A = \int \frac{-Rv}{W}\, dx + a \qquad \text{and} \qquad B = \int \frac{Ru}{W}\, dx + b \quad \text{where } W = \begin{vmatrix} u & v \\ u_1 & v_1 \end{vmatrix} = uv_1 - u_1v$$

Extension. The above method can be extended to linear equations of any order.

Consider, $$\frac{d^3y}{dx^3} + P\frac{d^2y}{dx^2} + Q\frac{dy}{dx} + Ry = S \qquad \text{...(1)}$$

Let $y = u$, $y = v$, $y = w$ be the solutions of the given equation when $S = 0$.

Let the complete solution of (1) be

$$y = Au + Bv + Cw \quad \text{where A, B, C are some suitable functions of } x.$$

The conditions to determine A, B, C are

$$A_1u + B_1v + C_1w = 0 \qquad \text{...(2)}$$

$$A_1u_1 + B_1v_1 + C_1w_1 = 0 \qquad \text{...(3)}$$

and $$A_1u_2 + B_1v_2 + C_1w_2 = S \qquad \text{...(4)}$$

Solving (2), (3) and (4), we get A_1, B_1 and C_1 which by integration will give A, B and C.

As the solution is obtained by varying the arbitrary constants of the complementary function, the above method is known as that of **Variation of Parameters.**

ILLUSTRATIVE EXAMPLES

Example 1. *Solve by the method of variation of parameters :*

$$\frac{d^2y}{dx^2} + a^2 y = \sec ax. \qquad \text{[U.P.T.U. (SUM) 2008; U.K.T.U. 2012]}$$

Sol. Here, $u = \cos ax$, $v = \sin ax$ are two parts of C.F.

Also, $\quad R = \sec ax.$

Let the complete solution be

$$y = A \cos ax + B \sin ax \qquad ...(1)$$

where A and B are suitable functions of x.

To determine the values of A and B, we have

$$A = \int \frac{-Rv}{uv_1 - u_1 v} dx + c_1$$

$$= \int \frac{-\sec ax \,.\, \sin ax}{\{\cos ax \,.\, a \cos ax - (-a \sin ax) \sin ax\}} dx + c_1$$

$$= -\int \frac{\tan ax}{a} dx + c_1$$

$$\Rightarrow \qquad A = \frac{1}{a^2} \log \cos ax + c_1$$

where c_1 is an arbitrary constant of integration.

$$B = \int \frac{Ru}{uv_1 - u_1 v} dx + c_2$$

$$= \int \frac{\sec ax \,.\, \cos ax}{\{\cos ax \,.\, a \cos ax - (-a \sin ax) \sin ax\}} dx + c_2$$

$$= \frac{1}{a} \int dx + c_2 = \frac{x}{a} + c_2$$

where c_2 is an arbitrary constant of integration.

Hence the complete solution is given by

$$y = A \cos ax + B \sin ax$$

$$= \left(\frac{\log \cos ax}{a^2} + c_1 \right) \cos ax + \left(\frac{x}{a} + c_2 \right) \sin ax.$$

Example 2. *Solve by method of variation of parameters :*

$$\frac{d^2y}{dx^2} - 2\frac{dy}{dx} = e^x \sin x.$$

Sol. Parts of C.F. are 1 and e^{2x}.

Let $u = 1, v = e^{2x}$ Also, $R = e^x \sin x$

Let $y = A + Be^{2x}$ be the complete solution

where A and B are suitable functions of x determined by

$$A = \int \frac{-Rv}{uv_1 - u_1v} dx + c_1 = -\int \frac{e^x \sin x \,.\, e^{2x}}{1.2\,e^{2x}} dx + c_1$$

$$= -\frac{1}{2}\int e^x \sin x\, dx + c_1 = -\frac{1}{2}\left[\frac{e^x}{1+1}(\sin x - \cos x)\right] + c_1$$

$$= -\frac{e^x}{4}(\sin x - \cos x) + c_1$$

where c_1 is an arbitrary constant of integration.

$$B = \int \frac{Ru}{uv_1 - u_1v} dx + c_2 = \int \frac{e^x \sin x \,.\, 1}{1.2e^{2x}} dx + c_2$$

$$= \frac{1}{2}\int e^{-x} \sin x\, dx + c_2 = \frac{1}{2}\left[\frac{e^{-x}}{1+1}(-\sin x - \cos x)\right] + c_2$$

$$= -\frac{e^{-x}}{4}(\sin x + \cos x) + c_2$$

where c_2 is an arbitrary constant of integration.

The complete solution is

$$y = A + B\,e^{2x}$$

$$= \frac{e^x}{4}(\cos x - \sin x) + c_1 + \left[-\frac{e^{-x}}{4}(\sin x + \cos x) + c_2\right]e^{2x}$$

$$= \frac{e^x}{4}(\cos x - \sin x) + c_1 - \frac{e^x}{4}(\sin x + \cos x) + c_2\,e^{2x}$$

$$\Rightarrow \qquad y = c_1 + c_2\,e^{2x} - \frac{e^x}{2}\sin x$$

Example 3. *Apply the method of variation of parameters to solve the ordinary differential equations :*

(*i*) $\dfrac{d^2y}{dx^2} + y = \tan x$ [U.P.T.U. 2009; U.K.T.U. 2011]

(*ii*) $(D^2 - 1)y = 2(1 - e^{-2x})^{-1/2}$. [M.T.U. 2011; U.P.T.U. (SUM) 2009]

Sol. (*i*) Parts of C.F. are $u = \cos x$ and $v = \sin x$

Let $y = A\cos x + B\sin x$ be the complete solution of the given equation where A and B are determined as :

$$A = -\int \frac{Rv}{uv_1 - u_1v}\, dx + c_1$$

$$= -\int \frac{\tan x \,.\, \sin x}{\cos^2 x + \sin^2 x}\, dx + c_1 \qquad | \because \quad R = \tan x$$

$$= -\int \frac{1-\cos^2 x}{\cos x}\, dx + c_1 = -\int (\sec x - \cos x)\, dx + c_1$$

$\Rightarrow$ $$A = \sin x - \log(\sec x + \tan x) + c_1$$

and $$B = \int \frac{Ru}{uv_1 - u_1v}\, dx + c_2 = \int \frac{\tan x \,.\, \cos x}{1}\, dx + c_2$$

$\Rightarrow$ $$B = -\cos x + c_2$$

Hence the complete solution is

$$y = A\cos x + B\sin x$$

$$= [\sin x - \log(\sec x + \tan x) + c_1]\cos x + (-\cos x + c_2)\sin x$$

$\Rightarrow$ $$y = c_1 \cos x + c_2 \sin x - \cos x \log(\sec x + \tan x)$$

where c_1 and c_2 are arbitrary constants of integration.

(*ii*) Parts of C.F. are $u = e^x$ and $v = e^{-x}$

Let $y = A e^x + B e^{-x}$ be the complete solution of the given equation where A and B are determined as :

$$A = -\int \frac{Rv}{uv_1 - u_1v}\, dx + c_1$$

$$= -\int \frac{2(1-e^{-2x})^{-1/2} \,.\, e^{-x}}{e^x(-e^{-x}) - e^x \,.\, e^{-x}}\, dx + c_1 = -2\int \frac{e^{-x}}{-2\sqrt{1-e^{-2x}}}\, dx + c_1$$

$$= \int \frac{e^{-x}}{\sqrt{1-e^{-2x}}}\, dx + c_1 \qquad \text{Put } e^{-x} = t \quad \therefore \quad e^{-x}\, dx = -dt$$

$$= -\int \frac{dt}{\sqrt{1-t^2}} + c_1$$

$\Rightarrow$ $$A = -\sin^{-1}(e^{-x}) + c_1$$

and $$B = \int \frac{Ru}{uv_1 - u_1v}\, dx + c_2$$

$$= \int \frac{2(1-e^{-2x})^{-1/2} \,.\, e^x}{(-2)}\, dx + c_2 = -\int \frac{e^x}{\sqrt{1-e^{-2x}}}\, dx + c_2$$

$$= -\int \frac{e^{2x}}{\sqrt{e^{2x}-1}}\, dx + c_2 \qquad \text{Put } e^{2x} = t \Rightarrow e^{2x}\, dx = \frac{dt}{2}$$

$$= -\frac{1}{2}\int \frac{dt}{\sqrt{t-1}} + c_2 = -\frac{1}{2}\frac{(t-1)^{1/2}}{(1/2)} + c_2$$

$\Rightarrow$ $$B = -(e^{2x}-1)^{1/2} + c_2$$

Hence the complete solution is

$$y = \mathrm{A}\, e^{x} + \mathrm{B}\, e^{-x}$$

$$y = [-\sin^{-1}(e^{-x}) + c_1]\, e^{x} + [-(e^{2x} - 1)^{1/2} + c_2]\, e^{-x}$$

$$\Rightarrow \qquad y = c_1 e^{x} + c_2 e^{-x} - e^{x}\sin^{-1}(e^{-x}) - e^{-x}(e^{2x} - 1)^{1/2}$$

where c_1 and c_2 are arbitrary constants of integration.

Example 4. *Solve by the method of variation of parameters :*

$$\frac{d^2y}{dx^2} - y = \frac{2}{1+e^x}. \qquad \text{[G.B.T.U. (SUM) 2010]}$$

Sol. Here $u = e^x$, $v = e^{-x}$ which are parts of C.F. Also, $\mathrm{R} = \dfrac{2}{1+e^x}$

Let $y = \mathrm{A}e^x + \mathrm{B}e^{-x}$ be the complete solution of given equation, where A and B are determined as :

$$\mathrm{A} = \int \frac{-\mathrm{R}v}{uv_1 - u_1 v}\, dx + c_1 = \int \frac{-2\,.\,e^{-x}}{(1+e^x)\{e^x(-e^{-x}) - e^x\,.\,e^{-x}\}}\, dx + c_1$$

$$= -2\int \frac{e^{-x}}{(1+e^x)(-2)}\, dx + c_1 = \int \frac{e^{-x}}{1+e^x}\, dx + c_1$$

$$= \int \frac{e^{-2x}}{e^{-x}+1}\, dx + c_1 = \log\left(\frac{1+e^x}{e^x}\right) - e^{-x} + c_1$$

$$\mathrm{B} = \int \frac{\mathrm{R}u}{uv_1 - u_1 v}\, dx + c_2 = \int \frac{2\,e^x}{(1+e^x)\{e^x(-e^{-x}) - e^x\,.\,e^{-x}\}}\, dx + c_2$$

$$= -\int \frac{e^x}{1+e^x}\, dx + c_2 = -\log(1+e^x) + c_2$$

Hence complete solution is

$$y = \left[\log\left(\frac{1+e^x}{e^x}\right) - e^{-x} + c_1\right] e^x + [-\log(1+e^x) + c_2]\, e^{-x} \qquad |\ \because\ y = \mathrm{A}u + \mathrm{B}v$$

where c_1 and c_2 are arbitrary constants of integration.

Example 5. *Solve by the method of variation of parameters :*

$$\frac{d^2y}{dx^2} - 3\frac{dy}{dx} + 2y = \frac{e^x}{1+e^x}. \qquad \text{[M.T.U. (SUM) 2011]}$$

Sol. Here, parts of C.F. are $u = e^x$, $v = e^{2x}$. Also, $\mathrm{R} = \dfrac{e^x}{1+e^x}$

Let $y = \mathrm{A}e^x + \mathrm{B}e^{2x}$ be the complete solution of the given equation where A and B are suitable functions of x.

To determine A and B, we have

$$\mathrm{A} = \int \frac{-\mathrm{R}v}{uv_1 - u_1 v}\, dx + c_1 = -\int \frac{e^x\,.\,e^{2x}}{(1+e^x)(2e^{3x} - e^{3x})}\, dx + c_1$$

$$= -\int \frac{1}{1+e^x}\,dx + c_1 = -\int \frac{e^{-x}}{e^{-x}+1}\,dx + c_1 = \log(e^{-x}+1) + c_1$$

$$B = \int \frac{Ru}{uv_1 - u_1v}\,dx + c_2 = \int \frac{e^x \cdot e^x}{(1+e^x)\,e^{3x}}\,dx + c_2$$

$$= \int \frac{e^{-x}}{1+e^x}\,dx + c_2 = \int \frac{e^{-2x}}{e^{-x}+1}\,dx + c_2 = \log(1+e^{-x}) - (1+e^{-x}) + c_2$$

Hence the complete solution is

$$y = [\log(e^{-x}+1) + c_1]\,e^x + [\log(1+e^{-x}) - (1+e^{-x}) + c_2]\,e^{2x}$$

Example 6. *Solve by method of variation of parameters :*

$$\frac{d^2y}{dx^2} + 2\frac{dy}{dx} + y = e^{-x}\log x. \qquad \text{(U.P.T.U. 2008)}$$

Sol. Parts of C.F. are $u = e^{-x}$, $v = xe^{-x}$ and $R = e^{-x}\log x$

Let $y = Ae^{-x} + Bxe^{-x}$ be the complete solution where A and B are some suitable functions of x. To determine A and B, we have

$$A = -\int \frac{Rv}{uv_1 - u_1v}\,dx + c_1 = -\int \frac{e^{-x}\log x \cdot xe^{-x}}{e^{-x}(e^{-x} - xe^{-x}) + xe^{-2x}}\,dx + c_1$$

$$= -\int x\log x\,dx + c_1 = -\frac{x^2}{2}\log x + \frac{x^2}{4} + c_1$$

$$B = \int \frac{Ru}{uv_1 - u_1v}\,dx + c_2 = \int \frac{e^{-x}\log x \cdot e^{-x}}{e^{-2x}}\,dx + c_2$$

$$= \int \log x\,dx + c_2 = x\log x - x + c_2$$

Hence the complete solution is

$$y = Ae^{-x} + Bxe^{-x} = \left(-\frac{x^2}{2}\log x + \frac{x^2}{4} + c_1\right)e^{-x} + (x\log x - x + c_2)\,xe^{-x}$$

Example 7. *Use the variation of parameter method to solve the differential equation*

$$x^2y'' + xy' - y = x^2e^x. \qquad \text{(U.P.T.U. 2006)}$$

Sol. The given equation is

$$x^2y'' + xy' - y = x^2e^x \qquad ...(1)$$

$$\Rightarrow \qquad y'' + \frac{y'}{x} - \frac{y}{x^2} = e^x \qquad ...(2)$$

Here, $R = e^x$

Consider the equation $y'' + \frac{y'}{x} - \frac{y}{x^2} = 0$ for finding parts of C.F.

Put $x = e^z$ so that $z = \log x$ and Let $D \equiv \frac{d}{dz}$ then the above eqn. reduces to

$$[D(D-1) + D - 1]\, y = 0$$

$$\Rightarrow \qquad (D^2 - 1)\, y = 0 \qquad ...(3)$$

Auxiliary equation is $m^2 - 1 = 0 \Rightarrow m = \pm 1$

$$\therefore \qquad \text{C.F.} = c_1 e^z + c_2 e^{-z} = c_1 x + c_2 \cdot \frac{1}{x}$$

Hence parts of C.F. are x and $\frac{1}{x}$

Let $u = x$ and $v = \frac{1}{x}$

Let $y = Ax + \frac{B}{x}$ be the complete solution, where A and B are some suitable functions of x. A and B are determined as follows :

$$A = -\int \frac{Rv}{uv_1 - u_1 v}\, dx + c_1 = -\int \frac{e^x \cdot \frac{1}{x}}{x \cdot \left(\frac{-1}{x^2}\right) - 1 \cdot \left(\frac{1}{x}\right)}\, dx + c_1$$

$$= -\int \frac{e^x \cdot \frac{1}{x}}{\left(\frac{-2}{x}\right)}\, dx + c_1 = \frac{1}{2} e^x + c_1$$

and

$$B = \int \frac{Ru}{uv_1 - u_1 v}\, dx + c_2 = \int \frac{e^x \cdot x}{x\left(\frac{-1}{x^2}\right) - 1\left(\frac{1}{x}\right)}\, dx + c_2$$

$$= \int \frac{e^x \cdot x}{\left(\frac{-2}{x}\right)}\, dx + c_2 = -\frac{1}{2} \int x^2 e^x\, dx + c_2$$

$$= -\frac{1}{2}\left[x^2 e^x - \int 2x\, e^x\, dx\right] + c_2 = -\frac{1}{2}[x^2 e^x - 2(x-1)\, e^x] + c_2$$

$$= -\frac{1}{2} x^2 e^x + (x-1)\, e^x + c_2$$

Hence the complete solution is given by

$$y = Ax + \frac{B}{x} = \left(\frac{1}{2} e^x + c_1\right) x + \left[-\frac{1}{2} x^2 e^x + (x-1)\, e^x + c_2\right] \cdot \frac{1}{x}$$

$$\Rightarrow \qquad y = c_1 x + \frac{c_2}{x} + \left(1 - \frac{1}{x}\right) e^x$$

where c_1 and c_2 are arbitrary constants of integration.

Example 8. *Using variation of parameters method, solve :*

$$x^2 \frac{d^2y}{dx^2} + 2x \frac{dy}{dx} - 12y = x^3 \log x.$$

Sol. Consider the equation

$$x^2 \frac{d^2y}{dx^2} + 2x \frac{dy}{dx} - 12y = 0 \text{ for finding parts of C.F.}$$

Put $x = e^z$ so that $z = \log x$ and Let $D \equiv \frac{d}{dz}$ then the given equation reduces to

$$[D(D - 1) + 2D - 12]\, y = 0$$

$$\Rightarrow \qquad (D^2 + D - 12)\, y = 0$$

Auxiliary equation is

$$m^2 + m - 12 = 0 \;\Rightarrow\; m = 3, -4$$

$$\therefore \qquad \text{C.F.} = c_1 e^{3z} + c_2 e^{-4z} = c_1 x^3 + c_2 x^{-4}$$

Hence, parts of C.F. are x^3 and x^{-4}

Let $u = x^3$ and $v = x^{-4}$. Also, $R = x \log x$

Let $y = Au + Bv$ be the complete solution, where A and B are some suitable functions of x. A and B are determined as follows :

$$A = -\int \frac{Rv}{uv_1 - u_1 v}\, dx + c_1 = -\int \frac{x \log x \,.\, x^{-4}}{x^3 .(-4x^{-5}) - 3x^2 (x^{-4})}\, dx + c_1$$

$$= -\int \frac{x^{-3} \log x}{-7x^{-2}}\, dx + c_1 = \frac{1}{7}\int \frac{\log x}{x}\, dx + c_1 = \frac{1}{14} (\log x)^2 + c_1$$

and

$$B = \int \frac{Ru}{uv_1 - u_1 v}\, dx + c_2 = \int \frac{x \log x \,.\, x^3}{-7x^{-2}}\, dx + c_2$$

$$= -\frac{1}{7}\int x^6 \log x\; dx + c_2 = -\frac{1}{7}\left[\log x \,.\, \frac{x^7}{7} - \int \frac{1}{x} . \frac{x^7}{7}\, dx\right] + c_2$$

$$= -\frac{1}{7}\left[\frac{x^7 \log x}{7} - \frac{1}{7}\left(\frac{x^7}{7}\right)\right] + c_2 = \frac{x^7}{49}\left(\frac{1}{7} - \log x\right) + c_2$$

Hence the complete solution is given by

$$y = Ax^3 + Bx^{-4} = \left[\frac{1}{14} (\log x)^2 + c_1\right] x^3 + \left[\frac{x^7}{49}\left(\frac{1}{7} - \log x\right) + c_2\right] x^{-4}$$

where c_1 and c_2 are arbitrary constants of integration.

Example 9. *By the method of variation of parameters, solve the differential equation*

$$\frac{d^2y}{dx^2} + (1 - \cot x) \frac{dy}{dx} - y \cot x = \sin^2 x.$$

Sol. Take $y'' + (1 - \cot x)\, y' - y \cot x = 0$ ...(1)

Obviously, $y = e^{-x}$ is a part of C.F.

Let $y = ve^{-x}$ be the complete solution of (1)

$$\therefore \quad \frac{dy}{dx} = e^{-x}\frac{dv}{dx} - ve^{-x}$$

$$\therefore \quad \frac{d^2y}{dx^2} = ve^{-x} - 2e^{-x}\frac{dv}{dx} + e^{-x}\frac{d^2v}{dx^2}$$

Substituting above values in equation (1), we get

$$\frac{d^2v}{dx^2} - (1 + \cot x)\frac{dv}{dx} = 0$$

$$\Rightarrow \quad \frac{dp}{dx} - (1 + \cot x)\, p = 0, \qquad \text{where } p = \frac{dv}{dx}.$$

Its solution is given by

$$p = c_1 e^x \sin x$$

$$\therefore \quad \frac{dv}{dx} = c_1 e^x \sin x$$

Integration gives, $\quad v = c_1 \dfrac{e^x}{2}(\sin x - \cos x) + c_2$

Hence complete solution of (1) is

$$y = ve^{-x} = \frac{c_1}{2}(\sin x - \cos x) + c_2 e^{-x} \qquad ...(2)$$

Hence $u = e^{-x}$ and $v = \sin x - \cos x$ are the two parts of C.F.

To determine the values of A and B, we have

$$A = \int \frac{-\sin^2 x(\sin x - \cos x)}{e^{-x}(\cos x + \sin x) + e^{-x}(\sin x - \cos x)}\, dx + c_1$$

$$= -\int \frac{\sin^2 x(\sin x - \cos x)}{2e^{-x}\sin x}\, dx + c_1$$

$$= \frac{1}{2}\int e^x \sin x(\cos x - \sin x)\, dx + c_1$$

$$= \frac{e^x}{20}(3\sin 2x - \cos 2x - 5) + c_1$$

where c_1 is an arbitrary constant of integration.

$$B = \int \frac{\sin^2 x\, e^{-x}}{e^{-x}(\cos x + \sin x) + e^{-x}(\sin x - \cos x)}\, dx + c_2$$

$$= \frac{1}{2}\int \sin x\, dx + c_2 = \frac{-\cos x}{2} + c_2$$

where c_2 is an arbitrary constant of integration.

Hence the complete solution of the given differential equation is given by

$$y = Ae^{-x} + B(\sin x - \cos x)$$

$$= \left[\frac{e^x}{20}(3\sin 2x - \cos 2x - 5) + c_1\right]e^{-x} + \left(-\frac{\cos x}{2} + c_2\right)(\sin x - \cos x).$$

Example 10. *Apply the method of variation of parameters to solve*

$$\frac{d^3y}{dx^3} - 6\frac{d^2y}{dx^2} + 11\frac{dy}{dx} - 6y = e^{2x}.$$

Sol. Here, $u = e^x$, $v = e^{2x}$, $w = e^{3x}$ which are parts of C.F.

Let $y = Ae^x + Be^{2x} + Ce^{3x}$ be the complete solution of the given equation, where A, B and C are the suitable functions of x.

To determine the values of A, B and C, we have the equations

$$A_1(e^x) + B_1(e^{2x}) + C_1(e^{3x}) = 0 \quad ...(1)$$

$$A_1(e^x) + B_1(2e^{2x}) + C_1(3e^{3x}) = 0 \quad ...(2)$$

$$A_1(e^x) + B_1(4e^{2x}) + C_1(9e^{3x}) = e^{2x} \quad ...(3)$$

From (1) and (2), $\dfrac{A_1}{e^{5x}} = \dfrac{B_1}{-2e^{4x}} = \dfrac{C_1}{e^{3x}} = \lambda$ (say)

Substituting the values of A_1, B_1, C_1 in (3), we get

$$e^{2x} = \lambda(e^{6x} - 8e^{6x} + 9e^{6x}) = 2\lambda e^{6x}$$

$$\Rightarrow \qquad \lambda = \frac{1}{2}e^{-4x}$$

$$\therefore \qquad A_1 = \frac{1}{2}e^x, \; B_1 = -1, \; C_1 = \frac{1}{2}e^{-x}$$

Integrating, $\quad A = \dfrac{1}{2}e^x + a, \quad B = -x + b, \quad C = -\dfrac{1}{2}e^{-x} + c$

$\therefore$ The complete solution is

$$y = \frac{1}{2}e^{2x} + ae^x - xe^{2x} + be^{2x} - \frac{1}{2}e^{2x} + ce^{3x} = ae^x + be^{2x} + ce^{3x} - xe^{2x}$$

where a, b and c are arbitrary constants of integration.

TEST YOUR KNOWLEDGE

Solve the following differential equations by the method of variation of parameters :

1. $\dfrac{d^2y}{dx^2} + y = \text{cosec } x$

2. $y_2 + 4y = 4\tan 2x$

3. $\dfrac{d^2y}{dx^2} + y = x$

4. $\dfrac{d^2y}{dx^2} + y = \sec x \tan x$

5. $y_2 - 3y_1 + 2y = e^{2x} + x^2$

6. $(D^2 + 1)y = \tan^2 x$

7. $(D^2 + 1)\,y = \text{cosec } x \cot x$

8. (*i*) $\dfrac{d^2y}{dx^2} + y = x\cos x$ (*ii*) $\dfrac{d^2y}{dx^2} + y = x\sin x$

9. (*i*) $x^2\dfrac{d^2y}{dx^2} - 4x\dfrac{dy}{dx} + 6y = \sin(\log x)$ (*ii*) $x^2\dfrac{d^2y}{dx^2} - x\dfrac{dy}{dx} + y = x\log x$

10. (*i*) $\dfrac{d^2y}{dx^2} - 2\dfrac{dy}{dx} + 2y = e^x\tan x$ (*ii*) $\dfrac{d^2y}{dx^2} - 2\dfrac{dy}{dx} + y = e^x\log x$

11. $\frac{d^2y}{dx^2} - 3\frac{dy}{dx} + 2y = \sin e^{-x}$ (*M.T.U. 2012*)

12. $\frac{d^2y}{dx^2} + 4\frac{dy}{dx} + 4y = 3x\, e^{-x}$

13. $\frac{d^2y}{dx^2} - 6\frac{dy}{dx} + 9y = \frac{e^{3x}}{x^2}$

14. $x^2\frac{d^2y}{dx^2} + 4x\frac{dy}{dx} + 2y = e^x$ [*G.B.T.U. 2012*]

15. $x^2\frac{d^2y}{dx^2} + 4x\frac{dy}{dx} + 2y = x^2 + \frac{1}{x^2}$

16. $x^2\frac{d^2y}{dx^2} + x\frac{dy}{dx} - 9y = 48x^5$. [*G.B.T.U. (C.O.) 2010*]

Answers

1. $y = (a - x)\cos x + (b + \log \sin x)\sin x$

2. $y = c_1 \cos 2x + b \sin 2x - \cos 2x \log \tan\left(\frac{\pi}{4} + x\right)$

3. $y = c_1 \cos x + c_2 \sin x + x$

4. $y = c_1 \cos x + c_2 \sin x + x \cos x + \sin x \log \sec x - \sin x$

5. $y = c_1 e^x + c_2 e^{2x} + xe^{2x} + \frac{3}{2}x + \frac{7}{4} + \frac{1}{2}x^2 - e^{2x}$

6. $y = c_1 \cos x + c_2 \sin x - \cos x (\sec x + \cos x) + \sin x \log(\sec x + \tan x) + \sin^2 x$.

7. $y = c_1 \cos x + c_2 \sin x - \cos x \log \sin x - x \sin x - \sin x \cot x$

8. (*i*) $y = c_1 \cos x + \left(c_2 - \frac{1}{8}\right)\sin x + \frac{x^2}{4}\sin x + \frac{x}{4}\cos x$

   (*ii*) $y = c_1 \cos x + c_2 \sin x + \frac{x}{4}\sin x - \frac{x^2}{4}\cos x$

9. (*i*) $y = c_1x^2 + c_2x^3 + \frac{1}{10}(\sin \log x + \cos \log x)$ (*ii*) $y = c_1\, x \log x + c_2 x + \frac{1}{6}x(\log x)^3$

10. (*i*) $y = e^x(c_1 \cos x + c_2 \sin x) - e^x \cos x \log(\sec x + \tan x)$

    (*ii*) $y = (c_1 + c_2x)\, e^x + x^2 e^x\left(\frac{1}{2}\log x - \frac{3}{4}\right)$

11. $y = c_1e^x + c_2\, e^{2x} - e^{2x} \sin e^{-x}$

12. $y = c_1e^{-2x} + c_2x\, e^{-2x} + \frac{1}{2}x^3e^{-2x}$

13. $y = (c_1x + c_2)\, e^{3x} - e^{3x} \log x$

14. $y = (e^x + c_1)\frac{1}{x} + [(1 - x)\, e^x + c_2]\frac{1}{x^2}$

15. $y = \frac{c_1}{x} + \frac{c_2}{x^2} + \frac{1}{12}x^2 - \frac{1}{x^2}\log x$

16. $y = (4x^2 + c_1)\, x^3 + (c_2 - x^8)\, x^{-3}$.

1.34. EQUATIONS OF THE FORM $y'' = f(y)$

Steps for solution :

1. Multiply both sides by $2\frac{dy}{dx}$.

$$\Rightarrow \quad 2\frac{dy}{dx} \cdot \frac{d^2y}{dx^2} = 2\frac{dy}{dx} f(y) \qquad \text{...(1)}$$

2. Integrate (1) w.r.t. x,

$$\Rightarrow \qquad \left(\frac{dy}{dx}\right)^2 = 2\int f(y)\,dy = \psi(y) \qquad | \text{ say}$$

$$\Rightarrow \qquad \frac{dy}{dx} = \sqrt{\psi(y)} \qquad \ldots(2)$$

3. Integrate (2) w.r.t. x again

$$\int \frac{dy}{\sqrt{\psi(y)}} = x + c \qquad \ldots(3)$$

where c is an arbitrary constant of integration.

Solution (3) will be the required solution of the given differential equation.

ILLUSTRATIVE EXAMPLES

Example 1. *Solve :* $\frac{d^2y}{dx^2} = 2(y^3 + y)$ *under the conditions* $y = 0$, $y' = 1$ *at* $x = 0$.

Sol. $$\frac{d^2y}{dx^2} = 2(y^3 + y) \qquad \ldots(1)$$

Multiplying equation (1) by $2\frac{dy}{dx}$ and then integrating both sides w.r.t. x, we get

$$\left(\frac{dy}{dx}\right)^2 = y^4 + 2y^2 + a \qquad \ldots(2)$$

Since $y = 0$, $\frac{dy}{dx} = 1$ $\quad \therefore \quad$ From (2), $\quad a = 1$

$\therefore$ From (2), $$\left(\frac{dy}{dx}\right)^2 = y^4 + 2y^2 + 1 = (y^2 + 1)^2$$

$$\Rightarrow \qquad \frac{dy}{dx} = y^2 + 1$$

Integrating again w.r.t. x, we get

$$\int \frac{dy}{y^2 + 1} = x + b \qquad \Rightarrow \qquad \tan^{-1} y = x + b \qquad \ldots(3)$$

Again put $x = 0$, $\qquad y = 0$

$\therefore$ From (3), $\qquad 0 = 0 + b \qquad \Rightarrow \qquad b = 0$

$\therefore$ From (3), $\qquad y = \tan x.$

Example 2. *Solve* $\sin^3 y \frac{d^2y}{dx^2} = \cos y.$

Sol. The given differential equation may be written as,

$$\frac{d^2y}{dx^2} = \text{cosec}^2\, y \cot\, y$$

$\therefore \qquad 2\dfrac{dy}{dx}\dfrac{d^2y}{dx^2} = 2\operatorname{cosec}^2 y \cot y \dfrac{dy}{dx}$

Integration yields, $\qquad \left(\dfrac{dy}{dx}\right)^2 = -\cot^2 y + c_1$

$\Rightarrow \qquad \dfrac{dy}{dx} = \sqrt{c_1 - \cot^2 y}$

$\Rightarrow \qquad \dfrac{dy}{\sqrt{c_1 - \cot^2 y}} = dx$

$\Rightarrow \qquad \dfrac{\sin y\, dy}{\sqrt{c_1 \sin^2 y - \cos^2 y}} = dx$

$\Rightarrow \qquad \dfrac{\sin y\, dy}{\sqrt{c_1 - (1+c_1)\cos^2 y}} = dx$

Integrating, we get

$$-\frac{1}{\sqrt{1+c_1}} \sin^{-1}\left(\frac{\sqrt{1+c_1}}{c_1}\cos y\right) = x + c_2$$

or $\qquad \sin\left[(x+c_2)\sqrt{1+c_1}\right] + \dfrac{\sqrt{1+c_1}}{c_1}\cos y = 0$

Example 3. *Solve :* $\dfrac{d^2y}{dx^2} = \sec^2 y \tan y$ *under the boundary conditions* $y = 0$ *and* $\dfrac{dy}{dx} = 1$ *when* $x = 0$. [U.P.T.U. (SUM) 2009]

Sol. $\qquad \dfrac{d^2y}{dx^2} = \sec^2 y \tan y \qquad$ ...(1)

$\Rightarrow \qquad 2\dfrac{dy}{dx}\dfrac{d^2y}{dx^2} = 2\sec^2 y \tan y \dfrac{dy}{dx}$

Integration yields,

$$\left(\frac{dy}{dx}\right)^2 = 2\int \sec^2 y \tan y\, dy + c_1 = \tan^2 y + c_1 \qquad \text{...(2)}$$

Applying the condition $y = 0$, $\dfrac{dy}{dx} = 1$, when $x = 0$, we get $\quad 1 = c_1$

$\therefore \quad$ From (1), $\qquad \left(\dfrac{dy}{dx}\right)^2 = \sec^2 y$

$$\frac{dy}{dx} = \sec y$$

$$\cos y\, dy = dx$$

Integration yields,

$$\sin y = x + c_2 \qquad ...(3)$$

Applying the condition $y = 0$ when $x = 0$, we get

$$0 = 0 + c_2 \quad \Rightarrow \quad c_2 = 0$$

$\therefore$ From (3), $\quad y = \sin^{-1} x.$

1.35. AN EQUATION OF THE FORM $\frac{d^n y}{dx^n} = f(x)$

The equation can directly be integrated.

The first integration yields

$$\frac{d^{n-1}y}{dx^{n-1}} = \int f(x)\, dx + a_1, \quad \text{where } a_1 \text{ is arbitrary constant.}$$

Second gives, $\quad \frac{d^{n-2}y}{dx^{n-2}} = \iint f(x)\,(dx)^2 + a_1 x + a_2, \quad$ where a_2 is an arbitrary constant.

Integrating n times, we get

$$y = \iint \ldots\ldots \int f(x)\,(dx)^n + c_1 x^{n-1} + c_2 x^{n-2} + \ldots\ldots + c_n$$

where c_1, c_2, ..., c_n are arbitrary constants.

1.36. AN EQUATION WHICH DOES NOT CONTAIN *y* DIRECTLY

In such cases, the order of equation may be depressed by assuming as a dependent variable, the lowest derivative which presents itself in the given equation. Thus, when we write

$$\frac{dy}{dx} = p$$

$$\frac{d^2y}{dx^2} = \frac{dp}{dx}$$

$$\vdots \qquad \vdots$$

$$\frac{d^n y}{dx^n} = \frac{d^{n-1}p}{dx^{n-1}} \text{ in the general equation } f\left(\frac{d^n y}{dx^n}, \ldots\ldots, \frac{dy}{dx}, x\right) = 0,$$

the order of the equation is lowered and it takes the form

$$f\left(\frac{d^{n-1}p}{dx^{n-1}}, \ldots\ldots, p, x\right) = 0$$

which may possibly be solved for p.

1.37. AN EQUATION WHICH DOES NOT CONTAIN *x* DIRECTLY

In such cases, p is substituted for $\frac{dy}{dx}$.

Then writing

$$\frac{d^2y}{dx^2} = \frac{dp}{dx} = \frac{dp}{dy} \cdot \frac{dy}{dx} = p\,\frac{dp}{dy}$$

$$\frac{d^3y}{dx^3} = p^2\frac{d^2p}{dy^2} + p\left(\frac{dp}{dy}\right)^2, \ldots\ldots$$

the equation $f\left(\frac{d^ny}{dx^n}, \ldots\ldots, \frac{dy}{dx}, y\right) = 0$ is reduced to $f\left(\frac{d^{n-1}p}{dy^{n-1}}, \ldots\ldots, p, y\right) = 0$ which being an equation of $(n-1)$th order between y and p may possibly be solved for p.

1.38. EQUATION OF THE FORM $f\left(\frac{d^ny}{dx^n}, \frac{d^{n-1}y}{dx^{n-1}}, x\right) = 0$ WHERE DIFFERENTIAL COEFFICIENTS DIFFER IN ORDER BY 1

In such case, we write $q = \frac{d^{n-1}y}{dx^{n-1}}$ so that the equation reduces to $f\left(\frac{dq}{dx}, q, x\right) = 0$ which may be integrated for q being an equation of I order between q and x.

Thus if $q = \frac{d^{n-1}y}{dx^{n-1}} = \text{F}(x)$; we can find y by successive integration.

1.39. EQUATION OF THE FORM $f\left(\frac{d^ny}{dx^n}, \frac{d^{n-2}y}{dx^{n-2}}, x\right) = 0$, WHERE DIFFERENTIAL COEFFICIENTS DIFFER IN ORDER BY 2

In such cases, if we write $q = \frac{d^{n-2}y}{dx^{n-2}}$, the equation is reduced to $f\left(\frac{d^2q}{dx^2}, q, x\right) = 0$ from where q may be found. Thus if $q = \frac{d^{n-2}y}{dx^{n-2}} = \text{F}(x)$, we can find value of y by successive integration.

ILLUSTRATIVE EXAMPLES

Example 1. *Solve :* $\frac{d^2y}{dx^2} = \left[1 - \left(\frac{dy}{dx}\right)^2\right]^{1/2}$.

Sol. Put $\quad \frac{dy}{dx} = p \quad$ then $\quad \frac{d^2y}{dx^2} = \frac{dp}{dx}$

The given equation reduces to

$$\frac{dp}{dx} = \sqrt{1-p^2} \qquad \Rightarrow \qquad \frac{dp}{\sqrt{1-p^2}} = dx$$

Integrating, we get

$$\sin^{-1} p = x + c_1$$

$$\Rightarrow \qquad p = \sin(x + c_1)$$

$$\Rightarrow \qquad \frac{dy}{dx} = \sin(x + c_1)$$

Integrating again, $\quad y = -\cos(x + c_1) + c_2.$

Example 2. *Solve :* $\dfrac{d^4y}{dx^4} - \cot x \dfrac{d^3y}{dx^3} = 0.$

Sol. Put $\dfrac{d^3y}{dx^3} = z \quad$ then $\dfrac{d^4y}{dx^4} = \dfrac{dz}{dx}$

$\therefore$ (1) becomes,

$$\frac{dz}{dx} - z \cot x = 0$$

$$\Rightarrow \qquad \frac{dz}{z} = \cot x \, dx$$

Integration yields, $\log z = \log \sin x + \log c_1$

$$\Rightarrow \qquad z = c_1 \sin x \qquad \text{or} \qquad \frac{d^3y}{dx^3} = c_1 \sin x$$

$$\Rightarrow \qquad \frac{d^2y}{dx^2} = -c_1 \cos x + c_2 \qquad \text{| On integration}$$

$$\Rightarrow \qquad \frac{dy}{dx} = -c_1 \sin x + c_2 x + c_3 \qquad \text{| Again on integration}$$

or

$$y = c_1 \cos x + c_2 \frac{x^2}{2} + c_3 x + c_4. \qquad \text{| Again on integration}$$

Example 3. *Solve:* $x\dfrac{d^2y}{dx^2} + x\left(\dfrac{dy}{dx}\right)^2 - \dfrac{dy}{dx} = 0.$ (G.B.T.U. 2010)

Sol. Put $\dfrac{dy}{dx} = p$ then $\dfrac{d^2y}{dx^2} = \dfrac{dp}{dx}$

The given equation reduces to

$$x \frac{dp}{dx} + xp^2 - p = 0$$

$$\Rightarrow \qquad \frac{dp}{dx} - \frac{p}{x} = -p^2$$

$$\Rightarrow \qquad -\frac{1}{p^2}\frac{dp}{dx} + \frac{1}{px} = 1 \qquad \text{...(1)}$$

Put $\dfrac{1}{p} = t \quad \therefore \quad -\dfrac{1}{p^2}\dfrac{dp}{dx} = \dfrac{dt}{dx}$

Equation (1) becomes,

$$\frac{dt}{dx} + \frac{t}{x} = 1 \qquad ...(2)$$

$$\text{I.F.} = e^{\int \frac{1}{x} dx} = e^{\log x} = x$$

Solution to (2) is

$$tx = \int x\, dx + c_1 \quad \Rightarrow \quad tx = \frac{x^2}{2} + c_1$$

$$\Rightarrow \quad \frac{1}{p} = \frac{x}{2} + \frac{c_1}{x} \quad \Rightarrow \quad p = \frac{2x}{x^2 + 2c_1}$$

$$\Rightarrow \quad \frac{dy}{dx} = \frac{2x}{x^2 + 2c_1}$$

$$dy = \frac{2x}{x^2 + 2c_1} dx$$

Integration yields, $y = \log (x^2 + 2c_1) + c_2$

where c_1 and c_2 are arbitrary constants of integration.

1.40. APPLICATIONS OF DIFFERENTIAL EQUATIONS

Differential equations are of fundamental importance in engineering mathematics because many physical laws and relations appear mathematically in the form of such equations. Here, we shall consider various physical and geometrical problems that lead to differential equations and we will explain methods for solving such equations. The transition from the given physical problem to a corresponding mathematical model is called modelling. This is of great practical importance to the engineer, physicist and others. We will discuss here few striking applications of differential equations *e.g.*, motion of a particle in a resisting medium, simple electrical circuits, simple harmonic motion, deflection of beams, whirling of shaft, electrical transmission lines etc. Since electrical circuits are easier to assemble, less expensive and accurate measurements can be made of electrical quantities, we construct equivalent electrical models of complicated mechanical systems to study their displacements.

1.40.1. Motion in a Resisting Medium

When a body moves in a medium such as air, it experiences a resistance to its motion. When a particle falls under gravity in a resisting medium, the max. velocity, which it attains, is called **limiting** or **terminal velocity**—limiting velocity is the velocity when acceleration is zero.

ILLUSTRATIVE EXAMPLES

Example 1. *A particle of unit mass falls under gravity in a resisting medium whose resistance varies with velocity. Find the relation between distance and velocity if initially the particle starts from rest.* [U.P.T.U. (C.O.) 2009]

Sol. Let v be the velocity when the particle has fallen distance s in time t from rest so that the resistance due to velocity is kv per unit of mass. Hence the force of resistance on the particle of mass m is mkv against the direction of motion. Also, the force due to gravity, mg is acting vertically downwards.

Equation of motion of the particle is

$$m\frac{dv}{dt} = mg - mkv$$

$$\therefore \quad \frac{dv}{dt} = g - kv$$

$$\Rightarrow \quad \frac{dv}{g - kv} = dt$$

Integration gives,

$$-\frac{1}{k}\log(g - kv) = t + c_1 \quad \text{...(1)}$$

Since $v = 0$ when $t = 0$

$$\therefore \quad c_1 = -\frac{1}{k}\log g$$

$$\Rightarrow \quad \frac{1}{k}\log\frac{g}{g - kv} = t$$

$$\Rightarrow \quad v = \frac{ds}{dt} = \frac{g}{k}(1 - e^{-kt}) \quad \text{...(2)}$$

Integrating (2), we get

$$s = \frac{g}{k}t + \frac{g}{k^2}e^{-kt} + c_2$$

Since $s = 0$ when $t = 0$,

$$c_2 = -\frac{g}{k^2}$$

$$\therefore \quad s = \frac{g}{k}t + \frac{g}{k^2}(e^{-kt} - 1) \quad \text{...(3)}$$

Eliminating t between (2) and (3), we get

$$s = \frac{g}{k^2}\log\left(\frac{g}{g - kv}\right) - \frac{v}{k}$$

which gives a relation between distance and velocity.

Example 2. *Two particles fall freely, one in a medium whose resistance is equal to k times the velocity and the other in a medium whose resistance is equal to k times the square of the velocity. If V_1 and V_2 are their maximum velocities respectively, show that $V_1 = V_2^2$.*

Sol. Assume that the particle of mass m falls under gravity in a medium having resistance equal to m times the nth power of the velocity. Then the equation of motion is

$$m\frac{dv}{dt} = mg - mkv^n$$

$$\Rightarrow \quad \frac{dv}{dt} = g - kv^n \quad \text{...(1)}$$

For maximum velocity,

$$\frac{dv}{dt} = 0$$

$$\Rightarrow \quad g - kv^n = 0$$

$$\Rightarrow \quad v = \left(\frac{g}{k}\right)^{1/n}$$

For $n = 1$, $\quad V_1 = \frac{g}{k}$

For $n = 2$, $\quad V_2 = \left(\frac{g}{k}\right)^{1/2}$

Hence $\quad V_1 = V_2^2$

Example 3. *A body falling from rest is subjected to the force of gravity and an air resistance of* $\frac{n^2}{g}$ *times square of the velocity. Show that the distance travelled by the body in t seconds is* $\frac{g}{n^2}$ *log cosh nt.*

Sol. Equation of motion is

$$\frac{dv}{dt} = g - \frac{n^2}{g} v^2$$

$$\frac{dv}{g^2 - n^2v^2} = \frac{dt}{g}$$

$$\frac{dv}{\left(\frac{g}{n}\right)^2 - v^2} = \frac{n^2}{g}\, dt$$

Integrating, we get

$$\frac{n}{2g} \log\left(\frac{g + nv}{g - nv}\right) = \frac{n^2}{g} t + c_1 \qquad \text{...(1)}$$

When $t = 0$, $v = 0$ $\quad \therefore \quad$ From (1), $c_1 = 0$

$\therefore \quad$ From (1), $\quad \frac{g + nv}{g - nv} = e^{2nt}$

$$\Rightarrow \quad \frac{2nv}{2g} = \frac{e^{2nt} - 1}{e^{2nt} + 1} \qquad \text{| Applying C and D formula}$$

$$\Rightarrow \quad v = \frac{g}{n}\left(\frac{e^{nt} - e^{-nt}}{e^{nt} + e^{-nt}}\right)$$

$$\Rightarrow \quad \frac{ds}{dt} = \frac{g}{n} \tanh nt$$

$$ds = \frac{g}{n} \tanh nt\, dt$$

Integration yields,

$$s = \frac{g}{n^2} \log \cosh nt + c_2 \qquad \text{...(2)}$$

When $t = 0$, $s = 0$ $\therefore$ $c_2 = 0$

$\therefore$ From (2), $$s = \frac{g}{n^2} \log \cosh nt$$

Example 4. *A particle of mass m is projected vertically upwards under gravity, the resistance of the air being mk times the velocity. Show that the greatest height attained by the particle is* $\frac{V^2}{g}$ $[\lambda - \log (1 + \lambda)]$, *where V is the greatest velocity which the above mass will attain when it falls freely and* λV *is the initial velocity.*

Sol. Let v be the velocity of the particle at time t. The forces acting on the particle are

(*i*) its weight mg acting vertically downwards.

(*ii*) the resistance mkv of the air acting vertically downwards.

Accelerating force on the particle $= - mg - mkv$

$\therefore$ By Newton's second law, the equation of motion of the particle is

$$mv \frac{dv}{dx} = - mg - mkv$$

or $$v \frac{dv}{dx} = - g - kv \qquad ...(1)$$

When the particle falls freely (under gravity), equation (1) becomes (changing g to $- g$).

$$v \frac{dv}{dx} = g - kv \qquad ...(2)$$

When the particle attains the greatest velocity V, its acceleration is zero.

$\therefore$ From (2), $$0 = g - kV \quad \text{or} \quad k = \frac{g}{V}$$

Putting this value of k in (1), we have $v \frac{dv}{dx} = - g - \frac{g}{V} v = - \frac{g}{V} (V + v)$

or $$\frac{v}{V + v} dv = - \frac{g}{V} dx$$

Integrating,

$$\int \left(1 - \frac{V}{V + v}\right) dv = - \frac{g}{V} x + c$$

or $$v - V \log (V + v) = - \frac{g}{V} x + c \qquad ...(3)$$

Initially, when $x = 0$, $v = \lambda V$

$\therefore$ From (3), we have

$$\lambda V - V \log (V + \lambda V) = c$$

or $$c = V [\lambda - \log V (1 + \lambda)]$$

Substituting the value of c in (3),

$$v - V \log (V + v) = - \frac{g}{V} x + V [\lambda - \log V (1 + \lambda)] \qquad ...(4)$$

Let h be the greatest height attained by the particle, then $x = h$ when $v = 0$

$\therefore$ From (4), we have $- V \log V = - \frac{g}{V} h + V [\lambda - \log V (1 + \lambda)]$

or $$\frac{g}{V} h = V\lambda - V \log \frac{V(1+\lambda)}{V}$$

or $$h = \frac{V^2}{g} [\lambda - \log(1+\lambda)].$$

Example 5. *A body of mass m, falling from rest, is subject to the force of gravity and an air resistance proportional to the square of the velocity (i.e., kv^2). If it falls through a distance x and possesses a velocity v at that instant. Prove that* $\frac{2kx}{m} = \log \frac{a^2}{a^2 - v^2}$, *where* $mg = ka^2$.

[G.B.T.U. (AG) 2011]

Sol. The forces acting on the body are

(*i*) its weight mg acting vertically downwards.

(*ii*) the resistance kv^2 of the air acting vertically upwards.

Accelerating force on the body $= mg - kv^2 = ka^2 - kv^2 = k(a^2 - v^2)$ $[\because \ mg = ka^2]$

By Newton's second law, the equation of motion of the body is

$$mv \frac{dv}{dx} = k(a^2 - v^2)$$

or $$\frac{v}{a^2 - v^2} dv = \frac{k}{m} dx$$

Integrating,

$$-\frac{1}{2} \log(a^2 - v^2) = \frac{k}{m} x + c \qquad \text{...(1)}$$

Initially, when $x = 0, v = 0 \quad \therefore \quad c = -\frac{1}{2} \log a^2$

$\therefore$ From (1), we have $-\frac{1}{2} \log(a^2 - v^2) = \frac{k}{m} x - \frac{1}{2} \log a^2$

or $$\frac{2kx}{m} = \log a^2 - \log(a^2 - v^2)$$

or $$\frac{2kx}{m} = \log \frac{a^2}{a^2 - v^2}.$$

1.40.2. Application to Electric Circuits

If Q is the electrical charge on a condenser of capacity C and i is the current, then

(*a*) $i = \frac{dQ}{dt}$ or $Q = \int i \, dt$

(*b*) the potential drop across the resistance R is Ri.

(*c*) the potential drop across the inductance L is $L \frac{di}{dt}$.

(*d*) the potential drop across the capacitance C is $\frac{Q}{C}$.

Also, by Kirchhoff's Law, the total potential drop (voltage drop) in the circuit is equal to the applied voltage (E.M.F.).

ILLUSTRATIVE EXAMPLES

Example 1. *A constant electromotive force E volts is applied to a circuit containing a constant resistance R ohms in series and a constant inductance L henries. If the initial current is zero, show that the current builds up to half its theoretical maximum in (L log 2)/R seconds.*

Sol. Let i be the current in the circuit at any time t.

By Kirchhoff 's law, we have

$$\mathrm{L}\frac{di}{dt} + \mathrm{R}i = \mathrm{E}$$

or $$\frac{di}{dt} + \frac{\mathrm{R}}{\mathrm{L}}i = \frac{\mathrm{E}}{\mathrm{L}} \qquad ...(1)$$

which is Leibnitz's linear equation.

$$\text{I.F.} = e^{\int \frac{\mathrm{R}}{\mathrm{L}} dt} = e^{\frac{\mathrm{R}t}{\mathrm{L}}}$$

∴ The solution of equation (1) is

$$i \,.\, e^{\frac{\mathrm{R}t}{\mathrm{L}}} = \int \frac{\mathrm{E}}{\mathrm{L}} . e^{\frac{\mathrm{R}t}{\mathrm{L}}} \, dt + c = \frac{\mathrm{E}}{\mathrm{L}} . \frac{\mathrm{L}}{\mathrm{R}} e^{\frac{\mathrm{R}t}{\mathrm{L}}} + c$$

or $$i = \frac{\mathrm{E}}{\mathrm{R}} + ce^{-\frac{\mathrm{R}t}{\mathrm{L}}} \qquad ...(2)$$

Initially, when $t = 0$, $i = 0$ so that $c = -\frac{\mathrm{E}}{\mathrm{R}}$

Thus (2) becomes, $$i = \frac{\mathrm{E}}{\mathrm{R}}\left(1 - e^{-\frac{\mathrm{R}t}{\mathrm{L}}}\right) \qquad ...(3)$$

This equation gives the current in the circuit at any time t.

Clearly, i increases with t and attains the maximum value $\frac{\mathrm{E}}{\mathrm{R}}$.

Let the current in the circuit be half its theoretical maximum after a time T seconds. Then

$$\frac{1}{2} . \frac{\mathrm{E}}{\mathrm{R}} = \frac{\mathrm{E}}{\mathrm{R}}\left(1 - e^{-\frac{\mathrm{RT}}{\mathrm{L}}}\right) \text{ or } e^{-\frac{\mathrm{RT}}{\mathrm{L}}} = \frac{1}{2}$$

or $$-\frac{\mathrm{RT}}{\mathrm{L}} = \log\frac{1}{2} = -\log 2$$

∴ $$\mathrm{T} = (\mathrm{L} \log 2)/\mathrm{R}.$$

Example 2. *The equations of electromotive force interms of current i for an electrical circuit having resistance R and a condenser of capacity C, in series, is*

$$E = Ri + \int \frac{i}{C} dt$$

Find the current i at any time t, when $E = E_0 \sin wt$. (U.P.T.U. 2006)

Sol. The given equation is

$$Ri + \int \frac{i}{C} dt = E_0 \sin wt \quad ...(1)$$

Differentiating both sides w.r.t.t, we get

$$R \frac{di}{dt} + \frac{i}{C} = wE_0 \cos wt$$

$$\Rightarrow \quad \frac{di}{dt} + \frac{i}{RC} = \frac{wE_0}{R} \cos wt \quad ...(2)$$

$$\text{I.F.} = e^{\int \frac{1}{RC} dt} = e^{t/RC}$$

Solution of eqn. (2) is

$$ie^{t/RC} = \int \frac{wE_0}{R} \cos wt . e^{t/RC} dt + k$$

$$= \frac{wE_0}{R} \cdot \frac{e^{t/RC}}{\left(\frac{1}{R^2C^2} + w^2\right)} \left(\frac{1}{RC} \cos wt + w \sin wt\right) + k$$

$$\Rightarrow \quad ie^{t/RC} = \frac{wE_0 \, RC^2}{(1 + R^2C^2w^2)} \left(\frac{1}{RC} \cos wt + w \sin wt\right) e^{t/RC} + k$$

$$\Rightarrow \quad i = \frac{wE_0 \, C}{1 + R^2C^2w^2} (\cos wt + RCw \sin wt) + ke^{-t/RC}$$

where k is an arbitrary constant of integration.

Example 3. *An inductance L of 2.0 H and a resistance R of 20 Ω are connected in series with an e.m.f. E volt. If the current i is zero when t = 0, find the current i at the end of 0.01 second if E = 100 V, using the following differential equation*

$$L \frac{di}{dt} + Ri = E. \quad \text{(U.P.T.U. 2008)}$$

Sol. The given equation is

$$\frac{di}{dt} + \frac{R}{L} i = \frac{E}{L} \quad ...(1)$$

$$\text{I.F.} = e^{R/L \int dt} = e^{Rt/L}$$

Solution of (1) is

$$ie^{Rt/L} = \frac{E}{L} \int e^{Rt/L} dt = \frac{E}{R} e^{Rt/L} + c_1 \quad ...(2)$$

at $t = 0, i = 0$ $\therefore$ From (2), $c_1 = -\frac{E}{R}$

So, from (2), $$i = \frac{E}{R} (1 - e^{-Rt/L})$$

Putting the values of E, R, L and t, we get

$$i = \frac{100}{20} [1 - e^{-0.1}] = 0.4758 \text{ ampere.}$$

TEST YOUR KNOWLEDGE

1. A resistance R of 5 Ω and an inductance L of 0.1 H are connected in series with a battery of 12 V. Find the current i in the circuit as a function of time using the following differential equation

$$\text{R}i + \text{L}\frac{di}{dt} = \text{E}.$$ [*U.P.T.U. (SUM) 2008*]

2. A voltage E e^{-at} is applied at $t = 0$ to a circuit containing inductance L and resistance R. Show that the current at any time t is $\frac{\text{E}}{\text{R} - a\text{L}}(e^{-at} - e^{-\text{R}t/\text{L}})$

3. When a switch is closed in a circuit containing a battery E, a resistance R and an inductance L, the current i builds up at rate given by $\text{L}\frac{di}{dt} + \text{R}i = \text{E}$. Find i as a function of t. How long will it be, before the current has reached one-half its maximum value if E = 6 volts, R = 100 ohms and L = 0.1 henry ?

$\left[\textbf{Hint :} \text{T} = \frac{\text{L} \log 2}{\text{R}}\right]$

4. A particle falls in a vertical line under gravity (supposed constant) and the force of air resistance to its motion is proportional to its velocity. Show that its velocity cannot exceed a particular limit.

$\left[\textbf{Hint :} \frac{dv}{dt} = g - kv \;\Rightarrow\; v = \frac{g}{k}(1 - e^{-kt})\text{; limiting velocity} = g/k\right]$

5. An electric circuit contains an inductance L and a resistance R connected in series. If at any instant, the current in the circuit is I due to a battery having a periodic e.m.f. given by $\text{E}_0 \sin wt$, find the value of the current at any time t, if initially there is no current in the circuit. What is the value of the current in the steady state ?

[**Hint :** The steady state is reached as $t \to \infty$]

6. (*i*) When a resistance R ohms is connected in series with an inductance L henries, an e.m.f. of E volts, the current i amperes at time t is given by

$$\text{L}\frac{di}{dt} + \text{R}i = \text{E}.$$

If E = 10 sin t volts and $i = 0$ when $t = 0$, find i as a function of t.

(*ii*) An R-L-circuit has an e.m.f. given (in volts) by 4 sin t, a resistance of 100 ohms, an inductance of 4 henries with no initial current. Find the current at any time t.

[*G.B.T.U. 2012; G.B.T.U. (C.O.) 2011; M.T.U. (SUM) 2011*]

7. A body of mass m falls from rest under gravity in a field whose resistance is mk times the velocity of the body. Find the terminal velocity of the body and also the time taken to acquire one-half of its limiting speed.

8. The initial value problem governing the current i flowing in a series RL circuit when a voltage $v(t) = t$ is applied, is given by

$$\text{L}\frac{di}{dt} + \text{R}i = t\ ;\ t \ge 0\ ;\ i(0) = 0$$

Where R and L are constants. Find the current $i(t)$ at time t.

9. A decaying e.m.f. $E = 200\, e^{-5t}$ is connected in series with a 20 Ω resistor and 0.01 F capacitor. Assuming $Q = 0$ at $t = 0$, find the charge Q and current i at any time. Show that the charge reaches a maximum. Calculate it and find out when it is reached.

$$\left[\textbf{Hint: } 20\frac{dQ}{dt} + 100\,Q = 200\,e^{-5t}\right]$$

10. Solve : $L\dfrac{dI}{dt} + RI = E_0$ given that I_0 is the current flow initially. E_0 is the constant e.m.f. impressed on the circuit at $t = 0$.

11. An inductance L of 5.0 H and a resistance R of 25 Ω are connected in series with an e.m.f. E volt. If the current I is zero when $t = 0$, find the current I at the end of 1 second if E = 100 V using the differential equation $L\dfrac{dI}{dt} + IR = E$. *[G.B.T.U. (C.O.) 2010]*

12. (*i*) Find the steady state solution in R-L-C circuit equation consisting of inductance L = 0.05 H, resistance R = 5 ohms and a condenser of capacitance 4×10^{-4} farad, if $Q = I = 0$ when $t = 0$ and there is an alternating e.m.f. of $200 \cos 100t$. Find Q (t) and I (t). *(M.T.U. 2011)*

[**Hint:** Steady state solutions are obtained in the limiting case as $t \to \infty$]

(*ii*) An R-L-C circuit connected in series has R = 90 Ω, $C = \dfrac{1}{140}$ farad, L = 10 henries and an applied voltage $E(t) = 10 \cos t$. Assuming no initial charge on the capacitor but an initial current of 1 ampere at $t = 0$, when the voltage is first applied, find the subsequent charge on the capacitor and the amplitude of the steady state charge. *(M.T.U. 2012)*

Answers

1. $i = 2.4\left(1 - e^{-50t}\right)$ ampere

3. $i = \dfrac{E}{R}\left(1 - e^{-Rt/L}\right)$; 0.000693 sec

5. $I = \dfrac{E_0}{R^2 + w^2L^2}(R \sin wt - wL \cos wt) + \dfrac{E_0\, wL}{R^2 + w^2L^2} e^{-Rt/L}$; $I = \dfrac{E_0}{R^2 + w^2L^2}(R \sin wt - wL \cos wt)$

6. (*i*) $i = \dfrac{10}{L^2 + R^2}(R \sin t - L \cos t + Le^{-Rt/L})$ (*ii*) $i(t) = \dfrac{1}{626}(e^{-25t} - \cos t + 25 \sin t)$

7. $\dfrac{g}{k}, \dfrac{1}{k}\log 2$

8. $i(t) = \dfrac{t}{R} + \dfrac{L}{R^2}\left(e^{-\frac{Rt}{L}} - 1\right)$

9. $Q = 10t\,e^{-5t}$, $i = 10\,e^{-5t} - 50t\,e^{-5t}$; $Q_{max.} = \dfrac{2}{e}$ at $t = \dfrac{1}{5}$ sec

10. $I = \dfrac{E_0}{R} + \left(I_0 - \dfrac{E_0}{R}\right)e^{-Rt/L}$

11. 3.973 ampere

12. (*i*) $Q(t) = \frac{2}{85}(\sin 100\,t + 4\cos 100\,t)$; $I(t) = \frac{40}{17}(\cos 100t - 4\sin 100\,t)$

(*ii*) $q = \frac{3}{25}e^{-2t} - \frac{43}{250}e^{-7t} + \frac{1}{250}(9\sin t + 13\cos t)$; $\frac{\sqrt{10}}{50}$.

1.40.3. Simple Harmonic Motion (S.H.M.)

A particle is said to execute **simple harmonic motion** if it moves in a straight line such that its acceleration is always directed towards a fixed point in the line and is proportional to the distance of the particle from the fixed point.

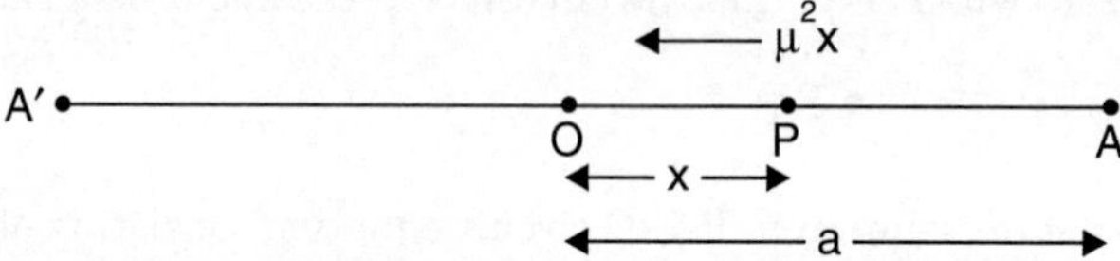

Let O be the fixed point in the line A'A. Let P be the position of the particle at any time t, where OP $= x$. Since the acceleration is always directed towards O, *i.e.*, the acceleration is in the direction opposite to that in which x increases, the equation of motion of the particle is

$$\frac{d^2x}{dt^2} = -\mu^2 x$$

or $$(D^2 + \mu^2)x = 0, \text{ where } D \equiv \frac{d}{dt} \qquad ...(1)$$

It is a linear differential equation with constant coefficients.

Its Auxiliary equation is $m^2 + \mu^2 = 0$ so that $m = \pm i\mu$

$\therefore$ The solution of (1) is $x = c_1 \cos \mu t + c_2 \sin \mu t$ ...(2)

Velocity of particle at P $= \frac{dx}{dt} = -c_1\mu \sin \mu t + c_2\mu \cos \mu t$ ...(3)

If the particle starts from rest at A, where OA $= a$

then from (2), (at $t = 0, x = a$) ; $c_1 = a$

and from (3), $\left(\text{at } t = 0, \frac{dx}{dt} = 0\right)$; $c_2 = 0$

$\therefore$ $$x = a \cos \mu t \qquad ...(4)$$

and $$\frac{dx}{dt} = -a\mu \sin \mu t \qquad ...(5)$$

$$= -a\mu\sqrt{1 - \cos^2 \mu t} = -a\mu\sqrt{1 - \frac{x^2}{a^2}} \qquad \left(\because \cos \mu t = \frac{x}{a}\right)$$

$$= -\mu\sqrt{a^2 - x^2} \qquad ...(6)$$

Equation (4) gives the displacement of the particle from the fixed point O at any time t.

Equation (6) gives the velocity of the particle at any time t, when its displacement from the fixed point O is x. Equation (6) also shows that the velocity is directed towards O and decreases as x increases.

Now, equations (4) and (5) remain unaltered, when t is replaced by $t + \frac{2\pi}{\mu}$ *i.e.*, when t is increased by $\frac{2\pi}{\mu}$ showing thereby that the particle occupies the same position and has the same velocity after a time $\frac{2\pi}{\mu}$. The quantity $\frac{2\pi}{\mu}$, usually denoted by T, is called the **particle time** *i.e.*, the time of complete oscillation.

Nature of motion. At A, $x = a$ and $v = 0$. Since acceleration is directed towards O, the particle moves towards O. The acceleration gradually decreases and vanishes at O, when the particle has acquired maximum velocity. Thus the particle moves further towards A′ under retardation and comes to rest at A′, where OA′ = OA. It moves back towards O under acceleration and acquires maximum velocity at O. Thus the particle moves further towards A under retardation and comes to rest at A. It retraces its path and goes on oscillating between A and A′. The point O is called the **centre of motion** or the **mean position**. The maximum distance a which the particle covers on either side of the mean position is called the **amplitude** of the motion.

The number of complete oscillations per second is called the **frequency** of motion. If n is the frequency, then

$$n = \frac{1}{T} = \frac{\mu}{2\pi}.$$

ILLUSTRATIVE EXAMPLES

Example 1. *A particle is executing simple harmonic motion with amplitude 20 cm and time 4 seconds. Find the time required by the particle in passing between points which are at distances 15 cm and 5 cm from the centre of force and are on the same side of it.*

Sol. Here $a = 20$ cm, T = 4 seconds

Since $$T = \frac{2\pi}{\mu} \quad \therefore \quad \mu = \frac{\pi}{2}$$

Let t_1 and t_2 seconds be the times when the particle is at distances 15 cm and 5 cm respectively from the centre of force.

Using $x = a \cos \mu t$, we have

$$15 = 20 \cos \frac{\pi}{2} t_1 \Rightarrow t_1 = \frac{2}{\pi} \cos^{-1} \frac{3}{4}$$

and $$5 = 20 \cos \frac{\pi}{2} t_2 \Rightarrow t_2 = \frac{2}{\pi} \cos^{-1} \frac{1}{4}$$

$$\text{Required time} = t_2 - t_1 = \frac{2}{\pi} \left(\cos^{-1} \frac{1}{4} - \cos^{-1} \frac{3}{4} \right) = 0.38 \text{ sec.}$$

Example 2. *A particle moving in a straight line with S.H.M. has velocities v_1 and v_2 when its distances from the centre are x_1 and x_2 respectively. Show that the period of motion is*

$$2\pi\sqrt{\frac{x_1^2 - x_2^2}{v_2^2 - v_1^2}}.$$

Sol. The velocity v of the particle, when it is at a distance x from the mean position is given by

$$v^2 = \mu^2(a^2 - x^2), \quad \text{where } a \text{ is the amplitude.}$$

$$\therefore \quad v_1^2 = \mu^2(a^2 - x_1^2) \qquad ...(1)$$

and $$v_2^2 = \mu^2(a^2 - x_2^2) \qquad ...(2)$$

Subtracting (1) from (2), we get

$$v_2^2 - v_1^2 = \mu^2(x_1^2 - x_2^2)$$

or $$\mu^2 = \frac{v_2^2 - v_1^2}{x_1^2 - x_2^2}$$

Periodic time $$T = \frac{2\pi}{\mu} = 2\pi\sqrt{\frac{x_1^2 - x_2^2}{v_2^2 - v_1^2}}.$$

Example 3. *At the end of three successive seconds, the distances of a point moving with S.H.M. from its mean position are x_1, x_2, x_3 respectively. Show that the time of a complete oscillation is $2\pi / \cos^{-1}\left(\frac{x_1 + x_3}{2x_2}\right)$.*

Sol. Let the moving point be at distances x_1, x_2, x_3 from the mean position at the end of t, $t + 1$, $t + 2$ seconds respectively.

Using $x = a \cos \mu t$, we have

$$x_1 = a \cos \mu t \qquad ...(1)$$

$$x_2 = a \cos \mu(t + 1) \qquad ...(2)$$

$$x_3 = a \cos \mu(t + 2) \qquad ...(3)$$

Adding (1) and (3), we get

$$x_1 + x_3 = a[\cos \mu(t + 2) + \cos \mu t]$$

$$= a \cdot 2 \cos \frac{\mu(t+2) + \mu t}{2} \cos \frac{\mu(t+2) - \mu t}{2}$$

$$= 2a \cos \mu(t + 1) \cos \mu = 2x_2 \cos \mu \qquad \text{[Using (2)]}$$

$$\Rightarrow \quad \mu = \cos^{-1}\left(\frac{x_1 + x_3}{2x_2}\right)$$

Hence the time of a complete oscillation $= \frac{2\pi}{\mu} = 2\pi / \cos^{-1}\left(\frac{x_1 + x_3}{2x_2}\right)$.

Example 4. *A particle moves with S.H.M. in a straight line. In the first second, starting from rest, it travels a distance 'a' and in the next second, it travels a distance 'b' in the same direction. Prove that the amplitude of motion is $\frac{2a^2}{3a - b}$.*

Sol. Let A be the amplitude of motion.

According to the problem

$$A - a = A \cos \mu \qquad ...(1)$$

$$A - a - b = A \cos 2\mu \qquad ...(2)$$

Now, $$A - a - b = A\,(2\cos^2 \mu - 1)$$

$$= A\left[2\left(\frac{A-a}{A}\right)^2 - 1\right] = \frac{2}{A}\,(A^2 + a^2 - 2Aa) - A$$

$$A - a - b = 2A + \frac{2a^2}{A} - 4a - A$$

$$3a - b = \frac{2a^2}{A}$$

$$\Rightarrow \qquad A = \frac{2a^2}{3a - b}.$$

Example 5. *A point moves in a straight line towards a centre of force with an acceleration $\frac{\mu}{(distance)^3}$, starting from rest at a distance 'a' from the centre of force. Show that the time of reaching a point distant 'b' from the centre of force is $\frac{a}{\sqrt{\mu}}\sqrt{a^2 - b^2}$ and that its velocity then is $\frac{\sqrt{\mu}}{ab} \cdot \sqrt{a^2 - b^2}$.*

Sol. O is the centre of force and the point starts from P, where OP = a.

We have to find out the time of reaching from P to Q and velocity at Q, where OQ = b.

Given : $$\frac{d^2x}{dt^2} = -\frac{\mu}{x^3} \qquad ...(1)$$

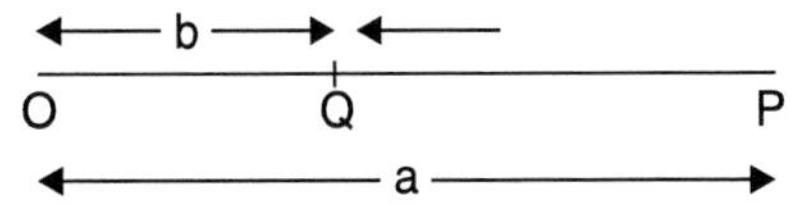

Multiplying (1) both sides by $2\frac{dx}{dt}$, we get

$$2\frac{dx}{dt} \cdot \frac{d^2x}{dt^2} = -\frac{\mu}{x^3} \cdot 2\frac{dx}{dt}$$

Integrating both sides, we get

$$\left(\frac{dx}{dt}\right)^2 = \int\left(\frac{-\mu}{x^3}\right) \cdot 2\frac{dx}{dt} \cdot dt + c$$

$$\Rightarrow \qquad \left(\frac{dx}{dt}\right)^2 = \frac{\mu}{x^2} + c \qquad ...(2)$$

Also, velocity $\frac{dx}{dt} = 0$, when $x = a$ (Given)

$\therefore$ By (2), $$c = -\mu a^{-2}$$

$$\therefore \qquad \left(\frac{dx}{dt}\right)^2 = \mu\,(x^{-2} - a^{-2}) = \mu\left(\frac{a^2 - x^2}{a^2x^2}\right) \qquad ...(3)$$

$\therefore$ Velocity towards O at Q *i.e.*, at $x = b$ is

$$\left(\frac{dx}{dt}\right)_{x=b} = \frac{\sqrt{\mu}}{ab}\sqrt{a^2 - b^2} \qquad \text{[From (3)]}$$

Again, separating the variables in equation (3)

$$\frac{-ax}{\sqrt{a^2-x^2}}\,dx = \sqrt{\mu}\,dt$$

where (–) ve sign is taken because point is moving towards O.

Integrating both sides, we get

$$\int \frac{-ax}{\sqrt{a^2-x^2}}\,dx = \int \sqrt{\mu}\,dt + A$$

$$\Rightarrow \qquad a\sqrt{a^2-x^2} = \sqrt{\mu}\;t + A$$

Now, $t = 0$ when $x = a$ (given) ...(4)

$\therefore$ From (4), A = 0. $\therefore$ At Q (when $x = b$), $t = \frac{a}{\sqrt{\mu}}\sqrt{a^2-b^2}$.

Example 6. *A particle of unit mass is acted upon by a force $\mu(x + a^4x^{-3})$ towards the origin ; if it starts from rest at a distance a, show that it will arrive at the origin in time $\frac{\pi}{4\sqrt{\mu}}$.*

Sol. O is the centre of force and the particle starts from P where OP = a. Equation of motion is

$$\frac{d^2x}{dt^2} = -\mu(x + a^4x^{-3}) \qquad ...(1)$$

Multiplying (1) both sides by $2\frac{dx}{dt}$, we get

$$2\frac{dx}{dt}\frac{d^2x}{dt^2} = -2\mu\left(x + \frac{a^4}{x^3}\right)\frac{dx}{dt}$$

Integrating both sides, we get

$$\left(\frac{dx}{dt}\right)^2 = -\mu x^2 + \mu\frac{a^4}{x^2} + c_1 \qquad ...(2)$$

Initially when $x = a$, $\frac{dx}{dt} = 0$

$$\therefore \qquad 0 = -\mu a^2 + \mu a^2 + c_1 \Rightarrow c_1 = 0$$

Hence, from (2),

$$\left(\frac{dx}{dt}\right)^2 = \frac{\mu}{x^2}(a^4 - x^4)$$

$$\Rightarrow \qquad \frac{dx}{dt} = \frac{-\sqrt{\mu}}{x}\sqrt{a^4-x^4} \qquad | \text{ Since particle is moving towards O}$$

$$\Rightarrow \qquad \frac{-x\,dx}{\sqrt{a^4-x^4}} = \sqrt{\mu}\,dt$$

Integrating both sides,

$$-\int \frac{x\,dx}{\sqrt{a^4 - x^4}} = \sqrt{\mu}\, t + c_2$$

$$-\frac{1}{2}\sin^{-1}\left(\frac{x^2}{a^2}\right) = \sqrt{\mu}\, t + c_2 \qquad ...(3)$$

Initially when $t = 0$, $x = a$ $\therefore$ From (3),

$$-\frac{\pi}{4} = c_2$$

Hence from (3),

$$-\frac{1}{2}\sin^{-1}\left(\frac{x^2}{a^2}\right) = \sqrt{\mu} t - \frac{\pi}{4} \qquad ...(4)$$

Let the particle arrive at the origin O (*i.e.*, where $x = 0$) at time t_1.

From (4), $$0 = \sqrt{\mu}\, t_1 - \frac{\pi}{4}$$

$\Rightarrow$ $$t_1 = \frac{\pi}{4\sqrt{\mu}}.$$

Example 7. *A particle is performing a simple harmonic motion of period T about a centre O and it passes through a point P, where OP = b with velocity v in the direction OP. Prove that the time which elapses before it returns to P is*

$$\frac{T}{\pi} \tan^{-1}\left(\frac{vT}{2\pi b}\right).$$

Sol. Let the amplitude be a.

Required time = time taken from P to N + time taken from N to P

= 2(time taken from N to P) ...(1)

For the motion from N to P, we have

M O b P N (with v → at P)

$$\frac{dx}{dt} = -\mu\sqrt{a^2 - x^2}$$

$\Rightarrow$ $$dt = \frac{-dx}{\mu\sqrt{a^2 - x^2}} \qquad ...(2)$$

Let t_1 be the time from N to P. Then at N, $t = 0$, $x = a$ and at P, $t = t_1$, $x = b$

$\therefore$ Integrating (2), we get

$$\int_0^{t_1} dt = \frac{1}{\mu}\int_a^b \frac{-dx}{\sqrt{a^2 - x^2}}$$

$$t_1 = \frac{1}{\mu}\left[\cos^{-1}\left(\frac{x}{a}\right)\right]_a^b = \frac{1}{\mu}\cos^{-1}\left(\frac{b}{a}\right)$$

From (1) Required time $= \dfrac{2}{\mu}\cos^{-1}\left(\dfrac{b}{a}\right) = \dfrac{2}{\mu}\tan^{-1}\left(\dfrac{\sqrt{a^2 - b^2}}{b}\right)$

$$= \frac{2}{\mu} \tan^{-1}\left(\frac{v}{b\mu}\right) \quad \left| \begin{array}{l} \because \quad \dfrac{dx}{dt} = -\mu\sqrt{a^2 - x^2} \\ \text{At P, } x = b, \dfrac{dx}{dt} = v \\ \therefore \quad v = -\mu\sqrt{a^2 - b^2} \text{ \{Neglect (–) ve sign\}} \end{array} \right.$$

$$= \frac{2}{\left(\frac{2\pi}{T}\right)} \tan^{-1}\left\{\frac{v}{b\left(\frac{2\pi}{T}\right)}\right\} = \frac{T}{\pi}\tan^{-1}\left(\frac{vT}{2\pi b}\right). \quad \left| \because \quad T = \frac{2\pi}{\mu} \right.$$

Example 8. *A particle executes S.H.M such that in two of its positions, velocities are u, v and the two corresponding accelerations are α, β. Show that the distance between two positions is* $\frac{v^2 - u^2}{\alpha + \beta}$.

Sol. Let the particle be at distances x_1 and x_2 from the centre at times t_1 and t_2.

$$u^2 = \mu^2 (a^2 - x_1^2) \quad \text{...(1)}$$

$$v^2 = \mu^2 (a^2 - x_2^2) \quad \text{...(2)}$$

Subtracting (1) from (2), we get

$$v^2 - u^2 = \mu^2 (x_1^2 - x_2^2) = -\mu^2 (x_2 + x_1)(x_2 - x_1) \quad \text{...(3)}$$

Also, we have, $\alpha = -\mu^2 x_1$

$$\beta = -\mu^2 x_2$$

$\therefore$ $\alpha + \beta = -\mu^2 (x_1 + x_2)$

Hence from (3),

$$x_2 - x_1 = \frac{v^2 - u^2}{\alpha + \beta}.$$

Example 9. *A particle moves with S.H.M. in a straight line under the action of a force which is proportional to the distance of the particle from x = 0. If it starts at x = 5 cm with a velocity of 10 cm/sec and it reaches an extreme position x = 10 cm, at what speed does it pass through the origin?*

Sol.

$$v^2 = \mu^2 (a^2 - x^2) \quad \text{...(1)}$$

$$x = 5, v = 10$$

$\therefore$

$$(10)^2 = \mu^2(a^2 - 25) \quad \text{...(2)}$$

Dividing (1) by (2), we get

$$\frac{v^2}{100} = \frac{a^2 - x^2}{a^2 - 25}$$

$$\Rightarrow \quad \frac{v^2}{100} = \frac{100 - x^2}{100 - 25} \quad | \text{ Here } a = 10$$

$$\Rightarrow \quad v^2 = \frac{4}{3}(100 - x^2)$$

At $x = 0$,

$$v^2 = \frac{400}{3} = 133.33$$

$$\therefore \qquad v = \sqrt{133.33} = 11.546 \text{ cm/sec}$$

Hence the required speed is 11.546 cm/sec.

Example 10. *A particle of mass m is oscillating in a straight line about a centre of force O towards which the force is mn^2r when at a distance r. The particle receives a blow in the direction of motion which generates a velocity na, when it is at a distance $\frac{a\sqrt{3}}{2}$ from O, a is the amplitude of oscillation. If this velocity is away from O, show that the new amplitude is $a\sqrt{3}$.*

Sol. Equation of motion is

$$m\frac{dv}{dt} = -mn^2r$$

$$\Rightarrow \qquad mv\frac{dv}{dr} = -mn^2r$$

$$\Rightarrow \qquad v\,dv = -n^2r\,dr$$

Integration yields,

$$\frac{v^2}{2} = -n^2\frac{r^2}{2} + \frac{c_1}{2} \qquad \text{...(1)}$$

At $r = a$, $v = 0$, $\therefore$ From (1),

$$0 = -n^2\frac{a^2}{2} + \frac{c_1}{2}$$

$$\Rightarrow \qquad c_1 = n^2a^2$$

Hence, from (1), $\quad v^2 = n^2(a^2 - r^2) \qquad$ ...(2)

At $r = \frac{a\sqrt{3}}{2}$, $\quad v^2 = n^2\left(a^2 - \frac{3a^2}{4}\right) = \frac{n^2a^2}{4}$

$$\therefore \qquad v = \frac{na}{2}$$

After the blow, the new velocity $(v) = \frac{na}{2} + na = \frac{3na}{2}$

From (1), we have, $\quad v^2 = -n^2r^2 + c_1$

$$\left(\frac{3na}{2}\right)^2 = -n^2\left(\frac{\sqrt{3}a}{2}\right)^2 + c_1 \qquad \Big| \text{ At } r = \frac{a\sqrt{3}}{2}$$

$$\frac{9n^2a^2}{4} = \frac{-3n^2a^2}{4} + \text{C}$$

$$c_1 = \frac{9n^2a^2}{4} + \frac{3n^2a^2}{4} = 3n^2a^2$$

Hence, again from (1),

$$v^2 = -n^2r^2 + 3n^2a^2 \qquad \text{...(3)}$$

New amplitude will be the value of r when $v = 0$.

Hence, from (3), $\quad 0 = -n^2r^2 + 3n^2a^2$

$$\Rightarrow \qquad r^2 = 3a^2$$

$$\Rightarrow \qquad r = a\sqrt{3}.$$

TEST YOUR KNOWLEDGE

1. A point executing S.H.M. passes through two points A and B, 2 metres apart, with the same velocity having occupied 4 seconds in passing from A to B. After another 4 seconds, it returns to B. Find the period and amplitude.
2. A particle of mass of 4 gm executing S.H.M has velocities 8 cm/sec and 6 cm/sec respectively when it is at distances 3 cm and 4 cm from the centre of its path. Find its period and amplitude. Find also the force acting on the particle when it is a distance 1 cm from the centre.
3. At the end of three successive seconds, the distances of a point moving with S.H.M. from its mean position, measured in the same direction are 1, 5, 5. Show that the period of complete oscillation is $\frac{2\pi}{\theta}$, where $\cos\theta = \frac{3}{5}$.
4. A particle begins to move from a distance 'a' towards a fixed centre which repels it with retardation μx. If its initial velocity is $a\sqrt{\mu}$, show that it will continually approach the fixed centre but will never reach it. *[U.P.T.U. (SUM) 2007]*

   [Hint : $\ddot{x} = \mu x$; $t = 0$, $x = a$, $\dot{x} = a\sqrt{\mu}$ so that $x = ae^{\sqrt{\mu}\,t}$]
5. At what distance from the centre, the velocity in a S.H.M will be one fourth of the maximum?
6. A particle of mass m moves in a straight line under the action of force mn^2x which is always directed towards a fixed point O on the line. Determine the displacement $x(t)$ if the resistance to the motion is $2\lambda mnv$ given that initially $x = 0$, $\frac{dx}{dt} = 0$ $(0 < \lambda < 1)$. *(G.B.T.U. 2010)*

   [Hint : Equation of motion is $m\ddot{x} = -2\lambda mn\dot{x} - mn^2x$]

Answers

1. 16 sec, $\sqrt{2}$ m   2. π sec, 5 cm, 16 dynes   5. $x = \pm\frac{\sqrt{15}\,a}{4}$

6. $x(t) = \frac{x_0}{n\omega}e^{-\lambda nt}\sin n\omega t$, where $\omega = \sqrt{1-\lambda^2}$.

1.41. APPLICATIONS OF II ORDER DIFFERENTIAL EQUATIONS TO MECHANICAL AND ELECTRICAL OSCILLATORY CIRCUITS

1.41.1. Free Oscillations

(*i*) *Mechanical system.* Consider a spring OA suspended vertically from a fixed support at O. Let a body of mass m be suspended from the end A, the mass of the body being so large in comparison with the mass of the spring, that the latter may be neglected. Let $e(=\text{AB})$ be the elongation produced by the mass m hanging in equilibrium, then B is called the position of **static equilibrium** and e is called the **static extension.**

Let k be the stiffness of the spring, *i.e.*, the restoring force per unit stretch of the spring due to elasticity.

For equilibrium at B, $mg = \text{T} = ke$ ...(1)

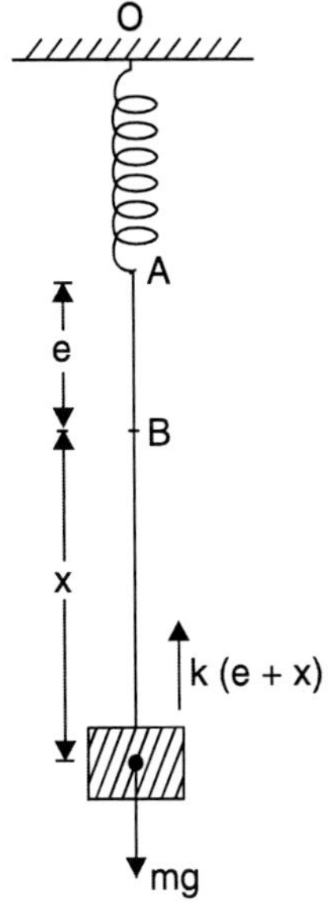

Let the mass be displaced through a further distance x from the equilibrium position. The acceleration of the mass m at this position is $\frac{d^2x}{dt^2}$ and the forces acting upon it are its weight mg downwards and the restoring force $k(e + x)$ upwards.

∴ The equation of motion of mass m is

$$m \frac{d^2x}{dt^2} = mg - k(e + x) = -kx \qquad \text{[Using (1)]}$$

or
$$\frac{d^2x}{dt^2} + \frac{k}{m} x = 0$$

Writing $\omega^2 = \frac{k}{m}$, it becomes $\frac{d^2x}{dt^2} + \omega^2 x = 0$ ...(2)

(ii) Equivalent electrical circuit (L-C circuit). Consider an electrical circuit containing an inductance L and capacitance C. Let q be the electrical charge on the condenser plate and i be the current in the circuit at any time t. The voltage drops across L and C being $L \frac{di}{dt}$ and $\frac{q}{C}$ respectively and since there is no applied E.M.F. in the circuit, we have by Kirchhoff's Law,

C

L

$$L \frac{di}{dt} + \frac{q}{C} = 0 \qquad ...(3)$$

Since $i = \frac{dq}{dt}$, equation (3) becomes

$$L \frac{d^2q}{dt^2} + \frac{q}{C} = 0 \quad \text{or} \quad \frac{d^2q}{dt^2} + \frac{q}{LC} = 0$$

Writing $\omega^2 = \frac{1}{LC}$, it becomes $\frac{d^2q}{dt^2} + \omega^2 q = 0$ ...(4)

which is of the same form as equation (2).

Solution and its Physical Interpretation :

The solution of equation (2) is $x = c_1 \cos \omega t + c_2 \sin \omega t$ which can also be written as

$$x = A \cos (\omega t + B) \qquad ...(5)$$

where c_1, c_2 or A, B are arbitrary constants to be determined from initial conditions of the problem, electrical or mechanical.

Equation (5) represents oscillatory variations of the variable x with amplitude A and period $T = \frac{2\pi}{\omega}$. In mechanical system, it represents the S.H.M. of the mass m with period

$$2\pi \sqrt{\frac{m}{k}} = 2\pi \sqrt{\frac{e}{g}} \qquad \left(\text{Since } \omega^2 = \frac{k}{m} \text{ and } mg = ke\right)$$

In electrical circuit, it represents an oscillatory current with period $2\pi \sqrt{LC}$, since $\omega^2 = \frac{1}{LC}$.

1.41.2. Damped Free Oscillations

(*i*) *Mechanical system.* If the motion of the mass m is subjected to an additional force of resistance, proportional to the instantaneous velocity of the mass, say $\lambda \frac{dx}{dt}$, produced by a damper, the oscillations are said to be **damped.**

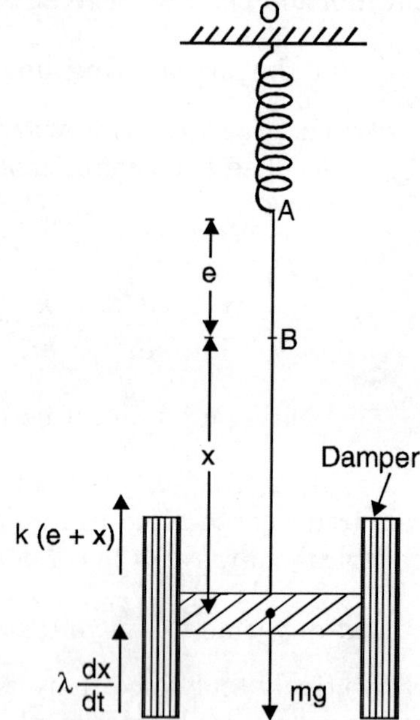

The equation of motion of the mass m is

$$m \frac{d^2x}{dt^2} = mg - k(e + x) - \lambda \frac{dx}{dt}$$

$$= -kx - \lambda \frac{dx}{dt} \qquad (\because \quad ke = mg)$$

or
$$\frac{d^2x}{dt^2} + \frac{\lambda}{m}\frac{dx}{dt} + \frac{k}{m} x = 0$$

Writing $\frac{\lambda}{m} = 2p$ and $\frac{k}{m} = \omega^2$, it becomes

$$\frac{d^2x}{dt^2} + 2p \frac{dx}{dt} + \omega^2 x = 0 \qquad ...(1)$$

(*ii*) *Equivalent electrical circuit (L-C-R circuit).* Consider the discharge of a condenser C through an inductance L and the resistance R. Let q be the charge and i the current in the circuit at any time t. The voltage drops across L, C and R are respectively

$$L \frac{d^2q}{dt^2}, \ \frac{q}{C} \text{ and } R \frac{dq}{dt}$$

$\therefore$ By Kirchhoff's Law, we have

$$L \frac{d^2q}{dt^2} + R \frac{dq}{dt} + \frac{q}{C} = 0$$

or
$$\frac{d^2q}{dt^2} + \frac{R}{L}\frac{dq}{dt} + \frac{1}{LC} q = 0$$

Writing $\frac{R}{L} = 2p$ and $\frac{1}{LC} = \omega^2$, it becomes

$$\frac{d^2q}{dt^2} + 2p \frac{dq}{dt} + \omega^2 q = 0 \qquad ...(2)$$

which is of the same form as equation (1).

Solution and its Physical Interpretation:

Equation (1) is a linear differential equation with constant coefficients.

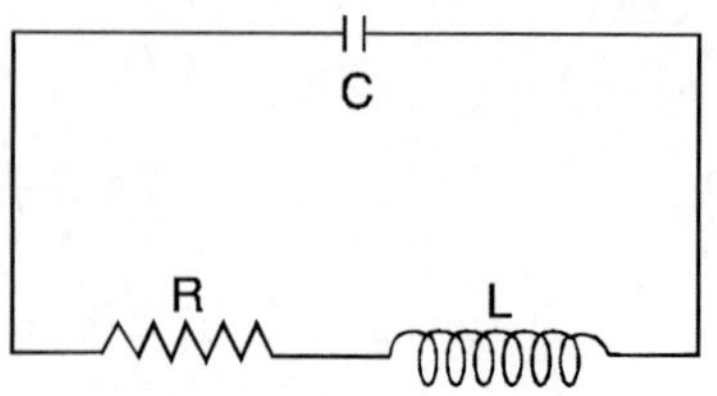

Auxiliary eqn. of (1) is $\quad m^2 + 2pm + \omega^2 = 0$

$$\Rightarrow \qquad m = -p \pm \sqrt{p^2 - \omega^2}.$$

Thus the general solution of equation (1) depends upon the relative values of p and ω.

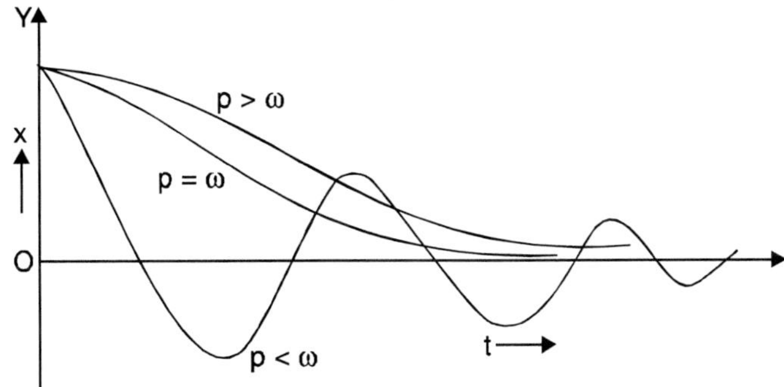

Case I. When $p > \omega$, the roots of the auxiliary equation are real and distinct.

The solution of equation (1) is $x = c_1 e^{(-p+\sqrt{p^2-\omega^2})t} + c_2 e^{(-p-\sqrt{p^2-\omega^2})t}$

or $$x = e^{-pt}\left(c_1 e^{\sqrt{p^2-\omega^2}\,t} + c_2 e^{-\sqrt{p^2-\omega^2}\,t}\right)$$

where c_1, c_2 are arbitrary constants to be determined from the initial conditions of the given problem.

The solution shows that x is always positive and hence the motion is non-oscillatory. Further, as $t \to \infty$, $x \to 0$; the restoring force in this case is so great that the non-oscillatory motion is called **over-damped** or **dead-beat motion.**

Case II. When $p = \omega$, the roots of the auxiliary equation are equal, each being equal to $-p$.

The solution of equation (1) is $x = (c_1 + c_2 t)e^{-pt}$

Here also x is always positive and the motion is non-oscillatory.

Further, as $t \to \infty$, $x \to 0$. The motion of the mass m in this case is called **critically damped motion,** because it separates the non-oscillatory motion of case I from the oscillatory motion of case III.

Case III. When $p < \omega$, the roots of the auxiliary equation are imaginary *i.e.*,

$$m = -p \pm i\sqrt{\omega^2 - p^2}$$

The solution of equation (1) is $x = e^{-pt}\left(c_1 \cos\sqrt{\omega^2 - p^2}\; t + c_2 \sin\sqrt{\omega^2 - p^2}\; t\right)$

where c_1 and c_2 are constants.

The variation of x is now oscillatory due to the presence of the trigonometric factor.

The periodic time of the oscillation is $T = \dfrac{2\pi}{\sqrt{\omega^2 - p^2}}$ which is greater than the periodic time in case of free oscillations (without damping) which is $\dfrac{2\pi}{\omega}$. Thus, the effect of damping is to increase the period of oscillation and the motion ultimately dies away. Such a motion is called **damped oscillatory motion.**

1.41.3. Forced Oscillations (*Without damping*)

If the point of the support of the spring is also vibrating with some external periodic force, then the resulting motion is called **forced oscillatory motion.**

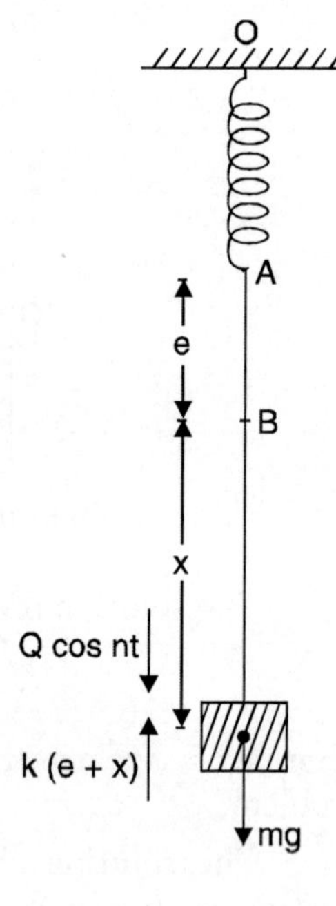

(*i*) *Mechanical system.* Consider the motion of the mass m as in 1.30.1 with an external periodic force Q cos nt impressed upon the system. This force is applied to the support of the spring so that now the support is not steady. The equation of motion of mass m is

$$m\frac{d^2x}{dt^2} = mg - k(e + x) + Q\cos nt$$

Since $mg = ke$, it becomes

$$m\frac{d^2x}{dt^2} = -kx + Q\cos nt$$

or
$$\frac{d^2x}{dt^2} + \frac{k}{m}x = \frac{Q}{m}\cos nt$$

Writing $\omega^2 = \frac{k}{m}$ and $E = \frac{Q}{m}$, it becomes

$$\frac{d^2x}{dt^2} + \omega^2x = E\cos nt \qquad ...(1)$$

(*ii*) *Equivalent electrical circuit* (*L-C circuit with e.m.f. Q cos nt*). As in 1.41.1, the equation for an L-C circuit now becomes

$$L\frac{di}{dt} + \frac{q}{C} = Q\cos nt$$

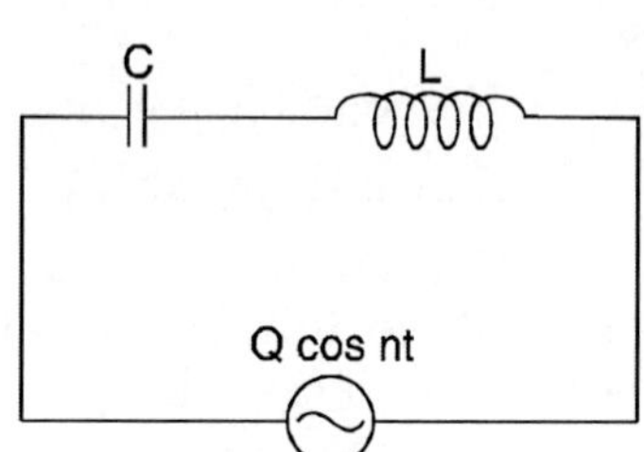

Since $i = \frac{dq}{dt}$, it becomes

$$L\frac{d^2q}{dt^2} + \frac{q}{C} = Q\cos nt$$

or
$$\frac{d^2q}{dt^2} + \frac{1}{LC}q = \frac{Q}{L}\cos nt$$

Writing $\omega^2 = \frac{1}{LC}$ and $E = \frac{Q}{L}$, it becomes

$$\frac{d^2q}{dt^2} + \omega^2q = E\cos nt \qquad ...(2)$$

which is of the same form as equation (1).

Solution and its Physical Interpretation:

Equation (1) is a linear differential equation with constant coefficients.

Its A.E. is $m^2 + \omega^2 = 0$ which gives $m = \pm\, i\omega$

Its $\qquad$ C.F. $= c_1\cos\omega t + c_2\sin\omega t$

and $\qquad$ P.I. $= E\,\frac{1}{D^2 + \omega^2}\cos nt$

Evaluation of P.I. depends upon the relative values of ω and n.

Thus, we have to consider two cases : $\omega \neq n$ and $\omega = n$.

Case I. When $\omega \neq n$

$$\text{P.I.} = \frac{E}{\omega^2 - n^2} \cos nt$$

$\therefore$ The complete solution of (1) is $x = c_1 \cos \omega t + c_2 \sin \omega t + \dfrac{E}{\omega^2 - n^2} \cos nt$

which may be written as $x = A \cos (\omega t + B) + \dfrac{E}{\omega^2 - n^2} \cos nt$

This shows that the variation of x consists of two oscillatory motions : the one due to the C.F. gives free oscillations of period $\dfrac{2\pi}{\omega}$ and the second due to the P.I. gives forced oscillations of period $\dfrac{2\pi}{n}$.

Also, if the frequency of free oscillations is very high, *i.e.*, ω is large, then the amplitude $\dfrac{E}{\omega^2 - n^2}$ of the forced oscillations is small.

Case II. When $\omega = n$

$$\text{P.I.} = Et \frac{1}{2D} \cos \omega t = \frac{Et}{2} \int \cos \omega t \, dt = \frac{Et}{2\omega} \sin \omega t$$

$\therefore$ The complete solution of (1) is

$$x = c_1 \cos \omega t + c_2 \sin \omega t + \frac{Et}{2\omega} \sin \omega t$$

$$= c_1 \cos \omega t + \left(c_2 + \frac{Et}{2\omega}\right) \sin \omega t \qquad ...(3)$$

Let $\quad c_1 = r \sin \phi \quad$ and $\quad c_2 + \dfrac{Et}{2\omega} = r \cos \phi$

then $\quad r = \sqrt{c_1^2 + \left(c_2 + \dfrac{Et}{2\omega}\right)^2} \quad$ and $\quad \phi = \tan^{-1} \left(\dfrac{c_1}{c_2 + \dfrac{Et}{2\omega}}\right)$

Equation (3) reduces to $x = r \sin (\omega t + \phi)$ which shows that motion is oscillatory with period $\dfrac{2\pi}{\omega}$ and amplitude $= \sqrt{c_1^2 + \left(c_2 + \dfrac{Et}{2\omega}\right)^2}$.

Clearly, amplitude increases with time, so that after a long time the amplitude becomes abnormally large. This phenomenon in which the impressed frequency due to external periodic force becomes equal to the natural frequency of the system is known as **resonance**. A practical instance of the case of resonance is the soldiers breaking step while marching over a bridge, for the simple reason that, if by chance the steps be in rhythm with the natural frequency of the bridge, it may collapse due to resonance.

1.41.4. Forced Oscillations (*with damping*)

(*i*) *Mechanical system.* In the above case, if in addition, there is a damping force, which is proportional to the instantaneous velocity of the mass, say $\lambda \frac{dx}{dt}$, then the equation of motion of mass m is

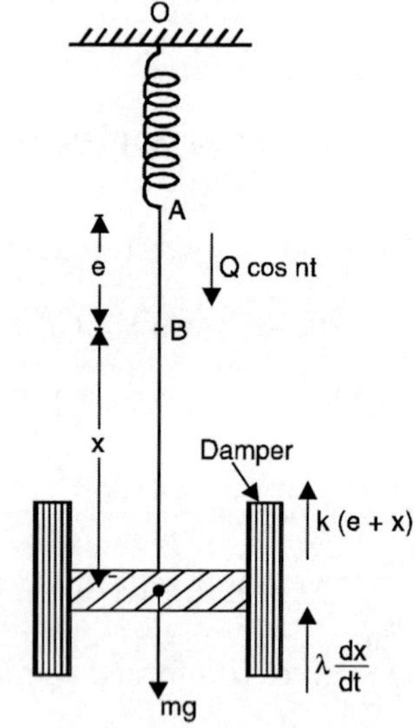

$$m\frac{d^2x}{dt^2} = mg - k(e + x) - \lambda \frac{dx}{dt} + Q \cos nt$$

Since $mg = ke$, it becomes

$$m\frac{d^2x}{dt^2} = - kx - \lambda \frac{dx}{dt} + Q \cos nt$$

or
$$\frac{d^2x}{dt^2} + \frac{\lambda}{m}\frac{dx}{dt} + \frac{k}{m}x = \frac{Q}{m}\cos nt$$

Writing $\frac{\lambda}{m} = 2p$, $\frac{k}{m} = \omega^2$ and $\frac{Q}{m} = E$, it becomes

$$\frac{d^2x}{dt^2} + 2p\frac{dx}{dt} + \omega^2 x = E \cos nt$$

(*ii*) *Equivalent electrical system (L-C-R circuit with e.m.f. Q cos nt).*

The differential equation of the L-C-R circuit which contains an alternating e.m.f. Q cos *nt* can be written as

$$L\frac{d^2q}{dt^2} + R\frac{dq}{dt} + \frac{q}{C} = Q \cos nt$$

or
$$\frac{d^2q}{dt^2} + \frac{R}{L}\frac{dq}{dt} + \frac{1}{LC}q = \frac{Q}{L}\cos nt$$

Writing $\frac{R}{L} = 2p$, $\frac{1}{LC} = \omega^2$ and $\frac{Q}{L} = E$, it becomes

$$\frac{d^2q}{dt^2} + 2p\frac{dq}{dt} + \omega^2 q = E \cos nt \qquad ...(1)$$

C R L

Q cos nt

which is of the same form as equation (1).

Solution and its Physical Interpretation :

Equation (1) is a linear differential equation with constant coefficients.

Its A.E. is $m^2 + 2pm + \omega^2 = 0 \Rightarrow m = -p \pm \sqrt{p^2 - \omega^2}$

$\therefore$
$$\text{C.F.} = e^{-pt}\left(c_1 e^{\sqrt{p^2-\omega^2}\,t} + c_2 e^{-\sqrt{p^2-\omega^2}\,t}\right)$$

$$\text{P.I.} = E \cdot \frac{1}{D^2 + 2pD + \omega^2}\cos nt = E \cdot \frac{1}{-n^2 + 2pD + \omega^2}\cos nt$$

$$= E \cdot \frac{1}{(\omega^2 - n^2) + 2pD} \cos nt = E \cdot \frac{(\omega^2 - n^2) - 2pD}{(\omega^2 - n^2)^2 - 4p^2D^2} \cos nt$$

$$= E \cdot \frac{(\omega^2 - n^2)\cos nt + 2pn \sin nt}{(\omega^2 - n^2)^2 + 4p^2n^2}$$

Now, let $\omega^2 - n^2 = r \cos \phi$ and $2pn = r \sin \phi$ so that

$$r = \sqrt{(\omega^2 - n^2)^2 + 4p^2n^2} \quad \text{and} \quad \phi = \tan^{-1}\left(\frac{2pn}{\omega^2 - n^2}\right)$$

$\therefore$ $$\text{P.I.} = E \cdot \frac{r \cos(nt - \phi)}{r^2} = \frac{E}{r} \cos(nt - \phi)$$

$\therefore$ The complete solution of equation (1) is

$$x = e^{-pt}\left(c_1 e^{\sqrt{p^2 - \omega^2}\, t} + c_2 e^{-\sqrt{p^2 - \omega^2}\, t}\right) + \frac{E \cos\left\{nt - \tan^{-1}\left(\frac{2pn}{\omega^2 - n^2}\right)\right\}}{\sqrt{(\omega^2 - n^2)^2 + 4p^2n^2}}$$

The C.F. represents free oscillations of the system which die out as $t \to \infty$ due to the presence of the factor e^{-pt}.

The P.I. represents the forced oscillations of the system having a constant amplitude

$$= \frac{E}{\sqrt{(\omega^2 - n^2)^2 + 4p^2n^2}}$$

and the period $= \frac{2\pi}{n}$ which is the same as that of the impressed force.

Thus as t increases, the free oscillations (given by the C.F.) die out while the forced oscillations (given by the P.I.) persist giving the steady state of motion.

ILLUSTRATIVE EXAMPLES

Example 1. *Show that the frequency of free vibrations in a closed electrical circuit with inductance L and capacity C in series is* $\frac{30}{\pi\sqrt{LC}}$ *per minute.*

Sol. Let i be the current and q the charge in the condenser plate at any time t. The voltage drops across L and C are $L\frac{di}{dt} = L\frac{d^2q}{dt^2}$ and $\frac{q}{C}$ respectively. Since there is no applied E.M.F. in the circuit, we have by Kirchhoff's Law,

$$L\frac{d^2q}{dt^2} + \frac{q}{C} = 0 \quad \text{or} \quad \frac{d^2q}{dt^2} = -\frac{1}{LC}q$$

Writing $\frac{1}{LC} = \omega^2$, it becomes $\frac{d^2q}{dt^2} = -\omega^2 q$

It represents oscillatory current with period $\frac{2\pi}{\omega} = 2\pi\sqrt{LC}$.

$\therefore$ Frequency $= \frac{1}{T}$ per second $= \frac{60}{2\pi\sqrt{LC}}$ per minute $= \frac{30}{\pi\sqrt{LC}}$ per minute.

Example 2. *An uncharged condenser of capacity C is charged by applying an e.m.f. E sin* $\frac{t}{\sqrt{LC}}$ *, through leads of self-inductance L and negligible resistance. Prove that at time t, the charge on one of the plates is*

$$\frac{EC}{2}\left[\sin\frac{t}{\sqrt{LC}} - \frac{t}{\sqrt{LC}}\cos\frac{t}{\sqrt{LC}}\right].$$

Sol. Let q be the charge on the condenser at any time t. The differential equation for the circuit is

$$L\frac{d^2q}{dt^2} + \frac{q}{C} = E\sin\frac{t}{\sqrt{LC}} \qquad ...(1)$$

Its A.E. is $\quad Lm^2 + \frac{1}{C} = 0 \quad$ or $\quad m^2 = -\frac{1}{LC}$ so that $m = \pm\frac{i}{\sqrt{LC}}$

$$\text{C.F.} = c_1\cos\frac{t}{\sqrt{LC}} + c_2\sin\frac{t}{\sqrt{LC}}$$

and

$$\text{P.I.} = \frac{1}{LD^2 + \frac{1}{C}}E\sin\frac{t}{\sqrt{LC}} \qquad \text{(Case of failure)}$$

$$= Et\,.\frac{1}{2LD}\sin\frac{t}{\sqrt{LC}} = \frac{Et}{2L}\left(-\sqrt{LC}\cos\frac{t}{\sqrt{LC}}\right)$$

$$= -\frac{Et}{2}\sqrt{\frac{C}{L}}\cos\frac{t}{\sqrt{LC}}$$

$\therefore$ The complete solution of (1) is $q = c_1\cos\frac{t}{\sqrt{LC}} + c_2\sin\frac{t}{\sqrt{LC}} - \frac{Et}{2}\sqrt{\frac{C}{L}}\cos\frac{t}{\sqrt{LC}}$ ...(2)

Initially, when $t = 0, q = 0 \quad \therefore \quad c_1 = 0$

Differentiating (2) w.r.t. t

$$\frac{dq}{dt} = -\frac{c_1}{\sqrt{LC}}\sin\frac{t}{\sqrt{LC}} + \frac{c_2}{\sqrt{LC}}\cos\frac{t}{\sqrt{LC}} - \frac{E}{2}\sqrt{\frac{C}{L}}\left[\cos\frac{t}{\sqrt{LC}} - \frac{t}{\sqrt{LC}}\sin\frac{t}{\sqrt{LC}}\right]$$

Initially, $\frac{dq}{dt} = i = 0$, when $t = 0$

$$\therefore \qquad \frac{c_2}{\sqrt{LC}} - \frac{E}{2}\sqrt{\frac{C}{L}} = 0 \quad \text{or} \quad c_2 = \frac{EC}{2}.$$

Substituting the values of c_1 and c_2 in equation (2), the charge q on the condenser plate, at any time t, is given by

$$q = \frac{EC}{2}\sin\frac{t}{\sqrt{LC}} - \frac{Et}{2}\sqrt{\frac{C}{L}}\cos\frac{t}{\sqrt{LC}}$$

or $$q = \frac{EC}{2}\left[\sin\frac{t}{\sqrt{LC}} - \frac{t}{\sqrt{LC}}\cos\frac{t}{\sqrt{LC}}\right].$$

Example 3. *In an L-C-R circuit, the charge q on a plate of the condenser is given by* $L\frac{d^2q}{dt^2} + R\frac{dq}{dt} + \frac{q}{C} = E\sin\omega t$, *where* $i = \frac{dq}{dt}$. *The circuit is tuned to resonance so that* $\omega^2 = \frac{1}{LC}$.

If $R^2 < \frac{4L}{C}$ *and* $q = 0 = i$, *when* $t = 0$, *show that*

$$q = \frac{E}{R\omega}\left[-\cos\omega t + e^{-\frac{Rt}{2L}}\left(\cos pt + \frac{R}{2Lp}\sin pt\right)\right]$$

and $$i = \frac{E}{R}\left[\sin\omega t - \frac{1}{p\sqrt{LC}}e^{-\frac{Rt}{2L}}\sin pt\right], \text{ where } p^2 = \frac{1}{LC} - \frac{R^2}{4L^2}.$$

Sol. The given equation is $L\frac{d^2q}{dt^2} + R\frac{dq}{dt} + \frac{q}{C} = E\sin\omega t$ ...(1)

Auxiliary equation is

$Lm^2 + Rm + \frac{1}{C} = 0$

$$\Rightarrow \quad m = \frac{-R \pm \sqrt{R^2 - \frac{4L}{C}}}{2L} = \frac{-R \pm i\sqrt{\frac{4L}{C} - R^2}}{2L}, \text{ since } R^2 < \frac{4L}{C}$$

$$\Rightarrow \quad m = -\frac{R}{2L} \pm i\sqrt{\frac{1}{LC} - \frac{R^2}{4L^2}} = -\frac{R}{2L} \pm ip, \text{ since } \frac{1}{LC} - \frac{R^2}{4L^2} = p^2$$

$$\therefore \quad \text{C.F.} = e^{-\frac{Rt}{2L}}(c_1\cos pt + c_2\sin pt)$$

and $$\text{P.I.} = \frac{1}{LD^2 + RD + \frac{1}{C}}E\sin\omega t$$

$$= E\,.\frac{1}{-L\omega^2 + RD + \frac{1}{C}}\sin\omega t = \frac{E}{R}.\frac{1}{D}\sin\omega t \qquad \Big|\because\ \omega^2 = \frac{1}{LC}$$

$$= -\frac{E}{R\omega}\cos\omega t$$

$\therefore$ The complete solution of equation (1) is

$$q = e^{-\frac{Rt}{2L}}(c_1\cos pt + c_2\sin pt) - \frac{E}{R\omega}\cos\omega t \qquad ...(2)$$

Initially, when $t = 0, q = 0 \quad \therefore \quad c_1 = \frac{E}{R\omega}$

Differentiating (2) w.r.t. t

$$\frac{dq}{dt} = e^{-\frac{Rt}{2L}}(-pc_1 \sin pt + pc_2 \cos pt) - \frac{R}{2L}\, e^{-\frac{Rt}{2L}}(c_1 \cos pt + c_2 \sin pt) + \frac{E}{R}\sin \omega t$$

Initially, when $t = 0$, $\frac{dq}{dt} = i = 0$

$$\therefore \quad pc_2 - \frac{R}{2L} c_1 = 0 \quad \text{or} \quad c_2 = \frac{R}{2pL} \cdot \frac{E}{R\omega} = \frac{E}{2pL\omega}$$

Substituting the values of c_1 and c_2 in equation (2), we get

$$q = e^{-\frac{Rt}{2L}}\left(\frac{E}{R\omega}\cos pt + \frac{E}{2pL\omega}\sin pt\right) - \frac{E}{R\omega}\cos \omega t$$

or
$$q = \frac{E}{R\omega}\left[-\cos \omega t + e^{-\frac{Rt}{2L}}\left(\cos pt + \frac{R}{2Lp}\sin pt\right)\right] \qquad \ldots(3)$$

Differentiating (3), w.r.t. t

$$\frac{dq}{dt} = \frac{E}{R\omega}\left[\omega \sin \omega t - \frac{R}{2L} e^{-\frac{Rt}{2L}}\left(\cos pt + \frac{R}{2Lp}\sin pt\right) + e^{-\frac{Rt}{2L}}\left(-p \sin pt + \frac{R}{2L}\cos pt\right)\right]$$

or
$$i = \frac{E}{R\omega}\left[\omega \sin \omega t - e^{-\frac{Rt}{2L}}\left(\frac{R^2}{4L^2 p} + p\right)\sin pt\right] = \frac{E}{R\omega}\left[\omega \sin \omega t - e^{-\frac{Rt}{2L}} \cdot \frac{R^2 + 4L^2p^2}{4L^2 p}\sin pt\right]$$

$$= \frac{E}{R}\left[\sin \omega t - e^{-\frac{Rt}{2L}} \frac{1}{LCp\omega}\sin pt\right] \text{ since } \frac{R^2 + 4L^2p^2}{4L^2} = \frac{1}{LC}$$

or
$$i = \frac{E}{R}\left[\sin \omega t - \frac{1}{p\sqrt{LC}}\, e^{-\frac{Rt}{2L}} \sin pt\right]. \qquad \Big|\because \omega^2 = \frac{1}{LC}$$

Example 4. *In an L-C-R circuit, the charge q on a plate of a condenser is given by* $L\frac{d^2q}{dt^2} + R\frac{dq}{dt} + \frac{q}{C} = E \sin pt$. *The circuit is turned to resonance so that* $p^2 = \frac{1}{LC}$. *If initially the current i and the charge q be zero, show that, for small values of* $\frac{R}{L}$, *the current in the circuit at time t is given by*

$$\left\{\frac{Et}{2L}\right\} \sin pt.$$

Sol. The given equation is

$$\left(LD^2 + RD + \frac{1}{C}\right) q = E \sin pt; \quad D \equiv \frac{d}{dt} \qquad \ldots(1)$$

Auxiliary equation is

$$Lm^2 + Rm + \frac{1}{C} = 0$$

$$\Rightarrow \qquad m = \frac{-R \pm \sqrt{R^2 - \frac{4L}{C}}}{2L} = -\frac{R}{2L} \pm \frac{1}{2}\sqrt{\frac{R^2}{L^2} - \frac{4}{LC}}$$

$$= -\frac{R}{2L} \pm \frac{1}{2}\sqrt{\frac{-4}{LC}} \qquad \left(\text{Neglecting the term } \frac{R^2}{L^2}\right)$$

$$\Rightarrow \qquad m = -\frac{R}{2L} \pm \frac{i}{\sqrt{LC}} = -\frac{R}{2L} \pm pi \qquad \left(\because\ p = \frac{1}{\sqrt{LC}}\right)$$

$$\therefore \qquad \text{C.F.} = e^{-\frac{Rt}{2L}} (C_1 \cos pt + C_2 \sin pt)$$

$$= \left(1 - \frac{Rt}{2L}\right) (C_1 \cos pt + C_2 \sin pt)$$

$$\text{P.I.} = \frac{1}{LD^2 + RD + \frac{1}{C}} (E \sin pt)$$

$$= E \cdot \frac{1}{-Lp^2 + RD + \frac{1}{C}} \sin pt$$

$$= E \cdot \frac{1}{RD} \sin pt = -\frac{E}{Rp} \cos pt. \qquad \left(\because\ p^2 = \frac{1}{LC}\right)$$

Complete solution of equation (1) is

$$q = \left(1 - \frac{Rt}{2L}\right) (C_1 \cos pt + C_2 \sin pt) - \frac{E}{Rp} \cos pt \qquad ...(2)$$

$$\therefore \qquad i = \frac{dq}{dt} = \left(1 - \frac{Rt}{2L}\right) (-pC_1 \sin pt + pC_2 \cos pt)$$

$$- \frac{R}{2L} (C_1 \cos pt + C_2 \sin pt) + \frac{E}{R} \sin pt \qquad ...(3)$$

when $t = 0$, $q = 0$ and $i = 0$, then

From (2), $\qquad 0 = C_1 - \frac{E}{Rp} \qquad \Rightarrow \quad C_1 = \frac{E}{Rp}$

and from (3), $\qquad 0 = C_2 p - \frac{R}{2L} C_1 \quad \Rightarrow \quad C_2 = \frac{E}{2Lp^2}.$

Putting the values of C_1 and C_2 in (3), we get

$$i = \left(1 - \frac{Rt}{2L}\right)\left(-\frac{E}{R} \sin pt + \frac{E}{2Lp} \cos pt\right) - \frac{R}{2L}\left(\frac{E}{Rp} \cos pt + \frac{E}{2Lp^2} \sin pt\right) + \frac{E}{R} \sin pt$$

$$= \frac{Et}{2L} \sin pt - \frac{ERt}{4pL^2} \cos pt - \frac{ER}{4L^2 p^2} \sin pt$$

$$= \frac{Et}{2L} \sin pt \ ; \ \frac{R}{L} \text{ being small.}$$

Example 5. *The voltage V and the current i at a distance x from the sending end of the transmission line satisfy the equations*

$$-\frac{dV}{dx} = Ri \text{ and } -\frac{di}{dx} = GV, \quad \text{where R and G are constants.}$$

If $V = V_0$ *at the sending end (x = 0) and V = 0 at the receiving end (x = l) ; show that*

$$V = V_0\left[\frac{\sinh n\,(l - x)}{\sinh nl}\right], \text{ where } n^2 = RG.$$

Sol.
$$-\frac{di}{dx} = GV$$

$$\Rightarrow \quad -\frac{d}{dx}\left(-\frac{1}{R}\frac{dV}{dx}\right) = GV$$

$$\Rightarrow \quad \frac{d^2V}{dx^2} - RGV = 0$$

Auxiliary equation is

$$m^2 - RG = 0$$

$$\Rightarrow \quad m^2 - n^2 = 0 \qquad (\because \ RG = n^2)$$

$$\Rightarrow \quad m = \pm n$$

$$\therefore \quad \text{C.F.} = c_1 e^{nx} + c_2 e^{-nx}$$

$$\text{P.I.} = 0$$

$$\therefore \quad V = c_1 e^{nx} + c_2 e^{-nx} \qquad ...(1)$$

At $x = 0, \ V = V_0 \quad \therefore \quad V_0 = c_1 + c_2$ ...(2)

At $x = l, \ V = 0 \quad \therefore \quad 0 = c_1 e^{nl} + c_2 e^{-nl}$ ...(3)

Solving (2) and (3), we get

$$c_1 = \frac{V_0}{1 - e^{2nl}}, \ c_2 = \frac{-V_0 e^{2nl}}{1 - e^{2nl}}$$

From (1),
$$V = \frac{V_0}{1 - e^{2nl}}\left[e^{nx} - e^{2nl - nx}\right]$$

$$= \frac{V_0\,[e^{(nl - nx)} - e^{-(nl - nx)}]}{e^{nl} - e^{-nl}} = V_0\left\{\frac{\sinh n\,(l - x)}{\sinh nl}\right\}.$$

Example 6. *The differential equation* $\frac{d^2x}{dt^2} + 2k\frac{dx}{dt} + n^2x = 0$ *; (k < n) represents the damped harmonic oscillations of a particle. Solve this equation and show that the ratio of the amplitude of any oscillation to that of the preceding one is constant i.e., its amplitude form a G.P.*

Sol. We have,

$$(D^2 + 2kD + n^2)\,x = 0\,; \quad D \equiv \frac{d}{dt} \qquad ...(1)$$

Auxiliary equation is

$$m^2 + 2km + n^2 = 0$$

$$m = -k \pm \sqrt{k^2 - n^2} = -k \pm \sqrt{n^2 - k^2}\, i \qquad | \because \quad k < n$$

$\therefore$ $$\text{C.F.} = e^{-kt}(c_1 \cos \sqrt{n^2 - k^2}\, t + c_2 \sin \sqrt{n^2 - k^2}\, t)$$

Also, $$\text{P.I} = 0$$

Hence $$x = e^{-kt}(c_1 \cos \sqrt{n^2 - k^2}\, t + c_2 \sin \sqrt{n^2 - k^2}\, t) \qquad ...(2)$$

which is the reqd. solution.

At time t, amplitude $= e^{-kt}$

At time $t + 1$, amplitude $= e^{-k(t+1)}$

At time $t + 2$, amplitude $= e^{-k(t+2)}$ and so on.

Ratio of amplitude of any oscillation to the preceding one $= e^{-k}$ (a constant)

Hence the amplitudes of successive vibrations are in G.P.

Example 7. *A spring of negligible weight which stretches 1 inch under tension of 2 lb is fixed at one end and is attached to a weight of ω lb at the other. It is found that resonance occurs when an axial periodic force 2 cos 2t lb acts on the weight. Show that when the free vibrations have died out, the forced vibrations are given by x = ct sin 2t and find the values of ω and c.*

Sol. When a weight of 2 lb is attached to A, spring stretches by $\frac{1}{12}$ ft.

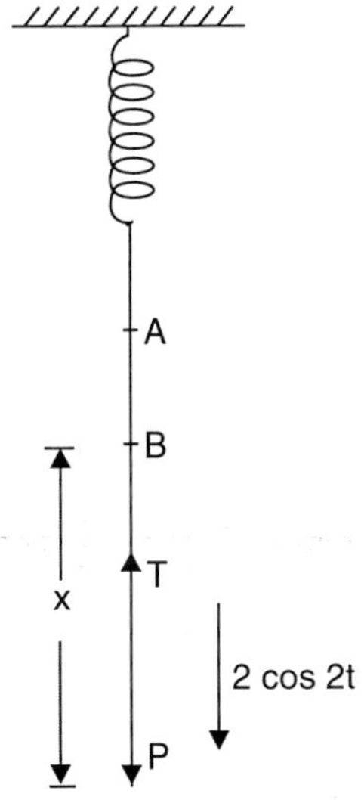

$\therefore$ $$2 = k \cdot \frac{1}{12} \Rightarrow k = 24 \text{ lb/ft.}$$

Let B be the equation position of the weight w attached to A then,

$$\omega = k \times \text{AB} \Rightarrow \text{AB} = \frac{\omega}{24} \text{ ft.}$$

At any time t, Let the weight be at P where BP $= x$

Tension at P, $$\text{T}_\text{P} = k \times \text{AP} = 24\left(\frac{\omega}{24} + x\right) = \omega + 24x$$

Its equation of motion is

$$\frac{\omega}{g}\frac{d^2x}{dt^2} = -\text{T} + \omega + 2\cos 2t = -\omega - 24x + \omega + 2\cos 2t$$

$$\Rightarrow \omega \frac{d^2x}{dt^2} + 24gx = 2g \cos 2t \qquad ...(1)$$

The phenomenon of resonance occurs when the period of free oscillations is equal to the period of forced oscillations.

From (1), $$\frac{d^2x}{dt^2} + \mu^2 x = \frac{2g}{\omega}\cos 2t \qquad \left|\ \text{where } \mu^2 = \frac{24g}{\omega}\right.$$

$\therefore$ The period of free oscillations is $\frac{2\pi}{\mu}$ and the period of the force $\left(\frac{2g}{\omega}\right)\cos 2t$ is π.

$\therefore$ $$\frac{2\pi}{\mu} = \pi \Rightarrow \mu = 2$$

Hence $$4 = \frac{24g}{\omega} \Rightarrow \omega = 6g \qquad ...(2)$$

Again from (1), $$\frac{d^2x}{dt^2} + 4x = \frac{1}{3}\cos 2t \qquad ...(3) \mid \because \omega = 6g \text{ and } \mu = 2$$

we know that the free oscillations are given by the C.F. and the forced oscillations are given by P.I. Thus, when the free oscillations have died out, the forced oscillations are given by the P.I. of (3)

$$\therefore \quad \text{P.I.} = \frac{1}{3}\cdot\left(\frac{1}{D^2+4}\cos 2t\right) = \frac{1}{3}t\cdot\frac{1}{2D}\cos 2t = \frac{t}{12}\sin 2t$$

Hence, $$c = \frac{1}{12}.$$

Example 8. *A mass M suspended from the end of a helical spring is subjected to a periodic force $f = F\sin\omega t$ in the direction of its length. The force f is measured positive vertically downwards and at zero time M is at rest. If the spring stiffness is S, prove that the displacement of M at time t from the commencement of motion is given by* $x = \frac{F}{M(p^2-\omega^2)}\left(\sin\omega t - \frac{\omega}{p}\sin pt\right)$, *where* $p^2 = \frac{S}{M}$ *and damping effects are neglected.*

Sol. Let x be the displacement from the equilibrium position at any time t, then the equation of motion of the mass M is

$$M\frac{d^2x}{dt^2} = -Sx + F\sin\omega t$$

or $$\frac{d^2x}{dt^2} + \frac{S}{M}x = \frac{F}{M}\sin\omega t$$

or $$\frac{d^2x}{dt^2} + p^2x = \frac{F}{M}\sin\omega t \qquad ...(1) \quad \left(\because \frac{S}{M} = p^2\right)$$

Its A.E. is $m^2 + p^2 = 0 \Rightarrow m = \pm ip$

$$\therefore \quad \text{C.F.} = c_1\cos pt + c_2\sin pt$$

and $$\text{P.I.} = \frac{F}{M}\cdot\frac{1}{D^2+p^2}\sin\omega t = \frac{F}{M}\cdot\frac{1}{p^2-\omega^2}\sin\omega t$$

$\therefore$ Complete solution of equation (1) is

$$x = c_1\cos pt + c_2\sin pt + \frac{F}{M}\cdot\frac{1}{p^2-\omega^2}\sin\omega t \qquad ...(2)$$

Initially, when $t = 0, x = 0 \quad \therefore \quad c_1 = 0$

Differentiating (2) w.r.t. t,

$$\frac{dx}{dt} = -pc_1\sin pt + pc_2\cos pt + \frac{F}{M}\cdot\frac{\omega}{p^2-\omega^2}\cos\omega t$$

Since $\frac{dx}{dt} = 0$, when $t = 0$

$$\therefore \quad pc_2 + \frac{F}{M}\cdot\frac{\omega}{p^2-\omega^2} = 0$$

or $$c_2 = -\frac{\omega}{p} \cdot \frac{F}{M(p^2 - \omega^2)}.$$

Substituting the values of c_1 and c_2 in (2), the displacement of the mass at any time t is given by

$$x = -\frac{\omega}{p} \cdot \frac{F}{M(p^2 - \omega^2)} \sin pt + \frac{F}{M} \cdot \frac{1}{p^2 - \omega^2} \sin \omega t$$

or $$x = \frac{F}{M(p^2 - \omega^2)} \left(\sin \omega t - \frac{\omega}{p} \sin pt \right).$$

Example 9. *A spring which stretches by an amount e under a force mk^2e is suspended from a support P and has a mass m at its lower end. At time $t = 0$, the mass is at rest in its equilibrium position at a point A below P. A vertical oscillation is now given to the support P such that at any time $t(> 0)$ its displacement below its initial position is a sin nt. Show that the displacement x of the mass below A is given by $\frac{d^2x}{dt^2} + k^2x = k^2 a \sin nt$. Hence show that if $n \neq k$, the displacement is given by $x = \frac{ka}{k^2 - n^2}(k \sin nt - n \sin kt)$. What happens, when $n = k$?*

Sol. If λ is the restoring force, then $mk^2e = \lambda e$ so that $\lambda = mk^2$

If e is the elongation produced by the mass m hanging in equilibrium, then $mg = \lambda e$.

Due to vertical oscillation of the support, if at any time t (> 0) the mass is at B, where AB = x, then the stretch of the spring is $(e + x - a \sin nt)$

The equation of motion is

$$m \frac{d^2x}{dt^2} = mg - \lambda(e + x - a \sin nt)$$

$$= -\lambda x + \lambda a \sin nt \qquad (\because \; mg = \lambda e)$$

$$= -mk^2x + mk^2 a \sin nt$$

or $$\frac{d^2x}{dt^2} + k^2x = k^2 a \sin nt \qquad ...(1)$$

Its A.E. is $m^2 + k^2 = 0 \quad \Rightarrow \quad m = \pm ik$

$$\text{C.F.} = c_1 \cos kt + c_2 \sin kt$$

$$\text{P.I.} = \frac{1}{D^2 + k^2} k^2 a \sin nt$$

Case I. When $n \neq k$

$$\text{P.I.} = k^2a \cdot \frac{1}{k^2 - n^2} \sin nt$$

$\therefore$ The complete solution of (1) is

$$x = c_1 \cos kt + c_2 \sin kt + \frac{k^2a}{k^2 - n^2} \sin nt \qquad ...(2)$$

Initially, when $t = 0$, $x = 0 \Rightarrow c_1 = 0$

Differentiating (2) w.r.t. t,

$$\frac{dx}{dt} = -kc_1 \sin kt + kc_2 \cos kt + \frac{k^2an}{k^2 - n^2} \cos nt$$

Since $\frac{dx}{dt} = 0$, when $t = 0$, we have

$$kc_2 + \frac{k^2an}{k^2 - n^2} = 0 \quad \text{or} \quad c_2 = -\frac{kan}{k^2 - n^2}$$

Substituting the values of c_1 and c_2 in (2), the displacement of the mass at any time t is given by

$$x = -\frac{kan}{k^2 - n^2} \sin kt + \frac{k^2a}{k^2 - n^2} \sin nt$$

or

$$x = \frac{ka}{k^2 - n^2} (k \sin nt - n \sin kt).$$

Case II. When $n = k$

$$\text{P.I.} = n^2a \cdot \frac{1}{D^2 + a^2} \sin nt = n^2a \cdot t \cdot \frac{1}{2D} \sin nt = -\frac{nat}{2} \cos nt$$

$\therefore$ Complete solution of (1) is

$$x = c_1 \cos nt + c_2 \sin nt - \frac{nat}{2} \cos nt \text{ (since } k = n) \qquad \ldots(3)$$

Initially, when $t = 0, x = 0 \Rightarrow c_1 = 0$

Differentiating (3) w.r.t. t,

$$\frac{dx}{dt} = -nc_1 \sin nt + nc_2 \cos nt - \frac{na}{2} (\cos nt - nt \sin nt)$$

Since $\frac{dx}{dt} = 0$, when $t = 0$, we have $nc_2 - \frac{na}{2} = 0 \quad \therefore \quad c_2 = \frac{a}{2}$

Substituting the values of c_1 and c_2 in (3), the displacement of the mass at any time t is given by

$$x = \frac{a}{2} \sin nt - \frac{na}{2} \cos nt$$

or

$$x = \frac{a}{2} (\sin nt - nt \cos nt) = \frac{ar}{2} \sin (nt - \phi),$$

where $r = \sqrt{1 + n^2t^2}$, $\phi = \tan^{-1} nt$

The amplitude $\frac{ar}{2} = \frac{a}{2}\sqrt{1 + n^2t^2}$ involves t and increases with t.

Thus the phenomenon of resonance occurs.

TEST YOUR KNOWLEDGE

1. A circuit consists of an inductance L and a condenser of capacity C in series. An alternating e.m.f. E sin nt is applied to the circuit at time $t = 0$, the initial current and the charge on the condenser being zero. Prove that the current at time t is $i = \dfrac{nE}{L(n^2 - \omega^2)}(\cos \omega t - \cos nt)$, where $CL\omega^2 = 1$.

2. The differential equation for a circuit in which self-inductance and capacitance neutralize each other is
$$L\frac{d^2 i}{dt^2} + \frac{i}{C} = 0$$
Find the current i as a function of t, given that I is the maximum current and $i = 0$ when $t = 0$.

3. Solve the equation $\dfrac{d^2x}{dt^2} + 2h\dfrac{dx}{dt} + (h^2 + p^2)x = ke^{-ht} \cos pt$ completely. Show that the particular integral represents an oscillation of variable amplitude which is maximum when $ht = 1$.

4. The damped LCR circuit is governed by the equation $L\dfrac{d^2Q}{dt^2} + R\dfrac{dQ}{dt} + \left(\dfrac{1}{C}\right)Q = 0$, where L, R, C are positive constants. Find the conditions under which the circuit is overdamped, underdamped and critically damped. Find also the critical resistance. *[U.P.T.U. (C.O.) 2008]*

5. A constant e.m.f. E at $t = 0$ is applied to a circuit consisting of an inductance L, resistance R and capacitance C in series. The initial values of the current and the charge being zero, find the current at any time t, if $CR^2 < 4L$. Show that the amplitudes of the successive vibrations are in geometrical progression.

6. An e.m.f. E sin pt is applied at $t = 0$ to a circuit containing a capacitance C and inductance L. The current i satisfies the equation $L\dfrac{di}{dt} + \dfrac{1}{C}\displaystyle\int i\, dt = E \sin pt$. If $p^2 = \dfrac{1}{LC}$ and initially the current i and the charge q are zero, show that the current at time t is $\dfrac{Et}{2L} \sin pt$, where $i = \dfrac{dq}{dt}$.

Answers

2. $i = I \sin \dfrac{t}{\sqrt{LC}}$

3. $x = e^{-ht}(c_1 \cos pt + c_2 \sin pt) + \dfrac{k}{2p} te^{-ht} \sin pt$

4. For over damping, $R^2 > \dfrac{4L}{C}$; For critical damping, $R^2 = \dfrac{4L}{C}$; For under damping, $R^2 < \dfrac{4L}{C}$; critical resistance $= 2\sqrt{\dfrac{L}{C}}$

1.42. DEFINITIONS

(1) Beam or Bar. A rod of a circular or rectangular cross-section with its length very large than its thickness is called a beam.

(2) Supported beam. If a beam may just rest on support like a knife edge then it is called a supported beam.

(3) Fixed beam. If one of the ends of a beam is firmly fixed then it is called a fixed beam.

(4) Cantilever. If the beam is fixed only at one end and loaded at the other, it is called a cantilever.

(5) Strut. A beam of homogeneous isotropic material subject to compressive stress is called strut.

1.43. DEFLECTION OF BEAMS

Consider a uniform beam as made up of fibres running lengthwise. When the beam is deflected, the fibres in some region are elongated and those in some region are contracted. In between these two, there is a region of the beam where the fibres are neither compressed nor stretched. This region is called the ***neutral surface*** of the beam and the curve of any particular fibre in this surface is called the ***elastic curve*** or ***deflection curve*** of the beam. The line in which any plane section of the beam cuts the neutral surface is called the ***neutral axis*** of that section.

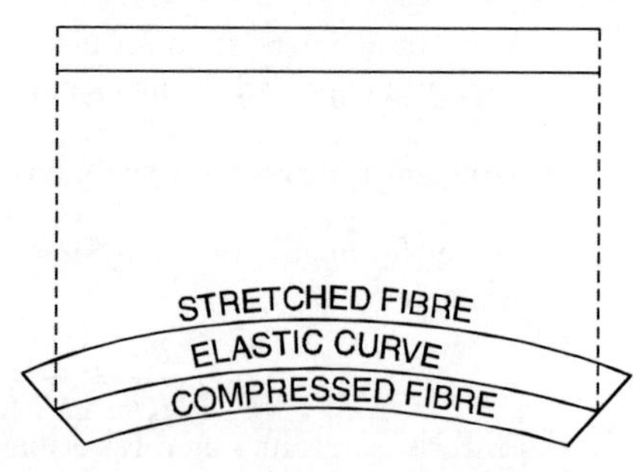

Consider a cross-section of the beam cutting the elastic curve in P and the neutral surface in the line AB, the neutral axis of this section.

It is well-known from the mechanics of structure that the forces above and below the neutral surface acting in opposite directions have a tendency to restore the beam to its original position ; creating an interval bending moment M given by $\frac{EI}{R}$,

where E = modulus of elasticity of the material of the beam

I = moment of inertia of the cross-section of the beam about the neutral axis AB

R = radius of curvature of the elastic curve at P(x, y).

Now,
$$R = \frac{\left[1+\left(\frac{dy}{dx}\right)^2\right]^{3/2}}{\frac{d^2y}{dx^2}}$$

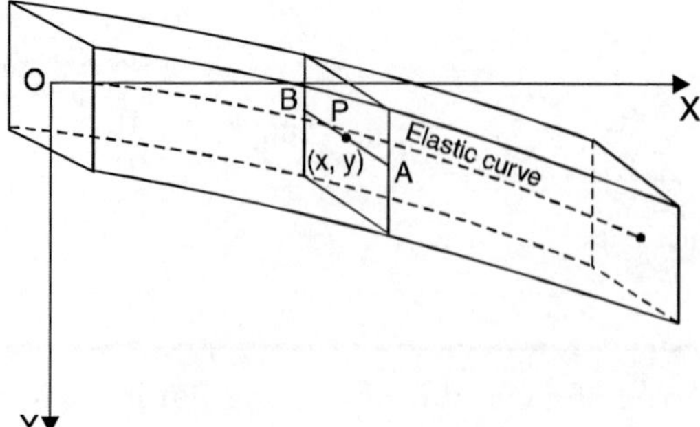

If the deflection (slope) of the beam is small, $\left(\frac{dy}{dx}\right)^2$ is very small and can be neglected, so that

$$R = \frac{1}{\frac{d^2y}{dx^2}}$$

Thus
$$\boxed{M = EI\,\frac{d^2y}{dx^2}} \qquad ...(1)$$

which is the differential equation of the elastic curve.

Note 1. The moment M with respect to AB of all external forces acting on either of the two segments into which the beam is separated by the cross-section is independent of the segment considered.

Note 2. The amount M is the algebraic sum of the moments of the external forces acting on the segment of the beam about the line AB. The upward forces give positive moments and the downward forces give negative moments.

1.44. BOUNDARY CONDITIONS

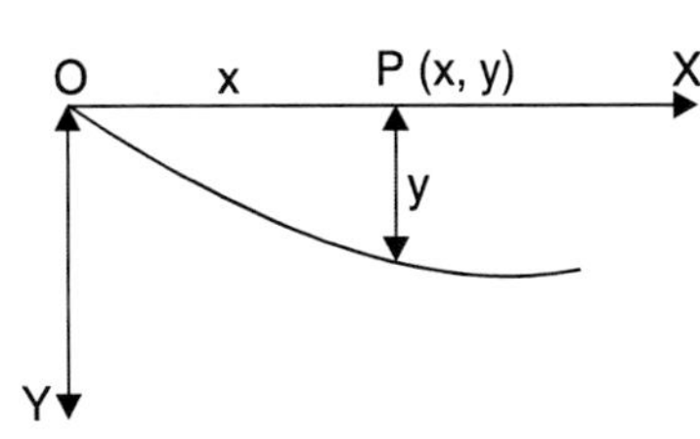

The general solution of the differential equation (1) will contain two arbitrary constants which, in any particular problem, are to be determined from the boundary (or end) conditions given below :

(*i*) *End freely supported.* At the freely supported end O, there is no deflection of the beam, so that $y = 0$. Also there is no bending moment at this end, so that $\frac{d^2y}{dx^2} = 0$.

Hence, at the freely supported end

$$y = 0 \quad \text{and} \quad \frac{d^2y}{dx^2} = 0.$$

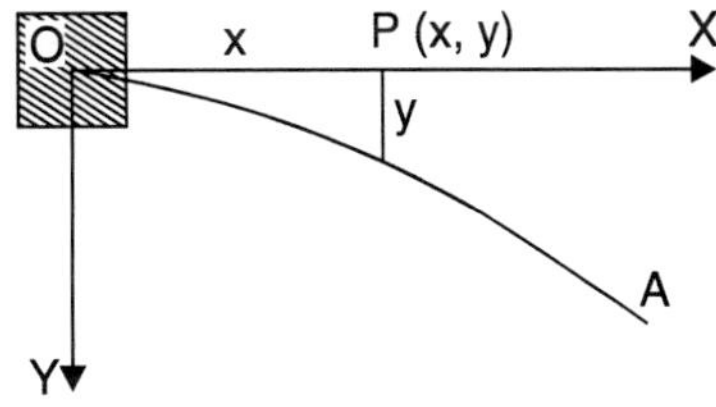

(*ii*) *End fixed horizontal.* At the end fixed horizontally, the deflection and the slope of the beam are zero.

$$\therefore \qquad y = 0 \quad \text{and} \quad \frac{dy}{dx} = 0.$$

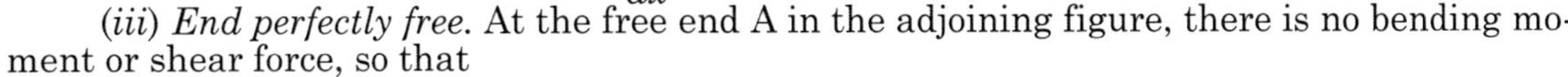

(*iii*) *End perfectly free.* At the free end A in the adjoining figure, there is no bending moment or shear force, so that

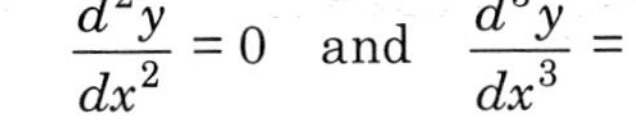

$$\frac{d^2y}{dx^2} = 0 \quad \text{and} \quad \frac{d^3y}{dx^3} = 0.$$

1.45. WHIRLING OF SHAFTS

All rotating shafts deflect during rotation.

The magnitude of this deflection depends upon

(*i*) Stiffness of shaft and its support
(*ii*) Total mass of shaft and attached parts
(*iii*) Imbalanceness
(*iv*) Amount of damping in system

At a certain speed, rotating shafts fracture due to large deflection. These dangerous speeds are called whirling or critical speeds of the shaft.

The differential equation for whirling of shaft is

$$\frac{d^4y}{dx^4} - a^4y = 0 \qquad ...(1)$$

where $a^4 = \frac{W\omega^2}{gEI}$. Here W is weight of shaft per unit length and ω is angular velocity through which it rotates in radian/sec.

Solution to (1) is $y = c_1 \cosh ax + c_2 \sinh ax + c_3 \cos ax + c_4 \sin ax$

To determine arbitrary constants, boundary conditions are

(1) In case of short or flexible bearings. There is no deflection and no bending moment. Boundary conditions are

$$y = 0, \frac{d^2y}{dx^2} = 0.$$

(2) In case of long bearings. The deflection and the slope of the shaft both will be zero. Boundary conditions are

$$y = 0, \frac{dy}{dx} = 0.$$

(3) When end of shaft is perfectly free. There is no bending moment and no shear force. Boundary conditions are

$$\frac{d^2y}{dx^2} = 0 \quad \text{and} \quad \frac{d^3y}{dx^3} = 0.$$

ILLUSTRATIVE EXAMPLES

Example 1. *The deflection of a strut of length l with one end (x = 0) built in and the other supported and subjected to end thrust P, satisfies the equation* $\frac{d^2y}{dx^2} + a^2y = \frac{a^2R}{P}(l - x)$. *Prove that deflection curve is* $y = \frac{R}{P}\left(\frac{\sin ax}{a} - l \cos ax + l - x\right)$, *where* $al = \tan al$.

Sol. The given equation is

$$\frac{d^2y}{dx^2} + a^2y = \frac{a^2R}{P}(l - x) \quad ...(1)$$

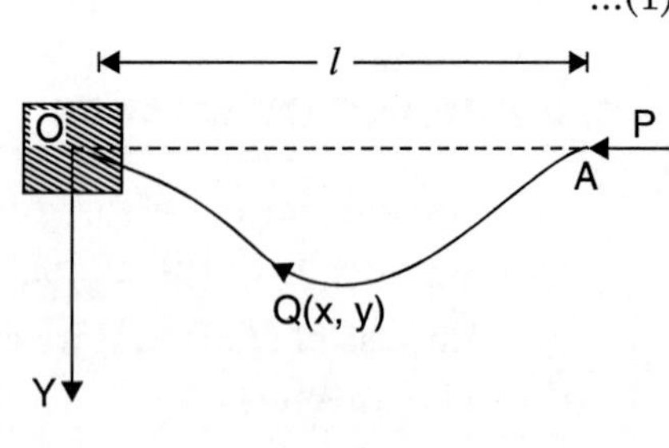

Auxiliary equation is

$$m^2 + a^2 = 0 \text{ so that } m = \pm ia$$

$\therefore$ $$\text{C.F.} = c_1 \cos ax + c_2 \sin ax$$

and $$\text{P.I.} = \frac{1}{D^2 + a^2} \frac{a^2R}{P}(l - x)$$

$$= \frac{a^2R}{P} \cdot \frac{1}{a^2\left(1 + \frac{D^2}{a^2}\right)}(l - x)$$

$$= \frac{R}{P}\left(1 + \frac{D^2}{a^2}\right)^{-1}(l - x)$$

$$= \frac{R}{P}\left(1 - \frac{D^2}{a^2} + ...\right)(l - x) = \frac{R}{P}(l - x)$$

$\therefore$ The complete solution of (1) is $y = c_1 \cos ax + c_2 \sin ax + \frac{R}{P}(l - x)$ ...(2)

Differentiating (2) w.r.t. x $\quad \frac{dy}{dx} = -ac_1 \sin ax + ac_2 \cos ax - \frac{R}{P}$ ...(3)

Since the end O is build in, $\quad y = 0$ and $\frac{dy}{dx} = 0$ at $x = 0$

$\therefore$ From (2), $\quad 0 = c_1 + \frac{Rl}{P} \Rightarrow c_1 = -\frac{Rl}{P}$

From (3), $\quad 0 = ac_2 - \frac{R}{P} \Rightarrow c_2 = \frac{R}{aP}$

Substituting the values of c_1 and c_2 in (2), we have

$$y = \frac{R}{P}\left(\frac{\sin ax}{a} - l \cos ax + l - x\right) \quad ...(4)$$

which is the equation of the deflection curve.

Also, at the end A, $\quad y = 0$ when $x = l$.

$\therefore$ From (4), $\quad 0 = \frac{R}{P}\left(\frac{\sin al}{a} - l \cos al\right)$

or $\quad \frac{\sin al}{a} = l \cos al \quad \therefore \quad al = \tan al.$

Example 2. *A light horizontal strut AB of length l is freely pinned at A and B and is under the action of equal and opposite compressive forces P at each of its ends and carries a load W at its centre.*

Prove that the deflection at the centre is $\frac{W}{2P}\left(\frac{l}{n} \tan \frac{nl}{2} - \frac{l}{2}\right)$, *where* $n^2 = \frac{P}{EI}$.

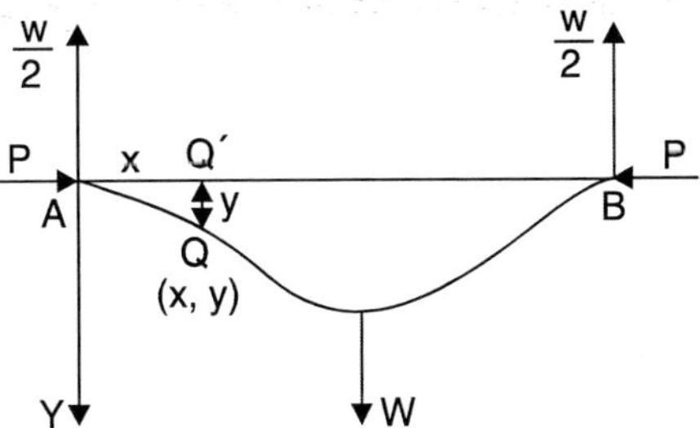

Sol. At each end there is a vertical reaction $\frac{W}{2}$. At any point Q(x, y) of the beam, the interval bending moment is EI $\frac{d^2y}{dx^2}$ and this must be equal to the moment of external forces taken to the left (or right) of the section QQ′.

$\therefore$ The differential equation for the elastic curve of the beam is

$$EI \frac{d^2y}{dx^2} = -\frac{W}{2}x - Py$$

or
$$\frac{d^2y}{dx^2} + \frac{P}{EI}y = -\frac{W}{2EI}x$$

or
$$\frac{d^2y}{dx^2} + n^2y = -\frac{n^2W}{2P}x \quad ...(1) \quad \left(\because \frac{P}{EI} = n^2\right)$$

Its A.E. is $m^2 + n^2 = 0$ so that $m = \pm in$.

$$\therefore \qquad \text{C.F.} = c_1 \cos nx + c_2 \sin nx$$

and
$$\text{P.I.} = \frac{1}{D^2 + n^2}\left(-\frac{n^2 W}{2P} x\right)$$

$$= -\frac{n^2 W}{2P} \cdot \frac{1}{n^2\left(1 + \frac{D^2}{n^2}\right)} x = -\frac{W}{2P}\left(1 + \frac{D^2}{n^2}\right)^{-1} x$$

$$= -\frac{W}{2P}\left(1 - \frac{D^2}{n^2} + \ldots\ldots\right) x = -\frac{Wx}{2P}$$

$\therefore$ The complete solution of (1) is $y = c_1 \cos nx + c_2 \sin nx - \frac{W}{2P} x$ ...(2)

Differentiating (2) w.r.t. x, $\frac{dy}{dx} = -nc_1 \sin nx + nc_2 \cos nx - \frac{W}{2P}$ ...(3)

At the end A, $x = 0, y = 0$ $\therefore$ From (2), $c_1 = 0$

At $x = \frac{l}{2}, \frac{dy}{dx} = 0$.

$\therefore$ From (3), $0 = nc_2 \cos \frac{nl}{2} - \frac{W}{2P} \Rightarrow c_2 = \frac{W}{2Pn \cos \frac{nl}{2}}$ $(\because c_1 = 0)$

Substituting the values of c_1 and c_2 in (2), we have

$$y = \frac{W}{2Pn \cos \frac{nl}{2}} \sin nx - \frac{W}{2P} x$$

Deflection at the centre $y_{x = l/2} = \frac{W}{2P}\left(\frac{\sin \frac{nl}{2}}{n \cos \frac{nl}{2}} - \frac{l}{2}\right) = \frac{W}{2P}\left(\frac{1}{n} \tan \frac{nl}{2} - \frac{l}{2}\right)$.

Example 3. *The differential equation satisfied by a beam uniformly loaded (W kg/m) with one end fixed and the other end subjected to tensile force P is given by*

$$EI \frac{d^2 y}{dx^2} = Py - \frac{1}{2} Wx^2$$

Show that the elastic curve for the beam with conditions $y = 0 = \frac{dy}{dx}$ *at* $x = 0$ *is given by*

$$y = \frac{W}{Pn^2}(1 - \cosh nx) + \frac{Wx^2}{2P}, \quad \text{where } n^2 = \frac{P}{EI}.$$

Sol. The given differential equation is

$$\frac{d^2 y}{dx^2} - \frac{P}{EI} y = -\frac{W}{2EI} x^2 \qquad \ldots(1)$$

Auxiliary equation is

$$m^2 - \frac{P}{EI} = 0$$

$$\Rightarrow \qquad m^2 - n^2 = 0 \quad \Rightarrow \quad m = \pm n$$

$$\therefore \qquad \text{C.F.} = c_1 e^{nx} + c_2\, e^{-nx}$$

$$\text{P.I.} = \frac{1}{D^2 - n^2}\left(-\frac{W}{2EI}x^2\right) = -\frac{W}{2EI}\left(-\frac{1}{n^2}\right)\left(1 - \frac{D^2}{n^2}\right)^{-1}(x^2)$$

$$= \frac{W}{2EIn^2}\left(1 + \frac{D^2}{n^2}\right)(x^2) = \frac{W}{2EIn^2}\left(x^2 + \frac{2}{n^2}\right)$$

$$\therefore \qquad y = c_1\, e^{nx} + c_2\, e^{-nx} + \frac{W}{2EIn^2}\left(x^2 + \frac{2}{n^2}\right) \qquad ...(2)$$

Differentiating (2) w.r.t. x, we get

$$\frac{dy}{dx} = nc_1 e^{nx} - nc_2 e^{-nx} + \frac{W}{2EIn^2}(2x) \qquad ...(3)$$

Putting $x = 0$, $\frac{dy}{dx} = 0$ in (3), we have

$$0 = nc_1 - nc_2 \Rightarrow c_1 = c_2 \qquad ...(4)$$

Putting $x = 0$, $y = 0$ in (2), we have

$$0 = c_1 + c_2 + \frac{W}{2EIn^2}\left(\frac{2}{n^2}\right) = 2c_1 + \frac{W}{EIn^4} \qquad | \text{ From (4)}$$

$$\Rightarrow \qquad c_1 = -\frac{W}{2EIn^4} = -\frac{W}{2n^2P} = c_2$$

$$\therefore \qquad y = -\frac{W}{2n^2P}(e^{nx} + e^{-nx}) + \frac{W}{2P}\left(x^2 + \frac{2}{n^2}\right)$$

$$= -\frac{W}{n^2P}\cosh nx + \frac{W}{2P}x^2 + \frac{W}{Pn^2}$$

$$\Rightarrow \qquad y = \frac{W}{Pn^2}(1 - \cosh nx) + \frac{W}{2P}x^2.$$

Example 4. *Solve the differential equation*

$$EI\frac{d^2y}{dx^2} + Py = -\frac{Wl^2}{8}\, sin\, \frac{\pi x}{l}$$

for a strut of length l, freely hinged at each end. Prove that bending moment at the centre is $-\frac{Wl^2}{8}\left(\frac{Q}{Q-P}\right)$, *where* $Q = EI\frac{\pi^2}{l^2}$.

Sol. The differential equation is

$$\frac{d^2y}{dx^2} + \frac{P}{EI}\, y = -\frac{Wl^2}{8EI} \sin\frac{\pi x}{l}$$

$$\Rightarrow \qquad \frac{d^2y}{dx^2} + \frac{P\pi^2}{Ql^2}\, y = \frac{-W\pi^2}{8Q} \sin\frac{\pi x}{l} \qquad ...(1)$$

Auxiliary equation is

$$m^2 + \frac{P\pi^2}{Ql^2} = 0 \;\Rightarrow\; m = \pm \frac{\pi}{l}\sqrt{\frac{P}{Q}}\, i$$

$$\therefore \qquad \text{C.F.} = c_1 \cos\frac{\pi}{l}\sqrt{\frac{P}{Q}}\, x + c_2 \sin\frac{\pi}{l}\sqrt{\frac{P}{Q}}\, x$$

$$\text{P.I.} = \frac{1}{D^2 + \frac{P\pi^2}{Ql^2}}\left(-\frac{W\pi^2}{8Q}\sin\frac{\pi x}{l}\right) = -\frac{W\pi^2}{8Q} \cdot \frac{1}{\left(-\frac{\pi^2}{l^2} + \frac{P\pi^2}{Ql^2}\right)} \sin\frac{\pi x}{l}$$

$$= \frac{W\pi^2}{8Q} \cdot \frac{l^2}{\pi^2} \cdot \frac{1}{\left(1 - \frac{P}{Q}\right)} \sin\frac{\pi x}{l} = \frac{Wl^2}{8} \cdot \frac{1}{(Q-P)} \sin\frac{\pi x}{l}$$

$$\therefore \qquad y = c_1 \cos\frac{\pi}{l}\sqrt{\frac{P}{Q}}\, x + c_2 \sin\frac{\pi}{l}\sqrt{\frac{P}{Q}}\, x + \frac{Wl^2}{8(Q-P)} \sin\frac{\pi x}{l} \qquad ...(2)$$

Since ends are freely hinged $\therefore$ conditions are

when $x = 0$, $y = 0$ and $\frac{d^2y}{dx^2} = 0$ and when $x = l$, $y = 0$ and $\frac{d^2y}{dx^2} = 0$

Putting $x = 0, y = 0$ in (2), we get $c_1 = 0$

Putting $x = l, y = 0$ in (2), we get $c_2 = 0$

$$\therefore \qquad y = \frac{Wl^2}{8(Q-P)} \sin\frac{\pi x}{l}$$

Bending moment,

$$M = EI\frac{d^2y}{dx^2} = -Py - \frac{Wl^2}{8}\sin\frac{\pi x}{l}$$

$$= -\frac{Wl^2}{8}\left(\frac{P}{Q-P}\right)\sin\frac{\pi x}{l} - \frac{Wl^2}{8}\sin\frac{\pi x}{l} = -\frac{Wl^2}{8} \cdot \left(\frac{Q}{Q-P}\right)\sin\frac{\pi x}{l}$$

$$\text{M(at the centre)} = \text{M}\left(\text{at } x = \frac{l}{2}\right)$$

$$= -\frac{Wl^2}{8} \cdot \frac{Q}{Q-P}\sin\frac{\pi}{2} = -\frac{Wl^2}{8} \cdot \left(\frac{Q}{Q-P}\right).$$

Example 5. *A horizontal tie-rod of length 2l with concentrated load W at the centre and ends freely hinged, satisfies the differential equation*

$$EI\frac{d^2y}{dx^2} = Py - \frac{W}{2}x \quad \text{with conditions } x = 0,\ y = 0 \text{ and } x = l,\ \frac{dy}{dx} = 0.$$

Prove that the deflection δ and bending moment M at the centre (x = l) are

$$\delta = \frac{W}{Pn}(nl - \tanh nl) \quad \text{and} \quad M = -\frac{W}{2n}\tanh nl, \text{ where } n^2 EI = P.$$

Sol. The differential equation is

$$\frac{d^2y}{dx^2} - \frac{P}{EI}y = -\frac{Wx}{2EI} \qquad \text{...(1)}$$

Auxiliary equation is $m^2 - \frac{P}{EI} = 0$

$\Rightarrow \qquad m^2 - n^2 = 0 \;\Rightarrow\; m = \pm n$

$\therefore \qquad \text{C.F.} = c_1 e^{nx} + c_2 e^{-nx}$

$$\text{P.I.} = \frac{1}{D^2 - n^2}\left(-\frac{Wx}{2EI}\right) = \frac{1}{D^2 - n^2}\left(-\frac{Wn^2}{2P}\right)x$$

$$= -\frac{Wn^2}{2P}\cdot\left(-\frac{1}{n^2}\right)\left(1 - \frac{D^2}{n^2}\right)^{-1}(x) = \frac{W}{2P}x$$

$\therefore$ Solution to (1) is

$$y = c_1 e^{nx} + c_2 e^{-nx} + \frac{Wx}{2P} \qquad \text{...(2)}$$

Differentiating (2), we get

$$\frac{dy}{dx} = nc_1 e^{nx} - nc_2 e^{-nx} + \frac{W}{2P} \qquad \text{...(3)}$$

Using conditions $x = 0, y = 0\ ;\ x = l, \frac{dy}{dx} = 0$

$$c_1 + c_2 = 0 \Rightarrow c_2 = -c_1 \qquad | \text{ From (2)}$$

and from (3), $\quad 0 = c_1 n\, e^{nl} + c_1 n\, e^{-nl} + \frac{W}{2P} \;\Rightarrow\; c_1 = \frac{-W}{2Pn(e^{nl} + e^{-nl})}$

From (2), $\quad y = \frac{-W e^{nx}}{2Pn(e^{nl} + e^{-nl})} + \frac{W e^{-nx}}{2Pn(e^{nl} + e^{-nl})} + \frac{Wx}{2P}$

$$= \frac{W}{2Pn}\left[nx - \left(\frac{e^{nx} - e^{-nx}}{e^{nl} + e^{-nl}}\right)\right]$$

Deflection y (*at* $x = l$),

$$\delta = \frac{W}{2Pn}\left[nl - \left(\frac{e^{nl} - e^{-nl}}{e^{nl} + e^{-nl}}\right)\right] = \frac{W}{2Pn}(nl - \tanh nl) \qquad \text{...(4)}$$

Bending moment,

$$M = EI\frac{d^2y}{dx^2} = Py - \frac{Wx}{2}$$ | From the given equation

$\therefore$ M (at the centre) = M (at $x = l$)

$$= P \cdot \frac{W}{2Pn}(nl - \tanh nl) - \frac{Wl}{2}$$

$$= \frac{W}{2n}(nl - \tanh nl) - \frac{Wl}{2} = -\frac{W}{2n}\tanh nl.$$

Example 6. *A beam of length l metres is fixed horizontally at one end. Find the equation of the elastic curve and the maximum deflection, if there is uniform load W Newtons/m along the length and load W Newtons at the free end.*

Sol. Let the end O of beam be fixed horizontally and end A be free. Consider segment PA of the beam.

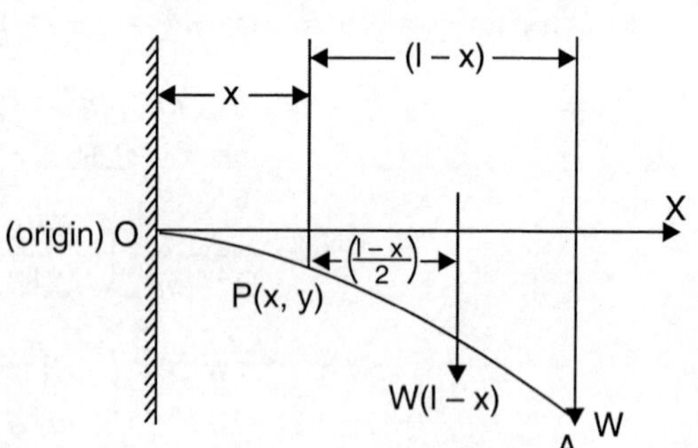

Taking moments about point P(x, y), we have

$$EI\frac{d^2y}{dx^2} = -W(l-x)\left(\frac{l-x}{2}\right) - W(l-x)$$

$$\Rightarrow \quad EI\frac{d^2y}{dx^2} = -\frac{W}{2}(l^2 - 2lx + x^2) - W(l-x)$$

Integrating, we get

$$EI\frac{dy}{dx} = -\frac{W}{2}\left(l^2x - lx^2 + \frac{x^3}{3}\right) - W\left(lx - \frac{x^2}{2}\right) + c_1 \quad ...(1)$$

Again integrating, we get

$$EIy = -\frac{W}{2}\left(\frac{l^2x^2}{2} - \frac{lx^3}{3} + \frac{x^4}{12}\right) - W\left(\frac{lx^2}{2} - \frac{x^3}{6}\right) + c_1x + c_2 \quad ...(2)$$

Putting $x = 0, y = 0$ in (2), we get $c_2 = 0$

Putting $\frac{dy}{dx} = 0, x = 0$ in (1), we get $c_1 = 0$

$\therefore$ From (2),

$$EIy = -\frac{W}{24}(6l^2x^2 - 4lx^3 + x^4 + 12lx^2 - 4x^3)$$

$$y = \frac{W}{24EI}[-x^4 + 4lx^3 + 4x^3 - 12lx^2 - 6l^2x^2]$$

which is required equation of the beam.

Maximum deflection (at $x = l$),

$$y = \frac{W}{24EI}(-l^4 + 4l^4 + 4l^3 - 12l^3 - 6l^4)$$

$$= \frac{W}{24EI}(-3l^4 - 8l^3) = \frac{Wl^3}{24EI}(3l + 8). \quad | \text{ Numerically}$$

(Neglecting (–) sign)

Example 7. *The differential equation for the displacement y of a whirling shift when the weight of the shaft is taken into account is*

$$EI\frac{d^4y}{dx^4} - \frac{Ww^2}{g}y = W$$

Taking the shaft of length 2l with the origin at the centre and short bearings at both ends, show that the maximum deflection of the shaft is

$$\frac{g}{2w^2}(\text{sech } al + \sec al - 2).$$

Sol. The differential equation is

$$\frac{d^4y}{dx^4} - a^4y = \frac{W}{EI}, \quad \text{where } a^4 = \frac{Ww^2}{EIg} \quad \text{...(1)}$$

$\therefore$

$$\text{C.F.} = c_1 \cosh ax + c_2 \sinh ax + c_3 \cos ax + c_4 \sin ax$$

$$\text{P.I.} = \frac{1}{D^4 - a^4}\left(\frac{W}{EI}\right) = -\frac{W}{EI\,a^4} = -\frac{g}{w^2}$$

Complete solution is, $y = c_1 \cosh ax + c_2 \sinh ax + c_3 \cos ax + c_4 \sin ax - \dfrac{g}{w^2}$ ...(2)

Differentiating, we get

$$\frac{1}{a}\frac{dy}{dx} = c_1 \sinh ax + c_2 \cosh ax - c_3 \sin ax + c_4 \cos ax$$

and

$$\frac{1}{a^2}\frac{d^2y}{dx^2} = c_1 \cosh ax + c_2 \sinh ax - c_3 \cos ax - c_4 \sin ax \quad \text{...(3)}$$

At end A, the shaft is in short bearings

$\therefore$ when $\quad x = l, \quad y = 0, \dfrac{d^2y}{dx^2} = 0$

From (2) and (3),

$$0 = c_1 \cosh al + c_2 \sinh al + c_3 \cos al + c_4 \sin al - \frac{g}{w^2} \quad \text{...(4)}$$

and

$$0 = c_1 \cosh al + c_2 \sinh al - c_3 \cos al - c_4 \sin al \quad \text{...(5)}$$

Similarly at end B, $\quad x = -l, y = 0$ and $\dfrac{d^2y}{dx^2} = 0$

From (2) and (3), we get

$$0 = c_1 \cosh al - c_2 \sinh al + c_3 \cos al - c_4 \sin al - \frac{g}{w^2} \qquad ...(6)$$

and

$$0 = c_1 \cosh al - c_2 \sinh al - c_3 \cos al + c_4 \sin al \qquad ...(7)$$

Adding (4), (6) and (5), (7), we get

$$c_1 \cosh al + c_3 \cos al = \frac{g}{w^2}$$

and

$$c_1 \cosh al - c_3 \cos al = 0$$

$$\therefore \quad c_1 = \frac{g}{2w^2 \cosh al} \quad \text{and} \quad c_3 = \frac{g}{2w^2 \cos al}$$

Again, subtracting (6) from (4) and (7) from (5), we get

$$c_2 \sinh al + c_4 \sin al = 0$$

and

$$c_2 \sinh al - c_4 \sin al = 0$$

$$\Rightarrow \quad c_2 = 0, c_4 = 0$$

$$\therefore \quad y = \frac{g}{2w^2}\left[\frac{\cosh ax}{\cosh al} + \frac{\cos ax}{\cos al} - 2\right]$$

Thus, Maximum deflection = Value of y at the centre (at $x = 0$)

$$= \frac{g}{2w^2}(\text{sech } al + \sec al - 2).$$

ASSIGNMENT-I

(2 Marks Questions for Section–A)

1. Find the general solution of $(2D + 1)^2 y = 0$ where $D = \dfrac{d}{dt}$. *(G.B.T.U. 2012)*

2. Find the particular integral of $\dfrac{d^2y}{dx^2} - y = x^2$. *(G.B.T.U. 2012)*

3. Prove that if M and N in $M(x, y)\, dx + N(x, y)\, dy = 0$ satisfy the equation $\dfrac{\partial M}{\partial y} + \dfrac{3}{y} M = \dfrac{\partial N}{\partial x}$ then y^3 is an integrating factor. *(M.T.U. 2012)*

4. $y = (c_1 + c_2 x + c_3 x^2)\, e^x$ is the solution of the differential equation ..., c_1, c_2, c_3 are constants. *(M.T.U. 2012)*

5. Solve: $y'' + y = 0;\ y(0) = 1,\ y(\pi/2) = 2$.

6. Solve: $(D^4 - 6D^3 + 12D^2 - 8D)y = 0;\ D \equiv \dfrac{d}{dx}$.

7. Solve: $(D^2 - 2D + 5)^2 y = 0,\ D \equiv \dfrac{d}{dx}$.

8. Find the particular integral of $(D^2 + a^2)\, y = \sin ax,\ a \neq 0$. [*G.B.T.U. (Pharm) SUM 2010*]

9. Form a differential equation whose general solution is $y = e^{-x}\,(c_1 \cos \sqrt{3}x + c_2 \sin \sqrt{3}x) + c_3\, e^{2x}$.

10. Solve: $\dfrac{d^2y}{dx^2} - 3\dfrac{dy}{dx} + 2y = e^{3x}$.

11. Find the P.I. of $(D^3 - D)\, y = e^x + e^{-x}$.

12. Find the P.I. of $\dfrac{d^2y}{dx^2} + \dfrac{dy}{dx} = x^2 + 2x + 4$.

13. A particular executing simple harmonic motion of amplitude 5 cm has a speed of 8 cm/sec. when at a distance of 3 cm from the centre of the path. Find the period of the motion of the particle.

14. Find the periodic time of the motion described by the differential equation $\dfrac{d^2x}{dt^2} + \mu x = 0$.

15. Find the differential equation which represents the family of straight lines passing through the origin?

16. Form a differential eqn. which satisfies the relation $y = A\cos\,(mt - \alpha)$

17. Find the parts of C.F. of the differential eqn. $x^2y'' + xy' - y = 0$.

18. Solve: $\dot{x}(t) = y,\ \dot{y}(t) = -x;\ x(0) = 0,\ y(0) = 0$.

19. What is the order of the differential eqn. $x^2 \left(\dfrac{dy}{dx}\right)^2 + xy\dfrac{dy}{dx} - 6y^2 = 0$.

[*G.B.T.U. (AG) S.U.M. 2010*]

20. Find the complementary function of $\dfrac{d^2y}{dx^2} - 2\dfrac{dy}{dx} + 2y = 0$. [*M.T.U. (B.Pharm) 2011*]

21. Find the P.I. of $(D^2 - 2D + 1)\, y = \sin x$. [*M.T.U. (B.Pharm) 2011*]

22. Solve: $\dfrac{d^2y}{dx^2} - 2\dfrac{dy}{dx} + y = 0$. [*M.T.U. (B.Pharm) 2011*]

23. Find a particular integral of the differential eqn. $(D^2 + D)\, y = x^2 + 2x + 1$.

[*M.T.U. (SUM) 2011*]

24. A condenser of capacity C is charged through an inductance L and resistance R in series where charge q satisfies the equation

$L\dfrac{d^2q}{dt^2} + A\dfrac{dq}{dt} + Bq = 0$. Here find A and B. [*M.T.U. (SUM) 2011*]

25. Find the roots of the auxiliary equation of the differential equation $\dfrac{d^2y}{dt^2} - 6\dfrac{dy}{dt} + 9y = 4e^{3t}$.

(*G.B.T.U. 2011*)

26. Solve: $x\, dy - y\, dx = 0$

27. Find the integrating factor of $\dfrac{dy}{dx} - \dfrac{y}{x+1} = e^{3x}\,(x+1)$.

28. Solve: $\dfrac{d^3y}{dx^3} - 3\dfrac{d^2y}{dx} + 4y = 0$.

29. Find the P.I. of $(D^2 - 4)\ y = \sin 2x$.

30. Find the P.I. of $(D^2 + 6D + 5)\ y = 4e^{-x}$.

31. Find the C.F. of the differential eqn. $x^2y'' - xy' + y = \log x$.

32. Solve: $x^2 \dfrac{d^2y}{dx^2} + x\dfrac{dy}{dx} = 0$.

33. Find the P.I. of $\dfrac{d^2y}{dx^2} + y = \cosh 3x$.

34. Find the differential eqn. whose auxiliary eqn. has the roots 0, – 1 and – 1.

35. In the eqn. $\dfrac{d^2y}{dx^2} + P\dfrac{dy}{dx} + Qy = R$, if we obtain $1 + \dfrac{P}{2} + \dfrac{Q}{4} = 0$ then find one part of C.F.

36. Find the order and degree of

(*i*) $\left(\dfrac{d^3y}{dx^3}\right)^4 - 6x^2\left(\dfrac{dy}{dx}\right)^2 + e^x = \sin xy$ (*U.P.T.U. 2009*)

(*ii*) $\left(\dfrac{d^3y}{dx^3}\right)^4 - 6x^2\left(\dfrac{dy}{dx}\right)^8 = 0$ (*G.B.T.U. 2010*)

(*iii*) $\dfrac{d^2y}{dx^2} + \sqrt{1+\left(\dfrac{dy}{dx}\right)^3} = 0$ [*G.B.T.U. (SUM) 2010*]

(*iv*) $\left[1+\left(\dfrac{dy}{dx}\right)^2\right]^{3/2} = \dfrac{d^2y}{dx^2}$ [*G.B.T.U. (BT) SUM 2010*]

37. Solve: $\dfrac{dy}{dx} = \dfrac{1}{2}(y^2 - 1)\ ;\ y(0) = 2$. (*U.P.T.U. 2009*)

38. Solve: $\dfrac{d^5y}{dx^5} - \dfrac{d^3y}{dx^3} = 0$. (*U.P.T.U. 2009*)

39. Solve: $\dfrac{d^2y}{dx^2} = \sec^2 y \tan y\ ;\ y(0) = 0,\ \dfrac{dy}{dx} = 1$ at $x = 0$. [*U.P.T.U. (SUM) 2009*]

40. The population of the bacteria in a certain region doubles in 50 days. Assuming that the rate of increase is proportional to the number of inhabitants, how many days will it take to triple its population? [*U.P.T.U. (SUM) 2009*]

41. Form a differential equation if its general solution is $y = Ae^x + Be^{-x}$. [*U.P.T.U. (B.Pharm) SUM 2009*]

42. Solve: $x^2\dfrac{dy}{dx} = 2$. [*U.P.T.U. (B.Pharm) SUM 2009*]

43. Solve: $\dfrac{d^2y}{dx^2} + 3\dfrac{dy}{dx} + 2y = 0$. [*U.P.T.U. (B.Pharm) SUM 2009*]

44. Solve: $\dfrac{d^3y}{dx^3} - 7\dfrac{dy}{dx} - 6y = 0$. [*G.B.T.U. (SUM) 2010*]

45. Solve: $\dfrac{d^2y}{dx^2} = 0$. [*G.B.T.U. (Pharm) SUM 2010*]

46. Solve: $\dfrac{d^4y}{dx^4} + 2\dfrac{d^2y}{dx^2} + y = 0$. [*G.B.T.U. (BT) SUM 2010*]

47. Form a differential equation whose solution is $y = a \sin x$. [*M.T.U. (B.Pharm) 2011*]

48. Find the P.I. of $(D^2 - 4D + 4)\, y = \sin 2x$. *(G.B.T.U. 2011)*

49. In the RC-circuit where C = 0.01 F, R = 20 Ω, E_0 = 10 V, find the current I(t), assuming that capacitor is completely uncharged. *(M.T.U. 2011)*

50. Find the differential equation whose solution is $xy = ae^x + be^{-x} + x^2$. *(M.T.U. 2011)*

Answers

1. $y = (c_1 + c_2 t)\, e^{-t/2}$ **2.** $-(x^2 + 2)$ **4.** $(D - 1)^3 y = 0;\ D \equiv \frac{d}{dx}$

5. $y = \cos x + 2 \sin x$ **6.** $y = c_1 + (c_2 + c_3 x + c_4 x^2)\, e^{2x}$

7. $y = e^x [(c_1 + c_2 x) \cos 2x + (c_3 + c_4 x) \sin 2x]$

8. $-\frac{x}{2a} \cos ax$ **9.** $\frac{d^3y}{dx^3} - 8y = 0$ **10.** $y = c_1 e^x + c_2 e^{2x} + \frac{1}{2} e^{3x}$

11. $\frac{1}{2} x(e^x + e^{-x})$ **12.** $\frac{x^3}{3} + 4x$ **13.** π sec.

14. $\frac{2\pi}{\sqrt{\mu}}$ **15.** $y\, dx - x dy = 0$ **16.** $\frac{d^2y}{dt^2} = -m^2 y$

17. $x, \frac{1}{x}$ **18.** $x = 0,\ y = 0$ **19.** 1

20. $e^x (c_1 \cos x + c_2 \sin x)$ **21.** $\frac{1}{2} \cos x$ **22.** $y = (c_1 + c_2 x)\, e^x$

23. $\frac{x^3}{3} + x$ **24.** $A = R,\ B = C^{-1}$ **25.** 3, 3

26. $y = cx$ **27.** $\frac{1}{x+1}$ **28.** $y = c_1 e^{-x} + (c_2 + c_3 x)\, e^{2x}$

29. $-\frac{1}{8} \sin 2x$ **30.** xe^{-x} **31.** C.F. $y = c_1 x + c_2 x \log x$

32. $y = c_1 + c_2 \log x$ **33.** $\frac{1}{10} \cosh 3x$ **34.** $\frac{d^3y}{dx^3} + 2\frac{d^2y}{dx^2} + \frac{dy}{dx} = 0$

35. e^{2x} **36.** (*i*) 3, 4 (*ii*) 3, 4 (*iii*) 2, 2, (*iv*) 2, 2

37. $y = \frac{3 + e^t}{3 - e^t}$ **38.** $y = c_1 + c_2 x + c_3 x^2 + c_4 e^x + c_5 e^{-x}$

39. $y = \sin^{-1} x$ **40.** 79 days **41.** $\frac{d^2y}{dx^2} - y = 0$

42. $y = -\frac{2}{x} + c_1$ **43.** $y = c_1 e^{-x} + c_2 e^{-2x}$ **44.** $y = c_1 e^{-x} + c_2 e^{-2x} + c_3 e^{3x}$

45. $y = c_1 + c_2 x$ **46.** $y = (c_1 + c_2 x) \cos x + (c_3 + c_4 x) \sin x$

47. $\frac{dy}{dx} = y \cot x$ **48.** $\frac{1}{8} \cos 2x$ **49.** $\frac{1}{2} e^{-5t}$

50. $x \frac{d^2y}{dx^2} + 2\frac{dy}{dx} - xy = 2 - x^2$

UNIT 2

Series Solution of Ordinary Differential Equations and Special Functions

2.1. INTRODUCTION

The solution of ordinary linear differential equations of second order with variable coefficients in the form of an infinite convergent series is called *solution in series* or *integration in series.*

The series solution of certain differential equations give rise to *special functions* such as Bessel's function, Legendre's polynomials, Laguerre's polynomial, Hermite's polynomial, Chebyshev polynomials. These special functions have wide applications in engineering.

In this unit, we will discuss methods of solution of second order linear differential equations with variable coefficients in series along with Bessel's function, Legendre's polynomial and their properties.

2.2. DEFINITIONS

2.2.1. Power Series

An infinite series of the form

$$\sum_{n=0}^{\infty} a_n (x - x_0)^n = a_0 + a_1 (x - x_0) + a_2 (x - x_0)^2 + \ldots$$

is called a power series in ascending powers of $x - x_0$.

In particular, a power series in ascending powers of x is an infinite series

$$\sum_{n=0}^{\infty} a_n x^n = a_0 + a_1 x + a_2 x^2 + \ldots$$

e.g.,
$$e^x = \sum_{n=0}^{\infty} \frac{x^n}{n!} = 1 + x + \frac{x^2}{2!} + \frac{x^3}{3!} + \ldots$$

2.2.2. Analytic Function

A function $f(x)$ defined on an interval containing the point $x = x_0$ is called analytic at x_0 if its Taylor series $\sum_{n=0}^{\infty} \frac{f^{(n)}(x_0)}{n!} (x - x_0)^n$ exists and converges to $f(x)$ for all x in the interval of convergence of Taylor's series.

Note 1. A rational function is analytic except at those values of x at which its denominator is zero. *e.g.,* Rational function $\frac{x}{x^2 - 5x + 6}$ is analytic everywhere except at $x = 2$ and $x = 3$.

Note 2. All polynomial functions e^x, $\sin x$, $\cos x$, $\sinh x$ and $\cosh x$ are analytic everywhere.

2.2.3. Ordinary Point

A point $x = x_0$ is called an ordinary point of the equation

$$\frac{d^2y}{dx^2} + P(x)\frac{dy}{dx} + Q(x)\,y = 0 \qquad ...(1)$$

if both the functions P(x) and Q (x) are analytic at $x = x_0$.

2.2.4. Regular and Irregular Singular Points

If the point $x = x_0$ is not an ordinary point of the differential equation (1), then it is called a singular point of equation (1). There are two types of singular points :

(*i*) Regular singular point.

(*ii*) Irregular singular point.

A singular point $x = x_0$ of the differential equation (1) is called a regular singular point of (1) if both $(x - x_0)$ P(x) and $(x - x_0)^2$ Q(x) are analytic at $x = x_0$.

A singular point which is not regular is called an irregular singular point.

Remark 1. When $x = 0$ is an ordinary point of equation (1), its every solution can be expressed as a series of the form

$$y = a_0 + a_1x + a_2x^2 + a_3x^3 + ... = \sum_{n=0}^{\infty} a_n x^n .$$

Remark 2. When $x = 0$ is a regular singular point of equation (1), at least one of its solution can be expressed as

$$y = a_0x^m + a_1x^{m+1} + a_2x^{m+2} + ... = x^m (a_0 + a_1x + a_2x^2 + ...) = \sum_{n=0}^{\infty} a_n x^{m+n}$$

where m may be a positive or negative integer or a fraction.

Remark 3. If $x = 0$ is an irregular singular point of equation (1), then discussion of solution of the equation is beyond the scope of this book.

2.3. SOME IMPORTANT DIFFERENTIAL EQUATIONS

(*i*) Legendre's differential equation

The differential equation of the form

$$(1 - x^2)\frac{d^2y}{dx^2} - 2x\frac{dy}{dx} + n(n + 1)\,y = 0$$

or

$$\frac{d}{dx}\left\{(1 - x^2)\frac{dy}{dx}\right\} + n(n + 1)\,y = 0$$

is called Legendre's differential equation, where n is a real number.

(*ii*) **Bessel's differential equation**

The differential equation of the form

$$x^2 \frac{d^2y}{dx^2} + x\frac{dy}{dx} + (x^2 - n^2)\, y = 0$$

is called Bessel's differential equation of order n, where n is a positive constant.

(*iii*) **Chebyshev's differential equation**

The differential equation of the form

$$(1 - x^2) \frac{d^2y}{dx^2} - x\frac{dy}{dx} + n^2y = 0$$

is called Chebyshev's differential equation.

2.4. POWER SERIES SOLUTION, WHEN $x = 0$ IS AN ORDINARY POINT OF THE EQUATION $\frac{d^2y}{dx^2} + P(x)\frac{dy}{dx} + Q(x)\, y = 0$

Steps for solution :

1. Assume its solution to be of the form $y = a_0 + a_1x + a_2x^2 + ... + a_nx^n + ...$ ...(1)
2. Find $\frac{dy}{dx}$ (or y') and $\frac{d^2y}{dx^2}$ (or y'') from y.
3. Substitute the values of y, $\frac{dy}{dx}$ and $\frac{d^2y}{dx^2}$ in the given differential equation.
4. Equate to zero the coefficients of various powers of x and find $a_2, a_3, a_4, a_5, ...$ in terms of a_0 and a_1.
5. Equate to zero, the coefficient of x^n. The relation so obtained is called the *recurrence relation.* It helps us in finding the values of other constants easily.
6. Give different values to n in the recurrence relation to determine various a_i's in terms of a_0 and a_1.
7. Substitute the values of $a_2, a_3, a_4, ...$ in assumed solution (1) above to get the series solution of the given equation having a_0 and a_1 as arbitrary constants.

ILLUSTRATIVE EXAMPLES

Example 1. *Solve in series the differential equation*

$$\frac{d^2y}{dx^2} + xy = 0.$$ [G.B.T.U. (SUM) 2010]

Sol. Comparing the given equation with the form $\frac{d^2y}{dx^2} + P(x)\frac{dy}{dx} + Q(x)\, y = 0$,

we get $\quad P(x) = 0,\ Q(x) = x$

At $x = 0$, Both P(x) and Q(x) are analytic, hence $x = 0$ is an *ordinary point.*

Assume its solution to be

$$y = a_0 + a_1x + a_2x^2 + a_3x^3 + ... + a_nx^n + ... \qquad ...(1)$$

Then, $\dfrac{dy}{dx} = a_1 + 2a_2x + 3a_3x^2 + 4a_4x^3 + \dots + n\,a_nx^{n-1} + \dots$

and $\dfrac{d^2y}{dx^2} = 2.1\,a_2 + 3.2\,a_3x + 4.3\,a_4x^2 + 5.4\,a_5x^3 + \dots + n(n-1)\,a_nx^{n-2} + \dots$

Substituting these values in the given differential equation, we get

$$[2.1.\,a_2 + 3.2\,.\,a_3x + 4.3\,.\,a_4x^2 + 5.4\,.\,a_5x^3 + \dots + n(n-1)\,a_nx^{n-2} + \dots]$$
$$+ x\,[a_0 + a_1x + a_2x^2 + a_3x^3 + \dots + a_nx^n + \dots] = 0$$

$$2.1\,.\,a_2 + (3.2\,a_3 + a_0)\,x + (4.3\,.\,a_4 + a_1)x^2 + (5.4\,.\,a_5 + a_2)x^3 + \dots$$
$$+ \{(n+2)(n+1)\,a_{n+2} + a_{n-1}\}x^n + \dots = 0$$

Equating to zero, the various powers of x as,

Coefficient of $x^0 = 0$

$\Rightarrow \quad 2.1\,.\,a_2 = 0 \quad \Rightarrow \quad \boxed{a_2 = 0}$

Coefficient of $x = 0$

$\Rightarrow \quad 3.2\,.\,a_3 + a_0 = 0$

$\Rightarrow \quad a_3 = -\dfrac{a_0}{3.2} \quad \Rightarrow \quad \boxed{a_3 = -\dfrac{a_0}{3!}}$

Coefficient of $x^2 = 0$

$\Rightarrow \quad 4.3\,.\,a_4 + a_1 = 0$

$\Rightarrow \quad a_4 = -\dfrac{a_1}{4.3} \quad$ or $\quad \boxed{a_4 = -\dfrac{2a_1}{4!}}$

Coefficient of $x^3 = 0$

$\Rightarrow \quad 5.4\,.\,a_5 + a_2 = 0$

$\Rightarrow \quad a_5 = -\dfrac{a_2}{5.4} \quad$ or $\quad \boxed{a_5 = 0}$

Coefficient of $x^4 = 0$

$\Rightarrow \quad 6.5\,.\,a_6 + a_3 = 0$

$\Rightarrow \quad a_6 = -\dfrac{a_3}{6.5} - \dfrac{a_0}{6.5.3!} \quad$ or $\quad \boxed{a_6 = \dfrac{4a_0}{6!}}$

and so on.

Coefficient of $x^n = 0$

$\Rightarrow \quad (n+2)(n+1)\,a_{n+2} + a_{n-1} = 0$

$\Rightarrow \quad \boxed{a_{n+2} = -\dfrac{a_{n-1}}{(n+2)(n+1)}}$

which is the recurrence relation.

Putting $n = 5, 6, 7, \dots$, successively in recurrence relation, we obtain

$$a_7 = \frac{5.2a_1}{7!},\ a_8 = 0,\ a_9 = \frac{-7.4}{9!}\,a_0 \text{ and so on.}$$

Substituting these values in (1), we get

$$y = a_0 + a_1x - \frac{a_0}{3!}\,x^3 - \frac{2a_1}{4!}\,x^4 + \frac{4a_0}{6!}\,x^6 + \frac{5.2\,a_1}{7!}\,x^7 - \frac{7.4}{9!}\,a_0\,x^9 + \dots$$

$$\Rightarrow \qquad y = a_0\left[1 - \frac{x^3}{3!} + \frac{1.4}{6!}x^6 - \frac{1.4.7}{9!}x^9 + \ldots\right] + a_1\left[x - \frac{2}{4!}x^4 + \frac{2.5}{7!}x^7 - \ldots\right]$$

where a_0 and a_1 are constants.

Example 2. *Solve in series the differential equation*

$$(1 + x^2)\frac{d^2y}{dx^2} + x\frac{dy}{dx} - y = 0 \textit{ about the point } x = 0.$$

Sol. Comparing the given differential equation with the form

$$\frac{d^2y}{dx^2} + P(x)\frac{dy}{dx} + Q(x)\,y = 0, \text{ we get}$$

$$P(x) = \frac{x}{1+x^2} \quad \text{and} \quad Q(x) = \frac{-1}{1+x^2}.$$

Both P(x) and Q(x) are analytic at $x = 0$

$\therefore$ $x = 0$ is an *ordinary point* of the given differential equation.

Assume the solution to be

$$y = a_0 + a_1x + a_2x^2 + a_3x^3 + \ldots + a_nx^n + \ldots \qquad \ldots(1)$$

Then,
$$\frac{dy}{dx} = a_1 + 2a_2x + 3a_3x^2 + \ldots + na_nx^{n-1} + \ldots$$

and
$$\frac{d^2y}{dx^2} = 2.1.\,a_2 + 3.2.\,a_3x + \ldots + n(n-1)a_n\,x^{n-2} + \ldots$$

Substituting these values in given equation, we get

$$(1 + x^2)\,[2.1.\,a_2 + 3.2.\,a_3x + 4.3.a_4x^2 + \ldots + n(n-1)\,a_nx^{n-2} + \ldots]$$
$$+ x\,[a_1 + 2a_2x + 3a_3x^2 + 4a_4x^3 + \ldots + n\,a_nx^{n-1} + \ldots]$$
$$- [a_0 + a_1x + a_2x^2 + a_3x^3 + \ldots + a_nx^n + \ldots] = 0$$

Coefficient of $x^0 = 0$

$$\Rightarrow \quad 2.1.\,a_2 - a_0 = 0 \qquad \Rightarrow \quad \boxed{a_2 = \frac{a_0}{2}}$$

Coefficient of $x = 0$

$$\Rightarrow \quad 3.2\,a_3 + a_1 - a_1 = 0 \qquad \Rightarrow \quad \boxed{a_3 = 0}$$

Coefficient of $x^2 = 0$

$$\Rightarrow \quad 2.1\,.\,a_2 + 4.3.a_4 + 2a_2 - a_2 = 0$$

$$\Rightarrow \quad 4.3\,a_4 + 3a_2 = 0$$

$$\Rightarrow \quad a_4 = -\frac{a_2}{4} = -\frac{a_0}{8} \quad \text{or} \quad \boxed{a_4 = -\frac{a_0}{8}}$$

Coefficient of $x^3 = 0$

$$\Rightarrow \quad 5.4.\,a_5 + 3.2.\,a_3 + 3a_3 - a_3 = 0$$

$$\Rightarrow \quad 20a_5 + 8a_3 = 0 \qquad \Rightarrow \quad \boxed{a_5 = 0}$$

Coefficient of $x^4 = 0$

$\Rightarrow \quad 6.5 \,.\, a_6 + 4.3 \,.\, a_4 + 4a_4 - a_4 = 0$

$\Rightarrow \quad 30a_6 + 15a_4 = 0$

$$\Rightarrow \quad a_6 = -\frac{a_4}{2} = \frac{a_0}{16} \quad \text{or} \quad \boxed{a_6 = \frac{a_0}{16}}$$

Similarly, $a_7 = 0, a_9 = 0, a_{11} = 0$ and so on.

Also, coefficient of $x^n = 0$

$$(n + 2)(n + 1)\, a_{n+2} + n(n - 1)a_n + na_n - a_n = 0$$

$$\Rightarrow \quad a_{n+2} = -\left(\frac{n-1}{n+2}\right) a_n \qquad | \because \; n + 1 \neq 0$$

Putting $n = 6, 8, 10, \ldots$, we get

$$a_8 = -\frac{5}{8} a_6 = -\frac{5a_0}{128}$$

$$a_{10} = -\frac{7}{10} a_8 = \frac{7a_0}{256} \text{ and so on.}$$

Substituting these values in (1), we get

$$y = a_0 + a_1 x + \frac{a_0}{2} x^2 - \frac{a_0}{8} x^4 + \frac{a_0}{16} x^6 - \frac{5a_0}{128} x^8 + \frac{7a_0}{256} x^{10} - \ldots$$

$$\Rightarrow \quad y = a_0 \left(1 + \frac{x^2}{2} - \frac{x^4}{8} + \frac{x^6}{16} - \frac{5x^8}{128} + \frac{7x^{10}}{256} - \ldots\right) + a_1 x$$

where a_0 and a_1 are constants.

Example 3. *Solve in series Chebyshev's differential equation (when n = 2)*

Or

Solve : $(1 - x^2)y'' - xy' + 4y = 0$ in series. [G.B.T.U. 2012; U.P.T.U. 2006]

Sol. Comparing the given differential equation with the form

$y'' + P(x)\, y' + Q(x)\, y = 0$, we get

$$P(x) = \frac{-x}{1-x^2}, \; Q(x) = \frac{4}{1-x^2}$$

Since both $P(x)$ and $Q(x)$ are analytic at $x = 0$, hence $x = 0$ is an *ordinary point* of the given equation.

Assume the solution to be

$$y = a_0 + a_1 x + a_2 x^2 + a_3 x^3 + \ldots + a_n x^n + \ldots \qquad \ldots(1)$$

Then, $\quad y' = a_1 + 2.a_2 x + 3.a_3 x^2 + \ldots + na_n x^{n-1} + \ldots$

and $\quad y'' = 2.1.\, a_2 + 3.2.a_3 x + \ldots + n(n - 1)a_n x^{n-2} + \ldots$

Substituting these values in given equation, we get

$$(1 - x^2)\,[2.1.\, a_2 + 3.2.\, a_3 x + 4.3.\, a_4 x^2 + \ldots + n(n - 1)\, a_n x^{n-2} + \ldots]$$
$$- x\,[a_1 + 2a_2 x + 3a_3 x^2 + \ldots + na_n x^{n-1} + \ldots] + 4\,[a_0 + a_1 x + a_2 x^2 + a_3 x^3 + \ldots + a_n x^n + \ldots] = 0$$

Coefficient of $x^0 = 0$

$\Rightarrow \quad 2.1.\, a_2 + 4a_0 = 0 \quad \Rightarrow \quad \boxed{a_2 = -2a_0}$

Coefficient of $x = 0$

$\Rightarrow \quad 3.2\, a_3 - a_1 + 4a_1 = 0 \quad \Rightarrow \quad \boxed{a_3 = -\frac{a_1}{2}}$

Coefficient of $x^2 = 0$

$\Rightarrow \quad 4.3.\, a_4 - 2.1\, a_2 - 2a_2 + 4a_2 = 0 \quad \Rightarrow \quad \boxed{a_4 = 0}$

Coefficient of $x^3 = 0$

$\Rightarrow \quad 5.4\, a_5 - 3.2\, a_3 - 3a_3 + 4a_3 = 0$

$$\Rightarrow \quad a_5 = \frac{a_3}{4} = \frac{1}{4}\left(\frac{-a_1}{2}\right) = -\frac{a_1}{8}$$

$\Rightarrow \quad \boxed{a_5 = -\frac{a_1}{8}}$ and so on.

Substituting these values in assumed solution (1), we get

$$y = a_0 + a_1 x - 2a_0 x^2 - \frac{a_1}{2} x^3 - \frac{a_1}{8} x^5 + \ldots$$

$$\Rightarrow \quad y = a_0 (1 - 2x^2) + a_1 x \left(1 - \frac{x^2}{2} - \frac{x^4}{8} - \ldots\right)$$

where a_0 and a_1 are constants.

Example 4. *Find the power series solution of the following differential equation about $x = 0$*

$$(1 - x^2) \frac{d^2y}{dx^2} - 2x \frac{dy}{dx} + 2y = 0.$$

Sol. Comparing the given differential equation with the form

$$\frac{d^2y}{dx^2} + P(x) \frac{dy}{dx} + Q(x)y = 0, \text{ we get}$$

$$P(x) = \frac{-2x}{1 - x^2}, \; Q(x) = \frac{2}{1 - x^2}$$

Since both P(x) and Q(x) are analytic at $x = 0$, hence $x = 0$ is an *ordinary point* of the given equation.

Assume the solution to be

$$y = a_0 + a_1 x + a_2 x^2 + a_3 x^3 + \ldots + a_n x^n + \ldots \qquad \ldots(1)$$

Then, $$y' = a_1 + 2a_2 x + 3a_3 x^2 + 4a_4 x^3 + \ldots + n\, a_n\, x^{n-1} + \ldots$$

and $$y'' = 2.1.\, a_2 + 3.2.\, a_3\, x + 4.3.\, a_4\, x^2 + \ldots + n(n-1) a_n\, x^{n-2} + \ldots$$

Substituting these values in given equation, we get

$$(1 - x^2)\,[2.1.\, a_2 + 3.2.\, a_3 x + 4.3.\, a_4 x^2 + \ldots + n(n-1)\, a_n x^{n-2} + \ldots]$$
$$- 2x\,[a_1 + 2a_2 x + 3a_3 x^2 + 4a_4 x^3 + \ldots + n\, a_n\, x^{n-1} + \ldots]$$
$$+ 2\,[a_0 + a_1 x + a_2 x^2 + a_3 x^3 + \ldots + a_n\, x^n + \ldots] = 0$$

Coefficient of $x^0 = 0$

$\Rightarrow \quad 2.1.\, a_2 + 2a_0 = 0 \quad \Rightarrow \quad \boxed{a_2 = -a_0}$

Coefficient of $x = 0$

$\Rightarrow \quad 3.2.\, a_3 - 2a_1 + 2a_1 = 0 \quad \Rightarrow \quad \boxed{a_3 = 0}$

Coefficient of $x^2 = 0$

$\Rightarrow \quad 4.3.a_4 - 2.1.\ a_2 - 4a_2 + 2a_2 = 0$

$\Rightarrow \quad 12a_4 - 4a_2 = 0 \quad \Rightarrow \quad a_4 = \frac{a_2}{3} = -\frac{a_0}{3} \quad \Rightarrow \quad \boxed{a_4 = -\frac{a_0}{3}}$

Coefficient of $x^3 = 0$

$\Rightarrow \quad 5.4.a_5 - 3.2.\ a_3 - 6a_3 + 2a_3 = 0$

$\Rightarrow \quad 20a_5 - 10a_3 = 0 \quad \Rightarrow \quad \boxed{a_5 = 0}$

Coefficient of $x^4 = 0$

$\Rightarrow \quad 6.5.a_6 - 4.3.\ a_4 - 8a_4 + 2a_4 = 0$

$\Rightarrow \quad 30a_6 - 18a_4 = 0 \quad \Rightarrow \quad a_6 = \frac{3}{5}a_4 \quad \Rightarrow \quad \boxed{a_6 = -\frac{a_0}{5}}$

Also, $a_7 = 0$, $a_9 = 0$ and so on.

Substituting these values in assumed solution (1), we get

$$y = a_0 + a_1x - a_0x^2 - \frac{a_0}{3}x^4 - \frac{a_0}{5}x^6 - \ldots\ldots$$

$$\Rightarrow \quad y = a_0\left(1 - x^2 - \frac{x^4}{3} - \frac{x^6}{5} - \ldots\right) + a_1x$$

where a_0 and a_1 are constants.

Example 5. *Solve in series the Legendre's differential equation*

$$(1 - x^2)\frac{d^2y}{dx^2} - 2x\frac{dy}{dx} + p(p+1)y = 0. \qquad \text{[G.B.T.U. (C.O.) 2010]}$$

Sol. Here, $\quad \mathrm{P}(x) = \frac{-2x}{1-x^2},\ \mathrm{Q}(x) = \frac{p(p+1)}{1-x^2}$

Since both P(x) and Q(x) are analytic at $x = 0$ $\therefore$ $x = 0$ is an *ordinary point* of the given differential equation.

Let the solution be $\quad y = a_0 + a_1x + a_2x^2 + \ldots\ldots + a_nx^n + \ldots\ldots = \sum_{n=0}^{\infty} a_n x^n \qquad \ldots(1)$

$$\therefore \quad \frac{dy}{dx} = \sum_{n=0}^{\infty} n\,a_n\,x^{n-1} \qquad \ldots(2)$$

$$\frac{d^2y}{dx^2} = \sum_{n=0}^{\infty} n(n-1)\,a_n\,x^{n-2} \qquad \ldots(3)$$

Substituting the above values in the given equation, we get

$$(1 - x^2)\sum_{n=0}^{\infty} n(n-1)\,a_n\,x^{n-2} - 2x\sum_{n=0}^{\infty} n\,a_n\,x^{n-1} + p(p+1)\sum_{n=0}^{\infty} a_n\,x^n = 0$$

$$\Rightarrow \quad \sum_{n=0}^{\infty} n(n-1)\,a_n\,x^{n-2} - \sum_{n=0}^{\infty} a_n[n(n-1) + 2n - p(p+1)]x^n = 0$$

$$\Rightarrow \quad \sum_{n=0}^{\infty} n(n-1)\,a_n\,x^{n-2} - \sum_{n=0}^{\infty} a_n(n-p)(n+p+1)x^n = 0$$

This is an identity in x.

Coefficient of $x^n = 0$

$$\Rightarrow \quad (n+2)(n+1)\, a_{n+2} - (n-p)(n+p+1)\, a_n = 0$$

$$\therefore \quad a_{n+2} = \frac{(n-p)(n+p+1)}{(n+2)(n+1)}\, a_n$$

Putting $n = 0, 2, 4, \ldots..$ etc., we get

$$a_2 = \frac{-p(p+1)}{2.1}\, a_0$$

$$a_4 = \frac{(2-p)(3+p)}{4.3}\, a_2 = \frac{(p-2)(p)(p+1)(p+3)}{4!}\, a_0 \text{ etc.}$$

Again, putting $n = 1, 3, 5, \ldots\ldots$ etc., we get

$$a_3 = \frac{(1-p)(p+2)}{3.2}\, a_1 = -\frac{(p-1)(p+2)}{3!}\, a_1$$

$$a_5 = \frac{(3-p)(p+4)}{5.4}\, a_3 = \frac{(p-3)(p-1)(p+2)(p+4)}{5!}\, a_1 \text{ etc.}$$

Substituting these values in eqn. (1), we get

$$y = a_0\left[1 - \frac{p(p+1)}{2!}x^2 + \frac{(p-2)p(p+1)(p+3)}{4!}x^4 - \ldots\ldots\right]$$

$$+ a_1\left[x - \frac{(p-1)(p+2)}{3!}x^3 + \frac{(p-3)(p-1)(p+2)(p+4)}{5!}x^5 + \ldots\ldots\right]$$

Note. Above method is an *aliter* to the method of solution in series discussed before and preferred when, we get the recurrence relation in between a_n and a_{n+2}.

Example 6. *Solve the differential equation*

$$y'' + (x-1)^2 y' - 4(x-1)\, y = 0$$

in series about the ordinary point $x = 1$.

Sol. Put $x = t + 1$ (or $x - 1 = t$)

$$\frac{dy}{dx} = \frac{dy}{dt}\cdot\frac{dt}{dx} = \frac{dy}{dt} \qquad \left(\because \frac{dt}{dx} = 1\right)$$

$$\Rightarrow \quad \frac{d}{dx} \equiv \frac{d}{dt}$$

$$\frac{d^2y}{dx^2} = \frac{d}{dx}\left(\frac{dy}{dx}\right) = \frac{d}{dt}\left(\frac{dy}{dt}\right) = \frac{d^2y}{dt^2}$$

$\therefore$ The given equation becomes,

$$\frac{d^2y}{dt^2} + t^2y' - 4ty = 0 \qquad \ldots(1)$$

Now, $t = 0$ is an *ordinary point.* | given

Assume the solution to be

$$y = a_0 + a_1t + a_2t^2 + a_3t^3 + \ldots + a_nt^n + \ldots \qquad \ldots(2)$$

then $\quad y' = a_1 + 2a_2t + 3a_3t^2 + \ldots + n\, a_n\, t^{n-1} + \ldots$

and $\quad y'' = 2a_2 + 3.2.\, a_3t + \ldots + n\,(n-1)\, a_n\, t^{n-2} + \ldots$

Substituting these values in eqn. (1), we get

$$[2a_2 + 3.2.\ a_3 t + 4.3.\ a_4 t^2 + \ldots + n(n-1)\ a_n\ t^{n-2} + \ldots]$$
$$+ t^2\ [a_1 + 2a_2 t + 3a_3\ t^2 + 4a_4 t^3 + \ldots + n\ a_n t^{n-1} + \ldots]$$
$$- 4t\ [a_0 + a_1 t + a_2 t^2 + a_3 t^3 + \ldots + a_n t^n + \ldots] = 0$$

Coefficient of $t^0 = 0$

$\Rightarrow \quad 2a_2 = 0 \quad \Rightarrow \quad \boxed{a_2 = 0}$

Coefficient of $t = 0$

$\Rightarrow \quad 3.2.\ a_3 - 4a_0 = 0 \quad \Rightarrow \quad \boxed{a_3 = \dfrac{2a_0}{3}}$

Coefficient of $t^2 = 0$

$\Rightarrow \quad 4.3.\ a_4 + a_1 - 4a_1 = 0$

$\Rightarrow \quad 12a_4 = 3a_1 \quad \Rightarrow \quad \boxed{a_4 = \dfrac{a_1}{4}}$

Coefficient of $t^3 = 0$

$\Rightarrow \quad 5.4.\ a_5 + 2a_2 - 4a_2 = 0 \quad \Rightarrow \quad \boxed{a_5 = 0}$

Coefficient of $t^4 = 0$

$\Rightarrow \quad 6.5.\ a_6 + 3a_3 - 4a_3 = 0$

$$a_6 = \frac{a_3}{6.5} = \frac{2a_0}{6.5.3} \quad \Rightarrow \quad \boxed{a_6 = \frac{a_0}{45}}$$

Now, coefficient of $t^n = 0$

$\Rightarrow \quad (n+2)(n+1)\ a_{n+2} + (n-1)\ a_{n-1} - 4a_{n-1} = 0$

$$\Rightarrow \quad a_{n+2} = -\frac{(n-5)}{(n+2)(n+1)} a_{n-1}$$

Putting $n = 5, 6, 7, 8, \ldots$, we get

$$a_7 = 0$$

$$a_8 = \frac{-1}{8.7} a_5 = 0$$

$$a_9 = \frac{-2}{9.8} a_6 = \frac{-2}{9.8} \frac{a_0}{45} = -\frac{a_0}{1620}$$

and so on.

Substituting these values in (2), we get

$$y = a_0 + a_1 t + \frac{2}{3} a_0\ t^3 + \frac{a_1}{4} t^4 + \frac{a_0}{45} t^6 - \frac{a_0}{1620} t^9 + \ldots$$

$$= a_0 \left(1 + \frac{2}{3} t^3 + \frac{1}{45} t^6 - \frac{1}{1620} t^9 + \ldots\right) + a_1 \left(t + \frac{t^4}{4}\right)$$

$$\Rightarrow \quad y = a_0 \left[1 + \frac{2}{3}(x-1)^3 + \frac{1}{45}(x-1)^6 - \frac{1}{1620}(x-1)^9 + \ldots\right] + a_1 \left[(x-1) + \frac{(x-1)^4}{4}\right]$$

where a_0 and a_1 are constants.

TEST YOUR KNOWLEDGE

Solve the following equations in series : [Dashes denote differentiation w.r.t. x]

1. $\dfrac{d^2y}{dx^2} - y = 0$

2. $y'' + x^2y = 0$

3. (*i*) $y'' + xy' + y = 0$ (*ii*) $y'' - xy' + y = 0$

4. (*i*) $y'' - xy' + x^2y = 0$ (*ii*) $y'' + xy' + x^2y = 0$

5. $(1 - x^2)\, y'' + 2xy' + y = 0$

6. $(2 + x^2)\, y'' + xy' + (1 + x)\, y = 0$

7. $(x^2 + 1)\, y'' + xy' - xy = 0$ [*U.P.T.U.(C.O.) 2008*]

8. (*i*) $(x^2 - 1)\, y'' + 4xy' + 2y = 0$ (*ii*) $(x^2 - 1)\, y'' + xy' - y = 0$

9. (*i*) $y'' + xy' + (x^2 + 2)\, y = 0$ (*ii*) $(x^2 - 1)y'' + 3xy' + xy = 0$; $y(0) = 4$, $y'(0) = 6$.

10. (*i*) $y'' - xy' + 2y = 0$ near $x = 1$ (*ii*) $y'' + (x - 3)\, y' + y = 0$ near $x = 2$.

Answers

1. $y = a_0\left(1 + \dfrac{x^2}{2!} + \dfrac{x^4}{4!} + \dfrac{x^6}{6!} + \ldots\right) + a_1\left(x + \dfrac{x^3}{3!} + \dfrac{x^5}{5!} + \ldots\right) = a_0 \cosh x + a_1 \sinh x$

2. $y = a_0\left(1 - \dfrac{x^4}{3.4} + \dfrac{x^8}{3.4.7.8} - \ldots\right) + a_1\left(x - \dfrac{x^5}{4.5} + \dfrac{x^9}{4.5.8.9} - \ldots\right)$

3. (*i*) $y = a_0\left(1 - \dfrac{x^2}{2} + \dfrac{x^4}{2.4} - \dfrac{x^6}{2.4.6} + \ldots\right) + a_1\left(x - \dfrac{x^3}{3} + \dfrac{x^5}{3.5} - \dfrac{x^7}{3.5.7} + \ldots\right)$

(*ii*) $y = a_0\left(1 - \dfrac{x^2}{2!} - \dfrac{x^4}{4!} - \dfrac{3}{6!}x^6 - \dfrac{3.5}{8!}x^8 + \ldots\right) + a_1x$

4. (*i*) $y = a_0\left(1 - \dfrac{x^4}{12} - \dfrac{x^6}{90} - \ldots\right) + a_1\left(x + \dfrac{x^3}{6} - \dfrac{x^5}{40} - \dfrac{x^7}{144} + \ldots\right)$

(*ii*) $y = a_0\left(1 - \dfrac{x^4}{12} + \dfrac{x^6}{90} - \ldots\right) + a_1\left(x - \dfrac{x^3}{6} - \dfrac{x^5}{40} - \ldots\right)$

5. $y = a_0\left(1 - \dfrac{x^2}{2} + \dfrac{x^4}{8} + \ldots\right) + a_1\left(x - \dfrac{x^3}{2} + \dfrac{x^5}{40} + \ldots\right)$

6. $y = a_0\left(1 - \dfrac{x^2}{4} - \dfrac{x^3}{12} + \dfrac{5x^4}{96} + \ldots\right) + a_1\left(x - \dfrac{x^3}{6} - \dfrac{x^4}{24} + \ldots\right)$

7. $y = a_0\left(1 + \dfrac{x^3}{6} - \dfrac{3x^5}{40} + \ldots\right) + a_1\left(x - \dfrac{x^3}{6} + \dfrac{x^4}{12} + \dfrac{3x^5}{40} - \ldots\right)$

8. (*i*) $y = a_0\,(1 + x^2 + x^4 + \ldots) + a_1\,(x + x^3 + x^5 + \ldots)$ (*ii*) $y = a_0\left(1 + \dfrac{x^2}{2} + \dfrac{x^4}{4} + \ldots\right) + a_1x$

9. (*i*) $y = c_0\left(1 - x^2 + \dfrac{x^4}{4} + \ldots\right) + c_1\left(x - \dfrac{x^3}{2} + \dfrac{3}{40}x^5 - \ldots\right)$

(*ii*) $y = 4 + 6x + \dfrac{11}{3}x^3 + \dfrac{1}{2}x^4 + \dfrac{11}{4}x^5 + \ldots$

10. (*i*) $y = a_0\left[1-(x-1)^2 - \frac{1}{3}(x-1)^3 - \ldots\right] + a_1\left[(x-1) + \frac{1}{2}(x-1)^2 - \ldots\right]$

(*ii*) $y = a_0\left[1-\frac{1}{2}(x-2)^2 - \frac{1}{6}(x-2)^3 - \frac{1}{12}(x-2)^4 + \ldots\right]$

$$+ a_1\left[(x-2) + \frac{1}{2}(x-2)^2 - \frac{1}{6}(x-2)^3 - \frac{1}{6}(x-2)^4 + \ldots\right]$$

2.5. FROBENIUS METHOD : SERIES SOLUTION WHEN $X = 0$ IS A REGULAR SINGULAR POINT OF THE DIFFERENTIAL EQUATION

$$\frac{d^2y}{dx^2} + P(x)\frac{dy}{dx} + Q(x)y = 0$$

Steps for solution :

1. Assume $y = a_0 x^m + a_1x^{m+1} + a_2x^{m+2} + \ldots$ ...(1)
2. Substitute from (1) for $y, \frac{dy}{dx}, \frac{d^2y}{dx^2}$ in given equation.
3. Equate to zero the coefficient of *lowest power* of x. This gives a quadratic equation in m which is known as the *Indicial equation.*
4. Equate to zero, the coefficients of other powers of x to find $a_1, a_2, a_3, \ldots$ interms of a_0.
5. Substitute the values of $a_1, a_2, a_3, \ldots$in (1) to get the series solution of the given equation having a_0 as arbitrary constant. Obviously, this is not the complete solution of given equation since the complete solution must have two independent arbitrary constants.

   The method of complete solution depends on the nature of roots of the indicial equation.

2.5.1. Case I. When Roots are Distinct and do not Differ by an Integer

e.g., $$m_1 = \frac{1}{2}, m_2 = 1$$

Let m_1 and m_2 be the roots then complete solution is

$$\boxed{y = c_1 (y)_{m_1} + c_2 (y)_{m_2}}$$

ILLUSTRATIVE EXAMPLES

Example 1. *Solve in series the differential equation*

$$2x(1-x)\frac{d^2y}{dx^2} + (5-7x)\frac{dy}{dx} - 3y = 0.$$

Sol. Comparing the given equation with

$$\frac{d^2y}{dx^2} + P(x)\frac{dy}{dx} + Q(x)y = 0, \text{ we get}$$

$$P(x) = \frac{5-7x}{2x(1-x)},\ Q(x) = \frac{-3}{2x(1-x)}$$

At $x = 0$, Both P(x) and Q(x) are not analytic, hence $x = 0$ is a *singular point.*

Now, $$x\,P(x) = \frac{5-7x}{2(1-x)}$$

$$x^2\,Q(x) = \frac{-3x}{2(1-x)}$$

At $x = 0$, both x P(x) and x^2 Q(x) are analytic, hence $x = 0$ is a *regular singular* point.

Let us assume

$$y = a_0 x^m + a_1 x^{m+1} + a_2 x^{m+2} + a_3 x^{m+3} + \ldots \quad \ldots(1)$$

Then, $$y' = ma_0 x^{m-1} + (m+1)\,a_1 x^m + (m+2)\,a_2 x^{m+1} + (m+3)\,a_3 x^{m+2} + \ldots$$

and $$y'' = m(m-1)\,a_0 x^{m-2} + (m+1)\,m\,a_1 x^{m-1} + (m+2)(m+1)\,a_2 x^m + (m+3)(m+2)\,a_3 x^{m+1} + \ldots..$$

Substituting these values in given equation, we get

$$2x(1-x)[m(m-1)\,a_0 x^{m-2} + (m+1)\,ma_1 x^{m-1} + (m+2)(m+1)\,a_2 x^m + (m+3)(m+2)\,a_3 x^{m+1} + \ldots]$$
$$+ (5-7x)[m\,a_0 x^{m-1} + (m+1)\,a_1 x^m + (m+2)\,a_2 x^{m+1} + (m+3)\,a_3 x^{m+2} + \ldots]$$
$$- 3[a_0 x^m + a_1 x^{m+1} + a_2 x^{m+2} + a_3 x^{m+3} + \ldots] = 0$$

Now, coefficient of lowest power of $x = 0$

$\Rightarrow$ Coefficient of $x^{m-1} = 0$

$\Rightarrow$ $2m(m-1)\,a_0 + 5m\,a_0 = 0$

$\Rightarrow$ $(2m^2 + 3m)\,a_0 = 0$

$\Rightarrow$ $2m^2 + 3m = 0$ $(\because\ a_0 \neq 0)$

This is called indicial equation

$$m(2m+3) = 0$$

$$\Rightarrow \quad \boxed{m = 0,\ -3/2}$$

Roots are distinct and do not differ by an integer.

Now, Coefficient of $x^m = 0$

$\Rightarrow$ $2(m+1)\,m\,a_1 - 2m(m-1)\,a_0 + 5(m+1)\,a_1 - 7ma_0 - 3a_0 = 0$

$\Rightarrow$ $(m+1)(2m+5)\,a_1 = (2m^2 - 2m + 7m + 3)\,a_0$

$$a_1 = \frac{(m+1)(2m+3)}{(m+1)(2m+5)}\,a_0$$

$$\Rightarrow \quad \boxed{a_1 = \frac{2m+3}{2m+5}\,a_0}$$

Coefficient of $x^{m+1} = 0$

$\Rightarrow$ $2(m+2)(m+1)\,a_2 - 2(m+1)\,m\,a_1 + 5(m+2)\,a_2 - 7(m+1)\,a_1 - 3a_1 = 0$

$\Rightarrow$ $(m+2)(2m+7)\,a_2 = (2m^2 + 2m + 7m + 7 + 3)\,a_1$

$$= (2m^2 + 9m + 10)\,a_1 = (2m+5)(m+2)\,a_1$$

$$\Rightarrow \quad a_2 = \frac{2m+5}{2m+7}\,a_1 = \frac{2m+5}{2m+7}\cdot\frac{2m+3}{2m+5}\,a_0$$

$\Rightarrow$ $$\boxed{a_2 = \frac{2m+3}{2m+7}\, a_0}$$

Similarly, $$a_3 = \frac{2m+7}{2m+9}\, a_2 = \frac{2m+7}{2m+9} \cdot \frac{2m+3}{2m+7}\, a_0$$

$\Rightarrow$ $$\boxed{a_3 = \frac{2m+3}{2m+9}\, a_0}$$

and so on.

Hence, from (1),

$$y = x^m \left[a_0 + \frac{2m+3}{2m+5}\, a_0\, x + \frac{2m+3}{2m+7}\, a_0\, x^2 + \frac{2m+3}{2m+9}\, a_0\, x^3 + \ldots \right]$$

$\Rightarrow$ $$y = a_0\, x^m \left[1 + \left(\frac{2m+3}{2m+5}\right) x + \left(\frac{2m+3}{2m+7}\right) x^2 + \left(\frac{2m+3}{2m+9}\right) x^3 + \ldots \right] \quad \ldots(2)$$

Now, $$y_1 = (y)_{m=0}$$

$$\boxed{y_1 = a_0 \left[1 + \frac{3}{5}\, x + \frac{3}{7}\, x^2 + \frac{3}{9}\, x^3 + \ldots \right]} \quad \ldots(3)$$

Also, $$y_2 = (y)_{m=-3/2} = a_0\, x^{-3/2}\, (1 + 0 \,.\, x + 0 \,.\, x^2 + 0 \,.\, x^3 + \ldots)$$

$$\boxed{y_2 = a_0\, x^{-3/2}} \quad \ldots(4)$$

Hence the complete solution is given by

$$y = c_1\, y_1 + c_2\, y_2 = c_1\, a_0 \left(1 + \frac{3}{5}\, x + \frac{3}{7}\, x^2 + \frac{3}{9}\, x^3 + \ldots \right) + c_2 a_0\, x^{-3/2}$$

$\Rightarrow$ $$y = \mathrm{A} \left(1 + \frac{3}{5}\, x + \frac{3}{7}\, x^2 + \frac{3}{9}\, x^3 + \ldots \right) + \mathrm{B}x^{-3/2}$$

where A and B are constants.

Example 2. *Solve in series the differential equation*

$$2x^2\, \frac{d^2y}{dx^2} + (2x^2 - x)\, \frac{dy}{dx} + y = 0.$$

Sol. Comparing the given equation with $\frac{d^2y}{dx^2} + \mathrm{P}(x)\, \frac{dy}{dx} + \mathrm{Q}(x)\, y = 0$, we get

$$\mathrm{P}(x) = \frac{2x^2 - x}{2x^2} = 1 - \frac{1}{2x} \quad \text{and} \quad \mathrm{Q}(x) = \frac{1}{2x^2}$$

At $x = 0$, Both P(x) and Q(x) are not analytic, hence $x = 0$ is a *singular point.*

Now, $$x\, \mathrm{P}(x) = x - \frac{1}{2} \quad \text{and} \quad x^2\, \mathrm{Q}(x) = \frac{1}{2}$$

Since both x P(x) and x^2 Q(x) are analytic at $x = 0$, hence $x = 0$ is a *regular singular point.*

Let us assume

$$y = a_0\, x^m + a_1\, x^{m+1} + a_2\, x^{m+2} + a_3\, x^{m+3} + \ldots \quad \ldots(1)$$

Then, $y' = m\,a_0\,x^{m-1} + (m+1)\,a_1\,x^m + (m+2)\,a_2\,x^{m+1} + (m+3)\,a_3\,x^{m+2} + \ldots$

and $y'' = m(m-1)\,a_0\,x^{m-2} + (m+1)\,m\,a_1\,x^{m-1} + (m+2)(m+1)\,a_2\,x^m + (m+3)(m+2)\,a_3\,x^{m+1} + \ldots$

Substituting these values in given equation, we get

$$2x^2\,[m(m-1)\,a_0\,x^{m-2} + (m+1)m\,a_1\,x^{m-1} + (m+2)(m+1)\,a_2x^m + (m+3)(m+2)\,a_3\,x^{m+1} + \ldots] + (2x^2 - x)\,[m\,a_0\,x^{m-1} + (m+1)\,a_1\,x^m + (m+2)\,a_2\,x^{m+1} + (m+3)\,a_3\,x^{m+2} + \ldots] + [a_0\,x^m + a_1\,x^{m+1} + a_2\,x^{m+2} + a_3\,x^{m+3} + \ldots] = 0$$

Now, coeff. of lowest power of $x = 0$ *i.e.,* coeff. of $x^m = 0$

$$2m\,(m-1)\,a_0 - m\,a_0 + a_0 = 0$$

$$\Rightarrow \quad (2m^2 - 3m + 1)\,a_0 = 0$$

$$\Rightarrow \quad (2m-1)\,(m-1) = 0 \text{ (since } a_0 \neq 0)$$

which is indicial equation.

Its roots are $\boxed{m = 1, \frac{1}{2}}$

Roots are distinct and donot differ by an integer.

Now, coeff. of $x^{m+1} = 0$

$$\Rightarrow \quad 2m\,(m+1)\,a_1 + 2m\,a_0 - (m+1)\,a_1 + a_1 = 0$$

$$\Rightarrow \quad (2m^2 + m)\,a_1 + 2m\,a_0 = 0$$

$$\Rightarrow \quad \boxed{a_1 = -\frac{2}{2m+1}a_0} \qquad | \because \; m \neq 0$$

Coefficient of $x^{m+2} = 0$

$$\Rightarrow \quad 2(m+2)\,(m+1)\,a_2 + 2(m+1)\,a_1 - (m+2)\,a_2 + a_2 = 0$$

$$\Rightarrow \quad (2m^2 + 5m + 3)\,a_2 + 2(m+1)\,a_1 = 0$$

$$\Rightarrow \quad (2m+3)\,(m+1)\,a_2 + 2(m+1)\,a_1 = 0$$

$$\Rightarrow \quad a_2 = \frac{-2}{2m+3}a_1 = \frac{(-2)}{2m+3}\cdot\frac{(-2)}{2m+2}a_0$$

$$\Rightarrow \quad \boxed{a_2 = \frac{4}{(2m+1)(2m+3)}a_0}$$

Similarly, we can find

$$a_3 = \frac{-8}{(2m+1)(2m+3)(2m+5)}a_0$$

$$a_4 = \frac{16}{(2m+1)(2m+3)(2m+5)(2m+7)}a_0$$

and so on.

$$\therefore \quad y = a_0\,x^m\left[1 - \frac{2}{2m+1}x + \frac{4}{(2m+1)(2m+3)}x^2 - \frac{8}{(2m+1)(2m+3)(2m+5)}x^3 + \ldots\right] \quad \ldots(2)$$

Now, $y_1 = (y)_{m=1}$

$$y_1 = a_0\, x \left[1 - \frac{2}{3}x + \frac{4}{3.5}x^2 - \frac{8}{3.5.7}x^3 + \ldots\right]$$

or
$$y_1 = a_0\, x \left(1 - \frac{2}{3}x + \frac{2^2}{3.5}x^2 - \frac{2^3}{3.5.7}x^3 + \ldots\right) \quad \ldots(3)$$

and $y_2 = (y)_{m=1/2}$

$$y_2 = a_0\, x^{1/2} \left[1 - x + \frac{1}{2}x^2 - \frac{1}{6}x^3 + \ldots\right] \quad \ldots(4)$$

Hence the complete solution is

$$y = c_1 y_1 + c_2 y_2$$

$$= c_1 a_0\, x \left(1 - \frac{2}{3}x + \frac{2^2}{3.5}x^2 - \frac{2^3}{3.5.7}x^3 + \ldots\right) + c_2 a_0 \sqrt{x}\left(1 - x + \frac{1}{2}x^2 - \frac{1}{6}x^3 + \ldots\right)$$

$$\Rightarrow \quad y = \text{A}x \left(1 - \frac{2}{3}x + \frac{2^2}{3.5}x^2 - \frac{2^3}{3.5.7}x^3 + \ldots\right) + \text{B}\sqrt{x}\left(1 - x + \frac{1}{2}x^2 - \frac{1}{6}x^3 + \ldots\right)$$

where A and B are constants.

TEST YOUR KNOWLEDGE

Solve in series :

1. $9x(1 - x)\dfrac{d^2y}{dx^2} - 12\dfrac{dy}{dx} + 4y = 0$

2. $x(2 + x^2)\dfrac{d^2y}{dx^2} - \dfrac{dy}{dx} - 6xy = 0$

3. $3x\dfrac{d^2y}{dx^2} + 2\dfrac{dy}{dx} + y = 0$

4. $2x^2\dfrac{d^2y}{dx^2} - x\dfrac{dy}{dx} + (1 - x^2)\,y = 0$ [*G.B.T.U. (C.O.) 2011*]

5. $2x^2 y'' + xy' - (x + 1)\,y = 0$ (*G.B.T.U. 2011*)

6. $2x(1 - x)\dfrac{d^2y}{dx^2} + (1 - x)\dfrac{dy}{dx} + 3y = 0$ (*G.B.T.U. 2010*)

7. $2x^2\dfrac{d^2y}{dx^2} - x\dfrac{dy}{dx} + (x - 5)y = 0$

8. $y'' + \dfrac{1}{4x}y' + \dfrac{1}{8x^2}y = 0$

9. $2x^2\dfrac{d^2y}{dx^2} - x\dfrac{dy}{dx} + (x^2 + 1)\,y = 0$

10. $4x\dfrac{d^2y}{dx^2} + 2(1 - x)\dfrac{dy}{dx} - y = 0.$

Answers

1. $y = \text{A}\left(1 + \frac{1}{3}x + \frac{1.4}{3.6}x^2 + \frac{1.4.7}{3.6.9}x^3 + \ldots\right) + \text{B}x^{7/3}\left(1 + \frac{8}{10}x + \frac{8.11}{10.13}x^2 + \frac{8.11.14}{10.13.16}x^3 + \ldots\right)$

2. $y = A\left(1 + 3x^2 + \frac{3}{5}x^4 - \frac{1}{15}x^6 + \dots\right) + Bx^{3/2}\left(1 + \frac{3}{8}x^2 - \frac{3.1}{8.16}x^4 + \frac{5.3.1}{8.16.24}x^6 - \dots\right)$

3. $y = A\left(1 - \frac{x}{2} + \frac{x^2}{20} - \frac{x^3}{480} + \dots\right) + Bx^{1/3}\left(1 - \frac{x}{4} + \frac{x^2}{56} - \frac{x^3}{1680} + \dots\right)$

4. $y = Ax\left(1 + \frac{x^2}{2.5} + \frac{x^4}{2.4.5.9} + \dots\right) + Bx^{1/2}\left(1 + \frac{x^2}{2.3} + \frac{x^4}{2.4.3.7} + \dots\right)$

5. $y = Ax\left(1 + \frac{1}{5}x + \frac{1}{70}x^2 + \dots\right) + Bx^{-1/2}\left(1 - x - \frac{1}{2}x^2 + \dots\right)$

6. $y = A\left(1 - 3x + \frac{3x^2}{1.3} + \frac{3x^3}{3.5} + \frac{3x^4}{5.7} + \dots\right) + B\sqrt{x}\,(1 - x)$

7. $y = c_1x^{5/2}\left(1 - \frac{x}{9} + \frac{x^2}{198} - \frac{x^3}{7722} + \dots\right) + c_2x^{-1}\left(1 + \frac{x}{5} + \frac{x^2}{30} + \frac{x^3}{90} + \dots\right)$

8. $y = A\sqrt{x} + Bx^{1/4}$

9. $y = Ax\left(1 - \frac{x^2}{10} + \frac{x^4}{360} - \dots\right) + Bx^{1/2}\left(1 - \frac{x^2}{6} + \frac{x^4}{168} - \dots\right)$

10. $y = A\left(1 + \frac{x}{2.1!} + \frac{x^2}{2^2.2!} + \frac{x^3}{2^3.3!} + \dots\right) + B\sqrt{x}\left(1 + \frac{x}{1.3} + \frac{x^2}{1.3.5} + \frac{x^3}{1.3.5.7} + \dots\right).$

2.5.2. Case II. When Roots are Equal e.g., $m_1 = m_2 = 0$

Complete solution is

$$y = c_1\,(y)_{m_1} + c_2\left(\frac{\partial y}{\partial m}\right)_{m_1}$$

ILLUSTRATIVE EXAMPLES

Example 1. *Solve in series :*

$$x\,(x-1)\,\frac{d^2y}{dx^2} + (3x-1)\,\frac{dy}{dx} + y = 0.$$

Sol. Comparing the given equation with

$$\frac{d^2y}{dx^2} + P(x)\,\frac{dy}{dx} + Q(x)\,y = 0, \text{ we get}$$

$$P(x) = \frac{3x-1}{x(x-1)} \text{ and } Q(x) = \frac{1}{x(x-1)}$$

At $x = 0$, Both P(x) and Q(x) are not analytic, hence $x = 0$ is a *singular point.*

Now, $\quad x\,P(x) = \frac{3x-1}{x-1}$ and $x^2\,Q(x) = \frac{x}{x-1}$

Both x P(x) and x^2 Q(x) are analytic at $x = 0$, hence $x = 0$ is a *regular singular point.*

Let us assume

$$y = a_0x^m + a_1x^{m+1} + a_2x^{m+2} + a_3x^{m+3} + \dots \qquad \dots(1)$$

Then, $\quad y' = m\,a_0\,x^{m-1} + (m+1)\,a_1\,x^m + (m+2)\,a_2\,x^{m+1} + (m+3)\,a_3\,x^{m+2} + \dots$

and $$y'' = m(m-1)a_0 x^{m-2} + (m+1)m a_1 x^{m-1} + (m+2)(m+1)a_2 x^m + (m+3)(m+2)a_3 x^{m+1} + \dots$$

Substituting these values in given equation, we get

$$x(x-1)[m(m-1)a_0 x^{m-2} + (m+1)m a_1 x^{m-1} + (m+2)(m+1)a_0 x^m + (m+3)(m+2)a_3 x^{m+1} + \dots]$$
$$+ (3x-1)[m a_0 x^{m-1} + (m+1)a_1 x^m + (m+2)a_2 x^{m+1} + (m+3)a_3 x^{m+2} + \dots]$$
$$+ [a_0 x^m + a_1 x^{m+1} + a_2 x^{m+2} + a_3 x^{m+3} + \dots] = 0$$

Now, coefficient of lowest power of $x = 0$

$\Rightarrow$ coefficient of $x^{m-1} = 0$

$\Rightarrow$ $-m(m-1)a_0 - m a_0 = 0 \Rightarrow -m^2 a_0 = 0$

$m^2 = 0$ $(\because a_0 \neq 0)$

which is *Indicial equation*

Its roots are $\boxed{m = 0, 0}$

Roots are equal.

Now, coefficient of $x^m = 0$

$\Rightarrow$ $m(m-1)a_0 - (m+1)m a_1 + 3m a_0 - (m+1)a_1 + a_0 = 0$

$\Rightarrow$ $(m+1)^2 a_0 - (m+1)^2 a_1 = 0$

$\Rightarrow$ $\boxed{a_1 = a_0}$ $(\because m \neq -1)$

Coefficient of $x^{m+1} = 0$

$\Rightarrow$ $(m+1)m a_1 - (m+2)(m+1)a_2 + 3(m+1)a_1 - (m+2)a_2 + a_1 = 0$

$\Rightarrow$ $(m+2)^2 a_1 - (m+2)^2 a_2 = 0$

$\Rightarrow$ $a_2 = a_1$ $(\because m \neq -2)$

$\Rightarrow$ $\boxed{a_2 = a_0}$

Similarly, we can show that

$a_3 = a_0$

$a_4 = a_0$ and so on.

$\therefore$ $y = a_0 x^m (1 + x + x^2 + x^3 + \dots)$ | From (1)

Now, $y_1 = (y)_{m=0} = a_0 x^0 (1 + x + x^2 + x^3 + \dots) = a_0 (1 + x + x^2 + x^3 + \dots)$

$$y_2 = \left(\frac{\partial y}{\partial m}\right)_{m=0} = [a_0 (1 + x + x^2 + x^3 + \dots) x^m \log x]_{m=0}$$
$$= a_0 \log x (1 + x + x^2 + x^3 + \dots)$$

Hence the complete solution is given by

$$y = c_1 y_1 + c_2 y_2 = c_1 a_0 (1 + x + x^2 + x^3 + \dots) + c_2 a_0 \log x (1 + x + x^2 + x^3 + \dots)$$
$$y = (A + B \log x)(1 + x + x^2 + x^3 + \dots)$$

where A and B are constants.

Example 2. *Solve in series the differential equation :*

$$x \frac{d^2y}{dx^2} + \frac{dy}{dx} - y = 0.$$

Sol. Comparing with the equation

$$\frac{d^2y}{dx^2} + P(x)\frac{dy}{dx} + Q(x)\,y = 0, \text{ we get}$$

$$P(x) = \frac{1}{x} \text{ and } Q(x) = -\frac{1}{x}$$

Since at $x = 0$, both $P(x)$ and $Q(x)$ are not analytic $\therefore$ $x = 0$ is a *singular point.*

Also, $x\,P(x) = 1$ and $x^2\,Q(x) = -x$

Both $x\,P(x)$ and $x^2\,Q(x)$ are analytic at $x = 0$ $\therefore$ $x = 0$ is a *regular singular point.*

Let us assume

$$y = a_0\,x^m + a_1\,x^{m+1} + a_2x^{m+2} + a_3\,x^{m+3} + \ldots \qquad \ldots(1)$$

Then, $y' = m\,a_0\,x^{m-1} + (m+1)\,a_1x^m + (m+2)\,a_2\,x^{m+1} + (m+3)\,a_3\,x^{m+2} + \ldots$

and $y'' = m(m-1)\,a_0\,x^{m-2} + (m+1)\,m\,a_1\,x^{m-1} + (m+2)\,(m+1)\,a_2\,x^m + (m+3)\,(m+2)\,a_3\,x^{m+1} + \ldots$

Substituting these values in the given equation, we get

$$x\,[m\,(m-1)\,a_0\,x^{m-2} + (m+1)m\,a_1\,x^{m-1} + (m+2)\,(m+1)\,a_2x^m + (m+3)\,(m+2)\,a_3\,x^{m+1} + \ldots]$$
$$+ [m\,a_0\,x^{m-1} + (m+1)\,a_1\,x^m + (m+2)\,a_2\,x^{m+1} + (m+3)\,a_3\,x^{m+2} + \ldots]$$
$$- [a_0\,x^m + a_1\,x^{m+1} + a_2\,x^{m+2} + a_3x^{m+3} + \ldots] = 0$$

Now, coefficient of $x^{m-1} = 0$

$\Rightarrow$ $m(m-1)\,a_0 + ma_0 = 0$

$\Rightarrow$ $m^2a_0 = 0 \;\Rightarrow\; m^2 = 0$ $(\because\; a_0 \neq 0)$

which is Indicial equation.

Its roots are $\boxed{m = 0, 0}$ *which are equal.*

Coefficient of $x^m = 0$

$\Rightarrow$ $(m+1)\,ma_1 + (m+1)a_1 - a_0 = 0 \;\Rightarrow\; (m+1)^2\,a_1 = a_0$

$$\Rightarrow \quad \boxed{a_1 = \frac{a_0}{(m+1)^2}}$$

Coefficient of $x^{m+1} = 0$

$\Rightarrow$ $(m+2)\,(m+1)\,a_2 + (m+2)\,a_2 - a_1 = 0 \;\Rightarrow\; (m+2)^2\,a_2 = a_1$

$$\Rightarrow \quad a_2 = \frac{a_1}{(m+2)^2} \;\Rightarrow\; \boxed{a_2 = \frac{a_0}{(m+1)^2\,(m+2)^2}}$$

Similarly, $a_3 = \dfrac{a_0}{(m+1)^2\,(m+2)^2\,(m+3)^2}$ and so on.

$$\therefore \text{ From (1), } y = a_0x^m\left[1 + \frac{x}{(m+1)^2} + \frac{x^2}{(m+1)^2\,(m+2)^2} + \frac{x^3}{(m+1)^2\,(m+2)^2\,(m+3)^2} + \ldots\right] \qquad \ldots(2)$$

Now, $$y_1 = (y)_{m=0} = a_0\left[1 + x + \frac{x^2}{(2\,!)^2} + \frac{x^3}{(3\,!)^2} + \ldots\right] \qquad \ldots(3)$$

To get the second independent solution, differentiate (1) partially w.r.t. m.

$$\frac{\partial y}{\partial m} = a_0 x^m \log x \left[1 + \frac{x}{(m+1)^2} + \frac{x^2}{(m+1)^2 (m+2)^2} + \frac{x^3}{(m+1)^2 (m+2)^2 (m+3)^2} + \ldots\right]$$

$$+ a_0 x^m \left[-\frac{2x}{(m+1)^3} - \frac{2}{(m+1)^2 (m+2)^2}\left\{\frac{1}{m+1} + \frac{1}{m+2}\right\} x^2\right.$$

$$\left. - \frac{2}{(m+1)^2 (m+2)^2 (m+3)^2}\left\{\frac{1}{m+1} + \frac{1}{m+2} + \frac{1}{m+3}\right\} x^3 - \ldots\right]$$

The second solution is $y_2 = \left(\frac{\partial y}{\partial m}\right)_{m=0} = a_0 \log x \left[1 + x + \frac{x^2}{(2!)^2} + \frac{x^3}{(3!)^2} + \ldots\right]$

$$- 2a_0 \left[x + \frac{1}{(2!)^2}\left(1 + \frac{1}{2}\right) x^2 + \frac{1}{(3!)^2}\left(1 + \frac{1}{2} + \frac{1}{3}\right) x^3 + \ldots\right]$$

$$= y_1 \log x - 2a_0 \left[x + \frac{1}{(2!)^2} + \left(1 + \frac{1}{2}\right) x^2 + \frac{1}{(3!)^2}\left(1 + \frac{1}{2} + \frac{1}{3}\right) x^3 + \ldots\right]$$

Hence the complete solution is

$$y = c_1 y_1 + c_2 y_2 = (c_1 a_0 + c_2 a_0 \log x)\left[1 + x + \frac{x^2}{(2!)^2} + \frac{x^3}{(3!)^2} + \ldots\right]$$

$$- 2c_2 a_0 \left[x + \frac{1}{(2!)^2}\left(1 + \frac{1}{2}\right) x^2 + \frac{1}{(3!)^2}\left(1 + \frac{1}{2} + \frac{1}{3}\right) x^3 + \ldots\right]$$

$$\Rightarrow \qquad y = (\text{A} + \text{B} \log x)\left[1 + x + \frac{x^2}{(2!)^2} + \frac{x^3}{(3!)^2} + \ldots\right]$$

$$- 2\text{B} \left[x + \frac{1}{(2!)^2}\left(1 + \frac{1}{2}\right) x^2 + \frac{1}{(3!)^2}\left(1 + \frac{1}{2} + \frac{1}{3}\right) x^3 + \ldots\right]$$

where $c_1 a_0 = \text{A}$, $c_2 a_0 = \text{B}$.

TEST YOUR KNOWLEDGE

Solve in series :

1. (*i*) $xy'' + (1 + x) y' + 2y = 0$ (*ii*) $x \frac{d^2y}{dx^2} + \frac{dy}{dx} - xy = 0$ (*M.T.U. 2012*)
2. $x^2 \frac{d^2y}{dx^2} + x(x-1) \frac{dy}{dx} + (1 - x) y = 0$ [*M.T.U. 2011 ; U.P.T.U. (SUM) 2008*]
3. $(x - x^2) \frac{d^2y}{dx^2} + (1 - 5x) \frac{dy}{dx} - 4y = 0$
4. $(x - x^2) y'' + (1 - x) y' - y = 0$
5. $x^2 y'' - x(1 + x) y' + y = 0$
6. $xy'' + y' + x^2 y = 0$ (*U.P.T.U. 2007*)
7. $xy'' + y' + xy = 0.$ (*Bessel's equation of order zero*)

Answers

1. (i) $y = A\left(1 - 2x + \frac{3}{2!}x^2 - \frac{4}{3!}x^3 + \ldots\right) + B\left[y_1 \log x + a_0\left(3x - \frac{13}{4}x^2 + \ldots\right)\right]$

(ii) $y = (A + B\log x)\left(1 + \frac{x^2}{2^2} + \frac{x^4}{2^2 . 4^2} + \ldots\right) - B\left(\frac{x^2}{2^2} + \frac{3x^4}{2 . 4^3} + \ldots\right)$

2. $y = Ax + B\left[x \log x - x + \frac{x^2}{4} - \ldots\right]$

3. $y = A(1^2 + 2^2x + 3^2x^2 + 4^2x^3 + \ldots) + B[y_1 \log x - 2a_0(1.2x + 2.3x^2 + 3.4x^3 + \ldots)]$

4. $y = A\left(1 + x + \frac{2}{4}x^2 + \frac{2.5}{4.9}x^3 + \ldots\right) + B\left[y_1 \log x + a_0\left(-2x - x^2 - \frac{14}{27}x^3 - \ldots\right)\right]$

5. $y = Ax\left(1 + x + \frac{1}{2}x^2 + \frac{1}{2.3}x^3 + \ldots\right) + B\left[y_1 \log x + a_0 x^2\left(-1 - \frac{3}{4}x + \ldots\right)\right]$

6. $y = A\left[1 - \frac{x^3}{3^2} + \frac{x^6}{3^4(2!)^2} - \frac{x^9}{3^6(3!)^2} + \ldots\right] + B\left[y_1 \log x + 2a_0\left\{\frac{x^3}{3^3} - \frac{1}{3^5(2!)^2}\left(1 + \frac{1}{2}\right)x^6 + \ldots\right\}\right]$

7. $y = A\left(1 - \frac{x^2}{2^2} + \frac{x^4}{2^2 . 4^2} - \frac{x^6}{2^2 . 4^2 . 6^2} + \ldots\right) + B\left[y_1 \log x + a_0\left\{\frac{x^2}{2^2} - \frac{1}{2^2 . 4^2}\left(1 + \frac{1}{2}\right)x^4\right.\right.$

$$\left.\left. + \frac{1}{2^2 . 4^2 . 6^2}\left(1 + \frac{1}{2} + \frac{1}{3}\right)x^6 - \ldots\right\}\right].$$

2.5.3. Case III. When Roots are Distinct, Differ by Integer and Making a Coefficient of y Infinite

Let m_1 and m_2 be the roots such that $m_1 > m_2$.

In this case, if some of the coefficients of y become infinite when $m = m_2$, we modify the form of y by replacing a_0 by $b_0(m - m_2)$.

Complete solution is

$$y = c_1 (y)_{m_1} + c_2 \left(\frac{\partial y}{\partial m}\right)_{m_2}.$$

Remark. We can also obtain two independent solutions by putting $m = m_2$ (value of m for which some coefficients of y become infinite) in modified form of y and $\frac{\partial y}{\partial m}$. The result of putting $m = m_1$ in y will give a numerical multiple of that obtained by putting $m = m_2$.

ILLUSTRATIVE EXAMPLES

Example 1. *Obtain the series solution of the Bessel's equation of order two*

$$x^2 \frac{d^2y}{dx^2} + x\frac{dy}{dx} + (x^2 - 4)y = 0 \quad \textit{near } x = 0.$$

Sol. Comparing the given equation with the form

$$\frac{d^2y}{dx^2} + P(x)\frac{dy}{dx} + Q(x)y = 0, \text{ we get}$$

$$P(x) = \frac{1}{x} \quad \text{and} \quad Q(x) = \frac{x^2 - 4}{x^2} = 1 - \frac{4}{x^2}$$

At $x = 0$, both P(x) and Q(x) are not analytic.

Therefore $x = 0$ is a *singular point.*

Also, $x\,P(x) = 1$ and $x^2\,Q(x) = x^2 - 4$

Both x P(x) and x^2 Q(x) are analytic at $x = 0$

$\therefore$ $x = 0$ is a *regular singular point.*

Let us assume,

$$y = a_0 x^m + a_1 x^{m+1} + a_2 x^{m+2} + a_3 x^{m+3} + \ldots \qquad \ldots(1)$$

Then, $$\frac{dy}{dx} = m\,a_0 x^{m-1} + (m+1)\,a_1 x^m + (m+2)\,a_2 x^{m+1} + (m+3)\,a_3 x^{m+2} + \ldots$$

and $$\frac{d^2y}{dx^2} = m(m-1)\,a_0\,x^{m-2} + (m+1)\,ma_1\,x^{m-1} + (m+2)(m+1)\,a_2\,x^m + (m+3)(m+2)\,a_3 x^{m+1} + \ldots$$

Substituting these values in the given equation, we get

$$x^2\,[m(m-1)\,a_0\,x^{m-2} + (m+1)\,ma_1\,x^{m-1} + (m+2)(m+1)\,a_2\,x^m + (m+3)(m+2)\,a_3\,x^{m+1} + \ldots]$$
$$+ x\,[m\,a_0\,x^{m-1} + (m+1)\,a_1\,x^m + (m+2)\,a_2\,x^{m+1} + (m+3)\,a_3\,x^{m+2} + \ldots]$$
$$+ (x^2 - 4)\,[a_0\,x^m + a_0\,x^{m+1} + a_2\,x^{m+2} + a_3\,x^{m+3} + \ldots] = 0$$

Now, coefficient of lowest power of $x = 0$

$\Rightarrow$ Coefficient of $x^m = 0$

$\Rightarrow$ $m(m-1)a_0 + m\,a_0 - 4a_0 = 0$ $\Rightarrow$ $(m^2 - 4)\,a_0 = 0$

$\Rightarrow$ $m^2 - 4 = 0$ *(Indicial equation)* | $\because$ $a_0 \neq 0$

$$\boxed{m = -2,\, 2}$$

Roots are distinct and differ by integer.

Now, coefficient of $x^{m+1} = 0$

$(m+1)m\,a_1 + (m+1)\,a_1 - 4a_1 = 0$

$\Rightarrow$ $(m^2 + 2m - 3)\,a_1 = 0$ $\Rightarrow$ $(m+3)(m-1)\,a_1 = 0$

$\Rightarrow$ $\boxed{a_1 = 0}$ | Since $m \neq 1$, and $m \neq -3$

Coefficient of $x^{m+2} = 0$

$\Rightarrow$ $(m+2)(m+1)\,a_2 + (m+2)\,a_2 + a_0 - 4a_2 = 0$

$\Rightarrow$ $(m^2 + 4m)\,a_2 + a_0 = 0$

$\Rightarrow$ $$\boxed{a_2 = \frac{-a_0}{m\,(m+4)}}$$

Coefficient of $x^{m+3} = 0$

$\Rightarrow$ $(m+3)(m+2)\,a_3 + (m+3)\,a_3 + a_1 - 4a_3 = 0$

$\Rightarrow$ $(m+1)(m+5)\,a_3 = -a_1$

$$\Rightarrow \qquad \boxed{a_3 = 0} \qquad \Big|\because\ a_1 = 0$$

Also, coefficient of $x^{m+4} = 0$

$$(m+2)(m+6)\,a_4 + a_2 = 0$$

$$\Rightarrow \qquad a_4 = \frac{-a_2}{(m+2)(m+6)} = \frac{a_0}{m(m+2)(m+4)(m+6)}$$

$$\therefore \qquad \boxed{a_4 = \frac{a_0}{m(m+2)(m+4)(m+6)}}$$

Similarly, $a_5 = a_7 = a_9 = \ldots = 0$

$$a_6 = \frac{-a_0}{m(m+2)(m+4)^2(m+6)(m+8)} \text{ etc.}$$

Substituting above obtained values in assumed y given by eqn. (1), we get

$$y = a_0x^m\left[1 - \frac{x^2}{m(m+4)} + \frac{x^4}{m(m+2)(m+4)(m+6)} - \frac{x^6}{m(m+2)(m+4)^2(m+6)(m+8)} + \ldots\right] \qquad \ldots(2)$$

Putting $m = 2$ (the greater of the two roots) in (2), the first solution is

$$y_1 = a_0x^2\left(1 - \frac{x^2}{2.6} + \frac{x^4}{2.4.6.8} - \frac{x^6}{2.4.6^2.8.10} + \ldots\right)$$

If we put $m = -2$ in (1), the coefficients become infinite due to the presence of the factor $(m+2)$ in the denominator. To overcome this difficulty, let $a_0 = b_0(m+2)$ so that

$$y = b_0x^m\left[(m+2) - \frac{(m+2)x^2}{m(m+4)} + \frac{x^4}{m(m+4)(m+6)} - \frac{x^6}{m(m+4)^2(m+6)(m+8)} + \ldots\right]$$

Differentiating partially w.r.t. m, we get

$$\frac{\partial y}{\partial m} = b_0x^m \log x\left[(m+2) - \frac{(m+2)x^2}{m(m+4)} + \frac{x^4}{m(m+4)(m+6)} - \ldots\right]$$

$$+ b_0x^m\left[1 - \frac{(m+2)}{m(m+4)}\left\{\frac{1}{m+2} - \frac{1}{m} - \frac{1}{m+4}\right\}x^2 + \frac{1}{m(m+4)(m+6)}\left\{-\frac{1}{m} - \frac{1}{m+4} - \frac{1}{m+6}\right\}x^4 \ldots\right]$$

The second solution is $y_2 = \left(\dfrac{\partial y}{\partial m}\right)_{m=-2}$

$$= b_0x^{-2}\log x\left[\frac{x^4}{(-2)(2)(4)} - \frac{x^6}{(-2)(2)^2(4)(6)} \ldots\right]$$

$$+ b_0x^{-2}\left[1 - \frac{x^2}{(-2)(2)} + \frac{1}{(-2)(2)(4)}\left(\frac{1}{2} - \frac{1}{2} - \frac{1}{4}\right)x^4 \ldots\right]$$

$$= b_0 x^2 \log x \left[-\frac{1}{2^2.4} + \frac{x^2}{2^3.4.6} \ldots \right] + b_0 x^{-2} \left[1 + \frac{x^2}{2^2} + \frac{x^4}{2^2.4^2} + \ldots \right]$$

Hence the complete solution is

$$y = c_1 y_1 + c_2 y_2$$

$$= \text{A}x^2 \left[\left(1 - \frac{x^2}{2.6} + \frac{x^4}{2.4.6.8} - \frac{x^6}{2.4.6^2.8.10} + \ldots \right) \right] + \text{B} \left[x^2 \log x \left(-\frac{1}{2^2.4} + \frac{x^2}{2^3.4.6} \ldots \right) + x^{-2} \left(1 + \frac{x^2}{2^2} + \frac{x^4}{2^2.4^2} + \ldots \right) \right]$$

where $\text{A} = c_1 a_0$, $\text{B} = c_2 b_0$.

Example 2. *Solve in series the differential equation* $x^2 \dfrac{d^2y}{dx^2} + 5x \dfrac{dy}{dx} + x^2 y = 0$.

Sol. Comparing the given equation with the form

$$\frac{d^2y}{dx^2} + \text{P}(x) \frac{dy}{dx} + \text{Q}(x)\, y = 0, \text{ we get}$$

$$\text{P}(x) = \frac{5}{x}, \quad \text{Q}(x) = 1$$

At $x = 0$, since $\text{P}(x)$ is not analytic $\therefore$ $x = 0$ is a *singular point.*

Also, $x\,\text{P}(x) = 5$

$x^2\,\text{Q}(x) = 0$

Since both $x\,\text{P}(x)$ and $x^2\,\text{Q}(x)$ are analytic at $x = 0$ $\therefore$ $x = 0$ is a *regular singular point.*

Let us assume

$$y = a_0 x^m + a_1 x^{m+1} + a_2 x^{m+2} + a_3 x^{m+3} + \ldots \quad \ldots(1)$$

$$\therefore \quad \frac{dy}{dx} = m\, a_0 x^{m-1} + (m+1)\, a_1 x^m + (m+2)\, a_2 x^{m+1} + \ldots \quad \ldots(2)$$

and

$$\frac{d^2y}{dx^2} = m(m-1)\, a_0 x^{m-2} + (m+1)\, m\, a_1 x^{m-1} + (m+2)(m+1)\, a_2 x^m + \ldots \quad \ldots(3)$$

Substituting the above values in given equation, we get

$$x^2 [m(m-1)\, a_0 x^{m-2} + (m+1)\, m a_1 x^{m-1} + (m+2)(m+1)\, a_2 x^m + \ldots]$$
$$+ 5x [m a_0 x^{m-1} + (m+1)\, a_1 x^m + (m+2)\, a_2 x^{m+1} + \ldots]$$
$$+ x^2 [a_0 x^m + a_1 x^{m+1} + a_2 x^{m+2} + \ldots] = 0 \quad \ldots(4)$$

Equating the coefficient of lowest power of x to zero, we get

$$m(m-1)\, a_0 + 5m a_0 = 0 \qquad [\text{Coeff. of } x^m = 0]$$

$$\Rightarrow \quad (m^2 + 4m)\, a_0 = 0$$

$$\Rightarrow \quad m(m+4) = 0 \qquad \text{(Indicial equation)} \qquad (\because \; a_0 \neq 0)$$

$$\Rightarrow \quad \boxed{m = 0, -4}$$

Hence *the roots are distinct and differing by an integer*. Equating to zero, the coefficients of successive powers of x, we get

$$\text{coefficient of } x^{m+1} = 0$$

$$(m + 1)\, m\, a_1 + 5(m + 1)\, a_1 = 0$$

$$\Rightarrow \quad (m + 5)(m + 1)a_1 = 0 \Rightarrow \boxed{a_1 = 0} \quad ...(5) \qquad | \because \; m \neq -5, -1$$

$$\text{coefficient of } x^{m+2} = 0$$

$$(m + 2)(m + 1)\, a_2 + 5(m + 2)a_2 + a_0 = 0$$

$$(m + 2)(m + 6)\, a_2 + a_0 = 0$$

$$\boxed{a_2 = \frac{-a_0}{(m+2)(m+6)}} \quad ...(6)$$

Again, $\quad$ coefficient of $x^{m+3} = 0$

$$(m + 3)(m + 2)\, a_3 + 5(m + 3)\, a_3 + a_1 = 0$$

$$(m + 3)(m + 7)\, a_3 + a_1 = 0$$

$$\Rightarrow \quad a_3 = \frac{-a_1}{(m+3)(m+7)}$$

$$\Rightarrow \quad \boxed{a_3 = 0} \quad ...(7)$$

Similarly, $\quad a_5 = a_7 = a_9 = ... = 0$

Now, $\quad$ coefficient of $x^{m+4} = 0$

$$(m + 4)(m + 3)\, a_4 + 5(m + 4)\, a_4 + a_2 = 0$$

$$\Rightarrow \quad (m + 4)(m + 8)\, a_4 = -a_2$$

$$a_4 = \frac{-a_2}{(m+4)(m+8)} = \frac{a_0}{(m+2)(m+4)(m+6)(m+8)} \text{ etc.} \quad ...(8)$$

These give $\quad y = a_0 x^m \left[1 - \dfrac{x^2}{(m+2)(m+6)} + \dfrac{x^4}{(m+2)(m+4)(m+6)(m+8)} - ...\right] \quad ...(9)$

Putting $\quad m = 0$ in (9), we get

$$y_1 = (y)_{m=0} = a_0 \left[1 - \frac{x^2}{2.6} + \frac{x^4}{2.4.6.8} - ...\right] \quad ...(10)$$

If we put $m = -4$ in the series given by eqn. (9), the coefficients become infinite. To avoid this difficulty, we put $a_0 = b_0\,(m + 4)$, so that

$$y = b_0\, x^m \left[(m+4) - \frac{(m+4)\, x^2}{(m+2)(m+6)} + \frac{x^4}{(m+2)(m+6)(m+8)} - ...\right] \quad ...(11)$$

Now, $\quad \dfrac{\partial y}{\partial m} = y \log x + b_0 x^m \left[1 + \dfrac{m^2 + 8m + 20}{(m^2 + 8m + 12)^2}\, x^2 - \dfrac{(3m^2 + 32m + 76)}{(m^3 + 16m^2 + 76m + 96)^2}\, x^4 + ...\right]$

Second solution is given by

$$y_2 = \left(\frac{\partial y}{\partial m}\right)_{m=-4} = (y)_{m=-4} \log x + b_0\, x^{-4} \left(1 + \frac{x^2}{4} - \frac{x^4}{4} + ...\right)$$

$$= b_0 x^{-4} \log x \left[0 - 0 + \frac{x^4}{(-2)(2)(4)} - \frac{x^6}{16} + ...\right] + b_0\, x^{-4} \left(1 + \frac{x^2}{4} - \frac{x^4}{4} + ...\right)$$

$$= b_0 x^{-4} \log x \left(\frac{-x^4}{16} - \frac{x^6}{16} - \dots \right) + b_0 x^{-4} \left(1 + \frac{x^2}{4} - \frac{x^4}{4} + \dots \right)$$

Hence the complete solution is given by

$y = c_1 y_1 + c_2 y_2$

$$= c_1 a_0 \left(1 - \frac{x^2}{12} + \frac{x^4}{384} - \dots \right) + c_2 b_0 x^{-4} \log x \left(-\frac{x^4}{16} - \frac{x^6}{16} - \dots \right) + c_2 b_0 x^{-4} \left(1 + \frac{x^2}{4} - \frac{x^4}{4} + \dots \right)$$

$$\therefore \; y = \text{A} \left(1 - \frac{x^2}{12} + \frac{x^4}{384} - \dots \right) + \text{B} x^{-4} \left(1 + \frac{x^2}{4} - \frac{x^4}{4} + \dots \right) - \text{B} \log x \left(\frac{1}{16} + \frac{x^2}{16} + \dots \right)$$

where $\text{A} = c_1 a_0$ and $\text{B} = c_2 b_0$.

TEST YOUR KNOWLEDGE

Solve in series :

1. $x(1-x)\dfrac{d^2y}{dx^2} - 3x\dfrac{dy}{dx} - y = 0$

2. $x^2 \dfrac{d^2y}{dx^2} + x\dfrac{dy}{dx} + (x^2 - 1)y = 0$ [*M.T.U. (SUM) 2011*]

(*Bessel's equation of order one*)

3. $(x + x^2 + x^3)\dfrac{d^2y}{dx^2} + 3x^2 \dfrac{dy}{dx} - 2y = 0$

4. $x(1-x)\dfrac{d^2y}{dx^2} - (1+3x)\dfrac{dy}{dx} + y = 0$.

Answers

1. $y = (\text{A} + \text{B} \log x)(x + 2x^2 + 3x^3 + 4x^4 + \dots) + \text{B}(1 + x + x^2 + x^3 + \dots)$

2. $y = \text{A}x \left(1 - \dfrac{x^2}{2.4} + \dfrac{x^4}{2.4^2.6} - \dots \right) + \text{B}x^{-1} \log x \left(-\dfrac{x^2}{2} + \dfrac{x^4}{2^2.4} - \dots \right) + \text{B}x^{-1} \left[1 + \dfrac{x^2}{2^2} - \dfrac{3}{2^2.2^3} x^4 + \dots \right]$

3. $y = \text{A}x \left[1 + x - \dfrac{1}{2}x^2 - \dfrac{1}{2}x^3 + \dots \right] + \text{B} \log x\,(2x + 2x^2 - x^3 + \dots) + \text{B}(1 - x - 5x^2 - x^3 + \dots)$

4. $y = (\text{A} + \text{B} \log x)(1.2\,x^2 + 2.3x^3 + 3.4x^4 + \dots) + \text{B}(-1 + x + 5x^2 + 11x^3 + \dots)$.

2.5.4. Case IV. When Roots are Distinct, Differ by Integer and Making One or More Coefficients Indeterminate

Let the roots be m_1 and m_2. If one of the coefficients (suppose a_1) become indeterminate when $m = m_2$, the *complete solution is given by putting $m = m_2$ in y* which then contains two arbitrary constants.

Note. The result contained by putting $m = m_1$ in y merely gives a numerical multiple of one of the series contained in the first solution. Hence we reject the solution obtained by putting $m = m_1$.

Example. *Solve in series the differential equation : $xy'' + 2y' + xy = 0$.*

Sol. Comparing the given equation with the form

$$\frac{d^2y}{dx^2} + \text{P}(x)\frac{dy}{dx} + \text{Q}(x)\,y = 0, \text{ we get}$$

$$P(x) = \frac{2}{x} \quad \text{and} \quad Q(x) = 1$$

At $x = 0$, P(x) is not analytic $\therefore$ $x = 0$ is a *singular point.*

Also, $x P(x) = 2$ and $x^2 Q(x) = x^2$

At $x = 0$, since x P(x) and x^2 Q(x) are analytic $\therefore$ $x = 0$ is a *regular singular point.*

Let us assume

$$y = a_0 x^m + a_1 x^{m+1} + a_2 x^{m+2} + a_3 x^{m+3} + \ldots \qquad \ldots(1)$$

Then, $$\frac{dy}{dx} = ma_0 x^{m+1} + (m+1) a_1 x^m + (m+2) a_2 x^{m+1} + (m+3) a_3 x^{m+2} + \ldots$$

and $$\frac{d^2y}{dx^2} = m(m-1) a_0 x^{m-2} + (m+1) m a_1 x^{m-1} + (m+2)(m+1) a_2 x^m + (m+3)(m+2) a_3 x^{m+1} + \ldots$$

Substituting these values in the given equation, we get

$$x [m(m-1) a_0 x^{m-2} + (m+1) m a_1 x^{m-1} + (m+2)(m+1) a_2 x^m + (m+3)(m+2) a_3 x^{m+1} + \ldots]$$
$$+ 2 [m a_0 x^{m-1} + (m+1) a_1 x^m + (m+2) a_2 x^{m+1} + \ldots]$$
$$+ x [a_0 x^m + a_1 x^{m+1} + a_2 x^{m+2} + a_3 x^{m+3} + \ldots] = 0$$

Now, coefficient of $x^{m-1} = 0$

$\Rightarrow$ $m(m-1) a_0 + 2m a_0 = 0$

$(m^2 + m) a_0 = 0$

$\Rightarrow$ $m^2 + m = 0$ (Indicial equation) $\quad | \because a_0 \neq 0$

$\Rightarrow$ $\boxed{m = 0, -1}$

Hence *roots are distinct and differ by an integer.*

coefficient of $x^m = 0$

$\Rightarrow$ $(m+1) m a_1 + 2(m+1) a_1 = 0$

$\Rightarrow$ $(m+1)(m+2) a_1 = 0$

$\Rightarrow$ $(m+1) a_1 = 0$ $\quad | \because m + 2 \neq 0$

Since $m + 1$ may be zero, hence a_1 *is arbitrary* (or takes the form $\frac{0}{0}$). In other words, a_1 becomes indeterminate.

Hence the solution will contain a_0 and a_1 as arbitrary constants. The complete solution will be given by putting $m = -1$ in y.

Now, coefficient of $x^{m+1} = 0$

$\Rightarrow$ $(m+2)(m+1) a_2 + 2(m+2) a_2 + a_0 = 0$

$\Rightarrow$ $(m+2)(m+3) a_2 + a_0 = 0$

$$\boxed{a_2 = \frac{-a_0}{(m+2)(m+3)}}$$

coefficient of $x^{m+2} = 0$

$\Rightarrow$ $(m+3)(m+2) a_3 + 2(m+3) a_3 + a_1 = 0$

$(m+3)(m+4) a_3 + a_4 = 0$

$$\boxed{a_3 = \frac{-a_1}{(m+3)(m+4)}}$$

coefficient of $x^{m+3} = 0$

$\Rightarrow$ $(m + 4)(m + 3) a_4 + 2(m + 4) a_4 + a_2 = 0$

$\Rightarrow$ $(m + 4)(m + 5) a_4 = - a_2$

$\Rightarrow$ $$a_4 = \frac{-a_2}{(m+4)(m+5)}$$

$\Rightarrow$ $$\boxed{a_4 = \frac{a_0}{(m+2)(m+3)(m+4)(m+5)}}$$

coefficient of $x^{m+4} = 0$

$(m + 5)(m + 4) a_5 + 2(m + 5) a_5 + a_3 = 0$

$(m + 5)(m + 6) a_5 = - a_3$

$$\boxed{a_5 = \frac{a_1}{(m+3)(m+4)(m+5)(m+6)}}$$

and so on.

Substituting these values in eqn. (1), we get

$$y = x^m \left[a_0 + a_1 x - \frac{a_0}{(m+2)(m+3)} x^2 - \frac{a_1}{(m+3)(m+4)} x^3 + \frac{a_0}{(m+2)(m+3)(m+4)(m+5)} x^4 + \frac{a_1}{(m+3)(m+4)(m+5)(m+6)} x^5 + \ldots \right]$$

$$y = x^m \left[a_0 \left\{ 1 - \frac{x^2}{(m+2)(m+3)} + \frac{x^4}{(m+2)(m+3)(m+4)(m+5)} - \ldots \right\} + a_1 \left\{ x - \frac{x^3}{(m+3)(m+4)} + \frac{x^5}{(m+3)(m+4)(m+5)(m+6)} - \ldots \right\} \right]$$

Now, $$(y)_{m=-1} = x^{-1} \left[a_0 \left(1 - \frac{x^2}{1.2} + \frac{x^4}{1.2.3.4} - \ldots \right) + a_1 \left(x - \frac{x^3}{2.3} + \frac{x^5}{2.3.4.5} - \ldots \right) \right]$$

$$= x^{-1} [a_0 \cos x + a_1 \sin x]$$

Hence complete solution is given by

$$y = (y)_{m=-1}$$

$\Rightarrow$ $$y = \frac{1}{x} (a_0 \cos x + a_1 \sin x).$$

Note. All those problems, in which $x = 0$ was an ordinary point of $y'' + P(x) y' + Q(x) y = 0$, can also be solved by Frobenius method as given in *Art. 2.5.4* and explained in above illustrative example.

TEST YOUR KNOWLEDGE

Solve in series :

1. $x^2 \frac{d^2y}{dx^2} + 4x \frac{dy}{dx} + (x^2 + 2) y = 0$

2. $(1 - x^2) \frac{d^2y}{dx^2} - x \frac{dy}{dx} + 4y = 0$ *(U.P.T.U. 2006)*

3. $(1 - x^2) \frac{d^2y}{dx^2} - 2x \frac{dy}{dx} + n(n + 1) y = 0.$

Answers

1. $y = x^{-2} (a_0 \cos x + a_1 \sin x)$

2. $y = a_0 (1 - 2x^2) + a_1 \left(x - \frac{x^3}{2} - \frac{x^5}{8} + \frac{x^7}{16} - \ldots \right)$

3. $y = a_0 \left[1 - \frac{n(n+1)}{2!} x^2 + \frac{(n-2)\, n(n+1)(n+3)}{4!} x^4 - \ldots \right]$

$$+ a_1 \left[x - \frac{(n-1)(n+2)}{3!} x^3 + \frac{(n-3)(n-1)(n+2)(n+4)}{5!} x^5 + \ldots \right].$$

2.6. LEGENDRE'S DIFFERENTIAL EQUATION

The differential equation $$(1 - x^2) \frac{d^2y}{dx^2} - 2x \frac{dy}{dx} + n(n + 1)y = 0 \quad \ldots(1)$$
where n is real number, is called Legendre's differential equation. This equation is of considerable importance in applied mathematics, particularly in boundary value problems involving spherical configurations.

Though n is a real number, in most physical applications, only integral values of n are required. Also, equation (1) can be solved in series of ascending or descending powers of x. The solution in descending powers of x is more important than the one in ascending powers.

Let $$y = \sum_{k=0}^{\infty} a_k x^{m-k}$$

then $$\frac{dy}{dx} = \sum_{k=0}^{\infty} (m-k)\, a_k x^{m-k-1} \text{ and } \frac{d^2y}{dx^2} = \sum_{k=0}^{\infty} (m-k)(m-k-1)\, a_k x^{m-k-2}$$

Substituting for y, $\frac{dy}{dx}$ and $\frac{d^2y}{dx^2}$ in (1), we get

$$(1 - x^2) \sum_{k=0}^{\infty} (m-k)(m-k-1)\, a_k x^{m-k-2} - 2x \sum_{k=0}^{\infty} (m-k) a_k x^{m-k-1} + n(n+1) \sum_{k=0}^{\infty} a_k x^{m-k} = 0$$

or $$\sum_{k=0}^{\infty} (m-k)(m-k-1)\, a_k x^{m-k-2} - \sum_{k=0}^{\infty} [(m-k)(m-k-1) + 2(m-k) - n(n+1)]\, a_k x^{m-k} = 0$$

or $$\sum_{k=0}^{\infty} (m-k)(m-k-1)\, a_k x^{m-k-2} - \sum_{k=0}^{\infty} (m-k)^2 - n^2 + (m-k) - n]\, a_k x^{m-k} = 0$$

or $$\sum_{k=0}^{\infty} (m-k)(m-k-1)\, a_k\, x^{m-k-2} - \sum_{k=0}^{\infty} [(m-k-n)(m-k+n+1)\, a_k\, x^{m-k} = 0.$$

Equating to zero the coefficient of highest power of x, *i.e.*, x^m, we get the indicial equation

$$(m-n)(m+n+1)\, a_0 = 0$$

whence $m = n$ or $m = -(n+1)$ since $a_0 \neq 0$

Equating to zero the coefficient of the next lower power of x, *i.e.*, x^{m-1}, we get

$$(m+n)(m-n-1)\, a_1 = 0 \text{ or } a_1 = 0,$$

since $(m+n)$ and $(m-n-1)$ are not zero for $m = n$ or $-(n+1)$.

Equating to zero the coefficient of x^{m-k}, we get the recurrence relation

$$[m-(k-2)]\,[m-(k-2)-1]\, a_{k-2} - (m-k-n)(m-k+n+1)\, a_k = 0$$

or $$\boxed{a_k = -\frac{(m-k+2)(m-k+1)}{(n-m+k)(n+m-k+1)}\, a_{k-2}} \qquad ...(2)$$

Since $a_1 = 0$, therefore, from (2), we get $a_3 = a_5 = a_7 = \ldots\ldots = 0$.

Case I. When $m = n$, the recurrence relation (2) reduces to

$$a_k = -\frac{(n-k+2)(n-k+1)}{k(2n-k+1)}\, a_{k-2}$$

Putting $k = 2, 4, 6, \ldots\ldots$, we get $a_2 = -\dfrac{n(n-1)}{2(2n-1)} a_0$,

$$a_4 = -\frac{(n-2)(n-3)}{4(2n-3)}\, a_2 = \frac{n(n-1)(n-2)(n-3)}{2.4.(2n-1)(2n-3)}\, a_0, \text{ etc.}$$

Therefore, one solution of Legendre's equation is given by

$$y_1 = a_0 \left[x^n - \frac{n(n-1)}{2(2n-1)} x^{n-2} + \frac{n(n-1)(n-2)(n-3)}{2.4.(2n-1)(2n-3)} x^{n-4} - \ldots \right] \qquad ...(3)$$

Case II. When $m = -(n+1)$, the recurrence relation (2) reduces to

$$a_k = \frac{(n+k-1)(n+k)}{k(2n+k+1)}\, a_{k-2}$$

Putting $k = 2, 4, 6, \ldots\ldots$, we get

$$a_2 = \frac{(n+1)(n+2)}{2(2n+3)} a_0,$$

$$a_4 = \frac{(n+3)(n+4)}{4(2n+5)} a_2 = \frac{(n+1)(n+2)(n+3)(n+4)}{2.4.(2n+3)(2n+5)}\, a_0, \text{ etc.}$$

Therefore, the second solution of Legendre's equation is given by

$$y_2 = a_0 \left[x^{-n-1} + \frac{(n+1)(n+2)}{2(2n+3)} x^{-n-3} + \frac{(n+1)(n+2)(n+3)(n+4)}{2.4.(2n+3)(2n+5)} x^{-n-5} + \ldots \right] \qquad ...(4)$$

2.7. LEGENDRE'S FUNCTION OF FIRST KIND $P_n(x)$

When n is a positive integer and $a_0 = \dfrac{1.3.5 \ldots\ldots (2n-1)}{n!}$,

the first solution given by (3) is denoted by $P_n(x)$ and is called Legendre's function of first kind.

Thus,
$$P_n(x) = \frac{1.3.5 \ldots\ldots (2n-1)}{n!}\left[x^n - \frac{n(n-1)}{2(2n-1)}x^{n-2} + \frac{n(n-1).(n-2)(n-3)}{2.4.(2n-1)(2n-3)}x^{n-4} - \ldots\right]$$

$P_n(x)$ is a terminating series. R.H.S. is known as Zonal Harmonic. $P_n(x)$ gives Legendre's polynomials for different values of n such that $P_n(1) = 1$.

Now, two cases arise :

Case I. When *n* is even :

No. of terms in the series within bracket $= \dfrac{n}{2} + 1$

$$\text{Last term} = (-1)^{n/2} \cdot \frac{\{n(n-1)(n-2)(n-3) \ldots\ldots 2.1\}}{(2.4.6 \ldots n)\{(2n-1)(2n-3) \ldots (n+1)\}}.$$

Case II. When *n* is odd :

No. of terms in the series within bracket $= \dfrac{n+1}{2}$

$$\text{Last term} = (-1)^{\frac{n-1}{2}} \cdot \frac{n(n-1)(n-2)(n-3) \ldots 3.2}{\{2.4.6 \ldots (n-1)\}\{(2n-1)(2n-3) \ldots (n+2)\}}.$$

2.8. LEGENDRE'S FUNCTION OF SECOND KIND $Q_n(x)$

When n is a positive integer and $a_0 = \dfrac{n!}{1.3.5 \ldots (2n+1)}$,

the second solution is denoted by $Q_n(x)$ and is called Legendre's function of second kind.

Thus,
$$Q_n(x) = \frac{n!}{1.3.5 \ldots (2n+1)}\left[x^{-n-1} + \frac{(n+1)(n+2)}{2.(2n+3)}x^{-n-3} + \frac{(n+1)(n+2)(n+3)(n+4)}{2.4.(2n+3)(2n+5)}x^{-n-5} + \ldots\right]$$

It is a non-terminating series so there is no last term.

2.9. SOLUTION OF LEGENDRE'S EQUATION

Since $y = P_n(x)$ and $y = Q_n(x)$ both are the solutions of the given equation hence the most general solution is given by

$$\boxed{y = AP_n(x) + BQ_n(x)}$$

where A and B are arbitrary constants.

2.10. GENERATING FUNCTION FOR $P_n(x)$

We shall show that $P_n(x)$ is the coefficient of h^n in the expansion of $(1 - 2xh + h^2)^{-1/2}$ in ascending powers of h.

i.e.,
$$\boxed{(1 - 2xh + h^2)^{-1/2} = \sum_{n=0}^{\infty} P_n(x) \,.\, h^n}$$

Using Binomial theorem,

$$(1-t)^{-1/2} = 1 + \frac{1}{2}t + \frac{\frac{1}{2}\cdot\frac{3}{2}}{2!}t^2 + \frac{\frac{1}{2}\cdot\frac{3}{2}\cdot\frac{5}{2}}{3!}t^3 + \ldots$$

$$= 1 + \frac{1}{2}t + \frac{1.3}{2.4}t^2 + \frac{1.3.5}{2.4.6}t^3 + \ldots + \frac{1.3.5\ldots\ldots(2n-1)}{2.4.6\ldots\ldots 2n}t^n + \ldots$$

$$\therefore \quad (1 - 2xh + h^2)^{-1/2} = [1 - h(2x - h)]^{-1/2}$$

$$= 1 + \frac{1}{2}h(2x-h) + \frac{1.3}{2.4}h^2(2x-h)^2 + \ldots$$

$$+ \frac{1.3.5\ldots\ldots(2n-5)}{2.4.6\ldots\ldots(2n-4)}h^{n-2}(2x-h)^{n-2} + \frac{1.3.5\ldots\ldots(2n-3)}{2.4.6\ldots\ldots(2n-2)}h^{n-1}(2x-h)^{n-1}$$

$$+ \frac{1.3.5\ldots\ldots(2n-1)}{2.4.6\ldots\ldots(2n)}h^n(2x-h)^n + \ldots$$

Now, the coefficient of h^n in $\dfrac{1.3.5\ldots\ldots(2n-1)}{2.4.6\ldots\ldots(2n)}h^n(2x-h)^n$ is

$$= \frac{1.3.5\ldots\ldots(2n-1)}{2.4.6\ldots\ldots(2n)}(2x)^n = \frac{1.3.5\ldots\ldots(2n-1)}{2^n\,(n)!}(2x)^n = \frac{1.3.5\ldots\ldots(2n-1)}{n!}x^n$$

The coefficient of h^n in $\dfrac{1.3.5\ldots\ldots(2n-3)}{2.4.6\ldots\ldots(2n-2)}h^{n-1}(2x-h)^{n-1}$ is

$$= \frac{1.3.5\ldots\ldots(2n-3)}{2.4.6\ldots\ldots(2n-2)}[-\,{}^{n-1}C_1(2x)^{n-2}] = -\frac{1.3.5\ldots\ldots(2n-3)}{2.4.6\ldots\ldots(2n-2)}(n-1)\,2^{n-2}\,.\,x^{n-2}$$

$$= -\frac{1.3.5\ldots\ldots(2n-3)}{2^{n-1}(n-1)!}(n-1)\,2^{n-2}\,.\,x^{n-2}$$

$$= -\frac{1.3.5\ldots\ldots(2n-3)(2n-1)}{2\,(n)!}\cdot\frac{n(n-1)}{2n-1}x^{n-2}$$

$$= -\frac{1.3.5\ldots\ldots(2n-1)}{n!}\cdot\frac{n(n-1)}{2(2n-1)}x^{n-2}$$

Similarly, the coefficient of h^n in $\dfrac{1.3.5\ldots\ldots(2n-5)}{2.4.6\ldots\ldots(2n-4)}h^{n-2}(2x-h)^{n-2}$ is

$$= \frac{1.3.5\ldots\ldots(2n-1)}{n!}\cdot\frac{n(n-1)(n-2)(n-3)}{2.4.(2n-1)(2n-3)}x^{n-4} \text{ and so on.}$$

$\therefore$ The coefficient of h^n in $(1 - 2xh + h^2)^{-1/2}$ is given by

$$\frac{1.3.5\ldots\ldots(2n-1)}{n!}\left[x^n - \frac{n(n-1)}{2(2n-1)}x^{n-2} + \frac{n(n-1)(n-2)(n-3)}{2.4.(2n-1)(2n-3)}x^{n-4} - \ldots\right] = \mathrm{P}_n(x)$$

Thus, in the expansion of $(1 - 2xh + h^2)^{-1/2}$, $\mathrm{P}_1(x)$, $\mathrm{P}_2(x)$, $\mathrm{P}_3(x)$, ..., $\mathrm{P}_n(x)$, ... are the coefficients of $h, h^2, h^3, \ldots\ldots, h^n, \ldots..$ respectively.

$$\therefore \qquad (1 - 2xh + h^2)^{-1/2} = 1 + \mathrm{P}_1(x).h + \mathrm{P}_2(x).h^2 + \ldots + \mathrm{P}_n(x).h^n + \ldots = \sum_{n=0}^{\infty} \mathrm{P}_n(x).h^n$$

The function $(1 - 2xh + h^2)^{-1/2}$ is called the **generating function for $\mathbf{P}_n(x)$.**

ILLUSTRATIVE EXAMPLES

Example 1. *Show that*

(i) $P_n(1) = 1$ *(ii)* $P_n(-x) = (-1)^n P_n(x)$ *(iii)* $P'_n(-x) = (-1)^{n+1} P'_n(x)$.

(G.B.T.U. 2012)

Sol. We know that $\displaystyle\sum_{n=0}^{\infty} h^n \mathrm{P}_n(x) = (1 - 2xh + h^2)^{-1/2}$ ...(1)

(*i*) Putting $x = 1$ in eqn. (1), we get

$$\sum_{n=0}^{\infty} h^n \mathrm{P}_n(1) = (1 - 2h + h^2)^{-1/2} = (1-h)^{-1}$$

$$= 1 + h + h^2 + \ldots\ldots + h^n + \ldots\ldots = \sum_{n=0}^{\infty} h^n$$

Equating the coefficients of h^n, we have $\mathrm{P}_n(1) = 1$.

(*ii*) Replacing x by $(-x)$ in eqn. (1), we get

$$\sum_{n=0}^{\infty} h^n \mathrm{P}_n(-x) = (1 + 2xh + h^2)^{-1/2} \qquad \ldots(2)$$

Again, replacing h by $(-h)$ in eqn. (1), we have

$$\sum_{n=0}^{\infty} (-h)^n \mathrm{P}_n(x) = (1 + 2xh + h^2)^{-1/2}$$

or

$$\sum_{n=0}^{\infty} (-1)^n h^n \mathrm{P}_n(x) = (1 + 2xh + h^2)^{-1/2} \qquad \ldots(3)$$

From (2) and (3), $\displaystyle\sum_{n=0}^{\infty} h^n \mathrm{P}_n(-x) = \sum_{n=0}^{\infty} (-1)^n h^n \mathrm{P}_n(x)$

Equating the coefficients of h^n, we have

$$\mathrm{P}_n(-x) = (-1)^n \mathrm{P}_n(x).$$

(*iii*) We have, $\mathrm{P}_n(-x) = (-1)^n \mathrm{P}_n(x)$ | Proved in (*ii*)

Differentiating w.r.t. x, we get

$$-\mathrm{P}'_n(-x) = (-1)^n \mathrm{P}'_n(x)$$

$$\therefore \qquad \mathrm{P}'_n(-x) = (-1)^{n+1} \mathrm{P}'_n(x).$$

Example 2. *Show that*

(*i*) $P_{2n}(0) = (-1)^n \dfrac{2n!}{2^{2n}(n!)^2}$ [U.P.T.U. 2008 ; U.P.T.U. (C.O.) 2009]

(*ii*) $P_{2n+1}(0) = 0.$ [U.P.T.U. (C.O.) 2009]

Sol. We know that $\sum_{n=0}^{\infty} h^n P_n(x) = (1 - 2xh + h^2)^{-1/2}$

Putting $x = 0$, we get $\sum_{n=0}^{\infty} h^n P_n(0) = (1 + h^2)^{-1/2}$

$$= 1 - \frac{1}{2}h^2 + \frac{1.3}{2.4}h^4 - ...... + (-1)^r . \frac{1.3.5......(2r-1)}{2.4.6......(2r)} h^{2r} + ...$$

(*i*) Equating the coefficients of h^{2n} on both sides, we get

$$P_{2n}(0) = (-1)^n \frac{1.3.5......(2n-1)}{2.4.6......(2n)} = (-1)^n \frac{1.2.3.4......(2n-1)(2n)}{[2.4.6......(2n)]^2}$$

$$= (-1)^n \frac{(2n)!}{[2^n\ 1.2.3......n]^2} = (-1)^n \frac{(2n)!}{2^{2n}(n!)^2}.$$

(*ii*) Equating the coefficients of h^{2n+1} on both sides, we get $P_{2n+1}(0) = 0$, since the right-hand side contains only even power of h.

Example 3. *Prove that :*

(*i*) $\sum_{n=0}^{\infty} P_n(x) = \dfrac{1}{\sqrt{2-2x}}$ (M.T.U. 2012) (*ii*) $P_n(-1) = (-1)^n$.

Sol. We know that,

$$(1 - 2x\,h + h^2)^{-1/2} = \sum_{n=0}^{\infty} h^n P_n(x) \quad ...(1)$$

(*i*) Put $h = 1$ in (1), we get

$$(1 - 2x + 1)^{-1/2} = \sum_{n=0}^{\infty} P_n(x)$$

$$\Rightarrow \quad \frac{1}{\sqrt{2-2x}} = \sum_{n=0}^{\infty} P_n(x)$$

(*ii*) We have already proved in example 1 (*ii*) that

$$P_n(-x) = (-1)^n P_n(x)$$

Put $x = 1$ in above relation, we get

$$P_n(-1) = (-1)^n P_n(1) = (-1)^n \quad | \because \; P_n(1) = 1$$

Example 4. *Prove that :*

$$\frac{1 - z^2}{(1 - 2xz + z^2)^{3/2}} = \sum_{n=0}^{\infty} (2n+1) P_n z^n.$$

Sol. We know that

$$(1 - 2zx + z^2)^{-1/2} = \sum_{n=0}^{\infty} z^n P_n(x) \quad ...(1)$$

Differentiating (1) w.r.t. z, we get

$$-\frac{1}{2}(1-2zx+z^2)^{-3/2}.(2z-2x)=\sum_{n=0}^{\infty} nz^{n-1}\,P_n(x)$$

$$\Rightarrow \qquad (x-z)(1-2zx+z^2)^{-3/2}=\sum_{n=0}^{\infty} nz^{n-1}\,P_n(x) \qquad ...(2)$$

Multiplying both sides of eqn. (2) by $2z$, we get

$$2z(x-z)(1-2zx+z^2)^{-3/2}=\sum_{n=0}^{\infty} 2nz^{n}\,P_n(x) \qquad ...(3)$$

Adding (1) and (3), we get

$$(1-2zx+z^2)^{-3/2}(2zx-2z^2+1-2zx+z^2)=\sum_{n=0}^{\infty}(2n+1)z^n\,P_n(x)$$

$$\Rightarrow \qquad \frac{1-z^2}{(1-2zx+z^2)^{3/2}}=\sum_{n=0}^{\infty}(2n+1)z^n\,P_n(x).$$

Example 5. *Prove that :* $\dfrac{1+z}{z\sqrt{1-2xz+z^2}}-\dfrac{1}{z}=\displaystyle\sum_{n=0}^{\infty}(P_n+P_{n+1})\,z^n.$

Sol. R.H.S. $=\displaystyle\sum_{n=0}^{\infty} P_n z^n+\sum_{n=0}^{\infty} P_{n+1}z^n$

$$=\sum_{n=0}^{\infty} P_n z^n+\frac{1}{z}\sum_{n=0}^{\infty} P_{n+1}z^{n+1}$$

$$=\sum_{n=0}^{\infty} P_n z^n+\frac{1}{z}(P_1z+P_2z^2+P_3z^3+\ldots+P_nz^n+\ldots)$$

$$=\sum_{n=0}^{\infty} P_n z^n+\frac{1}{z}\{-P_0+P_0z^0+P_1z+P_2z^2+\ldots+P_nz^n+\ldots\} \qquad |\because\ P_0=1$$

$$=\sum_{n=0}^{\infty} P_n z^n-\frac{1}{z}+\frac{1}{z}\sum_{n=0}^{\infty} P_n z^n=\left(1+\frac{1}{z}\right)\sum_{n=0}^{\infty} P_n z^n-\frac{1}{z} \qquad ...(1)$$

$$\text{L.H.S.}=\frac{1+z}{z\sqrt{1-2xz+z^2}}-\frac{1}{z}=\left(1+\frac{1}{z}\right)(1-2xz+z^2)^{-1/2}-\frac{1}{z}$$

$$=\left(1+\frac{1}{z}\right)\sum_{n=0}^{\infty} z^n P_n-\frac{1}{z} \qquad ...(2)$$

Hence the proof. | Since L.H.S. = R.H.S.

Example 6. *Prove that :*

(i) $P_n'(1)=\dfrac{n(n+1)}{2}$ *(ii)* $P_n'(-1)=(-1)^{n-1}.\dfrac{n(n+1)}{2}$ *Or* $P_n'(-1)=(-1)^{n+1}.\dfrac{n(n+1)}{2}.$

Sol. Legendre's differential equation is

$$(1 - x^2) \frac{d^2y}{dx^2} - 2x \frac{dy}{dx} + n(n + 1) y = 0$$

$y = P_n(x)$ is a solution of it. So,

$$(1 - x^2) P_n''(x) - 2x P_n'(x) + n(n + 1) P_n(x) = 0 \quad \ldots(1)$$

(*i*) Put $x = 1$ in (1), $\quad -2P_n'(1) + n(n + 1) P_n(1) = 0$

$$\Rightarrow \quad P_n'(1) = \frac{n(n+1)}{2} \quad \mid \because \; P_n(1) = 1$$

(*ii*) Put $x = -1$ in (1),

$$2P_n'(-1) + n(n + 1) P_n(-1) = 0$$

$$\Rightarrow \quad 2P_n'(-1) + n(n + 1)(-1)^n = 0 \quad \mid \text{See Ex. 3 } (ii)$$

$$\Rightarrow \quad 2P_n'(-1) = -n(n + 1)(-1)^n$$

Case I. $2P_n'(-1) = (-1)^1 . n(n + 1)(-1)^n = (-1)^{n+1} . n(n + 1)$

$$\Rightarrow \quad P_n'(-1) = (-1)^{n+1} . \frac{n(n+1)}{2}.$$

Case II. $2P_n'(-1) = (-1)^{-1} . n(n + 1) . (-1)^n = (-1)^{n-1} . n(n + 1)$

$$\Rightarrow \quad P_n'(-1) = (-1)^{n-1} . \frac{n(n+1)}{2}$$

2.11. RODRIGUE'S FORMULA

[U.P.T.U. 2007 ; U.P.T.U. (C.O.) 2008 ; G.B.T.U. (C.O.) 2010]

The relation $\quad P_n(x) = \dfrac{1}{2^n n!} \dfrac{d^n}{dx^n} (x^2 - 1)^n$ is known as Rodrigue's formula.

To prove it, let $\quad v = (x^2 - 1)^n$ then $v_1 = \dfrac{dv}{dx} = n(x^2 - 1)^{n-1} . 2x$

Multiplying both sides by $(x^2 - 1)$, we get

$$(x^2 - 1)v_1 = 2nx (x^2 - 1)^n = 2nxv$$

or
$$(1 - x^2)v_1 + 2nxv = 0$$

Differentiating $(n + 1)$ times by Leibnitz's theorem, we have

$$\left[(1-x^2)v_{n+2} + (n+1)(-2x)v_{n+1} + \frac{(n+1)n}{2!}(-2)v_n\right] + 2n\,[xv_{n+1} + (n + 1) v_n] = 0$$

or
$$(1 - x^2)v_{n+2} - 2xv_{n+1} + n(n + 1)v_n = 0$$

or
$$(1 - x^2) \frac{d^2(v_n)}{dx^2} - 2x \frac{d(v_n)}{dx} + n(n + 1)v_n = 0$$

which is Legendre's equation and v_n is its solution. But the solutions of Legendre's equation are $P_n(x)$ and $Q_n(x)$.

Since $v_n = \dfrac{d^n}{dx^n}(x^2 - 1)^n$ contains only positive powers of x, it must be a constant multiple of $P_n(x)$.

i.e.,
$$v_n = cP_n(x)$$

or
$$cP_n(x) = \frac{d^n}{dx^n} (x^2 - 1)^n$$

$$= \frac{d^n}{dx^n} [(x-1)^n (x+1)^n] \qquad ...(1)$$

$$= (x-1)^n \frac{d^n}{dx^n} (x+1)^n + {}^nC_1 \,.\, n(x-1)^{n-1} \frac{d^{n-1}}{dx^{n-1}} (x+1)^n + ...$$

$$+ (x+1)^n \frac{d^n}{dx^n} (x-1)^n$$

$$= (x-1)^n \,.\, n\,! + {}^nC_1 \,.\, n(x-1)^{n-1} \,.\, \frac{d^{n-1}}{dx^{n-1}} (x+1)^n + ... + (x+1)^n \, n\,!$$

$$= n\,! \,(x+1)^n + \text{terms containing powers of } (x-1)$$

Putting $x = 1$ on both sides, we get

$$cP_n(1) = n\,! \,.\, 2^n \quad \text{or} \quad c = 2^n \, n\,!, \text{ since } P_n(1) = 1$$

Substituting in (1), we get

$$\boxed{P_n(x) = \frac{1}{2^n \, n!} \frac{d^n}{dx^n} (x^2-1)^n}$$

Putting $n = 0, 1, 2, 3, ...$ in Rodrigue's formula, we get Legendre's polynomials. Thus

$$P_0(x) = 1$$

$$P_1(x) = \frac{1}{2} \frac{d}{dx} (x^2-1) = x$$

$$P_2(x) = \frac{1}{2^2 (2)!} \frac{d^2}{dx^2} (x^2-1)^2 = \frac{1}{8} \frac{d^2}{dx^2} (x^4 - 2x^2 + 1) = \tfrac{1}{2} (3x^2 - 1)$$

$$P_3(x) = \frac{1}{2^3 (3)!} \frac{d^3}{dx^3} (x^2-1)^3 = \frac{1}{48} \frac{d^3}{dx^3} (x^6 - 3x^4 + 3x^2 - 1) = \tfrac{1}{2} (5x^3 - 3x)$$

Similarly, $P_4(x) = \dfrac{1}{8} (35x^4 - 30x^2 + 3)$

$$P_5(x) = \frac{1}{8} (63x^5 - 70x^3 + 15x)$$

$$P_6(x) = \frac{1}{6} (231x^6 - 351x^4 + 105x^2 - 5) \text{ etc.}$$

ILLUSTRATIVE EXAMPLES

Example 1. *Show that* $x^4 = \dfrac{1}{35} [8P_4(x) + 20P_2(x) + 7P_0(x)]$.

Sol. We know that $P_4(x) = \tfrac{1}{8} (35x^4 - 30x^2 + 3)$

$$P_2(x) = \tfrac{1}{2} (3x^2 - 1), \; P_0(x) = 1$$

$$\therefore \quad \frac{1}{35} [8P_4(x) + 20P_2(x) + 7P_0(x)] = \frac{1}{35} [35x^4 - 30x^2 + 3) + 10(3x^2 - 1) + 7] = x^4.$$

Example 2. *Express* $f(x) = x^3 - 5x^2 + x + 2$ *in terms of Legendre's polynomials.*

Sol. We know that $P_3(x) = \tfrac{1}{2}(5x^3 - 3x)$

$$\therefore \quad x^3 = \frac{2}{5} P_3(x) + \frac{3}{5} x$$

$$\therefore \quad f(x) = \left[\frac{2}{3} P_3(x) + \frac{3}{5}(x)\right] - 5x^2 + x + 2 = \frac{2}{5} P_3(x) - 5x^2 + \frac{8}{5}x + 2$$

$$= \frac{2}{5} P_3(x) - 5\left[\frac{2}{3} P_2(x) + \frac{1}{3}\right] + \frac{8}{5}x + 2 \qquad \left[\because \ P_2(x) = \tfrac{1}{2}(3x^2 - 1) \ \therefore \ x^2 = \tfrac{2}{3} P_2(x) + \tfrac{1}{3}\right]$$

$$= \frac{2}{5} P_3(x) - \frac{10}{3} P_2(x) + \frac{8}{5}x + \frac{1}{3}$$

$$= \frac{2}{5} P_3(x) - \frac{10}{3} P_2(x) + \frac{8}{5} P_1(x) + \frac{1}{3} P_0(x) \qquad [\because \ x = P_1(x) \text{ and } 1 = P_0(x)]$$

Example 3. *Prove that :*

$$\int_{-1}^{1} P_n(x)\, dx = \begin{matrix} 0, & n \neq 0 \\ 2, & n = 0 \end{matrix}\Bigg\}. \qquad \text{[U.P.T.U. (SUM) 2009]}$$

Sol. We know by Rodrigue's formula, $P_n(x) = \dfrac{1}{2^n\, n!} \dfrac{d^n}{dx^n}\{(x^2 - 1)^n\}$

Integrating, we get

$$\int_{-1}^{1} P_n(x)\, dx = \frac{1}{2^n\, n!} \int_{-1}^{1} \frac{d^n}{dx^n} (x^2 - 1)^n\, dx$$

$$= \frac{1}{2^n\, n!} \left[\frac{d^{n-1}}{dx^{n-1}} (x^2 - 1)^n\right]_{-1}^{1} = 0$$

when $n = 0$, $\displaystyle\int_{-1}^{1} P_0(x)\, dx = \int_{-1}^{1} 1\, dx = 2.$ $\qquad | \because \ P_0(x) = 1$

Example 4. *Express $4x^3 + 6x^2 + 7x + 2$ in terms of Legendre's polynomials.*

Sol. Let $\quad 4x^3 + 6x^2 + 7x + 2 \equiv \alpha P_3(x) + \beta P_2(x) + \gamma P_1(x) + \xi P_0(x) \qquad \ldots(1)$

$$\equiv \alpha\left(\frac{5x^3 - 3x}{2}\right) + \beta\left(\frac{3x^2 - 1}{2}\right) + \gamma(x) + \xi(1)$$

$$\equiv \frac{5\alpha}{2}x^3 + \frac{3\beta}{2}x^2 + \left(\gamma - \frac{3\alpha}{2}\right)x + \left(\xi - \frac{\beta}{2}\right)$$

Equating the coefficients of like powers of x, we get

$$\frac{5\alpha}{2} = 4 \quad \Rightarrow \quad \alpha = \frac{8}{5}$$

$$6 = \frac{3\beta}{2} \quad \Rightarrow \quad \beta = 4$$

$$7 = \gamma - \frac{3\alpha}{2} \quad \Rightarrow \quad 7 = \gamma - \frac{12}{5} \quad \Rightarrow \quad \gamma = \frac{47}{5}$$

$$2 = \xi - \frac{\beta}{2} \quad \Rightarrow \quad 2 = \xi - 2 \quad \Rightarrow \quad \xi = 4$$

Hence from (1),

$$4x^3 + 6x^2 + 7x + 2 = \frac{8}{5} P_3(x) + 4P_2(x) + \frac{47}{5} P_1(x) + 4P_0(x).$$

Example 5. *Prove that :*

$$P_n\left(-\frac{1}{2}\right) = P_0\left(-\frac{1}{2}\right) P_{2n}\left(\frac{1}{2}\right) + P_1\left(-\frac{1}{2}\right) P_{2n-1}\left(\frac{1}{2}\right) + \ldots + P_{2n}\left(-\frac{1}{2}\right) P_0\left(\frac{1}{2}\right).$$

Sol. We know that,

$$\sum_{n=0}^{\infty} h^n \mathrm{P}_n(x) = (1 - 2hx + h^2)^{-1/2} \qquad ...(1)$$

Put $x = \frac{1}{2}$ in (1),

$$\sum_{n=0}^{\infty} h^n \mathrm{P}_n\left(\frac{1}{2}\right) = (1 - h + h^2)^{-1/2} \qquad ...(2)$$

Put $x = -\frac{1}{2}$ in (1),

$$\sum_{n=0}^{\infty} h^n \mathrm{P}_n\left(-\frac{1}{2}\right) = (1 + h + h^2)^{-1/2} \qquad ...(3)$$

Replacing h by h^2 in (3), we get

$$\sum_{n=0}^{\infty} h^{2n} \mathrm{P}_n\left(-\frac{1}{2}\right) = (1 + h^2 + h^4)^{-1/2} = [(1 + h^2)^2 - h^2]^{-1/2}$$

$$= (1 + h^2 + h)^{-1/2}\,(1 + h^2 - h)^{-1/2}$$

$$= \sum_{n=0}^{\infty} h^n \mathrm{P}_n\left(-\frac{1}{2}\right) . \sum_{n=0}^{\infty} h^n \mathrm{P}_n\left(\frac{1}{2}\right) \qquad \text{| From (2) and (3)}$$

$$\Rightarrow \quad \sum_{n=0}^{\infty} h^{2n} \mathrm{P}_n\left(-\frac{1}{2}\right) = \left[\mathrm{P}_0\left(-\frac{1}{2}\right) + h\,\mathrm{P}_1\left(-\frac{1}{2}\right) + \ldots + h^{2n-1}\,\mathrm{P}_{2n-1}\left(-\frac{1}{2}\right) + h^{2n}\,\mathrm{P}_{2n}\left(-\frac{1}{2}\right) + \ldots\right]$$

$$\left[\mathrm{P}_0\left(\frac{1}{2}\right) + h\mathrm{P}_1\left(\frac{1}{2}\right) + \ldots\ldots + h^{2n-1}\,\mathrm{P}_{2n-1}\left(\frac{1}{2}\right) + h^{2n}\,\mathrm{P}_{2n}\left(\frac{1}{2}\right) + \ldots\right]$$

Equating the coefficients of h^{2n} from both sides of the above equation, we get the required result.

$$\mathrm{P}_n\left(-\frac{1}{2}\right) = \mathrm{P}_0\left(-\frac{1}{2}\right).\mathrm{P}_{2n}\left(\frac{1}{2}\right) + \mathrm{P}_1\left(-\frac{1}{2}\right)\mathrm{P}_{2n-1}\left(\frac{1}{2}\right) + \ldots\ldots + \mathrm{P}_{2n}\left(-\frac{1}{2}\right)\mathrm{P}_0\left(\frac{1}{2}\right).$$

Example 6. *Let $P_n(x)$ be the Legendre polynomial of degree n. Show that for any function f(x), for which the nth derivative is continuous*

$$\int_{-1}^{1} f(x)\, P_n(x)\, dx = \frac{(-1)^n}{2^n\, n!} \int_{-1}^{1} (x^2 - 1)^n f^{(n)}(x)\, dx. \qquad \text{[U.P.T.U. (SUM) 2008]}$$

Sol. $\int_{-1}^{1} f(x)\,\mathrm{P}_n(x)\, dx = \int_{-1}^{1} f(x) . \frac{1}{2^n\, n!} \frac{d^n}{dx^n} (x^2 - 1)^n\, dx$ | Using Rodrigue's formula

$$= \frac{1}{2^n\, n!} \int_{-1}^{1} f(x) . \frac{d^n}{dx^n} (x^2 - 1)^n\, dx$$

$$= \frac{1}{2^n\, n!} \left[\left\{f(x) \frac{d^{n-1}}{dx^{n-1}} (x^2 - 1)^n\right\}_{-1}^{1} - \int_{-1}^{1} f'(x) \frac{d^{n-1}}{dx^{n-1}} (x^2 - 1)^n\, dx\right]$$

| Integrating by parts

$$= \frac{1}{2^n n!}\left[0 - \int_{-1}^{1} f'(x) \frac{d^{n-1}}{dx^{n-1}}(x^2-1)^n \, dx\right]$$

$$= \frac{(-1)^1}{2^n n!}\int_{-1}^{1} f'(x) \frac{d^{n-1}}{dx^{n-1}}(x^2-1)^n \, dx$$

$$= \frac{(-1)^2}{2^n n!}\int_{-1}^{1} f''(x) \frac{d^{n-2}}{dx^{n-2}}(x^2-1)^n \, dx$$ | Integrating by parts again

$$= \frac{(-1)^n}{2^n n!}\int_{-1}^{1} f^{(n)}(x)\,(x^2-1)^n \, dx.$$ | Integrating by parts $(n-2)$ times

2.12. RECURRENCE RELATIONS

1. $$\boxed{n\,P_n(x) = (2n-1)\,x\,P_{n-1}(x) - (n-1)\,P_{n-2}(x)}$$

Or

$$(n+1)\,P_{n+1}(x) = (2n+1)\,x\,P_n(x) - n\,P_{n-1}(x)$$ *(U.P.T.U. 2007, M.T.U. 2012)*

We know that,

$$(1-2xh+h^2)^{-1/2} = \sum_{n=0}^{\infty} h^n P_n(x) \qquad ...(1)$$

Differentiating both sides w.r.t. h, we get

$$-\frac{1}{2}(1-2xh+h^2)^{-3/2}(2h-2x) = \sum_{0}^{\infty} n\,h^{n-1} P_n(x)$$

$$\Rightarrow \qquad (x-h)(1-2xh+h^2)^{-1/2} = (1-2xh+h^2)\sum_{0}^{\infty} n\,h^{n-1} P_n(x)$$

$$\Rightarrow \qquad (x-h)\sum_{0}^{\infty} h^n P_n(x) = (1-2xh+h^2)\sum_{0}^{\infty} n\,h^{n-1} P_n(x)$$

Equating coefficient of h^{n-1} on both sides,

$$x\,P_{n-1}(x) - P_{n-2}(x) = n\,P_n(x) - 2x(n-1)\,P_{n-1}(x) + (n-2)\,P_{n-2}(x)$$

$$\Rightarrow \qquad n\,P_n(x) = (2n-1)\,x\,P_{n-1}(x) - (n-1)\,P_{n-2}(x)$$

Replacing n by $(n+1)$, we get the other form.

2. $$\boxed{n\,P_n(x) = x\,P_n'(x) - P'_{n-1}(x)}$$

[U.P.T.U. 2006, 2009; G.B.T.U. (C.O.) 2011]

We know that, $$(1-2h\,x+h^2)^{-1/2} = \sum_{n=0}^{\infty} h^n P_n(x) \qquad ...(1)$$

Differentiating both sides of (1) w.r.t. h, we get

$$-\frac{1}{2}(1-2xh+h^2)^{-3/2}\,.\,(-2x+2h) = \sum_{0}^{\infty} n\,h^{n-1} P_n(x)$$

$$\Rightarrow \qquad (x-h)(1-2hx+h^2)^{-3/2} = \sum_0^{\infty} n h^{n-1} P_n(x) \qquad ...(2)$$

Differentiating both sides of (1) w.r.t. x, we get

$$-\frac{1}{2}(1-2hx+h^2)^{-3/2}.(-2h) = \sum_0^{\infty} h^n P_n'(x)$$

$$\Rightarrow \qquad (x-h)(1-2hx+h^2)^{-3/2} = (x-h)\sum_0^{\infty} h^{n-1} P_n'(x) \qquad ...(3)$$

Equating eqns. (2) and (3), we get

$$\sum_0^{\infty} n h^{n-1} P_n(x) = (x-h)\sum_0^{\infty} h^{n-1} P_n'(x)$$

Comparing the coefficient of h^{n-1} on both sides, we get

$$n P_n(x) = x P_n'(x) - P'_{n-1}(x)$$

3. $\boxed{(2n+1) P_n(x) = P'_{n+1}(x) - P'_{n-1}(x)}$

[U.P.T.U. (C.O.) 2009; U.P.T.U. (SUM) 2008]

From Recurrence relation (1),

$$(2n+1)\, x P_n(x) = (n+1) P_{n+1}(x) + n P_{n-1}(x)$$

Differentiating w.r.t. x, we get

$$(2n+1)[x P_n'(x) + P_n(x)] = (n+1) P'_{n+1}(x) + n P'_{n-1}(x) \qquad ...(1)$$

From Recurrence relation (2), $\quad x P_n'(x) = n P_n(x) + P'_{n-1}(x)$

From (1),

$$(2n+1)[n P_n(x) + P'_{n-1}(x) + P_n(x)] = (n+1) P'_{n+1}(x) + n P'_{n-1}(x)$$

$$\Rightarrow \qquad (2n+1)(n+1) P_n(x) = (n+1) P'_{n+1}(x) - (n+1) P'_{n-1}(x)$$

$$\Rightarrow \qquad (2n+1) P_n(x) = P'_{n+1}(x) - P'_{n-1}(x)$$

4. $\boxed{(n+1) P_n(x) = P'_{n+1}(x) - x P_n'(x)}$ *(G.B.T.U. 2010)*

From Recurrence relation (3), we have

$$(2n+1) P_n(x) = P'_{n+1}(x) - P'_{n-1}(x) \qquad ...(1)$$

From Recurrence relation (2), we have

$$n P_n(x) = x P_n'(x) - P'_{n-1}(x) \qquad ...(2)$$

Subtraction yields, $\quad (n+1) P_n(x) = P'_{n+1}(x) - x P'_n(x)$

5. $\boxed{(1-x^2) P'_n(x) = n[P_{n-1}(x) - xP_n(x)]}$ *(U.P.T.U. 2007)*

From Recurrence relation (4), we have

$$P_n'(x) - xP'_{n-1}(x) = nP_{n-1}(x) \qquad ...(1)$$

From Recurrence relation (2), we have

$$x P_n'(x) - P'_{n-1}(x) = n P_n(x) \qquad ...(2)$$

Multiplying (2) by x and subtracting from (1), we get

$$(1-x^2) P_n'(x) = n[P_{n-1}(x) - xP_n(x)]$$

6. $$(1 - x^2)\, P'_n(x) = (n + 1)\,[xP_n(x) - P_{n+1}(x)]$$

Recurrence relation (1) may be written as

$$(\overline{n + 1} + \overline{n})\, xP_n(x) = (n + 1)\, P_{n+1}(x) + nP_{n-1}(x)$$

$$\Rightarrow \quad (n + 1)\, xP_n(x) + nxP_n(x) = (n + 1)\, P_{n+1}(x) + nP_{n-1}(x)$$

or $$(n + 1)\,[xP_n(x) - P_{n+1}(x)] = n[P_{n-1}(x) - xP_n(x)]$$

$$= (1 - x^2)\, P_n'(x) \qquad | \text{ Using recurrence relation (5)}$$

$$\therefore \quad (1 - x^2)\, P_n'(x) = (n + 1)\,[xP_n(x) - P_{n+1}(x)].$$

2.13. BELTRAMI'S RESULT

$$\mathbf{(2n + 1)\,(x^2 - 1)\,P_n' = n(n + 1)\,(P_{n+1} - P_{n-1})}$$

From Recurrence relation (5), we have

$$n(P_{n-1} - xP_n) = (1 - x^2)\, P_n' \qquad \text{...(1)}$$

From Recurrence relation (6), we have

$$(n + 1)(xP_n - P_{n+1}) = (1 - x^2)\, P_n' \qquad \text{...(2)}$$

From eqn. (1), $$nP_{n-1} - nx\, P_n = (1 - x^2)\, P_n'$$

$$\Rightarrow \quad xP_n = \frac{nP_{n-1} - (1 - x^2)\, P_n'}{n} \qquad \text{...(3)}$$

From eqn. (2) $$xP_n - P_{n+1} = \frac{(1 - x^2)\, P_n'}{n + 1}$$

$$\Rightarrow \quad xP_n = P_{n+1} + \frac{(1 - x^2)\, P_n'}{n + 1} \qquad \text{...(4)}$$

From (3) and (4),

$$\frac{nP_{n-1} - (1 - x^2)P_n'}{n} = P_{n+1} + \frac{(1 - x^2)\, P_n'}{n + 1}$$

$$= \frac{(n + 1)\, P_{n+1} + (1 - x^2)P_n'}{n + 1}$$

$$\Rightarrow \quad (n + 1)\,\{nP_{n-1} - (1 - x^2)\, P_n'\} = n\{(n + 1)\, P_{n+1} + (1 - x^2)\, P_n'\}$$

$$\Rightarrow \quad (2n + 1)\,(1 - x^2)\, P_n' = n\,(n + 1)\,\{P_{n-1} - P_{n+1}\}$$

$$\Rightarrow \quad (2n + 1)\,(x^2 - 1)\, P_n' = n(n + 1)\,\{P_{n+1} - P_{n-1}\}.$$

2.14. ORTHOGONALITY OF LEGENDRE POLYNOMIALS

We shall show that

$$\int_{-1}^{1} P_m(x)\, P_n(x)\, dx = \begin{cases} 0 & , \quad \text{if } m \neq n \\ \dfrac{2}{2n + 1}, & \text{if } m = n \end{cases}$$

Case I. When $m \neq n$ [*U.P.T.U. 2008 ; U.P.T.U. (SUM) 2007*]

We know that $P_m(x)$ and $P_n(x)$ are the solutions of the equations

$$(1 - x^2)u'' - 2xu' + m(m + 1)u = 0 \quad ...(1)$$

and

$$(1 - x^2)v'' - 2xv' + n(n + 1)v = 0 \quad ...(2)$$

Multiplying (1) by v and (2) by u and subtracting, we get

$$(1 - x^2)(u''v - v''u) - 2x(u'v - v'u) + [m(m + 1) - n(n + 1)]\, uv = 0$$

or

$$\frac{d}{dx}[(1 - x^2)(u'v - v'u)] + (m - n)(m + n + 1)uv = 0$$

or

$$(n - m)(n + m + 1)\, uv = \frac{d}{dx}[(1 - x^2)(u'v - v'u)]$$

Integrating w.r.t. x from -1 to 1, we get

$$(n - m)(n + m + 1)\int_{-1}^{1} uv\, dx = \left[(1 - x^2)(u'v - v'u)\right]_{-1}^{1} = 0$$

Hence $\int_{-1}^{1} P_m(x)\, P_n(x)\, dx = 0$, since $m \neq n$.

Case II. When $m = n$ [*U.P.T.U. 2008 ; G.B.T.U. (C.O.) 2011*]

We know that $\quad (1 - 2xh + h^2)^{-1/2} = \sum_{n=0}^{\infty} h^n P_n(x)$

Squaring both sides, we get

$$(1 - 2xh + h^2)^{-1} = \sum_{n=0}^{\infty} [h^n P_n(x)]^2 = \sum_{n=0}^{\infty} h^{2n} [P_n(x)]^2 + 2\sum_{\substack{m=0 \\ (m \neq n)}}^{\infty} \sum_{n=0}^{\infty} h^{m+n} P_m(x)\, P_n(x)$$

Integrating w.r.t. x between the limits -1 to 1, we have

$$\sum_{n=0}^{\infty} \int_{-1}^{1} h^{2n} [P_n(x)]^2\, dx + 2\sum_{\substack{m=0 \\ (m \neq n)}}^{\infty} \sum_{n=0}^{\infty} \int_{-1}^{1} h^{m+n} P_m(x)\, P_n(x)\, dx = \int_{-1}^{1} \frac{dx}{1 - 2xh + h^2}$$

or

$$\sum_{n=0}^{\infty} \int_{-1}^{1} h^{2n} [P_n(x)]^2\, dx = \int_{-1}^{1} \frac{dx}{1 - 2xh + h^2}$$

| Since other integrals on the L.H.S. vanish by Case I as $m \neq n$

$$= -\frac{1}{2h}\left[\log(1 - 2xh + h^2)\right]_{-1}^{1} = -\frac{1}{2h}[\log(1 - h)^2 - \log(1 + h)^2]$$

$$= \frac{1}{h}[\log(1 + h) - \log(1 - h)] = \frac{1}{h}\left[\left(h - \frac{h^2}{2} + \frac{h^3}{3} - \frac{h^4}{4} + \ldots\right) + \left(h + \frac{h^2}{2} + \frac{h^3}{3} + \frac{h^4}{4} + \ldots\right)\right]$$

$$= \frac{2}{h}\left[h + \frac{h^3}{3} + \frac{h^5}{5} + \ldots\right]$$

or
$$\sum_{n=0}^{\infty} h^{2n} \int_{-1}^{1} [P_n(x)]^2 \, dx = 2\left(1+\frac{h^2}{3}+\frac{h^4}{5}+\ldots\ldots+\frac{h^{2n}}{2n+1}+\ldots\ldots\right)$$

Equating the coefficients of h^{2n} on the two sides, we get

$$\boxed{\int_{-1}^{1} [P_n(x)]^2 \, dx = \frac{2}{2n+1}.}$$

2.15. LAPLACE'S INTEGRAL OF FIRST KIND

$$\boxed{\mathbf{P}_n(x) = \frac{1}{\pi}\int_0^{\pi} \{x \pm \sqrt{x^2-1}\cos\phi\}^n \, d\phi.}$$

We know that,

$$\int_0^{\pi} \frac{d\phi}{a \pm b\cos\phi} = \frac{\pi}{\sqrt{a^2-b^2}}; \; a > b \qquad \ldots(1)$$

Replace a by $(1 - xz)$ and b by $z\sqrt{x^2-1}$

$\therefore$
$$a^2 - b^2 = (1 - xz)^2 - z^2(x^2 - 1) = 1 - 2xz + z^2$$

Then (1) becomes

$$\int_0^{\pi} \frac{d\phi}{1 - xz \pm z\sqrt{x^2-1}\cos\phi} = \frac{\pi}{\sqrt{1-2xz+z^2}}$$

$$\Rightarrow \quad \int_0^{\pi} \frac{d\phi}{1 - z\{x \mp \sqrt{x^2-1}\cos\phi\}} = \pi(1 - 2xz + z^2)^{-1/2}$$

Let $z\{x \mp \sqrt{x^2-1}\cos\phi\} = t$, then

$$\int_0^{\pi} \frac{d\phi}{1-t} = \pi \sum_{n=0}^{\infty} z^n P_n(x) \qquad \ldots(2)$$

If $|t| < 1$, then $\quad (1-t)^{-1} = \sum_{n=0}^{\infty} t^n$

$\therefore$ From (2), $\quad \int_0^{\pi} \sum_{n=0}^{\infty} [z^n \{x \mp \sqrt{x^2-1}\cos\phi\}^n] d\phi = \pi \sum_{n=0}^{\infty} z^n P_n(x)$

Equating the coefficient of z^n on both sides, we get

$$P_n(x) = \frac{1}{\pi}\int_0^{\pi} \{x \pm \sqrt{x^2-1}\cos\phi\}^n \, d\phi.$$

2.16. LAPLACE'S INTEGRAL OF SECOND KIND

$$\mathbf{P}_n(x) = \frac{1}{\pi}\int_0^{\pi} \frac{d\phi}{\{x \pm \sqrt{x^2-1}\cos\phi\}^{n+1}}.$$

We know that

$$\int_0^{\pi} \frac{d\phi}{a \pm b\cos\phi} = \frac{\pi}{\sqrt{a^2-b^2}} \; ; a > b \qquad ...(1)$$

Put $a = xz - 1$ and $b = z\sqrt{x^2-1}$ so that

$$a^2 - b^2 = (xz-1)^2 - z^2(x^2-1) = 1 - 2xz + z^2$$

With above substitutions, (1) becomes,

$$\int_0^{\pi} \frac{d\phi}{xz - 1 \pm z\sqrt{x^2-1}\cos\phi} = \frac{\pi}{\sqrt{1-2xz+z^2}}$$

$$= \frac{\pi}{z\sqrt{1-2\left(\frac{1}{z}\right)x+\left(\frac{1}{z}\right)^2}} = \frac{\pi}{z}\sum_{n=0}^{\infty}\frac{1}{z^n}\mathrm{P}_n(x)$$

$$\therefore \quad \int_0^{\pi} \frac{d\phi}{z\{x \pm \sqrt{x^2-1}\cos\phi\} - 1} = \frac{\pi}{z^{n+1}}\sum_{n=0}^{\infty}\mathrm{P}_n(x)$$

$$\Rightarrow \quad \int_0^{\pi}\frac{d\phi}{t-1} = \frac{\pi}{z^{n+1}}\sum_{n=0}^{\infty}\mathrm{P}_n(x) \qquad ...(2) \quad \text{where } t = z\,\{x \pm \sqrt{x^2-1}\cos\phi\}$$

Now,

$$\text{L.H.S.} = \int_0^{\pi}\frac{d\phi}{t\left(1-\frac{1}{t}\right)} = \int_0^{\pi}\frac{1}{t}\left(1-\frac{1}{t}\right)^{-1} d\phi$$

If $\left|\frac{1}{t}\right| < 1$, then

$$\text{L.H.S.} = \int_0^{\pi}\frac{1}{t}\left(1+\frac{1}{t}+\frac{1}{t^2}+\ldots\ldots+\frac{1}{t^n}+\ldots\ldots\right)d\phi = \int_0^{\pi}\sum_{n=0}^{\infty}\frac{1}{t^{n+1}}\,d\phi$$

$$= \int_0^{\pi}\sum_{n=0}^{\infty}\frac{1}{z^{n+1}\{x \pm \sqrt{x^2-1}\cos\phi\}^{n+1}}\,d\phi$$

Now, comparing and equating the coefficients of $\frac{1}{z^{n+1}}$ on both sides of eqn.(2), we get

$$\mathrm{P}_n(x) = \frac{1}{\pi}\int_0^{\pi}\frac{d\phi}{\{x \pm \sqrt{x^2-1}\cos\phi\}^{n+1}}.$$

2.17. CRISTOFFEL'S EXPANSION FORMULA

$$\mathbf{P_n'(x) = (2n - 1)\, P_{n-1}(x) + (2n - 5)\, P_{n-3}(x) + (2n - 9)\, P_{n-5}(x) + \ldots\ldots + \text{Last term.}}$$

where Last term = $\left\{\begin{matrix} \mathbf{3P_1}\,; & \textbf{when } \boldsymbol{n} \textbf{ is even} \\ \mathbf{P_0}\,; & \textbf{when } \boldsymbol{n} \textbf{ is odd} \end{matrix}\right\}$.

From Recurrence relation (3), we know that,

$$(2n + 1)\, P_n = P'_{n+1} - P'_{n-1}$$

$$\Rightarrow \qquad P'_{n+1} = (2n + 1)\, P_n + P'_{n-1} \qquad \ldots(1)$$

Replace n by $(n - 1)$, then

$$P_n' = (2n - 1)\, P_{n-1} + P'_{n-2} \qquad \ldots(2)$$

Now replace n by $(n - 2)$ in (2), we get

$$P'_{n-2} = (2n - 5)\, P_{n-3} + P'_{n-4} \qquad \ldots(3)$$

$$\therefore \quad \text{From (2),} \qquad P_n' = (2n - 1)\, P_{n-1} + (2n - 5)\, P_{n-3} + P'_{n-4}$$

Proceeding in this manner, for the last term, two cases arise :

Case I. When *n* is even :

$$P_2' = 3P_1 + P_0' = 3P_1 \qquad \left|\because P_0 = 1 \text{ and } P_0' = 0\right.$$

so, last term = $3P_1$

Case II. When *n* is odd :

$$P_3' = 5P_2 + P_1' \qquad \left|\because P_1 = x \;\therefore\; P_1' = 1 = P_0\right.$$

$$= 5P_2 + P_0$$

so, last term = P_0.

2.18. CRISTOFFEL'S SUMMATION FORMULA

The sum of first (*n* + 1) terms of the series

$$\sum_{m=0}^{\infty} (2m + 1)\, P_m(x)\, P_m(y) \text{ is } = \frac{(n + 1)\,[P_{n+1}(x)\, P_n(y) - P_n(x)\, P_{n+1}(y)]}{x - y}$$

By Recurrence relation (1),

$$(2m + 1)\, xP_m(x) = (m + 1)\, P_{m+1}(x) + mP_{m-1}(x) \qquad \ldots(1)$$

Similarly, $(2m + 1)\; yP_m(y) = (m + 1)\, P_{m+1}(y) + mP_{m-1}(y)$ ...(2)

Multiplying (1) by $P_m(y)$ and (2) by $P_m(x)$ and then subtracting (2) from (1), we get

$$(2m + 1)\,(x - y)\, P_m(x)\, P_m(y) = (m + 1)\, P_{m+1}(x)\, P_m(y) + mP_{m-1}(x)\, P_m(y)$$
$$- (m + 1)\, P_{m+1}(y)\, P_m(x) - mP_{m-1}(y)\, P_m(x)$$
$$= (m + 1)\,[P_{m+1}(x)\, P_m(y) - P_{m+1}(y)\, P_m(x)] - m\,[P_{m-1}(y)\, P_m(x) - P_{m-1}(x)\, P_m(y)]$$

Put 0, 1, 2, 3, ..., n for m in succession, we get

$$(x-y)\, P_0(x)\, P_0(y) = P_1(x)\, P_0(y) - P_1(y)\, P_0(x)$$

$$3(x-y)\, P_1(x)\, P_1(y) = 2\{P_2(x)\, P_1(y) - P_2(y)\, P_1(x)\} - \{P_0(y)\, P_1(x) - P_0(x)\, P_1(y)\}$$

$$5(x-y)\, P_2(x)\, P_2(y) = 3\,\{P_3(x)\, P_2(y) - P_3(y)\, P_2(x)\} - 2\{P_1(y)\, P_2(x) - P_1(x)\, P_2(y)\}$$

$$\vdots \qquad\qquad \vdots \qquad\qquad \vdots$$

$$\vdots \qquad\qquad \vdots \qquad\qquad \vdots$$

$$(2n+1)\,(x-y)\, P_n(x)\, P_n(y) = (n+1)\,[P_{n+1}(x)\, P_n(y) - P_{n+1}(y)\, P_n(x)] - n\,[P_{n-1}(y)\, P_n(x) - P_{n-1}(x)\, P_n(y)]$$

Adding simultaneously, we get

$$(x-y)\,[P_0(x)\, P_0(y) + 3P_1(x)\, P_1(y) + 5P_2(x)\, P_2(y) + \ldots\ldots + (2n+1)\, P_n(x)\, P_n(y)] = (n+1)\,[P_{n+1}(x)\, P_n(y) - P_{n+1}(y)\, P_n(x)]$$

$$\Rightarrow \qquad P_0(x)\, P_0\,(y) + 3P_1(x)\, P_1(y) + \ldots + (2n+1)\, P_n(x)\, P_n(y) = \left(\frac{n+1}{x-y}\right)\{P_{n+1}(x)\, P_n(y) - P_{n+1}(y)\, P_n(x)\}$$

$\therefore$ Sum of first n terms of the series

$$\sum_{m=0}^{\infty} (2m+1)\, P_m(x)\, P_m(y) = \frac{(n+1)\,\{P_{n+1}(x)\, P_n(y) - P_{n+1}(y)\, P_n(x)\}}{x-y}.$$

2.19. EXPANSION OF A FUNCTION IN A SERIES OF LEGENDRE POLYNOMIALS (FOURIER-LEGENDRE SERIES)

The orthogonal property of Legendre polynomials enables us to expand a function $f(x)$, defined from $x = -1$ to $x = 1$ in a series of Legendre polynomials.

Let
$$f(x) = \sum_{n=0}^{\infty} a_n\, P_n(x) = a_0 P_0\,(x) + a_1 P_1(x) + a_2 P_2(x) + \ldots \qquad \ldots(1)$$

To determine a_n, multiplying both sides of (1) by $P_n(x)$ and integrating w.r.t. x from -1 to 1, we have

$$\int_{-1}^{1} f(x)\, P_n(x)\, dx = a_n \int_{-1}^{1} P_n^{\,2}(x)\, dx = a_n \left(\frac{2}{2n+1}\right)$$

$$\Rightarrow \qquad \boxed{a_n = \left(n + \frac{1}{2}\right) \int_{-1}^{1} f(x)\, P_n(x)\, dx}$$

Expansion of $f(x)$ given by (1) is known as *Fourier-Legendre series.*

ILLUSTRATIVE EXAMPLES

Example 1. *Prove that :*

$$\int_{-1}^{1} (1-x^2)\, P'_m\, P'_n\, dx = 0$$

where m and n are distinct positive integers and $m \neq n$. (U.P.T.U. 2006)

Sol. $\int_{-1}^{1} (1-x^2)\, P_m{}'P_n{}'\, dx$

$$= \left[(1-x^2)\, P_m{}'\, P_n\right]_{-1}^{1} - \int_{-1}^{1} P_n \left[\frac{d}{dx}\{(1-x^2)\, P_m{}'\}\right] dx \qquad | \text{ Integrating by parts}$$

$$= -\int_{-1}^{1} P_n \frac{d}{dx}\{(1-x^2)\, P_m{}'\}\, dx$$

$$= -\int_{-1}^{1} P_n\{-m\,(m+1)\, P_m\}\, dx \qquad | \text{ From Legendre's differential equation}$$

$$= m(m+1)\int_{-1}^{1} P_n\, P_m\, dx = m(m+1)\,.\,0 = 0$$

Note. We can also prove that

$$\int_{-1}^{1} (1-x^2)\,(P_n{}')^2\, dx = n\,(n+1)\,.\,\frac{2}{2n+1}.$$

Above is same as Ex. 1 with $m = n$.

Example 2. *Prove that :*

$$\int_{-1}^{1} x^2\, P_{n-1}(x)\, P_{n+1}(x)\, dx = \frac{2n\,(n+1)}{(2n-1)(2n+1)(2n+3)}.$$

Sol. Recurrence relation (1) is

$$(n+1)\, P_{n+1} = (2n+1)\, xP_n - n\, P_{n-1}$$

$$\Rightarrow \qquad (2n+1)\, xP_n = (n+1)\, P_{n+1} + nP_{n-1} \qquad ...(1)$$

Replacing n by $n + 1$ and $n - 1$ respectively in (1), we get

$$(2n+3)\, xP_{n+1} = (n+2)\, P_{n+2} + (n+1)\, P_n \qquad ...(2)$$

and

$$(2n-1)\, xP_{n-1} = nP_n + (n-1)\, P_{n-2} \qquad ...(3)$$

Multiplying (2) and (3) and integrating within limits -1 and 1, we get

$$(2n+3)\,(2n-1)\int_{-1}^{1} x^2 P_{n+1}P_{n-1}\, dx = n\,(n+1)\int_{-1}^{1} P_n{}^2 dx$$

$$+\, n(n+2)\int_{-1}^{1} P_n\, P_{n+2} dx + (n^2-1)\int_{-1}^{1} P_{n-2}\, P_n\, dx + (n+2)\,(n-1)\int_{-1}^{1} P_{n-2}\, P_{n+2}\, dx$$

$$= n(n+1)\,.\,\frac{2}{2n+1} \qquad [\text{Using orthogonal properties}]$$

$$\therefore \quad \int_{-1}^{1} x^2\, P_{n+1}\, P_{n-1}\, dx = \frac{2n\,(n+1)}{(2n+1)(2n-1)(2n+3)}.$$

Example 3. *Prove that :*

$$\int_0^1 P_n^2(x)\,dx = \frac{1}{2n+1}.$$

Sol. We know that by orthogonal property, $\int_{-1}^{1} P_n^2(x)\,dx = \frac{2}{2n+1}$

$$\Rightarrow \qquad \int_{-1}^{0} P_n^2(x)\,dx + \int_0^1 P_n^2(x)\,dx = \frac{2}{2n+1}$$

Put $x = -y$ in first integral, then $dx = -dy$

$$-\int_1^0 P_n^2(-y)\,dy + \int_0^1 P_n^2(x)\,dx = \frac{2}{2n+1}$$

$$\Rightarrow \qquad \int_0^1 P_n^2(-x)\,dx + \int_0^1 P_n^2(x)\,dx = \frac{2}{2n+1}$$

$$\Rightarrow \qquad \int_0^1 (-1)^{2n} P_n^2(x)dx + \int_0^1 P_n^2(x)\,dx = \frac{2}{2n+1}$$

$$\Rightarrow \qquad 2\int_0^1 P_n^2(x)\,dx = \frac{2}{2n+1}$$

$$\Rightarrow \qquad \int_0^1 P_n^2(x)\,dx = \frac{1}{2n+1}.$$

Example 4. *Prove that :*

$$\int_{-1}^{1} P_n(x)(1-2xt+t^2)^{-1/2}\,dx = \frac{2t^n}{2n+1}$$

where n is a positive integer.

Sol. $\int_{-1}^{1} P_n(x)(1-2xt+t^2)^{-1/2}\,dx$

$$= \int_{-1}^{1} P_n(x)\{\Sigma\, t^n P_n(x)\}\,dx$$

$$= t^n \int_{-1}^{1} P_n^2(x)\,dx$$

| All other terms vanish since $\int_{-1}^{1} P_m(x)\,P_n(x)\,dx = 0\,;\, m \neq n$

$$= t^n \cdot \frac{2}{2n+1}.$$

| By II orthogonal property

Example 5. *Prove that :*

$$\int_{-1}^{1} x^m P_n(x)\,dx = 0, \text{ if } m < n.$$

Sol. $\int_{-1}^{1} x^m P_n(x)\,dx = \int_{-1}^{1} x^m \frac{1}{2^n n!}\frac{d^n}{dx^n}(x^2-1)^n\,dx$ (Using Rodrigue's Formula)

$$= \frac{1}{2^n n!}\int_{-1}^{1} x^m \frac{d^n}{dx^n}(x^2-1)^n\,dx$$

Integrating by parts, we get

$$= \frac{1}{2^n n!}\left[\left\{x^m \frac{d^{n-1}}{dx^{n-1}}(x^2-1)^n\right\}_{-1}^{1} - \int_{-1}^{1} mx^{m-1}\frac{d^{n-1}}{dx^{n-1}}(x^2-1)^n\, dx\right]$$

$$= 0 - \frac{m}{2^n n!}\int_{-1}^{1} x^{m-1}\frac{d^{n-1}}{dx^{n-1}}(x^2-1)^n\, dx$$

Similarly, $\int_{-1}^{1} x^m \mathrm{P}_n(x)\, dx = (-1)^2 \frac{m(m-1)}{2^n n!}\int_{-1}^{1} x^{m-2}\frac{d^{n-2}}{dx^{n-2}}(x^2-1)^n\, dx$

Integrating $(m-2)$ times in all, we get

$$\mathrm{I} = (-1)^m \frac{m(m-1)\ldots 1}{2^n n!}\int_{-1}^{1}\frac{d^{n-m}}{dx^{n-m}}(x^2-1)^n\, dx$$

$$= \frac{(-1)^m\, m!}{2^n\, n!}\int_{-1}^{1}\frac{d^{n-m}}{dx^{n-m}}(x^2-1)^n\, dx$$

$$= \frac{(-1)^m\, m!}{2^n\, n!}\left[\frac{d^{n-m-1}}{dx^{n-m-1}}(x^2-1)^n\right]_{-1}^{1} = 0.$$

Example 6. *Prove that :*

$$\frac{P_{n+1} - P_{n-1}}{2n+1} = \int P_n\, dx + c.$$

Sol. From Recurrence relation (3), we have

$$\mathrm{P}'_{n+1} - \mathrm{P}'_{n-1} = (2n+1)\,\mathrm{P}_n$$

Integrating both sides w.r.t. x, we get

$$\frac{\mathrm{P}_{n+1} - \mathrm{P}_{n-1}}{2n+1} = \int \mathrm{P}_n\, dx + c.$$

Example 7. *Prove that :*

$$xP'_n = nP_n + (2n-3)\,P_{n-2} + (2n-7)\,P_{n-4} + \ldots$$

Sol. From Recurrence relation (2),

$$x\mathrm{P}'_n = n\,\mathrm{P}_n + \mathrm{P}'_{n-1} \qquad \ldots(1)$$

From Recurrence relation (3),

$$\mathrm{P}'_{n+1} = (2n+1)\,\mathrm{P}_n + \mathrm{P}'_{n-1} \qquad \ldots(2)$$

Replacing n by $n-2$ in (2), we get

$$\mathrm{P}'_{n-1} = (2n-3)\,\mathrm{P}_n + \mathrm{P}'_{n-3} \qquad \ldots(3)$$

Replacing n by $n-4$ in (2), we get

$$\mathrm{P}'_{n-3} = (2n-7)\,\mathrm{P}_{n-4} + \mathrm{P}'_{n-5} \qquad \ldots(4)$$

$\therefore$ From (1), (3) and (4),

$$x\mathrm{P}'_n = n\mathrm{P}_n + (2n \quad 3)\,\mathrm{P}_n + (2n-7)\,\mathrm{P}_{n-4} + \ldots$$

Example 8. *Prove that :*

$$\int_{-1}^{1} xP_nP'_n\, dx = \frac{2n}{2n+1}.$$

Sol. $\int_{-1}^{1} P_n(xP_n')\,dx = \int_{-1}^{1} P_n[nP_n + (2n-3)P_{n-2} + (2n-7)P_{n-4} + \ldots]\,dx$

$$= \int_{-1}^{1} nP_n^2\,dx + (2n-3)\int_{-1}^{1} P_n P_{n-2}\,dx + (2n-7)\int_{-1}^{1} P_n P_{n-4}\,dx + \ldots$$

$$= n \cdot \frac{2}{2n+1} + 0 + 0 + \ldots \qquad | \text{ Using orthogonal property}$$

$$= \frac{2n}{2n+1}$$

Example 9. *Prove that :*

$$\int_{-1}^{1} (x^2 - 1) P_{n+1} P_n'\,dx = \frac{2n(n+1)}{(2n+1)(2n+3)}.$$

Sol. From Recurrence relation (5),

$$n(P_{n-1} - xP_n) = (1 - x^2) P_n'$$

$$\Rightarrow \quad (x^2 - 1) P_n' = n(xP_n - P_{n-1}) \qquad \ldots(1)$$

Now, $\int_{-1}^{1} (x^2 - 1) P_{n+1} P_n'\,dx = \int_{-1}^{1} \{(x^2 - 1)P_n'\} P_{n+1}\,dx$

$$= \int_{-1}^{1} n(xP_n - P_{n-1}) P_{n+1}\,dx = n\int_{-1}^{1} xP_n P_{n+1}\,dx - n\int_{-1}^{1} P_{n-1} P_{n+1}\,dx$$

$$= n\int_{-1}^{1} xP_n P_{n+1}\,dx \qquad \ldots(2) \qquad \Big|\ \because \int_{-1}^{1} P_{n-1} P_{n+1}\,dx = 0$$

From Recurrence relation (1),

$$(2n+1)\,xP_n = (n+1)\,P_{n+1} + nP_{n-1}$$

$$\Rightarrow \quad xP_n = \frac{(n+1)P_{n+1} + nP_{n-1}}{(2n+1)}$$

$\therefore$ From (2), $\int_{-1}^{1} (x^2 - 1)P_{n+1} P_n'\,dx = n\int_{-1}^{1} \left[\frac{(n+1)\,P_{n+1} + n\,P_{n-1}}{2n+1}\right] . P_{n+1}\,dx$

$$= \frac{n(n+1)}{2n+1}\int_{-1}^{1} P'_{n+1}\,dx + \frac{n^2}{2n+1}\int_{-1}^{1} P_{n-1} P_{n+1}\,dx$$

$$= \frac{n(n+1)}{(2n+1)} \cdot \frac{2}{2(n+1)+1} + 0 = \frac{2n(n+1)}{(2n+1)(2n+3)}.$$

Example 10. *Prove that :*

$$\sum_{n=0}^{\infty} \frac{x^{n+1}}{n+1} P_n(x) = \frac{1}{2} \log\left(\frac{1+x}{1-x}\right).$$

Sol. We know that

$$\sum_{n=0}^{\infty} h^n\, P_n(x) = (1 - 2xh + h^2)^{-1/2}$$

Integrating both sides w.r.t. h from 0 to h, we get

$$\sum_{n=0}^{\infty} \frac{h^{n+1}}{n+1} P_n(x) = \int_0^h \frac{dh}{\sqrt{1 - 2hx + h^2}} = \int_0^h \frac{dh}{\sqrt{(h-x)^2 + (1-x^2)}} \text{ ; if } |x| < 1$$

$$= \log \frac{(h-x) + \sqrt{h^2 - 2hx + 1}}{1-x}$$

Putting $h = x$ in the expression, we get

$$\sum_{n=0}^{\infty} \frac{x^{n+1}}{n+1} P_n(x) = \log\left(\frac{\sqrt{1-x^2}}{1-x}\right) = \frac{1}{2}\log\left(\frac{1+x}{1-x}\right).$$

Example 11. *If* $f(x) = \left.\begin{matrix} 0\ , & -1 < x < 0 \\ x\ , & 0 < x < 1 \end{matrix}\right\}$ *show that :*

$$f(x) = \frac{1}{4} P_0(x) + \frac{1}{2} P_1(x) + \frac{5}{16} P_2(x) - \frac{3}{32} P_4(x) + \ldots$$

Sol. We know that

$$f(x) = \sum_{n=0}^{\infty} a_n P_n(x) \qquad \ldots(1)$$

where $a_n = \left(n + \frac{1}{2}\right)\int_{-1}^{1} f(x) P_n(x)\, dx$

$$= \left(\frac{2n+1}{2}\right)\left[\int_{-1}^{0} f(x) P_n(x)\, dx + \int_0^1 f(x) P_n(x)\, dx\right]$$

$$= \left(\frac{2n+1}{2}\right)\int_0^1 f(x) P_n(x)\, dx \qquad \ldots(2)$$

Putting $n = 0, 1, 2, 3, 4, \ldots$ successively in (2), we get

$$a_0 = \frac{1}{2}\int_0^1 x P_0(x)\, dx = \frac{1}{2}\left(\frac{x^2}{2}\right)_0^1 = \frac{1}{4}$$

$$a_1 = \frac{3}{2}\int_0^1 x P_1(x)\, dx = \frac{3}{2}\left(\frac{x^3}{3}\right)_0^1 = \frac{1}{2}$$

$$a_2 = \frac{5}{2}\int_0^1 x P_2(x)\, dx = \frac{5}{2}\int_0^1 x\left(\frac{3x^2-1}{2}\right) dx = \frac{5}{16}$$

$$a_3 = \frac{7}{2}\int_0^1 x P_3(x)\, dx = \frac{7}{2}\int_0^1 x\left(\frac{5x^3-3x}{2}\right) dx = 0$$

$$a_4 = \frac{9}{2}\int_0^1 x P_4(x)\, dx = \frac{9}{2}\int_0^1 x\left(\frac{35x^4-30x^2+3}{8}\right) dx = \frac{-3}{32} \text{ and so on.}$$

Putting these values in (1), we get

$$f(x) = \frac{1}{4} P_0(x) + \frac{1}{2} P_1(x) + \frac{5}{16} P_2(x) - \frac{3}{32} P_4(x) + \ldots$$

Example 12. *Compute the first three non-vanishing terms in the Fourier-Legendre series over the interval (– 1, 1) of the function*

$$f(x) = \begin{cases} \dfrac{1}{2\varepsilon}, & |x| < \varepsilon \\ 0\ , & \varepsilon < |x| < 1 \end{cases}.$$

Sol. Let the Fourier-Legendre series be

$$f(x) = \sum_{n=0}^{\infty} a_n P_n(x) \qquad \text{...(1)}$$

where, $$a_n = \frac{2n+1}{2}\int_{-1}^{1} f(x)\, \mathrm{P}_n(x)\, dx = \frac{2n+1}{2}\int_{-\varepsilon}^{\varepsilon} f(x)\, \mathrm{P}_n(x)\, dx \qquad \text{...(2)}$$

Putting $n = 0, 1, 2, 3, \ldots$ successively in (2), we get

$$a_0 = \frac{1}{2}\int_{-\varepsilon}^{\varepsilon} \frac{1}{2\varepsilon}\mathrm{P}_0(x)\, dx = \frac{1}{4\varepsilon}(2\varepsilon) = \frac{1}{2} \qquad | \because \ \mathrm{P}_0(x) = 1$$

$$a_1 = \frac{3}{2}\int_{-\varepsilon}^{\varepsilon} \frac{1}{2\varepsilon}\mathrm{P}_1(x)\, dx = \frac{3}{4\varepsilon}\int_{-\varepsilon}^{\varepsilon} x\, dx = 0$$

Therefore $a_n = 0$ for all n odd.

Now, $$a_2 = \frac{5}{2}\int_{-\varepsilon}^{\varepsilon} \frac{1}{2\varepsilon}\mathrm{P}_2(x)\, dx = \frac{5}{4\varepsilon}\int_{-\varepsilon}^{\varepsilon}\left(\frac{3x^2-1}{2}\right) dx = \frac{5}{8\varepsilon}\left(x^3 - x\right)_{-\varepsilon}^{\varepsilon}$$

$\Rightarrow$ $$a_2 = \frac{5}{4\varepsilon}(\varepsilon^3 - \varepsilon) = \frac{5}{4}(\varepsilon^2 - 1)$$

Also, $$a_4 = \frac{9}{2}\int_{-\varepsilon}^{\varepsilon} \frac{1}{2\varepsilon}\mathrm{P}_4(x)\, dx$$

$$= \frac{9}{4\varepsilon}\int_{-\varepsilon}^{\varepsilon}\left(\frac{35x^4 - 30x^2 + 3}{8}\right) dx = \frac{9}{32\varepsilon}\left(7x^5 - 10x^3 + 3x\right)_{-\varepsilon}^{\varepsilon}$$

$\Rightarrow$ $$a_4 = \frac{9}{16}(7\varepsilon^5 - 10\varepsilon^2 + 3)$$

and so on ......

Hence the Fourier-Legendre series is

$$f(x) = \frac{1}{2}\mathrm{P}_0(x) + \frac{5}{4}(\varepsilon^2 - 1)\,\mathrm{P}_2(x) + \frac{9}{16}(7\varepsilon^5 - 10\varepsilon^2 + 3)\,\mathrm{P}_4(x) + \ldots\ldots .$$

Example 13. *Prove that :*

$$\sum_{r=0}^{n} (2r+1)\, P_r = P'_n + P'_{n+1}. \qquad \text{[M.T.U. (SUM) 2011]}$$

Sol. From Recurrence relation (3), we have

$$(2n + 1)\, \mathrm{P}_n = \mathrm{P}'_{n+1} - \mathrm{P}'_{n-1}$$

Putting $n = 1, 2, 3, ..., n$, we get

$$3P_1 = P_2' - P_0'$$
$$5P_2 = P_3' - P_1'$$
$$7P_3 = P_4' - P_2'$$
$$\vdots \qquad \vdots$$
$$(2n-1)\,P_{n-1} = P_n' - P'_{n-2}$$
$$(2n+1)\,P_n = P'_{n+1} - P'_{n-1}$$

Adding simultaneously, we get

$$3P_1 + 5P_2 + 7P_3 + ... + (2n+1)\,P_n = P'_{n+1} + P_n' - P_0' - P_1'$$
$$= P'_{n+1} + P_n' - 1 = P'_{n+1} + P_n' - P_0$$

$$\Rightarrow \quad P_0 + 3P_1 + 5P_2 + 7P_3 + ... + (2n+1)\,P_n = P'_{n+1} + P_n'$$

$$\Rightarrow \quad \sum_{r=0}^{n} (2r+1)\,P_r = P'_{n+1} + P_n'.$$

Example 14. *If $P_n(x)$ is a Legendre polynomial of degree n and α is such that $P_n(\alpha) = 0$. Show that $P_{n-1}(\alpha)$ and $P_{n+1}(\alpha)$ are of opposite signs.*

Sol. From Recurrence relation (1), we have

$$(2n+1)\,xP_n(x) = (n+1)\,P_{n+1}(x) + nP_{n-1}(x) \qquad ...(1)$$

Given that $P_n(\alpha) = 0$ ...(2)

$\therefore$ Put $x = \alpha$ in (1) and using (2), we get

$$(2n+1)\,\alpha\,.\,0 = (n+1)\,P_{n+1}(\alpha) + nP_{n-1}(\alpha)$$

$$\Rightarrow \quad \frac{P_{n+1}(\alpha)}{P_{n-1}(\alpha)} = -\frac{n}{n+1} \qquad ...(3)$$

Since n is a positive integer so R.H.S. of (3) is negative. Hence (3) shows that $P_{n+1}(\alpha)$ and $P_{n-1}(\alpha)$ are of opposite signs.

Example 15. *Show that all the roots of $P_n(x) = 0$ are real and lie between – 1 and 1.*

Sol. Let $$f(x) = (x^2-1)^n = (x-1)^n\,(x+1)^n \qquad ...(1)$$

From (1), we see that $f(x)$ vanishes for $x = 1$ and $x = -1$ hence by Rolle's theorem, $f'(x)$ must vanish at least once for some value α of x lying between – 1 and 1.

From (1), we have

$$f'(x) = n(x-1)^{n-1}\,(x+1)^n + n(x-1)^n\,(x+1)^{n-1}$$

which shows that $f'(x)$ vanishes at $x = 1$ and $x = -1$.

Again, we have already shown that $f'(x)$ vanishes at $x = \alpha$. Now applying Rolle's theorem to $f'(x)$ two times, we conclude that $f''(x)$ must vanish at $x = \beta$ between α and 1.

Proceeding in this manner, we conclude that $f^{(n)}(x) = 0$ must have n real roots lying between – 1 and 1.

By Rodrigue's formula and eqn. (1), we have

$$P_n(x) = \frac{1}{2^n\, n!} f^{(n)}(x)$$

Hence we see that $P_n(x) = 0$ must have n real roots lying between -1 and 1.

Example 16. *Prove that :*

$$\int_x^1 P_n(x)\, dx = (P_{n-1} - P_{n+1})/(2n+1).$$

Sol. From Recurrence relation (3), we have

$$(2n+1)\, P_n(x) = P'_{n+1}(x) - P'_{n+1}(x)$$

$$\Rightarrow \qquad P_n(x) = \frac{1}{2n+1} \frac{d}{dx} [P_{n+1}(x) - P_{n-1}(x)]$$

Integrating w.r.t. x between limits x to 1, we get

$$\int_x^1 P_n(x)\, dx = \frac{1}{2n+1} \Big[P_{n+1}(x) - P_{n-1}(x) \Big]_x^1$$

$$= \frac{1}{2n+1} [\{P_{n+1}(1) - P_{n-1}(1)\} - \{P_{n+1}(x) - P_{n-1}(x)\}]$$

$$= \frac{1}{2n+1} \{P_{n-1}(x) - P_{n+1}(x)\}. \qquad \left| \begin{array}{l} \because \;\; P_{n+1}(1) = 1 \\ \text{and } \; P_{n-1}(1) = 1 \end{array} \right.$$

Example 17. *Prove that :*

$$\int_{-1}^1 x^2 P_n^2\, dx = \frac{1}{8(2n-1)} + \frac{3}{4(2n+1)} + \frac{1}{8(2n+3)}. \qquad \text{(G.B.T.U. 2010)}$$

Sol. From Recurrence relation (1),

$$(2n+1) x P_n = (n+1)\, P_{n+1} + n P_{n-1}$$

Squaring both sides, we get

$$(2n+1)^2\, x^2 P_n^{\,2} = (n+1)^2\, P^2_{n+1} + n^2\, P^2_{n-1} + 2n(n+1)\, P_{n-1} P_{n+1}$$

Integrating w.r.t. x between limits -1 to 1, we get

$$(2n+1)^2 \int_{-1}^1 x^2\, P_n^{\,2}\, dx = (n+1)^2 \int_{-1}^1 P^2_{n+1}\, dx + n^2 \int_{-1}^1 P^2_{n-1}\, dx + 2n\,(n+1) \int_{-1}^1 P_{n-1} P_{n+1}\, dx$$

$$= (n+1)^2 \cdot \frac{2}{[2(n+1)+1]} + n^2 \cdot \frac{2}{[2(n-1)+1]} + 0$$

$$\Rightarrow \qquad \int_{-1}^1 x^2\, P_n^{\,2}\, dx = \frac{2}{(2n+1)^2} \left[\frac{(n+1)^2}{2n+3} + \frac{n^2}{2n-1} \right]$$

$$= \frac{1}{8(2n-1)} + \frac{3}{4(2n+1)} + \frac{1}{8(2n+3)}$$

(on resolving into partial fractions)

Example 18. *Show that :*

$$\int_{-1}^{1} xP_n(x)\, P_{n-1}(x)\, dx = \frac{2n}{4n^2 - 1}.$$ [G.B.T.U. (SUM) 2010]

Sol. Recurrence relation (1) is

$$nP_n = (2n - 1)\, x\, P_{n-1} - (n - 1)\, P_{n-2} \quad ...(1)$$

From (1), $$x\, P_{n-1} = \frac{1}{2n-1}\, [nP_n + (n-1)\, P_{n-2}]$$

Therefore, $$\int_{-1}^{1} xP_n(x)\, P_{n-1}(x)\, dx$$

$$= \frac{1}{2n-1}\int_{-1}^{1} [nP_n^{\ 2} + (n-1)\, P_n\, P_{n-2}]\, dx$$

$$= \frac{n}{2n-1}\left(\frac{2}{2n+1}\right)$$ | Using orthogonal property

$$= \frac{2n}{4n^2 - 1}.$$

Example 19. *Prove that :*

$$\int_{-1}^{1} [P_n'(x)]^2\, dx = n(n+1).$$

Sol. $$\int_{-1}^{1} [P_n'(x)]^2\, dx$$

$$= \int_{-1}^{1} [(2n-1)P_{n-1} + (2n-5)\, P_{n-3} + (2n-9)\, P_{n-5} + \ldots]^2\, dx$$ | By Cristoffel's expansion formula

$$= \int_{-1}^{1} (2n-1)^2\, P^2{}_{n-1}\, dx + \int_{-1}^{1} (2n-5)^2\, P^2{}_{n-3}\, dx + \int_{-1}^{1} (2n-9)^2\, P^2{}_{n-5}\, dx + \ldots$$

$$+ 2\int_{-1}^{1} (2n-1)(2n-5)\, P_{n-1} P_{n-3} dx + 2\int_{-1}^{1} (2n-1)(2n-9)\, P_{n-1} P_{n-5}\, dx + \ldots$$

$$= (2n-1)^2 \cdot \frac{2}{2(n-1)+1} + (2n-5)^2 \cdot \frac{2}{2(n-3)+1}$$

$$+ (2n-9)^2 \cdot \frac{2}{2(n-5)+1} + \ldots\ldots + 0 + 0 + 0 + \ldots$$

| By orthogonal properties

$$= (2n-1)^2 \cdot \frac{2}{2n-1} + (2n-5)^2 \cdot \frac{2}{2n-5} + (2n-9)^2 \cdot \frac{2}{2n-9} + \ldots$$

$$= 2\, [(2n-1) + (2n-5) + (2n-9) + \ldots + 1]$$

Here $l = a + (N - 1)d$

$$1 = (2n - 1) + (N - 1)(-4) \Rightarrow N = \frac{n+1}{2}$$

$\therefore$ No. of terms in above series $= \dfrac{n+1}{2}$

$$\therefore \quad S_{\frac{n+1}{2}} = 2 \cdot \frac{1}{2}\left(\frac{n+1}{2}\right)[(2n - 1) + 1] = n(n + 1) \qquad \Big| \because S_n = \frac{n}{2}(a + l)$$

Hence, $\int_{-1}^{1} [P_n'(x)]^2 \, dx = n(n + 1)$.

Example 20. *Prove that $(1 - 2xz + z^2)^{-1/2}$ is a solution of the equation*

$$z \frac{\partial^2}{\partial z^2}(z\text{v}) + \frac{\partial}{\partial x}\left[(1 - x^2)\frac{\partial \text{v}}{\partial x}\right] = 0.$$

Sol. We have, $\quad \text{v} = (1 - 2xz + z^2)^{-1/2} = \sum_{n=0}^{\infty} z^n P_n(x)$

or
$$z\text{v} = \sum_{n=0}^{\infty} z^{n+1} P_n(x)$$

$$\therefore \quad z \frac{\partial^2}{\partial z^2}(z\text{v}) = \sum_{n=0}^{\infty} (n + 1) n z^n P_n(x) \qquad \text{...(1)}$$

Also,
$$\frac{\partial \text{v}}{\partial x} = \sum_{n=0}^{\infty} z^n P_n'(x)$$

$$\therefore \quad \frac{\partial}{\partial x}\left\{(1 - x^2)\frac{\partial \text{v}}{\partial x}\right\} = \frac{\partial}{\partial x}\left[(1 - x^2)\sum_{n=0}^{\infty} z^n P_n'(x)\right]$$

$$= (1 - x^2)\sum_{n=0}^{\infty} z^n P_n''(x) - 2x \sum_{n=0}^{\infty} z^n P_n'(x) \qquad \text{...(2)}$$

Substituting in L.H.S. of the given equation, we have

$$\sum_{n=0}^{\infty} [(n + 1)n\, z^n P_n(x) + (1 - x^2) z^n P_n''(x) - 2xz^n P_n'(x)]$$

$$= \sum_{n=0}^{\infty} z^n [(1 - x^2) P_n''(x) - 2x P_n'(x) + n(n + 1) P_n(x)]$$

$= 0.$ $\quad | \because P_n(x)$ is a solution of Legendre's equation

TEST YOUR KNOWLEDGE

1. Show that :

(*i*) $x^2 = \frac{1}{3} P_0(x) + \frac{2}{3} P_2(x)$

(*ii*) $x^3 = \frac{2}{5} P_3(x) + \frac{3}{5} P_1(x)$

(*iii*) $x^5 = \frac{8}{63}\left[P_5(x) + \frac{7}{2} P_3(x) + \frac{27}{8} P_1(x)\right]$.

2. Express the following in terms of Legendre's polynomials :

(*i*) $1 + x - x^2$

(*ii*) $x^4 + 3x^3 - x^2 + 5x - 2$ (*G.B.T.U. 2012*)

(*iii*) $5x^3 + x$

(*iv*) $x^3 - 5x^2 + 6x + 1$

(*v*) $4x^3 - 2x^2 - 3x + 8$ (*U.P.T.U. 2009 ; M.T.U. 2011*)

(*vi*) $x^4 + 2x^3 + 2x^2 - x - 3$. [*M.T.U. (SUM) 2011*]

3. Expand $x^4 - 3x^2 + x$ in a series of the form $\Sigma C_r P_r(x)$.

4. Expand $f(x)$ in a series of Legendre polynomials if $f(x) = \left.\begin{matrix} 0, & -1 \le x < 0 \\ 2x+1, & 0 < x \le 1 \end{matrix}\right\}$.

5. Obtain the Legendre expansion of $f(x)$ defined as

$$f(x) = \left.\begin{matrix} 0, & -1 < x < 0 \\ 1, & 0 < x < 1 \end{matrix}\right\}.$$

(*G.B.T.U. 2011*)

6. Express the function

$$f(x) = \left.\begin{matrix} 0, & -1 < x \le 0 \\ x^2, & 0 < x < 1 \end{matrix}\right\} \text{ in Fourier-Legendre expansion.}$$

7. Expand $f(x) = \cos \frac{\pi x}{2}$ in Fourier-Legendre series.

8. Prove that :

(*i*) $\int_0^1 P_{2n}(x) P_{2n+1}(x)\, dx = \int_0^1 P_{2n}(x) P_{2n-1}(x)\, dx$

(*ii*) $\int_{-2}^1 x^6 P_4(x)\, dx = \frac{16}{231}$

(*iii*) $\int_0^1 P_{2n+1}(x)\, dx = (-1)^n$.

9. Prove that :

(*i*) $\int_0^1 P_n(x) dx = \frac{1}{n+1} P_{n-1}(0)$

(*ii*) $\int_{-1}^1 P_3^2(x) = \frac{2}{7}$

(*iii*) $\int_{-1}^1 P'_{n-1}(x) P'_{n+1}(x)\, dx = n(n-1)$

(*iv*) $\int_0^1 P_{2n}(x)\, dx = 0$.

Answers

2. (*i*) $\frac{2}{3} P_0(x) + P_1(x) - \frac{2}{3} P_2(x)$

(*ii*) $\frac{8}{35} P_4(x) + \frac{6}{5} P_3(x) - \frac{2}{21} P_2(x) + \frac{34}{5} P_1(x) - \frac{224}{105} P_0(x)$

(*iii*) $2P_3(x) + 4P_1(x)$

(*iv*) $\frac{2}{5} P_3(x) - \frac{10}{3} P_2(x) + \frac{33}{5} P_1(x) - \frac{2}{3} P_0(x)$

(*v*) $\frac{22}{3} P_0(x) - \frac{3}{5} P_1(x) - \frac{4}{3} P_2(x) + \frac{8}{5} P_3(x)$

(*vi*) $\frac{8}{35} P_4(x) + \frac{4}{5} P_3(x) + \frac{40}{21} P_2(x) + \frac{1}{5} P_1(x) - \frac{224}{105} P_0(x)$

3. $-\frac{4}{5}P_0(x) + P_1(x) - \frac{10}{7}P_2(x) + \frac{8}{35}P_4(x)$ **4.** $P_0(x) + \frac{7}{4}P_1(x) + \frac{5}{8}P_2(x) - \frac{7}{16}P_3(x) + \ldots$

5. $\frac{1}{2}P_0(x) + \frac{3}{4}P_1(x) - \frac{7}{16}P_3(x) + \ldots$ **6.** $\frac{1}{6}P_0(x) + \frac{3}{8}P_1(x) + \frac{1}{3}P_2(x) + \frac{7}{48}P_3(x) + \ldots$

7. $\cos\frac{\pi x}{2} = 0.6366\,P_0 - 0.6871\,P_2 + .0518\,P_4 - .0013\,P_6 + \ldots$

2.20. BESSEL'S DIFFERENTIAL EQUATION

The differential equation

$$x^2\frac{d^2y}{dx^2} + x\frac{dy}{dx} + (x^2 - n^2)y = 0$$

is called Bessel's differential equation of order n, where n is a positive constant.

This equation can also be put in the form

$$x\frac{d}{dx}\left(x\frac{dy}{dx}\right) + (x^2 - n^2)\,y = 0$$

The particular solutions of this equation are called Bessel's functions of order n.

2.21. SOLUTION OF BESSEL'S EQUATION

[U.P.T.U. (SUM) 2007 ; U.P.T.U. (C.O.) 2009]

Bessel's equation is

$$x^2\frac{d^2y}{dx^2} + x\frac{dy}{dx} + (x^2 - n^2)y = 0 \qquad \ldots(1)$$

Comparing equation (1) with the form

$$\frac{d^2y}{dx^2} + P(x)\frac{dy}{dx} + Q(x)\,y = 0, \text{ we get}$$

$$P(x) = \frac{1}{x} \text{ and } Q(x) = 1 - \frac{n^2}{x^2}$$

At $x = 0$, both $P(x)$ and $Q(x)$ are not analytic $\therefore$ $x = 0$ is a singular point.

Also, $xP(x) = 1$ and $x^2\,Q(x) = x^2 - n^2$

Since both $xP(x)$ and $x^2\,Q(x)$ are analytic at $x = 0$

$\therefore$ $x = 0$ is a regular singular point.

Assume $$y = \sum_{k=0}^{\infty} a_k\,x^{m+k}$$

Then $$\frac{dy}{dx} = \sum_{k=0}^{\infty} (m+k)a_k\,x^{m+k-1}$$

and $$\frac{d^2y}{dx^2} = \sum_{k=0}^{\infty} (m+k)(m+k-1)\,a_k\,x^{m+k-2}$$

Substituting for y, $\frac{dy}{dx}$ and $\frac{d^2y}{dx^2}$ in (1), we get

$$x^2 \sum_{k=0}^{\infty} (m+k)(m+k-1)a_k x^{m+k-2} + x \sum_{k=0}^{\infty} (m+k)a_k x^{m+k-1} + (x^2 - n^2) \sum_{k=0}^{\infty} a_k x^{m+k} = 0$$

or
$$\sum_{k=0}^{\infty} [(m+k)^2 - (m+k) + (m+k) - n^2] a_k x^{m+k} + \sum_{k=0}^{\infty} a_k x^{m+k+2} = 0$$

or
$$\sum_{k=0}^{\infty} [(m+k)^2 - n^2] a_k x^{m+k} + \sum_{k=0}^{\infty} a_k x^{m+k+2} = 0$$

The lowest power of x is x^m corresponding to $k = 0$. Equating to zero the coefficient of x^m, we get the indicial equation

$$m^2 - n^2 = 0, \text{ since } a_0 \neq 0 \quad \text{whence } m = \pm n$$

Equating to zero the coefficient of next term *i.e.,* x^{m+1}, we get

$$[(m+1)^2 - n^2]a_1 = 0$$

$\Rightarrow$ $a_1 = 0$, since $(m+1)^2 - n^2 \neq 0$ for $m = \pm n$

Equating to zero the coefficient of x^{m+k+2}, we get the recurrence relation

$$[(m+k+2)^2 - n^2]\, a_{k+2} + a_k = 0$$

or
$$a_{k+2} = -\frac{a_k}{(m-n+k+2)(m+n+k+2)}$$

Putting $k = 1, 3, 5, \ldots\ldots$, we get $a_3 = a_5 = a_7 = \ldots\ldots = 0$

Putting $k = 0, 2, 4, \ldots\ldots$, we get

$$a_2 = -\frac{a_0}{(m-n+2)(m+n+2)}$$

$$a_4 = -\frac{a_2}{(m-n+4)(m+n+4)} = \frac{a_0}{(m-n+4)(m+n+4)(m-n+2)(m+n+2)}$$

and so on.

$$\therefore \quad \boxed{y = a_0 x^m \left[1 - \frac{x^2}{(m+2)^2 - n^2} + \frac{x^4}{[(m+2)^2 - n^2][(m+4)^2 - n^2]} - \ldots\right]} \quad \ldots(2)$$

Depending upon the values of n, we get different types of solutions.

Case I. When $n \neq 0$ or $n \neq$ an integer.

In this case, we get two independent solutions for $m = n$ and $m = -n$.

For $m = n$, we get

$$y_1 = a_0 x^n \left[1 - \frac{x^2}{2(2n+2)} + \frac{x^4}{2\,.\,4(2n+2)(2n+4)} - \ldots\ldots\right]$$

$$= a_0 x^n \left[1 + (-1)^1 \frac{x^2}{2^2 (1)!\,(n+1)} + (-1)^2 \frac{x^4}{2^4 (2)!\,(n+1)(n+2)} + \ldots\right]$$

$$= a_0 x^n \sum_{k=0}^{\infty} \frac{(-1)^k}{2^{2k} (k)!\,(n+1)(n+2)\ldots\ldots(n+k)} x^{2k}$$

$$\Rightarrow \quad y_1 = a_0 x^n \sum_{k=0}^{\infty} \frac{(-1)^k \Gamma(n+1)}{2^{2k} \cdot k! \Gamma(n+k+1)} x^{2k} \quad \text{...(3)}$$

Replacing n by $-n$, the second independent solution corresponding to $m = -n$ is

$$y_2 = a_0 x^n \sum_{k=0}^{\infty} \frac{(-1)^k \Gamma(-n+1)}{2^{2k} (k)! \Gamma(-n+k+1)} x^{2k} \quad \text{...(4)}$$

$\therefore$ The complete solution of equation (1) is $y = c_1 y_1 + c_2 y_2$

Since a_0 is arbitrary, we can choose it in any manner.

Choose $a_0 = \dfrac{1}{2^n \Gamma(n+1)}$, then (3) takes the form

$$y_1 = \frac{x^n}{2^n \Gamma(n+1)} \sum_{k=0}^{\infty} \frac{(-1)^k \Gamma(n+1)}{2^{2k} \cdot k! \Gamma(n+k+1)} x^{2k} = \sum_{k=0}^{\infty} \frac{(-1)^k}{(k)! \Gamma(n+k+1)} \left(\frac{x}{2}\right)^{n+2k}$$

This is called **Bessel function of the first kind of order n** and is denoted by $\mathbf{J_n(x)}$.

Thus,

$$\boxed{J_n(x) = \sum_{k=0}^{\infty} \frac{(-1)^k}{(k)! \Gamma(n+k+1)} \left(\frac{x}{2}\right)^{n+2k}}$$

The solution corresponding to $m = -n$ is

$$\boxed{J_{-n}(x) = \sum_{k=0}^{\infty} \frac{(-1)^k}{(k)! \Gamma(-n+k+1)} \left(\frac{x}{2}\right)^{-n+2k}}$$

which is called **Bessel function of the first kind of order – n.**

When n is not an integer, $J_{-n}(x)$ is distinct from $J_n(x)$. Hence the complete solution of the Bessel's equation may be expressed as

$\boxed{y = AJ_n(x) + BJ_{-n}(x)}$, where A and B are arbitrary constants.

Case II. When $n = 0$, the Bessel's equation (1) takes the form

$$x \frac{d^2y}{dx^2} + \frac{dy}{dx} + xy = 0.$$

This is called **Bessel's equation of order zero.**

The two roots of the indicial equation are equal, each = 0.

From equation (2), putting $n = 0$, we have (assuming $a_0 = 1$)

$$y = x^m \left[1 - \frac{x^2}{(m+2)^2} + \frac{x^4}{(m+2)^2 (m+4)^2} - \frac{x^6}{(m+2)^2 (m+4)^2 (m+6)^2} + \ldots\ldots \right]$$

which is a solution if $m = 0$.

The first solution is given by

$$\boxed{J_0(x) = \sum_{k=0}^{\infty} \frac{(-1)^k}{(k!)^2} \left(\frac{x}{2}\right)^{2k}} \quad , \quad \text{since } \Gamma(k+1) = k\,!$$

which is **Bessel function of the first kind of order zero.**

Now, $\dfrac{\partial y}{\partial m} = x^m \log x \left[1 - \dfrac{x^2}{(m+2)^2} + \dfrac{x^4}{(m+2)^2 (m+4)^2} - \ldots\ldots\right]$

$$+ x^m \left[\frac{x^2}{(m+2)^2} \cdot \frac{2}{m+2} - \frac{x^4}{(m+2)^2 (m+4)^2} \left\{\frac{2}{m+2} + \frac{2}{m+4}\right\} + \ldots\ldots\right]$$

The second independent solution is given by $\left(\dfrac{\partial y}{\partial m}\right)_{m=0}$

$$= J_0(x) \log x + \left[\frac{1}{2^2} x^2 - \frac{1}{2^2 . 4^2}\left(1 + \frac{1}{2}\right) x^4 + \frac{1}{2^2 . 4^2 . 6^2}\left(1 + \frac{1}{2} + \frac{1}{3}\right) x^6 - \ldots\ldots\right]$$

$$= J_0(x) \log x + \left[\left(\frac{x}{2}\right)^2 - \frac{1}{(2!)^2}\left(1 + \frac{1}{2}\right)\left(\frac{x}{2}\right)^4 + \frac{1}{(3!)^2}\left(1 + \frac{1}{2} + \frac{1}{3}\right)\left(\frac{x}{2}\right)^6 - \ldots\ldots\right]$$

$$= J_0(x) \log x + \sum_{k=1}^{\infty} \frac{(-1)^{k+1}}{(k!)^2}\left(1 + \frac{1}{2} + \frac{1}{3} + \ldots\ldots + \frac{1}{k}\right)\left(\frac{x}{2}\right)^{2k}$$

It is denoted by $Y_0(x)$ and is called **Bessel function of the second kind of order zero or Neumann function.**

Thus the complete solution of the Bessel's equation of order zero is

$$\boxed{y = AJ_0(x) + BY_0(x)}$$

Case III. When *n* is an integer, the two functions $J_n(x)$ and $J_{-n}(x)$ are not independent but are connected by the relation

$$\mathbf{J_{-n}(x) = (-1)^n J_n(x).}$$

Now, when n is an integer, y_2 fails to give a solution for positive values of n and y_1 fails to give a solution for negative values of n. Let us find an independent solution of Bessel's equation (1), when n is an integer.

Let $y = u(x) J_n(x)$ be a solution of (1) when n is integral.

Then $\dfrac{dy}{dx} = u' J_n + uJ_n'$ and $\dfrac{d^2y}{dx^2} = u'' J_n + 2u' J_n' + uJ_n''$

Substituting the values of y, $\dfrac{dy}{dx}$ and $\dfrac{d^2y}{dx^2}$ in (1), we get

$$x^2(u''J_n + 2u'J_n' + uJ_n'') + x(u'J_n + uJ_n') + (x^2 - n^2)uJ_n = 0$$

or $$u[x^2J_n'' + xJ_n' + (x^2 - n^2)J_n] + x^2u''J_n + 2x^2u'J_n' + xu'J_n = 0$$

or $$x^2u''J_n + 2x^2u'J_n' + xu'J_n = 0 \text{ since } J_n \text{ is a solution of (1).}$$

Dividing throughout by $x^2u'J_n$, we get

$$\frac{u''}{u'} + 2\frac{J_n'}{J_n} + \frac{1}{x} = 0$$

Integrating w.r.t. x, we get

$$\log (u'J_n^2 x) = \log B$$

or $$u' J_n^2 x = B$$

or $$u' = \frac{B}{xJ_n^2} \quad \text{or} \quad u = B \int \frac{dx}{xJ_n^2} + A$$

Substituting the value of u in the assumed solution $y = u(x)\, J_n(x)$, we have

$$y = \left[B \int \frac{dx}{x J_n^2(x)} + A \right] J_n(x)$$

or
$$y = AJ_n(x) + BY_n(x), \text{ where } \quad Y_n(x) = J_n(x) \int \frac{dx}{x J_n^2(x)}$$

The function $Y_n(x)$ is called the **Bessel function of the second kind of order *n* or Neumann function.**

2.22. SERIES REPRESENTATION OF BESSEL FUNCTIONS

Since
$$J_n(x) = \sum_{k=0}^{\infty} \frac{(-1)^k}{k!\,\Gamma(n+k+1)} \left(\frac{x}{2}\right)^{n+2k}$$

$\therefore$
$$J_0(x) = \sum_{k=0}^{\infty} \frac{(-1)^k}{k!\,\Gamma(k+1)} \left(\frac{x}{2}\right)^{2k} = \sum_{k=0}^{\infty} \frac{(-1)^k}{(k!)^2} \left(\frac{x}{2}\right)^{2k}, \qquad \because \ \Gamma(k+1) = k!$$

$$= 1 - \left(\frac{x}{2}\right)^2 + \frac{1}{(2!)^2}\left(\frac{x}{2}\right)^4 - \frac{1}{(3!)^2}\left(\frac{x}{2}\right)^6 + \ldots\ldots$$

$$= 1 - \frac{x^2}{2^2} + \frac{x^4}{2^2 . 4^2} - \frac{x^6}{2^2 . 4^2 . 6^2} + \ldots\ldots$$

$$J_1(x) = \sum_{k=0}^{\infty} \frac{(-1)^k}{k!\,\Gamma(k+2)} \left(\frac{x}{2}\right)^{1+2k} = \sum_{k=0}^{\infty} \frac{(-1)^k}{k!\,(k+1)!} \left(\frac{x}{2}\right)^{1+2k}$$

$$= \frac{x}{2} - \frac{1}{2!}\left(\frac{x}{2}\right)^3 + \frac{1}{2!\,3!}\left(\frac{x}{2}\right)^5 - \ldots\ldots = \frac{x}{2} - \frac{x^3}{2^2 . 4} + \frac{x^5}{2^2 . 4^2 . 6} - \ldots\ldots$$

In particular, $J_0(0) = 1$ and $J_1(0) = 0$.

The values of $J_0(x)$ and $J_1(x)$ are given in 'Jahnke Emde's tables' to four decimal places at intervals of 0.1.

2.23. RECURRENCE RELATIONS FOR $J_n(X)$

1. $\boxed{x J_n' = nJ_n - x J_{n+1}}$ *[G.B.T.U. (C.O.) 2010]*

We know that,

$$J_n = \sum_{r=0}^{\infty} \frac{(-1)^r}{r!\,\Gamma n + r + 1} \left(\frac{x}{2}\right)^{n+2r}$$

Differentiating w.r.t. x, we get

$$J_n' = \sum_{r=0}^{\infty} \frac{(-1)^r (n+2r)}{r!\,\Gamma n + r + 1} \cdot \frac{1}{2} \left(\frac{x}{2}\right)^{n+2r-1}$$

Multiplying both sides by x and breaking it into two terms

$$xJ_n' = n\sum_{r=0}^{\infty}\frac{(-1)^r}{r!\,\Gamma n+r+1}\left(\frac{x}{2}\right)^{n+2r} + x\sum_{r=1}^{\infty}\frac{(-1)^r}{(r-1)!\,\Gamma n+r+1}\left(\frac{x}{2}\right)^{n+2r-1}$$

$$= nJ_n + x\sum_{s=0}^{\infty}\frac{(-1)^{s+1}}{s!\,\Gamma n+s+2}\left(\frac{x}{2}\right)^{n+2s+1} \qquad |\ \text{Here } r = s+1$$

$$= nJ_n - x\sum_{s=0}^{\infty}\frac{(-1)^s}{s!\,\Gamma n+s+2}\left(\frac{x}{2}\right)^{(n+1)+2s}$$

$$\Rightarrow \qquad x\,J_n' = nJ_n - xJ_{n+1} \qquad \text{...(1)}$$

2. $\boxed{\mathbf{xJ_n' = -nJ_n + xJ_{n-1}}}$ *(U.P.T.U. 2006)*

We know that

$$xJ_n' = \sum_{r=0}^{\infty}\frac{(-1)^r\,(n+2r)}{r!\,\Gamma n+r+1}\left(\frac{x}{2}\right)^{n+2r} = \sum_{r=0}^{\infty}\frac{(-1)^r\,(2n+2r-n)}{r!\,\Gamma n+r+1}\left(\frac{x}{2}\right)^{n+2r}$$

$$= -n\sum_{r=0}^{\infty}\frac{(-1)^r}{r!\,\Gamma n+r+1}\left(\frac{x}{2}\right)^{n+2r} + x\sum_{r=0}^{\infty}\frac{(-1)^r\,(n+r)}{r!\,\Gamma n+r+1}\left(\frac{x}{2}\right)^{n+2r-1}$$

$$= -nJ_n + x\sum_{r=0}^{\infty}\frac{(-1)^r}{r!\,\Gamma n+r}\left(\frac{x}{2}\right)^{n+2r-1}$$

$$= -nJ_n + x\sum_{r=0}^{\infty}\frac{(-1)^r}{r!\,\Gamma(n-1)+r+1}\left(\frac{x}{2}\right)^{n-1+2r}$$

$$xJ_n' = -nJ_n + xJ_{n-1} \qquad \text{...(2)}$$

3. $\boxed{\mathbf{2J_n' = J_{n-1} - J_{n+1}}}$

Adding equations (1) and (2), we get

$$2xJ_n' = x\,(J_{n-1} - J_{n+1})$$

$$\Rightarrow \qquad 2J_n' = J_{n-1} - J_{n+1} \qquad \text{...(3)}$$

4. $\boxed{\mathbf{2nJ_n = x(J_{n-1} + J_{n+1})}}$ *[U.P.T.U. 2007 ; U.P.T.U. (SUM) 2007]*

Subtracting (2) from (1), we get

$$0 = 2n\,J_n - x\,J_{n-1} - xJ_{n+1}$$

$$\Rightarrow \qquad 2nJ_n = x\,(J_{n-1} + J_{n+1}) \qquad \text{...(4)}$$

5. $\boxed{\mathbf{\frac{d}{dx}(x^{-n}\,J_n) = -x^{-n}\,J_{n+1}}}$ *[U.P.T.U. (SUM) 2007]*

Multiplying cqn. (1) by x^{-n-1}, we get

$$x^{-n}\,J_n' = nx^{-n-1}\,J_n - x^{-n}\,J_{n+1}$$

$$\Rightarrow \quad x^{-n}\,J_n' - x^{-n-1}\,.\,nJ_n = -x^{-n}\,J_{n+1}$$

$$\frac{d}{dx}(x^{-n}\,J_n) = -x^{-n}\,J_{n+1} \qquad \text{...(5)}$$

6. $\boxed{\dfrac{d}{dx}(x^n J_n) = x^n J_{n-1}}$ [*G.B.T.U. 2011, 2012 ; U.P.T.U. (C.O.) 2008*]

Multiplying eqn. (2) by x^{n-1}, we get

$$x^n J_n' = -n x^{n-1} J_n + x^n J_{n-1}$$

$$\Rightarrow \quad x^n J_n' + nx^{n-1} J_n = x^n J_{n-1}$$

$$\Rightarrow \quad \frac{d}{dx}(x^n J_n) = x^n J_{n-1} \quad \ldots(6)$$

ILLUSTRATIVE EXAMPLES

Example 1. *Prove that :*

$$J_{-n}(x) = (-1)^n J_n(x).$$

Sol. Since $\Gamma - p$ is infinity ($p > 0$), we get terms in $J_{-n}(x)$ equal to zero till $r + 1 - n \geq 1$ so that the series begins when $r \geq n$

Hence we can write,

$$J_{-n}(x) = \sum_{r=n}^{\infty} \frac{(-1)^r}{r!\,\Gamma - n + r + 1}\left(\frac{x}{2}\right)^{-n+2r}$$

Putting $r = n + s$, we get

$$J_{-n}(x) = \sum_{s=0}^{\infty} \frac{(-1)^{n+s}}{(n+s)!\,\Gamma s + 1}\left(\frac{x}{2}\right)^{n+2s}$$

$$= (-1)^n \sum_{r=0}^{\infty} \frac{(-1)^r}{(n+r)!\,\Gamma r + 1}\left(\frac{x}{2}\right)^{n+2r} = (-1)^n \sum_{r=0}^{\infty} \frac{(-1)^r}{\Gamma n + r + 1\; r!}\left(\frac{x}{2}\right)^{n+2r}$$

$$\Rightarrow \quad J_{-n}(x) = (-1)^n J_n(x).$$

Example 2. *Prove that :* $J_0'(x) = -J_1(x)$.

Sol. We know that

$$\frac{d}{dx}[x^{-n} J_n(x)] = -x^{-n} J_{n+1}(x)$$

Putting $n = 0$, we get

$$\frac{d}{dx}[J_0(x)] = -J_1(x)$$

$$\Rightarrow \quad J_0'(x) = -J_1(x).$$

Example 3. *Prove that :*

(*i*) $J_{1/2}(x) = \sqrt{\dfrac{2}{\pi x}}\sin x$ [U.P.T.U. 2009, U.P.T.U. (SUM) 2008] (*ii*) $J_{-1/2}(x) = \sqrt{\dfrac{2}{\pi x}}\cos x$.

Sol. We know that,

$$J_n(x) = \frac{x^n}{2^n\,\Gamma n + 1}\left[1 - \frac{x^2}{2(2n+2)} + \frac{x^4}{2.4.(2n+2)(2n+4)} - \ldots\ldots\right] \quad \ldots(1)$$

(*i*) Putting $n = \frac{1}{2}$ in (1),

$$J_{1/2}(x) = \frac{\sqrt{x}}{\sqrt{2}\,\Gamma 3/2}\left[1 - \frac{x^2}{3!} + \frac{x^4}{5!} - \ldots\right]$$

$$= \frac{\sqrt{x}}{\sqrt{2}\,.\,\frac{1}{2}\sqrt{\pi}} \cdot \frac{1}{x}\left[x - \frac{x^3}{3!} + \frac{x^3}{5!} - \ldots\right] = \sqrt{\frac{2}{\pi x}}\sin x$$

(*ii*) Putting $n = -\frac{1}{2}$ in (1),

$$J_{-1/2}(x) = \frac{x^{-1/2}}{2^{-1/2}\,\Gamma 1/2}\left(1 - \frac{x^2}{2!} + \frac{x^4}{4!} - \ldots\right) = \sqrt{\frac{2}{\pi x}}\cos x\,.$$

Example 4. *Prove that :*

$$\frac{d}{dx}[J_n^{\,2}(x) + J^2_{n+1}(x)] = 2\left[\frac{n}{x}J_n^{\,2}(x) - \frac{n+1}{x}J^2_{n+1}(x)\right].$$ [M.T.U. (SUM) 2011]

Sol. L.H.S. $= 2J_n J_n' + 2J_{n+1} J'_{n+1}$ ...(1)

But $xJ_n' = nJ_n - xJ_{n+1}$ | Recurrence relation (1)

$\therefore$ $J_n' = \frac{n}{x}J_n - J_{n+1}$ ...(2)

and also, $xJ_n' = -nJ_n + xJ_{n-1}$ | Recurrence relation (2)

$\therefore$ $J_n' = -\frac{n}{x}J_n + J_{n-1}$

or $J'_{n+1} = -\left(\frac{n+1}{x}\right)J_{n+1} + J_n$ ...(3)

Substituting these values of J_n' and J'_{n+1} from (2) and (3) in eqn. (1), we get

$$\text{L.H.S.} = 2J_n\left(\frac{n}{x}J_n - J_{n+1}\right) + 2J_{n+1}\left(-\frac{n+1}{x}J_{n+1} + J_n\right)$$

$$= 2\,\frac{n}{x}J_n^{\,2} - 2\left(\frac{n+1}{x}\right)J^2_{n+1} = \text{R.H.S.}$$

Hence the result.

Example 5. *Prove that :*

(*i*) $J_{3/2}(x) = \sqrt{\frac{2}{\pi x}}\left(\frac{\sin x}{x} - \cos x\right)$ [G.B.T.U. (SUM) 2010 ; U.P.T.U. (SUM) 2009]

(*ii*) $J_{-3/2}(x) = \sqrt{\frac{2}{\pi x}}\left(\frac{-\cos x}{x} - \sin x\right).$

Sol. By Recurrence relation (4), we have,

$$2n\,J_n(x) = x\,[J_{n-1}(x) + J_{n+1}(x)] \qquad \ldots(1)$$

$$\Rightarrow \quad J_{n+1}(x) = \frac{2n}{x}J_n(x) - J_{n-1}(x) \qquad \ldots(2)$$

(*i*) Putting $n = 1/2$ in (2), we get

$$J_{3/2}(x) = \frac{1}{x} J_{1/2}(x) - J_{-1/2}(x)$$

$$= \sqrt{\frac{2}{\pi x}}\left[\frac{\sin x}{x} - \cos x\right] \qquad \text{| Using results of Ex. 3}$$

(*ii*) From equation (1),

$$J_{n-1}(x) = \frac{2n}{x} J_n(x) - J_{n+1}(x) \qquad ...(3)$$

Putting $n = -1/2$ in (3), we get

$$J_{-3/2}(x) = -\frac{1}{x} J_{-1/2}(x) - J_{1/2}(x)$$

$$= \sqrt{\frac{2}{\pi x}}\left[\frac{-\cos x}{x} - \sin x\right] \qquad \text{| Using results of Ex. 3}$$

Example 6. *Prove that :*

$$J_{5/2}(x) = \sqrt{\frac{2}{\pi x}}\left[\left(\frac{3-x^2}{x^2}\right)\sin x - \frac{3\cos x}{x}\right]. \qquad \text{[G.B.T.U. (C.O.) 2011]}$$

Sol. From Recurrence relation (4),

$$2nJ_n(x) = x[J_{n-1}(x) + J_{n+1}(x)]$$

$$\Rightarrow \quad J_{n+1}(x) = \frac{2n}{x} J_n(x) - J_{n-1}(x) \qquad ...(1)$$

Putting $n = 1/2, 3/2$ in (1), we get

$$J_{3/2}(x) = \frac{1}{x} J_{1/2}(x) - J_{-1/2}(x) \qquad ...(2)$$

$$J_{5/2}(x) = \frac{3}{x} J_{3/2}(x) - J_{1/2}(x) \qquad ...(3)$$

From (2) and (3),

$$J_{5/2}(x) = \frac{3}{x}\left[\frac{1}{x} J_{1/2}(x) - J_{-1/2}(x)\right] - J_{1/2}(x)$$

$$= \left(\frac{3}{x^2} - 1\right) J_{1/2}(x) - \frac{3}{x} J_{-1/2}(x)$$

$$= \left(\frac{3-x^2}{x^2}\right)\sqrt{\frac{2}{\pi x}}\sin x - \frac{3}{x}.\sqrt{\frac{2}{\pi x}}\cos x$$

$$= \sqrt{\frac{2}{\pi x}}\left[\left(\frac{3-x^2}{x^2}\right)\sin x - \frac{3}{x}\cos x\right].$$

Example 7. *Prove that :*

$$J_4(x) = \left(\frac{48}{x^3} - \frac{8}{x}\right) J_1(x) + \left(1 - \frac{24}{x^2}\right) J_0(x).$$

Hence or otherwise find $J_6(x)$ in terms of $J_0(x)$ and $J_1(x)$. (U.P.T.U. 2009)

Sol. From Recurrence relation (4),

$$2n\text{J}_n(x) = x[\text{J}_{n-1}(x) + \text{J}_{n+1}(x)]$$

$$\Rightarrow \quad \text{J}_{n+1}(x) = \frac{2n}{x}\text{J}_n(x) - \text{J}_{n-1}(x) \quad \text{...(1)}$$

Putting $n = 1, 2, 3$ in eqn. (1), we get

$$\text{J}_2(x) = \frac{1}{x}[2\text{J}_1(x) - x\text{J}_0(x)] \quad \text{...(2)}$$

$$\text{J}_3(x) = \frac{1}{x}[4\text{J}_2(x) - x\text{J}_1(x)] \quad \text{...(3)}$$

$$\text{J}_4(x) = \frac{1}{x}[6\text{J}_3(x) - x\text{J}_2(x)] \quad \text{...(4)}$$

From (2) and (3),

$$\text{J}_3(x) = \frac{8}{x^2}\text{J}_1(x) - \frac{4}{x}\text{J}_0(x) - \text{J}_1(x) = \left(\frac{8-x^2}{x^2}\right)\text{J}_1(x) - \frac{4}{x}\text{J}_0(x) \quad \text{...(5)}$$

Again from (4) and (5),

$$\text{J}_4(x) = \left(\frac{48-6x^2}{x^3}\right)\text{J}_1(x) - \frac{24}{x^2}\text{J}_0(x) - \frac{2}{x}\text{J}_1(x) + \text{J}_0(x)$$

$$= \left(\frac{48}{x^3} - \frac{8}{x}\right)\text{J}_1(x) + \left(1 - \frac{24}{x^2}\right)\text{J}_0(x). \quad \text{...(6)}$$

Again, putting $n = 4, 5$ in eqn. (1), we get

$$\text{J}_5(x) = \frac{8}{x}\text{J}_4(x) - \text{J}_3(x) \quad \text{...(7)}$$

$$\text{J}_6(x) = \frac{10}{x}\text{J}_5(x) - \text{J}_4(x) \quad \text{...(8)}$$

From (7) and (8),

$$\text{J}_6(x) = \frac{10}{x}\left[\frac{8}{x}\text{J}_4(x) - \text{J}_3(x)\right] - \text{J}_4(x)$$

$$= \left(\frac{80}{x^2} - 1\right)\text{J}_4(x) - \frac{10}{x}\text{J}_3(x)$$

$$= \left(\frac{80}{x^2} - 1\right)\left[\left(\frac{48}{x^3} - \frac{8}{x}\right)\text{J}_1(x) + \left(1 - \frac{24}{x^2}\right)\text{J}_0(x)\right]$$

$$- \frac{10}{x}\left[\left(\frac{8}{x^2} - 1\right)\text{J}_1(x) - \frac{4}{x}\text{J}_0(x)\right] \quad \text{| Using eqn. (5) and (6)}$$

$$\Rightarrow \quad \text{J}_6(x) = \left(\frac{3840}{x^5} - \frac{768}{x^3} + \frac{18}{x}\right)\text{J}_1(x) + \left(\frac{144}{x^2} - \frac{1920}{x^4} - 1\right)\text{J}_0(x).$$

Example 8. *Prove that :*

$$\int J_3(x)\,dx + J_2(x) + \frac{2}{x}J_1(x) = 0.$$

Sol. We know that,

$$\frac{d}{dx}[x^{-n} J_n(x)] = -x^{-n} J_{n+1}(x)$$

$$\therefore \int x^{-n} J_{n+1}(x)\,dx = -x^{-n} J_n(x) \qquad ...(1)$$

Now, $\int J_3(x)\,dx = \int x^2 [x^{-2} J_3(x)]\,dx$

$$= x^2 . [-x^{-2} J_2(x)] - \int 2x . [-x^{-2} J_2(x)]\,dx$$

$$= -J_2(x) + 2\int x^{-1} J_2(x) dx$$

$$= -J_2(x) + 2[-x^{-1} J_1(x)] = -J_2(x) - \frac{2}{x} J_1(x)$$

or $\int J_3(x)\,dx + J_2(x) + \frac{2}{x} J_1(x) = 0.$

Example 9. *Prove that :*

$$\int xJ_0^2(x)\,dx = \frac{1}{2}x^2 [J_0^2(x) + J_1^2(x)] + c. \qquad \text{(M.T.U. 2012)}$$

Sol. $\int xJ_0^2(x)\,dx = J_0^2(x) . \frac{x^2}{2} - \int 2J_0(x) J_0'(x) . \frac{x^2}{2}\,dx + c$

$$= \frac{x^2}{2} J_0^2(x) - \int x^2 J_0(x) \{-J_1(x)\}\,dx + c \qquad [\because \; J_0'(x) = -J_1(x)]$$

$$= \frac{x^2}{2} J_0^2(x) + \int xJ_1(x) . xJ_0(x)\,dx + c$$

$$= \frac{x^2}{2} J_0^2(x) + \int xJ_1(x) . \frac{d}{dx}[xJ_1(x)]\,dx + c$$

| Using Recurrence relation

$$= \frac{x^2}{2} J_0^2(x) + \frac{[xJ_1(x)]^2}{2} + c = \frac{x^2}{2}[J_0^2(x) + J_1^2(x)] + c.$$

Example 10. *Prove that :*

$$4J_n''(x) = J_{n-2}(x) - 2J_n(x) + J_{n+2}(x).$$

[U.P.T.U. (C.O.) 2009 ; G.B.T.U. (C.O.) 2011]

Sol. From Recurrence relation (3), we have

$$2J_n' = J_{n-1} - J_{n+1} \qquad ...(1)$$

Differentiating, $2J_n'' = J'_{n-1} - J'_{n+1}$

or $4J_n'' = 2J'_{n-1} - 2J'_{n+1} = (J_{n-2} - J_n) - (J_n - J_{n+2})$ | Using (1)

$\Rightarrow$ $4J_n'' = J_{n-2} - 2J_n + J_{n+2}$

Example 11. *Prove that :*

$$4J_0'''(x) + 3J_0'(x) + J_3(x) = 0. \qquad \text{[U.P.T.U. (SUM) 2008]}$$

Sol. We know that

$$J_0' = -J_1$$

Diff. gives, $J_0'' = -J_1' = -\frac{1}{2}(J_0 - J_2)$ [By Recurrence relation $2J_n' = J_{n-1} - J_{n+1}$]

Diff. again, $J_0''' = -\frac{1}{2}(J_0' - J_2') = -\frac{1}{2}J_0' + \frac{1}{2}\cdot\frac{1}{2}[J_1 - J_3]$

$$= -\frac{1}{2}J_0' + \frac{1}{4}J_1 - \frac{1}{4}J_3 = -\frac{1}{2}J_0' - \frac{1}{4}J_0' - \frac{1}{4}J_3 \qquad | \because \; J_1 = -J_0'$$

$$= -\frac{3}{4}J_0' - \frac{1}{4}J_3$$

$\Rightarrow \qquad 4J_0''' + 3J_0' + J_3 = 0.$

Example 12. *Prove that :*

$$\frac{d}{dx}[xJ_n(x)\,J_{n+1}(x)] = x\,[J_n^2(x) - J_{n+1}^2(x)].$$

Sol. L.H.S. $= \frac{d}{dx}[x^{-n}J_n(x)\,.\,x^{n+1}J_{n+1}(x)]$

$$= x^{-n}J_n(x)\frac{d}{dx}[x^{n+1}J_{n+1}(x)] + x^{n+1}J_{n+1}(x)\,.\,\frac{d}{dx}[x^{-n}J_n(x)]$$

$$= x^{-n}J_n(x)\,.\,x^{n+1}J_n(x) + x^{n+1}J_{n+1}(x)\,[-x^{-n}J_{n+1}(x)]$$

$$| \because \; \frac{d}{dx}(x^nJ_n) = x^nJ_{n-1}$$

$$= xJ_n^2(x) - xJ_{n+1}^2 = x\,[J_n^2(x) - J_{n+1}^2] = \text{R.H.S.}$$

Example 13. *Prove that :*

$$\lim_{x\to 0}\frac{J_n(x)}{x^n} = \frac{1}{2^n\,\Gamma n+1} \quad ; (n > -1).$$

Sol. We know that

$$J_n(x) = \frac{x^n}{2^n\,\Gamma n+1}\left[1 - \frac{x^2}{2\,.\,(2n+2)} + \frac{x^4}{2\,.\,4\,.\,(2n+2)\,(2n+4)} - \ldots\ldots\right]$$

$$\therefore \quad \lim_{x\to 0}\frac{J_n(x)}{x^n} = \lim_{x\to 0}\frac{1}{2^n\,\Gamma n+1}\left[1 - \frac{x^2}{2\,.\,(2n+2)} + \frac{x^4}{2\,.\,4\,.\,(2n+2)(2n+4)} - \ldots\ldots\right]$$

$$= \frac{1}{2^n\,\Gamma n+1}.$$

Example 14. *Prove that :*

$$J_2'(x) = \left(1 - \frac{4}{x^2}\right)J_1(x) + \frac{2}{x}J_0(x). \qquad \text{(U.P.T.U. 2008)}$$

Sol. By Recurrence relation (2), we have

$$xJ_n' = -nJ_n + xJ_{n-1} \qquad \ldots(1)$$

Putting $n = 2$, $\quad xJ_2' = -2J_2 + xJ_1$

$$\Rightarrow \qquad J_2' = -\frac{2}{x}J_2 + J_1 \qquad \ldots(2)$$

By Recurrence relation (1), we have

$$xJ_n' = nJ_n - xJ_{n+1} \qquad \ldots(3)$$

From (1) and (3), we have

$$-nJ_n + xJ_{n-1} = nJ_n - xJ_{n+1}$$

Putting $n = 1, -J_1 + xJ_0 = J_1 - xJ_2$

$$\Rightarrow \qquad J_2 = \frac{2}{x} J_1 - J_0 \qquad \ldots(4)$$

$$\therefore \text{ From (2),} \qquad J_2' = -\frac{2}{x}\left(\frac{2}{x} J_1 - J_0\right) + J_1 = \left(1 - \frac{4}{x^2}\right) J_1 + \frac{2}{x} J_0.$$

Example 15. *Prove that :*

$$J_{n+3} + J_{n+5} = \frac{2}{x} (n + 4) J_{n+4}. \qquad \text{[U.P.T.U. 2007 ; G.B.T.U. (C.O.) 2010]}$$

Sol. By Recurrence relation (4), we have

$$2nJ_n = x (J_{n-1} + J_{n+1})$$

Replacing n by $n + 4$, we get

$$\frac{2}{x} (n + 4) J_{n+4} = J_{n+3} + J_{n+5}.$$

Example 16. *Prove that $J_n(x) = 0$ has no repeated root except at $x = 0$.*

Sol. Suppose, if possible, α is a double root of $J_n(x) = 0$

Then, $\qquad J_n(\alpha) = 0 \quad \text{and} \quad J_n'(\alpha) = 0 \qquad \ldots(1)$

From Recurrence relations, we know that

$$J_{n+1}(x) = \frac{n}{x} J_n(x) - J_n'(x)$$

and

$$J_{n-1}(x) = \frac{n}{x} J_n(x) + J_n'(x)$$

Using (1), we get $\quad J_{n+1}(\alpha) = 0 \quad$ and $\quad J_{n-1}(\alpha) = 0$

which is inadmissible as power series cannot have the same sum function.

Hence $J_n(x)$ has no repeated root except $\qquad x = 0$.

Example 17. *Prove that :*

$$x^2 J_n''(x) = (n^2 - n - x^2) J_n(x) + x J_{n+1}(x) \; ; n = 0, 1, 2. \qquad \text{(U.P.T.U. 2006, 2007)}$$

Sol. We have

$$xJ_n' = nJ_n - xJ_{n+1} \qquad \ldots(1) \quad | \text{By R.R. (1)}$$

$$\text{Diff.,} \qquad xJ_n'' + J_n' = nJ_n' - xJ'_{n+1} - J_{n+1}$$

$$\Rightarrow \qquad x^2 J_n'' = (n - 1) x J_n' - x^2 J'_{n+1} - xJ_{n+1} \qquad \ldots(2)$$

By Recurrence relation (2),

$$xJ_n' = -nJ_n + xJ_{n-1}$$

$$\Rightarrow \qquad xJ'_{n+1} = -(n + 1) J_{n+1} + xJ_n \qquad \ldots(3)$$

$$\therefore \text{ From (2),} \qquad x^2 J_n'' = (n - 1) [nJ_n - xJ_{n+1}] - x [-(n + 1) J_{n+1} + xJ_n] - xJ_{n+1}$$

$$\Rightarrow \qquad x^2 J_n'' = (n^2 - n - x^2) J_n + x J_{n+1}.$$

Example 18. *Prove that :*

$$\frac{x}{2} J_n = (n + 1) J_{n+1} - (n + 3) J_{n+3} + (n + 5) J_{n+5} - \ldots..$$

Sol. By Recurrence relation (4), we have

$$2nJ_n = x(J_{n-1} + J_{n+1})$$

$$\Rightarrow \qquad 2(n + 1) J_{n+1} = x (J_n + J_{n+2}) \qquad | \text{ Replacing } n \text{ by } (n + 1)$$

$$\Rightarrow \qquad \frac{x}{2} J_n = (n+1) J_{n+1} - \frac{x}{2} J_{n+2} \qquad ...(1)$$

$$\Rightarrow \qquad \frac{x}{2} J_{n+2} = (n+3) J_{n+3} - \frac{x}{2} J_{n+4} \qquad ...(2)$$

$\therefore$ From (1) and (2),

$$\frac{x}{2} J_n = (n+1) J_{n+1} - (n+3) J_{n+3} + \frac{x}{2} J_{n+4}$$

Continuing this way,

$$\frac{x}{2} J_n = (n+1) J_{n+1} - (n+3) J_{n+3} + (n+5) J_{n+5} - .....$$

Example 19. *If $n > -1$, show that :*

$$\int_0^x x^{-n} J_{n+1}(x)\, dx = \frac{1}{2^n \Gamma n+1} - x^{-n} J_n(x).$$

Sol. We know that,

$$\frac{d}{dx}[x^{-n} J_n(x)] = -x^{-n} J_{n+1}(x) \qquad | \text{ Recurrence relation}$$

Integrating it between 0 and x, we get

$$\int_0^x x^{-n} J_{n+1}(x)\, dx = -\left[x^{-n} J_n(x)\right]_0^x = -x^{-n} J_n(x) + \underset{x \to 0}{\text{Lt}} \left[\frac{J_n(x)}{x^n}\right]$$

$$= -x^{-n} J_n(x) + \frac{1}{2^n \Gamma n+1}.$$

Example 20. *Prove that :*

$$J_n' = \frac{2}{x}\left[\frac{n}{2} J_n - (n+2) J_{n+2} + (n+4) J_{n+1} - ......\right].$$

Sol. From Recurrence formula (2), we have

$$J_n' = -\frac{n}{x} J_n + J_{n-1}$$

$$= -\frac{n}{x} J_n + \frac{2}{x}[nJ_n - (n+2) J_{n+2} + ...] \qquad | \text{Using example 18}$$

$$= \frac{2}{x}\left[\frac{n}{2} J_n - (n+2) J_{n+2} + ...\right].$$

2.24. GENERATING FUNCTION FOR $J_n(x)$

The function $e^{\frac{x}{2}\left(z - \frac{1}{z}\right)}$ is called generating function.

Prove that

$$(i) \qquad \boxed{e^{\frac{x}{2}\left(z - \frac{1}{z}\right)} = \sum_{n=-\infty}^{\infty} z^n J_n(x)}$$

i.e., $J_n(x)$ is the coefficient of z^n in the expansion of $e^{\frac{x}{2}\left(z - \frac{1}{z}\right)}$.

(*ii*)
$$e^{\frac{x}{2}\left(z-\frac{1}{z}\right)} = \sum_{n=-\infty}^{\infty} (-1)^n \, J_n(x)\, z^{-n}$$

i.e., $(-1)^n J_n(x)$ is the coefficient of z^{-n} in the expansion of $e^{\frac{x}{2}\left(z-\frac{1}{z}\right)}$.

Note. Above results are true if n is an integer.

Proof. We have,

$$e^{\frac{x}{2}\left(z-\frac{1}{z}\right)} = e^{\frac{xz}{2}} e^{-\frac{x}{2z}}$$
$$= \left[1+\frac{xz}{2}+\left(\frac{x}{2}\right)^2\frac{z^2}{2!}+\ldots..\right]\left[1-\frac{x}{2z}+\left(\frac{x}{2z}\right)^2\frac{1}{2!}-\ldots..\right]$$

(*i*) Coeff. of z^n in this product

$$= \left(\frac{x}{2}\right)^n \frac{1}{n!} - \left(\frac{x}{2}\right)^{n+2} \cdot \frac{1}{(n+1)!} + \left(\frac{x}{2}\right)^{n+4} \cdot \frac{1}{(n+2)!} \cdot \frac{1}{2!} + \ldots\ldots$$

$$= \sum_{r=0}^{\infty} \frac{(-1)^r}{r!\,(n+r)!}\left(\frac{x}{2}\right)^{n+2r} = J_n$$

(*ii*) Coeff. of z^{-n} in this product

$$= \left(-\frac{x}{2}\right)^n \frac{1}{n!} - \left(-\frac{x}{2}\right)^{n+2} \cdot \frac{1}{(n+1)!} + \left(-\frac{x}{2}\right)^{n+4} \cdot \frac{1}{(n+2)!} \cdot \frac{1}{2!} + \ldots\ldots$$
$$= (-1)^n \sum_{r=0}^{\infty} \frac{(-1)^r}{r!\,(n+r)!}\left(\frac{x}{2}\right)^{n+2r} = (-1)^n J_n.$$

2.25. INTEGRAL FORM OF BESSEL FUNCTION

We know that $e^{\frac{x}{2}\left(t-\frac{1}{t}\right)} = \sum_{n=-\infty}^{\infty} t^n J_n(x)$

$$= J_0(x) + tJ_1(x) + t^2J_2(x) + t^3J_3(x) + \ldots\ldots + t^{-1}J_{-1}(x) + t^{-2}J_{-2}(x) + t^{-3}J_{-3}(x) + \ldots\ldots$$
$$= J_0(x) + tJ_1(x) + t^2J_2(x) + t^3J_3(x) + \ldots\ldots - t^{-1}J_1(x) + t^{-2}J_2(x) - t^{-3}J_3(x) + \ldots\ldots$$

$[\because \; J_{-n}(x) = (-1)^n J_n(x)]$

$$= J_0(x) + \left(t-\frac{1}{t}\right)J_1(x) + \left(t^2+\frac{1}{t^2}\right)J_2(x) + \left(t^3-\frac{1}{t^3}\right)J_3(x) + \ldots\ldots \quad \ldots(1)$$

Put $t = \cos\theta + i\sin\theta$

$\therefore \quad t^n = \cos n\theta + i \sin n\theta \quad$ and $\quad \dfrac{1}{t^n} = \cos n\theta - i\sin n\theta \qquad$ | By De-Moivre's theorem

so that $t^n + \dfrac{1}{t^n} = 2\cos n\theta \quad$ and $\quad t^n - \dfrac{1}{t^n} = 2i\sin n\theta$

Substituting these values in (1), we have

$$e^{ix \sin \theta} = J_0(x) + 2i \sin \theta J_1(x) + 2 \cos 2\theta\, J_2(x) + 3i \sin 3\theta\, J_3(x) + \ldots\ldots \quad \ldots(2)$$

Since $e^{ix \sin \theta} = \cos(x \sin \theta) + i \sin(x \sin \theta)$

∴ Equating the real and imaginary parts in (2), we get

$$\mathbf{\cos(x \sin \theta) = J_0(x) + 2[J_2(x) \cos 2\theta + J_4(x) \cos 4\theta + \ldots\ldots]} \quad \ldots(3)$$

$$\mathbf{\sin(x \sin \theta) = 2[J_1(x) \sin \theta + J_3(x) \sin 3\theta + \ldots\ldots]} \quad \ldots(4)$$

These are known as **Jacobi series.**

Multiplying both sides of (3) by $\cos n\theta$ and integrating w.r.t. θ between the limits 0 and π (when n is odd, all terms on the R.H.S. vanish ; when n is even, all terms on the R.H.S. except the one containing $\cos n\theta$ vanish), we get

$$\int_0^\pi \cos(x \sin \theta) \cos n\theta \, d\theta = \begin{cases} 0, & \text{when } n \text{ is odd} \\ \pi J_n(x), & \text{when } n \text{ is even} \end{cases}$$

Similarly, multiplying (4) by $\sin n\theta$ and integrating w.r.t. θ between the limits 0 and π, we get

$$\int_0^\pi \sin(x \sin \theta) \sin n\theta \, d\theta = \begin{cases} \pi J_n(x), & \text{when } n \text{ is odd} \\ 0, & \text{when } n \text{ is even} \end{cases}$$

Adding, we get $\int_0^\pi [\cos(x \sin \theta) \cos n\theta + \sin(x \sin \theta) \sin n\theta] \, d\theta = \pi J_n(x)$

$$\Rightarrow \quad J_n(x) = \frac{1}{\pi} \int_0^\pi \cos(n\theta - x \sin \theta) \, d\theta \quad \text{for all integral values of } n.$$

(G.B.T.U. 2011)

ILLUSTRATIVE EXAMPLES

Example 1. *Use Jacobi series to prove that*

$$[J_0(x)]^2 + 2[J_1(x)]^2 + 2[J_2(x)]^2 + 2[J_3(x)]^2 + \ldots\ldots = 1. \quad \text{(U.P.T.U. 2008)}$$

Sol. The Jacobi series are

$$J_0(x) + 2J_2(x) \cos 2\theta + 2J_4(x) \cos 4\theta + \ldots\ldots = \cos(x \sin \theta) \quad \ldots(1)$$

and

$$2J_1(x) \sin \theta + 2J_3(x) \sin 3\theta + \ldots\ldots = \sin(x \sin \theta) \quad \ldots(2)$$

Squaring (1) and (2) and integrating w.r.t. θ between the limits 0 and π, and remembering that if m, n are integers then

$$\int_0^\pi \cos^2 n\theta \, d\theta = \int_0^\pi \sin^2 n\theta \, d\theta = \frac{\pi}{2}$$

and $\int_0^\pi \cos m\theta \cos n\theta \, d\theta = \int_0^\pi \sin m\theta \sin n\theta \, d\theta = 0, \; m \neq n$, we get

$$[J_0(x)]^2 \pi + 2[J_2(x)]^2 \pi + 2[J_4(x)]^2 \pi + \ldots\ldots = \int_0^\pi \cos^2(x \sin \theta) \, d\theta$$

$$2[J_1(x)]^2 \pi + 2[J_3(x)]^2 \pi + \ldots\ldots = \int_0^\pi \sin^2(x \sin \theta) \, d\theta$$

Adding, we have $\pi\{[J_0(x)]^2 + 2[J_1(x)]^2 + 2[J_2(x)]^2 + \ldots\ldots\}$

$$= \int_0^\pi [\cos^2(x \sin \theta) + \sin^2(x \sin \theta)] \, d\theta = \int_0^\pi d\theta = \pi.$$

$$\therefore \quad [J_0(x)]^2 + 2[J_1(x)]^2 + 2[J_2(x)]^2 + \ldots\ldots = 1.$$

Example 2. *Prove that :*

$$J_0(x) = \frac{1}{\pi}\int_0^{\pi} \cos(x\cos\phi)\, d\phi.$$

Sol. We know that

$$e^{x.\frac{1}{2}\left(z-\frac{1}{z}\right)} = J_0 + \left(z - \frac{1}{z}\right)J_1 + \left(z^2 + \frac{1}{z^2}\right)J_2 + \left(z^3 - \frac{1}{z^3}\right)J_3 + \ldots \qquad \ldots(1)$$

Putting $z = e^{i\theta}$ so that $\frac{1}{z} = e^{-i\theta}$

and $$z + \frac{1}{z} = 2\cos\theta\,; \quad z - \frac{1}{z} = 2i\sin\theta,$$

Eqn. (1) becomes,

$$e^{ix\sin\theta} = J_0 + (2i\sin\theta)\, J_1 + (2\cos 2\theta)\, J_2 + (2i\sin 3\theta)\, J_3 + (2\cos 4\theta)\, J_4 + \ldots\ldots$$

Equating real parts,

$$\cos(x\sin\theta) = J_0 + 2\cos 2\theta\, J_2 + 2\cos 4\theta\, J_4 + \ldots\ldots \qquad \ldots(2)$$

Putting $\theta = \frac{\pi}{2} + \phi$ in (2), we get

$$\cos(x\cos\phi) = J_0 + 2\cos(\pi + 2\phi)J_2 + 2\cos 4\left(\frac{\pi}{2} + \phi\right)J_4 + \ldots\ldots.$$

$$= J_0 + (-\,2\cos 2\phi)\, J_2 + (2\cos 4\phi)J_4 + \ldots\ldots..$$

$$\therefore \quad \int_0^{\pi} \cos(x\cos\phi)\, d\phi = J_0\int_0^{\pi} d\phi - 2J_2\int_0^{\pi} \cos 2\phi\, d\phi + 2J_4\int_0^{\pi} \cos 4\phi\, d\phi - \ldots = \pi J_0$$

$$\therefore \quad J_0 = \frac{1}{\pi}\int_0^{\pi} \cos(x\cos\phi)\, d\phi.$$

TEST YOUR KNOWLEDGE

1. Show that

(*i*) $J_{1/2}(x) = J_{-1/2}(x)\cot x$

(*ii*) $J_{-5/2}(x) = \sqrt{\frac{2}{\pi x}}\left[\frac{3}{x}\sin x + \left(\frac{3 - x^2}{x^2}\right)\cos x\right]$

(*iii*) $[J_{1/2}(x)]^2 + [J_{-1/2}(x)]^2 = \frac{2}{\pi x}$

(*iv*) $J_{7/2}(x) = \sqrt{\frac{2}{\pi x}}\left[\left(\frac{15 - 6x^2}{x^3}\right)\sin x - \left(\frac{15}{x^2} - 1\right)\cos x\right].$

2. Show that

(*i*) $J_0'' = \frac{1}{2}(J_2 - J_0)$

(*ii*) $J_2 = J_0'' - x^{-1}J_0'$

(*iii*) $\frac{J_2}{J_1} = \frac{1}{x} - \frac{J_0''}{J_0'}$

(*iv*) $J_1''(x) = -\,J_1(x) + \frac{1}{x}J_2(x).$

(G.B.T.U. 2010 ; M.T.U. 2011)

3. Prove that

(*i*) $\frac{d}{dx}[x^n J_n(ax)] = ax^n J_{n-1}(ax)$ (*ii*) $\frac{d}{dx}[J_n^2(x)] = \frac{x}{2n}[J^2_{n-1}(x) - J^2_{n+1}(x)]$.

4. Prove that

(*i*) $\int J_0(x) J_1(x)\, dx = -\frac{1}{2} J_0^2(x)$ (*ii*) $\int x^2 J_0(x) J_1(x)\, dx = \frac{1}{2} x^2 J_1^2(x)$

(*iii*) $\int \frac{J_4(x)}{x}\, dx = -\frac{1}{x} J_3(x) - \frac{2}{x^2} J_2(x)$ (*iv*) $\int J_5(x)\, dx = -J_4(x) - \frac{4}{x} J_3(x) - \frac{8}{x^2} J_2(x)$

(*v*) $\int x^3 J_0(x)\, dx = x^3 J_1(x) - 2x^2 J_2(x)$ (*vi*) $\int_0^{\alpha} x J_0(\lambda x)\, dx = \frac{\alpha}{\lambda} J_1(\alpha\lambda)$.

5. Prove that

(*i*) $J_n(x) = \frac{1}{2\pi}\int_0^{2\pi} \cos(x \sin\theta - n\theta)\, d\theta$

(*ii*) $\cos x = J_0 - 2J_2 + 2J_4 - \ldots\ldots$; $\sin x = 2J_1 - 2J_3 + 2J_5 - \ldots\ldots.$

[**Hint :** Put $\theta = \pi/2$ in Jacobi series]

(*iii*) $\cos(x\cos\theta) = J_0 - 2J_2 \cos 2\theta + 2J_4 \cos 4\theta - \ldots\ldots.$

$\sin(x\cos\theta) = 2J_1 \cos\theta - 2J_3 \cos 3\theta + 2J_5 \cos 5\theta - \ldots\ldots.$

[**Hint :** Replace θ by $\left(\frac{\pi}{2} - \theta\right)$ in Jacobi series]

(*iv*) $J_0(x) = \frac{1}{\pi}\int_0^{\pi} \cos(x\sin\theta)\, d\theta = \frac{2}{\pi}\int_0^{\pi/2} \cos(x\sin\theta)\, d\theta = \frac{2}{\pi}\int_0^{\pi/2} \cos(x\cos\theta)\, d\theta$

(*v*) $J_0 + 2J_2 + 2J_4 + 2J_6 + \ldots\ldots = 1$ (*vi*) $\int_0^{\pi/2} \sqrt{\pi x}\, J_{1/2}(2x)\, dx = 1.$ (*G.B.T.U. 2012*)

6. Show that Bessel's function $J_n(x)$ is an even function when n is even and is an odd function when n is odd. [**Hint :** $J_n(-x) = (-1)^n J_n(x)$] [*U.P.T.U. 2009 ; U.P.T.U. (SUM) 2009*]

7. (*i*) Express $J_6(x)$ in terms of $J_0(x)$ and $J_1(x)$. (*U.P.T.U. 2009*)

(*ii*) Express $J_5(x)$ in terms of $J_0(x)$ and $J_1(x)$.

(*iii*) Show that $J_3(x) = \left(\frac{8}{x^2} - 1\right) J_1(x) - \frac{4}{x} J_0(x)$ (*M.T.U. 2012*)

8. Show that

(*i*) $\int x^2 J_1(x)\, dx = 2x J_1(x) - x^2 J_0(x) + c$ (*M.T.U. 2011*)

(*ii*) $\int x^3 J_3(x)\, dx = -x^3 J_2(x) - 5x^2 J_1(x) - 15x J_0(x) + 15\int J_0(x)\, dx$.

9. Evaluate $\int x^4 J_1(x)\, dx$. (*G.B.T.U. 2011*)

Answers

7. (*i*) $J_6(x) = \left(\frac{3840}{x^5} \quad \frac{768}{x^3} + \frac{18}{x}\right) J_1(x) + \left(\frac{144}{x^2} - \frac{1920}{x^4} - 1\right) J_0(x).$

(*ii*) $J_5(x) = \left(\frac{384}{x^4} - \frac{72}{x^2} - 1\right) J_1(x) + \left(\frac{12}{x} - \frac{192}{x^3}\right) J_0(x).$

9. $(8x^2 - x^4) J_0(x) + (4x^3 - 16x) J_1(x).$

2.26. EQUATIONS REDUCIBLE TO BESSEL'S EQUATION

A number of second order differential equations with variable coefficients can be reduced to Bessel's equation by a suitable transformation and, hence, can be solved in terms of Bessel functions.

Consider the differential equation

$$x^2 \frac{d^2y}{dx^2} + (1 - 2\alpha)x \frac{dy}{dx} + [\beta^2\gamma^2 x^{2\gamma} + (\alpha^2 - n^2\gamma^2)]y = 0 \quad ...(1)$$

where α, β, γ and n are constants.

Putting $X = \beta x^\gamma$ and $Y = x^{-\alpha}y$, equation (1) reduces to

$$X^2 \frac{d^2Y}{dX^2} + X\frac{dY}{dX} + (X^2 - n^2)\,Y = 0 \quad ...(2)$$

which is Bessel's equation.

When n is not an integer, the solution of (2) is

$$\boxed{Y = c_1J_n\,(X) + c_2J_{-n}\,(X)}$$

and, hence, the solution of (2) is

$$x^{-\alpha}\,y = c_1J_n\,(\beta x^\gamma) + c_2J_{-n}\,(\beta x^\gamma)$$

or
$$\boxed{y = x^\alpha\,[c_1J_n\,(\beta x^\gamma) + c_2J_{-n}(\beta x^\gamma)]}$$

When n is an integer, the solution of (2) is

$$Y = c_1J_n\,(X) + c_2Y_n\,(X)$$

and, hence, the solution of (2) is

$$\boxed{y = x^\alpha\,[c_1J_n\,(\beta x^\gamma) + c_2Y_n\,(\beta x^\gamma)].}$$

Equation (1) is a general form of Bessel's equation with α, β, γ and n as parameters. Comparing the given equation with (1), we get specific values of the parameters and hence the solution.

ILLUSTRATIVE EXAMPLES

Example 1. *Solve the following differential equations in terms of Bessel functions :*

(*i*) $y'' - \frac{2}{x}y' + 4\left(x^2 - \frac{1}{x^2}\right)y = 0$ (*ii*) $xy'' - 3y' + xy = 0.$

Sol. (*i*) The given equation is $x^2y'' - 2xy' + (4x^4 - 4)y = 0$

Comparing with the general form, we get

$$1 - 2\alpha = -2,\ \beta^2\gamma^2 = 4,\ 2\gamma = 4,\ \alpha^2 - n^2\gamma^2 = -4$$

i.e.,
$$\alpha = \tfrac{3}{2},\ \beta = 1,\ \gamma = 2,\ n = \tfrac{5}{4}.$$

Here n is not an integer and the solution is

$$y = x^{3/2}\,[c_1J_{5/4}\,(x^2) + c_2J_{-5/4}\,(x^2)]$$

(*ii*) Multiplying by x, the given equation becomes

$$x^2y'' - 3xy' + x^2y = 0$$

Comparing with the general form, we get

$$1 - 2\alpha = -3,\ \beta^2\gamma^2 = 1,\ 2\gamma = 2,\ \alpha^2 - n^2\gamma^2 = 0$$

i.e., $$\alpha = 2,\ \beta = \gamma = 1,\ n = 2$$

Here n is integer and the solution is $y = x^2[c_1 J_2(x) + c_2 Y_2(x)]$.

Example 2. *Obtain in terms of Bessel functions, the solution of differential equation*

$$\frac{d^2y}{dx^2} + \left(9x - \frac{20}{x^2}\right)y = 0.$$

Sol. The given equation on multiplying by x^2 is

$$x^2\frac{d^2y}{dx^2} + (9x^3 - 20)y = 0$$

Comparing this with the standard transformed equation

$$x^2y'' + (1 - 2\alpha)xy' + \{\beta^2\gamma^2 x^{2\gamma} + (\alpha^2 - n^2\gamma^2)\}y = 0,$$

we get $$1 - 2\alpha = 0,\ \beta^2\gamma^2 = 9,\ 2\gamma = 3, \quad \text{and} \quad \alpha^2 - n^2\gamma^2 = -20$$

This gives, $$\alpha = \frac{1}{2},\ \gamma = \frac{3}{2},\ \beta = 2,\ n = 3$$

Here n is an integer.

Hence the solution is $$y = \sqrt{x}\,[c_1 J_3(2x^{3/2}) + c_2 Y_3(2x^{3/2})]$$

Example 3. *Solve the differential equation*

$$y'' + \frac{y'}{x} + 4\left(x^2 - \frac{n^2}{x^2}\right)y = 0 \quad \textit{in terms of Bessel's functions.}$$

Sol. The given equation is

$$x^2y'' + xy' + 4(x^4 - n^2)y = 0 \qquad ...(1)$$

Comparing with the general form, we get

$$1 - 2\alpha = 1 \qquad ...(2)$$

$$\beta^2\gamma^2 = 4 \qquad ...(3)$$

$$2\gamma = 4 \qquad ...(4)$$

$$\alpha^2 - m^2\gamma^2 = -4n^2 \qquad ...(5)$$

From (2), $\alpha = 0$

From (4), $\gamma = 2$

From (3), $\beta^2 = 1 \quad \Rightarrow \quad \beta = 1$

From (5), $0 - m^2(4) = -4n^2 \quad \Rightarrow \quad m = n$

when n is not an integer, solution to (1) is

$$y = x^{\alpha}[c_1 J_m(\beta x^{\gamma}) + c_2 J_{-m}(\beta x^{\gamma})]$$

$$= x^0[c_1 J_n(x^2) + c_2 J_{-n}(x^2)] = c_1 J_n(x^2) + c_2 J_{-n}(x^2)$$

when n is an integer, solution to (1) is

$$y = x^{\alpha} [c_1 J_m (\beta x^{\gamma}) + c_2 Y_m (\beta x^{\gamma})]$$
$$= x^0 [c_1 J_n (x^2) + c_2 Y_n (x^2)] = c_1 J_n (x^2) + c_2 Y_n (x^2).$$

2.27. MODIFIED BESSEL'S EQUATION

The differential equation $x^2 \frac{d^2y}{dx^2} + x\frac{dy}{dx} - (x^2 + n^2)\, y = 0$ ...(1)

is called modified Bessel's equation of order n.

Equation (1) can be re-written as $x^2 \frac{d^2y}{dx^2} + x\frac{dy}{dx} + (i^2x^2 - n^2)\, y = 0$

When n is not an integer, its solution is given by $y = c_1 J_n (ix) + c_2 J_{-n} (ix)$

Now $$J_n (ix) = \sum_{k=0}^{\infty} \frac{(-1)^k}{k!\,\Gamma(n+k+1)} \left(\frac{ix}{2}\right)^{n+2k}$$

$$= i^n \sum_{r=0}^{\infty} \frac{1}{k!\,\Gamma(n+k+1)} \left(\frac{x}{2}\right)^{n+2k} \qquad [\because\ (-1)^k (i)^{2k} = i^{2k} . i^{2k} = i^{4k} = 1]$$

The series $\sum_{k=0}^{\infty} \frac{1}{k!\,\Gamma(n+k+1)} \left(\frac{x}{2}\right)^{n+2k}$ is a real function with all terms positive. It is denoted by $I_n (x)$ and is called the **modified Bessel function of the first kind of order *n*.**

Thus $I_n(x) = i^{-n} J_n (ix)$

Since i^{-n} is a constant, $I_n (x)$ is also a solution of (1).

If n is not an integer, a second independent solution of (1) is $I_{-n} (x)$,

where $$I_{-n} (x) = \sum_{r=0}^{\infty} \frac{1}{k!\,\Gamma(-n+k+1)} \left(\frac{x}{2}\right)^{-n+2k}$$

Thus, if n is not an integer, the complete solution of (1) is given by

$$y = c_1 I_n (x) + c_2 I_{-n} (x)$$

If n is a non-zero integer, a second independent solution of (1) is given by

$$K_n (x) = \frac{\pi/2}{\sin n\pi} [I_{-n} (x) - J_n (x)]$$

and is called **modified Bessel function of second kind of order *n*.**

In this case, the complete solution of (1) is given by

$$y = c_1 I_n(x) + c_2 K_n(x).$$

2.28. BER AND BEI FUNCTIONS

Consider the differential equation $x\frac{d^2y}{dx^2} + \frac{dy}{dx} - ixy = 0$ ...(1)

Comparing it with equation (1) of Art. 2.26, we have

$$\alpha = 0,\ n = 0,\ \gamma = 1 \text{ and } \beta^2 = -i \quad \text{or} \quad \beta^2 = i^3 \quad \text{so that} \quad \beta = i^{3/2}.$$

Hence a solution of (1) is given by $J_0 (i^{3/2} x)$

Replacing x by $i^{3/2}\, x$ in the series for $J_0\,(x)$, we have

$$J_0\,(i^{3/2}\,x) = 1 - \frac{i^3 x^2}{2^2} + \frac{i^6 x^4}{(2!)^2\,.\,2^4} - \frac{i^9 x^6}{(3!)^2\,.\,2^6} + \frac{i^{12}\,x^8}{(4!)^2\,.\,2^8} - \ldots\ldots$$

$$= \left[1 - \frac{x^4}{2^2\,.\,4^2} + \frac{x^8}{2^2\,.\,4^4\,.\,6^2\,.\,8^2} - \ldots\ldots\right] + i\left[\frac{x^2}{2^2} - \frac{x^6}{2^2\,.\,4^2\,.\,6^2} + \frac{x^{10}}{2^2\,.\,4^2\,.\,6^2\,.\,8^2\,.\,10^2} - \ldots\ldots\right]$$

Thus $J_0\,(i^{2/3}\,x)$ is a complex function for real values of x. The real and the imaginary parts are denoted by ber (x) (Bessel-real) and bei (x) (Bessel-imaginary) respectively. Thus

$$\text{ber}(x) = 1 + \sum_{k=1}^{\infty} \frac{(-1)^k\,x^{4k}}{2^2\,.\,4^2\,.\,6^2\,\ldots\ldots\,(4k)^2}$$

and

$$\text{bei}(x) = 1 - \sum_{k=1}^{\infty} \frac{(-1)^k\,x^{4k-2}}{2^2\,.\,4^2\,.\,6^2\,\ldots\ldots\,(4k-2)^2}$$

Hence a solution of (1) is $y = J_0(i^{3/2}\,x) = \text{ber}\,(x) + i\,\text{bei}\,(x)$.

Example. *Show that :*

$$(a)\ \frac{d}{dx}\,[x\,ber'(x)] = -\,x\,bei\,(x) \quad (b)\ \frac{d}{dx}\,[x\,bei'(x)] = x\,ber\,(x).$$

Sol. We know that

$$\text{ber}\,(x) = 1 - \frac{x^4}{2^2\,.\,4^2} + \frac{x^8}{2^2\,.\,4^2\,.\,6^2\,.\,8^2} - \ldots\ldots$$

$$\text{bei}\,(x) = \frac{x^2}{2^2} - \frac{x^6}{2^2\,.\,4^2\,.\,6^2} + \frac{x^{10}}{2^2\,.\,4^2\,.\,6^2\,.\,8^2\,.\,10^2} - \ldots\ldots$$

(*a*) Now
$$\text{ber}'\,(x) = -\frac{x^3}{2^2\,.\,4} + \frac{x^7}{2^2\,.\,4^2\,.\,6^2\,.\,8} - \ldots\ldots$$

$\therefore$
$$x\,\text{ber}'\,(x) = -\frac{x^4}{2^2\,.\,4} + \frac{x^8}{2^2\,.\,4^2\,.\,6^2\,.\,8} - \ldots\ldots$$

$$\frac{d}{dx}\,[x\,\text{ber}'\,(x)] = -\frac{x^3}{2^2} + \frac{x^7}{2^2\,.\,4^2\,.\,6^2} - \ldots\ldots$$

$$= -\,x\left(\frac{x^2}{2^2} - \frac{x^6}{2^2\,.\,4^2\,.\,6^2} + \ldots\ldots\right) = -\,x\,\text{bei}\,(x).$$

(*b*) Also
$$\text{bei}'\,(x) = \frac{x}{2} - \frac{x^5}{2^2\,.\,4^2\,.\,6} + \frac{x^9}{2^2\,.\,4^2\,.\,6^2\,.\,8^2\,.\,10} - \ldots\ldots$$

$\therefore$
$$x\,\text{bei}'\,(x) = \frac{x^2}{2} - \frac{x^6}{2^2\,.\,4^2\,.\,6} + \frac{x^{10}}{2^2\,.\,4^2\,.\,6^2\,.\,8^2\,.\,10} - \ldots\ldots$$

$$\frac{d}{dx}\,[x\,\text{bci}'\,(x)] = x - \frac{x^5}{2^2\,.\,4^2} + \frac{x^9}{2^2\,.\,4^2\,.\,6^2\,.\,8^2}\ \ldots\ldots$$

$$= x\left(1 - \frac{x^4}{2^2\,.\,4^2} + \frac{x^8}{2^2\,.\,4^2\,.\,6^2\,.\,8^2} - \ldots\ldots\right) = x\,\text{ber}\,(x).$$

2.29. ORTHOGONALITY OF BESSEL FUNCTIONS [*U.P.T.U. (SUM) 2009*]

If α and β are the roots of $J_n(x) = 0$, then

$$\int_0^1 x\, J_n(\alpha x) . J_n(\beta x)\, dx = \begin{cases} 0, & \text{when } \alpha \neq \beta \\ \frac{1}{2} J^2{}_{n+1}(\alpha), & \text{when } \alpha = \beta \end{cases}$$

Consider the Bessel's equations

$$x^2 u'' + xu' + (\alpha^2 x^2 - n^2) u = 0 \qquad ...(1)$$

and

$$x^2 v'' + xv' + (\beta^2 x^2 - n^2)\, v = 0 \qquad ...(2)$$

Their solutions are $u = J_n(\alpha x)$ and $v = J_n(\beta x)$ respectively.

Multiplying (1) by $\frac{v}{x}$ and (2) by $\frac{u}{x}$ and subtracting, we get

$$x(u''v - uv'') + (u'v - uv') + (\alpha^2 - \beta^2)\, xuv = 0$$

or

$$\frac{d}{dx}[x(u'v - uv')] = (\beta^2 - \alpha^2)\, xuv$$

Integrating both sides w.r.t. x between the limits 0 and 1, we get

$$(\beta^2 - \alpha^2) \int_0^1 xuv\, dx = \Big[x\,(u'v - uv') \Big]_0^1 = \Big[u'v - uv' \Big]_{x=1} \qquad ...(3)$$

Since $u = J_n(\alpha x)$

$$\therefore \quad u' = \frac{d}{dx}[J_n(\alpha x)] = \frac{d}{d(\alpha x)}(J_n(\alpha x)] . \frac{d(\alpha x)}{dx} = \alpha J_n{}'(\alpha x)$$

Similarly, $v = J_n(\beta x) \Rightarrow v' = \beta J_n{}'(\beta x)$

Substituting for u, v, u' and v' in (3), we get

$$\int_0^1 x J_n(\alpha x)\, J_n(\beta x)\, dx = \frac{\alpha J_n'(\alpha)\, J_n(\beta) - \beta J_n(\alpha)\, J_n'(\beta)}{\beta^2 - \alpha^2} \qquad ...(4)$$

If α and β are *distinct* roots of $J_n(x) = 0$, then $J_n(\alpha) = 0$ and $J_n(\beta) = 0$.

Hence, from (4), we have

$$\int_0^1 x J_n(\alpha x)\, J_n(\beta x)\, dx = 0$$

However, if $\alpha = \beta$, the value of the integral is $\frac{0}{0}$, which is indeterminate.

To evaluate the integral, we assume that α is a root of $J_n(x) = 0$ so that $J_n(\alpha) = 0$ and β is a variable approaching α. Thus, from (4), we have

$$\operatorname*{Lt}_{\beta \to \alpha} \int_0^1 x J_n(\alpha x)\, J_n(\beta x)\, dx = \operatorname*{Lt}_{\beta \to \alpha} \frac{\alpha J_n'(\alpha)\, J_n(\beta)}{\beta^2 - \alpha^2}$$

or

$$\int_0^1 x J_n^2(\alpha x)\, dx = \operatorname*{Lt}_{\beta \to \alpha} \frac{\alpha J_n'(\alpha)\, J_n(\beta)}{2\beta} \qquad \text{[by L-Hospital's rule]}$$

$$= \frac{1}{2}[J_n'(\alpha)]^2 \qquad ...(5)$$

But $\quad x J_n'(x) = n J_n(x) - x J_{n+1}(x)$

$\therefore \quad x J_n'(\alpha) = n J_n(\alpha) - \alpha J_{n+1}(\alpha) = -\alpha J_{n+1}(\alpha)$, since $J_n(\alpha) = 0$

$$\Rightarrow \qquad J_n'(\alpha) = -J_{n+1}(\alpha)$$

Hence, from (5), we get $\int_0^1 xJ_n^2(\alpha x)\,dx = \frac{1}{2} J^2_{n+1}(\alpha)$.

Note. If the interval is from 0 to a, it can be shown that

$$\int_0^a xJ_n^2(\alpha x)\,dx = \frac{a^2}{2} J_{n+1}^2(\alpha a), \quad \text{where } \alpha \text{ is a root of } J_n(\alpha a) = 0.$$

2.30. FOURIER-BESSEL EXPANSION OF $f(x)$

From the orthogonal property of Bessel functions, we can expand a function $f(x)$ in Fourier-Bessel series in the range 0 to a.

Let $\quad f(x) = c_1 J_n(\lambda_1 x) + c_2 J_n(\lambda_2 x) + \ldots\ldots + c_n J_n(\lambda_n x) + \ldots\ldots = \sum_{i=1}^{\infty} c_1 J_n(\lambda_i x) \quad \ldots(1)$

where $\lambda_1, \lambda_2, \ldots\ldots$ are the roots of the equation $J_n(\lambda a) = 0$.

To determine c_i, we multiply both sides of (1) by $xJ_n(\lambda_i x)$ and integrate w.r.t. x between the limits 0 to a. From the orthogonal property of Bessel functions, all integrals on the right hand side will vanish except the one containing c_i and we have

$$\int_0^a xf(x)\,J_n(\lambda_i x)\,dx = c_i \int_0^a xJ_n^2(\lambda_i x)\,dx = c_i \cdot \frac{a^2}{2} J^2_{n+1}(\lambda_i a)$$

$$\therefore \qquad c_i = \frac{2}{a^2 J^2_{n+1}(\lambda_{ia})} \int_0^a xf(x)\,J_n(\lambda_i x)\,dx$$

Putting $i = 1, 2, 3, \ldots\ldots$ we can find $c_1, c_2, c_3, \ldots\ldots$ and hence the function $f(x)$.

ILLUSTRATIVE EXAMPLES

Example 1. *If $\alpha_1, \alpha_2, \ldots\ldots, \alpha_n$ are the positive roots of $J_0(x) = 0$, prove that*

$$\frac{1}{2} = \sum_{n=1}^{\infty} \frac{J_0(\alpha_n x)}{\alpha_n J_1(\alpha_n)}.$$

Sol. We know that if $f(x) = \sum_{i=1}^{\infty} c_i J_n(\alpha_i x) \quad \ldots(1)$

then
$$c_i = \frac{2}{a^2 J^2_{n+1}(\alpha_i a)} \int_0^a xf(x)\,J_n(\alpha_i x)\,dx$$

Taking $f(x) = 1$, $a = 1$ and $n = 0$, we get

$$c_i = \frac{2}{J_1^2(\alpha_i)} \int_0^1 xJ_0(\alpha_i x)\,dx = \frac{2}{J_1^2(\alpha_i)} \left[\frac{xJ_1(\alpha_i x)}{\alpha_i}\right]_0^1 = \frac{2}{\alpha_i J_1(\alpha_i)}$$

$\therefore$ From (1), we have $1 = \sum_{i=1}^{\infty} \frac{2}{\alpha_i J_1(\alpha_i)} J_0(\alpha_i x)$

or
$$\frac{1}{2} = \sum_{n=1}^{\infty} \frac{J_0(\alpha_n x)}{\alpha_n J_1(\alpha_n)}.$$

Example 2. *Show that the Fourier-Bessel series in $J_2(\lambda_n x)$ for $f(x) = x^2$ $(0 < x < a)$, where $\lambda_n a$ are positive roots of $J_2(x) = 0$, is*

$$x^2 = 2a^2 \sum_{n=1}^{\infty} \frac{J_2(\lambda_n x)}{a\lambda_n J_3(\lambda_n a)}.$$

Sol. Let the Fourier-Bessel series representing $f(x) = x^2$ be given by

$$x^2 = \sum_{n=1}^{\infty} c_n J_2(\lambda_n x)$$

Multiplying both sides by $xJ_2(\lambda_n x)$ and integrating w.r.t. x between the limits 0 to a, we get

$$\int_0^a x^3 J_2(\lambda_n x)\, dx = c_n \int_0^a x J_2^2(\lambda_n x)\, dx$$

or
$$\left[\frac{x^3 J_3(\lambda_n x)}{\lambda_n}\right]_0^a = c_n \cdot \frac{a^2}{2} J_3^2(\lambda_n a)$$

or
$$\frac{a^3 J_3(\lambda_n a)}{\lambda_n} = c_n \cdot \frac{a^2}{2} J_3^2(\lambda_n a)$$

$\therefore$
$$c_n = \frac{2a^2}{a\lambda_n} \cdot \frac{1}{J_3(\lambda_n a)}$$

Hence
$$x^2 = 2a^2 \sum_{n=1}^{\infty} \frac{J_2(\lambda_n x)}{a\lambda_n J_3(\lambda_n a)}.$$

TEST YOUR KNOWLEDGE

1. Solve the following differential equations in terms of Bessel functions :

   (*i*) $xy'' + y = 0$

   (*ii*) $xy'' - y' + 4x^3 y = 0$

   (*iii*) $y'' + \frac{1}{x}y' + 4\left(1 - \frac{1}{x^2}\right) y = 0$

   (*iv*) $y'' + \frac{1}{x}y' + \left(3 - \frac{1}{4x^2}\right) y = 0$

   (*v*) $y'' + \left(9 - \frac{20}{x^2}\right) y = 0.$

   (*vi*) $x^2 y'' - xy' + 4x^2 y = 0$

   (*vii*) $y'' + \frac{1}{x}y' + \left(8 - \frac{1}{x^2}\right) y = 0$ (*G.B.T.U. 2012*)

   (*viii*) $4y'' + 9xy = 0$

   (*ix*) $xy'' + y' + \frac{1}{4}y = 0$

2. Expand $f(x) = 1$ over the interval $0 < x < 3$ in terms of the functions $J_0(\lambda_n x)$, where λ_n are determined by $J_0(3\lambda) = 0$.

3. Expand $f(x) = 4x - x^3$ over the interval (0, 2) in terms of Bessel functions of first kind of order one which satisfy the condition $[J_1(\lambda x)]_{x=2} = 0$.

4. If $\alpha_1, \alpha_2, \ldots\ldots, \alpha_n, \ldots\ldots$ are the positive roots of $J_1(x) = 0$, prove that

(i) $x^2 = \dfrac{1}{2} + 4 \displaystyle\sum_{n=1}^{\infty} \dfrac{J_0(\alpha_n x)}{\alpha_n^2 J_0(\alpha_n)}$ (ii) $(1 - x^2)^2 = \dfrac{1}{3} - 64 \displaystyle\sum_{n=1}^{\infty} \dfrac{J_0(\alpha_n x)}{\alpha_n^2 J_0(\alpha_n)}$.

5. If a is the root of the equation $J_0(x) = 0$, show that

(i) $\displaystyle\int_0^1 J_1(ax)\, dx = \dfrac{1}{a}$ (ii) $\displaystyle\int_0^a J_1(x)\, dx = 1$.

Answers

1. (i) $y = \sqrt{x}\,[c_1 J_1(2\sqrt{x}) + c_2 Y_1(2\sqrt{x})]$ (ii) $y = x\,[c_1 J_{1/2}(x^2) + c_2 J_{-1/2}(x^2)]$

(iii) $y = c_1 J_2(2x) + c_2 Y_2(2x)$ (iv) $y = c_1 J_{1/2}(\sqrt{3}x) + c_2 J_{-1/2}(\sqrt{3}x)$

(v) $y = \sqrt{x}\,[c_1 J_{9/2}(3x) + c_2 J_{-9/2}(3x)]$ (vi) $y = x[c_1 J_1(2x) + c_2 Y_1(2x)]$

(vii) $y = c_1 J_2(4\sqrt{2x}) + c_2 Y_2(4\sqrt{2x})$ (viii) $y = x^{1/2}\,[c_1 J_{1/3}(x^{3/2}) + c_2 J_{-1/3}(x^{3/2})]$

(ix) $y = c_1 J_0(\sqrt{x}) + c_2 Y_0(\sqrt{x})$

2. $1 = \dfrac{2}{3} \displaystyle\sum_{n=1}^{\infty} \dfrac{J_0(\lambda_n x)}{\lambda_n J_1(3\lambda_n)}$

3. $4x - x^3 = 8 \displaystyle\sum_{n=1}^{\infty} \dfrac{J_3(2\lambda_n)}{\lambda_n^2 J_2^2(2\lambda_n)} \cdot J_1(\lambda_n x)$.

ASSIGNMENT-II

(2 Marks Questions for Section–A)

1. Evaluate $\displaystyle\int_{-1}^{1} x^2 P_2(x)\, dx$. *(G.B.T.U. 2012)*

2. Evaluate $\displaystyle\int_0^{\pi/2} \sqrt{\pi x}\, J_{1/2}(2x)\, dx$. *(G.B.T.U. 2012)*

3. Classify the singular points of the differential equation. $x^2 \dfrac{d^2y}{dx^2} + ax\dfrac{dy}{dx} + by = 0$ where a and b are constants. *(M.T.U. 2012)*

4. Show that $\displaystyle\sum_{n=0}^{\infty} P_n(x) = \dfrac{1}{\sqrt{2}} \cdot \dfrac{1}{\sqrt{1-x}}$. *(M.T.U. 2012)*

5. What is the generating function for $P_n(x)$? *[G.B.T.U. (SUM) 2010]*

6. State Rodrigue's formula for Legendre polynomial $P_n(x)$. *[(U.P.T.U. 2009, G.B.T.U. 2010]*

7. Express $2x^2 + x + 3$ interms of Legendre polynomials.

8. Legendre polynomial is $P_5(x) = \lambda\left(x^5 - \dfrac{70}{63}x^3 + \dfrac{15}{63}x\right)$. Here find the value of λ.

9. Let $P_n(x)$ be Legendre polynomial of degree $n > 1$ then find $\int_{-1}^{1} (1+x)\, P_n(x)\, dx$ ·

10. Find $\int_{-1}^{1} (2x+1)\, P_3(x)$.

11. Evaluate $\int_{0}^{\pi} [J_{-2}(x) - J_2(x)]\, dx$.

12. If $3x^2 = m\ P_2(x) + nP_0(x)$, then find m and n. *(G.B.T.U. 2011)*

13. If $J_{1/2}(x) = \sqrt{\dfrac{m}{\pi x}}\ \sin kx$, then find m and k. *[M.T.U. (SUM) 2011]*

14. If $\dfrac{d}{dx}[J_0(x)] = nJ_1(x)$, then find n. *(M.T.U. 2011)*

15. What are the roots of the indicial equation for the power series solution of the differential equation. $2x^2y'' + xy' + (x^2 - 3)y = 0$. *(M.T.U. 2011)*

16. If $P_3(x) = \dfrac{1}{2}\ (mx^3 - nx)$, then find the value of m and n. *[M.T.U. (SUM) 2011]*

17. Evaluate: $\int_{-1}^{1} P_n^2(x)\, dx$

18. Evaluate: $\dfrac{d}{dx}[x^n\ J_n(x)]$

19. Evaluate: $\int_{0}^{1} xJ_n(\alpha x)\, J_n(\beta x)\, dx\ (\alpha \neq \beta)$

20. Evaluate: $P_{2n+1}(0)$.

Answers

1. $\dfrac{4}{15}$ **2.** 1

3. $x = 0$ is a regular singular point **5.** $(1 - 2hx + h^2)^{-1/2}$

6. $P_n(x) = \dfrac{1}{n!\, 2^n} \dfrac{d^n}{dx^n} (x^2 - 1)^n$ **7.** $\dfrac{1}{3}\ (4P_2 + 3P_1 + 11P_0)$

8. $\dfrac{63}{8}$ **9.** 0 **10.** 0

11. 0 **12.** $m = 2, n = 1$ **13.** $m = 2, k = 1$

14. -1 **15.** $-1, \dfrac{3}{2}$ **16.** 5, 3

17. $\dfrac{2}{2n+1}$ **18.** $x^nJ_{n-1}(x)$ **19.** 0

20. 0

UNIT 3
Laplace Transform

3.1. INTRODUCTION

A transformation is a mathematical device which converts one function into another. For example, when the differential operator D $\left(\equiv \dfrac{d}{dx}\right)$ operates on $f(x) = \sin x$, it gives a new function $g(x) = \mathrm{D}\, f(x) = \cos x$.

Laplace transform or Laplace transformation is widely used by scientists and engineers. It is particularly effective in solving linear differential equations—ordinary as well as partial. It reduces an ordinary differential equation into an algebraic equation.

Laplace transform directly gives the solution of differential equations with given initial conditions without the necessity of first finding the general solution and then evaluating the arbitrary constants.

French Mathematician Pierre De Laplace (1749–1827) used this transform much earlier in 1799 while developing the theory of probability.

3.2. DEFINITION

Let $\mathrm{F}(t)$ be a function of t defined for all $t \geq 0$. Then the *Laplace transform* of $\mathrm{F}(t)$, denoted by $\mathrm{L}\{\mathrm{F}(t)\}$, is defined by

$$\boxed{\mathrm{L}\{\mathrm{F}(t)\} = f(p) = \int_0^\infty e^{-pt}\,\mathrm{F}(t)\, dt}$$

provided that the integral exists, 'p' is a parameter which may be real or complex.

$\mathrm{L}\{\mathrm{F}(t)\}$ is said to exist if the above integral converges for some value of p otherwise not.

The function $f(p)$ is called the Laplace transform or the image of the object function $\mathrm{F}(t)$.

Remark 1. Some authors use the letter s for the parameter instead of p. Therefore, we may also write

$$\mathrm{L}\,\{\mathrm{F}(t)\} = \int_0^\infty e^{-st}\,\mathrm{F}(t)\, dt = f(s).$$

Remark 2. In general, we will denote the object function by a capital letter and its transform by the same letter in lower case. But other notations that distinguish between functions and their transforms are sometimes preferable

e.g., $\mathrm{L}\{\mathrm{F}(t)\} = \phi(p)$ or $\mathrm{L}\{y(t)\} = \bar{y}(p)$ or $\mathrm{L}\{f(t)\} = \bar{f}(p)$ etc.

3.3. LINEARITY PROPERTY

If c_1, c_2 are constants and f, g are functions of t, then

$$L\{c_1 f(t) + c_2 g(t)\} = c_1 L\{f(t)\} + c_2 L\{g(t)\}$$

By definition, $L\{c_1 f(t) + c_2 g(t)\} = \int_0^\infty e^{-pt} \{c_1 f(t) + c_2 g(t)\}\, dt$

$$= c_1 \int_0^\infty e^{-pt} f(t)\, dt + c_2 \int_0^\infty e^{-pt}\, g(t)\, dt = c_1 L\{f(t)\} + c_2 L\{g(t)\}$$

The result can easily be generalised.

3.4. LAPLACE TRANSFORM OF SOME ELEMENTARY FUNCTIONS

(1) $\mathbf{L\{1\} = \frac{1}{p}}$, $p > 0$

$$L\{1\} = \int_0^\infty e^{-pt} . 1\, dt = \left[-\frac{e^{-pt}}{p} \right]_0^\infty = \frac{1}{p}, \text{ if } p > 0.$$

(2) $\mathbf{L\{t^n\} = \frac{n!}{p^{n+1}}}$, where n is a positive integer.

$$L\{t^n\} = \int_0^\infty e^{-pt} . t^n\, dt = \int_0^\infty e^{-x} \left(\frac{x}{p}\right)^n \frac{dx}{p}, \text{ on putting } pt = x$$

$$= \frac{1}{p^{n+1}} \int_0^\infty x^n e^{-x}\, dx = \frac{\Gamma(n+1)}{p^{n+1}} \quad \text{provided that } p > 0 \text{ and } n + 1 > 0 \text{ i.e., } n > -1.$$

If n is a positive integer, $\Gamma(n + 1) = n\,!$

$$\therefore \qquad L\{t^n\} = \frac{n!}{p^{n+1}}.$$

Note. For $n = 1$, $L(t) = \frac{1}{p^2}$.

(3) $\mathbf{L\{e^{at}\} = \frac{1}{p - a}}$, $p > a$

$$L\{e^{at}\} = \int_0^\infty e^{-pt} . e^{at}\, dt = \int_0^\infty e^{-(p-a)t}\, dt = \left[-\frac{e^{-(p-a)t}}{p-a} \right]_0^\infty = \frac{1}{p-a}, \text{ if } p > a.$$

(4) $\mathbf{L\{\sin at\} = \frac{a}{p^2 + a^2}}$, $p > 0$

$$L\{\sin at\} = \int_0^\infty e^{-pt} \sin at\, dt = \left[\frac{e^{-pt}}{p^2 + a^2} (-\, p \sin at - a \cos at) \right]_0^\infty = \frac{a}{p^2 + a^2}.$$

(5) $\mathbf{L\{\cos at\} = \frac{p}{p^2 + a^2}}$, $p > 0$.

$$L\{\cos at\} = \int_0^\infty e^{-pt} . \cos at\, dt = \left[\frac{e^{-pt}}{p^2 + a^2} (-\, p \cos at + a \sin at) \right]_0^\infty = \frac{p}{p^2 + a^2}.$$

(6) **L{sinh *at*}** $= \dfrac{a}{p^2 - a^2}$, $p > |a|$.

$$\text{L}[\sinh at] = \int_0^\infty e^{-pt} \sinh at \, dt = \int_0^\infty e^{-pt} . \left[\frac{e^{at} - e^{-at}}{2}\right] dt$$

$$= \frac{1}{2}\left[\int_0^\infty e^{-(p-a)t} \, dt - \int_0^\infty e^{-(p+a)t} \, dt\right]$$

$$= \frac{1}{2}\left[\frac{1}{p-a} - \frac{1}{p+a}\right] = \frac{a}{p^2 - a^2}, \text{ for } p > |a|.$$

Note. We can also prove it by using linearity property.

Thus $\text{L}\{\sinh at\} = \text{L}\{\frac{1}{2}(e^{at} - e^{-at})\} = \frac{1}{2}\text{L}(e^{at}) - \frac{1}{2}\text{L}(e^{-at})$

$$= \frac{1}{2}\left(\frac{1}{p-a}\right) - \frac{1}{2}\left(\frac{1}{p+a}\right) = \frac{a}{p^2 - a^2}$$

(7) **L{cosh *at*}** $= \dfrac{p}{p^2 - a^2}$, $p > |a|$.

$$\text{L}\{\cosh at\} = \text{L}\{\tfrac{1}{2}(e^{at} + e^{-at})\} = \tfrac{1}{2}\text{L}\{e^{at}\} + \tfrac{1}{2}\text{L}\{e^{-at}\}$$

$$= \frac{1}{2}\left(\frac{1}{p-a}\right) + \frac{1}{2}\left(\frac{1}{p+a}\right) = \frac{p}{p^2 - a^2}, \text{ for } p > |a|.$$

For ready reference, the Laplace transforms of various elementary functions have been listed in the following table:

F(t)	*L[F(t)] = f(p)*
1	$\frac{1}{p}, p > 0$
t	$\frac{1}{p^2}, p > 0$
t^n, *n is a positive integer*	$\frac{n!}{p^{n+1}}, p > 0$
$t^n, n > -1$	$\frac{\Gamma(n+1)}{p^{n+1}}, p > 0$
e^{at}	$\frac{1}{p-a}, p > a$
e^{-at}	$\frac{1}{p+a}$
$\sin at$	$\frac{a}{p^2 + a^2}, p > 0$
$\cos at$	$\frac{p}{p^2 + a^2}, p > 0$
$\sinh at$	$\frac{a}{p^2 - a^2}, p > \|a\|$
$\cosh at$	$\frac{p}{p^2 - a^2}, p > \|a\|$

3.5. TRANSFORMS OF DISCONTINUOUS FUNCTIONS

The Laplace transform of F(t) will exist even if the object function F(t) is discontinuous, provided the integral in the definition of L{F(t)} exists.

3.6. FIRST TRANSLATION PROPERTY OR FIRST SHIFTING PROPERTY

If $\mathbf{L\{F(t)\} = f(p)}$ **then** $\mathbf{L\{e^{at}\,F(t)\} = f(p - a)}$. [*G.B.T.U. (C.O.) 2010, 2011*]

$$L\{e^{at}\,F(t)\} = \int_0^\infty e^{-pt} . e^{at}\,F(t)\,dt \qquad \text{| By definition}$$

$$= \int_0^\infty e^{-(p-a)t}\,F(t)\,dt = f(p-a).$$

Remark 1. $L\{e^{-at}\,F(t)\} = f(p+a)$.

Remark 2. $L\{e^{at}\,F(bt)\} = \frac{1}{b} f\left(\frac{p-a}{b}\right)$.

Applying this property to the elementary functions of Art. 3.4, we get the following useful results:

(1) $\mathbf{L\{e^{at}\,t^n\} = \dfrac{n!}{(p-a)^{n+1}}}$ **; n is a positive integer.**

(2) $\mathbf{L\{e^{at}\sin bt\} = \dfrac{b}{(p-a)^2 + b^2}}$ (3) $\mathbf{L\{e^{at}\cos bt\} = \dfrac{p-a}{(p-a)^2 + b^2}}$

(4) $\mathbf{L\{e^{at}\sinh bt\} = \dfrac{b}{(p-a)^2 - b^2}}$ (5) $\mathbf{L\{e^{at}\cosh bt\} = \dfrac{p-a}{(p-a)^2 - b^2}}$.

3.7. SECOND TRANSLATION PROPERTY OR HEAVISIDE'S SHIFTING THEOREM

If $\mathbf{L\{F(t)\} = f(p)}$ **and** $\mathbf{G(t) = \begin{cases} F(t-a), & t > a \\ 0, & t < a \end{cases}}$

[*U.P.T.U. 2006, 2008; U.P.T.U. (C.O.) 2009; M.T.U. 2012*]

then, $\mathbf{L\{G(t)\} = e^{-ap} f(p)}$.

$$L\{G(t)\} = \int_0^\infty e^{-pt} . G(t)\,dt = \int_0^a e^{-pt}\,G(t)\,dt + \int_a^\infty e^{-pt}\,G(t)\,dt$$

$$= 0 + \int_a^\infty e^{-pt} . F(t-a)\,dt = \int_a^\infty e^{-pt} . F(t-a)\,dt$$

Put $t - a = u \Rightarrow dt = du$

$$= \int_0^\infty e^{-p(u+a)}\,F(u)\,du = e^{-pa} \int_0^\infty e^{-pu}\,F(u)\,du$$

$$= e^{-ap} \int_0^\infty e^{-pt} F(t)\,dt = e^{-ap} f(p).$$

3.8. CHANGE OF SCALE PROPERTY

[*U.P.T.U. (SUM) 2008*]

If $\mathbf{L\{F(t)\} = f(p)}$ **then** $\mathbf{L\{F(at)\} = \dfrac{1}{a} f\left(\dfrac{p}{a}\right)}$.

$$L\{F(at)\} = \int_0^\infty e^{-pt} F(at)\,dt$$

Put $at = u \Rightarrow dt = \dfrac{du}{a}$

$$= \int_0^\infty e^{-p\frac{u}{a}} F(u) \frac{du}{a} = \frac{1}{a}\int_0^\infty e^{-\left(\frac{p}{a}\right)u} F(u)\, du$$

$$= \frac{1}{a}\int_0^\infty e^{-\left(\frac{p}{a}\right)t} F(t)\, dt = \frac{1}{a} f\left(\frac{p}{a}\right).$$

ILLUSTRATIVE EXAMPLES

Example 1. *Find the Laplace transform of* $7e^{2t} + 9e^{-2t} + 5\cos t + 7t^3 + 5\sin 3t + 2$.

Sol. $L(7e^{2t} + 9e^{-2t} + 5\cos t + 7t^3 + 5\sin 3t + 2)$

$$= 7\,L(e^{2t}) + 9\,L(e^{-2t}) + 5\,L(\cos t) + 7\,L(t^3) + 5\,L(\sin 3t) + 2\,L(1)$$

$$= 7 \cdot \frac{1}{p-2} + 9 \cdot \frac{1}{p+2} + 5 \cdot \frac{p}{p^2+1} + 7 \cdot \frac{3!}{p^4} + 5 \cdot \frac{3}{p^2+9} + 2 \cdot \frac{1}{p}$$

$$= \frac{7}{p-2} + \frac{9}{p+2} + \frac{5p}{p^2+1} + \frac{42}{p^4} + \frac{15}{p^2+9} + \frac{2}{p}.$$

Example 2. *Find the Laplace transforms of*

(*i*) *sin 2t cos 3t* (*ii*) *sin³ 2t*

(*iii*) *cosh³ 2t* (*iv*) $(1 + te^{-t})^3$.

Sol. (*i*) Since $\sin 2t \cos 3t = \frac{1}{2}(2\cos 3t \sin 2t) = \frac{1}{2}(\sin 5t - \sin t)$

$$\therefore \quad L\{\sin 2t \cos 3t\} = L\{\tfrac{1}{2}(\sin 5t - \sin t)\} = \tfrac{1}{2}[L\{\sin 5t\} - L\{\sin t\}]$$

$$= \frac{1}{2}\left[\frac{5}{p^2+5^2} - \frac{1}{p^2+1^2}\right] = \frac{2(p^2-5)}{(p^2+25)(p^2+1)}$$

(*ii*) Since $\sin 6t = 3\sin 2t - 4\sin^3 2t$

$$\Rightarrow \quad \sin^3 2t = \frac{3}{4}\sin 2t - \frac{1}{4}\sin 6t$$

$$\therefore \quad L\{\sin^3 2t\} = L\left\{\frac{3}{4}\sin 2t - \frac{1}{4}\sin 6t\right\} = \frac{3}{4}L\{\sin 2t\} - \frac{1}{4}L\{\sin 6t\}$$

$$= \frac{3}{4} \cdot \frac{2}{p^2+2^2} - \frac{1}{4} \cdot \frac{6}{p^2+6^2} = \frac{48}{(p^2+4)(p^2+36)}.$$

(*iii*) Since $\cosh 6t = 4\cosh^3 2t - 3\cosh 2t$

$$\Rightarrow \quad \cosh^3 2t = \frac{3}{4}\cosh 2t + \frac{1}{4}\cosh 6t$$

$$\therefore \quad L\{\cosh^3 2t\} = L\left\{\frac{3}{4}\cosh 2t + \frac{1}{4}\cosh 6t\right\} = \frac{3}{4}L\{\cosh 2t\} + \frac{1}{4}L\{\cosh 6t\}$$

$$= \frac{3}{4} \cdot \frac{p}{p^2-2^2} + \frac{1}{4} \cdot \frac{p}{p^2-6^2} = \frac{p(p^2-28)}{(p^2-4)(p^2-36)}.$$

(*iv*) $(1 + te^{-t})^3 = 1 + t^3 e^{-3t} + 3te^{-t}(1 + te^{-t}) = 1 + t^3 e^{-3t} + 3te^{-t} + 3t^2 e^{-2t}$

$$L\{(1 + te^{-t})^3\} = L(1) + L(t^3 e^{-3t}) + 3L(te^{-t}) + 3L(t^2 e^{-2t}) \qquad \text{...(1)}$$

Determination of $L(t^3 e^{-3t})$:

$$L(t^3) = \frac{3!}{p^4}$$

$$\therefore \quad L(e^{-3t} t^3) = \frac{3!}{(p+3)^4} = \frac{6}{(p+3)^4} \qquad | \text{Using first shifting property}$$

Determination of $L(t e^{-t})$:

$$L(t) = \frac{1}{p^2}$$

$$\therefore \quad L(e^{-t} . t) = \frac{1}{(p+1)^2} \qquad | \text{Using first shifting property}$$

Determination of $L(t^2 e^{-2t})$:

$$L(t^2) = \frac{2!}{p^3}$$

$$\therefore \quad L(e^{-2t} . t^2) = \frac{2!}{(p+2)^3} = \frac{2}{(p+2)^3} \qquad | \text{Using first shifting property}$$

Also, $\quad L(1) = \dfrac{1}{p}$

Now, from (1), $\quad L\{(1 + t e^{-t})^3\} = \dfrac{1}{p} + \dfrac{6}{(p+3)^4} + \dfrac{3}{(p+1)^2} + \dfrac{6}{(p+2)^3}$.

Example 3. *Find the Laplace transform of e^{-3t} (cos 4t + 3 sin 4t).*

Sol. $\quad L(\cos 4t + 3 \sin 4t) = L(\cos 4t) + 3L(\sin 4t)$

$$= \frac{p}{p^2+16} + \frac{12}{p^2+16} = \frac{p+12}{p^2+16}$$

$$\therefore \quad L\{e^{-3t}(\cos 4t + 3 \sin 4t)\} = \frac{(p+3)+12}{(p+3)^2+16} \qquad | \text{ Using first shifting property}$$

$$= \frac{p+15}{p^2+6p+25}.$$

Example 4. *Find the Laplace transform of*

(*i*) $\left(\sqrt{t} + \dfrac{1}{\sqrt{t}}\right)^3$ (*ii*) *cosh at sin bt* (*iii*) *$\sinh^2 2t$*

(*iv*) e^{-t} *cos t cos 2t* (*v*) $e^t \, t^{-\frac{1}{2}}$.

Sol. (*i*) $\left(\sqrt{t} + \dfrac{1}{\sqrt{t}}\right)^3 = (\sqrt{t})^3 + \left(\dfrac{1}{\sqrt{t}}\right)^3 + 3\sqrt{t} . \dfrac{1}{\sqrt{t}}\left(\sqrt{t} + \dfrac{1}{\sqrt{t}}\right) = t^{3/2} + t^{-3/2} + 3\,t^{1/2} + 3t^{-1/2}$

$$\therefore\ L\left\{\left(\sqrt{t}+\frac{1}{\sqrt{t}}\right)^3\right\} = L(t^{3/2} + t^{-3/2} + 3t^{1/2} + 3t^{-1/2}) = L(t^{3/2}) + L(t^{-3/2}) + 3\,L(t^{1/2}) + 3\,L\,(t^{-1/2})$$

$$= \frac{\Gamma(\frac{5}{2})}{p^{5/2}} + \frac{\Gamma(-\frac{1}{2})}{p^{-1/2}} + 3\,\frac{\Gamma(\frac{3}{2})}{p^{3/2}} + 3\,\frac{\Gamma(\frac{1}{2})}{p^{1/2}}$$

$$= \frac{\frac{3}{2}\cdot\frac{1}{2}\sqrt{\pi}}{p^{5/2}} + \frac{(-2\sqrt{\pi})}{p^{-1/2}} + 3\,.\,\frac{\frac{1}{2}\sqrt{\pi}}{p^{3/2}} + 3\,\frac{\sqrt{\pi}}{p^{1/2}} \qquad \left|\ \because\ \Gamma\left(-\frac{1}{2}\right) = -2\sqrt{\pi}\right.$$

$$= \sqrt{\pi}\left[\frac{3}{4p^{5/2}} - 2\sqrt{p} + \frac{3}{2p^{3/2}} + \frac{3}{\sqrt{p}}\right]$$

(*ii*) $\because\ \cosh at \sin bt = \left(\dfrac{e^{at}+e^{-at}}{2}\right)\sin bt$

$$\therefore\quad L\,(\cosh at \sin bt) = \frac{1}{2}\left[L(e^{at}\sin bt) + L\,(e^{-at}\sin bt)\right] = \frac{1}{2}\left[\frac{b}{(p-a)^2+b^2} + \frac{b}{(p+a)^2+b^2}\right]$$

| Using first shifting property

(*iii*)
$$\sinh^2 2t = \left(\frac{e^{2t}-e^{-2t}}{2}\right)^2 = \frac{1}{4}(e^{4t}+e^{-4t}-2)$$

$$\therefore\quad L(\sinh^2 2t) = \frac{1}{4}\left[L(e^{4t}) + L(e^{-4t}) - L(2)\right]$$

$$= \frac{1}{4}\left[\frac{1}{p-4} + \frac{1}{p+4} - \frac{2}{p}\right] = \frac{1}{2}\left[\frac{p}{p^2-16} - \frac{1}{p}\right]$$

(*iv*)
$$\cos t \cos 2t = \frac{1}{2}\,(\cos 3t + \cos t)$$

$$\therefore\ L\{e^{-t}\cos t\cos 2t\} = \frac{1}{2}\left[L(e^{-t}\cos 3t) + L(e^{-t}\cos t)\right] = \frac{1}{2}\left[\frac{p+1}{(p+1)^2+9} + \frac{p+1}{(p+1)^2+1}\right]$$

| Using first shifting property

(*v*)
$$L(t^{-1/2}) = \frac{\Gamma(\frac{1}{2})}{p^{1/2}} = \frac{\sqrt{\pi}}{\sqrt{p}}$$

$$\therefore\quad L\,(e^t\, t^{-1/2}) = \frac{\sqrt{\pi}}{\sqrt{p-1}}.$$ | Using first shifting property

Example 5. *Find the Laplace transform of f(t) defined as*

$$f(t) = \begin{cases} \dfrac{t}{T}, & \text{when } 0 < t < T \\ 1, & \text{when } t > T. \end{cases}$$

Sol.
$$L\{f(t)\} = \int_0^\infty e^{-pt} f(t)\,dt = \int_0^T e^{-pt}\,.\,\frac{t}{T}\,dt + \int_T^\infty e^{-pt}\,.\,1\,dt$$

$$= \frac{1}{T}\left[\left| t.\frac{e^{-pt}}{-p}\right|_0^T - \int_0^T 1.\frac{e^{-pt}}{-p}dt\right] + \left[\frac{e^{-pt}}{-p}\right]_T^\infty$$

$$= \frac{1}{T}\left[-\frac{T}{p}e^{-pT} + \frac{1}{p}\left\{\frac{e^{-pt}}{-p}\right\}_0^T\right] + \frac{e^{-pT}}{p} = -\frac{e^{-pT}}{p} - \left(\frac{e^{-pT}-1}{Tp^2}\right) + \frac{e^{-pT}}{p} = \frac{1-e^{-pT}}{Tp^2}.$$

Example 6. *Find the Laplace transform of*

(i) $F(t) = \begin{cases} \cos t, & 0 < t < \pi \\ 0, & t > \pi \end{cases}$ (ii) $F(t) = \begin{cases} 1, & 0 \le t < 1 \\ t, & 1 \le t < 2 \\ t^2, & 2 \le t < \infty \end{cases}.$

(iii) $F(t) = \begin{cases} t^2, & 0 < t < 2 \\ t-1, & 2 < t < 3 \\ 7, & t > 3 \end{cases}.$ (U.P.T.U. 2007)

Sol. (i) $L\{F(t)\} = \int_0^\infty e^{-pt}.F(t)\,dt = \int_0^\pi e^{-pt}.\cos t\,dt + \int_\pi^\infty e^{-pt}.0\,dt$

$$= \left[\frac{e^{-pt}}{p^2+1}(-p\cos t + \sin t)\right]_0^\pi = \left[\frac{e^{-p\pi}}{p^2+1}p - \frac{1}{p^2+1}(-p)\right]$$

$$= \frac{p(1+e^{-p\pi})}{p^2+1}$$

(ii) $L\{F(t)\} = \int_0^\infty e^{-pt}.F(t)\,dt = \int_0^1 e^{-pt}\,dt + \int_1^2 t\,e^{-pt}\,dt + \int_2^\infty t^2 e^{-pt}\,dt$

$$= \left(\frac{e^{-pt}}{-p}\right)_0^1 + \left(t\frac{e^{-pt}}{-p} - \frac{e^{-pt}}{p^2}\right)_1^2 + \left(t^2\frac{e^{-pt}}{-p}\right)_2^\infty - \int_2^\infty 2t.\frac{e^{-pt}}{-p}dt$$

$$= \left(\frac{1-e^{-p}}{p}\right) + \left(\frac{-2}{p}e^{-2p} - \frac{e^{-2p}}{p^2}\right) - \left(\frac{e^{-p}}{-p} - \frac{e^{-p}}{p^2}\right) + \frac{4}{p}e^{-2p} + \frac{2}{p}\int_2^\infty t\,e^{-pt}\,dt$$

$$= \frac{1}{p} + \frac{2}{p}e^{-2p} + \frac{e^{-p}}{p^2} - \frac{e^{-2p}}{p^2} + \frac{2}{p}\left[\left(t\frac{e^{-pt}}{-p}\right)_2^\infty - \int_2^\infty 1.\frac{e^{-pt}}{-p}dt\right]$$

$$= \frac{1}{p} + \frac{2}{p}e^{-2p} + \frac{e^{-p}}{p^2} - \frac{e^{-2p}}{p^2} + \frac{2}{p}\left[\frac{2}{p}e^{-2p} + \frac{1}{p}\left(\frac{e^{-pt}}{-p}\right)_2^\infty\right]$$

$$= \frac{1}{p} + \frac{2}{p}e^{-2p} + \frac{e^{-p}}{p^2} + \frac{3}{p^2}e^{-2p} + \frac{2}{p^3}e^{-2p}.$$

(iii) $L\{F(t)\} = \int_0^\infty e^{-pt}.F(t)\,dt$

$$= \int_0^2 t^2 e^{-pt}\,dt + \int_2^3 (t-1)e^{-pt}\,dt + \int_3^\infty 7e^{-pt}\,dt$$

$$= \left\{t^2\frac{e^{-pt}}{(-p)}\right\}_0^2 - \int_0^2 2t\frac{e^{-pt}}{(-p)}dt + \left\{(t-1)\frac{e^{-pt}}{(-p)}\right\}_2^3 - \int_2^3 \frac{e^{-pt}}{(-p)}dt + 7\left(\frac{e^{-pt}}{-p}\right)_3^\infty$$

$$= -\frac{4}{p}e^{-2p} + \frac{2}{p}\left[\left\{t\,\frac{e^{-pt}}{(-p)}\right\}_0^2 - \int_0^2 1.\frac{e^{-pt}}{(-p)}\,dt\right] + \frac{1}{p}e^{-2p} - \frac{2}{p}e^{-3p} + \frac{1}{p}\left(\frac{e^{-pt}}{-p}\right)_2^3 + \frac{7}{p}e^{-3p}$$

$$= -\frac{4}{p}e^{-2p} - \frac{2}{p^2}(2e^{-2p}) + \frac{2}{p^2}\left[\frac{e^{-pt}}{(-p)}\right]_0^2 + \frac{1}{p}e^{-2p} - \frac{2}{p}e^{-3p} - \frac{1}{p^2}e^{-3p} + \frac{1}{p^2}e^{-2p} + \frac{7}{p}e^{-3p}$$

$$= -\frac{4}{p}e^{-2p} - \frac{4}{p^2}e^{-2p} + \frac{2}{p^3} - \frac{2e^{-2p}}{p^3} + \frac{1}{p}e^{-2p} - \frac{2}{p}e^{-3p} - \frac{1}{p^2}e^{-3p} + \frac{1}{p^2}e^{-2p} + \frac{7}{p}e^{-3p}$$

$$= \frac{2}{p^3} - \frac{e^{-2p}}{p^3}(2 + 3p + 3p^2) + \frac{e^{-3p}}{p^2}(5p - 1)$$

Example 7. *Find L{F(t)} if*

(*i*) $F(t) = \begin{cases} \sin\left(t - \frac{\pi}{3}\right), & t > \frac{\pi}{3} \\ 0, & t < \frac{\pi}{3} \end{cases}$ (*ii*) $F(t) = \begin{cases} (t-1)^2, & t > 1 \\ 0, & 0 < t < 1 \end{cases}$.

Sol. (*i*) $L\{F(t)\} = e^{-p\frac{\pi}{3}} L(\sin t)$ $\quad\Big|\because\ a = \frac{\pi}{3}$

$= e^{-p\frac{\pi}{3}} . \frac{1}{p^2 + 1}$ | Using second shifting property

(*ii*) $L\{F(t)\} = e^{-p}\, L(t^2)$ $\quad|\because\ a = 1$

$= e^{-p} . \frac{2}{p^3}$. | Using second shifting property

Example 8. *If* $L(\cos^2 t) = \frac{p^2 + 2}{p(p^2 + 4)}$, *find* $L(\cos^2 at)$. (U.P.T.U. 2006)

Sol. By change of scale property,

$$L(\cos^2 at) = \frac{1}{a}\left[\frac{\left(\frac{p}{a}\right)^2 + 2}{\frac{p}{a}\left\{\left(\frac{p}{a}\right)^2 + 4\right\}}\right] = \frac{p^2 + 2a^2}{p(p^2 + 4a^2)}$$

Example 9. *Given that* $L\left(\frac{\sin t}{t}\right) = \tan^{-1}\left(\frac{1}{p}\right)$, *find* $L\left(\frac{\sin at}{t}\right)$.

Sol. By change of scale property,

$$L\left(\frac{\sin at}{at}\right) = \frac{1}{a}\tan^{-1}\left(\frac{1}{p/a}\right)$$

$$\frac{1}{a}L\left(\frac{\sin at}{t}\right) = \frac{1}{a}\tan^{-1}\left(\frac{a}{p}\right)$$

$$\Rightarrow \quad L\left(\frac{\sin at}{t}\right) = \tan^{-1}\left(\frac{a}{p}\right).$$

Example 10. *If* $L\{J_0(\sqrt{t})\} = \dfrac{e^{-\frac{1}{4p}}}{p}$, *find* $L\{J_0(2\sqrt{t})\}$.

Sol. By change of scale property,

$$L\{J_0(\sqrt{4t})\} = \frac{1}{4}\cdot\left\{\frac{e^{-\frac{1}{4(p/4)}}}{(p/4)}\right\}$$

$$\Rightarrow \qquad L\{J_0(2\sqrt{t})\} = \frac{1}{p}e^{-1/p}.$$

TEST YOUR KNOWLEDGE

Find the Laplace transforms of (1–12) :

1. $\cosh at - \cos at$ 2. $\cos(at + b)$ 3. $\sin at \sin bt$
4. $\sin^2 3t$ 5. $\cos^3 2t$ 6. $\sinh^3 2t$
7. $e^{-\alpha t}\cos \beta t$ [*G.B.T.U. (C.O.) 2010*] 8. $t^3 e^{-3t}$ 9. $\cosh at \cos at$
10. $e^{-3t}(2\cos 5t - 3\sin 5t)$ 11. (*i*) $(\sin t - \cos t)^2$ (*ii*) $(5e^{2t} - 3)^2$
12. (*i*) $\sinh\dfrac{t}{2}\sin\dfrac{\sqrt{3}\,t}{2}$ (*ii*) 3^t (*iii*) $\cos t\cos 2t\cos 3t$
13. Find the Laplace transform of F(*t*) defined as $F(t) = |t - 1| + |t + 1|, t \geq 0$.

    $\left[\textbf{Hint}: F(t) = \begin{cases} 2, & 0 \leq t \leq 1 \\ 2t, & t > 1 \end{cases}\right]$
14. Show that (*i*) $L\{\sin kt \sinh kt\} = \dfrac{2k^2 p}{p^4 + 4k^4}$ (*ii*) $L(\sin^3 t) = \dfrac{6}{(p^2+1)(p^2+9)}$.
15. If $L\{F(t)\} = f(p)$, show that $L\left\{F\left(\dfrac{t}{a}\right)\right\} = af(ap)$.
16. Find the Laplace transform of F(*t*) defined as

    (*i*) $F(t) = \begin{cases} t, & 0 < t < 4 \\ 5, & t > 4 \end{cases}$ (*ii*) $F(t) = \begin{cases} \sin t, & 0 < t < \pi \\ 0, & t > \pi \end{cases}$ [*U.P.T.U. (C.O.) 2009*]

    (*iii*) $F(t) = \begin{cases} \cos t, & 0 < t < 2\pi \\ 0, & t > 2\pi \end{cases}$ (*iv*) $F(t) = \begin{cases} e^t, & 0 < t < 1 \\ 0, & t > 1 \end{cases}$
17. Find the Laplace transform of the following functions :

    (*i*) $F(t) = \dfrac{e^{-at}t^{n-1}}{(n-1)!}$ (*ii*) $f(t) = \begin{cases} t/w, & 0 < t < w \\ 1 - \dfrac{t}{w}, & w < t < 2w \\ 1, & 2w < t < \infty \end{cases}$ [*G.B.T.U. (C.O.) 2010*]

    (*iii*) $F(t) = \sinh kt \cos kt$.
18. Find the Laplace transform of the functions given below :

    (*i*) $F(t) = \begin{cases} e^{t-a}, & t > a \\ 0, & t < a \end{cases}$ [*U.P.T.U. 2008; M.T.U. 2012*] (*ii*) $F(t) = \begin{cases} \cos\left(t - \dfrac{2\pi}{3}\right), & t > \dfrac{2\pi}{3} \\ 0, & t < \dfrac{2\pi}{3} \end{cases}$

19. (*i*) If $L\{F(t)\} = \dfrac{e^{-1/p}}{p}$, show that $L\{F(3t)\} = \dfrac{e^{-3/p}}{p}$. Also find $L\{e^{-t} F(3t)\}$.

(*ii*) If $L\{F(t)\} = \dfrac{p^2 - p + 1}{(2p+1)^2 (p-1)}$, show that $L\{F(2t)\} = \dfrac{p^2 - 2p + 4}{4(p+1)^2 (p-2)}$.

20. If $L\{J_0(t)\} = \dfrac{1}{\sqrt{1+p^2}}$, find $L\{J_0(at)\}$.

21. Find the Laplace transform of

(*i*) $F(t) = e^{3t} t^{7/2}$ (*ii*) $F(t) = \sinh at \sin at$

(*iii*) $F(t) = e^{-t} \sin^2 t$ (*iv*) $F(t) = (t+2)^2 e^t$.

22. Find the Laplace transform of

(*i*) $F(t) = e^{4t} \cos t \sin 2t$ (*ii*) $F(t) = e^{2t} \sin^4 t$ (*iii*) $F(t) = e^{-2t} \sin^3 t$.

Answers

1. $\dfrac{2a^2 p}{p^4 - a^4}$ **2.** $\dfrac{p \cos b - a \sin b}{p^2 + a^2}$ **3.** $\dfrac{2abp}{[p^2 + (a+b)^2][p^2 + (a-b)^2]}$

4. $\dfrac{18}{p(p^2 + 36)}$ **5.** $\dfrac{p(p^2 + 28)}{(p^2+4)(p^2+36)}$ **6.** $\dfrac{48}{(p^2-4)(p^2-36)}$

7. $\dfrac{p+\alpha}{(p+\alpha)^2 + \beta^2}$ **8.** $\dfrac{6}{(p+3)^4}$ **9.** $\dfrac{1}{2}\left[\dfrac{p-a}{(p-a)^2 + a^2} + \dfrac{p+a}{(p+a)^2 + a^2}\right]$

10. $\dfrac{2p-9}{p^2 + 6p + 34}$ **11.** (*i*) $\dfrac{1}{p} - \dfrac{2}{p^2+4}$ (*ii*) $\dfrac{25}{p-4} - \dfrac{30}{p-2} + \dfrac{9}{p}$, $p > 4$

12. (*i*) $\dfrac{\sqrt{3}p}{2(p^4 + p^2 + 1)}$ (*ii*) $\dfrac{1}{p - \log 3}$

(*iii*) $\dfrac{1}{4}\left[\dfrac{p}{p^2+36} + \dfrac{p}{p^2+16} + \dfrac{p}{p^2+4} + \dfrac{1}{p}\right]$ **13.** $\dfrac{2}{p}\left(1 + \dfrac{e^{-p}}{p}\right)$

16. (*i*) $\dfrac{1}{p^2} + e^{-4p}\left(\dfrac{1}{p} - \dfrac{1}{p^2}\right)$ (*ii*) $\dfrac{1 + e^{-\pi p}}{p^2 + 1}$ (*iii*) $\dfrac{p(1 - e^{-2\pi p})}{p^2+1}$ (*iv*) $\dfrac{e^{1-p} - 1}{1-p}$

17. (*i*) $\dfrac{1}{(p+a)^n}$ (*ii*) $\dfrac{1}{p}\left[\dfrac{1}{pw} - e^{-pw}\left(1 + \dfrac{2}{pw}\right) + e^{-2pw}\left(2 + \dfrac{1}{pw}\right)\right]$ (*iii*) $\dfrac{k(p^2 - 2k^2)}{p^4 + 4k^4}$

18. (*i*) $\dfrac{e^{-ap}}{p-1}$, $p > 1$ (*ii*) $e^{-(2\pi/3)p} \cdot \dfrac{p}{p^2+1}$ **19.** (*i*) $\dfrac{e^{-\{3/(p+1)\}}}{p+1}$ **20.** $\dfrac{1}{\sqrt{p^2 + a^2}}$

21. (*i*) $\dfrac{105}{16} \dfrac{\sqrt{\pi}}{(p-3)^{9/2}}$ (*ii*) $\dfrac{2a^2 p}{p^4 + 4a^4}$ (*iii*) $\dfrac{2}{(p+1)(p^2 + 2p + 5)}$ (*iv*) $\dfrac{4p^2 - 4p + 2}{(p-1)^3}$

22. (*i*) $\dfrac{1}{2}\left[\dfrac{3}{(p-4)^2 + 9} + \dfrac{1}{(p-4)^2 + 1}\right]$ (*ii*) $\dfrac{1}{8}\left[\dfrac{3}{p-2} - \dfrac{4(p-2)}{(p-2)^2 + 4} + \dfrac{p-2}{(p-2)^2 + 16}\right]$

(*iii*) $\dfrac{3}{4}\left[\dfrac{1}{p^2 + 4p + 5} - \dfrac{1}{p^2 + 4p + 13}\right]$.

3.9. FUNCTIONS OF EXPONENTIAL ORDER

A function F(t) is said to be of exponential order as $t \to \infty$, if there exist constants M and b and a fixed value t_0 of t such that

$$| \text{F}(t) | < \text{M}\, e^{bt}, \text{ for } t \geq t_0$$

we also write $\text{F}(t) = \text{O}\,(e^{bt}),\ t \to \infty$ to mean that F(t) is of exponential order.

From the definition, it is clear that if a constant b exists, such that $\lim\limits_{t \to \infty} e^{-bt}\, \text{F}(t)$ exists or the value of limit is finite then the function F(t) is of exponential order.

3.10. A FUNCTION OF CLASS 'A'

A function which is sectionally (or piecewise) continuous over every finite interval in the range $t \geq 0$ and is of exponential order as $t \to \infty$ is termed as a function of class A. A function F(t) is said to be piecewise continuous in any interval $[a, b]$ if it is defined on that interval and is such that the interval can be broken up into a finite number of sub-intervals in each of which F(t) is continuous.

3.11. EXISTENCE THEOREM

(U.K.T.U. 2011; M.T.U. 2012)

If F(t) is sectionally continuous for $t \geq 0$ and is of exponential order b, then L{F(t)} = f (p) exists for $p > b$.

In other words, if F(t) is a function of class A, L {F(t)} exists.

$$\int_0^\infty e^{-pt}\, \text{F}(t)\, dt = \int_0^{t_0} e^{-pt}\,.\,\text{F}(t)\, dt + \int_{t_0}^\infty e^{-pt}\,.\,\text{F}(t)\, dt = \text{I}_1 + \text{I}_2 \qquad \text{(say)}$$

I_1 exists since F(t) is sectionally continuous in every finite interval $0 \leq t \leq t_0$.

$$| \text{I}_2 | \leq \int_{t_0}^\infty | e^{-pt}\,.\,\text{F}(t) |\, dt \leq \int_0^\infty | e^{-pt}\,.\,\text{F}(t) |\, dt$$

$$\leq \int_0^\infty e^{-pt}\,.\,\text{M}e^{bt}\, dt \qquad \text{as F}(t) \text{ is of exponential order } b$$

$$\leq \int_0^\infty e^{-(p-b)t}\,.\,\text{M}\, dt = \frac{\text{M}}{p-b}.$$

Thus the Laplace transform exists for $p > b$.

Note. The conditions of the theorem are sufficient but not necessary for the existence of Laplace transform.

ILLUSTRATIVE EXAMPLES

Example 1. *Prove that t^n is of exponential order as $t \to \infty$.*

Sol.
$$\lim_{t \to \infty} (e^{-bt}\,.\,t^n) = \lim_{t \to \infty} \frac{t^n}{e^{bt}}$$

$$= \lim_{t \to \infty} \frac{nt^{n-1}}{be^{bt}} = \lim_{t \to \infty} \frac{n\,(n-1)t^{n-2}}{b^2 e^{bt}} = \lim_{t \to \infty} \frac{n\,!}{b^n e^{bt}} = 0$$

$\because$ $t^n = \text{O}\,(e^{bt}),\ t \to \infty$ for any fixed positive value of b

$\therefore$ t^n is of exponential order.

Example 2. *Show that e^{t^2} is not of exponential order as $t \to \infty$.*

Sol. $$\lim_{t \to \infty} (e^{-bt} e^{t^2}) = \lim_{t \to \infty} \left(\frac{e^{t^2}}{e^{bt}} \right) = \lim_{t \to \infty} e^{t^2 - bt}$$

If $b \le 0$, this limit is infinite

If $b > 0$, $\lim\limits_{t \to \infty} e^{t(t-b)} = \infty$

Thus, whatever be the value of b, this limit is not finite hence we cannot find a number M such that

$$e^{t^2} < Me^{bt}.$$

$\therefore$ e^{t^2} is not of exponential order as $t \to \infty$.

3.12. LAPLACE TRANSFORM OF DERIVATIVES

Theorem 1. *If F(t) is continuous for all $t \ge 0$ and of exponential order b as $t \to \infty$, and if F′(t) is of class A, then Laplace transform of the derivative F′(t) exists when $p > b$ and*

$$L\{F'(t)\} = pL\{F(t)\} - F(0) = pf(p) - F(0). \qquad | \text{ If } L\{F(t)\} = f(p)$$

Proof. $$L\{F'(t)\} = \int_0^\infty e^{-pt}.F'(t)\,dt \qquad ...(1)$$

$$= \left[e^{-pt}.F(t) \right]_0^\infty + p\int_0^\infty e^{-pt}.F(t)\,dt \qquad | \text{ Integrating by parts}$$

$$= \lim_{t \to \infty} e^{-pt}\,F(t) - F(0) + pL\{F(t)\} \qquad ...(2)$$

Since F(t) is of exponential order b as $t \to \infty$ then for $p > b$, e^{-pt} F(t) $\to 0$ as $t \to \infty$

$\therefore$ From (2), $L\{F'(t)\} = pL\{F(t)\} - F(0) = pf(p) - F(0)$ | if $L\{F(t)\} = f(p)$

Note. If F(t) fails to be continuous at $t = 0$ but

$\lim\limits_{t \to 0} F(t) = F(0 + 0)$ exists, then $L\{F'(t)\} = pL\{F(t)\} - F(0 + 0)$.

Theorem 2. *If F(t) is continuous, except for an ordinary discontinuity at $t = a(a > 0)$ as given in figure :*

Then,

$$L\{F'(t)\} = pL\,\{F(t)\} - F(0) - e^{-ap}\,[F(a + 0) - F(a - 0)]$$

where F(a + 0) and F(a – 0) are the limits of F at t = a as t approaches a from right and from left respectively. The quantity F (a + 0) – F(a – 0) is called the jump at the discontinuity t = a, and e^{-pt} F(t) $\to$ 0 as $t \to \infty$.

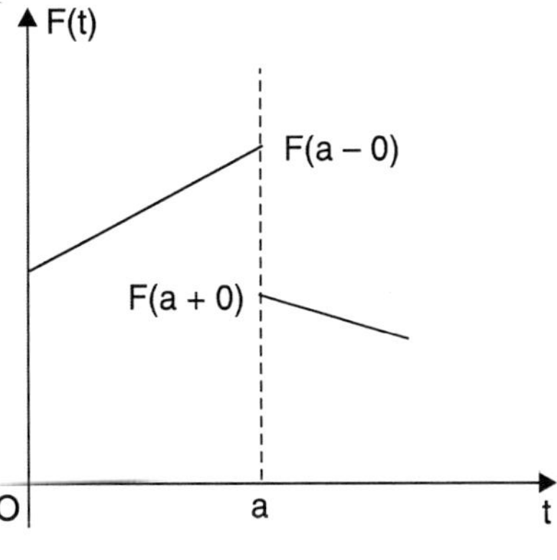

Proof. $$L\{F'(t)\} = \int_0^\infty e^{-pt}.F'(t)\,dt$$

$$= \int_0^a e^{-pt}.F'(t)\,dt + \int_a^\infty e^{-pt}.F'(t)\,dt$$

$$= \left[e^{-pt} \, . \mathrm{F}(t) \right]_0^a + p \int_0^a e^{-pt} \, . \mathrm{F}(t) \, dt + \left\{ e^{-pt} \, . \mathrm{F}(t) \right\}_a^\infty + p \int_a^\infty e^{-pt} \, . \mathrm{F}(t) \, dt$$

$$= e^{-ap} \, \mathrm{F}(a - 0) - \mathrm{F}(0) + p \int_0^\infty e^{-pt} \, . \mathrm{F}(t) \, dt + \lim_{t \to \infty} e^{-pt} \, \mathrm{F}(t) - e^{-ap} \, \mathrm{F}(a + 0)$$

$$\mathrm{L}\{\mathrm{F}'(t)\} = p\mathrm{L}\{\mathrm{F}(t)\} - \mathrm{F}(0) - e^{-ap} \, [\mathrm{F}(a + 0) - \mathrm{F}(a - 0)]. \qquad \because \operatorname*{Lt}_{t \to \infty} e^{-pt} \, \mathrm{F}(t) = 0$$

3.12.1. Generalization

If $\mathrm{F}(t)$ and its first $(n - 1)$ derivatives are continuous functions for all $t \geq 0$ and are of exponential order b as $t \to \infty$ and if $\mathrm{F}^{(n)}(t)$ is of class A then Laplace transform of $\mathrm{F}^{(n)}(t)$ exists when $p > b$ given by

$$\boxed{\mathrm{L}\{\mathrm{F}^{(n)}(t)\} = p^n \mathrm{L}\{\mathrm{F}(t)\} - p^{n-1} \, \mathrm{F}(0) - p^{n-2} \, \mathrm{F}'(0) - \ldots\ldots - \mathrm{F}^{(n-1)}(0).}$$

Proof. $\mathrm{L}\{\mathrm{F}''(t)\} = p\mathrm{L}\{\mathrm{F}'(t)\} - \mathrm{F}'(0)$ (Applying Theorem 1)

$$= p[p\mathrm{L}\{\mathrm{F}(t)\} - \mathrm{F}(0)] - \mathrm{F}'(0)$$
$$= p^2\mathrm{L}\{\mathrm{F}(t)\} - p\mathrm{F}(0) - \mathrm{F}'(0)$$

Again $\mathrm{L}\{\mathrm{F}'''(t)\} = p\mathrm{L}\{\mathrm{F}''(t)\} - \mathrm{F}''(0)$

$$= p\,[p^2\mathrm{L}\{\mathrm{F}(t)\} - p\mathrm{F}(0) - \mathrm{F}'(0)] - \mathrm{F}''(0)$$
$$= p^3\mathrm{L}\{\mathrm{F}(t)\} - p^2\mathrm{F}(0) - p\mathrm{F}'(0) - \mathrm{F}''(0)$$

Proceeding, we get

$$\mathrm{L}\{\mathrm{F}^{(n)}(t)\} = p^n\mathrm{L}\{\mathrm{F}(t)\} - p^{n-1} \, \mathrm{F}(0) - p^{n-2} \, \mathrm{F}'(0) - \ldots\ldots - p\mathrm{F}^{(n-2)}(0) - \mathrm{F}^{(n-1)}(0).$$

3.13. INITIAL-VALUE THEOREM

If $\mathrm{F}(t)$ is continuous for all $t \geq 0$ and is of exponential order as $t \to \infty$ and if $\mathrm{F}'(t)$ is of class A then

$$\boxed{\lim_{t \to 0} \mathrm{F}(t) = \lim_{p \to \infty} p\mathrm{L}\{\mathrm{F}(t)\}.}$$

3.14. FINAL-VALUE THEOREM

If $\mathrm{F}(t)$ is continuous for all $t \geq 0$ and is of exponential order as $t \to \infty$ and if $\mathrm{F}'(t)$ is of class A then

$$\boxed{\lim_{t \to \infty} \mathrm{F}(t) = \lim_{p \to 0} p\mathrm{L}\{\mathrm{F}(t)\}.}$$

Example. *If* $L\,\{F\,(t)\} = \dfrac{1}{p\,(p + \beta)}$ *then, find*

(*i*) $\lim_{t \to \infty} F(t)$ (*ii*) $\lim_{t \to 0} F(t)$.

Sol. (*i*) By final-value theorem,

$$\lim_{t \to \infty} \mathrm{F}(t) = \lim_{p \to 0} p\mathrm{L}\{\mathrm{F}(t)\} = \lim_{p \to 0} \frac{1}{p + \beta} = \frac{1}{\beta}$$

(*ii*) By initial-value theorem,

$$\lim_{t \to 0} \mathrm{F}(t) = \lim_{p \to \infty} p\mathrm{L}\{\mathrm{F}(t)\} = \lim_{p \to \infty} \frac{p}{p\,(p + \beta)} = \lim_{p \to \infty} \frac{1}{p + \beta} = 0.$$

3.15. LEIBNITZ RULE

To develop the theory of Laplace transforms further, we state the following result for differentiation under the integral sign.

Let $$\phi(\alpha) = \int_{u_1}^{u_2} f(x, \alpha)\, dx,\ a \le \alpha \le b$$

where u_1 and u_2 may depend on the parameter α then,

$$\frac{d\phi}{d\alpha} = \int_{u_1}^{u_2} \frac{\partial f}{\partial \alpha} dx + f(u_2, \alpha)\frac{du_2}{d\alpha} - f(u_1, \alpha)\frac{du_1}{d\alpha} \quad ...(1)$$

for $a \le \alpha \le b$ if $f(x, \alpha)$ and $\frac{\partial f}{\partial \alpha}$ are continuous in both x and α in some region of $x\alpha$ plane including $u_1 \le x \le u_2$, $a \le \alpha \le b$ and u_1, u_2 are continuous and have continuous derivatives in interval (a, b).

Note. If u_1, u_2 are constants, the last two terms in (1) are zero and so

$$\frac{d\phi}{d\alpha} = \int_{u_1}^{u_2} \frac{\partial f}{\partial \alpha} dx.$$

3.16. LAPLACE TRANSFORM OF INTEGRALS

If $\quad L\{F(t)\} = f(p)$, then $L\left\{\int_0^t F(t)\, dt\right\} = \frac{1}{p} f(p)$

Let $$G(t) = \int_0^t F(t)\, dt, \text{ then}$$

$$G'(t) = F(t) \quad \text{and} \quad G(0) = 0$$

Taking Laplace transform, we get

$$L\{G'(t)\} = pL\{G(t)\} - G(0) = pL\{G(t)\}$$

$$\therefore \quad L\{G(t)\} = \frac{1}{p} L\{G'(t)\} = \frac{1}{p} L\{F(t)\} = \frac{1}{p} f(p)$$

i.e., $$L\left[\int_0^t F(t)\, dt\right] = \frac{1}{p} f(p)$$

3.17. MULTIPLICATION BY t^n

If $L\{F(t)\} = f(p)$, then $\quad L\{t^n F(t)\} = (-1)^n \frac{d^n}{dp^n}[f(p)]$, where $n = 1, 2, 3, ...$

We prove the theorem by mathematical induction

$$L\{F(t)\} = f(p) \quad \Rightarrow \quad \int_0^\infty e^{-pt} F(t)\, dt = f(p)$$

Differentiating both sides w.r.t. p (using Leibnitz's rule for differentiation under the integral sign), we have

$$\frac{d}{dp}\int_0^\infty e^{-pt} F(t)\, dt = \frac{d}{dp}[f(p)]$$

or $$\int_0^\infty \frac{\partial}{\partial p}[e^{-pt} F(t)]\, dt = \frac{d}{dp}[f(p)]$$

or $$\int_0^\infty -t\, e^{-pt} \mathrm{F}(t)\, dt = \frac{d}{dp}[f(p)]$$

or $$\int_0^\infty e^{-pt}\, [t\, \mathrm{F}(t)]\, dt = -\frac{d}{dp}[f(p)]$$

or $$\mathrm{L}\{t\, \mathrm{F}(t)\} = -\frac{d}{dp}[f(p)]$$

which confirms the truth of the theorem for $n = 1$.

Now assume the theorem to be true for $n = m$, so that

$$\mathrm{L}\{t^m\, \mathrm{F}(t)\} = (-1)^m \frac{d^m}{dp^m}[f(p)]$$

or $$\int_0^\infty e^{-pt}\, t^m\, \mathrm{F}(t)\, dt = (-1)^m \frac{d^m}{dp^m}[f(p)]$$

Differentiating both sides w.r.t. p, we have

$$\frac{d}{dp}\int_0^\infty e^{-pt}\, t^m\, \mathrm{F}(t)\, dt = (-1)^m \frac{d^{m+1}}{dp^{m+1}}[f(p)]$$

or $$\int_0^\infty \frac{\partial}{\partial p}[e^{-pt}\, t^m\, \mathrm{F}(t)]\, dt = (-1)^m \frac{d^{m+1}}{dp^{m+1}}[f(p)]$$

or $$\int_0^\infty -te^{-pt}\, t^m\, \mathrm{F}(t)\, dt = (-1)^m \frac{d^{m+1}}{dp^{m+1}}[f(p)]$$

or $$\int_0^\infty e^{-pt}[t^{m+1}\, \mathrm{F}(t)]\, dt = (-1)^{m+1} \frac{d^{m+1}}{dp^{m+1}}[f(p)]$$

or $$\mathrm{L}\{t^{m+1}\, \mathrm{F}(t)\} = (-1)^{m+1} \frac{d^{m+1}}{dp^{m+1}}[f(p)]$$

which shows that the theorem is true for $n = m + 1$.

Hence by mathematical induction, the theorem is true for all positive integer n.

3.18. DIVISION BY t *(U.P.T.U. 2007)*

If L{F(t)} = $f(p)$, then $\mathrm{L}\left\{\frac{1}{t}\mathrm{F}(t)\right\} = \int_p^\infty f(p)\, dp$ **provided the integral exists.**

We have $$f(p) = \int_0^\infty e^{-pt}\, \mathrm{F}(t)\, dt$$

Integrating both sides w.r.t. p from p to ∞, we have

$$\int_p^\infty f(p)\, dp = \int_p^\infty \left[\int_0^\infty e^{-pt}\, \mathrm{F}(t)\, dt\right] dp$$

Since p and t are independent, changing the order of integration on the right-hand side, we have

$$\int_p^\infty f(p)\, dp = \int_0^\infty \left[\int_p^\infty e^{-pt}\, dp\right] \mathrm{F}(t)\, dt$$

$$= \int_0^\infty \left[\frac{e^{-pt}}{-t}\right]_p^\infty \mathrm{F}(t)\, dt = \int_0^\infty e^{-pt}\, \frac{\mathrm{F}(t)}{t}\, dt = \mathrm{L}\left\{\frac{1}{t}\mathrm{F}(t)\right\}.$$

ILLUSTRATIVE EXAMPLES

Example 1. *If* $L\{t \sin \omega t\} = \dfrac{2\omega p}{(p^2+\omega^2)^2}$, *evaluate*

(*i*) $L\{\omega t \cos \omega t + \sin \omega t\}$ (*ii*) $L\{2 \cos \omega t - \omega t \sin \omega t\}$.

Sol. Let $F(t) = t \sin \omega t,$

then $F'(t) = \omega t \cos \omega t + \sin \omega t$

and $F''(t) = 2\omega \cos \omega t - \omega^2 t \sin \omega t$

Also $F(0) = 0,\ F'(0) = 0,\ F''(0) = 2\omega$

Given : $$f(p) = \frac{2\omega p}{(p^2+\omega^2)^2}$$

(*i*) $$L\{F'(t)\} = pf(p) - F(0)$$

$$\Rightarrow \quad L\{\omega t \cos \omega t + \sin \omega t\} = p \cdot \frac{2\omega p}{(p^2+\omega^2)^2} - 0 = \frac{2\omega p^2}{(p^2+\omega^2)^2}.$$

(*ii*) $$L\{F''(t)\} = p^2 f(p) - pF(0) - F'(0)$$

$$\Rightarrow \quad L\{2\omega \cos \omega t - \omega^2 t \sin \omega t\} = p^2 \cdot \frac{2\omega p}{(p^2+\omega^2)^2} - p \cdot 0 - 0 = \frac{2\omega p^3}{(p^2+\omega^2)^2}$$

$$\therefore \quad L\{2\cos \omega t - \omega t \sin \omega t\} = \frac{2p^3}{(p^2+\omega^2)^2}.$$

Example 2. *If* $F(t) = \dfrac{e^{at} - \cos bt}{t}$, *find the Laplace transform of F(t).*

Sol. $$L(e^{at}) = \frac{1}{p-a}$$

$$L(\cos bt) = \frac{p}{p^2+b^2}$$

$$\therefore \quad L(e^{at} - \cos bt) = \frac{1}{p-a} - \frac{p}{p^2+b^2}$$

Now, $$L\left(\frac{e^{at} - \cos bt}{t}\right) = \int_p^\infty \left(\frac{1}{p-a} - \frac{p}{p^2+b^2}\right) dp$$

$$= \left[\log (p-a) - \frac{1}{2}\log (p^2+b^2)\right]_p^\infty$$

$$= \frac{1}{2}\left[\log (p-a)^2 - \log (p^2+b^2)\right]_p^\infty$$

$$= \frac{1}{2}\left[\log \frac{(p-a)^2}{p^2+b^2}\right]_p^\infty = \frac{1}{2}\left[\log \frac{\left(1-\dfrac{a}{p}\right)^2}{\left(1+\dfrac{b^2}{p^2}\right)}\right]_p^\infty$$

$$= -\frac{1}{2}\log \frac{(p-a)^2}{p^2+b^2} = \frac{1}{2}\log \left\{\frac{p^2+b^2}{(p-a)^2}\right\}.$$

Example 3. *Find the Laplace transform of* $\frac{\sin at}{t}$. *Does the Laplace transform of* $\frac{\cos at}{t}$ *exist?*

Sol. Since $\lim_{t \to 0} \frac{\sin at}{t} = a$, the Laplace transform of $\frac{\sin at}{t}$ exists.

Now,
$$L(\sin at) = \frac{a}{p^2 + a^2}$$

$$\therefore \quad L\left(\frac{\sin at}{t}\right) = \int_p^\infty \frac{a}{p^2 + a^2}\, dp = \left[\tan^{-1}\left(\frac{p}{a}\right)\right]_p^\infty = \frac{\pi}{2} - \tan^{-1}\left(\frac{p}{a}\right)$$

$$= \cot^{-1}\left(\frac{p}{a}\right) = \tan^{-1}\left(\frac{a}{p}\right)$$

The function $\frac{\cos at}{t}$ is discontinuous at $t = 0$, so its Laplace transform does not exist.

Example 4. *Find the Laplace transform of*

(*i*) $t^3 e^{-3t}$ (*ii*) $t \sin^2 3t$ (*iii*) $\frac{1 - \cos t}{t^2}$.

Sol. (*i*)
$$L(e^{-3t}) = \frac{1}{p+3}$$

$$\therefore \quad L(t^3 e^{-3t}) = (-1)^3 \frac{d^3}{dp^3}\left(\frac{1}{p+3}\right) = -\frac{(-1)^3\, 3!}{(p+3)^4} = \frac{6}{(p+3)^4}.$$

Aliter :
$$L(t^3) = \frac{6}{p^4}$$

$$\therefore \quad L(e^{-3t}\, t^3) = \frac{6}{(p+3)^4}.$$

(*ii*)
$$\sin^2 3t = \frac{1 - \cos 6t}{2}$$

$$\therefore \quad L(\sin^2 3t) = \frac{1}{2}[L(1) - L(\cos 6t)] = \frac{1}{2}\left(\frac{1}{p} - \frac{p}{p^2 + 36}\right) = \frac{18}{p(p^2 + 36)}$$

$$\therefore \quad L(t \sin^2 3t) = -\frac{d}{dp}\left[\frac{18}{p(p^2 + 36)}\right]$$

$$= (-18)(-1)(p^3 + 36p)^{-2}(3p^2 + 36) = \frac{54(p^2 + 12)}{p^2(p^2 + 36)^2}.$$

(*iii*)
$$L(1 - \cos t) = \frac{1}{p} - \frac{p}{p^2 + 1}$$

$$L\left(\frac{1 - \cos t}{t}\right) = \int_p^\infty \left(\frac{1}{p} - \frac{p}{p^2 + 1}\right) dp$$

$$= \left[\log p - \frac{1}{2}\log(p^2+1)\right]_p^\infty = \frac{1}{2}\left[\log\left(\frac{p^2}{p^2+1}\right)\right]_p^\infty$$

$$= \frac{1}{2}\left[\log\left(\frac{1}{1+\dfrac{1}{p^2}}\right)\right]_p^\infty = -\frac{1}{2}\log\left(\frac{p^2}{p^2+1}\right) = \frac{1}{2}\log\left(\frac{p^2+1}{p^2}\right)$$

Now, $$\mathrm{L}\left(\frac{1-\cos t}{t^2}\right) = \int_p^\infty \frac{1}{2}\log\left(\frac{p^2+1}{p^2}\right)dp = \frac{1}{2}\int_p^\infty [\log(p^2+1) - 2\log p]\,dp$$

$$= \frac{1}{2}\left[\{\log(p^2+1) - 2\log p\}\,.\,p - \int\left(\frac{2p}{p^2+1} - \frac{2}{p}\right).\,p\,dp\right]_p^\infty$$

$$= \left[\frac{p}{2}\log\left(\frac{p^2+1}{p^2}\right)\right]_p^\infty + \int_p^\infty \frac{dp}{p^2+1} = -\frac{p}{2}\log\left(1+\frac{1}{p^2}\right) + \frac{\pi}{2} - \tan^{-1}p$$

$$\Rightarrow \qquad \mathrm{L}\left(\frac{1-\cos t}{t^2}\right) = \cot^{-1}p - \frac{p}{2}\log\left(1+\frac{1}{p^2}\right).$$

Example 5. *Given* $L\left(2\sqrt{\dfrac{t}{\pi}}\right) = \dfrac{1}{p^{3/2}}$, *show that* $L\left(\dfrac{1}{\sqrt{\pi t}}\right) = \dfrac{1}{\sqrt{p}}$.

Sol. Let $\mathrm{F}(t) = 2\sqrt{\dfrac{t}{\pi}}$ $\quad\therefore\quad$ $\mathrm{F}'(t) = \dfrac{1}{\sqrt{\pi t}}$. Also $\mathrm{F}(0) = 0$

$$\therefore \qquad \mathrm{L}\{\mathrm{F}'(t)\} = p\,\mathrm{L}\{\mathrm{F}(t)\} - \mathrm{F}(0) = p\,.\,\frac{1}{p^{3/2}} - 0$$

$$\therefore \qquad \mathrm{L}\left(\frac{1}{\sqrt{\pi t}}\right) = \frac{1}{\sqrt{p}}.$$

Example 6. *Find the Laplace transform of*

(*i*) $\dfrac{e^{-at} - e^{-bt}}{t}$ (*ii*) $\dfrac{\cos at - \cos bt}{t}$. (U.K.T.U. 2012)

Sol. (*i*) Since $\mathrm{L}\{e^{-at} - e^{-bt}\} = \dfrac{1}{p+a} - \dfrac{1}{p+b}$

$$\therefore \qquad \mathrm{L}\left\{\frac{e^{-at} - e^{-bt}}{t}\right\} = \int_p^\infty \left(\frac{1}{p+a} - \frac{1}{p+b}\right)dp$$

$$= \left[\log(p+a) - \log(p+b)\right]_p^\infty = \left[\log\frac{p+a}{p+b}\right]_p^\infty = \left[\log\frac{1+\dfrac{a}{p}}{1+\dfrac{b}{p}}\right]_p^\infty$$

$$= \log 1 - \log\frac{1+\dfrac{a}{p}}{1+\dfrac{b}{p}} = 0 - \log\frac{p+a}{p+b} = \log\frac{p+b}{p+a}.$$

(*ii*) Since $L\{\cos at - \cos bt\} = \frac{p}{p^2+a^2} - \frac{p}{p^2+b^2}$

$$\therefore \quad L\left\{\frac{\cos at - \cos bt}{t}\right\} = \int_p^\infty \left(\frac{p}{p^2+a^2} - \frac{p}{p^2+b^2}\right) dp = \left[\frac{1}{2}\log(p^2+a^2) - \frac{1}{2}\log(p^2+b^2)\right]_p^\infty$$

$$= \frac{1}{2}\left[\log\frac{p^2+a^2}{p^2+b^2}\right]_p^\infty = \frac{1}{2}\left[\log\frac{1+\frac{a^2}{p^2}}{1+\frac{b^2}{p^2}}\right]_p^\infty$$

$$= \frac{1}{2}\left[\log 1 - \log\frac{p^2+a^2}{p^2+b^2}\right] = \frac{1}{2}\log\frac{p^2+b^2}{p^2+a^2}.$$

Example 7. *Find the Laplace transform of the following functions :*

(*i*) *t sin 3t cos 2t* (*ii*) *te^{-t} cosh t* (*iii*) *$t^2 e^{-2t}$ cos t.*

Sol. (*i*) $L(\sin 3t \cos 2t) = \frac{1}{2} L(\sin 5t + \sin t) = \frac{1}{2}\left(\frac{5}{p^2+5^2} + \frac{1}{p^2+1}\right)$

$$\Rightarrow \quad L(t \sin 3t \cos 2t) = -\frac{d}{dp}\left[\frac{1}{2}\left(\frac{5}{p^2+25} + \frac{1}{p^2+1}\right)\right]$$

$$= -\frac{1}{2}\left[\frac{-5}{(p^2+25)^2}(2p) - \frac{1}{(p^2+1)^2}(2p)\right] = \frac{5p}{(p^2+25)^2} + \frac{p}{(p^2+1)^2}.$$

(*ii*) $$L(e^{-t}\cosh t) = L\left[e^{-t}\left(\frac{e^t+e^{-t}}{2}\right)\right] = \frac{1}{2}L(1+e^{-2t}) = \frac{1}{2}\left(\frac{1}{p} + \frac{1}{p+2}\right)$$

$$\Rightarrow \quad L(te^{-t}\cosh t) = -\frac{d}{dp}\left[\frac{1}{2}\left(\frac{1}{p} + \frac{1}{p+2}\right)\right] = -\frac{1}{2}\left[-\frac{1}{p^2} - \frac{1}{(p+2)^2}\right] = \frac{1}{2}\left[\frac{1}{p^2} + \frac{1}{(p+2)^2}\right]$$

(*iii*) $$L(e^{-2t}\cos t) = \frac{p+2}{(p+2)^2+1} = \frac{p+2}{p^2+4p+5}$$

$$\Rightarrow \quad L(t^2e^{-2t}\cos t) = (-1)^2\frac{d^2}{dp^2}\left[\frac{p+2}{p^2+4p+5}\right] = \frac{d}{dp}\left[-\frac{p^2+4p+3}{(p^2+4p+5)^2}\right]$$

$$= \frac{2(p^3+6p^2+9p+2)}{(p^2+4p+5)^3}.$$

Example 8. *Find the Laplace transform of the following functions :*

(*i*) $\frac{e^{-t}\sin t}{t}$ (G.B.T.U. 2012) (*ii*) $\frac{1-\cos 2t}{t}$.

Sol. (*i*) $$L(e^{-t}\sin t) = \frac{1}{(p+1)^2+1}$$

$$\Rightarrow \quad L\left(\frac{e^{-t}\sin t}{t}\right) = \int_p^{\infty} \frac{1}{(p+1)^2+1}\,dp = \Big[\tan^{-1}(p+1)\Big]_p^{\infty}$$

$$= \frac{\pi}{2} - \tan^{-1}(p+1) = \cot^{-1}(p+1).$$

(*ii*) $$L(1-\cos 2t) = \frac{1}{p} - \frac{p}{p^2+2^2}$$

$$\Rightarrow \quad L\left(\frac{1-\cos 2t}{t}\right) = \int_p^{\infty}\left(\frac{1}{p} - \frac{p}{p^2+4}\right)dp$$

$$= \left[\log p - \frac{1}{2}\log(p^2+4)\right]_p^{\infty} = \frac{1}{2}\left[\log \frac{p^2}{p^2+4}\right]_p^{\infty}$$

$$= \frac{1}{2}\left[\lim_{p\to\infty} \log \frac{1}{1+\frac{4}{p^2}} - \log \frac{p^2}{p^2+4}\right]$$

$$= \frac{1}{2}\left[\log 1 + \log \frac{p^2+4}{p^2}\right] = \frac{1}{2}\log\left(\frac{p^2+4}{p^2}\right).$$

Example 9. *Evaluate :*

(*i*) $\int_0^{\infty} t^3 e^{-t}\, \sin t\, dt$ [G.B.T.U. (SUM) 2010]

(*ii*) $\int_0^{\infty} \frac{e^{-t}\, \sin^2 t}{t}\, dt.$ [U.P.T.U. 2008; G.B.T.U. (C.O.) 2010, 2011]

Sol. (*i*) $$L(\sin t) = \frac{1}{p^2+1}$$

$$L(t^3 \sin t) = (-1)^3 \frac{d^3}{dp^3}\left(\frac{1}{p^2+1}\right)$$

$$= \frac{d^2}{dp^2}\left[\frac{2p}{(p^2+1)^2}\right] = \frac{d}{dp}\left[\frac{2(1-3p^2)}{(p^2+1)^3}\right]$$

$$L(t^3 \sin t) = \frac{24p(p^2-1)}{(p^2+1)^4} \qquad \text{...(1)}$$

By definition, $\int_0^{\infty} e^{-pt}\,.\,t^3 \sin t\, dt = \frac{24p(p^2-1)}{(p^2+1)^4}$

Put $p = 1$

$$\int_0^{\infty} e^{-t}\, t^3 \sin t\, dt = 0.$$

(*ii*) $$L(\sin^2 t) = \frac{1}{2}L(1-\cos 2t) = \frac{1}{2}\left(\frac{1}{p} - \frac{p}{p^2+4}\right)$$

$$L\left(\frac{\sin^2 t}{t}\right) = \frac{1}{2}\int_p^\infty \left(\frac{1}{p} - \frac{p}{p^2+4}\right) dp = \frac{1}{4}\log\left(\frac{p^2+4}{p^2}\right)$$

By definition, $\displaystyle\int_0^\infty e^{-pt} \cdot \frac{\sin^2 t}{t}\, dt = \frac{1}{4}\log\left(\frac{p^2+4}{p^2}\right)$

Put $p = 1$

$$\int_0^\infty e^{-t}\, \frac{\sin^2 t}{t}\, dt = \frac{1}{4}\log 5.$$

Example 10. *Find the Laplace transform of*

(i) $\displaystyle\int_0^t e^{-t} \cos t\, dt$ *(ii)* $\displaystyle\int_0^t \frac{\sin t}{t}\, dt$ (U.P.T.U. 2007)

(iii) $\displaystyle\int_0^t e^t\, \frac{\sin t}{t}\, dt.$

Sol. (*i*) $\displaystyle L(\cos t) = \frac{p}{p^2+1}$

$$L(e^{-t}\cos t) = \frac{p+1}{(p+1)^2+1} = f(p) \quad \text{(say)}$$

$$\therefore \quad L\left(\int_0^t e^{-t}\cos t\, dt\right) = \frac{1}{p} f(p) = \frac{p+1}{p(p^2+2p+2)}.$$

(*ii*) $\displaystyle L(\sin t) = \frac{1}{p^2+1}$

$$L\left(\frac{\sin t}{t}\right) = \int_p^\infty \frac{1}{p^2+1}\, dp = \frac{\pi}{2} - \tan^{-1} p = \cot^{-1} p$$

$$\therefore \quad L\left(\int_0^t \frac{\sin t}{t}\, dt\right) = \frac{1}{p}\cot^{-1} p.$$

(*iii*) $\displaystyle L\left(\frac{\sin t}{t}\right) = \cot^{-1} p$ | as done in part (*ii*)

$$\therefore \quad L\left(e^t\, \frac{\sin t}{t}\right) = \cot^{-1}(p-1)$$

$$\therefore \quad L\left(\int_0^t e^t\, \frac{\sin t}{t}\, dt\right) = \frac{1}{p}\cot^{-1}(p-1).$$

Example 11. *Find the value of*

(i) $\displaystyle\int_0^\infty e^{-st}\, t^3 \cos t\, dt$ *(ii)* $\displaystyle\int_0^\infty e^{-3t}\, t \sin t\, dt.$

Sol. (*i*) $\displaystyle L(\cos t) = \frac{p}{p^2+1}$

$$L(t^3\cos t) = (-1)^3\, \frac{d^3}{dp^3}\left(\frac{p}{p^2+1}\right)$$

$$= -\frac{d^2}{dp^2}\left\{\frac{1-p^2}{(p^2+1)^2}\right\} = -\frac{d}{dp}\left[\frac{2p^3-bp}{(1+p^2)^3}\right] = \frac{6(p^4-6p^2+1)}{(1+p^2)^4}$$

$$\Rightarrow \quad \int_0^\infty e^{-pt}\,.\,t^3\cos t\,dt = \frac{6(p^4-6p^2+1)}{(1+p^2)^4} \qquad \text{| By definition}$$

Replacing p by s, we get

$$\int_0^\infty e^{-st}\,.\,t^3\cos t\,dt = \frac{6(s^4-6s^2+1)}{(1+s^2)^4}$$

(ii)

$$L(\sin t) = \frac{1}{p^2+1}$$

$$L(t\sin t) = -\frac{d}{dp}\left(\frac{1}{p^2+1}\right) = \frac{2p}{(p^2+1)^2}$$

$$\int_0^\infty e^{-pt}\,.\,t\sin t\,dt = \frac{2p}{(p^2+1)^2} \qquad \text{| By definition}$$

Put $p = 3$

$$\int_0^\infty e^{-3t}\,.\,t\sin t\,dt = \frac{6}{100} = \frac{3}{50}.$$

Example 12. *Find the Laplace transform of*

(i) $\sin\sqrt{t}$ *; Hence find* $L\left(\frac{\cos\sqrt{t}}{\sqrt{t}}\right)$ *(ii)* $\int_0^{t/2}\frac{1-e^{-2x}}{x}\,dx.$

Sol. *(i)*

$$\sin\sqrt{t} = \sqrt{t} - \frac{(\sqrt{t})^3}{3!} + \frac{(\sqrt{t})^5}{5!} - \ldots\ldots = t^{1/2} - \frac{t^{3/2}}{3!} + \frac{t^{5/2}}{5!} - \ldots\ldots$$

$$\therefore \quad L(\sin\sqrt{t}) = L\left(t^{1/2} - \frac{t^{3/2}}{3!} + \frac{t^{5/2}}{5!} - \ldots\ldots\right) = \frac{\Gamma 3/2}{p^{3/2}} - \frac{\Gamma 5/2}{3!\,p^{5/2}} + \frac{\Gamma 7/2}{5!\,p^{7/2}} - \ldots\ldots$$

$$= \frac{\sqrt{\pi}}{2p^{3/2}}\left\{1 - \left(\frac{1}{2^2p}\right) + \frac{1}{2!}\left(\frac{1}{2^2p}\right)^2 - \ldots\ldots\right\}$$

$$\Rightarrow \quad L(\sin\sqrt{t}) = \frac{\sqrt{\pi}}{2p^{3/2}}\,e^{-(1/4p)}$$

Now, $L\left[\frac{d}{dt}(\sin\sqrt{t})\right] = p\,L(\sin\sqrt{t}) - 0$ | $\because$ F(0) = 0

$$L\left(\frac{\cos\sqrt{t}}{2\sqrt{t}}\right) = \frac{\sqrt{\pi}}{2\sqrt{p}}\,e^{-\left(\frac{1}{4p}\right)}$$

$$L\left(\frac{\cos\sqrt{t}}{\sqrt{t}}\right) = \sqrt{\frac{\pi}{p}}\,e^{-\left(\frac{1}{4p}\right)}.$$

(*ii*) $\int_0^{t/2} \left(\frac{1-e^{-2x}}{x}\right) dx$

Put $2x = u$ so that $2dx = du$ $\therefore$ Integral becomes $\int_0^t \left(\frac{1-e^{-u}}{u}\right) du$

Now, $$L(1 - e^{-u}) = \frac{1}{p} - \frac{1}{p+1}$$

$$L\left(\frac{1-e^{-u}}{u}\right) = \int_p^{\infty}\left(\frac{1}{p} - \frac{1}{p+1}\right) dp = \left[\log\left(\frac{p}{p+1}\right)\right]_p^{\infty}$$

$$= 0 - \log\left(\frac{p}{p+1}\right) = \log\left(\frac{p+1}{p}\right)$$

$$\therefore \quad L\left[\int_0^t \left(\frac{1-e^{-u}}{u}\right) du\right] = \frac{1}{p}\log\left(\frac{p+1}{p}\right) = \frac{1}{p}\log\left(1+\frac{1}{p}\right).$$

Example 13. *Find the Laplace transform of*

(*i*) $t\,e^{-t} \sin 2t$ [G.B.T.U. (SUM) 2010] (*ii*) $t^2 e^t \sin 4t$ [G.B.T.U. (C.O.) 2011]

Sol. (*i*) $$L(\sin 2t) = \frac{2}{p^2+4}$$

$$L(t \sin 2t) = -\frac{d}{dp}\left(\frac{2}{p^2+4}\right) = \frac{2}{(p^2+4)^2} \cdot 2p = \frac{4p}{(p^2+4)^2}$$

$$\therefore \quad L(te^{-t} \sin 2t) = \frac{4(p+1)}{\left[(p+1)^2+4\right]^2} = \frac{4p+4}{(p^2+2p+5)^2}$$

(*ii*) $$L(\sin 4t) = \frac{4}{p^2+16}$$

$$L(t^2 \sin 4t) = (-1)^2 \frac{d^2}{dp^2}\left(\frac{4}{p^2+16}\right) = \frac{d}{dp}\left\{\frac{-8p}{(p^2+16)^2}\right\}$$

$$= -8\left[\frac{(p^2+16)^2 \cdot 1 - p \cdot 2(p^2+16) \cdot 2p}{(p^2+16)^4}\right] = -8\left[\frac{16-3p^2}{(p^2+16)^3}\right]$$

$$\therefore \quad L(e^t \cdot t^2 \sin 4t) = -8\left[\frac{16-3(p-1)^2}{\left\{(p-1)^2+16\right\}^3}\right] = \frac{8(3p^2-6p-13)}{(p^2-2p+17)^3}$$

Example 14. *Using Laplace transform, evaluate the following integrals :*

[U.P.T.U. (SUM) 2007]

(*i*) $\int_0^\infty \frac{e^{-t}\sin\sqrt{3}t}{t}\,dt$ (*ii*) $\int_0^\infty \left(\frac{e^{-2t}-e^{-4t}}{t}\right)dt$

Sol. (*i*) $$\mathrm{L}\,(\sin\sqrt{3}\,t) = \frac{\sqrt{3}}{p^2+3}$$

$$\mathrm{L}\left(\frac{\sin\sqrt{3}t}{t}\right) = \int_p^\infty \frac{\sqrt{3}}{p^2+3}\,dp = \left[\tan^{-1}\left(\frac{p}{\sqrt{3}}\right)\right]_p^\infty$$

$$= \frac{\pi}{2} - \tan^{-1}\left(\frac{p}{\sqrt{3}}\right) = \cot^{-1}\left(\frac{p}{\sqrt{3}}\right)$$

$$\Rightarrow \quad \int_0^\infty e^{-pt}\,\frac{\sin\sqrt{3}t}{t}\,dt = \cot^{-1}\left(\frac{p}{\sqrt{3}}\right)$$

Putting $p = 1$, we get

$$\int_0^\infty e^{-t}\,\frac{\sin\sqrt{3}t}{t}\,dt = \cot^{-1}\left(\frac{1}{\sqrt{3}}\right) = \frac{\pi}{3}$$

(*ii*) $$\mathrm{L}\,(e^{-2t} - e^{-4t}) = \frac{1}{p+2} - \frac{1}{p+4}$$

$$\mathrm{L}\left(\frac{e^{-2t}-e^{-4t}}{t}\right) = \int_p^\infty \left(\frac{1}{p+2} - \frac{1}{p+4}\right)dp = \left[\log\frac{p+2}{p+4}\right]_p^\infty = \log\frac{p+4}{p+2}$$

$$\Rightarrow \int_0^\infty e^{-pt}\left(\frac{e^{-2t}-e^{-4t}}{t}\right)dt = \log\left(\frac{p+4}{p+2}\right)$$

Putting $p = 0$, we get

$$\int_0^\infty \left(\frac{e^{-2t}-e^{-4t}}{t}\right)dt = \log 2$$

Example 15. *Prove that* $\int_{t=0}^\infty \int_{u=0}^t e^{-t}\,\frac{\sin u}{u}\,du\,dt = \frac{\pi}{4}$. (M.T.U. 2011)

Sol. $$\mathrm{L}\,(\sin u) = \frac{1}{p^2+1}$$

$$\mathrm{L}\left(\frac{\sin u}{u}\right) = \int_p^\infty \frac{1}{p^2+1}\,dp = \tan^{-1}\left(\frac{1}{p}\right)$$

$$L\left(\int_0^t \frac{\sin u}{u}\,du\right) = \frac{1}{p}\tan^{-1}\left(\frac{1}{p}\right)$$

$$\Rightarrow \quad \int_0^\infty e^{-pt}\left(\int_o^t \frac{\sin u}{u}\,du\right)dt = \frac{1}{p}\tan^{-1}\left(\frac{1}{p}\right)$$

Putting $p = 1$, we get

$$\int_0^\infty \int_0^t e^{-t}\frac{\sin u}{u}\,du\,dt = \tan^{-1}(1) = \frac{\pi}{4}$$

TEST YOUR KNOWLEDGE

1. Find the Laplace transforms of

(i) $t \sinh at$ (ii) $t^2 \sin 2t$

(iii) $t^2 e^{-2t}$ (iv) $t\, e^{at} \sin at$ (U.K.T.U. 2012)

(v) $t \sin^2 t$ (vi) $t \cosh 3t$

(vii) $t\,(3 \sin 2t - 2 \cos 2t)$ (viii) $\sin at - at \cos at$

(ix) $t^n e^{at}$, $p > a$; n is a positive integer (x) $(t^2 - 3t + 2) \sin 3t$.

2. If $L\{F(t)\} = f(p)$, show that $L\{t^2 F(t)\} = \frac{d^2}{dp^2}\{f(p)\}$. Use this result to obtain $L(t^2 \cos at)$.

3. If $L\left(\frac{1-\cos at}{a^2}\right) = \frac{1}{p\,(p^2+a^2)}$, show that $L\left\{\frac{t(1-\cos at)}{a^2}\right\} = \frac{3p^2+a^2}{p^2\,(p^2+a^2)^2}$.

4. Find the Laplace transform of

(i) $\frac{\sin 2t}{t}$ (ii) $\frac{1-e^t}{t}$ (iii) $\frac{\cos 2t - \cos 3t}{t}$ (iv) $\frac{\sin^2 t}{t}$

(v) $\frac{\sinh t}{t}$ (vi) $\frac{e^t - \cos t}{t}$ (vii) $\frac{1-e^{-t}}{t}$ (viii) $\frac{\sin 3t \cos t}{t}$.

5. Evaluate :

(i) $\int_0^\infty \frac{\sin t}{t}\,dt$ (U.P.T.U. 2009) (ii) $\int_0^\infty \frac{\sin^2 t}{t^2}\,dt$ (iii) $\int_0^\infty \frac{e^{-at} - e^{-bt}}{t}\,dt$

[U.P.T.U. (SUM) 2008 ; G.B.T.U. 2011]

(iv) $\int_0^\infty \frac{e^{-3t} - e^{-6t}}{t}\,dt$ (v) $\int_0^\infty \frac{\cos 6t - \cos 4t}{t}\,dt$ (vi) $\int_0^\infty e^{-t}\frac{\sin t}{t}\,dt$.

(M.T.U. 2012)

6. Find the Laplace transform of

(i) $\int_0^t e^{-t}\frac{\sin t}{t}\,dt$ (ii) $\int_0^t \frac{e^{-at} - e^{-bt}}{t}\,dt$

(iii) $\int_0^t \frac{1-\cos 2t}{t}\,dt$ (iv) $\int_0^t \frac{\cos at - \cos bt}{t}\,dt$.

7. Find the Laplace transform of

(i) $\int_0^t \int_0^t \int_0^t \cos at \, dt \, dt \, dt$ [U.P.T.U. (SUM) 2009]

(ii) $\int_0^t te^{-t} \sin 4t \, dt$ (iii) $e^{-4t} \int_0^t \frac{\sin 3t}{t} dt$

8. Show that :

(i) $\int_0^\infty t^2 e^{-4t} \sin 2t \, dt = \frac{11}{500}$ (ii) $\int_0^\infty e^{-2t} \sin^3 t \, dt = \frac{6}{65}$

(iii) $\int_0^\infty e^{-2t} \left(\frac{2 \sin t - 3 \sinh t}{t} \right) dt = 2 \cot^{-1}(2) + \frac{3}{2} \log \left(\frac{1}{3} \right).$

Answers

1. (i) $\frac{2ap}{(p^2 - a^2)^2}$ (ii) $\frac{4(3p^2 - 4)}{(p^2 + 4)^3}$ (iii) $\frac{2}{(p + 2)^3}$

(iv) $\frac{2a(p - a)}{(p^2 - 2ap + 2a^2)^2}$ (v) $\frac{2(3p^2 + 4)}{p^2(p^2 + 4)^2}$ (vi) $\frac{p^2 + 9}{(p^2 - 9)^2}$ (vii) $\frac{8 + 12p - 2p^2}{(p^2 + 4)^2}$

(viii) $\frac{2a^3}{(p^2 + a^2)^2}$ (ix) $\frac{n!}{(p - a)^{n+1}}$ (x) $\frac{6p^4 - 18p^3 + 126p^2 - 162p + 432}{(p^2 + 9)^3}$

2. $\frac{2p(p^2 - 3a^2)}{(p^2 + a^2)^3}$

4. (i) $\cot^{-1}\left(\frac{p}{2}\right)$ (ii) $\log\left(\frac{p - 1}{p}\right)$ (iii) $\frac{1}{2}\log\left(\frac{p^2 + 9}{p^2 + 4}\right)$ (iv) $\frac{1}{4}\log\left\{\frac{p^2 + 4}{p^2}\right)$

(v) $\frac{1}{2}\log\left(\frac{p + 1}{p - 1}\right)$ (vi) $\frac{1}{2}\log\left\{\frac{p^2 + 1}{(p - 1)^2}\right\}$ (vii) $\log\left(1 + \frac{1}{p}\right)$

(viii) $\frac{1}{2}\left[\pi - \tan^{-1}\left(\frac{p}{4}\right) - \tan^{-1}\left(\frac{p}{2}\right)\right]$

5. (i) $\pi/2$ (ii) $\pi/2$ (iii) $\log\left(\frac{b}{a}\right)$ (iv) $\log 2$

(v) $\log \frac{2}{3}$ (vi) $\pi/4$

6. (i) $\frac{1}{p}\cot^{-1}(p + 1)$ (ii) $\frac{1}{p}\log\left(\frac{p + b}{p + a}\right)$ (iii) $\frac{1}{2p}\log\left(1 + \frac{4}{p^2}\right)$ (iv) $\frac{1}{2p}\log\left(\frac{p^2 + b^2}{p^2 + a^2}\right)$

7. (i) $\frac{1}{p^2(p^2 + a^2)}$ (ii) $\frac{8(p + 1)}{p(p^2 + 2p + 17)^2}$ (iii) $\frac{1}{(p + 4)}\cot^{-1}\left(\frac{p + 4}{3}\right).$

3.19. LAPLACE TRANSFORM OF SOME SPECIAL FUNCTIONS

(1) The error function. The error function denoted by erf $\sqrt{t}$ is defined as

$$\text{erf } \sqrt{t} = \frac{2}{\sqrt{\pi}} \int_0^{\sqrt{t}} e^{-\eta^2} \, d\eta$$

Note. $\lim\limits_{x \to 0} \text{erf } x = 0$ and $\lim\limits_{x \to \infty} \text{erf } x = 1$.

Example. *Find L (erf $\sqrt{t}$) and hence prove that*

$$L\,(t.\ erf\ 2\sqrt{t}) = \frac{3p+8}{p^2(p+4)^{3/2}}\,.$$

Sol. By definition,

$$\text{erf}\sqrt{t} = \frac{2}{\sqrt{\pi}} \int_0^{\sqrt{t}} e^{-\eta^2}\, d\eta \qquad \text{...(1)}$$

$$\therefore \qquad \text{erf}\sqrt{t} = \frac{2}{\sqrt{\pi}} \int_0^{\sqrt{t}} \left(1-\eta^2+\frac{\eta^4}{2!}-\frac{\eta^6}{3!}+\ldots\ldots\right) d\eta$$

$$= \frac{2}{\sqrt{\pi}} \left(t^{1/2}-\frac{1}{3}t^{3/2}+\frac{1}{5.2!}t^{5/2}-\frac{1}{7.3!}t^{7/2}+\ldots\ldots\right)$$

$$\therefore \qquad \text{L}\,(\text{erf}\,\sqrt{t}) = \frac{2}{\sqrt{\pi}}\left[\frac{\Gamma(3/2)}{p^{3/2}}-\frac{\Gamma(5/2)}{3p^{5/2}}+\frac{\Gamma(7/2)}{5.2!\,p^{7/2}}-\frac{\Gamma(9/2)}{7.3!\,p^{9/2}}+\ldots\ldots\right]$$

$$= \frac{1}{p^{3/2}}-\frac{1}{2}.\frac{1}{p^{5/2}}+\frac{1.3}{2.4}.\frac{1}{p^{7/2}}-\frac{1.3.5}{2.4.6}.\frac{1}{p^{9/2}}+\ldots\ldots$$

$$= \frac{1}{p^{3/2}}\left[1-\frac{1}{2}.\frac{1}{p}+\frac{1.3}{2.4}.\frac{1}{p^2}-\frac{1.3.5}{2.4.6}.\frac{1}{p^3}+\ldots\ldots\right]$$

$$= \frac{1}{p^{3/2}}\left(1+\frac{1}{p}\right)^{-1/2} = \frac{1}{p\sqrt{p+1}}$$

Now,
$$\text{L}(\text{erf}\ 2\sqrt{t}) = \frac{1}{4}\cdot\frac{1}{\frac{p}{4}\sqrt{\frac{p}{4}+1}} = \frac{2}{p\sqrt{p+4}}$$

$$\therefore \qquad \text{L}(t\ \text{erf}\ 2\sqrt{t}) = -\frac{d}{dp}\left[\frac{2}{(p^3+4p^2)^{1/2}}\right] = \frac{p\,(3p+8)}{p^3\,(p+4)^{3/2}} = \frac{3p+8}{p^2\,(p+4)^{3/2}}\,.$$

(2) The Bessel function. Bessel function of order n is given by

$$\text{J}_n\,(x) = \frac{x^n}{2^n\,\Gamma(n+1)}\left[1-\frac{x^2}{2.(2n+2)}+\frac{x^4}{2.4(2n+2)(2n+4)}-\ldots\ldots\right]$$

$$= \sum_{r=0}^{\infty} \frac{(-1)^r}{r!\,\Gamma(n+r+1)}\left(\frac{x}{2}\right)^{n+2r}$$

Bessel function of order zero is given by

$$\text{J}_0\,(x) = 1-\frac{x^2}{2^2}+\frac{x^4}{2^2.4^2}-\frac{x^6}{2^2.4^2.6^2}+\ldots\ldots$$

Example. *Find $L[J_0\,(t)]$, where $J_0\,(t)$ is the Bessel function of order zero. Hence or otherwise obtain $L[J_1\,(t)]$.*

Sol. By definition, $\text{J}_0(t) = 1-\dfrac{t^2}{2^2}+\dfrac{t^4}{2^2.4^2}-\dfrac{t^6}{2^2.4^2.6^2}+\ldots\ldots$ ...(1)

$$\therefore \quad L[J_0(t)] = \frac{1}{p} - \frac{1}{2^2}\cdot\frac{2!}{p^3} + \frac{1}{2^2.4^2}\cdot\frac{4!}{p^5} - \frac{1}{2^2.4^2.6^2}\cdot\frac{6!}{p^7} + \ldots\ldots$$

$$= \frac{1}{p}\left[1 - \frac{1}{2}\cdot\left(\frac{1}{p^2}\right) + \frac{1.3}{2.4}\left(\frac{1}{p^4}\right) - \frac{1.3.5}{2.4.6}\left(\frac{1}{p^6}\right) + \ldots\ldots\right]$$

$$= \frac{1}{p}\left[\left(1 + \frac{1}{p^2}\right)^{-1/2}\right] = \frac{1}{\sqrt{1+p^2}}$$

We know by the recurrence relation,

$$J_0'(t) = -J_1(t)$$

where $J_1(t)$ is the Bessel function of order one.

$$\therefore \quad L[J_1(t)] = -L[J_0'(t)] = -[pL\{J_0(t)\} - 1] = 1 - p\frac{1}{\sqrt{1+p^2}}$$

$$\Rightarrow \quad L(J_1(t)] = 1 - \frac{p}{\sqrt{1+p^2}}.$$

(3) The sine integral. The sine integral, denoted by $S_i(t)$ is defined as

$$S_i(t) = \int_0^t \frac{\sin y}{y}\, dy$$

(4) The cosine integral. The cosine integral, denoted by $C_i(t)$, is defined as

$$C_i(t) = \int_t^\infty \frac{\cos u}{u}\, du.$$

Example. *Find* $L\{C_i(t)\}$, *where* $C_i(t) = \int_t^\infty \frac{\cos u}{u}\, du.$

Sol. Let $$F(t) = \int_t^\infty \frac{\cos u}{u}\, du = -\int_\infty^t \frac{\cos u}{u}\, du$$

so that, $$F'(t) = -\frac{\cos t}{t} \quad \Rightarrow \quad t\,F'(t) = -\cos t$$

$$\therefore \quad L\{tF'(t)\} = -\frac{p}{p^2+1}$$

$$\Rightarrow \quad -\frac{d}{dp}[L\{F'(t)\}] = -\frac{p}{p^2+1}$$

$$\Rightarrow \quad \frac{d}{dp}[p\,f(p) - F(0)] = \frac{p}{p^2+1}$$

$$\Rightarrow \quad \frac{d}{dp}\{p\,f(p)\} = \frac{p}{p^2+1} \qquad (\because \ F(0) \text{ is constant})$$

Integration yields, $pf(p) = \frac{1}{2}\log(p^2+1) + c$ ...(1)

But from the final-value theorem,

$$\underset{p\to 0}{\text{Lt}}\ pf(p) = \underset{t\to\infty}{\text{Lt}}\ F(t) = 0$$

$\therefore$ From (1), as $p \to 0$, we have $c = 0$

$$\therefore \quad pf(p) = \frac{1}{2}\log(p^2+1)$$

$$\Rightarrow \qquad f(p) = \frac{1}{2p} \log (p^2 + 1)$$

(5) The complementary error function. The complementary error function is defined as

$$\text{erf}_c(t) = 1 - \text{erf } t = \frac{2}{\sqrt{\pi}} \int_t^\infty e^{-u^2}\, du.$$

Example. *Evaluate : L(erf$_c$ $\sqrt{t}$).*

Sol. $\text{L}(\text{erf}_c \sqrt{t}) = \text{L}\{1 - \text{erf}(\sqrt{t})\} = \text{L}(1) - \text{L}\{\text{erf}(\sqrt{t})\} = \frac{1}{p} - \frac{1}{p\sqrt{p+1}}.$

(6) The exponential integral function. The exponential integral is defined as

$$\text{E}_i(t) = \int_t^\infty \frac{e^{-u}}{u}\, du.$$

Example. *Evaluate : L {E$_i$ (t)}, where* $E_i(t) = \int_t^\infty \frac{e^{-u}}{u}\, du.$

Sol. $\text{L}\{\text{E}_i(t)\} = \text{L}\left\{\int_t^\infty \frac{e^{-u}}{u}\, du\right\}$ Put $u = tv$ so that $\frac{du}{u} = \frac{dv}{v}$

$$= \text{L}\left\{\int_1^\infty \frac{e^{-tv}}{v}\, dv\right\}$$

$$= \int_0^\infty e^{-pt} \left\{\int_1^\infty \frac{e^{-tv}}{v}\, dv\right\} dt$$

$$= \int_1^\infty \frac{1}{v} \left\{\int_0^\infty e^{-pt} \,.\, e^{-tv}\, dt\right\} dv \qquad |\text{ On changing the order of integration}$$

$$= \int_1^\infty \frac{1}{v} \cdot \frac{1}{p+v}\, dv = \int_1^\infty \frac{1}{p}\left(\frac{1}{v} - \frac{1}{p+v}\right) dv$$

$$= \frac{1}{p}\Big[\log v - \log(p+v)\Big]_1^\infty = \frac{1}{p}\left[-\log\left(\frac{p}{v}+1\right)\right]_1^\infty = \frac{1}{p}\log(p+1)$$

(7) Laguerre polynomial. This polynomial is defined as

$$\text{L}_n(x) = \frac{e^x}{n!} \frac{d^n}{dx^n} (e^{-x} x^n).$$

Example. *Evaluate : L {L$_n$(t)}, where L$_n$(t) is Laguerre polynomial and n is a (+)ve integer.*

Sol. $\text{L}\{\text{L}_n(t)\} = \int_0^\infty e^{-pt} \left\{\frac{e^t}{n!} \frac{d^n}{dt^n} (e^{-t}\, t^n)\right\} dt$

$$= \frac{1}{n!} \int_0^\infty e^{-(p-1)t} \frac{d^n}{dt^n} (e^{-t}\, t^n)\, dt$$

$$= \frac{1}{n!}\left[\left\{e^{-(p-1)t} \frac{d^{n-1}}{dt^{n-1}} (e^{-t}\, t^n)\right\}_0^\infty - \int_0^\infty \{-(p-1)\, e^{-(p-1)t}\} \frac{d^{n-1}}{dt^{n-1}} (e^{-t}\, t^n)\, dt\right]$$

$$= \frac{1}{n!}\left[(p-1)\int_0^\infty e^{-(p-1)t}\,\frac{d^{n-1}}{dt^{n-1}}(e^{-t}\,t^n)\,dt\right]$$

$$= \frac{(p-1)^2}{n!}\int_0^\infty e^{-(p-1)t}\,\frac{d^{n-2}}{dt^{n-2}}(e^{-t}\,t^n)\,dt$$

$$\vdots \qquad \vdots \qquad \vdots \qquad \vdots \qquad \vdots$$

$$= \frac{(p-1)^n}{n!}\int_0^\infty e^{-(p-1)t}\,e^{-t}\,t^n\,dt = \frac{(p-1)^n}{n!}\int_0^\infty e^{-pt}\,t^n\,dt$$

$$= \frac{(p-1)^n}{n!}\cdot\frac{n!}{p^{n+1}} = \frac{(p-1)^n}{p^{n+1}}\,; \quad p > 1.$$

(8) Unit Step Function (or Heaviside's Unit Step Function)

The unit step function $u(t-a)$ is defined as

$$u(t-a) = \begin{cases} 0, & \text{for } t < a \\ 1, & \text{for } t \geq a \end{cases}, \text{ where } a \geq 0.$$

As a particular case, $u(t) = \begin{cases} 0, & \text{for } t < 0 \\ 1, & \text{for } t \geq 0 \end{cases}$

The product $\mathrm{F}(t)\,.\,u(t-a) = \begin{cases} 0, & \text{for } t < a \\ \mathrm{F}(t), & \text{for } t \geq a \end{cases}$

The function $\mathrm{F}(t-a)\,.\,u(t-a)$ represents the graph of $\mathrm{F}(t)$ shifted through a distance 'a' to the right.

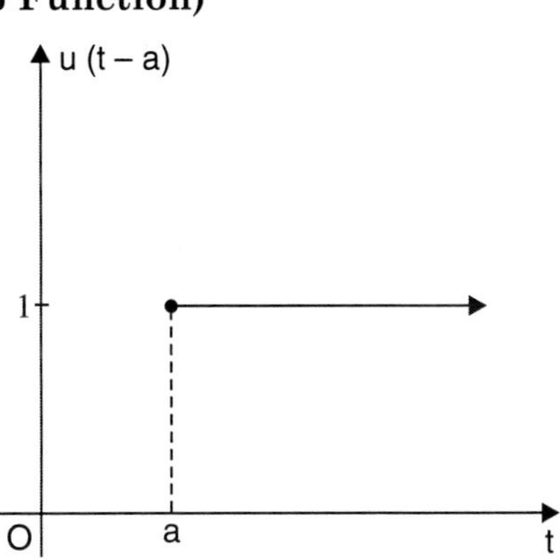

Laplace Transform of Unit Step Function

$$\mathrm{L}\{u(t-a)\} = \int_0^\infty e^{-pt}\,u(t-a)\,dt$$

$$= \int_0^a e^{-pt}\,.\,0\,dt + \int_a^\infty e^{-pt}\,.\,1\,dt = 0 + \left[\frac{e^{-pt}}{-p}\right]_a^\infty = \frac{1}{p}\,e^{-ap}$$

In particular, $\mathrm{L}\{u(t)\} = \dfrac{1}{p}$.

Second Shifting Theorem

If $\mathrm{L}\{\mathrm{F}(t)\} = f(p)$, then $\mathrm{L}\{\mathrm{F}(t-a)\,.\,u(t-a)\} = e^{-ap}\,f(p)$.

$$\mathrm{L}\{\mathrm{F}(t-a)\,.\,u(t-a)\} = \int_0^\infty e^{-pt}\,\mathrm{F}(t-a)\,.\,u(t-a)\,dt$$

$$= \int_a^\infty e^{-pt}\,\mathrm{F}(t-a)\,dt = \int_0^\infty e^{-p(u+a)}\,\mathrm{F}(u)\,du, \text{ where } u = t-a$$

$$= e^{-ap}\int_0^\infty e^{-pu}\,\mathrm{F}(u)\,du = e^{-ap}\,f(p)$$

Note. If $a = 0$, $\mathrm{L}\{\mathrm{F}(t)\,u(t)\} = f(p) = \mathrm{L}\{\mathrm{F}(t)\}$.

ILLUSTRATIVE EXAMPLES

Example 1. *Express the following functions interms of Heaviside's unit step function :*

(*i*) $F(t) = \begin{cases} \sin t\ , & 0 < t < \pi \\ \sin 2t, & \pi < t < 2\pi \\ \sin 3t, & t > 2\pi \end{cases}$ (*ii*) $F(t) = \begin{cases} e^{-t}\ , & 0 < t < 3 \\ 0\ \ , & t > 3 \end{cases}$

(*iii*) $F(t) = \begin{cases} \sin t\ , & t > \pi \\ \cos t\ , & 0 < t < \pi \end{cases}$.

Sol. (*i*)
$$F(t) = \sin t\{u(t) - u(t-\pi)\} + \sin 2t\{u(t-\pi) - u(t-2\pi)\} + \sin 3t\, u(t-2\pi)$$
$$= \sin t\, u(t) + (\sin 2t - \sin t)\, u(t-\pi) + (\sin 3t - \sin 2t)\, u(t-2\pi)$$

(*ii*)
$$F(t) = e^{-t}\{u(t) - u(t-3)\} + 0\{u(t-3)\}$$
$$= e^{-t}\{u(t) - u(t-3)\}$$

(*iii*)
$$F(t) = \sin t\, u(t-\pi) + \cos t\{u(t) - u(t-\pi)\}$$
$$= \cos t\, u(t) + (\sin t - \cos t)\, u(t-\pi)$$

Example 2. *Find the Laplace transform of the functions :*

(*i*) $F(t) = \begin{cases} 2 & \text{if } 0 < t < \pi \\ 0 & \text{if } \pi < t < 2\pi \\ \sin t & \text{if } t > 2\pi \end{cases}$ [U.P.T.U. (C.O.) 2009]

(*ii*) $F(t) = \begin{cases} 1, & 0 < t < 1 \\ 2, & 1 < t < 2 \\ 3, & 2 < t < 3 \\ \ldots\ldots & \ldots\ldots\ldots\ldots \\ \ldots\ldots & \ldots\ldots\ldots\ldots \end{cases}$ (*Staircase function*)

(*iii*) $F(t) = \begin{cases} 1, & 0 < t < 2 \\ 2, & 2 < t < 4 \\ 3, & 4 < t < 6 \\ 0, & t > 6 \end{cases}$ (*iv*) $F(t) = \begin{cases} 0\ , & 0 < t < \pi/2 \\ \sin t\ , & t > \pi/2 \end{cases}$

Sol. (*i*)
$$F(t) = 2\{u(t) - u(t-\pi)\} + \sin t\ \{u(t-2\pi)\}$$
$$= 2\{u(t) - u(t-\pi)\} + \sin(t - 2\pi + 2\pi)\, u(t-2\pi)$$

$\Rightarrow$
$$F(t) = 2\{u(t) - u(t-\pi)\} + \sin(t-2\pi)\, u(t-2\pi)$$

Taking Laplace transform, we get

$$L\{F(t)\} = 2\left(\frac{1}{p} - \frac{e^{-\pi p}}{p}\right) + e^{-2\pi p}\, L(\sin t) \quad | \text{ Using second shifting theorem}$$

$\Rightarrow$
$$f(p) = 2\left(\frac{1 - e^{-\pi p}}{p}\right) + \frac{e^{-2\pi p}}{p^2 + 1}$$

(*ii*)
$$F(t) = 1\{u(t) - u(t-1)\} + 2\{u(t-1) - u(t-2)\}$$
$$+ 3\{u(t-2) - u(t-3)\} + \ldots\ldots$$

$\Rightarrow$
$$F(t) = u(t) + u(t-1) + u(t-2) + u(t-3) + \ldots.$$

$\therefore$
$$L\{F(t)\} = \frac{1}{p} + \frac{e^{-p}}{p} + \frac{e^{-2p}}{p} + \frac{e^{-3p}}{p} + \ldots..$$

$\Rightarrow$
$$f(p) = \frac{1}{p}\left(\frac{1}{1 - e^{-p}}\right).$$

(*iii*) $$\begin{aligned} F(t) &= 1\{u(t) - u(t-2)\} + 2\{u(t-2) - u(t-4)\} \\ &\quad + 3\{u(t-4) - u(t-6)\} \\ &= u(t) + u(t-2) + u(t-4) - 3u(t-6) \end{aligned}$$

$$\therefore \quad L\{F(t)\} = \frac{1}{p} + \frac{e^{-2p}}{p} + \frac{e^{-4p}}{p} - \frac{3e^{-6p}}{p}$$

$$\Rightarrow \quad f(p) = \frac{1}{p}\,(1 + e^{-2p} + e^{-4p} - 3e^{-6p})$$

(*iv*) $$F(t) = \sin t\, u(t - \pi/2)$$

$$= \sin\left(t - \frac{\pi}{2} + \frac{\pi}{2}\right) u\left(t - \frac{\pi}{2}\right) = \cos\left(t - \frac{\pi}{2}\right) u\left(t - \frac{\pi}{2}\right)$$

$$\therefore \quad L\{F(t)\} = e^{-\frac{\pi}{2}p}\, L(\cos t)$$ | Using second shifting theorem

$$\Rightarrow \quad f(p) = \frac{pe^{-(\pi p/2)}}{p^2 + 1}.$$

Example 3. *Find the Laplace transform of*

(*i*) $(t-1)^2\, u(t-1)$ (U.P.T.U. 2008) (*ii*) $\sin t\, u(t-\pi)$ (U.P.T.U. 2008)

(*iii*) $e^{-3t}\, u(t-2)$ (*iv*) $e^{-t}\{1 - u(t-2)\}$.

Sol. (*i*) Comparing $(t-1)^2 u(t-1)$ with $F(t-a)\, u(t-a)$, we have

$$a = 1 \text{ and } F(t) = t^2$$

$$\therefore \quad f(p) = L\{F(t)\} = \frac{2}{p^3}$$

$$\therefore \quad L\{(t-1)^2 u(t-1)\} = e^{-p} f(p)$$ | By second shifting property

$$= \frac{2e^{-p}}{p^3}.$$

(*ii*) Expressing $\sin t$ as a function of $(t - \pi)$, we have

$$\sin t = \sin[(t-\pi) + \pi] = -\sin(t-\pi)$$

Comparing $-\sin(t-\pi)\, u(t-\pi)$ with $F(t-a)\, u(t-a)$, we get

$$a = \pi \text{ and } F(t) = -\sin t$$

$$\therefore \quad f(p) = L\{F(t)\} = -\frac{1}{p^2+1}$$

$$\therefore \quad L[\sin t\, u(t-\pi)\} = e^{-\pi p} f(p)$$ | By second shifting property

$$= \frac{-e^{-\pi p}}{p^2+1}.$$

(*iii*) $$\mathrm{L}\,\{u\,(t-2)\} = \frac{e^{-2p}}{p}$$

$\therefore$ $$\mathrm{L}\left\{e^{-3t}\,u\,(t-2)\right\} = \frac{e^{-2(p+3)}}{p+3}$$ | By first shifting property

(*iv*) $$\mathrm{L}\,[1-u\,(t-2)] = \frac{1}{p} - \frac{e^{-2p}}{p}$$

$$\therefore \quad \mathrm{L}\left[e^{-t}\,\{1-u\,(t-2)\}\right] = \frac{1}{p+1} - \frac{e^{-2(p+1)}}{p+1}$$ | By first shifting property

Example 4. *Express the function shown in the diagram in terms of unit step function and obtain its Laplace transform.* (U.P.T.U. 2009)

Sol. Here,

$$\mathrm{F}(t) = \begin{cases} t-1 & , \quad 1<t<2 \\ 3-t & , \quad 2<t<3 \end{cases}$$

$$\therefore \quad \mathrm{F}(t) = (t-1)\,\{u(t-1) - u(t-2)\} + (3-t)\,\{u(t-2) - u\,(t-3)\}$$

$$= (t-3)\,u(t-3) - 2(t-2)\,u(t-2) + (t-1)\,u(t-1)$$

Hence, $$\mathrm{L}\{\mathrm{F}(t)\} = \mathrm{L}\{(t-3)\,u(t-3)\} - 2\,\mathrm{L}\{(t-2)\,u(t-2)\} + \mathrm{L}\{(t-1)\,u(t-1)\}$$

$$= \frac{e^{-3p}}{p^2} - \frac{2\,e^{-2p}}{p^2} + \frac{e^{-p}}{p^2}$$ | By second shifting property

$$= \frac{e^{-p}\,(1-e^{-p})^2}{p^2}.$$

Example 5. *Express the following function interms of unit step function and find its Laplace transform :*

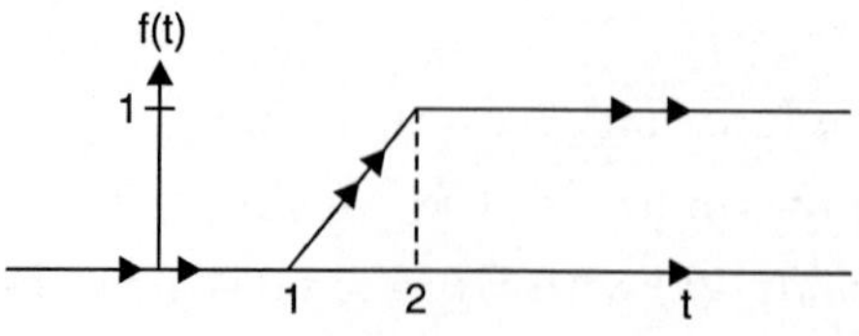

Sol. Here, $$f(t) = \left.\begin{matrix} 0 & , & 0<t<1 \\ t-1 & , & 1<t<2 \\ 1 & , & t>2 \end{matrix}\right\}$$

or $$f(t) = (t-1)\{u(t-1) - u(t-2)\} + u(t-2)$$

$$= (t-1)\,u(t-1) - (t-2)\,u(t-2)$$

By second shifting theorem,

If $\mathrm{L}\{f(t)\} = \bar{f}\,(p)$, then $\mathrm{L}\{f(t-a)\,u(t-a)\} = e^{-ap}\,\bar{f}\,(p)$

Here, $$L\{f(t)\} = L(t) = \frac{1}{p^2}$$

$\therefore$ $$L\{(t-1)\,u(t-1)\} = e^{-p}\,.\,\frac{1}{p^2} \quad \text{and} \quad L\{(t-2)\,u\,(t-2)\} = e^{-2p}\,.\,\frac{1}{p^2}$$

Hence, $$L\{(t-1)\,u(t-1) - (t-2)\,u(t-2)\} = \frac{e^{-p} - e^{-2p}}{p^2}.$$

Example 6. *Sketch the following functions and express them interms of unit step functions. Hence obtain the Laplace transform.*

$$(i)\ f(t) = \begin{cases} t^2 , & 0 < t \le 2 \\ 4t , & t > 2 \end{cases} \qquad (ii)\ f(t) = \begin{cases} \cos(\omega t + \phi) , & 0 < t < T \\ 0 , & t > T. \end{cases}$$

Sol. (*i*) The graph is shown. In terms of unit-step function,

$$f(t) = t^2\{u(t) - u(t-2)\} + 4t\ u(t-2)$$
$$= t^2\,u(t) + (4t - t^2)\,u(t-2)$$

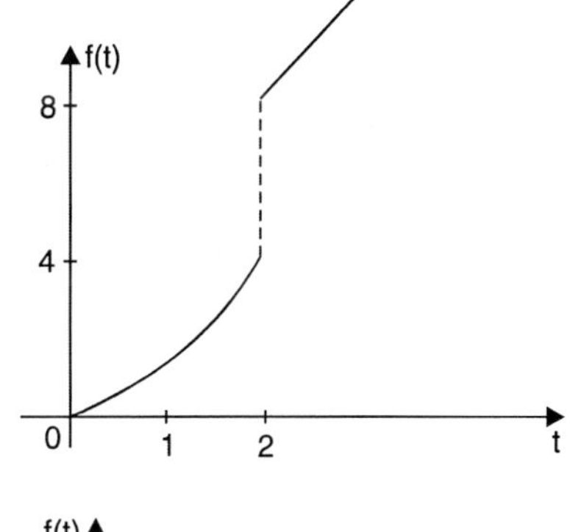

$$\therefore\ L\{f(t)\} = L\{t^2\,u(t)\} + L[\{4 - (t-2)^2\}\,u(t-2)]$$
$$= \frac{2}{p^3} + e^{-2p}\,L(4 - t^2)$$
$$= \frac{2}{p^3} + e^{-2p}\left(\frac{4}{p} - \frac{2}{p^3}\right)$$
$$= \frac{2(1 - e^{-2p})}{p^3} + \frac{4e^{-2p}}{p}.$$

(*ii*) The graph of the function is shown.

In terms of unit step function,

$$f(t) = \cos(\omega t + \phi)\,\{u(t) - u(t - T)\}$$
$$\therefore\ L\{f(t)\} = L\{\cos(\omega t + \phi)\} - e^{-pT}\,L\{\cos(\omega t + \omega T + \phi)\}$$
$$= \cos\phi\left(\frac{p}{p^2 + \omega^2}\right) - \sin\phi\,.\left(\frac{\omega}{p^2 + \omega^2}\right)$$
$$- e^{-pT}\,L\{\cos\omega t\ \cos(\omega T + \phi) - \sin\omega t\,\sin(\omega T + \phi)\}$$
$$= \frac{p\cos\phi - \omega\sin\phi}{p^2 + \omega^2} - e^{-pT}\,.\left\{\frac{p\cos(\omega T + \phi) - \omega\sin(\omega T + \phi)}{p^2 + \omega^2}\right\}.$$

Example 7. *A periodic square wave function F(t) in terms of unit step functions, is written as*

$$F(t) = k[u_0(t) - 2u_a(t) + 2u_{2a}(t) - 2u_{3a}(t) + \ldots]$$

Find its Laplace transform.

Sol. $\mathrm{L}[\mathrm{F}(t)] = k[\mathrm{L}\{u_0(t)\} - 2\mathrm{L}\{u_a(t)\} + 2\mathrm{L}\{u_{2a}(t)\} - 2\mathrm{L}\{u_{3a}(t)\} + ...]$

$$= k\left[\frac{1}{p} - \frac{2\,e^{-ap}}{p} + 2\frac{e^{-2ap}}{p} - 2\frac{e^{-3ap}}{p} + \ldots\right]$$

$$= \frac{k}{p}\,[1 - 2(e^{-ap} - e^{-2ap} + e^{-3ap} - \ldots\ldots)]$$

$$= \frac{k}{p}\left[1 - 2\left(\frac{e^{-ap}}{1 + e^{-ap}}\right)\right] = \frac{k}{p}\left(\frac{1 - e^{-ap}}{1 + e^{-ap}}\right)$$

$$= \frac{k}{p}\left(\frac{e^{ap/2} - e^{-ap/2}}{e^{ap/2} + e^{-ap/2}}\right) = \frac{k}{p}\tanh\frac{ap}{2}.$$

(9) Unit Impulse Function (or Dirac-delta Function)

In mechanics, we come across problems where a very large force acts for a very small time. In the study of bending of beams, we have point loads which is equivalent to large pressure acting over a very small area. To deal with such problems, we introduce the unit impulse function or Dirac-delta function.

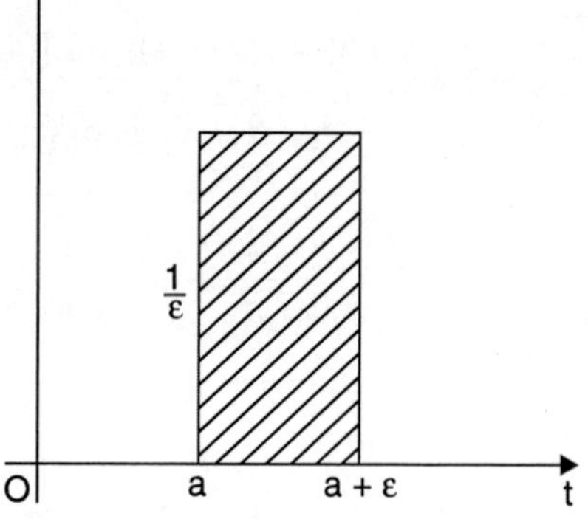

Unit impulse function is considered as the limiting form of the function

$$\delta_\varepsilon(t - a) = \begin{cases} 0, & \text{for} \quad t < a \\ \dfrac{1}{\varepsilon}, & \text{for} \quad a \le t \le a + \varepsilon \\ 0, & \text{for} \quad t > a \end{cases}$$

This function is represented in the figure. Integrating this function, we get

$$\int_0^\infty \delta_\varepsilon(t - a)\, dt = \int_a^{a+\varepsilon} \frac{1}{\varepsilon}\, dt = \frac{1}{\varepsilon}\,(a + \varepsilon - a) = 1$$

As $\varepsilon \to 0$, the function $\delta_\varepsilon(t - a)$ tends to be infinite at $x = a$ and zero elsewhere, with the characteristic property that its integral across $t = a$ is unity. If $\delta_\varepsilon(t - a)$ represents a force acting for short duration ε at time $t = a$, then the integral

$$\underset{\varepsilon \to 0}{\mathrm{Lt}} \int_0^{a+\varepsilon} \delta_\varepsilon(t - a)\, dt = 1$$

represents unit impulse at $t = a$. Hence the limiting form of $\delta_\varepsilon(t - a)$ as $\varepsilon \to 0$ is expressed as unit impulse function denoted by $\delta(t - a)$.

Thus the unit impulse function $\delta(t - a)$ is defined as follows :

$$\delta(t - a) = \begin{cases} \infty, & \text{for} \quad t = a \\ 0, & \text{for} \quad t \ne a \end{cases}$$

such that $$\int_0^\infty \delta(t - a)\;\, dt = 1.$$

Laplace Transform of Unit Impulse Function

If $f(t)$ is a function of t continuous at $t = a$, then

$$\int_0^\infty f(t)\,\delta_\varepsilon\,(t - a)\, dt = \int_a^{a+\varepsilon} f(t)\,.\,\frac{1}{\varepsilon}\,dt$$

$$= (a + \varepsilon - a)\, f(c) \,.\, \frac{1}{\varepsilon} = f(c), \text{ where } a < c < a + \varepsilon$$

(by mean value theorem for integrals)

As $\varepsilon \to 0$, we get $\displaystyle\int_0^\infty f(t)\, \delta(t - a)\, dt = f(a).$

Cor. 1. $\displaystyle L\{\delta(t - a)\} = \int_0^\infty e^{-pt}\, \delta(t - a)\, dt = e^{-pa}.$

Cor. 2. $L\{\delta(t)\} = e^0 = 1.$

ILLUSTRATIVE EXAMPLES

Example 1. *Evaluate :*

(*i*) $\displaystyle\int_0^\infty e^{-4t}\, \delta(t - 3)\, dt$ (*ii*) $\displaystyle\int_0^\infty \phi(t)\, \delta'(t - a)\, dt.$

Sol. (*i*) $\displaystyle\int_0^\infty e^{-4t}\, \delta(t - 3)\, dt = [e^{-4t}]_{t=3} = e^{-12}$

(*ii*)
$$\int_0^\infty \phi(t)\, \delta'(t - a)\, dt = \Big[\phi(t)\, \delta(t - a)\Big]_0^\infty - \int_0^\infty \phi'(t)\, \delta(t - a)\, dt$$
$$= 0 - 0 - \phi'(a) = -\phi'(a).$$

Example 2. *Find the Laplace transform of*

(*i*) $t^3\, \delta(t - 5)$ (*ii*) $\cos t \log t\, \delta(t - \pi).$

Sol. (*i*) $\displaystyle L[t^3\, \delta(t - 5)] = \int_0^\infty e^{-pt} \,.\, t^3\, \delta(t - 5)\, dt = (5)^3\, e^{-5p}$ | By definition

(*ii*) $\displaystyle L\{\cos t \log t\, \delta(t - \pi)\} = \int_0^\infty e^{-pt} \,.\, \cos t \log t\, \delta(t - \pi)\, dt$ | By definition

$$= \cos \pi \log \pi\, e^{-p\pi} = -\log \pi\, e^{-p\pi}.$$

(10) Periodic Functions. *If $f(t)$ is a periodic function with period T, i.e., $f(t + T) = f(t)$, then*

$$L\{f(t)\} = \frac{1}{1 - e^{-pT}} \int_0^T e^{-pt} f(t)\, dt.$$

[U.P.T.U. (C.O.) 2009; G.B.T.U (C.O.) 2010]

Here, $\displaystyle L\{f(t)\} = \int_0^\infty e^{-pt} f(t)\, dt = \int_0^T e^{-pt} f(t)\, dt + \int_T^{2T} e^{-pt} f(t)\, dt + \int_{2T}^{3T} e^{-pt} f(t)\, dt + \ldots\ldots$

Putting $t = u,\ t = u + T,\ t = u + 2T, \ldots\ldots$ in the successive integrals

$$L\{f(t)\} = \int_0^T e^{-pu} f(u)\, du + \int_0^T e^{-p(u+T)} f(u + T)\, du + \int_0^T e^{-p(u+2T)} f(u + 2T)\, du + \ldots\ldots$$

Since $f(u) = f(u + T) = f(u + 2T) = \ldots\ldots$, we have

$$L\{f(t)\} = \int_0^T e^{-pu} f(u)\, du + e^{-pT} \int_0^T e^{-pu} f(u)\, du + e^{-2pT} \int_0^T e^{-pu} f(u)\, du + \ldots$$
$$= (1 + e^{-pT} + e^{-2pT} + \ldots) \int_0^T e^{-pu} f(u)\, du = \frac{1}{1 - e^{-pT}} \int_0^T e^{-pt} f(t)\, dt.$$

ILLUSTRATIVE EXAMPLES

Example 1. *Find the Laplace transform of the following periodic functions :*

(i) $f(t) = t/T$, *for* $0 < t < T$ *(saw-tooth wave of period T)* (U.K.T.U. 2011)

(ii) $f(t) = \sin\left(\frac{\pi t}{a}\right)$ *for* $0 < t < a$. *(Rectified sine wave of period a)*

Sol. *(i)* Here,
$$L\{f(t)\} = \frac{1}{1-e^{-pT}} \int_0^T e^{-pt} f(t)\, dt = \frac{1}{1-e^{-pT}} \int_0^T e^{-pt} \cdot \frac{t}{T}\, dt$$

$$= \frac{1}{T(1-e^{-pT})}\left[\left(\frac{te^{-pt}}{-p}\right)_0^T - \int_0^T 1 . \frac{e^{-pt}}{-p}\, dt\right]$$

$$= \frac{1}{1-e^{-pT}}\left[-\frac{e^{-pT}}{p} + \frac{1-e^{-pT}}{p^2 T}\right] = \frac{1}{p^2 T} - \frac{e^{-pT}}{p(1-e^{-pT})}$$

(ii)
$$L\{f(t)\} = \frac{1}{1-e^{-ap}} \int_0^a e^{-pt} . \sin\left(\frac{\pi t}{a}\right) dt \quad ...(1)$$

Let
$$I = \int_0^a e^{-pt} . \sin\left(\frac{\pi t}{a}\right) dt$$

$$= \left[\frac{e^{-pt}}{p^2 + \frac{\pi^2}{a^2}}\left(-p \sin\frac{\pi t}{a} - \frac{\pi}{a}\cos\frac{\pi t}{a}\right)\right]_0^a$$

$$= \left[\frac{e^{-ap}}{p^2 + \frac{\pi^2}{a^2}}\left(\frac{\pi}{a}\right)\right] - \left[\frac{1}{p^2 + \frac{\pi^2}{a^2}} \cdot \left(-\frac{\pi}{a}\right)\right] = \frac{(1+e^{-ap})\, a\pi}{a^2 p^2 + \pi^2}$$

$\therefore$ From (1),
$$L\{f(t)\} = \frac{(1+e^{-ap})\, a\pi}{(1-e^{-ap})(a^2 p^2 + \pi^2)}$$

$$= \left(\frac{e^{ap/2} + e^{-ap/2}}{e^{ap/2} - e^{-ap/2}}\right)\left(\frac{a\pi}{a^2 p^2 + \pi^2}\right) = \frac{a\pi \coth \frac{ap}{2}}{a^2 p^2 + \pi^2}.$$

Example 2. *Draw the graph and find the Laplace transform of the triangular wave function of period 2c given by*

$$f(t) = \begin{cases} t & , \quad 0 < t \le c \\ 2c - t & , \quad c < t < 2c \end{cases}.$$
[U.P.T.U. (SUM) 2007, 2008]

Sol.
$$L\{f(t)\} = \frac{1}{1-e^{-2cp}} \int_0^{2c} e^{-pt} f(t)\, dt = \frac{1}{1-e^{-2cp}}\left[\int_0^c e^{-pt} . t\, dt + \int_c^{2c} e^{-pt}(2c - t)\, dt\right]$$

$$= \frac{1}{1-e^{-2cp}}\left[\left\{t\,.\frac{e^{-pt}}{-p} - 1.\frac{e^{-pt}}{p^2}\right\}_0^c + \left\{(2c-t)\,.\frac{e^{-pt}}{-p} - (-1).\frac{e^{-pt}}{p^2}\right\}_c^{2c}\right]$$

$$= \frac{1}{1-e^{-2cp}}\left[\left\{-\frac{ce^{-cp}}{p} - \frac{e^{-cp}}{p^2} + \frac{1}{p^2}\right\} + \left\{\frac{e^{-2cp}}{p^2} + \frac{ce^{-cp}}{p} - \frac{e^{-cp}}{p^2}\right\}\right]$$

$$= \frac{1}{1-e^{-2cp}}\left(\frac{1-2e^{-cp}+e^{-2cp}}{p^2}\right) = \frac{1}{p^2}\cdot\frac{(1-e^{-cp})^2}{(1+e^{-cp})(1-e^{-cp})} = \frac{1}{p^2}\cdot\frac{1-e^{-cp}}{1+e^{-cp}}$$

$$= \frac{1}{p^2}\left(\frac{e^{cp/2}-e^{-cp/2}}{e^{cp/2}+e^{-cp/2}}\right) = \frac{1}{p^2}\tanh\frac{cp}{2}\,.$$

The graph of the given function is shown below :

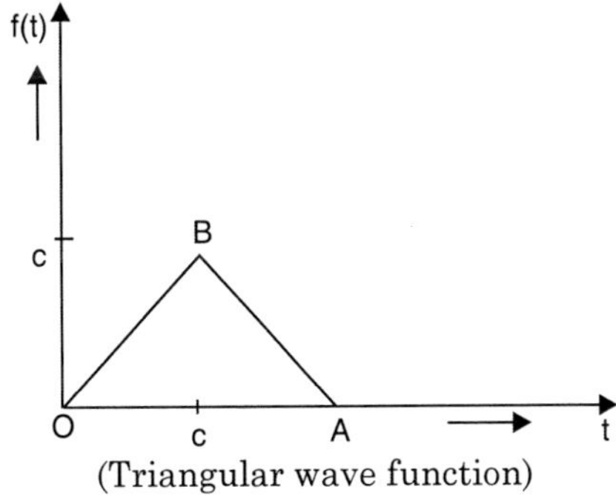

(Triangular wave function)

Example 3. *Find the Laplace transform of the rectified semi-wave function defined by*

$$f(t) = \begin{cases} \sin \omega t\,, & 0 < t \le \dfrac{\pi}{\omega} \\ 0\,, & \dfrac{\pi}{\omega} < t < \dfrac{2\pi}{\omega} \end{cases}.$$ (G.B.T.U. 2010; M.T.U. 2011)

Or

Find the Laplace transform of following periodic function

[U.P.T.U. (SUM) 2009]

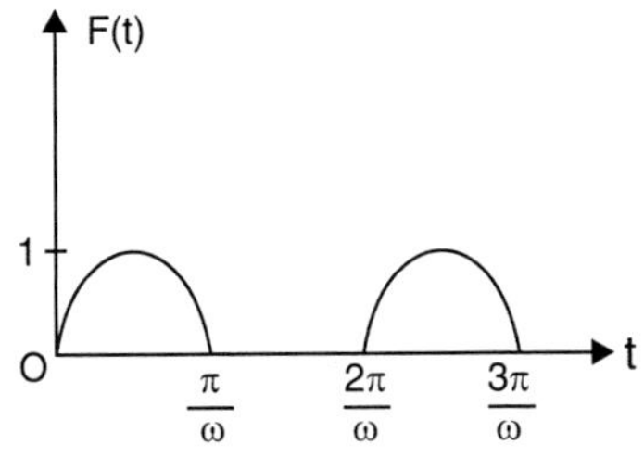

(Half-wave rectifier)

Sol. Here $f(t)$ is a periodic function with period $\frac{2\pi}{\omega}$

$$\therefore \text{L}\{f(t)\} = \frac{1}{1-e^{-\frac{2\pi p}{\omega}}}\int_0^{2\pi/\omega} e^{-pt} f(t)\,dt = \frac{1}{1-e^{-\frac{2\pi p}{\omega}}}\left[\int_0^{\pi/\omega} e^{-pt}\sin\omega t\,dt + \int_{\pi/\omega}^{2\pi/\omega} e^{-pt}\,.\,0\,dt\right]$$

$$= \frac{1}{1-e^{-\frac{2\pi p}{\omega}}}\left[\frac{e^{-pt}(-p\sin\omega t - \omega\cos\omega t)}{p^2+\omega^2}\right]_0^{\pi/\omega}$$

$$= \frac{\omega e^{-\frac{\pi p}{\omega}} + \omega}{\left(1-e^{-\frac{\pi p}{\omega}}\right)\left(1+e^{-\frac{\pi p}{\omega}}\right)(p^2+\omega^2)} = \frac{\omega}{\left(1-e^{-\frac{\pi p}{\omega}}\right)(p^2+\omega^2)}.$$

Example 4. *Find the Laplace transform of the square-wave function of period a defined as :*

$$f(t) = \begin{cases} 1 \;, & 0 \le t \le \dfrac{a}{2} \\ -1 \;, & \dfrac{a}{2} < t < a \end{cases}.$$

Sol.

$$\text{L}\{f(t)\} = \frac{1}{1-e^{-ap}}\int_0^a e^{-pt} f(t)\,dt = \frac{1}{1-e^{-ap}}\left[\int_0^{a/2} e^{-pt}\,.\,1\,dt + \int_{a/2}^a e^{-pt}(-1)\,dt\right]$$

$$= \frac{1}{1-e^{-ap}}\left[\left(\frac{e^{-pt}}{-p}\right)_0^{a/2} + \left(\frac{e^{-pt}}{p}\right)_{a/2}^a\right] = \frac{1}{p(1-e^{-ap})}\,[1 - e^{-ap/2} + e^{-ap} - e^{-ap/2}]$$

$$= \frac{1}{p(1-e^{-ap})}(1-e^{-ap/2})^2 = \frac{1}{p}\cdot\left(\frac{1-e^{-ap/2}}{1+e^{-ap/2}}\right) = \frac{1}{p}\left(\frac{e^{ap/4}-e^{-ap/4}}{e^{ap/4}+e^{-ap/4}}\right)$$

$$= \frac{1}{p}\tanh\left(\frac{ap}{4}\right).$$

TEST YOUR KNOWLEDGE

1. Find the Laplace transform of

   (*i*) $e^{t-2}\,u(t-2)$ (*ii*) $t^2\,u(t-3)$ (*iii*) $\sin 2t\,u(t-\pi)$.

2. Express the following functions interms of unit step function and find its Laplace transform :

   (*i*) $f(t) = \begin{cases} 8, & t < 2 \\ 6, & t > 2 \end{cases}$ (*ii*) $f(t) = \begin{cases} \text{E}, & a < t < b \\ 0, & t > b \end{cases}$

   (*iii*) $f(t) = \begin{cases} \sin t, & 0 < t < \pi \\ \sin 2t, & \pi < t \end{cases}$ (*iv*) $f(t) = \begin{cases} \sin 2t, & 2\pi < t < 4\pi \\ 0, & \text{otherwise} \end{cases}$

   [*G.B.T.U. (C.O.) 2011*]

   (*v*) $f(t) = \begin{cases} 4, & 0 < t < 1 \\ -2, & 1 < t < 3 \\ 5, & t > 3 \end{cases}$ (*vi*) $f(t) = \begin{cases} 2t, & \text{for } 0 \le t \le 5 \\ 10, & \text{for } t > 5 \end{cases}.$

3. Find the Laplace transform of the periodic function

$$F(t) = \begin{cases} 1 & \text{for } 0 \le t \le 1,\ 2 < t \le 3,\ 4 < t \le 5, \\ 0 & \text{for } 1 < t \le 2,\ 3 < t \le 4,\ 5 < t \le 6, \end{cases} \ldots\ldots$$

[**Hint:** The period of the given function is 2.]

4. Find L{F(t)}, where F(t) is defined by

(*i*) $F(t) = t,\ 0 < t < a$ and $F(t + a) = F(t)$

(*ii*) $F(t) = \begin{cases} \sin t, & 0 < t < \pi \\ 0, & \pi < t < 2\pi \end{cases}$ and $F(t + 2\pi) = F(t)$

(*iii*) $F(t) = \begin{cases} t, & 0 < t < 1 \\ 0, & 1 < t < 2 \end{cases}$, where F($t$) has period 2

(*iv*) $F(t) = \begin{cases} 1, & 0 \le t < 2 \\ -1, & 2 \le t < 4 \end{cases}$ and $F(t + 4) = F(t)$. (*U.P.T.U. 2009*)

5. (*i*) Find the Laplace transform of a periodic function $f(t)$ with period τ. [*G.B.T.U. (C.O.) 2010*]

(*ii*) Find the Laplace transform of "saw-tooth wave" function $f(t)$ which is periodic with period 1 and defined as $f(t) = kt$ in $0 < t < 1$. [*U.P.T.U. (SUM) 2007*]

6. Evaluate :

(*i*) $L[e^{t-1}\, u(t-1)]$ (*ii*) $L\{t^2 u(t-1) + \delta(t-1)\}$.

7. Draw the graph and find the Laplace transform of the following function of period $2a$:

$$f(t) = \begin{cases} \dfrac{h}{a} t, & 0 < t < a \\ \dfrac{h}{a}(2a - t), & a < t < 2a \end{cases}$$

(*G.B.T.U. 2011*)

Answers

1. (*i*) $\dfrac{e^{-2p}}{p-1}$ (*ii*) $\dfrac{e^{-3p}\,(2 + 6p + 9p^2)}{p^3}$ (*iii*) $\dfrac{2e^{-\pi p}}{p^2 + 4}$

2. (*i*) $\dfrac{8}{p} - 2\,\dfrac{e^{-2p}}{p}$ (*ii*) $E\left(\dfrac{e^{-ap} - e^{-bp}}{p}\right)$ (*iii*) $\dfrac{1 + e^{-\pi p}}{p^2 + 1} + \dfrac{2e^{-\pi p}}{p^2 + 4}$

(*iv*) $(e^{-2\pi p} - e^{-4\pi p}) \cdot \dfrac{2}{p^2 + 4}$ (*v*) $\dfrac{4 - 6e^{-p} + 7e^{-3p}}{p}$ (*vi*) $\dfrac{2}{p^2}(1 - e^{-5p})$

3. $\dfrac{1}{p(1 + e^{-p})}$

4. (*i*) $\dfrac{1}{p^2} + \dfrac{a}{2p}\left(1 - \coth\dfrac{ap}{2}\right)$ (*ii*) $\dfrac{1}{(1 - e^{-\pi p})(1 + p^2)}$ (*iii*) $\dfrac{1 - e^{-p}(p + 1)}{p^2(1 - e^{-2p})}$

(*iv*) $\dfrac{(1 - e^{-2p})}{p(1 + e^{-2p})}$

5. (*i*) $\dfrac{1}{1 - e^{-p\tau}} \displaystyle\int_0^{\tau} e^{-pt} f(t)\, dt$ (*ii*) $\dfrac{k}{p^2} - \dfrac{ke^{-p}}{p(1 - e^{-p})}$

6. (*i*) $\dfrac{e^{-p}}{p-1}$ (*ii*) $e^{-p}\,\dfrac{(2 + 2p + p^2 + p^3)}{p^3}$ 7. $\dfrac{h}{ap^2}\tanh\dfrac{ap}{2}$

3.20. INVERSE LAPLACE TRANSFORM

If $L\{F(t)\} = f(p)$, then $F(t)$ is called the inverse Laplace transform of $f(p)$ and is denoted by

$$L^{-1}\{f(p)\} = F(t)$$

Here L^{-1} denotes the inverse Laplace transform operator.

e.g., Since $L\{e^{5t}\} = \dfrac{1}{p-5}$ $\therefore$ $L^{-1}\left\{\dfrac{1}{p-5}\right\} = e^{5t}$

The inverse Laplace transforms given below follow at once from the results of Laplace transforms given earlier :

(1) $L^{-1}\left\{\dfrac{1}{p}\right\} = 1$

(2) $L^{-1}\left\{\dfrac{1}{p-a}\right\} = e^{at}$

(3) $L^{-1}\left\{\dfrac{1}{p^n}\right\} = \dfrac{t^{n-1}}{(n-1)!}$, **if *n* is a positive integer.** $\left[\textbf{otherwise} = \dfrac{t^{n-1}}{G(n)}\right]$

(4) $L^{-1}\left\{\dfrac{1}{(p-a)^n}\right\} = e^{at}\dfrac{t^{n-1}}{(n-1)!}$

(5) $L^{-1}\left\{\dfrac{1}{p^2+a^2}\right\} = \dfrac{1}{a}\sin at$

(6) $L^{-1}\left\{\dfrac{p}{p^2+a^2}\right\} = \cos at$

(7) $L^{-1}\left\{\dfrac{1}{p^2-a^2}\right\} = \dfrac{1}{a}\sinh at$

(8) $L^{-1}\left\{\dfrac{p}{p^2-a^2}\right\} = \cosh at.$

All the above results must be remembered.

3.21. LINEARITY PROPERTY

If c_1 and c_2 are constants and $L\{F_1(t)\} = f_1(p)$ and $L\{F_2(t)\} = f_2(p)$, then

$$L^{-1}\{c_1f_1(p) + c_2f_2(p)\} = c_1 L^{-1}\{f_1(p)\} + c_2 L^{-1}\{f_2(p)\}.$$

By definition,

$$L\{c_1 F_1(t) + c_2 F_2(t)\} = \int_0^\infty e^{-pt}\{c_1 F_1(t) + c_2 F_2(t)\}\, dt$$

$$= c_1\int_0^\infty e^{-pt}\,.\,F_1(t)\,dt + c_2\int_0^\infty e^{-pt}\,.\,F_2(t)\,dt = c_1f_1(p) + c_2 f_2(p)$$

$$\Rightarrow \quad L^{-1}\{c_1f_1(p) + c_2f_2(p)\} = c_1 F_1(t) + c_2 F_2(t) = c_1 L^{-1}\{f_1(p)\} + c_2 L^{-1}\{f_2(p)\}$$

The above result can be extended to more than two functions.

3.22. FIRST TRANSLATION OR SHIFTING PROPERTY

If $\quad L^{-1}\{f(p)\} = F(t)$, **then** $\quad L^{-1}\{f(p-a)\} = e^{at}\,F(t)$

$$f(p) = \int_0^\infty e^{-pt}\,.\,F(t)\,dt \qquad \text{| By definition}$$

$\therefore \qquad f(p-a) = \int_0^\infty e^{-(p-a)t} \,.\, \mathrm{F}(t)\, dt$

$$= \int_0^\infty e^{-pt} \,.\, e^{at}\, \mathrm{F}(t)\, dt = \mathrm{L}\{e^{at}\, \mathrm{F}(t)\}$$

$\therefore \qquad \mathrm{L}^{-1}\{f(p-a)\} = e^{at}\, \mathrm{F}(t).$

3.23. SECOND TRANSLATION OR SHIFTING PROPERTY

If $\quad \mathbf{L^{-1}\{\mathit{f(p)}\} = F(\mathit{t})}$**, then**

$$\mathbf{L^{-1}\{e^{-ap} f(p)\} = G(t) \quad \text{where} \quad G(t) = \begin{cases} F(t-a), & t > a \\ 0 \quad , & t < a \end{cases}}.$$

$$f(p) = \int_0^\infty e^{-pt} \,.\, \mathrm{F}(t) dt \qquad \text{| By definition}$$

$\therefore \qquad e^{-ap} f(p) = \int_0^\infty e^{-ap} \,.\, e^{-pt} \,.\, \mathrm{F}(t)\, dt = \int_0^\infty e^{-p(t+a)} \,.\, \mathrm{F}(t)\, dt$

Put $t + a = u \quad \therefore \quad dt = du$

$$= \int_a^\infty e^{-pu} \,.\, \mathrm{F}(u-a) du = \int_a^\infty e^{-pt} \,.\, \mathrm{F}(t-a)\, dt$$

$$= \int_0^a e^{-pt} \,.\, 0\, dt + \int_a^\infty e^{-pt} \,.\, \mathrm{F}(t-a)\, dt = \int_0^\infty e^{-pt} \,.\, \mathrm{G}(t)\, dt = \mathrm{L}\{\mathrm{G}(t)\}$$

Hence the result.

Remark. We may write $\mathrm{G}(t)$ interms of Heaviside's unit step function as $\mathrm{F}(t-a)\, \mathrm{U}(t-a)$ or $\mathrm{F}(t-a)\, \mathrm{H}(t-a)$

$\therefore$ The theorem can be restated as

If $\quad \mathrm{L}^{-1}\{f(p)\} = \mathrm{F}(t)$, then $\mathrm{L}^{-1}\{e^{-ap} f(p)\} = \mathrm{F}(t-a)\, \mathrm{U}(t-a)$.

3.24. CHANGE OF SCALE PROPERTY

If $\mathbf{L^{-1}\{\mathit{f(p)}\} = F(\mathit{t})}$**, then** $\quad \mathbf{L^{-1}\{\mathit{f(ap)}\} = \dfrac{1}{\mathit{a}} F\left(\dfrac{\mathit{t}}{\mathit{a}}\right)}.$

$$f(p) = \int_0^\infty e^{-pt} \,.\, \mathrm{F}(t)\, dt \qquad \text{| By definition}$$

$\therefore \qquad f(ap) = \int_0^\infty e^{-apt} \,.\, \mathrm{F}(t)\, dt \qquad$ Put $\; at = u \quad \therefore \quad dt = \dfrac{du}{a}$

$$= \int_0^\infty e^{-pu} \,.\, \mathrm{F}\left(\frac{u}{a}\right) \frac{du}{a} = \frac{1}{a} \int_0^\infty e^{-pt} \,.\, \mathrm{F}\left(\frac{t}{a}\right) dt$$

$$= \int_0^\infty e^{-pt} \left\{\frac{1}{a} \mathrm{F}\left(\frac{t}{a}\right)\right\} dt = \mathrm{L}\left\{\frac{1}{a} \mathrm{F}\left(\frac{t}{a}\right)\right\}$$

$\therefore \qquad \mathrm{L}^{-1}\{f(ap)\} = \dfrac{1}{a} \mathrm{F}\left(\dfrac{t}{a}\right).$

3.25. USE OF PARTIAL FRACTIONS

Whenever it is convenient to break an expression into partial fractions, it becomes easier to manipulate inversion term by term.

ILLUSTRATIVE EXAMPLES

Example 1. *Find the inverse Laplace transform of*

(*i*) $\dfrac{3(p^2-1)^2}{2p^5}$ (*ii*) $\dfrac{2p+1}{p^2-4}$ [U.P.T.U. (SUM) 2009]

(*iii*) $\dfrac{4p+15}{16p^2-25}$ (*iv*) $\dfrac{p+1}{p^2+p+1}$.

Sol. (*i*) $$\frac{3(p^2-1)^2}{2p^5}=\frac{3p^4-6p^2+3}{2p^5}=\frac{3}{2}\cdot\frac{1}{p}-3\cdot\frac{1}{p^3}+\frac{3}{2}\cdot\frac{1}{p^5}$$

$$\therefore \quad L^{-1}\left\{\frac{3(p^2-1)^2}{2p^5}\right\}=\frac{3}{2}L^{-1}\left\{\frac{1}{p}\right\}-3L^{-1}\left\{\frac{1}{p^3}\right\}+\frac{3}{2}L^{-1}\left\{\frac{1}{p^5}\right\}$$

$$=\frac{3}{2}(1)-3\left\{\frac{t^2}{2!}\right\}+\frac{3}{2}\left\{\frac{t^4}{4!}\right\}=\frac{3}{2}-\frac{3}{2}t^2+\frac{1}{16}t^4.$$

(*ii*) $$L^{-1}\left(\frac{2p+1}{p^2-4}\right)=2L^{-1}\left(\frac{p}{p^2-4}\right)+\frac{1}{2}L^{-1}\left(\frac{2}{p^2-4}\right)=2\cosh 2t+\frac{1}{2}\sinh 2t.$$

(*iii*) $$\frac{4p+15}{16p^2-25}=\frac{4p+15}{16\left(p^2-\frac{25}{16}\right)}=\frac{1}{4}\cdot\frac{p}{p^2-(\frac{5}{4})^2}+\frac{15}{16}\cdot\frac{1}{p^2-(\frac{5}{4})^2}$$

$$\therefore \quad L^{-1}\left\{\frac{4p+15}{16p^2-25}\right\}=\frac{1}{4}L^{-1}\left[\frac{p}{p^2-(\frac{5}{4})^2}\right]+\frac{15}{16}L^{-1}\left[\frac{1}{p^2-(\frac{5}{4})^2}\right]$$

$$=\frac{1}{4}\cosh\left(\frac{5}{4}t\right)+\frac{15}{16}\cdot\frac{1}{\frac{5}{4}}\sinh\left(\frac{5}{4}t\right)=\frac{1}{4}\cosh\left(\frac{5}{4}t\right)+\frac{3}{4}\sinh\left(\frac{5}{4}t\right).$$

(*iv*) $$\frac{p+1}{p^2+p+1}=\frac{(p+\frac{1}{2})+\frac{1}{2}}{(p+\frac{1}{2})^2+\frac{3}{4}}=\frac{p+\frac{1}{2}}{\left(p+\frac{1}{2}\right)^2+\left(\frac{\sqrt{3}}{2}\right)^2}+\frac{1}{2}\cdot\frac{1}{\left(p+\frac{1}{2}\right)^2+\left(\frac{\sqrt{3}}{2}\right)^2}$$

$$\therefore \quad L^{-1}\left\{\frac{p+1}{p^2+p+1}\right\} = L^{-1}\left[\frac{p+\frac{1}{2}}{\left(p+\frac{1}{2}\right)^2+\left(\frac{\sqrt{3}}{2}\right)^2}\right] + \frac{1}{2}L^{-1}\left(\frac{1}{\left(p+\frac{1}{2}\right)^2+\left(\frac{\sqrt{3}}{2}\right)^2}\right)$$

$$= e^{-(t/2)}\cos\left(\frac{\sqrt{3}}{2}t\right) + \frac{1}{2}\cdot\frac{1}{\frac{\sqrt{3}}{2}}e^{-(t/2)}\sin\left(\frac{\sqrt{3}}{2}t\right)$$

$$= \frac{1}{\sqrt{3}}e^{-(t/2)}\left(\sqrt{3}\cos\frac{\sqrt{3}}{2}t + \sin\frac{\sqrt{3}}{2}t\right).$$

Example 2. *Find the inverse Laplace transform of*

(*i*) $\frac{6}{2p-3} - \frac{3+4p}{9p^2-16} + \frac{8-6p}{16p^2+9}$ (*ii*) $\frac{p^3}{p^4-a^4}$

(*iii*) $\frac{1}{p^{3/2}} + \frac{4}{p-2} + \frac{2p-18}{p^2-9}$ (*iv*) $\frac{2p+9}{p^2+9} + \frac{12}{4-3p} + \frac{1}{\sqrt{p}}$.

Sol. (*i*) $L^{-1}\left(\frac{6}{2p-3} - \frac{3+4p}{9p^2-16} + \frac{8-6p}{16p^2+9}\right)$

$$= 3L^{-1}\left(\frac{1}{p-3/2}\right) - \frac{1}{3}L^{-1}\left\{\frac{1}{p^2-\left(\frac{4}{3}\right)^2}\right\} - \frac{4}{9}L^{-1}\left\{\frac{p}{p^2-\left(\frac{4}{3}\right)^2}\right\}$$

$$+ \frac{1}{2}L^{-1}\left\{\frac{1}{p^2+\left(\frac{3}{4}\right)^2}\right\} - \frac{3}{8}L^{-1}\left\{\frac{p}{p^2+\left(\frac{3}{4}\right)^2}\right\}$$

$$= 3e^{\frac{3}{2}t} - \frac{1}{3}\cdot\frac{3}{4}\sinh\frac{4}{3}t - \frac{4}{9}\cdot\cosh\frac{4}{3}t + \frac{1}{2}\cdot\frac{4}{3}\sin\frac{3}{4}t - \frac{3}{8}\cos\frac{3}{4}t$$

$$= 3e^{\frac{3}{2}t} - \frac{1}{4}\sinh\frac{4}{3}t - \frac{4}{9}\cosh\frac{4}{3}t + \frac{2}{3}\sin\frac{3t}{4} - \frac{3}{8}\cos\frac{3}{4}t.$$

(*ii*) $L^{-1}\left(\frac{p^3}{p^4-a^4}\right) = L^{-1}\left[p\left\{\frac{p^2}{(p^2-a^2)(p^2+a^2)}\right\}\right]$

$$= L^{-1}\left[\frac{p}{2}\left(\frac{1}{p^2-a^2} + \frac{1}{p^2+a^2}\right)\right] = \frac{1}{2}L^{-1}\left(\frac{p}{p^2-a^2} + \frac{p}{p^2+a^2}\right)$$

$$= \frac{1}{2}(\cosh at + \cos at).$$

(*iii*) $L^{-1}\left(\frac{1}{p^{3/2}}+\frac{4}{p-2}+\frac{2p-18}{p^2-9}\right)$

$$= L^{-1}\left(\frac{1}{p^{3/2}}\right) + 4L^{-1}\left(\frac{1}{p-2}\right) + 2L^{-1}\left(\frac{p}{p^2-9}\right) - 18L^{-1}\left(\frac{1}{p^2-9}\right)$$

$$= \frac{t^{1/2}}{\Gamma(3/2)} + 4e^{2t} + 2\cosh 3t - 6\sinh 3t$$

$$= 2\sqrt{\frac{t}{\pi}} + 4e^{2t} + 2\cosh 3t - 6\sinh 3t. \qquad \because\ \Gamma(3/2)=\frac{\sqrt{\pi}}{2}$$

(*iv*) $L^{-1}\left\{\frac{2p+9}{p^2+9}+\frac{12}{4-3p}+\frac{1}{\sqrt{p}}\right\}$

$$= L^{-1}\left(\frac{2p+9}{p^2+9}\right) - L^{-1}\left(\frac{12}{3p-4}\right) + L^{-1}\left(\frac{1}{\sqrt{p}}\right)$$

$$= 2L^{-1}\left(\frac{p}{p^2+9}\right) + 3L^{-1}\left(\frac{3}{p^2+9}\right) - 4L^{-1}\left(\frac{1}{p-\frac{4}{3}}\right) + L^{-1}\left(\frac{1}{\sqrt{p}}\right)$$

$$= 2\cos 3t + 3\sin 3t - 4e^{\frac{4}{3}t} + \frac{1}{\sqrt{\pi t}}.$$

Example 3. *Find the Inverse Laplace transform of*

(*i*) $\frac{2p+1}{p\,(p+1)}$ (*ii*) $\left(\frac{\sqrt{p}-1}{p}\right)^2$ (*iii*) $\frac{p}{p^4+4a^4}$ (*iv*) $\frac{1}{\sqrt{2p+3}}$.

Sol. (*i*) $L^{-1}\left[\frac{2p+1}{p\,(p+1)}\right] = L^{-1}\left\{\frac{p+(p+1)}{p\,(p+1)}\right\} = L^{-1}\left(\frac{1}{p+1}+\frac{1}{p}\right) = e^{-t}+1.$

(*ii*) $L^{-1}\left(\frac{\sqrt{p}-1}{p}\right)^2 = L^{-1}\left(\frac{p+1-2\sqrt{p}}{p^2}\right) = L^{-1}\left(\frac{1}{p}+\frac{1}{p^2}-\frac{2}{p^{3/2}}\right)$

$$= L^{-1}\left(\frac{1}{p}\right) + L^{-1}\left(\frac{1}{p^2}\right) - 2L^{-1}\left(\frac{1}{p^{3/2}}\right)$$

$$= 1 + t - 2\,\frac{t^{1/2}}{\Gamma(3/2)} = 1 + t - 4\sqrt{\frac{t}{\pi}}.$$

(*iii*) $p^4 + 4a^4 = (p^2+2a^2)^2 - (2ap)^2 = (p^2-2ap+2a^2)(p^2+2ap+2a^2)$

$$= \{(p-a)^2+a^2\}\,\{(p+a)^2+a^2)\}$$

$$\frac{p}{p^4+4a^4} = \frac{p}{\{(p-a)^2+a^2\}\{(p+a)^2+a^2\}}$$

$$= \frac{1}{4a}\left[\frac{1}{(p-a)^2+a^2} - \frac{1}{(p+a)^2+a^2}\right]$$

$$\therefore \quad L^{-1}\left(\frac{p}{p^4+4a^4}\right) = \frac{1}{4a}\left[L^{-1}\left\{\frac{1}{(p-a)^2+a^2}\right\} - L^{-1}\left\{\frac{1}{(p+a)^2+a^2}\right\}\right]$$

$$= \frac{1}{4a}\left[\frac{1}{a}e^{at}\sin at - e^{-at}\,.\frac{1}{a}\sin at\right]$$

$$= \frac{1}{2a^2}\sin at\left(\frac{e^{at}-e^{-at}}{2}\right) = \frac{1}{2a^2}\sin at \sinh at.$$

(iv)
$$L^{-1}\left(\frac{1}{\sqrt{2p+3}}\right) = L^{-1}\left(\frac{1}{\sqrt{2}\sqrt{p+3/2}}\right) = \frac{1}{\sqrt{2}}L^{-1}\left(\frac{1}{\sqrt{p+3/2}}\right)$$

$$= \frac{1}{\sqrt{2}}e^{-(3/2)t}L^{-1}\left(\frac{1}{\sqrt{p}}\right) = \frac{1}{\sqrt{2\pi t}}e^{-(3/2)t}.$$

Example 4. *Find the Inverse Laplace transform of*

(i) $\frac{1}{\sqrt{p+a}}$ *(ii)* $\frac{15}{p^2+4p+13}$

(iii) $\frac{p+8}{p^2+4p+5}$ *(iv)* $\frac{p^2+2a^2}{p^4+4a^4}$.

Sol. *(i)*
$$L^{-1}\left(\frac{1}{\sqrt{p+a}}\right) = e^{-at}L^{-1}\left(\frac{1}{\sqrt{p}}\right)$$ | By first shifting property

$$= e^{-at}\,.\,\frac{t^{-1/2}}{\Gamma(1/2)} = \frac{e^{-at}}{\sqrt{\pi t}}.$$

(ii)
$$L^{-1}\left(\frac{15}{p^2+4p+13}\right) = L^{-1}\left\{\frac{15}{(p+2)^2+9}\right\}$$

$$= e^{-2t}L^{-1}\left(\frac{15}{p^2+9}\right)$$ | By first shifting property

$$= e^{-2t}\,.\,15\,.\,\frac{1}{3}\sin 3t = 5e^{-2t}\sin 3t.$$

(iii)
$$L^{-1}\left(\frac{p+8}{p^2+4p+5}\right) = L^{-1}\left\{\frac{(p+2)+6}{(p+2)^2+1}\right\} = L^{-1}\left\{\frac{p+2}{(p+2)^2+1}\right\} + 6\,L^{-1}\left\{\frac{1}{(p+2)^2+1}\right\}$$

$$= e^{-2t}L^{-1}\left(\frac{p}{p^2+1}\right) + 6\,e^{-2t}L^{-1}\left(\frac{1}{p^2+1}\right)$$

$$= e^{-2t}\cos t + 6\,e^{-2t}\sin t = e^{-2t}(\cos t + 6\sin t)\,.$$

(iv)
$$\frac{p^2+2a^2}{p^4+4a^4} = \frac{1}{2}\left[\frac{1}{(p-a)^2+a^2} + \frac{1}{(p+a)^2+a^2}\right]$$

$$\therefore \quad L^{-1}\left(\frac{p^2+2a^2}{p^4+4a^4}\right)=\frac{1}{2}L^{-1}\left[\frac{1}{(p-a)^2+a^2}+\frac{1}{(p+a)^2+a^2}\right]$$

$$=\frac{1}{2}\left[\frac{1}{a}e^{at}\sin at+\frac{1}{a}e^{-at}\sin at\right]=\frac{1}{a}\left(\frac{e^{at}+e^{-at}}{2}\right)\sin at$$

$$=\frac{1}{a}\sin at\cosh at.$$

Example 5. *Evaluate :*

(*i*) $L^{-1}\left(\frac{e^{-2p}}{p^2}\right)$ (*ii*) $L^{-1}\left(\frac{e^{-p}-3e^{-3p}}{p^2}\right)$ (*iii*) $L^{-1}\left(\frac{pe^{-ap}}{p^2-\omega^2}\right)$; $a > 0$

(*iv*) $L^{-1}\left(\frac{e^{-p}}{\sqrt{p+1}}\right)$ (*v*) $L^{-1}\left(\frac{pe^{-p/2}+\pi e^{-p}}{p^2+\pi^2}\right)$ (*vi*) $L^{-1}\left[\frac{e^{-2\pi p}}{p(p^2+1)}\right]$

(G.B.T.U. 2011)

Sol. (*i*) We have

$$L^{-1}\left(\frac{1}{p^2}\right)=t=F(t) \qquad | \text{ say}$$

$$\therefore \quad L^{-1}\left(e^{-2p}\cdot\frac{1}{p^2}\right)=\begin{cases}t-2, & t>2\\ 0, & t<2\end{cases}=(t-2)\,u\,(t-2).$$

| By second shifting theorem

(*ii*)
$$L^{-1}\left(e^{-p}\cdot\frac{1}{p^2}\right)=\begin{cases}t-1, & t>1\\ 0, & t<1\end{cases}=(t-1)\,u\,(t-1)$$

$$L^{-1}\left(e^{-3p}\cdot\frac{1}{p^2}\right)=\begin{cases}t-3, & t>3\\ 0, & t<3\end{cases}=(t-3)\,u\,(t-3)$$

Hence $L^{-1}\left(\frac{e^{-p}-3e^{-3p}}{p^2}\right)=(t-1)\,u\,(t-1)-3(t-3)\,u\,(t-3).$

| By second shifting theorem

(*iii*)
$$L^{-1}\left(\frac{p}{p^2-\omega^2}\right)=\cosh \omega t=F(t)$$

$$\therefore \quad L^{-1}\left(\frac{pe^{-ap}}{p^2-\omega^2}\right)=\left.\begin{matrix}\cosh\omega(t-a), & t>a\\ 0, & t<a\end{matrix}\right\}=\cosh\omega(t-a)\,u(t-a)$$

| By second shifting theorem

(*iv*) We have, $L^{-1}\left(\frac{1}{\sqrt{p+1}}\right)=e^{-t}L^{-1}\left(\frac{1}{\sqrt{p}}\right)=\frac{1}{\sqrt{\pi t}}e^{-t}$

$$\therefore \quad L^{-1}\left(\frac{e^{-p}}{\sqrt{p+1}}\right)=\left.\begin{matrix}\frac{e^{-(t-1)}}{\sqrt{\pi(t-1)}}, & t>1\\ 0, & t<1\end{matrix}\right\}=\frac{e^{-(t-1)}}{\sqrt{\pi(t-1)}}u\,(t-1).$$

| By second shifting theorem

(*v*) $$L^{-1}\left(\frac{p}{p^2+\pi^2}\right) = \cos \pi t \text{ and } L^{-1}\left(\frac{\pi}{p^2+\pi^2}\right) = \sin \pi t$$

$\therefore$ $$L^{-1}\left(\frac{p\, e^{-p/2}}{p^2+\pi^2}\right) = \cos \pi\left(t-\frac{1}{2}\right) u\left(t-\frac{1}{2}\right) = \sin \pi t\, u\left(t-\frac{1}{2}\right)$$

and $$L^{-1}\left(\frac{\pi\, e^{-p}}{p^2+\pi^2}\right) = \sin \pi(t-1)\, u(t-1) = -\sin \pi t\, u(t-1)$$

$\therefore$ $$L^{-1}\left[\frac{p\, e^{-p/2}+\pi\, e^{-p}}{p^2+\pi^2}\right] = \sin \pi t\left[u\left(t-\frac{1}{2}\right) - u\,(t-1)\right].$$ | By second shifting theorem

(*vi*) $$L^{-1}\left[\frac{1}{p(p^2+1)}\right] = L^{-1}\left(\frac{1}{p} - \frac{p}{p^2+1}\right) = 1 - \cos t$$

$\therefore$ $$L^{-1}\left[\frac{e^{-2\pi p}}{p(p^2+1)}\right] = 1 - \cos\,(t-2\pi)\, u(t-2\pi) = 1 - \cos t\, u(t-2\pi)$$

Example 6. *Find the inverse Laplace transform of*

(*i*) $\dfrac{p^2+2p-3}{p\,(p-3)\,(p+2)}$ (*ii*) $\dfrac{1}{(p-\alpha)\,(p-\beta)}$

(*iii*) $\dfrac{p}{(p^2-1)^2}$ (*iv*) $\dfrac{p-1}{p^2(p-7)}$ [G.B.T.U. (C.O.) 2011]

Sol. (*i*) $$\frac{p^2+2p-3}{p(p-3)\,(p+2)} = \frac{1}{2p} + \frac{4}{5(p-3)} - \frac{3}{10(p+2)}$$

$$\therefore\ L^{-1}\left\{\frac{p^2+2p-3}{p(p-3)\,(p+2)}\right\} = \frac{1}{2}L^{-1}\left(\frac{1}{p}\right) + \frac{4}{5}\, L^{-1}\left(\frac{1}{p-3}\right) - \frac{3}{10}\, L^{-1}\left(\frac{1}{p+2}\right)$$

$$= \frac{1}{2} + \frac{4}{5}\, e^{3t} - \frac{3}{10}\, e^{-2t}.$$

(*ii*) $$\frac{1}{(p-\alpha)\,(p-\beta)} = \frac{1}{\alpha-\beta}\left(\frac{1}{p-\alpha} - \frac{1}{p-\beta}\right)$$

$\therefore$ $$L^{-1}\left[\frac{1}{(p-\alpha)\,(p-\beta)}\right] = \frac{1}{\alpha-\beta}\, L^{-1}\left(\frac{1}{p-\alpha} - \frac{1}{p-\beta}\right) = \frac{1}{\alpha-\beta}\,(e^{\alpha t} - e^{\beta t}).$$

(*iii*) $$\frac{1}{(p^2-1)^2} = \frac{1}{(p-1)^2\,(p+1)^2} = \frac{1}{4p}\left\{\frac{1}{(p-1)^2} - \frac{1}{(p+1)^2}\right\}$$

$$\frac{p}{(p^2-1)^2} = \frac{1}{4}\left\{\frac{1}{(p-1)^2} - \frac{1}{(p+1)^2}\right\}$$

$$L^{-1}\left\{\frac{p}{(p^2-1)^2}\right\} - \frac{1}{4}\left[L^{-1}\left\{\frac{1}{(p-1)^2}\right\} - L^{-1}\left\{\frac{1}{(p+1)^2}\right\}\right]$$

$$= \frac{1}{4}\{e^t\,.\,t - e^{-t}\,.\,t\} = \frac{t}{2}\,\sinh t.$$

(*iv*) $$\frac{p-1}{p^2(p-7)} = \frac{A}{p} + \frac{B}{p^2} + \frac{C}{p-7}$$

$\Rightarrow$ $$p - 1 = A(p^2 - 7p) + B(p - 7) + Cp^2 = (A + C)p^2 + (B - 7A)\,p - 7B$$

Comparison gives

$$A + C = 0,\ B - 7A = 1,\ -7B = -1$$

$\Rightarrow$ $$A = -\frac{6}{49},\ B = \frac{1}{7},\ C = \frac{6}{49}$$

$\therefore$ $$L^{-1}\left[\frac{p-1}{p^2(p-7)}\right] = \frac{-6}{49} L^{-1}\left(\frac{1}{p}\right) + \frac{1}{7} L^{-1}\left(\frac{1}{p^2}\right) + \frac{6}{49} L^{-1}\left(\frac{1}{p-7}\right)$$

$$= -\frac{6}{49} + \frac{1}{7} t + \frac{6}{49} e^{7t}$$

Example 7. *Find the inverse Laplace transform of the following functions :*

(*i*) $\dfrac{2p^2 - 1}{(p^2+1)(p^2+4)}$ (*ii*) $\dfrac{2p^2 - 6p + 5}{p^3 - 6p^2 + 11p - 6}$ (*iii*) $\dfrac{5p+3}{(p-1)(p^2+2p+5)}$

Sol. (*i*) $$\frac{2p^2-1}{(p^2+1)(p^2+4)} = \frac{2m-1}{(m+1)(m+4)} \qquad \Big|\ p^2 = m \text{ (say)}$$

Now, $$\frac{2m-1}{(m+1)(m+4)} = \frac{-1}{m+1} + \frac{3}{m+4}$$

$\therefore$ $$\frac{2p^2-1}{(p^2+1)(p^2+4)} = \frac{-1}{p^2+1} + \frac{3}{p^2+4}$$

$\therefore$ $$L^{-1}\left[\frac{2p^2-1}{(p^2+1)(p^2+4)}\right] = L^{-1}\left(\frac{-1}{p^2+1}\right) + L^{-1}\left(\frac{3}{p^2+4}\right) = -\sin t + \frac{3}{2}\sin 2t$$

(*ii*) $$\frac{2p^2-6p+5}{p^3-6p^2+11p-6} = \frac{2p^2-6p+5}{(p-1)(p-2)(p-3)} = \frac{1}{2(p-1)} - \frac{1}{p-2} + \frac{5}{2(p-3)}$$

$\therefore$ $$L^{-1}\left[\frac{2p^2-6p+5}{(p-1)(p-2)(p-3)}\right] = L^{-1}\left[\frac{1}{2(p-1)}\right] - L^{-1}\left(\frac{1}{p-2}\right) + L^{-1}\left[\frac{5}{2(p-3)}\right]$$

$$= \frac{1}{2}e^t - e^{2t} + \frac{5}{2}e^{3t}.$$

(*iii*) Let $$\frac{5p+3}{(p-1)(p^2+2p+5)} = \frac{A}{p-1} + \frac{Bp+C}{p^2+2p+5} \qquad \ldots(1)$$

$\Rightarrow$ $$5p + 3 = A(p^2 + 2p + 5) + (Bp + C)(p - 1)$$
$$= p^2(A + B) + p(2A + C - B) + (5A - C)$$

Comparing the coefficients on both sides, we get

$$A + B = 0, \quad 2A - B + C = 5, \quad 5A - C = 3$$

$$\Rightarrow \qquad A = 1, B = -1, C = 2$$

$\therefore$ Form (1),

$$\frac{5p+3}{(p-1)(p^2+2p+5)} = \frac{1}{p-1} - \frac{p-2}{p^2+2p+5}$$

Hence,

$$L^{-1}\left[\frac{5p+3}{(p-1)(p^2+2p+5)}\right] = L^{-1}\left(\frac{1}{p-1}\right) - L^{-1}\left(\frac{p-2}{p^2+2p+5}\right)$$

$$= e^t - L^{-1}\left[\frac{(p+1)-3}{(p+1)^2+4}\right] = e^t - e^{-t}\left(\cos 2t - \frac{3}{2}\sin 2t\right)$$

Example 8. *Prove that :*

$$L^{-1}\left(\frac{p}{p^4+p^2+1}\right) = \frac{2}{\sqrt{3}} \sinh \frac{t}{2} \sin \frac{\sqrt{3}}{2}t.$$

Sol.

$$\frac{1}{p^4+p^2+1} = \frac{1}{(p^2+1)^2 - p^2}$$

$$= \frac{1}{(p^2-p+1)(p^2+p+1)} = \frac{1}{2p}\left[\frac{1}{p^2-p+1} - \frac{1}{p^2+p+1}\right]$$

$$\therefore \quad \frac{p}{p^4+p^2+1} = \frac{1}{2}\left(\frac{1}{p^2-p+1} - \frac{1}{p^2+p+1}\right)$$

$$L^{-1}\left(\frac{p}{p^4+p^2+1}\right) = \frac{1}{2}\left[L^{-1}\left(\frac{1}{p^2-p+1}\right) - L^{-1}\left(\frac{1}{p^2+p+1}\right)\right]$$

$$= \frac{1}{2}\left[L^{-1}\left\{\frac{1}{\left(p-\frac{1}{2}\right)^2 + \left(\frac{\sqrt{3}}{2}\right)^2}\right\} - L^{-1}\left\{\frac{1}{\left(p+\frac{1}{2}\right)^2 + \left(\frac{\sqrt{3}}{2}\right)^2}\right\}\right]$$

$$= \frac{1}{2}\left[e^{t/2} \cdot \frac{2}{\sqrt{3}} \sin \frac{\sqrt{3}}{2} t - e^{-t/2} \cdot \frac{2}{\sqrt{3}} \sin \frac{\sqrt{3}}{2} t\right] = \frac{2}{\sqrt{3}} \sin \frac{\sqrt{3}}{2} t \sinh \frac{t}{2}.$$

Example 9. *Find the inverse Laplace transform of following functions :*

(*i*) $\dfrac{14p+10}{49p^2+28p+13}$ [U.P.T.U. (SUM) 2007]

(*ii*) $\dfrac{p^2+2p+3}{(p^2+2p+2)(p^2+2p+5)}$

(*iii*) $\dfrac{a(p^2-2a^2)}{p^4+4a^4}$.

Sol. (*i*) $$\frac{14p+10}{49p^2+28p+13} = \frac{14p+10}{(7p+2)^2+9} = \frac{14\left(p+\frac{2}{7}\right)+6}{49\left(p+\frac{2}{7}\right)^2+9}$$

$$\therefore \quad L^{-1}\left(\frac{14p+10}{49p^2+28p+13}\right) = L^{-1}\left[\frac{14\left(p+\frac{2}{7}\right)+6}{49\left(p+\frac{2}{7}\right)^2+9}\right] = e^{-\frac{2t}{7}} L^{-1}\left(\frac{14p+6}{49p^2+9}\right)$$

$$= e^{-\frac{2t}{7}}\left[\frac{14}{49} L^{-1}\left(\frac{p}{p^2+\frac{9}{49}}\right) + \frac{6}{49} L^{-1}\left(\frac{1}{p^2+\frac{9}{49}}\right)\right]$$

$$= e^{-\frac{2t}{7}}\left[\frac{2}{7}\cos\frac{3}{7}t + \frac{6}{49}\cdot\frac{7}{3}\sin\frac{3}{7}t\right]$$

$$= \frac{2}{7} e^{-\frac{2t}{7}}\left(\cos\frac{3}{7}t + \sin\frac{3}{7}t\right)$$

(*ii*) $$\frac{p^2+2p+3}{(p^2+2p+2)(p^2+2p+5)} = \frac{1}{3}\left[\frac{1}{p^2+2p+2} + \frac{2}{p^2+2p+5}\right]$$

$$\therefore \quad L^{-1}\left[\frac{p^2+2p+3}{(p^2+2p+2)(p^2+2p+5)}\right] = \frac{1}{3} L^{-1}\left[\frac{1}{p^2+2p+2} + \frac{2}{p^2+2p+5}\right]$$

$$= \frac{1}{3} L^{-1}\left[\frac{1}{(p+1)^2+1} + \frac{2}{(p+1)^2+4}\right]$$

$$= \frac{1}{3}(e^{-t}\sin t + e^{-t}\sin 2t) = \frac{e^{-t}}{3}(\sin t + \sin 2t)$$

(*iii*) $$p^4 + 4a^4 = (p^2+2a^2)^2 - 4a^2p^2 = (p^2 - 2ap + 2a^2)(p^2 + 2ap + 2a^2)$$

$$= \left\{(p-a)^2 + a^2\right\}\left\{(p+a)^2 + a^2\right\}$$

$$\frac{2a(p^2-2a^2)}{p^4+4a^4} = \frac{p-a}{(p-a)^2+a^2} - \frac{p+a}{(p+a)^2+a^2}$$

$$\therefore \quad L^{-1}\left[\frac{a(p^2-2a^2)}{p^4+4a^4}\right] = \frac{1}{2}\left[L^{-1}\left\{\frac{p-a}{(p-a)^2+a^2}\right\} - L^{-1}\left\{\frac{p+a}{(p+a)^2+a^2}\right\}\right]$$

$$= \frac{1}{2}\left[e^{at}\cos at - e^{-at}\cos at\right]$$

$$= \cos at\left(\frac{e^{at}-e^{-at}}{2}\right) = \cos at \sinh at$$

Example 10. *If* $L^{-1}\left(\frac{e^{-1/p}}{\sqrt{p}}\right) = \frac{\cos 2\sqrt{t}}{\sqrt{\pi t}}$, *find* $L^{-1}\left\{\frac{e^{-a/p}}{\sqrt{p}}\right\}$.

Sol. Replacing p by kp, we get

$$L^{-1}\left(\frac{e^{-\frac{1}{kp}}}{\sqrt{kp}}\right) = \frac{1}{k} \cdot \frac{\cos 2\sqrt{\frac{t}{k}}}{\sqrt{\pi \frac{t}{k}}} = \frac{1}{\sqrt{k}}\ \frac{\cos 2\sqrt{\frac{t}{k}}}{\sqrt{\pi t}}$$

$$\Rightarrow \quad L^{-1}\left(\frac{e^{-\frac{1}{kp}}}{\sqrt{p}}\right) = \frac{\cos 2\sqrt{\frac{t}{k}}}{\sqrt{\pi t}}$$

Putting $k = \frac{1}{a}$, we get $\quad L^{-1}\left(\frac{e^{-a/p}}{\sqrt{p}}\right) = \frac{\cos 2\sqrt{at}}{\sqrt{\pi t}}$.

TEST YOUR KNOWLEDGE

Find the inverse Laplace transforms of (1–20) :

1. $\left(\frac{1-\sqrt{p}}{p^2}\right)^2$ **2.** $\frac{2p+6}{p^2+4}$ **3.** $\frac{p+2}{p^2-4p+13}$

4. $\frac{4p+12}{p^2+8p+16}$ **5.** $\frac{p}{(p+a)^2}$ **6.** $\frac{p+1}{p^2+2p}$

7. (*i*) $\frac{3p+1}{(p+1)^4}$ (*ii*) $\frac{72}{p^5} - \frac{3\sqrt{\pi}}{2p^{5/2}} + \frac{6}{p}$ **8.** $\frac{p}{(p^2+1)(p^2+4)}$

9. (*i*) $\frac{3p+7}{p^2-2p-3}$ (*ii*) $\frac{p}{p^2+6p+25}$ (*G.B.T.U. 2011*) (*iii*) $\frac{p+1}{p^2-6p+25}$ (*G.B.T.U. 2010*)

10. (*i*) $\frac{p+1}{p^2+6p+25}$ (*ii*) $\frac{1}{p^2+2p+5}$ (*iii*) $\frac{1}{p(p^2+4)}$

11. $\frac{p^2+1}{p^3+3p^2+2p}$ **12.** (*i*) $\frac{(p+1)\,e^{-\pi p}}{p^2+p+1}$ (*ii*) $\frac{5e^{-3p}}{p} - \frac{e^{-p}}{p}$

13. (*i*) $\dfrac{21p-33}{(p+1)(p-2)^3}$ (*ii*) $\dfrac{2p^2-4}{(p+1)(p-2)(p-3)}$

14. (*i*) $\dfrac{3p+1}{(p-1)(p^2+1)}$ (*ii*) $\dfrac{4p+5}{(p-1)^2(p+2)}$ **15.** $\dfrac{p+2}{p^2(p+3)}$

16. $\dfrac{1}{(p+1)(p^2+2p+2)}$ **17.** $\dfrac{p}{(p+1)^2\,(p^2+1)}$

18. (*i*) $\dfrac{1}{p^2(p^2+a^2)}$ (*ii*) $\dfrac{1}{(p^2+4)(p+1)^2}$

19. (*i*) $\dfrac{p+2}{(p^2+4p+5)^2}$ (*ii*) $\dfrac{p+3}{(p^2+6p+13)^2}$ (*iii*) $\dfrac{1}{p^3-a^3}$

20. (*i*) $\dfrac{e^{-\pi p}}{p^2+1}$ (*ii*) $\dfrac{p\,e^{-2p}}{p^2-1}$ (*iii*) $\dfrac{e^{-cp}}{p^2\,(p+a)}$, $c>0$

21. If $L^{-1}\left(\dfrac{e^{-\sqrt{p}}}{\sqrt{p}}\right)=\dfrac{e^{-\frac{1}{4t}}}{\sqrt{\pi t}}$, show that $L^{-1}\left(\dfrac{e^{-K\sqrt{p}}}{\sqrt{p}}\right)=\dfrac{e^{-K^2/4t}}{\sqrt{\pi t}}$.

Answers

1. $\dfrac{t^3}{6}+\dfrac{t^2}{2}-\dfrac{16}{15\sqrt{\pi}}t^{5/2}$ **2.** $2\cos 2t+3\sin 2t$ **3.** $e^{2t}\cos 3t+\dfrac{4}{3}e^{2t}\sin 3t$

4. $4e^{-4t}\,(1-t)$ **5.** $(1-at)e^{-at}$ **6.** $\dfrac{1}{2}(1+e^{-2t})$

7. (*i*) $e^{-t}\left(\dfrac{3}{2}t^2-\dfrac{1}{3}t^3\right)$ (*ii*) $3t^4-2t^{3/2}+6$ **8.** $\dfrac{1}{3}(\cos t-\cos 2t)$

9. (*i*) $4e^{3t}-e^{-t}$ (*ii*) $e^{-3t}\left(\cos 4t-\dfrac{3}{4}\sin 4t\right)$ (*iii*) $e^{3t}\,(\cos 4t+\sin 4t)$

10. (*i*) $e^{-3t}\left(\cos 4t-\dfrac{1}{2}\sin 4t\right)$ (*ii*) $\dfrac{1}{2}e^{-t}\sin 2t$ (*iii*) $\dfrac{1}{4}(1-\cos 2t)$

11. $\dfrac{1}{2}-2e^{-t}+\dfrac{5}{2}e^{-2t}$

12. (*i*) $\dfrac{e^{-\left(\frac{t-\pi}{2}\right)}}{\sqrt{3}}\left\{\sqrt{3}\cos\dfrac{\sqrt{3}(t-\pi)}{2}+\sin\dfrac{\sqrt{3}(t-\pi)}{2}\right\}u(t-\pi)$ (*ii*) $5u(t-3)-u(t-1)$

13. (*i*) $2(e^{-t}-e^{2t})+6t\,e^{2t}+\dfrac{3}{2}\,t^2\,e^{2t}$ (*ii*) $-\dfrac{1}{6}\,e^{-t}-\dfrac{4}{3}e^{2t}+\dfrac{7}{2}\,e^{3t}$

14. (*i*) $2e^t-2\cos t+\sin t$ (*ii*) $\dfrac{1}{3}\,e^t+3te^t-\dfrac{1}{3}e^{-2t}$ **15.** $\dfrac{1}{9}+\dfrac{2t}{3}-\dfrac{1}{9}\,e^{-3t}$

16. $e^{-t}\,(1-\cos t)$ **17.** $\dfrac{1}{2}(\sin t-t\,e^{-t})$

18. (*i*) $\dfrac{1}{a^3}(at-\sin at)$ (*ii*) $\dfrac{2}{25}\,e^{-t}+\dfrac{1}{5}\,t\,e^{-t}-\dfrac{2}{25}\cos 2t-\dfrac{3}{50}\sin 2t$

19. (*i*) $\dfrac{1}{2}\,te^{-2t}\sin t$ (*ii*) $\dfrac{1}{4}te^{-3t}\sin 2t$ (*iii*) $\dfrac{1}{3a^2}\left[e^{at}-e^{-\frac{1}{2}at}\left\{\cos\dfrac{\sqrt{3}}{2}\,at+\sqrt{3}\sin\dfrac{\sqrt{3}}{2}\,at\right\}\right]$

20. (*i*) $-\sin t\,.\,u(t-\pi)$ (*ii*) $\cosh\,(t-2)\,u\,(t-2)$ (*iii*) $\dfrac{1}{a^2}\,[a\,(t-c)-1+e^{-a(t-c)}]\,u(t-c)$.

3.26. INVERSE LAPLACE TRANSFORM OF DERIVATIVES

If $\quad L^{-1}\{f(p)\} = F(t)$, **then**

$$L^{-1}\{f^{(n)}(p)\} = L^{-1}\left[\frac{d^n}{dp^n}\{f(p)\}\right] = (-1)^n t^n F(t).$$

We have, $\quad L\{t^n F(t)\} = (-1)^n \left\{\frac{d^n}{dp^n} f(p)\right\} = (-1)^n f^{(n)}(p)$

$\therefore \quad L^{-1}\{f^{(n)}(p)\} = (-1)^n t^n F(t).$

3.27. MULTIPLICATION BY *p*

If $\quad L^{-1}\{f(p)\} = F(t)$ **and** $F(0) = 0$, **then** $L^{-1}\{pf(p)\} = F'(t)$.

We have,

$$L\{F'(t)\} = pf(p) - F(0) = pf(p) \qquad | \because F(0) = 0$$

$\therefore \quad L^{-1}\{p f(p)\} = F'(t).$

Note 1. If $F(0) \neq 0$, then

$$L^{-1}\{pf(p) - F(0)\} = F'(t) \quad \text{or} \quad L^{-1}\{pf(p)\} = F'(t) + F(0)\,\delta(t)$$

where $\delta(t)$ is the unit impulse function.

Note 2. Generalizations to $L^{-1}\{p^n f(p)\}$ are also possible for $n = 2, 3, \ldots$.

3.28. DIVISION BY *p*

If $L^{-1}\{f(p)\} = F(t)$, then

$$L^{-1}\left\{\frac{f(p)}{p}\right\} = \int_0^t F(u)\,du$$

Also, $$L^{-1}\left\{\frac{f(p)}{p^2}\right\} = \int_0^t \int_0^t F(u)\,du\,du$$

$$L^{-1}\left\{\frac{f(p)}{p^3}\right\} = \int_0^t \int_0^t \int_0^t F(u)\,du\,du\,du$$

$$\therefore \quad L^{-1}\left\{\frac{f(p)}{p^n}\right\} = \int_0^t \int_0^t \cdots\cdots \underbrace{\int_0^t}_{(n \text{ times})} F(u)\,du \cdots\cdots \underbrace{du}_{(n \text{ times})}$$

3.29. HEAVISIDE EXPANSION FORMULA FOR INVERSE LAPLACE TRANSFORM

If $F(p)$ and $G(p)$ are two polynomials in p and the degree of $F(p)$ is less than the degree of $G(p)$ and if $G(p) = (p - \alpha_1)(p - \alpha_2) \ldots\ldots (p - \alpha_n)$ where $\alpha_1, \alpha_2, \ldots\ldots, \alpha_n$ are distinct constants, real or complex, then

$$L^{-1}\left\{\frac{F(p)}{G(p)}\right\} = \sum_{r=1}^{n} \frac{F(\alpha_r)}{G'(\alpha_r)} e^{\alpha_r t}$$

By the method of partial fractions, let

$$\frac{F(p)}{G(p)} = \frac{A_1}{p-\alpha_1} + \frac{A_2}{p-\alpha_2} + \ldots\ldots + \frac{A_r}{p-\alpha_r} + \ldots\ldots + \frac{A_n}{p-\alpha_n}$$

Multiplying both sides by $p - \alpha_r$ and allowing $p \to \alpha_r$, we obtain,

$$A_r = \lim_{p\to\alpha_r} \frac{F(p)(p-\alpha_r)}{G(p)} = \lim_{p\to\alpha_r} F(p) \, . \lim_{p\to\alpha_r} \frac{p-\alpha_r}{G(p)}$$

$$= \lim_{p\to\alpha_r} F(p) \, . \lim_{p\to\alpha_r} \frac{1}{G'(p)} = \frac{F(\alpha_r)}{G'(\alpha_r)}$$

$$\therefore \quad \frac{F(p)}{G(p)} = \frac{F(\alpha_1)}{G'(\alpha_1)} \cdot \frac{1}{p-\alpha_1} + \ldots\ldots + \frac{F(\alpha_r)}{G'(\alpha_r)} \cdot \frac{1}{p-\alpha_r} + \ldots\ldots + \frac{F(\alpha_n)}{G'(\alpha_n)} \cdot \frac{1}{p-\alpha_n}$$

$$\therefore \quad L^{-1}\left\{\frac{F(p)}{G(p)}\right\} = \frac{F(\alpha_1)}{G'(\alpha_1)} e^{\alpha_1 t} + \ldots\ldots + \frac{F(\alpha_r)}{G'(\alpha_r)} e^{\alpha_r t} + \ldots\ldots + \frac{F(\alpha_n)}{G'(\alpha_n)} e^{\alpha_n t}$$

$$= \sum_{r=1}^{n} \frac{F(\alpha_r)}{G'(\alpha_r)} e^{\alpha_r t} .$$

3.30. CONVOLUTION THEOREM

[*U.P.T.U. 2006, 2007; U.P.T.U. (C.O.) 2009, 2010; U.K.T.U. 2011; M.T.U. 2012*]

If $\quad L^{-1}\{f(p)\} = F(t)$ **and** $L^{-1}\{g(p)\} = G(t)$**, then**

$$L^{-1}\{f(p)\, g(p)\} = F * G = \int_0^t F(u)\, G(t-u)\, du$$

Let $\quad \phi(t) = \int_0^t F(u)\, G(t-u)\, du$ then

$$L\{\phi(t)\} = \int_0^\infty e^{-pt} \left[\int_0^t F(u)\, G(t-u)\, du\right] dt = \int_0^\infty \int_0^t e^{-pt}\, F(u)\, G(t-u)\, du\, dt$$

On changing the order of integration, we get

$$L\{\phi(t)\} = \int_0^\infty \int_u^\infty e^{-pt}\, F(u)\, G(t-u)\, dt\, du$$

$$= \int_0^\infty e^{-pu}\, F(u) \left[\int_u^\infty e^{-p(t-u)}\, G(t-u)\, dt\right] du$$

$$= \int_0^\infty e^{-pu}\, F(u) \left[\int_0^\infty e^{-pv} G(v)\, dv\right] du$$

on putting $t - u = v$

$$= \int_0^\infty e^{-pu}\, F(u)\, g(p)\, du = g(p) \int_0^\infty e^{-pu}\, F(u)\, du$$

$$= g(p) \, . \, f(p) = f(p)\, g(p)$$

$$\Rightarrow \quad L^{-1}\{f(p)\, g(p)\} = \phi(t) = \int_0^t F(u)\, G(t-u)\, du.$$

We call F ∗ G, the convolution of F and G and the theorem is called the convolution theorem or the convolution property.

ILLUSTRATIVE EXAMPLES

Example 1. *Find the inverse Laplace transform of*

(*i*) $log\left(1+\frac{1}{p^2}\right)$ (*ii*) $log\left(\frac{p+1}{p-1}\right)$

(U.K.T.U. 2012; U.P.T.U. 2009)

(*iii*) $cot^{-1}\left(\frac{p+3}{2}\right)$ (*iv*) $tan^{-1}\left(\frac{2}{p^2}\right)$

(*v*) $cot^{-1}\left(\frac{p}{2}\right)$ (*vi*) $L^{-1}\left[log\left(\frac{p^2+4p+5}{p^2+2p+5}\right)\right]$

[M.T.U. (SUM) 2011]

Sol. (*i*) Let $$\mathrm{L}^{-1}\left\{\log\left(1+\frac{1}{p^2}\right)\right\} = \mathrm{F}(t) \quad | \text{ say}$$

$$\therefore \quad \mathrm{L}^{-1}\left[\frac{d}{dp}\left\{\log\left(1+\frac{1}{p^2}\right)\right\}\right] = -t\,\mathrm{F}(t) \quad | \text{ By Art. 3.26}$$

$$\Rightarrow \quad \mathrm{L}^{-1}\left[\frac{1}{1+\frac{1}{p^2}}\left(\frac{-2}{p^3}\right)\right] = -t\,\mathrm{F}(t)$$

$$\Rightarrow \quad \mathrm{L}^{-1}\left[\frac{-2}{p(p^2+1)}\right] = -t\,\mathrm{F}(t)$$

$$\Rightarrow \quad \mathrm{L}^{-1}\left(\frac{1}{p}-\frac{p}{p^2+1}\right) = \frac{t}{2}\,\mathrm{F}(t)$$

$$\Rightarrow \quad 1-\cos t = \frac{t}{2}\,\mathrm{F}(t)$$

$$\therefore \quad \mathrm{F}(t) = \frac{2(1-\cos t)}{t}$$

(*ii*) Let $$\mathrm{L}^{-1}\left\{\log\left(\frac{p+1}{p-1}\right)\right\} = \mathrm{F}(t) \quad | \text{ say}$$

$$\therefore \quad \mathrm{L}^{-1}\left[\frac{d}{dp}\{\log(p+1)-\log(p-1)\}\right] = -t\,\mathrm{F}(t) \quad | \text{ By Art. 3.26}$$

$$\Rightarrow \quad \mathrm{L}^{-1}\left[\frac{1}{p+1}-\frac{1}{p-1}\right] = -t\,\mathrm{F}(t)$$

$$\Rightarrow \quad e^{-t}-e^{t} = -t\,\mathrm{F}(t)$$

$$\therefore \quad \mathrm{F}(t) = \frac{e^{t}-e^{-t}}{t} = \frac{2\sinh t}{t}$$

(*iii*) Let $$L^{-1}\left\{\cot^{-1}\left(\frac{p+3}{2}\right)\right\} = F(t)$$ | say

$$\therefore \quad L^{-1}\left[\frac{d}{dp}\left\{\cot^{-1}\left(\frac{p+3}{2}\right)\right\}\right] = -t\,F(t)$$ | By Art. 3.26

$$\Rightarrow \quad L^{-1}\left[\frac{-1}{1+\left(\frac{p+3}{2}\right)^2}\cdot\frac{1}{2}\right] = -t\,F(t)$$

$$\Rightarrow \quad L^{-1}\left[\frac{-2}{(p+3)^2+4}\right] = -t\,F(t)$$

$$\Rightarrow \quad -e^{-3t}\sin 2t = -t\,F(t)$$

$$\Rightarrow \quad F(t) = \frac{e^{-3t}\sin 2t}{t}$$

(*iv*) Let $$f(p) = \tan^{-1}\left(\frac{2}{p^2}\right) = \tan^{-1}\left(\frac{2}{1+p^2-1}\right)$$

$$= \tan^{-1}\left\{\frac{2}{1+(p-1)(p+1)}\right\} = \tan^{-1}\frac{1}{p-1} - \tan^{-1}\frac{1}{p+1}$$

$$\therefore \quad L^{-1}\{f(p)\} = L^{-1}\left\{\tan^{-1}\left(\frac{1}{p-1}\right)\right\} - L^{-1}\left\{\tan^{-1}\left(\frac{1}{p+1}\right)\right\}$$

$$= e^{t}\,L^{-1}\left(\tan^{-1}\frac{1}{p}\right) - e^{-t}\,L^{-1}\left(\tan^{-1}\frac{1}{p}\right)$$

$$= 2\sinh t\,L^{-1}\left(\tan^{-1}\frac{1}{p}\right) = 2\sinh t\,.\,\frac{\sin t}{t}$$

$$\Rightarrow \quad F(t) = \frac{2}{t}\sin t\sinh t.$$

(*v*) Let $$L^{-1}\left\{\cot^{-1}\left(\frac{p}{2}\right)\right\} = F(t)$$ | say

$$\therefore \quad L^{-1}\left[\frac{d}{dp}\left\{\cot^{-1}\left(\frac{p}{2}\right)\right\}\right] = -t\,F(t)$$ | By Art. 3.26

$$\Rightarrow \quad L^{-1}\left(\frac{-1}{1+\frac{p^2}{4}}\cdot\frac{1}{2}\right) = -t\,F(t)$$

$$\Rightarrow \quad L^{-1}\left(\frac{-2}{p^2+4}\right) = -t\,F(t)$$

$$\Rightarrow \quad -\sin 2t = -t\,F(t)$$

$$\therefore \quad F(t) = \frac{\sin 2t}{t}$$

(*vi*) Let $$L^{-1}\left[\log\left(\frac{p^2+4p+5}{p^2+2p+5}\right)\right] = F(t)$$ | say

$$\therefore \quad L^{-1}\left[\frac{d}{dp}\left\{\log(p^2+4p+5)-\log(p^2+2p+5)\right\}\right] = -t\,F(t)$$ | By Art. 3.26

$$\Rightarrow \quad L^{-1}\left[\frac{2p+4}{p^2+4p+5}-\frac{2p+2}{p^2+2p+5}\right] = -t\,F(t)$$

$$\Rightarrow \quad L^{-1}\left[\frac{2(p+2)}{(p+2)^2+1}-\frac{2(p+1)}{(p+1)^2+4}\right] = -t\,F(t)$$

$$\Rightarrow \quad 2e^{-2t}\,L^{-1}\left(\frac{p}{p^2+1}\right)-2e^{-t}\,L^{-1}\left(\frac{p}{p^2+4}\right) = -t\,F(t)$$

$$\Rightarrow \quad 2(e^{-2t}\cos t-e^{-t}\cos 2t) = -t\,F(t)$$

$$\Rightarrow \quad F(t) = \frac{2}{t}(e^{-t}\cos 2t-e^{-2t}\cos t)$$

Example 2. *Find the inverse Laplace transforms of*

(*i*) $\dfrac{1}{p^3(p^2+a^2)}$ (*ii*) $\dfrac{1}{p(p+1)^3}$.

Sol. (*i*) Since $L^{-1}\left[\dfrac{1}{p^2+a^2}\right] = \dfrac{1}{a}\sin at$

therefore, by Art. 3.28, we have

$$L^{-1}\left[\frac{1}{p(p^2+a^2)}\right] = \int_0^t \frac{1}{a}\sin au\,du = -\frac{1}{a^2}\left[\cos au\right]_0^t = \frac{1}{a^2}(1-\cos at)$$

$$L^{-1}\left[\frac{1}{p^2(p^2+a^2)}\right] = \int_0^t \frac{1}{a^2}(1-\cos au)\,du = \frac{1}{a^2}\left[u-\frac{\sin au}{a}\right]_0^t = \frac{1}{a^2}\left[t-\frac{\sin at}{a}\right]$$

$$L^{-1}\left[\frac{1}{p^3(p^2+a^2)}\right] = \int_0^t \frac{1}{a^2}\left(u-\frac{\sin au}{a}\right)du = \frac{1}{a^2}\left[\frac{u^2}{2}+\frac{\cos au}{a^2}\right]_0^t = \frac{1}{a^2}\left[\frac{t^2}{2}+\frac{\cos at}{a^2}-\frac{1}{a^2}\right].$$

(*ii*) Since $L^{-1}\left[\dfrac{1}{(p+1)^3}\right] = \dfrac{e^{-t}\,.\,t^2}{2!}$ | By first shifting property

$$\therefore \quad L^{-1}\left[\frac{1}{p(p+1)^3}\right] = \frac{1}{2}\int_0^t t^2e^{-t}\,dt = \frac{1}{2}\left[t^2(-e^{-t})-2t(e^{-t})+2(-e^{-t})\right]_0^t$$

$$= \frac{1}{2}[(-t^2-2t-2)e^{-t}+2] = 1-e^{-t}\left(1+t+\frac{t^2}{2}\right).$$

Example 3. *Find* (*i*) $L^{-1}\left(\frac{1}{p\sqrt{p+4}}\right)$ (*ii*) $L^{-1}\left\{\frac{1}{p(p^2+a^2)}\right\}$.

Sol. (*i*) $$L^{-1}\left(\frac{1}{\sqrt{p+4}}\right) = e^{-4t}\, L^{-1}\left(\frac{1}{\sqrt{p}}\right) = e^{-4t} \cdot \frac{t^{-1/2}}{\Gamma 1/2} = \frac{e^{-4t}}{\sqrt{\pi t}}$$

$$\therefore \quad L^{-1}\left(\frac{1}{p\sqrt{p+4}}\right) = \int_0^t \frac{e^{-4u}}{\sqrt{\pi u}}\, du = \frac{1}{\sqrt{\pi}} \int_0^t e^{-4u}\, u^{-1/2}\, du$$

Put $2\sqrt{u} = x \quad \therefore \quad u^{-1/2}\, du = dx$

$$= \frac{1}{\sqrt{\pi}} \int_0^{2\sqrt{t}} e^{-x^2}\, dx = \frac{1}{2} \cdot \left(\frac{2}{\sqrt{\pi}} \int_0^{2\sqrt{t}} e^{-x^2}\, dx\right) = \frac{1}{2}\, \text{erf}\,(2\sqrt{t}).$$

(*ii*) $$L^{-1}\left(\frac{1}{p^2+a^2}\right) = \frac{1}{a} \sin at$$

$$\therefore \quad L^{-1}\left\{\frac{1}{p(p^2+a^2)}\right\} = \int_0^t \frac{1}{a} \sin au\, du = \frac{1}{a^2}(1 - \cos at).$$

Example 4. *Find the inverse Laplace transform of*

(*i*) $\frac{p^2 - a^2}{(p^2+a^2)^2}$ (*ii*) $\frac{2ap}{(p^2+a^2)^2}$

(*iii*) $\frac{1}{(p^2+a^2)^2}$ (*iv*) $\frac{1}{p^4+4}$. [U.P.T.U. (SUM) 2007]

Sol. (*i*) $$L^{-1}\left(\frac{p}{p^2+a^2}\right) = \cos at$$

$$\therefore \quad L^{-1}\left[\frac{d}{dp}\left(\frac{p}{p^2+a^2}\right)\right] = -\, t\cos at$$

$$\Rightarrow \quad L^{-1}\left[\frac{a^2 - p^2}{(p^2+a^2)^2}\right] = -\, t\cos at$$

$$\therefore \quad L^{-1}\left[\frac{p^2 - a^2}{(p^2+a^2)^2}\right] = t\cos at.$$

(*ii*) $$L^{-1}\left(\frac{a}{p^2+a^2}\right) = \sin at$$

$$\therefore \quad L^{-1}\left[\frac{d}{dp}\left\{\frac{a}{p^2+a^2}\right\}\right] = -\, t\sin at$$

$$\Rightarrow \quad L^{-1}\left\{\frac{-\,2ap}{(p^2+a^2)^2}\right\} = -\, t\sin at$$

or $$L^{-1}\left\{\frac{2ap}{(p^2+a^2)^2}\right\} = t \sin at.$$

(*iii*) $$L^{-1}\left(\frac{1}{p^2+a^2}\right) = \frac{1}{a}\sin at$$

∴ $$L^{-1}\left\{\frac{d}{da}\left(\frac{1}{p^2+a^2}\right)\right\} = \frac{d}{da}\left(\frac{\sin at}{a}\right)$$

⇒ $$L^{-1}\left\{\frac{-2a}{(p^2+a^2)^2}\right\} = \frac{at\cos at - \sin at}{a^2}$$

or $$L^{-1}\left\{\frac{1}{(p^2+a^2)^2}\right\} = -\frac{1}{2a^3}(at\cos at - \sin at) = \frac{\sin at - at\cos at}{2a^3}.$$

(*iv*) $$p^4 + 4 = (p^2+2)^2 - (2p)^2 = (p^2 - 2p + 2)(p^2 + 2p + 2)$$

∴ $$\frac{1}{p^4+4} = \frac{1}{(p^2-2p+2)(p^2+2p+2)}$$

$$= \frac{1}{4p}\left[\frac{1}{p^2-2p+2} - \frac{1}{p^2+2p+2}\right] \quad ...(1)$$

Now, $$L^{-1}\left(\frac{1}{p^2-2p+2}\right) = L^{-1}\left[\frac{1}{(p-1)^2+1}\right] = e^t \sin t$$

and $$L^{-1}\left(\frac{1}{p^2+2p+2}\right) = L^{-1}\left[\frac{1}{(p+1)^2+1}\right] = e^{-t}\sin t$$

∴ $$\frac{1}{4}L^{-1}\left(\frac{1}{p^2-2p+2} - \frac{1}{p^2+2p+2}\right) = \frac{1}{4}(e^t - e^{-t})\sin t$$

Hence

$$L^{-1}\left[\frac{1}{4p}\left(\frac{1}{p^2-2p+2} - \frac{1}{p^2+2p+2}\right)\right] = \frac{1}{4}\int_0^t (e^t - e^{-t})\sin t\, dt$$

⇒ $$L^{-1}\left(\frac{1}{p^4+4}\right) = \frac{1}{4}\left[\frac{e^t}{2}(\sin t - \cos t) - \frac{e^{-t}}{2}(-\sin t - \cos t)\right]$$

$$= \frac{1}{4}\left[\sin t\left(\frac{e^t + e^{-t}}{2}\right) - \cos t\left(\frac{e^t - e^{-t}}{2}\right)\right]$$

or, $$L^{-1}\left(\frac{1}{p^4+4}\right) = \frac{1}{4}[\sin t \cosh t - \cos t \sinh t]$$

Example 5. *Evaluate :*

(*i*) $\int_0^\infty e^{-x^2}\, dx$ (*ii*) $\int_0^\infty \sin x^2\, dx$ (*iii*) $L^{-1}\left(\frac{e^{-1/p}}{p}\right)$.

Sol. (*i*) Let $$G(t) = \int_0^\infty e^{-tx^2}\, dx \quad ...(1)$$

$$\therefore \quad L\{G(t)\} = \int_0^\infty \frac{dx}{p + x^2} = \left[\frac{1}{\sqrt{p}} \tan^{-1}\left(\frac{x}{\sqrt{p}}\right)\right]_0^\infty = \frac{\pi}{2\sqrt{p}}$$

$$\therefore \quad G(t) = L^{-1}\left(\frac{\pi}{2\sqrt{p}}\right)$$

$$\Rightarrow \quad \int_0^\infty e^{-tx^2}\, dx = \frac{\pi}{2} \cdot \frac{1}{\sqrt{\pi t}} = \frac{1}{2}\sqrt{\frac{\pi}{t}}$$

If $t = 1$, $$\int_0^\infty e^{-x^2}\, dx = \frac{1}{2}\sqrt{\pi}$$

(*ii*) Let $$G(t) = \int_0^\infty \sin tx^2\, dx$$

$$\therefore \quad L\{G(t)\} = \int_0^\infty \frac{x^2}{p^2 + x^4}\, dx \qquad \text{Put } x^2 = p \tan\theta \Rightarrow dx = \frac{\sqrt{p}\sec^2\theta\, d\theta}{2\sqrt{\tan\theta}}$$

$$= \frac{1}{2\sqrt{p}} \int_0^{\pi/2} \sqrt{\tan\theta}\, d\theta = \frac{1}{2\sqrt{p}} \int_0^{\pi/2} \sin^{1/2}\theta \cos^{-1/2}\theta\, d\theta$$

$$= \frac{1}{2\sqrt{p}} \cdot \frac{\Gamma(3/4)\,\Gamma(1/4)}{2\,\Gamma(1)} = \frac{1}{4\sqrt{p}} \cdot \frac{\pi}{\sin \pi/4}$$

$$L\{G(t)\} = \frac{\pi}{2\sqrt{2p}} \quad \Rightarrow \quad G(t) = L^{-1}\left(\frac{\pi}{2\sqrt{2p}}\right)$$

$$\Rightarrow \quad \int_0^\infty \sin tx^2\, dx = \frac{\pi}{2\sqrt{2}} \cdot \frac{1}{\sqrt{\pi t}} = \frac{1}{2}\sqrt{\frac{\pi}{2t}}$$

If $t = 1$, $$\int_0^\infty \sin x^2\, dx = \frac{1}{2}\sqrt{\frac{\pi}{2}}.$$

(*iii*) $$\frac{1}{p} e^{-1/p} = \frac{1}{p}\left\{1 - \frac{1}{p} + \frac{1}{2!\,p^2} - \frac{1}{3!\,p^3} + \ldots\ldots\right\}$$

$$= \frac{1}{p} - \frac{1}{p^2} + \frac{1}{2!\,p^3} - \frac{1}{3!\,p^4} + \ldots\ldots$$

$$\therefore \quad L^{-1}\left(\frac{1}{p} e^{-1/p}\right) = 1 - t + \frac{t^2}{(2!)^2} - \frac{t^3}{(3!)^2} + \ldots\ldots = 1 - t + \frac{t^2}{1^2 . 2^2} - \frac{t^3}{1^2 . 2^2 . 3^2} + \ldots\ldots$$

$$= 1 - \frac{(2\sqrt{t})^2}{2^2} + \frac{(2\sqrt{t})^4}{2^2 . 4^2} - \frac{(2\sqrt{t})^6}{2^2 . 4^2 . 6^2} + \ldots\ldots = J_0(2\sqrt{t}).$$

Example 6. *Apply Heaviside expansion theorem to obtain*

(*i*) $L^{-1}\left(\dfrac{2p^2+5p-4}{p^3+p^2-2p}\right)$ (*ii*) $L^{-1}\left\{\dfrac{3p+1}{(p-1)(p^2+1)}\right\}$.

Sol. (*i*)

$$F(p) = 2p^2 + 5p - 4$$

$$G(p) = p^3 + p^2 - 2p = p(p-1)(p+2)$$

$$G(p) = 0 \quad \text{gives} \quad p = 0, 1, -2$$

$$\therefore \quad \alpha_1 = 0, \quad \alpha_2 = 1, \quad \alpha_3 = -2$$

$$F(\alpha_1) = -4, \quad F(\alpha_2) = 3, \quad F(\alpha_3) = -6$$

$$G'(p) = 3p^2 + 2p - 2,$$

$$G'(\alpha_1) = -2, G'(\alpha_2) = 3, \quad G'(\alpha_3) = 6$$

$$\therefore \quad L^{-1}\left(\frac{2p^2+5p-4}{p^3+p^2-2p}\right) = \frac{F(\alpha_1)}{G'(\alpha_1)}e^{\alpha_1 t} + \frac{F(\alpha_2)}{G'(\alpha_2)}e^{\alpha_2 t} + \frac{F(\alpha_3)}{G'(\alpha_3)}e^{\alpha_3 t}$$

$$= \left(\frac{-4}{-2}\right)e^{0t} + \left(\frac{3}{3}\right)e^{t} + \left(\frac{-6}{6}\right)e^{-2t} = 2 + e^t - e^{-2t}.$$

(*ii*)

$$F(p) = 3p + 1$$

$$G(p) = (p-1)(p^2+1) = (p-1)(p+i)(p-i)$$

$$G(p) = 0 \quad \text{gives} \quad p = 1, i, -i$$

$$\therefore \quad \alpha_1 = 1, \quad \alpha_2 = i, \quad \alpha_3 = -i$$

$$F(\alpha_1) = 4, \quad F(\alpha_2) = 3i + 1, \quad F(\alpha_3) = 1 - 3i$$

$$G'(p) = (p-1) . (2p) + p^2 + 1 = 3p^2 - 2p + 1$$

$$G'(\alpha_1) = 2, \quad G'(\alpha_2) = -2 - 2i, \quad G'(\alpha_3) = 2i - 2$$

$$\therefore \quad L^{-1}\left\{\frac{3p+1}{(p-1)(p^2+1)}\right\} = \left(\frac{4}{2}\right)e^t + \left(\frac{3i+1}{-2-2i}\right)e^{it} + \left(\frac{1-3i}{2i-2}\right)e^{-it}$$

$$= 2e^t - \left(\frac{i}{2}+1\right)e^{it} + \left(\frac{i}{2}-1\right)e^{-it} = 2e^t - \frac{i}{2}(e^{it} - e^{-it}) - (e^{it} + e^{-it})$$

$$= 2e^t - \frac{i}{2} . 2i \sin t - 2\cos t = 2e^t + \sin t - 2\cos t.$$

Example 7. *State convolution theorem and hence evaluate*

(*i*) $L^{-1}\left\{\dfrac{p}{(p^2+1)(p^2+4)}\right\}$ (*ii*) $L^{-1}\left\{\dfrac{1}{p(p^2-a^2)}\right\}$

(*iii*) $L^{-1}\left\{\dfrac{1}{p(p+1)(p+2)}\right\}$. [U.P.T.U. (SUM) 2008]

Sol. If $\quad L^{-1}\{f(p)\} = F(t)$ and $L^{-1}\{g(p)\} = G(t)$, then

$$L^{-1}\{f(p)\,.\,g(p)\} = F * G = \int_0^t F(u)\,.\,G(t-u)\,du$$

(*i*) Let
$$f(p) = \frac{1}{p^2+4} \quad \text{and} \quad g(p) = \frac{p}{p^2+1}$$

$$\therefore \quad F(t) = \frac{1}{2}\sin 2t \quad \text{and} \quad G(t) = \cos t$$

$$\therefore \quad F(u) = \frac{1}{2}\sin 2u,\ G(t-u) = \cos(t-u)$$

$$\therefore \quad L^{-1}\left\{\frac{p}{(p^2+1)(p^2+4)}\right\} = \int_0^t \frac{1}{2}\sin 2u\,.\,\cos(t-u)\,du$$

$$= \frac{1}{4}\int_0^t [\sin(u+t) + \sin(3u-t)]\,du$$

$$= \frac{1}{4}\left[-\cos(u+t) - \frac{\cos(3u-t)}{3}\right]_0^t$$

$$= \frac{1}{4}\left[\left(-\cos 2t - \frac{\cos 2t}{3}\right) - \left(-\cos t - \frac{\cos t}{3}\right)\right]$$

$$= \frac{1}{4}\left[-\frac{4}{3}\cos 2t + \frac{4}{3}\cos t\right] = \frac{1}{3}(\cos t - \cos 2t).$$

(*ii*) Let
$$f(p) = \frac{1}{p^2-a^2} \quad \text{and} \quad g(p) = \frac{1}{p}$$

$$\therefore \quad F(t) = \frac{1}{a}\sinh at \quad \text{and} \quad G(t) = 1$$

$$\therefore \quad F(u) = \frac{1}{a}\sinh au \quad \text{and} \quad G(t-u) = 1$$

$$\therefore \quad L^{-1}\left\{\frac{1}{p(p^2-a^2)}\right\} = \int_0^t \frac{1}{a}\sinh au\,.\,1\,du$$

$$= \frac{1}{a}\left(\frac{\cosh au}{a}\right)_0^t = \frac{1}{a^2}(\cosh at - 1).$$

(*iii*) Let
$$f(p) = \frac{1}{p(p+1)} \text{ and } g(p) = \frac{1}{p+2}$$

$$\therefore \quad F(t) = L^{-1}\left\{\frac{1}{p(p+1)}\right\} = L^{-1}\left(\frac{1}{p} - \frac{1}{p+1}\right) = 1 - e^{-t}$$

and
$$G(t) = L^{-1}\left(\frac{1}{p+2}\right) = e^{-2t}$$

Now, $F(u) = 1 - e^{-u},\ G(t-u) = e^{-2(t-u)}$

$\therefore$ By convolution theorem, we get

$$L^{-1}\left\{\frac{1}{p(p+1)(p+2)}\right\} = \int_0^t (1-e^{-u})\, e^{-2(t-u)}\, du$$

$$= e^{-2t}\int_0^t (e^{2u} - e^{u})\, du = e^{-2t}\left(\frac{e^{2u}}{2} - e^{u}\right)_0^t$$

$$= e^{-2t}\left[\left(\frac{e^{2t}}{2} - e^{t}\right) - \left(\frac{1}{2} - 1\right)\right] = e^{-2t}\left(\frac{e^{2t}}{2} - e^{t} + \frac{1}{2}\right)$$

$$= \frac{1}{2} - e^{-t} + \frac{1}{2}e^{-2t}$$

Example 8. *Use convolution theorem to evaluate :*

(*i*) $L^{-1}\left\{\frac{p}{(p^2+4)^2}\right\}$ (G.B.T.U. 2010)

(*ii*) $L^{-1}\left\{\frac{p^2}{(p^2+a^2)(p^2+b^2)}\right\}$. (U.K.T.U. 2011; U.P.T.U. 2006)

Sol. (*i*) $$\frac{p}{(p^2+4)^2} = \frac{1}{p^2+4}\cdot\frac{p}{p^2+4}$$

Let, $f(p) = \frac{1}{p^2+4}$ and $g(p) = \frac{p}{p^2+4}$

$\therefore$ $$F(t) = L^{-1}\{f(p)\} = L^{-1}\left(\frac{1}{p^2+4}\right) = \frac{1}{2}\sin 2t$$

and $$G(t) = L^{-1}\{g(p)\} = L^{-1}\left(\frac{p}{p^2+4}\right) = \cos 2t$$

Now, $F(u) = \frac{1}{2}\sin 2u,\ G(t-u) = \cos 2(t-u)$

$\therefore$ By convolution theorem, we have

$$L^{-1}\left\{\frac{p}{(p^2+4)^2}\right\} = \int_0^t \frac{1}{2}\sin 2u.\cos 2(t-u)\, du = \frac{1}{4}\int_0^t [\sin 2t + \sin(4u-2t)]\, du$$

$$= \frac{1}{4}\left[u\sin 2t - \frac{\cos(4u-2t)}{4}\right]_0^t = \frac{t}{4}\sin 2t$$

(*ii*) $$\frac{p^2}{(p^2+a^2)(p^2+b^2)} = \frac{p}{p^2+a^2}\cdot\frac{p}{p^2+b^2}$$

Let, $f(p) = \frac{p}{p^2+a^2}$ and $g(p) = \frac{p}{p^2+b^2}$

$$\therefore \qquad F(t) = L^{-1}\{f(p)\} = L^{-1}\left(\frac{p}{p^2+a^2}\right) = \cos at$$

and
$$G(t) = L^{-1}\{g(p)\} = L^{-1}\left(\frac{p}{p^2+b^2}\right) = \cos bt$$

Now, $\qquad F(u) = \cos au$

$$G(t-u) = \cos b(t-u)$$

$\therefore$ By convolution theorem, we have

$$L^{-1}\left\{\frac{p^2}{(p^2+a^2)(p^2+b^2)}\right\} = \int_0^t \cos au . \cos b(t-u)\, du$$

$$= \frac{1}{2}\int_0^t [\cos\{(a-b)u+bt\} + \cos\{(a+b)u-bt\}]\, du$$

$$= \frac{1}{2}\left[\frac{\sin\{(a-b)u+bt\}}{a-b} + \frac{\sin\{(a+b)u-bt\}}{a+b}\right]_0^t$$

$$= \frac{1}{2}\left[\frac{\sin at - \sin bt}{a-b} + \frac{\sin at + \sin bt}{a+b}\right] = \frac{a\sin at - b\sin bt}{a^2-b^2}.$$

Example 9. *Prove that*

(i) $F * G = G * F$ $\qquad$ *(ii)* $L^{-1}\left\{\frac{1}{(p-1)\sqrt{p}}\right\} = e^t \operatorname{erf}\sqrt{t}$.

Sol. (*i*) By convolution theorem, we have

$$F * G = L^{-1}\{f(p) . g(p)\} = \int_0^t F(u) . G(t-u)\, du$$

Putting $t - u = v$ or $u = t - v$, this gives

$$F * G = \int_t^0 F(t-v) . G(v)\,(-dv) = \int_0^t G(v)\, F(t-v)\, dv = G * F$$

This shows that the convolution of F and G obeys the commutative law of Algebra.

(*ii*) Let $\qquad f(p) = \frac{1}{\sqrt{p}}$ and $g(p) = \frac{1}{p-1}$, then

$$F(t) = L^{-1}\{f(p)\} = \frac{1}{\sqrt{\pi t}} \quad \text{and} \quad G(t) = L^{-1}\{g(p)\} = e^t$$

Hence by convolution theorem, we have

$$L^{-1}\left\{\frac{1}{(p-1)\sqrt{p}}\right\} = \int_0^t F(u) . G(t-u)\, du$$

$$= \int_0^t \frac{1}{\sqrt{\pi u}}\, e^{t-u}\, du = \frac{e^t}{\sqrt{\pi}} \int_0^t \frac{e^{-u}}{\sqrt{u}}\, du$$

Put $\sqrt{u} = x \quad \therefore \quad \frac{du}{2\sqrt{u}} = dx$

$$= e^t . \left(\frac{2}{\sqrt{\pi}} \int_0^{\sqrt{t}} e^{-x^2}\, dx\right) = e^t \operatorname{erf}\sqrt{t}.$$

Example 10. *Show that* $1 * 1 * 1 = \dfrac{t^2}{2}$ *hence evaluate* $1 * 1 * 1 * ...... * 1$ *(n times).*

Sol. For $1 * 1$, we have $F(t) = 1$ and $G(t) = 1$

$\therefore$ By convolution theorem, we have

$$1 * 1 = \int_0^t 1 \,.\, 1 \, du = t \qquad | \because \ F(u) = 1 \text{ and } G(t-u) = 1$$

Using the convolution theorem again, we obtain

$$1 * 1 * 1 = t * 1 = \int_0^t u \,.\, 1 \, du = \left(\frac{u^2}{2}\right)_0^t = \frac{t^2}{2}$$

Similarly, $1 * 1 * 1 * 1 = \dfrac{t^3}{3!}$

Hence $1 * 1 * 1 * ...... * 1$ (n times) $= \dfrac{t^{n-1}}{(n-1)!}$.

Example 11. *Using the convolution theorem, evaluate* $\int_0^t \sin u \cos (t-u) \, du.$

Sol. By convolution theorem, we have

$$\int_0^t \sin u \cos (t-u) \, du = \sin t * \cos t \qquad ...(1)$$

Here, $F(t) = \sin t, \quad G(t) = \cos t$

$\therefore$ $f(p) = L\{F(t)\} = L(\sin t) = \dfrac{1}{p^2+1}$

and $g(p) = L\{G(t)\} = L(\cos t) = \dfrac{p}{p^2+1}$

$$\sin t * \cos t = L^{-1}\{f(p) \,.\, g(p)\} = L^{-1}\left\{\frac{p}{(p^2+1)^2}\right\} \qquad ...(2)$$

Now, $L^{-1}\left(\dfrac{p}{p^2+a^2}\right) = \cos at$

Differentiating this w.r.t. a, we get

$$L^{-1}\left\{\frac{-2ap}{(p^2+a^2)^2}\right\} = -t \sin at$$

If $a = 1$, $L^{-1}\left\{\dfrac{p}{(p^2+1)^2}\right\} = \dfrac{t}{2} \sin t$

From (1) and (2), $\int_0^t \sin u \cos (t-u) \, du = \dfrac{1}{2} t \sin t.$

Example 12. *Prove that :*

$$\beta(m, n) = \int_0^1 x^{m-1} (1-x)^{n-1}\, dx = \frac{\Gamma m\, \Gamma n}{\Gamma(m+n)} \; ; \; m, n > 0.$$

Sol. Let
$$\phi(t) = \int_0^t x^{m-1} (t-x)^{n-1}\, dx \qquad ...(1)$$

By convolution theorem, we have

$$\int_0^t x^{m-1} (t-x)^{n-1}\, dx = t^{m-1} * t^{n-1} \qquad ...(2)$$

Here, $F(t) = t^{m-1}$, $G(t) = t^{n-1}$

$$\therefore \quad f(p) = L\{F(t)\} = L(t^{m-1}) = \frac{\Gamma(m)}{p^m}$$

$$g(p) = L\{G(t)\} = L(t^{n-1}) = \frac{\Gamma(n)}{p^n}$$

$$t^{m-1} * t^{n-1} = L^{-1}\{f(p) \,.\, g(p)\}$$

$$= L^{-1}\left(\frac{\Gamma(m)\,\Gamma(n)}{p^{m+n}}\right) = \Gamma(m)\,\Gamma(n) \,.\, \frac{t^{m+n-1}}{\Gamma(m+n)}$$

$\therefore$ From (1) and (2), $\phi(t) = \int_0^t x^{m-1} (t-x)^{n-1}\, dx = \Gamma(m)\,\Gamma(n) \,.\, \frac{t^{m+n-1}}{\Gamma(m+n)}$

Letting $t = 1$, we get

$$\int_0^1 x^{m-1} (1-x)^{n-1}\, dx = \frac{\Gamma(m)\,\Gamma(n)}{\Gamma(m+n)}.$$

Example 13. *Apply convolution theorem to show that*

(*i*) $\int_0^t J_0(u)\, J_1(t-u)\, du = J_0(t) - \cos t$ (*ii*) $\int_0^t J_0(u) \sin(t-u)\, du = t\, J_1(t).$

Sol. (*i*) By convolution theorem, we have

$$\int_0^t J_0(u)\, J_1(t-u)\, du = J_0(t) * J_1(t)$$

Here, $F(t) = J_0(t)$, $G(t) = J_1(t)$

$$\therefore \quad f(p) = L\{F(t)\} = L\{J_0(t)\} = \frac{1}{\sqrt{p^2+1}}$$

and
$$g(p) = L\{G(t)\} = L[J_1(t)] = 1 - \frac{p}{\sqrt{p^2+1}}$$

$$\therefore \quad J_0(t) * J_1(t) = L^{-1}\{f(p) \,.\, g(p)\} = L^{-1}\left(\frac{1}{\sqrt{p^2+1}} - \frac{p}{p^2+1}\right) = J_0(t) - \cos t.$$

(*ii*) By convolution theorem, we have

$$\int_0^t J_0(u) \sin(t-u)\, du = J_0(t) * \sin t$$

Here, $F(t) = J_0(t)$, $G(t) = \sin t$

$$\therefore \qquad f(p) = \text{L}\{\text{F}(t)\} = \text{L}\{\text{J}_0(t)\} = \frac{1}{\sqrt{p^2+1}}$$

and
$$g(p) = \text{L}\{\text{G}(t)\} = \text{L}(\sin t) = \frac{1}{p^2+1}$$

$$\therefore \qquad \text{J}_0(t) * \sin t = \text{L}^{-1}\{f(p)\,.\,g(p)\}$$

$$= \text{L}^{-1}\left\{\frac{1}{\sqrt{p^2+1}}\cdot\frac{1}{p^2+1}\right\} = \text{L}^{-1}\left\{\frac{1}{(p^2+1)^{3/2}}\right\} \qquad ...(1)$$

Now, we know that,

$$\text{L}\{\text{J}_0(at)\} = \frac{1}{\sqrt{p^2+a^2}}$$

Differentiating w.r.t. 'a' we find

$$\text{L}\left\{\frac{d}{da}\text{J}_0(at)\right\} = \frac{-a}{(p^2+a^2)^{3/2}}$$

$$\Rightarrow \qquad \text{L}\{t\,\text{J}_0'(at)\} = \frac{-a}{(p^2+a^2)^{3/2}}$$

$$\therefore \qquad \text{L}^{-1}\left\{\frac{1}{(p^2+a^2)^{3/2}}\right\} = -\frac{t}{a}\text{J}_0'(at) = \frac{t}{a}\text{J}_1(at) \qquad \Big|\because\ \text{J}_0'(t) = -\text{J}_1(t)$$

Put $a = 1$,

$$\therefore \qquad \text{L}^{-1}\left\{\frac{1}{(p^2+1)^{3/2}}\right\} = t\,\text{J}_1(t)$$

$\therefore$ From (1), $\text{J}_0(t) * \sin t = t\,\text{J}_1(t)$.

Example 14. *Prove that :*

$$L^{-1}\left\{\frac{1}{(p^2+1)^3}\right\} = \frac{1}{8}\,[(3-t^2)\sin t - 3t\cos t].$$

Sol. We have

$$\text{L}^{-1}\left(\frac{1}{p^2+a^2}\right) = \frac{1}{a}\sin at$$

Diff. w.r.t. a, we get

$$\therefore \qquad \text{L}^{-1}\left\{\frac{d}{da}\left(\frac{1}{p^2+a^2}\right)\right\} = \frac{d}{da}\left(\frac{\sin at}{a}\right)$$

$$\Rightarrow \qquad \text{L}^{-1}\left\{\frac{-2a}{(p^2+a^2)^2}\right\} = -\frac{1}{a^2}\sin at + \frac{t}{a}\cos at$$

$$\Rightarrow \qquad \text{L}^{-1}\left\{\frac{1}{(p^2+a^2)^2}\right\} = \frac{1}{2a^2}\sin at - \frac{t}{2a^2}\cos at$$

Differentiating again w.r.t. a, we get

$$\text{L}^{-1}\left\{\frac{-4a}{(p^2+a^2)^3}\right\} = -\frac{3}{2a^4}\sin at + \frac{t}{2a^3}\cos at + \frac{t}{a^3}\cos at + \frac{t^2}{2a^2}\sin at$$

Letting $a = 1$, this readily yields

$$L^{-1}\left\{\frac{1}{(p^2+1)^3}\right\} = \frac{1}{8}\,[3\,(\sin t - t\cos t) - t^2 \sin t]$$

$$= \frac{1}{8}\,[(3 - t^2)\sin t - 3\,t\cos t].$$

TEST YOUR KNOWLEDGE

1. Find the inverse Laplace transforms of :

(i) $\cot^{-1}\left(\frac{p}{a}\right)$ (ii) $\tan^{-1}\left(\frac{2}{p}\right)$ (iii) $\cot^{-1}(p+1)$

(iv) $\log\frac{p(p+1)}{p^2+4}$ (v) $\log\left(1+\frac{1}{p}\right)$ (U.P.T.U. 2007) (vi) $\log\left(\frac{p+a}{p+b}\right)$

(vii) $\log\left(\frac{p-1}{p}\right)$ (viii) $\log\left(\frac{p^2-1}{p^2}\right)$ (ix) $\log\left(1+\frac{\alpha^2}{p^2}\right)$

(x) $\frac{1}{2}\log\left\{\frac{p^2+\beta^2}{(p-\alpha)^2}\right\}$ (xi) $\log\left\{\frac{p^2+1}{p(p+1)}\right\}$ (xii) $\log\left\{\frac{p+1}{(p+2)(p+3)}\right\}$

(xiii) $\frac{1}{2}\log\left(\frac{p^2+b^2}{p^2+a^2}\right)$ (xiv) $\log\left(1-\frac{a^2}{p^2}\right)$ (xv) $p\log\left(\frac{p-1}{p+1}\right)$.

[U.P.T.U. (C.O.) 2009]

2. Show that :

(i) $L^{-1}\left(\frac{1}{p}\sin\frac{1}{p}\right) = t - \frac{t^3}{(3\,!)^2} + \frac{t^5}{(5\,!)^2} - \frac{t^7}{(7\,!)^2} + \ldots\ldots$

(ii) $L^{-1}\left(\frac{1}{p}\cos\frac{1}{p}\right) = 1 - \frac{t^2}{(2\,!)^2} + \frac{t^4}{(4\,!)^2} - \frac{t^6}{(6\,!)^2} + \ldots\ldots$

3. Apply Heaviside's expansion formula to evaluate :

(i) $L^{-1}\left\{\frac{2p-1}{p(p-1)(p+1)}\right\}$ (ii) $L^{-1}\left\{\frac{2(p^2-2)}{(p+1)(p-2)(p-3)}\right\}$

(iii) $L^{-1}\left(\frac{3p+16}{p^2-p-6}\right)$ (iv) $L^{-1}\left\{\frac{p^2-6}{p(p+1)(p+3)}\right\}$.

4. Evaluate :

(i) $L^{-1}\left\{\frac{1}{(p+a)(p+b)}\right\}$ (ii) $L^{-1}\left\{\frac{1}{(p+1)(p^2+1)}\right\}$

(iii) $L^{-1}\left\{\frac{1}{p(p+a)^3}\right\}$ (U.K.T.U. 2012) (iv) $L^{-1}\left\{\frac{1}{p^2(p^2+1)}\right\}$. [U.P.T.U. (SUM) 2009]

(v) $L^{-1}\left[\frac{p^2}{(p^2+\omega^2)^2}\right]$ [G.B.T.U.(C.O.) 2010] (vi) $L^{-1}\left[\frac{1}{(p^2+2p+5)^2}\right]$

5. Apply convolution theorem to evaluate :

(*i*) $L^{-1}\left[\dfrac{p^2}{(p^2+4)^2}\right]$ (*ii*) $L^{-1}\left[\dfrac{1}{p(p^2+4)}\right]$

(*iii*) $L^{-1}\left\{\dfrac{1}{p^4(p^2+1)}\right\}$ (*iv*) $L^{-1}\left[\dfrac{p^2}{p^4-a^4}\right]$.

6. Apply convolution theorem to show that

(*i*) $\int_0^t J_0(u)\, J_0(t-u)\, du = \sin t$ (*ii*) $t * t * t = \dfrac{t^5}{5!}$

(*iii*) $\int_0^t u^2 \cos(t-u)\, du = 2t - 2\sin t.$

7. Evaluate :

(*i*) $\int_0^\infty \cos x^2\, dx$ (*ii*) $\int_0^\infty \dfrac{\sin x}{x}\, dx$

(*iii*) $\int_0^\infty x \cos x^3\, dx$ (*iv*) $\int_0^\infty \dfrac{x \sin tx}{1+x^2}\, dx,\ t > 0$

8. Prove that :

(*i*) $L^{-1}\left(\dfrac{1}{p^3+1}\right) = \dfrac{1}{3}\left[e^{-t} - e^{t/2}\left(\cos\dfrac{\sqrt{3}}{2}t - \sqrt{3}\sin\dfrac{\sqrt{3}}{2}t\right)\right]$

(*ii*) $L^{-1}\left[\dfrac{1}{p^{3/2}(p-1)}\right] = e^t \operatorname{erf}(\sqrt{t}) - 2\sqrt{\dfrac{t}{\pi}}$.

9. State convolution theorem for the inverse Laplace transform. Hence or otherwise, find the inverse Laplace transform of the function $\dfrac{8p}{(p^2+16)(p^2+1)^2}$. [*U.P.T.U. (C.O.) 2009*]

10. Evaluate :

(*i*) $L^{-1}\left(\dfrac{2p^2-6p+5}{p^3-6p^2+11p-6}\right)$ (*ii*) $L^{-1}\left(\dfrac{1}{\sqrt{p^2-4p+20}}\right)$

(*iii*) $L^{-1}\left[\dfrac{11p^3-47p^2+56p+4}{(p-2)^3(p+2)}\right]$ (*iv*) $L^{-1}\left(\dfrac{p^3+16p-24}{p^4+20p^2+64}\right)$.

11. Using convolution theorem, prove that

(*i*) $L^{-1}\left[\dfrac{1}{p^3(p^2+1)}\right] = \dfrac{t^2}{2} + \cos t - 1$ (*G.B.T.U. 2012*)

(*ii*) $L^{-1}\left[\dfrac{1}{(p^2+a^2)^2}\right] = \dfrac{1}{2a^3}(\sin at - at\cos at)$ [*U.P.T.U. (SUM) 2007 ; U.P.T.U. 2009*]

12. Use convolution theorem to find

(*i*) $L^{-1}\left[\dfrac{1}{(p^2+4)(p+2)}\right]$ (*ii*) $L^{-1}\left[\dfrac{16}{(p-2)(p+2)^2}\right]$ (*M.T.U. 2011*)

(*iii*) $L^{-1}\left[\dfrac{p}{(p^2+a^2)^3}\right]$ (*M.T.U. 2012; U.P.T.U. 2008*)

Answers

1. (*i*) $\dfrac{\sin at}{t}$ (*ii*) $\dfrac{\sin 2t}{t}$ (*iii*) $e^{-t}\dfrac{\sin t}{t}$

(*iv*) $\dfrac{2\cos 2t - e^{-t} - 1}{t}$ (*v*) $\dfrac{1-e^{-t}}{t}$ (*vi*) $\dfrac{e^{-bt} - e^{-at}}{t}$

(*vii*) $\dfrac{1-e^{t}}{t}$ (*viii*) $\dfrac{2}{t}(1-\cosh t)$ (*ix*) $\dfrac{2(1-\cos \alpha t)}{t}$

(*x*) $\dfrac{e^{\alpha t} - \cos \beta t}{t}$ (*xi*) $\dfrac{-2\cos t + 1 + e^{-t}}{t}$ (*xii*) $\dfrac{-e^{-t} + e^{-2t} + e^{-3t}}{t}$

(*xiii*) $\dfrac{\cos at - \cos bt}{t}$ (*xiv*) $\dfrac{2}{t}(1-\cosh at)$ (*xv*) $\dfrac{2}{t^2}(\sinh t - t\cosh t)$

3. (*i*) $1 + \dfrac{1}{2}e^{t} - \dfrac{3}{2}e^{-t}$ (*ii*) $-\dfrac{1}{6}e^{-t} - \dfrac{4}{3}e^{2t} + \dfrac{7}{2}e^{3t}$ (*iii*) $5e^{3t} - 2e^{-2t}$

(*iv*) $-2 + \dfrac{5}{2}e^{-t} + \dfrac{1}{2}e^{-3t}$

4. (*i*) $\dfrac{e^{-at} - e^{-bt}}{b-a}$ (*ii*) $\dfrac{1}{2}(\sin t - \cos t + e^{-t})$ (*iii*) $\dfrac{1}{a^3} - \dfrac{1}{a^3}e^{-at}\left(1 + at + \dfrac{a^2t^2}{2}\right)$

(*iv*) $t - \sin t$ (*v*) $\dfrac{1}{2\omega}\sin \omega t + \dfrac{t}{2}\cos \omega t$ (*vi*) $\dfrac{1}{16}e^{-t}(\sin 2t - 2t\cos 2t)$

5. (*i*) $\dfrac{1}{4}(\sin 2t + 2t\cos 2t)$ (*ii*) $\dfrac{1}{4}(1-\cos 2t)$ (*iii*) $\dfrac{t^3}{6} + \sin t - t$

(*iv*) $\dfrac{1}{2a}(\sinh at + \sin at)$

7. (*i*) $\dfrac{1}{2}\sqrt{\dfrac{\pi}{2}}$ (*ii*) $\dfrac{\pi}{2}$ (*iii*) $\dfrac{\pi}{3\sqrt{3}\,\Gamma 1/3}$ (*iv*) $\dfrac{\pi}{2}e^{-t}$

9. $\dfrac{60t\sin t - 8\cos t + 8\cos 4t}{225}$

10. (*i*) $\dfrac{1}{2}e^{t} - e^{2t} + \dfrac{5}{2}e^{3t}$ (*ii*) $e^{2t}J_0(4t)$ (*iii*) $(2t^2 - t + 5)e^{2t} + 6e^{-2t}$

(*iv*) $\dfrac{1}{2}\sin 4t + \cos 2t - \sin 2t$

12. (*i*) $\dfrac{1}{8}(\sin 2t - \cos 2t + e^{-2t})$ (*ii*) $e^{2t} - e^{-2t}(1+4t)$ (*iii*) $\dfrac{t}{8a^3}(\sin at - at\cos at)$.

3.31. APPLICATIONS TO DIFFERENTIAL EQUATIONS

1. Solution of ordinary linear differential equations with constant coefficients. Laplace transforms can be used to solve ordinary linear differential equations with constant coefficients. The advantage of this method is that it yields the particular solution directly without the necessity of first finding the general solution and then evaluating the arbitrary constants.

Steps :

1. Take Laplace transform of both sides of the given differential equation, using initial conditions. This gives an algebraic equation.
2. Solve the algebraic equation to get $\bar{y}$ in terms of p.
3. Take Inverse Laplace transform of both sides. This gives y as a function of t which is the desired solution.

Remember. $L\{F^{(n)}(t)\} = p^n f(p) - p^{n-1} F(0) - p^{n-2} F'(0) - \ldots\ldots - pF^{(n-2)}(0) - F^{(n-1)}(0)$; if $L\{F(t)\} = f(p)$.

ILLUSTRATIVE EXAMPLES

Example 1. *Solve the differential equation :*

$$\frac{d^3y}{dt^3} + 2\frac{d^2y}{dt^2} - \frac{dy}{dt} - 2y = 0, \text{ where } y = 1, \frac{dy}{dt} = 2, \frac{d^2y}{dt^2} = 2 \text{ at } t = 0.$$

Sol. The given equation is $y''' + 2y'' - y' - 2y = 0$

Taking Laplace transform on both sides, we get

$$[p^3\bar{y} - p^2y(0) - py'(0) - y''(0)] + 2[p^2\bar{y} - py(0) - y'(0)] - [p\bar{y} - y(0)] - 2\bar{y} = 0 \quad \ldots(1)$$

Using the given conditions $y(0) = 1, y'(0) = 2, y''(0) = 2$, equation (1) reduces to

$$(p^3 + 2p^2 - p - 2)\bar{y} = p^2 + 4p + 5$$

$$\therefore \quad \bar{y} = \frac{p^2+4p+5}{p^3+2p^2-p-2} = \frac{p^2+4p+5}{(p-1)(p+1)(p+2)}$$

$$= \frac{5}{3(p-1)} - \frac{1}{p+1} + \frac{1}{3(p+2)} \quad \text{(Partial Fractions)}$$

Taking the Inverse Laplace transforms of both sides, we get

$$y = \frac{5}{3}L^{-1}\left\{\frac{1}{p-1}\right\} - L^{-1}\left\{\frac{1}{p+1}\right\} + \frac{1}{3}L^{-1}\left\{\frac{1}{p+2}\right\} = \frac{5}{3}e^t - e^{-t} + \frac{1}{3}e^{-2t}$$

Example 2. *Solve the differential equation*

$$y'' - 3y' + 2y = 4t + e^{3t}, \text{ where } y(0) = 1 \text{ and } y'(0) = -1.$$

Sol. Taking Laplace transform of both sides, we get

$$[p^2\bar{y} - py(0) - y'(0)] - 3[p\bar{y} - y(0)] + 2\bar{y} = \frac{4}{p^2} + \frac{1}{p-3}$$

Using the given conditions, it reduces to

$$(p^2 - 3p + 2)\bar{y} - p + 1 + 3 = \frac{4}{p^2} + \frac{1}{p-3}$$

or

$$(p^2 - 3p + 2)\bar{y} = \frac{4}{p^2} + \frac{1}{p-3} + p - 4$$

$$\therefore \quad \bar{y} = \frac{p^4 - 7p^3 + 13p^2 + 4p - 12}{p^2(p-1)(p-2)(p-3)}$$

$$= \frac{3}{p} + \frac{2}{p^2} - \frac{1}{2(p-1)} - \frac{2}{p-2} + \frac{1}{2(p-3)} \quad \text{(Partial Fractions)}$$

Taking the Inverse Laplace transforms on both sides, we get

$$y = 3L^{-1}\left\{\frac{1}{p}\right\} + 2L^{-1}\left\{\frac{1}{p^2}\right\} - \frac{1}{2}L^{-1}\left\{\frac{1}{p-1}\right\} - 2L^{-1}\left\{\frac{1}{p-2}\right\} + \frac{1}{2}L^{-1}\left\{\frac{1}{p-3}\right\}$$

$$\Rightarrow \quad y = 3 + 2t - \tfrac{1}{2}e^{t} - 2e^{2t} + \tfrac{1}{2}e^{3t}$$

Example 3. *Using Laplace transform, solve the following differential equation :*

$$\frac{d^2x}{dt^2} + 2\frac{dx}{dt} + 5x = e^{-t} \sin t, \text{ where } x(0) = 0 \text{ and } x'(0) = 1.$$

[U.P.T.U. 2008; U.P.T.U. (SUM) 2009; M.T.U. 2011]

Sol. The given equation is $x'' + 2x' + 5x = e^{-t} \sin t$

Taking Laplace transform of both sides, we get

$$[p^2\bar{x} - px(0) - x'(0)] + 2[p\bar{x} - x(0)] + 5\bar{x} = \frac{1}{(p+1)^2 + 1}$$

Using the given conditions, it reduces to

$$(p^2 + 2p + 5)\bar{x} - 1 = \frac{1}{p^2 + 2p + 2}$$

or
$$\bar{x} = \frac{1}{(p^2 + 2p + 2)(p^2 + 2p + 5)} + \frac{1}{p^2 + 2p + 5}$$

$$= \frac{1}{3}\left[\frac{1}{p^2 + 2p + 2} - \frac{1}{p^2 + 2p + 5}\right] + \frac{1}{p^2 + 2p + 5}$$

$$= \frac{1}{3}\left[\frac{1}{p^2 + 2p + 2} + \frac{2}{p^2 + 2p + 5}\right] = \frac{1}{3}\left[\frac{1}{(p+1)^2 + 1} + \frac{2}{(p+1)^2 + 2^2}\right]$$

Taking Inverse Laplace transform of both sides, we get

$$x = \frac{1}{3}L^{-1}\left\{\frac{1}{(p+1)^2 + 1} + 2 \cdot \frac{1}{(p+1)^2 + 2^2}\right\} = \frac{1}{3}\left[e^{-t} \sin t + 2 \cdot \tfrac{1}{2}e^{-t} \sin 2t\right]$$

or
$$x = \frac{1}{3}e^{-t}(\sin t + \sin 2t).$$

Example 4. *Using Laplace transformation, solve the differential equation*

$$\frac{d^2x}{dt^2} + 9x = \cos 2t, \text{ if } x(0) = 1, x\left(\frac{\pi}{2}\right) = -1.$$

Sol. The given equation is

$$x'' + 9x = \cos 2t$$

Taking the Laplace transform of both sides, we get

$$L(x'') + 9L(x) = L(\cos 2t)$$

$$[p^2\bar{x} - px(0) - x'(0)] + 9\bar{x} = \frac{p}{p^2 + 4}$$

$$\Rightarrow \quad (p^2 + 9)\bar{x} - p - A = \frac{p}{p^2 + 4} \qquad | \text{ where } x'(0) = A \text{ (say)}$$

$$\Rightarrow \quad \bar{x} = \frac{p}{(p^2 + 4)(p^2 + 9)} + \frac{p}{p^2 + 9} + \frac{A}{p^2 + 9}$$

$$\Rightarrow \quad \bar{x} = \frac{1}{5}\left(\frac{p}{p^2+4} - \frac{p}{p^2+9}\right) + \frac{p}{p^2+9} + \frac{A}{p^2+9}$$

Taking the Inverse Laplace transform of both sides, we get

$$x = \frac{1}{5}(\cos 2t - \cos 3t) + \cos 3t + \frac{A}{3}\sin 3t$$

But $x\left(\frac{\pi}{2}\right) = -1$

$$\Rightarrow \quad -1 = \frac{1}{5}(-1-0) + 0 + \frac{A}{3}(-1) \Rightarrow -1 = -\frac{1}{5} - \frac{A}{3} \Rightarrow A = \frac{12}{5}$$

$$\therefore \quad x(t) = \frac{1}{5}(\cos 2t - \cos 3t) + \cos 3t + \frac{4}{5}\sin 3t$$

$$= \frac{1}{5}(\cos 2t + 4\cos 3t + 4\sin 3t).$$

Example 5. *Solve the following differential equation by Laplace transform :*
$(D^2 + n^2)x = a \sin(nt + \alpha)$; $x = Dx = 0$ at $t = 0$.

Sol. The given equation is

$$(D^2 + n^2)x = a\sin(nt + \alpha)$$

Taking Laplace transform of both sides, we get

$$L(x'') + n^2 L(x) = L\{a \sin(nt + \alpha)\}$$

$$\Rightarrow \quad [p^2\bar{x} - px(0) - x'(0)] + n^2\bar{x} = a\cos\alpha \cdot \frac{n}{p^2+n^2} + a\sin\alpha \cdot \frac{p}{p^2+n^2}$$

$$\Rightarrow \quad (p^2+n^2)\bar{x} = \frac{an\cos\alpha}{p^2+n^2} + \frac{ap\sin\alpha}{p^2+n^2}$$

$$\Rightarrow \quad \bar{x} = \frac{an\cos\alpha}{(p^2+n^2)^2} + \frac{ap\sin\alpha}{(p^2+n^2)^2} \quad \text{...(1)}$$

Taking the Inverse Laplace transform of both sides, we get

$$x = (a\cos\alpha)\, L^{-1}\left[\frac{n}{(p^2+n^2)^2}\right] + (a\sin\alpha)\, L^{-1}\left[\frac{p}{(p^2+n^2)^2}\right] \quad \text{...(2)}$$

We know that $L^{-1}\left(\frac{1}{p^2+n^2}\right) = \frac{1}{n}\sin nt$ ...(3)

$$L^{-1}\left[\frac{d}{dn}\left\{\frac{1}{(p^2+n^2)}\right\}\right] = \frac{nt\cos nt - \sin nt}{n^2}$$

$$L^{-1}\left[\frac{-2n}{(p^2+n^2)^2}\right] = \frac{nt\cos nt - \sin nt}{n^2}$$

$$L^{-1}\left[\frac{n}{(p^2+n^2)^2}\right] = \frac{1}{2n^2}(\sin nt - nt\cos nt]$$

Again, from (3), $L^{-1}\left[\frac{d}{dp}\left(\frac{1}{(p^2+n^2)}\right)\right] = -t \cdot \frac{1}{n}\sin nt$

$$\Rightarrow \quad L^{-1}\left[\frac{-2p}{(p^2+n^2)^2}\right] = -\frac{t}{n}\sin nt$$

$$\Rightarrow \quad L^{-1}\left[\frac{p}{(p^2+n^2)^2}\right] = \frac{t}{2n}\sin nt$$

$\therefore$ From (2), $x = (a\cos\alpha) \cdot \frac{1}{2n^2}(\sin nt - nt\cos nt) + (a\sin\alpha) \cdot \frac{t}{2n}\sin nt$

$$= \frac{a}{2n^2}[\cos\alpha\sin nt - nt\cos(\alpha + nt)].$$

Example 6. *Solve the following equation by Laplace transform*

$$y''' - 2y'' + 5y' = 0\ ;\ y = 0,\ y' = 1 \text{ at } t = 0 \text{ and } y = 1 \text{ at } t = \frac{\pi}{8}.$$

Sol. Taking Laplace transform on both sides, we get

$$L(y''') - 2L(y'') + 5L(y') = L(0)$$

$$\Rightarrow \quad p^3\bar{y} - p^2y(0) - py'(0) - y''(0) - 2[p^2\bar{y} - py(0) - y'(0)] + 5[p\bar{y} - y(0)] = 0$$

$$\Rightarrow \quad (p^3 - 2p^2 + 5p)\bar{y} - p - A + 2 = 0 \qquad | \text{ Let } y''(0) = A \text{ (say)}$$

$$\Rightarrow \quad \bar{y} = \frac{(A-2)+p}{p(p^2-2p+5)}$$

$$= \left(\frac{A-2}{5}\right)\left(\frac{1}{p} - \frac{p-2}{p^2-2p+5}\right) + \frac{1}{p^2-2p+5}$$

$$= \left(\frac{A-2}{5}\right)\frac{1}{p} - \left(\frac{A-2}{5}\right)\left\{\frac{(p-1)-1}{(p-1)^2+4}\right\} + \frac{1}{(p-1)^2+4}$$

$$\Rightarrow \quad \bar{y} = \left(\frac{A-2}{5}\right)\frac{1}{p} - \left(\frac{A-2}{5}\right)\left[\frac{p-1}{(p-1)^2+4}\right] + \left(\frac{A+3}{10}\right) \cdot \left\{\frac{2}{(p-1)^2+4}\right\}$$

Taking Inverse Laplace transform on both sides, we get

$$y = \left(\frac{A-2}{5}\right) - \left(\frac{A-2}{5}\right)e^t\cos 2t + \left(\frac{A+3}{10}\right)e^t\sin 2t$$

Since $\quad y\left(\frac{\pi}{8}\right) = 1$

$$\therefore \quad 1 = \left(\frac{A-2}{5}\right) - \left(\frac{A-2}{5}\right)e^{\pi/8} \cdot \frac{1}{\sqrt{2}} + \left(\frac{A+3}{10}\right)e^{\pi/8} \cdot \frac{1}{\sqrt{2}}$$

$$\Rightarrow \quad A = 7 \qquad \text{(on simplification)}$$

Hence required solution is $y = 1 + e^t(\sin 2t - \cos 2t)$.

Example 7. *Using Laplace transform, find the solution of the initial value problem*

$$\frac{d^2y}{dt^2} + 9y = 6\cos 3t;\ y(0) = 2,\ y'(0) = 0 \qquad \text{(U.P.T.U. 2006)}$$

Sol. The given differential equation is

$$y'' + 9y = 6\cos 3t \qquad ...(1)$$

Taking Laplace transform on both sides of eqn. (1), we get

$$L(y'') + 9L(y) = 6L(\cos 3t)$$

$$\Rightarrow \quad \left[p^2\bar{y} - py(0) - y'(0)\right] + 9\bar{y} = 6\frac{p}{p^2+9} \qquad | \text{ Here } \bar{y} = L(y)$$

$$\Rightarrow \quad (p^2 + 9)\,\bar{y} - 2p = \frac{6p}{p^2+9} \qquad | \because \; y(0) = 2,\, y'(0) = 0$$

$$\Rightarrow \quad \bar{y} = \frac{6p}{(p^2+9)^2} + \frac{2p}{p^2+9} \qquad ...(2)$$

Taking Inverse Laplace transform on both sides of (2), we get

$$y(t) = t\sin 3t + 2\cos 3t \qquad | \because \; L^{-1}\left\{\frac{p}{(p^2+a^2)^2}\right\} = \frac{t}{2a}\sin at$$

Example 8. *Solve, using Laplace transform method*

$$y''(t) + 4y'(t) + 4y(t) = 6e^{-t}\,;\, y(0) = -2,\, y'(0) = 8. \qquad \text{[U.P.T.U. 2007]}$$

Sol. The given differential equation is

$$y'' + 4y' + 4y = 6e^{-t} \qquad ...(1)$$

Taking Laplace transform on both sides of eqn. (1), we get

$$L(y'') + 4L(y') + 4L(y) = 6L(e^{-t})$$

$$\Rightarrow \quad [p^2\bar{y} - py(0) - y'(0)] + 4\,[p\bar{y} - y(0)] + 4\bar{y} = \frac{6}{p+1} \qquad | \text{ Here } \bar{y} = L(y)$$

$$\Rightarrow \quad (p^2 + 4p + 4)\,\bar{y} + 2p - 8 + 8 = \frac{6}{p+1} \qquad | \because \; y(0) = -2 \text{ and } y'(0) = 8$$

$$\Rightarrow \quad \bar{y} = \frac{6}{(p+1)(p+2)^2} - \frac{2p}{(p+2)^2}$$

$$= 6\left[\frac{1}{p+1} - \frac{1}{p+2} - \frac{1}{(p+2)^2}\right] - \frac{2\{(p+2)-2\}}{(p+2)^2}$$

$$= \frac{6}{p+1} - \frac{6}{p+2} - \frac{6}{(p+2)^2} - \frac{2}{p+2} + \frac{4}{(p+2)^2}$$

$$= \frac{6}{p+1} - \frac{8}{p+2} - \frac{2}{(p+2)^2}$$

Taking inverse Laplace transform on both sides, we get

$$y = 6e^{-t} - 8e^{-2t} - 2t\,e^{-2t}.$$

Example 9. *Solve the following differential equation using Laplace transform*

$$\frac{d^3y}{dt^3} - 3\frac{d^2y}{dt^2} + 3\frac{dy}{dt} - y = t^2e^t$$

where $\quad y(0) = 1,\ \left(\frac{dy}{dt}\right)_{t=0} = 0,\ \left(\frac{d^2y}{dt^2}\right)_{t=0} = -2.$ [U.P.T.U. (SUM) 2008]

Sol. The given equation is

$$y''' - 3y'' + 3y' - y = t^2 e^t \qquad ...(1)$$

Taking Laplace transform on both sides of eqn. (1), we get

$$L(y''') - 3L(y'') + 3L(y') - L(y) = L(t^2 e^t)$$

$$\Rightarrow \left[p^3\bar{y} - p^2 y(0) - py'(0) - y''(0)\right] - 3\left[p^2\bar{y} - py(0) - y'(0)\right]$$

$$+ 3\,[p\bar{y} - y(0)] - \bar{y} = \frac{2}{(p-1)^3} \qquad \mid \text{ where } \bar{y} = L(y)$$

$$\Rightarrow \quad (p^3\bar{y} - p^2 + 2) - 3(p^2\bar{y} - p) + 3(p\bar{y} - 1) - \bar{y} = \frac{2}{(p-1)^3}$$

$$\Rightarrow \quad (p^3 - 3p^2 + 3p - 1)\,\bar{y} - p^2 + 3p - 1 = \frac{2}{(p-1)^3}$$

$$\Rightarrow \quad (p-1)^3\,\bar{y} = p^2 - 3p + 1 + \frac{2}{(p-1)^3}$$

$$\Rightarrow \quad \bar{y} = \frac{(p-1)^2}{(p-1)^3} - \frac{p}{(p-1)^3} + \frac{2}{(p-1)^6}$$

$$= \frac{1}{p-1} - \frac{(p-1)+1}{(p-1)^3} + \frac{2}{(p-1)^6}$$

$$= \frac{1}{p-1} - \frac{1}{(p-1)^2} - \frac{1}{(p-1)^3} + \frac{2}{(p-1)^6} \qquad ...(2)$$

Taking inverse Laplace transform on both sides of eqn.(2), we get

$$y = e^t - t\,e^t - \frac{t^2}{2}e^t + \frac{t^5 e^t}{60} = \left(1 - t - \frac{t^2}{2} + \frac{t^5}{60}\right)e^t$$

Example 10. *Solve by Laplace transform :*

$$\frac{d^2y}{dt^2} + y = t\cos 2t,\ t > 0 \text{ given that } y = \frac{dy}{dt} = 0 \text{ for } t = 0. \qquad \text{(U.K.T.U. 2012)}$$

Sol. The given equation is

$$y'' + y = t\cos 2t \qquad ...(1)$$

Taking Laplace transform on both sides of eqn. (1), we get

$$L(y'') + L(y) = L(t\cos 2t)$$

$$\Rightarrow \quad \left[p^2\bar{y} - py(0) - y'(0)\right] + \bar{y} = -\frac{d}{dp}\left(\frac{p}{p^2+4}\right) \qquad \mid \text{where } \bar{y} = L(y)$$

$$\Rightarrow \quad (p^2 + 1)\,\bar{y} = \frac{p^2 - 4}{(p^2+4)^2}$$

$$\Rightarrow \quad \bar{y} = \frac{p^2 - 4}{(p^2+1)(p^2+4)^2}$$

$$= -\frac{5}{9}\frac{1}{(p^2+1)} + \frac{5}{9}\cdot\frac{1}{(p^2+4)} + \frac{8}{3(p^2+4)^2} \qquad ...(2)$$

Taking inverse Laplace transform on both sides of (2), we get

$$y = -\frac{5}{9}\sin t + \frac{5}{18}\sin 2t + \frac{8}{3}\cdot\frac{1}{16}(\sin 2t - 2t\cos 2t)$$

$$\Big| \because \quad L^{-1}\left\{\frac{1}{(p^2+a^2)^2}\right\} = \frac{1}{2a^3}(\sin at - at\cos at)$$

$$= -\frac{5}{9}\sin t + \frac{4}{9}\sin 2t - \frac{t}{3}\cos 2t.$$

Example 11. *Voltage Ee^{-at} is applied at $t = 0$ to a circuit of inductance L and resistance R. Show that the current at time t is $\frac{E}{R-aL}(e^{-at} - e^{-Rt/L})$.* [U.P.T.U. (SUM) 2007]

Sol. Let I be the current in the circuit at any time t, then by Kirchhoff 's law, we have

$$L\frac{dI}{dt} + RI = Ee^{-at}, \text{ where } I(0) = 0$$

Taking Laplace transform of both sides,

$$L[p\bar{I} - I(0)] + R\bar{I} = \frac{E}{p+a}$$

Using the given condition, it reduces to

$$(Lp + R)\bar{I} = \frac{E}{p+a}$$

or

$$\bar{I} = \frac{E}{(p+a)(Lp+R)} = \frac{E}{R-aL}\left(\frac{1}{p+a} - \frac{L}{Lp+R}\right) = \frac{E}{R-aL}\left(\frac{1}{p+a} - \frac{1}{p+R/L}\right)$$

Taking the Inverse Laplace transforms of both sides, we get

$$I = \frac{E}{R-aL}L^{-1}\left\{\frac{1}{p+a} \quad \frac{1}{p+R/L}\right\} - \frac{E}{R-aL}[e^{-at} - e^{-Rt/L}].$$

2. Solution of simultaneous ordinary differential equations. Laplace transform technique can also be used in solving two or more simultaneous ordinary differential equations.

This procedure is illustrated as follows.

Example 12. *Solve the simultaneous equations :*

$$\frac{dx}{dt} - y = e^t, \; \frac{dy}{dt} + x = \sin t, \quad \textit{given } x(0) = 1, y(0) = 0.$$

[U.P.T.U. 2006; G.B.T.U. (SUM) 2010; U.K.T.U. 2011]

Sol. Taking Laplace transform of the given equations, we get

$$[p\bar{x} - x(0)] - \bar{y} = \frac{1}{p-1}$$

i.e., $$p\bar{x} - 1 - \bar{y} = \frac{1}{p-1} \qquad [\because\ x(0) = 1]$$

i.e., $$p\bar{x} - \bar{y} = \frac{p}{p-1} \qquad ...(1)$$

and $$[p\bar{y} - y(0)] + \bar{x} = \frac{1}{p^2+1}$$

i.e., $$\bar{x} + p\bar{y} = \frac{1}{p^2+1} \qquad ...(2) \qquad [\because\ y(0) = 0]$$

Solving (1) and (2) for $\bar{x}$ and $\bar{y}$, we have

$$\bar{x} = \frac{p^2}{(p-1)(p^2+1)} + \frac{1}{(p^2+1)^2} = \frac{1}{2}\left[\frac{1}{p-1} + \frac{p}{p^2+1} + \frac{1}{p^2+1}\right] + \frac{1}{(p^2+1)^2}$$

and $$\bar{y} = \frac{p}{(p^2+1)^2} - \frac{p}{(p-1)(p^2+1)} = \frac{p}{(p^2+1)^2} - \frac{1}{2}\left[\frac{1}{p-1} - \frac{p}{p^2+1} + \frac{1}{p^2+1}\right]$$

Taking Inverse Laplace transform of both sides, we get

$$x = \frac{1}{2}\mathrm{L}^{-1}\left[\frac{1}{p-1} + \frac{p}{p^2+1} + \frac{1}{p^2+1}\right] + \mathrm{L}^{-1}\left[\frac{1}{(p^2+1)^2}\right]$$

$$= \frac{1}{2}[e^t + \cos t + \sin t] + \tfrac{1}{2}(\sin t - t\cos t)$$

$$\left[\because\ \mathrm{L}^{-1}\left[\frac{1}{(p^2+a^2)^2}\right] = \frac{1}{2a^3}(\sin at - at\cos at)\right]$$

$$= \frac{1}{2}[e^t + \cos t + 2\sin t - t\cos t)$$

$$y = \mathrm{L}^{-1}\left[\frac{p}{(p^2+1)^2}\right] - \frac{1}{2}\mathrm{L}^{-1}\left[\frac{1}{p-1} - \frac{p}{p^2+1} + \frac{1}{p^2+1}\right]$$

$$= \tfrac{1}{2}t\sin t - \tfrac{1}{2}[e^t - \cos t + \sin t] \qquad \left[\because\ \mathrm{L}^{-1}\left[\frac{p}{(p^2+a^2)^2}\right] = \frac{1}{2a}t\sin at\right]$$

$$= \tfrac{1}{2}[t\sin t - e^t + \cos t - \sin t]$$

Hence $$x = \tfrac{1}{2}(e^t + \cos t + 2\sin t - t\cos t)$$

$$y = \tfrac{1}{2}(t\sin t - e^t + \cos t - \sin t).$$

Example 13. *Solve the simultaneous equations*

$$(D^2 - 3)x - 4y = 0$$

$$x + (D^2 + 1)y = 0$$

for $t > 0$, *given that* $x = y = \frac{dy}{dt} = 0$ *and* $\frac{dx}{dt} = 2$ *at* $t = 0$.

Sol. Taking Laplace transform of the given equations, we get

$$p^2\bar{x} - px(0) - x'(0) - 3\bar{x} - 4\bar{y} = 0$$

i.e., $$(p^2 - 3)\bar{x} - 4\bar{y} = 2 \qquad ...(1)\ [\because\ x(0) = 0,\ x'(0) = 2]$$

and $$\bar{x} + p^2\bar{y} - py(0) - y'(0) + \bar{y} = 0$$

i.e., $$\bar{x} + (p^2+1)\bar{y} = 0 \qquad ...(2)\ [\because\ y(0) = y'(0) = 0]$$

Solving (1) and (2) for $\bar{x}$ and $\bar{y}$, we get

$$\bar{x} = \frac{2(p^2+1)}{(p^2-1)^2} = \frac{1}{(p-1)^2} + \frac{1}{(p+1)^2}$$

and
$$\bar{y} = -\frac{2}{(p^2-1)^2} = -\frac{1}{2}\left[\frac{1}{p+1} - \frac{1}{p-1} - \frac{1}{(p+1)^2} + \frac{1}{(p-1)^2}\right]$$

Taking Inverse Laplace transform of both sides, we get

$$x = \mathrm{L}^{-1}\left[\frac{1}{(p-1)^2} + \frac{1}{(p+1)^2}\right] = te^t + te^{-t} = 2t\left(\frac{e^t + e^{-t}}{2}\right) = 2t \cosh t$$

and
$$y = -\frac{1}{2}\mathrm{L}^{-1}\left(\frac{1}{p+1} - \frac{1}{p-1} - \frac{1}{(p+1)^2} + \frac{1}{(p-1)^2}\right)$$

$$= -\tfrac{1}{2}(e^{-t} - e^t - te^{-t} + te^t) = \frac{e^t - e^{-t}}{2} - t\left(\frac{e^t - e^{-t}}{2}\right) = (1-t)\sinh t$$

Hence $\quad x = 2t \cosh t, \quad y = (1-t)\sinh t.$

Example 14. *Solve the simultaneous equations*

$$\frac{d^2x}{dt^2} + 5\frac{dy}{dt} - x = t, \quad 2\frac{dx}{dt} - \frac{d^2y}{dt^2} + 4y = 2$$

given that when $t = 0$, $x = 0$, $y = 0$, $\frac{dx}{dt} = 0$, $\frac{dy}{dt} = 0$.

Sol. Let $\quad \mathrm{L}\{x(t)\} = \bar{x}(p)$ and $\mathrm{L}\{y(t)\} = \bar{y}(p)$

then, taking Laplace transform of given equations, we get

$$\{p^2\bar{x} - px(0) - x'(0)\} + 5\{p\bar{y} - y(0)\} - \bar{x} = \frac{1}{p^2}$$

and
$$2\{p\bar{x} - x(0)\} - \{p^2\bar{y} - py(0) - y'(0)\} + 4\bar{y} = \frac{2}{p}$$

Using the given initial conditions, these equations reduce to

$$(p^2-1)\bar{x} + 5p\bar{y} = \frac{1}{p^2} \qquad \text{...(1)}$$

and
$$2p\bar{x} - (p^2-4)\bar{y} = \frac{2}{p} \qquad \text{...(2)}$$

Eliminating $\bar{y}$ between (1) and (2), we find that

$$\{(p^2-1)(p^2-4) + 10p^2\}\bar{x} = \frac{p^2-4}{p^2} + 10$$

$$\therefore \quad \bar{x} = \frac{11p^2-4}{p^2(p^2+1)(p^2+4)} = -\frac{1}{p^2} + \frac{5}{p^2+1} - \frac{4}{p^2+4}$$

Taking Inverse Laplace transform, we get

$$x = -t + 5\sin t - 2\sin 2t \qquad \text{...(3)}$$

Again eliminating $\bar{x}$ between (1) and (2), we have

$$\{10p^2 + (p^2-1)(p^2-4)\}\bar{y} = \frac{2}{p} - \frac{2(p^2-1)}{p}$$

$$\therefore \qquad \bar{y} = \frac{4-2p^2}{p(p^2+1)(p^2+4)} = \frac{1}{p} - \frac{2p}{p^2+1} + \frac{p}{p^2+4}$$

Taking Inverse Laplace transform, we get

$$y = 1 - 2\cos t + \cos 2t \qquad ...(4)$$

Thus (3) and (4) together constitute the desired solution.

Example 15. *The co-ordinates (x, y) of a particle moving along a plane curve at any time t are given by* $\frac{dy}{dt} + 2x = \sin 2t$, $\frac{dx}{dt} - 2y = \cos 2t$; $(t > 0)$. *It is given that at* $t = 0$, $x = 1$ *and* $y = 0$. *Show using transforms that the particle moves along the curve* $4x^2 + 4xy + 5y^2 = 4$.

[M.T.U. (SUM) 2011]

Sol. The given equations are

$$\frac{dy}{dt} + 2x = \sin 2t \qquad ...(1)$$

$$\frac{dx}{dt} - 2y = \cos 2t \qquad ...(2)$$

Above equations may be rewritten as

$$2x + Dy = \sin 2t$$

$$Dx - 2y = \cos 2t, \qquad \text{where } D \equiv \frac{d}{dt}$$

Taking Laplace transform of eqn. (1) on both sides, we get

$$2\bar{x} + p\bar{y} - y(0) = \frac{2}{p^2+4}, \qquad \text{where } \bar{x} = L(x) \text{ and } \bar{y} = L(y)$$

$$\Rightarrow \qquad 2\bar{x} + p\bar{y} = \frac{2}{p^2+4} \qquad ...(3) \quad | \because \ y(0) = 0$$

Again, taking Laplace transform of eqn. (2) on both sides, we get

$$p\bar{x} - x(0) - 2\bar{y} = \frac{p}{p^2+4}, \quad \text{where } \bar{x} = L(x) \text{ and } \bar{y} = L(y)$$

$$\Rightarrow \qquad p\bar{x} - 2\bar{y} = \frac{p}{p^2+4} + 1 \qquad ...(4) \quad | \because \ x(0) = 0$$

Multiplying equation (3) by 2 and equation (4) by p and then adding, we get

$$4\bar{x} + p^2\bar{x} = \frac{4}{p^2+4} + \frac{p^2}{p^2+4} + p$$

$$\Rightarrow \qquad (4 + p^2)\bar{x} = 1 + p$$

$$\bar{x} = \frac{1+p}{4+p^2} = \frac{1}{p^2+4} + \frac{p}{p^2+4}$$

Taking Inverse Laplace transform, we get

$$x = \frac{1}{2}\sin 2t + \cos 2t \qquad ...(5)$$

Again, Multiplying eqn. (3) by p and eqn. (4) by 2 then subtracting eqn. (4) from (3), we get

$$p^2\bar{y} + 4\bar{y} = \frac{2p}{p^2+4} - \frac{2p}{p^2+4} - 2$$

$$\Rightarrow \qquad \bar{y} = \frac{-2}{p^2+4}$$

Taking Inverse Laplace transform, we get $y = -\sin 2t$ ...(6)

Now, $$4x^2 = 4\left[\frac{1}{4}\sin^2 2t + \cos^2 2t + \sin 2t \cos 2t\right]$$

$$5y^2 = 5\sin^2 2t$$

$$4xy = 4\left[\left(\frac{1}{2}\sin 2t + \cos 2t\right).(-\sin 2t)\right] = -(2\sin^2 2t + 4\sin 2t\cos 2t)$$

$$\therefore \qquad 4x^2 + 5y^2 + 4xy = 4\sin^2 2t + 4\cos^2 2t = 4$$

Hence the result.

Example 16. *Use Laplace transform to solve :* $\frac{dx}{dt} + y = \sin t,\ \frac{dy}{dt} + x = \cos t$ *given that* $x = 2,\ y = 0$ *at* $t = 0.$ (G.B.T.U. 2012)

Sol. Taking Laplace transform of the given equations, we get

$$p\bar{x} - x(0) + \bar{y} = \frac{1}{p^2+1}$$

$$\Rightarrow \qquad p\bar{x} + \bar{y} = \frac{1}{p^2+1} + 2 \qquad ...(1)$$

and $$p\bar{y} - y(0) + \bar{x} = \frac{p}{p^2+1}$$

$$\Rightarrow \qquad \bar{x} + p\bar{y} = \frac{p}{p^2+1} \qquad ...(2)$$

Solving (1) and (2) for $\bar{x}$ and $\bar{y}$, we get

$$\bar{x} = \frac{2p}{p^2-1} \quad \text{and} \quad \bar{y} = \frac{1}{1+p^2} + \frac{2}{1-p^2}$$

$$\Rightarrow \qquad \bar{x} = \frac{1}{p+1} + \frac{1}{p-1} \quad \text{and} \quad \bar{y} = \frac{1}{1+p^2} + \frac{1}{p+1} - \frac{1}{p-1}$$

Taking Inverse Laplace transform on both sides, we get

$$x = e^{-t} + e^{t} \qquad ...(3)$$

and $$y = \sin t + e^{-t} - e^{t} \qquad ...(4)$$

Equations (3) and (4), when taken together, give the complete solution.

Example 17. *Solve the following simultaneous differential equations by Laplace transform*

$\frac{dx}{dt} + 4\frac{dy}{dt} - y = 0;\ \frac{dx}{dt} + 2y = e^{-t}$ *with conditions* $x(0) = y(0) = 0.$ (U.P.T.U. 2008)

Sol. The given equations are

$$\frac{dx}{dt} + 4\frac{dy}{dt} - y = 0 \qquad ...(1)$$

and $$\frac{dx}{dt} + 2y = e^{-t} \qquad ...(2)$$

Taking Laplace transform on both sides of eqn. (1), we get

$$L(x') + 4L(y') - L(y) = L(0)$$

$$\Rightarrow \quad p\bar{x} - x(0) + 4[p\bar{y} - y(0)] - \bar{y} = 0 \qquad | \text{ where } \bar{x} = L(x) \text{ and } \bar{y} = L(y)$$

$$\Rightarrow \quad p\bar{x} + (4p - 1)\,\bar{y} = 0 \qquad ...(3)$$

Similarly, taking Laplace transform on both sides of eqn. (2), we get

$$L(x') + 2L(y) = L(e^{-t})$$

$$p\bar{x} - x(0) + 2\bar{y} = \frac{1}{p+1}$$

$$p\bar{x} + 2\bar{y} = \frac{1}{p+1} \qquad ...(4)$$

Subtracting (4) from (3), we get

$$(4p - 3)\,\bar{y} = -\frac{1}{p+1}$$

$$\Rightarrow \quad \bar{y} = -\frac{1}{(p+1)(4p-3)} = \frac{1}{7}\left(\frac{1}{p+1} - \frac{1}{p-3/4}\right)$$

Taking inverse Laplace transform on both sides, we get

$$y = \frac{1}{7}\left(e^{-t} - e^{\frac{3t}{4}}\right) \qquad ...(5)$$

Substituting $\bar{y}$ in (4), we get

$$p\bar{x} + \frac{2}{7}\left(\frac{1}{p+1} - \frac{1}{p-3/4}\right) = \frac{1}{p+1}$$

$$p\bar{x} = \frac{5}{7(p+1)} + \frac{2}{7(p-3/4)}$$

$$\bar{x} = \frac{5}{7p(p+1)} + \frac{2}{7p(p-3/4)}$$

$$= \frac{5}{7}\left(\frac{1}{p} - \frac{1}{p+1}\right) + \frac{8}{21}\left(\frac{1}{p-3/4} - \frac{1}{p}\right)$$

$$= \frac{1}{3p} - \frac{5}{7(p+1)} + \frac{8}{21(p-3/4)}$$

Taking Inverse Laplace transform on both sides, we get

$$x = \frac{1}{3} - \frac{5}{7}e^{-t} + \frac{8}{21}e^{\frac{3t}{4}} \qquad ...(6)$$

Equation (5) and (6), when taken together, give the complete solution.

Example 18. *Solve the following simultaneous differential equations by Laplace transform*

$3\frac{dx}{dt} - y = 2t,\ \frac{dx}{dt} + \frac{dy}{dt} - y = 0$ *with the conditions* $x(0) = y(0) = 0.$ [U.P.T.U. (SUM) 2008]

Sol. The given equations are

$$3\frac{dx}{dt} - y = 2t \quad \text{...(1)}$$

and

$$\frac{dx}{dt} + \frac{dy}{dt} - y = 0 \quad \text{...(2)}$$

Taking Laplace transform on both sides of eqn. (1), we get

$$3L(x') - L(y) = L(2t)$$

$$3\left[p\bar{x} - x(0)\right] - \bar{y} = \frac{2}{p^2} \qquad | \text{ where } L(x) = \bar{x} \text{ and } L(y) = \bar{y}$$

$$3p\bar{x} - \bar{y} = \frac{2}{p^2} \quad \text{...(3)}$$

Similarly, taking Laplace transform on both sides of eqn. (2), we get

$$L(x') + L(y') - L(y) = L(0)$$

$$\Rightarrow \quad \left[p\bar{x} - x(0)\right] + \left[p\bar{y} - y(0)\right] - \bar{y} = 0$$

$$\Rightarrow \quad p\bar{x} + (p-1)\,\bar{y} = 0 \quad \text{...(4)}$$

Multiplying equation (4) by 3, we get

$$3p\bar{x} + 3(p-1)\,\bar{y} = 0 \quad \text{...(5)}$$

Subtracting equation (3) from (5), we get

$$(3p-2)\,\bar{y} = -\frac{2}{p^2}$$

$$\bar{y} = -\frac{2}{p^2\,(3p-2)} = \frac{1}{p^2} + \frac{3}{2p} - \frac{3}{2(p-2/3)}$$

Taking inverse Laplace transform on both sides, we get

$$y = t + \frac{3}{2} - \frac{3}{2}e^{2t/3} \quad \text{...(6)}$$

Substituting $\bar{y}$ in (3), we get

$$3p\bar{x} - \frac{1}{p^2} - \frac{3}{2p} + \frac{3}{2(p-2/3)} = \frac{2}{p^2}$$

$$3p\bar{x} = \frac{3}{p^2} + \frac{3}{2p} - \frac{3}{2(p-2/3)}$$

$$\bar{x} = \frac{1}{p^3} + \frac{1}{2p^2} - \frac{1}{2p\,(p-2/3)}$$

$$\bar{x} = \frac{1}{p^3} + \frac{1}{2p^2} - \frac{3}{4}\left(\frac{1}{p-2/3} - \frac{1}{p}\right)$$

Taking inverse Laplace transform on both sides, we get

$$x = \frac{t^2}{2} + \frac{t}{2} - \frac{3}{4}e^{2t/3} + \frac{3}{4} \quad \text{...(7)}$$

Equation (6) and (7), when taken together, give the complete solution.

3. Solution of ordinary differential equations with variable coefficients. The method is illustrated as follows :

Example 19. *Solve :* $\dfrac{d^2y(t)}{dt^2}+t\,\dfrac{dy(t)}{dt}-y(t)=0$ *if* $y(0)=0$, $\left(\dfrac{dy}{dt}\right)_{t=0}=1.$

Sol. Taking the Laplace transform of both sides of the given equation, we get

$$L(y'') + L(ty') - L(y) = L(0)$$

$$\Rightarrow \quad \{p^2\bar{y} - py(0) - y'(0)\} - \frac{d}{dp}L(y') - \bar{y} = 0$$

$$\Rightarrow \quad p^2\bar{y} - 1 - \frac{d}{dp}\{p\bar{y} - y(0)\} - \bar{y} = 0$$

$$\Rightarrow \quad p^2\bar{y} - 1 - \frac{d}{dp}(p\bar{y}) - \bar{y} = 0$$

$$\Rightarrow \quad -p\frac{d\bar{y}}{dp} + (p^2-2)\bar{y} = 1$$

$$\frac{d\bar{y}}{dp} + \left(\frac{2}{p} - p\right)\bar{y} = -\frac{1}{p} \quad \text{which is linear.}$$

$$\text{I.F.} = e^{\int\left(\frac{2}{p}-p\right)dp} = p^2e^{-p^2/2}$$

Solution of equation is

$$\bar{y}p^2e^{-p^2/2} = \int\left(\frac{-1}{p}\right)p^2e^{-p^2/2}\,dp + c$$

$$= -\int pe^{-p^2/2}\,dp + c = c + e^{-p^2/2} \qquad | \text{ where } c \text{ is a constant}$$

c must vanish if $\bar{y}$ is a transform since $\bar{y} \to 0$ as $p \to \infty$

$$\therefore \quad \bar{y} = \frac{1}{p^2}$$

or $$y = L^{-1}\left(\frac{1}{p^2}\right) = t.$$

Example 20. *Solve the problem*

$$t\frac{d^2y}{dt^2} + \frac{dy}{dt} + 4ty = 0 \text{ given that } y = 3 \text{ and } \frac{dy}{dt} = 0 \text{ when } t = 0.$$

Sol. Taking Laplace transform on both sides of the given equation, we have

$$L(ty'') + L(y') + 4L(ty) = L(0)$$

$$\Rightarrow \quad -\frac{d}{dp}L(y'') + L(y') - 4\frac{d}{dp}L(y) = 0$$

$$\Rightarrow \quad -\frac{d}{dp}\{p^2\bar{y} - py(0) - y'(0)\} + \{p\bar{y} - y(0)\} - 4\frac{d\bar{y}}{dp} = 0$$

$$\Rightarrow \quad (p^2+4)\frac{d\bar{y}}{dp} + p\bar{y} = 0 \qquad \text{...(1)}$$

Separating the variables, we have

$$\frac{d\bar{y}}{\bar{y}} + \frac{p\,dp}{p^2+4} = 0 \qquad ...(2)$$

Integration yields $\log \bar{y} + \frac{1}{2}\log (p^2 + 4) = \log c$

$$\Rightarrow \qquad \bar{y} = \frac{c}{\sqrt{p^2+4}} \qquad ...(3)$$

Taking Inverse Laplace transform, we get

$$y = c\mathrm{J}_0(2t) \qquad ...(4)$$

Since $y(0) = 3$, from (4), $\quad y(0) = c\mathrm{J}_0(0) = c$

$\therefore \quad c = 3$

Hence the required solution is $\quad y = 3\mathrm{J}_0(2t)$.

Example 21. *Using Laplace transform, solve the differential equation $y'' + 2ty' - y = t$, when $y(0) = 0$ and $y'(0) = 1$.*

Sol. Taking Laplace transform on both sides, we get

$$\mathrm{L}(y'') + 2\,\mathrm{L}(ty') - \mathrm{L}(y) = \mathrm{L}(t) \qquad ...(1)$$

$$\Rightarrow \quad p^2\bar{y} - py(0) - y'(0) + 2\left[-\frac{d}{dp}\mathrm{L}(y')\right] - \bar{y} = \frac{1}{p^2}, \qquad \text{where } \bar{y} = \mathrm{L}(y)$$

$$\Rightarrow \quad p^2\bar{y} - 1 - 2\frac{d}{dp}\{p\bar{y} - y(0)\} - \bar{y} = \frac{1}{p^2} \qquad \because y(0) = 0 \text{ and } y'(0) = 1$$

$$\Rightarrow \quad p^2\bar{y} - 1 - 2\left(p\frac{d\bar{y}}{dp} + \bar{y}\right) - \bar{y} = \frac{1}{p^2} \qquad \because y(0) = 0$$

$$\Rightarrow \quad -2p\frac{d\bar{y}}{dp} + \bar{y}(p^2 - 3) = \frac{1}{p^2} + 1$$

$$\frac{d\bar{y}}{dp} + \left(\frac{3-p^2}{2p}\right)\bar{y} = -\frac{1}{2p^3} - \frac{1}{2p} \qquad ...(2)$$

which is a linear diff. equation of I order in $\bar{y}$ and p.

$$\text{I.F.} = e^{\frac{1}{2}\int\left(\frac{3}{p} - p\right)dp} = e^{\frac{1}{2}\left(3\log p - \frac{p^2}{2}\right)} = e^{-(p^2/4)}\,p^{3/2}$$

Solution to eqn. (2) is

$$\bar{y}\,.\,e^{-p^2/4}\,p^{3/2} = -\frac{1}{2}\int\left(\frac{1}{p^3} + \frac{1}{p}\right)p^{3/2}\,e^{-(p^2/4)}\,dp = -\frac{1}{2}\int\left(\sqrt{p} + \frac{1}{p^{3/2}}\right)e^{-p^2/4}\,dp$$

Put $p^2 = 4t \Rightarrow p = 2\sqrt{t}$ so that $dp = \frac{dt}{\sqrt{t}}$

$$\Rightarrow \bar{y}\,.\,p^{3/2}\,e^{-p^2/4} = -\frac{1}{2}\int\left(\sqrt{2}\,t^{1/4} + \frac{1}{2\sqrt{2}}t^{-3/4}\right)e^{-t}\frac{dt}{\sqrt{t}}$$

$$= -\frac{1}{\sqrt{2}}\int\left(t^{-1/4} + \frac{1}{4}t^{-5/4}\right)e^{-t}\,dt$$

$$= -\frac{1}{\sqrt{2}}\left[t^{-1/4}\frac{e^{-t}}{(-1)} + \int\left(\frac{-1}{4}\right)t^{-5/4}\,e^{-t}\,dt + \frac{1}{4}\int t^{-5/4}\,e^{-t}\,dt\right]$$

$$= \frac{1}{\sqrt{2}} e^{-t} t^{-1/4} = \frac{1}{\sqrt{2}} e^{-(p^2/4)} \left(\frac{p^2}{4}\right)^{-1/4} = \frac{1}{\sqrt{p}} e^{-(p^2/4)}$$

$$\Rightarrow \qquad \bar{y} = \frac{1}{p^2} + c, \text{ where } c \text{ is a constant.}$$

c must vanish if $\bar{y}$ is a transform since $\bar{y} \to 0$ as $p \to \infty$

$$\therefore \qquad \bar{y} = \frac{1}{p^2}$$

Taking Inverse Laplace transform, we get

$$y = L^{-1}\left(\frac{1}{p^2}\right) = t$$

which is the required solution.

4. Solution of integral equations. An equation in which an unknown function occurs inside an integral is called an **integral equation.**

Thus an equation of the form,

$$Y(t) = F(t) + \int_a^b Y(u)\, K(u, t)\, du \qquad ...(1)$$

in which $F(t)$ and $K(u, t)$ are known functions and $Y(t)$ is the unknown function is an integral equation. Here a and b are either constants or functions of t.

The function $K(u, t)$ is often called the kernel of the integral equation.

If a and b are constants, eqn. (1) is called **Fredholm integral equation.** If a is a constant while $b = t$, it is called a **Volterra integral equation.**

A special integral equation of convolution type is

$$\boxed{Y(t) = F(t) + \int_0^t Y(u) \,.\, G(t - u)\, du}$$

The Laplace transform is an excellent tool for solving such integral equations of convolution type. The method is illustrated as follows :

Example 1. *Solve the integral equation*

$$y(t) = t^2 + \int_0^t y(u) \,.\, \sin (t - u)\, du.$$

Sol. We have

$$y(t) = t^2 + y(t) * \sin t \qquad ...(1)$$

Let $L\{y(t)\} = \bar{y}(p)$ then taking Laplace transform and using convolution theorem, we find that

$$\bar{y} = \frac{2}{p^3} + \bar{y} \,.\, \frac{1}{p^2 + 1}$$

$$\Rightarrow \quad \bar{y}\left(1 - \frac{1}{p^2 + 1}\right) = \frac{2}{p^3} \quad \Rightarrow \quad \bar{y}\left(\frac{p^2}{p^2 + 1}\right) = \frac{2}{p^3}$$

$$\Rightarrow \qquad \bar{y} = \frac{2(p^2+1)}{p^5} = \frac{2}{p^3} + \frac{2}{p^5} \qquad \text{...(2)}$$

Taking Inverse Laplace transform, we get

$$y = t^2 + \frac{t^4}{12}.$$

Example 23. *A function f (t) obeys the equation*

$$f(t) + 2\int_0^t f(t)\,dt = \cosh 2t$$

Find the Laplace transform of f(t). [U.P.T.U. 2006]

Sol. Taking the Laplace transform of the given equation,

We have $\mathrm{L}\{f(t)\} + 2\mathrm{L}\left(\int_0^t f(t)\,dt\right) = \mathrm{L}\,(\cosh 2t)$

$$\Rightarrow \qquad \bar{f}(p) + \frac{2}{p}\bar{f}(p) = \frac{p}{p^2-4} \quad \text{where } \bar{f}(p) = \mathrm{L}\{f(t)\}$$

$$\Rightarrow \qquad \left(\frac{p+2}{p}\right)\bar{f}(p) = \frac{p}{p^2-4}$$

$$\Rightarrow \qquad \bar{f}(p) = \frac{p^2}{(p+2)(p^2-4)} = \frac{p^2}{(p+2)^2(p-2)}$$

or,

$$\mathrm{L}\{f(t)\} = \frac{p^2}{(p+2)^2(p-2)}$$

Example 24. *Solve for y(t) the equation* $y(t) = 1 + \int_0^t y(\tau)\cos(t-\tau)\,d\tau$. (U.P.T.U. 2007)

Sol. We have the equation

$$y(t) = 1 + (y(t) * \cos t) \qquad \text{...(1)}$$

Taking Laplace transform on both sides of eqn. (1), we get

$$\bar{y} = \frac{1}{p} + \bar{y}\,.\,\frac{p}{p^2+1} \qquad | \text{ where } \mathrm{L}(y) = \bar{y}$$

$$\Rightarrow \qquad \bar{y}\left(1 - \frac{p}{p^2+1}\right) = \frac{1}{p}$$

$$\Rightarrow \qquad \bar{y} = \frac{p^2+1}{p^2-p+1} = \frac{1}{p} + \frac{1}{p^2-p+1}$$

$$= \frac{1}{p} + \frac{1}{\left(p-\frac{1}{2}\right)^2 + \frac{3}{4}} \qquad \text{...(2)}$$

Taking inverse Laplace transform on both sides of (2), we get

$$y = 1 + e^{t/2}\,\mathrm{L}^{-1}\left(\frac{1}{p^2+3/4}\right)$$

$$\Rightarrow \qquad y = 1 + \frac{2}{\sqrt{3}}e^{t/2}\sin\frac{\sqrt{3}}{2}t.$$

TEST YOUR KNOWLEDGE

Solve the following equations by Laplace transform (1 – 17) :

1. $(D^2 - 2D + 2)x = 0$, $x = Dx = 1$ at $t = 0$

2. $(D^2 - 2D + 1)\,x = e^t$; $x = 2$, $Dx = -1$ at $t = 0$.

3. $y'' + 4y' + 3y = e^{-t}$, $y(0) = y'(0) = 1$.

4. $x'' - 3x' + 2x = 1 - e^{2t}$, $x(0) = 1$, $x'(0) = 0$.

5. $y'' + y' - 2y = t$, $y(0) = 1$, $y'(0) = 0$.

6. $(D^2 - D - 2)x = 20 \sin 2t$, $x(0) = -1$, $x'(0) = 2$.

7. $\dfrac{d^2x}{dt^2} + 9x = \sin 2t$, $x(0) = 1$, $x'(0) = 0$. [*G.B.T.U. (C.O.) 2011*]

8. (*i*) $\dfrac{d^2y}{dx^2} + n^2y = a \sin (nx + 2)$, given: $y(0) = 0$ and $y'(0) = 0$. [*G.B.T.U. (C.O.) 2010*]

(*ii*) $\dfrac{d^2y}{dt^2} + 9y = \sin 3t$, given: $y = 0$, $\dfrac{dy}{dt} = 0$ at $t = 0$ (*M.T.U. 2012*)

9. $(D^3 - D^2 + 4D - 4)x = 68\, e^t \sin 2t$; $x = 1$, $Dx = -19$, $D^2x = -37$ at $t = 0$.

10. $y'' + y = e^{-2t} \sin t$, $y(0) = 0$, $y'(0) = 0$.

11. $\dfrac{d^2x}{dt^2} + 6\dfrac{dx}{dt} + 8x = e^{-3t} - e^{-5t}$; $x(0) = 0$, $x'(0) = 0$ [*U.P.T.U. (C.O.) 2009*]

12. (*i*) $\dfrac{d^2y}{dt^2} + \dfrac{dy}{dt} - 2y = 3 \cos 3t - 11 \sin 3t$ given that $y(0) = 0$ and $y'(0) = 6$.

(*ii*) $y'' + 3y' + 2y = t\, e^{-t}$; $y(0) = 1$, $y'(0) = 0$ (*G.B.T.U. 2012*)

13. (*i*) $y'' + 2y' + y = t\, e^{-t}$; $y(0) = 1$, $y'(0) = 2$ [*M.T.U. (SUM) 2011*]

(*ii*) $y'' - 8y' + 15y = 9te^{2t}$; $y(0) = 5$, $y'(0) = 10$.

14. $(D^3 + D)x = 2$, $x = 3$, $Dx = 1$, $D^2x = -2$ at $t = 0$.

15. $(D^4 - 16)y = 30 \sin t$; $y(0) = 0$, $y'(0) = 2$, $y''(\pi) = 0$, $y'''(\pi) = -18$

16. $(D^3 - D^2 - D + 1)y = 8te^{-t}$; $y(0) = 0$, $y'(0) = 1$, $y''(0) = 0$.

17. $y'' + y = \sin t \sin 2t$; $y(0) = 1$, $y'(0) = 0$.

18. (*i*) $\dfrac{d^2x}{dt^2} + 3\dfrac{dx}{dt} + 2x = r(t)$ where, $r(t) = \begin{cases} e^t, & 0 < t < 2 \\ 0, & t > 2 \end{cases}$

and $x(0) = 1$, $x'(0) = -2$ [*G.B.T.U.(C.O.) 2010*]

(*ii*) $\dfrac{d^2y}{dt^2} + 9y = r(t)$ with initial conditions $y(0) = 0$ and $y'(0) = 4$ where $r(t) = \begin{cases} 8 \sin t, & 0 < t < \pi \\ 0, & t > \pi \end{cases}$

(*G.B.T.U. 2011*)

19. A particle moves in a line so that its displacement x from a fixed point 0 at any time t, is given by

$$\frac{d^2x}{dt^2} + 4\frac{dx}{dt} + 5x = 80 \sin 5t.$$

Using Laplace transform, find its displacement at any time t if initially particle is at rest at $x = 0$.

[*U.P.T.U. (C.O.) 2009*]

20. An alternating e.m.f. $E \sin \omega t$ is applied to circuit with an inductance L and a capacitance C in series. Show that the current in the circuit is

$$\frac{E\omega}{(n^2 - \omega^2)\,L} (\cos \omega t - \cos nt) \quad \text{where } n^2 = \frac{1}{LC}.$$ (*G.B.T.U. 2010*)

21. Constant voltage E is applied at $t = 0$ to a circuit with an inductance L, capacitance C and resistance R. Find the current I at time t, if the initial current and charge are zero.

Solve the following simultaneous equations by using Laplace transform (22–27) :

22. $\frac{dx}{dt} + y = 0$; $\frac{dy}{dt} - x = 0$ under the conditions $x(0) = 1$, $y(0) = 0$.

23. $\frac{dx}{dt} + \frac{dy}{dt} + x + y = 1$, $\frac{dy}{dt} = 2x + y$; $x(0) = 0$, $y(0) = 1$ [*M.T.U. (SUM) 2011*]

24. $D^2x + y = -5 \cos 2t$, $D^2y + x = 5 \cos 2t$, where $x(0) = x'(0) = y'(0) = 1$ and $y(0) = -1$.

25. $2\frac{dx}{dt} + \frac{dy}{dt} - x - y = e^{-t}$, $\frac{dx}{dt} + \frac{dy}{dt} + 2x + y = e^{t}$; $y(0) = 1$, $x(0) = 2$.

26. $\frac{dx}{dt} - 2x + 3y = 0$, $\frac{dy}{dt} + 2x - y = 0$ given that $x(0) = 8$ and $y(0) = 3$.

27. $(D - 2)x - (D + 1)y = 6e^{3t}$

$(2D - 3)x + (D - 3)y = 6e^{3t}$; Given : $x = 3$, $y = 0$ when $t = 0$.

28. (*i*) The currents i_1 and i_2 in mesh are given by the differential equations :

$$\frac{di_1}{dt} - \omega i_2 = a \cos pt, \quad \frac{di_2}{dt} + \omega i_1 = a \sin pt.$$

Find the currents i_1 and i_2 by Laplace transform, if $i_1 = i_2 = 0$ at $t = 0$.

(*ii*) A mechanical system, with two degrees of freedom, satisfies the equations :

$$2\frac{d^2x}{dt^2} + 3\frac{dy}{dt} = 4, \quad 2\frac{d^2y}{dt^2} - 3\frac{dx}{dt} = 0.$$

Use Laplace transform to determine x and y at any instant, given that x, y, $\frac{dx}{dt}$, $\frac{dy}{dt}$ all vanish at $t = 0$.

29. Solve the following integral equations :

(*i*) $\int_0^t \frac{y(u)}{\sqrt{t-u}}\, du = 1 + t + t^2$

(*ii*) $\int_0^t y(u) \, . \, y(t-u)\, du = 16 \sin 4t$.

(*iii*) $y(t) = e^{-t} - 2\int_0^t y(u) \, . \cos (t-u)\, du$

(*iv*) $y(t) = 1 - \sinh t + \int_0^t (1+u)\, y(t-u)\, du$ [*G.B.T.U. (C.O.) 2011*]

30. Solve the differential equation using Laplace transform method :

$$\frac{\partial y}{\partial t} = 3\frac{\partial^2 y}{\partial x^2} \text{ where } y\left(\frac{\pi}{2}, t\right) = 0, \left(\frac{\partial y}{\partial x}\right)_{x=0} = 0 \quad \text{and} \quad y(x, 0) = 30 \cos 5x.$$

Answers

1. $x = e^t \cos t$

2. $x = (2 - 3t + \frac{1}{2}t^2)e^t$

3. $y = \frac{7}{4}e^{-t} - \frac{3}{4}e^{-3t} - \frac{1}{2}te^{-t}$

4. $x = \frac{1}{2} + (\frac{1}{2} - t)\, e^{2t}$

5. $y = e^t + \frac{1}{4}(e^{-2t} - 1) - \frac{1}{2}t$

6. $x = 2e^{2t} - 4e^{-t} + \cos 2t - 3 \sin 2t$

7. $x = \cos 3t + \frac{1}{5} \sin 2t - \frac{2}{15} \sin 3t$

8. (*i*) $y = \frac{a}{2n^2}$ $[\cos 2 \sin nx - nx \cos (nx + 2)]$ (*ii*) $y = \frac{1}{18}(\sin 3t - 3t \cos 3t)$

9. $x = \frac{1}{5}(e^t + 14 \cos 2t - 3 \sin 2t) - 2e^t (\cos 2t + 4 \sin 2t)$

10. $y = \frac{1}{8}(\sin t - \cos t) + \frac{e^{-2t}}{8}(\sin t + \cos t)$

11. $x = \frac{1}{3}(e^{-2t} - e^{-5t}) - e^{-3t} + e^{-4t}$

12. (*i*) $y = e^t - e^{-2t} + \sin 3t$ (*ii*) $y = 3e^{-t} - 2e^{-2t} + e^{-t}\left(\frac{t^2}{2} - t\right)$

13. (*i*) $y = e^{-t}\left(1 + 3t + \frac{t^3}{6}\right)$ (*ii*) $y = 4e^{2t} + 3t\,e^{2t} + 3e^{3t} - 2e^{5t}$

14. $x = 1 + 2t + 2\cos t - \sin t$

15. $y = 2(\sin 2t - \sin t)$

16. $y = e^{-t}(1 + 2t + t^2) - e^t(1 - t)$

17. $y = \frac{15}{16}\cos t + \frac{t}{4}\sin t + \frac{1}{16}\cos 3t$

18. (*i*) $x = \frac{4}{3}e^{-2t} + \frac{1}{6}e^t[1 - u(t-2)] - \frac{1}{2}e^{-t} + \frac{1}{2}e^{4-t}\,u(t-2) - \frac{1}{3}e^{6-2t}\,u(t-2)$

(*ii*) $y = \sin 3t + \sin t + \left[\sin(t - \pi) - \frac{1}{3}\sin 3(t - \pi)\right]u(t - \pi)$

19. $x = e^{-2t}(2\cos t + 14\sin t) - 2\cos 5t - 2\sin 5t$

21. $I = \frac{E}{R}(1 - e^{-Rt/L})$

22. $x = \cos t,\ y = \sin t$

23. $x = e^{-t} - 1,\ y = 2 - e^{-t}$

24. $x = \sin t + \cos 2t,\ y = \sin t - \cos 2t$

25. $x = 2\cos t + 8\sin t,\ y = \cos t - 13\sin t + \sinh t$

26. $x = 5e^{-t} + 3e^{4t},\ y = 5e^{-t} - 2e^{4t}$

27. $y = \sinh t + \cosh t - e^{-3t} - te^t$; $x = e^t + 2t\,e^t + 2e^{3t}$.

28. (*i*) $i_1 = \frac{a}{p + \omega}(\sin \omega t + \sin pt),\ i_2 = \frac{a}{p + \omega}(\cos \omega t - \cos pt)$

(*ii*) $x = \frac{8}{9}\left(1 - \cos\frac{3}{2}t\right),\ y = \frac{8}{9}\left(\frac{3}{2}t - \sin\frac{3}{2}t\right)$

29. (*i*) $y = \frac{t^{-1/2}}{3\pi}(3 + 6t + 8t^2)$ (*ii*) $y = \pm 8J_0(4t)$ (*iii*) $y = e^{-t}(1 - t)^2$

(*iv*) $y(t) = \cosh t$

30. $y(x, t) = 30\,e^{-75t}\cos 5x$.

ASSIGNMENT-III

(2 Marks Questions for Section–A)

1. Find the Laplace transform of $f(t) = t^4 e^{2t}$. (*G.B.T.U. 2012*)
2. Find the function whose Laplace transform is $\frac{e^{-\pi p}}{p^2 + 2}$. (*G.B.T.U. 2012*)
3. State the conditions for the existence of Laplace transform. (*M.T.U. 2012*)
4. State convolution theorem. (*M.T.U. 2012*)
5. Evaluate: $L^{-1}\left\{\frac{1}{(p + a)^2}\right\}$
6. Evaluate: $L(te^{at}\sin at)$
7. Evaluate: $L(te^{-t}\cosh 2t)$
8. Evaluate: $L\,[t\,u(t - 2)]$

9. Evaluate: $L^{-1}\left[\frac{1}{p(p^2+1)}\right]$.

10. Evaluate: $L^{-1}\left(\frac{e^{-4p}}{p^3}\right)$.

11. Evaluate: $L^{-1}\left(\frac{e^{-2p}-e^{-3p}}{p}\right)$.

12. Find the inverse Laplace transform of 1.

13. Find $L^{-1}\left(\frac{\lambda e^{-bp}}{p^2+\lambda^2}\right)$.

14. Find $L\left\{\frac{\delta(t-\pi)}{t}\right\}$.

15. Find the Laplace of transform of

$$F(t) = \left.\begin{matrix} 1, & 0 \le t < 2 \\ -1, & 2 \le t < 4 \end{matrix}\right\} ; \ F(t+4) = F(t)$$

16. Find $L^{-1}\left[\log\left(\frac{p+1}{p-1}\right)\right]$ *(U.P.T.U. 2009)*

17. Find $L^{-1}\left(\frac{e^{-p}}{p^2}\right)$.

18. Find $L^{-1}\left[\frac{p^2}{(p^2+4)^2}\right]$.

19. Find $L\,[t^2\, u\,(t-3)]$

20. Find $L^{-1}\left(\frac{1}{p^{3/2}}\right)$ *(M.T.U. 2011)*

21. If $L\,[F(t)] = \frac{e^{-1/p}}{p}$ then find $L\,[e^{-t}\, F(3t)]$ *(M.T.U. 2011)*

22. Find the Laplace transform of $u(t-a)$ *[G.B.T.U. (SUM) 2010]*

23. Find $L^{-1}\left[\frac{1}{(p+2)^2}\right]$.

24. Using Laplace transform, evaluate: $\int_0^\infty e^{-2t}\cos 3t\, dt$

25. Find $L^{-1}\left(\frac{1}{p^2+4p+13}\right)$.

26. Find $L^{-1}\left[\frac{p}{(2p+3)^2}\right]$.

27. Find $L\,(e^{2t}\cos 2t)$.

28. Find $L^{-1}\left[\frac{1}{(p+3)^5}\right]$.

29. Find the Laplace transform of $\int_0^t\int_0^t\int_0^t \cos au\, du\, du\, du$ *[U.P.T.U. (SUM) 2009]*

30. Find $L^{-1}\left(\frac{2p+1}{p^2-4}\right)$. *[U.P.T.U. (SUM) 2009]*

31. Find $L^{-1}\,[\cot^{-1}(1+p)]$.

32. Find $L^{-1}\left[\frac{1}{(p-2)(p^2+1)}\right]$.

33. Find $L^{-1}\left[\frac{3p+1}{(p-1)(p^2+1)}\right]$.

34. Find $L^{-1}\left[\dfrac{2}{(p-1)(p-2)}\right]$. (G.B.T.U. 2011)

35. Find $L^{-1}\left(\dfrac{1}{\sqrt{p}}\right)$ [M.T.U. (SUM) 2011]

36. Find $L(e^{2t-3})$ [M.T.U. (SUM) 2011]

37. Find $L(t^3 e^{-3t})$ [G.B.T.U. (SUM) 2010]

38. Find the Laplace transform of $F(t) = \left.\begin{matrix} 0, & 0 < t < 5 \\ t-3, & t > 5 \end{matrix}\right\}$.

Answers

1. $\dfrac{24}{(p-2)^5}$

2. $\dfrac{1}{\sqrt{2}} \sin \sqrt{2}\,(t - \pi)\; u(t - \pi)$

5. te^{-at}

6. $\dfrac{2a\,(p-a)}{[(p-a)^2 + a^2]^2}$

7. $\dfrac{p^2 + 2p + 5}{(p^2 + 2p - 3)^2}$

8. $\left(\dfrac{1}{p^2} + \dfrac{2}{p}\right) e^{-2p}$

9. $1 - \cos t$

10. $\dfrac{(t-4)^2}{2} u(t-4)$

11. $F(t) = \left.\begin{matrix} 1, & 2 < t < 3 \\ 0, & \text{otherwise} \end{matrix}\right\}$

12. $\delta(t)$

13. $\sin \lambda\,(t - b)\; u(t - b)$

14. $\dfrac{e^{-p\pi}}{\pi}$

15. $\dfrac{1 - e^{-2p}}{p(1 + e^{-2p})}$

16. $\dfrac{2}{t} \sinh t$

17. $(t - 1)\; u_1(t)$

18. $\dfrac{1}{4} \sin 2t + \dfrac{t}{2} \cos 2t$

19. $e^{-3p}\left(\dfrac{2}{p^3} + \dfrac{6}{p^2} + \dfrac{9}{p}\right)$

20. $2\sqrt{\dfrac{t}{\pi}}$

21. $\dfrac{1}{p+1} e^{-3/(p+1)}$

22. $\dfrac{e^{-ap}}{p}$

23. $t\, e^{-2t}$

24. $\dfrac{2}{13}$

25. $\dfrac{1}{3} e^{-2t} \sin 3t$

26. $\dfrac{1}{8}(2 - 3t)\, e^{-3t/2}$

27. $\dfrac{p-2}{p^2 - 4p + 8}$

28. $e^{-3t}\, \dfrac{t^4}{24}$

29. $\dfrac{1}{p^2\,(p^2 + a^2)}$

30. $2 \cosh 2t + \dfrac{1}{2} \sinh 2t$

31. $\dfrac{e^{-t} \sin t}{t}$

32. $\dfrac{1}{5} e^{2t} - \dfrac{1}{5} \cos t - \dfrac{2}{5} \sin t$

33. $e^t - 2 \cos t + \sin t$

34. $2(e^{2t} - e^t)$

35. $\dfrac{1}{\sqrt{\pi t}}$

36. $\dfrac{e^{-3}}{p-2}$

37. $\dfrac{6}{(p+3)^4}$

38. $e^{-5p}\left(\dfrac{1}{p^2} + \dfrac{2}{p}\right)$

UNIT 4

Fourier Series and Partial Differential Equations

4.1. PERIODIC FUNCTIONS

A function $f(x)$ which satisfies the relation $f(x + T) = f(x)$ for all real x and some fixed T is called a periodic function. The *smallest positive number* T, for which this relation holds, is called the **period** of $f(x)$.

If T is the period of $f(x)$, then $f(x) = f(x + T) = f(x + 2T) = ... = f(x + nT) = ...$

Also $f(x) = f(x - T) = f(x - 2T) = ... = f(x - nT) = ...$

$\therefore \; f(x) = f(x \pm nT)$, where n is a positive integer.

Thus, $f(x)$ repeats itself after periods of T.

For example, sin x, cos x, sec x and cosec x are periodic functions with period 2π.

Since $$\tan(\theta + \pi) = \frac{\sin(\pi + \theta)}{\cos(\pi + \theta)} = \frac{-\sin\theta}{-\cos\theta} = \tan\theta$$

and $$\cot(\theta + \pi) = \frac{\cos(\pi + \theta)}{\sin(\pi + \theta)} = \frac{-\cos\theta}{-\sin\theta} = \cot\theta.$$

Therefore tan θ and cot θ are periodic functions with period π.

The functions sin nx and cos nx are periodic with period $\frac{2\pi}{n}$.

The sum of a number of periodic functions is also periodic. If T_1 and T_2 are the periods of $f(x)$ and $g(x)$, then the period of $a\,f(x) + b\,g(x)$ is the least common multiple of T_1 and T_2.

For example, cos x, cos $2x$, cos $3x$ are periodic functions with periods 2π, π and $\frac{2\pi}{3}$ respectively.

$\therefore \; f(x) = \cos x + \frac{1}{2}\cos 2x + \frac{1}{3}\cos 3x$ is also periodic with period 2π, the L.C.M. of 2π, π and $\frac{2\pi}{3}$.

4.2. FOURIER SERIES

Expansion of a function $f(x)$ in a series of sines and cosines of multiples of x was developed by French Mathematician and physicist Jacques Fourier.

We have seen how a function can be expanded inpowers of x by Maclaurin's theorem but that expansion was possible only when the function and its derivatives are continuous. A need arises to expand functions which have discontinuities in their values or derivatives.

By Fourier series, we can expand both type of functions under certain conditions as an infinite series of sines and cosines of x and its integral multiples.

Fourier series for the function $f(x)$ in the interval $c < x < c + 2\pi$ is given by

$$f(x) = \frac{a_0}{2} + \sum_{n=1}^{\infty} a_n \cos nx + \sum_{n=1}^{\infty} b_n \sin nx$$

where
$$a_0 = \frac{1}{\pi}\int_c^{c+2\pi} f(x)\, dx$$
$$a_n = \frac{1}{\pi}\int_c^{c+2\pi} f(x) \cos nx\, dx$$
$$b_n = \frac{1}{\pi}\int_c^{c+2\pi} f(x) \sin nx\, dx$$

Above formulae are also called **Euler's formulae.** Constants a_0, a_n and b_n are called **Fourier coefficients** of $f(x)$.

Remark. To write $\frac{a_0}{2}$ instead of a_0 is a conventional device to be able to get more symmetric formulae for the coefficients.

Note. To determine a_0, a_n and b_n, we shall need the following results : (m and n are integers)

(*i*) $\int_c^{c+2\pi} \sin nx\, dx = \left(\frac{-\cos nx}{n}\right)_c^{c+2\pi} = 0, n \neq 0$; $\int_c^{c+2\pi} \cos nx\, dx = \left(\frac{\sin nx}{n}\right)_c^{c+2\pi} = 0, n \neq 0$

(*ii*) $\int_c^{c+2\pi} \sin mx \cos nx\, dx = 0, m \neq n$ (*iii*) $\int_c^{c+2\pi} \cos mx \cos nx\, dx = 0, m \neq n$

(*iv*) $\int_c^{c+2\pi} \sin mx \sin nx\, dx = 0, m \neq n$

(*v*) $\int_c^{c+2\pi} \cos^2 nx\, dx = \pi, n \neq 0$; $\int_c^{c+2\pi} \sin^2 nx\, dx = \pi, n \neq 0$

(*vi*) $\int_c^{c+2\pi} \sin nx \cos nx\, dx = \frac{1}{2}\int_c^{c+2\pi} \sin 2nx\, dx = 0, n \neq 0$

(*vii*) $\int e^{ax} \sin bx\, dx = \frac{e^{ax}}{a^2 + b^2}(a \sin bx - b \cos bx) + c$

(*viii*) $\int e^{ax} \cos bx\, dx = \frac{e^{ax}}{a^2 + b^2}(a \cos bx + b \sin bx) + c$

(*ix*) To integrate the product of two functions, one of which is a power of x, we apply the *generalised rule of integration by parts.* If dashes denote differentiation and suffixes denote integration w.r.t. x, the rule can be stated as follows :

$$\int uv\, dx = uv_1 - u' v_2 + u'' v_3 - u''' v_4 + \ldots\ldots, \text{ where } u \text{ and } v \text{ are functions of } x.$$

i.e., Integral of the product of two functions

= I function × integral of II – go on differentiating I, integrating II, signs alternately +ve and –ve.

[Simplification should be done only when the integration is over.]

e.g.,
$$\int x^2 \cos nx \, dx = x^2\left(\frac{\sin nx}{n}\right) - 2x\left(\frac{-\cos nx}{n^2}\right) + 2\left(-\frac{\sin nx}{n^3}\right)$$
$$= \frac{x^2}{n}\sin nx + \frac{2x}{n^2}\cos nx - \frac{2}{n^3}\sin nx.$$

(*x*) $\sin n\pi = 0$ and $\cos n\pi = (-1)^n$

$$\sin\left(n+\frac{1}{2}\right)\pi = (-1)^n \text{ and } \cos\left(n+\frac{1}{2}\right)\pi = 0,$$ where n is an integer.

(*xi*) **Even and Odd Functions** [U.P.T.U. 2009 ; U.P.T.U. (SUM) 2009]

A function $f(x)$ is said to be *even* if $f(-x) = f(x)$ *e.g.,* x^2, $\cos x$, $\sin^2 x$ are even functions.

The graph of an even function is symmetrical about the y-axis.

Here y-axis is a mirror for the reflection of the curve.

$$\int_{-\pi}^{\pi} f(x)\, dx = 2\int_0^{\pi} f(x)\, dx$$

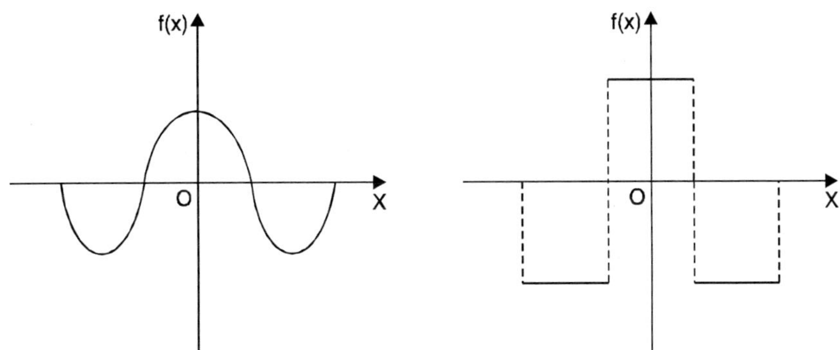

Graphs of even functions

A function $f(x)$ is said to be *odd* if $f(-x) = -f(x)$ *e.g.,* x^3, $\sin x$, $\tan^3 x$ are odd functions.

The graph of an odd function is symmetrical about the origin.

$$\int_{-\pi}^{\pi} f(x)\, dx = 0$$

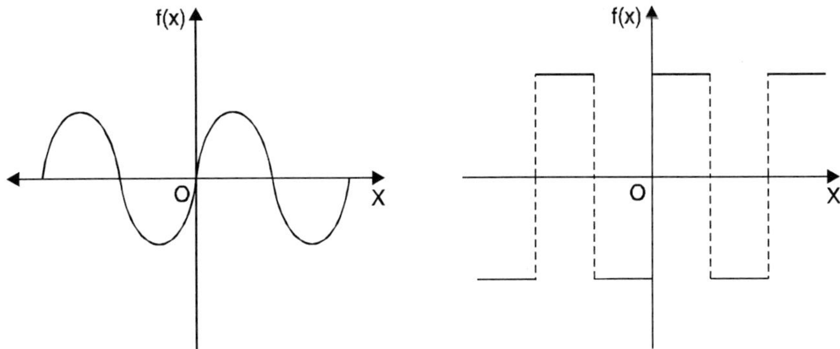

Graphs of odd functions

The product of two even functions or two odd functions is an even function while the product of an even function and an odd function is an odd function.

4.3. EULER'S FORMULAE

The Fourier series for the function $f(x)$ in the interval $c < x < c + 2\pi$ is given by

$$f(x) = \frac{a_0}{2} + \sum_{n=1}^{\infty} a_n \cos nx + \sum_{n=1}^{\infty} b_n \sin nx \qquad \ldots(1)$$

In finding the coefficients a_0, a_n and b_n, we assume that the series on the right hand side of eqn. (1) is uniformly convergent for $c < x < c + 2\pi$ and it can be integrated term by term in the given interval.

To find a_0, integrate both sides of (1) w.r.t. x between the limits c to $c + 2\pi$.

$$\int_c^{c+2\pi} f(x)\, dx = \frac{a_0}{2}\int_c^{c+2\pi} dx + \int_c^{c+2\pi}\left(\sum_{n=1}^{\infty} a_n \cos nx\right) dx + \int_c^{c+2\pi}\left(\sum_{n=1}^{\infty} b_n \sin nx\right) dx$$

$$= \frac{a_0}{2}(c + 2\pi - c) + 0 + 0 \qquad \text{[By formula } (i) \text{ above]}$$

$$= a_0\pi$$

$$\therefore \qquad \boxed{a_0 = \frac{1}{\pi}\int_c^{c+2\pi} f(x)\, dx}$$

To find a_n, multiply both sides of (1) by $\cos nx$ and integrate w.r.t. x between the limits c to $c + 2\pi$.

$$\int_c^{c+2\pi} f(x)\cos nx\, dx = \frac{a_0}{2}\int_c^{c+2\pi} \cos nx\, dx + \int_c^{c+2\pi}\left(\sum_{n=1}^{\infty} a_n \cos nx\right)\cos nx\, dx$$

$$+ \int_c^{c+2\pi}\left(\sum_{n=1}^{\infty} b_n \sin nx\right)\cos nx\, dx$$

$$= 0 + a_n\pi + 0 \qquad \text{[By formulae } (i), (v) \text{ and } (vi)]$$

$$= a_n\pi$$

$$\therefore \qquad \boxed{a_n = \frac{1}{\pi}\int_c^{c+2\pi} f(x)\cos nx\, dx}$$

To find b_n, multiply both sides of (1) by $\sin nx$ and integrate w.r.t. x between the limits c to $c + 2\pi$.

$$\int_c^{c+2\pi} f(x)\sin nx\, dx = \frac{a_0}{2}\int_c^{c+2\pi} \sin nx\, dx + \int_c^{c+2\pi}\left(\sum_{n=1}^{\infty} a_n \cos nx\right)\sin nx\, dx$$

$$+ \int_c^{c+2\pi}\left(\sum_{n=1}^{\infty} b_n \sin nx\right)\sin nx\, dx$$

$$= 0 + 0 + b_n\pi \qquad \text{[By formulae } (i), (vi) \text{ and } (v)]$$

$$= b_n\pi$$

$\therefore$ $$b_n = \frac{1}{\pi}\int_c^{c+2\pi} f(x)\sin nx\, dx$$

These values of a_0, a_n and b_n are called **Euler's formulae.**

Cor. 1. *If c = 0, the interval becomes $0 < x < 2\pi$, and the formulae reduce to*

$$a_0 = \frac{1}{\pi}\int_0^{2\pi} f(x)\, dx\,;\quad a_n = \frac{1}{\pi}\int_0^{2\pi} f(x)\cos nx\, dx\,;\quad b_n = \frac{1}{\pi}\int_0^{2\pi} f(x)\sin nx\, dx$$

Cor. 2. *If c = $-\pi$, the interval becomes $-\pi < x < \pi$, and the formulae reduce to*

$$a_0 = \frac{1}{\pi}\int_{-\pi}^{\pi} f(x)\, dx\,; a_n = \frac{1}{\pi}\int_{-\pi}^{\pi} f(x)\cos nx\, dx\,; b_n = \frac{1}{\pi}\int_{-\pi}^{\pi} f(x)\sin nx\, dx$$

Cor. 3. When *f(x)* is an odd function $a_0 = \frac{1}{\pi}\int_{-\pi}^{\pi} f(x)\, dx = 0$

Since cos nx is an even function, therefore, $f(x)$ cos nx is an odd function.

$\therefore$ $$a_n = \frac{1}{\pi}\int_{-\pi}^{\pi} f(x)\cos nx\, dx = 0$$

Since sin nx is an odd function, therefore, $f(x)$ sin nx is an even function.

$\therefore$ $$b_n = \frac{1}{\pi}\int_{-\pi}^{\pi} f(x)\sin nx\, dx = \frac{2}{\pi}\int_0^{\pi} f(x)\sin nx\, dx$$

Hence, **if a periodic function *f(x)* is odd, its Fourier expansion contains only sine terms.**

i.e., $$f(x) = \sum_{n=1}^{\infty} b_n \sin nx, \quad \text{where} \quad b_n = \frac{2}{\pi}\int_0^{\pi} f(x)\sin nx\, dx$$

Cor. 4. When *f(x)* is an even function $a_0 = \frac{1}{\pi}\int_{-\pi}^{\pi} f(x)\, dx = \frac{2}{\pi}\int_0^{\pi} f(x)\, dx$

Since cos nx is an even function, therefore, $f(x)$ cos nx is an even function.

$\therefore$ $$a_n = \frac{1}{\pi}\int_{-\pi}^{\pi} f(x)\cos nx\, dx = \frac{2}{\pi}\int_0^{\pi} f(x)\cos nx\, dx$$

Since sin nx is an odd function, therefore, $f(x)$ sin nx is an odd function.

$\therefore$ $$b_n = \frac{1}{\pi}\int_{-\pi}^{\pi} f(x)\sin nx\, dx = 0$$

Hence, **if a periodic function *f(x)* is even, its Fourier expansion contains only cosine terms.**

i.e., $$f(x) = \frac{a_0}{2} + \sum_{n=1}^{\infty} a_n \cos nx, \text{ where } a_0 = \frac{2}{\pi}\int_0^{\pi} f(x)\, dx \text{ and } a_n = \frac{2}{\pi}\int_0^{\pi} f(x)\cos nx\, dx$$

4.4. DIRICHLET'S CONDITIONS

The sufficient conditions for the uniform convergence of a Fourier series are called Dirichlet's conditions (after Dirichlet, a German mathematician). All the functions that normally arise in engineering problems satisfy these conditions and hence they can be expressed as a Fourier series.

Any function f(x) can be expressed as a Fourier series $\frac{a_0}{2}+\sum_{n=1}^{\infty} a_n \cos nx+\sum_{n=1}^{\infty} b_n \sin nx$

where a_0, a_n, b_n *are constants, provided*

(*i*) *f(x) is periodic, single valued and finite*

(*ii*) *f(x) has a finite number of finite discontinuities in any one period.*

(*iii*) *f(x) has a finite number of maxima and minima.*

When these conditions are satisfied, the Fourier series converges to *f*(*x*) at every point of continuity. At a point of discontinuity, the sum of the series is equal to the mean of the limits on the right and left

i.e., $\frac{1}{2}[f(x+0)+f(x-0)]$

where $f(x+0)$ and $f(x-0)$ denote the limit on the right and the limit on the left respectively.

ILLUSTRATIVE EXAMPLES

Example 1. *Obtain the Fourier series to represent* $f(x)=\frac{1}{4}(\pi-x)^2$ *in the interval* $0 \le x \le 2\pi$. *Hence obtain the following relations :* [U.P.T.U. (SUM) 2008]

(*i*) $\frac{1}{1^2}+\frac{1}{2^2}+\frac{1}{3^2}+\frac{1}{4^2}+\ldots=\frac{\pi^2}{6}$ (*ii*) $\frac{1}{1^2}-\frac{1}{2^2}+\frac{1}{3^2}-\frac{1}{4^2}+\ldots=\frac{\pi^2}{12}$

(*iii*) $\frac{1}{1^2}+\frac{1}{3^2}+\frac{1}{5^2}+\ldots=\frac{\pi^2}{8}$.

Sol. Let $f(x)=\frac{1}{4}(\pi-x)^2=\frac{a_0}{2}+\sum_{n=1}^{\infty} a_n \cos nx+\sum_{n=1}^{\infty} b_n \sin nx$ ...(1)

By Euler's formulae, we have

$$a_0=\frac{1}{\pi}\int_0^{2\pi} f(x)\,dx=\frac{1}{\pi}\int_0^{2\pi}\frac{1}{4}(\pi-x)^2\,dx=\frac{1}{4\pi}\left[\frac{(\pi-x)^3}{-3}\right]_0^{2\pi}=-\frac{1}{12\pi}[-\pi^3-\pi^3]=\frac{\pi^2}{6}$$

$$a_n=\frac{1}{\pi}\int_0^{2\pi} f(x)\cos nx\,dx=\frac{1}{\pi}\int_0^{2\pi}\frac{1}{4}(\pi-x)^2\cos nx\,dx$$

$$=\frac{1}{4\pi}\left[\left\{(\pi-x)^2\frac{\sin nx}{n}\right\}_0^{2\pi}+\int_0^{2\pi}2(\pi-x)\frac{\sin nx}{n}\,dx\right]$$

$$= \frac{1}{4\pi} \cdot \frac{2}{n} \left[\left\{ (\pi - x) \left(\frac{-\cos nx}{n} \right) \right\}_0^{2\pi} - \int_0^{2\pi} (-1) \left(\frac{-\cos nx}{n} \right) dx \right]$$

$$= \frac{-1}{2\pi n^2} (-\pi - \pi) = \frac{1}{n^2} \qquad | \because \cos 2n\pi = 1 \text{ and } \sin 2n\pi = 0, n \in I$$

$$b_n = \frac{1}{\pi} \int_0^{2\pi} f(x) \sin nx \, dx = \frac{1}{\pi} \int_0^{2\pi} \frac{1}{4} (\pi - x)^2 \sin nx \, dx$$

$$= \frac{1}{4\pi} \left[\left\{ (\pi - x)^2 \left(\frac{-\cos nx}{n} \right) \right\}_0^{2\pi} - \int_0^{2\pi} 2(\pi - x) \frac{\cos nx}{n} dx \right]$$

$$= \frac{1}{4\pi} \left[\left(-\frac{\pi^2}{n} + \frac{\pi^2}{n} \right) - \frac{2}{n} \int_0^{2\pi} (\pi - x) \cos nx \, dx \right]$$

$$= -\frac{1}{2\pi n} \left[\left\{ (\pi - x) \frac{\sin nx}{n} \right\}_0^{2\pi} - \int_0^{2\pi} (-1) \frac{\sin nx}{n} dx \right]$$

$$= -\frac{1}{2\pi n^2} \left(\frac{-\cos nx}{n} \right)_0^{2\pi} = 0 \qquad | \because \cos 2n\pi = 1, n \in I \text{ and } \cos 0 = 1$$

$$\therefore \quad f(x) = \frac{\pi^2}{12} + \sum_{n=1}^{\infty} \frac{\cos nx}{n^2} = \frac{\pi^2}{12} + \frac{\cos x}{1^2} + \frac{\cos 2x}{2^2} + \frac{\cos 3x}{3^2} + \ldots\ldots \qquad \ldots(2)$$

(*i*) Putting $x = 0$ in eqn. (2), we get

$$\frac{\pi^2}{4} = \frac{\pi^2}{12} + \left(\frac{1}{1^2} + \frac{1}{2^2} + \frac{1}{3^2} + \frac{1}{4^2} + \ldots \right)$$

$$\Rightarrow \quad \frac{\pi^2}{6} = \frac{1}{1^2} + \frac{1}{2^2} + \frac{1}{3^2} + \frac{1}{4^2} + \ldots \qquad \ldots(3)$$

(*ii*) Putting $x = \pi$ in eqn. (2), we get

$$0 = \frac{\pi^2}{12} + \left[\left(\frac{-1}{1^2} \right) + \frac{1}{2^2} + \left(\frac{-1}{3^2} \right) + \frac{1}{4^2} + \ldots \right]$$

$$\Rightarrow \quad \frac{\pi^2}{12} = \frac{1}{1^2} - \frac{1}{2^2} + \frac{1}{3^2} - \frac{1}{4^2} + \ldots \qquad \ldots(4)$$

(*iii*) Adding equations (3) and (4), we get

$$\frac{\pi^2}{6} + \frac{\pi^2}{12} = 2 \left(\frac{1}{1^2} + \frac{1}{3^2} + \frac{1}{5^2} + \ldots \right)$$

$$\Rightarrow \quad \frac{\pi^2}{4} = 2 \left(\frac{1}{1^2} + \frac{1}{3^2} + \frac{1}{5^2} + \ldots \right)$$

$$\Rightarrow \quad \frac{\pi^2}{8} = \frac{1}{1^2} + \frac{1}{3^2} + \frac{1}{5^2} + \ldots$$

Example 2. *Obtain the Fourier series for $f(x) = e^{-x}$ in the interval $0 < x < 2\pi$.*

Sol. Let $f(x) = e^{-x} = \dfrac{a_0}{2} + \sum_{n=1}^{\infty} a_n \cos nx + \sum_{n=1}^{\infty} b_n \sin nx$

Here,
$$a_0 = \frac{1}{\pi}\int_0^{2\pi} f(x)\,dx = \frac{1}{\pi}\int_0^{2\pi} e^{-x}\,dx = \frac{1}{\pi}\Big[-e^{-x}\Big]_0^{2\pi} = \frac{1-e^{-2\pi}}{\pi}$$

$$a_n = \frac{1}{\pi}\int_0^{2\pi} f(x)\cos nx\,dx = \frac{1}{\pi}\int_0^{2\pi} e^{-x}\cos nx\,dx$$

$$= \frac{1}{\pi}\left[\frac{e^{-x}}{1+n^2}(-\cos nx + n\sin nx)\right]_0^{2\pi} = \frac{1-e^{-2\pi}}{\pi(1+n^2)}$$

$$b_n = \frac{1}{\pi}\int_0^{2\pi} f(x)\sin nx\,dx = \frac{1}{\pi}\int_0^{2\pi} e^{-x}\sin nx\,dx$$

$$= \frac{1}{\pi}\left[\frac{e^{-x}}{1+n^2}(-\sin nx - n\cos nx)\right]_0^{2\pi} = \frac{1-e^{-2\pi}}{\pi}\cdot\frac{n}{1+n^2}$$

$$\therefore \quad e^{-x} = \frac{1-e^{-2\pi}}{2\pi} + \frac{1-e^{-2\pi}}{\pi}\sum_{n=1}^{\infty}\frac{\cos nx}{1+n^2} + \frac{1-e^{-2\pi}}{\pi}\sum_{n=1}^{\infty}\frac{n\sin nx}{1+n^2}.$$

Example 3. *Expand $f(x) = x \sin x$, $0 < x < 2\pi$ as a Fourier series.*

[G.B.T.U. (SUM) 2010]

Sol. Let $f(x) = x\sin x = \dfrac{a_0}{2} + \sum_{n=1}^{\infty} a_n \cos nx + \sum_{n=1}^{\infty} b_n \sin nx$

By Euler's formulae, we have

$$a_0 = \frac{1}{\pi}\int_0^{2\pi} f(x)\,dx = \frac{1}{\pi}\int_0^{2\pi} x\sin x\,dx$$

$$= \frac{1}{\pi}\Big[x(-\cos x) - 1.(-\sin x)\Big]_0^{2\pi} = \frac{1}{\pi}[-2\pi] = -2$$

$$a_n = \frac{1}{\pi}\int_0^{2\pi} f(x)\cos nx\,dx = \frac{1}{\pi}\int_0^{2\pi} x\sin x\cos nx\,dx = \frac{1}{2\pi}\int_0^{2\pi} x(2\cos nx\sin x)\,dx$$

$$= \frac{1}{2\pi}\int_0^{2\pi} x[\sin(n+1)x - \sin(n-1)x]\,dx$$

$$= \frac{1}{2\pi}\left[x\left\{-\frac{\cos(n+1)x}{n+1} + \frac{\cos(n-1)x}{n-1}\right\} - 1.\left\{-\frac{\sin(n+1)x}{(n+1)^2} + \frac{\sin(n-1)x}{(n-1)^2}\right\}\right]_0^{2\pi}$$

$$= \frac{1}{2\pi}\left[2\pi\left\{-\frac{\cos 2(n+1)\pi}{n+1} + \frac{\cos 2(n-1)\pi}{n-1}\right\}\right]$$

$$= -\frac{1}{n+1} + \frac{1}{n-1} = \frac{2}{n^2-1},\ n \neq 1$$

When $n = 1$, we have

$$a_1 = \frac{1}{\pi}\int_0^{2\pi} x \sin x \cos x \, dx = \frac{1}{2\pi}\int_0^{2\pi} x \sin 2x \, dx$$

$$= \frac{1}{2\pi}\left[x\left(-\frac{\cos 2x}{2}\right) - 1.\left(-\frac{\sin 2x}{4}\right)\right]_0^{2\pi} = \frac{1}{2\pi}[-\pi] = -\frac{1}{2}$$

$$b_n = \frac{1}{\pi}\int_0^{2\pi} f(x) \sin nx \, dx = \frac{1}{\pi}\int_0^{2\pi} x \sin x \sin nx \, dx$$

$$= \frac{1}{2\pi}\int_0^{2\pi} x(2 \sin nx \sin x) \, dx = \frac{1}{2\pi}\int_0^{2\pi} x\,[\cos (n-1)\, x - \cos (n+1)\, x] \, dx$$

$$= \frac{1}{2\pi}\left[x\left\{\frac{\sin (n-1)\, x}{n-1} - \frac{\sin (n+1)\, x}{n+1}\right\} - 1.\left\{-\frac{\cos (n-1)\, x}{(n-1)^2} + \frac{\cos (n+1)\, x}{(n+1)^2}\right\}\right]_0^{2\pi}$$

$$= \frac{1}{2\pi}\left[\frac{\cos 2(n-1)\,\pi}{(n-1)^2} - \frac{\cos 2(n+1)\,\pi}{(n+1)^2} - \frac{1}{(n-1)^2} + \frac{1}{(n+1)^2}\right]$$

$$= \frac{1}{2\pi}\left[\frac{1}{(n-1)^2} - \frac{1}{(n+1)^2} - \frac{1}{(n-1)^2} + \frac{1}{(n+1)^2}\right] = 0, \quad n \neq 1$$

When $n = 1$, we have

$$b_1 = \frac{1}{\pi}\int_0^{2\pi} x \sin x \sin x \, dx = \frac{1}{2\pi}\int_0^{2\pi} x(1 - \cos 2x) \, dx$$

$$= \frac{1}{2\pi}\left[x\left(x - \frac{\sin 2x}{2}\right) - 1.\left(\frac{x^2}{2} + \frac{\cos 2x}{4}\right)\right]_0^{2\pi}$$

$$= \frac{1}{2\pi}\left[2\pi(2\pi) - \frac{4\pi^2}{2} - \frac{1}{4} + \frac{1}{4}\right] = \frac{1}{2\pi}(2\pi^2) = \pi$$

$$\therefore\; f(x) = \frac{a_0}{2} + a_1 \cos x + b_1 \sin x + \sum_{n=2}^{\infty} a_n \cos nx + \sum_{n=2}^{\infty} b_n \sin nx$$

$$= -1 - \frac{1}{2}\cos x + \pi \sin x + \sum_{n=2}^{\infty} \frac{2}{n^2 - 1} \cos nx$$

Example 4. *Find the Fourier series to represent e^{ax} in the interval $-\pi < x < \pi$.*

Sol. Let $f(x) = e^{ax} = \dfrac{a_0}{2} + \sum_{n=1}^{\infty} a_n \cos nx + \sum_{n=1}^{\infty} b_n \sin nx$

Here, $$a_0 = \frac{1}{\pi}\int_{-\pi}^{\pi} f(x) \, dx = \frac{1}{\pi}\int_{-\pi}^{\pi} e^{ax} \, dx = \frac{1}{\pi}\left[\frac{e^{ax}}{a}\right]_{-\pi}^{\pi} = \frac{1}{\pi a}(e^{a\pi} - e^{-a\pi}) = \frac{2 \sinh a\pi}{\pi a}$$

$$a_n = \frac{1}{\pi}\int_{-\pi}^{\pi} f(x) \cos nx \, dx = \frac{1}{\pi}\int_{-\pi}^{\pi} e^{ax} \cos nx \, dx$$

$$= \frac{1}{\pi}\left[\frac{e^{ax}}{a^2 + n^2}(a \cos nx + n \sin nx)\right]_{-\pi}^{\pi}$$

$$= \frac{1}{\pi(a^2+n^2)}[ae^{a\pi}\cos n\pi - ae^{-a\pi}\cos n\pi]$$

$$= \frac{a\cos n\pi\,(e^{a\pi}-e^{-a\pi})}{\pi(a^2+n^2)} = \frac{2a(-1)^n \sinh a\pi}{\pi(a^2+n^2)}$$

Similarly, $b_n = \dfrac{2n(-1)^n \sinh a\pi}{\pi(a^2+n^2)}$

$$\therefore \quad e^{ax} = \frac{\sinh a\pi}{a\pi} + \sum_{n=1}^{\infty} \frac{2a(-1)^n \sinh a\pi}{\pi(a^2+n^2)}\cos nx + \sum_{n=1}^{\infty} \frac{2n(-1)^n \sinh a\pi}{\pi(a^2+n^2)}\sin nx$$

Example 5. *Find a Fourier series to represent $x - x^2$ from $x = -\pi$ to $x = \pi$. Hence show that*

$$\frac{1}{1^2} - \frac{1}{2^2} + \frac{1}{3^2} - \frac{1}{4^2} + \ldots\ldots = \frac{\pi^2}{12}.$$ (G.B.T.U. (A.G.) 2012)

Sol. Let $x - x^2 = \dfrac{a_0}{2} + \displaystyle\sum_{n=1}^{\infty} a_n \cos nx + \sum_{n=1}^{\infty} b_n \sin nx$

By Euler's formulae, we have

$$a_0 = \frac{1}{\pi}\int_{-\pi}^{\pi}(x-x^2)\,dx = \frac{1}{\pi}\left[\int_{-\pi}^{\pi} x\,dx - \int_{-\pi}^{\pi} x^2\,dx\right]$$

$$= -\frac{2}{\pi}\int_0^{\pi} x^2\,dx = -\frac{2}{\pi}\left(\frac{x^3}{3}\right)_0^{\pi} = -\frac{2}{3}\pi^2$$

$$a_n = \frac{1}{\pi}\int_{-\pi}^{\pi}(x-x^2)\cos nx\,dx = \frac{1}{\pi}\left[\int_{-\pi}^{\pi} x\cos nx\,dx - \int_{-\pi}^{\pi} x^2\cos nx\,dx\right]$$

$$= -\frac{2}{\pi}\int_0^{\pi} x^2\cos nx\,dx = -\frac{2}{\pi}\left[\left(x^2\frac{\sin nx}{n}\right)_0^{\pi} - \int_0^{\pi} 2x\frac{\sin nx}{n}\,dx\right]$$

$$= \frac{4}{\pi n}\int_0^{\pi} x\sin nx\,dx = \frac{4}{\pi n}\left[\left\{x\left(\frac{-\cos nx}{n}\right)\right\}_0^{\pi} - \int_0^{\pi}\left(\frac{-\cos nx}{n}\right)dx\right]$$

$$= -\frac{4}{\pi n^2}(\pi\cos n\pi) = -\frac{4}{n^2}(-1)^n \qquad \mid \because \cos n\pi = (-1)^n,\ n \in \mathrm{I}$$

$$b_n = \frac{1}{\pi}\int_{-\pi}^{\pi}(x-x^2)\sin nx\,dx = \frac{1}{\pi}\left[\int_{-\pi}^{\pi} x\sin nx\,dx - \int_{-\pi}^{\pi} x^2\sin nx\,dx\right]$$

$$= \frac{2}{\pi}\int_0^{\pi} x\sin nx\,dx = \frac{2}{\pi}\left[\left\{x\left(\frac{-\cos nx}{n}\right)\right\}_0^{\pi} - \int_0^{\pi} 1.\left(\frac{-\cos nx}{n}\right)dx\right]$$

$$= -\frac{2}{n}\cos n\pi = -\frac{2}{n}(-1)^n \qquad \mid \because \sin n\pi = 0,\ n \in \mathrm{I}$$

$$\therefore \quad x - x^2 = -\frac{\pi^2}{3} - 4\sum_{n=1}^{\infty} \frac{(-1)^n}{n^2}\cos nx - 2\sum_{n=1}^{\infty} \frac{(-1)^n}{n}\sin nx$$

$$= -\frac{\pi^2}{3} - 4\left[-\frac{\cos x}{1^2} + \frac{\cos 2x}{2^2} - \frac{\cos 3x}{3^2} + \ldots\ldots\right] - 2\left[\frac{-\sin x}{1} + \frac{\sin 2x}{2} - \frac{\sin 3x}{3} + \ldots\ldots\right]$$

$$= -\frac{\pi^2}{3} + 4\left[\frac{\cos x}{1^2} - \frac{\cos 2x}{2^2} + \frac{\cos 3x}{3^2} - \ldots\ldots\right] + 2\left[\frac{\sin x}{1} - \frac{\sin 2x}{2} + \frac{\sin 3x}{3} - \ldots\ldots\right]$$

Putting $x = 0$, we get

$$0 = -\frac{\pi^2}{3} + 4\left(\frac{1}{1^2} - \frac{1}{2^2} + \frac{1}{3^2} - \frac{1}{4^2} + \ldots\ldots\right)$$

$$\Rightarrow \quad \frac{1}{1^2} - \frac{1}{2^2} + \frac{1}{3^2} - \frac{1}{4^2} + \ldots\ldots = \frac{\pi^2}{12}.$$

Example 6. *Find the Fourier series for the function* $f(x) = x + x^2$, $-\pi < x < \pi$.

[G.B.T.U. (AG) SUM 2010]

Hence show that

(*i*) $\dfrac{\pi^2}{6} = 1 + \dfrac{1}{2^2} + \dfrac{1}{3^2} + \dfrac{1}{4^2} + \ldots$ (U.K.T.U. 2011) (*ii*) $\dfrac{\pi^2}{12} = \dfrac{1}{1^2} - \dfrac{1}{2^2} + \dfrac{1}{3^2} - \dfrac{1}{4^2} + \ldots$

Sol. Let the Fourier series be

$$x + x^2 = \frac{a_0}{2} + \sum_{n=1}^{\infty} a_n \cos nx + \sum_{n=1}^{\infty} b_n \sin nx \quad \ldots(1)$$

Here, $$a_0 = \frac{1}{\pi}\int_{-\pi}^{\pi} (x + x^2)\, dx = \frac{1}{\pi}\left[\int_{-\pi}^{\pi} x\, dx + \int_{-\pi}^{\pi} x^2\, dx\right] = \frac{2}{\pi}\int_0^{\pi} x^2\, dx = \frac{2}{3}\pi^2$$

$$a_n = \frac{1}{\pi}\int_{-\pi}^{\pi} (x + x^2)\cos nx\, dx$$

$$= \frac{1}{\pi}\left[\int_{-\pi}^{\pi} x\cos nx\, dx + \int_{-\pi}^{\pi} x^2 \cos nx\, dx\right] = \frac{2}{\pi}\int_0^{\pi} x^2 \cos nx\, dx$$

$$= \frac{2}{\pi}\left[\left(x^2\frac{\sin nx}{n}\right)_0^{\pi} - \int_0^{\pi} 2x \cdot \frac{\sin nx}{n}\, dx\right] = -\frac{4}{n\pi}\int_0^{\pi} x\sin nx\, dx$$

$$= -\frac{4}{n\pi}\left[\left\{x \cdot \left(\frac{-\cos nx}{n}\right)\right\}_0^{\pi} - \int_0^{\pi} 1 \cdot \left(\frac{-\cos nx}{n}\right) dx\right]$$

$$= -\frac{4}{n\pi}\left(\frac{-\pi}{n}\cos n\pi\right) = \frac{4}{n^2}\cos n\pi = \frac{4}{n^2}(-1)^n$$

$$b_n = \frac{1}{\pi}\int_{-\pi}^{\pi} (x + x^2)\sin nx\, dx = \frac{2}{\pi}\int_0^{\pi} x\sin nx\, dx \quad \Bigg|\because \int_{-\pi}^{\pi} x^2 \sin nx\, dx = 0$$

$$= \frac{2}{\pi}\left(\frac{-\pi}{n}\cos n\pi\right) = -\frac{2}{n}(-1)^n \qquad \text{| as above}$$

$\therefore$ From (1), $x + x^2 = \dfrac{\pi^2}{3} + 4\sum_{n=1}^{\infty} \dfrac{(-1)^n}{n^2}\cos nx - 2\sum_{n=1}^{\infty}\dfrac{(-1)^n}{n}\sin nx$

$$\Rightarrow \quad f(x) = \frac{\pi^2}{3} + 4\left[\frac{-1}{1^2}\cos x + \frac{1}{2^2}\cos 2x - \frac{1}{3^2}\cos 3x + \ldots\right]$$

$$-2\left[\frac{-1}{1}\sin x + \frac{1}{2}\sin 2x - \frac{1}{3}\sin 3x + \ldots\right] \qquad \ldots(2)$$

We observe that the series on the R.H.S. given by eqn. (2) always represents $x + x^2$ for all values of x except the end points $-\pi$ or π.

At the point of discontinuity,

$$f(-\pi) = \frac{1}{2}\,(\text{L.H.L.} + \text{R.H.L.}) = \frac{1}{2}\,[f(-\pi - 0) + f(-\pi + 0)]$$

$$= \frac{1}{2}\,[f(\pi - 0) + f(-\pi + 0)] \qquad \text{| } \because \ f(x) \text{ is periodic with period } 2\pi$$

$$= \frac{1}{2}\,[\pi + \pi^2 + (-\pi) + (-\pi)^2] = \pi^2$$

Putting $x = -\pi$ in eqn. (2), we get

$$\pi^2 = \frac{\pi^2}{3} + 4\left[\frac{1}{1^2} + \frac{1}{2^2} + \frac{1}{3^2} + \frac{1}{4^2} + \ldots\right]$$

$$\Rightarrow \quad \frac{\pi^2}{6} = 1 + \frac{1}{2^2} + \frac{1}{3^2} + \frac{1}{4^2} + \ldots \qquad \ldots(3)$$

Again, putting $x = 0$ in eqn. (2), we get

$$0 = \frac{\pi^2}{3} + 4\left[\frac{-1}{1^2} + \frac{1}{2^2} - \frac{1}{3^2} + \frac{1}{4^2} - \ldots\right]$$

$$\Rightarrow \quad \frac{\pi^2}{12} = \frac{1}{1^2} - \frac{1}{2^2} + \frac{1}{3^2} - \frac{1}{4^2} + \ldots \qquad \ldots(4)$$

Example 7. *Express $f(x) = |\,x\,|$, $-\pi < x < \pi$, as Fourier series. Hence show that*

$$\frac{1}{1^2} + \frac{1}{3^2} + \frac{1}{5^2} + \ldots\ldots = \frac{\pi^2}{8}.$$

Sol. Since $f(-x) = |-x| = |\,x\,| = f(x)$

$\therefore$ $f(x)$ is an even function and hence $b_n = 0$

Let $\qquad f(x) = |\,x\,| = \dfrac{a_0}{2} + \sum_{n=1}^{\infty} a_n \cos nx$

where $\qquad a_0 = \dfrac{2}{\pi}\displaystyle\int_0^{\pi} f(x)\,dx = \dfrac{2}{\pi}\int_0^{\pi} |\,x\,|\,dx = \dfrac{2}{\pi}\int_0^{\pi} x\,dx = \dfrac{2}{\pi}\left[\dfrac{x^2}{2}\right]_0^{\pi} = \pi$

$$a_n = \frac{2}{\pi}\int_0^{\pi} f(x)\cos nx\,dx = \frac{2}{\pi}\int_0^{\pi} |\,x\,|\cos nx\,dx = \frac{2}{\pi}\int_0^{\pi} x\cos nx\,dx$$

$$= \frac{2}{\pi}\left[x\left(\frac{\sin nx}{n}\right) - 1.\left(-\frac{\cos nx}{n^2}\right)\right]_0^{\pi}$$

$$= \frac{2}{\pi}\left[\frac{\cos n\pi}{n^2} - \frac{1}{n^2}\right] = \frac{2}{\pi n^2}[(-1)^n - 1] = \begin{cases} 0 \quad , & \text{if } n \text{ is even} \\ \dfrac{-4}{\pi n^2}, & \text{if } n \text{ is odd} \end{cases}$$

$$\therefore \qquad |x| = \frac{\pi}{2} - \frac{4}{\pi}\left(\cos x + \frac{\cos 3x}{3^2} + \frac{\cos 5x}{5^2} + \ldots\ldots\right)$$

Putting $x = 0$ in the above result, we get $\dfrac{1}{1^2} + \dfrac{1}{3^2} + \dfrac{1}{5^2} + \ldots\ldots = \dfrac{\pi^2}{8}$.

Example 8. *Obtain the Fourier series for the function $f(x) = x^2$, $-\pi \le x \le \pi$. Sketch the graph of $f(x)$. Hence show that* (G.B.T.U. (AG) 2012)

(i) $\dfrac{1}{1^2} + \dfrac{1}{2^2} + \dfrac{1}{3^2} + \dfrac{1}{4^2} + \ldots.. = \displaystyle\sum_{n=1}^{\infty} \frac{1}{n^2} = \frac{\pi^2}{6}$

(ii) $\dfrac{1}{1^2} - \dfrac{1}{2^2} + \dfrac{1}{3^2} - \dfrac{1}{4^2} + \ldots.. = \dfrac{\pi^2}{12}$

(iii) $\dfrac{1}{1^2} + \dfrac{1}{3^2} + \dfrac{1}{5^2} + \ldots\ldots = \displaystyle\sum_{n=1}^{\infty} \frac{1}{(2n-1)^2} = \frac{\pi^2}{8}$.

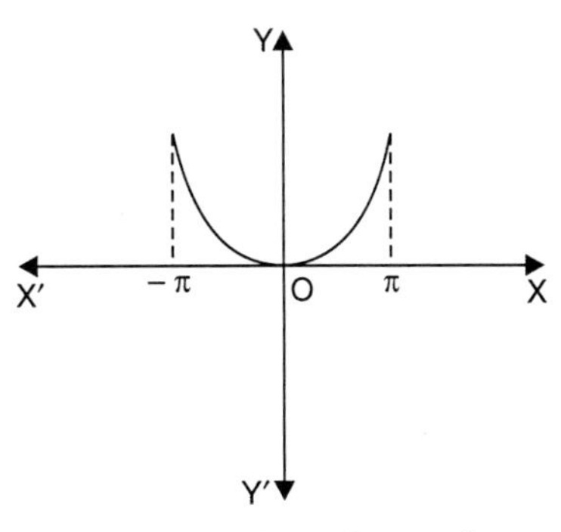

Graph of $f(x) = x^2$

Sol. Since $f(-x) = (-x)^2 = x^2 = f(x)$.

$\therefore$ $f(x)$ is an even function and hence $b_n = 0$

Let $$f(x) = x^2 = \frac{a_0}{2} + \sum_{n=1}^{\infty} a_n \cos nx$$

where $$a_0 = \frac{2}{\pi}\int_0^{\pi} f(x)\, dx = \frac{2}{\pi}\int_0^{\pi} x^2\, dx = \frac{2}{\pi}\left[\frac{x^3}{3}\right]_0^{\pi} = \frac{2}{3}\pi^2$$

$$a_n = \frac{2}{\pi}\int_0^{\pi} f(x)\cos nx\, dx = \frac{2}{\pi}\int_0^{\pi} x^2 \cos nx\, dx$$

$$= \frac{2}{\pi}\left[\left(x^2\,\frac{\sin nx}{n}\right)_0^{\pi} - \int_0^{\pi} 2x\,.\frac{\sin nx}{n}\, dx\right]$$

$$= -\frac{4}{\pi n}\int_0^{\pi} x \sin nx\, dx = -\frac{4}{\pi n}\left[\left\{x\left(\frac{-\cos nx}{n}\right)\right\}_0^{\pi} - \int_0^{\pi} 1.\left(\frac{-\cos nx}{n}\right) dx\right]$$

$$= \frac{4}{\pi n^2}(\pi \cos n\pi) = \frac{4}{n^2}(-1)^n$$

$$\therefore \qquad x^2 = \frac{\pi^2}{3} + 4\sum_{n=1}^{\infty} \frac{(-1)^n}{n^2}\cos nx$$

$$= \frac{\pi^2}{3} - 4\left(\frac{\cos x}{1^2} - \frac{\cos 2x}{2^2} + \frac{\cos 3x}{3^2} - \frac{\cos 4x}{4^2} + \ldots\ldots\right) \qquad \ldots(1)$$

Putting $x = \pi$ in (1), we get

$$\pi^2 = \frac{\pi^2}{3} - 4\left(-\frac{1}{1^2} - \frac{1}{2^2} - \frac{1}{3^2} - \frac{1}{4^2} + \ldots\ldots\right)$$

$$\Rightarrow \qquad \frac{2\pi^2}{3} = 4\left(\frac{1}{1^2} + \frac{1}{2^2} + \frac{1}{3^2} + \frac{1}{4^2} + \ldots\ldots\right)$$

$$\therefore \qquad \frac{1}{1^2} + \frac{1}{2^2} + \frac{1}{3^2} + \frac{1}{4^2} + \ldots\ldots = \frac{\pi^2}{6} \qquad \ldots(2)$$

Putting $x = 0$ in (1), we get

$$0 = \frac{\pi^2}{3} - 4\left(\frac{1}{1^2} - \frac{1}{2^2} + \frac{1}{3^2} - \frac{1}{4^2} + \ldots\ldots\right)$$

$$\therefore \qquad \frac{1}{1^2} - \frac{1}{2^2} + \frac{1}{3^2} - \frac{1}{4^2} + \ldots\ldots = \frac{\pi^2}{12} \qquad \ldots(3)$$

Adding (2) and (3), we get

$$2\left(\frac{1}{1^2} + \frac{1}{3^2} + \frac{1}{5^2} + \ldots\ldots\right) = \frac{\pi^2}{4}$$

$$\therefore \qquad \frac{1}{1^2} + \frac{1}{3^2} + \frac{1}{5^2} + \ldots\ldots = \frac{\pi^2}{8}.$$

Example 9. *Expand the function $f(x) = x \sin x$ as a Fourier series in the interval $-\pi \le x \le \pi$. Deduce that* $\frac{1}{1.3} - \frac{1}{3.5} + \frac{1}{5.7} - \frac{1}{7.9} + \ldots\ldots = \frac{\pi - 2}{4}$. (U.P.T.U. 2008)

Sol. Since $x \sin x$ is an even function of x, $b_n = 0$

Let $\qquad f(x) = x \sin x = \frac{a_0}{2} + \sum_{n=1}^{\infty} a_n \cos nx$

where $\qquad a_0 = \frac{2}{\pi}\int_0^\pi x \sin x \, dx = \frac{2}{\pi}\Big[x(-\cos x) - 1.(-\sin x)\Big]_0^\pi = \frac{2}{\pi}(-\pi \cos \pi) = 2$

$$a_n = \frac{2}{\pi}\int_0^\pi x \sin x \cos nx \, dx = \frac{1}{\pi}\int_0^\pi x(2 \cos nx \sin x) \, dx$$

$$= \frac{1}{\pi}\int_0^\pi x[\sin (n+1)x - \sin (n-1)x] \, dx$$

$$= \frac{1}{\pi}\left[x\left\{-\frac{\cos (n+1)x}{n+1} + \frac{\cos (n-1)x}{n-1}\right\} - 1.\left\{-\frac{\sin (n+1)x}{(n+1)^2} + \frac{\sin (n-1)x}{(n-1)^2}\right\}\right]_0^\pi$$

$$= \frac{1}{\pi}\left[\pi\left\{-\frac{\cos (n+1)\pi}{n+1} + \frac{\cos (n-1)\pi}{n-1}\right\}\right] = \frac{\cos (n-1)\pi}{n-1} - \frac{\cos (n+1)\pi}{n+1}, \ n \ne 1$$

When n is odd, $n \neq 1$, $n-1$ and $n+1$ are even

$$\therefore \qquad a_n = \frac{1}{n-1} - \frac{1}{n+1} = \frac{2}{n^2-1}$$

When n is even, $n-1$ and $n+1$ are odd

$$\therefore \qquad a_n = \frac{-1}{n-1} + \frac{1}{n+1} = \frac{-2}{n^2-1}$$

When $n = 1$, we have

$$a_1 = \frac{2}{\pi}\int_0^{\pi} x \sin x \cos x \, dx = \frac{1}{\pi}\int_0^{\pi} x \sin 2x \, dx$$

$$= \frac{1}{\pi}\left[x\left(-\frac{\cos 2x}{2}\right) - 1.\left(-\frac{\sin 2x}{4}\right)\right]_0^{\pi} = \frac{1}{\pi}\left[-\frac{\pi \cos 2\pi}{2}\right] = -\frac{1}{2}$$

$$\therefore \qquad x \sin x = 1 - \frac{1}{2}\cos x - 2\left(\frac{\cos 2x}{2^2-1} - \frac{\cos 3x}{3^2-1} + \frac{\cos 4x}{4^2-1} - \frac{\cos 5x}{5^2-1} + \ldots\ldots\right)$$

Putting $x = \frac{\pi}{2}$, we get

$$\frac{\pi}{2} = 1 - 2\left(\frac{-1}{2^2-1} + \frac{1}{4^2-1} - \frac{1}{6^2-1} + \ldots\ldots\right)$$

$$\Rightarrow \qquad \frac{\pi}{2} - 1 = 2\left(\frac{1}{3} - \frac{1}{15} + \frac{1}{35} - \ldots\ldots\right)$$

$$\Rightarrow \qquad \frac{\pi-2}{4} = \frac{1}{1.3} - \frac{1}{3.5} + \frac{1}{5.7} - \ldots\ldots$$

Example 10. *Show that for* $-\pi < x < \pi$,

$$\sin ax = \frac{2 \sin a\pi}{\pi}\left(\frac{\sin x}{1^2-a^2} - \frac{2\sin 2x}{2^2-a^2} + \frac{3 \sin 3x}{3^2-a^2} - \ldots\ldots\right).$$

Sol. Since $\sin ax$ is an odd function of x, $\therefore$ $a_0 = 0$ and $a_n = 0$

Let $\sin ax = \sum_{n=1}^{\infty} b_n \sin nx$

where
$$b_n = \frac{2}{\pi}\int_0^{\pi} \sin ax \sin nx \, dx = \frac{1}{\pi}\int_0^{\pi} [\cos (n-a)x - \cos (n+a)x] \, dx$$

$$= \frac{1}{\pi}\left[\frac{\sin (n-a)x}{n-a} - \frac{\sin (n+a)x}{n+a}\right]_0^{\pi} = \frac{1}{\pi}\left[\frac{\sin (n-a)\pi}{n-a} - \frac{\sin (n+a)\pi}{n+a}\right]$$

$$= \frac{1}{\pi}\left[\frac{(-1)^n(-\sin a\pi)}{n-a} - \frac{(-1)^n \sin a\pi}{n+a}\right] = -\frac{(-1)^n \sin a\pi}{\pi}\left[\frac{1}{n-a} + \frac{1}{n+a}\right]$$

$$= (-1)^{n+1} \cdot \frac{2n \sin a\pi}{\pi(n^2 - a^2)}$$

$$\therefore \qquad \sin ax = \frac{2 \sin a\pi}{\pi} \sum_{n=1}^{\infty} \frac{(-1)^{n+1}\, n}{n^2 - a^2} \sin nx$$

$$= \frac{2 \sin a\pi}{\pi} \left(\frac{\sin x}{1^2 - a^2} - \frac{2 \sin 2x}{2^2 - a^2} + \frac{3 \sin 3x}{3^2 - a^2} - \ldots\ldots \right).$$

TEST YOUR KNOWLEDGE

1. Expand in a Fourier series the function $f(x) = x$ in the interval $0 < x < 2\pi$.

2. Express $f(x) = \frac{1}{2}(\pi - x)$ in a Fourier series in the interval $0 < x < 2\pi$. Deduce that

$$\frac{\pi}{4} = 1 - \frac{1}{3} + \frac{1}{5} - \frac{1}{7} + \ldots$$ *(U.P.T.U. 2009)*

3. Prove that for all values of x between $-\pi$ and π, $\frac{1}{2}x = \sin x - \frac{1}{2}\sin 2x + \frac{1}{3}\sin 3x - \frac{1}{4}\sin 4x + \ldots\ldots$

4. Obtain the Fourier series to represent e^x in the interval $0 < x < 2\pi$.

5. Find the Fourier series to represent e^x in the interval $-\pi < x < \pi$.

6. Find the Fourier series to represent the function $f(x) = |\sin x|$, $-\pi < x < \pi$.

7. Expand $f(x) = |\cos x|$ as a Fourier series in the interval $-\pi < x < \pi$. *[M.T.U. (SUM) 2011]*

8. Prove that in the interval $-\pi < x < \pi$,

$$x \cos x = -\frac{1}{2}\sin x + 2\sum_{n=2}^{\infty} \frac{n(-1)^n}{n^2 - 1} \sin nx.$$ *[U.P.T.U. (SUM) 2008]*

9. Prove that for $-\pi < x < \pi$, $\frac{x(\pi^2 - x^2)}{12} = \frac{\sin x}{1^3} - \frac{\sin 2x}{2^3} + \frac{\sin 3x}{3^3} - \frac{\sin 4x}{4^3} + \ldots\ldots$

10. Obtain a Fourier series to represent $f(x) = x^2$ in the interval $(0, 2\pi)$ and hence deduce that

$$\frac{1}{1^2} - \frac{1}{2^2} + \frac{1}{3^2} - \frac{1}{4^2} + \ldots = \frac{\pi^2}{12}$$ *(U.P.T.U. 2008)*

11. Obtain a Fourier series to represent e^{-ax} from $x = -\pi$ to $x = \pi$. Hence derive series for $\frac{\pi}{\sinh \pi}$.

12. Prove that in the range $-\pi < x < \pi$, $\cosh ax = \frac{2a}{\pi} \sinh a\pi \left[\frac{1}{2a^2} + \sum_{n=1}^{\infty} \frac{(-1)^n}{n^2 + a^2} \cos nx \right]$.

13. Find Fourier series of $f(x) = x^3$ in $(-\pi, \pi)$. *[U.P.T.U. (SUM) 2009]*

14. Expand the function $f(x) = \frac{\pi^2}{12} - \frac{x^2}{4}$ in Fourier series in the interval $(-\pi, \pi)$.

15. Find the Fourier series expansion for $f(x) = x + \dfrac{x^2}{4}$, $-\pi \le x \le \pi$ (*U.P.T.U. 2009*)

16. Express $f(x) = \cos wx$, $-\pi < x < \pi$, where w is a fraction, as a Fourier series. Hence prove that

$$\cot\theta = \frac{1}{\theta} + \frac{2\theta}{\theta^2 - \pi^2} + \frac{2\theta}{\theta^2 - 4\pi^2} + \ldots\ldots$$

17. Find the Fourier series of $f(x) = \dfrac{3x^2 - 6\pi x + 2\pi^2}{12}$ in the interval $(0, 2\pi)$. Hence, deduce that

$$\frac{\pi^2}{6} = 1 + \frac{1}{2^2} + \frac{1}{3^2} + \ldots$$ (*M.T.U. 2012*)

Answers

1. $f(x) = \pi - 2\displaystyle\sum_{n=1}^{\infty} \frac{\sin nx}{n}$

2. $f(x) = \displaystyle\sum_{n=1}^{\infty} \frac{\sin nx}{n}$

4. $e^x = \dfrac{e^{2\pi} - 1}{2\pi} + \dfrac{e^{2\pi} - 1}{\pi} \displaystyle\sum_{n=1}^{\infty} \left(\frac{\cos nx}{1+n^2} - \frac{n}{1+n^2}\sin nx\right)$

5. $e^x = \dfrac{2\sinh\pi}{\pi}\left[\dfrac{1}{2} - \left(\dfrac{1}{2}\cos x - \dfrac{1}{5}\cos 2x + \dfrac{1}{10}\cos 3x - \ldots\ldots\right) - \left(\dfrac{1}{2}\sin x - \dfrac{2}{5}\sin 2x + \dfrac{3}{10}\sin 3x - \ldots\ldots\right)\right]$

6. $|\sin x| = \dfrac{2}{\pi} - \dfrac{4}{\pi}\left(\dfrac{\cos 2x}{3} + \dfrac{\cos 4x}{15} + \ldots\ldots + \dfrac{\cos 2nx}{4n^2 - 1} + \ldots\ldots\right)$

7. $|\cos x| = \dfrac{2}{\pi} + \dfrac{4}{\pi}\left(\dfrac{\cos 2x}{3} - \dfrac{\cos 4x}{15} + \ldots\ldots\right)$

10. $x^2 = \dfrac{4\pi^2}{3} + 4\displaystyle\sum_{n=1}^{\infty} \frac{\cos nx}{n^2} - 4\pi \sum_{n=1}^{\infty} \frac{\sin nx}{n}$

11. $e^{-ax} = \dfrac{2\sinh a\pi}{\pi}\left[\left(\dfrac{1}{2a} - \dfrac{a\cos x}{1^2 + a^2} + \dfrac{a\cos 2x}{2^2 + a^2} - \ldots\ldots\right) - \left(\dfrac{\sin x}{1^2 + a^2} - \dfrac{2\sin 2x}{2^2 + a^2} + \dfrac{3\sin 3x}{3^2 + a^2} - \ldots\ldots\right)\right]$

$$\frac{\pi}{\sinh\pi} = 2\left[\frac{1}{2^2 + 1} - \frac{1}{3^2 + 1} + \frac{1}{4^2 + 1} - \ldots\ldots\right]$$

13. $f(x) = 2\displaystyle\sum_{n=1}^{\infty} \left(\frac{6}{n^3} - \frac{\pi^2}{n}\right)(-1)^n \sin nx$

14. $f(x) = \displaystyle\sum_{n=1}^{\infty} (-1)^{n+1} \frac{\cos nx}{n^2}$

15. $f(x) = \dfrac{\pi^2}{12} + \displaystyle\sum_{n=1}^{\infty} \frac{(-1)^n}{n^2}\cos nx - 2\sum_{n=1}^{\infty} \frac{(-1)^n}{n}\sin nx$

16. $\cos wx = \dfrac{2w\sin w\pi}{\pi}\left(\dfrac{1}{2w^2} + \dfrac{\cos x}{1^2 - w^2} - \dfrac{\cos 2x}{2^2 - w^2} + \dfrac{\cos 3x}{3^2 - w^2} - \ldots\ldots\right)$

17. $f(x) = \displaystyle\sum_{n=1}^{\infty} \frac{\cos nx}{n^2}$.

4.5. FOURIER SERIES FOR DISCONTINUOUS FUNCTIONS

In art. 4.3, we derived Euler's formulae for a_0, a_n, b_n on the assumption that $f(x)$ is continuous in $(c, c + 2\pi)$. However, if $f(x)$ has finitely many points of finite discontinuity, even then it can be expressed as a Fourier series. The integrals for a_0, a_n, b_n are to be evaluated by breaking up the range of integration.

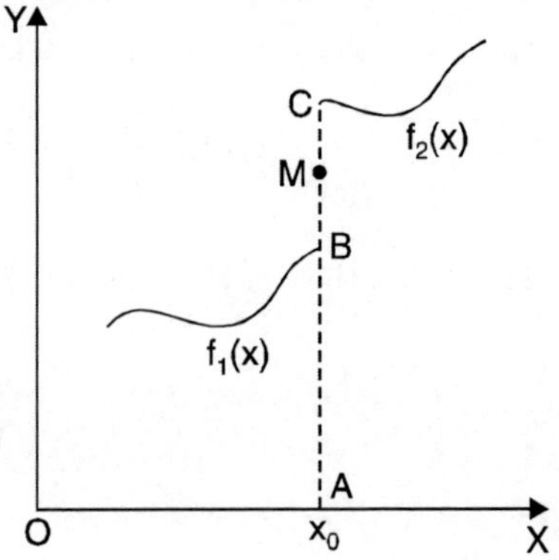

Let $f(x)$ be defined by $f(x) = \begin{cases} f_1(x), & c < x < x_0 \\ f_2(x), & x_0 < x < c + 2\pi \end{cases}$

where x_0 is the point of finite discontinuity in the interval $(c, c + 2\pi)$.

The values of a_0, a_n, b_n are given by

$$a_0 = \frac{1}{\pi}\left[\int_c^{x_0} f_1(x)\,dx + \int_{x_0}^{c+2\pi} f_2(x)\,dx\right]$$

$$a_n = \frac{1}{\pi}\left[\int_c^{x_0} f_1(x)\cos nx\,dx + \int_{x_0}^{c+2\pi} f_2(x)\cos nx\,dx\right]$$

$$b_n = \frac{1}{\pi}\left[\int_c^{x_0} f_1(x)\sin nx\,dx + \int_{x_0}^{c+2\pi} f_2(x)\sin nx\,dx\right]$$

At $x = x_0$, there is a finite jump in the graph of the function. Both the limits $f(x_0 - 0)$ and $f(x_0 + 0)$ exist but are unequal. The sum of the Fourier series $= \frac{1}{2}[f(x_0 - 0) + f(x_0 + 0)]$ $= \frac{1}{2}$ (AB + AC) = AM, where M is the mid-point of BC.

ILLUSTRATIVE EXAMPLES

Example 1. *Find the Fourier series to represent the function f(x) given by*

$$f(x) = \begin{cases} x & \text{for } 0 \le x \le \pi \\ 2\pi - x & \text{for } \pi \le x \le 2\pi \end{cases}$$

Deduce that $\frac{1}{1^2} + \frac{1}{3^2} + \frac{1}{5^2} + \ldots\ldots = \frac{\pi^2}{8}$. [G.B.T.U. (SUM) 2010]

Sol. Let $f(x) = \frac{a_0}{2} + \sum_{n=1}^{\infty} a_n \cos nx + \sum_{n=1}^{\infty} b_n \sin nx$, where

$$a_0 = \frac{1}{\pi}\int_0^{2\pi} f(x)\,dx = \frac{1}{\pi}\left[\int_0^{\pi} x\,dx + \int_{\pi}^{2\pi} (2\pi - x)\,dx\right]$$

$$= \frac{1}{\pi}\left[\left|\frac{x^2}{2}\right|_0^{\pi} + \left|2\pi x - \frac{x^2}{2}\right|_{\pi}^{2\pi}\right] = \frac{1}{\pi}\left[\frac{\pi^2}{2} + (4\pi^2 - 2\pi^2) - \left(2\pi^2 - \frac{\pi^2}{2}\right)\right] = \pi$$

$$a_n = \frac{1}{\pi}\int_0^{2\pi} f(x)\cos nx\,dx = \frac{1}{\pi}\left[\int_0^{\pi} x\cos nx\,dx + \int_{\pi}^{2\pi}(2\pi - x)\cos nx\,dx\right]$$

$$= \frac{1}{\pi}\left[\left(x\,\frac{\sin nx}{n}\right)_0^{\pi} - \int_0^{\pi} 1.\frac{\sin nx}{n}\,dx + \left\{(2\pi - x)\frac{\sin nx}{n}\right\}_{\pi}^{2\pi} + \int_{\pi}^{2\pi}\frac{\sin nx}{n}\,dx\right]$$

$$= \frac{1}{\pi}\left[\left(\frac{\cos nx}{n^2}\right)_0^{\pi} - \left(\frac{\cos nx}{n^2}\right)_{\pi}^{2\pi}\right]$$

$$= \frac{1}{\pi n^2}[(-1)^n - 1 - 1 + (-1)^n] = \frac{2}{\pi n^2}[(-1)^n - 1] = \begin{cases} -\dfrac{4}{\pi n^2}, & \text{if } n \text{ is odd} \\ 0, & \text{if } n \text{ is even}\end{cases}$$

$$b_n = \frac{1}{\pi}\int_0^{2\pi} f(x)\sin nx\,dx = \frac{1}{\pi}\left[\int_0^{\pi} x\sin nx\,dx + \int_{\pi}^{2\pi}(2\pi - x)\sin nx\,dx\right]$$

$$= \frac{1}{\pi}\left[\left\{x\left(\frac{-\cos nx}{n}\right)\right\}_0^{\pi} + \int_0^{\pi}\frac{\cos nx}{n}\,dx\right.$$

$$\left. + \left\{(2\pi - x)\left(\frac{-\cos nx}{n}\right)\right\}_{\pi}^{2\pi} - \int_{\pi}^{2\pi}(-1)\left(\frac{-\cos nx}{n}\right)dx\right]$$

$$= \frac{1}{\pi}\left[-\frac{\pi}{n}\cos n\pi + \frac{\pi}{n}\cos n\pi\right] = 0$$

$$\therefore \quad f(x) = \frac{\pi}{2} - \frac{4}{\pi}\left(\frac{\cos x}{1^2} + \frac{\cos 3x}{3^2} + \frac{\cos 5x}{5^2} + \ldots\ldots\right)$$

Putting $x = 0$, we get $0 = \dfrac{\pi}{2} - \dfrac{4}{\pi}\left(\dfrac{1}{1^2} + \dfrac{1}{3^2} + \dfrac{1}{5^2} + \ldots\ldots\right) \Rightarrow \dfrac{\pi^2}{8} = \dfrac{1}{1^2} + \dfrac{1}{3^2} + \dfrac{1}{5^2} + \ldots\ldots$

Example 2. *If* $f(x) = \left.\begin{matrix} 0, & -\pi \le x \le 0 \\ \sin x, & 0 \le x \le \pi \end{matrix}\right\}$

Prove that $f(x) = \dfrac{1}{\pi} + \dfrac{1}{2}\sin x - \dfrac{2}{\pi}\displaystyle\sum_{n=1}^{\infty}\frac{\cos 2nx}{4n^2 - 1}$. [G.B.T.U. (AG) 2012]

Hence show that

(i) $\dfrac{1}{1.3} + \dfrac{1}{3.5} + \dfrac{1}{5.7} + \ldots\ldots = \dfrac{1}{2}$ *(ii)* $\dfrac{1}{1.3} - \dfrac{1}{3.5} + \dfrac{1}{5.7} - \ldots\ldots = \dfrac{\pi - 2}{4}$.

Sol. Let $f(x) = \dfrac{a_0}{2} + \displaystyle\sum_{n=1}^{\infty} a_n\cos nx + \sum_{n=1}^{\infty} b_n\sin nx$

Then $a_0 = \dfrac{1}{\pi}\displaystyle\int_{-\pi}^{\pi} f(x)\,dx = \frac{1}{\pi}\left[\int_{-\pi}^{0} 0\,dx + \int_0^{\pi}\sin x\,dx\right] = \frac{2}{\pi}$

$$a_n = \frac{1}{\pi}\int_{-\pi}^{\pi} f(x)\cos nx\,dx = \frac{1}{\pi}\left[\int_{-\pi}^{0} 0\,dx + \int_0^{\pi}\sin x\cos nx\,dx\right]$$

$$= \frac{1}{2\pi}\int_0^{\pi} 2\cos nx\sin x\,dx = \frac{1}{2\pi}\int_0^{\pi}[\sin(n+1)x - \sin(n-1)x]\,dx$$

$$= \frac{1}{2\pi}\left[-\frac{\cos(n+1)x}{n+1} + \frac{\cos(n-1)x}{n-1}\right]_0^{\pi}, \; n \neq 1$$

$$= \frac{1}{2\pi}\left[-\frac{\cos(n+1)\pi}{n+1} + \frac{\cos(n-1)\pi}{n-1} + \frac{1}{n+1} - \frac{1}{n-1}\right]$$

$$= \frac{1}{2\pi}\left[-\frac{(-1)^{n+1}}{n+1} + \frac{(-1)^{n-1}}{n-1} + \frac{1}{n+1} - \frac{1}{n-1}\right]$$

$$= \begin{cases} \dfrac{1}{2\pi}\left(-\dfrac{1}{n+1} + \dfrac{1}{n-1} + \dfrac{1}{n+1} - \dfrac{1}{n-1}\right), & \text{when } n \text{ is odd} \\ \dfrac{1}{2\pi}\left(\dfrac{1}{n+1} - \dfrac{1}{n-1} + \dfrac{1}{n+1} - \dfrac{1}{n-1}\right), & \text{when } n \text{ is even} \end{cases}$$

$$= \begin{cases} 0, \text{ when } n \text{ is odd}, i.e., n = 3, 5, 7, \ldots.. \\ -\dfrac{2}{\pi(n^2-1)}, \text{ when } n \text{ is even} \end{cases}$$

When $n = 1$, we have

$$a_1 = \frac{1}{\pi}\int_0^{\pi} \sin x \cos x \, dx = \frac{1}{2\pi}\int_0^{\pi} \sin 2x \, dx = \frac{1}{2\pi}\left[-\frac{\cos 2x}{2}\right]_0^{\pi} = 0$$

$$b_n = \frac{1}{\pi}\int_{-\pi}^{\pi} f(x) \sin nx \, dx = \frac{1}{\pi}\left[\int_{-\pi}^{0} 0 \, dx + \int_0^{\pi} \sin x \sin nx \, dx\right]$$

$$= \frac{1}{2\pi}\int_0^{\pi} 2 \sin nx \sin x \, dx = \frac{1}{2\pi}\int_0^{\pi} [\cos (n-1)\, x - \cos (n+1)\, x] \, dx$$

$$= \frac{1}{2\pi}\left[\frac{\sin (n-1)x}{n-1} - \frac{\sin (n+1)x}{n+1}\right]_0^{\pi} = 0, \; n \neq 1$$

When $n = 1$, we have

$$b_1 = \frac{1}{\pi}\int_0^{\pi} \sin x \sin x \, dx = \frac{1}{2\pi}\int_0^{\pi} (1 - \cos 2x) \, dx = \frac{1}{2\pi}\left[x - \frac{\sin 2x}{2}\right]_0^{\pi} = \frac{1}{2}$$

$$\therefore \quad f(x) = \frac{1}{\pi} - \frac{2}{\pi}\left[\frac{\cos 2x}{2^2-1} + \frac{\cos 4x}{4^2-1} + \frac{\cos 6x}{6^2-1} + \ldots..\right] + \frac{1}{2}\sin x$$

$$= \frac{1}{\pi} + \frac{1}{2}\sin x - \frac{2}{\pi}\sum_{n=1}^{\infty} \frac{\cos 2nx}{(2n)^2 - 1} \qquad \ldots(1)$$

Putting $x = 0$ in (1), we have

$$0 = \frac{1}{\pi} - \frac{2}{\pi}\sum_{n=1}^{\infty} \frac{1}{4n^2-1}$$

$$\Rightarrow \quad \frac{1}{2} = \sum_{n=1}^{\infty} \frac{1}{4n^2-1} = \sum_{n=1}^{\infty} \frac{1}{(2n-1)(2n+1)} = \frac{1}{1.3} + \frac{1}{3.5} + \frac{1}{5.7} + \ldots..$$

Putting $x = \frac{\pi}{2}$ in (1), we have

$$1 = \frac{1}{\pi} + \frac{1}{2} - \frac{2}{\pi} \sum_{n=1}^{\infty} \frac{\cos n\pi}{4n^2 - 1}$$

$$\Rightarrow \quad \frac{1}{2} - \frac{1}{\pi} = -\frac{2}{\pi} \sum_{n=1}^{\infty} \frac{(-1)^n}{4n^2 - 1}$$

$$\Rightarrow \quad \frac{\pi - 2}{4} = -\sum_{n=1}^{\infty} \frac{(-1)^n}{(2n-1)(2n+1)} = -\left(-\frac{1}{1.3} + \frac{1}{3.5} - \frac{1}{5.7} + \ldots\ldots\right)$$

$$\Rightarrow \quad \frac{1}{1.3} - \frac{1}{3.5} + \frac{1}{5.7} - \ldots\ldots = \frac{\pi - 2}{4}.$$

Example 3. *Obtain Fourier series for the function*

$$f(x) = \begin{cases} x, & -\pi < x < 0 \\ -x, & 0 < x < \pi \end{cases}$$

and hence show that

$$\frac{1}{1^2} + \frac{1}{3^2} + \frac{1}{5^2} + \ldots\ldots = \frac{\pi^2}{8}.$$

[G.B.T.U. (C.O.) 2010 ; G.B.T.U. (AG) SUM 2010]

Sol. Let $$f(x) = \frac{a_0}{2} + \sum_{n=1}^{\infty} a_n \cos nx + \sum_{n=1}^{\infty} b_n \sin nx \qquad \ldots(1)$$

Then, $$a_0 = \frac{1}{\pi} \int_{-\pi}^{\pi} f(x)\, dx = \frac{1}{\pi}\left[\int_{-\pi}^{0} x\, dx + \int_{0}^{\pi} -x\, dx\right]$$

$$= \frac{1}{\pi}\left[\left(\frac{x^2}{2}\right)_{-\pi}^{0} - \left(\frac{x^2}{2}\right)_{0}^{\pi}\right] = \frac{1}{\pi}\left(0 - \frac{\pi^2}{2} - \frac{\pi^2}{2}\right) = -\pi$$

$$a_n = \frac{1}{\pi} \int_{-\pi}^{\pi} f(x) \cos nx\, dx = \frac{1}{\pi}\left[\int_{-\pi}^{0} x \cos nx\, dx + \int_{0}^{\pi} -x \cos nx\, dx\right]$$

$$= \frac{1}{\pi}\left[\left(x\frac{\sin nx}{n}\right)_{-\pi}^{0} - \int_{-\pi}^{0} 1.\frac{\sin nx}{n}\, dx + \left(-x.\frac{\sin nx}{n}\right)_{0}^{\pi} - \int_{0}^{\pi} (-1)\frac{\sin nx}{n}\, dx\right]$$

$$= \frac{1}{\pi}\left[\frac{1}{n^2}\left(\cos nx\right)_{-\pi}^{0} - \frac{1}{n^2}\left(\cos nx\right)_{0}^{\pi}\right] = \frac{1}{\pi}\left[\left\{\frac{1-(-1)^n}{n^2}\right\} - \left\{\frac{(-1)^n - 1}{n^2}\right\}\right]$$

$$= \frac{1}{\pi}\left[\frac{2\{1-(-1)^n\}}{n^2}\right] = \frac{2}{\pi n^2}\{1-(-1)^n\} = \left.\begin{matrix} 0, & \text{if } n \text{ is even} \\ \frac{4}{\pi n^2}, & \text{if } n \text{ is odd} \end{matrix}\right\}$$

$$b_n = \frac{1}{\pi} \int_{-\pi}^{\pi} f(x) \sin nx\, dx = \frac{1}{\pi}\left[\int_{-\pi}^{0} x \sin nx\, dx + \int_{0}^{\pi} (-x) \sin nx\, dx\right]$$

$$= \frac{1}{\pi}\left[\left\{x.\left(-\frac{\cos nx}{n}\right)\right\}_{-\pi}^{0} - \int_{-\pi}^{0} 1.\left(-\frac{\cos nx}{n}\right)dx\right.$$

$$\left. + \left\{(-x)\left(-\frac{\cos nx}{n}\right)\right\}_{0}^{\pi} - \int_{0}^{\pi} (-1).\left(-\frac{\cos nx}{n}\right)dx\right]$$

$$= \frac{1}{\pi}\left[\frac{-\pi}{n}(-1)^n + \frac{1}{n}.\pi(-1)^n\right] = 0$$

$\therefore$ From (1), $f(x) = -\frac{\pi}{2} + \frac{4}{\pi}\left[\frac{\cos x}{1^2} + \frac{\cos 3x}{3^2} + \frac{\cos 5x}{5^2} + ...\right]$ ...(2)

At the point of discontinuity,

$$f(0) = \frac{1}{2}\,[f(0-0) + f(0+0)] = \frac{1}{2}\,(0-0) = 0$$

Putting $x = 0$ is above expression, we get

$$0 = -\frac{\pi}{2} + \frac{4}{\pi}\left(\frac{1}{1^2} + \frac{1}{3^2} + \frac{1}{5^2} + ...\right)$$

$$\Rightarrow \quad \frac{1}{1^2} + \frac{1}{3^2} + \frac{1}{5^2} + ... = \frac{\pi^2}{8}.$$

Example 4. *Obtain Fourier series for the function f(x) given by*

$$f(x) = \begin{cases} 1 + \dfrac{2x}{\pi}, & -\pi \le x \le 0 \\ 1 - \dfrac{2x}{\pi}, & 0 \le x \le \pi \end{cases}$$ (U.K.T.U. 2011)

Hence deduce that $\frac{1}{1^2} + \frac{1}{3^2} + \frac{1}{5^2} + ... = \frac{\pi^2}{8}$.

Sol. When $\quad -\pi \le x \le 0, \qquad 0 \le -x \le \pi$

$$\therefore \quad f(-x) = 1 - \frac{2(-x)}{\pi} = 1 + \frac{2x}{\pi} = f(x)$$

When $\quad 0 \le x \le \pi, \qquad -\pi \le -x \le 0$

$$\therefore \quad f(-x) = 1 + \frac{2(-x)}{\pi} = 1 - \frac{2x}{\pi} = f(x)$$

$\Rightarrow$ $f(x)$ is an even function of x in $[-\pi, \pi]$. This is also clear from its graph which is symmetrical about the y-axis.

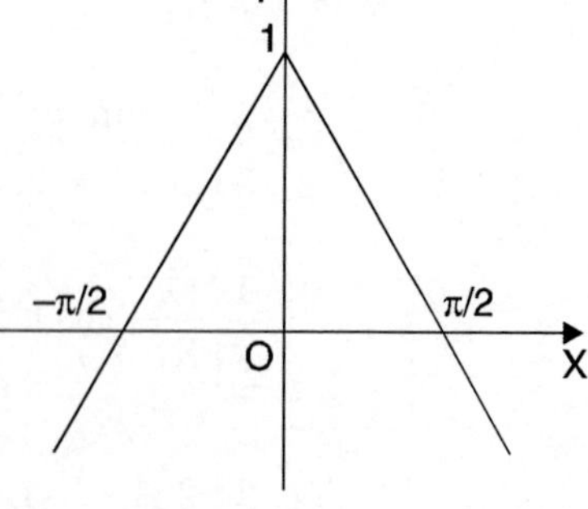

$$\therefore \quad b_n = 0$$

Let $\quad f(x) = \frac{a_0}{2} + \sum_{n=1}^{\infty} a_n \cos nx$

Here, $\quad a_0 = \frac{2}{\pi}\int_0^{\pi} f(x)\,dx = \frac{2}{\pi}\int_0^{\pi}\left(1 - \frac{2x}{\pi}\right)dx = \frac{2}{x}\left[x - \frac{x^2}{\pi}\right]_0^{\pi} = 0$

$$a_n = \frac{2}{\pi}\int_0^{\pi} f(x)\cos nx\,dx = \frac{2}{\pi}\int_0^{\pi}\left(1 - \frac{2x}{\pi}\right)\cos nx\,dx$$

$$= \frac{2}{\pi}\left[\left(1 - \frac{2x}{\pi}\right)\frac{\sin nx}{n} - \left(-\frac{2}{\pi}\right)\left(-\frac{\cos nx}{n^2}\right)\right]_0^{\pi}$$

$$= \frac{2}{\pi}\left[-\frac{2\cos n\pi}{\pi n^2} + \frac{2}{\pi n^2}\right] = \frac{4}{\pi^2 n^2}[1 - (-1)^n]$$

$$\therefore \quad f(x) = \frac{4}{\pi^2}\sum_{n=1}^{\infty}[1 - (-1)^n]\frac{\cos nx}{n^2}$$

$$= \frac{4}{\pi^2}\left(\frac{2\cos x}{1^2} + \frac{2\cos 3x}{3^2} + \frac{2\cos 5x}{5^2} + \ldots\ldots\right) = \frac{8}{\pi^2}\left(\frac{\cos x}{1^2} + \frac{\cos 3x}{3^2} + \frac{\cos 5x}{5^2} + \ldots\ldots\right)$$

Putting $x = 0$, we get $\frac{1}{1^2} + \frac{1}{3^2} + \frac{1}{5^2} + \ldots\ldots = \frac{\pi^2}{8}$ $\quad | \because f(0) = 1.$

TEST YOUR KNOWLEDGE

1. Find the Fourier series to represent the function

$$f(x) = \begin{cases} -k & \text{when} \quad -\pi < x < 0 \\ k & \text{where} \quad 0 < x < \pi \end{cases}$$

Also deduce that $\frac{\pi}{4} = 1 - \frac{1}{3} + \frac{1}{5} - \frac{1}{7} + \ldots\ldots$ *(G.B.T.U. 2010)*

2. (*i*) Find the Fourier series for the function

$$f(x) = \begin{cases} -1 \ , & -\pi < x < -\pi/2 \\ 0 \ , & -\frac{\pi}{2} < x < \frac{\pi}{2} \\ 1 \ , & \frac{\pi}{2} < x < \pi \end{cases}$$ *(G.B.T.U. 2012)*

Hence deduce that $\frac{\pi}{4} = 1 - \frac{1}{3} + \frac{1}{5} - \frac{1}{7} + \ldots\ldots$

(*ii*) Find a Fourier series for the function defined by :

$$f(x) = \begin{cases} -1 \ , & \text{for} \quad -\pi < x < 0 \\ 0 \ , & \text{for} \quad x = 0 \\ 1 \ , & \text{for} \quad 0 < x < \pi \end{cases}$$

Hence prove that $\frac{\pi}{4} = 1 - \frac{1}{3} + \frac{1}{5} - \frac{1}{7} + \frac{1}{9} - \ldots\ldots$

3. Find the Fourier series for the function

$$f(x) = \begin{cases} -\frac{\pi}{4} & \text{for} \quad -\pi < x < 0 \\ \frac{\pi}{4} & \text{for} \quad 0 < x < \pi \end{cases}$$

and $f(-\pi) = f(0) = f(\pi) = 0$, $f(x) = f(x + 2\pi)$ for all x.

Deduce that $\frac{\pi}{4} = 1 - \frac{1}{3} + \frac{1}{5} - \frac{1}{7} + \ldots\ldots$

4. (*i*) Obtain the Fourier series for the square waveform upto 4 terms as shown in the following figure: [*G.B.T.U. (C.O.) 2010*]

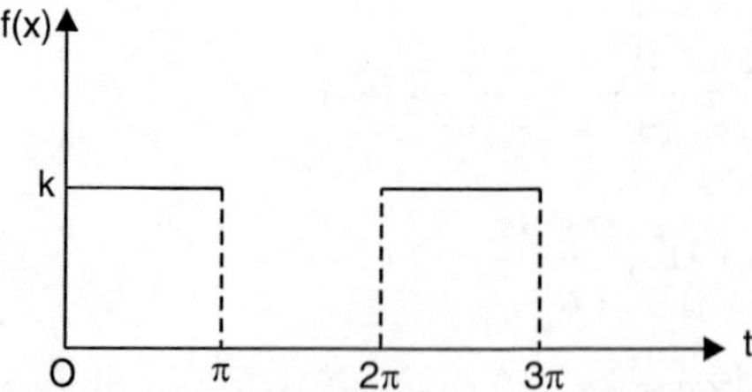

(*ii*) Obtain Fourier series of the function:

$$f(x) = \begin{cases} -\pi, & -\pi < x < 0 \\ x, & 0 < x < \pi \end{cases}$$

and deduce that $\dfrac{1}{1^2} + \dfrac{1}{3^2} + \dfrac{1}{5^2} + \ldots = \dfrac{\pi^2}{8}$. [*U.K.T.U. 2012 ; G.B.T.U. (AG) 2011*]

5. Find the Fourier series of the following function :

$$f(x) = \begin{cases} x^2, & -\pi < x < 0 \\ -x^2, & 0 < x < \pi \end{cases}$$ [*U.P.T.U. (C.O.) 2009*]

6. An alternating current after passing through a rectifier has the form

$$\begin{aligned} i &= I_0 \sin x \quad \text{for} \quad 0 \le x \le \pi \\ &= 0 \quad \text{for} \quad \pi \le x \le 2\pi \end{aligned}$$

where I_0 is the maximum current and the period is 2π. Express i as a Fourier series.

7. Find the Fourier series of the function defined as

$$f(x) = \begin{cases} x + \pi, & \text{for } 0 \le x \le \pi \\ -x - \pi, & \text{for } -\pi \le x < 0 \end{cases} \quad \text{and} \quad f(x + 2\pi) = f(x).$$ (*U.P.T.U. 2006*)

8. (*i*) Find the Fourier series for $f(x)$ in the interval $(-\pi, \pi)$ when

$$f(x) = \begin{cases} \pi + x, & -\pi < x < 0 \\ \pi - x, & 0 < x < \pi \end{cases}$$

(*ii*) Find the Fourier series for following periodic function :

$$f(x) = \begin{cases} \pi + x, & -\pi < x < 0 \\ -\pi - x, & 0 < x < \pi \end{cases}$$

9. Find the Fourier series expansion of $f(x)$ as shown in figure : [*M.T.U. (SUM) 2011*]

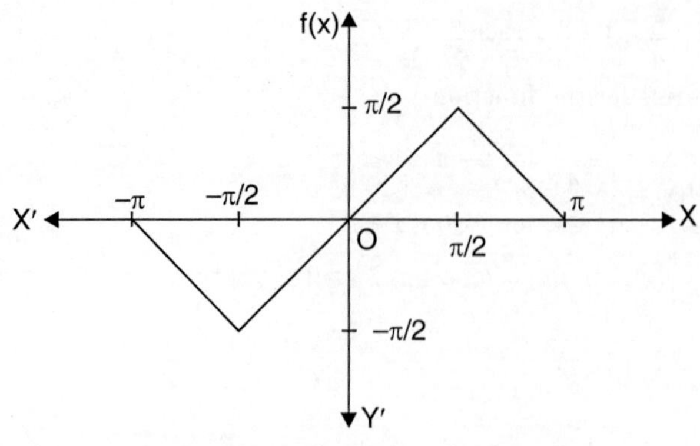

10. (*i*) Find the Fourier series of

$$f(x) = \begin{cases} 0, & \text{when } -\pi \le x \le 0 \\ x^2, & \text{when } 0 \le x \le \pi \end{cases}$$

which is assumed to be periodic with period 2π. (*M.T.U. 2011*)

(*ii*) Find the Fourier series of the periodic function $f(x)$ with period 2π defined as follows :

$$f(x) = \begin{cases} 0, & -\pi < x \le 0 \\ x, & 0 \le x \le \pi \end{cases}$$

Hence prove that $\sum_{n=1}^{\infty} \frac{1}{(2n-1)^2} = \frac{\pi^2}{8}$. [*G.B.T.U. (C.O.) 2011*]

Answers

1. $f(x) = \frac{4k}{\pi}\left(\sin x + \frac{\sin 3x}{3} + \frac{\sin 5x}{5} + \ldots\ldots\right)$

2. (*i*) $f(x) = \frac{2}{\pi}\left[\sin x - \sin 2x + \frac{\sin 3x}{3} - \ldots\right]$ (*ii*) $f(x) = \frac{4}{\pi}\left(\sin x + \frac{\sin 3x}{3} + \frac{\sin 5x}{5} + \ldots\ldots\right)$

3. $f(x) = \frac{\sin x}{1} + \frac{\sin 3x}{3} + \frac{\sin 5x}{5} + \frac{\sin 7x}{7} + \ldots$

4. (*i*) $f(t) = \frac{k}{2} + \frac{2k}{\pi}\left(\sin t + \frac{1}{3}\sin 3t + \frac{1}{5}\sin 5t + \ldots\right)$

(*ii*) $f(x) = -\frac{\pi}{4} - \frac{2}{\pi}\left[\frac{1}{1^2}\cos x + \frac{1}{3^2}\cos 3x + \frac{1}{5^2}\cos 5x + \ldots\right] + \sum_{n=1}^{\infty}\left(\frac{1 - 2\cos n\pi}{n}\right)\sin nx$

5. $f(x) = \frac{2}{\pi}\sum_{n=1}^{\infty}\left[\frac{\pi^2}{n}\cos n\pi + \frac{2}{n^3}(1 - \cos n\pi)\right]\sin nx$

6. $i = \frac{I_0}{\pi} + \frac{I_0}{2}\sin x - \frac{2I_0}{\pi}\left(\frac{\cos 2x}{2^2 - 1} + \frac{\cos 4x}{4^2 - 1} + \frac{\cos 6x}{6^2 - 1} + \ldots\ldots\right)$

7. $f(x) = \frac{\pi}{2} - \frac{4}{\pi}\left[\frac{\cos x}{1^2} + \frac{\cos 3x}{3^2} + \ldots\right] + 4\left[\frac{\sin x}{1} + \frac{\sin 3x}{3} + \ldots\right]$

8. (*i*) $f(x) = \frac{\pi}{2} + \frac{4}{\pi}\left(\frac{\cos x}{1^2} + \frac{\cos 3x}{3^2} + \frac{\cos 5x}{5^2} + \ldots\right)$

(*ii*) $f(x) = -\frac{\pi}{2} + \frac{4}{\pi}\left(\frac{\cos x}{1^2} + \frac{\cos 3x}{3^2} + \ldots\right) + 4\left(\frac{\sin x}{1} + \frac{\sin 3x}{3} + \ldots\right)$

9. $f(x) = \frac{4}{\pi}\sum_{n=1}^{\infty}\frac{1}{n^2}\sin\frac{n\pi}{2}\sin nx$

10. (*i*) $f(x) = \frac{\pi^2}{6} + 2\sum_{n=1}^{\infty}\frac{(-1)^n}{n^2}\cos nx + \sum_{n=1}^{\infty}\left[\frac{\pi}{n}(-1)^{n+1} + \frac{2\{(-1)^n - 1\}}{\pi n^3}\right]\sin nx$

(*ii*) $f(x) = \frac{\pi}{4} - \frac{2}{\pi}\sum_{\substack{n=1 \\ (n \text{ is odd})}}^{\infty}\frac{1}{n^2}\cos nx - \sum_{n=1}^{\infty}\frac{(-1)^n}{n}\sin nx$

4.6. CHANGE OF INTERVAL

In many engineering problems, it is desired to expand a function in a Fourier series over an interval of length $2l$ and not 2π. In order to apply foregoing theory, this interval must be transformed into an interval of length 2π. This can be achieved by a transformation of the variable.

Consider a periodic function $f(x)$ defined in the interval $c < x < c + 2l$. To change the interval into one of length 2π, we put

$$\frac{x}{l} = \frac{z}{\pi} \quad \text{or} \quad z = \frac{\pi x}{l} \text{ so that}$$

when $x = c$, $\quad z = \frac{\pi c}{l} = d$ (say)

and when $x = c + 2l$, $\quad z = \frac{\pi(c + 2l)}{l} = \frac{\pi c}{l} + 2\pi = d + 2\pi.$

Thus the function $f(x)$ of period $2l$ in $(c, c + 2l)$ is transformed to the function $f\left(\frac{lz}{\pi}\right) = F(z)$, say, of period 2π in $(d, d + 2\pi)$ and the latter function can be expressed as the Fourier series

$$F(z) = \frac{a_0}{2} + \sum_{n=1}^{\infty} a_n \cos nz + \sum_{n=1}^{\infty} b_n \sin nz \qquad ...(1)$$

where $a_0 = \frac{1}{\pi}\int_d^{d+2\pi} F(z)\, dz$; $a_n = \frac{1}{\pi}\int_d^{d+2\pi} F(z) \cos nz\, dz$; and $b_n = \frac{1}{\pi}\int_d^{d+2\pi} F(z) \sin nz\, dz$

Now making the inverse substitution $z = \frac{\pi x}{l}$, $dz = \frac{\pi}{l}\, dx$

When $z = d$, $x = c$ and when $z = d + 2\pi$, $x = c + 2l$.

The expression (1) becomes $F(z) = F\left(\frac{\pi x}{l}\right) = f(x) = \frac{a_0}{2} + \sum_{n=1}^{\infty} a_n \cos \frac{n\pi x}{l} + \sum_{n=1}^{\infty} b_n \sin \frac{n\pi x}{l}$

and the coefficients a_0, a_n, b_n from (2) reduce to

$$a_0 = \frac{1}{l}\int_c^{c+2l} f(x)\, dx\,; \quad a_n = \frac{1}{l}\int_c^{c+2l} f(x) \cos \frac{n\pi x}{l}\, dx\,; \quad \text{and} \quad b_n = \frac{1}{l}\int_c^{c+2l} f(x) \sin \frac{n\pi x}{l}\, dx$$

Hence the Fourier series $f(x)$ in the interval $c < x < c + 2l$ is given by

$$\boxed{f(x) = \frac{a_0}{2} + \sum_{n=1}^{\infty} a_n \cos \frac{n\pi x}{l} + \sum_{n=1}^{\infty} b_n \sin \frac{n\pi x}{l}}$$

where $a_0 = \frac{1}{l}\int_c^{c+2l} f(x)\, dx$, $a_n = \frac{1}{l}\int_c^{c+2l} f(x) \cos \frac{n\pi x}{l}\, dx$ and $b_n = \frac{1}{l}\int_c^{c+2l} f(x) \sin \frac{n\pi x}{l}\, dx.$

Cor. 1. If we put $c = 0$, the interval becomes $0 < x < 2l$ and the above results reduce to

$$a_0 = \frac{1}{l}\int_0^{2l} f(x)\, dx\,; \quad a_n = \frac{1}{l}\int_0^{2l} f(x) \cos \frac{n\pi x}{l}\, dx\,; \quad \text{and} \quad b_n = \frac{1}{l}\int_0^{2l} f(x) \sin \frac{n\pi x}{l}\, dx.$$

Cor. 2. If we put $c = -l$, the interval becomes $-l < x < l$ and the above results reduce to

$$a_0 = \frac{1}{l}\int_{-l}^{l} f(x)\,dx,\quad a_n = \frac{1}{l}\int_{-l}^{l} f(x)\cos\frac{n\pi x}{l}\,dx,\quad \text{and}\quad b_n = \frac{1}{l}\int_{-l}^{l} f(x)\sin\frac{n\pi x}{l}\,dx.$$

Cor. 3. If $f(x)$ is an even function, we have

$$a_0 = \frac{2}{l}\int_0^{l} f(x)\,dx,\quad a_n = \frac{2}{l}\int_0^{l} f(x)\cos\frac{n\pi x}{l}\,dx\quad \text{and}\quad b_n = 0$$

Cor. 4. If $f(x)$ is an odd function, we have $a_0 = 0,\ \ a_n = 0$ and $b_n = \dfrac{2}{l}\displaystyle\int_0^{l} f(x)\sin\frac{n\pi x}{l}\,dx.$

ILLUSTRATIVE EXAMPLES

Example 1. *Obtain the Fourier series expansion of*

$$f(x) = \left(\frac{\pi - x}{2}\right)\ \textit{for}\ \ 0 < x < 2$$ [U.P.T.U. (SUM) 2007 ; M.T.U. 2011]

Sol. Let $f(x) = \dfrac{a_0}{2} + \displaystyle\sum_{n=1}^{\infty} a_n \cos\frac{n\pi x}{l} + \sum_{n=1}^{\infty} b_n \sin\frac{n\pi x}{l}$

Here, $l = 1$

$$\therefore\quad \frac{\pi - x}{2} = \frac{a_0}{2} + \sum_{n=1}^{\infty} a_n \cos n\pi x + \sum_{n=1}^{\infty} b_n \sin n\pi x \qquad ...(1)$$

Here, $a_0 = \dfrac{1}{l}\displaystyle\int_0^{2l} f(x)\,dx = \int_0^2 \left(\frac{\pi - x}{2}\right)dx = \frac{1}{2}\left(\pi x - \frac{x^2}{2}\right)_0^2 = \frac{1}{2}(2\pi - 2) = \pi - 1$

$$a_n = \frac{1}{l}\int_0^{2l} f(x)\cos n\pi x\,dx = \int_0^2 \left(\frac{\pi - x}{2}\right)\cos n\pi x\,dx$$

$$= \frac{1}{2}\left[\left\{(\pi - x)\frac{\sin n\pi x}{n\pi}\right\}_0^2 - \int_0^2 (-1)\frac{\sin n\pi x}{n\pi}\,dx\right] = \frac{1}{2n\pi}\left(\frac{-\cos n\pi x}{n\pi}\right)_0^2 = 0$$

$$b_n = \frac{1}{l}\int_0^{2l} f(x)\sin n\pi x\,dx = \int_0^2 \left(\frac{\pi - x}{2}\right)\sin n\pi x\,dx$$

$$= \frac{1}{2}\left[\left\{(\pi - x)\left(\frac{-\cos n\pi x}{n\pi}\right)\right\}_0^2 - \int_0^2 (-1)\left(\frac{-\cos n\pi x}{n\pi}\right)dx\right]$$

$$= -\frac{1}{2n\pi}[(\pi - 2) - \pi] = \frac{1}{n\pi}$$

Hence, from (1),

$$\frac{\pi - x}{2} = \frac{(\pi - 1)}{2} + \frac{1}{\pi}\sum_{n=1}^{\infty} \frac{1}{n}\sin n\pi x$$

Example 2. *Find Fourier expansion for the function $f(x) = x - x^2$, $-1 < x < 1$.*

Sol. Let $f(x) = \dfrac{a_0}{2} + \sum_{n=1}^{\infty} a_n \cos n\pi x + \sum_{n=1}^{\infty} b_n \sin n\pi x$

Then $a_0 = \int_{-1}^{1} (x - x^2)\, dx = \int_{-1}^{1} x\, dx - \int_{-1}^{1} x^2\, dx = 0 - 2\int_0^1 x^2\, dx = -2\left[\dfrac{x^3}{3}\right]_0^1 = -\dfrac{2}{3}$

$$a_n = \int_{-1}^{1} (x - x^2) \cos n\pi x\, dx = \int_{-1}^{1} x \cos n\pi x\, dx - \int_{-1}^{1} x^2 \cos n\pi x\, dx$$

$$= 0 - 2\int_0^1 x^2 \cos n\pi x\, dx = -2\left[\left(x^2 \frac{\sin n\pi x}{n\pi}\right)_0^1 - \int_0^1 2x \cdot \frac{\sin n\pi x}{n\pi}\, dx\right]$$

$$= \frac{4}{n\pi}\int_0^1 x \sin n\pi x\, dx = \frac{4}{n\pi}\left[\left\{x \cdot \left(\frac{-\cos n\pi x}{n\pi}\right)\right\}_0^1 - \int_0^1 \left(\frac{-\cos n\pi x}{n\pi}\right) dx\right]$$

$$= -\frac{4}{n^2\pi^2} \cos n\pi = \frac{-4(-1)^n}{n^2\pi^2}$$

$$b_n = \int_{-1}^{1} (x - x^2) \sin n\pi x\, dx = \int_{-1}^{1} x \sin n\pi x\, dx - \int_{-1}^{1} x^2 \sin n\pi x\, dx$$

$$= 2\int_0^1 x \sin n\pi x\, dx - 0 = 2\left[x\left(-\frac{\cos n\pi x}{n\pi}\right) - 1 \cdot \left(-\frac{\sin n\pi x}{n^2\pi^2}\right)\right]_0^1$$

$$= 2\left[-\frac{\cos n\pi}{n\pi}\right] = \frac{-2(-1)^n}{n\pi}$$

$$\therefore\ x - x^2 = -\frac{1}{3} + \frac{4}{\pi^2}\left(\frac{\cos \pi x}{1^2} - \frac{\cos 2\pi x}{2^2} + \frac{\cos 3\pi x}{3^2} - \ldots\ldots\right)$$

$$+ \frac{2}{\pi}\left(\frac{\sin \pi x}{1} - \frac{\sin 2\pi x}{2} + \frac{\sin 3\pi x}{3} - \ldots\ldots\right)$$

Example 3. *Find the Fourier series to represent $f(x) = x^2 - 2$, when $-2 \le x \le 2$.*

Sol. Since $f(x)$ is an even function, $b_n = 0$.

Let $\qquad f(x) = x^2 - 2 = \dfrac{a_0}{2} + \sum_{n=1}^{\infty} a_n \cos \dfrac{n\pi x}{2}$

Then $\qquad a_0 = \dfrac{2}{2}\int_0^2 (x^2 - 2)\, dx = \left[\dfrac{x^3}{3} - 2x\right]_0^2 = \dfrac{8}{3} - 4 = -\dfrac{4}{3}$

$$a_n = \frac{2}{2}\int_0^2 (x^2 - 2) \cos \frac{n\pi x}{2}\, dx$$

$$= \left\{(x^2-2)\frac{\sin\frac{n\pi x}{2}}{\frac{n\pi}{2}}\right\}_0^2 - \int_0^2 (2x)\frac{\sin\frac{n\pi x}{2}}{\left(\frac{n\pi}{2}\right)}\,dx$$

$$= -\frac{4}{n\pi}\int_0^2 x\sin\frac{n\pi x}{2}\,dx$$

$$= -\frac{4}{n\pi}\left[\left\{x\left(\frac{-\cos\frac{n\pi x}{2}}{\frac{n\pi}{2}}\right)\right\}_0^2 - \int_0^2\left(\frac{-\cos\frac{n\pi x}{2}}{\frac{n\pi}{2}}\right)dx\right]$$

$$= \frac{8}{n^2\pi^2}(2\cos n\pi) = \frac{16\cos n\pi}{n^2\pi^2} = \frac{16(-1)^n}{n^2\pi^2}$$

$$\therefore \qquad x^2-2 = -\frac{2}{3}-\frac{16}{\pi^2}\left(\cos\frac{\pi x}{2}-\frac{1}{4}\cos\pi x+\frac{1}{9}\cos\frac{3\pi x}{2}-\ldots\ldots\right).$$

Example 4. *Expand $f(x) = e^{-x}$ as a Fourier series in the interval $(-l, l)$.*

Sol. Let $f(x) = e^{-x} = \frac{a_0}{2} + \sum_{n=1}^{\infty} a_n \cos\frac{n\pi x}{l} + \sum_{n=1}^{\infty} b_n \sin\frac{n\pi x}{l}$

Then $\quad a_0 = \frac{1}{l}\int_{-l}^{l} e^{-x}\,dx = \frac{1}{l}\left[-e^{-x}\right]_{-l}^{l} = \frac{1}{l}(e^l - e^{-l}) = \frac{2\sinh l}{l}$

$$a_n = \frac{1}{l}\int_{-l}^{l} e^{-x}\cos\frac{n\pi x}{l}\,dx = \frac{1}{l}\left[\frac{e^{-x}}{1+\left(\frac{n\pi}{l}\right)^2}\left(-\cos\frac{n\pi x}{l}+\frac{n\pi}{l}\sin\frac{n\pi x}{l}\right)\right]_{-l}^{l}$$

$$= \frac{l}{l^2+(n\pi)^2}\,[-e^{-l}\cos n\pi + e^{l}\cos n\pi] = \frac{2l\cos n\pi}{l^2+(n\pi)^2}\left(\frac{e^l-e^{-l}}{2}\right)$$

$$= \frac{2l(-1)^n\sinh l}{l^2+n^2\pi^2}$$

$$b_n = \frac{1}{l}\int_{-l}^{l} e^{-x}\sin\frac{n\pi x}{l}\,dx = \frac{1}{l}\left[\frac{e^{-x}}{1+\left(\frac{n\pi}{l}\right)^2}\left(-\sin\frac{n\pi x}{l}-\frac{n\pi}{l}\cos\frac{n\pi x}{l}\right)\right]_{-l}^{l}$$

$$= -\frac{l}{l^2+(n\pi)^2}\left[\frac{n\pi}{l}(e^{-l}-e^{l})\cos n\pi\right] = \frac{2n\pi\cos n\pi}{l^2+(n\pi)^2}\left(\frac{e^l-e^{-l}}{2}\right) = \frac{2n\pi(-1)^n\sinh l}{l^2+n^2\pi^2}$$

$$\therefore \quad e^{-x} = \frac{\sinh l}{l} + 2l \sinh l \sum_{n=1}^{\infty} \frac{(-1)^n}{l^2 + n^2\pi^2} \cos \frac{n\pi x}{l} + 2\pi \sinh l \sum_{n=1}^{\infty} \frac{n(-1)^n}{l^2 + n^2\pi^2} \sin \frac{n\pi x}{l}.$$

Example 5. *Obtain Fourier series for* $f(x) = \begin{cases} \pi x, & 0 \le x \le 1 \\ \pi(2-x), & 1 \le x \le 2 \end{cases}$. (U.P.T.U. 2007)

Sol. Let $f(x) = \dfrac{a_0}{2} + \sum_{n=1}^{\infty} a_n \cos n\pi x + \sum_{n=1}^{\infty} b_n \sin n\pi x$

Then $a_0 = \int_0^2 f(x)\,dx = \int_0^1 \pi x\,dx + \int_1^2 \pi(2-x)\,dx = \pi\left[\dfrac{x^2}{2}\right]_0^1 + \pi\left[2x - \dfrac{x^2}{2}\right]_1^2$

$$= \pi\left(\frac{1}{2}\right) + \pi\left[(4-2) - \left(2 - \frac{1}{2}\right)\right] = \pi$$

$$a_n = \int_0^2 f(x) \cos n\pi x\,dx = \int_0^1 \pi x \cos n\pi x\,dx + \int_1^2 \pi(2-x) \cos n\pi x\,dx$$

$$= \left[\pi x \cdot \frac{\sin n\pi x}{n\pi} - \pi\left(-\frac{\cos n\pi x}{n^2\pi^2}\right)\right]_0^1 + \left[\pi(2-x) \cdot \frac{\sin n\pi x}{n\pi} - (-\pi)\left(-\frac{\cos n\pi x}{n^2\pi^2}\right)\right]_1^2$$

$$= \left[\frac{\cos n\pi}{n^2\pi} - \frac{1}{n^2\pi}\right] + \left[-\frac{\cos 2n\pi}{n^2\pi} + \frac{\cos n\pi}{n^2\pi}\right] = \frac{2}{n^2\pi}(\cos n\pi - 1) = \frac{2}{n^2\pi}[(-1)^n - 1]$$

$= 0$ or $-\dfrac{4}{n^2\pi}$ according as n is even or odd.

$$b_n = \int_0^2 f(x) \sin n\pi x\,dx = \int_0^1 \pi x \sin n\pi x\,dx + \int_1^2 \pi(2-x) \sin n\pi x\,dx$$

$$= \left[\pi x\left(-\frac{\cos n\pi x}{n\pi}\right) - \pi\left(-\frac{\sin n\pi x}{n^2\pi^2}\right)\right]_0^1 + \left[\pi(2-x)\left(-\frac{\cos n\pi x}{n\pi}\right) - (-\pi)\left(-\frac{\sin n\pi x}{n^2\pi^2}\right)\right]_1^2$$

$$= \left[-\frac{\cos n\pi}{n}\right] + \left[\frac{\cos n\pi}{n}\right] = 0$$

$$f(x) = \frac{\pi}{2} - \frac{4}{\pi}\left(\frac{\cos \pi x}{1^2} + \frac{\cos 3\pi x}{3^2} + \frac{\cos 5\pi x}{5^2} + \ldots\ldots\right).$$

TEST YOUR KNOWLEDGE

1. Find a Fourier series for $f(t) = 1 - t^2$ when $-1 \le t \le 1$.
2. (*i*) Expand $f(x)$ in Fourier series in the interval $(-2, 2)$ when $f(x) = \begin{cases} 0, & -2 < x < 0 \\ 1, & 0 < x < 2. \end{cases}$

   (*ii*) Find the Fourier series of $f(x) = \begin{cases} 0, & \text{if } -2 \le x \le -1 \\ 1+x, & \text{if } -1 \le x \le 0 \\ 1-x, & \text{if } 0 \le x \le 1 \\ 0, & \text{if } 1 \le x \le 2 \end{cases}$ [**Hint.** $f(x)$ is an even function]

3. Develop $f(x)$ in a Fourier series in the interval (0, 2) if $f(x) = \begin{cases} x, & 0 < x < 1 \\ 0, & 1 < x < 2. \end{cases}$

4. (*i*) Find the Fourier expansion for $f(x) = \pi x$ from $x = -c$ to $x = c$.

(*ii*) Find the Fourier series expansion of $f(x) = 1 + |x|$ defined in $-3 < x < 3$.

[*M.T.U. (SUM) 2011*]

5. Find the Fourier expansion for the function $f(x) = x - x^3$ in the interval $-1 < x < 1$.

6. Find the Fourier series for the function given by $f(t) = \begin{cases} t, & 0 < t < 1 \\ 1 - t, & 1 < t < 2. \end{cases}$

Hence deduce that $\sum_{n=1}^{\infty} \frac{1}{(2n-1)^2} = \frac{\pi^2}{8}$ (*G.B.T.U. 2011*)

7. Find the Fourier series for the function $f(x) = \begin{cases} 0 & \text{when } -2 < x < -1 \\ k & \text{when } -1 < x < 1 \\ 0 & \text{when } 1 < x < 2 \end{cases}$.

8. A sinusoidal voltage E sin ωt is passed through a half-wave rectifier which clips the negative portion of the wave. Expand the resulting periodic function $u(t) = \begin{cases} 0 & \text{when } -\frac{T}{2} < t < 0 \\ E \sin \omega t & \text{when } 0 < t < \frac{T}{2} \end{cases}$

and $T = \frac{2\pi}{\omega}$, in a Fourier series.

9. Obtain Fourier series of the function $F(x) = \begin{cases} 1 + \frac{2x}{l}, & -l < x < 0 \\ 1 - \frac{2x}{l}, & 0 < x < l \end{cases}$

10. Find the Fourier series expansion of the periodic function whose definition in one period is $f(x) = 4 - x^2, -2 \le x \le 2$. Also prove that

$$1 - \frac{1}{2^2} + \frac{1}{3^2} - \frac{1}{4^2} + \ldots\ldots = \frac{\pi^2}{12}$$

Answers

1. $1 - t^2 = \frac{2}{3} + \frac{4}{\pi^2}\left(\cos \pi t - \frac{\cos 2\pi t}{2^2} + \frac{\cos 3\pi t}{3^2} - \ldots\ldots\right)$

2. (*i*) $f(x) = \frac{1}{2} + \frac{2}{\pi^2}\left(\sin \frac{\pi x}{2} + \frac{1}{3}\sin \frac{3\pi x}{2} + \frac{1}{5}\sin \frac{5\pi x}{2} + \ldots\ldots\right)$

(*ii*) $f(x) = \frac{1}{4} + \frac{4}{\pi^2}\sum_{n=1}^{\infty} \frac{\left(1 - \cos \frac{n\pi}{2}\right)}{n^2} \cos \frac{n\pi x}{2}$

3. $f(x) = \frac{1}{4} - \frac{2}{\pi^2}\left(\cos \pi x + \frac{\cos 3\pi x}{3^2} + \frac{\cos 5\pi x}{5^2} + \ldots\ldots\right) + \frac{1}{\pi}\left(\sin \pi x - \frac{\sin 2\pi x}{2} + \frac{\sin 3\pi x}{3} + \ldots\ldots\right)$

4. (*i*) $f(x) = 2c\left[\sin\left(\frac{\pi x}{c}\right) - \frac{1}{2}\sin\left(\frac{2\pi x}{c}\right) + \frac{1}{3}\sin\left(\frac{3\pi x}{c}\right) - \ldots\ldots\right]$

(*ii*) $f(x) = \frac{5}{2} - \frac{12}{\pi^2}\left[\frac{1}{1^2}\cos x + \frac{1}{3^2}\cos 3x + \frac{1}{5^2}\cos 5x + \ldots\right]$

5. $f(x) = \frac{12}{\pi^3}\left(\sin \pi x - \frac{\sin 2\pi x}{2^3} + \frac{\sin 3\pi x}{3^3} - \ldots\ldots\right)$

6. $f(t) = -\frac{4}{\pi^2}\left(\cos \pi t + \frac{\cos 3\pi t}{3^2} + \frac{\cos 5\pi t}{5^2} + ...\right) + \frac{2}{\pi}\left(\sin \pi t + \frac{\sin 3\pi t}{3} + ...\right)$

7. $f(x) = \frac{k}{2} + \frac{2k}{\pi}\left(\cos \frac{\pi x}{2} - \frac{1}{3}\cos \frac{3\pi x}{2} + \frac{1}{5}\cos \frac{5\pi x}{2} - ......\right)$

8. $u(t) = \frac{E}{\pi} + \frac{E}{2}\sin \omega t - \frac{2E}{\pi}\left(\frac{\cos 2\omega t}{1.3} + \frac{\cos 4\omega t}{3.5} + \frac{\cos 6\omega t}{5.7} + ...\right)$

9. $F(x) = \frac{4}{\pi^2}\sum_{n=1}^{\infty} \{1-(-1)^n\} \frac{\cos n \frac{\pi x}{l}}{n^2}$

10. $f(x) = \frac{8}{3} - \frac{16}{\pi^2}\sum_{n=1}^{\infty} \frac{(-1)^n}{n^2} \cos \frac{n\pi x}{2}$

4.7. HALF RANGE SERIES

Sometimes it is required to expand a function $f(x)$ in the range $(0, \pi)$ in a Fourier series of period 2π or more generally in the range $(0, l)$ in a Fourier series of period $2l$.

If it is required to expand $f(x)$ in the interval $(0, l)$, then it is immaterial what the function may be outside the range $0 < x < l$. We are free to choose it arbitrarily in the interval $(-l, 0)$.

If we extend the function $f(x)$ by reflecting it in the y-axis so that $f(-x) = f(x)$, then the extended function is even for which $b_n = 0$. The Fourier expansion of $f(x)$ will contain only cosine terms.

If we extend the function $f(x)$ by reflecting it in the origin so that $f(-x) = -f(x)$, then the extended function is odd for which $a_0 = a_n = 0$. The Fourier expansion of $f(x)$ will contain only sine terms.

For example, consider the function

$$f(x) = \begin{cases} x, & 0 < x < \frac{\pi}{2} \\ \pi - x, & \frac{\pi}{2} < x < \pi \end{cases}$$

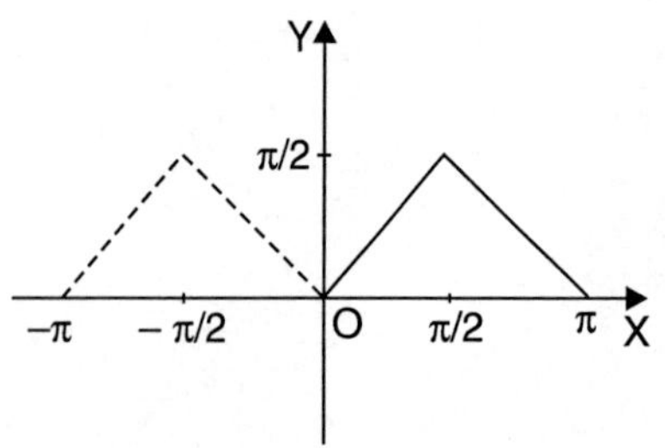

(Reflection in the y-axis)

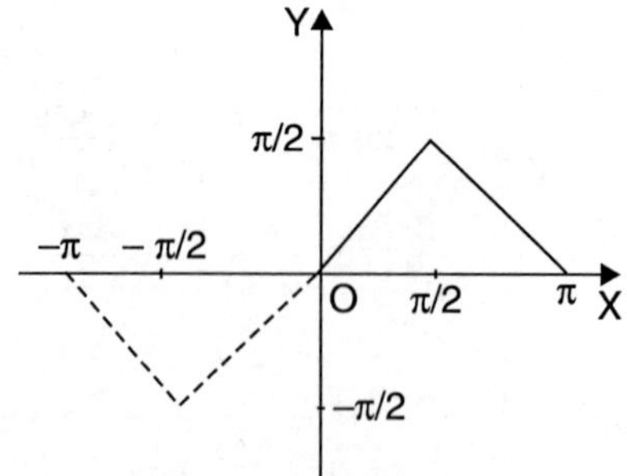

(Reflection in the origin)

Hence a function $f(x)$ defined over the interval $0 < x < l$ is capable of two distinct half-range series.

The half-range cosine series is

$$f(x) = \frac{a_0}{2} + \sum_{n=1}^{\infty} a_n \cos \frac{n\pi x}{l}$$

where $a_0 = \frac{2}{l}\int_0^l f(x)\, dx$; $a_n = \frac{2}{l}\int_0^l f(x) \cos \frac{n\pi x}{l}\, dx.$

The half-range sine series is

$$f(x) = \sum_{n=1}^{\infty} b_n \sin \frac{n\pi x}{l} \quad \text{where} \quad b_n = \frac{2}{l}\int_0^l f(x) \sin \frac{n\pi x}{l}\, dx.$$

Cor. If the range is $0 < x < \pi$, then

(*i*) The half-range cosine series is

$$f(x) = \frac{a_0}{2} + \sum_{n=1}^{\infty} a_n \cos nx$$

where $a_0 = \frac{2}{\pi}\int_0^{\pi} f(x)\, dx$; $a_n = \frac{2}{\pi}\int_0^{\pi} f(x) \cos nx\, dx.$

(*ii*) The half-range sine series is

$$f(x) = \sum_{n=1}^{\infty} b_n \sin nx \quad \text{where} \quad b_n = \frac{2}{\pi}\int_0^{\pi} f(x) \sin nx\, dx.$$

ILLUSTRATIVE EXAMPLES

Example 1. *Expand $\pi x - x^2$ in a half-range sine series in the interval $(0, \pi)$ up to the first three terms.*

Sol. Let $\pi x - x^2 = \sum_{n=1}^{\infty} b_n \sin nx$, where

$$b_n = \frac{2}{\pi}\int_0^{\pi} (\pi x - x^2) \sin nx\, dx$$

$$= \frac{2}{\pi}\left[\left\{(\pi x - x^2)\left(\frac{-\cos nx}{n}\right)\right\}_0^{\pi} - \int_0^{\pi} (\pi - 2x)\left(\frac{-\cos nx}{n}\right) dx\right]$$

$$= \frac{2}{\pi n}\int_0^{\pi} (\pi - 2x) \cos nx\, dx$$

$$= \frac{2}{\pi n}\left[\left\{(\pi - 2x)\frac{\sin nx}{n}\right\}_0^{\pi} - \int_0^{\pi} (-2)\frac{\sin nx}{n}\, dx\right]$$

$$= \frac{4}{\pi n^2}\left(\frac{-\cos nx}{n}\right)_0^{\pi} = \frac{4}{\pi n^3}\{1 - (-1)^n\}$$

$$= 0 \quad \text{or} \quad \frac{8}{\pi n^3} \quad \text{according as } n \text{ is even or odd.}$$

$$\therefore \quad \pi x - x^2 = \frac{8}{\pi}\left(\sin x + \frac{\sin 3x}{3^3} + \frac{\sin 5x}{5^3} + \ldots\ldots\right).$$

Example 2. *If* $f(x) = \begin{cases} x, & 0 < x < \dfrac{\pi}{2} \\ \pi - x, & \dfrac{\pi}{2} < x < \pi \end{cases}$

show that (i) $f(x) = \dfrac{4}{\pi}\left[\sin x - \dfrac{\sin 3x}{3^2} + \dfrac{\sin 5x}{5^2} - \ldots\ldots\right]$

(ii) $f(x) = \dfrac{\pi}{4} - \dfrac{2}{\pi}\left[\dfrac{\cos 2x}{1^2} + \dfrac{\cos 6x}{3^2} + \dfrac{\cos 10x}{5^2} + \ldots\ldots\right]$.

Sol. (*i*) **For the half-range sine series,**

Let $f(x) = \sum_{n=1}^{\infty} b_n \sin nx$

where, $b_n = \dfrac{2}{\pi}\int_0^{\pi} f(x) \sin nx\, dx = \dfrac{2}{\pi}\left[\int_0^{\pi/2} x \sin nx\, dx + \int_{\pi/2}^{\pi} (\pi - x) \sin nx\, dx\right]$

$$= \frac{2}{\pi}\left[x\left(-\frac{\cos nx}{n}\right) - 1.\left(-\frac{\sin nx}{n^2}\right)\right]_0^{\pi/2} + \frac{2}{\pi}\left[(\pi - x)\left(-\frac{\cos nx}{n}\right) - (-1)\left(-\frac{\sin nx}{n^2}\right)\right]_{\pi/2}^{\pi}$$

$$= \frac{2}{\pi}\left[-\frac{\pi}{2n}\cos\frac{n\pi}{2} + \frac{1}{n^2}\sin\frac{n\pi}{2}\right] + \frac{2}{\pi}\left[\frac{\pi}{2n}\cos\frac{n\pi}{2} + \frac{1}{n^2}\sin\frac{n\pi}{2}\right]$$

$$= \frac{2}{\pi}\left[\frac{2}{n^2}\sin\frac{n\pi}{2}\right] = \frac{4}{\pi n^2}\sin\frac{n\pi}{2}$$

When n is even, $b_n = 0$.

$$\therefore \quad f(x) = \frac{4}{\pi}\left[\sin x - \frac{\sin 3x}{3^2} + \frac{\sin 5x}{5^2} - \ldots\ldots\right]$$

(*ii*) **For the half-range cosine series,**

Let $f(x) = \dfrac{a_0}{2} + \sum_{n=1}^{\infty} a_n \cos nx$

Then $a_0 = \dfrac{2}{\pi}\int_0^{\pi} f(x)\, dx = \dfrac{2}{\pi}\left[\int_0^{\pi/2} x\, dx + \int_{\pi/2}^{\pi} (\pi - x)\, dx\right]$

$$= \frac{2}{\pi}\left[\left|\frac{x^2}{2}\right|_0^{\pi/2} + \left|\pi x - \frac{x^2}{2}\right|_{\pi/2}^{\pi}\right]$$

$$= \frac{2}{\pi}\left[\frac{\pi^2}{8} + \left(\pi^2 - \frac{\pi^2}{2}\right) - \left(\frac{\pi^2}{2} - \frac{\pi^2}{8}\right)\right] = \frac{2}{\pi}\left[\frac{\pi^2}{4}\right] = \frac{\pi}{2}$$

$$a_n = \frac{2}{\pi}\int_0^{\pi} f(x) \cos nx\, dx = \frac{2}{\pi}\left[\int_0^{\pi/2} x \cos nx\, dx + \int_{\pi/2}^{\pi} (\pi - x) \cos nx\, dx\right]$$

$$= \frac{2}{\pi}\left[x \cdot \frac{\sin nx}{n} - 1.\left(-\frac{\cos nx}{n^2}\right)\right]_0^{\pi/2} + \frac{2}{\pi}\left[(\pi - x) \cdot \frac{\sin nx}{n} - (-1)\left(-\frac{\cos nx}{n^2}\right)\right]_{\pi/2}^{\pi}$$

$$= \frac{2}{\pi}\left[\frac{\pi}{2n}\sin\frac{n\pi}{2} + \frac{1}{n^2}\cos\frac{n\pi}{2} - \frac{1}{n^2}\right] + \frac{2}{\pi}\left[-\frac{\cos n\pi}{n^2} - \frac{\pi}{2n}\sin\frac{n\pi}{2} + \frac{1}{n^2}\cos\frac{n\pi}{2}\right]$$

$$= \frac{2}{\pi}\left[\frac{2}{n^2}\cos\frac{n\pi}{2} - \frac{\cos n\pi}{n^2} - \frac{1}{n^2}\right] = \frac{2}{\pi n^2}\left[2\cos\frac{n\pi}{2} - \cos n\pi - 1\right]$$

$\therefore \quad a_1 = 0,\ a_2 = \dfrac{2}{\pi . 2^2}(2\cos\pi - \cos 2\pi - 1) = \dfrac{-2}{\pi . 1^2}$,

$a_3 = 0,\ a_4 = 0,\ a_5 = 0,\ a_6 = \dfrac{2}{\pi . 6^2}(2\cos 3\pi - \cos 6\pi - 1) = \dfrac{-2}{\pi . 3^2}$,

$a_7 = 0,\ a_8 = 0,\ a_9 = 0,\ a_{10} = \dfrac{2}{\pi . 10^2}(2\cos 5\pi - \cos 10\pi - 1) = \dfrac{-2}{\pi . 5^2}$, ...

Hence $\quad f(x) = \dfrac{\pi}{4} - \dfrac{2}{\pi}\left[\dfrac{\cos 2x}{1^2} + \dfrac{\cos 6x}{3^2} + \dfrac{\cos 10x}{5^2} + ...\right]$.

Example 3. *Find a series of cosines of multiples of x which will represent x sin x in the interval (0, π) and show that* $\dfrac{1}{1.3} - \dfrac{1}{3.5} + \dfrac{1}{5.7} - ...... = \dfrac{\pi - 2}{4}$.

Sol. Let $x \sin x = \dfrac{a_0}{2} + \displaystyle\sum_{n=1}^{\infty} a_n \cos nx$

Here, $\quad a_0 = \dfrac{2}{\pi}\displaystyle\int_0^\pi x \sin x\, dx = \dfrac{2}{\pi}\Big[x(-\cos x) - 1.(-\sin x)\Big]_0^\pi = \dfrac{2}{\pi}[-\pi\cos\pi] = 2$

$$a_n = \frac{2}{\pi}\int_0^\pi x \sin x \cos nx\, dx = \frac{1}{\pi}\int_0^\pi x\,(2\cos nx \sin x)\, dx$$

$$= \frac{1}{\pi}\int_0^\pi x\,[\sin(n+1)x - \sin(n-1)x]\, dx$$

$$= \frac{1}{\pi}\left[x\left\{-\frac{\cos(n+1)x}{n+1} + \frac{\cos(n-1)x}{n-1}\right\} - 1.\left\{-\frac{\sin(n+1)x}{(n+1)^2} - \frac{\sin(n-1)x}{(n-1)^2}\right\}\right]_0^\pi$$

$$= \frac{1}{\pi}\left[-\frac{\pi\cos(n+1)\pi}{n+1} + \frac{\pi\cos(n-1)\pi}{n-1}\right] \quad \text{when } n \neq 1$$

$$= -\frac{(-1)^{n+1}}{n+1} + \frac{(-1)^{n-1}}{n-1} = (-1)^{n-1}\left[\frac{1}{n-1} - \frac{1}{n+1}\right] = \frac{2(-1)^{n-1}}{(n-1)(n+1)}$$

When $n = 1$, we have

$$a_1 = \frac{2}{\pi}\int_0^\pi x \sin x \cos x\, dx = \frac{1}{\pi}\int_0^\pi x \sin 2x\, dx = \frac{1}{\pi}\left[x\left(-\frac{\cos 2x}{2}\right) - 1.\left(-\frac{\sin 2x}{2^2}\right)\right]_0^\pi$$

$$= \frac{1}{\pi}\left[-\frac{\pi\cos 2\pi}{2}\right] = -\frac{1}{2}$$

$$\therefore \quad x \sin x = 1 - \frac{1}{2}\cos x - 2\left(\frac{\cos 2x}{1.3} - \frac{\cos 3x}{2.4} + \frac{\cos 4x}{3.5} - ......\right).$$

Putting $x = \dfrac{\pi}{2}$, we get

$$\frac{\pi}{2} = 1 - 2\left(\frac{-1}{1.3} + \frac{1}{3.5} + \frac{-1}{5.7} - ......\right)$$

$$\Rightarrow \qquad 1+\frac{2}{1.3}-\frac{2}{3.5}+\frac{2}{5.7}-\ldots\ldots=\frac{\pi}{2}$$

$$\Rightarrow \qquad \frac{2}{1.3}-\frac{2}{3.5}+\frac{2}{5.7}-\ldots\ldots=\frac{\pi}{2}-1$$

Hence $$\frac{1}{1.3}-\frac{1}{3.5}+\frac{1}{5.7}-\ldots\ldots=\frac{\pi-2}{4}.$$

Example 4. *Obtain the half-range sine series for e^x in $0 < x < 1$.*

Sol. Let $$e^x=\sum_{n=1}^{\infty} b_n \sin n\pi x, \text{ (since } l=1)$$

Here, $$b_n=2\int_0^1 e^x \sin n\pi x\, dx = 2\left[\frac{e^x}{1+(n\pi)^2}(\sin n\pi x - n\pi\cos n\pi x)\right]_0^1$$

$$=2\left[\frac{e}{1+(n\pi)^2}(-n\pi\cos n\pi)-\frac{1}{1+(n\pi)^2}(-n\pi)\right]$$

$$=\frac{2}{1+n^2\pi^2}\,[-en\pi(-1)^n+n\pi]=\frac{2n\pi}{1+n^2\pi^2}\,[1-e(-1)^n]$$

Hence $$e^x=2\pi\sum_{n=1}^{\infty}\frac{n[1-e(-1)^n]}{1+n^2\pi^2}\sin n\pi x.$$

Example 5. *Develop $f(x) = \sin\left(\frac{\pi x}{l}\right)$ in half-range cosine series in the range $0 < x < l$. Graph the corresponding periodic continuation of $f(x)$.* [U.P.T.U. (SUM) 2007]

Sol. Let $$\sin\left(\frac{\pi x}{l}\right)=\frac{a_0}{2}+\sum_{n=1}^{\infty} a_n\cos\frac{n\pi x}{l}$$

where, $$a_0=\frac{2}{l}\int_0^l \sin\frac{\pi x}{l}\,dx=\frac{2}{l}\left[-\frac{\cos\frac{\pi x}{l}}{\frac{\pi}{l}}\right]_0^l=-\frac{2}{\pi}[\cos\pi-1]=\frac{4}{\pi}$$

$$a_n=\frac{2}{l}\int_0^l \sin\frac{\pi x}{l}\cos\frac{n\pi x}{l}\,dx$$

$$=\frac{1}{l}\int_0^l\left[\sin(n+1)\frac{\pi x}{l}-\sin(n-1)\frac{\pi x}{l}\right]dx$$

$$=\frac{1}{l}\left[-\frac{\cos(n+1)\frac{\pi x}{l}}{(n+1)\frac{\pi}{l}}+\frac{\cos(n-1)\frac{\pi x}{l}}{(n-1)\frac{\pi}{l}}\right]_0^l$$

$$=\frac{1}{\pi}\left[\left\{-\frac{\cos(n+1)\pi}{n+1}+\frac{\cos(n-1)\pi}{n-1}\right\}-\left\{-\frac{1}{n+1}+\frac{1}{n-1}\right\}\right]$$

$$=\frac{1}{\pi}\left[-\frac{(-1)^{n+1}}{n+1}+\frac{(-1)^{n-1}}{n-1}+\frac{1}{n+1}-\frac{1}{n-1}\right]$$

When n is odd, $$a_n = \frac{1}{\pi}\left[-\frac{1}{n+1}+\frac{1}{n-1}+\frac{1}{n+1}-\frac{1}{n-1}\right] = 0\ ;\ n \neq 1$$

When n is even, $$a_n = \frac{1}{\pi}\left[\frac{1}{n+1}-\frac{1}{n-1}+\frac{1}{n+1}-\frac{1}{n-1}\right]$$

$$= \frac{2}{\pi}\left[\frac{1}{n+1}-\frac{1}{n-1}\right] = -\frac{4}{\pi(n+1)(n-1)}$$

When $n = 1$, $$a_1 = \frac{2}{l}\int_0^l \sin\frac{\pi x}{l}\cos\frac{\pi x}{l}\,dx$$

$$= \frac{1}{l}\int_0^l \sin\frac{2\pi x}{l}\,dx = \frac{1}{l}\left(\frac{-\cos\frac{2\pi x}{l}}{\frac{2\pi}{l}}\right)_0^l = \frac{1}{2\pi}(1-\cos 2\pi) = 0$$

$$\therefore \quad \sin\left(\frac{\pi x}{l}\right) = \frac{2}{\pi} - \frac{4}{\pi}\left[\frac{\cos\frac{2\pi x}{l}}{1.3}+\frac{\cos\frac{4\pi x}{l}}{3.5}+\frac{\cos\frac{6\pi x}{l}}{5.7}+\ldots\ldots\right].$$

In $0 < x < l$, $f(x)$ is neither periodic nor odd nor even. So we construct

$$g(x) = \begin{cases} \sin\frac{\pi x}{l} & \text{in } 0 < x < l \\ -\sin\frac{\pi x}{l} & \text{in } -l < x < 0 \end{cases}$$

which is even, periodic with period $2l$.

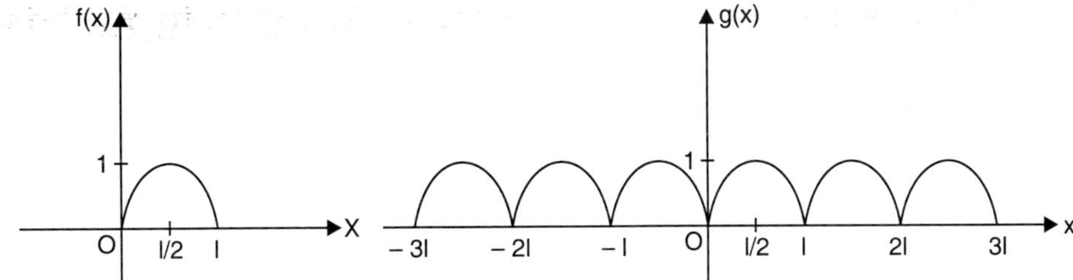

Example 6. *Obtain a half-range cosine series for*

$$f(x) = \begin{cases} kx, & \text{for } 0 < x < \frac{l}{2} \\ k(l-x), & \text{for } \frac{l}{2} \le x \le l \end{cases}.$$

Deduce the sum of the series $\frac{1}{1^2}+\frac{1}{3^2}+\frac{1}{5^2}+\ldots\ldots$

Sol. Let $$f(x) = \frac{a_0}{2} + \sum_{n=1}^{\infty} a_n \cos\frac{n\pi x}{l}$$

where, $$a_0 = \frac{2}{l}\int_0^l f(x)\,dx = \frac{2}{l}\left[\int_0^{l/2} kx\,dx + \int_{l/2}^{l} k(l-x)\,dx\right]$$

$$= \frac{2}{l}\left[\left|\frac{kx^2}{2}\right|_0^{l/2} + \left|k\left(lx - \frac{x^2}{2}\right)\right|_{l/2}^{l}\right]$$

$$= \frac{2}{l}\left[\frac{kl^2}{8} + k\left(l^2 - \frac{l^2}{2}\right) - k\left(\frac{l^2}{2} - \frac{l^2}{8}\right)\right] = \frac{2}{l}\left(\frac{kl^2}{4}\right) = \frac{kl}{2}$$

$$a_n = \frac{2}{l}\int_0^l f(x)\cos\frac{n\pi x}{l}\,dx = \frac{2}{l}\left[\int_0^{l/2} kx\,.\cos\frac{n\pi x}{l}\,dx + \int_{l/2}^{l} k(l-x)\,.\cos\frac{n\pi x}{l}\,dx\right]$$

$$= \frac{2}{l}\left[\left|kx\,.\frac{l}{n\pi}\sin\frac{n\pi x}{l} + k\,.\frac{l^2}{n^2\pi^2}\cos\frac{n\pi x}{l}\right|_0^{l/2}\right.$$

$$\left.+\left|k(l-x)\,.\frac{l}{n\pi}\sin\frac{n\pi x}{l} - k\,.\frac{l^2}{n^2\pi^2}\cos\frac{n\pi x}{l}\right|_{l/2}^{l}\right]$$

$$= \frac{2}{l}\left[\left|\frac{kl^2}{2n\pi}\sin\frac{n\pi}{2} + \frac{kl^2}{n^2\pi^2}\left(\cos\frac{n\pi}{2} - 1\right)\right|\right.$$

$$\left.+\left|\frac{-kl^2}{n^2\pi^2}\cos n\pi - \frac{kl^2}{2n\pi}\sin\frac{n\pi}{2} + \frac{kl^2}{n^2\pi^2}\cos\frac{n\pi}{2}\right|\right]$$

$$= \frac{2}{l}\left[\frac{2kl^2}{n^2\pi^2}\cos\frac{n\pi}{2} - \frac{kl^2}{n^2\pi^2} - \frac{kl^2}{n^2\pi^2}\cos n\pi\right] = \frac{2kl}{n^2\pi^2}\left[2\cos\frac{n\pi}{2} - 1 - \cos n\pi\right]$$

When n is odd, $\cos\frac{n\pi}{2} = 0$ and $\cos n\pi = -1$ $\quad\therefore\quad a_n = 0 \Rightarrow a_1 = a_3 = a_5 = \ldots\ldots = 0$

When n is even, $$a_2 = \frac{2kl}{2^2\pi^2}[2\cos\pi - 1 - \cos 2\pi] = -\frac{8kl}{2^2\pi^2}\;;$$

$$a_4 = \frac{2kl}{4^2\pi^2}[2\cos 2\pi - 1 - \cos 4\pi] = 0$$

$$a_6 = \frac{2kl}{6^2\pi^2}[2\cos 3\pi - 1 - \cos 6\pi]$$

$$= \frac{2kl}{6^2\pi^2}(-2-1-1) = -\frac{8kl}{6^2\pi^2} \text{ and so on.}$$

$$\therefore \quad f(x) = \frac{kl}{4} - \frac{8kl}{\pi^2}\left(\frac{1}{2^2}\cos\frac{2\pi x}{l} + \frac{1}{6^2}\cos\frac{6\pi x}{l} + \ldots\ldots\right) \qquad \ldots(1)$$

Putting $x = l$, $f(l) = 0$

$\therefore$ From (1), we have $0 = \frac{kl}{4} - \frac{8kl}{\pi^2}\left(\frac{1}{2^2} + \frac{1}{6^2} + \ldots\ldots\right)$

$$\Rightarrow \qquad \frac{1}{2^2}+\frac{1}{6^2}+\ldots\ldots=\frac{\pi^2}{32}$$

$$\Rightarrow \qquad \frac{1}{2^2}\left[\frac{1}{1^2}+\frac{1}{3^2}+\ldots\ldots\right]=\frac{\pi^2}{32}$$

Hence $$\frac{1}{1^2}+\frac{1}{3^2}+\ldots\ldots=\frac{\pi^2}{8}.$$

Example 7. *Let* $f(x)=\begin{cases}\omega x, & when \ \ 0\le x\le \dfrac{l}{2}\\ \omega(l-x), & when \ \ \dfrac{l}{2}\le x\le l\end{cases}$

Show that $$f(x)=\frac{4\omega l}{\pi^2}\sum_{n=0}^{\infty}\frac{(-1)^n}{(2n+1)^2}\sin\frac{(2n+1)\pi x}{l}$$

Hence obtain the sum of the series

$$1+\frac{1}{3^2}+\frac{1}{5^2}+\ldots\ldots$$ (G.B.T.U. 2011)

Sol. For half-range sine series,

Let $$f(x)=\sum_{n=1}^{\infty} b_n \sin\frac{n\pi x}{l} \qquad \ldots(1)$$

where, $$b_n=\frac{2}{l}\int_0^l f(x)\sin\frac{n\pi x}{l}\,dx$$

$$=\frac{2}{l}\left[\int_0^{l/2}\omega x\sin\frac{n\pi x}{l}\,dx+\int_{l/2}^{l}\omega(l-x)\sin\frac{n\pi x}{l}\,dx\right]$$

$$=\frac{2}{l}\left[\omega.\left\{x.\left(\frac{-\cos\frac{n\pi x}{l}}{\frac{n\pi}{l}}\right)\right\}_0^{l/2}-\int_0^{l/2}\omega.\left(\frac{-\cos\frac{n\pi x}{l}}{\frac{n\pi}{l}}\right)dx\right.$$

$$\left.+\,\omega\left\{(l-x).\left(\frac{-\cos\frac{n\pi x}{l}}{\frac{n\pi}{l}}\right)\right\}_{l/2}^{l}-\int_{l/2}^{l}(-\omega)\left(\frac{-\cos\frac{n\pi x}{l}}{\frac{n\pi}{l}}\right)dx\right]$$

$$=\frac{2}{l}\left[\omega.\frac{l}{2}.\frac{l}{n\pi}\left(-\cos\frac{n\pi}{2}\right)+\frac{\omega l}{n\pi}\left(\frac{\sin\frac{n\pi x}{l}}{\frac{n\pi}{l}}\right)_0^{l/2}\right.$$

$$\left.+\,\omega.\frac{l}{2}.\frac{l}{n\pi}\cos\frac{n\pi}{2}-\frac{\omega l}{n\pi}\left\{\sin\left(\frac{n\pi x}{l}\right)\Big/\frac{n\pi}{l}\right\}_{l/2}^{l}\right]$$

$$=\frac{2}{l}\left[\frac{\omega l^2}{n^2\pi^2}\sin\frac{n\pi}{2}-\frac{\omega l^2}{n^2\pi^2}\left(0-\sin\frac{n\pi}{2}\right)\right]=\frac{4\omega l}{n^2\pi^2}\sin\frac{n\pi}{2} \qquad \ldots(2)$$

$\therefore$ From (1), $f(x) = \dfrac{4\omega l}{\pi^2} \sum_{n=1}^{\infty} \dfrac{1}{n^2} \sin \dfrac{n\pi}{2} \sin \dfrac{n\pi x}{l}$

$$= \frac{4\omega l}{\pi^2} \sum_{n=0}^{\infty} \frac{1}{(2n+1)^2} \sin (2n+1) \frac{\pi}{2} \sin \frac{(2n+1)\pi x}{l}$$

$$= \frac{4\omega l}{\pi^2} \sum_{n=0}^{\infty} \frac{(-1)^n}{(2n+1)^2} \sin \frac{(2n+1)\pi x}{l} \quad \ldots(3)$$

Put $x = \dfrac{l}{2}$ in eqn.(3), we get

$$\frac{\omega l}{2} = \frac{4\omega l}{\pi^2} \sum_{n=0}^{\infty} \frac{(-1)^n}{(2n+1)^2} \sin (2n+1) \frac{\pi}{2} = \frac{4\omega l}{\pi^2} \sum_{n=0}^{\infty} \frac{(-1)^n}{(2n+1)^2} (-1)^n$$

$$\Rightarrow \quad \frac{\pi^2}{8} = \sum_{n=0}^{\infty} \frac{1}{(2n+1)^2}$$

or $\quad \dfrac{1}{1^2} + \dfrac{1}{3^2} + \dfrac{1}{5^2} + \ldots\ldots = \dfrac{\pi^2}{8}.$

Example 8. *Expand $f(x) = x$ as a half range*

(i) sine series in $0 < x < 2$ [U.P.T.U. 2007, U.K.T.U. 2011]

(ii) cosine series in $0 < x < 2$. [U.P.T.U. 2007]

Sol. (*i*) Let $\quad x = \sum_{n=1}^{\infty} b_n \sin \dfrac{n\pi x}{2} \quad \ldots(1)$

where, $\quad b_n = \displaystyle\int_0^2 x \sin \frac{n\pi x}{2}\, dx$

$$= \left\{ x \left(\frac{-\cos \frac{n\pi x}{2}}{\frac{n\pi}{2}} \right) \right\}_0^2 - \int_0^2 \left(\frac{-\cos \frac{n\pi x}{2}}{\frac{n\pi}{2}} \right) dx = -\frac{4}{n\pi} \cos n\pi = -\frac{4}{n\pi} (-1)^n$$

Hence from (1),

$$x = -\frac{4}{\pi} \sum_{n=1}^{\infty} \frac{(-1)^n}{n} \sin \frac{n\pi x}{2}$$

(*ii*) Let $\quad x = \dfrac{a_0}{2} + \sum_{n=1}^{\infty} a_n \cos \dfrac{n\pi x}{2} \quad \ldots(2)$

where, $\quad a_0 = \displaystyle\int_0^2 x\, dx = \left(\frac{x^2}{2} \right)_0^2 = 2$

and $\quad a_n = \displaystyle\int_0^2 x \cos \frac{n\pi x}{2}\, dx = \left(x \frac{\sin \frac{n\pi x}{2}}{\frac{n\pi}{2}} \right)_0^2 - \int_0^2 \frac{\sin \frac{n\pi x}{2}}{\frac{n\pi}{2}}\, dx$

$$= -\frac{2}{n\pi}\left(\frac{-\cos\frac{n\pi x}{2}}{\frac{n\pi}{2}}\right)_0^2 = \frac{4}{n^2\pi^2}(\cos n\pi - 1)$$

Hence, $$x = 1 + \frac{4}{\pi^2}\sum_{n=1}^{\infty}\frac{(\cos n\pi - 1)}{n^2}\cos\frac{n\pi x}{2}$$

TEST YOUR KNOWLEDGE

1. Obtain cosine and sine series for $f(x) = x$ in the interval $0 \le x \le \pi$. Hence show that $\frac{1}{1^2} + \frac{1}{3^2} + \frac{1}{5^2} + \ldots\ldots = \frac{\pi^2}{8}$.

2. Find Fourier half-range even expansion of the function $f(x) = \left(-\frac{x}{l}\right) + 1 \,;\, 0 \le x \le l$.

3. Find the half-range cosine series for the function $f(x) = (x-1)^2$ in the interval $0 < x < 1$. Hence show that

(*i*) $\frac{1}{1^2} + \frac{1}{2^2} + \frac{1}{3^2} + \frac{1}{4^2} + \ldots\ldots = \frac{\pi^2}{6}$ (*ii*) $\frac{1}{1^2} - \frac{1}{2^2} + \frac{1}{3^2} - \frac{1}{4^2} + \ldots\ldots = \frac{\pi^2}{12}$

(*iii*) $\frac{1}{1^2} + \frac{1}{3^2} + \frac{1}{5^2} + \frac{1}{7^2} + \ldots\ldots = \frac{\pi^2}{8}$.

4. Express $\sin x$ as a cosine series in $0 < x < \pi$.

5. Given the function $f(x) = x$, $0 < x < 1$, find:

(*i*) Fourier cosine series for $f(x)$ (*ii*) Fourier sine series for $f(x)$ [*G.B.T.U. (C.O.) 2011*]

6. (*i*) If

$$f(x) = \begin{cases} \frac{\pi}{3}, & 0 \le x \le \frac{\pi}{3} \\ 0, & \frac{\pi}{3} \le x \le \frac{2\pi}{3} \\ -\frac{\pi}{3}, & \frac{2\pi}{3} \le x \le \pi \end{cases}$$

then show that $f(x) = \frac{2}{\sqrt{3}}\left[\cos x - \frac{\cos 5x}{5} + \frac{\cos 7x}{7} - \ldots\ldots\right]$

(*ii*) If

$$f(x) = \begin{cases} mx, & 0 \le x \le \frac{\pi}{2} \\ m\,(\pi - x), & \frac{\pi}{2} \le x \le \pi \end{cases}$$

then show that $f(x) = \frac{4m}{\pi}\left[\frac{\sin x}{1^2} - \frac{\sin 3x}{3^2} + \frac{\sin 5x}{5^2} - \ldots\ldots\right]$.

7. Prove that for all values of x lying between $-\frac{\pi}{2}$ and $\frac{\pi}{2}$, $x = \frac{4}{\pi}\left[\sin x - \frac{\sin 3x}{3^2} + \frac{\sin 5x}{5^2} - \ldots\ldots\right]$.

8. (*i*) Obtain the half-range sine series for the function $f(x) = x^2$ is the interval $0 < x < 3$. [*G.B.T.U. (A.G.) SUM 2010*]

(*ii*) Expand $f(x) = k$ for $0 < x < 2$ in a half-range sine series. [*G.B.T.U. (A.G.) 2011*]

(*iii*) Find the half-range sine series of $f(x) = lx - x^2$ in the interval $(0, l)$. Hence, deduce that

$$\frac{\pi^3}{32} = 1 - \frac{1}{3^3} + \frac{1}{5^3} - \frac{1}{7^3} + \ldots$$ (*M.T.U. 2012*)

9. Show that the series $\frac{1}{\pi} \sum_{n=1}^{\infty} \frac{1}{n} \sin \frac{2n\pi x}{l}$ represents $\frac{l}{2} - x$ when $0 < x < l$.

10. (*i*) Find the half-range sine series for (*U.K.T.U. 2012*)

$$f(x) = \begin{cases} \frac{1}{4} - x, & 0 < x < \frac{1}{2} \\ x - \frac{3}{4}, & \frac{1}{2} < x < 1. \end{cases}$$

(*ii*) Represent the following function by Fourier sine series

$$f(x) = \begin{cases} 1 & \text{when } 0 < x < \frac{l}{2} \\ 0 & \text{when } \frac{l}{2} < x < l. \end{cases}$$

11. Find the half-range expansions of the function whose graph is given in followng figure. [*U.P.T.U. (C.O.) 2009*]

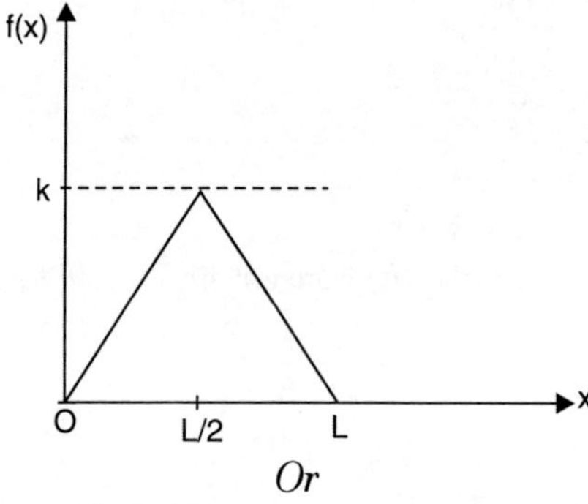

Or

Find the two half-range expansions of

$$f(x) = \begin{cases} \frac{2kx}{L} & \text{if } 0 < x < \frac{L}{2} \\ \frac{2k(L - x)}{L} & \text{if } \frac{L}{2} < x < L \end{cases}$$ [*U.P.T.U. (SUM) 2009*]

12. Find the half period sine series for $f(x)$ given in the range $(0, l)$ by the graph OPQ as shown in figure : (*U.P.T.U. 2009*)

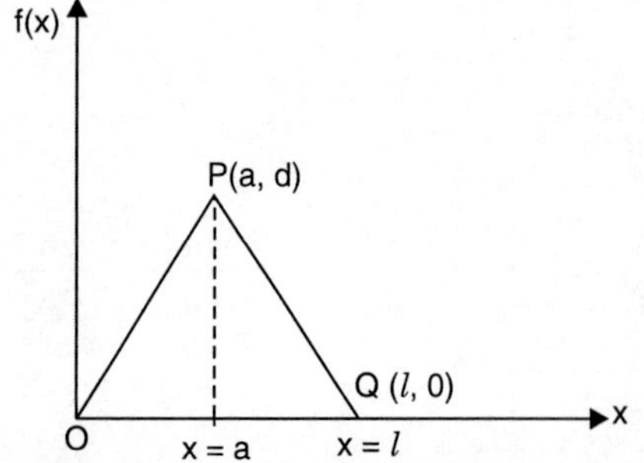

$$\left[\textbf{Hint: } f(x) = \begin{cases} \frac{dx}{a}, & 0 < x < a \\ \frac{d(l - x)}{l - a}, & a < x < l \end{cases} \right]$$

13. (*i*) Show that in the range $0 < x < \pi$, $c = \frac{4}{\pi}\left[\sin x + \frac{\sin 3x}{3} + \frac{\sin 5x}{5} + \ldots\ldots\right] c$; where c is the constant function.

(*ii*) Show that in the interval (0, 1), $\cos \pi x = \frac{8}{\pi}\sum_{n=1}^{\infty}\frac{n}{4n^2-1}\sin 2n\pi x$.

14. (*i*) Find the half-range cosine series for the function $f(x) = x(\pi - x)$; $0 < x < \pi$

(*ii*) Find the half-range sine series for the function $f(x) = 2x - 1$; $0 < x < 1$.

(*iii*) Find the half-range sine series for the function $f(t) = t - t^2$ in the interval $0 < t < 1$.

(M.T.U. 2011)

(*iv*) Find the half-range cosine series expansion of $f(x) = x - x^2$ in $0 < x < 1$. *(G.B.T.U. 2012)*

15. (*i*) Find the half range Fourier sine series of $f(x) = \begin{cases} \sin x, & 0 \le x \le \frac{\pi}{4} \\ \cos x, & \frac{\pi}{4} \le x \le \frac{\pi}{2} \end{cases}$. *[M.T.U. (SUM) 2011]*

(*ii*) Find the Fourier half-range cosine series of the function

$$F(t) = \begin{cases} 2t, & 0 < x < 1 \\ 2(2-t), & 1 < x < 2 \end{cases}$$

[G.B.T.U. (A.G.) 2011 ; U.P.T.U. 2006]

Answers

1. $f(x) = \frac{\pi}{2} - \frac{4}{\pi}\left(\cos x + \frac{\cos 3x}{3^2} + \frac{\cos 5x}{5^2} + \ldots\ldots\right)$; $f(x) = 2\left(\sin x - \frac{\sin 2x}{2} + \frac{\sin 3x}{3} - \frac{\sin 4x}{4} + \ldots\ldots\right)$

2. $f(x) = \frac{1}{2} + \frac{4}{\pi^2}\left[\frac{1}{1^2}\cos\frac{\pi x}{l} + \frac{1}{3^2}\cos\frac{3\pi x}{l} + \ldots\ldots\right]$

3. $f(x) = \frac{1}{3} + \frac{4}{\pi^2}\left(\cos \pi x + \frac{\cos 2\pi x}{2^2} + \frac{\cos 3\pi x}{3^2} + \ldots\ldots\right)$

4. $\sin x = \frac{2}{\pi} - \frac{4}{\pi}\left[\frac{\cos 2x}{1.3} + \frac{\cos 4x}{3.5} + \frac{\cos 6x}{5.7} + \ldots\ldots\right]$

5. (*i*) $f(x) = \frac{1}{2} - \frac{4}{\pi^2}\left[\frac{1}{1^2}\cos \pi x + \frac{1}{3^2}\cos 3\pi x + \frac{1}{5^2}\cos 5\pi x + \ldots\right]$

(*ii*) $f(x) = -\frac{2}{\pi}\sum_{n=1}^{\infty}\frac{(-1)^n}{n}\sin n\pi x$

8. (*i*) $f(x) = \sum_{n=1}^{\infty} b_n \sin\frac{n\pi x}{3}$, where $b_n = \frac{18}{n\pi}(-1)^{n+1} + \frac{36}{n^3\pi^3}[(-1)^n - 1]$

(*ii*) $f(x) = \frac{4k}{\pi}\left[\sin\frac{\pi x}{2} + \frac{1}{3}\sin\frac{3\pi x}{2} + \frac{1}{5}\sin\frac{5\pi x}{2} + \ldots\right]$

(*iii*) $f(x) = \frac{8l^2}{\pi^3}\sum_{\substack{n=1 \\ (n \text{ is odd})}}^{\infty}\frac{1}{n^3}\sin\frac{n\pi x}{l}$

10. (*i*) $f(x) = \left(\frac{1}{\pi} - \frac{4}{\pi^2}\right) \sin \pi x + \left(\frac{1}{3\pi} - \frac{4}{3^2 \pi^2}\right) \sin 3\pi x + \left(\frac{1}{5\pi} - \frac{4}{5^2 \pi^2}\right) \sin 5\pi x + \ldots$

(*ii*) $f(x) = \frac{2}{\pi}\left[\sin \frac{\pi x}{l} + \sin \frac{2\pi x}{l} + \frac{1}{3} \sin \frac{3\pi x}{l} + \frac{1}{5} \sin \frac{5\pi x}{l} + \ldots\ldots\right]$

11. (*i*) $f(x) = \frac{k}{2} + \frac{4k}{\pi^2} \sum_{n=1}^{\infty} \left(\frac{2 \cos \frac{n\pi}{2} - \cos n\pi - 1}{n^2}\right) \cos \frac{n\pi x}{L}$

(*ii*) $f(x) = \frac{8k}{\pi^2} \sum_{n=1}^{\infty} \frac{1}{n^2} \sin \frac{n\pi}{2} \sin \frac{n\pi x}{L}$

12. $f(x) = \sum_{n=1}^{\infty} \frac{2dl^2}{a(l-a)\, n^2 \pi^2} \sin \frac{n\pi a}{l} \sin \frac{n\pi x}{l}$

14. (*i*) $f(x) = \frac{\pi^2}{6} - 4\left(\frac{\cos 2x}{2^2} + \frac{\cos 4x}{4^2} + \ldots\ldots\right)$

(*ii*) $f(x) = -\frac{2}{\pi}\left(\sin 2\pi x + \frac{1}{2} \sin 4\pi x + \frac{1}{3} \sin 6\pi x + \ldots\ldots\right)$

(*iii*) $f(t) = \frac{8}{\pi^3}\left[\sin \pi t + \frac{1}{3^3} \sin 3\pi t + \frac{1}{5^3} \sin 5\pi t + \ldots\ldots\right]$

(*iv*) $f(x) = \frac{1}{6} - \frac{4}{\pi^2} \sum_{\substack{n=1 \\ (n \text{ is even})}}^{\infty} \frac{1}{n^2} \cos n\pi x$

15. (*i*) $f(x) = \frac{4\sqrt{2}}{\pi}\left[\frac{\sin 2x}{1.3} - \frac{\sin 6x}{5.7} + \frac{\sin 10x}{9.11} - \ldots\ldots\right]$

(*ii*) $F(t) = 1 + \frac{8}{\pi^2} \sum_{n=1}^{\infty} \frac{1}{n^2}\left(2 \cos \frac{n\pi}{2} - 1 - \cos n\pi\right) \cos \frac{n\pi t}{2}$

4.8. FOURIER SERIES OF DIFFERENT WAVEFORMS

Some typical waveforms usually met with in communication engineering are:

(1) **Square waveform.** This waveform is the extension of the function

$$f(x) = \begin{cases} -k, & -\pi < x < 0 \\ k, & 0 < x < \pi \end{cases}$$

where $f(x + 2\pi) = f(x)$ and k is a constant. It has the graph as shown in the diagram:

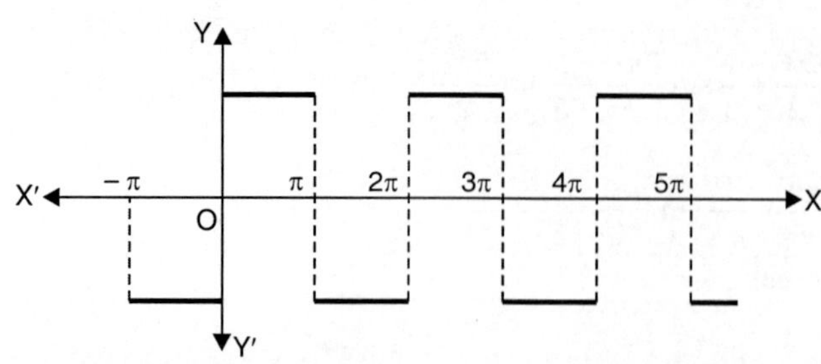

Fourier series is

$$f(x) = \frac{4k}{\pi}\left(\sin x + \frac{\sin 3x}{3} + \frac{\sin 5x}{5} + ...\right)$$

(2) **Saw-toothed waveform.** This waveform is the extension of the function

$$f(x) = x, \quad -\pi < x < \pi \quad ; \quad f(x + 2\pi) = f(x)$$

This function represents the discontinuous function called **saw-toothed waveform.** It has the graph as shown in the diagram:

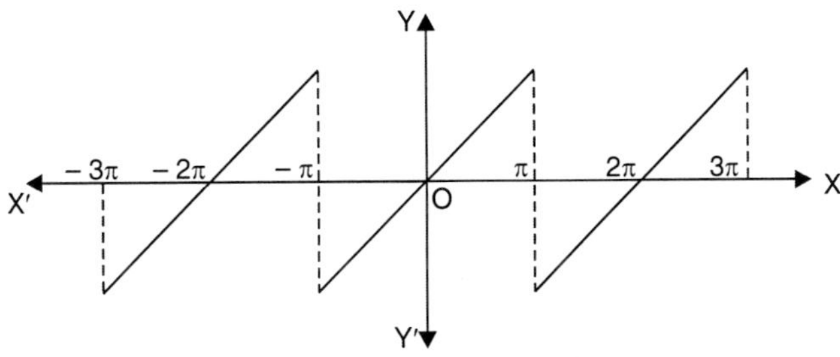

Fourier series is

$$f(x) = 2\left[\sin x - \frac{1}{2}\sin 2x + \frac{1}{3}\sin 3x - \frac{1}{4}\sin 4x + ...\right]$$

(3) **Modified saw-toothed waveform.** This wave is the extension of the function

$$f(x) = \begin{cases} 0, & -\pi < x \le 0 \\ x, & 0 \le x < \pi \end{cases}$$

It has the graph as shown in the diagram :

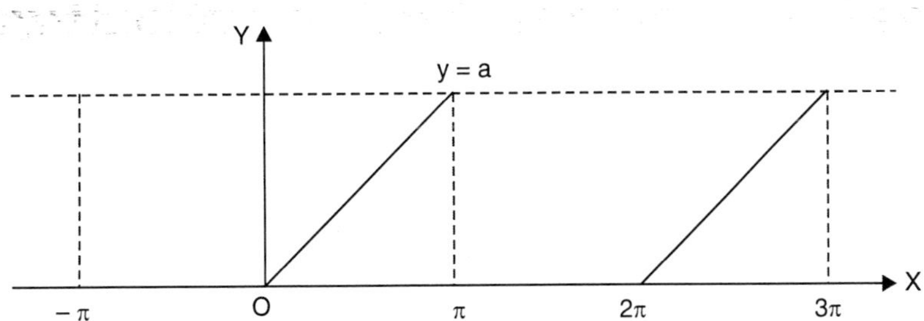

Fourier series is

$$F(x) = \frac{a}{4} - \frac{2a}{\pi^2}\left(\cos x + \frac{\cos 3x}{3^2} + \frac{\cos 5x}{5^2} + ...\right) + \frac{a}{\pi}\left(\sin x - \frac{\sin 2x}{2} + \frac{\sin 3x}{3} - ......\right)$$

(4) **Triangular waveform.** This waveform is the extension of the function

$$f(x) = \begin{cases} 1 + \left(\dfrac{2x}{\pi}\right), & -\pi \le x \le 0 \\ 1 - \left(\dfrac{2x}{\pi}\right), & 0 \le x \le \pi \end{cases}$$

It has the graph as shown in the diagram :

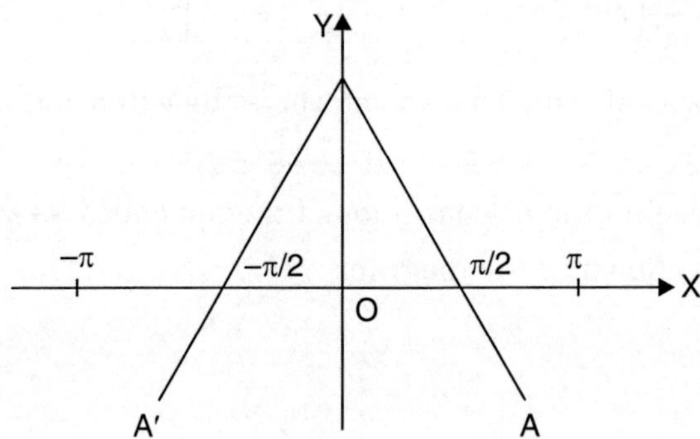

Fourier series is

$$f(x) = \frac{8}{\pi^2}\left[\frac{\cos x}{1^2} + \frac{\cos 3x}{3^2} + \frac{\cos 5x}{5^2} + \ldots\ldots\right]$$

(5) **Half-wave rectifier.** This wave rectifier is the extension of the function

$$f(x) = \begin{Bmatrix} I_0 \sin x, & 0 \le x \le \pi \\ 0, & \pi \le x \le 2\pi \end{Bmatrix}$$

where I_0 is the maximum current and the period is 2π.

It has the graph as shown in the diagram :

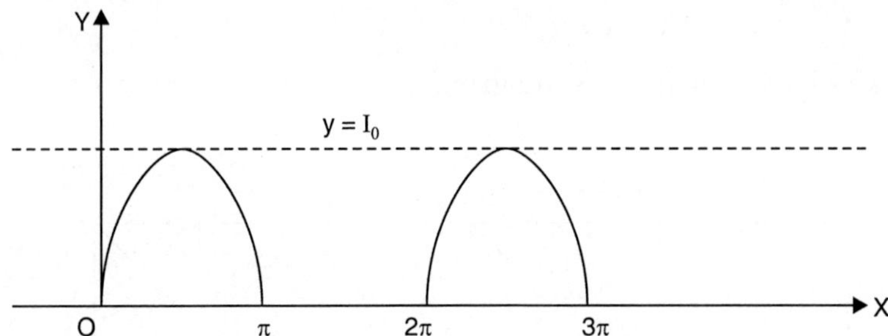

Fourier series is

$$f(x) = \frac{I_0}{\pi} + \frac{I_0}{2}\sin x - \frac{2I_0}{\pi}\left[\frac{\cos 2x}{2^2 - 1} + \frac{\cos 4x}{4^2 - 1} + \frac{\cos 6x}{6^2 - 1} + \ldots\ldots\right]$$

(6) **Full-wave rectifier**

This waveform is an extension of the function $f(x) = a \sin x$, $0 < x \le \pi$.

It has the graph as shown in the diagram :

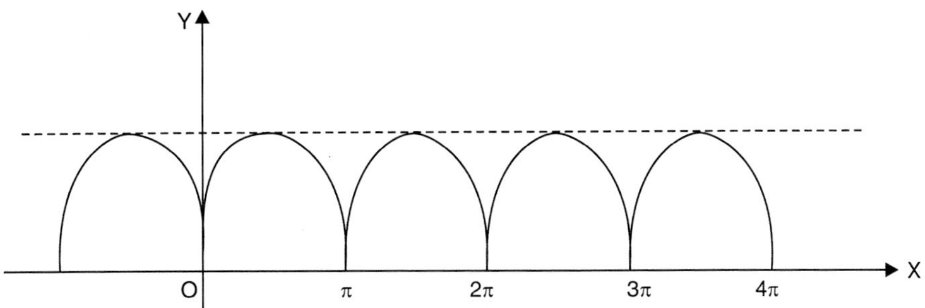

Fourier series is

$$f(x) = \frac{4a}{\pi}\left[\frac{1}{2} - \frac{1}{1.3}\cos 2x - \frac{1}{3.5}\cos 4x - \frac{1}{5.7}\cos 6x - \ldots\ldots\right].$$

4.9. PARSEVAL'S IDENTITY

If Fourier series for f(x) converges uniformly in (– π, π), then

$$\boxed{\int_{-\pi}^{\pi} [f(x)]^2\, dx = \pi\left[\frac{{a_0}^2}{2} + \sum_{n=1}^{\infty} ({a_n}^2 + {b_n}^2)\right]}$$

Proof. The Fourier series for $f(x)$ in $(-\pi, \pi)$ is

$$f(x) = \frac{a_0}{2} + \sum_{n=1}^{\infty} (a_n \cos nx + b_n \sin nx) \quad \ldots(1)$$

where

$$a_0 = \frac{1}{\pi}\int_{-\pi}^{\pi} f(x)\, dx \quad \ldots(2)$$

$$a_n = \frac{1}{\pi}\int_{-\pi}^{\pi} f(x)\cos nx\, dx \quad \ldots(3)$$

$$b_n = \frac{1}{\pi}\int_{-\pi}^{\pi} f(x)\sin nx\, dx \quad \ldots(4)$$

Multiplying both sides of (1) by $f(x)$ and integrating term by term from $-\pi$ to π, we get

$$\int_{-\pi}^{\pi} [f(x)]^2\, dx = \frac{a_0}{2}\int_{-\pi}^{\pi} f(x)\, dx + \sum_{n=1}^{\infty}\left[a_n\int_{-\pi}^{\pi} f(x)\cos nx\, dx + b_n\int_{-\pi}^{\pi} f(x)\sin nx\, dx\right]$$

$$= \frac{a_0}{2}(\pi a_0) + \sum_{n=1}^{\infty} [a_n(\pi a_n) + b_n(\pi b_n)] \qquad | \text{ Using (2), (3) and (4)}$$

$$\Rightarrow \int_{-\pi}^{\pi} [f(x)]^2\, dx = \pi\left[\frac{{a_0}^2}{2} + \sum_{n=1}^{\infty} ({a_n}^2 + {b_n}^2)\right].$$

Note. Similarly, we can obtain the following Parseval's formulae :

(1) If Fourier series for $f(x)$ converges uniformly in $(-l, l)$ then

$$\int_{-l}^{l} [f(x)]^2 \, dx = l\left[\frac{a_0^2}{2} + \sum_{n=1}^{\infty} (a_n^2 + b_n^2)\right].$$

(2) If Fourier series for $f(x)$ converges uniformly in $(0, 2l)$ then

$$\int_{0}^{2l} [f(x)]^2 \, dx = l\left[\frac{a_0^2}{2} + \sum_{n=1}^{\infty} (a_n^2 + b_n^2)\right].$$

(3) For half-range sine series in $(0, l)$, we have

$$\int_{0}^{l} [f(x)]^2 \, dx = \frac{l}{2} \sum_{n=1}^{\infty} b_n^2$$

(4) For half-range cosine series in $(0, l)$, we have

$$\int_{0}^{l} [f(x)]^2 \, dx = \frac{l}{2}\left[\frac{a_0^2}{2} + \sum_{n=1}^{\infty} a_n^2\right]$$

In all the above formulae, the left hand side terms are related to root mean square (rms) value.

4.10. ROOT MEAN SQUARE (RMS) VALUE

The root mean square value of the function $y = f(x)$ over an interval (a, b) is defined as

$$\bar{y} = \sqrt{\left\{\frac{\int_a^b [f(x)]^2 \, dx}{b - a}\right\}}$$

The use of root mean square value of a periodic function is frequently made in the theory of mechanical vibrations and in electric circuit theory.

Example. *Obtain the Fourier series for $y = x^2$ in $-\pi < x < \pi$ and hence show that*

$$\frac{1}{1^4} + \frac{1}{2^4} + \frac{1}{3^4} + \frac{1}{4^4} + \ldots\ldots = \sum_{n=1}^{\infty} \frac{1}{n^4} = \frac{\pi^4}{90}.$$

Sol. Since $y = x^2$ is an even function $\therefore\ b_n = 0$

Let $$y = \frac{a_0}{2} + \sum_{n=1}^{\infty} a_n \cos nx \qquad \ldots(1)$$

where, $$a_0 = \frac{1}{\pi}\int_{-\pi}^{\pi} x^2 \, dx = \frac{2}{\pi}\int_0^{\pi} x^2 \, dx = \frac{2}{3}\pi^2$$

$$a_n = \frac{1}{\pi}\int_{-\pi}^{\pi} x^2 \cos nx \, dx = \frac{2}{\pi}\int_0^{\pi} x^2 \cos nx \, dx$$

$$= \frac{2}{\pi}\left[\left(x^2 \frac{\sin nx}{n}\right)_0^{\pi} - \int_0^{\pi} 2x \,.\, \frac{\sin nx}{n} \, dx\right] = -\frac{4}{\pi n}\int_0^{\pi} x \sin nx \, dx$$

$$= -\frac{4}{\pi n}\left[\left\{x\left(\frac{-\cos nx}{n}\right)\right\}_0^{\pi} - \int_0^{\pi} 1.\left(\frac{-\cos nx}{n}\right) dx\right]$$

$$\Rightarrow \qquad a_n = \frac{4}{\pi n^2}(\pi \cos n\pi) = \frac{4}{n^2}(-1)^n \qquad \text{...(2)}$$

$$\therefore \quad \text{From (1),} \qquad x^2 = \frac{\pi^2}{3} + 4\sum_{n=1}^{\infty} \frac{(-1)^n}{n^2} \cos nx$$

Applying Parseval's identity, we get

$$\int_{-\pi}^{\pi} (x^2)^2\, dx = \pi\left[\frac{1}{2}\left(\frac{2\pi^2}{3}\right)^2 + \sum_{n=1}^{\infty} \frac{16}{n^4}(-1)^{2n}\right]$$

$$\Rightarrow \qquad 2\int_0^{\pi} x^4\, dx = \pi\left[\frac{2\pi^4}{9} + 16\sum_{n=1}^{\infty} \frac{1}{n^4}\right]$$

$$\Rightarrow \qquad \frac{2}{5}\pi^4 = \frac{2}{9}\pi^4 + 16\sum_{n=1}^{\infty} \frac{1}{n^4}$$

or

$$\sum_{n=1}^{\infty} \frac{1}{n^4} = \frac{\pi^4}{90}$$

TEST YOUR KNOWLEDGE

1. Using the Fourier series expansion of $f(x) = |x|$ in $(-\pi, \pi)$, show that

   (*i*) $\displaystyle\sum_{n=1}^{\infty} \frac{1}{(2n-1)^4} = \frac{\pi^4}{96}$ (*ii*) $\displaystyle\sum_{n=1}^{\infty} \frac{1}{n^4} = \frac{\pi^4}{90}$.

2. Using the Fourier series for $f(x) = x$ is $0 < x < 1$, show that $\displaystyle\sum_{n=1}^{\infty} \frac{1}{(2n-1)^4} = \frac{\pi^4}{96}$.

3. Expand $f(x) = x - \dfrac{x^2}{2}$ in (0, 2) as Fourier sine series and hence evaluate $\displaystyle\sum_{n=1}^{\infty} \frac{1}{(2n-1)^6}$.

4. By using the sine series for $f(x) = 1$ in $0 < x < \pi$, show that $\dfrac{\pi^2}{8} = 1 + \dfrac{1}{3^2} + \dfrac{1}{5^2} + \dfrac{1}{7^2} + \ldots\ldots$.

5. If $f(x) = \begin{cases} \pi x, & 0 < x < 1 \\ \pi(2-x), & 1 < x < 2 \end{cases}$, then using half range cosine series expansion, show that $\dfrac{1}{1^4} + \dfrac{1}{3^4} + \dfrac{1}{5^4} + \ldots = \dfrac{\pi^4}{96}$. *(U.P.T.U. 2007)*

Answer

3. $f(x) = \dfrac{16}{\pi^2}\displaystyle\sum_{n=1}^{\infty} \frac{1}{(2n-1)^3} \sin\frac{(2n-1)\pi x}{2}$; $\dfrac{\pi^4}{960}$.

4.11. PRACTICAL HARMONIC ANALYSIS [*G.B.T.U. (AG) SUM 2010*]

Sometimes the function is not given by a formula but by a graph or by a table of corresponding values. The process of finding Fourier series for a function given by such values of the function and independent variable is called **Harmonic Analysis.**

Fourier constants are evaluated by the following formulae :

(1) $$a_0 = \frac{1}{\pi}\int_0^{2\pi} f(x)\, dx = 2.\left[\frac{1}{2\pi - 0}\int_0^{2\pi} f(x)\, dx\right]$$

$$= 2\text{ [mean value of } f(x) \text{ in } (0, 2\pi)] \qquad \left| \because \text{ Mean} = \frac{1}{b-a}\int_a^b f(x)\, dx \right.$$

(2) $$a_n = \frac{1}{\pi}\int_0^{2\pi} f(x) \cos nx\, dx$$

$$= 2\,.\left[\frac{1}{2\pi - 0}\int_0^{2\pi} f(x)\cos nx\, dx\right]$$

$$= 2\text{ [mean value of } f(x) \cos nx \text{ in } (0, 2\pi)].$$

(3) $$b_n = \frac{1}{\pi}\int_0^{2\pi} f(x) \sin nx\, dx$$

$$= 2\,.\left[\frac{1}{2\pi - 0}\int_0^{2\pi} f(x)\sin nx\, dx\right] = 2\text{ [mean value of } f(x) \sin nx \text{ in } (0, 2\pi)]$$

Here mean value is also referred as 'average'.

The term ($a_1 \cos x + b_1 \sin x$) in Fourier series is called the **fundamental** or **first harmonic.** The term ($a_2 \cos 2x + b_2 \sin 2x$) in Fourier series is called the **second harmonic** and so on. Similarly, we can obtain the harmonics for Fourier series in $(0, 2l)$, half-range sine and cosine series.

ILLUSTRATIVE EXAMPLES

Example 1. *Obtain the first three coefficients in the Fourier cosine series for y, where y is given in the following table :*

x	0	1	2	3	4	5
y	4	8	15	7	6	2

Sol. Taking the interval as $\pi/3$, Fourier cosine series to represent y in (0, 5) *i.e.,* in $(0, 2\pi)$ is

$$y = \frac{a_0}{2} + a_1 \cos\frac{\pi x}{3} + a_2 \cos\frac{2\pi x}{3} + \ldots\ldots$$

where $$a_0 = 2\text{ [mean value of } y \text{ in } (0, 5)]$$

$$a_1 = 2\left[\text{mean value of } y \cos\frac{\pi x}{3} \text{ in } (0, 5)\right]$$

$$a_2 = 2\left[\text{mean value of } y \cos\frac{2\pi x}{3} \text{ in } (0, 5)\right]$$

Let us form the following table :

x	$\frac{\pi x}{3}$	$\cos \frac{\pi x}{3}$	$\cos \frac{2\pi x}{3}$	y	$y \cos \frac{\pi x}{3}$	$y \cos \frac{2\pi x}{3}$
0	0	1	1	4	4	4
1	$\frac{\pi}{3}$	$\frac{1}{2}$	$-\frac{1}{2}$	8	4	– 4
2	$\frac{2\pi}{3}$	$-\frac{1}{2}$	$-\frac{1}{2}$	15	– 7.5	– 7.5
3	π	– 1	1	7	– 7	7
4	$\frac{4\pi}{3}$	$-\frac{1}{2}$	$-\frac{1}{2}$	6	– 3	– 3
5	$\frac{5\pi}{3}$	$\frac{1}{2}$	$-\frac{1}{2}$	2	1	– 1
		Total		$\Sigma y = 42$	$\Sigma y \cos \frac{\pi x}{3} = -8.5$	$\Sigma y \cos \frac{2\pi x}{3} = -4.5$

Hence $a_0 = 2\left[\frac{42}{6}\right] = 14, \quad a_1 = 2\left[\frac{-8.5}{6}\right] = -2.83, \quad a_2 = 2\left[\frac{-4.5}{6}\right] = -1.5$

Hence the required series is

$$y = 7 - 2.83 \cos \frac{\pi x}{3} - 1.5 \cos \frac{2\pi x}{3}.$$

Example 2. *Find the Fourier series as far as the second harmonic to represent the function given by the following table :*

x	0	30°	60°	90°	120°	150°	180°	210°	240°	270°	300°	330°
$f(x)$	2.34	3.01	3.69	4.15	3.69	2.20	0.83	0.51	0.88	1.09	1.19	1.64

Sol.

x	$\sin x$	$\sin 2x$	$\cos x$	$\cos 2x$	$f(x)$	$f(x) \sin x$	$f(x) \sin 2x$	$f(x) \cos x$	$f(x) \cos 2x$
0	0	0	1	1	2.34	0	0	2.340	2.340
30°	0.50	0.87	.87	.5	3.01	1.505	2.619	2.619	1.505
60°	0.87	0.87	.50	– .5	3.69	3.210	3.210	1.845	– 1.845
90°	1	0	0	– 1	4.15	4.150	0	0	– 4.150
120°	0.87	– 0.87	– .50	– .5	3.69	3.210	– 3.210	– 1.845	– 1.845
150°	0.50	– 0.87	– .87	.5	2.20	1.100	– 1.914	– 1.914	1.100
180°	0	0	– 1	1	.83	0	0	– .830	.830
210°	– 0.50	0.87	– .87	.5	.51	– .255	.444	– .444	.255
240°	– 0.87	0.87	– .50	– .5	.88	– .766	.766	– .440	– .440
270°	– 1	0	0	– 1	1.09	– 1.090	0	0	– 1.090
300°	– .87	– 0.87	.50	– .5	1.19	– 1.035	– 1.035	.595	– .595
330°	– .50	– 0.87	.87	.5	1.64	– .820	– 1.427	1.427	.820
		Total	(Σ)	=	25.22	9.209	– .547	3.353	– 3.115

$$a_0 = 2 \text{ [Mean of } f(x)] = 2\left(\frac{25.22}{12}\right) = 4.203$$

$$a_1 = 2 \text{ [Mean of } f(x) \cos x] = 2\left(\frac{3.353}{12}\right) = .559$$

$$a_2 = 2 \text{ [Mean of } f(x) \cos 2x] = 2\left(\frac{-3.115}{12}\right) = -.519$$

$$b_1 = 2 \text{ [Mean of } f(x) \sin x] = 2\left(\frac{9.209}{12}\right) = 1.535$$

$$b_2 = 2 \text{ [Mean of } f(x) \sin 2x] = 2\left(\frac{-.547}{12}\right) = -.091$$

∴ Fourier series is

$$f(x) = \frac{a_0}{2} + (a_1 \cos x + b_1 \sin x) + (a_2 \cos 2x + b_2 \sin 2x) + \ldots$$

$$= 2.1015 + (.559 \cos x + 1.535 \sin x) + (-.519 \cos 2x - .091 \sin 2x) + \ldots\ldots$$

TEST YOUR KNOWLEDGE

1. A machine completes its cycle of operations every time as certain pulley completes a revolution. The displacement $f(x)$ of a point on a certain portion of the machine is given in the table given below for 12 positions of the pulley, x being the angle in degree turned through by the pulley. Find the Fourier series to represent $f(x)$ for all values of x

x	30°	60°	90°	120°	150°	180°	210°	240°	270°	300°	330°	360°
$f(x)$	7.976	8.026	7.204	5.676	3.674	1.764	0.552	0.262	0.904	2.492	4.736	6.824

2. Obtain the constant term and the coefficient of the first sine and cosine terms in the Fourier series of $f(x)$ as given in the following table : *(M.T.U. 2012)*

x	0	1	2	3	4	5
$f(x)$	9	18	24	28	26	20

3. The displacement y of a part of a mechanism is tabulated with corresponding angular movement $x°$ of the crank. Express y as a Fourier series neglecting the harmonics above the third :

$x°$	0	30	60	90	120	150	180	210	240	270	300	330
y	1.80	1.10	.30	.16	1.50	1.30	2.16	1.25	1.30	1.52	1.76	2.00

4. Following table gives the variations of periodic current over a period :

t (sec.)	0	T/6	T/3	T/2	$\frac{2T}{3}$	$\frac{5T}{6}$	T
A(amp.)	1.98	1.30	1.05	1.30	– 0.88	– 0.25	1.98

Show that there is a direct current part of 0.75 amp. in the variable current and obtain the amplitude of the first harmonic.

[**Hint.** Here length of interval is T ∴ $c = T/2$

Hence $A = \frac{a_0}{2} + \left(a_1 \cos \frac{2\pi t}{T} + b_1 \sin \frac{2\pi t}{T}\right) + \ldots\ldots$].

5. In a machine, the displacement y of a given point for a certain angle θ is as follows :

$\theta°$	0	30	60	90	120	150	180	210	240	270	300	330
y	7.8	8.1	7.4	5.7	3.6	2.1	1.1	0.4	0.9	1.9	3.8	6.2

Express y as a Fourier series neglecting the harmonics on and above the third.

6. The turning moment T on the crank-shaft of a steam engine for the crank angle θ degrees is given as follows :

θ	0	30	60	90	120	150	180
T	0	6.1	8.2	7.9	5.5	2.5	0

Find the coefficient of sin 2θ if T is expanded in a series of sines.

7. The turning moment T is given for a series of values of the crank angle θ degrees. Expand T in a half-range cosine series.

θ	0	30	60	90	120	150	180
T	0	52	81	79	55	27	0

8. Determine the first two harmonics of the Fourier series for the following values :

α	30	60	90	120	150	180	210	240	270	300	330	360
y	3.11	3.23	4	4.25	3.71	2.69	1.23	.87	.98	1.24	1.44	1.86

9. Analyse the following data harmonically and express y interms of a Fourier series :

[*G.B.T.U. (A.G.) 2010*]

x	0	$\pi/3$	$2\pi/3$	π	$4\pi/3$	$5\pi/3$	2π
y	1.0	1.4	1.9	1.7	1.5	1.2	1.0

10. In a machine, the displacement y of a given point is given for a certain angle θ as follows :

θ	0	30	60	90	120	150	180	210	240	270	300	330
y	7.9	8	7.2	5.6	3.6	1.7	0.5	0.2	0.9	2.5	4.7	6.8

Find the coefficient of sin 2θ in the Fourier series representing the above variation.

Answers

1. $f(x) = 4.17 + (2.45 \cos x + 3.16 \sin x) + (0.12 \cos 2x + 0.03 \sin 2x) + (0.08 \cos 3x + 0.01 \sin 3x) + \ldots$

2. $f(x) = 20.83 - \left(8.33 \cos \frac{\pi x}{3} + 1.156 \sin \frac{\pi x}{3}\right) + \ldots$

3. $y = 1.26 + (0.04 \cos x - 0.63 \sin x) + (0.53 \cos 2x - 0.23 \sin 2x) + (-0.1 \cos 3x + 0.085 \sin 3x)$.

4. 1.072.

5. $4.085 + (3.39 \cos \theta + 1.85 \sin \theta) + (-0.04 \cos 2\theta + 0.16 \sin 2\theta)$. **6.** 1.56

7. $42 + 9.93 \cos x - 30.71 \cos 2x + \ldots$

8. $(-0.25 \cos x + 1.63 \sin x)$; $(-0.08 \cos 2x - 0.32 \sin 2x)$.

9. $y = 1.45 + (-.37 \cos x + .17 \sin x) + (-.1 \cos 2x - .06 \sin 2x) + .03 \cos 3x + \ldots$ **10.** -0.0731.

PARTIAL DIFFERENTIAL EQUATIONS

4.12. INTRODUCTION

A differential equation containing partial derivatives of a function of two or more independent variables is called a partial differential equation. *e.g.*,

$$y\frac{\partial z}{\partial x} + x\frac{\partial z}{\partial y} = 0$$

$$\frac{\partial^2 z}{\partial x^2} + \frac{\partial^2 z}{\partial y^2} = 0$$

are the partial differential equations.

When we have a function z of two independent variables x and y, we use the alphabets p, q, r, s, t to denote the partial derivatives as follows :

$$p = \frac{\partial z}{\partial x}, \quad q = \frac{\partial z}{\partial y}$$

$$r = \frac{\partial^2 z}{\partial x^2} = \frac{\partial}{\partial x}\left(\frac{\partial z}{\partial x}\right) = \frac{\partial p}{\partial x}$$

$$s = \frac{\partial^2 z}{\partial x \partial y} = \frac{\partial^2 z}{\partial y \partial x} = \frac{\partial q}{\partial x} = \frac{\partial p}{\partial y}$$

and

$$t = \frac{\partial^2 z}{\partial y} = \frac{\partial}{\partial y}\left(\frac{\partial z}{\partial y}\right) = \frac{\partial q}{\partial y}$$

Partial differential equations generally occur in the problems of Physics and Engineering. Some of the important partial differential equations are

$$\frac{\partial^2 u}{\partial x^2} + \frac{\partial^2 u}{\partial y^2} + \frac{\partial^2 u}{\partial z^2} = 0 \qquad ...(1)$$

$$\frac{\partial^2 u}{\partial t^2} = c^2\left(\frac{\partial^2 u}{\partial x^2} + \frac{\partial^2 u}{\partial y^2} + \frac{\partial^2 u}{\partial z^2}\right) \qquad ...(2)$$

$$\frac{\partial u}{\partial t} = c^2\left(\frac{\partial^2 u}{\partial x^2} + \frac{\partial^2 u}{\partial y^2} + \frac{\partial^2 u}{\partial z^2}\right) \qquad ...(3)$$

Equations (1), (2) and (3) are respectively known as Laplace's equation, wave equation and heat conduction equation.

Sometimes for brevity, the partial differentiation with regard to a variable is denoted by a suffix. *e.g.*, Laplace's equation may be rewritten as $u_{xx} + u_{yy} + u_{zz} = 0$.

If u does not depend on z, then we get two dimensional Laplace's equation as $u_{xx} + u_{yy} = 0$.

4.13. ORDER AND DEGREE OF PARTIAL DIFFERENTIAL EQUATION

Order of a partial differential equation is the order of the highest ordered derivative present in the equation.

Degree of a partial differential equation is the greatest exponent (power) of the highest ordered derivative present in the equation when it has been made free from radical signs and fractional powers.

4.14. SOLUTION OF PARTIAL DIFFERENTIAL EQUATION

Solution is one which satisfies. The solution of a partial differential equation in a region D is a function having partial derivatives which satisfy the differential equation at every point in D.

The general solution of a p.d.e. contains arbitrary constants or arbitrary functions or both. Consequently, we can say that by the elimination of arbitrary constants or arbitrary functions, partial differential equations can be formed.

4.15. FORMATION OF PARTIAL DIFFERENTIAL EQUATION

(1) By the elimination of arbitrary constants

Let
$$f(x, y, z, a, b) = 0 \qquad \text{...(1)}$$
be the given function, where a, b are arbitrary constants. x and y are independent variables and z is a dependent variable. Differentiating eqn. (1) partially w.r.t. x, we get
$$\frac{\partial f}{\partial x} + \frac{\partial f}{\partial z} \cdot \frac{\partial z}{\partial x} = 0 \Rightarrow \frac{\partial f}{\partial x} + p\frac{\partial f}{\partial z} = 0 \qquad \text{...(2)}$$
Again differentiating eqn. (1) partially w.r.t. y, we get
$$\frac{\partial f}{\partial y} + \frac{\partial f}{\partial z} \cdot \frac{\partial z}{\partial y} = 0 \Rightarrow \frac{\partial f}{\partial y} + q\frac{\partial f}{\partial z} = 0 \qquad \text{...(3)}$$
Eliminating a, b from equations (1), (2) and (3), we get
$$F(x, y, z, p, q) = 0$$
which is a partial differential equation of first order.

Note. If the number of arbitrary constants is more than the number of independent variables, then the order of the partial differential equation obtained will be greater than 1.

(2) By the elimination of arbitrary functions

Let u, v be two known functions of x, y, z connected by the relation
$$\phi(u, v) = 0 \qquad \text{...(1)}$$
where ϕ is an arbitrary function.

Differentiating eqn. (1) partially w.r.t. x, we get
$$\frac{\partial \phi}{\partial u}\left(\frac{\partial u}{\partial x} + \frac{\partial u}{\partial z} \cdot \frac{\partial z}{\partial x}\right) + \frac{\partial \phi}{\partial v}\left(\frac{\partial v}{\partial x} + \frac{\partial v}{\partial z} \cdot \frac{\partial z}{\partial x}\right) = 0$$
$$\Rightarrow \quad \frac{\partial \phi}{\partial u}\left(\frac{\partial u}{\partial x} + p\frac{\partial u}{\partial z}\right) + \frac{\partial \phi}{\partial v}\left(\frac{\partial v}{\partial x} + p\frac{\partial v}{\partial z}\right) = 0$$
$$\Rightarrow \quad \frac{\partial \phi/\partial u}{\partial \phi/\partial v} = -\left(\frac{\dfrac{\partial v}{\partial x} + p\dfrac{\partial v}{\partial z}}{\dfrac{\partial u}{\partial x} + p\dfrac{\partial u}{\partial z}}\right) \qquad \text{...(2)}$$
Diff. (1) partially w.r.t. y, we get
$$\frac{\partial \phi}{\partial u}\left(\frac{\partial u}{\partial y} + \frac{\partial u}{\partial z}\frac{\partial z}{\partial y}\right) + \frac{\partial \phi}{\partial v}\left(\frac{\partial v}{\partial y} + \frac{\partial v}{\partial z}\frac{\partial z}{\partial y}\right) = 0$$
$$\Rightarrow \quad \frac{\partial \phi}{\partial u}\left(\frac{\partial u}{\partial y} + q\frac{\partial u}{\partial z}\right) + \frac{\partial \phi}{\partial v}\left(\frac{\partial v}{\partial y} + q\frac{\partial v}{\partial z}\right) = 0$$

$$\Rightarrow \qquad \frac{\partial\phi/\partial u}{\partial\phi/\partial v} = -\left(\frac{\dfrac{\partial v}{\partial y} + q\dfrac{\partial v}{\partial z}}{\dfrac{\partial u}{\partial y} + q\dfrac{\partial u}{\partial z}}\right) \qquad ...(3)$$

From eqns. (2) and (3), we get

$$\frac{\dfrac{\partial v}{\partial x} + p\dfrac{\partial v}{\partial z}}{\dfrac{\partial u}{\partial x} + p\dfrac{\partial u}{\partial z}} = \frac{\dfrac{\partial v}{\partial y} + q\dfrac{\partial v}{\partial z}}{\dfrac{\partial u}{\partial y} + q\dfrac{\partial u}{\partial z}}$$

$$\Rightarrow \qquad \left(\frac{\partial u}{\partial y}\frac{\partial v}{\partial z} - \frac{\partial u}{\partial z}\frac{\partial v}{\partial y}\right)p + \left(\frac{\partial u}{\partial z}\frac{\partial v}{\partial x} - \frac{\partial u}{\partial x}\frac{\partial v}{\partial z}\right)q = \frac{\partial u}{\partial x}\frac{\partial v}{\partial y} - \frac{\partial u}{\partial y}\frac{\partial v}{\partial x}$$

$$\Rightarrow \qquad \boxed{\mathrm{P}p + \mathrm{Q}q = \mathrm{R}} \qquad ...(4)$$

Eqn. (4) is a partial diff. equation of first degree (*i.e.* linear) in p and q.

Note. If the given relation between x, y, z contains two arbitrary functions, then the p.d.e. derived therefrom will be, in general of order greater than one.

ILLUSTRATIVE EXAMPLES

Example 1. *Form partial differential equations from the following equations by eliminating the arbitrary constants :*

(*i*) $z = ax + by + ab$ (*ii*) $z = ax + a^2y^2 + b$

(*iii*) $z = (x + a)(y + b)$ (*iv*) $az + b = a^2x + y$.

Sol. (*i*) Differentiating z partially w.r.t. x and y,

$$p = \frac{\partial z}{\partial x} = a, \quad q = \frac{\partial z}{\partial y} = b$$

Substituting for a and b in the given equation, we get

$$z = px + qy + pq$$

which is a partial differential equation.

(*ii*) Differentiating z partially w.r.t. x and y

$$p = \frac{\partial z}{\partial x} = a, \quad q = \frac{\partial z}{\partial y} = 2a^2y$$

Eliminating a between these results, we get $q = 2p^2y$

which is a partial differential equation.

(*iii*) Differentiating z partially w.r.t. x, we get

$$\frac{\partial z}{\partial x} = p = y + b \qquad ...(1)$$

Differentiating z partially w.r.t. y, we get

$$\frac{\partial z}{\partial y} = q = x + a \qquad ...(2)$$

Multiplying eqns. (1) and (2), we get

$$pq = (y + b)(x + a)$$

$$\Rightarrow \qquad pq = z$$

which is a partial differential equation.

(*iv*) Differentiating the given relation w.r.t. x partially, we get

$$a \frac{\partial z}{\partial x} = a^2$$

$$\Rightarrow \qquad \frac{\partial z}{\partial x} = p = a \qquad \text{...(1)}$$

Again differentiating the given relation w.r.t. y partially, we get

$$a \frac{\partial z}{\partial y} = 1$$

$$\Rightarrow \qquad \frac{\partial z}{\partial y} = q = \frac{1}{a} \qquad \text{...(2)}$$

Multiplying eqns.(1) and (2), we get $pq = 1$

which is a partial differential equation.

Example 2. *Form the partial differential equation by eliminating the arbitrary function(s) from the following :*

(*i*) $z = f(x^2 - y^2)$ (*ii*) $z = \phi(x) . \psi(y)$

(*iii*) $z = x + y + f(xy)$ (*iv*) $z = f(x + it) + g(x - it)$. (U.K.T.U. 2011)

Sol. (*i*) Differentiating z partially w.r.t. x, we get

$$\frac{\partial z}{\partial x} = p = f'(x^2 - y^2) . 2x \qquad \text{...(1)}$$

Differentiating z partially w.r.t. y, we get

$$\frac{\partial z}{\partial y} = q = f'(x^2 - y^2) . (-2y) \qquad \text{...(2)}$$

Dividing eqn. (1) by eqn. (2), we get

$$\frac{p}{q} = \frac{x}{(-y)} \quad \Rightarrow \quad py + qx = 0$$

which is a partial differential equation.

(*ii*) Differentiating z w.r.t. x, partially, we get

$$\frac{\partial z}{\partial x} = p = \phi'(x)\, \psi(y) \qquad \text{...(1)}$$

Differentiating z w.r.t. y partially, we get

$$\frac{\partial z}{\partial y} = q = \phi(x)\, \psi'(y) \qquad \text{...(2)}$$

Differentiating eqn. (1) partially w.r.t. y, we get

$$\frac{\partial^2 z}{\partial y \partial x} = s = \phi'(x)\, \psi'(y) \qquad \text{...(3)}$$

Multiplying eqns. (1) and (2), we get

$$pq = \phi(x)\, \psi(y)\, \phi'(x)\, \psi'(y) = zs \qquad | \text{ Using (3)}$$

$$\Rightarrow \qquad pq - zs = 0$$

which is a partial differential equation.

(*iii*) Differentiating z w.r.t. x, partially, we get

$$\frac{\partial z}{\partial x} = p = 1 + f'(xy) \cdot y \Rightarrow p - 1 = yf'(xy) \qquad ...(1)$$

Differentiating z w.r.t. y, partially, we get

$$\frac{\partial z}{\partial y} = q = 1 + f'(xy) \cdot x \Rightarrow q - 1 = x f'(xy) \qquad ...(2)$$

Dividing eqn. (1) by eqn. (2), we get

$$\frac{p-1}{q-1} = \frac{y}{x} \Rightarrow px - qy = x - y$$

which is a partial differential equation.

(*iv*) Given $z = f(x + it) + g(x - it)$

Differentiating z twice partially w.r.t. x and t, we have

$$\frac{\partial z}{\partial x} = f'(x + it) + g'(x - it)$$

$$\frac{\partial^2 z}{\partial x^2} = f''(x + it) + g''(x - it) \qquad ...(1)$$

$$\frac{\partial z}{\partial t} = i f'(x + it) - ig'(x - it)$$

$$\frac{\partial^2 z}{\partial t^2} = i^2 f''(x + it) + i^2 g''(x - it)$$

or

$$\frac{\partial^2 z}{\partial t^2} = - f''(x + it) - g''(x - it) \qquad ...(2)$$

Adding (1) and (2), we obtain $\frac{\partial^2 z}{\partial x^2} + \frac{\partial^2 z}{\partial t^2} = 0$

which is a partial differential equation of second order.

4.16. DEFINITIONS

The solution $f(x, y, z, a, b) = 0$ of a first order partial differential equation, which contains two arbitrary constants is called a *complete solution* or *complete integral*.

If in this solution, we put $b = \phi(a)$ and find the envelope of the family of surfaces $f(x, y, z, a, \phi(a)) = 0$, we get a solution involving an arbitrary function ϕ. This is called the *general solution* or *general integral*.

A solution obtained from the complete integral by giving particular values to the arbitrary constant is called a *particular solution* or *particular integral*.

A partial differential equation may have a large number of entirely different solutions. For example, $u = x^2 - y^2$, $u = \log(x^2 + y^2)$, $u = \sin kx \cosh ky$ are solutions of the Laplace equation $\frac{\partial^2 u}{\partial x^2} + \frac{\partial^2 u}{\partial y^2} = 0$. The unique solution of a partial differential equation corresponding to a physical problem must satisfy certain other conditions at the boundary of the region R. These are known as the *boundary conditions*.

If these conditions are given for the time $t = 0$, they are known as the *initial conditions*.

4.17. LINEAR HOMOGENEOUS PARTIAL DIFFERENTIAL EQUATION

A partial differential equation is said to be linear if it is of first degree in the dependent variable and its partial derivatives and also they are not multiplied together.

If, in addition, every term of the equation contains the dependent variable or its derivative, it is called a homogeneous equation.

Note. An equation which is not linear is called a non-linear partial differential equation.

4.18. QUASI-LINEAR PARTIAL DIFFERENTIAL EQUATIONS

A partial differential equation is said to be quasi-linear if degree of highest ordered derivative is one and no products of partial derivatives of the highest order are present.

e.g., $$z \frac{\partial^2 z}{\partial x^2} + \left(\frac{\partial z}{\partial y}\right)^2 = 0 \text{ is a quasi-linear p.d.e. of second order.}$$

The general form of a quasi-linear p.d.e. of the first order is

$$P(x, y, z) \frac{\partial z}{\partial x} + Q(x, y, z) \frac{\partial z}{\partial y} = R(x, y, z) \qquad ...(1)$$

If P and Q are independent of z and R is linear in z then eqn. (1) is linear partial differential equation.

4.19. EQUATIONS SOLVABLE BY DIRECT INTEGRATION

The equations which contain **only one** partial derivative can be solved by direct integration. However, in place of the constants of integration, we must use arbitrary functions of the variable kept constant.

ILLUSTRATIVE EXAMPLES

Example 1. *Solve : $t = \sin (xy)$.*

Sol. The given equation is

$$\frac{\partial^2 z}{\partial y^2} = \sin (xy)$$

Integrating w.r.t. y, we get

$$\frac{\partial z}{\partial y} = -\frac{1}{x} \cos (xy) + f(x)$$

The constant is being taken as a function of x.

Again integrating w.r.t. y, we get

$$z = -\frac{1}{x^2} \sin (xy) + yf(x) + \phi(x).$$

Example 2. *Solve :* $\frac{\partial^2 z}{\partial x^2} + z = 0$, *given that when* $x = 0$, $z = e^y$ *and* $\frac{\partial z}{\partial x} = 1$.

Sol. If z were *a* function of **x alone,** the solution would have been $z = c_1 \cos x + c_2 \sin x$, where c_1 and c_2 are arbitrary constants.

But here z is a function of x and y, therefore, c_1 and c_2 are arbitrary functions of y, the independent variable kept constant.

∴ The solution of the given equation is

$$z = f(y) \cos x + \phi(y) \sin x \text{ and } \frac{\partial z}{\partial x} = -f(y) \sin x + \phi(y) \cos x$$

When $x = 0$, $z = e^y$ ∴ $e^y = f(y)$

When $x = 0$, $\frac{\partial z}{\partial x} = 1$ ∴ $1 = \phi(y)$

∴ The required particular solution is $z = e^y \cos x + \sin x$.

4.20. LINEAR PARTIAL DIFFERENTIAL EQUATIONS OF THE FIRST ORDER

A differential equation involving first order partial derivatives p and q only is called a *partial differential equation of the first order*. If p and q both occur in the first degree only and are not multiplied together, then it is called *linear partial differential equation of the first order*.

4.21. LAGRANGE'S LINEAR EQUATION

The partial differential equation of the form $Pp + Qq = R$, where P, Q and R are functions of x, y, z is the standard form of a quasi-linear partial differential equation of the first order and is called *Lagrange's Equation*.

Now Lagrange's equation $Pp + Qq = R$ ...(1)

is obtained by eliminating an arbitrary function ϕ from $\phi(u, v) = 0$ ...(2)

where u, v are some definite functions of x, y, z.

Differentiating (2) partially w.r.t. x and y

$$\frac{\partial \phi}{\partial u}\left(\frac{\partial u}{\partial x} + \frac{\partial u}{\partial z} p\right) + \frac{\partial \phi}{\partial v}\left(\frac{\partial v}{\partial x} + \frac{\partial v}{\partial z} p\right) = 0$$

and

$$\frac{\partial \phi}{\partial u}\left(\frac{\partial u}{\partial y} + \frac{\partial u}{\partial z} q\right) + \frac{\partial \phi}{\partial v}\left(\frac{\partial v}{\partial y} + \frac{\partial v}{\partial z} q\right) = 0$$

Eliminating $\frac{\partial \phi}{\partial u}$ and $\frac{\partial \phi}{\partial v}$, we get

$$\left(\frac{\partial u}{\partial x} + \frac{\partial u}{\partial z} p\right)\left(\frac{\partial v}{\partial y} + \frac{\partial v}{\partial z} q\right) - \left(\frac{\partial v}{\partial x} + \frac{\partial v}{\partial z} p\right)\left(\frac{\partial u}{\partial y} + \frac{\partial u}{\partial z} q\right) = 0$$

or

$$\left(\frac{\partial u}{\partial y} \cdot \frac{\partial v}{\partial z} - \frac{\partial u}{\partial z} \cdot \frac{\partial v}{\partial y}\right) p + \left(\frac{\partial u}{\partial z} \cdot \frac{\partial v}{\partial x} - \frac{\partial u}{\partial x} \cdot \frac{\partial v}{\partial z}\right) q = \frac{\partial u}{\partial x} \cdot \frac{\partial v}{\partial y} - \frac{\partial u}{\partial y} \cdot \frac{\partial v}{\partial x}$$

which is the same as (1) with

$$P = \frac{\partial u}{\partial y} \cdot \frac{\partial v}{\partial z} - \frac{\partial u}{\partial z} \cdot \frac{\partial v}{\partial y}, Q = \frac{\partial u}{\partial z} \cdot \frac{\partial v}{\partial x} - \frac{\partial u}{\partial x} \cdot \frac{\partial v}{\partial z}, \quad R = \frac{\partial u}{\partial x} \cdot \frac{\partial v}{\partial y} - \frac{\partial u}{\partial y} \cdot \frac{\partial v}{\partial x}.$$

To determine u, v from P, Q, R, suppose $u = a$ and $v = b$, where a, b are constants, so that

$$\frac{\partial u}{\partial x} dx + \frac{\partial u}{\partial y} dy + \frac{\partial u}{\partial z} dz = du = 0$$

$$\frac{\partial v}{\partial x} dx + \frac{\partial v}{\partial y} dy + \frac{\partial v}{\partial z} dz = dv = 0$$

By cross-multiplication, we have

$$\frac{dx}{\frac{\partial u}{\partial y}\cdot\frac{\partial v}{\partial z} - \frac{\partial u}{\partial z}\cdot\frac{\partial v}{\partial y}} = \frac{dy}{\frac{\partial u}{\partial z}\cdot\frac{\partial v}{\partial x} - \frac{\partial u}{\partial x}\cdot\frac{\partial v}{\partial z}} = \frac{dz}{\frac{\partial u}{\partial x}\cdot\frac{\partial v}{\partial y} - \frac{\partial u}{\partial y}\cdot\frac{\partial v}{\partial x}}$$

or
$$\boxed{\frac{dx}{P} = \frac{dy}{Q} = \frac{dz}{R}} \qquad \text{...(3)}$$

The solutions of these equations are $u = a$ and $v = b$. Thus determining u, v from the simultaneous equations (3), we have the solution of the partial differential equation

$$Pp + Qq = R \text{ as } \phi(u, v) = 0 \quad \text{or} \quad v = f(u).$$

Note. Equations (3) are called **Lagrange's auxiliary equations** or **subsidiary equations**.

Remark. In the differential equation $Pp + Qq = R$, there are **two independent variables** x and y. To solve it, we have to find **two independent solutions** satisfying the equation $\frac{dx}{P} = \frac{dy}{Q} = \frac{dz}{R}$. This procedure can be extended to linear partial differential equations of the first order involving more than two independent variables.

If $u_1 = c_1$, $u_2 = c_2$, ..., $u_n = c_n$ are n independent solutions of the equations

$$\frac{dx_1}{P_1} = \frac{dx_2}{P_2} = \ldots\ldots = \frac{dx_n}{P_n} = \frac{dz}{R}$$

then the general solution of the partial differential equation

$$P_1 \frac{\partial z}{\partial x_1} + P_2 \frac{\partial z}{\partial x_2} + \ldots\ldots + P_n \frac{\partial z}{\partial x_n} = R$$

is $\phi(u_1, u_2, \ldots\ldots, u_n) = 0$, where ϕ is an arbitrary function.

4.22. WORKING RULE

To solve the equation $\qquad Pp + Qq = R$

(*i*) Form the auxiliary equations $\frac{dx}{P} = \frac{dy}{Q} = \frac{dz}{R}$

(*ii*) Solve the auxiliary equations by the method of grouping or the method of multipliers or both to get two independent solutions $u = a$ and $v = b$, where a, b are arbitrary constants.

(*iii*) Then $\phi(u, v) = 0$ or $v = f(u)$ is the general solution of the equation $Pp + Qq = R$.

ILLUSTRATIVE EXAMPLES

Example 1. *Solve the following partial differential equations :*

(*i*) $yzp - xzq = xy$ (*ii*) $y^2p - xyq = x(z - 2y)$ (*iii*) $x^2p + y^2q = (x + y)z$

Sol. (*i*) The given differential equation is $yzp - xzq = xy$ ...(1)

Comparing equation (1) with $Pp + Qq = R$, we get

$$P = yz, \; Q = -xz \quad \text{and} \quad R = xy$$

Lagrange's subsidiary equations are

$$\frac{dx}{P} = \frac{dy}{Q} = \frac{dz}{R}$$

$$\Rightarrow \quad \frac{dx}{yz} = \frac{dy}{-xz} = \frac{dz}{xy}$$

From first and second fractions, we get

$$\frac{dx}{yz} = \frac{dy}{-xz} \quad \Rightarrow \quad \frac{dx}{y} = \frac{dy}{-x}$$

$$\Rightarrow \quad x\,dx + y\,dy = 0$$

Integrating, we get

$$\frac{x^2}{2} + \frac{y^2}{2} = \frac{c_1}{2} \quad \Rightarrow \quad x^2 + y^2 = c_1 \qquad ...(2)$$

From first and third fractions, we get

$$\frac{dx}{yz} = \frac{dz}{xy} \quad \Rightarrow \quad \frac{dx}{z} = \frac{dz}{x} \quad \Rightarrow x\,dx - z\,dz = 0$$

Integrating, we get

$$\frac{x^2}{2} - \frac{z^2}{2} = \frac{c_2}{2} \quad \Rightarrow \quad x^2 - z^2 = c_2$$

Hence the general solution is $\phi(x^2 + y^2, x^2 - z^2) = 0$

(*ii*) Lagrange's subsidiary equations are

$$\frac{dx}{P} = \frac{dy}{Q} = \frac{dz}{R}$$

$$\Rightarrow \quad \frac{dx}{y^2} = \frac{dy}{-xy} = \frac{dz}{x(z - 2y)}$$

From first and second fractions, we have

$$\frac{dx}{y^2} = \frac{dy}{-xy}$$

$$\Rightarrow \quad x\,dx + y\,dy = 0$$

Integrating, we get

$$\frac{x^2}{2} + \frac{y^2}{2} = \frac{c_1}{2} \quad \Rightarrow \quad x^2 + y^2 = c_1 \qquad ...(1)$$

From second and third fractions, we have

$$\frac{dy}{-xy} = \frac{dz}{x(z - 2y)}$$

$$\Rightarrow \quad -z\,dy + 2y\,dy = y\,dz$$

$$\Rightarrow \quad 2y\,dy = y\,dz + z\,dy$$

Integrating, we get

$$y^2 = yz + c_2 \qquad ...(2)$$

Hence the general solution is $\phi\,(x^2 + y^2, y^2 - yz) = 0$.

(*iii*) Lagrange's subsidiary equations are

$$\frac{dx}{P} = \frac{dy}{Q} = \frac{dz}{R}$$

$$\Rightarrow \qquad \frac{dx}{x^2} = \frac{dy}{y^2} = \frac{dz}{(x+y)\,z} \qquad ...(1)$$

From first and second fractions, we have

$$\frac{dx}{x^2} = \frac{dy}{y^2}$$

Integrating, we get

$$-\frac{1}{x} = -\frac{1}{y} - c_1$$

$$\Rightarrow \qquad \frac{1}{x} - \frac{1}{y} = c_1 \qquad ...(2)$$

Again from (1),

$$\frac{dx - dy}{x^2 - y^2} = \frac{dz}{(x+y)\,z} \quad \Rightarrow \quad \frac{dx - dy}{x - y} = \frac{dz}{z}$$

Integrating, we get

$$\log(x - y) = \log z + \log c_2$$

$$\Rightarrow \qquad \frac{x - y}{z} = c_2 \qquad ...(3)$$

Hence the general solution is

$$\phi\left(\frac{1}{x} - \frac{1}{y}, \frac{x - y}{z}\right) = 0$$

Example 2. *Solve the following differential equations :*

(*i*) $\dfrac{y^2 z}{x}\,p + xzq = y^2$ (*ii*) $pz - qz = z^2 + (x+y)^2$

(*iii*) $(x^2 - yz)p + (y^2 - zx)q = z^2 - xy.$ [G.B.T.U. 2010 ; G.B.T.U. (AG) 2010]

Sol. (*i*) The given equation can be written as $y^2zp + x^2zq = xy^2$

Comparing with $Pp + Qq = R$, we have $P = y^2z, Q = x^2z, R = xy^2$

∴ Lagrange's subsidiary equations are

$$\frac{dx}{y^2 z} = \frac{dy}{x^2 z} = \frac{dz}{xy^2}$$

Taking the first two members, we have $x^2dx = y^2dy$

which on integration gives $x^3 - y^3 = c_1$ ...(1)

Again taking the first and third members, we have $xdx = zdz$

which on integration gives $x^2 - z^2 = c_2$ ...(2)

From (1) and (2), the general solution is

$$\phi(x^3 - y^3, x^2 - z^2) = 0.$$

(*ii*) Here Lagrange's subsidiary equations are

$$\frac{dx}{z}=\frac{dy}{-z}=\frac{dz}{z^2+(x+y)^2}$$

Taking the first two members, we have $dx + dy = 0$

which on integration gives $x + y = c_1$ ...(1)

Again taking the first and third members, we have

$$dx=\frac{zdz}{z^2+c_1^{\,2}}\text{ , since } x+y=c_1$$

or $$\frac{2z\,dz}{z^2+c_1^{\,2}}=2dx$$

which on integration gives

$$\log(z^2+c_1^{\,2})=2x+c_2$$

or $$\log[z^2+(x+y)^2]-2x=c_2 \qquad ...(2)$$

From (1) and (2), the general solution is

$$\phi[x+y,\ \log(x^2+y^2+z^2+2xy)-2x]=0.$$

(*iii*) Here Lagrange's subsidiary equations are

$$\frac{dx}{x^2-yz}=\frac{dy}{y^2-zx}=\frac{dz}{z^2-xy}$$

$$\therefore \quad \frac{dx-dy}{(x-y)(x+y+z)}=\frac{dy-dz}{(y-z)(x+y+z)}=\frac{dz-dx}{(z-x)(x+y+z)}$$

Taking the first two members, we have $\dfrac{dx-dy}{x-y}=\dfrac{dy-dz}{y-z}$

which on integration gives

$$\log(x-y)=\log(y-z)+\log a$$

or $$\log\left(\frac{x-y}{y-z}\right)=\log a \quad\text{or}\quad \frac{x-y}{y-z}=a \qquad ...(1)$$

Similarly, taking the last two members, we obtain

$$\frac{y-z}{z-x}=b \qquad ...(2)$$

From (1) and (2), the general solution is

$$\phi\left(\frac{x-y}{y-z},\frac{y-z}{z-x}\right)=0.$$

Example 3. *Solve the following differential equations :*

(*i*) $(mz-ny)p+(nx-lz)q=ly-mx$ [*G.B.T.U. (A.G.) 2012*]

(*ii*) $x^2(y-z)p+y^2(z-x)q=z^2(x-y)$. [*G.B.T.U. (AG) 2012*]

Sol. (*i*) Here Lagrange's subsidiary equations are

$$\frac{dx}{mz-ny}=\frac{dy}{nx-lz}=\frac{dz}{ly-mx}$$

Using x, y, z as multipliers, we get

$$\text{each fraction}=\frac{xdx+ydy+zdz}{0}$$

$$\therefore \quad xdx+ydy+zdz=0$$

which on integration gives $x^2+y^2+z^2=a$ ...(1)

Again using l, m, n as multipliers, we get

$$\text{each fraction} = \frac{ldx + mdy + ndz}{0}$$

$$\therefore \qquad ldx + mdy + ndz = 0$$

which on integration gives $lx + my + nz = b$ ...(2)

From (1) and (2), the general solution is

$$x^2 + y^2 + z^2 = f(lx + my + nz).$$

(*ii*) Here the auxiliary equations are

$$\frac{dx}{x^2(y-z)} = \frac{dy}{y^2(z-x)} = \frac{dz}{z^2(x-y)}$$

Using $\frac{1}{x^2}, \frac{1}{y^2}, \frac{1}{z^2}$ as multipliers, we get

$$\text{each fraction} = \frac{\frac{1}{x^2}dx + \frac{1}{y^2}dy + \frac{1}{z^2}dz}{0}$$

$$\therefore \qquad \frac{dx}{x^2} + \frac{dy}{y^2} + \frac{dz}{z^2} = 0$$

which on integration gives $\frac{1}{x} + \frac{1}{y} + \frac{1}{z} = a$ ...(1)

Again using $\frac{1}{x}, \frac{1}{y}, \frac{1}{z}$ as multipliers, we get

$$\text{each fraction} = \frac{\frac{1}{x}dx + \frac{1}{y}dy + \frac{1}{z}dz}{0}$$

$$\therefore \qquad \frac{dx}{x} + \frac{dy}{y} + \frac{dz}{z} = 0$$

which on integration gives

$$\log x + \log y + \log z = \log b$$

or $\log (xyz) = \log b$ or $xyz = b$ ...(2)

From (1) and (2), the general solution is

$$\phi\left(\frac{1}{x} + \frac{1}{y} + \frac{1}{z}, xyz\right) = 0.$$

Example 4. *Solve the partial differential equation*

$$x(y^2 + z)\, p - y(x^2 + z)\, q = z(x^2 - y^2) \textit{ where } p = \frac{\partial z}{\partial x} \textit{ and } q = \frac{\partial z}{\partial y}.$$ [U.P.T.U. 2008]

Sol. Lagrange's subsidiary equations are

$$\frac{dx}{x(y^2 + z)} = \frac{dy}{-y(x^2 + z)} = \frac{dz}{z(x^2 - y^2)} \qquad ...(1)$$

Using $x, y, -1$ as multipliers, we get

$$\text{each fraction} = \frac{x\,dx + y\,dy - dz}{x^2(y^2+z) - y^2(x^2+z) - z(x^2-y^2)} = \frac{x\,dx + y\,dy - dz}{0}$$

$\therefore \quad x\,dx + y\,dy - dz = 0$

Integrating, we get

$$\frac{x^2}{2} + \frac{y^2}{2} - z = \frac{c_1}{2}$$

$$\Rightarrow \quad x^2 + y^2 - 2z = c_1 \qquad \text{...(2)}$$

Again, using $\frac{1}{x}, \frac{1}{y}$ and $\frac{1}{z}$ as multipliers, we get

$$\text{each fraction} = \frac{\frac{1}{x}dx + \frac{1}{y}dy + \frac{1}{z}dz}{y^2+z-x^2-z+x^2-y^2} = \frac{\frac{1}{x}dx + \frac{1}{y}dy + \frac{1}{z}dz}{0}$$

$$\therefore \quad \frac{1}{x}dx + \frac{1}{y}dy + \frac{1}{z}dz = 0$$

Integrating, we get

$$\log x + \log y + \log z = \log c_2$$

$$\Rightarrow \quad xyz = c_2 \qquad \text{...(3)}$$

Hence the general solution is

$$\phi(x^2 + y^2 - 2z,\ xyz) = 0$$

Example 5. *Solve the following partial differential equation*

$x(y^2 - z^2)\,p + y(z^2 - x^2)\,q = z(x^2 - y^2)$ *where* $p = \frac{\partial z}{\partial x}$ *and* $q = \frac{\partial z}{\partial y}$, [U.P.T.U. (SUM) 2008]

Sol. Lagrange's subsidiary equations are

$$\frac{dx}{x(y^2-z^2)} = \frac{dy}{y(z^2-x^2)} = \frac{dz}{z(x^2-y^2)} \qquad \text{...(1)}$$

Using multipliers x, y, z, we get

$$\text{each fraction} = \frac{x\,dx + y\,dy + z\,dz}{x^2(y^2-z^2) + y^2(z^2-x^2) + z^2(x^2-y^2)} = \frac{x\,dx + y\,dy + z\,dz}{0}$$

$\therefore \quad x\,dx + y\,dy + z\,dz = 0$

Integrating, we get

$$\frac{x^2}{2} + \frac{y^2}{2} + \frac{z^2}{2} = \frac{c_1}{2}$$

$$\Rightarrow \quad x^2 + y^2 + z^2 = c_1 \qquad \text{...(2)}$$

Again using $\frac{1}{x}, \frac{1}{y}, \frac{1}{z}$ as multipliers, we get

$$\text{each fraction} = \frac{\frac{1}{x}dx + \frac{1}{y}dy + \frac{1}{z}dz}{y^2 - z^2 + z^2 - x^2 + x^2 - y^2} = \frac{\frac{1}{x}dx + \frac{1}{y}dy + \frac{1}{z}dz}{0}$$

$$\therefore \qquad \frac{1}{x}dx + \frac{1}{y}dy + \frac{1}{z}dz = 0$$

Integrating, we get

$$\log x + \log y + \log z = \log c_2$$

$$\Rightarrow \qquad xyz = c_2 \qquad \ldots(3)$$

Hence the general solution is

$$\phi\,(x^2 + y^2 + z^2, xyz) = 0$$

Example 6. *Solve :*

(*i*) $p + 3q = 5z + \tan(y - 3x)$ (*ii*) $(y^2 + z^2 - x^2)\,p - 2xyq + 2xz = 0$

(*iii*) $(y + zx)\,p - (x + yz)q = x^2 - y^2$

Sol. (*i*) Lagrange's subsidiary equations are

$$\frac{dx}{1} = \frac{dy}{3} = \frac{dz}{5z + \tan(y - 3x)} \qquad \ldots(1)$$

From first and second fractions, we have

$$\frac{dx}{1} = \frac{dy}{3}$$

Integrating, we get

$$y - 3x = c_1 \qquad \ldots(2)$$

Now, from first and last fractions, we have

$$\frac{dx}{1} = \frac{dz}{5z + \tan c_1}$$

Integrating, we get

$$x = \frac{1}{5}\log(5z + \tan c_1) - \frac{c_2}{5}$$

$$\Rightarrow \qquad \log\{5z + \tan(y - 3x)\} - 5x = c_2 \qquad \ldots(3)$$

Hence the general solution is

$$\phi\left[y - 3x, \log\{5z + \tan(y - 3x)\}\right] = 0$$

(*ii*) Lagrange's subsidiary equations are

$$\frac{dx}{y^2 + z^2 - x^2} = \frac{dy}{-2xy} = \frac{dz}{-2xz} \qquad \ldots(1)$$

Taking the last two fractions, we have

$$\frac{dy}{-2xy} = \frac{dz}{-2xz} \quad \Rightarrow \quad \frac{dy}{y} = \frac{dz}{z}$$

Integrating, we get

$$\log y = \log z + \log c_1$$

$$\Rightarrow \qquad \frac{y}{z} = c_1 \qquad \ldots(2)$$

Using x, y, z as multipliers, we have

$$\text{each fraction} = \frac{x\,dx + y\,dy + z\,dz}{xy^2 + xz^2 - x^3 - 2xy^2 - 2xz^2} = \frac{x\,dx + y\,dy + z\,dz}{-x(x^2 + y^2 + z^2)}$$

Let $$\frac{x\,dx + y\,dy + z\,dz}{-x(x^2 + y^2 + z^2)} = \frac{dz}{-2xz}$$

$$\Rightarrow \qquad \frac{2x\,dx + 2y\,dy + 2z\,dz}{x^2 + y^2 + z^2} = \frac{dz}{z}$$

Integrating, we get

$$\log\left(x^2 + y^2 + z^2\right) = \log z + \log c_2$$

$$\Rightarrow \qquad \frac{x^2 + y^2 + z^2}{z} = c_2$$

Hence the general solution is

$$\phi\left(\frac{y}{z}, \frac{x^2 + y^2 + z^2}{z}\right) = 0.$$

(*iii*) Lagrange's subsidiary equations are

$$\frac{dx}{y + zx} = \frac{dy}{-(x + yz)} = \frac{dz}{x^2 - y^2}$$

Using multipliers x, y and $-z$, we get

$$\text{each fraction} = \frac{x\,dx + y\,dy - z\,dz}{xy + x^2z - yx - y^2z - zx^2 + zy^2} = \frac{x\,dx + y\,dy - z\,dz}{0}$$

$$\therefore \qquad x\,dx + y\,dy - z\,dz = 0$$

Integrating, we get

$$\frac{x^2}{2} + \frac{y^2}{2} - \frac{z^2}{2} = \frac{c_1}{2}$$

$$\Rightarrow \qquad x^2 + y^2 - z^2 = c_1 \qquad \ldots(1)$$

Again, using multipliers $y, x, 1$; we get

$$\text{each fraction} = \frac{y\,dx + x\,dy + dz}{y^2 + yzx - x^2 - xyz + x^2 - y^2} = \frac{y\,dx + x\,dy + dz}{0}$$

$$\therefore \qquad y\,dx + x\,dy + dz = 0$$

Integrating, we get

$$xy + z = c_2 \qquad \text{...(2)}$$

Hence the general solution is

$$\phi(x^2 + y^2 - z^2, xy + z) = 0.$$

Example 7. *Solve :*

(*i*) $(x^2 - y^2 - yz) p + (x^2 - y^2 - zx) q = z (x - y)$

(*ii*) $(x^2 + xy) p - (xy + y^2) q = -(x - y)(2x + 2y + z)$

Sol. (*i*) Lagrange's subsidiary equations are

$$\frac{dx}{x^2 - y^2 - yz} = \frac{dy}{x^2 - y^2 - zx} = \frac{dz}{z(x - y)}$$

Using 1, – 1, – 1 as multipliers, we have

$$\text{each fraction} = \frac{dx - dy - dz}{x^2 - y^2 - yz - x^2 + y^2 + zx - zx + zy} = \frac{dx - dy - dz}{0}$$

$$\therefore \qquad dx - dy - dz = 0$$

Integrating, we get

$$x - y - z = c_1 \qquad \text{...(1)}$$

Again, from first and second, we have

$$\frac{x\,dx - y\,dy}{x^3 - xy^2 - xyz - yx^2 + y^3 + yzx} = \frac{dz}{z(x - y)}$$

$$\Rightarrow \qquad \frac{x\,dx - y\,dy}{x^3 - xy^2 - yx^2 + y^3} = \frac{dz}{z(x - y)}$$

$$\Rightarrow \qquad \frac{x\,dx - y\,dy}{(x - y)(x^2 - y^2)} = \frac{dz}{z(x - y)}$$

$$\Rightarrow \qquad \frac{x\,dx - y\,dy}{x^2 - y^2} = \frac{dz}{z}$$

Integrating, we get

$$\frac{1}{2}\log(x^2 - y^2) = \log z + \frac{1}{2}\log c_2$$

$$\Rightarrow \qquad \frac{x^2 - y^2}{z^2} = c_2 \qquad \text{...(2)}$$

Hence the general solution is

$$\phi\left(x - y - z, \frac{x^2 - y^2}{z^2}\right) = 0$$

(*ii*) Lagrange's subsidiary equations are

$$\frac{dx}{x(x + y)} = \frac{dy}{-y(x + y)} = \frac{dz}{-(x - y)(2x + 2y + z)}$$

Taking first and second fractions, we have

$$\frac{dx}{x} = \frac{dy}{-y}$$

Integrating, we get

$$\log x = -\log y + \log c_1$$

$\Rightarrow$ $$xy = c_1 \quad ...(1)$$

Again from first and second,

$$\frac{dx + dy}{(x - y)(x + y)} = \frac{dz}{-(x - y)(2x + 2y + z)}$$

$\Rightarrow$ $$(2x + 2y + z)(dx + dy) + (x + y)\,dz = 0$$

$\Rightarrow$ $$(x + y + z)\,d(x + y) + (x + y)(dx + dy) + (x + y)\,dz = 0$$

$\Rightarrow$ $$(x + y + z)\,d(x + y) + (x + y)\,d(x + y + z) = 0$$

$\Rightarrow$ $$d\{(x + y)(x + y + z)\} = 0$$

Integrating, we get

$$(x + y)(x + y + z) = c_2$$

Hence the general solution is

$$\phi\{xy, (x + y)(x + y + z)\} = 0$$

Example 8. *Solve the partial differential equations :*

(*i*) $\left(\frac{y - z}{yz}\right)p + \left(\frac{z - x}{zx}\right)q = \left(\frac{x - y}{xy}\right)$ (*ii*) $(y^2 + z^2)\,p - xyq = -zx$ (M.T.U. 2011)

[G.B.T.U. (AG) 2011]

Sol. (*i*) The given equation can also be written as

$$x(y - z)\,p + y(z - x)\,q = z(x - y) \quad ...(1)$$

Lagrange's subsidiary equations are

$$\frac{dx}{x(y - z)} = \frac{dy}{y(z - x)} = \frac{dz}{z(x - y)}$$

Using multipliers as $\frac{1}{x}, \frac{1}{y}, \frac{1}{z}$, we have

$$\text{each fraction} = \frac{\frac{1}{x}dx + \frac{1}{y}dy + \frac{1}{z}dz}{y - z + z - x + x - y} = \frac{\frac{1}{x}dx + \frac{1}{y}dy + \frac{1}{z}dz}{0}$$

$\therefore$ $$\frac{1}{x}dx + \frac{1}{y}dy + \frac{1}{z}dz = 0$$

Integrating, we get

$$\log x + \log y + \log z = \log c_1 \quad \Rightarrow \quad xyz = c_1 \quad ...(2)$$

Again, using 1, 1, 1 as multipliers, we get

$$\text{each fraction} = \frac{dx + dy + dz}{x(y - z) + y(z - x) + z(x - y)} = \frac{dx + dy + dz}{0}$$

$\therefore$ $$dx + dy + dz = 0$$

Integrating, we get

$$x + y + z = c_2$$

Hence the general solution is

$$\phi(xyz, x + y + z) = 0.$$

(*ii*) Lagrange's subsidiary eqns. are

$$\frac{dx}{y^2+z^2}=\frac{dy}{-xy}=\frac{dz}{-zx} \quad \ldots(1)$$

From second and third fractions,

$$\frac{dy}{y}=\frac{dz}{z}$$

Integrating, we get $\frac{y}{z}=c_1$

Now, using multipliers as x, y, z, we get

$$\text{each fraction} = \frac{x\,dx+y\,dy+z\,dz}{0}$$

$\therefore \quad x\,dx+y\,dy+z\,dz=0$

Integrating, we get

$$\frac{x^2}{2}+\frac{y^2}{2}+\frac{z^2}{2}=\frac{c_2}{2} \quad \Rightarrow \quad x^2+y^2+z^2=c_2$$

Hence the general solution is

$$\phi\left(\frac{y}{z}, x^2+y^2+z^2\right)=0.$$

TEST YOUR KNOWLEDGE

Solve the following partial differential equations :

1. $2p+3q=1$

2. $xp+yq=3z$

3. $(y-z)p+(x-y)q=z-x$

4. $p\tan x+q\tan y=\tan z$

5. $p\sqrt{x}+q\sqrt{y}=\sqrt{z}$

6. $(z-y)p+(x-z)q=y-x$

7. $yzp+zxq=xy$

8. $(y+z)p+(z+x)q=x+y$

9. $2yzp+zxq=3xy$

10. $z(xp-yq)=y^2-x^2$

11. $2xzp+2yzq=z^2-x^2-y^2$

12. $(3-2yz)\,p+x(2z-1)\,q=2x\,(y-3)$

13. $x\,(z-3y^3)\,p+y\,(3x^3-z)\,q=3\,(y^3-x^3)\,z$ [**Hint :** Multipliers $\to (x^2, y^2, 1/3)$ and $(1/x, 1/y, 1/z)$]

14. $(z^2-2yz-y^2)\,p+x(y+z)\,q=x\,(y-z)$

15. $y^2\,(x+y)\,p+x^2\,(x+y)\,q=(x^2+y^2)\,z$ [**Hint :** Multipliers $\to (1, 1, 0)$ and $(x^2, -y^2, 0)$]

16. $(x+2y^2+z)\,p+y\,(2x-1)\,q+2\,(x^2+y^2+xz)=0$ [**Hint :** Multipliers $\to (x, -y, 1/2)$ and $(y, x+z, y)$]

17. $yp+xq=xyz^2\,(x^2-y^2)$ [*G.B.T.U. 2011*]

18. $(x-y)\,y^2p+(y-x)\,x^2\,q=(x^2+y^2)z$ [*G.B.T.U. (AG) 2011, 2012*]

19. $x\frac{\partial u}{\partial x}+y\frac{\partial u}{\partial y}+z\frac{\partial u}{\partial z}=xyz$

20. $x_1p_1+2x_2p_2+3x_3p_3+4x_4p_4=0$

Answers

1. $\phi\,(3x - 2y,\, y - 3z) = 0$

2. $\phi\left(\frac{x}{y}, \frac{x^3}{z}\right) = 0$

3. $\phi\left(x + y + z, \frac{x^2}{2} + yz\right) = 0$

4. $\phi\left(\frac{\sin x}{\sin y}, \frac{\sin y}{\sin z}\right) = 0$

5. $\sqrt{x} - \sqrt{y} = f(\sqrt{x} - \sqrt{z})$

6. $x^2 + y^2 + z^2 = f\,(x + y + z)$

7. $\phi\,(x^2 - y^2,\, x^2 - z^2) = 0$

8. $\phi\left[\frac{x - y}{y - z}, (x - y)^2\,(x + y + z)\right] = 0$

9. $\phi\,(x^2 - 2y^2,\, 3y^2 - z^2) = 0$

10. $\phi\,(xy,\, x^2 + y^2 + z^2) = 0$

11. $\phi\left(\frac{y}{x}, \frac{x^2 + y^2 + z^2}{x}\right) = 0$

12. $\phi\,(y^2 - 6y - z^2 + z,\, x^2 + z^2 + 6y) = 0$

13. $\phi\,(x^3 + y^3 + z,\, xyz) = 0$

14. $\phi\,(x^2 + y^2 + z^2,\; y^2 - 2yz - z^2) = 0$

15. $\phi\left(x^3 - y^3, \frac{x + y}{z}\right) = 0$

16. $\phi\,(x^2 - y^2 + z,\, xy + yz) = 0$

17. $\phi\left\{x^2 - y^2, \frac{x^4}{4} - \frac{y^4}{4} + \frac{1}{z}\right\} = 0$

18. $\phi\left\{x^3 + y^3, \frac{x - y}{z}\right\} = 0$

19. $\phi\left(\frac{x}{y}, \frac{y}{z}, xyz - 3u\right) = 0$

20. $z = \phi\left(\frac{x_1^2}{x_2}, \frac{x_1^3}{x_3}, \frac{x_1^4}{x_4}\right)$

4.23. NON-LINEAR PDE OF FIRST ORDER

A partial differential equation which involves first order partial derivatives p and q with degree higher than one and the products of p and q is called a non-linear partial differential equation of the first order. The complete solution of such an equation involves only two arbitrary constants (*i.e.*, equal to the number of independent variables). There is a general method for solving such equations. Before giving this method, we shall deal with some special types of such equations which can be solved easily by methods other than the general method.

4.23.1. Equations of the Form $f(p, q) = 0$, *i.e.*,

equations involving only **p** *and* **q** *and no* **x, y, z**

The complete solution is $z = ax + by + c$ ...(1)

where a and b are connected by the relation

$$f(a, b) = 0 \qquad \text{...(2)} \qquad \left[\text{since } p = \frac{\partial z}{\partial x} = a \text{ and } q = \frac{\partial z}{\partial y} = b\right]$$

From (2), we can find b in terms of a. Let $b = \phi\,(a)$.

Putting this value of b in (1), the complete solution is

$$z = ax + \phi\,(a)y + c, \quad \text{where } a \text{ and } c \text{ are arbitrary constants.}$$

ILLUSTRATIVE EXAMPLES

Example 1. *Solve :*

(*i*) $\sqrt{p} + \sqrt{q} = 1$ (*ii*) $pq = p + q$.

Sol. (*i*) The equation is of the form $f(p, q) = 0$

The complete solution is $z = ax + by + c$ ...(1)

where $\sqrt{a} + \sqrt{b} = 1$ or $b = (1 - \sqrt{a})^2$

$\therefore$ From (1), the complete solution is

$$z = ax + (1 - \sqrt{a})^2 y + c$$

(*ii*) The equation is of the form $f(p, q) = 0$

The complete solution is $z = ax + by + c$ ...(1)

where $ab = a + b$ or $b = \dfrac{a}{a-1}$

$\therefore$ From (1), the complete solution is $z = ax + \dfrac{a}{a-1} y + c$.

Example 2. *Solve* $x^2p^2 + y^2q^2 = z^2$.

Sol. The given equation can be written as

$$\left(\frac{x}{z} \cdot \frac{\partial z}{\partial x}\right)^2 + \left(\frac{y}{z} \cdot \frac{\partial z}{\partial y}\right)^2 = 1 \quad ...(1)$$

Let $\dfrac{\partial x}{x} = \partial X$, $\dfrac{\partial y}{y} = \partial Y$, $\dfrac{\partial z}{z} = \partial Z$ then $X = \log x$, $Y = \log y$, $Z = \log z$

$$\frac{\partial Z}{\partial X} = \frac{x}{z} \cdot \frac{\partial z}{\partial x} \text{ and } \frac{\partial Z}{\partial Y} = \frac{y}{z} \cdot \frac{\partial z}{\partial y}$$

$\therefore$ Eqn. (1) can be written as $\left(\dfrac{\partial Z}{\partial X}\right)^2 + \left(\dfrac{\partial Z}{\partial Y}\right)^2 = 1$

or $P^2 + Q^2 = 1$, where $P = \dfrac{\partial Z}{\partial X}$ and $Q = \dfrac{\partial Z}{\partial Y}$

It is of the form $f(P, Q) = 0$

Its complete solution is $Z = aX + bY + c$ ...(2)

where $a^2 + b^2 = 1$ or $b = \sqrt{1 - a^2}$

$\therefore$ From (2), the complete solution is $\log z = a \log x + \sqrt{1 - a^2} \log y + c$.

Example 3. *Solve* $(y - x)(qy - px) = (p - q)^2$.

Sol. Let $x + y = X$ and $xy = Y$

so that $$p = \frac{\partial z}{\partial x} = \frac{\partial z}{\partial X} \cdot \frac{\partial X}{\partial x} + \frac{\partial z}{\partial Y} \cdot \frac{\partial Y}{\partial x} = \frac{\partial z}{\partial X} + y \frac{\partial z}{\partial Y}$$

and $$q = \frac{\partial z}{\partial y} = \frac{\partial z}{\partial X} \cdot \frac{\partial X}{\partial y} + \frac{\partial z}{\partial Y} \cdot \frac{\partial Y}{\partial y} = \frac{\partial z}{\partial X} + x \frac{\partial z}{\partial Y}$$

$\therefore \qquad qy - px = (y - x)\dfrac{\partial z}{\partial X}$ and $p - q = (y - x)\dfrac{\partial z}{\partial Y}$

$\therefore$ The given equation can be written as $\dfrac{\partial z}{\partial X} = \left(\dfrac{\partial z}{\partial Y}\right)^2$

or $\qquad P = Q^2$, where $P = \dfrac{\partial z}{\partial X}$ and $Q = \dfrac{\partial z}{\partial Y}$

It is of the form $f(P, Q) = 0$

Its complete solution is $z = aX + bY + c$ ...(1)

where $a = b^2$ or $b = \sqrt{a}$

$\therefore$ From (1), the complete solution is $z = a(x + y) + \sqrt{a}\ xy + c.$

4.23.2. Equations of the Form $z = px + qy + f(p, q)$

The complete solution is $z = ax + by + f(a, b)$ obtained by writing a for p and b for q.

ILLUSTRATIVE EXAMPLES

Example 1. *Solve:* $z = px + qy + \sqrt{1 + p^2 + q^2}$.

Sol. The given equation is of the form $z = px + qy + f(p, q)$

Its complete solution is $\qquad z = ax + by + \sqrt{1 + a^2 + b^2}$.

Example 2. *Find the singular integral of* $z = px + qy + pq$. [G.B.T.U. (AG) 2012]

Sol. The equation is of the form

$$z = px + qy + f(p, q)$$

Its complete integral is

$$z = ax + by + ab \qquad ...(1)$$

Diff. (1) partially w.r.t. a and b,

$$0 = x + b \quad \text{and} \quad 0 = y + a \qquad ...(2)$$

Eliminating a and b between eqns. (1) and (2), we get

$$z = -xy - xy + xy$$

$\Rightarrow \qquad z = -xy$

which is the required singular solution, for it satisfies the given equation.

Example 3. *Solve:* $4xyz = pq + 2px^2y + 2qxy^2$.

Sol. Let $\qquad x^2 = X$ and $y^2 = Y$

so that $\qquad p = \dfrac{\partial z}{\partial x} = \dfrac{\partial z}{\partial X}\cdot\dfrac{\partial X}{\partial x} = 2x\dfrac{\partial z}{\partial X}$ and $q = \dfrac{\partial z}{\partial y} = \dfrac{\partial z}{\partial Y}\cdot\dfrac{\partial Y}{\partial y} = 2y\dfrac{\partial z}{\partial Y}$

$\therefore$ The given equation becomes

$$4xyz = 4xy\,\frac{\partial z}{\partial X}\cdot\frac{\partial z}{\partial Y} + 4x^3y\,\frac{\partial z}{\partial X} + 4xy^3\,\frac{\partial z}{\partial Y}$$

or $$z = x^2\frac{\partial z}{\partial X} + y^2\frac{\partial z}{\partial Y} + \frac{\partial z}{\partial X}\cdot\frac{\partial z}{\partial Y} = X\frac{\partial z}{\partial X} + Y\frac{\partial z}{\partial Y} + \frac{\partial z}{\partial X}\cdot\frac{\partial z}{\partial Y}$$

or $$z = PX + QY + PQ, \quad \text{where } P = \frac{\partial z}{\partial X} \quad \text{and} \quad Q = \frac{\partial z}{\partial Y}$$

It is of the form $z = PX + QY + f(P, Q)$

Its complete solution is $z = aX + bY + ab$ or $z = ax^2 + by^2 + ab$.

4.23.3. Equations of the Form $f(z, p, q) = 0$,

i.e., equations not containing x and y.

Assume $z = \phi(x + ay) = \phi(u)$, where $u = x + ay$ as a trial solution of the given equation.

$$\therefore \quad p = \frac{\partial z}{\partial x} = \phi'(x + ay) = \phi'(u) = \frac{dz}{du}$$

$$q = \frac{dz}{dy} = \phi'(x + ay)a = a\phi'(u) = a\frac{dz}{du}$$

Substituting these values of p and q in the given equation, we get $f\left(z, \frac{dz}{du}, a\frac{dz}{du}\right) = 0$ which is an ordinary differential equation of the first order. Integrating it, we get the complete solution.

Method. (*i*) Assume $u = x + ay$ so that $p = \frac{dz}{du}$ and $q = a\frac{dz}{du}$.

(*ii*) Substitute these values of p and q in the given equation.

(*iii*) Solve the resulting ordinary differential equation in z and u.

(*iv*) Replace u by $x + ay$.

ILLUSTRATIVE EXAMPLES

Example 1. *Solve:* $z^2(p^2 + q^2 + 1) = a^2$.

Sol. The given equation is of the form $f(z, p, q) = 0$

Let $u = x + by$ (note the use of b instead of a, since a is a given constant)

so that $$p = \frac{dz}{du} \quad \text{and} \quad q = b\frac{dz}{du}.$$

Substituting these values of p and q in the given equation, we get

$$z^2\left[\left(\frac{dz}{du}\right)^2 + b^2\left(\frac{dz}{du}\right)^2 + 1\right] = a^2$$

or $$z^2(1 + b^2)\left(\frac{dz}{du}\right)^2 = a^2 - z^2$$

or $$z\sqrt{1+b^2}\,\frac{dz}{du} = \pm\sqrt{a^2 - z^2}$$

or $$\pm\sqrt{1+b^2}\,.\,\frac{z}{\sqrt{a^2 - z^2}}\,dz = du$$

Integrating, we have

$$\pm\sqrt{1+b^2}\,\sqrt{a^2 - z^2} = u + c$$

or $$(1 + b^2)(a^2 - z^2) = (x + by + c)^2$$

Example 2. *Solve:* $z^2 (p^2x^2 + q^2) = 1$.

Sol. The given equation can be written as

$$z^2 \left[\left(x \frac{\partial z}{\partial x} \right)^2 + \left(\frac{\partial z}{\partial y} \right)^2 \right] = 1 \quad \ldots(1)$$

Let $\quad X = \log x$

so that $\quad \frac{\partial z}{\partial x} = \frac{\partial z}{\partial X} \cdot \frac{\partial X}{\partial x} = \frac{\partial z}{\partial X} \cdot \frac{1}{x} \quad$ *i.e.,* $\quad x \frac{\partial z}{\partial x} = \frac{\partial z}{\partial X}$

$\therefore$ Equation (1) reduces to $z^2 \left[\left(\frac{\partial z}{\partial X} \right)^2 + \left(\frac{\partial z}{\partial y} \right)^2 \right] = 1$

or $$z^2 (P^2 + q^2) = 1, \text{ where } P = \frac{\partial z}{\partial X} \quad \ldots(2)$$

Let $\quad u = X + ay \quad$ so that $\quad P = \frac{dz}{du} \quad$ and $\quad q = a \frac{dz}{du}$

$\therefore$ From (2), we have $z^2 \left[\left(\frac{dz}{du} \right)^2 + a^2 \left(\frac{dz}{du} \right)^2 \right] = 1$

or $$(1 + a^2)z^2 \left(\frac{dz}{du} \right)^2 = 1 \quad \text{or} \quad \sqrt{1+a^2} \,.\, z\, dz = \pm\, du$$

Integrating, $\quad \sqrt{1+a^2} \,.\, \frac{z^2}{2} = \pm\, u + b$

or $\quad \sqrt{1+a^2} \,.\, z^2 = \pm\, 2(X + ay) + 2b$

or $\quad \sqrt{1+a^2} \,.\, z^2 = \pm\, 2\,(\log x + ay) + c$

4.23.4. Equations of the Form $f_1\,(x, p) = f_2\,(y, q)$

i.e., equations in which ***z*** *is absent and the terms involving* ***x*** *and* ***p*** *can be separated from those involving* ***y*** *and* ***q***.

As a trial solution, let us put each side equal to an arbitrary constant a. Then

$$f_1\,(x, p) = f_2\,(y, q) = a$$

Solving these equations for p and q, let $p = F_1\,(x)$ and $q = F_2\,(y)$

Since $\quad dz = \frac{\partial z}{\partial x}\, dx + \frac{\partial z}{\partial y}\, dy = p\,dx + q\,dy$

$\therefore \quad dz = F_1(x)\, dx + F_2(y)\, dy$

Integrating, $\quad z = \int F_1\,(x)\, dx + \int F_2\,(y)\, dy + b$

ILLUSTRATIVE EXAMPLES

Example 1. *Solve:* $p^2 - q^2 = x - y$.

Sol. The given equation is $p^2 - x = q^2 - y$ which is of the form $f_1(x, p) = f_2(y, q)$

Let $\quad p^2 - x = q^2 - y = a$

then $\quad p^2 = x + a$ and $q^2 = y + a$ *i.e.,* $p = \sqrt{x+a}$ and $q = \sqrt{y+a}$

Substituting these values of p and q in $dz = pdx + qdy$, we get

$$dz = \sqrt{x+a}\, dx + \sqrt{y+a}\, dy$$

Integrating, $z = \frac{2}{3}(x+a)^{3/2} + \frac{2}{3}(y+a)^{3/2} + b$

Example 2. *Solve:* $yp = 2yx + \log q$.

Sol. The given equation can be written as

$$p = 2x + \frac{1}{y}\log q \quad \text{or} \quad p - 2x = \frac{1}{y}\log q$$

which is of the form $f_1(x, p) = f_2(y, q)$.

Let $\quad p - 2x = \frac{1}{y}\log q = a$ then $p = 2x + a$ and $\log q = ay$, *i.e.,* $q = e^{ay}$

Substituting these values of p and q in $dz = pdx + qdy$, we get

$$dz = (2x + a)\, dx + e^{ay}\, dy$$

Integrating, $z = x^2 + ax + \frac{1}{a}e^{ay} + b$

TEST YOUR KNOWLEDGE

Solve the following equations :

1. $p^2 + q^2 = 2$
2. $p^3 - q^3 = 0$
3. $p^2 + p = q^2$
4. $p = e^q$
5. $(x + y)(p + q)^2 + (x - y)(p - q)^2 = 1$
6. $z = px + qy - 2\sqrt{pq}$
7. $z = px + qy + \sin(p + q)$
8. $(pq - p - q)(z - px - qy) = pq$
9. $p^2 = zq$
10. $p(1 + q^2) = q(z - a)$
11. $p(1 + q) = qz$
12. $z^2(p^2 + q^2 + 1) = 1$
13. $z = p^2 + q^2$
14. $p + q = z$
15. $z^2(p^2z^2 + q^2) = 1$
16. $9(p^2z + q^2) = 4$
17. $p^2 + q^2 = x + y$
18. $p - x^2 = q + y^2$
19. $\sqrt{p} + \sqrt{q} = x + y$
20. $\sqrt{p} + \sqrt{q} = 2x$
21. $pe^y = qe^x$
22. $q = xyp^2$
23. $q(p - \cos x) = \cos y$
24. $yp + xq + pq = 0$
25. $z(p^2 - q^2) = x - y$
26. $p + q = \sin x + \sin y$
27. $z^2(p^2 + q^2) = x^2 + y^2$.

Answers

1. $z = ax + \sqrt{2 - a^2}\, y + c$
2. $z = a(x + y) + c$
3. $z = ax + \sqrt{a^2 + a}\, y + c$
4. $z = ax + y\log a + c$
5. $z = a\sqrt{x+y} + \sqrt{1-a^2}\sqrt{x-y} + c$
6. $z = ax + by - 2\sqrt{ab}$
7. $z = ax + by + \sin(a + b)$
8. $z = ax + by + \dfrac{ab}{ab - a - b}$
9. $z = be^{ax + a^2y}$

10. $4(bz - ab - 1) = (x + by + c)^2$

11. $\log (az - 1) = x + ay + b$

12. $(1 + a^2)(1 - z^2) = (x + ay + b)^2$

13. $4z(1 + a^2) = (x + ay + b)^2$

14. $(1 + a) \log z = x + ay + b$

15. $(z^2 + a^2)^3 = 9(x + ay + b)^2$

16. $(z + a^2)^3 = (x + ay + b)^2$

17. $z = \frac{2}{3}(x + a)^{3/2} + \frac{2}{3}(y - a)^{3/2} + b$

18. $z = \frac{1}{3}(x^3 - y^3) + a(x + y) + b$

19. $z = \frac{1}{3}(x + a)^3 + \frac{1}{3}(y - a)^3 + b$

20. $z = \frac{1}{6}(2x + a)^3 + a^2 y + b$

21. $z = ae^x + ae^y + b$

22. $z = 2\sqrt{ax} + \frac{1}{2} ay^2 + b$

23. $z = ax + \sin x + \frac{1}{a} \sin y + b$

24. $2z = ax^2 - \frac{a}{a+1} y^2 + b$

25. $z^{3/2} = (x + a)^{3/2} + (y + a)^{3/2} + b$

26. $z = a(x - y) - (\cos x + \cos y) + c$

27. $z^2 = x\sqrt{x^2 + a} + y\sqrt{y^2 - a} + a \log \frac{x + \sqrt{x^2 + a}}{y + \sqrt{y^2 - a}} + c.$

4.24. CHARPIT'S METHOD

This is a general method for finding the complete solution of non-linear partial differential equations of the first order.

Let the given equation be $f(x, y, z, p, q) = 0$ ...(1)

If we can find another relation $F(x, y, z, p, q) = 0$ ...(2)

involving x, y, z, p and q, then we can solve (1) and (2) for p and q and substitute in

$$dz = p\,dx + q\,dy \qquad \text{...(3)}$$

Solution of (3), if it exists, is the complete solution of (1).

To determine F, we differentiate (1) and (2) partially w.r.t. x and y. Thus

$$\frac{\partial f}{\partial x} + \frac{\partial f}{\partial z} \cdot p + \frac{\partial f}{\partial p} \cdot \frac{\partial p}{\partial x} + \frac{\partial f}{\partial q} \cdot \frac{\partial q}{\partial x} = 0 \qquad \text{...(4)}$$

$$\frac{\partial F}{\partial x} + \frac{\partial F}{\partial z} \cdot p + \frac{\partial F}{\partial p} \cdot \frac{\partial p}{\partial x} + \frac{\partial F}{\partial q} \cdot \frac{\partial q}{\partial x} = 0 \qquad \text{...(5)}$$

$$\frac{\partial f}{\partial y} + \frac{\partial f}{\partial z} \cdot q + \frac{\partial f}{\partial p} \cdot \frac{\partial p}{\partial y} + \frac{\partial f}{\partial q} \cdot \frac{\partial q}{\partial y} = 0 \qquad \text{...(6)}$$

$$\frac{\partial F}{\partial y} + \frac{\partial F}{\partial z} \cdot q + \frac{\partial F}{\partial p} \cdot \frac{\partial p}{\partial y} + \frac{\partial F}{\partial q} \cdot \frac{\partial q}{\partial y} = 0 \qquad \text{...(7)}$$

Eliminating $\frac{\partial p}{\partial x}$ between (4) and (5), we get

$$\left(\frac{\partial f}{\partial x} \cdot \frac{\partial F}{\partial p} - \frac{\partial F}{\partial x} \cdot \frac{\partial f}{\partial p}\right) + \left(\frac{\partial f}{\partial z} \cdot \frac{\partial F}{\partial p} - \frac{\partial F}{\partial z} \cdot \frac{\partial f}{\partial p}\right) p + \left(\frac{\partial f}{\partial q} \cdot \frac{\partial F}{\partial p} - \frac{\partial F}{\partial q} \cdot \frac{\partial f}{\partial p}\right) \frac{\partial q}{\partial x} = 0 \qquad \text{...(8)}$$

Eliminating $\frac{\partial q}{\partial y}$ between (6) and (7), we get

$$\left(\frac{\partial f}{\partial y} \cdot \frac{\partial F}{\partial q} - \frac{\partial F}{\partial y} \cdot \frac{\partial f}{\partial q}\right) + \left(\frac{\partial f}{\partial z} \cdot \frac{\partial F}{\partial q} - \frac{\partial F}{\partial z} \cdot \frac{\partial f}{\partial q}\right) q + \left(\frac{\partial f}{\partial p} \cdot \frac{\partial F}{\partial q} - \frac{\partial F}{\partial p} \cdot \frac{\partial f}{\partial q}\right) \frac{\partial p}{\partial y} = 0 \qquad \text{...(9)}$$

Since $\frac{\partial q}{\partial x} = \frac{\partial^2 z}{\partial x \partial y} = \frac{\partial^2 z}{\partial y \partial x} = \frac{\partial p}{\partial y}$, the last terms in (8) and (9) differ in sign only. Adding (8) and (9), we get

$$\left(\frac{\partial f}{\partial x} + p\frac{\partial f}{\partial z}\right)\frac{\partial F}{\partial p} + \left(\frac{\partial f}{\partial y} + q\frac{\partial f}{\partial z}\right)\frac{\partial F}{\partial q} + \left(-p\frac{\partial f}{\partial p} - q\frac{\partial f}{\partial q}\right)\frac{\partial F}{\partial z} + \left(-\frac{\partial f}{\partial p}\right)\frac{\partial F}{\partial x} + \left(-\frac{\partial f}{\partial q}\right)\frac{\partial F}{\partial y} = 0 \quad ...(10)$$

which is a linear partial differential equation of the first order with x, y, z, p, q as independent variables and F as the dependent variable.

∴ The auxiliary equations are

$$\frac{dp}{\frac{\partial f}{\partial x} + p\frac{\partial f}{\partial z}} = \frac{dq}{\frac{\partial f}{\partial y} + q\frac{\partial f}{\partial z}} = \frac{dz}{-p\frac{\partial f}{\partial p} - q\frac{\partial f}{\partial q}} = \frac{dx}{-\frac{\partial f}{\partial p}} = \frac{dy}{-\frac{\partial f}{\partial q}} = \frac{dF}{0} \quad ...(11)$$

Any integral of (11) which involves p or q or both can be taken as the assumed relation (2). In practice, we choose the simplest of the integrals of (11).

ILLUSTRATIVE EXAMPLES

Example 1. *Solve:* $2zx - px^2 - 2pxy + pq = 0$.

Sol. Here $\quad f \equiv 2zx - px^2 - 2qxy + pq = 0 \quad ...(1)$

$$\therefore \quad \frac{\partial f}{\partial x} = 2z - 2px - 2qy, \frac{\partial f}{\partial y} = -2qx, \frac{\partial f}{\partial z} = 2x, \frac{\partial f}{\partial p} = -x^2 + q, \frac{\partial f}{\partial q} = -2xy + p$$

Charpit's auxiliary equations are

$$\frac{dp}{\frac{\partial f}{\partial x} + p\frac{\partial f}{\partial z}} = \frac{dq}{\frac{\partial f}{\partial y} + q\frac{\partial f}{\partial z}} = \frac{dz}{-p\frac{\partial f}{\partial p} - q\frac{\partial f}{\partial q}} = \frac{dx}{-\frac{\partial f}{\partial p}} = \frac{dy}{-\frac{\partial f}{\partial q}} = \frac{dF}{0}$$

or
$$\frac{dp}{2z - 2qy} = \frac{dq}{0} = \frac{dz}{px^2 - 2pq + 2qxy} = \frac{dx}{x^2 - q} = \frac{dy}{2xy - p} = \frac{dF}{0}$$

$$\therefore \quad dq = 0 \quad \text{or} \quad q = a$$

Putting $q = a$ in (1), we get $\quad p = \frac{2x(z - ay)}{x^2 - a}$

$$\therefore \quad dz = pdx + qdy = \frac{2x(z - ay)}{x^2 - a}dx + ady$$

or
$$\frac{dz - ady}{z - ay} = \frac{2x}{x^2 - a}dx$$

Integrating, $\log (z - ay) = \log (x^2 - a) + \log b$ or $z - ay = b(x^2 - a)$

∴ $\quad z = ay + b(x^2 - a)$ which is the required complete integral.

Example 2. *Solve:* $(p^2 + q^2)y = qz$.

Sol. Here $\quad f \equiv (p^2 + q^2)y - qz = 0 \quad ...(1)$

$$\therefore \quad \frac{\partial f}{\partial x} = 0, \frac{\partial f}{\partial y} = p^2 + q^2, \frac{\partial f}{\partial z} = -q, \frac{\partial f}{\partial p} = 2py, \frac{\partial f}{\partial q} = 2qy - z$$

Charpit's auxiliary equations are

$$\frac{dp}{\frac{\partial f}{\partial x}+p\frac{\partial f}{\partial z}}=\frac{dq}{\frac{\partial f}{\partial y}+q\frac{\partial f}{\partial z}}=\frac{dz}{-p\frac{\partial f}{\partial p}-q\frac{\partial f}{\partial q}}=\frac{dx}{-\frac{\partial f}{\partial p}}=\frac{dy}{-\frac{\partial f}{\partial q}}=\frac{dF}{0}$$

or
$$\frac{dp}{-pq}=\frac{dq}{p^2}=\frac{dz}{-qz}=\frac{dx}{-2py}=\frac{dy}{-2qy+z}=\frac{dF}{0}$$

From the first two members, we have $pdp + qdq = 0$

Integrating, $p^2 + q^2 = a^2$ ...(2)

Putting in (1), $q = \frac{a^2 y}{z}$

$\therefore$ From (2), $p=\sqrt{a^2-q^2}=\sqrt{a^2-\frac{a^4y^2}{z^2}}=\frac{a}{z}\sqrt{z^2-a^2y^2}$

$$\therefore \quad dz = pdx + qdy = \frac{a}{z}\sqrt{z^2-a^2y^2}\,dx+\frac{a^2y}{z}\,dy$$

or
$$zdz - a^2ydy = a\sqrt{z^2-a^2y^2}\,dx \text{ or } \frac{\frac{1}{2}d(z^2-a^2y^2)}{\sqrt{z^2-a^2y^2}} = a\,dx$$

Integrating, we get $\sqrt{z^2-a^2y^2} = ax + b$

or
$$z^2 = (ax + b)^2 + a^2y^2$$

TEST YOUR KNOWLEDGE

Solve the following equations by Charpit's method :

1. $pz + qy = pq$ [G.B.T.U. (AG) 2012]
2. $z^2 = pqxy$
3. $pxy + pq + qy = yz$
4. $z = p^2x + q^2y$
5. $2(z + xp + yp) = yp^2$
6. $q + xp = p^2$.

Answers

1. $az = \frac{1}{2}(y + ax)^2 + b$
2. $z = ax^b y^{1/b}$
3. $\log (z - ax) = y - a \log (a + y) + b$
4. $\sqrt{(1+a)z} = \sqrt{ax} + \sqrt{y} + b$
5. $z = \frac{ax}{y^2} - \frac{a^2}{4y^3} + \frac{b}{y}$
6. $z = axe^{-y} - \frac{1}{2}a^2e^{-2y} + b$.

4.25. PARTIAL DIFFERENTIAL EQUATIONS OF THE SECOND ORDER

An equation is said to be a partial differential equation of the second order when it includes at least one of the partial derivatives *r*, *s*, *t* but none of the higher order.

4.26. LINEAR PARTIAL DIFFERENTIAL EQUATION WITH CONSTANT COEFFICIENTS

A partial differential equation in which the dependent variable and its derivatives appear only in the first degree and are not multiplied together is called a linear partial differential equation.

General form of such an equation is

$$A_0 \frac{\partial^n z}{\partial x^n} + A_1 \frac{\partial^n z}{\partial x^{n-1} \partial y} + \ldots\ldots + A_n \frac{\partial^n z}{\partial y^n} + B_0 \frac{\partial^{n-1} z}{\partial x^{n-1}}$$

$$+ B_1 \frac{\partial^{n-1} z}{\partial x^{n-2} \partial y} + \ldots\ldots + B_{n-1} \frac{\partial^{n-1} z}{\partial y^{n-1}} + C_0 \frac{\partial z}{\partial x} + C_1 \frac{\partial z}{\partial y} + P_0 z = F(x, y) \quad \ldots(1)$$

where the coefficients $A_0, A_1, \ldots\ldots, A_n$; $B_0, B_1, \ldots\ldots, B_{n-1}$; C_0, C_1, P_0 are constants or functions of x and y.

If these coefficients are constants, then eqn. (1) is called as linear partial differential equation with constant coefficients.

If all the derivatives appearing in eqn. (1) are of the same order then the differential equation is called a linear homogeneous p.d.e. with constant coefficients while if all the derivatives are not of same order, then it is called a non-homogeneous linear p.d.e. with constant coefficients.

4.27. HOMOGENEOUS LINEAR PARTIAL DIFFERENTIAL EQUATIONS WITH CONSTANT COEFFICIENTS

An equation of the form $a_0 \frac{\partial^n z}{\partial x^n} + a_1 \frac{\partial^n z}{\partial x^{n-1} \partial y} + a_2 \frac{\partial^n z}{\partial x^{n-2} \partial y^2} + \ldots\ldots + a_n \frac{\partial^n z}{\partial y^n} = F(x, y)$

...(1)

where $a_0, a_1, a_2, \ldots\ldots, a_n$ are constants, is called a *homogeneous linear partial differential equation of the nth order with constant coefficients.*

Here, all the partial derivatives are of the nth order

Writing D for $\frac{\partial}{\partial x}$ and D′ for $\frac{\partial}{\partial y}$, eqn. (1) can be written as

$$(a_0 D^n + a_1 D^{n-1} D' + a_2 D^{n-2} D'^2 + \ldots + a_n D'^n) z = F(x, y)$$

or

$$\boxed{\phi(D, D')z = F(x, y)} \quad \ldots(2)$$

As in the case of ordinary linear differential equations with constant coefficients, the complete solution of (2) consists of two parts :

(*i*) the **complementary function** (C.F.) which is the complete solution of the equation $\phi(D, D')z = 0$. It must contain n arbitrary functions, where n is the order of the differential equation.

(*ii*) the **particular integral** (P.I.) which is a particular solution (free from arbitrary constants) of $\phi(D, D')\, z = F(x, y)$

The complete solution of (2) is $\boxed{z = \text{C.F.} + \text{P.I.}}$

4.28. RULES FOR FINDING C.F.

We explain the procedure for finding the complementary function of a differential equation of the second order. It can be easily extended to differential equations of higher order.

Consider the equation $\frac{\partial^2 z}{\partial x^2} + a_1 \frac{\partial^2 z}{\partial x \partial y} + a_2 \frac{\partial^2 z}{\partial y^2} = 0$

which in symbolic form is $(D^2 + a_1 DD' + a_2 D'^2) z = 0$ ...(1)

Its symbolic operator equated to zero, *i.e.*, $D^2 + a_1 DD' + a_2 D'^2 = 0$ ...(2)
is called the **auxiliary equation** (A.E.)

Considered as a quadratic in D/D′, let its roots be m_1, m_2.

Case I. When the A.E. has distinct roots *i.e.*, $m_1 \neq m_2$, then (2) can be written as

$$(D - m_1 D')(D - m_2 D')z = 0 \qquad ...(3)$$

Now the solution of $(D - m_2 D')z = 0$ will also be a solution of (3).

But $\qquad (D - m_2 D')z = 0 \Rightarrow p - m_2 q = 0$

which is of Lagrange's form and the auxiliary equations are $\dfrac{dx}{1} = \dfrac{dy}{-m_2} = \dfrac{dz}{0}$

The first two members give $dy + m_2 dx = 0$ or $y + m_2 x = a$

Also $\qquad dz = 0$ or $z = b$

$\therefore \quad z = f_2(y + m_2 x)$ is a solution of $(D - m_2 D')z = 0$

Similarly, (3) will also be satisfied by the solution of

$$(D - m_1 D')z = 0 \quad i.e., \quad \text{by } z = f_1(y + m_1 x).$$

Hence the complete solution of (2) is

$$\boxed{z = f_1(y + m_1 x) + f_2(y + m_2 x)}$$

Case II. When the A.E. has equal roots, each = m, then (2) can be written as

$$(D - mD')(D - mD')z = 0 \qquad ...(4)$$

Let $(D - mD')z = u$, then (4) becomes $(D - mD')u = 0$

Its solution is $u = f(y + mx)$, as proved in Case I.

$\therefore \qquad (D - mD')z = u$ takes the form $(D - mD')z = f(y + mx)$

or $\qquad p - mq = f(y + mx)$ [Lagrange's form]

The Auxiliary equations are $\dfrac{dx}{1} = \dfrac{dy}{-m} = \dfrac{dz}{f(y+mx)}$

Now $\qquad \dfrac{dx}{1} = \dfrac{dy}{-m}$ gives $dy + m\,dx = 0$ or $y + mx = a$

Also $\qquad \dfrac{dx}{1} = \dfrac{dz}{f(a)}$ gives $dz = f(a)\,dx$ or $z = f(a)\,x + b$ *i.e.*, $z - xf(y + mx) = b$

$\therefore$ The complete solution of eqn. (2) is

$$z - x f(y + mx) = \phi(y + mx)$$

or

$$\boxed{z = \phi(y + mx) + xf(y + mx)}$$

Note 1. Auxiliary eqn. of $\phi(D, D')z = F(x, y)$
is obtained by putting $D = m$ and $D' = 1$ in $\phi(D, D') = 0$.

Hence the A.E. is $\phi(m, 1) = 0$.

Note 2. Generalising the results of Case I and Case II, we have

(*i*) if the roots of A.E. are $m_1, m_2, m_3, \ldots\ldots$ (all distinct roots), then

$$\text{C.F.} = f_1(y + m_1 x) + f_2(y + m_2 x) + f_3(y + m_3 x) + \ldots\ldots$$

(*ii*) if the roots of A.E. are $m_1, m_1, m_2, \ldots$ (two equal roots), then

$$\text{C.F.} = f_1(y + m_1x) + xf_2(y + m_1x) + f_3(y + m_2x) + \ldots\ldots$$

(*iii*) if the roots of A.E. are $m_1, m_1, m_1, \ldots$ (three equal roots), then

$$\text{C.F.} = f_1(y + m_1x) + xf_2(y + m_1x) + x^2f_3(y + m_1x) + \ldots\ldots$$

Note 3. Corresponding to a non-repeated factor D′ on L.H.S., the part of C.F. is taken as $\phi(x)$ and for D'^2 on L.H.S., the part of C.F. is $y\,\phi(x) + \psi(x)$.

ILLUSTRATIVE EXAMPLES

Example 1. *Solve :*

(*i*) $\dfrac{\partial^2 z}{\partial x^2} - \dfrac{\partial^2 z}{\partial x \partial y} - 6\dfrac{\partial^2 z}{\partial y^2} = 0$ (*ii*) $(D + 2D')(D - 3D')^2 z = 0$ (*iii*) $4r - 12s + 9t = 0$.

Sol. (*i*) The given equation is

$$(D^2 - DD' - 6D'^2)z = 0, \quad \text{where } D \equiv \frac{\partial}{\partial x} \text{ and } D' \equiv \frac{\partial}{\partial y}$$

Auxiliary equation is

$$m^2 - m - 6 = 0$$

$$\Rightarrow \quad (m - 3)(m + 2) = 0 \Rightarrow m = 3, -2$$

$$\therefore \quad \text{C.F.} = f_1(y + 3x) + f_2(y - 2x)$$

$$\text{P.I.} = 0$$

Hence the complete solution is

$$z = \text{C.F.} + \text{P.I.} = f_1(y + 3x) + f_2(y - 2x)$$

where f_1 and f_2 are arbitrary functions.

(*ii*) Auxiliary equation is

$$(m + 2)(m - 3)^2 = 0 \Rightarrow m = -2, 3, 3$$

$$\therefore \quad \text{C.F.} = f_1(y - 2x) + f_2(y + 3x) + xf_3(y + 3x)$$

$$\text{P.I.} = 0$$

Hence the complete solution is

$$z = \text{C.F.} + \text{P.I.} = f_1(y - 2x) + f_2(y + 3x) + xf_3(y + 3x)$$

where f_1, f_2 and f_3 are arbitrary functions.

(*iii*) The given equation is

$$4\frac{\partial^2 z}{\partial x^2} - 12\frac{\partial^2 z}{\partial x \partial y} + 9\frac{\partial^2 z}{\partial y^2} = 0$$

$$\Rightarrow \quad (4D^2 - 12DD' + 9D'^2)z = 0$$

Auxiliary equation is $4m^2 - 12m + 9 = 0$

$$\Rightarrow \quad (2m - 3)^2 = 0 \Rightarrow m = \frac{3}{2}, \frac{3}{2}$$

$$\therefore \quad \text{C.F.} = f_1\left(y + \frac{3}{2}x\right) + x f_2\left(y + \frac{3}{2}x\right)$$

$$\text{P.I.} = 0$$

Hence the complete solution is

$$z = \text{C.F.} + \text{P.I.} = f_1\left(y + \frac{3}{2}x\right) + x f_2\left(y + \frac{3}{2}x\right)$$

where f_1 and f_2 are arbitrary functions.

Example 2. *Solve :*

(*i*) $\dfrac{\partial^3 z}{\partial x^3} - 3\dfrac{\partial^3 z}{\partial x^2 \partial y} + 2\dfrac{\partial^3 z}{\partial x \partial y^2} = 0$ (*ii*) $r = a^2 t$

(*iii*) $(D^3D'^2 + D^2D'^3)\, z = 0$ (*iv*) $\dfrac{\partial^4 z}{\partial x^4} - \dfrac{\partial^4 z}{\partial y^4} = 0.$

Sol. (*i*) The given equation is

$$(D^3 - 3D^2D' + 2DD'^2)z = 0$$

The auxiliary equation is $m^3 - 3m^2 + 2m = 0$

$\Rightarrow$ $m(m-1)(m-2) = 0$

$\Rightarrow$ $m = 0, 1, 2$

$\therefore$ $\text{C.F.} = f_1(y) + f_2(y + x) + f_3(y + 2x)$

$\text{P.I.} = 0$

Hence the complete solution is $z = \text{C.F.} + \text{P.I.} = f_1(y) + f_2(y + x) + f_3(y + 2x)$.

where f_1, f_2 and f_3 are arbitrary functions.

(*ii*) The given equation is $(D^2 - a^2D'^2)z = 0$

The auxiliary equation is $m^2 - a^2 = 0 \Rightarrow m = \pm a$

$\therefore$ $\text{C.F.} = f_1(y + ax) + f_2(y - ax)$

$\text{P.I.} = 0$

Hence the complete solution is

$$z = \text{C.F.} + \text{P.I.} = f_1(y + ax) + f_2(y - ax).$$

where f_1 and f_2 are arbitrary functions.

(*iii*) The given equation is $D^2D'^2(D + D')z = 0$

$\therefore$ $\text{C.F.} = f_1(y) + xf_2(y) + f_3(x) + yf_4(x) + f_5(y - x)$

$\text{P.I.} = 0$

Hence the complete solution is

$$z = \text{C.F.} + \text{P.I.} = f_1(y) + xf_2(y) + f_3(x) + yf_4(x) + f_5(y - x).$$

where f_1, f_2, f_3, f_4 and f_5 are arbitrary functions.

(*iv*) The given equation is $(D^4 - D'^4)z = 0$

The auxiliary equation is $m^4 - 1 = 0$

$\Rightarrow$ $(m^2 - 1)(m^2 + 1) = 0$

$\Rightarrow$ $m = \pm 1, \pm i$

$\therefore$ $\text{C.F.} = f_1(y + x) + f_2(y - x) + f_3(y + ix) + f_4(y - ix)$

$\text{P.I.} = 0$

$\therefore$ The complete solution is

$$z = \text{C.F.} + \text{P.I.} = f_1(y + x) + f_2(y - x) + f_3(y + ix) + f_4(y - ix).$$

where f_1, f_2, f_3 and f_4 are arbitrary functions.

Example 3. *Solve :*

(*i*) $(D^3 - 6D^2D' + 11DD'^2 - 6D'^3)z = 0$ (*ii*) $(D^3 - 6D^2D' + 12DD'^2 - 8D'^3)z = 0$

(*iii*) $r - 4s + 4t = 0.$ [G.B.T.U. (AG) 2010]

Sol. (*i*) Auxiliary equation is

$$m^3 - 6m^2 + 11m - 6 = 0$$

$$\Rightarrow \quad (m - 1)(m - 2)(m - 3) = 0$$

$$\Rightarrow \quad m = 1, 2, 3$$

$$\therefore \quad \text{C.F.} = f_1(y + x) + f_2(y + 2x) + f_3(y + 3x)$$

$$\text{P.I.} = 0$$

Hence the complete solution is

$$z = \text{C.F.} + \text{P.I.} = f_1(y + x) + f_2(y + 2x) + f_3(y + 3x)$$

where f_1, f_2 and f_3 are arbitrary functions.

(*ii*) Auxiliary equation is

$$m^3 - 6m^2 + 12m - 8 = 0$$

$$\Rightarrow \quad (m - 2)^3 = 0 \Rightarrow m = 2, 2, 2$$

$$\therefore \quad \text{C.F.} = f_1(y + 2x) + x\, f_2(y + 2x) + x^2 f_3(y + 2x)$$

$$\text{P.I.} = 0$$

Hence the complete solution is

$$z = \text{C.F.} + \text{P.I.} = f_1(y + 2x) + x\, f_2(y + 2x) + x^2 f_3(y + 2x)$$

where f_1, f_2 and f_3 are arbitrary functions.

(*iii*) Auxiliary equation is

$$m^2 - 4m + 4 = 0 \Rightarrow m = 2, 2$$

$$\therefore \quad \text{C.F.} = f_1(y + 2x) + x\, f_2(y + 2x)$$

$$\text{P.I.} = 0$$

Hence the complete solution is

$$z = \text{C.F.} + \text{P.I.} = f_1(y + 2x) + x\, f_2(y + 2x)$$

where f_1 and f_2 are arbitrary functions.

Example 4. *Solve the linear partial differential equation* $\dfrac{\partial^4 z}{\partial x^4} + \dfrac{\partial^4 z}{\partial y^4} = 0.$

Sol. The given equation is $(D^4 + D'^4)z = 0$

Auxiliary equation is $m^4 + 1 = 0$

$$\Rightarrow \quad m^4 + 1 + 2m^2 = 2m^2$$

$$\Rightarrow \quad (m^2 + 1)^2 \quad (m\sqrt{2})^2 = 0$$

$$\Rightarrow \quad (m^2 + \sqrt{2}\,m + 1)\,(m^2 - \sqrt{2}\,m + 1) = 0$$

so that $m^2 + \sqrt{2}\,m + 1 = 0$ or $m^2 - \sqrt{2}\,m + 1 = 0$

$\Rightarrow \qquad m = \dfrac{-1 \pm i}{\sqrt{2}}, \dfrac{1 \pm i}{\sqrt{2}}$

Let $\qquad z_1 = \dfrac{-1+i}{\sqrt{2}}$ and $z_2 = \dfrac{1+i}{\sqrt{2}}$

then, $\qquad m = z_1, \overline{z_1}, z_2, \overline{z_2}$

Here $\overline{z_1}$ and $\overline{z_2}$ denote complex conjugate of z_1 and z_2 respectively.

$\therefore \qquad \text{C.F.} = f_1(y + z_1 x) + f_2(y + \overline{z_1}\, x) + f_3(y + z_2 x) + f_4(y + \overline{z_2}\, x)$

$\text{P.I.} = 0$

Hence the complete solution is

$$z = \text{C.F.} + \text{P.I.} = f_1(y + z_1 x) + f_2(y + \overline{z_1}\, x) + f_3(y + z_2 x) + f_4(y + \overline{z_2}\, x)$$

where f_1, f_2, f_3 and f_4 are arbitrary functions.

TEST YOUR KNOWLEDGE

Solve the following partial differential equations :

1. $2\dfrac{\partial^2 z}{\partial x^2} + 5\dfrac{\partial^2 z}{\partial x\,\partial y} + 2\dfrac{\partial^2 z}{\partial y^2} = 0$

2. $\dfrac{\partial^3 z}{\partial x^3} - 4\dfrac{\partial^3 z}{\partial x^2\,\partial y} + 4\dfrac{\partial^3 z}{\partial x \partial y^2} = 0$

3. $\dfrac{\partial^2 z}{\partial x^2} + \dfrac{\partial^2 z}{\partial x\,\partial y} = 0$

4. $\dfrac{\partial^3 z}{\partial x^3} - 4\dfrac{\partial^3 z}{\partial x^2\,\partial y} + 3\dfrac{\partial^3 z}{\partial x \partial y^2} = 0$

5. $\dfrac{\partial^4 z}{\partial x^4} + \dfrac{\partial^4 z}{\partial y^4} = 2\dfrac{\partial^4 z}{\partial x^2\,\partial y^2}$

6. $\dfrac{\partial^3 z}{\partial x^3} + 3\dfrac{\partial^3 z}{\partial x^2\,\partial y} + 2\dfrac{\partial^3 z}{\partial x \partial y^2} = 0$

7. $\dfrac{\partial^2 z}{\partial x^2} + a^2\dfrac{\partial^2 z}{\partial y^2} = 0$

8. $\dfrac{\partial^2 z}{\partial x^2} - 3a\dfrac{\partial^2 z}{\partial x \partial y} + 2a^2\dfrac{\partial^2 z}{\partial y^2} = 0$

9. $25r - 40s + 16t = 0$

10. $r + 2s + t = 0.$

Answers

1. $z = f_1(y - 2x) + f_2\left(y - \dfrac{x}{2}\right)$

2. $z = f_1(y) + f_2(y + 2x) + xf_3(y + 2x)$

3. $z = f_1(y) + f_2(y - x)$

4. $z = f_1(y) + f_2(y + x) + f_3(y + 3x)$

5. $z = f_1(y - x) + x\,f_2(y - x) + f_3(y + x) + xf_4(y + x)$

6. $z = f_1(y) + f_2(y - x) + f_3(y - 2x)$

7. $z = f_1(y + aix) + f_2(y - aix)$

8. $z = f_1(y + ax) + f_2(y + 2ax)$

9. $z = f_1\left(y + \dfrac{4}{5}x\right) + x\,f_2\left(y + \dfrac{4}{5}x\right)$

10. $z = f_1(y - x) + x\,f_2(y - x).$

4.29. RULES FOR FINDING P.I.

P.I. of the equation $F(D, D')z = \phi(x, y)$ is given by $\dfrac{1}{F(D, D')}\,\phi(x, y)$.

Short methods :

4.30. WHEN $\phi(x, y)$ IS A FUNCTION OF $ax + by$

To find out P.I. of the equation

$$F(D, D')z = \phi(ax + by) \; ; \; F(a, b) \neq 0$$

where F(D, D′) is a homogeneous function of D and D′ of degree n.

Steps involved

Step 1. Replace D by a, D′ by b in F(D, D′) to get $F(a, b)$.

Step 2. Put $ax + by = u$ and integrate $\phi(u)$, n times w.r.t. u.

Then,
$$\text{P.I.} = \frac{1}{F(a, b)} \underbrace{\iiint \ldots\ldots \int}_{(n \text{ times})} \phi(u)\, \underbrace{du\, du\, du \ldots\ldots du}_{(n \text{ times})}.$$

Step 3. Replace u by $ax + by$ at last.

Remark. It should be noted that here $F(a, b) \neq 0$. If $F(a, b) = 0$, then method fails.

Cases of failure

(*i*) To find out P.I. of the equation

$$F(D, D')z = \phi(ax + by) \; ; \; F(a, b) = 0$$

where F(D, D′) is a homogeneous function of D and D′ of degree n.

Steps involved

Step 1. Differentiate F(D, D′) partially w.r.t. D and simultaneously multiply the expression by x.

Step 2. Check whether $F'(a, b) \neq 0$?

Then,
$$\text{P.I.} = \frac{1}{F(D, D')} \phi(ax + by) \; ; \; F(a, b) = 0$$

$$= x \cdot \frac{1}{\frac{\partial}{\partial D}\{F(D, D')\}} \phi(ax + by)$$

This method fails if $F'(a, b) = 0$.

(*ii*) To find out P.I. of the equation

$$F(D, D')z = \phi(ax + by) \; ; \; F'(a, b) = 0$$

where F(D, D′) is a homogeneous function of D and D′ of degree n.

Steps Involved :

Step 1. Repeat the procedure as again differentiate F′(D, D′) partially w.r.t. D and simultaneously multiply the expression by x.

Step 2. Check whether $F''(a, b) \neq 0$?

Then
$$\text{P.I.} = x \cdot \frac{1}{F'(D, D')} \phi(ax + by)$$

$$= x^2 \cdot \frac{1}{\frac{\partial}{\partial D}\{F'(D, D')\}} \phi(ax + by)$$

This method also fails if $F''(a, b) = 0$.

We proceed this method as long as the derivative of F(D, D′) vanishes when D is replaced by a and D′ by b.

If $F^r(a, b) \neq 0$, then $\dfrac{1}{F^r(D, D')}$ can be evaluated for particular integral.

4.30.1. As a Particular Case when in F(D, D′), Power of D′ in Highest Degree Terms is Greater than that of D and Case of Failure Occurs :

Step 1. Differentiate F(D, D′) partially w.r.t. D′ and simultaneously multiply the expression by y.

Step 2. Check whether $F'(a, b) \neq 0$?

Then,
$$\text{P.I.} = \frac{1}{F(D, D')} \cdot \phi(ax + by) \; ; \; F(a, b) \neq 0$$
$$= y \cdot \frac{1}{\dfrac{\partial}{\partial D'}\{F(D, D')\}} \phi(ax + by).$$

Step 3. This method fails if $F'(a, b) = 0$.

In such case, we follow the same procedure as given below:
$$\text{P.I.} = y \cdot \frac{1}{F'(D, D')} \phi(ax + by) \; ; \; F'(a, b) = 0$$
$$= y^2 \cdot \frac{1}{\dfrac{\partial}{\partial D'}\{F'(D, D')\}} \phi(ax + by).$$

Step 4. This method also fails if $F''(a, b) = 0$. We repeat the method as long as derivative of F(D, D′) vanishes when D is replaced by a and D′ by b.

ILLUSTRATIVE EXAMPLES

Example 1. *Solve the linar partial differential equation*
$$\frac{\partial^3 u}{\partial x^3} - 3\frac{\partial^3 u}{\partial x^2 \partial y} + 4\frac{\partial^3 u}{\partial y^3} = e^{x + 2y}$$
[G.B.T.U. (AG) 2011; U.P.T.U. 2007]

Sol. The given equation is
$$(D^3 - 3D^2D' + 4D'^3)\, u = e^{x + 2y} \text{ where } D \equiv \frac{\partial}{\partial x} \text{ and } D' \equiv \frac{\partial}{\partial y}$$

Auxiliary equation is
$$m^3 - 3m^2 + 4 = 0$$
$$m^2 (m + 1) - 4m (m + 1) + 4 (m + 1) = 0$$
$$(m - 2)^2 (m + 1) = 0$$
$$\Rightarrow \quad m = 2, 2, -1$$
$$\therefore \quad \text{C.F.} = f_1 (y - x) + f_2 (y + 2x) + x f_3 (y + 2x)$$

$$\text{P.I.} = \frac{1}{D^3 - 3D^2D' + 4D'^3} e^{x+2y}$$

$$= \frac{1}{(1)^3 - 3(1)^2(2) + 4(2)^3} \iiint e^u \, du\, du\, du \qquad \text{where } x + 2y = u$$

$$= \frac{1}{27} e^{x+2y}$$

Hence the complete solution is

$$u = \text{C.F.} + \text{P.I.} = f_1(y - x) + f_2(y + 2x) + x f_3(y + 2x) + \frac{1}{27} e^{x+2y}$$

where f_1, f_2 and f_3 are arbitrary functions.

Example 2. *Solve the linear partial differential equation*

$$\frac{\partial^2 z}{\partial x^2} + 3\frac{\partial^2 z}{\partial x \partial y} + 2\frac{\partial^2 z}{\partial y^2} = x + y. \qquad \text{[U.P.T.U. (C.O.) 2008]}$$

Sol. The given equation is

$$(D^2 + 3DD' + 2D'^2)\, z = x + y.$$

The auxiliary equation is $m^2 + 3m + 2 = 0$

$\Rightarrow$ $(m + 1)(m + 2) = 0$

$\Rightarrow$ $m = -1, -2$

$\therefore$ $\text{C.F.} = f_1(y - x) + f_2(y - 2x)$

$$\text{P.I.} = \frac{1}{D^2 + 3DD' + 2D'^2}(x + y)$$

$$= \frac{1}{(1)^2 + 3(1)(1) + 2(1)^2} \iint u \, du\, du \qquad \text{where } x + y = u$$

$$= \frac{1}{6} \cdot \frac{u^3}{6} = \frac{u^3}{36} = \frac{(x + y)^3}{36}$$

Hence the complete solution is

$$z = \text{C.F.} + \text{P.I.} = f_1(y - x) + f_2(y - 2x) + \frac{(x + y)^3}{36}$$

where f_1 and f_2 are arbitrary functions.

Example 3. *Solve the linear partial differential equation*

$$\frac{\partial^2 z}{\partial x^2} - 2\frac{\partial^2 z}{\partial x \partial y} + \frac{\partial^2 z}{\partial y^2} = \sin(2x + 3y). \qquad \text{(U.P.T.U. 2006)}$$

Sol. The given equation is

$$(D^2 - 2DD' + D'^2)\, z = \sin(2x + 3y)$$

The auxiliary equation is

$$m^2 - 2m + 1 = 0$$

$\Rightarrow$ $(m - 1)^2 = 0 \Rightarrow m = 1, 1.$

$\therefore$ $$\text{C.F.} = f_1(y + x) + xf_2(y + x)$$

$$\text{P.I.} = \frac{1}{D^2 - 2DD' + D'^2} \sin(2x + 3y) = \frac{1}{(D - D')^2} \sin(2x + 3y)$$

$$= \frac{1}{(2-3)^2} \iint \sin u \, du \, du \qquad \text{where } 2x + 3y = u$$

$$= -\sin u = -\sin(2x + 3y).$$

Hence the complete solution is

$$z = \text{C.F.} + \text{P.I.} = f_1(y + x) + xf_2(y + x) - \sin(2x + 3y)$$

where f_1 and f_2 are arbitrary functions.

Example 4. *Solve :* $(2D^2 - 5DD' + 2D'^2)z = 24(y - x)$.

Sol. The auxiliary equation is

$$2m^2 - 5m + 2 = 0$$

$\Rightarrow$ $$(2m - 1)(m - 2) = 0 \quad \Rightarrow \quad m = \tfrac{1}{2}, 2$$

Hence, $$\text{C.F.} = f_1\left(y + \frac{1}{2}x\right) + f_2(y + 2x) = \phi_1(2y + x) + f_2(y + 2x)$$

$$\text{P.I.} = \frac{1}{2D^2 - 5DD' + 2D'^2} 24(y - x) \qquad | \text{ Here } a = -1, b = 1$$

$$= \frac{24}{2(-1)^2 - 5(-1)(1) + 2(1)^2} \iint u \, du \, du \qquad \text{where } y - x = u$$

$$= \frac{4}{9} u^3 = \frac{4}{9}(y - x)^3$$

$\therefore$ Complete solution is

$$z = \text{C.F.} + \text{P.I.} = \phi_1(2y + x) + f_2(y + 2x) + \frac{4}{9}(y - x)^3.$$

where ϕ_1 and f_2 are arbitrary functions.

Example 5. *Solve :* $r + s - 2t = \sqrt{2x + y}$.

Sol. The given equation is

$$\frac{\partial^2 z}{\partial x^2} + \frac{\partial^2 z}{\partial x \partial y} - 2\frac{\partial^2 z}{\partial y^2} = (2x + y)^{1/2}$$

or $$(D^2 + DD' - 2D'^2) z = (2x + y)^{1/2}$$

Auxiliary equation is

$$m^2 + m - 2 = 0$$

$\Rightarrow$ $$(m - 1)(m + 2) = 0 \quad \Rightarrow \quad m = 1, -2$$

$\therefore$ $$\text{C.F.} = f_1(y + x) + f_2(y - 2x)$$

$$\text{P.I.} = \frac{1}{D^2 + DD' - 2D'^2} (2x + y)^{1/2} \qquad | \text{ Here } a = 2, b = 1$$

$$= \frac{1}{(2)^2 + (2)(1) - 2(1)^2} \iint \sqrt{u}\ du\ du \qquad \text{where } u = 2x + y$$

$$= \frac{1}{4} \cdot \frac{4}{15} u^{5/2} = \frac{1}{15}(2x + y)^{5/2}$$

Hence the required complete solution is

$$z = \text{C.F.} + \text{P.I.} = f_1(y + x) + f_2(y - 2x) + \frac{1}{15}(2x + y)^{5/2}.$$

where f_1 and f_2 are arbitrary functions.

Example 6. *Solve the linear partial differential equation*

$$\frac{\partial^2 z}{\partial x^2} + \frac{\partial^2 z}{\partial y^2} = \cos mx \cos ny + 30\,(2x + y).$$

[G.B.T.U. (AG) 2011, 2012 ; U.P.T.U. (SUM) 2008]

Sol. The given equation is

$$(D^2 + D'^2)z = \cos mx \cos ny + 30\,(2x + y).$$

Auxiliary equation is

$$m^2 + 1 = 0 \Rightarrow m = \pm i$$

$$\therefore \qquad \text{C.F.} = f_1(y + ix) + f_2(y - ix)$$

$$\text{P.I.} = \frac{1}{D^2 + D'^2}(\cos mx \cos ny) + \frac{1}{D^2 + D'^2} 30\,(2x + y) = P_1 + P_2$$

where $$P_1 = \frac{1}{D^2 + D'^2} \cos mx \cos ny$$

$$= \frac{1}{2} \frac{1}{D^2 + D'^2}[\cos(mx + ny) + \cos(mx - ny)]$$

$$= \frac{1}{2}\left[\frac{1}{D^2 + D'^2}\cos(mx + ny) + \frac{1}{D^2 + D'^2}\cos(mx - ny)\right]$$

$$= \frac{1}{2}\left[\frac{1}{m^2 + n^2}\iint \cos u\ du\ du + \frac{1}{m^2 + n^2}\iint \cos v\ dv\ dv\right]$$

$$= \frac{1}{2}\left[\frac{-1}{m^2 + n^2}\cos u - \frac{1}{m^2 + n^2}\cos v\right] \text{ where } \quad mx + ny = u \text{ and } mx - ny = v$$

$$= \frac{-1}{2(m^2 + n^2)}[\cos(mx + ny) + \cos(mx - ny)]$$

and $$P_2 = \frac{1}{D^2 + D'^2} 30\,(2x + y) = \frac{30}{(2)^2 + (1)^2}\iint \omega\ d\omega\ d\omega, \qquad \text{where } 2x + y = \omega$$

$$= 6\,\frac{\omega^3}{6} = \omega^3 = (2x + y)^3.$$

$$\therefore \quad \text{P.I.} = -\frac{1}{2(m^2 + n^2)}[\cos(mx + ny) + \cos(mx - ny)] + (2x + y)^3$$

$$= -\frac{1}{m^2 + n^2}\cos mx \cos ny + (2x + y)^3.$$

Hence the complete solution is

$$z = \text{C.F.} + \text{P.I.}$$

$$\Rightarrow \quad z = f_1(y + ix) + f_2(y - ix) - \frac{1}{m^2 + n^2} \cos mx \cos ny + (2x + y)^3$$

where f_1 and f_2 are arbitrary functions.

Example 7. *Solve :*

$$\frac{\partial^2 z}{\partial x^2} - 3\frac{\partial^2 z}{\partial x \partial y} + 2\frac{\partial^2 z}{\partial y^2} = e^{2x + 3y} + \sin(x - 2y).$$

Sol. The given equation is

$$(D^2 - 3DD' + 2D'^2)z = e^{2x + 3y} + \sin(x - 2y)$$

Auxiliary equation is

$$m^2 - 3m + 2 = 0$$

$$\Rightarrow \quad (m - 1)(m - 2) = 0 \quad \Rightarrow \quad m = 1, 2$$

$$\therefore \quad \text{C.F.} = f_1(y + x) + f_2(y + 2x)$$

$$\text{P.I.} = \frac{1}{(D^2 - 3DD' + 2D'^2)} e^{2x + 3y} + \frac{1}{(D^2 - 3DD' + 2D'^2)} \sin(x - 2y)$$

$$= P_1 + P_2$$

where

$$P_1 = \frac{1}{D^2 - 3DD' + 2D'^2} e^{2x + 3y}$$

$$= \frac{1}{(2)^2 - 3(2)(3) + 2(3)^2} \iint e^u \, du \, du, \qquad \text{where } 2x + 3y = u$$

$$= \frac{1}{4} e^u = \frac{1}{4} e^{2x + 3y}$$

$$P_2 = \frac{1}{D^2 - 3DD' + 2D'^2} \sin(x - 2y) = \frac{1}{(1)^2 - 3(1)(-2) + 2(-2)^2} \iint \sin v \, dv \, dv$$

where $x - 2y = v$

$$= \frac{1}{15}(-\sin v) = -\frac{1}{15} \sin(x - 2y)$$

$$\therefore \quad \text{P.I.} = P_1 + P_2 = \frac{1}{4} e^{2x + 3y} - \frac{1}{15} \sin(x - 2y)$$

Hence the complete solution is

$$z = \text{C.F.} + \text{P.I.} = f_1(y + x) + f_2(y + 2x) + \frac{1}{4} e^{2x + 3y} - \frac{1}{15} \sin(x - 2y)$$

where f_1 and f_2 are arbitrary functions.

Example 8. *Solve :* $\dfrac{\partial^2 z}{\partial x^2} - 2\dfrac{\partial^2 z}{\partial x \partial y} + \dfrac{\partial^2 z}{\partial y^2} = \sin x.$ (U.P.T.U. 2009)

Sol. The given equation is

$$(D^2 - 2DD' + D'^2)z = \sin x$$

Auxiliary equation is

$$m^2 - 2m + 1 = 0 \quad \Rightarrow \quad m = 1, 1$$

$\therefore \quad \text{C.F.} = f_1(y + x) + x\, f_2(y + x)$

$$\text{P.I.} = \frac{1}{(D - D')^2} \sin (x + 0.y)$$

$$= \frac{1}{(1-0)^2} \iint \sin u\, du\, du, \text{ where } x = u$$

$$= - \sin u = - \sin x$$

Hence the complete solution is

$$z = \text{C.F.} + \text{P.I.} = f_1\ (y + x) + x\, f_2\ (y + x) - \sin x$$

where f_1 and f_2 are arbitrary functions.

Example 9. *Solve the linear partial differential equation*

$$\frac{\partial^3 z}{\partial x^3} - 4\frac{\partial^3 z}{\partial x^2\, \partial y} + 4\frac{\partial^3 z}{\partial x\, \partial y^2} = 4 \sin (2x + y).$$

Sol. The given equation is

$$(D^3 - 4D^2 D' + 4DD'^2)z = 4 \sin (2x + y)$$

The auxiliary equation is $\quad m^3 - 4m^2 + 4m = 0$

$\Rightarrow \quad m\,(m^2 - 4m + 4) = 0$

$\Rightarrow \quad m = 0, 2, 2.$

$\therefore \quad \text{C.F.} = f_1\ (y) + f_2\ (y + 2x) + x\, f_3\ (y + 2x)$

$$\text{P.I.} = \frac{1}{D^3 - 4D^2D' + 4DD'^2}\ 4 \sin (2x + y)$$

$$= \frac{4}{D}\left[\frac{1}{D^2 - 4DD' + 4D'^2} \sin (2x + y)\right] = \frac{4}{D}\left[\frac{1}{(D - 2D')^2} \sin (2x + y)\right]$$

$$= x \cdot \frac{4}{D}\left[\frac{1}{2(D - 2D')} \sin (2x + y)\right] = 4x^2 \cdot \frac{1}{D}\left[\frac{1}{2} \sin (2x + y)\right]$$

$$= 2x^2 \frac{1}{D} \sin (2x + y) = - 2x^2 \frac{\cos(2x + y)}{2} = - x^2 \cos (2x + y).$$

Hence the complete solution is

$$z = \text{C.F.} + \text{P.I.} = f_1\ (y) + f_2\ (y + 2x) + x\, f_3\ (y + 2x) - x^2 \cos (2x + y)$$

where f_1, f_2 and f_3 are arbitrary functions.

Example 10. *Solve the linear partial differential equation*

$$2\frac{\partial^2 z}{\partial x^2} - 5\frac{\partial^2 z}{\partial x\, \partial y} + 2\frac{\partial^2 z}{\partial y^2} = 5 \sin (2x + y).$$

Sol. The given equation is

$$(2D^2 - 5DD' + 2D'^2)\ z = 5 \sin (2x + y)$$

The auxiliary equation is

$$2m^2 - 5m + 2 = 0 \quad \Rightarrow \quad m = \frac{1}{2}, 2.$$

$\therefore \quad \text{C.F.} = f_1\left(y + \frac{1}{2}x\right) + f_2\ (y + 2x)$

$$\text{P.I.} = \frac{1}{2D^2 - 5DD' + 2D'^2} 5 \sin (2x + y)$$
$$= 5x \cdot \frac{1}{4D - 5D'} \sin (2x + y)$$
$$= 5x \cdot \frac{1}{4(2) - 5(1)} \int \sin u \, du, \quad \text{where } 2x + y = u$$
$$= 5x \cdot \frac{1}{3} (-\cos u) = -\frac{5x}{3} \cos (2x + y).$$

Hence the complete solution is

$$z = \text{C.F.} + \text{P.I.} = f_1 \left(y + \frac{1}{2} x \right) + f_2 (y + 2x) - \frac{5x}{3} \cos (2x + y)$$

where f_1 and f_2 are arbitrary functions.

Example 11. *Solve :* $(D^2 + 5DD' + 6D'^2) z = \dfrac{1}{y - 2x}$.

Sol. Auxiliary equation is $m^2 + 5m + 6 = 0$

$\Rightarrow$ $(m + 2)(m + 3) = 0$

$\Rightarrow$ $m = -2, -3$

$\therefore$ C.F. $= f_1 (y - 2x) + f_2 (y - 3x)$

$$\text{P.I.} = \frac{1}{D^2 + 5DD' + 6D'^2} \left(\frac{1}{y - 2x} \right)$$
$$= x \cdot \frac{1}{2D + 5D'} \left(\frac{1}{y - 2x} \right)$$
$$= x \cdot \frac{1}{2(-2) + 5(1)} \int \frac{1}{u} du, \quad \text{where } y - 2x = u$$
$$= x \log u = x \log (y - 2x)$$

Hence the complete solution is

$$z = \text{C.F.} + \text{P.I.} = f_1 (y - 2x) + f_2 (y - 3x) + x \log (y - 2x)$$

where f_1 and f_2 are arbitrary functions.

Example 12. *Solve the linear partial differential equations :*

(*i*) $\dfrac{\partial^2 z}{\partial x^2} - \dfrac{\partial^2 z}{\partial x \partial y} = \sin x \cos y$ [G.B.T.U. (SUM) 2010]

(*ii*) $\dfrac{\partial^2 z}{\partial x^2} - 2 \dfrac{\partial^2 z}{\partial x \partial y} = \sin x \cos 2y$ (U.P.T.U. 2008)

(*iii*) $(D^2 - DD')z = \cos 2y(\sin x + \cos x)$. (G.B.T.U. 2010)

Sol. (*i*) The given equation is

$$(D^2 - DD') z = \sin x \cos y$$

The auxiliary equation is $m^2 - m = 0 \Rightarrow m = 0, 1$.

$\therefore \quad \text{C.F.} = f_1(y) + f_2(y + x)$

$$\text{P.I.} = \frac{1}{D^2 - DD'} \sin x \cos y$$

$$= \frac{1}{2(D^2 - DD')} [\sin (x + y) + \sin (x - y)]$$

$$= \frac{1}{2}\left[\frac{1}{D^2 - DD'} \sin (x + y) + \frac{1}{D^2 - DD'} \sin (x - y)\right] = \frac{1}{2}[P_1 + P_2]$$

where $$P_1 = \frac{1}{D^2 - DD'} \sin (x + y)$$

$$= x \cdot \frac{1}{2D - D'} \sin (x + y) = x \cdot \frac{1}{2(1) - (1)} \int \sin u \, du, \qquad \text{where } x + y = u$$

$$= x \cdot (- \cos u) = - x \cos (x + y)$$

$$P_2 = \frac{1}{D^2 - DD'} \sin (x - y)$$

$$= \frac{1}{(1)^2 - (1)(-1)} \iint \sin \omega \, d\omega \, d\omega, \qquad \text{where } x - y = \omega$$

$$= \frac{1}{2} (- \sin \omega) = - \frac{1}{2} \sin (x - y).$$

$$\therefore \quad \text{P.I.} = \frac{1}{2}\left[- x \cos (x + y) - \frac{1}{2} \sin (x - y)\right].$$

Hence the complete solution is

$$z = \text{C.F.} + \text{P.I.} = f_1(y) + f_2(y + x) - \frac{x}{2} \cos (x + y) - \frac{1}{4} \sin (x - y)$$

where f_1 and f_2 are arbitrary functions.

(*ii*) The given equation is

$$(D^2 - 2DD') z = \sin x \cos 2y$$

Auxiliary equation is

$$m^2 - 2m = 0 \quad \Rightarrow \quad m = 0, 2$$

$\therefore \quad \text{C.F.} = f_1(y) + f_2(y + 2x)$

$$\text{P.I.} = \frac{1}{D^2 - 2DD'} \sin x \cos 2y$$

$$= \frac{1}{2(D^2 - 2DD')} [\sin (x + 2y) + \sin (x - 2y)]$$

$$= \frac{1}{2}\left[\frac{1}{D^2 - 2DD'} \sin (x + 2y) + \frac{1}{D^2 - 2DD'} \sin (x - 2y)\right]$$

$$= \frac{1}{2} (P_1 + P_2) \qquad \text{...(1)}$$

where, $$P_1 = \frac{1}{D^2 - 2DD'} \sin (x + 2y)$$

$$= \frac{1}{(1)^2 - 2(1)(2)} \iint \sin u \, du \, du \qquad \text{where } x + 2y = u$$

$$= -\frac{1}{3}(-\sin u) = \frac{1}{3}\sin(x + 2y)$$

$$P_2 = \frac{1}{D^2 - 2DD'} \sin(x - 2y)$$

$$= \frac{1}{(1)^2 - 2(1)(-2)} \iint \sin v \, dv \, dv \qquad \text{where } x - 2y = v$$

$$= -\frac{1}{5}\sin v = -\frac{1}{5}\sin(x - 2y)$$

$\therefore$ From (1),

$$\text{P.I.} = \frac{1}{6}\sin(x + 2y) - \frac{1}{10}\sin(x - 2y)$$

Hence the complete solution is

$$z = \text{C.F.} + \text{P.I.} = f_1(y) + f_2(y + x) + \frac{1}{6}\sin(x + 2y) - \frac{1}{10}\sin(x - 2y)$$

where f_1 and f_2 are arbitrary functions.

(*iii*) Auxiliary equation is

$$m^2 - m = 0 \quad \Rightarrow \quad m = 0, 1$$

$$\therefore \qquad \text{C.F.} = f_1(y) + f_2(y + x)$$

$$\text{P.I.} = \frac{1}{D^2 - DD'} \cos 2y (\sin x + \cos x)$$

$$= \frac{1}{2}\left[\frac{1}{D^2 - DD'}\{\sin(x + 2y) + \sin(x - 2y)\} + \frac{1}{D^2 - DD'}\{\cos(x + 2y) + \cos(x - 2y)\}\right]$$

$$= \frac{1}{2}\left[\frac{1}{D^2 - DD'}\{\sin(x + 2y) + \cos(x + 2y)\} + \frac{1}{D^2 - DD'}\{\sin(x - 2y) + \cos(x - 2y)\}\right]$$

$$= \frac{1}{2}\left[\frac{1}{(1)^2 - (1)(2)} \iint (\sin u + \cos u)\, du\, du + \frac{1}{(1)^2 - (1)(-2)} \iint (\sin v + \cos v)\, dv\, dv\right]$$

where $x + 2y = u$ and $x - 2y = v$

$$= \frac{1}{2}\left[\sin(x + 2y) + \cos(x + 2y) - \frac{1}{3}\sin(x - 2y) - \frac{1}{3}\cos(x - 2y)\right]$$

$$= \frac{1}{2}[\sin(x + 2y) + \cos(x + 2y)] - \frac{1}{6}[\sin(x - 2y) + \cos(x - 2y)]$$

Hence the complete solution is

$$z = \text{C.F.} + \text{P.I.} = f_1(y) + f_2(y + x) + \frac{1}{2}[\sin(x + 2y) + \cos(x + 2y)]$$

$$- \frac{1}{6}[\sin(x - 2y) + \cos(x - 2y)]$$

where f_1 and f_2 are arbitrary functions.

Example 13. *Solve :*

(*i*) $4r - 4s + t = 16 \log (x + 2y)$ (*ii*) $r + 2s + t = 2(y - x) + \sin (x - y)$

[M.T.U. (SUM) 2011]

(*iii*) $2r - s - 3t = 5 \dfrac{e^x}{e^y}$ (*iv*) $(D - D')^2 z = x + \phi(x + y)$.

Sol. (*i*) The given equation is

$$(4D^2 - 4DD' + D'^2)z = 16 \log (x + 2y)$$

Auxiliary equation is $4m^2 - 4m + 1 = 0 \Rightarrow m = \dfrac{1}{2}, \dfrac{1}{2}$

$$\therefore \quad \text{C.F.} = f_1\left(y + \frac{1}{2}x\right) + x f_2\left(y + \frac{1}{2}x\right)$$

$$\text{P.I.} = \frac{1}{(2D - D')^2} 16 \log (x + 2y)$$

$$= 16 . x . \frac{1}{2(2D - D').2} \log (x + 2y) = 4x . \frac{1}{2D - D'} \log (x + 2y)$$

$$= 4x^2 . \frac{1}{2} \log (x + 2y) = 2x^2 \log (x + 2y)$$

Hence the complete solution is

$$z = \text{C.F.} + \text{P.I.} = f_1\left(y + \frac{1}{2}x\right) + x f_2\left(y + \frac{1}{2}x\right) + 2x^2 \log (x + 2y)$$

where f_1 and f_2 are arbitrary functions.

(*ii*) The given equation is

$$(D^2 + 2DD' + D'^2) z = 2(y - x) + \sin (x - y)$$

Auxiliary equation is $m^2 + 2m + 1 = 0$

$\Rightarrow$ $m = -1, -1$

$$\therefore \quad \text{C.F.} = f_1 (y - x) + x f_2 (y - x)$$

$$\text{P.I.} = \frac{1}{(D + D')^2} 2(y - x) + \frac{1}{(D + D')^2} \sin (x - y) = P_1 + P_2$$

where

$$P_1 = \frac{1}{(D + D')^2} . 2(y - x) = 2 . x . \frac{1}{2(D + D')} (y - x)$$

$$= x . \frac{1}{D + D'} (y - x) = x^2 . (y - x)$$

$$P_2 = \frac{1}{(D + D')^2} \sin (x - y) = x . \frac{1}{2(D + D')} \sin (x - y) = x^2 . \frac{1}{2} \sin (x - y)$$

$$\therefore \quad \text{P.I.} = x^2 (y - x) + \frac{x^2}{2} \sin (x - y)$$

Hence the complete solution is

$$z = \text{C.F.} + \text{P.I.} = f_1(y-x) + x f_2(y-x) + x^2(y-x) + \frac{x^2}{2}\sin(x-y)$$

where f_1 and f_2 are arbitrary functions.

(*iii*) The given equation is

$$(2D^2 - DD' - 3D'^2)z = 5e^{x-y}$$

Auxiliary equation is $\quad 2m^2 - m - 3 = 0 \Rightarrow m = -1, 3/2$

$$\therefore \quad \text{C.F.} = f_1(y-x) + f_2\left(y + \frac{3}{2}x\right)$$

$$\text{P.I.} = \frac{1}{2D^2 - DD' - 3D'^2}(5e^{x-y}) = 5x \cdot \frac{1}{4D - D'} e^{x-y}$$

$$= 5x \cdot \frac{1}{4(1) - (-1)} \int e^u \, du = xe^{x-y} \qquad \text{where } x - y = u$$

Hence the complete solution is

$$z = \text{C.F.} + \text{P.I.} = f_1(y-x) + f_2\left(y + \frac{3}{2}x\right) + x\,e^{x-y}$$

where f_1 and f_2 are arbitrary functions.

(*iv*) The given equation is $\quad (D - D')^2 z = x + \phi(x+y)$

Auxiliary equation is $\quad (m-1)^2 = 0, \Rightarrow m = 1, 1$

$$\therefore \quad \text{C.F.} = f_1(y+x) + x f_2(y+x)$$

$$\text{P.I.} = \frac{1}{(D-D')^2}x + \frac{1}{(D-D')^2}\phi(x+y) = P_1 + P_2$$

where

$$P_1 = \frac{1}{(D-D')^2}(x + 0.y) = \frac{1}{(1-0)^2}\iint u \, du \, du, \qquad \text{where } x = u$$

$$= \frac{u^3}{6} = \frac{x^3}{6}$$

$$P_2 = \frac{1}{(D-D')^2}\phi(x+y) = x \cdot \frac{1}{2(D-D')}\phi(x+y) = \frac{x^2}{2}\phi(x+y)$$

$$\therefore \quad \text{P.I.} = P_1 + P_2 = \frac{x^3}{6} + \frac{x^2}{2}\phi(x+y)$$

Hence the complete solution is

$$z = \text{C.F.} + \text{P.I.} = f_1(y+x) + x f_2(y+x) + \frac{x^3}{6} + \frac{x^2}{2}\phi(x+y)$$

where f_1 and f_2 are arbitrary functions.

Example 14. *Solve the differential equation :*

$$\frac{\partial^3 z}{\partial x^2 \partial y} - 2\frac{\partial^3 z}{\partial x \partial y^2} + \frac{\partial^3 z}{\partial y^3} = \frac{1}{x^2}.$$

Sol. The given equation is

$$(D^2D' - 2DD'^2 + D'^3)\, z = \frac{1}{x^2}$$

$$\Rightarrow \qquad D'(D^2 - 2DD' + D'^2)z = \frac{1}{x^2}$$

Part of C.F. corresponding to $D'\left(\equiv \frac{\partial}{\partial y}\right)$ is $f_1(x)$

Auxiliary equation of the remaining factor is

$$m^2 - 2m + 1 = 0 \quad \Rightarrow \quad m = 1, 1$$

$\therefore$ Another part of C.F. $= f_2(y + x) + x f_3(y + x)$

$\therefore$ Complete C.F. $= f_1(x) + f_2(y + x) + x f_3(y + x)$

$$\text{P.I.} = \frac{1}{D'^3 + D^2D' - 2DD'^2}\left(\frac{1}{x^2}\right) \qquad | \; x^{-2} = (x + 0.y)^{-2}$$

$$= y \cdot \frac{1}{3D'^2 + D^2 - 4DD'}\left(\frac{1}{x^2}\right) \qquad | \text{ Using art. 4.30.1}$$

$$= y \cdot \frac{1}{3(0)^2 + (1)^2 - 4(1)(0)} \iint \frac{1}{u^2}\, du\, du, \qquad \text{where } x = u$$

$$= y \int \frac{-1}{u}\, du = y\,(-\log u) = -\,y \log x$$

Hence the complete solution is

$$z = \text{C.F.} + \text{P.I.} = f_1(x) + f_2(y + x) + x f_3(y + x) - y \log x$$

where f_1, f_2 and f_3 are arbitrary functions.

Example 15. *Solve :* $\frac{\partial^3 z}{\partial x^3} - 7\frac{\partial^3 z}{\partial x \partial y^2} - 6\frac{\partial^3 z}{\partial y^3} = \sin(x + 2y) + e^{3x+y}$.

Sol. The given equation is

$$(D^3 - 7DD'^2 - 6D'^3)z = \sin(x + 2y) + e^{3x+y}$$

Auxiliary equation is

$$m^3 - 7m - 6 = 0 \quad \Rightarrow \quad m = -1, -2, 3$$

$$\therefore \qquad \text{C.F.} = f_1(y - x) + f_2(y - 2x) + f_3(y + 3x)$$

$$\text{P.I.} = \frac{1}{D^3 - 7DD'^2 - 6D'^3}\sin(x + 2y) + \frac{1}{D^3 - 7DD'^2 - 6D'^3}e^{3x+y}.$$

P.I. corresponding to $\sin(x + 2y)$

$$= \frac{1}{(1)^3 - 7(1)(2)^2 - 6(2)^3}\iiint \sin u\, du\, du\, du, \quad \text{where } x + 2y = u$$

$$= -\frac{1}{75}\cos u = -\frac{1}{75}\cos(x + 2y)$$

P.I. corresponding to e^{3x+y}

$$= \frac{1}{D^3 - 7DD'^2 - 6D'^3}(e^{3x+y})$$

$$= x \cdot \frac{1}{\frac{\partial}{\partial D}(D^3 - 7DD'^2 - 6D'^3)} e^{3x+y} = x \cdot \frac{1}{3D^2 - 7D'^2} e^{3x+y}$$

$$= x \cdot \frac{1}{3(3)^2 - 7(1)^2} e^{3x+y} = x \cdot \frac{1}{20} e^{3x+y}$$

∴ Required P.I. $= -\frac{1}{75}\cos(2y + x) + \frac{x}{20} e^{3x+y}$

∴ Complete solution is

$$z = \text{C.F.} + \text{P.I.} = f_1(y - x) + f_2(y - 2x) + f_3(y + 3x) - \frac{1}{75}\cos(x + 2y) + \frac{x}{20} e^{3x+y}$$

where f_1, f_2 and f_3 are arbitrary functions.

TEST YOUR KNOWLEDGE

Solve the following partial differential equations :

1. (*i*) $\frac{\partial^2 z}{\partial x^2} - 7\frac{\partial^2 z}{\partial x\,\partial y} + 12\frac{\partial^2 z}{\partial y^2} = e^{x-y}$ (*ii*) $(D^2 + 2DD' + D'^2)\,z = e^{2x+3y}$ [*G.B.T.U. (A.G.) 2012*]

2. (*i*) $\frac{\partial^2 z}{\partial x^2} + \frac{\partial^2 z}{\partial x\,\partial y} - 6\frac{\partial^2 z}{\partial y^2} = \cos(3x + y)$ (*ii*) $(D^3 - 4D^2D' + 4DD'^2)z = 6\sin(3x + 2y)$ [*U.K.T.U. 2012*]

3. $(D^2 - 4DD' + 4D'^2)\,z = e^{2x+y}$ [*G.B.T.U. (C.O.) 2010*]

4. $\frac{\partial^2 V}{\partial x^2} + \frac{\partial^2 V}{\partial y^2} = 12(x + y)$

5. $(D^2 - 8DD' + 7D'^2)z = \sin(7x + y)$ [*U.P.T.U. (C.O.) 2009*]

6. $\frac{\partial^2 z}{\partial x^2} - \frac{\partial^2 z}{\partial x\partial y} = \cos x \cos 2y$

7. $(D^2 - 6DD' + 9D'^2)z = 6x + 2y$

8. $(D^2 - 2DD' + D'^2)z = e^{x+y}$

9. $4r + 12s + 9t = e^{3x-2y}$

10. $\frac{\partial^3 z}{\partial x^2\partial y} - 5\frac{\partial^3 z}{\partial x\partial y^2} + 6\frac{\partial^3 z}{\partial y^3} = e^x$

11. (*i*) $r + s - 6t = \cos(2x + y)$ (*ii*) $(D^2 - 5DD' + 4D'^2)z = \sin(4x + y)$ [*G.B.T.U. (AG) 2011*]

12. (*i*) $(D - D')^2\,z = \tan(y + x)$ (*ii*) $(D^2 - DD')z = \sin(x + 2y)$ [*G.B.T.U. (AG) 2012*]

13. $(D^2 + 3DD' - 4D'^2)z = x + \sin y$

14. $(D^3 - 4D^2D' + 5DD'^2 - 2D'^3)z = e^{y+2x} + (y + x)^{1/2}$

15. $(D^2 - 3DD' + 2D'^2)\,z = e^{2x-y} + e^{x+y} + \cos(x + 2y)$ (*G.B.T.U. 2012*)

Answers

1. (*i*) $z = f_1(y + 3x) + f_2(y + 4x) + \frac{1}{20} e^{x-y}$ (*ii*) $z = f_1(y - x) + x f_2(y - x) + \frac{1}{25} e^{2x + 3y}$

2. (*i*) $z = f_1(y - 3x) + f_2(y + 2x) - \frac{1}{6} \cos(3x + y)$ (*ii*) $z = f_1(y) + f_2(y + 2x) + x f_3(y + 2x) + 2\cos(3x + 2y)$

3. $z = f_1(y + 2x) + x f_2(y + 2x) + \frac{x^2}{2} e^{2x + y}$ 4. $V = f_1(y + ix) + f_2(y - ix) + (x + y)^3$.

5. $z = f_1(y + x) + f_2(y + 7x) - \frac{x}{6} \cos(7x + y)$ 6. $z = f_1(y) + f_2(y + x) + \frac{1}{2}\cos(x + 2y) - \frac{1}{6}\cos(x - 2y)$

7. $z = f_1(y + 3x) + x f_2(y + 3x) + x^2(3x + y)$ 8. $z = f_1(y + x) + x f_2(y + x) + \frac{1}{2} x^2 e^{x + y}$

9. $z = f_1(2y - 3x) + x f_2(2y - 3x) + \frac{1}{8} x^2 e^{3x-2y}$ 10. $z = f_1(x) + f_2(y + 2x) + f_3(y + 3x) + ye^x$

11. (*i*) $z = f_1(y - 3x) + f_2(y + 2x) + \frac{x}{5} \sin(2x + y)$ (*ii*) $z = f_1(y + x) + f_2(y + 4x) - \frac{x}{3} \cos(4x + y)$

12. (*i*) $z = f_1(y + x) + x f_2(y + x) + \frac{x^2}{2} \tan(y + x)$ (*ii*) $z = f_1(y) + f_2(y + x) + \sin(x + 2y)$

13. $z = f_1(y + x) + f_2(y - 4x) + \frac{x^3}{6} + \frac{1}{4} \sin y$

14. $z = f_1(y + x) + x f_2(y + x) + f_3(y + 2x) + x e^{y+x} - \frac{x^2}{3}(y + x)^{3/2}$

15. $z = f_1(y + x) + f_2(y + 2x) + \frac{1}{12} e^{2x-y} - x e^{x+y} - \frac{1}{3} \cos(x + 2y)$

4.31. WHEN $\phi(x, y)$ IS OF THE FORM $x^m y^n$ OR A RATIONAL INTEGRAL ALGEBRAIC FUNCTION OF x AND y

In this case, P.I. is obtained by expanding F(D, D′) in an infinite series of ascending powers of D or D′ or $\frac{D'}{D}$. It is to be noted that the difference in the two answers of P.I. is immaterial because it can be incorporated in the arbitrary functions occurring in C.F. of the given equation.

ILLUSTRATIVE EXAMPLES

Example 1. *Solve* : $\frac{\partial^3 z}{\partial x^3} - \frac{\partial^3 z}{\partial y^3} = x^3 y^3$.

Sol. The given equation is $(D^3 - D'^3)z = x^3 y^3$

Auxiliary equation is $m^3 - 1 = 0$

$\Rightarrow$ $m = 1, \omega, \omega^2$

where ω is one of the cube roots of unity.

$\therefore$ $\text{C.F.} = f_1(y + x) + f_2(y + \omega x) + f_3(y + \omega^2 x)$

$$\text{P.I.} = \frac{1}{D^3 - D'^3}(x^3y^3) = \frac{1}{D^3\left(1 - \frac{D'^3}{D^3}\right)}(x^3y^3)$$

$$= \frac{1}{D^3}\left(1 - \frac{D'^3}{D^3}\right)^{-1}(x^3y^3) = \frac{1}{D^3}\left(1 + \frac{D'^3}{D^3}\right)(x^3y^3)$$

$$= \frac{1}{D^3}\left[x^3y^3 + \frac{1}{D^3}D'^3(x^3y^3)\right] = \frac{1}{D^3}\left[x^3y^3 + \frac{1}{D^3}(6x^3)\right]$$

$$= \frac{1}{D^3}(x^3y^3) + \frac{1}{D^6}(6x^3) = \frac{x^6y^3}{6.5.4} + \frac{6x^9}{4.5.6.7.8.9} = \frac{x^6y^3}{120} + \frac{x^9}{10080}$$

Hence the complete solution is

$$z = \text{C.F.} + \text{P.I.} = f_1(y + x) + f_2(y + \omega x) + f_3(y + \omega^2 x) + \frac{x^6y^3}{120} + \frac{x^9}{10080}.$$

where f_1, f_2 and f_3 are arbitrary functions.

Example 2. *Find a real function V of x and y, reducing to zero when y = 0 and satisfying*

$$\frac{\partial^2 V}{\partial x^2} + \frac{\partial^2 V}{\partial y^2} = -4\pi(x^2 + y^2).$$

Sol. The given equation is $(D^2 + D'^2)\,V = -4\pi(x^2 + y^2)$

The auxiliary equation is $m^2 + 1 = 0$

$\Rightarrow$ $m = \pm i$

$\therefore$ C.F. $= f_1(y + ix) + f_2(y - ix)$, which is imaginary.

Now,
$$\text{P.I.} = \frac{1}{D^2 + D'^2}[-4\pi(x^2 + y^2)] = -\frac{4\pi}{D^2}\left(1 + \frac{D'^2}{D^2}\right)^{-1}(x^2 + y^2)$$

$$= -\frac{4\pi}{D^2}\left(1 - \frac{D'^2}{D^2}\right)(x^2 + y^2) = -\frac{4\pi}{D^2}\left[x^2 + y^2 - \frac{1}{D^2}(2)\right]$$

$$= -\frac{4\pi}{D^2}\{x^2 + y^2 - x^2\} = -\frac{4\pi}{D^2}(y^2)$$

$$= -\frac{4\pi}{D}(xy^2) = -4\pi\left(\frac{x^2}{2}y^2\right)$$

P.I. $= -2\pi x^2y^2$

Since V is a real function, hence $V = -2\pi x^2y^2$.

Example 3. *Solve : $(D^2 - 6DD' + 9D'^2)\,z = 12x^2 + 36xy$.*

Sol. Auxiliary equation is

$$m^2 - 6m + 9 = 0$$

$\Rightarrow$ $m = 3, 3$

$\therefore$ C.F. $= f_1(y + 3x) + x\,f_2(y + 3x)$

$$\text{P.I.} = \frac{1}{D^2 - 6DD' + 9D'^2}12x^2 + \frac{1}{D^2 - 6\,DD' + 9D'^2}(36\,xy) = P_1 + P_2$$

where
$$P_1 = \frac{1}{D^2 - 6DD' + 9D'^2}(12x^2)$$

$$= \frac{12}{(1)^2 - 6(1)(0) + 9(0)^2} \iint u^2 \, du \, du, \qquad \text{where } x = u$$

$$= 12 \, \frac{u^4}{12} = u^4 = x^4$$

$$P_2 = \frac{1}{D^2 - 6DD' + 9D'^2} (36xy)$$

$$= \frac{36}{(D - 3D')^2} (xy) = \frac{36}{D^2} \left(1 - \frac{3D'}{D}\right)^{-2} (xy)$$

$$= \frac{36}{D^2} \left(1 + \frac{6D'}{D}\right) (xy) \qquad \text{| Leaving higher power terms}$$

$$= \frac{36}{D^2} \left[xy + \frac{6}{D} (x) \right] = \frac{36}{D^2} (xy + 3x^2)$$

$$= 36 \left(\frac{x^3}{6} y + \frac{x^4}{4} \right) = 6x^3y + 9x^4$$

$\therefore \qquad$ P.I. $= P_1 + P_2 = 6x^3y + 10x^4$

Hence the complete solution is

$$z = \text{C.F.} + \text{P.I.} = f_1(y + 3x) + xf_2\,(y + 3x) + 6x^3y + 10x^4$$

where f_1 and f_2 are arbitrary functions.

TEST YOUR KNOWLEDGE

Solve :

1. $\dfrac{\partial^2 z}{\partial x^2} + 3\dfrac{\partial^2 z}{\partial x \, \partial y} + 2\dfrac{\partial^2 z}{\partial y^2} = 12\,xy$

2. $\dfrac{\partial^2 z}{\partial x^2} + 2\dfrac{\partial^2 z}{\partial x \, \partial y} + \dfrac{\partial^2 z}{\partial y^2} = x^2 + xy + y^2$

3. $\dfrac{\partial^3 z}{\partial x^3} - 2\dfrac{\partial^3 z}{\partial x^2 \, \partial y} = 2e^{2x} + 3x^2y$

4. $(D^2 - a^2 D'^2)z = x$

5. $[D^2 + (a + b)\, DD' + ab\, D'^2]z = xy$ [*G.B.T.U. (AG) 2011*]

6. $(D^2 - 2DD' + D'^2)z = e^{x + 2y} + x^3$.

Answers

1. $z = f_1\,(y - x) + f_2(y - 2x) + 2x^3y - \dfrac{3}{2}x^4$

2. $z = f_1\,(y - x) + x\,f_2\,(y - x) + \dfrac{1}{4}\,(x^4 - 2x^3y + 2x^2y^2)$

3. $z = f_1(y) + x\,f_2(y) + f_3\,(y + 2x) + \dfrac{1}{4}\,e^{2x} + \dfrac{1}{60}\,(3x^5y + x^6)$

4. $z = f_1\,(y + ax) + f_2\,(y - ax) + \dfrac{x^3}{6}$

5. $z = f_1\,(y - ax) + f_2\,(y - bx) + \dfrac{1}{6}\,x^3y - \left(\dfrac{a + b}{24}\right)x^4$

6. $z = f_1\,(y + x) + x\,f_2\,(y + x) + e^{x + 2y} + \dfrac{x^5}{20}$.

4.32. GENERAL METHOD TO FIND THE P.I.

$\phi(x, y)$ is not always of the form given above. The general method is applicable to all cases, where $\phi(x, y)$ is not of the form given above.

Now, F(D, D′) can be factorised, in general, into n linear factors.

$$\therefore \quad \text{P.I.} = \frac{1}{F(D, D')} \phi(x, y)$$

$$= \frac{1}{(D - m_1 D')(D - m_2 D')\dots(D - m_n D')} \phi(x, y)$$

$$= \frac{1}{D - m_1 D'} \cdot \frac{1}{D - m_2 D'} \cdots\cdots \frac{1}{D - m_n D'} \phi(x, y)$$

Let us evaluate $\dfrac{1}{D - mD'} \phi(x, y)$

Consider the equation,

$$(D - mD')z = \phi(x, y) \quad \text{or} \quad p - mq = \phi(x, y) \qquad \text{[Lagrange's form]}$$

The subsidiary equations are $\dfrac{dx}{1} = \dfrac{dy}{-m} = \dfrac{dz}{\phi(x, y)}$

From the first two members $dy + mdx = 0$ or $y + mx = c$

From the first and last members, we have

$$dz = \phi(x, y)dx = \phi(x, c - mx)dx$$

$$\therefore \quad z = \int \phi(x, c - mx)dx$$

or

$$\boxed{\frac{1}{D - mD'} \phi(x, y) = \int \phi(x, c - mx)\, dx}$$

where c is replaced by $y + mx$ after integration.

By repeated application of the above rule, the P.I. can be evaluated.

ILLUSTRATIVE EXAMPLES

Example 1. *Solve the linear partial differential equation*

$$\frac{\partial^2 z}{\partial x^2} + \frac{\partial^2 z}{\partial x \partial y} - 6 \frac{\partial^2 z}{\partial y^2} = y \cos x.$$

Sol. The given equation is

$$(D^2 + DD' - 6D'^2)z = y \cos x$$

The auxiliary equation is

$$m^2 + m - 6 = 0$$

$$\Rightarrow \quad (m - 2)(m + 3) = 0$$

$$\Rightarrow \quad m = 2, -3.$$

$$\therefore \quad \text{C.F.} = f_1(y + 2x) + f_2(y - 3x)$$

$$\text{P.I.} = \frac{1}{D^2 + DD' - 6D'^2}\, y \cos x = \frac{1}{(D - 2D')(D + 3D')}\, y \cos x$$

$$= \frac{1}{D - 2D'} \int (c + 3x) \cos x \, dx, \quad \text{where } y = c + 3x$$

$$= \frac{1}{D - 2D'} \{c \sin x + 3 \int x \cos x \, dx\}$$

$$= \frac{1}{D - 2D'} [c \sin x + 3 \{x \sin x - \int 1 \,.\, \sin x \, dx\}]$$

$$= \frac{1}{D - 2D'} [(c + 3x) \sin x + 3 \cos x]$$

$$= \frac{1}{D - 2D'} (y \sin x + 3 \cos x), \quad \text{where } c = y - 3x$$

$$= \int (b - 2x) \sin x \, dx + 3 \sin x, \quad \text{where } y = b - 2x$$

$$= -\, b \cos x - 2 \{x (-\cos x) - \int 1 \,.\, (-\cos x) \, dx\} + 3 \sin x$$

$$= -\, b \cos x + 2x \cos x - 2 \sin x + 3 \sin x$$

$$= -\, (b - 2x) \cos x + \sin x$$

$$= -\, y \cos x + \sin x, \quad \text{where } b = y + 2x$$

Hence the complete solution is

$$z = \text{C.F.} + \text{P.I.} = f_1 (y + 2x) + f_2 (y - 3x) - y \cos x + \sin x$$

where f_1 and f_2 are arbitrary functions.

Example 2. *Solve the linear partial differential equation*

$$\frac{\partial^2 z}{\partial x^2} + \frac{\partial^2 z}{\partial x \partial y} - 2 \frac{\partial^2 z}{\partial y^2} = (y - 1)\, e^x.$$

Sol. The given equation is

$$(D^2 + DD' - 2D'^2)\, z = (y - 1)\, e^x$$

The auxiliary equation is

$$m^2 + m - 2 = 0$$

$$\Rightarrow \quad (m - 1)(m + 2) = 0$$

$$\Rightarrow \quad m = 1, -2$$

$$\text{C.F.} = f_1 (y + x) + f_2 (y - 2x)$$

$$\text{P.I.} = \frac{1}{D^2 + DD' - 2D'^2} (y - 1)\, e^x$$

$$= \frac{1}{(D - D')(D + 2D')} (y - 1)\, e^x$$

$$= \frac{1}{D - D'} \int (c + 2x - 1)\, e^x \, dx, \quad \text{where } y = c + 2x$$

$$= \frac{1}{D - D'} [(c - 1)\, e^x + 2\, (x - 1)\, e^x]$$

$$= \frac{1}{D - D'} [(c + 2x)\, e^x - 3e^x]$$

$$= \frac{1}{D - D'} (ye^x - 3e^x), \qquad \text{where } c = y - 2x$$
$$= \int (b - x)\, e^x\, dx - 3e^x, \qquad \text{where } y = b - x$$
$$= be^x - (x - 1)\, e^x - 3e^x$$
$$= (b - x - 2)\, e^x = (y - 2)\, e^x, \qquad \text{where } b = y + x$$

Hence the complete solution is

$$z = \text{C.F.} + \text{P.I.} = f_1 (y + x) + f_2 (y - 2x) + (y - 2)\, e^x$$

where f_1 and f_2 are arbitrary functions.

Example 3. *Solve the partial differential equation :*

$$r - t = \tan^3 x \tan y - \tan x \tan^3 y.$$

Sol. The given equation is

$$\frac{\partial^2 z}{\partial x^2} - \frac{\partial^2 z}{\partial y^2} = \tan x \tan y\, (\sec^2 x - \sec^2 y).$$

Auxiliary equation is $\quad m^2 - 1 = 0 \quad \Rightarrow \quad m = \pm 1.$

$$\text{C.F.} = f_1 (y + x) + f_2 (y - x)$$

$$\text{P.I.} = \frac{1}{D^2 - D'^2} \tan x \tan y\, (\sec^2 x - \sec^2 y)$$

$$= \frac{1}{D + D'} \left[\frac{1}{D - D'} (\tan x \sec^2 x \tan y - \tan x \tan y \sec^2 y) \right]$$

$$= \frac{1}{D + D'} \left[\int \tan x \sec^2 x \tan (c - x)\, dx - \int \tan x \tan (c - x) \sec^2 (c - x)\, dx \right]$$

where $y = c - x$

$$= \frac{1}{D + D'} \left[\tan (c - x) \frac{\tan^2 x}{2} + \int \sec^2 (c - x) \frac{\tan^2 x}{2} dx \right.$$
$$\left. + \tan x \,.\, \frac{\tan^2 (c - x)}{2} - \int \sec^2 x \frac{\tan^2 (c - x)}{2} dx \right]$$

$$= \frac{1}{2(D + D')} [\tan (c - x) \tan^2 x + \tan x \tan^2 (c - x]$$
$$+ \int \sec^2 (c - x) (\sec^2 x - 1)\, dx - \int \sec^2 x \{\sec^2 (c - x) - 1\}\, dx]$$

$$= \frac{1}{2(D + D')} [\tan (c - x) \tan^2 x + \tan x \tan^2 (c - x) + \int \{\sec^2 x - \sec^2 (c - x)\}\, dx]$$

$$= \frac{1}{2(D + D')} [\tan (c - x) \tan^2 x + \tan x \tan^2 (c - x) + \tan x + \tan (c - x)]$$

$$= \frac{1}{2(D + D')} [\tan x \sec^2 (c - x) + \tan (c - x) \sec^2 x]$$

$$= \frac{1}{2(D + D')} (\tan x \sec^2 y + \tan y \sec^2 x) \quad \text{where } c = y + x$$

$$= \frac{1}{2}\,[\textstyle\int \tan x \sec^2 (b+x)\, dx + \int \tan (b+x) \sec^2 x\, dx], \quad \text{where } y = b + x$$

$$= \frac{1}{2}\,[\tan x \,.\, \tan (b+x) - \textstyle\int \sec^2 x \,.\, \tan (b+x)\, dx + \int \tan (b+x) \sec^2 x\, dx]$$

$$= \frac{1}{2} \tan x \tan (b+x) = \frac{1}{2} \tan x \tan y \quad \text{where } b = y - x.$$

Hence the complete solution is

$$z = \text{C.F.} + \text{P.I.} = f_1 (y+x) + f_2 (y-x) + \frac{1}{2} \tan x \tan y$$

where f_1 and f_2 are arbitrary functions.

Example 4. *Solve :* $r - s - 2t = (2x^2 + xy - y^2) \sin xy - \cos xy.$

Sol. The given equation is

$$(D^2 - DD' - 2D'^2)z = (2x^2 + xy - y^2) \sin xy - \cos xy$$

Auxiliary equation is $\quad m^2 - m - 2 = 0$

$\Rightarrow \quad (m+1)(m-2) = 0 \;\Rightarrow\; m = -1, 2$

$\therefore \quad \text{C.F.} = f_1(y - x) + f_2(y + 2x)$

$$\text{P.I.} = \frac{1}{(D+D')(D-2D')}\,[(2x-y)(x+y) \sin xy - \cos xy]$$

$$= \frac{1}{(D+D')} \int [(4x-c)(c-x) \sin (cx - 2x^2) - \cos (cx - 2x^2)]\, dx, \text{ where } y = c - 2x$$

$$= \frac{1}{(D+D')} \int [(x-c)(c-4x) \sin (cx - 2x^2) - \cos (cx - 2x^2)]\, dx$$

$$= \frac{1}{(D+D')} \left[(x-c)\{-\cos (cx - 2x^2)\} + \int \cos (cx - 2x^2)\, dx - \int \cos (cx - 2x^2)\, dx\right]$$

$$= \frac{1}{(D+D')} (c - x) \cos \{x (c - 2x)\}$$

$$= \frac{1}{D+D'} (y+x) \cos xy, \qquad \text{where } c = y + 2x$$

$$= \int (b + 2x) \cos (bx + x^2)\, dx, \qquad \text{where } y = b + x$$

$$= \sin (bx + x^2) = \sin xy, \qquad \text{where } b = y - x$$

$\therefore$ Complete solution is

$$z = \text{C.F.} + \text{P.I.} = f_1(y - x) + f_2(y + 2x) + \sin xy$$

where f_1 and f_2 are arbitrary functions.

Example 5. *Solve :* $(D^2 + 2DD' + D'^2)z = 2 \cos y - x \sin y.$

Sol. Auxiliary equation is

$$m^2 + 2m + 1 = 0$$

$\Rightarrow \quad m = -1, -1$

$\therefore \quad \text{C.F.} = f_1 (y - x) + x f_2 (y - x)$

$$\text{P.I.} = \frac{1}{(D+D')^2} 2\cos y - \frac{1}{(D+D')^2}(x \sin y) = P_1 - P_2$$

where $$P_1 = \frac{1}{(D+D')^2} 2\cos y = \frac{2}{(0+1)^2} \iint \cos u \, du \, du, \text{ where } y = u$$

$$= 2(-\cos y) = -2\cos y$$

$$P_2 = \frac{1}{(D+D')^2} x \sin y = \frac{1}{D+D'} \int x \sin(c+x)\, dx, \text{ where } y = c + x$$

$$= \frac{1}{D+D'}\left[x\{-\cos(c+x)\} - \int 1.\{-\cos(c+x)\}\, dx\right]$$

$$= \frac{1}{D+D'}[-x\cos(c+x) + \sin(c+x)]$$

$$= \frac{1}{D+D'}(-x\cos y + \sin y), \quad \text{where } c = y - x$$

$$= \int -x\cos(b+x)\, dx + \int \sin(b+x)\, dx, \quad \text{where } y = b + x$$

$$= (-x).\sin(b+x) - \int (-1).\sin(b+x)\, dx + \int \sin(b+x)\, dx$$

$$= -x\sin(b+x) - 2\cos(b+x)$$

$$= -x\sin y - 2\cos y, \quad \text{where } b = y - x$$

$\therefore$ P.I. $= P_1 - P_2 = -2\cos y + x\sin y + 2\cos y = x \sin y$

Hence the complete solution is

$$z = \text{C.F.} + \text{P.I.} = f_1(y-x) + x f_2(y-x) + x\sin y$$

where f_1 and f_2 are arbitrary functions.

TEST YOUR KNOWLEDGE

Solve :

1. $(D^2 - DD' - 2D'^2)z = (y-1)e^x$
2. $(D - D')(D + 2D')z = (y+1)e^x$
3. $(D^3 + 2D^2D' - DD'^2 - 2D'^3)z = (y+2)e^x$
4. $r - 4t = \dfrac{4x}{y^2} - \dfrac{y}{x^2}$
5. $(D^3 + D^2D' - DD'^2 - D'^3)z = e^x \cos 2y$
6. $(D^2 + DD' - 6D'^2)z = y \sin x$ *[M.T.U. (SUM) 2011; M.T.U. 2012]*

Answers

1. $z = f_1(y-x) + f_2(y+2x) + ye^x$
2. $z = f_1(y+x) + f_2(y-2x) + ye^x$
3. $z = f_1(y+x) + f_2(y-x) + f_3(y-2x) + ye^x$
4. $z = f_1(y+2x) + f_2(y-2x) + x\log y + y\log x + 3x$
5. $z = f_1(y-x) + x f_2(y-x) + f_3(y+x) + \dfrac{e^x}{25}(\cos 2y + 2\sin 2y)$
6. $z = f_1(y+2x) + f_2(y-3x) - y\sin x - \cos x.$

4.33. NON-HOMOGENEOUS LINEAR PARTIAL DIFFERENTIAL EQUATIONS WITH CONSTANT COEFFICIENTS

In the equation $\phi(D, D')z = F(x, y)$ ...(1)

if the polynomial $\phi(D, D')$ in D, D′ is not homogeneous, then (1) is called a non-homogeneous linear partial differential equation.

Its complete solution is $z = \text{C.F.} + \text{P.I.}$

4.34. METHODS FOR FINDING OUT C.F.

(*a*) We resolve $\phi(D, D')$ into linear factors of the form $\mathbf{D - mD' - a}$.

Now consider the equation $(D - mD' - a)z = 0$ ...(2)

or $$p - mq = az$$

Lagrange's auxiliary equations are

$$\frac{dx}{1} = \frac{dy}{-m} = \frac{dz}{az}$$

From the first two members $dy + mdx = 0 \quad \therefore \quad y + mx = b$

From the first and last members $\dfrac{dz}{z} = adx \quad \therefore \quad \log z = ax + \log c$ or $z = ce^{ax}$

$\therefore$ The complete solution of (2) is $z = e^{ax} f(y + mx)$

Hence the C.F. of (1), *i.e.*, the complete solution of

$$(D - m_1D' - a_1)(D - m_2D' - a_2)......(D - m_nD' - a_n)z = 0 \text{ is}$$

$$z = e^{a_1x} f_1(y + m_1x) + e^{a_2x} f_2(y + m_2x) + ... + e^{a_nx} f_n(y + m_nx).$$

4.34.1. In the Case of Repeated Factors, *e.g.*, $(D - mD' - a)^3z = 0$

We have $z = e^{ax} f_1(y + mx) + xe^{ax} f_2(y + mx) + x^2e^{ax} f_3(y + mx)$.

4.34.2. If the Equation is of the Form

$$(\alpha D + \beta D' + \gamma)z = 0 \qquad ...(3)$$

$$\Rightarrow \qquad \alpha p + \beta q = -\gamma z$$

It is of Lagrange's form.

Lagrange's subsidiary equations are

$$\frac{dx}{\alpha} = \frac{dy}{\beta} = \frac{dz}{-\gamma z} \qquad ...(4)$$

First two will give $\alpha y - \beta x = c_1$ ...(5)

First and last will give, $\dfrac{dz}{z} = -\dfrac{\gamma}{\alpha} dx$

Integration gives, $\log z = -\dfrac{\gamma}{\alpha} x + \log c_2$

$$\Rightarrow \qquad z = c_2 \, e^{-\frac{\gamma}{\alpha}x} = \phi(c_1) \, e^{-\frac{\gamma}{\alpha}x}$$

$$\Rightarrow \qquad z = e^{-\frac{\gamma}{\alpha}x}\,\phi(\alpha y - \beta x)$$

where ϕ is an arbitrary function.

Note. The above result is not applicable in the absence of the first term *i.e.,* D or αD and also when $\alpha = 0$.

Remark 1. Corresponding to each non-repeated factor $(aD' + b)$, the part of C.F. is $e^{-(by/a)}\,\phi(ax)$ when $a \neq 0$.

Remark 2. Corresponding to repeated factor $(aD' + b)^r$, the part of C.F. is

$$e^{-\left(\frac{by}{a}\right)}\,[\phi_1(ax) + y\,\phi_2(ax) + y^2\,\phi_3(ax) + \ldots\ldots + y^{r-1}\,\phi_r(ax)].$$

Remark 3. As a particular case of remark 1 with $b = 0$, $a = 1$, corresponding to non-repeated factor D$'$, the part of C.F. $= \phi_1(x)$.

Remark 4. As a particular case of remark 2 with $b = 0$, $a = 1$, corresponding to repeated factor D'^r, part of C.F. $= \phi_1(x) + y\,\phi_2(x) + y^2\,\phi_3(x) + \ldots\ldots + y^{r-1}\,\phi_r(x)$

(*b*) When F(D, D$'$) cannot be factorized into linear factors :

In such cases, we use a trial method.

Let the equation be $\qquad (D - D'^2)z = 0$ $\qquad$ ...(1)

Let the trial solution of (1) be $\qquad z = Ae^{hx+ky}$, where A, h and k are constants. $\qquad$ ...(2)

From (2), $\qquad Dz = \dfrac{\partial z}{\partial x} = Ahe^{hx+ky}$

$$D'z = \frac{\partial z}{\partial y} = A\,ke^{hx+ky}$$

$$D'^2z = \frac{\partial^2 z}{\partial y^2} = A\,k^2\,e^{hx+ky}$$

Putting in (1), we get $Ahe^{hx+ky} - A\,k^2\,e^{hx+ky} = 0$

$$\Rightarrow \qquad A(h - k^2)\,e^{hx+ky} = 0$$

or $\qquad h = k^2$ $\qquad$ ...(3)

Equation (2) gives, $\qquad z = Ae^{k^2x + ky}$ $\qquad$ ...(4)

Since all values of k will satisfy eqn. (1), a more general solution of (1) is given by

$$z = \Sigma\,Ae^{k^2x + ky}$$

where A and k are arbitrary constants and Σ denotes that any number of terms may be taken.

ILLUSTRATIVE EXAMPLES

Example 1. *Solve the linear partial differential equation*

$$(D + D' - 1)\,(D + 2D' - 2)z = 0.$$

Sol. The given equation is

$$(D + D' - 1)\,(D + 2D' - 2)z = 0.$$

Its $\quad$ C.F. $= e^x f_1(y - x) + e^{2x} f_2(y - 2x)$

and $\quad$ P.I. $= 0$

Hence complete solution is

$$z = \text{C.F.} + \text{P.I.} = e^{x} f_1 (y - x) + e^{2x} f_2 (y - 2x)$$

where f_1 and f_2 are arbitrary functions.

Example 2. *Solve : $DD'(D + 2D' + 1)z = 0$.*

Sol. The given equation is

$$DD'(D + 2D' + 1)z = 0$$

Corresponding to the factor D, part of C.F. $= f_1(y)$

Corresponding to the factor D′, part of C.F. $= f_2(x)$

Corresponding to the factor $(D + 2D' + 1)$ part of C.F. $= e^{-x} f_3 (y - 2x)$

Hence combined C.F. $= f_1(y) + f_2(x) + e^{-x} f_3 (y - 2x)$

P.I. $= 0$

Hence complete solution is

$$z = \text{C.F.} + \text{P.I.} = f_1(y) + f_2(x) + e^{-x} f_3 (y - 2x)$$

where f_1, f_2 and f_3 are arbitrary functions.

Example 3. *Solve : $r + 2s + t + 2p + 2q + z = 0$.*

Sol. The given equation is

$$[D^2 + 2DD' + D'^2 + 2D + 2D' + 1]z = 0$$

$$\Rightarrow \quad \{(D + D')^2 + 2(D + D') + 1\}z = 0$$

$$\Rightarrow \quad (D + D' + 1)^2 z = 0$$

Its C.F. $= e^{-x} f_1 (y - x) + x\, e^{-x} f_2 (y - x)$

P.I. $= 0$

Hence complete solution is

$$z = \text{C.F.} + \text{P.I.} = e^{-x} f_1 (y - x) + x\, e^{-x} f_2 (y - x)$$

where f_1 and f_2 are arbitrary functions.

Example 4. *Solve :*

(*i*) $r - t + p - q = 0$ (*ii*) $(D + 4D' + 5)^2 z = 0$

(*iii*) $(D^2 - DD' - 2D)z = 0$ (*iv*) $(D + 1)(D + D' - 1)z = 0$.

Sol. (*i*) The given equation is

$$(D^2 - D'^2 + D - D')z = 0$$

$$\Rightarrow \quad (D - D')(D + D' + 1)z = 0$$

Its C.F. $= f_1 (y + x) + e^{-x} f_2 (y - x)$

P.I. $= 0$

Hence complete solution is

$$z = \text{C.F.} + \text{P.I.} = f_1 (y + x) + e^{-x} f_2 (y - x)$$

where f_1 and f_2 are arbitrary functions.

(*ii*) The given equation is

$$(D + 4D' + 5)^2 z = 0$$

Its C.F. $= e^{-5x} f_1 (y - 4x) + x\, e^{-5x} f_2 (y - 4x)$

P.I. $= 0$

Hence complete solution is

$$z = \text{C.F.} + \text{P.I.} = e^{-5x} f_1 (y - 4x) + x\, e^{-5x} f_2 (y - 4x)$$

where f_1 and f_2 are arbitrary functions.

(*iii*) The given equation is

$$(D^2 - DD' - 2D)z = 0$$

$\Rightarrow$ $$D(D - D' - 2)z = 0$$

Its $\quad \text{C.F.} = f_1(y) + e^{2x} f_2 (y + x)$

$\text{P.I.} = 0$

Hence complete solution is

$$z = \text{C.F.} + \text{P.I.} = f_1(y) + e^{2x} f_2 (y + x)$$

where f_1 and f_2 are arbitrary functions.

(*iv*) The given equation is

$$(D + 1)(D + D' - 1)z = 0$$

Its $\quad \text{C.F.} = e^{-x} f_1(y) + e^{x} f_2 (y - x)$

$\text{P.I.} = 0$

Hence complete solution is

$$z = \text{C.F.} + \text{P.I.} = e^{-x} f_1(y) + e^{x} f_2 (y - x)$$

where f_1 and f_2 are arbitrary functions.

Example 5. *Solve :* (*i*) $(D^2 - D'^2 + D + 3D' - 2)z = 0$

(*ii*) $(D^2 - DD' - 2D'^2 + 2D + 2D')z = 0.$

Sol. (*i*) The given equation is

$$(D^2 - D'^2 + D + 3D' - 2)z = 0$$

$\Rightarrow$ $$(D^2 - D'^2 + 2D - D + 2D' + D' - 2 + DD' - DD')z = 0$$

$\Rightarrow$ $$[D^2 - DD' + 2D + DD' - D'^2 + 2D' - D + D' - 2]z = 0$$

$\Rightarrow$ $$(D - D' + 2)(D + D' - 1)z = 0$$

Its $\quad \text{C.F.} = e^{-2x} f_1 (y + x) + e^{x} f_2 (y - x)$

$\text{P.I.} = 0$

Hence complete solution is $\quad z = \text{C.F.} + \text{P.I.} = e^{-2x} f_1 (y + x) + e^{x} f_2 (y - x)$

where f_1 and f_2 are arbitrary functions.

(*ii*) The given equation is

$$(D^2 - DD' - 2D'^2 + 2D + 2D')z = 0$$

$\Rightarrow$ $$(D + D')(D - 2D') + 2(D + D')]z = 0$$

$\Rightarrow$ $$(D + D')(D - 2D' + 2)z = 0$$

Its $\quad \text{C.F.} = f_1 (y - x) + e^{-2x} f_2 (y + 2x)$

$\text{P.I.} = 0$

Hence complete solution is

$$z = \text{C.F.} + \text{P.I.} = f_1 (y - x) + e^{-2x} f_2 (y + 2x)$$

where f_1 and f_2 are arbitrary functions.

Example 6. *Solve :* $(D^2 + D'^2 - p^2)z = 0.$

Sol. Here $D^2 + D'^2 - p^2$ cannot be resolved into linear factors in D and D′.

Let $z = Ae^{hx+ky}$

$\therefore$ $D^2z = Ah^2 e^{hx+ky}$

$D'^2z = Ak^2 e^{hx+ky}$

$\therefore$ $(D^2 + D'^2 - p^2)z = A(h^2 + k^2 - p^2) e^{hx+ky}$

Then, $(D^2 + D'^2 - p^2)z = 0$

$\Rightarrow$ $A(h^2 + k^2 - p^2) e^{hx+ky} = 0$

$\Rightarrow$ $h^2 + k^2 - p^2 = 0$ or $h^2 + k^2 = p^2$

$\therefore$ C.F. $= \Sigma Ae^{hx+ky}$, where $h^2 + k^2 - p^2 = 0$

P.I. = 0

$\therefore$ $z = \Sigma Ae^{hx+ky}$, where $h^2 + k^2 - p^2 = 0$

Now, h may be taken as $p \cos \alpha$ and k may be taken as $p \sin \alpha$. Therefore

The complete solution is

$$z = \Sigma Ae^{p(x \cos \alpha + y \sin \alpha)}$$

where A is arbitrary constant and Σ denotes that any number of terms may be taken.

TEST YOUR KNOWLEDGE

Solve the following partial differential equations :

1. $(D + D' - 1)(D + 2D' - 3)z = 0$

2. $r - 3s + 2t - p + 2q = 0$

3. $DD'(D - 2D' - 3)z = 0$

4. $t + s + q = 0$

5. $(D^2 - a^2D'^2 + 2abD + 2a^2bD')z = 0$

6. $(D - 2D' - 1)(D - 2D'^2 - 1)z = 0$

7. $(2D^4 - 3D^2D' + D'^2)z = 0$

8. $(D^3 - 3DD' + D' + 4)z = 0$

9. $2s + t - 3q = 0$

10. $(DD' + aD + bD' + ab)z = 0.$

Answers

1. $z = e^x f_1(y - x) + e^{3x} f_2(y - 2x)$

2. $z = f_1(y + 2x) + e^x f_2(y + x)$

3. $z = f_1(y) + f_2(x) + e^{3x} f_3(y + 2x)$

4. $z = f_1(x) + e^{-x} f_2(y - x)$

5. $z = f_1(y - ax) + e^{-2abx} f_2(y + ax)$

6. $z = e^x f_1(y + 2x) + \Sigma Ae^{(2k^2 + 1)x+ky}$

7. $z = \Sigma Ae^{hx + h^2y} + \Sigma A'e^{h'x + h'^2 y}$

8. $z = \Sigma A e^{hx+ky}$, where $h^3 - 3hk + k + 4 = 0$

9. $z = f_1(y) + e^{(3x/2)} f_2(2y - x).$

10. $z = e^{-ay} f_1(x) + e^{-bx} f_2(y)$

4.35. P.I. OF NON-HOMOGENEOUS LINEAR PARTIAL DIFFERENTIAL EQUATION WITH CONSTANT COEFFICIENTS

Let the given equation be $\phi(D, D')z = F(x, y)$

then
$$\text{P.I.} = \frac{1}{\phi(D, D')} F(x, y)$$

The methods of finding out P.I. of these equations quite resemble to those of ordinary linear differential equation with constant coefficients.

4.35.1 Case I. When $F(x, y) = e^{ax+by}$ and $\phi(a, b) \neq 0$

$$\text{P.I.} = \frac{1}{\phi(D, D')} e^{ax+by}$$

$$= \frac{1}{\phi(a, b)} e^{ax+by} \qquad \text{| Replacing D by } a \text{ and D}' \text{ by } b$$

ILLUSTRATIVE EXAMPLES

Example 1. *Solve :* $s + ap + bq + abz = e^{mx+ny}$.

Sol. The given equation is

$$(DD' + aD + bD' + ab)z = e^{mx+ny}$$

$$\Rightarrow \qquad (D + b)(D' + a)z = e^{mx+ny}$$

Its $\quad \text{C.F.} = e^{-bx} f_1(y) + e^{-ay} f_2(x)$

$$\text{P.I.} = \frac{1}{(D+b)(D'+a)} e^{mx+ny} = \frac{e^{mx+ny}}{(m+b)(n+a)}$$

Hence complete solution is

$$z = \text{C.F.} + \text{P.I.} = e^{-bx} f_1(y) + e^{-ay} f_2(x) + \frac{e^{mx+ny}}{(m+b)(n+a)}$$

where f_1 and f_2 are arbitrary functions.

Example 2. *Solve :* $(D^3 - 3DD' + D' + 4)z = e^{2x+y}$.

Sol. Here $D^3 - 3DD' + D' + 4$ cannot be resolved into linear factors in D and D′.

Let $\quad z = Ae^{hx+ky}$

$\therefore \quad (D^3 - 3DD' + D' + 4)z = A(h^3 - 3hk + k + 4)\, e^{hx+ky}$

Then $\quad (D^3 - 3DD' + D' + 4)z = 0$ iff $h^3 - 3hk + k + 4 = 0$

$\therefore$ The C.F. is $z = \Sigma\, Ae^{hx+ky}$, where $h^3 - 3hk + k + 4 = 0$

$$\text{P.I.} = \frac{1}{D^3 - 3DD' + D' + 4} e^{2x+y} = \frac{e^{2x+y}}{2^3 - 3(2)(1) + 1 + 4} = \frac{1}{7} e^{2x+y}$$

Hence complete solution is $z = \Sigma\, Ae^{hx+ky} + \frac{1}{7} e^{2x+y}$, where $h^3 - 3hk + k + 4 = 0$.

Example 3. *Solve :* $D(D - 2D' - 3)z = e^{x+2y}$.

Sol. $\quad \text{C.F.} = f_1(y) + e^{3x} f_2(y + 2x)$

$$\text{P.I.} = \frac{1}{D(D - 2D' - 3)} e^{x+2y} = \frac{e^{x+2y}}{1\{1 - 2(2) - 3\}} = -\frac{1}{6} e^{x+2y}$$

Hence the complete solution is

$$z = \text{C.F.} + \text{P.I.} = f_1(y) + e^{3x} f_2(y + 2x) - \frac{1}{6} e^{x+2y}$$

where f_1 and f_2 are arbitrary functions.

TEST YOUR KNOWLEDGE

Solve :

1. $(D^3 - 3DD' + D + 1)z = e^{2x+3y}$
2. $(D^2 - 4DD' + D - 1)z = e^{3x-2y}$
3. $(D^2 - D'^2 - 3D + 3D')z = e^{x-2y}$
4. $(D - D' - 1)(D + D' - 2)z = e^{2x-y}$
5. $(D^2 - D'^2 + D - D')z = e^{2x+3y}$.

Answers

1. $z = \Sigma\, Ae^{hx+ky} - \frac{1}{7}e^{2x+3y}$, where $h^3 - 3hk + h + 1 = 0$
2. $z = \Sigma\, Ae^{hx+ky} + \frac{1}{35}e^{3x-2y}$, where $h^2 - 4hk + h - 1 = 0$
3. $z = f_1(y + x) + e^{3x} f_2(y - x) - \frac{1}{12}e^{x-2y}$
4. $z = e^x f_1(y + x) + e^{2x} f_2(y - x) - \frac{1}{2}e^{2x-y}$
5. $z = f_1(y + x) + e^{-x} f_2(y - x) - \frac{1}{6}e^{2x+3y}$.

4.35.2. Case II. When $F(x, y) = \sin(ax + by)$ or $\cos(ax + by)$

$$\text{P.I.} = \frac{1}{\phi(D, D')}\{\sin(ax + by) \text{ or } \cos(ax + by)\}$$

$$= \frac{1}{\phi(D^2, DD', D'^2)}\{\sin(ax + by) \text{ or } \cos(ax + by)\}$$

$$= \frac{1}{\phi(-a^2, -ab, -b^2)}\{\sin(ax + by) \text{ or } \cos(ax + by)\}$$

where $\phi(-a^2, -ab, -b^2) \neq 0$. It is to be noted that here D^2 is replaced by $-a^2$, DD' is replaced by $-ab$ and D'^2 is replaced by $-b^2$.

If $\phi(D, D') = \phi(D^2, DD', D'^2, D, D')$, then

$$\text{P.I.} = \frac{1}{\phi(-a^2, -ab, -b^2, D, D')}\{\sin(ax + by) \text{ or } \cos(ax + by)\}$$

which can be evaluated further by operating N^r and D^r by the suitable conjugate operator.

ILLUSTRATIVE EXAMPLES

Example 1. *Solve : $(D^2 - DD' + D' - 1)z = \sin(x + 2y)$.*

Sol. The given equation is $(D^2 - DD' + D' - 1)z = \sin(x + 2y)$

$\Rightarrow \quad \{(D + 1)(D - 1) - D'(D - 1)\}z = \sin(x + 2y)$

$\Rightarrow \quad (D - 1)(D - D' + 1)z = \sin(x + 2y)$

$\therefore \quad \text{C.F.} = e^x f_1(y) + e^{-x} f_2(y + x)$

$$\text{P.I.} = \frac{1}{D^2 - DD' + D' - 1} \sin(x + 2y) = \frac{1}{-1 + 2 + D' - 1} \sin(x + 2y)$$

$$= \frac{1}{D'} \sin(x + 2y) = -\frac{\cos(x + 2y)}{2}$$

Hence complete solution is

$$z = \text{C.F.} + \text{P.I.} = e^x f_1(y) + e^{-x} f_2(y + x) - \frac{\cos(x + 2y)}{2}$$

where f_1 and f_2 are arbitrary functions.

Example 2. *Solve : $(D - D' - 1)(D - D' - 2)z = \sin(2x + 3y)$.* (U.K.T.U. 2011)

Sol. $\text{C.F.} = e^x f_1(y + x) + e^{2x} f_2(y + x)$

$$\text{P.I.} = \frac{1}{(D - D' - 1)(D - D' - 2)} \sin(2x + 3y)$$

$$= \frac{1}{D^2 - 2DD' + D'^2 - 3D + 3D' + 2} \sin(2x + 3y)$$

$$= \frac{1}{-4 + 12 - 9 - 3D + 3D' + 2} \sin(2x + 3y)$$

$$= \frac{1}{-3D + 3D' + 1} \sin(2x + 3y)$$

$$= -\left[\frac{(3D - 3D') + 1}{\{(3D - 3D') + 1\}\{3D - 3D' - 1\}} \sin(2x + 3y)\right]$$

$$= -\left[\frac{(3D - 3D') + 1}{9D^2 + 9D'^2 - 18DD' - 1} \sin(2x + 3y)\right]$$

$$= -\left[\frac{3D - 3D' + 1}{-36 - 81 + 108 - 1} \sin(2x + 3y)\right]$$

$$= \frac{1}{10}(3D - 3D' + 1)\sin(2x + 3y)$$

$$= \frac{1}{10}[6\cos(2x + 3y) - 9\cos(2x + 3y) + \sin(2x + 3y)]$$

$$= \frac{1}{10}[\sin(2x + 3y) - 3\cos(2x + 3y)]$$

Hence the complete solution is

$$z = \text{C.F.} + \text{P.I.} = e^x f_1(y + x) + e^{2x} f_2(y + x) + \frac{1}{10}[\sin(2x + 3y) - 3\cos(2x + 3y)]$$

where f_1 and f_2 are arbitrary functions.

Example 3. *Find the particular integral of $2s + t - 3q = 5\cos(3x - 2y)$.*

Sol. The given equation is

$$(2DD' + D'^2 - 3D')z = 5\cos(3x - 2y)$$

$$\text{P.I.} = \frac{1}{2DD' + D'^2 - 3D'} 5\cos(3x - 2y)$$

$$= \frac{1}{2(6) + (-4) - 3D'} 5\cos(3x - 2y) = \frac{1}{(8 - 3D')} 5\cos(3x - 2y)$$

$$= 5\left[\frac{8 + 3D'}{64 - 9D'^2}\cos(3x - 2y)\right] = 5\left[\frac{8 + 3D'}{64 - 9(-4)}\cos(3x - 2y)\right]$$

$$= \frac{1}{20}[8\cos(3x - 2y) + 6\sin(3x - 2y)]$$

$$= \frac{1}{10}[4\cos(3x - 2y) + 3\sin(3x - 2y)].$$

TEST YOUR KNOWLEDGE

Solve the following partial differential equations :

1. $(D^2 - DD' + D' - 1)z = \cos(x + 2y)$
2. $(D^2 - DD' - 2D'^2 + 2D + 2D')z = \sin(2x + y)$ *(G.B.T.U. 2011)*
3. $(D^2 + DD' + D' - 1)z = \sin(x + 2y)$ *(G.B.T.U. 2010)*
4. $(D^2 - DD' - 2D)z = \sin(3x + 4y) - e^{2x+y}$
5. $(D - D'^2)z = \cos(x - 3y)$
6. $(D^2 + 2DD' + D'^2 - 2D - 2D')z = \sin(x + 2y)$.

Answers

1. $z = e^x f_1(y) + e^{-x} f_2(y + x) + \frac{1}{2}\sin(x + 2y)$
2. $z = f_1(y - x) + e^{-2x} f_2(2x + y) - \frac{1}{6}\cos(2x + y)$
3. $z = e^{-x} f_1(y) + e^x f_2(y - x) - \frac{1}{10}[2\sin(x + 2y) + \cos(x + 2y)]$
4. $z = f_1(y) + e^{2x} f_2(y + x) + \frac{1}{15}[\sin(3x + 4y) + 2\cos(3x + 4y)] + \frac{1}{2}e^{2x+y}$
5. $z = \Sigma\, Ae^{k^2x + ky} + \frac{1}{82}[\sin(x - 3y) + 9\cos(x - 3y)]$
6. $z = f_1(y - x) + e^{2x} f_2(y - x) + \frac{1}{39}[2\cos(x + 2y) - 3\sin(x + 2y)]$.

4.35.3. Case III. When $F(x, y) = x^m y^n$ where m and n being positive integers

$$\text{P.I.} = \frac{1}{\phi(D, D')} x^m y^n = [\phi(D, D')]^{-1}(x^m y^n)$$

which can be evaluated after expanding $[\phi(D, D')]^{-1}$ in ascending powers of $\frac{D'}{D}$ (when $m > n$) or $\frac{D}{D'}$ (when $m < n$) or D or D′ as the case may be.

If a separate constant is present in $\phi(D, D')$ then it should be given preference in taking the term outside the bracket. It is to be noted that if P.I. is obtained by expanding $\phi(D, D')$ in two or more different ways, then difference in P.I. will be immaterial.

ILLUSTRATIVE EXAMPLES

Example 1. *Solve the linear partial differential equation*

$$(D - D' - 1)(D - D' - 2)z = e^{3x-y} + x.$$

Sol. $\quad$ C.F. $= e^{x} f_1 (y + x) + e^{2x} f_2 (y + x)$

$$\text{P.I.} = \frac{1}{(D - D' - 1)(D - D' - 2)} e^{3x - y} + \frac{1}{(D - D' - 1)(D - D' - 2)} (x) = P_1 + P_2$$

where

$$P_1 = \frac{1}{(D - D' - 1)(D - D' - 2)} e^{3x - y} = \frac{1}{(3 + 1 - 1)(3 + 1 - 2)} e^{3x - y} = \frac{1}{6} e^{3x - y},$$

$$P_2 = \frac{1}{(D - D' - 1)(D - D' - 2)} (x) = \frac{1}{(1 - D + D')(2 - D + D')} (x)$$

$$= \frac{1}{\{1 - (D - D')\} 2 \left\{1 - \left(\frac{D - D'}{2}\right)\right\}} (x)$$

$$= \frac{1}{2}\left[\{1 - (D - D')\}^{-1} \left\{1 - \left(\frac{D - D'}{2}\right)\right\}^{-1}\right] (x)$$

$$= \frac{1}{2}\left[(1 + D - D')\left(1 + \frac{D - D'}{2}\right)\right] (x) \qquad | \text{ Leaving higher powers}$$

$$= \frac{1}{2}\left[1 + \frac{D}{2} - \frac{D'}{2} + D + \frac{D^2}{2} - \frac{DD'}{2} - D' - \frac{D'D}{2} + \frac{D'^2}{2}\right] (x)$$

$$= \frac{1}{2}\left[x + \frac{1}{2} - 0 + 1 + 0 - 0 - 0 - 0 - 0 + 0\right] = \frac{1}{2}\left(x + \frac{3}{2}\right)$$

$$\therefore \qquad \text{P.I.} = \frac{1}{6} e^{3x-y} + \frac{1}{2}\left(x + \frac{3}{2}\right).$$

Hence the complete solution is

$$z = \text{C.F.} + \text{P.I.} = e^{x} f_1 (y + x) + e^{2x} f_2 (y + x) + \frac{1}{6} e^{3x-y} + \frac{1}{2}\left(x + \frac{3}{2}\right)$$

where f_1 and f_2 are arbitrary functions.

Example 2. *Solve the linear partial differential equation*

$$(D + D' - 1)(D + 2D' - 3)z = 4 + 3x + 6y.$$

Sol. C.F. $= e^x f_1(y - x) + e^{3x} f_2(y - 2x)$

$$\text{P.I.} = \frac{1}{(D + D' - 1)(D + 2D' - 3)}(4 + 3x + 6y)$$

$$= \frac{1}{(1 - D - D')(3 - D - 2D')}(4 + 3x + 6y)$$

$$= \frac{1}{\{1 - (D + D')\}\, 3\left\{1 - \left(\frac{D + 2D'}{3}\right)\right\}}(4 + 3x + 6y)$$

$$= \frac{1}{3}\left[\{1 - (D + D')\}^{-1}\left\{1 - \left(\frac{D + 2D'}{3}\right)\right\}^{-1}\right](4 + 3x + 6y)$$

$$= \frac{1}{3}\left[(1 + D + D')\left(1 + \frac{D}{3} + \frac{2D'}{3}\right)\right](4 + 3x + 6y)$$

$$= \frac{1}{3}\left[1 + \frac{4D}{3} + \frac{5D'}{3} + \frac{D^2}{3} + DD' + \frac{2D'^2}{3}\right](4 + 3x + 6y)$$

$$= \frac{1}{3}\left[(4 + 3x + 6y) + \frac{4}{3}(3) + \frac{5}{3}(6) + 0 + 0 + 0\right] = 6 + x + 2y.$$

Hence the complete solution is

$$z = \text{C.F.} + \text{P.I.} = e^x f_1(y - x) + e^{3x} f_2(y - 2x) + 6 + x + 2y$$

where f_1 and f_2 are arbitrary functions.

Example 3. *Solve the partial differential equation*

$$(D^2 - D'^2 - 3D + 3D')z = xy + e^{x+2y}.$$ [G.B.T.U. (C.O.) 2011]

Sol. The given equation is

$$(D^2 - D'^2 - 3D + 3D')\, z = 0$$

$$(D - D')(D + D' - 3)z = 0$$

$\therefore$ C.F. $= f_1(y + x) + e^{3x} f_2(y - x)$

P.I. corresponding to $xy = \dfrac{1}{(D - D')(D + D' - 3)}(xy)$

$$= -\frac{1}{3D}\left(1 - \frac{D'}{D}\right)^{-1}\left(1 - \frac{D}{3} - \frac{D'}{3}\right)^{-1}(xy)$$

$$= -\frac{1}{3D}\left(1 + \frac{D'}{D} + \ldots\right)\left(1 + \frac{D}{3} + \frac{D'}{3} + \frac{2DD'}{9} + \ldots\right)(xy)$$

$$= -\frac{1}{3D}\left(1 + \frac{D}{3} + \frac{D'}{3} + \frac{D'}{D} + \frac{D'}{3} + \frac{2DD'}{9} + \ldots\right)(xy)$$

$$= -\frac{1}{3D}\left(xy + \frac{y}{3} + \frac{2}{3}x + \frac{x^2}{2} + \frac{2}{9}\right) \qquad | \text{ Leaving higher powers}$$

$$= -\frac{1}{3}\left[\frac{x^2}{2}y + \frac{xy}{3} + \frac{x^2}{3} + \frac{x^3}{6} + \frac{2}{9}x\right]$$

P.I. corresponding to e^{x+2y}

$$= \frac{1}{(D-D')(D+D'-3)}e^{x+2y} = \frac{1}{(1-2)(D+D'-3)}e^{x+2y}$$

$$= -e^{x+2y} \cdot \frac{1}{D+1+D'+2-3}(1) = -e^{x+2y} \cdot \frac{1}{D+D'}e^{0x+0y}$$

$$= -e^{x+2y} \cdot x\, e^{0x+0y} = -x\, e^{x+2y}$$

$$\therefore \qquad \text{P.I.} = -\frac{1}{3}\left[\frac{x^2y}{2} + \frac{xy}{3} + \frac{x^2}{3} + \frac{x^3}{6} + \frac{2x}{9}\right] - x\, e^{x+2y}$$

Hence the complete solution is

$$z = \text{C.F.} + \text{P.I.} = f_1(y+x) + e^{3x} f_2(y-x) - \frac{1}{3}\left[\frac{x^2y}{2} + \frac{xy}{3} + \frac{x^2}{3} + \frac{x^3}{6} + \frac{2x}{9}\right] - x\, e^{x+2y}$$

where f_1 and f_2 are arbitrary funtions.

Example 4. *Solve* : $s + p - q = z + xy$.

Sol. The given equation is

$$(DD' + D - D' - 1)z = xy$$

$$\Rightarrow \qquad (D-1)(D'+1)z = xy$$

$$\therefore \qquad \text{C.F.} = e^x f_1(y) + e^{-y} f_2(x)$$

$$\text{P.I.} = \frac{1}{(D-1)(D'+1)}(xy) = -[(1-D)^{-1}(1+D')^{-1}](xy)$$

$$= -[(1 + D + D^2 + \ldots\ldots)(1 - D' + \ldots\ldots)](xy)$$

$$= -(1 + D - D' - DD')\, xy \qquad | \text{ Leaving higher powers}$$

$$= -(xy + y - x - 1) = x + 1 - xy - y$$

Hence the complete solution is

$$z = \text{C.F.} + \text{P.I.} = e^x f_1(y) + e^{-y} f_2(x) + x + 1 - xy - y$$

where f_1 and f_2 are arbitrary functions.

Example 5. *Solve :*

(*a*) $r - s + p = 1$ (*b*) $D(D + D' - 1)(D + 3D' - 2)z = x^2 - 4xy + 2y^2$.

Sol. (*a*) The given equation is

$$(D^2 - DD' + D)z = 1$$

$$\Rightarrow \qquad D(D - D' + 1)z = 1$$

$$\therefore \qquad \text{C.F} = f_1(y) + e^{-x} f_2(y + x)$$

$$\text{P.I.} = \frac{1}{D(D-D'+1)}(1) = \frac{1}{D}[1+(D-D')]^{-1}(1) = \frac{1}{D}(1) = x$$

∴ Complete solution is

$$z = \text{C.F} + \text{P.I.} = f_1(y) + e^{-x} f_2(y+x) + x$$

where f_1 and f_2 are arbitrary functions.

(*b*) $\text{C.F.} = f_1(y) + e^x f_2(y-x) + e^{2x} f_3(y-3x)$

$$\text{P.I.} = \frac{1}{D(D+D'-1)(D+3D'-2)}(x^2 - 4xy + 2y^2)$$

$$= \frac{1}{2D}\{1-(D+D')\}^{-1}\left\{1-\frac{D+3D'}{2}\right\}^{-1}(x^2-4xy+2y^2)$$

$$= \frac{1}{2D}\{1+D+D'+(D+D')^2+\ldots\}.\left\{1+\frac{D+3D'}{2}+\left(\frac{D+3D'}{2}\right)^2+\ldots\right\}(x^2-4xy+2y^2)$$

$$= \frac{1}{2D}\left[1+\frac{3D}{2}+\frac{5D'}{2}+\frac{7D^2}{4}+\frac{19D'^2}{4}+\frac{11DD'}{2}+\ldots\right](x^2-4xy+2y^2)$$

$$= \frac{1}{2D}\left[x^2-4xy+2y^2+3(x-2y)+5(2y-2x)+\frac{7}{2}+19-22\right]$$

$$= \frac{1}{2D}\left(x^2-4xy+2y^2-7x+4y+\frac{1}{2}\right) = \frac{1}{2}\left(\frac{x^3}{3}-2x^2y+2y^2x-\frac{7x^2}{2}+4yx+\frac{x}{2}\right)$$

Hence the complete solution is

$$z = \text{C.F.} + \text{P.I.} = f_1(y) + e^x f_2(y-x) + e^{2x} f_3(y-3x) + \frac{1}{6}x^3 - x^2y + xy^2 - \frac{7}{4}x^2 + 2xy + \frac{x}{4}$$

where f_1, f_2 and f_3 are arbitrary functions.

TEST YOUR KNOWLEDGE

Solve :

1. $(D - D' - 1)(D - D' - 2)z = e^{2x-y} + x$
2. $(D + D' - 1)(D + 2D' - 3)z = 2x + 3y$
3. $(D^2 - D' - 1)z = x^2y$
4. $(D + D' - 1)^2 z = xy$ [*G.B.T.U. (AG) 2011*]
5. $(D^2 - DD' - 2D'^2 + 2D + 2D')z = e^{2x+3y} + \sin(2x+y) + xy.$

Answers

1. $z = e^x f_1(y+x) + e^{2x} f_2(y+x) + \dfrac{e^{2x-y}}{2} + \dfrac{2x+3}{4}$
2. $z = e^x f_1(y-x) + e^{3x} f_2(y-2x) + \dfrac{2}{3}x + y + \dfrac{23}{9}$
3. $z = \Sigma\, A e^{hx+(h^2-1)y} + x^2 - x^2y - 2y + 4$

4. $z = e^x f_1(y - x) + xe^x f_2(y - x) + xy + 2y + 2x + 6$

5. $z = f_1(y - x) + e^{-2x} f_2(y + 2x) - \frac{1}{10} e^{2x+3y} - \frac{1}{6} \cos(2x + y) + \frac{x^2 y}{4} - \frac{xy}{4} - \frac{x^3}{12} + \frac{3x^2}{8} - \frac{x}{2}.$

4.35.4. Case IV. When $F(x, y) = e^{ax+by}$. V where V is a function of x and y

$$\text{P.I.} = \frac{1}{\phi(D, D')} e^{ax+by} . V = e^{ax+by} . \frac{1}{\phi(D + a, D' + b)} V$$

which can be evaluated further by using any one of the previous cases discussed.

Remark. V can be either

(i) $e^{a_1 x + b_1 y}$ (ii) $\sin(ax + by)$ or $\cos(ax + by)$

(iii) $x^m y^n$ (iv) constant (say 1)

or any other function of x and y in some special cases.

ILLUSTRATIVE EXAMPLES

Example 1. *Solve : $(D - 3D' - 2)^3 z = 6e^{2x} \sin(3x + y)$.* [G.B.T.U. (SUM) 2010]

Sol. Here C.F. $= e^{2x} f_1(y + 3x) + xe^{2x} f_2(y + 3x) + x^2 e^{2x} f_3(y + 3x)$

$$\text{P.I.} = \frac{1}{(D - 3D' - 2)^3} 6e^{2x} \sin(3x + y)$$

$$= 6e^{2x} \frac{1}{(D + 2 - 3D' - 2)^3} \sin(3x + y) = 6e^{2x} \frac{1}{(D - 3D')^3} \sin(3x + y)$$

$$= 6e^{2x} . \frac{x^3}{6} \sin(3x + y) = x^3 e^{2x} \sin(3x + y)$$

Hence complete solution is

$$z = e^{2x} f_1(y + 3x) + xe^{2x} f_2(y + 3x) + x^2 e^{2x} f_3(y + 3x) + x^3 e^{2x} \sin(3x + y)$$

where f_1, f_2 and f_3 are arbitrary functions.

Example 2. *Solve : $(D - 3D' - 2)^2 z = 2e^{2x} \tan(y + 3x)$.*

Sol. C.F. $= e^{2x} f_1(y + 3x) + xe^{2x} f_2(y + 3x)$

$$\text{P.I.} = \frac{1}{(D - 3D' - 2)^2} 2e^{2x} \tan(y + 3x)$$

$$= 2e^{2x} . \frac{1}{(D + 2 - 3D' - 2)^2} \tan(y + 3x) = 2e^{2x} . \left[\frac{1}{(D - 3D')^2} \tan(y + 3x)\right]$$

$$= 2e^{2x} . \left[x . \frac{1}{2(D - 3D')} \tan(y + 3x)\right] = 2e^{2x} . x^2 . \frac{1}{2} \tan(y + 3x)$$

$$= x^2 e^{2x} \tan(y + 3x)$$

Hence complete solution is

$$z = \text{C.F.} + \text{P.I.} = e^{2x} f_1(y + 3x) + xe^{2x} f_2(y + 3x) + x^2 e^{2x} \tan(y + 3x)$$

where f_1 and f_2 are arbitrary functions.

Example 3. *Solve the linear partial differential equation*

$$(D^2 - DD' + D' - 1)\, z = \cos(x + 2y) + e^y.$$

Sol. The given equation is

$$(D^2 - DD' + D' - 1)z = \cos(x + 2y) + e^y$$

$$\Rightarrow \quad (D - 1)(D - D' + 1)z = \cos(x + 2y) + e^y$$

$$\text{C.F.} = e^x f_1(y) + e^{-x} f_2(y + x)$$

$$\text{P.I.} = \frac{1}{D^2 - DD' + D' - 1} \cos(x + 2y) + \frac{1}{(D - D' + 1)(D - 1)} e^y = P_1 + P_2$$

where

$$P_1 = \frac{1}{D^2 - DD' + D' - 1} \cos(x + 2y)$$

$$= \frac{1}{-(1)^2 - (-2) + D' - 1} \cos(x + 2y) = \frac{1}{D'} \cos(x + 2y) = \frac{\sin(x + 2y)}{2}$$

and

$$P_2 = \frac{1}{D - D' + 1}\left[\frac{1}{D - 1} e^y\right] = \frac{1}{D - D' + 1}\left[\frac{1}{0 - 1} e^y\right]$$

$$= \frac{1}{D - D' + 1}(-e^y) = -e^y \cdot \frac{1}{(D + 0) - (D' + 1) + 1} (1)$$

$$= -e^y \cdot \frac{1}{D - D'}(1) = -e^y \cdot \frac{1}{D - D'}(e^{0x + 0y}) = -e^y \cdot x \cdot e^{0x+0y} = -xe^y.$$

$$\therefore \quad \text{P.I.} = \frac{1}{2} \sin(x + 2y) - xe^y.$$

Hence the complete solution is

$$z = \text{C.F.} + \text{P.I.} = e^x f_1(y) + e^{-x} f_2(y + x) + \frac{1}{2} \sin(x + 2y) - xe^y$$

where f_1 and f_2 are arbitrary functions.

Example 4. *Solve :* $r - 4s + 4t + p - 2q = e^{x+y}$.

Sol. The given equation is

$$(D^2 - 4DD' + 4D'^2 + D - 2D')z = e^{x+y}$$

$$\Rightarrow \quad [(D - 2D')^2 + (D - 2D')]z = e^{x+y}$$

$$\Rightarrow \quad (D - 2D')(D - 2D' + 1)z = e^{x+y}$$

$$\therefore \quad \text{C.F.} = f_1(y + 2x) + e^{-x} f_2(y + 2x)$$

$$\text{P.I.} = \frac{1}{(D - 2D')(D - 2D' + 1)} e^{x+y} = \frac{1}{D - 2D' + 1}\left[\frac{1}{D - 2D'} e^{x+y}\right]$$

$$= \frac{1}{D - 2D' + 1}\left[\frac{1}{1 - 2} \int e^u \, du\right] \qquad \text{where } x + y = u$$

$$= -\left[\frac{1}{D - 2D' + 1} e^{x+y}\right] = - e^{x+y} \cdot \frac{1}{D + 1 - 2(D' + 1) + 1} (1)$$

$$= - e^{x+y}\left[\frac{1}{D - 2D'}(1)\right] = - e^{x+y}\left[\frac{1}{D - 2D'}(e^{0x + 0y})\right]$$

$$= - xe^{x+y}.$$

Hence the complete solution is

$$z = \text{C.F.} + \text{P.I.} = f_1 (y + 2x) + e^{-x} f_2 (y + 2x) - xe^{x+y}$$

where f_1 and f_2 are arbitrary functions.

Example 5. *Find the particular integral of* $(D^2 - D')z = xe^{ax+a^2y}$.

Sol.
$$\text{P.I.} = \frac{1}{D^2 - D'}(xe^{ax + a^2y}) = e^{ax + a^2y} \cdot \frac{1}{(D + a)^2 - (D' + a^2)} (x)$$

$$= e^{ax + a^2y} \cdot \frac{1}{D^2 + 2aD - D'}(x) = e^{ax + a^2y} \cdot \frac{1}{2aD}\left(1 + \frac{D}{2a} - \frac{D'}{2aD}\right)^{-1}(x)$$

$$= e^{ax + a^2y} \cdot \frac{1}{2aD}\left\{1 - \left(\frac{D}{2a} - \frac{D'}{2aD}\right) + \ldots\right\} x = e^{ax + a^2y} \cdot \frac{1}{2aD}\left(x - \frac{1}{2a}\right)$$

$$= e^{ax + a^2y} \cdot \left(\frac{x^2}{4a} - \frac{x}{4a^2}\right).$$

TEST YOUR KNOWLEDGE

Solve the following partial differential equations :

1. $(3D^2 - 2D'^2 + D - 1)z = 4e^{x+y} \cos (x + y)$
2. $(D^2 + DD' + D + D' - 1)z = e^{-2x} (x^2 + y^2)$
3. $(D + D' - 1)(D + D' - 3)(D + D')z = e^{x+y} \sin (2x + y)$
4. $(D^2 - DD' + D' - 1)z = \cos (x + 2y) + e^x$.

Answers

1. $z = \Sigma\, Ae^{hx+ky} + \frac{4}{3} e^{x+y} \sin (x + y)$, where $3h^2 - 2k^2 + h - 1 = 0$
2. $z = \Sigma\, Ae^{hx+ky} + \frac{1}{27} e^{-2x} (9x^2 + 9y^2 + 18x + 6y + 14)$, where $h^2 + hk + h + k + 1 = 0$
3. $z = e^x f_1 (y - x) + e^{3x} f_2 (y - x) + f_3 (y - x) + \frac{1}{130} [3 \cos (2x + y) - 2 \sin (2x + y)]\, e^{x+y}$
4. $z = e^x f_1 (y) + e^{-x} f_2 (y + x) + \frac{1}{2} \sin (x + 2y) + \frac{1}{2} xe^x$.

4.36. EQUATIONS REDUCIBLE TO PARTIAL DIFFERENTIAL EQUATIONS WITH CONSTANT COEFFICIENTS

An equation in which the coefficient of derivative of any order say k is a multiple of the variables of the degree k then it can be reduced to partial differential equation with constant coefficients in the following way.

Let $$x = e^{X},\ y = e^{Y} \text{ so that } X = \log x,\ Y = \log y$$

$$\frac{\partial z}{\partial x} = \frac{\partial z}{\partial X} \cdot \frac{\partial X}{\partial x} = \frac{1}{x}\frac{\partial z}{\partial X}$$

or $$x\frac{\partial z}{\partial x} = \frac{\partial z}{\partial X} \quad \therefore \quad x\frac{\partial}{\partial x} = D\left(\equiv \frac{\partial}{\partial X}\right)$$

Now $$x\frac{\partial}{\partial x}\left(x^{k-1}\frac{\partial^{k-1} z}{\partial x^{k-1}}\right) = x^k\frac{\partial^k z}{\partial x^k} + (k-1)x^{k-1}\frac{\partial^{k-1} z}{\partial x^{k-1}}$$

or $$x^k\frac{\partial^k z}{\partial x^k} = \left(x\frac{\partial}{\partial x} - k + 1\right)x^{k-1}\frac{\partial^{k-1} z}{\partial x^{k-1}}$$

Putting $k = 2, 3, \ldots\ldots$, we get

$$x^2\frac{\partial^2 z}{\partial x^2} = (D-1)x\frac{\partial z}{\partial x} = (D-1)Dz$$

$$x^3\frac{\partial^3 z}{\partial x^3} = (D-2)x^2\frac{\partial^2 z}{\partial x^2} = (D-2)(D-1)Dz \text{ etc.}$$

Similarly, $$y\frac{\partial z}{\partial y} = D'z,\quad y^2\frac{\partial^2 z}{\partial y^2} = (D'-1)D'z,\quad y^3\frac{\partial^3 z}{\partial y^3} = (D'-2)(D'-1)D'z \text{ etc.}$$

and $$xy\frac{\partial^2 z}{\partial x \partial y} = DD'z \ldots\ldots$$

Substituting in the given equation, it reduces to $\psi(D, D')z = V$ which is an equation with constant coefficients.

ILLUSTRATIVE EXAMPLES

Example 1. *Solve the linear partial differential equation*

$$x^2\frac{\partial^2 z}{\partial x^2} - 4xy\frac{\partial^2 z}{\partial x \partial y} + 4y^2\frac{\partial^2 z}{\partial y^2} + 6y\frac{\partial z}{\partial y} = x^3y^4.$$

Sol. Put $x = e^{X}$, $y = e^{Y}$ so that $X = \log x$ and $Y = \log y$ and Let $D \equiv \frac{\partial}{\partial X}$, $D' \equiv \frac{\partial}{\partial Y}$

and $DD' \equiv \frac{\partial^2}{\partial X \partial Y}$ then the given equation reduces to

$$[D (D - 1) - 4DD' + 4D' (D' - 1) + 6D']z = e^{3X+4Y}$$

$$\Rightarrow \quad [(D^2 - 4DD' + 4D'^2) - (D - 2D')]z = e^{3X+4Y}$$

$$\Rightarrow \quad (D - 2D')(D - 2D' - 1)z = e^{3X+4Y}$$

Its
$$\text{C.F.} = f_1 (Y + 2X) + e^X f_2 (Y + 2X)$$
$$= f_1 (\log y + 2 \log x) + x f_2 (\log y + 2 \log x)$$
$$= f_1 (\log yx^2) + x f_2 (\log yx^2) = g_1 (yx^2) + x g_2 (yx^2)$$

$$\text{P.I.} = \frac{1}{D - 2D' - 1}\left[\frac{1}{D - 2D'} e^{3X+4Y}\right]$$

$$= \frac{1}{D - 2D' - 1}\left[\frac{1}{3 - 8} \int e^u \, du\right] \text{ where } 3X + 4Y = u$$

$$= \frac{1}{D - 2D' - 1}\left[-\frac{1}{5} e^{3X+4Y}\right] = -\frac{1}{5}\left[\frac{1}{D - 2D' - 1} e^{3X+4Y}\right]$$

$$= -\frac{1}{5}\left[\frac{1}{3 - 8 - 1} e^{3X+4Y}\right] = \frac{1}{30} e^{3X+4Y} = \frac{1}{30} x^3 y^4.$$

Hence the complete solution is

$$z = \text{C.F.} + \text{P.I.} = g_1 (yx^2) + x g_2 (yx^2) + \frac{1}{30} x^3 y^4$$

where g_1 and g_2 are arbitrary functions.

Example 2. *Solve :* $x^2r - y^2t + px - qy = \log x.$

Sol. Let $x = e^X$, $y = e^Y$ so that $X = \log x$ and $Y = \log y$ and let $D \equiv \frac{\partial}{\partial X}$ and $D' \equiv \frac{\partial}{\partial Y}$, then the given equation reduces to

$$[D(D - 1) - D' (D' - 1) + D - D'] z = X$$

$$\Rightarrow \quad (D^2 - D'^2)z = X \qquad ...(1)$$

which is a homogeneous linear p.d.e. with constant coefficients.

$$\therefore \quad \text{C.F.} = \phi_1(Y + X) + \phi_2(Y - X)$$

and
$$\text{P.I.} = \frac{1}{D^2 - D'^2} (X) = \frac{1}{(1)^2 - (0)^2} \iint u \, du \, du \qquad \text{where } X = u$$

$$= \int \frac{u^2}{2} du = \frac{u^3}{6} = \frac{X^3}{6}$$

Hence solution to (1) is

$$z = \phi_1(Y + X) + \phi_2(Y - X) + \frac{X^3}{6}$$

$$= \phi_1(\log y + \log x) + \phi_2(\log y - \log x) + \frac{(\log x)^3}{6}.$$

Therefore the complete solution to the given differential equation is

$$z = \phi_1(\log xy) + \phi_2\left(\log \frac{y}{x}\right) + \frac{1}{6}(\log x)^3$$

$$z = f_1(xy) + f_2\left(\frac{y}{x}\right) + \frac{1}{6}(\log x)^3$$

where f_1 and f_2 are arbitrary functions.

Example 3. *Solve :*

(*i*) $x^2 \dfrac{\partial^2 z}{\partial x^2} - y^2 \dfrac{\partial^2 z}{\partial y^2} = xy$ (*ii*) $(x^2 D^2 + 2xy DD' + y^2 D'^2)z = x^m y^n$.

Sol. (*i*) Let $x = e^X$, $y = e^Y$ so that $X = \log x$ and $Y = \log y$ and Let $D \equiv \dfrac{\partial}{\partial X}$, $D' \equiv \dfrac{\partial}{\partial Y}$ and $DD' \equiv \dfrac{\partial^2}{\partial X \partial Y}$ then the given equation reduces to

$$[D(D-1) - D'(D'-1)]z = e^{X+Y}$$

$$\Rightarrow \quad (D^2 - D'^2 - D + D')z = e^{X+Y}$$

$$\Rightarrow \quad (D - D')(D + D' - 1)z = e^{X+Y}$$

$$\text{C.F.} = f_1(Y + X) + e^X f_2(Y - X)$$

$$= f_1(\log y + \log x) + x f_2(\log y - \log x) = g_1(xy) + x\, g_2\left(\frac{y}{x}\right)$$

$$\text{P.I.} = \frac{1}{(D - D')(D + D' - 1)} e^{X+Y} = \frac{1}{D - D'}\left[\frac{1}{1 + 1 - 1} e^{X+Y}\right]$$

$$= \frac{1}{D - D'} e^{X+Y} = X.e^{X+Y} = xy \log x$$

Hence the complete solution is

$$z = \text{C.F.} + \text{P.I.} = g_1(xy) + x\, g_2\left(\frac{y}{x}\right) + xy \log x$$

where g_1 and g_2 are arbitrary functions.

(*ii*) Let $x = e^X$, $y = e^Y$ so that $X = \log x$, $Y = \log y$ and Let $D \equiv \dfrac{\partial}{\partial X}$, $D' \equiv \dfrac{\partial}{\partial Y}$ and $DD' \equiv \dfrac{\partial^2}{\partial X \partial Y}$ then the given equation reduces to

$$[D(D-1) + 2DD' + D'(D'-1)]z = e^{mX+nY}$$

$$\Rightarrow \quad (D^2 + 2DD' + D'^2 - D - D')z = e^{mX+nY}$$

$$\Rightarrow \quad [(D + D')^2 - (D + D')]z = e^{mX+nY}$$

$$\Rightarrow \quad (D + D')(D + D' - 1)z = e^{mX+nY}$$

$$\therefore \quad \text{C.F.} = f_1(Y - X) + e^X f_2(Y - X)$$

$$= f_1(\log y - \log x) + x f_2(\log y - \log x)$$

$$= f_1\left(\log \frac{y}{x}\right) + x f_2\left(\log \frac{y}{x}\right) = g_1\left(\frac{y}{x}\right) + x\, g_2\left(\frac{y}{x}\right)$$

$$\text{P.I.} = \frac{1}{(D + D')(D + D' - 1)} e^{mX+nY}$$

$$= \frac{1}{(m+n)(m+n-1)} e^{mX+nY} = \frac{x^m y^n}{(m+n)(m+n-1)}$$

Hence complete solution is

$$z = \text{C.F.} + \text{P.I.} = g_1\ (y/x) + x\, g_2\ (y/x) + \frac{x^m y^n}{(m+n)(m+n-1)}$$

where g_1 and g_2 are arbitrary functions.

ASSIGNMENT-IV

(2 Marks Questions for Section–A)

1. Find the constant term if the function $f(x) = x + x^2$ is expanded in Fourier series defined in $(-1, 1)$. *(G.B.T.U. 2012)*
2. Find the particular integral of $(D^2 + DD')z = \sin(x + y)$ where $D = \frac{\partial}{\partial x}$, $D' = \frac{\partial}{\partial y}$. *(G.B.T.U. 2012)*
3. Define periodic functions and find the period of $f(x) = \cos x + \frac{1}{2} \cos 2x + \frac{1}{3} \cos 3x$. *[G.B.T.U. (AG) 2012]*
4. For an even function defined in the interval $(0, 2\pi)$, write down the Fourier series. *[G.B.T.U. (AG) 2012]*
5. Form the partial differential equation by eliminating a and b from $z = (x^2 + a)(y^2 + b)$. *[G.B.T.U. (AG) 2012]*
6. Show that $z = f(x^2 + y^2)$ is a solution of $y\frac{\partial z}{\partial x} - x\frac{\partial z}{\partial y} = 0$. *[G.B.T.U. (AG) 2012]*
7. State Dirichlet's conditions for the expansion of $f(x)$ in Fourier series. *(M.T.U. 2012)*
8. Solve: $r = t$
9. Solve: $\frac{\partial^4 z}{\partial x^4} = 0$
10. Find the P.I. of $(D^2 - D'^2)z = \cos(x + y)$.
11. Find the P.I. of $(2D^2 - 3DD' + D'^2)z = e^{x+2y}$. *[M.T.U. (SUM) 2011, G.B.T.U. 2011]*
12. Find the period of $\sin nx$. *(G.B.T.U. 2011)*
13. Solve: $(D^2 + DD')z = 0$
14. Form a partial differential equation from $z = (a + x)^2 + y$.
15. Find the solution of $xp + yq = z$.
16. Solve: $p + q = z$.
17. Solve: $(y - z)\, p + (z - x)\, q = x - y$.
18. Solve: $\frac{\partial^3 z}{\partial x^3} = 0$.
19. Find Fourier half-range sine series for the function $f(x) = x$, $0 < x < 2$. *[G.B.T.U. (SUM) 2010]*
20. What does the Fourier coefficient a_0 in Fourier series expansion of a function represent? *(G.B.T.U. 2010)*
21. Write down the auxiliary equations for the differential equation of the type $Pq + Qq = R$. *[G.B.T.U. (AG) 2010]*

22. Find the particular integral of $(D^2 - 2DD' + D'^2)z = e^{x + 2y}$ *[G.B.T.U. (AG) 2011]*

23. If $F(x) = x \sin x$ in $(-\pi, \pi)$ then find b_n.

24. What is the smallest period of the function $f(x) = \sin\left(\frac{2n\pi x}{k}\right)$.

25. If $F(x) = x^2$ in $-2 < x < 2$ and $F(x + 4) = F(x)$, then find the value of a_n.

26. Solve: $(D^3 + D^2D' - DD'^2 - D'^3)z = 0$.

27. Find the order of the partial differential eqn. obtained by eliminating F from $z = F(x^2 + y^2)$.

28. Solve: $(D^3 - 3D^2D' + 2DD'^2)z = 0$.

29. Solve: $r + 6s + 9t = 0$

30. Form a partial differential equation by eliminating the constants a and b from $z = (x + a)(y + b)$. *[M.T.U. (SUM) 2011]*

31. Solve: $p - 2q = \sin(x + 2y)$. *[U.P.T.U. (SUM) 2009]*

32. What is the general solution of I order equation $Pq + Qq = R$. *[G.B.T.U. (AG) 2011, U.P.T.U (SUM) 2009]*

33. Solve: $p - q = \log(x + y)$ *(M.T.U. 2011)*

34. What is the product of two odd functions. *(G.B.T.U. 2011)*

35. If $F(x) = x$ is expanded in a Fourier sine series in $(0, \pi)$ then find b_n. *[M.T.U. (SUM) 2011]*

36. Solve: $\frac{\partial^2 z}{\partial x \partial y} = 0$ *[G.B.T.U. (AG) 2010]*

37. If $F(x) = x \cos x$ is expanded in a Fourier series in $(-\pi, \pi)$ then find a_0. *[G.B.T.U. (AG) 2011]*

38. Write the complementary function of the partial differential equation $\frac{\partial^2 z}{\partial x^2} - \frac{\partial^2 z}{\partial y^2} = \frac{1}{x^2}$ *[G.B.T.U. (AG) 2011]*

39. Find the partial differential equation of all spheres whose centres lie on z-axis and given by equations $x^2 + y^2 + (z - a)^2 = b^2$; a and b being constants *(U.P.T.U. 2009)*

40. If $F(x) = \left.\begin{matrix} -x, & -\pi < x < 0 \\ x, & 0 < x < \pi \end{matrix}\right\}$, then find F(0). *[M.T.U. (SUM) 2011]*

Answers

1. $\frac{2}{3}$

2. $-\frac{1}{2}\sin(x + y)$

3. 2π

4. $F(x) = \frac{a_0}{2} + \sum_{n=1}^{\infty} a_n \cos nx + \sum_{n=1}^{\infty} b_n \sin nx$

5. $pq = 4xyz$

8. $z = f_1(y + x) + f_2(y - x)$

9. $z = f_1(y) + xf_2(y) + x^2f_3(y) + x^3f_4(y)$

10. $\frac{x}{2}\sin(x + y)$

11. $-\frac{x}{2}e^{x + 2y}$

12. $\frac{2\pi}{n}$

13. $z = f_1(y) + f_2(y - x)$

14. $z = \frac{1}{4}\left(\frac{\partial z}{\partial x}\right)^2 + y$

15. $f\left(\frac{x}{y}, \frac{y}{z}\right) = 0$

16. $f(x - y, y - \log z) = 0$

17. $f(x + y + z) = x^2 + y^2 + z^2$

18. $z = f_1(y) + xf_2(y) + x^2 f_3(y)$

19. $x = -\frac{4}{\pi}\sum_{n=1}^{\infty}\frac{(-1)^n}{n}\sin\frac{n\pi x}{2}$

20. Mean value of the function

21. $\frac{dx}{P} = \frac{dy}{Q} = \frac{dz}{R}$

22. $e^{x + 2y}$

23. 0

24. $\frac{k}{n}$

25. $\int_0^2 x^2 \cos\frac{n\pi x}{2}\, dx$

26. $z = f_1(y + x) + f_2(y - x) + xf_3(y - x)$

27. First

28. $z = f_1(y) + f_2(y + x) + f_3(y + 2x)$.

29. $z = f_1(y - 3x) + xf_2(y - 3x)$.

30. $z = pq$

31. $3z = \cos(x + 2y)$

32. $\phi(u, v) = 0$; $u = f_1(x, y, z)$, $v = f_2(x, y, z)$

33. $\phi[x + y, z - x \log(x + y)] = 0$

34. Even function

35. $-\frac{2}{n}(-1)^n$

36. $z = \phi(y) + \psi(x)$

37. 0

38. $z = f_1(y + x) + f_2(y - x)$

39. $x\frac{\partial z}{\partial y} - y\frac{\partial z}{\partial x} = 0$

40. 0.

UNIT 5

Classification and Applications of Partial Differential Equations

5.1. INTRODUCTION

Many physical and engineering problems when formulated in the mathematical language give rise to partial differential equations. Besides these, partial differential equations also play an important role in the theory of Elasticity, Hydraulics etc.

Since the general solution of a partial differential equation in a region R contains arbitrary constants or arbitrary functions, the unique solution of a partial differential equation corresponding to a physical problem will satisfy certain other conditions at the boundary of the region R. These are known as *boundary conditions.* When these conditions are specified for the time $t = 0$, they are known as *initial conditions.* A partial differential equation together with boundary conditions constitutes a *boundary value problem.*

In the applications of ordinary linear differential equations, we first find the general solution and then determine the arbitrary constants from the initial values. But the same method is not applicable to problems involving partial differential equations. Most of the boundary value problems involving linear partial differential equations can be solved by the method of separation of variables. In this method, right from the beginning, we try to find the particular solutions of the partial differential equation which satisfy all or some of the boundary conditions and then adjust them till the remaining conditions are also satisfied. A combination of these particular solutions gives the solution of the problem.

Fourier series is a powerful aid in determining the arbitrary functions.

5.2. CLASSIFICATION OF LINEAR PARTIAL DIFFERENTIAL EQUATIONS OF SECOND ORDER [*G.B.T.U. (C.O.) 2010; U.P.T.U. 2007*]

5.2.1. Consider the Differential Equation of Second Order in Two Independent Variables x and y as

$$A\frac{\partial^2 u}{\partial x^2} + B\frac{\partial^2 u}{\partial x \partial y} + C\frac{\partial^2 u}{\partial y^2} + f\left(x, y, u, \frac{\partial u}{\partial x}, \frac{\partial u}{\partial y}\right) = 0 \qquad ...(1)$$

where A, B, C are constants or continuous functions of x and y possessing continuous partial derivatives and A is positive.

Now equation (1) is

(*i*) **elliptic** if $B^2 - 4AC < 0$

(*ii*) **hyperbolic** if $B^2 - 4AC > 0$

(*iii*) **parabolic** if $B^2 - 4AC = 0$

e.g., one dimensional wave equation $z_{xx} = z_{tt}$ is a hyperbolic equation.

One dimensional heat flow equation $u_t = u_{xx}$ is parabolic type.
while the two dimensional heat flow equation in steady state given by $z_{xx} + z_{yy} = 0$ is elliptic in nature.

Remark 1. If A, B, C in the given eqn. (1) are constants, then nature of eqn. (1) will be the same in whole region *i.e.*, for all values of x and y.

Remark 2. If A, B, C are functions of x and y in the given eqn. (1), then nature of eqn. (1) will not be the same in the whole region *i.e.*, for all values of x and y.

ILLUSTRATIVE EXAMPLES

Example 1. *Classify the following operators :*

(*i*) $\frac{\partial^2 u}{\partial x^2} + \frac{\partial^2 u}{\partial x \partial t} + \frac{\partial^2 u}{\partial t^2}$ (*ii*) $4\frac{\partial^2 u}{\partial x^2} + 4\frac{\partial^2 u}{\partial x\,\partial t} + \frac{\partial^2 u}{\partial t^2}$ (*iii*) $5\frac{\partial^2 u}{\partial x^2} - 9\frac{\partial^2 u}{\partial x\,\partial t} + 4\frac{\partial^2 u}{\partial t^2}$.

Sol. (*i*) Here the dependent variable u is a function of two independent variables x and t only.

Here $\qquad A = 1, B = 1, C = 1$

$\therefore \qquad B^2 - 4AC = (1)^2 - 4(1)(1) = 1 - 4 = -3 < 0$

Hence the given operator is elliptic.

(*ii*) Here $\qquad A = 4, B = 4, C = 1$

$\therefore \qquad B^2 - 4AC = (4)^2 - 4(4)(1) = 16 - 16 = 0$

Hence the given operator is parabolic.

(*iii*) Here $\qquad A = 5, B = -9, C = 4$

$\therefore \qquad B^2 - 4AC = (-9)^2 - 4(5)(4) = 81 - 80 = 1 > 0$

Hence the given operator is hyperbolic.

Note. Coefficient of $\frac{\partial^2 u}{\partial t^2}$ or u_{tt} may be taken as A.

Example 2. *Find whether the following operators are hyperbolic, parabolic and elliptic ?*

(*i*) $x^2\frac{\partial^2 u}{\partial t^2} - \frac{\partial^2 u}{\partial x^2} + u$ (*ii*) $t\frac{\partial^2 u}{\partial t^2} + 2\frac{\partial^2 u}{\partial x\,\partial t} + x\frac{\partial^2 u}{\partial x^2} + \frac{\partial u}{\partial x}$

(*iii*) $x\frac{\partial^2 u}{\partial x^2} + t\frac{\partial^2 u}{\partial x\,\partial t} + \frac{\partial^2 u}{\partial t^2}$.

Sol. (*i*) Here $\qquad A = x^2, B = 0, C = -1$

Now, $\qquad B^2 - 4AC = (0)^2 - 4x^2(-1) = 4x^2$

$\therefore$ The operator is hyperbolic if $4x^2 > 0$ *i.e.*, $x > 0$

parabolic if $4x^2 = 0$ *i.e.*, $x = 0$

Since $4x^2$ being a square, cannot be negative hence operator cannot be elliptic.

(*ii*) Here $\qquad A = t, B = 2, C = x$

Now, $\qquad B^2 - 4AC = 4 - 4tx$

$\therefore$ The operator is hyperbolic if $4 - 4tx > 0$ *i.e.*, $tx < 1$

elliptic if $4 - 4tx < 0$ *i.e.*, $tx > 1$

and parabolic if $4 - 4tx = 0$ *i.e.*, $tx = 1$.

(*iii*) Here $\qquad A = x, B = t, C = 1$

Now $\qquad B^2 - 4AC = (t)^2 - 4(x)(1) = t^2 - 4x$

∴ The operator is hyperbolic if $t^2 - 4x > 0$ *i.e.*, $t^2 > 4x$

elliptic if $t^2 - 4x < 0$ *i.e.*, $t^2 < 4x$

and parabolic if $t^2 - 4x = 0$ *i.e.*, $t^2 = 4x$.

Example 3. *Classify the following differential equation as to type in the second quadrant of xy-plane*

$$\sqrt{y^2 + x^2}\, u_{xx} + 2(x - y)\, u_{xy} + \sqrt{y^2 + x^2}\, u_{yy} = 0.$$

Sol. Here $A = \sqrt{y^2 + x^2}$, $B = 2(x - y)$, $C = \sqrt{y^2 + x^2}$

Now $B^2 - 4AC = 4(x - y)^2 - 4(y^2 + x^2) = -8xy$

In second quadrant, y is +ve while x is –ve

∴ $B^2 - 4AC = +\text{ve} > 0$

∴ Differential equation is hyperbolic.

Example 4. *Show that the equation* $\dfrac{\partial^2 u}{\partial t^2} = c^2 \dfrac{\partial^2 u}{\partial x^2}$ *is hyperbolic.*

Sol. The given differential equation is

$$\frac{\partial^2 u}{\partial t^2} - c^2 \frac{\partial^2 u}{\partial x^2} = 0$$

Here, $A = 1,\ B = 0,\ C = -c^2$

Now, $B^2 - 4AC = (0)^2 - 4\,(1)\,(-c^2) = 4c^2$

which is always greater than zero.

Hence, $B^2 - 4AC > 0$

∴ The given equation is hyperbolic.

Example 5. *Classify the partial differential equation*

$$\frac{\partial^2 u}{\partial t^2} + t\frac{\partial^2 u}{\partial x\, \partial t} + x\frac{\partial^2 u}{\partial x^2} + 2\frac{\partial u}{\partial t} + \frac{\partial u}{\partial x} + 6u = 0.$$

Sol. Here, $A = 1,\ B = t,\ C = x.$

Now, $B^2 - 4AC = t^2 - 4(1)(x) = t^2 - 4x.$

The equation is elliptic if $t^2 - 4x < 0.$

The equation is parabolic if $t^2 - 4x = 0.$

The equation is hyperbolic if $t^2 - 4x > 0.$

Example 6. *Classify the partial differential equation*

$$x^2\frac{\partial^2 u}{\partial t^2} + 3\frac{\partial^2 u}{\partial x\, \partial t} + x\frac{\partial^2 u}{\partial x^2} + 17\frac{\partial u}{\partial t} = 100u.$$

Sol. Here, $A = x^2,\ B = 3,\ C = x.$

Now, $B^2 - 4AC = (3)^2 - 4x^2.x = 9 - 4x^3.$

The equation is elliptic if $9 - 4x^3 < 0.$

The equation is parabolic if $9 - 4x^3 = 0.$

The equation is hyperbolic if $9 - 4x^3 > 0.$

Example 7. (*i*) *Show that the equation* $u_{xx} + xu_{yy} + u_y = 0$ *is elliptic for* $x > 0$ *and hyperbolic for* $x < 0$.

(*ii*) *Show that the equation* $z_{xx} + 2xz_{xy} + (1 - y^2)\, z_{yy} = 0$ *is elliptic for values of x and y in the region* $x^2 + y^2 < 1$, *parabolic on the boundary and hyperbolic outside this region.*

(U.K.T.U. 2011)

Sol. (*i*) Here, $A = 1,\ B = 0,\ C = x$

Now, $B^2 - 4AC = -4x$

Equation is elliptic if $B^2 - 4AC < 0$

i.e., if $-4x < 0$ or if $x > 0$

and equation is hyperbolic if $B^2 - 4AC > 0$

i.e., if $-4x > 0$ or if $x < 0$

(*ii*) Here, $A = 1,\ B = 2x,\ C = 1 - y^2$

Now, $B^2 - 4AC = 4x^2 - 4(1 - y^2) = 4(x^2 + y^2 - 1)$

Equation is elliptic if $B^2 - 4AC < 0$

i.e., if $4(x^2 + y^2 - 1) < 0$ or if $x^2 + y^2 < 1$

Parabolic if $B^2 - 4AC = 0$

i.e., if $4(x^2 + y^2 - 1) = 0$ or if $x^2 + y^2 = 1$ (on the boundary)

and hyperbolic if $B^2 - 4AC > 0$

i.e., if $4(x^2 + y^2 - 1) > 0$ or if $x^2 + y^2 > 1$

TEST YOUR KNOWLEDGE

1. Classify the following operators :

(*i*) $4\dfrac{\partial^2 u}{\partial x^2} - 4\dfrac{\partial^2 u}{\partial x\,\partial t} + \dfrac{\partial^2 u}{\partial t^2}$ (*ii*) $t\dfrac{\partial^2 u}{\partial t^2} + 3\dfrac{\partial^2 u}{\partial x\,\partial t} + x\dfrac{\partial^2 u}{\partial x^2} + 17\dfrac{\partial u}{\partial x}$.

2. Classify the following differential equations :

(*a*) $z_{xx} = z_{yy}$ (*b*) $z_{xx} + z_{yy} = 0$ (*c*) $z_{xx} = z_y$ (*d*) $u_{xx} + 3u_{xy} + u_{yy} = 0$. (*M.T.U. 2012*)

3. Classify the equation : $(1 - x^2)\dfrac{\partial^2 z}{\partial x^2} - 2xy\dfrac{\partial^2 z}{\partial x\,\partial y} + (1 - y^2)\dfrac{\partial^2 z}{\partial y^2} + x\dfrac{\partial z}{\partial x} + 3x^2y\dfrac{\partial z}{\partial y} - 2z = 0$.

4. Classify the equation : $y^2r - 2xys + x^2t = \dfrac{y^2}{z}p + \dfrac{x^2}{y}q$.

5. Characterize the following partial differential equations into elliptic, parabolic and hyperbolic equations $A\dfrac{\partial^2 u}{\partial x^2} + 2B\dfrac{\partial^2 u}{\partial x\partial y} + C\dfrac{\partial^2 u}{\partial y^2} = F(x, y, u, u_x, u_y)$. Here A, B, C may be functions of x and y.

(*U.P.T.U. 2007*)

6. Give a consize description of the classification of linear partial differential equations of second order with constant coefficients. Give examples of each type of partial differential equations.

[*G.B.T.U. (C.O.) 2010*]

Answers

1. (*i*) parabolic (*ii*) hyperbolic if $xt < \dfrac{9}{4}$, parabolic if $xt = \dfrac{9}{4}$, elliptic if $xt > \dfrac{9}{4}$

2. (*a*) hyperbolic (*b*) elliptic (*c*) parabolic (*d*) hyperbolic

3. hyperbolic in the region $x^2 + y^2 > 1$, parabolic at points on $x^2 + y^2 = 1$, and elliptic in the region $x^2 + y^2 < 1$

4. parabolic.

5.2.2. Consider a Linear P.D.E. of II Order in Three Independent Variables x, y, z as

$$a_{11}\frac{\partial^2 u}{\partial x^2}+a_{12}\frac{\partial^2 u}{\partial x\,\partial y}+a_{13}\frac{\partial^2 u}{\partial x\,\partial z}+a_{21}\frac{\partial^2 u}{\partial y\,\partial x}+a_{22}\frac{\partial^2 u}{\partial y^2}+a_{23}\frac{\partial^2 u}{\partial y\,\partial z}+a_{31}\frac{\partial^2 u}{\partial z\,\partial x}+a_{32}\frac{\partial^2 u}{\partial z\,\partial y}$$

$$+a_{33}\frac{\partial^2 u}{\partial z^2}+b_1\frac{\partial u}{\partial x}+b_2\frac{\partial u}{\partial y}+b_3\frac{\partial u}{\partial z}+cu=0 \qquad ...(1)$$

where a_{ij}, b_i and c are constants or some functions of x, y, z.

Eqn. (1) may be rewritten in the form

$$\sum_{i,j=1}^{3} a_{ij}\frac{\partial^2 u}{\partial x_i\,\partial x_j}+\sum_{i=1}^{3} b_i\frac{\partial u}{\partial x_i}+cu=0 \qquad ...(2)$$

In general, when there are n independent variables $x_1, x_2, x_3, \ldots\ldots, x_n$; we may write as

$$\sum_{i,j=1}^{n} a_{ij}\frac{\partial^2 u}{\partial x_i\,\partial x_j}+\sum_{i=1}^{n} b_i\frac{\partial u}{\partial x_i}+cu=0 \qquad ...(3)$$

Now, let $\delta_i \equiv \dfrac{\partial}{\partial x_i}$ $(1 \le i \le n)$ and $\delta_i\delta_j \equiv \dfrac{\partial^2}{\partial x_i\,\partial x_j}$ $(1 \le i \le n,\ 1 \le j \le n)$

Consider $\phi = \displaystyle\sum_{i=1}^{n}\sum_{j=1}^{n} a_{ij}\,\delta_i\delta_j$ for all real values of δ_i positive or negative.

At any point $x_1, x_2, \ldots\ldots, x_n$; differential equation (3) is said to be

(*i*) parabolic if Δ vanishes, where $\Delta = \begin{vmatrix} a_{11} & a_{12} \ldots\ldots & a_{1n} \\ a_{21} & a_{22} \ldots\ldots & a_{2n} \\ \vdots & \vdots \quad \vdots & \vdots \\ \vdots & \vdots \quad \vdots & \vdots \\ a_{n1} & a_{n2} \ldots\ldots & a_{nn} \end{vmatrix}$.

(*ii*) elliptic if ϕ is positive for all real values of δ_i and it reduces to zero only when all δ_i's are zero.

(*iii*) hyperbolic if ϕ can be both positive or negative.

Note. If a_{ij} are functions of $x_1, x_2, \ldots, x_n$ the same differential equation can be elliptic, hyperbolic and parabolic at different points while if a_{ij} are constant, the equation will have the same nature throughout.

ILLUSTRATIVE EXAMPLES

Example 1. *Classify the following equation* : $\dfrac{\partial^2 u}{\partial x^2}+\dfrac{\partial^2 u}{\partial y^2}+\dfrac{\partial^2 u}{\partial z^2}=\dfrac{1}{c^2}\dfrac{\partial u}{\partial t}$.

Sol. Here,
$$a_{11}=1,\ a_{22}=1,\ a_{33}=1,\ a_{44}=0$$
$$a_{13}=a_{23}=a_{31}=a_{24}=a_{34}=0, \text{ etc.}$$

$$\Delta=\begin{vmatrix} 1 & 0 & 0 & 0 \\ 0 & 1 & 0 & 0 \\ 0 & 0 & 1 & 0 \\ 0 & 0 & 0 & 0 \end{vmatrix}=0$$

Hence the given differential equation is parabolic.

Example 2. *Classify the equation :* $u_{xx} + 2u_{yy} + u_{zz} = 2u_{xy} + 2u_{yz}$.

Sol. Here, $a_{11} = 1, a_{12} = -2, a_{13} = 0, a_{21} = 0, a_{22} = 2,$
$a_{23} = -2, a_{31} = 0, a_{32} = 0, a_{33} = 1$

$$\therefore \quad \Delta = \begin{vmatrix} 1 & -2 & 0 \\ 0 & 2 & -2 \\ 0 & 0 & 1 \end{vmatrix} \neq 0$$

$$\therefore \quad \phi = \delta_1^2 - 2\delta_1\delta_2 + 2\delta_2^2 - 2\delta_2\delta_3 + \delta_3^2 = (\delta_1 - \delta_2)^2 + (\delta_2 - \delta_3)^2$$

which is definite positive for all real values of $\delta_1, \delta_2, \delta_3$.

Hence the equation is elliptic.

TEST YOUR KNOWLEDGE

Classify the following equations :

1. $u_{xx} + u_{yy} + u_{zz} = 0$
2. $u_{xx} + u_{yy} = u_z$
3. $u_{xx} + u_{yy} = u_{zz}$
4. $u_{xx} + u_{yy} + u_{zx} + 2u_{yz} = 0.$

Answers

1. Elliptic
2. Parabolic
3. Hyperbolic
4. Parabolic.

5.3. METHOD OF SEPARATION OF VARIABLES (*M.T.U. 2012; U.P.T.U. 2007*)

In this method, we assume the solution to be the product of two functions, each of which involves only one of the variables. The following examples explain the method.

ILLUSTRATIVE EXAMPLES

Example 1. *Use the method of separation of variables to solve the equation*

$$\frac{\partial u}{\partial x} = 2\frac{\partial u}{\partial t} + u, \text{ given that } u(x, 0) = 6e^{-3x}.$$

[G.B.T.U. (SUM) 2010; G.B.T.U. (AG) 2011; U.P.T.U. 2006]

Sol. The given equation is

$$\frac{\partial u}{\partial x} = 2\frac{\partial u}{\partial t} + u \quad \text{...(1)}$$

Let $u = XT$ ...(2)

where X is a function of x only and T is a function of t only

Then,
$$\frac{\partial u}{\partial x} = \frac{\partial}{\partial x}(XT) = T\frac{dX}{dx}$$
$$\frac{\partial u}{\partial t} = \frac{\partial}{\partial t}(XT) = X\frac{dT}{dt}.$$

Substituting in eqn. (1), we get

$$T\frac{dX}{dx} = 2X\frac{dT}{dt} + XT$$

$$\Rightarrow \quad TX' = 2XT' + XT$$

$$\Rightarrow \quad TX' = X(2T' + T)$$

$$\Rightarrow \qquad \frac{X'}{X} = \frac{2T'}{T} + 1 = -p^2 \text{ (say)}$$

(*i*)
$$\frac{X'}{X} = -p^2$$

$$\frac{dX}{dx} + p^2X = 0$$

$$\frac{dX}{X} = -p^2\,dx$$

Integration yields

$$\log X = -p^2x + \log c_1$$

$$\Rightarrow \qquad X = c_1\,e^{-p^2x} \qquad \text{...(3)}$$

(*ii*)
$$\frac{2T'}{T} = -(p^2 + 1)$$

$$\frac{dT}{T} = -\left(\frac{p^2+1}{2}\right)dt.$$

Integration yields, $\log T = -\left(\frac{p^2+1}{2}\right)t + \log c_2$

$$T = c_2\,e^{-\left(\frac{p^2+1}{2}\right)t} \qquad \text{...(4)}$$

From (2), (3) and (4), we get

$$u = XT = c_1c_2\,e^{-p^2x-\left(\frac{p^2+1}{2}\right)t}$$

or
$$u(x, t) = c_1c_2\,e^{-p^2x-\left(\frac{p^2+1}{2}\right)t} \qquad \text{...(5)}$$

$$u(x, 0) = c_1c_2\,e^{-p^2x}.$$

$$\Rightarrow \qquad 6e^{-3x} = c_1c_2\,e^{-p^2x}$$

Comparison gives, $c_1c_2 = 6$ and $p^2 = 3$.

Hence from (5), we get

$$u(x, t) = 6e^{-3x-2t}.$$

Example 2. *Use the method of separation of variables to solve the equation*

$$\frac{\partial^2 u}{\partial x^2} - 2\frac{\partial u}{\partial x} + \frac{\partial u}{\partial y} = 0.$$

[U.P.T.U. 2009; G.B.T.U. (A.G.) 2012]

Sol. Let
$$u = XY \qquad \text{...(1)}$$

where X is a function of x only and Y is a function of y only.

$$\frac{\partial u}{\partial x} = \frac{\partial}{\partial x}(XY) = Y\frac{dX}{dx}$$

$$\frac{\partial u}{\partial y} = \frac{\partial}{\partial y}(XY) = X\frac{dY}{dy}$$

$$\frac{\partial^2 u}{\partial x^2} = \frac{\partial^2}{\partial x^2}(XY) = Y\frac{d^2X}{dx^2}.$$

Substituting these values in (1), we get

$$Y\frac{d^2X}{dx^2} - 2Y\frac{dX}{dx} + X\frac{dY}{dy} = 0$$

$$\Rightarrow \qquad YX'' - 2YX' + XY' = 0$$

$$\Rightarrow \qquad \frac{X'' - 2X'}{X} + \frac{Y'}{Y} = 0$$

$$\Rightarrow \qquad \frac{X'' - 2X'}{X} = -\frac{Y'}{Y} = -p^2 \text{ (say)}$$

(*i*)
$$\frac{X'' - 2X'}{X} = -p^2$$

$$\Rightarrow \qquad X'' - 2X' + p^2 X = 0.$$

Auxiliary equation is $m^2 - 2m + p^2 = 0$

$$\Rightarrow \qquad m = \frac{2 \pm \sqrt{4 - 4p^2}}{2} = 1 \pm \sqrt{1 - p^2}$$

$$\therefore \qquad \text{C.F.} = c_1 e^{(1+\sqrt{1-p^2})x} + c_2 e^{(1-\sqrt{1-p^2})x}$$

$$\text{P.I.} = 0.$$

Hence, $X = \text{C.F.} + \text{P.I.} = c_1 e^{(1+\sqrt{1-p^2})x} + c_2 e^{(1-\sqrt{1-p^2})x}$ ...(2)

(*ii*)
$$-\frac{Y'}{Y} = -p^2 \Rightarrow \frac{dY}{dy} = p^2 Y \Rightarrow \frac{dY}{Y} = p^2 dy.$$

Integration yields, $\log Y = p^2 y + \log c_3$

$$Y = c_3 e^{p^2 y} \qquad ...(3)$$

$$\therefore \qquad u(x, y) = [c_1 e^{(1+\sqrt{1-p^2})x} + c_2 e^{(1-\sqrt{1-p^2})x}]\, c_3 e^{p^2 y}.$$

Example 3. *Use the method of separation of variables to solve the equation*

$$\frac{\partial^2 u}{\partial x^2} = \frac{\partial u}{\partial y} + 2u.$$

Sol. Let $u = XY$ ...(1)

where X is a function of x only and Y is a function of y only.

$$\frac{\partial u}{\partial y} = \frac{\partial}{\partial y}(XY) = X\frac{dY}{dy}$$

$$\frac{\partial^2 u}{\partial x^2} = \frac{\partial^2}{\partial x^2}(XY) = Y\frac{d^2X}{dx^2}.$$

From (1),
$$Y\frac{d^2X}{dx^2} = X\frac{dY}{dy} + 2XY$$

$\Rightarrow \qquad YX'' = XY' + 2XY = X(Y' + 2Y)$

$\Rightarrow \qquad \dfrac{X''}{X} = \dfrac{Y'}{Y} + 2 = -p^2$ (say)

(*i*) $\qquad \dfrac{X''}{X} = -p^2 \Rightarrow \dfrac{d^2X}{dx^2} + p^2X = 0$

Auxiliary eqn. is $m^2 + p^2 = 0$

$m = \pm pi$

$\therefore \qquad$ C.F. $= c_1 \cos px + c_2 \sin px$

P.I. $= 0$

$\therefore \qquad X = c_1 \cos px + c_2 \sin px \qquad ...(2)$

(*ii*) $\qquad \dfrac{Y'}{Y} + 2 = -p^2$

$\dfrac{Y'}{Y} = -(p^2 + 2)$

$\dfrac{dY}{Y} = -(p^2 + 2)\, dy.$

Integration yields, $\log Y = -(p^2 + 2)\, y + \log c_3$

$\Rightarrow \qquad Y = c_3\, e^{-(p^2+2)y} \qquad ...(3)$

$\therefore \qquad u(x, y) = (c_1 \cos px + c_2 \sin px)\, c_3\, e^{-(p^2+2)y}.$

Example 4. *Solve by the method of separation of variables :*

$$4\frac{\partial u}{\partial t} + \frac{\partial u}{\partial x} = 3u, \quad u = 3e^{-x} - e^{-5x}, \quad \textit{when } t = 0.$$

Sol. Let $\qquad u = XT \qquad ...(1)$

where X is a function of x only and T is a function of t only.

$\therefore \qquad \dfrac{\partial u}{\partial t} = \dfrac{\partial}{\partial t}(XT) = X\dfrac{dT}{dt} = XT'$ (say)

$\dfrac{\partial u}{\partial x} = \dfrac{\partial}{\partial x}(XT) = T\dfrac{dX}{dx} = TX'$ (say)

$\therefore$ From the given equation

$4XT' + TX' = 3XT$

$\dfrac{4T'}{T} + \dfrac{X'}{X} = 3$

$\dfrac{4T'}{T} - 3 = -\dfrac{X'}{X} = p^2$ (say) $\qquad ...(2)$

(*i*) $\qquad \dfrac{4T'}{T} = p^2 + 3$

$$\frac{dT}{T} = \left(\frac{3+p^2}{4}\right) dt$$

Integration yields,

$$\log T = \left(\frac{3+p^2}{4}\right) t + \log c_1 \quad \Rightarrow \quad T = c_1 e^{\left(\frac{3+p^2}{4}\right)t} \qquad \text{...(3)}$$

(ii) $$\frac{-X'}{X} = p^2 \quad \Rightarrow \quad \frac{X'}{X} = -p^2 \quad \Rightarrow \quad \frac{dX}{X} = -p^2\, dx$$

Integration yields,

$$\log X = -p^2 x + \log c_2$$

$$X = c_2\, e^{-p^2 x} \qquad \text{...(4)}$$

From (1), we get

$$u = XT = c_1 c_2\, e^{-p^2 x + \left(\frac{3+p^2}{4}\right)t}$$

or $$u(x, t) = b_n\, e^{-p^2 x + \left(\frac{3+p^2}{4}\right)t}$$

Most general solution is

$$u(x, t) = \sum_{n=1}^{\infty} b_n\, e^{-p^2 x + \left(\frac{3+p^2}{4}\right)t} \qquad \text{...(5)}$$

when $t = 0$, $$u(x, 0) = 3e^{-x} - e^{-5x} = \sum_{n=1}^{\infty} b_n\, e^{-p^2 x}$$

Comparing, when $p^2 = 1,\ b_1 = 3$ and when $p^2 = 5,\ b_2 = -1$

Hence, from (5), general solution is

$$u(x, t) = 3e^{-x+t} - e^{-5x+2t}$$

Example 5. *Use the method of separation of variables to solve the equation*

$\frac{\partial^2 v}{\partial x^2} = \frac{\partial v}{\partial t}$ *given that $v = 0$ when $t \to \infty$ as well as $v = 0$ at $x = 0$ and $x = l$.*

Sol. Let $v = XT$ ...(1)

where X is a function of x only and T is a function of t only.

$$\frac{\partial v}{\partial t} = \frac{\partial}{\partial t}(XT) = X\frac{dT}{dt} = XT' \text{ (say)}$$

$$\frac{\partial^2 v}{\partial x^2} = \frac{\partial^2}{\partial x^2}(XT) = T\frac{d^2X}{dx^2} = TX'' \text{ (say)}$$

From the given equation

$$TX'' = XT'$$

$$\Rightarrow \quad \frac{T'}{T} = \frac{X''}{X} = -p^2 \text{ (say)} \qquad \text{...(2)}$$

(*i*) $$\frac{T'}{T} = -p^2 \Rightarrow \frac{dT}{T} = -p^2\, dt$$

Integration yields,

$$\log T = -p^2t + \log c_1 \Rightarrow T = c_1 e^{-p^2t} \quad ...(3)$$

(*ii*) $$\frac{X''}{X} = -p^2 \Rightarrow X'' + p^2X = 0$$

Auxiliary eqn. is $m^2 + p^2 = 0 \Rightarrow m = \pm pi$

$$\text{C.F.} = c_2 \cos px + c_3 \sin px$$

$$\text{P.I.} = 0$$

$\therefore$ $$X = c_2 \cos px + c_3 \sin px \quad ...(4)$$

Hence $$v = XT = c_1 e^{-p^2t} (c_2 \cos px + c_3 \sin px) \quad ...(5)$$

Putting $x = 0$, $v = 0$ in (5), we get

$$0 = c_1\, e^{-p^2t} \cdot c_2$$

$\therefore$ $$c_2 = 0 \quad (\because \ c_1 \neq 0)$$

Hence from (5), $$v = c_1c_3e^{-p^2t} \sin px \quad ...(6)$$

At $x = l$, $v = 0$

$\therefore$ From (6), $$0 = c_1c_3e^{-p^2t} \sin pl$$

$\Rightarrow$ $$\sin pl = 0 = \sin n\pi \quad (\because \ c_3 \neq 0)$$

$$p = \frac{n\pi}{l},\ n \in I$$

$\therefore$ From (6), $$v = c_1c_3\, e^{-\frac{n^2\pi^2t}{l^2}} \sin \frac{n\pi x}{l} = b_n \sin \frac{n\pi x}{l} \cdot e^{-\left(\frac{n^2\pi^2}{l^2}\right)t} \quad ...(7)$$

The above equation (7) satisfies the given conditions for all values of n. Hence the most general solution is

$$v = \sum_{n=1}^{\infty} b_n\, e^{-\left(\frac{n^2\pi^2}{l^2}\right)t} \sin \frac{n\pi x}{l}.$$

Example 6. *Solve the following equation by the method of separation of variables*

$$\frac{\partial^2 u}{\partial x\, \partial t} = e^{-t} \cos x$$

given that $u = 0$ *when* $t = 0$ *and* $\frac{\partial u}{\partial t} = 0$ *when* $x = 0$.

[U.P.T.U. (SUM) 2008; G.B.T.U. 2012; G.B.T.U. (A.G.) 2012)]

Sol. Let $$u = XT \quad ...(1)$$

where X is a function of x only and T is a function of t only.

Then, $$\frac{\partial u}{\partial t} = \frac{\partial}{\partial t}(XT) = X\frac{dT}{dt}$$

$\therefore$ $$\frac{\partial^2 u}{\partial x \partial t} = \frac{\partial}{\partial x}\left(X\frac{dT}{dt}\right) = \frac{dT}{dt} \cdot \frac{dX}{dx} \quad ...(2)$$

Substituting (2) in the given equation, we get

$$\frac{dT}{dt}\frac{dX}{dx} = e^{-t}\cos x$$

$$e^{t}\frac{dT}{dt} = \frac{\cos x}{\left(\frac{dX}{dx}\right)} = -p^2 \text{ (say)} \qquad ...(3)$$

Now, $$e^{t}\frac{dT}{dt} = -p^2$$

$\Rightarrow$ $$dT = -p^2e^{-t}\,dt$$

Integration yields,

$$T = p^2e^{-t} + c_1 \qquad ...(4)$$

Also, $$\frac{dX}{dx} = -\frac{1}{p^2}\cos x$$

$$dX = -\frac{1}{p^2}\cos x\,dx$$

Integration yields,

$$X = -\frac{1}{p^2}\sin x + c_2 \qquad ...(5)$$

Using (4) and (5), we get from (1),

$$u(x, t) = XT = \left(-\frac{1}{p^2}\sin x + c_2\right)(p^2e^{-t} + c_1) \qquad ...(6)$$

Applying the condition $u = 0$ when $t = 0$ in (6), we get

$$0 = \left(-\frac{1}{p^2}\sin x + c_2\right)(p^2 + c_1)$$

$\Rightarrow$ $$p^2 + c_1 = 0 \Rightarrow c_1 = -p^2$$

From (6), $$\frac{\partial u}{\partial t} = \left(-\frac{1}{p^2}\sin x + c_2\right)(-p^2e^{-t}) \qquad ...(7)$$

Applying the condition $\frac{\partial u}{\partial t} = 0$ when $x = 0$ in (7), we get

$$0 = c_2(-p^2e^{-t})$$

$\Rightarrow$ $$c_2 = 0$$

Substituting the values of c_1 and c_2 in (6), we get

$$u(x, t) = -\frac{1}{p^2}\sin x\,(p^2e^{-t} - p^2) = \sin x\,(1 - e^{-t})$$

Example 7. *Solve the P.D.E. by separation of variables method,*

$$u_{xx} = u_y + 2u,\ u(0, y) = 0,\ \frac{\partial}{\partial x} u(0, y) = 1 + e^{-3y}.$$

(G.B.T.U. 2010; U.P.T.U. 2009)

Sol. Let $\qquad u = XY \qquad$ ...(1)

where X is a function of x only and Y is a function of y only.

$$\therefore \qquad \frac{\partial u}{\partial y} = \frac{\partial}{\partial y}(XY) = X\frac{dY}{dy} = XY'$$

$$\frac{\partial^2 u}{\partial x^2} = \frac{\partial^2}{\partial x^2}(XY) = Y\frac{d^2X}{dx^2} = YX''$$

From the given equation,

$$YX'' = XY' + 2XY$$

$$\frac{X''}{X} = \frac{Y' + 2Y}{Y}$$

$$\Rightarrow \qquad \frac{X''}{X} = \frac{Y'}{Y} + 2 = k(\text{say}) \qquad \text{...(2)}$$

(*i*) $\qquad \dfrac{X''}{X} = k$

$$\Rightarrow \qquad X'' - kX = 0$$

Auxiliary equation is

$$m^2 - k = 0$$

$$\Rightarrow \qquad m = \pm\sqrt{k}$$

$$\therefore \qquad \text{C.F.} = C_1 e^{\sqrt{k}x} + C_2 e^{-\sqrt{k}x}$$

$$\text{P.I.} = 0$$

$$\therefore \qquad X = C_1 e^{\sqrt{k}x} + C_2 e^{-\sqrt{k}x} \qquad \text{...(3)}$$

(*ii*) $\qquad \dfrac{Y'}{Y} + 2 = k$

$$\Rightarrow \qquad \frac{Y'}{Y} = k - 2$$

$$\Rightarrow \qquad \frac{dY}{Y} = (k-2)\,dy$$

Integration yields,

$$\log Y = (k-2)y + \log C_3$$

$$\Rightarrow \qquad Y = C_3 e^{(k-2)y} \qquad \text{...(4)}$$

Hence from (1),

$$u(x, y) = (C_1 e^{\sqrt{k}x} + C_2 e^{-\sqrt{k}x})\, C_3 e^{(k-2)y} \qquad \text{...(5)}$$

Applying the condition $u(0, y) = 0$ in (5), we get

$$u(0, y) = 0 = (C_1 + C_2)\, C_3 e^{(k-2)y}$$

$$\Rightarrow \qquad C_1 + C_2 = 0 \;\Rightarrow\; C_2 = -C_1 \qquad ...(6)$$

From (5), most general solution is

$$u(x, y) = \Sigma\, C_1C_3(e^{\sqrt{k}x} - e^{-\sqrt{k}x})\, e^{(k-2)y} \qquad ...(7)$$

$$\frac{\partial u}{\partial x} = \Sigma\, C_1C_3\sqrt{k}(e^{\sqrt{k}x} + e^{-\sqrt{k}x})\, e^{(k-2)y}$$

$$\left(\frac{\partial u}{\partial x}\right)_{x=0} = 1 + e^{-3y} = \Sigma C_1C_3\sqrt{k}(2)\, e^{(k-2)y} = \sum_{n=1}^{\infty} b_n\, e^{(k-2)y}$$

Comparing the coefficients, we get

(*i*) $b_1 = 1, \quad k - 2 = 0$

$$2C_1C_3\sqrt{k} = 1, \quad k = 2$$

$$\therefore \qquad C_1C_3 = \frac{1}{2\sqrt{2}}$$

(*ii*) $b_3 = -1, \quad k - 2 = -3$

$$2C_1C_3\sqrt{k} = 1, \quad k = -1$$

$$\therefore \qquad C_1C_3 = \frac{1}{2i}$$

Hence from (6), the particular solution is

$$u(x, y) = \frac{1}{2\sqrt{2}}(e^{\sqrt{2}x} - e^{-\sqrt{2}x}) + \frac{1}{2i}(e^{ix} - e^{-ix})\, e^{-3y}$$

$$\Rightarrow \qquad u(x, y) = \frac{1}{\sqrt{2}} \sinh \sqrt{2}\, x + e^{-3y} \sin x.$$

TEST YOUR KNOWLEDGE

Solve by the method of separation of variables :

1. $3\dfrac{\partial u}{\partial x} + 2\dfrac{\partial u}{\partial y} = 0;\ u(x, 0) = 4e^{-x}$
2. $\dfrac{\partial u}{\partial x} = 4\dfrac{\partial u}{\partial y};\ u(0, y) = 8e^{-3y}$ (*U.P.T.U. 2008*)
3. $4\dfrac{\partial u}{\partial x} + \dfrac{\partial u}{\partial y} = 3u;\ u(0, y) = 4e^{-y} - e^{-5y}$ (*U.K.T.U. 2012*)
4. $\dfrac{\partial u}{\partial t} = \dfrac{\partial u}{\partial x} - 2u;\ u(x, 0) = 10e^{-x} - 6e^{-4x}$
5. $y^3\dfrac{\partial u}{\partial x} + x^2\dfrac{\partial u}{\partial y} = 0$ (*G.B.T.U. 2011*)
6. $\dfrac{\partial^2 u}{\partial x^2} - \dfrac{\partial u}{\partial y} = 0.$ [*U.P.T.U. (SUM) 2007*]
7. $\dfrac{\partial u}{\partial x} = \dfrac{\partial u}{\partial y}$ (*G.B.T.U. 2012*)
8. $\dfrac{\partial z}{\partial x} + \dfrac{\partial^2 z}{\partial y^2} = 0;\ z(x, 0) = 0,\ z(x, \pi) = 0,\ z(0, y) = 4 \sin 3y$ (*M.T.U. 2012*)

Answers

1. $u(x, y) = 4e^{-x+\frac{3}{2}y}$
2. $u(x, y) = 8e^{-3y-12x}$
3. $u(x, y) = 4e^{x-y} - e^{2x-5y}$
4. $u(x, t) = 10\, e^{-(x+3t)} - 6e^{-2(2x+3t)}$
5. $u(x, y) = c_1c_2\, e^{p^2\left(\frac{y^4}{4}-\frac{x^3}{3}\right)}$
6. $u(x, y) = c_1\, e^{-p^2y}(c_2 \cos px + c_3 \sin px)$
7. $u(x, y) = c_1c_2e^{k(x+y)}$
8. $z(x, y) = 4\, e^{9x} \sin 3y.$

5.4. VIBRATIONS OF A STRETCHED STRING, ONE DIMENSIONAL WAVE EQUATION $\frac{\partial^2 y}{\partial t^2} = c^2 \frac{\partial^2 y}{\partial x^2}$ *(U.P.T.U. 2007)*

Consider a uniform elastic string of length l stretched tightly between two points O and A and displaced slightly from its equilibrium position OA. Taking the end O as the origin, OA as the x-axis and a perpendicular line through O as the y-axis, we shall find the displacement y as a function of the distance x and the time t.

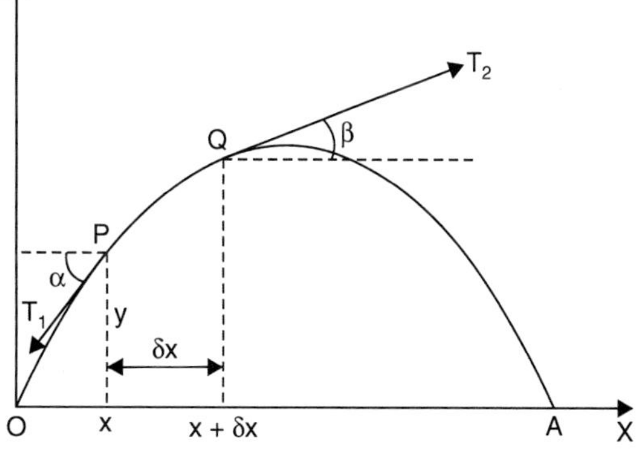

We shall obtain the equation of motion for the string under the following assumptions :

(*i*) The motion takes place entirely in the xy-plane and each particle of the string moves perpendicular to the equilibrium position OA of the string.

(*ii*) The string is perfectly flexible and does not offer resistance to bending.

(*iii*) The tension in the string is so large that the forces due to weight of the string can be neglected.

(*iv*) The displacement y and the slope $\frac{\partial y}{\partial x}$ are small, so that their higher powers can be neglected.

Let m be the mass per unit length of the string. Consider the motion of an element PQ of length δs. Since the string does not offer resistance to bending (by assumption), the tensions T_1 and T_2 at P and Q respectively are tangential to the curve.

Since, there is no motion in the horizontal direction, we have

$$T_1 \cos \alpha = T_2 \cos \beta = T \text{ (constant)} \qquad ...(1)$$

Mass of element PQ is $m\delta s$. By Newton's second law of motion, the equation of motion in the vertical direction is

$$m\delta s \frac{\partial^2 y}{\partial t^2} = T_2 \sin \beta - T_1 \sin \alpha$$

or

$$\frac{m\delta s}{T} \frac{\partial^2 y}{\partial t^2} = \frac{T_2 \sin \beta}{T_2 \cos \beta} - \frac{T_1 \sin \alpha}{T_1 \cos \alpha} \qquad \text{[By using (1)]}$$

or $$\frac{\partial^2 y}{\partial t^2} = \frac{T}{m\delta s}(\tan\beta - \tan\alpha)$$

or $$\frac{\partial^2 y}{\partial t^2} = \frac{T}{m\delta x}\left[\left(\frac{\partial y}{\partial x}\right)_{x+\delta x} - \left(\frac{\partial y}{\partial x}\right)_x\right]$$

[Since $\delta s = \delta x$ to a first approximation and $\tan\alpha$ and $\tan\beta$ are the slopes of the curve of the string at x and $x + \delta x$]

or $$\frac{\partial^2 y}{\partial t^2} = \frac{T}{m}\left[\frac{\left(\frac{\partial y}{\partial x}\right)_{x+\delta x} - \left(\frac{\partial y}{\partial x}\right)_x}{\delta x}\right] = \frac{T}{m}\frac{\partial^2 y}{\partial x^2}, \text{ as } \delta x \to 0$$

or $$\boxed{\frac{\partial^2 y}{\partial t^2} = c^2\frac{\partial^2 y}{\partial x^2}} \quad \text{where } c^2 = \frac{T}{m}$$

This is the partial differential equation giving the transverse vibrations of the string. It is also called the **one dimensional wave equation.**

The *boundary conditions* which the equation $\frac{\partial^2 y}{\partial t^2} = c^2\frac{\partial^2 y}{\partial x^2}$ has to satisfy are :

(*i*) $y = 0$ when $x = 0$
(*ii*) $y = 0$ when $x = l$
. These should be satisfied for every value of t.

If the string is made to vibrate by pulling it into a curve $y = f(x)$ and then releasing it, the *initial conditions* are

(*i*) $y = f(x)$ when $t = 0$ (*ii*) $\frac{\partial y}{\partial t} = 0$ when $t = 0$.

5.5. SOLUTION OF THE WAVE EQUATION

The wave equation is

$$\frac{\partial^2 y}{\partial t^2} = c^2\frac{\partial^2 y}{\partial x^2} \quad ...(1)$$

Let $$y = XT \quad ...(2)$$

where X is a function of x only and T is a function of t only, be a solution of (1)

Then, $$\frac{\partial^2 y}{\partial t^2} = XT'' \quad\text{and}\quad \frac{\partial^2 y}{\partial x^2} = X''T$$

Substituting in (1), we have $XT'' = c^2X''T$

Separating the variables, we get $$\frac{X''}{X} = \frac{1}{c^2}\cdot\frac{T''}{T} \quad ...(3)$$

Now the L.H.S of (3) is a function of x only and the R.H.S is a function of t only. Since x and t are independent variables, this equation can hold only when both sides reduce to a constant, say k. Then equation (3) leads to the ordinary linear differential equations.

$$X''k - X = 0 \quad\text{and}\quad T'' - kc^2T = 0 \quad ...(4)$$

Solving equations (4), we get

(*i*) *When k is positive* and $= p^2$, say

$$X = c_1 e^{px} + c_2 e^{-px}, \quad T = c_3 e^{cpt} + c_4 e^{-cpt}$$

(*ii*) *When k is negative* and $= -p^2$, say

$$X = c_1 \cos px + c_2 \sin px, \qquad T = c_3 \cos cpt + c_4 \sin cpt$$

(*iii*) *When* $k = 0$

$$X = c_1 x + c_2 \qquad T = c_3 t + c_4$$

Thus the various possible solutions of the wave equation (1) are :

$$y = (c_1 e^{px} + c_2 e^{-px})(c_3 e^{cpt} + c_4 e^{-cpt})$$
$$y = (c_1 \cos px + c_2 \sin px)(c_3 \cos cpt + c_4 \sin cpt)$$
$$y = (c_1 x + c_2)(c_3 t + c_4)$$

Of these three solutions, we have to choose that solution which is consistent with the physical nature of the problem. Since, we are dealing with a problem on vibrations, y must be a periodic function of x and t. Therefore, the solution must involve trigonometric terms.

Accordingly $y(x, t) = (c_1 \cos px + c_2 \sin px)(c_3 \cos cpt + c_4 \sin cpt)$ ...(5)

is the only suitable solution of the wave equation and it corresponds to $k = -p^2$.

Now, applying boundary conditions that

$$y = 0 \text{ when } x = 0 \quad \text{and} \quad y = 0 \text{ when } x = l, \text{ we get}$$

$$0 = c_1(c_3 \cos cpt + c_4 \sin cpt) \qquad ...(6)$$

and $$0 = (c_1 \cos pl + c_2 \sin pl)(c_3 \cos cpt + c_4 \sin cpt) \qquad ...(7)$$

From (6), we have $c_1 = 0$ and equation (7) reduces to

$$c_2 \sin pl\,(c_3 \cos cpt + c_4 \sin cpt) = 0$$

which is satisfied when $\sin pl = 0$ or $pl = n\pi$ or $p = \frac{n\pi}{l}$, where $n = 1, 2, 3, ...$

$\therefore$ A solution of the wave equation satisfying the boundary conditions is

$$y = c_2\left(c_3 \cos\frac{n\pi ct}{l} + c_4 \sin\frac{n\pi ct}{l}\right)\sin\frac{n\pi x}{l}$$
$$= \left(a_n \cos\frac{n\pi ct}{l} + b_n \sin\frac{n\pi ct}{l}\right)\sin\frac{n\pi x}{l}$$

on replacing c_2c_3 by a_n and c_2c_4 by b_n.

Adding up the solutions for different values of n, we get

$$y = \sum_{n=1}^{\infty}\left(a_n \cos\frac{n\pi ct}{l} + b_n \sin\frac{n\pi ct}{l}\right)\sin\frac{n\pi x}{l} \qquad ...(8)$$

which is also a solution.

Now applying the initial conditions

$$y = f(x) \quad \text{and} \quad \frac{\partial y}{\partial t} = 0, \text{ when } t = 0, \text{ we have}$$

$$f(x) = \sum_{n=1}^{\infty} a_n \sin\frac{n\pi x}{l} \qquad ...(9)$$

and $$0 = \sum_{n=1}^{\infty} \frac{n\pi c}{l} b_n \sin\frac{n\pi x}{l} \qquad ...(10)$$

Since equation (9) represents Fourier series for $f(x)$, we have

$$a_n = \frac{2}{l}\int_0^l f(x) \sin \frac{n\pi x}{l}\, dx \qquad ...(11)$$

From (10), $b_n = 0$, for all n

Hence (8) reduces to $$y = \sum_{n=1}^{\infty} a_n \cos \frac{n\pi ct}{l} \sin \frac{n\pi x}{l} \qquad ...(12)$$

where a_n is given by (11) when $f(x)$ *i.e.*, $y(x, 0)$ is known.

ILLUSTRATIVE EXAMPLES

Example 1. *A string is stretched and fastened to two points l apart. Motion is started by displacing the string in the form* $y = A \sin \frac{\pi x}{l}$ *from which it is released at time t = 0. Show that the displacement of any point at a distance x from one end at time t is given by*

$y(x, t) = A \sin \frac{\pi x}{l} \cos \frac{\pi ct}{l}$. [U.P.T.U. 2009; U.P.T.U. (SUM) 2009; U.K.T.U. 2011, 2012]

Sol. The equation of the string is

$$\frac{\partial^2 y}{\partial t^2} = c^2 \frac{\partial^2 y}{\partial x^2} \qquad ...(1)$$

Since, the string is stretched between two fixed points (0, 0) and (l, 0) hence the displacement of the string at these points will be zero

$$\therefore \quad y(0, t) = 0 \qquad ...(2)$$

and $$y(l, t) = 0 \qquad ...(3)$$

Since, the string is released from rest hence its initial velocity will be zero

$$\therefore \quad \frac{\partial y}{\partial t} = 0 \quad \text{at} \quad t = 0 \qquad ...(4)$$

Since, the string is displaced from its initial position at time $t = 0$ hence the initial displacement is

$$y(x, 0) = A \sin \frac{\pi x}{l} \qquad ...(5)$$

Conditions (2), (3), (4) and (5) are the boundary conditions.

Let us now proceed to solve equation (1),

Let $$y = XT. \qquad ...(6)$$

where X is a function of x only and T is a function of t only.

$$\frac{\partial y}{\partial t} = \frac{\partial}{\partial t}(XT) = X\frac{dT}{dt}$$

$$\frac{\partial^2 y}{\partial t^2} = \frac{\partial}{\partial t}\left(X\frac{dT}{dt}\right) = X\frac{d^2T}{dt^2}.$$

Similarly, $\quad \dfrac{\partial^2 y}{\partial x^2} = \mathrm{T}\dfrac{d^2\mathrm{X}}{dx^2}.$

Substituting the above in equation (1), we get

$$\mathrm{X}\frac{d^2\mathrm{T}}{dt^2} = c^2\mathrm{T}\frac{d^2\mathrm{X}}{dx^2} \quad \Rightarrow \quad \mathrm{XT}'' = c^2\mathrm{TX}''$$

Case I. $\quad \dfrac{1}{c^2}\dfrac{\mathrm{T}''}{\mathrm{T}} = \dfrac{\mathrm{X}''}{\mathrm{X}} = -p^2$ (say)

(*i*) $\quad \dfrac{1}{c^2}\dfrac{\mathrm{T}''}{\mathrm{T}} = -p^2$

$$\frac{d^2\mathrm{T}}{dt^2} + c^2p^2\mathrm{T} = 0.$$

Auxiliary equation is $\quad m^2 + c^2p^2 = 0$

$$m^2 = c^2p^2i^2$$

$$m = \pm\, cpi$$

$\therefore \quad$ C.F. $= c_1 \cos cpt + c_2 \sin cpt$

P.I. $= 0$

$\therefore \quad \mathrm{T} = \text{C.F.} + \text{P.I.} = c_1 \cos cpt + c_2 \sin cpt$ ...(7)

(*ii*) $\quad \dfrac{\mathrm{X}''}{\mathrm{X}} = -p^2 \quad \Rightarrow \quad \dfrac{d^2\mathrm{X}}{dx^2} + p^2\mathrm{X} = 0.$

Auxiliary equation is $\quad m^2 + p^2 = 0$

$$m = \pm\, pi$$

C.F. $= c_3 \cos px + c_4 \sin px$

P.I. $= 0$

$\therefore \quad \mathrm{X} = c_3 \cos px + c_4 \sin px$ ...(8)

Hence, $\quad y(x, t) = (c_1 \cos cpt + c_2 \sin cpt)(c_3 \cos px + c_4 \sin px)$ ...(9)

Case II. $\quad \dfrac{1}{c^2}\dfrac{\mathrm{T}''}{\mathrm{T}} = \dfrac{\mathrm{X}''}{\mathrm{X}} = p^2$ (say)

(*i*) $\quad \dfrac{1}{c^2}\dfrac{\mathrm{T}''}{\mathrm{T}} = p^2 \quad \Rightarrow \quad \dfrac{d^2\mathrm{T}}{dt^2} - p^2c^2\mathrm{T} = 0$

Auxiliary equation is $\quad m^2 - p^2c^2 = 0 \quad \Rightarrow \quad m = \pm\, pc$

$\therefore \quad$ C.F. $= c_5\, e^{pct} + c_6\, e^{-pct}$

P.I. $= 0$

$\therefore \quad \mathrm{T} = c_5\, e^{pct} + c_6\, e^{-pct}.$

(*ii*) $\quad \dfrac{\mathrm{X}''}{\mathrm{X}} = p^2 \quad \Rightarrow \quad \dfrac{d^2\mathrm{X}}{dx^2} - p^2\mathrm{X} = 0$

Auxiliary equation is

$$m^2 - p^2 = 0 \quad \Rightarrow \quad m = \pm\, p$$

$\therefore \quad$ C.F. $= c_7\, e^{px} + c_8\, e^{-px}$

$$\text{P.I.} = 0$$

$\therefore$ $$X = c_7 e^{px} + c_8 e^{-px}$$

Hence, $$y(x, t) = (c_5 e^{pct} + c_6 e^{-pct})(c_7 e^{px} + c_8 e^{-px}) \qquad ...(10)$$

Case III. $$\frac{1}{c^2}\frac{T''}{T} = \frac{X''}{X} = 0 \text{ (say)}$$

(*i*) $$\frac{1}{c^2}\frac{T''}{T} = 0 \;\Rightarrow\; T'' = 0 \text{ or } \frac{d^2T}{dt^2} = 0$$

Auxiliary equation is

$$m^2 = 0 \;\Rightarrow\; m = 0, 0$$

$\therefore$ $$\text{C.F.} = c_9 + c_{10}\, t$$

$$\text{P.I.} = 0$$

$\therefore$ $$T = c_9 + c_{10}\, t$$

(*ii*) $$\frac{X''}{X} = 0 \;\Rightarrow\; X'' = 0 \text{ or } \frac{d^2X}{dx^2} = 0$$

Auxiliary equation is

$$m^2 = 0 \;\Rightarrow\; m = 0, 0$$

$\therefore$ $$\text{C.F.} = c_{11} + c_{12}x$$

$$\text{P.I.} = 0$$

$\therefore$ $$X = c_{11} + c_{12}x$$

Hence, $$y(x, t) = (c_9 + c_{10}\, t)\,(c_{11} + c_{12}x) \qquad ...(11)$$

Out of these three above solutions (9), (10) and (11), we have to choose the solution which is consistent with the physical nature of the problem. Since, we are dealing with a problem on vibrations, the solution must contain periodic functions. Hence the solution which contains trigonometric terms must be the required solution.

Hence solution (9) is the general solution of one dimensional wave equation given by equation (1).

Now, $$y(x, t) = (c_1 \cos cpt + c_2 \sin cpt)\,(c_3 \cos px + c_4 \sin px)$$

Applying the boundary condition,

$$y(0, t) = 0 = (c_1 \cos cpt + c_2 \sin cpt)\, c_3$$

$\Rightarrow$ $$c_3 = 0.$$

$\therefore$ From (9), $$y(x, t) = (c_1 \cos cpt + c_2 \sin cpt)\, c_4 \sin px \qquad ...(12)$$

Again, $$y(l, t) = 0 = (c_1 \cos cpt + c_2 \sin cpt)\, c_4 \sin pl$$

$\Rightarrow$ $$\sin pl = 0 = \sin n\pi \;(n \in I)$$

$\therefore$ $$p = \frac{n\pi}{l}.$$

Hence from (12), $$y(x, t) = \left(c_1 \cos \frac{n\pi ct}{l} + c_2 \sin \frac{n\pi ct}{l}\right) c_4 \sin \frac{n\pi x}{l} \qquad ...(13)$$

$$\frac{\partial y}{\partial t} = \frac{n\pi c}{l}\left[-\,c_1 \sin \frac{n\pi ct}{l} + c_2 \cos \frac{n\pi ct}{l}\right] c_4 \sin \frac{n\pi x}{l}$$

At $t = 0$,

$$\left(\frac{\partial y}{\partial t}\right)_{t=0} = 0 = \frac{n\pi c}{l}\left[c_2 c_4 \sin \frac{n\pi x}{l}\right]$$

$\Rightarrow \qquad c_2 = 0,$

$\therefore$ From (13), $\quad y(x, t) = c_1c_4 \cos \dfrac{n\pi ct}{l} \sin \dfrac{n\pi x}{l}$ ...(14)

$$y(x, 0) = \text{A} \sin \frac{\pi x}{l} = c_1c_4 \sin \frac{n\pi x}{l}$$

$\Rightarrow \qquad c_1c_4 = \text{A},\ n = 1.$ | Comparing

Hence from (14), $\quad y(x, t) = \text{A} \cos \dfrac{\pi ct}{l} \sin \dfrac{\pi x}{l}$

which is the required solution.

Example 2. *Show how the wave equation*

$$c^2 \frac{\partial^2 y}{\partial x^2} = \frac{\partial^2 y}{\partial t^2}$$

can be solved by the method of separation of variables. If the initial displacement and velocity of a string stretched between $x = 0$ and $x = l$ are given by $y = f(x)$ and $\dfrac{\partial y}{\partial t} = g(x)$, determine the constants in the series solution. [U.P.T.U. (C.O.) 2008]

Sol. The wave equation is

$$\frac{\partial^2 y}{\partial t^2} = c^2 \frac{\partial^2 y}{\partial x^2} \qquad ...(1)$$

Let $\qquad y = \text{XT}$ ...(2)

where X is a function of x only and T is a function of t only.

$$\frac{\partial y}{\partial t} = \frac{\partial}{\partial t}(\text{XT}) = \text{X} \frac{d\text{T}}{dt}$$

$$\frac{\partial^2 y}{\partial t^2} = \text{X} \frac{d^2\text{T}}{dt^2}$$

Similarly, $\qquad \dfrac{\partial^2 y}{\partial x^2} = \text{T} \dfrac{d^2\text{X}}{dx^2}.$

Substituting in (1), we get

$$\text{X}\frac{d^2\text{T}}{dt^2} = c^2\text{T} \frac{d^2\text{X}}{dx^2} \quad \Rightarrow \quad \text{XT}'' = c^2\text{TX}''$$

$$\Rightarrow \qquad \frac{1}{c^2} \frac{\text{T}''}{\text{T}} = \frac{\text{X}''}{\text{X}} \qquad ...(3)$$

Case I. When $\qquad \dfrac{1}{c^2} \dfrac{\text{T}''}{\text{T}} = \dfrac{\text{X}''}{\text{X}} = p^2$ (say)

(*i*) $\qquad \dfrac{1}{c^2} \dfrac{\text{T}''}{\text{T}} = p^2 \quad \Rightarrow \quad \dfrac{d^2\text{T}}{dt^2} - p^2c^2\text{T} = 0.$

Auxiliary equation is

$$m^2 - p^2c^2 = 0$$

$$m = \pm\, pc$$

$$\text{C.F.} = c_1\, e^{pct} + c_2\, e^{-pct}$$

$$\text{P.I.} = 0$$

$\therefore$ $$\text{T} = \text{C.F.} + \text{P.I.} = c_1\, e^{pct} + c_2\, e^{-pct}$$

(*ii*) $$\frac{\text{X}''}{\text{X}} = p^2 \;\Rightarrow\; \frac{d^2\text{X}}{dx^2} - p^2\text{X} = 0.$$

Auxiliary equation is

$$m^2 - p^2 = 0$$

$$m = \pm\, p$$

$$\text{C.F.} = c_3\, e^{px} + c_4\, e^{-px}$$

$$\text{P.I.} = 0.$$

$\therefore$ $$\text{X} = \text{C.F.} + \text{P.I.} = c_3\, e^{px} + c_4\, e^{-px}.$$

Hence, the solution is

$$y = \text{XT} = (c_1\, e^{pct} + c_2\, e^{-pct})(c_3\, e^{px} + c_4\, e^{-px}). \quad ...(4)$$

Case II. When

$$\frac{1}{c^2}\frac{\text{T}''}{\text{T}} = \frac{\text{X}''}{\text{X}} = -\,p^2 \text{ (say)}$$

(*i*) $$\frac{1}{c^2}\frac{\text{T}''}{\text{T}} = -\,p^2 \;\Rightarrow\; \frac{d^2\text{T}}{dt^2} + p^2c^2\text{T} = 0.$$

Auxiliary equation is

$$m^2 + p^2c^2 = 0 \;\Rightarrow\; m = \pm\, pci$$

$\therefore$ $$\text{C.F.} = (c_5 \cos pct + c_6 \sin cpt)$$

$$\text{P.I.} = 0.$$

$\therefore$ $$\text{T} = \text{C.F.} + \text{P.I.} = c_5 \cos cpt + c_6 \sin cpt$$

(*ii*) $$\frac{\text{X}''}{\text{X}} = -\,p^2 \;\Rightarrow\; \frac{d^2\text{X}}{dx^2} + p^2\text{X} = 0.$$

Auxiliary equation is

$$m^2 + p^2 = 0 \;\Rightarrow\; m = \pm\, pi$$

$\therefore$ $$\text{C.F.} = c_7 \cos px + c_8 \sin px$$

$$\text{P.I.} = 0$$

$\therefore$ $$\text{X} = c_7 \cos px + c_8 \sin px.$$

Hence, the solution is

$$y = \text{XT} = (c_5 \cos cpt + c_6 \sin cpt)(c_7 \cos px + c_8 \sin px) \quad ...(5)$$

Case III. When, $\frac{1}{c^2}\frac{\text{T}''}{\text{T}} = \frac{\text{X}''}{\text{X}} = 0$

(*i*) $$\frac{1}{c^2}\frac{\text{T}''}{\text{T}} = 0 \;\Rightarrow\; \frac{d^2\text{T}}{dt^2} = 0$$

$\Rightarrow$ $$\text{T} = c_9 + c_{10}t$$

(*ii*) $$\frac{\text{X}''}{\text{X}} = 0 \;\Rightarrow\; \frac{d^2\text{X}}{dx^2} = 0$$

$\Rightarrow$ $$\text{X} = c_{11} + c_{12}\, x.$$

Hence, the solution is

$$y(x, t) = (c_9 + c_{10}t)(c_{11} + c_{12}x) \quad ...(6)$$

Of the above three solutions given by (4), (5) and (6), we have to choose the solution which is consistent with the physical nature of the problem. Since, we are dealing with a problem on vibrations, y must be a periodic function of x and t therefore the solution must involve trigonometric terms hence solution (5) is the required solution.

Boundary conditions are

$$y(0, t) = 0, \qquad y(l, t) = 0$$

$$y = f(x) \qquad \text{when } t = 0$$

$$\frac{\partial y}{\partial t} = g(x) \qquad \text{when } t = 0$$

From equation (5), $y(0, t) = (c_5 \cos cpt + c_6 \sin cpt)\, c_7$

$$0 = (c_5 \cos cpt + c_6 \sin cpt)\, c_7$$

$$\Rightarrow \quad c_7 = 0.$$

Hence from (5), $y(x, t) = (c_5 \cos cpt + c_6 \sin cpt)\, c_8 \sin px$ ...(7)

$$y(l, t) = 0 = (c_5 \cos cpt + c_6 \sin cpt)\, c_8 \sin pl$$

$$\Rightarrow \quad \sin pl = 0 = \sin n\pi \ (n \in \text{I}) \quad \Rightarrow \quad p = \frac{n\pi}{l}.$$

$\therefore$ From (7),

$$y(x, t) = \left(c_5 \cos \frac{n\pi ct}{l} + c_6 \sin \frac{n\pi ct}{l}\right) c_8 \sin \frac{n\pi x}{l} \qquad ...(8)$$

$$= \left(a_n \cos \frac{n\pi ct}{l} + b_n \sin \frac{n\pi ct}{l}\right) \sin \frac{n\pi x}{l}$$

where $c_5 c_8 = a_n$ and $c_6 c_8 = b_n$

The general solution is

$$y(x, t) = \sum_{n=1}^{\infty} \left(a_n \cos \frac{n\pi ct}{l} + b_n \sin \frac{n\pi ct}{l}\right) \sin \frac{n\pi x}{l} \qquad ...(9)$$

$$y(x, 0) = f(x) = \sum_{1}^{\infty} a_n \sin \frac{n\pi x}{l}$$

where

$$a_n = \frac{2}{l} \int_0^l f(x) . \sin \frac{n\pi x}{l}\, dx \qquad ...(10)$$

From (9),

$$\frac{\partial y}{\partial t} = \frac{\pi c}{l} \sum_{1}^{\infty} \left(-n\, a_n \sin \frac{n\pi ct}{l} + n\, b_n \cos \frac{n\pi ct}{l}\right) \sin \frac{n\pi x}{l}$$

At $t = 0$,

$$\left(\frac{\partial y}{\partial t}\right)_{t=0} = g(x) = \frac{\pi c}{l} \sum_{1}^{\infty} n b_n \sin \frac{n\pi x}{l}$$

where

$$\frac{n\pi c}{l} b_n = \frac{2}{l} \int_0^l g(x) . \sin \frac{n\pi x}{l}\, dx$$

$$\Rightarrow \quad b_n = \frac{2}{n\pi c} \int_0^l g(x) . \sin \frac{n\pi x}{l}\, dx. \qquad ...(11)$$

Hence, the required solution is

$$y(x, t) = \sum_{n=1}^{\infty} \left(a_n \cos \frac{n\pi ct}{l} + b_n \sin \frac{n\pi ct}{l} \right) \sin \frac{n\pi x}{l}$$

where $$a_n = \frac{2}{l} \int_0^l f(x) . \sin \frac{n\pi x}{l}\, dx$$

and $$b_n = \frac{2}{n\pi c} \int_0^l g(x) \sin \frac{n\pi x}{l}\, dx.$$

Example 3. *A tightly stretched string with fixed end points $x = 0$ and $x = l$ is initially in a position given by $y = y_0 \sin^3 \frac{\pi x}{l}$. If it is released from rest from this position, find the displacement $y(x, t)$.* [G.B.T.U. (C.O.) 2011]

Sol. The equation of the string is

$$\frac{\partial^2 y}{\partial t^2} = c^2 \frac{\partial^2 y}{\partial x^2} \quad ...(1)$$

The solution of eqn. (1) is

$$y(x, t) = (c_1 \cos cpt + c_2 \sin cpt)(c_3 \cos px + c_4 \sin px) \quad ...(2)$$

| Refer Sol. of Ex. 1

Boundary conditions are

$$y(0, t) = 0 \quad ...(3)$$

$$y(l, t) = 0 \quad ...(4)$$

$$\left(\frac{\partial y}{\partial t}\right)_{t=0} = 0 \quad ...(5)$$

$$y(x, 0) = y_0 \sin^3 \frac{\pi x}{l} \quad ...(6)$$

Applying boundary condition in (2),

$$y(0, t) = 0 = (c_1 \cos cpt + c_2 \sin cpt)\, c_3$$

$\Rightarrow$ $$c_3 = 0$$

$\therefore$ From (2), $$y(x, t) = (c_1 \cos cpt + c_2 \sin cpt)\, c_4 \sin px \quad ...(7)$$

Again, $$y(l, t) = 0 = (c_1 \cos cpt + c_2 \sin cpt)\, c_4 \sin pl$$

$\Rightarrow$ $$\sin pl = 0 = \sin n\pi \quad (n \in I)$$

$\therefore$ $$p = \frac{n\pi}{l}$$

Hence, from (7),

$$y(x, t) = \left(c_1 \cos \frac{n\pi ct}{l} + c_2 \sin \frac{n\pi ct}{l} \right) c_4 \sin \frac{n\pi x}{l} \quad ...(8)$$

$$\frac{\partial y}{\partial t} = \frac{n\pi c}{l} \left[-c_1 \sin \frac{n\pi ct}{l} + c_2 \cos \frac{n\pi ct}{l} \right] c_4 \sin \frac{n\pi x}{l}$$

At $t = 0$,

$$\left(\frac{\partial y}{\partial t}\right)_{t=0} = 0 = \frac{n\pi c}{l} c_2 c_4 \sin \frac{n\pi x}{l}$$

$\Rightarrow$ $$c_2 = 0.$$

∴ From (8),

$$y(x, t) = c_1 c_4 \sin \frac{n\pi x}{l} \cos \frac{n\pi ct}{l} = b_n \sin \frac{n\pi x}{l} \cos \frac{n\pi ct}{l}$$

Most general solution is

$$y(x, t) = \sum_{n=1}^{\infty} b_n \sin \frac{n\pi x}{l} \cos \frac{n\pi ct}{l} \qquad ...(9)$$

$$y(x, 0) = y_0 \sin^3 \frac{\pi x}{l} = \sum_{n=1}^{\infty} b_n \sin \frac{n\pi x}{l}$$

$$\Rightarrow \quad y_0 \left(\frac{3 \sin \frac{\pi x}{l} - \sin \frac{3\pi x}{l}}{4} \right) = b_1 \sin \frac{\pi x}{l} + b_2 \sin \frac{2\pi x}{l} + b_3 \sin \frac{3\pi x}{l} + ...$$

Comparing, we get

$$b_1 = \frac{3y_0}{4}, \; b_2 = 0, \; b_3 = \frac{-y_0}{4}, \; b_4 = b_5 = ... = 0$$

Hence, from (9),

$$y(x, t) = \frac{3y_0}{4} \sin \frac{\pi x}{l} \cos \frac{\pi ct}{l} - \frac{y_0}{4} \sin \frac{3\pi x}{l} \cos \frac{3\pi ct}{l}.$$

Example 4. *A tightly stretched flexible string has its ends fixed at x = 0 and x = l. At time t = 0, the string is given a shape defined by F(x) = μx(l – x), μ is a constant and then released. Find the displacement y(x, t) of any point x of the string at any time t > 0.*

Sol. The wave equation is

$$\frac{\partial^2 y}{\partial t^2} = c^2 \frac{\partial^2 y}{dx^2} \qquad ...(1)$$

The solution of equation (1) is

$$y(x, t) = (c_1 \cos cpt + c_2 \sin cpt)(c_3 \cos px + c_4 \sin px) \qquad ...(2) \text{ (Refer sol. of Ex. 1)}$$

Boundary conditions are

$$y(0, t) = 0 \qquad ...(3)$$

$$y(l, t) = 0 \qquad ..(4)$$

$$\frac{\partial y}{\partial t} = 0 \text{ at } t = 0 \qquad ...(5)$$

and

$$y(x, 0) = \mu x(l - x) \qquad ...(6)$$

From (2), $y(0, t) = 0 = (c_1 \cos cpt + c_2 \sin cpt)c_3$

$\Rightarrow$ $c_3 = 0.$

∴ From (2), $y(x, t) = (c_1 \cos cpt + c_2 \sin cpt)\, c_4 \sin px$ ...(7)

$y(l, t) = 0 = (c_1 \cos cpt + c_2 \sin cpt)\, c_4 \sin pl$

$\Rightarrow$ $\sin pl = 0 = \sin n\pi \; (n \in I)$

$$p = \frac{n\pi}{l}.$$

From (7),

$$y(x, t) = \left(c_1 \cos \frac{n\pi ct}{l} + c_2 \sin \frac{n\pi ct}{l} \right) c_4 \sin \frac{n\pi x}{l} \qquad ...(8)$$

Now from (7), $$\frac{\partial y}{\partial t} = \frac{n\pi c}{l}\left[-c_1 \sin\frac{n\pi ct}{l} + c_2 \cos\frac{n\pi ct}{l}\right].c_4 \sin\frac{n\pi x}{l}$$

At $t = 0$, $$\left(\frac{\partial y}{\partial t}\right)_{t=0} = 0 = \frac{n\pi c}{l} c_2 c_4 \sin\frac{n\pi x}{l}$$

$\Rightarrow$ $$c_2 = 0.$$

$\therefore$ From (8), $$y(x, t) = c_1 c_4 \cos\frac{n\pi ct}{l} \sin\frac{n\pi x}{l}$$

$\Rightarrow$ $$y(x, t) = b_n \cos\frac{n\pi ct}{l} \sin\frac{n\pi x}{l} \text{ where } c_1c_4 = b_n.$$

The most general solution is

$$y(x, t) = \sum_1^\infty b_n \cos\frac{n\pi ct}{l} \sin\frac{n\pi x}{l} \qquad ...(9)$$

$$y(x, 0) = \mu(lx - x^2) = \sum_1^\infty b_n \sin\frac{n\pi x}{l}$$

where $$b_n = \frac{2}{l}\int_0^l \mu\,(lx - x^2) \sin\frac{n\pi x}{l}\,dx$$

$$= \frac{2\mu}{l}\left[\left\{(lx - x^2)\left(\frac{-\cos\frac{n\pi x}{l}}{\frac{n\pi}{l}}\right)\right\}_0^l - \int_0^l (l - 2x)\left(\frac{-\cos\frac{n\pi x}{l}}{\frac{n\pi}{l}}\right)dx\right]$$

$$= \frac{2\mu}{l}\left[\frac{l}{n\pi}\int_0^l (l - 2x)\cos\frac{n\pi x}{l}\,dx\right]$$

$$= \frac{2\mu}{n\pi}\left[\left\{(l - 2x)\frac{\sin\frac{n\pi x}{l}}{\frac{n\pi}{l}}\right\}_0^l - \int_0^l (-2)\frac{\sin\frac{n\pi x}{l}}{\frac{n\pi}{l}}\,dx\right] = \frac{2\mu}{n\pi}.\frac{2l}{n\pi}\int_0^l \sin\frac{n\pi x}{l}\,dx$$

$$= \frac{4\mu l}{n^2\pi^2}\left(\frac{-\cos\frac{n\pi x}{l}}{\frac{n\pi}{l}}\right)_0^l = \frac{4\mu l^2}{n^3\pi^3}(-\cos n\pi + 1) = \frac{4\mu l^2}{n^3\pi^3}[1 - (-1)^n].$$

$\therefore$ From (9), $$y(x, t) = \frac{4\mu l^2}{\pi^3}\sum_1^\infty \frac{[1 - (-1)^n]}{n^3} \cos\frac{n\pi ct}{l} \sin\frac{n\pi x}{l}$$

$$= \frac{8\mu l^2}{\pi^3}\sum_{n=1}^\infty \frac{1}{(2n - 1)^3} \sin\frac{(2n - 1)\pi x}{l} \cos\frac{(2n - 1)\pi ct}{l}.$$

Example 5. *A string is stretched between two fixed points (0, 0) and (l, 0) and released at rest from the initial deflection given by*

and $$f(x) = \begin{cases} \left(\dfrac{2k}{l}\right)x & , \ 0 < x < \dfrac{l}{2} \\ \left(\dfrac{2k}{l}\right)(l - x), & \dfrac{l}{2} < x < l \end{cases}$$

Find the deflection of the string at any time.

Sol. The equation for the vibrations of the string is

$$\frac{\partial^2 y}{\partial t^2} = c^2 \frac{\partial^2 y}{dx^2} \qquad \text{...(1)}$$

The solution of eqn. (1) is

$y(x, t) = (c_1 \cos cpt + c_2 \sin cpt)(c_3 \cos px + c_4 \sin px)$ ...(2) [Refer Sol. of Ex. 1]

Boundary conditions are, $y(0, t) = 0$, $y(l, t) = 0$

$$\frac{\partial y}{\partial t} = 0 \quad \text{at} \quad t = 0$$

$$y(x, 0) = \begin{cases} \dfrac{2k}{l}x & , \ 0 < x < \dfrac{l}{2} \\ \dfrac{2k}{l}(l - x), & \dfrac{l}{2} < x < l \end{cases}$$

From (2), $y(0, t) = (c_1 \cos cpt + c_2 \sin cpt)\, c_3$

$0 = (c_1 \cos cpt + c_2 \sin cpt)\, c_3$

$\Rightarrow$ $c_3 = 0.$

$\therefore$ From (2), $y(x, t) = (c_1 \cos cpt + c_2 \sin cpt)\, c_4 \sin px$ ...(3)

$y(l, t) = 0 = (c_1 \cos cpt + c_2 \sin cpt)\, c_4 \sin pl$

$\Rightarrow$ $\sin pl = 0 = \sin n\pi \ ; \ n \in I$

$$p = \frac{n\pi}{l}.$$

$\therefore$ From (3), $$y(x, t) = \left(c_1 \cos \frac{n\pi ct}{l} + c_2 \sin \frac{n\pi ct}{l}\right) c_4 \sin \frac{n\pi x}{l} \qquad \text{...(4)}$$

$$\frac{\partial y}{\partial t} = \frac{n\pi c}{l}\left[- c_1 \sin \frac{n\pi ct}{l} + c_2 \cos \frac{n\pi ct}{l}\right) c_4 \sin \frac{n\pi x}{l}$$

At $t = 0$, $$\left(\frac{\partial y}{\partial t}\right)_{t=0} = 0 = \frac{n\pi c}{l}\left[c_2 c_4 \sin \frac{n\pi x}{l}\right]$$

$\Rightarrow$ $c_2 = 0.$

$\therefore$ From (4), $$y(x, t) = c_1 c_4 \cos \frac{n\pi ct}{l} \sin \frac{n\pi x}{l}$$

$$= b_n \cos \frac{n\pi ct}{l} \sin \frac{n\pi x}{l} \qquad \text{(where } c_1 c_4 = b_n\text{)} \quad \text{...(5)}$$

The most general solution is

$$y(x, t) = \sum_{n=1}^{\infty} b_n \cos \frac{n\pi ct}{l} \sin \frac{n\pi x}{l} \qquad \text{...(6)}$$

$$y(x, 0) = \sum_{1}^{\infty} b_n \sin \frac{n\pi x}{l} \qquad \text{[From (6)]}$$

where
$$b_n = \frac{2}{l} \int_0^l y(x, 0) \sin \frac{n\pi x}{l}\, dx$$

$$= \frac{2}{l}\left[\int_0^{l/2} \frac{2k}{l} x \sin \frac{n\pi x}{l}\, dx + \int_{l/2}^{l} \frac{2k}{l}(l - x) \sin \frac{n\pi x}{l}\, dx\right]$$

$$= \frac{4k}{l^2}\left[\int_0^{l/2} x \sin \frac{n\pi x}{l}\, dx + \int_{l/2}^{l} (l - x) \sin \frac{n\pi x}{l}\, dx\right]$$

$$= \frac{4k}{l^2}\left[x\left(\frac{-\cos \frac{n\pi x}{l}}{\frac{n\pi}{l}}\right)_0^{l/2} - \int_0^{l/2} 1.\left(\frac{-\cos \frac{n\pi x}{l}}{\frac{n\pi}{l}}\right) dx \right.$$

$$\left. + \left\{(l - x)\left(\frac{-\cos \frac{n\pi x}{l}}{\frac{n\pi}{l}}\right)\right\}_{l/2}^{l} - \int_{l/2}^{l} (-1).\left(\frac{-\cos \frac{n\pi x}{l}}{\frac{n\pi}{l}}\right) dx\right]$$

$$= \frac{4k}{l^2}\left[-\frac{l}{n\pi}.\frac{l}{2}\cos\frac{n\pi}{2} + \frac{l}{n\pi}\left(\frac{\sin \frac{n\pi x}{l}}{\frac{n\pi}{l}}\right)_0^{l/2} + \frac{l}{2}.\frac{l}{n\pi}\cos\frac{n\pi}{2} - \frac{l}{n\pi}\left(\frac{\sin \frac{n\pi x}{l}}{\frac{n\pi}{l}}\right)_{l/2}^{l}\right]$$

$$= \frac{4k}{l^2}\left[\frac{l^2}{n^2\pi^2}\sin\frac{n\pi}{2} - \frac{l^2}{n^2\pi^2}\left(\sin n\pi - \sin\frac{n\pi}{2}\right)\right]$$

$$= \frac{4k}{l^2}\left[\frac{2l^2}{n^2\pi^2}\sin\frac{n\pi}{2}\right] = \frac{8k}{n^2\pi^2}\sin\frac{n\pi}{2}.$$

$\therefore$ From (6),
$$y(x, t) = \frac{8k}{\pi^2}\sum_{1}^{\infty}\frac{1}{n^2}\sin\frac{n\pi}{2}\cos\frac{n\pi ct}{l}\sin\frac{n\pi x}{l}.$$

Example 6. *A tightly stretched violin string of length l and fixed at both ends is plucked at $x = \frac{l}{3}$ and assumes initially the shape of a triangle of height a. Find the displacement y at any distance x and any time t after the string is released from rest.*

Sol. One Dimensional wave equation is

$$\frac{\partial^2 y}{\partial t^2} = c^2 \frac{\partial^2 y}{\partial x^2} \qquad \text{...(1)}$$

The solution of eqn. (1) is

$$y(x, t) = (c_1 \cos cpt + c_2 \sin cpt)(c_3 \cos px + c_4 \sin px) \quad ...(2) \quad \text{(Refer Sol. of Ex. 1)}$$

Eqn. of line OC is $y - 0 = \dfrac{a - 0}{\dfrac{l}{3} - 0}(x - 0)$

$$y = \frac{3a}{l} x \quad ...(3)$$

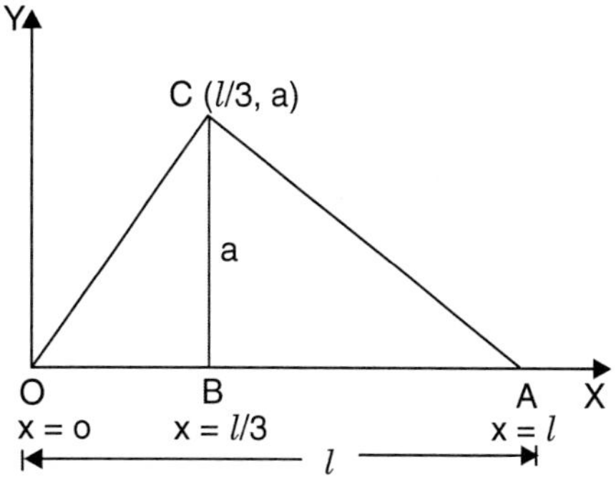

Eqn. of line CA is $y - a = \dfrac{0 - a}{l - l/3}\left(x - \dfrac{l}{3}\right)$

$$y - a = \frac{-a}{\left(\frac{2l}{3}\right)}\left(x - \frac{l}{3}\right) = -\frac{3a}{2l}\left(x - \frac{l}{3}\right)$$

$$y - a = -\frac{3ax}{2l} + \frac{a}{2}$$

$$y = -\frac{3ax}{2l} + \frac{3a}{2} = \frac{3a}{2}\left(1 - \frac{x}{l}\right) \quad ...(4)$$

Hence the boundary conditions are

$$y(0, t) = 0 \quad ...(5)$$

$$y(l, t) = 0 \quad ...(6)$$

$$\frac{\partial y}{\partial t} = 0 \text{ at } t = 0 \quad ...(7)$$

and

$$y(x, 0) = \begin{cases} \dfrac{3ax}{l}, & 0 < x < l/3 \\ \dfrac{3a}{2}\left(1 - \dfrac{x}{l}\right), & \dfrac{l}{3} < x < l \end{cases} \quad ...(8)$$

From (2), $y(0, t) = 0 = (c_1 \cos cpt + c_2 \sin cpt)\, c_3$

$\Rightarrow$ $c_3 = 0.$

$\therefore$ From (2), $y(x, t) = (c_1 \cos cpt + c_2 \sin cpt)\, c_4 \sin px \quad ...(9)$

$y(l, t) = 0 = (c_1 \cos cpt + c_2 \sin cpt)\, c_4 \sin pl$

$\Rightarrow$ $\sin pl = 0 = \sin n\pi (n \in \text{I}).$

$\Rightarrow$ $p = \dfrac{n\pi}{l}.$

$\therefore$
$$y(x, t) = \left(c_1 \cos \frac{n\pi ct}{l} + c_2 \sin \frac{n\pi ct}{l}\right) c_4 \sin \frac{n\pi x}{l} \quad ...(10)$$

$$\frac{\partial y}{\partial t} = \frac{n\pi c}{l}\left[-c_1 \sin \frac{n\pi ct}{l} + c_2 \cos \frac{n\pi ct}{l}\right] c_4 \sin \frac{n\pi x}{l}.$$

At $t = 0$,

$$\left(\frac{\partial y}{\partial t}\right)_{t=0} = 0 = \frac{n\pi c}{l}\left[c_2 c_4 \sin \frac{n\pi x}{l}\right]$$

$\Rightarrow$ $c_2 = 0.$

$\therefore$
$$y(x, t) = c_1 c_4 \cos \frac{n\pi ct}{l} \sin \frac{n\pi x}{l} = b_n \cos \frac{n\pi ct}{l} \sin \frac{n\pi x}{l}.$$

The most general solution is

$$y(x, t) = \sum_{1}^{\infty} b_n \cos \frac{n\pi ct}{l} \sin \frac{n\pi x}{l} \qquad \text{...(11)}$$

From (11), $y(x, 0) = \sum_{1}^{\infty} b_n \sin \frac{n\pi x}{l}$, where

$$b_n = \frac{2}{l} \int_0^l y(x, 0) \sin \frac{n\pi x}{l}\, dx$$

$$= \frac{2}{l} \left[\int_0^{l/3} \frac{3ax}{l} \sin \frac{n\pi x}{l}\, dx + \int_{l/3}^{l} \frac{3a}{2} \left(1 - \frac{x}{l}\right) \sin \frac{n\pi x}{l}\, dx \right]$$

$$= \frac{2}{l} \left[\frac{3a}{l} \int_0^{l/3} x \sin \frac{n\pi x}{l}\, dx + \frac{3a}{2} \int_{l/3}^{l} \left(1 - \frac{x}{l}\right) \sin \frac{n\pi x}{l}\, dx \right]$$

$$= \frac{6a}{l^2} \left[\left(x \left\{ \frac{-\cos \frac{n\pi x}{l}}{\frac{n\pi}{l}} \right\} \right)_0^{l/3} - \int_0^{l/3} 1 . \left(\frac{-\cos \frac{n\pi x}{l}}{\frac{n\pi}{l}} \right) dx \right]$$

$$+ \frac{3a}{l} \left[\left(\left(1 - \frac{x}{l}\right) \left(\frac{-\cos \frac{n\pi x}{l}}{\frac{n\pi}{l}} \right) \right)_{l/3}^{l} - \int_{l/3}^{l} \left(-\frac{1}{l}\right) \left(\frac{-\cos \frac{n\pi x}{l}}{\frac{n\pi}{l}} \right) dx \right]$$

$$= \frac{6a}{l^2} \left[-\frac{l}{n\pi} . \frac{l}{3} \cos \frac{n\pi}{3} + \frac{l}{n\pi} \left(\frac{\sin \frac{n\pi x}{l}}{\frac{n\pi}{l}} \right)_0^{l/3} \right] + \frac{3a}{l} \left[\frac{l}{n\pi} . \frac{2}{3} \cos \frac{n\pi}{3} - \frac{1}{n\pi} . \left(\frac{\sin \frac{n\pi x}{l}}{\frac{n\pi}{l}} \right)_{l/3}^{l} \right]$$

$$= \frac{6a}{l^2} \left[-\frac{l^2}{3n\pi} \cos \frac{n\pi}{3} + \frac{l^2}{n^2\pi^2} \sin \frac{n\pi}{3} \right] + \frac{3a}{l} \left[\frac{2l}{3n\pi} \cos \frac{n\pi}{3} - \frac{l}{n^2\pi^2} \left(0 - \sin \frac{n\pi}{3}\right) \right]$$

$$= \frac{6a}{n\pi} \left[\frac{-1}{3} \cos \frac{n\pi}{3} + \frac{1}{n\pi} \sin \frac{n\pi}{3} \right] + \frac{6a}{n\pi} \left[\frac{1}{3} \cos \frac{n\pi}{3} \right] + \frac{3a}{n^2\pi^2} \sin \frac{n\pi}{3}$$

$$\Rightarrow \qquad b_n = \frac{9a}{n^2\pi^2} \sin \frac{n\pi}{3}$$

$\therefore$ From (11), $y(x, t) = \frac{9a}{\pi^2} \sum_{1}^{\infty} \frac{1}{n^2} \sin \frac{n\pi}{3} \cos \frac{n\pi ct}{l} \sin \frac{n\pi x}{l}$.

Example 7. *The points of trisection of a string are pulled aside through the same distance on opposite sides of the position of equilibrium and the string is released from rest. Derive an expression for the displacement of the string at subsequent time and show that the mid-point of the string always remains at rest.*

Sol. The equation for the vibration of the string is

$$\frac{\partial^2 y}{\partial t^2} = c^2 \frac{\partial^2 y}{\partial x^2} \qquad ...(1)$$

The solution of eqn. (1) is

$$y(x, t) = (c_1 \cos cpt + c_2 \sin cpt)(c_3 \cos px + c_4 \sin px) \qquad ...(2)$$

Let l be the length of string (Refer Sol. of Ex. 1)

Eqn. of OB is,

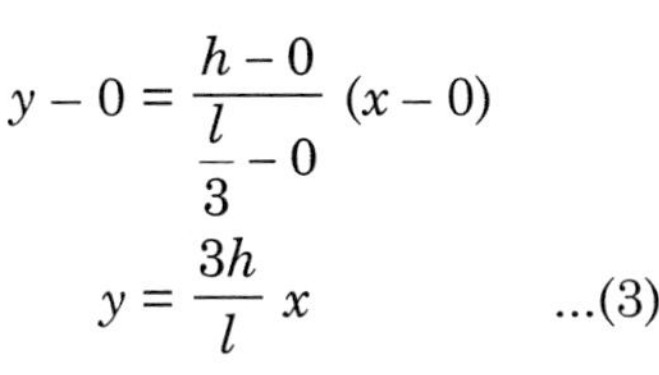

$$y - 0 = \frac{h - 0}{\frac{l}{3} - 0}(x - 0)$$

$$\Rightarrow \qquad y = \frac{3h}{l}x \qquad ...(3)$$

Eqn. of BC is,

$$y - h = \frac{-h-h}{\frac{2l}{3} - \frac{l}{3}}\left(x - \frac{l}{3}\right)$$

$$= \frac{-2h}{\left(\frac{l}{3}\right)}\left(x - \frac{l}{3}\right) = -\frac{6h}{l}\left(x - \frac{l}{3}\right)$$

$$y - h = -\frac{6hx}{l} + 2h$$

$$y = 3h - \frac{6hx}{l} = 3h\left(1 - \frac{2x}{l}\right) \qquad ...(4)$$

Eqn. of CA is,

$$y + h = \frac{0 + h}{l - \frac{2l}{3}}\left(x - \frac{2l}{3}\right) = \frac{3h}{l}\left(x - \frac{2l}{3}\right) = \frac{3hx}{l} - 2h$$

$$y = \frac{3hx}{l} - 3h = 3h\left(\frac{x}{l} - 1\right) \qquad ...(5)$$

Hence Boundary conditions are

$$y(0, t) = 0, \; y(l, t) = 0$$

$$\frac{\partial y}{\partial t} = 0 \qquad \text{when } t = 0$$

and

$$y(x, 0) = \begin{cases} \frac{3h}{l}x & , \; 0 \le x \le l/3 \\ \frac{3h}{l}(l - 2x), & \frac{l}{3} \le x \le \frac{2l}{3} \\ \frac{3h}{l}(x - l) & , \; \frac{2l}{3} \le x \le l \end{cases}$$

From (2), $y(0, t) = 0 = (c_1 \cos cpt + c_2 \sin cpt)\, c_3$

$\Rightarrow$ $c_3 = 0$.

$\therefore$ From (2),

$$y(x, t) = (c_1 \cos cpt + c_2 \sin cpt)\, c_4 \sin px \qquad \text{...(6)}$$

$$y(l, t) = 0 = (c_1 \cos cpt + c_2 \sin cpt)\, c_4 \sin pl$$

$\Rightarrow$ $$\sin pl = 0 = \sin n\pi \ (n \in \mathrm{I})$$

$\therefore$ $$p = \frac{n\pi}{l}.$$

$\therefore$ From (6), $$y(x, t) = \left(c_1 \cos \frac{n\pi ct}{l} + c_2 \sin \frac{n\pi ct}{l}\right) c_4 \sin \frac{n\pi x}{l} \qquad \text{...(7)}$$

$$\frac{\partial y}{\partial t} = \frac{n\pi c}{l}\left(-c_1 \sin \frac{n\pi ct}{l} + c_2 \cos \frac{n\pi ct}{l}\right) c_4 \sin \frac{n\pi x}{l}.$$

At $t = 0$, $$\left(\frac{\partial y}{\partial t}\right)_{t=0} = 0 = \frac{n\pi c}{l} c_2 c_4 \sin \frac{n\pi x}{l}$$

$\Rightarrow$ $$c_2 = 0$$

$\therefore$ From (7), $$y(x, t) = c_1 c_4 \cos \frac{n\pi ct}{l} \sin \frac{n\pi x}{l} = b_n \cos \frac{n\pi ct}{l} \sin \frac{n\pi x}{l}.$$

The most general solution is

$$y(x, t) = \sum_{1}^{\infty} b_n \cos \frac{n\pi ct}{l} \sin \frac{n\pi x}{l} \qquad \text{...(8)}$$

$$y(x, 0) = \sum_{1}^{\infty} b_n \sin \frac{n\pi x}{l}, \text{ where}$$

$$b_n = \frac{2}{l}\int_0^l y(x, 0) \sin \frac{n\pi x}{l}\, dx$$

$$= \frac{2}{l}\left[\int_0^{l/3} \frac{3h}{l} x \sin \frac{n\pi x}{l}\, dx + \int_{l/3}^{2l/3} \frac{3h}{l}(l - 2x) \sin \frac{n\pi x}{l}\, dx + \int_{2l/3}^{l} \frac{3h}{l}(x - l) \sin \frac{n\pi x}{l}\, dx\right]$$

$$= \frac{2}{l}\cdot\frac{3h}{l}\int_0^{l/3} x \sin \frac{n\pi x}{l}\, dx + \frac{2}{l}\cdot\frac{3h}{l}\int_{l/3}^{2l/3} (l - 2x) \sin \frac{n\pi x}{l}\, dx + \frac{2}{l}\cdot\frac{3h}{l}\int_{2l/3}^{l} (x - l) \sin \frac{n\pi x}{l}\, dx$$

$$= \frac{6h}{l^2}\left[\left\{x\left(\frac{-\cos \frac{n\pi x}{l}}{\frac{n\pi}{l}}\right)\right\}_0^{l/3} - \int_0^{l/3} 1.\left(\frac{-\cos \frac{n\pi x}{l}}{\frac{n\pi}{l}}\right) dx\right]$$

$$+ \frac{6h}{l^2}\left[\left\{(l - 2x)\left(\frac{-\cos \frac{n\pi x}{l}}{\frac{n\pi}{l}}\right)\right\}_{l/3}^{2l/3} - \int_{l/3}^{2l/3} (-2)\left(\frac{-\cos \frac{n\pi x}{l}}{\frac{n\pi}{l}}\right) dx\right]$$

$$+ \frac{6h}{l^2}\left[\left\{(x - l)\left(\frac{-\cos \frac{n\pi x}{l}}{\frac{n\pi}{l}}\right)\right\}_{2l/3}^{l} - \int_{2l/3}^{l} 1.\left(\frac{-\cos \frac{n\pi x}{l}}{\frac{n\pi}{l}}\right) dx\right]$$

$$= \frac{6h}{l^2}\left[\frac{-l}{n\pi}\cdot\frac{l}{3}\cos\frac{n\pi}{3} + \frac{l}{n\pi}\left(\frac{\sin\frac{n\pi x}{l}}{\frac{n\pi}{l}}\right)_0^{l/3}\right]$$

$$+ \frac{6h}{l^2}\left[\frac{-l}{3}\cdot\frac{l}{n\pi}\left(-\cos\frac{2n\pi}{3}\right) + \left(\cos\frac{n\pi}{3}\right)\frac{l}{3}\cdot\frac{l}{n\pi} - \frac{2l}{n\pi}\left(\frac{\sin\frac{n\pi x}{l}}{\frac{n\pi}{l}}\right)_{l/3}^{2l/3}\right]$$

$$+ \frac{6h}{l^2}\left[\frac{-l}{3}\cdot\frac{l}{n\pi}\cos\frac{2n\pi}{3} + \frac{l}{n\pi}\left(\frac{\sin n\pi x/l}{n\pi/l}\right)_{2l/3}^{l}\right]$$

$$= \frac{-2h}{n\pi}\cos\frac{n\pi}{3} + \frac{6h}{n^2\pi^2}\sin\frac{n\pi}{3} + \frac{2h}{n\pi}\cos\frac{2n\pi}{3}$$

$$+ \frac{2h}{n\pi}\cos\frac{n\pi}{3} - \frac{12h}{n^2\pi^2}\left(\sin\frac{2n\pi}{3} - \sin\frac{n\pi}{3}\right) - \frac{2h}{n\pi}\cos\frac{2n\pi}{3} + \frac{6h}{n^2\pi^2}\left(0 - \sin\frac{2n\pi}{3}\right)$$

$$= \frac{18h}{n^2\pi^2}\sin\frac{n\pi}{3} - \frac{18h}{n^2\pi^2}\sin\frac{2n\pi}{3} = \frac{18h}{n^2\pi^2}\sin\frac{n\pi}{3} - \frac{18h}{n^2\pi^2}\sin\left(n\pi - \frac{n\pi}{3}\right)$$

$$= \frac{18h}{n^2\pi^2}\sin\frac{n\pi}{3} + \frac{18h}{n^2\pi^2}\sin\frac{n\pi}{3}\cos n\pi$$

$$= \begin{cases} \dfrac{36h}{n^2\pi^2}\sin\dfrac{n\pi}{3}, & \text{when } n \text{ is even} \\ 0, & \text{when } n \text{ is odd} \end{cases}$$

$\therefore$ From (8), $$y(x, t) = \frac{36h}{\pi^2}\sum_{n=2,4,\ldots}^{\infty}\frac{1}{n^2}\sin\frac{n\pi}{3}\cos\frac{n\pi ct}{l}\sin\frac{n\pi x}{l}$$

$$y(x, t) = \frac{9h}{\pi^2}\sum_{m=1,2,\ldots}^{\infty}\frac{1}{m^2}\sin\frac{2m\pi}{3}\cos\frac{2m\pi ct}{l}\sin\frac{2m\pi x}{l} \qquad \ldots(9)$$

(where $n = 2m$)

Putting $x = \dfrac{l}{2}$ in eqn. (6), we get

$$y\left(\frac{l}{2}, t\right) = \frac{9h}{\pi^2}\sum_{m=1}^{\infty}\sin\left(\frac{2m\pi}{3}\right)\cdot\frac{1}{m^2}\cdot\cos\frac{2m\pi ct}{l}\cdot\sin m\pi = 0.$$

Hence, mid point of the string is always at rest.

Example 8. *If a string of length l is initially at rest in equilibrium position and each of its points is given the velocity* $\left(\dfrac{\partial y}{\partial t}\right)_{t-0} = b\sin^3\dfrac{\pi x}{l}$, *find the displacement y (x, t).*

(U.P.T.U. 2006)

Sol. The equation for the vibrations of the string is

$$\frac{\partial^2 y}{\partial t^2} = c^2 \frac{\partial^2 y}{\partial x^2} \quad ...(1)$$

The solution of equation (1) is

$y(x, t) = (c_1 \cos cpt + c_2 \sin cpt)(c_3 \cos px + c_4 \sin px)$ ...(2) [Refer Sol. of Ex. 1]

Boundary conditions are,

$$y(0, t) = 0 \quad ...(3)$$

$$y(l, t) = 0 \quad ...(4)$$

$$y(x, 0) = 0 \quad ...(5)$$

$$\left(\frac{\partial y}{\partial t}\right) = b \sin^3 \frac{\pi x}{l} \text{ at } t = 0 \quad ...(6)$$

From eqn. (2), $y(0, t) = 0 = (c_1 \cos cpt + c_2 \sin cpt)\, c_3$

$\Rightarrow$ $c_3 = 0.$

$\therefore$ From (2), $y(x, t) = (c_1 \cos cpt + c_2 \sin cpt)\, c_4 \sin px$ ...(7)

$y(l, t) = 0 = (c_1 \cos cpt + c_2 \sin cpt)\, c_4 \sin pl$

$\Rightarrow$ $\sin pl = 0 = \sin n\pi \ (n \in \text{I})$

$\therefore$ $p = \frac{n\pi}{l}.$

$\therefore$ From (7), $$y(x, t) = \left(c_1 \cos \frac{n\pi ct}{l} + c_2 \sin \frac{n\pi ct}{l}\right) c_4 \sin \frac{n\pi x}{l} \quad ...(8)$$

$$y(x, 0) = 0 = c_1 c_4 \sin \frac{n\pi x}{l}$$

$\Rightarrow$ $c_1 = 0.$

$\therefore$ From (8), $$y(x, t) = c_2 c_4 \sin \frac{n\pi ct}{l} \sin \frac{n\pi x}{l}$$

$$= b_n \sin \frac{n\pi ct}{l} \sin \frac{n\pi x}{l} \text{ where } c_2 c_4 = b_n$$

The general solution is

$$y(x, t) = \sum_1^\infty b_n \sin \frac{n\pi ct}{l} \sin \frac{n\pi x}{l} \quad ...(9)$$

$$\frac{\partial y}{\partial t} = \sum_1^\infty b_n \cdot \frac{n\pi c}{l} \cos \frac{n\pi ct}{l} \sin \frac{n\pi x}{l}$$

At $t = 0$, $$\left(\frac{\partial y}{\partial t}\right)_{t=0} = \sum_1^\infty b_n \cdot \frac{n\pi c}{l} \sin \frac{n\pi x}{l}$$

$$b \sin^3 \frac{\pi x}{l} = \sum_1^\infty b_n \cdot \frac{n\pi c}{l} \sin \frac{n\pi x}{l}$$

$$\frac{b}{4}\left[3 \sin \frac{\pi x}{l} - \sin \frac{3\pi x}{l}\right] = b_1 \frac{\pi c}{l} \sin \frac{\pi x}{l} + \frac{2b_2 \pi c}{l} \sin \frac{2\pi x}{l} + 3b_3 \frac{\pi c}{l} \sin \frac{3\pi x}{l} + \ldots$$

$$\Rightarrow \qquad b_1 \frac{\pi c}{l} = \frac{3b}{4} \quad \Rightarrow \quad b_1 = \frac{3bl}{4\pi c}$$

$$b_2 = 0 \quad \text{and} \quad \frac{3b_3\pi c}{l} = -\frac{b}{4} \quad \Rightarrow \quad b_3 = -\frac{bl}{12\pi c}$$

Also, $\qquad b_4 = 0 = b_5 = \ldots$ etc.

Hence from (9), $\quad y(x, t) = \dfrac{3bl}{4\pi c} \sin \dfrac{\pi ct}{l} \sin \dfrac{\pi x}{l} - \dfrac{bl}{12\pi c} \sin \dfrac{3\pi ct}{l} \sin \dfrac{3\pi x}{l}$

$$= \frac{bl}{12\pi c}\left[9 \sin \frac{\pi x}{l} \sin \frac{\pi ct}{l} - \sin \frac{3\pi x}{l} \sin \frac{3\pi ct}{l}\right].$$

Example 9. *A tightly stretched string with fixed end points $x = 0$ and $x = l$ is initially at rest in its equilibrium position. If it is set vibrating by giving to each of its points an initial velocity $\lambda x(l - x)$, find the displacement of the string at any distance x from one end at any time t.* [M.T.U. (SUM) 2011]

Sol. Here the boundary conditions are $\quad y(0, t) = y(l, t) = 0$

$$y(x, t) = \sum_{n=1}^{\infty} \left(a_n \cos \frac{n\pi ct}{l} + b_n \sin \frac{n\pi ct}{l}\right) \sin \frac{n\pi x}{l} \qquad \ldots(1)$$ | Refer Sol. of Ex. 2

Since the string was at rest initially, $y(x, 0) = 0$

$\therefore$ From (1), $\qquad 0 = \sum\limits_{n=1}^{\infty} a_n \sin \dfrac{n\pi x}{l} \quad \Rightarrow \quad a_n = 0$

$$\therefore \qquad y(x, t) = \sum_{n=1}^{\infty} b_n \sin \frac{n\pi ct}{l} \sin \frac{n\pi x}{l} \qquad \ldots(2)$$

and $\qquad \dfrac{\partial y}{\partial t} = \sum\limits_{n=1}^{\infty} \dfrac{n\pi c}{l} b_n \cos \dfrac{n\pi ct}{l} \sin \dfrac{n\pi x}{l} = \dfrac{\pi c}{l} \sum\limits_{n=1}^{\infty} nb_n \cos \dfrac{n\pi ct}{l} \sin \dfrac{n\pi x}{l}$

But $\qquad \dfrac{\partial y}{\partial t} = \lambda x(l - x) \quad$ when $t = 0$

$$\therefore \qquad \lambda x(l - x) = \frac{\pi c}{l} \sum_{n=1}^{\infty} nb_n \sin \frac{n\pi x}{l}$$

$$\Rightarrow \qquad \frac{\pi c}{l} nb_n = \frac{2}{l} \int_0^l \lambda x(l - x) \sin \frac{n\pi x}{l}\, dx$$

$$= \frac{2\lambda}{l}\left[x(l - x)\left(-\frac{l}{n\pi} \cos \frac{n\pi x}{l}\right) - (l - 2x)\left(-\frac{l^2}{n^2\pi^2} \sin \frac{n\pi x}{l}\right) + (-2)\left(\frac{l^3}{n^3\pi^3} \cos \frac{n\pi x}{l}\right)\right]_0^l$$

$$= \frac{4\lambda l^2}{n^3\pi^3}(1 - \cos n\pi) = \frac{4\lambda l^2}{n^3\pi^3}[1 - (-1)^n]$$

$$= \begin{cases} 0 & , \text{ when } n \text{ is even} \\ \dfrac{8\lambda l^2}{n^3\pi^3}, & \text{when } n \text{ is odd} \end{cases} \quad i.e., \ \frac{8\lambda l^2}{\pi^3 (2m - 1)^3}, \text{ taking } n = 2m - 1$$

$$\Rightarrow \quad b_n = \frac{8\lambda l^3}{c\pi^4 (2m - 1)^4}$$

$\therefore$ From (2), the required solution is

$$y(x, t) = \frac{8\lambda l^3}{c\pi^4} \sum_{m=1}^{\infty} \frac{1}{(2m-1)^4} \sin \frac{(2m-1)\pi ct}{l} \sin \frac{(2m-1)\pi x}{l}.$$

Example 10. *Transform the equation*

$$\frac{\partial^2 y}{\partial t^2} = c^2 \frac{\partial^2 y}{\partial x^2}$$

to its normal form using the transformation $u = x + ct$, $v = x - ct$ and hence solve it. Show that the solution may be put in the form $y = \frac{1}{2}[f(x + ct) + f(x - ct)]$.

Assume initial conditions $y = f(x)$ and $(\partial y/\partial t) = 0$ at $t = 0$.

Sol. One dimensional wave equation is

$$\frac{\partial^2 y}{\partial t^2} = c^2 \frac{\partial^2 y}{\partial x^2} \qquad ...(1)$$

Let us introduce two new independent variables

$$u = x + ct \qquad ...(2)$$

and

$$v = x - ct \qquad ...(3)$$

so that y becomes a function of u and v.

Then, $$\frac{\partial y}{\partial x} = \frac{\partial y}{\partial u} \cdot \frac{\partial u}{\partial x} + \frac{\partial y}{\partial v} \cdot \frac{\partial v}{\partial x} = \frac{\partial y}{\partial u} + \frac{\partial y}{\partial v} \qquad ...(4) \quad \text{[Using (2) and (3)]}$$

Also, $$\frac{\partial}{\partial x} \equiv \frac{\partial}{\partial u} + \frac{\partial}{\partial v} \qquad ...(5)$$

$\therefore$ $$\frac{\partial^2 y}{\partial x^2} = \frac{\partial}{\partial x}\left(\frac{\partial y}{\partial x}\right) = \left(\frac{\partial}{\partial u} + \frac{\partial}{\partial v}\right)\left(\frac{\partial y}{\partial u} + \frac{\partial y}{\partial v}\right)$$

$$= \frac{\partial^2 y}{\partial u^2} + 2\frac{\partial^2 y}{\partial u \partial v} + \frac{\partial^2 y}{\partial v^2} \qquad ...(6)$$

Also, $$\frac{\partial y}{\partial t} = \frac{\partial y}{\partial u} \cdot \frac{\partial u}{\partial t} + \frac{\partial y}{\partial v} \cdot \frac{\partial v}{\partial t} = c\frac{\partial y}{\partial u} + \frac{\partial y}{\partial v}(-c) = c\left(\frac{\partial y}{\partial u} - \frac{\partial y}{\partial v}\right) \qquad ...(7)$$

$\Rightarrow$ $$\frac{\partial}{\partial t} \equiv c\left(\frac{\partial}{\partial u} - \frac{\partial}{\partial v}\right) \qquad ...(8)$$

$\therefore$ $$\frac{\partial^2 y}{\partial t^2} = \frac{\partial}{\partial t}\left(\frac{\partial y}{\partial t}\right) = c\left(\frac{\partial}{\partial u} - \frac{\partial}{\partial v}\right) c\left(\frac{\partial y}{\partial u} - \frac{\partial y}{\partial v}\right)$$

$$= c^2\left(\frac{\partial^2 y}{\partial u^2} - 2\frac{\partial^2 y}{\partial u \partial v} + \frac{\partial^2 y}{\partial v^2}\right) \qquad ...(9)$$

From (1), (6) and (9), we have

$$c^2\left(\frac{\partial^2 y}{\partial u^2} - 2\frac{\partial^2 y}{\partial u \partial v} + \frac{\partial^2 y}{\partial v^2}\right) = c^2\left(\frac{\partial^2 y}{\partial u^2} + 2\frac{\partial^2 y}{\partial u \partial v} + \frac{\partial^2 y}{\partial v^2}\right)$$

$\Rightarrow$ $$-4c^2 \frac{\partial^2 y}{\partial u \partial v} = 0$$

$\Rightarrow$ $$\frac{\partial^2 y}{\partial u \partial v} = 0 \quad ...(10) \quad (\because \ c^2 \neq 0)$$

Integrating eqn. (10) partially, w.r.t. u, we get

$$\frac{\partial y}{\partial v} = f_1(v).$$

Integrating again w.r.t. v partially, we get

$$y = \int f_1(v)\, \partial v + \psi(u) = \phi(v) + \psi(u)$$

$\Rightarrow$ $$y(x, t) = \phi(x - ct) + \psi(x + ct) \quad ...(11)$$

which is *d'* Alembert's solution of wave equation.

Applying initial conditions $y = f(x)$ and $\frac{\partial y}{\partial t} = 0$ at $t = 0$ in (11), we get

$$f(x) = \phi(x) + \psi(x) \text{ and } 0 = -\phi'(x) + \psi'(x)$$

Hence, $$\phi(x) = \psi(x) = \frac{1}{2} f(x)$$

$\therefore$ $$y = \frac{1}{2}[f(x + ct) + f(x - ct)].$$

Example 11. *A tightly stretched string with fixed end points $x = 0$ and $x = \pi$ is initially at rest in its equilibrium position. If it is set vibrating by giving to each of its points an initial velocity*

$$\left(\frac{\partial y}{\partial t}\right)_{t=0} = 0.03 \sin x - 0.04 \sin 3x$$

then find the displacement $y(x, t)$ at any point of string at any time t.

Sol. The equation for the vibrations of a string is

$$\frac{\partial^2 y}{\partial t^2} = c^2 \frac{\partial^2 y}{\partial x^2} \quad ...(1)$$

Its solution is

$$y(x, t) = (c_1 \cos pct + c_2 \sin pct)(c_3 \cos px + c_4 \sin px) \quad ...(2)$$

Boundary conditions are

$$y(0, t) = 0 = y(\pi, t)$$
$$y(x, 0) = 0$$

and $$\left(\frac{\partial y}{\partial t}\right)_{t=0} = 0.03 \sin x - 0.04 \sin 3x.$$

From (2), $$y(0, t) = 0 = (c_1 \cos pct + c_2 \sin pct)\, c_3$$

$\Rightarrow$ $$c_3 = 0$$

From (2), $$y(x, t) = (c_1 \cos pct + c_2 \sin pct)\, c_4 \sin px \quad ...(3)$$

$$y(\pi, t) = 0 = (c_1 \cos pct + c_2 \sin pct)\, c_4 \sin p\pi$$

$\Rightarrow$ $$\sin p\pi = 0 = \sin n\pi \ (n \in \text{I})$$

$\Rightarrow$ $$p = n$$

From (3), $$y(x, t) = (c_1 \cos nct + c_2 \sin nct)\, c_4 \sin nx \quad ...(4)$$

$$y(x, 0) = 0 = c_1 c_4 \sin nx$$

$\Rightarrow$ $$c_1 = 0.$$

$\therefore$ From (4), $$y(x, t) = c_2 c_4 \sin nct \sin nx = b_n \sin nct \sin nx \quad ...(5)$$

where $$c_2 c_4 = b_n$$

The most general solution is

$$y(x, t) = \sum_{n=1}^{\infty} b_n \sin nct \sin nx$$

$$\frac{\partial y}{\partial t} = \sum_{n=1}^{\infty} nc\, b_n \cos nct \sin nx$$

At $t = 0$,

$$\left(\frac{\partial y}{\partial t}\right)_{t=0} = \sum_{n=1}^{\infty} nc\, b_n \sin nx$$

$$0.03 \sin x - 0.04 \sin 3x = cb_1 \sin x + 2cb_2 \sin 2x + 3cb_3 \sin 3x + \ldots$$

$\Rightarrow$ $$cb_1 = 0.03 \Rightarrow b_1 = \frac{0.03}{c}$$

$$b_2 = 0$$

and $$3cb_3 = -0.04 \Rightarrow b_3 = \frac{-0.0133}{c}.$$

$\therefore$ From (6), $$y(x, t) = \frac{0.03}{c} \sin ct \sin x - \frac{0.0133}{c} \sin 3ct \sin 3x$$

$$= \frac{1}{c}[0.03 \sin x \sin ct - 0.0133 \sin 3x \sin 3ct].$$

TEST YOUR KNOWLEDGE

1. Find the deflection $y(x, t)$ of the vibrating string of length π and ends fixed, corresponding to zero initial velocity and initial deflection $f(x) = k(\sin x - \sin 2x)$ given $c^2 = 1$.

2. Solve : $y_{tt} = 4y_{xx}$; $y(0, t) = 0 = y(5, t)$, $y(x, 0) = 0$ $\left(\frac{\partial y}{\partial t}\right)_{t=0} = f(x)$

if (*i*) $f(x) = 5 \sin \pi x$ (*ii*) $f(x) = 3 \sin 2\pi x - 2 \sin 5\pi x$.

3. Find the deflection of the vibrating string which is fixed at the ends $x = 0$ and $x = 2$ and the motion is started by displacing the string into the form $\sin^3\left(\frac{\pi x}{2}\right)$ and releasing it with zero initial velocity at $t = 0$. (*M.T.U. 2012*)

4. Find the solution of the equation of a vibrating string of length l satisfying the initial conditions :

$$y = F(x) \quad \text{when } t = 0$$

and $$\frac{\partial y}{\partial t} = \phi(x) \quad \text{when } t = 0$$

It is assumed that the equation of a vibrating string is $y_{tt} = a^2 y_{xx}$.

5. The vibrations of an elastic string is governed by the partial differential equation

$$\frac{\partial^2 u}{\partial t^2} = \frac{\partial^2 u}{\partial x^2}$$

The length of the string is π and ends are fixed. The initial velocity is zero and the initial deflection is $u(x, 0) = 2(\sin x + \sin 3x)$. Find the deflection $u(x, t)$ of the vibrating string at any time t.

6. A tight string of length 20 cms fastened at both ends is displaced from its position of equilibrium by imparting to each of its points an initial velocity given by

$$v = \left.\begin{matrix} x\,; & 0 \le x \le 10 \\ 20 - x\,; & 10 \le x \le 20 \end{matrix}\right\}\,;$$

x being the distance from one end. Determine the displacement at any subsequent time.

7. Using d' Alembert's method, find the deflection of a vibrating string of unit length having fixed ends, with initial velocity zero and initial deflection $f(x) = a(x - x^3)$.

8. Reduce the equation $u_{xx} - 2u_{xy} + u_{yy} = 0$ to its normal form using the transformation $v = x$, $z = x + y$ and solve it.

9. Solve the equation $\dfrac{\partial^2 u}{\partial x^2} + \dfrac{\partial^2 u}{\partial x \partial y} - 2\dfrac{\partial^2 u}{\partial y^2} = 0$ using the transformation $v = x + y$, $z = 2x - y$.

10. The ends of a tightly stretched string of length l are fixed at $x = 0$ and $x = l$. The string is at rest with the point $x = b$ drawn aside through a small distance d and released at time $t = 0$. Show that

$$y(x, t) = \frac{2dl^2}{\pi^2 b(l - b)} \sum_{n=1}^{\infty} \frac{1}{n^2} \sin \frac{n\pi b}{l} \sin \frac{n\pi x}{l} \cos \frac{n\pi ct}{l}.$$

11. Find the deflection of the vibrating string of unit length whose end points are fixed if the initial velocity is zero and the initial deflection is given by $u(x, 0) = \begin{Bmatrix} 1, & 0 \le x \le \dfrac{1}{2} \\ -1, & \dfrac{1}{2} < x \le 1 \end{Bmatrix}$ *(G.B.T.U. 2012)*

Answers

1. $y(x, t) = k(\cos t \sin x - \cos 2t \sin 2x)$

2. (*i*) $y(x, t) = \dfrac{5}{2\pi} \sin \pi x \sin 2\pi t$ (*ii*) $y(x, t) = \dfrac{3}{4\pi} \sin 2\pi x \sin 4\pi t - \dfrac{1}{5\pi} \sin 5\pi x \sin 10\pi t$

3. $y(x, t) = \dfrac{3}{4} \sin \dfrac{\pi x}{2} \cos \dfrac{\pi ct}{2} - \dfrac{1}{4} \sin \dfrac{3\pi x}{2} \cos \dfrac{3\pi ct}{2}$

4. $y(x, t) = \displaystyle\sum_{n=1}^{\infty} \sin \frac{n\pi x}{l} \left(a_n \cos \frac{n\pi at}{l} + b_n \sin \frac{n\pi at}{l} \right)$

where $a_n = \dfrac{2}{l} \displaystyle\int_0^l \mathrm{F}(x) \sin \frac{n\pi x}{l}\, dx$ and $b_n = \dfrac{2}{na\pi} \displaystyle\int_0^l \phi(x) \sin \frac{n\pi x}{l}\, dx$

5. $y(x, t) = 2[\cos t \sin x + \cos 3t \sin 3x]$

6. $y(x, t) = \dfrac{1600}{a\pi^3} \left[\sin \dfrac{\pi x}{20} \sin \dfrac{\pi at}{20} - \dfrac{1}{3^3} \sin \dfrac{3\pi x}{20} \sin \dfrac{3\pi at}{20} + \ldots\ldots \right]$

7. $y(x, t) = ax(1 - x^2 - 3c^2t^2)$

8. $\dfrac{\partial^2 u}{\partial v^2} = 0$; $u = xf_1(x + y) + f_2(x + y)$.

9. $\dfrac{\partial^2 u}{\partial v \partial z} = 0$; $u = f_1(x + y) + f_2(2x - y)$

11. $y(x, t) = \dfrac{2}{\pi} \displaystyle\sum_{n=1}^{\infty} \frac{1}{n} \left(1 + \cos n\pi - 2 \cos \frac{n\pi}{2} \right) \sin n\pi x \cos n\pi ct$

5.6. VIBRATING MEMBRANE—TWO-DIMENSIONAL WAVE EQUATION

We shall now obtain the equation for the vibrations of a tightly stretched membrane (such as the membrane of a drum). We shall assume that the membrane is uniform and the tension in it per unit length is the same at every point in all directions. Let T be the tension per unit length and m be the mass of the membrane per unit area.

Consider the forces on an element $\delta x \delta y$ of the membrane. Due to its displacement u, perpendicular to the xy-plane, the forces $T\delta y$ (tangential to the membrane) on its opposite edges of length δy act at angles α and β to the horizontal. So their vertical component

$= (T\delta y) \sin \beta - (T\delta y) \sin \alpha = T\delta y(\tan \beta - \tan \alpha)$ approximately, since α and β are small

$$= T\delta y \left[\left(\frac{\partial u}{\partial x} \right)_{x + \delta x} - \left(\frac{\partial u}{\partial x} \right)_x \right] = T\delta y \delta x \left[\frac{\left(\frac{\partial u}{\partial x} \right)_{x + \delta x} - \left(\frac{\partial u}{\partial x} \right)_x}{\delta x} \right]$$

$$= T\delta x \delta y \frac{\partial^2 u}{\partial x^2} \text{ upto a first order of approximation.}$$

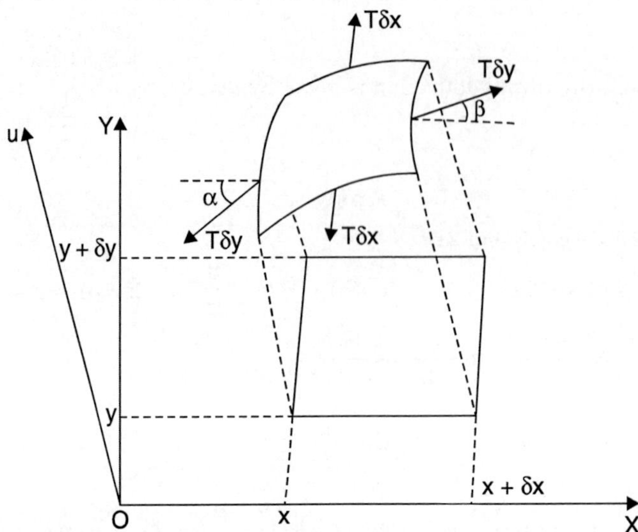

Similarly, the forces $T\delta x$ acting on the edges of length δx have the vertical component $T\delta x \delta y \dfrac{\partial^2 u}{\partial y^2}$.

Hence the equation of motion of the element is

$$(m\delta x \delta y) \frac{\partial^2 u}{\partial t^2} = T \left(\frac{\partial^2 u}{\partial x^2} + \frac{\partial^2 u}{\partial y^2} \right) \delta x \delta y$$

or
$$\boxed{\frac{\partial^2 u}{\partial t^2} = c^2 \left(\frac{\partial^2 u}{\partial x^2} + \frac{\partial^2 u}{\partial y^2} \right)} \quad \text{where } c^2 = \frac{T}{m}.$$

This is the wave equation in two dimensions.

5.7. SOLUTION OF TWO-DIMENSIONAL WAVE EQUATION

Two-dimensional wave equation is

$$\frac{\partial^2 u}{\partial t^2} = c^2 \left(\frac{\partial^2 u}{\partial x^2} + \frac{\partial^2 u}{\partial y^2} \right) \qquad ...(1)$$

Let $\qquad u = \text{XYT} \qquad ...(2)$

where X is a function of x only, Y is a function of y only and T is a function of t only, be a solution of (1).

Then $\qquad \frac{\partial^2 u}{\partial t^2} = \text{XYT}'', \frac{\partial^2 u}{\partial x^2} = \text{X}''\text{YT}$ and $\frac{\partial^2 u}{\partial y^2} = \text{XY}''\text{T}$

Substituting in (1), we have $\frac{1}{c^2}\text{XYT}'' = \text{X}''\text{YT} + \text{XY}''\text{T}$

Dividing by XYT, we have $\qquad \frac{1}{c^2}\frac{\text{T}''}{\text{T}} = \frac{\text{X}''}{\text{X}} + \frac{\text{Y}''}{\text{Y}} \qquad ...(3)$

This will be true only when *each member is a constant.* Choosing the constants suitably, we have

$$\frac{d^2\text{X}}{dx^2} + k^2\text{X} = 0, \quad \frac{d^2\text{Y}}{dy^2} + l^2\text{Y} = 0 \quad \text{and} \quad \frac{d^2\text{T}}{dt^2} + (k^2 + l^2)\, c^2\text{T} = 0$$

The solutions of these equations are respectively

$$\text{X} = c_1 \cos kx + c_2 \sin kx$$

$$\text{Y} = c_3 \cos ly + c_4 \sin ly$$

and $\qquad \text{T} = c_5 \cos \sqrt{(k^2 + l^2)}\, ct + c_6 \sin \sqrt{(k^2 + l^2)}\, ct$

Hence from (2), a solution of (1) is

$$u(x, y, t) = (c_1 \cos kx + c_2 \sin kx)(c_3 \cos ly + c_4 \sin ly)$$

$$[c_5 \cos \sqrt{(k^2 + l^2)}\, ct + c_6 \sin \sqrt{(k^2 + l^2)}\, ct] \qquad ...(4)$$

Now let us suppose that the membrane is rectangular and is stretched between the lines

$$x = 0,\ x = a,\ y = 0,\ y = b.$$

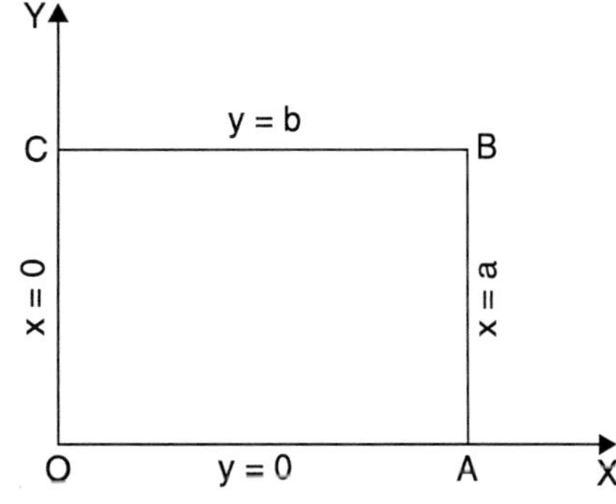

Then the boundary conditions are :

(*i*) $u = 0$, when $x = 0$

(*ii*) $u = 0$, when $x = a$

(*iii*) $u = 0$, when $y = 0$

(*iv*) $u = 0$, when $y = b$ for all t.

Applying the condition (*i*), we have

$$0 = c_1(c_3 \cos ly + c_4 \sin ly)[c_5 \cos \sqrt{(k^2 + l^2)}\, ct + c_6 \sin \sqrt{(k^2 + l^2)}\, ct]$$

i.e., $\qquad c_1 = 0$

Putting $c_1 = 0$ in (3) and applying the condition (*ii*), we have $\sin ka = 0$ or $k = \frac{m\pi}{a}$, where m is an integer.

Similarly, applying the conditions (*iii*) and (*iv*), we get

$$c_3 = 0 \quad \text{or} \quad l = \frac{n\pi}{b}, \text{ where } n \text{ is an integer.}$$

Therefore, the solution (3) becomes

$$u(x, y, t) = c_2 c_4 \sin \frac{m\pi x}{a} \sin \frac{n\pi y}{b} (c_5 \cos pt + c_6 \sin pt)$$

where $p = \pi c \sqrt{\frac{m^2}{a^2} + \frac{n^2}{b^2}}$

Replacing the arbitrary constants suitably, we can write the general solution as

$$u(x, y, t) = \sum_{m=1}^{\infty} \sum_{n=1}^{\infty} \sin \frac{m\pi x}{a} \sin \frac{n\pi y}{b} (A_{mn} \cos pt + B_{mn} \sin pt) \qquad \text{...(5)}$$

Now suppose the membrane starts from rest from the initial position $u = f(x, y)$ *i.e.*, $u(x, y, 0) = f(x, y)$.

Then applying the condition : $\frac{\partial u}{\partial t} = 0$ when $t = 0$, we get $B_{mn} = 0$.

Also using the condition : $u = f(x, y)$ when $t = 0$, we get

$$f(x, y) = \sum_{m=1}^{\infty} \sum_{n=1}^{\infty} A_{mn} \sin \frac{m\pi x}{a} \sin \frac{n\pi y}{b} \qquad \text{...(6)}$$

This is a double Fourier series. Multiplying both sides by $\sin \frac{m\pi x}{a} \sin \frac{n\pi y}{b}$ and integrating from $x = 0$ to $x = a$ and $y = 0$ to $y = b$, every term on the right except one becomes zero. Thus, we get

$$\int_0^a \int_0^b f(x, y) \sin \frac{m\pi x}{a} \sin \frac{n\pi y}{b} \, dy \, dx = \frac{ab}{4} A_{mn}$$

i.e.,

$$A_{mn} = \frac{4}{ab} \int_0^a \int_0^b f(x, y) \sin \frac{m\pi x}{b} \sin \frac{n\pi y}{a} \, dy \, dx \qquad \text{...(7)}$$

Hence, from (5), the required solution is

$$u(x, y, t) = \sum_{m=1}^{\infty} \sum_{n=1}^{\infty} A_{mn} \sin \frac{m\pi x}{a} \sin \frac{n\pi y}{b} \cos pt$$

where A_{mn} is given by (7) and $p = \pi c \sqrt{\frac{m^2}{a^2} + \frac{n^2}{b^2}}$.

ILLUSTRATIVE EXAMPLES

Example 1. *Find the deflection $u(x, y, t)$ of the square membrane with $a = b = c = 1$, if the initial velocity is zero and the initial deflection $f(x, y) = A \sin \pi x \sin 2\pi y$.*

Sol. The vibrations of the square membrane are governed by two dimensional wave equation

$$\frac{\partial^2 u}{\partial t^2} = c^2 \left(\frac{\partial^2 u}{\partial x^2} + \frac{\partial^2 u}{\partial y^2} \right) \qquad ...(1)$$

Here the boundary conditions are,

$$u(0, y, t) = 0, u(1, y, t) = 0, \quad u(x, 0, t) = 0, u(x, 1, t) = 0$$

and the initial conditions are

$$u(x, y, 0) = f(x, y) = \text{A} \sin \pi x \sin 2\pi y \quad \text{and} \quad \left(\frac{\partial u}{\partial t} \right)_{t=0} = 0$$

To solve eqn. (1), let $u = \text{XYT}$ ...(2)

where X is function of x only, Y is a function of y only, and T is a function of t only.

$$\frac{\partial^2 u}{\partial t^2} = \frac{\partial^2}{\partial t^2} (\text{XYT}) = \text{XY} \frac{d^2\text{T}}{dt^2}$$

$$\frac{\partial^2 u}{\partial x^2} = \frac{\partial^2}{\partial x^2} (\text{XYT}) = \text{YT} \frac{d^2\text{X}}{dx^2}$$

$$\frac{\partial^2 u}{\partial y^2} = \frac{\partial^2}{\partial y^2} (\text{XYT}) = \text{XT} \frac{d^2\text{Y}}{dy^2},$$

From (1), $\quad \text{XYT}'' = (\text{YTX}'' + \text{XTY}'')c^2$

$$\Rightarrow \quad \frac{1}{c^2} \frac{\text{T}''}{\text{T}} = \frac{\text{X}''}{\text{X}} + \frac{\text{Y}''}{\text{Y}}$$

This will be true only when each member is a constant. Choosing the constant suitably, we have

$$\frac{d^2\text{X}}{dx^2} + k^2\text{X} = 0, \; \frac{d^2\text{Y}}{dy^2} + l^2\text{Y} = 0 \quad \text{and} \quad \frac{d^2\text{T}}{dt^2} + (k^2 + l^2) c^2\text{T} = 0.$$

The solutions of these equations are respectively,

$$\text{X} = c_1 \cos kx + c_2 \sin kx$$

$$\text{Y} = c_3 \cos ly + c_4 \sin ly$$

and

$$\text{T} = c_5 \cos \sqrt{k^2 + l^2} \; ct + c_6 \sin \sqrt{k^2 + l^2} \; ct.$$

$$\therefore \quad u(x, y, t) = (c_1 \cos kx + c_2 \sin kx)(c_3 \cos ly + c_4 \sin y)$$

$$[c_5 \cos \sqrt{k^2 + l^2} \; ct + c_6 \sin \sqrt{k^2 + l^2} \; ct] \qquad ...(3)$$

From (3), $u(0, y, t) = 0 = c_1(c_3 \cos ly + c_4 \sin ly)(c_5 \cos \sqrt{k^2 + l^2}\, ct + c_6 \sin \sqrt{k^2 + l^2}\, ct)$

$\Rightarrow \quad c_1 = 0.$

$\therefore$ From (3),

$$u(x, y, t) = c_2 \sin kx(c_3 \cos ly + c_4 \sin ly)(c_5 \cos \sqrt{k^2 + l^2}\, ct + c_6 \sin \sqrt{k^2 + l^2}\, ct) \quad ...(4)$$

$$u(1, y, t) = 0 = c_2 \sin k(c_3 \cos ly + c_4 \sin ly)(c_5 \cos \sqrt{k^2 + l^2}\, ct + c_6 \sin \sqrt{k^2 + l^2}\, ct)$$

$\Rightarrow \quad \sin k = 0 = \sin m\pi \ (m \in \mathrm{I})$

$k = m\pi.$

$\therefore$ From (4), $u(x, y, t) = c_2 \sin m\pi x(c_3 \cos ly + c_4 \sin ly)$

$$(c_5 \cos \sqrt{k^2 + l^2}\, ct + c_6 \sin \sqrt{k^2 + l^2}\, ct) \quad ...(5)$$

$$u(x, 0, t) = 0 = c_2 \sin m\pi x \,.\, c_3(c_5 \cos \sqrt{k^2 + l^2}\, ct + c_6 \sin \sqrt{k^2 + l^2}\, ct]$$

$\Rightarrow \quad c_3 = 0.$

$\therefore$ From (5), $u(x, y, t) = c_2c_4 \sin m\pi x \sin ly\, (c_5 \cos \sqrt{k^2 + l^2}\, ct + c_6 \sin \sqrt{k^2 + l^2}\, ct)$ ...(6)

$$u(x, 1, t) = 0 = c_2c_4 \sin m\pi x \sin l\, (c_5 \cos \sqrt{k^2 + l^2}\, ct + c_6 \sin \sqrt{k^2 + l^2}\, ct)$$

$\Rightarrow \quad \sin l = 0 = \sin n\pi \ (n \in \mathrm{I})$

$\Rightarrow \quad l = n\pi.$

$\therefore$ From (6), $u(x, y, t) = c_2c_4 \sin m\pi x \sin n\pi y\, (c_5 \cos \sqrt{k^2 + l^2}\, ct + c_6 \sin \sqrt{k^2 + l^2}\, ct)$

$$u(x, y, t) = \sin m\pi x \sin n\pi y\, (\mathrm{A}_{mn} \cos pt + \mathrm{B}_{mn} \sin pt) \quad ...(7)$$

where $p = \pi c \sqrt{m^2 + n^2}$.

The most general solution is

$$u(x, y, t) = \sum_{m=1}^{\infty} \sum_{n=1}^{\infty} \sin m\pi x \sin n\pi y\, (\mathrm{A}_{mn} \cos pt + \mathrm{B}_{mn} \sin pt) \quad ...(8)$$

Applying the condition,

$$\frac{\partial u}{\partial t} = 0 \text{ at } t = 0$$

we get $\mathrm{B}_{mn} = 0$ ...(9)

Also, using the condition $u = f(x, y) = \mathrm{A} \sin \pi x \sin 2\pi y$ when $t = 0$, we get

$$\mathrm{A} \sin \pi x \sin 2\pi y = \sum_{m=1}^{\infty} \sum_{n=1}^{\infty} \mathrm{A}_{mn} \sin m\pi x \sin n\pi y$$

This is a double Fourier Series.

$$\mathrm{A}_{mn} = \frac{2}{1} \cdot \frac{2}{1} \int_0^1 \int_0^1 \mathrm{A} \sin \pi x \sin 2\pi y \sin m\pi x \sin n\pi y \, dx\, dy$$

Obviously, $\mathrm{A}_{m1} = \mathrm{A}_{m3} = \mathrm{A}_{m4} = \ldots\ldots = 0$

But, $$A_{m2} = 4A \int_0^1 \int_0^1 \sin \pi x \sin m\pi x \sin^2 2\pi y \, dx\, dy$$
$$= 2A \int_0^1 \int_0^1 \sin \pi x \sin m\pi x \, (1 - \cos 4\pi y) \, dx\, dy$$
$$= 2A \int_0^1 \sin \pi x \sin m\pi x \left(y - \frac{\sin 4\pi y}{4\pi} \right)_0^1 dx$$
$$= 2A \int_0^1 \sin \pi x \sin m\pi x \, dx$$

Again, obviously,
$$A_{22} = A_{32} = A_{42} = \ldots = 0$$

But, $$A_{12} = 2A \int_0^1 \sin^2 \pi x \, dx = A \int_0^1 (1 - \cos 2\pi x) \, dx$$
$$= A \left(x - \frac{\sin 2\pi x}{2\pi} \right)_0^1 = A \qquad \ldots(10)$$

$\therefore$ From (8), (9) and (10), we get
$$u(x, y, t) = A \sin \pi x \sin 2\pi y \cos pt \qquad \ldots(11)$$

where $$p = \pi c \sqrt{m^2 + n^2} = \pi(1) \sqrt{1+4} = \pi\sqrt{5}.$$

$\therefore$ From (11), $u(x, y, t) = A \cos \pi\sqrt{5}\, t \sin \pi x \sin 2\pi y$.

Example 2. *Find the deflection $u(x, y, t)$ of a rectangular membrane $(0 \le x \le a, 0 \le y \le b)$ whose boundary is fixed ; given that it starts from rest and $u(x, y, 0) = xy(a - x)(b - y)$. Show that the deflection u is given by*

$$u(x, y, t) = \sum_{m=1}^{\infty} \sum_{n=1}^{\infty} A_{mn} \cos ckt \sin \frac{m\pi x}{a} \sin \frac{n\pi y}{b}$$

where $$A_{mn} = \frac{16a^2b^2}{m^3 n^3 \pi^6}(1 - \cos m\pi)(1 - \cos n\pi) \quad \text{and} \quad k^2 = \pi^2 \left(\frac{m^2}{a^2} + \frac{n^2}{b^2} \right).$$

Sol. Proceeding as in Art. 5.7, we have

$$u(x, y, t) = \sum_{m=1}^{\infty} \sum_{n=1}^{\infty} A_{mn} \sin \frac{m\pi x}{a} \sin \frac{n\pi y}{b} \cos pt$$

where $$p = \pi c \sqrt{\frac{m^2}{a^2} + \frac{n^2}{b^2}} \qquad \ldots(1)$$

From (1), $$u(x, y, 0) = \sum_{m=1}^{\infty} \sum_{n=1}^{\infty} A_{mn} \sin \frac{m\pi x}{a} \sin \frac{n\pi y}{b}$$

$$xy\,(a - x)(b - y) = \sum_{m=1}^{\infty} \sum_{n=1}^{\infty} A_{mn} \sin \frac{m\pi x}{a} \sin \frac{n\pi y}{b}$$

where $$A_{mn} = \frac{2}{a} \cdot \frac{2}{b} \int_0^a \int_0^b xy\,(a-x)(b-y) \sin \frac{m\pi x}{a} \sin \frac{n\pi y}{b}\, dy\, dx$$

$$= \frac{4}{ab} \int_0^a x(a-x) \sin \frac{m\pi x}{a}\, dx \, . \int_0^b y(b-y) \sin \frac{n\pi y}{b}\, dy$$

$$= \frac{4}{ab} \left[x(a-x) \left(\frac{-\cos \frac{m\pi x}{a}}{\frac{m\pi}{a}} \right) - (a-2x) \left(\frac{-\sin \frac{m\pi x}{a}}{\frac{m^2\pi^2}{a^2}} \right) + (-2) \left(\frac{\cos \frac{m\pi x}{a}}{\frac{m^3\pi^3}{a^3}} \right) \right]_0^a$$

$$\times \left[y(b-y) \left(\frac{-\cos \frac{n\pi y}{b}}{\frac{n\pi}{b}} \right) - (b-2y) \left(\frac{-\sin \frac{n\pi y}{b}}{\frac{n^2\pi^2}{b^2}} \right) + (-2) \left(\frac{\cos \frac{n\pi y}{b}}{\frac{n^3\pi^3}{b^3}} \right) \right]_0^b$$

$$= \frac{4}{ab} \left[\frac{-2a^3}{m^3\pi^3} \cos m\pi + \frac{2a^3}{m^3\pi^3} \right] \left[\frac{-2b^3}{n^3\pi^3} \cos n\pi + \frac{2b^3}{n^3\pi^3} \right]$$

$$= \frac{4}{ab} \cdot \frac{2a^3}{m^3\pi^3} \cdot \frac{2b^3}{n^3\pi^3} [1-(-1)^n]\,[1-(-1)^m]$$

$$A_{mn} = \frac{16a^2b^2}{m^3n^3\pi^6} [1-(-1)^n]\,[1-(-1)^m].$$

Hence from (1),

$$u(x, y, t) = \frac{16a^2b^2}{\pi^6} \sum_{m=1}^{\infty} \sum_{n=1}^{\infty} \frac{[1-(-1)^n][1-(-1)^m]}{m^3n^3} \sin \frac{m\pi x}{a} \sin \frac{n\pi y}{b} \cos pt$$

where $$p = \pi c \sqrt{\frac{m^2}{a^2} + \frac{n^2}{b^2}} \qquad \text{...(2)}$$

Expression (2) may also be put in as,

$$u(x, y, t) = \sum_{m=1}^{\infty} \sum_{n=1}^{\infty} A_{mn} \cos ckt \sin \frac{m\pi x}{a} \sin \frac{n\pi y}{b}$$

where $$A_{mn} = \frac{16a^2b^2}{m^3\pi^6n^3} (1-\cos m\pi)(1-\cos n\pi) \quad \text{and} \quad k^2 = \pi^2 \left(\frac{m^2}{a^2} + \frac{n^2}{b^2} \right).$$

Example 3. *A tightly stretched unit square membrane starts vibrating from rest and its initial displacement is k sin 2πx sin πy. Show that the deflection at any instant is*

$$k \sin 2\pi x \sin \pi y \cos (\sqrt{5}\, \pi ct).$$

Sol. Here we have to solve the equation $\dfrac{\partial^2 u}{\partial t^2} = c^2 \left(\dfrac{\partial^2 u}{\partial x^2} + \dfrac{\partial^2 u}{\partial y^2} \right)$

with boundary conditions $u(0, y, t) = u(1, y, t) = u(x, 0, t) = u(x, 1, t) = 0$

and the initial conditions $u(x, y, 0) = f(x, y) = k \sin 2\pi x \sin \pi y$

$$\frac{\partial u}{\partial t} = 0 \quad \text{when } t = 0$$

Proceeding as in Ex. 1, we have

$$u(x, y, t) = \sum_{m=1}^{\infty} \sum_{n=1}^{\infty} A_{mn} \sin m\pi x \sin n\pi y \cos pt \qquad \text{...(1)}$$

Since, $a = b = 1$, where $p = \pi c \sqrt{m^2 + n^2}$

and
$$A_{mn} = \frac{4}{1 \times 1} \int_0^1 \int_0^1 k \sin 2\pi x \sin \pi y \sin m\pi x \sin n\pi y \, dy dx$$

$$= 4k \int_0^1 \sin m\pi x \sin 2\pi x \, dx \int_0^1 \sin n\pi y \sin \pi y \, dy$$

$$= 0 \quad \text{for } m \neq 2 \quad \text{or} \quad n \neq 1$$

$$\therefore \quad A_{21} = 4k(\tfrac{1}{2})(\tfrac{1}{2}) = k \quad \text{and} \quad p = \pi c \sqrt{(2)^2 + (1)^2} = \sqrt{5}\, \pi c$$

Hence solution (1) reduces to $u(x, y, t) = k \sin 2\pi x \sin \pi y \cos (\sqrt{5}\, \pi ct)$.

TEST YOUR KNOWLEDGE

1. Find the deflecting $u(x, y, t)$ of a rectangular membrane $(0 < x < 1, 0 < y < 2)$ whose boundary is fixed, given that it starts from rest and $u(x, y, 0) = xy(1 - x)(2 - y)$.
2. Find the deflection $u(x, y, t)$ of a rectangular membrane $(0 < x < a, 0 < y < b)$ whose boundary is fixed, given that it starts from rest and $u(x, y, 0) = xy(a^2 - x^2)(b^2 - y^2)$.
3. Find the deflection $u(x, y, t)$ of the tightly stretched rectangular membrane with sides a and b having wave velocity $c = 1$ if the initial velocity is zero and the initial deflection is

$$f(x, y) = \sin \frac{2\pi x}{a} \sin \frac{3\pi y}{b}. \qquad (G.B.T.U.\ 2011)$$

Answers

1. $u(x, y, t) = \sum_{m=1}^{\infty} \sum_{n=1}^{\infty} A_{mn} \sin m\pi x \sin \frac{n\pi y}{2} \cos pt$, where $A_{mn} = \frac{256}{m^3 n^3 \pi^6}$, both m, n odd and $p = \pi c \sqrt{m^2 + \frac{n^2}{4}}$
2. $u(x, y, t) = \sum_{m=1}^{\infty} \sum_{n=1}^{\infty} A_{mn} \sin \frac{m\pi x}{a} \sin \frac{n\pi y}{b} \cos pt$, where $A_{mn} = \frac{144 a^3 b^3}{m^3 n^3 \pi^6}$ and $p = \pi c \sqrt{\frac{m^2}{a^2} + \frac{n^2}{b^2}}$.
3. $u(x, y, t) = \sin \frac{2\pi x}{a} \sin \frac{3\pi y}{b} \cos pt$ where $p = \pi \sqrt{\frac{4}{a^2} + \frac{9}{b^2}}$.

5.8. ONE-DIMENSIONAL HEAT FLOW $\frac{\partial u}{\partial t} = c^2 \frac{\partial^2 u}{\partial x^2}$ [U.P.T.U. (C.O). 2009]

Consider the flow of heat by conducting in a uniform bar. It is assumed that the sides of the bar are insulated and the loss of heat from the sides by conduction or radiation is negligible. Take one end of the bar as origin and the direction of flow as the positive x-axis. The temperature

u at any point of the bar depends on the distance x of the point from one end and the time t. Also, the temperature of all points of any cross-section is the same.

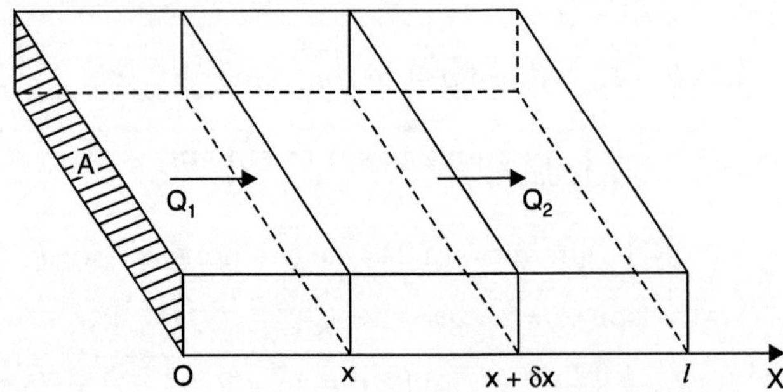

The amount of heat crossing any section of the bar per second depends on the area A of the cross-section, the conductivity K of the material of the bar and the temperature gradient $\frac{\partial u}{\partial x}$ *i.e.*, rate of change of temperature w.r.t. distance normal to the area.

$\therefore$ Q_1, the quantity of heat flowing into the section at a distance x

$$= -KA \left(\frac{\partial u}{\partial x}\right)_x \text{ per sec.}$$

(the negative sign on the right is attached because as x increases, u decreases).

Q_2, the quantity of heat flowing out of the section at a distance $x + \delta x$

$$= -KA \left(\frac{\partial u}{\partial x}\right)_{x+\delta x} \text{ per sec.}$$

Hence the amount of heat retained by the slab with thickness δx is

$$Q_1 - Q_2 = KA \left[\left(\frac{\partial u}{\partial x}\right)_{x+\delta x} - \left(\frac{\partial u}{\partial x}\right)_x\right] \text{ per sec.} \quad ...(1)$$

But the rate of increase of heat in the slab $= S\rho A\, \delta x \frac{\partial u}{\partial t}$ ...(2)

where S is the specific heat and ρ, the density of the material.

$\therefore$ From (1) and (2), $S\rho A\, \delta x \frac{\partial u}{\partial t} = KA \left[\left(\frac{\partial u}{\partial x}\right)_{x+\delta x} - \left(\frac{\partial u}{\partial x}\right)_x\right]$

or

$$S\rho \frac{\partial u}{\partial t} = K \left[\frac{\left(\frac{\partial u}{\partial x}\right)_{x+\delta x} - \left(\frac{\partial u}{\partial x}\right)_x}{\delta x}\right]$$

Taking the limit as $\delta x \to 0$, we have

$$S\rho \frac{\partial u}{\partial t} = K \frac{\partial^2 u}{\partial x^2} \quad \text{or} \quad \frac{\partial u}{\partial t} = \frac{K}{S\rho} \frac{\partial^2 u}{\partial x^2}$$

or $$\boxed{\frac{\partial u}{\partial t} = c^2 \frac{\partial^2 u}{\partial x^2}}$$, where $c^2 = \dfrac{K}{S\rho}$ is known as diffusivity of the material of the bar.

5.9. SOLUTION OF THE HEAT EQUATION

[*G.B.T.U. (C.O.) 2011; U.P.T.U. 2007*]

The heat equation is $$\frac{\partial u}{\partial t} = c^2 \frac{\partial^2 u}{\partial x^2} \quad ...(1)$$

Let $$u = XT \quad ...(2)$$

where X is a function of x only and T is a function of t only, be a solution of (1).

Then $$\frac{\partial u}{\partial t} = XT' \quad \text{and} \quad \frac{\partial^2 u}{\partial x^2} = X''T$$

Substituting in (1), we have $$XT' = c^2X''T$$

Separating the variables, we get $$\frac{X''}{X} = \frac{1}{c^2}\frac{T'}{T} \quad ...(3)$$

Now the L.H.S. of (3) is a function of x only and the R.H.S. is a function of t only. Since x and t are independent variables, this equation can hold only when both sides reduce to a constant, say k. The equation (3) leads to the ordinary differential equations

$$\frac{d^2X}{dx^2} - kX = 0 \quad \text{and} \quad \frac{dT}{dt} - kc^2T = 0 \quad ...(4)$$

Solving equations (4), we get

(*i*) *When k is positive* and $= p^2$, say

$$X = c_1e^{px} + c_2e^{-px},\ T = c_3\ e^{c^2p^2t}$$

(*ii*) *When k is negative* and $= -p^2$, say

$$X = c_1 \cos px + c_2 \sin px,\ T = c_3\ e^{-c^2p^2t}$$

(*iii*) *When k = 0*

$$X = c_1x + c_2,\ T = c_3.$$

Thus the various possible solutions of the heat equation (1) are :

$$u = (c_1\ e^{px} + c_2\ e^{-px})\ .\ c_3\ e^{c^2p^2t} \quad ...(5)$$

$$u = (c_1 \cos px + c_2 \sin px)\ .\ c_3e^{-c^2p^2t} \quad ...(6)$$

$$u = (c_1x + c_2)\ c_3 \quad ...(7)$$

Of these three solutions, we have to choose that solution which is consistent with the physical nature of the problem. Since u decreases as time t increases, the only suitable solution of the heat equation is

$$u = (c_1 \cos px + c_2 \sin px)\ c_3\ e^{-c^2p^2t}.$$

Solution (5) is rejected since $u \to \infty$ as $t \to \infty$.

Also, solution (7) is rejected as it gives a non-zero temperature at all times.

ILLUSTRATIVE EXAMPLES

Example 1. *A rod of length l with insulated sides is initially at a uniform temperature u_0. Its ends are suddenly cooled to 0°C and are kept at that temperature. Find the temperature function u(x, t).* [G.B.T.U. (SUM) 2010; G.B.T.U. 2011]

Sol. The temperature function $u(x, t)$ satisfies the differential equation

$$\frac{\partial u}{\partial t} = c^2 \frac{\partial^2 u}{\partial x^2}$$

As proved in Art. 5.9, we have

$$u(x, t) = (c_1 \cos px + c_2 \sin px)\, c_3 e^{-c^2p^2t} \qquad ...(1)$$

Since the ends $x = 0$ and $x = l$ are cooled to 0°C and kept at that temperature throughout, the boundary conditions are $u(0, t) = u(l, t) = 0$ for all t

Also $u(x, 0) = u_0$ is the initial condition.

Since $u(0, t) = 0$, we have from (1),

$$0 = c_1 c_3 e^{-c^2p^2t} \quad \Rightarrow \quad c_1 = 0$$

$\therefore$ From (1), $\quad u(x, t) = c_2 c_3 \sin px.\, e^{-c^2p^2t} \qquad ...(2)$

Since $u(l, t) = 0$, we have from (2),

$$0 = c_2 c_3 \sin pl \,.\, e^{-c^2p^2t}$$

$$\Rightarrow \qquad \sin pl = 0 \quad \Rightarrow \quad pl = n\pi$$

$$\therefore \qquad p = \frac{n\pi}{l}, \; n \text{ being an integer}$$

Solution (2) reduces to $u(x, t) = b_n \sin \frac{n\pi x}{l} \cdot e^{\frac{-c^2n^2\pi^2t}{l^2}}$ on replacing c_2c_3 by b_n.

The most general solution is obtained by adding all such solutions for $n = 1, 2, 3,......$

$$\therefore \qquad u(x, t) = \sum_{n=1}^{\infty} b_n \sin \frac{n\pi x}{l} . e^{\frac{-c^2n^2\pi^2t}{l^2}} \qquad ...(3)$$

Since $u(x, 0) = u_0$, we have $\quad u_0 = \sum_{n=1}^{\infty} b_n \sin \frac{n\pi x}{l}$

which is half-range since series for u_0.

$$b_n = \frac{2}{l}\int_0^l u_0 \sin \frac{n\pi x}{l}\, dx = \begin{cases} 0 \;, & \text{when } n \text{ is even} \\ \dfrac{4u_0}{n\pi}, & \text{when } n \text{ is odd} \end{cases}$$

Hence the temperature function

$$u(x, t) = \frac{4u_0}{\pi} \sum_{n=1, 3, 5 ......}^{\infty} \frac{1}{n} \sin \frac{n\pi x}{l}\, e^{-\frac{c^2n^2\pi^2t}{l^2}}$$

$$= \frac{4u_0}{\pi} \sum_{n=1}^{\infty} \frac{1}{2n-1} \sin \frac{(2n-1)\pi x}{l}\, e^{-\frac{c^2(2n-1)^2\pi^2t}{l^2}}.$$

Example 2. *Find the temperature in a bar of length 2 whose ends are kept at zero and lateral surface insulated if the initial temperature is* $\sin \frac{\pi x}{2} + 3 \sin \frac{5\pi x}{2}$.

[M.T.U. 2011; U.P.T.U. (C.O.) 2007; U.P.T.U. 2009]

Sol. Let $u(x, t)$ be the temperature in the bar. The boundary conditions are

$$u(0, t) = 0 = u(2, t) \text{ for any } t. \quad \ldots(1)$$

The initial condition is

$$u(x, 0) = \sin \frac{\pi x}{2} + 3 \sin \frac{5\pi x}{2} \quad \ldots(2)$$

One-dimensional heat flow equation is

$$\frac{\partial u}{\partial t} = c^2 \frac{\partial^2 u}{\partial x^2} \quad \ldots(3)$$

Its solution is

$$u(x, t) = (c_1 \cos px + c_2 \sin px)\, c_3\, e^{-c^2p^2t} \quad \ldots(4)$$

$$u(0, t) = 0 = c_1 c_3 e^{-c^2p^2t} \quad | \text{ Using (1)}$$

$\Rightarrow$ $c_1 = 0$

$\therefore$ From (4),

$$u(x, t) = c_2 c_3 \sin px\, e^{-c^2p^2t} \quad \ldots(5)$$

$$u(2, t) = 0 = c_2 c_3 \sin 2p\, e^{-c^2p^2t} \quad | \text{ Using (1)}$$

$\Rightarrow$ $\sin 2p = 0 = \sin n\pi$

$\therefore$ $p = \frac{n\pi}{2},\ n \in I$

Hence from (5),

$$u(x, t) = b_n \sin \frac{n\pi x}{2}\, e^{-\frac{n^2\pi^2c^2t}{4}} \quad | \because\ c_2c_3 = b_n$$

The most general solution is

$$u(x, t) = \sum_{n=1}^{\infty} b_n \sin \frac{n\pi x}{2}\, e^{-\frac{n^2\pi^2c^2t}{4}} \quad \ldots(6)$$

$$u(x, 0) = \sin\left(\frac{\pi x}{2}\right) + 3\sin\left(\frac{5\pi x}{2}\right) = \sum_{n=1}^{\infty} b_n \sin \frac{n\pi x}{2}$$

$$= b_1 \sin\left(\frac{\pi x}{2}\right) + b_2 \sin\left(\frac{2\pi x}{2}\right) + \ldots + b_5 \sin\left(\frac{5\pi x}{2}\right) + \ldots$$

Comparing, we get

$$b_1 = 1 \text{ and } b_5 = 3$$

Hence from (6),

$$u(x,\, t) = \sin\left(\frac{\pi x}{2}\right)\, e^{-\pi^2 c^2 t/4} + 3\,\sin\left(\frac{5\pi x}{2}\right)\, e^{-25\pi^2 c^2 t/4}.$$

Example 3. *An insulated rod of length l has its ends A and B maintained at 0°C and 100°C respectively until steady state conditions prevail. If B is suddenly reduced to 0°C and maintained at 0°C, find the temperature at a distance x from A at time t.*

[G.B.T.U. (A.G.) 2011, U.K.T.U. 2011]

Find also the temperature if the change consists of raising the temperature of A to 20°C and reducing that of B to 80°C.

Sol. Initial temperature distribution in the rod is

$$u_1 = 0 + \left(\frac{100-0}{l}\right)x = \frac{100}{l}\,x$$

Final temperature distribution (*i.e.*, in steady state) is

$$u_2 = 0 + \left(\frac{0-0}{l}\right)x = 0$$

To get u in the intermediate period,

$$u = u_2(x) + u_1(x,\, t)$$

where $u_2(x)$ is the steady state temperature distribution in the rod. $u_1(x, t)$ is the transient temperature distribution which tends to zero as t increases.

$u_1(x, t)$ satisfies one dimensional heat flow equation

$$\therefore \qquad u(x,\, t) = \sum_{n=1}^{\infty} (a_n \cos px + b_n \sin px)\, e^{-c^2 p^2 t} \qquad ...(1)$$

In steady state, $u(0, t) = 0 = u(l, t)$ ...(2)

$$\therefore \text{ From (1), } \qquad u(0,\, t) = 0 = \sum_{n=1}^{\infty} a_n e^{-c^2 p^2 t} \;\Rightarrow\; a_n = 0 \qquad ...(3)$$

$$\text{Also, } \qquad u(l,\, t) = 0 = \sum_{n=1}^{\infty} b_n \sin pl\, e^{-c^2 p^2 t} \qquad | \text{ using (3)}$$

$$\Rightarrow \qquad \sin pl = 0 = \sin n\pi,\; n \in \mathrm{I}$$

$$\text{or} \qquad p = \frac{n\pi}{l} \qquad ...(4)$$

$$\therefore \text{ From (1), (3) and (4), } u(x,\, t) = \sum_{n=1}^{\infty} b_n \sin \frac{n\pi x}{l}\, e^{-\left(\frac{n\pi}{l}\right)^2 c^2 t} \qquad ...(5)$$

Using initial condition,

$$u(x,\, 0) = \frac{100}{l}\, x = \sum_{n=1}^{\infty} b_n \sin \frac{n\pi x}{l}$$

which is half-range sine series for $\dfrac{100}{l}\, x$.

$\therefore \qquad b_n = \frac{2}{l}\int_0^l \frac{100}{l} x \sin\frac{n\pi x}{l}\, dx$

$$= \frac{200}{l^2}\left[\left\{x.\left(\frac{-\cos\frac{n\pi x}{l}}{\frac{n\pi}{l}}\right)\right\}_0^l - \int_0^l 1.\left(\frac{-\cos\frac{n\pi x}{l}}{\frac{n\pi}{l}}\right)dx\right]$$

$$= \frac{200}{l^2}\left[\frac{-l^2}{n\pi}\cos n\pi + \frac{l}{n\pi}\left(\frac{\sin\frac{n\pi x}{l}}{\frac{n\pi}{l}}\right)_0^l\right] = \frac{-200}{n\pi}(-1)^n$$

Hence the temperature function

$$u(x, t) = -\frac{200}{\pi}\sum_{n=1}^{\infty}\frac{(-1)^n}{n}\sin\frac{n\pi x}{l}\, e^{-\frac{n^2\pi^2c^2t}{l^2}}$$

In the second part, the initial condition remains the same as in first part *i.e.,*

$$u(x, 0) = \frac{100}{l}x.$$

Boundary conditions are $u(0, t) = 20$ and $u(l, t) = 80$ for all values of t then, final temperature distribution is

$$u_2 = 20 + \left(\frac{80-20}{l}\right)x = 20 + \frac{60}{l}x$$

Then, $\qquad u = u_2(x) + u_1(x, t)$

$$u = 20 + \frac{60}{l}x + \sum_{n=1}^{\infty}(a_n\cos px + b_n\sin px)\, e^{-c^2p^2t} \qquad ...(6)$$

$$u(0, t) = 20 = 20 + \sum_{n=1}^{\infty} a_n e^{-c^2p^2t} \qquad | \text{ From } (6)$$

$\Rightarrow \qquad a_n = 0$

$\therefore$ From (6),

$$u = 20 + \frac{60}{l}x + \sum_{n=1}^{\infty} b_n \sin px\, e^{-c^2p^2t} \qquad ...(7)$$

$$u(l, t) = 80 = 20 + \frac{60}{l}l + \sum_{n=1}^{\infty} b_n \sin pl\, e^{-c^2p^2t} \qquad | \text{ From } (7)$$

$\Rightarrow \qquad 0 = \sum_{n=1}^{\infty} b_n \sin pl\, e^{-c^2p^2t}$

$$\sin pl = 0 = \sin n\pi,\ n \in \text{I}$$

$\therefore \qquad p = \frac{n\pi}{l} \qquad ...(8)$

From (7) and (8),

$$u = 20 + \frac{60}{l}x + \sum_{n=1}^{\infty} b_n \sin\frac{n\pi x}{l}\, e^{-\left(\frac{n\pi c}{l}\right)^2 t} \qquad ...(9)$$

Using initial condition,

$$u(x, 0) = \frac{100}{l} x = 20 + \frac{60}{l} x + \sum_{n=1}^{\infty} b_n \sin \frac{n\pi x}{l}$$

$$\Rightarrow \qquad \frac{40}{l} x - 20 = \sum_{n=1}^{\infty} b_n \sin \frac{n\pi x}{l}$$

where

$$b_n = \frac{2}{l} \int_0^l \left(\frac{40}{l} x - 20 \right) \sin \frac{n\pi x}{l} \, dx$$

$$= \frac{2}{l} \left[\left\{ \left(\frac{40}{l} x - 20 \right) \left(\frac{-\cos \frac{n\pi x}{l}}{\frac{n\pi}{l}} \right) \right\}_0^l - \int_0^l \frac{40}{l} \cdot \left(\frac{-\cos \frac{n\pi x}{l}}{\frac{n\pi}{l}} \right) dx \right]$$

$$= \frac{2}{l} \left[\frac{-20l}{n\pi} \cos n\pi - \frac{20l}{n\pi} + \frac{40}{n\pi} \left(\frac{\sin \frac{n\pi x}{l}}{\frac{n\pi}{l}} \right)_0^l \right]$$

$$= \frac{-40}{n\pi} (1 + \cos n\pi) = \begin{cases} 0 & , \text{ when } n \text{ is odd} \\ \dfrac{-80}{n\pi} & , \text{ when } n \text{ is even} \end{cases}$$

Hence equation (9) becomes,

$$u(x, t) = 20 + \frac{60}{l} x - \frac{80}{\pi} \sum_{\substack{n = 2, 4, \ldots \\ (n \text{ is even})}}^{\infty} \frac{1}{n} \sin \frac{n\pi x}{l} e^{-\left(\frac{n\pi c}{l}\right)^2 t}$$

$$= 20 + \frac{60}{l} x - \frac{40}{\pi} \sum_{m=1}^{\infty} \frac{1}{m} \sin \frac{2m\pi x}{l} e^{-\frac{4c^2 m^2 \pi^2 t}{l^2}}. \qquad \text{(taking } n = 2m\text{)}$$

Example 4. *The ends A and B of a rod of length 20 cm are at temperatures 30°C and 80°C until steady state prevails. Then the temperature of the rod ends are changed to 40°C and 60°C respectively. Find the temperature distribution function u(x, t). The specific heat, density and the thermal conductivity of the material of the rod are such that the combination* $\frac{k}{\rho\sigma} = c^2 = 1$.

Sol. Initial temperature distribution in the rod is

$$u_1 = 30 + \left(\frac{80 - 30}{20} \right) x = 30 + \frac{5}{2} x$$

Final temperature distribution (*i.e.*, in steady state) is

$$u_2 = 40 + \left(\frac{60 - 40}{20} \right) x = 40 + x$$

To get u in the intermediate period,

$$u = u_1(x, t) + u_2(x)$$

where $u_2(x)$ is the steady state temperature distribution in the rod $u_1(x, t)$ is the transient temperature distribution which tends to zero as t increases.

$\because$ $u_1(x, t)$ satisfies one dimensional heat flow equation.

$$\therefore \qquad u = 40 + x + \sum_{n=1}^{\infty} (a_n \cos px + b_n \sin px)\, e^{-p^2 t} \qquad \text{...(1)}$$

In steady state,

$$u(0, t) = 40 \qquad \text{...(2)}$$
$$u(20, t) = 60 \qquad \text{...(3)}$$

From (1), and (2), $u(0, t) = 40 = 40 + \sum_{1}^{\infty} a_n\, e^{-p^2 t}$ | From (2)

$$0 = \sum_{1}^{\infty} a_n\, e^{-p^2 t} \quad \Rightarrow \quad a_n = 0 \qquad \text{...(4)}$$

$\therefore$ From (1),

$$u = 40 + x + \sum_{n=1}^{\infty} b_n \sin px\, e^{-p^2 t}$$

Again, $u(20, t) = 60 = 60 + \sum_{n=1}^{\infty} b_n \sin 20\,p\, e^{-p^2 t}$

$$\Rightarrow \qquad 0 = \sum_{1}^{\infty} b_n \sin 20\,p\, e^{-p^2 t}$$

$$\sin 20p = 0 = \sin n\pi,\ n \in \text{I}$$

$$\Rightarrow \qquad p = \frac{n\pi}{20}$$

$$\therefore \qquad u = 40 + x + \sum_{n=1}^{\infty} b_n \sin \frac{n\pi x}{20} e^{-\left(\frac{n\pi}{20}\right)^2 t} \qquad \text{...(5)}$$

Using initial condition,

$$u(x, 0) = 30 + \frac{5}{2}x \quad \text{in eqn. (5), we get}$$

$$\Rightarrow \qquad 30 + \frac{5}{2}x = 40 + x + \sum_{n=1}^{\infty} b_n \sin \frac{n\pi x}{20}$$

$$\Rightarrow \qquad \frac{3}{2}x - 10 = \sum_{n=1}^{\infty} b_n \sin \frac{n\pi x}{20}$$

where $$b_n = \frac{2}{20}\int_0^{20} \left(\frac{3}{2}x - 10\right) \sin \frac{n\pi x}{20}\, dx = -\frac{20}{n\pi}\,[2(-1)^n + 1]$$

From (5), $$u(x, t) = 40 + x - \frac{20}{\pi}\sum_{n=1}^{\infty} \left\{\frac{2(-1)^n + 1}{n}\right\} \sin \frac{n\pi x}{20} e^{-\left(\frac{n\pi}{20}\right)^2 t}.$$

Example 5. *The temperature distribution in a bar of length π which is perfectly insulated at ends x = 0 and x = π is governed by partial differential equation*

$$\frac{\partial u}{\partial t} = \frac{\partial^2 u}{\partial x^2}$$

Assuming the initial temperature distribution as u(x, 0) = f(x) = cos 2x, find the temperature distribution at any instant of time. (M.T.U. 2011)

Sol. $$\frac{\partial u}{\partial t} = \frac{\partial^2 u}{\partial x^2} \quad ...(1)$$

Its solution is $$u(x, t) = c_1 e^{-p^2 t} (c_2 \cos px + c_3 \sin px) \quad ...(2)$$

Since ends of bar are insulated, no heat can pass from either sides and boundary conditions are

$$\frac{\partial u}{\partial x} = 0 \quad \text{at } x = 0 \quad ...(3)$$

and $$\frac{\partial u}{\partial x} = 0 \quad \text{at } x = \pi \quad ..(4)$$

From (2), $$\frac{\partial u}{\partial x} = c_1 e^{-p^2 t} (-pc_2 \sin px + pc_3 \cos px)$$

At $x = 0$,

$$0 = c_1 e^{-p^2 t} \; pc_3 \quad \Rightarrow \quad c_3 = 0$$

$\therefore$ From (2), $$u(x, t) = c_1 c_2 \, e^{-p^2 t} \cos px \quad ...(5)$$

Again $$\frac{\partial u}{\partial x} = -pc_1 c_2 \, e^{-p^2 t} \sin px$$

At $x = \pi$,

$$0 = -pc_1 c_2 e^{-p^2 t} \sin p\pi$$

$\Rightarrow$ $$\sin p\pi = 0 = \sin n\pi \; (n \in \text{I})$$

$$p\pi = n\pi \quad \Rightarrow \quad p = n$$

$\therefore$ From (5), $u(x, t) = b_n \, e^{-n^2 t} \cos nx$, where $c_1 c_2 = b_n$

Most general solution is

$$u(x, t) = \sum_{n=1}^{\infty} b_n \, e^{-n^2 t} \cos nx \quad ...(6)$$

$$u(x, 0) = \cos 2x = \sum_{n=1}^{\infty} b_n \cos nx$$

Comparing, we get $b_2 = 1$ and $n = 2$. All other b_i's are zero.

$\therefore$ From (6), $u(x, t) = e^{-4t} \cos 2x$.

Example 6. *Solve the equation* $\frac{\partial u}{\partial t} = \frac{\partial^2 u}{\partial x^2}$ *with boundary condition u(x, 0) = 3 sin nπx, u(0, t) = 0, u (l, t) = 0, where 0 < x < l.*

Sol. The solution to the equation

$$\frac{\partial u}{\partial t} = \frac{\partial^2 u}{\partial x^2} \quad ...(1)$$

is given by $$u(x, t) = c_1 e^{-p^2 t} (c_2 \cos px + c_3 \sin px) \qquad ...(2)$$

From (2), $u(0, t) = c_1 c_2 e^{-p^2 t}$

$\Rightarrow$ $0 = c_1 c_2 e^{-p^2 t}$

$\Rightarrow$ $c_2 = 0.$

$\therefore$ From (2), $$u(x, t) = c_1 c_3 e^{-p^2 t} \sin px \qquad ...(3)$$

$u(l, t) = 0 = c_1 c_3 e^{-p^2 t} \sin pl$

$\Rightarrow$ $\sin pl = 0 = \sin n\pi (n \in \text{I})$

$\therefore$ $p = \dfrac{n\pi}{l}.$

From (3), $$u(x, t) = c_1 c_3 e^{-\frac{n^2\pi^2}{l^2} t} \sin \frac{n\pi x}{l} = b_n e^{-\frac{n^2\pi^2 t}{l^2}} \sin \frac{n\pi x}{l}$$

The most general solution is

$$u(x, t) = \sum_{n=1}^{\infty} b_n e^{-(n^2\pi^2 t/l^2)} \sin \frac{n\pi x}{l} \qquad ...(4)$$

$\therefore$ From (4), $$u(x, 0) = \sum_{1}^{\infty} b_n \sin \frac{n\pi x}{l}$$

$\Rightarrow$ $$3 \sin n\pi x = \sum_{1}^{\infty} b_n \sin \frac{n\pi x}{l}.$$

Comparison gives, $b_n = 3, l = 1.$

Hence from (4), the required solution is

$$u(x, t) = 3 \sum_{n=1}^{\infty} e^{-n^2\pi^2 t} \sin n\pi x.$$

Example 7. *A bar with insulated sides is initially at a temperature 0°C throughout. The end x = 0 is kept at 0°C, and heat is suddenly applied at the end x = l so that* $\dfrac{\partial u}{\partial x} = A$ *for x = l, where A is a constant. Find the temperature function u(x, t).*

Sol. One dimensional heat flow equation is

$$\frac{\partial u}{\partial t} = c^2 \frac{\partial^2 u}{\partial x^2} \qquad ...(1)$$

Its solution is

$$u(x, t) = c_1 e^{-p^2 c^2 t} (c_2 \cos px + c_3 \sin px)$$

or $$u(x, t) = (\text{A}_1 \cos px + \text{B} \sin px)\, e^{-p^2 c^2 t} \qquad ...(2)$$

Applying the zero end conditions as,

$u(0, t) = 0 = \text{A}_1 e^{-p^2 c^2 t}$

$\Rightarrow$ $\text{A}_1 = 0.$

$\therefore$ From (2), $u(x, t) = \text{B} \sin pxe^{-p^2c^2t}$ ...(3)

From (3), $\frac{\partial u}{\partial x} = p\text{B} \cos pxe^{-p^2c^2t}$.

At $x = l$, $\left(\frac{\partial u}{\partial x}\right)_{x=l} = 0 = p\text{B} \cos ple^{-p^2c^2t}$

$\Rightarrow$ $\cos pl = 0 = \cos\left(n\pi - \frac{\pi}{2}\right)$; $n \in \text{I}$ or $pl = (2n-1)\frac{\pi}{2}$

$\Rightarrow$ $p = (2n-1)\frac{\pi}{2l}$.

$\therefore$ From (3), $u(x, t) = \text{B} \sin pxe^{-p^2c^2t}$ ...(4) where $p = (2n-1)\frac{\pi}{2l}$

The most general solution is

$$u(x, t) = \sum_{n=1}^{\infty} \text{B}_n \sin px\, e^{-p^2c^2t} \quad \text{...(5)} \quad \text{where } p = (2n-1)\frac{\pi}{2l}.$$

The end conditions given for this problem are

(*i*) $u = 0$ at $x = 0$ (*ii*) $\frac{\partial u}{\partial x} = \text{A}$ at $x = l$ ...(6)

These conditions are different from the zero end conditions. So we add to (5) the solution

$$u = \text{A}_1 x + \text{B}$$

Choosing A_1 and B so that (6) is satisfied.

This gives, $0 = \text{B}$ and $\text{A}_1 = \text{A}$

$$\therefore \quad u(x, t) = \text{A}x + \sum_{n=1}^{\infty} \text{B}_n \sin px\, e^{-p^2c^2t} \quad \text{...(7)} \quad \text{where } p = (2n-1)\frac{\pi}{2l}.$$

Applying the condition that $u = 0$ at $t = 0$, we have

$$0 = \text{A}x + \sum_{n=1}^{\infty} \text{B}_n \sin px$$

or

$$-\text{A}x = \sum_{n=1}^{\infty} \text{B}_n \sin px$$

where

$$\text{B}_n = \frac{2}{l}\int_0^l (-\text{A}x) \sin px\, dx, \text{ where } p = (2n-1)\frac{\pi}{2l}$$

$$= \frac{-2\text{A}}{l}\left[\left\{x\left(\frac{-\cos px}{p}\right)\right\}_0^l - \int_0^l 1.\left(\frac{-\cos px}{p}\right)dx\right]$$

$$= -\frac{2\text{A}}{l}\left[\frac{-l\cos pl}{p} + \frac{1}{p}\left(\frac{\sin px}{p}\right)_0^l\right]$$

$$= \frac{-2A}{l}\left[\frac{-l\cos pl}{p}+\frac{1}{p^2}\sin pl\right] = -\frac{2A(2l)^2}{l(2n-1)^2\pi^2}\sin(2n-1)\frac{\pi}{2}$$

$(\because \quad \cos pl = 0)$

$$= \frac{-8Al}{\pi^2(2n-1)^2}\sin\left(n\pi-\frac{\pi}{2}\right) = \frac{8Al}{\pi^2(2n-1)^2}(-1)^n \qquad ...(8)$$

$\therefore$ From (7),
$$u(x,t) = Ax + \frac{8Al}{\pi^2}\sum_{n=1}^{\infty}\left[\frac{(-1)^n}{(2n-1)^2}\right]\sin(2n-1)\frac{\pi x}{2l}\, e^{-\left[\frac{(2n-1)^2\pi^2c^2t}{4l^2}\right]}$$

Example 8. *Solve :* $\frac{\partial u}{\partial t} = k\frac{\partial^2 u}{\partial x^2}$ *under the conditions*

(*i*) $u \neq \infty$ *if* $t \to \infty$ (*ii*) $\frac{\partial u}{\partial x} = 0$ *for* $x = 0$ *and* $x = l$

(*iii*) $u = lx - x^2$ *for* $t = 0$ *between* $x = 0$ *and* $x = l$.

Sol. Solution to $\frac{\partial u}{\partial t} = k\frac{\partial^2 u}{\partial x^2}$ is

$$u(x,t) = c_1 e^{-c^2kt}(c_2\cos cx + c_3\sin cx) \qquad ...(1)$$

Eqn. (1) satisfies the condition $u \neq \infty$ if $t \to \infty$

Applying $\frac{\partial u}{\partial x} = 0$ for $x = 0$ and $x = l$ to (1), we get

$$c_3 = 0$$

and
$$c = \frac{n\pi}{l},\ n \in I$$

$\therefore$
$$u = c_1c_2\, e^{-\left(\frac{n^2\pi^2kt}{l^2}\right)}\cos\frac{n\pi x}{l} = a_n\cos\frac{n\pi x}{l}\, e^{-\left(\frac{n^2\pi^2kt}{l^2}\right)} \qquad ...(2)$$

Again, the second possible solution is

$$u = c_1(c_2x + c_3) \qquad ...(3) \quad | \text{ if } c^2 = 0$$

Applying $\frac{\partial u}{\partial x} = 0$ for $x = 0$ and $x = l$ to (3), we get $c_2 = 0$

$\therefore$
$$u = c_1c_3 = \frac{a_0}{2}\ \text{(say)} \qquad ...(4) \quad | \text{ From (3)}$$

$\therefore$ The general solution is the sum of solutions (2) and (4) for various n.

$\therefore$
$$u(x,t) = \frac{a_0}{2} + \sum_{n=1}^{\infty} a_n\cos\frac{n\pi x}{l}\, e^{-\left(\frac{n^2\pi^2kt}{l^2}\right)} \qquad ...(5)$$

Now applying $u = lx - x^2$ for $t = 0$ to eqn. (5), we get

$$lx - x^2 = \frac{a_0}{2} + \sum_{n=1}^{\infty} a_n\cos\frac{n\pi x}{l}$$

Here,
$$a_0 = \frac{2}{l}\int_0^l (lx - x^2)\,dx = \frac{l^2}{3}$$

$$a_n = \frac{2}{l}\int_0^l (lx - x^2)\cos\frac{n\pi x}{l}\,dx$$

$$= \begin{cases} -\dfrac{4l^2}{n^2\pi^2}; & \text{when } n \text{ is even} \\ 0\;; & \text{when } n \text{ is odd} \end{cases}$$ | On simplification

$\therefore$ $$u = \frac{l^2}{6} - \frac{4l^2}{\pi^2}\sum_{n=2,4,\ldots}^{\infty}\frac{1}{n^2}\cos\frac{n\pi x}{l}\,e^{-\left(\frac{n^2\pi^2 kt}{l^2}\right)}$$

Put $n = 2m$, we get

$$u(x, t) = \frac{l^2}{6} - \frac{l^2}{\pi^2}\sum_{m=1}^{\infty}\frac{1}{m^2}\cos\frac{2m\pi x}{l}\,e^{-\left(\frac{4m^2\pi^2 kt}{l^2}\right)}$$

TEST YOUR KNOWLEDGE

1. (*i*) Solve: $\dfrac{\partial u}{\partial t} = \alpha\dfrac{\partial^2 u}{\partial x^2}$; α constant, subject to the boundary conditions $u(0, t) = 0$, $u(\pi, t) = 0$ and the initial condition $u(x, 0) = \sin 2x$. (*M.T.U. 2012*)

(*ii*) Solve: $\dfrac{\partial u}{\partial t} = a^2\dfrac{\partial^2 u}{\partial x^2}$ given that

(*a*) $u = 0$ when $x = 0$ and $x = l$ for all t (*b*) $u = 3\sin\dfrac{\pi x}{l}$ when $t = 0$ for all x.

2. (*i*) Determine the solution of one-dimensional heat equation $\dfrac{\partial u}{\partial t} = c^2\dfrac{\partial^2 u}{\partial x^2}$ where the boundary conditions are $u(0, t) = 0$, $u(l, t) = 0$ $(t > 0)$ and the initial condition $u(x, 0) = x$: l being the length of the bar. (*U.P.T.U. 2006*)

(*ii*) Find the temperature distribution in a rod of length 2 m whose end points are fixed at temperature zero and the initial temperature distribution is $f(x) = 100x$. (*G.B.T.U. 2012*)

3. The heat flow in a bar of length 10 cm of homogeneous material is governed by partial diff. eqn. $u_t = c^2 u_{xx}$. The ends of the bar are kept at temp. 0°C and initial temp. is $f(x) = x(10 - x)$. Find the temp. in the bar at any instant of time.

4. Find the temperature $u(x, t)$ in a homogeneous bar of heat conducting material of length L cm. with its ends kept at zero temperature and initial temperature given by $\dfrac{x(\mathrm{L} - x)\,d}{\mathrm{L}^2}$.

[*U.P.T.U. (SUM) 2009*]

5. A homogeneous rod of conducting material of length 100 cm has its ends kept at zero temperature and the temperature initially is $u(x, 0) = \begin{cases} x, & 0 \le x \le 50 \\ 100 - x, & 50 \le x \le 100 \end{cases}$

Find the temperature $u(x, t)$ at any time.

6. Find the temperature $u(x, t)$ in a slab whose ends $x = 0$ and $x = \mathrm{L}$ are kept at zero temperature and whose initial temperature $f(x)$ is given by

$$f(x) = \begin{cases} k, & \text{when } 0 < x < \frac{1}{2}\mathrm{L} \\ 0, & \text{when } \frac{1}{2}\mathrm{L} < x < \mathrm{L} \end{cases}.$$ [*G.B.T.U. 2010 ; G.B.T.U. (C.O.) 2010*]

7. Solve : $u_t = a^2 u_{xx}$ under the conditions $u_x(0, t) = 0 = u_x(\pi, t)$ and $u(x, 0) = x^2 (0 < x < \pi)$.

8. Find the temperature in a thin metal rod of length L with both ends insulated (so that there is no passage of heat through the ends) and with initial temperature $\sin \frac{\pi x}{L}$ in the rod. *[U.P.T.U. (SUM) 2009]*

$$\left[\textbf{Hint: } (u_x)_{x=0} = 0 = (u_x)_{x=L} \; ; \; u(x, 0) = \sin \frac{\pi x}{L} \right]$$

9. (*i*) The temperature of a bar 50 cm long with insulated sides is kept at 0° at one end and 100° at the other end until steady conditions prevail. The two end are then suddenly insulated so that the temperature gradient is zero at each end thereafter. Find the temperature distribution.

(*ii*) A bar 10 cm long, with insulated sides, has its ends A and B maintained at temperatures 50°C and 100°C respectively, until steady-state conditions prevail. The temperature at A is suddenly raised to 90°C and at the same time that at B is lowered to 60°C. Find the temperature distribution in the bar at time t.

10. A homogeneous rod of conducting material of length '1' has its ends kept at zero temperature. The temperature at the centre is T and falls uniformly to zero at the two ends. Find the temperature distribution. *(U.K.T.U. 2012)*

$$\left[\textbf{Hint: } u(x, 0) = \begin{cases} 2Tx, & 0 \le x \le \frac{1}{2} \\ 2T(1-x), & \frac{1}{2} \le x \le 1 \end{cases} \right]$$

11. Solve $\frac{\partial \theta}{\partial t} = k \frac{\partial^2 \theta}{\partial x^2}$, such that

(*i*) θ is finite when $t \to \infty$, (*ii*) $\frac{\partial \theta}{\partial x} = 0$ when $x = 0$ and $\theta = 0$ when $x = l$ for all t,

(*iii*) $\theta = \theta_0$ when $t = 0$ for all values of x between 0 and l.

12. Find a solution of the heat conduction equation $\frac{\partial u}{\partial t} = \alpha \frac{\partial^2 u}{\partial x^2}$ such that

(*i*) u is finite when $t \to \infty$, (*ii*) $u = 100$ when $x = 0$ or π for all values of t,

(*iii*) $u = 0$ when $t = 0$ for all values of x between 0 and π.

(Here, the initially ice-cold rod has its ends in boiling water.)

Answers

1. (*i*) $u(x, t) = \sin 2x \, e^{-4\alpha t}$ (*ii*) $u(x, t) = 3 \sin \frac{\pi x}{l} e^{-(a^2 \pi^2 t / l^2)}$

2. (*i*) $u(x, t) = -\frac{2l}{\pi} \sum_{n=1}^{\infty} \frac{\cos n\pi}{n} \sin \frac{n\pi x}{l} e^{-\left(\frac{c^2 n^2 \pi^2 t}{l^2}\right)}$

(*ii*) $u(x, t) = -\frac{400}{\pi} \sum_{n=1}^{\infty} \frac{\cos n\pi}{n} \sin \frac{n\pi x}{2} e^{-\left(\frac{c^2 n^2 \pi^2 t}{4}\right)}$

3. $u(x, t) = \dfrac{800}{\pi^3} \sum_{n=1}^{\infty} \dfrac{1}{(2n-1)^3} \sin \dfrac{(2n-1)\pi x}{10} e^{-\left[\frac{(2n-1)^2 \pi^2 c^2 t}{100}\right]}$.

4. $u(x, t) = \dfrac{8d}{\pi^3} \sum_{n=1}^{\infty} \dfrac{1}{(2n-1)^3} \sin \dfrac{(2n-1)\pi x}{L} e^{-\frac{(2n-1)^2 \pi^2 c^2 t}{L^2}}$.

5. $u(x, t) = \dfrac{400}{\pi^2} \sum_{m=0}^{\infty} \dfrac{(-1)^m}{(2m+1)^2} \sin \dfrac{(2m+1)\pi x}{100} e^{-\left[\frac{(2m+1) c\pi}{100}\right]^2 t}$

6. $u(x, t) = \dfrac{4k}{\pi} \sum_{n=1}^{\infty} \dfrac{1}{n} \sin^2 \dfrac{n\pi}{4} \sin \dfrac{n\pi x}{L} e^{-\left(\frac{c^2 n^2 \pi^2 t}{L^2}\right)}$

7. $u(x, t) = \dfrac{\pi^3}{3} + 4 \sum_{n=1}^{\infty} \dfrac{(-1)^n}{n^2} \cos nx \, e^{-a^2 n^2 t}$

8. $u(x, t) = \dfrac{2}{\pi} - \dfrac{4}{\pi} \sum_{m=1}^{\infty} \dfrac{1}{(4m^2-1)} \cos\left(\dfrac{2m\pi x}{L}\right) e^{-\frac{4m^2 \pi^2 c^2 t}{L^2}}$

9. (i) $u(x, t) = \dfrac{200}{\pi} \sum_{n=1}^{\infty} \dfrac{(-1)^{n+1}}{n} \sin \dfrac{n\pi x}{50} e^{-\left(\frac{n^2 \pi^2 kt}{2500}\right)}$

(ii) $u(x, t) = 90 - 3x - \dfrac{80}{\pi} \sum_{n=1}^{\infty} \dfrac{1}{n} \sin \dfrac{n\pi x}{5} e^{-\left(\frac{c^2 n^2 \pi^2 t}{25}\right)}$

10. $u(x, t) = \dfrac{8T}{\pi^2} \sum_{m=1}^{\infty} \dfrac{(-1)^{m+1}}{(2m-1)^2} \sin (2m-1)\pi x \, e^{-[(2m-1)^2 \pi^2 c^2 t]}$

11. $\theta = \dfrac{4\theta_0}{\pi} \left[e^{-(\pi/2l)^2 kt} \cos \dfrac{\pi x}{2l} - \dfrac{1}{3} e^{-\left(\frac{3\pi}{2l}\right)^2 kt} \cos \dfrac{3\pi x}{2l} + \dfrac{1}{5} e^{-\left(\frac{5\pi}{2l}\right)^2 kt} \cos \dfrac{5\pi x}{2l} - \ldots \right]$

12. $u(x, t) = 100 - \dfrac{400}{\pi} \sum_{m=1}^{\infty} \dfrac{\sin (2m-1) x}{2m-1} e^{-(2m-1)^2 \alpha t}$

5.10. TWO-DIMENSIONAL HEAT FLOW

Consider the flow of heat in a metal plate, in the XOY plane. If the temperature at any point is independent of the z-coordinate and depends on x, y and t only, then the flow is called two dimensional and the heat-flow lies in the plane XOY only and is zero along the normal to the plane XOY.

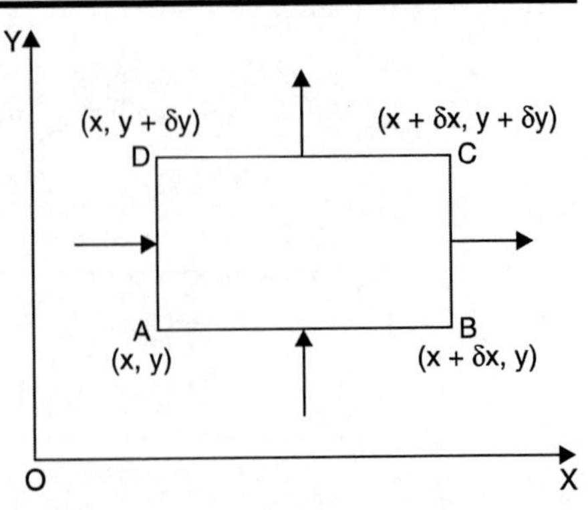

Take a rectangular element of the plate with sides δx and δy and thickness α. As discussed in the one-dimensional heat flow along a bar, the quantity of heat that enters the plate per second from the sides AB and AD is given by

$$-k\alpha\,\delta x\left(\frac{\partial u}{\partial y}\right)_y \quad\text{and}\quad -k\alpha\,\delta y\left(\frac{\partial u}{\partial x}\right)_x$$

respectively and that which flows out through the sides CD and BC per second is

$$-k\alpha\,\delta x\left(\frac{\partial u}{\partial y}\right)_{y+\delta y} \quad\text{and}\quad -k\alpha\,\delta y\left(\frac{\partial u}{\partial x}\right)_{x+\delta x} \text{ respectively.}$$

Therefore, the total gain of heat by the rectangular plate ABCD per second

$$= -k\alpha\delta x\left(\frac{\partial u}{\partial y}\right)_y - k\alpha\delta y\left(\frac{\partial u}{\partial x}\right)_x + k\alpha\delta x\left(\frac{\partial u}{\partial y}\right)_{y+\delta y} + k\alpha\delta y\left(\frac{\partial u}{\partial x}\right)_{x+\delta x}$$

$$= k\alpha\delta x\delta y\left[\frac{\left(\frac{\partial u}{\partial x}\right)_{x+\delta x}-\left(\frac{\partial u}{\partial x}\right)_x}{\delta x}+\frac{\left(\frac{\partial u}{\partial y}\right)_{y+\delta y}-\left(\frac{\partial u}{\partial y}\right)_y}{\delta y}\right] \quad ...(1)$$

The rate of gain of heat by the plate is also given by

$$s\rho\delta x\delta y\,\frac{\partial u}{\partial t} \quad ...(2)$$

where s = specific heat and ρ = density of the metal plate.

Equating (1) and (2), we obtain

$$k\alpha\delta x\delta y\left[\frac{\left(\frac{\partial u}{\partial x}\right)_{x+\delta x}-\left(\frac{\partial u}{\partial x}\right)_x}{\delta x}+\frac{\left(\frac{\partial u}{\partial y}\right)_{y+\delta y}-\left(\frac{\partial u}{\partial y}\right)_y}{\delta y}\right] = s\rho\delta x\delta y\,\frac{\partial u}{\partial t}$$

Dividing both sides by $\alpha\delta x\delta y$ and taking the limit as $\delta x \to 0$, $\delta y \to 0$, we get

$$k\left(\frac{\partial^2 u}{\partial x^2}+\frac{\partial^2 u}{\partial y^2}\right) = s\rho\,\frac{\partial u}{\partial t}$$

or

$$\boxed{c^2\left(\frac{\partial^2 u}{\partial x^2}+\frac{\partial^2 u}{\partial y^2}\right) = \frac{\partial u}{\partial t}} \quad \text{where } c^2 = \frac{k}{s\rho} \quad ...(3)$$

Equation (3) gives the temperature distribution of the plate in the transient state.

Note 1. In steady state, u is independent of t, so that $\frac{\partial u}{\partial t} = 0$ and the above equation reduces to

$$\frac{\partial^2 u}{\partial x^2}+\frac{\partial^2 u}{\partial y^2} = 0 \quad ...(4)$$

which is known as **Laplace's Equation in two dimensions.**

Note 2. The equation of heat flow in a solid (Three-dimensional heat flow) can similarly be derived as

$$c^2\left(\frac{\partial^2 u}{\partial x^2}+\frac{\partial^2 u}{\partial y^2}+\frac{\partial^2 u}{\partial z^2}\right) = \frac{\partial u}{\partial t}$$

In the steady state, it reduces to $\frac{\partial^2 u}{\partial x^2} + \frac{\partial^2 u}{\partial y^2} + \frac{\partial^2 u}{\partial z^2} = 0$

which is **Laplace's Equation in three dimensions.**

5.11. SOLUTION OF LAPLACE'S EQUATION IN TWO DIMENSIONS

[*G.B.T.U. 2011 ; G.B.T.U. (C.O.) 2010*]

Laplace's equation in two dimensions is

$$\frac{\partial^2 u}{\partial x^2} + \frac{\partial^2 u}{\partial y^2} = 0 \qquad \text{...(1)}$$

Let $u = XY$ ...(2)

where X is a function of x only and Y is a function of y only, be a solution of (1).

Then $\frac{\partial^2 u}{\partial x^2} = X''Y$ and $\frac{\partial^2 u}{\partial y^2} = XY''$

Substituting in (1), we have $X''Y + XY'' = 0$ or $\frac{X''}{X} = -\frac{Y''}{Y}$ ...(3)

Now the L.H.S. of (3) is a function of x only and the R.H.S is a function of y only. Since x and y are independent variables, this equation can hold only when both sides reduce to a constant, say k. Then equation (3) leads to the ordinary differential equations

$$\frac{d^2X}{dx^2} - kX = 0 \quad \text{and} \quad \frac{d^2Y}{dy^2} + kY = 0 \qquad \text{...(4)}$$

Solving equations (4), we get

(*i*) *When k is positive* and $= p^2$, say

$$X = c_1 e^{px} + c_2 e^{-px}, \; Y = c_3 \cos py + c_4 \sin py$$

(*ii*) *When k is negative* and $= -p^2$, say

$$X = c_1 \cos px + c_2 \sin px, \; Y = c_3 e^{py} + c_4 e^{-py}$$

(*iii*) *When $k = 0$*

$$X = c_1 x + c_2, \; Y = c_3 y + c_4$$

Thus, the various possible solutions of Laplace's equation (1) are :

$$u = (c_1 e^{px} + c_2 e^{-px})(c_3 \cos py + c_4 \sin py) \qquad \text{...(5)}$$

$$u = (c_1 \cos px + c_2 \sin px)(c_3 e^{py} + c_4 e^{-py}) \qquad \text{...(6)}$$

$$u = (c_1 x + c_2)(c_3 y + c_4) \qquad \text{...(7)}$$

Of these three solutions, we have to choose that solution which is consistent with the physical nature of the problem and the given boundary conditions. Solution (6) is the required solution.

$$\boxed{u(x, y) = (c_1 \cos px + c_2 \sin px)\,(c_3\, e^{py} + c_4 e^{-py}).}$$

ILLUSTRATIVE EXAMPLES

Example 1. *Use separation of variables method to solve the equation*

$$\frac{\partial^2 u}{\partial x^2}+\frac{\partial^2 u}{\partial y^2}=0$$

subject to the boundary conditions $u(0, y) = u(l, y) = u(x, 0) = 0$ *and* $u(x, a) = \sin \frac{n\pi x}{l}$.

[U.P.T.U. (C.O.) 2009; G.B.T.U. (A.G.) 2012]

Sol. The given equation is

$$\frac{\partial^2 u}{\partial x^2}+\frac{\partial^2 u}{\partial y^2}=0 \quad ...(1)$$

Let $u = XY$ ...(2)

where X is a function of x only and Y is a function of y only then,

$$\frac{\partial^2 u}{\partial x^2}=\frac{\partial^2}{\partial x^2}(XY)=Y\frac{d^2X}{dx^2} \quad \text{and} \quad \frac{\partial^2 u}{\partial y^2}=\frac{\partial^2}{\partial y^2}(XY)=X\frac{d^2Y}{dy^2}$$

$\therefore$ From (1), $YX'' + XY'' = 0$

$\Rightarrow$ $\frac{X''}{X}+\frac{Y''}{Y}=0$

Case I. When $\frac{X''}{X}=-\frac{Y''}{Y}=p^2$ (say)

(*i*) $\frac{X''}{X}=p^2$

$X'' - p^2X = 0$

Auxiliary equation is $m^2 - p^2 = 0$

$m = \pm p$

$\therefore$ C.F. $= c_1e^{px} + c_2e^{-px}$

P.I. $= 0$

$\therefore$ $X = c_1e^{px} + c_2e^{-px}$

(*ii*) $\frac{-Y''}{Y}=p^2 \Rightarrow Y'' + p^2Y = 0$

Auxiliary equation is $m^2 + p^2 = 0 \Rightarrow m = \pm pi$

$\therefore$ C.F. $= c_3 \cos py + c_4 \sin py$

P.I. $= 0$

$\therefore$ $y = c_3 \cos py + c_4 \sin py$

Now, $X(0) = 0$

$\Rightarrow$ $c_1 + c_2 = 0 \Rightarrow c_2 = -c_1$

$X(l) = 0$

$\Rightarrow$ $c_1e^{pl} + c_2e^{-pl} = 0 \Rightarrow c_1 (e^{pl} - e^{-pl}) = 0$

$\Rightarrow$ $c_1 = 0$ | Since $e^{pl} - e^{-pl} \neq 0$ (as $p \neq 0 \neq l$)

$\therefore$ $c_2 = 0$

$\therefore$ $X = 0 \Rightarrow u = XY = 0$ which is impossible

Hence we reject case I.

Case II. When $\frac{X''}{X} = -\frac{Y''}{Y} = 0$ (say)

(*i*) $\frac{X''}{X} = 0$

$\Rightarrow$ $X'' = 0 \Rightarrow X = c_5 x + c_6$

(*ii*) $\frac{-Y''}{Y} = 0$

$\Rightarrow$ $Y'' = 0 \Rightarrow Y = c_7 y + c_8$

Now, $X(0) = 0 \Rightarrow c_6 = 0$

$X(l) = 0$

$\Rightarrow$ $c_5 l + c_6 = 0 \Rightarrow c_5 l = 0$

$\Rightarrow$ $c_5 = 0$ (Since $l \neq 0$)

$\therefore$ $X = 0$

$\therefore$ $u = XY = 0$ which is impossible

Hence we also reject case II.

Case III. When $\frac{X''}{X} = -\frac{Y''}{Y} = -p^2$ (say)

(*i*) $\frac{X''}{X} = -p^2$

$\Rightarrow$ $X'' + p^2 X = 0 \Rightarrow \frac{d^2X}{dx^2} + p^2 X = 0.$

Auxiliary equation is $m^2 + p^2 = 0 \Rightarrow m = \pm pi$

$$\text{C.F.} = c_9 \cos px + c_{10} \sin px$$

$$\text{P.I.} = 0$$

$$X = c_9 \cos px + c_{10} \sin px$$

(*ii*) $-\frac{Y''}{Y} = -p^2$

$\Rightarrow$ $\frac{Y''}{Y} = p^2 \Rightarrow \frac{d^2Y}{dy^2} - p^2 Y = 0.$

Auxiliary equation is

$$m^2 - p^2 = 0$$

$$m = \pm p.$$

$\therefore$ $\text{C.F.} = c_{11} e^{py} + c_{12} e^{-py}$

$$\text{P.I.} = 0$$

Hence, $Y = c_{11}\, e^{py} + c_{12}\, e^{-py}.$

Now, $X(0) = 0 \Rightarrow c_9 = 0$

$\therefore$ $X = c_{10} \sin px$

$X(l) = 0$

$c_{10} \sin pl = 0$

$\Rightarrow$ $\sin pl = 0 = \sin n\pi,\ n \in I$

$\therefore$ $p = \frac{n\pi}{l}$

$\therefore \qquad X = c_{10} \sin \frac{n\pi x}{l}$ ...(3)

Again, $\qquad Y(0) = 0$

$\Rightarrow \qquad c_{11} + c_{12} = 0 \Rightarrow c_{12} = -c_{11}$

$$Y = c_{11}(e^{py} - e^{-py}) = c_{11}\left(e^{\frac{n\pi y}{l}} - e^{-\frac{n\pi y}{l}}\right) \qquad ...(4)$$

$$\therefore \qquad u = XY = c_{10}c_{11} \sin \frac{n\pi x}{l} [e^{(n\pi y/l)} - e^{(-n\pi y/l)}]$$

or $$u(x, y) = b_n \sin \frac{n\pi x}{l} [e^{(n\pi y/l)} - e^{(-n\pi y/l)}] \qquad ...(5)$$

Now, $$u(x, a) = \sin \frac{n\pi x}{l} = b_n \sin \frac{n\pi x}{l} [e^{(n\pi a/l)} - e^{-(n\pi a/l)}]$$

$$\Rightarrow \qquad b_n = \frac{1}{e^{\frac{n\pi a}{l}} - e^{-\frac{n\pi a}{l}}} = \frac{1}{2\sin h\left(\frac{n\pi a}{l}\right)}$$

$$\therefore \qquad u(x, y) = \frac{e^{(n\pi y/l)} - e^{-(n\pi y/l)}}{2\sinh\left(\frac{n\pi a}{l}\right)} \sin \frac{n\pi x}{l} = \frac{\sinh\left(\frac{n\pi y}{l}\right)}{\sinh\left(\frac{n\pi a}{l}\right)} \sin \frac{n\pi x}{l}.$$

Example 2. *A rectangular plate with insulated surfaces is 8 cm wide and so long compared to its width that it may be considered infinite in length without introducing an appreciable error. If the temperature along one short edge y = 0 is given by*

$$u(x, 0) = 100 \sin \frac{\pi x}{8}, \quad 0 < x < 8$$

while the two long edges x = 0 and x = 8 as well as the other short edge are kept at 0°C, show that the steady state temperature at any point of the plate is given by

$$u(x, y) = 100e^{-\frac{\pi y}{8}} \sin \frac{\pi x}{8}.$$

Sol. Let $u(x, y)$ be the temperature at any point P of the plate.

Two dimensional heat flow equation in steady state is given by

$$\frac{\partial^2 u}{\partial x^2} + \frac{\partial^2 u}{\partial y^2} = 0 \qquad ...(1)$$

Its solution is $\qquad u(x, y) = (c_1 \cos px + c_2 \sin px)(c_3 e^{py} + c_4 e^{-py})$ ...(2)

Boundary conditions are

$$u(0, y) = 0 = u(8, y)$$

$$\underset{y \to \infty}{\text{Lt}}\ u(x, y) = 0$$

$$u(x, 0) = 100 \sin \frac{\pi x}{8}, \quad 0 < x < 8$$

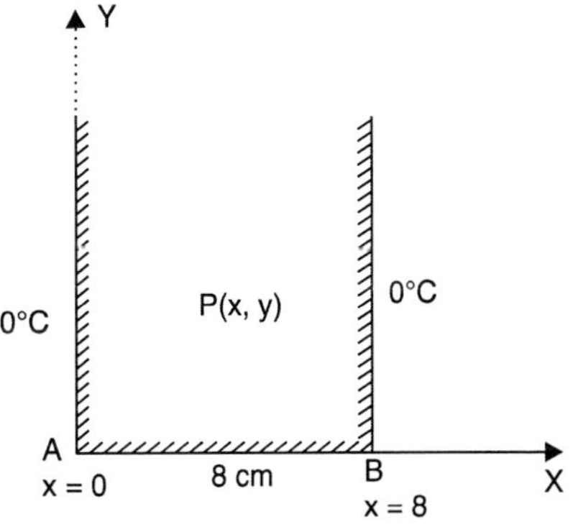

From (2),

$$u(0, y) = 0 = c_1 (c_3 e^{py} + c_4 e^{-py})$$

$\Rightarrow \qquad c_1 = 0.$

∴ From (2),

$$u(x, y) = c_2 \sin px\,(c_3\, e^{py} + c_4 e^{-py}) \qquad ...(3)$$

$$u(8, y) = 0 = c_2 \sin 8p(c_3\, e^{py} + c_4\, e^{-py})$$

⇒ $\sin 8p = 0 = \sin n\pi$

⇒ $p = \dfrac{n\pi}{8} \quad (n \in \mathrm{I})$

∴ From (3),

$$u(x, y) = c_2 \sin \frac{n\pi x}{8}\left(c_3 e^{\frac{n\pi y}{8}} + c_4 e^{-\frac{n\pi y}{8}}\right) \qquad ...(4)$$

$$\underset{y \to \infty}{\mathrm{Lt}}\; u(x, y) = 0 = c_2 \sin \frac{n\pi x}{8} \lim_{y \to \infty}\left(c_3 e^{\frac{n\pi y}{8}} + c_4 e^{-\frac{n\pi y}{8}}\right)$$

which is satisfied only when

$$c_3 = 0.$$

∴ From (4), $u(x, y) = c_2 c_4 \sin \dfrac{n\pi x}{8} e^{-\frac{n\pi y}{8}} = b_n \sin \dfrac{n\pi x}{8} e^{-\frac{n\pi y}{8}}$ ...(5)

From (5), $u(x, 0) = 100 \sin \dfrac{\pi x}{8} = b_n \sin \dfrac{n\pi x}{8}$

⇒ $b_n = 100,\ n = 1.$

∴ From (5), $u(x, y) = 100 \sin \left(\dfrac{\pi x}{8}\right) e^{-(\pi y/8)}$

which is the required steady state temperature at any point of the plate.

Example 3. *An infinitely long plane uniform plate is bounded by two parallel edges and an end at right angles to them. The breadth is π. This end is maintained at temperature u_0 at all points and the other edges are at zero temperature. Determine the temperature at any point of the plate in the steady state.* (G.B.T.U. 2012)

Sol. In steady state, two dimensional heat flow equation is

$$\frac{\partial^2 u}{\partial x^2} + \frac{\partial^2 u}{\partial y^2} = 0 \qquad ...(1)$$

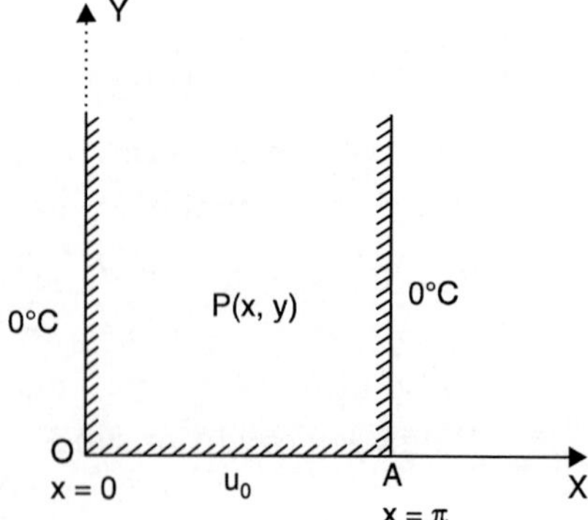

Boundary conditions are,

$$u(0, y) = 0 = u(\pi, y)$$

$$\underset{y \to \infty}{\mathrm{Lt}}\; u(x, y) = 0 \; (0 < x < \pi)$$

and $u(x, 0) = u_0 \; (0 < x < \pi)$

Solution to equation (1) is

$u(x, t) = (c_1 \cos px + c_2 \sin px)(c_3 e^{py} + c_4 e^{-py})$ ...(2)

From (2), $u(0, y) = 0 = c_1(c_3\, e^{py} + c_4 e^{-py})$

⇒ $c_1 = 0.$

From (2), $u(x, y) = c_2 \sin px(c_3\, e^{py} + c_4\, e^{-py})$

$$u(\pi, y) = 0 = c_2 \sin p\pi(c_3\, e^{py} + c_4\, e^{-py})$$

⇒ $\sin p\pi = 0 = \sin n\pi \; (n \in \mathrm{I})$ ...(3)

∴ $p = n.$

$\therefore$ From (3), $\quad u(x, y) = c_2 \sin nx\,(c_3 e^{ny} + c_4 e^{-ny})$ ...(4)

$$\lim_{y \to \infty} u(x, y) = 0 = c_2 \sin nx \lim_{y \to \infty} (c_3 e^{ny} + c_4 e^{-ny})$$

which is satisfied only when $c_3 = 0$.

$\therefore$ From (4), $\quad u(x, y) = c_2 c_4 e^{-ny} \sin nx = b_n e^{-ny} \sin nx,$ where $c_2 c_4 = b_n$

The most general solution is

$$u(x, y) = \sum_{n=1}^{\infty} b_n e^{-ny} \sin nx \qquad \text{...(5)}$$

$$u(x, 0) = u_0 = \sum_{n=1}^{\infty} b_n \sin nx$$

where
$$b_n = \frac{2}{\pi} \int_0^{\pi} u_0 \sin nx \, dx$$

$$= \frac{2u_0}{\pi} \left(\frac{-\cos nx}{n} \right)_0^{\pi} = \frac{2u_0}{n\pi} \{1 - (-1)^n\} = \begin{cases} \dfrac{4u_0}{n\pi}; & \text{if } n \text{ is odd} \\ 0 \;; & \text{if } n \text{ is even} \end{cases}$$

$\therefore$ From (5),
$$u(x, y) = \frac{4u_0}{\pi} \sum_{n=1,3,5,\ldots}^{\infty} \frac{\sin nx}{n} e^{-ny} \qquad (n \text{ is odd})$$

or
$$u(x, y) = \frac{4u_0}{\pi} \sum_{n=1}^{\infty} \frac{1}{(2n-1)} \sin (2n-1)\, x\, e^{-(2n-1)y}.$$

Example 4. *A rectangular plate with insulated surfaces is 10 cm wide and so long compared to its width that it may be considered infinite in length without introducing an appreciable error. If the temperature along the short edge y = 0 is given by*

and
$$u(x, y) = \begin{cases} 20x &, \quad 0 < x \le 5 \\ 20(10 - x), & 5 < x < 10 \end{cases}$$

and the two long edges x = 0 and x = 10 as well as other short edge are kept at 0°C. Find the temperature u at any point P(x, y).

Sol. In steady state, two dimensional heat flow equation is

$$\frac{\partial^2 u}{\partial x^2} + \frac{\partial^2 u}{\partial y^2} = 0 \qquad \text{...(1)}$$

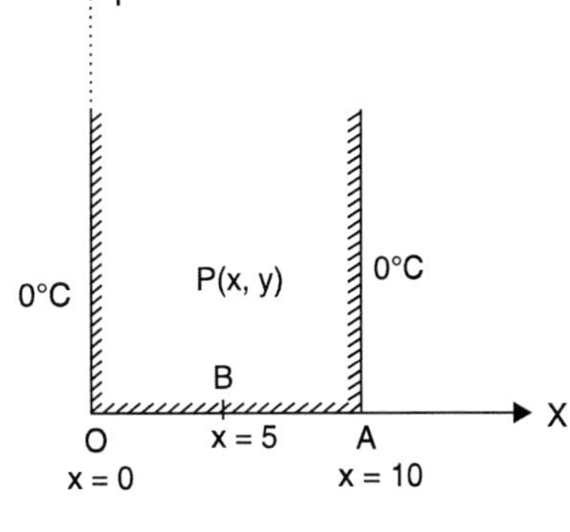

Its solution is

$u(x, y) = (c_1 \cos px + c_2 \sin px)(c_3\, e^{py} + c_4\, e^{-py})$ ...(2)

Boundary conditions are $u(0, y) = 0$

$$u(10, y) = 0$$

$$\lim_{y \to \infty} u(x, y) = u(x, \infty) = 0$$

and
$$u(x, 0) = \begin{cases} 20x, & 0 < x \le 5 \\ 20(10 - x), & 5 < x \le 10 \end{cases}$$

From (2), $\quad u(x, y) = 0 = c_1 (c_3 e^{py} + c_4 e^{-py}) \;\Rightarrow\; c_1 = 0$

From (2), $u(x, y) = c_2 \sin px\,(c_3 e^{py} + c_4 e^{-py})$ ...(3)

$$u(10, y) = 0 = c_2 \sin 10p\,(c_3 e^{py} + c_4 e^{-py})$$

$\Rightarrow$ $\sin 10p = 0 = \sin n\pi$

or $10p = n\pi \; (n \in I)$

$\Rightarrow$ $p = \dfrac{n\pi}{10}$.

$\therefore$ From (3), $u(x, y) = c_2 \sin \dfrac{n\pi x}{10}\left(c_3 e^{\frac{n\pi y}{10}} + c_4 e^{-\frac{n\pi y}{10}}\right)$ ...(4)

$$\lim_{y \to \infty} u(x, y) = c_2 \sin \frac{n\pi x}{10} \lim_{y \to \infty}\left(c_3 e^{\frac{n\pi y}{10}} + c_4 e^{-\frac{n\pi y}{10}}\right)$$

which is satisfied only when $c_3 = 0$.

Hence from (4), $u(x, y) = c_2 c_4 \sin \dfrac{n\pi x}{10} e^{-\frac{n\pi y}{10}} = b_n \sin \dfrac{n\pi x}{10} e^{-\frac{n\pi y}{10}}$ ...(5)

The most general solution is

$$u(x, y) = \sum_{n=1}^{\infty} b_n \sin \frac{n\pi x}{10} e^{-\frac{n\pi y}{10}} \quad ...(6)$$

$$u(x, 0) = \sum_{n=1}^{\infty} b_n \sin \frac{n\pi x}{10},$$

where $b_n = \dfrac{2}{10}\displaystyle\int_0^{10} u(x, 0) \sin \frac{n\pi x}{10}\, dx$

$$= \frac{1}{5}\left[\int_0^5 20x \sin \frac{n\pi x}{10} dx + \int_5^{10} 20\,(10 - x) \sin \frac{n\pi x}{10}\, dx\right]$$

$$= 4\left[\left\{x\left(\frac{-\cos \frac{n\pi x}{10}}{\frac{n\pi}{10}}\right)\right\}_0^5 - \int_0^5 1\left(\frac{-\cos \frac{n\pi x}{10}}{\frac{n\pi}{10}}\right) dx + \left\{(10 - x)\left(\frac{-\cos \frac{n\pi x}{10}}{\frac{n\pi}{10}}\right)\right\}_5^{10} - \int_5^{10} (-1)\left(\frac{-\cos \frac{n\pi x}{10}}{\frac{n\pi}{10}}\right) dx\right]$$

$$= 4\left[\frac{10}{n\pi}(-5)\cos \frac{n\pi}{2} + \frac{10}{n\pi}\left(\frac{\sin \frac{n\pi x}{10}}{\frac{n\pi}{10}}\right)_0^5 + \frac{50}{n\pi}\cos \frac{n\pi}{2} - \frac{10}{n\pi}\left(\frac{\sin \frac{n\pi x}{10}}{\frac{n\pi}{10}}\right)_5^{10}\right]$$

$$= 4\left[\frac{-50}{n\pi}\cos \frac{n\pi}{2} + \frac{100}{n^2\pi^2}\sin \frac{n\pi}{2} + \frac{50}{n\pi}\cos \frac{n\pi}{2} - \frac{100}{n^2\pi^2}\left(0 - \sin \frac{n\pi}{2}\right)\right]$$

$$= \frac{800}{n^2\pi^2} \sin \frac{n\pi}{2}.$$

From (6), $$u(x, y) = \frac{800}{\pi^2} \sum_{1}^{\infty} \frac{\sin n\pi/2}{n^2} \sin \frac{n\pi x}{10} e^{-\frac{n\pi y}{10}}.$$

Example 5. *Solve* $\frac{\partial^2 u}{\partial x^2} + \frac{\partial^2 u}{\partial y^2} = 0$, $0 < x < \pi$, $0 < y < \pi$, *which satisfies the conditions :*

$$u(0, y) = u(\pi, y) = u(x, \pi) = 0 \text{ and } u(x, 0) = \sin^2 x. \qquad \text{(U.K.T.U. 2011)}$$

Sol. The given equation is $$\frac{\partial^2 u}{\partial x^2} + \frac{\partial^2 u}{\partial y^2} = 0 \qquad ...(1)$$

Its solution consistent with boundary conditions is

$$u(x, y) = (c_1 \cos px + c_2 \sin px)(c_3 e^{py} + c_4 e^{-py}) \qquad ...(2)$$

From (2), $u(0, y) = 0 = c_1(c_3 e^{py} + c_4 e^{-py})$

$\Rightarrow$ $c_1 = 0.$

$\therefore$ From (2), $$u(x, y) = c_2 \sin px \,(c_3 e^{py} + c_4 e^{-py}) \qquad ...(3)$$

$u(\pi, y) = 0 = c_2 \sin p\pi(c_3 e^{py} + c_4 e^{-py})$

$\Rightarrow$ $\sin p\pi = 0 = \sin n\pi \; (n \in \text{I})$

$\therefore$ $p = n.$

Hence from (3), $$u(x, y) = c_2 \sin nx \,(c_3 e^{ny} + c_4 e^{-ny}) = \sin nx \,(\text{A}e^{ny} + \text{B}e^{-ny}) \qquad ...(4)$$

where $c_2 c_3 = \text{A}$ and $c_2 c_4 = \text{B}$.

From (4), $u(x, \pi) = \sin nx(\text{A}e^{n\pi} + \text{B}e^{-n\pi})$

$0 = \sin nx(\text{A}e^{n\pi} + \text{B}e^{-n\pi})$

$\Rightarrow$ $0 = \text{A}e^{n\pi} + \text{B}e^{-n\pi}$

$\Rightarrow$ $\text{A}e^{n\pi} = -\text{B}e^{-n\pi} = -\frac{1}{2}\text{B}_n$ (say)

then (4) becomes, $$u(x, y) = \sin nx \left[-\frac{1}{2}\text{B}_n e^{-n\pi} e^{ny} + \frac{1}{2}\text{B}_n e^{n\pi} e^{-ny}\right]$$

$$= \frac{1}{2}\text{B}_n[e^{n(\pi-y)} - e^{-n(\pi-y)}] \sin nx = \text{B}_n \sin hn\,(\pi - y) \sin nx.$$

The most general solution is

$$u(x, y) = \sum_{n=1}^{\infty} \text{B}_n \sin hn\,(\pi - y) \sin nx \qquad ...(5)$$

$$u(x, 0) = \sin^2 x = \sum_{n=1}^{\infty} \text{B}_n \sin h\,n\pi \sin nx$$

where $$\text{B}_n \sin hn\pi = \frac{2}{\pi}\int_0^{\pi} \sin^2 x \sin nx \, dx$$

$$= \frac{1}{\pi}\int_0^{\pi} (1 - \cos 2x) \sin nx \, dx$$

$$= \frac{1}{\pi}\int_0^{\pi} \left[\sin nx - \frac{1}{2}\{\sin (n+2)\,x + \sin (n-2)\,x\}\right] dx$$

$$= \frac{1}{\pi}\left[\frac{-\cos nx}{n} + \frac{\cos (n+2)x}{2(n+2)} + \frac{\cos (n-2)\,x}{2(n-2)}\right]_0^{\pi}$$

$$= \frac{1}{2\pi}\left[\left(\frac{1}{n+2}+\frac{1}{n-2}-\frac{2}{n}\right)\{(-1)^n - 1\}\right], \text{ when } n \neq 2$$

$$B_n \sinh n\pi = \begin{cases} \dfrac{-8}{\pi n(n^2-4)}, & \text{when } n \text{ is odd} \\ 0 \quad , & \text{when } n \text{ is even and} \neq 2 \end{cases}$$

when $n = 2$,

$$B_2 \sinh 2\pi = \frac{2}{\pi}\int_0^\pi \sin^2 x \sin 2x\, dx$$

$$= \frac{1}{\pi}\int_0^\pi (1-\cos 2x)\sin 2x\, dx = \frac{1}{\pi}\int_0^\pi \left(\sin 2x - \frac{1}{2}\sin 4x\right) dx$$

$$= \frac{1}{\pi}\left(\frac{-\cos 2x}{2} + \frac{1}{8}\cos 4x\right)_0^\pi = 0$$

$\therefore$ $B_2 = 0$.

Hence the solution (5) becomes,

$$u(x, y) = \frac{-8}{\pi}\sum_{n=1,3,5,\ldots}^{\infty} \frac{\sin nx \sinh n(\pi - y)}{n(n^2-4)\sinh n\pi}$$

or

$$u(x, y) = -\frac{8}{\pi}\sum_{m=1,2,3,\ldots}^{\infty} \frac{\sin(2m-1)x \sinh(2m-1)(\pi-y)}{(2m-1)\{(2m-1)^2-4\}\sinh(2m-1)\pi}.$$

Example 6. *Solve* $\frac{\partial^2 u}{\partial x^2} + \frac{\partial^2 u}{\partial y^2} = 0$, *with the rectangle* $0 \le x \le a$, $0 \le y \le b$ *; given that* $u(x, b) = u(0, y) = u(a, y) = 0$ *and* $u(x, 0) = x(a - x)$.

Sol. The equation is

$$\frac{\partial^2 u}{\partial x^2} + \frac{\partial^2 u}{\partial y^2} = 0 \qquad \ldots(1)$$

Its solution is

$$u(x, y) = (c_1 \cos px + c_2 \sin px)(c_3 e^{py} + c_4 e^{-py}) \qquad \ldots(2)$$

$$u(0, y) = 0 = c_1(c_3 e^{py} + c_4 e^{-py})$$

$\Rightarrow$ $c_1 = 0$.

$\therefore$ From (2), $u(x, y) = c_2 \sin px\,(c_3 e^{py} + c_4 e^{-py})$ ...(3)

$$u(a, y) = 0 = c_2 \sin ap\,(c_3 e^{py} + c_4 e^{-py})$$

$\Rightarrow$ $\sin ap = 0 = \sin n\pi \ (n \in I)$

$\Rightarrow$ $ap = n\pi$ or $p = \frac{n\pi}{a}$.

$\therefore$ From (3), $u(x, y) = c_2 \sin \frac{n\pi x}{a}\left(c_3 e^{\frac{n\pi y}{a}} + c_4 e^{-\frac{n\pi y}{a}}\right)$

$$u(x, y) = \sin \frac{n\pi x}{a}\left(A e^{\frac{n\pi y}{a}} + B e^{-\frac{n\pi y}{a}}\right) \qquad \ldots(4)$$

where $c_2 c_3 = A$ and $c_2 c_4 = B$

$$u(x, b) = \sin \frac{n\pi x}{a}\left(A e^{\frac{n\pi b}{a}} + B e^{-\frac{n\pi b}{a}}\right)$$

$$0 = \sin \frac{n\pi x}{a}(Ae^{\frac{n\pi b}{a}} + Be^{-\frac{n\pi b}{a}})$$

$$\Rightarrow \quad Ae^{\frac{n\pi b}{a}} + Be^{-\frac{n\pi b}{a}} = 0$$

$$Ae^{\frac{n\pi b}{a}} = -Be^{-\frac{n\pi b}{a}} = -\frac{1}{2}B_n \text{ (say)}.$$

Then (4) becomes,

$$u(x, y) = \sin \frac{n\pi x}{a}\left[\frac{-1}{2}B_n e^{-\frac{n\pi b}{a}} e^{\frac{n\pi y}{a}} + \frac{1}{2}B_n e^{\frac{n\pi b}{a}} e^{-\frac{n\pi y}{a}}\right]$$

$$= \frac{1}{2}B_n \sin \frac{n\pi x}{a}[e^{\frac{n\pi}{a}(b-y)} - e^{-\frac{n\pi}{a}(b-y)}]$$

$$= \frac{1}{2}B_n \sin \frac{n\pi x}{a}.2\sinh \frac{n\pi}{a}(b-y) = B_n \sin \frac{n\pi x}{a}\sinh \frac{n\pi}{a}(b-y).$$

The most general solution is

$$u(x, y) = \sum_{n=1}^{\infty} B_n \sin \frac{n\pi x}{a}\sinh \frac{n\pi}{a}(b-y) \qquad ...(5)$$

Applying to this the condition $u(x, 0) = x(a-x)$, we get

From (5), $$u(x, 0) = \sum_{n=1}^{\infty} B_n \sinh \frac{n\pi b}{a}\sin \frac{n\pi x}{a}$$

$$\Rightarrow \quad x(a-x) = \sum_{n=1}^{\infty} B_n \sinh \frac{n\pi b}{a}\sin \frac{n\pi x}{a}$$

where $$B_n \sin h\frac{n\pi}{a}b = \frac{2}{a}\int_0^a x(a-x)\sin \frac{n\pi}{a}x\,dx$$

$$= \frac{2}{a}\left[\left\{(ax-x^2)\left(\frac{-\cos \frac{n\pi}{a}x}{\frac{n\pi}{a}}\right)\right\}_0^a - \int_0^a (a-2x).\left(\frac{-\cos \frac{n\pi}{a}x}{\frac{n\pi}{a}}\right)dx\right]$$

$$= \frac{2}{a}.\frac{a}{n\pi}\int_0^a (a-2x).\cos \frac{n\pi}{a}x\,dx$$

$$= \frac{2}{n\pi}\left[\left\{(a-2x)\frac{\sin \frac{n\pi}{a}x}{\frac{n\pi}{a}}\right\}_0^a - \int_0^a (-2)\left(\frac{\sin \frac{n\pi}{a}x}{\frac{n\pi}{a}}\right)dx\right]$$

$$= \frac{4}{n\pi}.\frac{a}{n\pi}\left(\frac{-\cos \frac{n\pi}{a}x}{\frac{n\pi}{a}}\right)_0^a = \frac{4a}{n^2\pi^2}.\frac{a}{n\pi}(1-\cos n\pi)$$

$$= \frac{4a^2}{n^3\pi^3}[1-(-1)^n] = \begin{cases} \dfrac{8a^2}{n^3\pi^3} & , \text{ when } n \text{ is odd} \\ 0 & , \text{ when } n \text{ is even} \end{cases}$$

$$\therefore \qquad B_n = \begin{cases} \dfrac{8a^2}{\sinh\left(\dfrac{n\pi}{a}b\right)(n^3\pi^3)} & , \text{ when } n \text{ is odd} \\ 0 & , \text{ when } n \text{ is even} \end{cases}$$

$\therefore$ From (5),

$$u(x, y) = \frac{8a^2}{\pi^3} \sum_{\substack{n=1, 3, 5, \ldots \\ (n \text{ is odd})}}^{\infty} \frac{\sin \dfrac{n\pi x}{a}}{n^3 \sinh \dfrac{n\pi}{a} b} . \sinh \frac{n\pi}{a}(b-y)$$

or

$$u(x, y) = \frac{8a^2}{\pi^3} \sum_{n=0}^{\infty} \frac{1}{(2n+1)^3} \sin (2n+1)\frac{\pi x}{a} . \frac{\sinh \dfrac{(2n+1)\pi}{a}(b-y)}{\sinh \dfrac{(2n+1)\pi}{a} b}$$

Example 7. *A thin rectangular plate whose surface is impervious to heat flow has at $t = 0$ an arbitrary distribution of temperature $f(x, y)$. Its four edges $x = 0$, $x = a$, $y = 0$, $y = b$ are kept at zero temperature. Determine the temperature at a point of a plate as t increases.*

Sol. Two dimensional heat flow equation is

$$\frac{\partial^2 u}{\partial x^2} + \frac{\partial^2 u}{\partial y^2} = \frac{1}{c^2}\frac{\partial u}{\partial t}. \qquad \ldots(1)$$

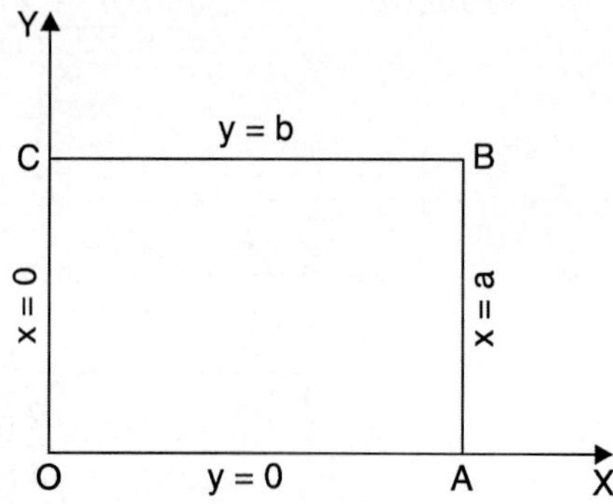

Boundary conditions are

$$u(0, y, t) = 0 = u(a, y, t)$$
$$u(x, 0, t) = 0 = u(x, b, t)$$

and $\qquad u(x, y, t) = f(x, y)$ at $t = 0$.

Let the solution be $\quad u = XYT$

where X is a function of x only, Y is a function of y only and T is a function of t only.

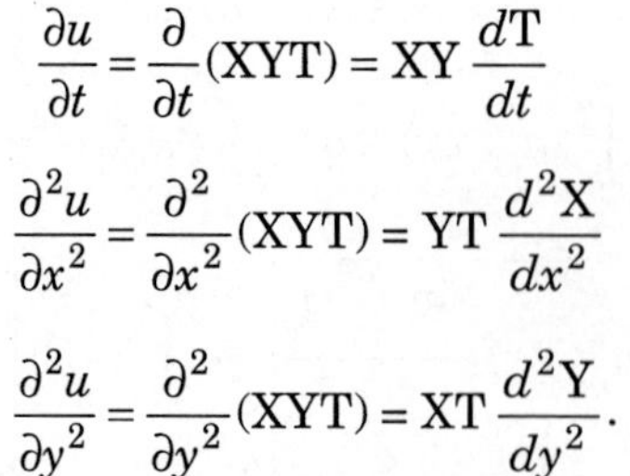

$$\frac{\partial u}{\partial t} = \frac{\partial}{\partial t}(XYT) = XY\frac{dT}{dt}$$

$$\frac{\partial^2 u}{\partial x^2} = \frac{\partial^2}{\partial x^2}(XYT) = YT\frac{d^2X}{dx^2}$$

$$\frac{\partial^2 u}{\partial y^2} = \frac{\partial^2}{\partial y^2}(XYT) = XT\frac{d^2Y}{dy^2}.$$

From (1), $YTX'' + XTY'' = \dfrac{1}{c^2}(XYT')$

$$\Rightarrow \qquad \frac{X''}{X} + \frac{Y''}{Y} = \frac{T'}{c^2T} \qquad \ldots(2)$$

There are three possibilities :

(*i*) $\frac{X''}{X} = 0, \quad \frac{Y''}{Y} = 0, \quad \frac{T'}{c^2T} = 0$

(*ii*) $\frac{X''}{X} = K_1^2, \quad \frac{Y''}{Y} = K_2^2, \quad \frac{T'}{c^2T} = K^2$

(*iii*) $\frac{X''}{X} = -K_1^2, \quad \frac{Y''}{Y} = -K_2^2, \quad \frac{T'}{c^2T} = -K^2$

where $K^2 = K_1^2 + K_2^2.$

Of these three solutions, we have to select the solution which is consistent with the physical nature of the problem.

The solution satisfying the given boundary conditions will be given by (*iii*).

Then,
$$X = c_1 \cos K_1x + c_2 \sin K_1x$$
$$Y = c_3 \cos K_2y + c_4 \sin K_2y$$
$$T = c_5e^{-c^2K^2t}$$

$\therefore$
$$u = XYT$$

$\Rightarrow$
$$u(x, y, t) = (c_1 \cos K_1x + c_2 \sin K_1x)(c_3 \cos K_2y + c_4 \sin K_2y)(c_5e^{-c^2K^2t}) \quad ...(3)$$

$$u(0, y, t) = 0 = c_1(c_3 \cos K_2y + c_4 \sin K_2y)c_5e^{-c^2K^2t}$$

$\Rightarrow$
$$c_1 = 0.$$

$\therefore$ From (3),
$$u(x, y, t) = c_2 \sin K_1x(c_3 \cos K_2y + c_4 \sin K_2y)(c_5e^{-c^2K^2t})$$
$$= c_6 \sin K_1x\,(c_3 \cos K_2y + c_4 \sin K_2y)(e^{-c^2K^2t}) \quad ...(4)$$

where
$$c_2c_5 = c_6$$

From (4),
$$u(a, y, t) = 0 = c_6 \sin K_1a(c_3 \cos K_2y + c_4 \sin K_2y)e^{-c^2K^2t}$$

$\Rightarrow$
$$\sin K_1a = 0 = \sin n\pi \ (n \in I)$$

$\therefore$
$$K_1 = \frac{n\pi}{a}.$$

From (4),
$$u(x, y, t) = c_6 \sin \frac{n\pi x}{a}\,(c_3 \cos K_2y + c_4 \sin K_2y)\,(e^{-c^2K^2t}) \quad ...(5)$$

$$u(x, 0, t) = 0 = c_6 \sin \frac{n\pi x}{a} . c_3\, e^{-c^2K^2t}$$

$\Rightarrow$
$$c_3 = 0.$$

$\therefore$ From (5),
$$u(x, y, t) = c_6c_4 \sin \frac{n\pi x}{a} \sin K_2y e^{-c^2K^2t} \quad ...(6)$$

$$u(x, b, t) = 0 = c_6c_4 \sin \frac{n\pi x}{a} \sin K_2b e^{-c^2K^2t}$$

$\Rightarrow$
$$\sin K_2b = 0 = \sin m\pi \ (m \in I)$$
$$K_2b = m\pi$$

$\Rightarrow$
$$K_2 = \frac{m\pi}{b}.$$

$\therefore$ From (6), $u(x, y, t) = c_6c_4 \sin \dfrac{n\pi x}{a} \sin \dfrac{m\pi y}{b} e^{-c^2K^2t}$

$$= A_{mn} \sin \frac{n\pi x}{a} \sin \frac{m\pi y}{b} e^{-c^2K^2t} \quad ...(7) \quad | \text{ where } c_6c_4 = A_{mn}$$

But, $$K^2 = K_1^2 + K_2^2 = \frac{n^2\pi^2}{a^2} + \frac{m^2\pi^2}{b^2}$$

or $$K^2_{mn} = \pi^2\left(\frac{n^2}{a^2} + \frac{m^2}{b^2}\right).$$

By using K_{mn}, equation (7) becomes,

$$u(x, y, t) = \sum_{m=1}^{\infty}\sum_{n=1}^{\infty} A_{mn} \sin \frac{n\pi x}{a} \sin \frac{m\pi y}{b} e^{-c^2K^2_{mn}t} \quad ...(8)$$

which is the most general solution.

$$u(x, y, 0) = f(x, y) = \sum_{m=1}^{\infty}\sum_{n=1}^{\infty} A_{mn} \sin \frac{n\pi x}{a} \sin \frac{m\pi y}{b}$$

which is the double Fourier half-range sine series for $f(x, y)$.

where $$A_{mn} = \frac{2}{a}\cdot\frac{2}{b}\int_{x=0}^{a}\int_{y=0}^{b} \sin \frac{n\pi x}{a} \sin \frac{m\pi y}{b} f(x, y)dx\, dy.$$

Example 8. *Solve the Laplace equation* $\dfrac{\partial^2 u}{\partial x^2} + \dfrac{\partial^2 u}{\partial y^2} = 0$ *in a rectangle in the xy-plane with* $u(x, 0) = 0$, $u(x, b) = 0$, $u(0, y) = 0$ *and* $u(a, y) = f(y)$ *parallel to y-axis.*

[U.P.T.U. (SUM) 2008]

Sol. The given equation is

$$\frac{\partial^2 u}{\partial x^2} + \frac{\partial^2 u}{\partial y^2} = 0 \quad ...(1)$$

Let $$u = XY \quad ...(2)$$

where X is a function of x only and Y is a function of y only. Then,

$$\frac{\partial^2 u}{\partial x^2} = \frac{\partial^2}{\partial x^2}(XY) = YX''$$

and $$\frac{\partial^2 u}{\partial y^2} = \frac{\partial^2}{\partial y^2}(XY) = XY''$$

$\therefore$ From (1), $YX'' + XY'' = 0 \Rightarrow \dfrac{Y''}{Y} = -\dfrac{X''}{X}$ ...(3)

Case I. When $$\frac{Y''}{Y} = -\frac{X''}{X} = p^2 \text{ (say)}$$

(*i*) $$\frac{Y''}{Y} = p^2$$

$\Rightarrow$ $$Y'' - p^2Y = 0$$

Auxiliary equation is

$$m^2 - p^2 = 0 \quad \Rightarrow \quad m = \pm p$$

$\therefore$ $\quad$ $\text{C.F.} = c_1 e^{py} + c_2 e^{-py}$

$\text{P.I.} = 0$

$\therefore$ $\quad$ $\text{Y} = c_1 e^{py} + c_2 e^{-py}$

(*ii*) $\quad$ $-\dfrac{\text{X}''}{\text{X}} = p^2$

$\Rightarrow$ $\quad$ $\text{X}'' + p^2\text{X} = 0$

Auxiliary equation is

$$m^2 + p^2 = 0 \quad \Rightarrow \quad m = \pm pi$$

$\therefore$ $\quad$ $\text{C.F.} = c_3 \cos px + c_4 \sin px$

$\text{P.I.} = 0$

$\therefore$ $\quad$ $\text{X} = c_3 \cos px + c_4 \sin px$

Now, $\quad$ $\text{Y}(0) = 0$

$\Rightarrow$ $\quad$ $c_1 + c_2 = 0 \quad \Rightarrow \quad c_2 = -c_1$

$\text{Y}(b) = 0$

$\Rightarrow$ $\quad$ $c_1 e^{pb} + c_2 e^{-pb} = 0$

$\Rightarrow$ $\quad$ $c_1(e^{pb} - e^{-pb}) = 0$

$\Rightarrow$ $\quad$ $c_1 = 0$ $\quad$ | Since $e^{pb} - e^{-pb} \neq 0$ (as $p \neq 0 \neq b$)

$\therefore$ $\quad$ $\text{Y} = 0 \quad \Rightarrow \quad u = \text{XY} = 0$ $\quad$ which is impossible.

Hence, we reject case I.

Case II. When $\quad$ $\dfrac{\text{Y}''}{\text{Y}} = -\dfrac{\text{X}''}{\text{X}} = 0$ (say)

(*i*) $\quad$ $\dfrac{\text{Y}''}{\text{Y}} = 0$

$\Rightarrow$ $\quad$ $\text{Y}'' = 0 \quad \Rightarrow \quad \text{Y} = c_5 + c_6 y$

(*ii*) $\quad$ $-\dfrac{\text{X}''}{\text{X}} = 0$

$\Rightarrow$ $\quad$ $\text{X}'' = 0 \quad \Rightarrow \quad \text{X} = c_7 + c_8 x$

Now, $\quad$ $\text{Y}(0) = 0 \quad \Rightarrow \quad c_5 = 0$

$\text{Y}(b) = 0 \quad \Rightarrow \quad c_6 b = 0 \quad \Rightarrow \quad c_6 = 0$ $\quad$ | $\because$ $b \neq 0$

$\therefore$ $\quad$ $\text{Y} = 0$

$\therefore$ $\quad$ $u = \text{XY} = 0$ which is impossible

Hence, we also reject case II.

Case III. When $\quad$ $\dfrac{\text{Y}''}{\text{Y}} = -\dfrac{\text{X}''}{\text{X}} = -p^2$ (say)

(*i*) $\quad$ $\dfrac{\text{Y}''}{\text{Y}} = -p^2$

$\Rightarrow$ $\quad$ $\text{Y}'' + p^2\text{Y} = 0$

Auxiliary equation is

$$m^2 + p^2 = 0 \quad \Rightarrow \quad m = \pm pi$$

$\therefore$ $$\text{C.F.} = c_9 \cos py + c_{10} \sin py$$

$$\text{P.I.} = 0$$

$\therefore$ $$\text{Y} = c_9 \cos py + c_{10} \sin py$$

(ii) $$-\frac{\text{X}''}{\text{X}} = -p^2 \quad \Rightarrow \quad \text{X}'' - p^2\text{X} = 0$$

Auxiliary equation is

$$m^2 - p^2 = 0 \quad \Rightarrow \quad m = \pm p$$

$\therefore$ $$\text{C.F.} = c_{11}\, e^{px} + c_{12}\, e^{-px}$$

$$\text{P.I.} = 0$$

$\therefore$ $$\text{X} = c_{11}\, e^{px} + c_{12}\, e^{-px}$$

Now, $$\text{Y}(0) = 0 \quad \Rightarrow \quad c_9 = 0$$

$$\text{Y}(b) = 0 \quad \Rightarrow \quad c_{10} \sin bp = 0$$

$\therefore$ $$\sin bp = 0 = \sin n\pi,\ n \in \text{I}$$

$$p = \frac{n\pi}{b}$$

Hence, $$u = \text{XY} = c_{10} \sin \frac{n\pi y}{b} \left(c_{11}\, e^{\frac{n\pi x}{b}} + c_{12} e^{-\frac{n\pi x}{b}} \right) \qquad ...(4)$$

Now, $$u(0, y) = 0 = c_{10} \sin \frac{n\pi y}{b}\, (c_{11} + c_{12})$$

$\Rightarrow$ $$c_{11} + c_{12} = 0 \quad \Rightarrow \quad c_{12} = -\, c_{11}$$

$\therefore$ From (4), $$u(x, y) = c_{10}\, c_{11} \sin \frac{n\pi y}{b} \left(e^{\frac{n\pi x}{b}} - e^{-\frac{n\pi x}{b}} \right)$$

$$= b_n \sin \frac{n\pi y}{b} \sinh \frac{n\pi x}{b} \qquad ...(5)$$

| where $b_n = 2\, c_{10}\, c_{11}$

Most general solution is

$$u(x, y) = \sum_{n=1}^{\infty} b_n \sin \frac{n\pi y}{b} \sinh \frac{n\pi x}{b} \qquad ...(6)$$

Now, $$u(a, y) = f(y) = \sum_{n=1}^{\infty} b_n \sin \frac{n\pi y}{b} \sinh \frac{n\pi a}{b}$$

where $$\left(\sinh \frac{n\pi a}{b} \right) b_n = \frac{2}{b} \int_0^b f(y) \sin \frac{n\pi y}{b}\, dy$$

$\Rightarrow$ $$b_n = \frac{2}{b \sinh \left(\frac{n\pi a}{b} \right)} \int_0^b f(y) \sin \frac{n\pi y}{b}\, dy. \qquad ...(7)$$

Example 9. *Find the steady state temperature distribution in a rectangular thin plate with its two surfaces insulated and with the conditions $u(0, y) = 0$, $u(x, 0) = 0$, $u(a, y) = g(y)$, $u(x, b) = f(x)$.* [U.P.T.U. (SUM) 2007]

Sol. Superposition applied to boundary conditions dismantles the given problem to solution of two simpler problems each of which can easily be solved by the method of separation of variables.

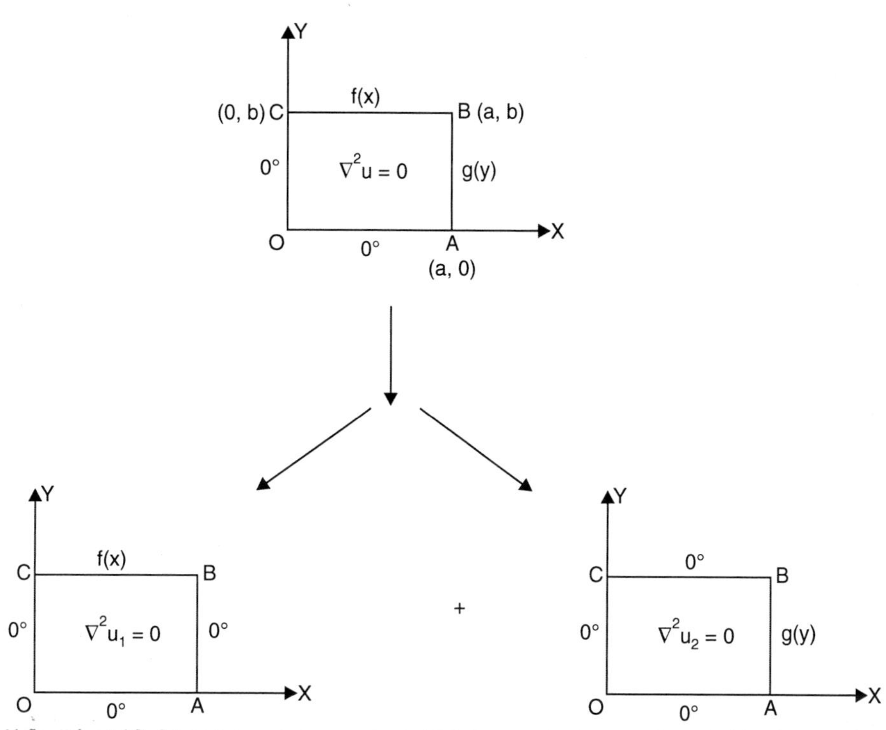

Now, the following two problems are required to be solved :

Problem 1. $\dfrac{\partial^2 u_1}{\partial x^2} + \dfrac{\partial^2 u_1}{\partial y^2} = 0$ subject to conditions

$$u_1(0, y) = 0,\ u_1(a, y) = 0,\ u_1(x, 0) = 0,\ u_1(x, b) = f(x)$$

Problem 2. $\dfrac{\partial^2 u_2}{\partial x^2} + \dfrac{\partial^2 u_2}{\partial y^2} = 0$ subject to conditions

$$u_2(0, y) = 0,\ u_2(x, 0) = 0,\ u_2(x, b) = 0,\ u_2(a, y) = g(y)$$

Let us now proceed to solve problem 1.

$$u_1(x, y) = (c_1 \cos px + c_2 \sin px)\,(c_3 e^{py} + c_4\, e^{-py}) \quad ...(1)$$

$$u_1(0, y) = 0 = c_1\,(c_3 e^{py} + c_4 e^{-py})$$

$$\Rightarrow \quad c_1 = 0$$

$$\therefore \quad u_1(x, y) = c_2 \sin px\,(c_3 e^{py} + c_4 e^{-py}) \quad ...(2)$$

$$u_1(a, y) = 0 = c_2 \sin pa\,(c_3 e^{py} + c_4 e^{-py})$$

$$\Rightarrow \quad \sin ap = 0 = \sin n\pi \quad (n \in I)$$

$$p = \frac{n\pi}{a}$$

Hence, from (2), $u_1(x, y) = c_2 \sin \frac{n\pi x}{a} \left(c_3 \, e^{\frac{n\pi y}{a}} + c_4 \, e^{-\frac{n\pi y}{a}} \right)$ ...(3)

$$u_1(x, 0) = 0 = c_2 \sin \frac{n\pi x}{a} (c_3 + c_4)$$

$\Rightarrow$ $c_3 + c_4 = 0 \Rightarrow c_4 = -c_3$

$\therefore$ $u_1(x, y) = c_2 c_3 \sin \frac{n\pi x}{a} \left(e^{\frac{n\pi y}{a}} - e^{-\frac{n\pi y}{a}} \right) = 2\, c_2 c_3 \sin \frac{n\pi x}{a} \sinh \frac{n\pi y}{a}$

$$= b_n \sin \frac{n\pi x}{a} \sinh \frac{n\pi y}{a} \text{ where } b_n = 2c_2 c_3$$

Most general solution to problem 1 is

$$u_1(x, y) = \sum_{n=1}^{\infty} b_n \sin \frac{n\pi x}{a} \sinh \frac{n\pi y}{a} \quad ...(4)$$

Now, $u_1(x, b) = f(x) = \sum_{n=1}^{\infty} b_n \sin \frac{n\pi x}{a} \sinh \frac{n\pi b}{a}$

where $b_n \sinh \frac{n\pi b}{a} = \frac{2}{a} \int_0^a f(x) \sin \frac{n\pi x}{a} \, dx$

$\Rightarrow$ $b_n = \frac{2}{a \sinh\left(\frac{n\pi b}{a}\right)} \int_0^a f(x) \sin \frac{n\pi x}{a} \, dx$ ...(5)

Similarly, the most general solution to problem 2 is

$$u_2(x, y) = \sum_{n=1}^{\infty} B_n \sin\left(\frac{n\pi y}{b}\right) \sinh\left(\frac{n\pi x}{b}\right) \quad ...(6)$$

where $B_n = \frac{2}{b \sinh\left(\frac{n\pi a}{b}\right)} \int_0^b g(y) \sin\left(\frac{n\pi y}{b}\right) dy$ ...(7)

| Interchanging x by y, a by b and $f(x)$ by $g(y)$

Hence, the required solution to the given original problem is

$$u(x, y) = u_1(x, y) + u_2(x, y)$$

$$= \sum_{n=1}^{\infty} \left[b_n \sin\left(\frac{n\pi x}{a}\right) \sinh\left(\frac{n\pi y}{a}\right) + B_n \sin\left(\frac{n\pi y}{b}\right) \sinh\left(\frac{n\pi x}{b}\right) \right]$$

where $b_n = \frac{2}{a \sinh\left(\frac{n\pi b}{a}\right)} \int_0^a f(x) \sin \frac{n\pi x}{a} \, dx$

and $B_n = \frac{2}{b \sinh\left(\frac{n\pi a}{b}\right)} \int_0^b g(y) \sin \frac{n\pi y}{b} \, dy.$

TEST YOUR KNOWLEDGE

1. A long rectangular plate of width a cm with insulated surface has its temperature v equal to zero on both the long sides and one of the short sides so that $v(0, y) = 0$, $v(a, y) = 0$,

$$\lim_{y \to \infty} v(x, y) = 0 \quad \text{and} \quad v(x, 0) = kx$$

Show that the steady-state temperature within the plate is

$$v(x, y) = \frac{2ak}{\pi} \sum_{n=1}^{\infty} \frac{(-1)^{n+1}}{n} e^{-\left(\frac{n\pi y}{a}\right)} \sin \frac{n\pi x}{a}.$$

2. A square plate is bounded by the lines $x = 0$, $y = 0$, $x = 20$ and $y = 20$. Its faces are insulated. The temperature along the upper horizontal edge is given by $u(x, 20) = x(20 - x)$ when $0 < x < 20$ while other three edges are kept at 0°C. Find the steady state temperature in the plate.

3. A rectangular plate has sides a and b. Let the side of length a be taken along OX and that of length b along OY and the other sides along $x = a$ and $y = b$. The sides $x = 0$, $x = a$ and $y = b$ are insulated and the edge $y = 0$ is kept at temperature $u_0 \cos \frac{\pi x}{a}$. Find the steady-state temperature at any point (x, y).

[**Hint:** Boundary conditions are $(u_x)_{x=0} = 0$, $(u_x)_{x=a} = 0$, $(u_y)_{y=b} = 0$ and $u(x, 0) = u_0 \cos (\pi x/a)$]

4. The temperature u is maintained at 0° along three edges of a square plate of length 100 cm and the fourth edge is maintained at 100° until steady-state conditions prevail. Find an expression for the temperature u at any point (x, y).

Hence, show that the temperature at the centre of the plate

$$= \frac{200}{\pi} \left[\frac{1}{\cosh \frac{\pi}{2}} - \frac{1}{3 \cosh \frac{3\pi}{2}} + \frac{1}{5 \cosh \frac{5\pi}{2}} - \ldots \right].$$

5. A rectangular plate is bounded by the lines $x = 0$, $y = 0$, $x = a$, $y = b$. Its surfaces are insulated and the temperature along the upper horizontal edge is 100°C while the other three edges are kept at 0°C. Find the steady state temperature function $u(x, y)$ and also the temperature at the point $\left(\frac{1}{2} a, \frac{1}{2} b\right)$.

6. Solve the following Laplace equation $\frac{\partial^2 u}{\partial x^2} + \frac{\partial^2 u}{\partial y^2} = 0$ in a rectangle with $u(0, y) = 0$, $u(a, y) = 0$, $u(x, b) = 0$ and $u(x, 0) = f(x)$ along x-axis. *(U.P.T.U. 2008)*

7. Solve the boundary value problem:

$$\frac{\partial^2 u}{\partial x^2} + \frac{\partial^2 u}{\partial y^2} = 0, \; 0 \le x \le a, \; 0 \le y \le b$$

with the boundary conditions:

$$u_x(0, y) = u_x(a, y) = u_y(x, 0) = 0 \text{ and } u_y(x, b) = f(x)$$ *[M.T.U. (SUM) 2011]*

Answers

2. $u(x, y) = \dfrac{3200}{\pi^3} \displaystyle\sum_{n=1}^{\infty} \dfrac{\sin \dfrac{(2n-1)\pi x}{20} \sin \dfrac{(2n-1)\pi y}{20}}{(2n-1)^3 \sinh (2n-1)\pi}$

3. $u(x, y) = u_0 \cos \dfrac{\pi x}{a} \cosh \dfrac{\pi}{a}(b-y) \operatorname{sech} \dfrac{\pi b}{a}$

5. $u(x, y) = \dfrac{400}{\pi} \displaystyle\sum_{n=1}^{\infty} \dfrac{\sin \left\{(2m-1)\dfrac{\pi x}{a}\right\} \sinh \left\{(2m-1)\dfrac{\pi y}{a}\right\}}{(2m-1) \sinh \left\{(2m-1)\dfrac{\pi b}{a}\right\}}$;

$$u\left(\frac{1}{2}a, \frac{1}{2}a\right) = \frac{200}{\pi}\left[\frac{1}{\cosh\left(\dfrac{\pi b}{2a}\right)} - \frac{1}{3\cosh\left(\dfrac{3\pi b}{2a}\right)} + \ldots\right]$$

6. $u(x, y) = \displaystyle\sum_{n=1}^{\infty} B_n \sin\left(\dfrac{n\pi x}{a}\right) \sinh \dfrac{n\pi}{a}(b-y)$, where $B_n = \dfrac{2}{a \sinh\left(\dfrac{n\pi b}{a}\right)} \displaystyle\int_0^a f(x) \sin \dfrac{n\pi x}{a}\, dx$

7. $u(x, y) = \displaystyle\sum_{n=1}^{\infty} b_n \cos \dfrac{n\pi x}{a}\left(e^{\frac{n\pi y}{a}} - e^{-\frac{n\pi y}{a}}\right)$ where, $b_n = \dfrac{1}{n\pi \cosh \dfrac{n\pi}{a} b} \displaystyle\int_0^a f(x) \cos \dfrac{n\pi x}{a}\, dx$.

5.12. LAPLACE EQUATION

Laplace's equation has wide applications in Physics and engineering. The theory of its solutions is called the *potential theory* and its solutions are called *harmonic functions.* The solution of Laplace's equation, subject to certain boundary conditions, is simplified by a proper choice of coordinate system.

Note 1. If the problem involves *rectangular boundaries,* we prefer to take Laplace's equation in *cartesian coordinates given by* $\dfrac{\partial^2 u}{\partial x^2} + \dfrac{\partial^2 u}{\partial y^2} = 0$ and $\dfrac{\partial^2 u}{\partial x^2} + \dfrac{\partial^2 u}{\partial y^2} + \dfrac{\partial^2 u}{\partial z^2} = 0.$

Note 2. If the problem involves circular boundaries, we prefer to take Laplace's equation in polar coordinates given by

$$\frac{\partial^2 u}{\partial r^2} + \frac{1}{r}\frac{\partial u}{\partial r} + \frac{1}{r^2}\frac{\partial^2 u}{\partial \theta^2} = 0.$$

This equations can be obtained from $u_{xx} + u_{yy} = 0$ by putting $x = r\cos\theta$, $y = r\sin\theta$, thus changing the independent variables from (x, y) to (r, θ).

Note 3. If the problem involves *cylindrical boundaries,* we prefer to take Laplace's equation in *cylindrical coordinates* given by

$$\frac{\partial^2 u}{\partial r^2} + \frac{1}{r}\frac{\partial u}{\partial r} + \frac{1}{r^2}\frac{\partial^2 u}{\partial \theta^2} + \frac{\partial^2 u}{\partial z^2} = 0.$$

This equation can be obtained from $u_{xx} + u_{yy} + u_{zz} = 0$ by putting $x = r\cos\theta$, $y = r\sin\theta$, $z = z$, thus changing the independent variables (x, y, z) to (r, θ, z).

Note 4. If the problem involves *spherical boundaries,* we prefer to take Laplace's equation in *spherical polar coordinates* given by

$$\frac{\partial^2 u}{\partial r^2}+\frac{2}{r}\frac{\partial u}{\partial r}+\frac{1}{r^2}\frac{\partial^2 u}{\partial \theta^2}+\frac{\cot\theta}{r^2}\frac{\partial u}{\partial \theta}+\frac{1}{r^2\sin^2\theta}\frac{\partial^2 u}{\partial \phi^2}=0.$$

This equation can be obtained from $u_{xx}+u_{yy}+u_{zz}=0$ by putting,

$$x=r\sin\theta\cos\phi,\ y=r\sin\theta\sin\phi,\ z=r\cos\theta,$$

thus changing the independent variables (x, y, z) to (r, θ, ϕ).

5.13. SOLUTIONS OF LAPLACE'S EQUATION

(a) Solution of Laplace's Equation in Two-dimensional Cartesian Form

We have already discussed the solution of $\frac{\partial^2 u}{\partial x^2}+\frac{\partial^2 u}{\partial y^2}=0$ in Art. 5.11.

(b) Solution of Laplace's Equation in Polar Coordinates

Laplace's equation in polar coordinates is $r^2\frac{\partial^2 u}{\partial r^2}+r\frac{\partial u}{\partial r}+\frac{\partial^2 u}{\partial \theta^2}=0$ ...(1)

Let $u(r, \theta)=R(r)F(\theta)$ or simply $u=RF$ ...(2)

where R is a function of r only and F is a function of θ only, be a solution of (1).

Substituting it in (1), we get

$$r^2R''F+rR'F+RF''=0 \quad \text{or} \quad (r^2R''+rR')F+RF''=0$$

Separating the variables, $\frac{r^2R''+rR'}{R}=-\frac{F''}{F}=\text{constant}=k$ (say)

Thus, we get ordinary differential equations

$$r^2\frac{d^2R}{dr^2}+r\frac{dR}{dr}-kR=0 \quad \text{...(3)}$$

and

$$\frac{d^2F}{d\theta^2}+kF=0 \quad \text{...(4)}$$

Now (3) is a homogeneous linear differential equation.

Putting $r=e^z$, (3) reduces to $\frac{d^2R}{dr^2}-kR=0$ ...(5)

Solving (5) and (4), we get

(*i*) *When k is positive and* $=p^2$, *say*

$$R=c_1e^{pz}+c_2e^{-pz}=c_1r^p+c_2r^{-p},$$
$$F=c_3\cos p\theta+c_4\sin p\theta.$$

(*ii*) *When k is negative and* $=-p^2$, *say*

$$R=c_1\cos pz+c_2\sin pz=c_1\cos(p\log r)+c_2\sin(p\log r)$$
$$F=c_3e^{p\theta}+c_4e^{-p\theta}$$

(*iii*) *When* $k=0$

$$R=c_1z+c_2=c_1\log r+c_2$$
$$F=c_3\theta+c_4$$

Thus the three possible solution of (1) are

$$u=(c_1r^p+c_2r^{-p})(c_3\cos p\theta+c_4\sin p\theta) \quad \text{...(6)}$$
$$u=[c_1\cos(p\log r)+c_2\sin(p\log r)]\,(c_3e^{p\theta}+c_4e^{-p\theta}) \quad \text{...(7)}$$
$$u=(c_1\log r+c_2)(c_3\theta+c_4) \quad \text{...(8)}$$

Of these solutions, we choose the one which is consistent with the physical nature of the problem.

Note. Usually we require a solution extending up to the origin.

Since u must be finite at the origin, we reject solutions (7) and (8). Also from (6), $c_2 = 0$.

$\therefore$ In this case, the solution may be written as

$$u = (\text{A} \cos p\theta + \text{B} \sin p\theta) r^p$$

The general solution will consist of a sum of similar terms with different (arbitrary) values of A, B and p.

(*c*) Solution of Laplace's Equation in Three-dimensional Cartesian Form

Laplace's equation in three-dimensional cartesian form is

$$\frac{\partial^2 u}{\partial x^2} + \frac{\partial^2 u}{\partial y^2} + \frac{\partial^2 u}{\partial z^2} = 0 \qquad ...(1)$$

Let $u(x, y, z) = \text{X}(x)\,\text{Y}(y)\,\text{Z}(z)$ or simply $u = \text{XYZ}$ ...(2) be a solution of (1).

Substituting it in (1), we get $\text{X}''\text{YZ} + \text{XY}''\text{Z} + \text{XYZ}'' = 0$

Dividing to XYZ, we get $$\frac{\text{X}''}{\text{X}} + \frac{\text{Y}''}{\text{Y}} + \frac{\text{Z}''}{\text{Z}} = 0$$

or $$\frac{1}{\text{X}} \cdot \frac{d^2\text{X}}{dx^2} + \frac{1}{\text{Y}} \cdot \frac{d^2\text{Y}}{dy^2} + \frac{1}{\text{Z}} \cdot \frac{d^2\text{Z}}{dz^2} = 0 \qquad ...(3)$$

which is of the form $\text{F}_1(x) + \text{F}_2(y) + \text{F}_3(z) = 0$.

Since x, y, z are independent, this is possible only when $\text{F}_1, \text{F}_2, \text{F}_3$ are constants. Assuming these constants to be k^2, l^2 and $-(k^2 + l^2)$ respectively, (3) gives rise to the following equations :

$$\frac{d^2\text{X}}{dx^2} - k^2\text{X} = 0, \quad \frac{d^2\text{Y}}{dy^2} - l^2\text{Y} = 0, \quad \frac{d^2\text{Z}}{dz^2} + (k^2 + l^2)\text{Z} = 0$$

Their solutions are $\text{X} = c_1 e^{kx} + c_2 e^{-kx}$, $\text{Y} = c_3 e^{ly} + c_4 e^{-ly}$

$$\text{Z} = c_5 \cos \sqrt{(k^2 + l^2)}\, z + c_6 \sin \sqrt{(k^2 + l^2)}\, z$$

Hence a solution of (1) is

$$u = (c_1 e^{kx} + c_2 e^{-kx})(c_3 e^{ly} + c_4 e^{-ly})[c_5 \cos \sqrt{(k^2 + l^2)}\, z + c_6 \sin \sqrt{(k^2 + l^2)}\, z]$$

Since, the three constants could have been taken as $-k^2$, $-l^2$ and $k^2 + l^2$, and alternative solution of (1) is

$$u = (c_1 \cos kx + c_2 \sin kx)(c_3 \cos ly + c_4 \sin ly)\,[c_5 e^{\sqrt{(k^2 + l^2)}\, z} + c_6 e^{-\sqrt{(k^2 + l^2)}\, z}]$$

The choice of the constants and hence the general solution depends on the given initial and boundary conditions.

(*d*) Solution of Laplace's Equation in Cylindrical Coordinates

Laplace's equation in cylindrical coordinates is

$$\frac{\partial^2 u}{\partial r^2} + \frac{1}{r}\frac{\partial u}{\partial r} + \frac{1}{r^2}\frac{\partial^2 u}{\partial \theta^2} + \frac{\partial^2 u}{\partial z^2} = 0 \qquad ...(1)$$

Let $u(r, \theta, z) = \text{R}(r)\text{F}(\theta)\text{Z}(z)$

or simply $u = \text{RFZ}$ ...(2) be a solution of (1).

Substituting it in (1), we get $\text{R}''\text{FZ} + \dfrac{1}{r}\text{R}'\text{FZ} + \dfrac{1}{r^2}\text{RF}''\text{Z} + \text{RFZ}'' = 0$

Dividing by RFZ, we get

$$\frac{1}{R}\left(\frac{d^2R}{dr^2}+\frac{1}{r}\frac{dR}{dr}\right)+\frac{1}{r^2F}\frac{d^2F}{d\theta^2}+\frac{1}{z}\frac{d^2Z}{dz^2}=0 \quad ...(3)$$

Assuming $$\frac{d^2F}{d\theta^2}=-n^2F \text{ and } \frac{d^2Z}{dz^2}=k^2Z \quad ...(4)$$

Equation (3) reduces to $$\frac{1}{R}\left(\frac{d^2R}{dr^2}+\frac{1}{r}\frac{dR}{dz}\right)-\frac{n^2}{r^2}+k^2=0$$

or $$r^2\frac{d^2R}{dr^2}+r\frac{dR}{dz}+(k^2r^2-n^2)R=0$$

This is Bessel's equation. Its solution is $R = c_1J_n(kr) + c_2Y_n(kr)$

The solutions of equations (3) are $F = c_3 \cos n\theta + c_4 \sin n\theta$, $Z = c_5e^{kz} + c_6e^{-kz}$

Hence a solution of (1) is $u = [c_1J_n(kr) + c_2Y_n(kr)]\,(c_3 \cos n\theta + c_4 \sin n\theta)(c_5e^{kz} + c_6e^{-kz})$ which is known as a *cylindrical harmonic*.

(*e*) **Solution of Laplace's Equation in Spherical Coordinates**

Laplace's equation is spherical coordinates is

$$\frac{\partial^2u}{\partial r^2}+\frac{2}{r}\frac{\partial u}{\partial r}+\frac{1}{r^2}\frac{\partial^2u}{\partial\theta^2}+\frac{\cot\theta}{r^2}\frac{\partial u}{\partial\theta}+\frac{1}{r^2\sin^2\theta}\frac{\partial^2u}{\partial\phi^2}=0 \quad ...(1)$$

Let $u(r, \theta, \phi) = R(r)G(\theta)H(\phi)$.

or simply $u = RGH$ ...(2) be a solution of (1).

Substituting it in (1), we get

$$R''GH+\frac{2}{r}R'GH+\frac{1}{r^2}RG''H+\frac{\cot\theta}{r^2}RG'H+\frac{1}{r^2\sin^2\theta}RGH''=0$$

Dividing by RGH, we get

$$\frac{1}{R}\left(r^2\frac{d^2R}{dr^2}+2r\frac{dR}{dr}\right)+\frac{1}{G}\left(\frac{d^2G}{d\theta^2}+\cot\theta\frac{dG}{d\theta}\right)+\frac{1}{H\sin^2\theta}\frac{d^2H}{d\phi^2}=0 \quad ...(3)$$

Putting $$\frac{1}{R}\left(r^2\frac{d^2R}{dr^2}+2r\frac{dR}{dr}\right)=n(n+1) \quad ...(4)$$

and $$\frac{1}{H}\frac{d^2H}{d\phi^2}=-m^2 \quad ...(5)$$

Equation (3) reduces to $$\frac{d^2G}{d\theta^2}+\cot\theta\frac{dG}{d\theta}+[n(n+1)-m^2\operatorname{cosec}^2\theta]\,G=0$$

This is associated Legendre's equation and its solution is

$$G = c_1P_n^m(\cos\theta) + c_2\,Q_n^m(\cos\theta)$$

The solution of (5) is $H = c_3 \cos m\phi + c_4 \sin m\phi$

To solve (4), assume that $R = r^k$ so that

$$k(k-1)+2k=n(n+1) \quad \text{or} \quad (k^2-n^2)+(k-n)=0$$

or $$(k - n)(k + n + 1) = 0 \quad \therefore \quad k = n \text{ or } - n - 1$$

Thus $$\text{R} = c_5 r^n + c_6 r^{-n-1}$$

Hence, the general solution of (1) is

$$u = \sum_{n=0}^{\infty} \sum_{m=0}^{\infty} [c_1 \text{P}_n^m (\cos \theta) + c_2 \text{Q}_n^m (\cos \theta)] (c_3 \cos m\phi + c_4 \sin m\phi)(c_5 r^n + c_6 r^{-n-1})$$

Any solution of (1) is known as a *spherical harmonic.*

ILLUSTRATIVE EXAMPLES

Example 1. *The diameter of a semi-circular plate of radius a is kept at 0°C and the temperature at the semi-circular boundary is T°C. Show that the steady state temperature in the plate is given by*

$$u(r, \theta) = \frac{4T}{\pi} \sum_{n=1}^{\infty} \frac{1}{2n-1} \left(\frac{r}{a}\right)^{2n-1} \sin (2n - 1)\, \theta. \qquad \text{[G.B.T.U. (C.O.) 2011]}$$

Sol. Take the centre of the circle as the pole and the bounding diameter as the initial line. Let the steady state temperature at any point P(r, θ) be $u(r, \theta)$, so that u satisfies the equation

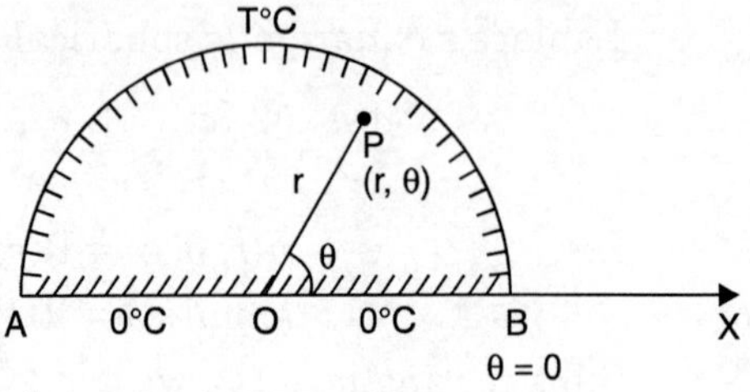

$$r^2 \frac{\partial^2 u}{\partial r^2} + r \frac{\partial u}{\partial r} + \frac{\partial^2 u}{\partial \theta^2} = 0 \qquad ...(1)$$

Let $$u = \text{RT} \qquad ...(2)$$

where R is a function of r only and T is a function of θ only.

$$\frac{\partial u}{\partial r} = \frac{\partial}{\partial r}(\text{RT}) = \text{T}\frac{d\text{R}}{dr}$$

$$\frac{\partial^2 u}{\partial r^2} = \frac{\partial}{\partial r}\left(\text{T}\frac{d\text{R}}{dr}\right) = \text{T}\frac{d^2\text{R}}{dr^2}$$

$$\frac{\partial^2 u}{\partial \theta^2} = \frac{\partial^2}{\partial \theta^2}(\text{RT}) = \text{R}\frac{d^2\text{T}}{d\theta^2}.$$

$\therefore$ From (1), $$r^2\text{TR}'' + r\text{TR}' + \text{RT}'' = 0$$

$$\frac{r^2\text{R}'' + r\text{R}'}{\text{R}} + \frac{\text{T}''}{\text{T}} = 0 \Rightarrow \frac{r^2\text{R}'' + r\text{R}'}{\text{R}} = -\frac{\text{T}''}{\text{T}}$$

Case I. When $$\frac{r^2\text{R}'' + r\text{R}'}{\text{R}} = -\frac{\text{T}''}{\text{T}} = p^2 \text{ (say)}$$

(*i*) $$\frac{r^2\text{R}'' + r\text{R}'}{\text{R}} = p^2 \Rightarrow r^2\text{R}'' + r\text{R}' - p^2\text{R} = 0.$$

Put $r = e^z$ so that $z = \log r$ and let $\text{D} \equiv \frac{d}{dz}$ then above equation reduces to

$$\{D(D-1) + D - p^2\} R = 0$$

$$(D^2 - p^2)R = 0$$

Auxiliary equation is $m^2 - p^2 = 0 \Rightarrow m = \pm p$

$$\text{C.F.} = c_1 e^{pz} + c_2 e^{-pz} = c_1 e^{p \log r} + c_2 e^{-p \log r} = c_1 r^p + c_2 r^{-p}$$

$$\text{P.I.} = 0.$$

$\therefore$ $$R = c_1 r^p + c_2 r^{-p}$$

(*ii*) $$-\frac{T''}{T} = p^2$$

$$\frac{d^2T}{d\theta^2} + p^2 T = 0.$$

Auxiliary equation is $m^2 + p^2 = 0$

$\Rightarrow$ $$m = \pm pi$$

$\therefore$ $$\text{C.F.} = c_3 \cos p\theta + c_4 \sin p\theta$$

$$\text{P.I.} = 0$$

$\therefore$ $$T = c_3 \cos p\theta + c_4 \sin p\theta$$

$\therefore$ $$u(r, \theta) = (c_1 r^p + c_2 r^{-p})(c_3 \cos p\theta + c_4 \sin p\theta) \qquad \text{...(3)}$$

Case II. When $\dfrac{r^2R'' + rR'}{R} = -\dfrac{T''}{T} = -p^2$ (say)

(*i*) $$\frac{r^2R'' + rR'}{R} = -p^2$$

$\Rightarrow$ $$r^2R'' + rR' + p^2R = 0$$

Put $r = e^z$ so that $z = \log r$ and let $D \equiv \dfrac{d}{dz}$ then above equation reduces to

$$[D(D-1) + D + p^2] R = 0$$

$$(D^2 + p^2)R = 0.$$

Auxiliary equation is $m^2 + p^2 = 0$

$$m = \pm pi$$

$$\text{C.F.} = (c_5 \cos pz + c_6 \sin pz)$$

$$\text{P.I.} = 0$$

$\therefore$ $$R = c_5 \cos pz + c_6 \sin pz$$

$$= c_5 \cos (p \log r) + c_6 \sin (p \log r).$$

(*ii*) $$-\frac{T''}{T} = -p^2$$

$\Rightarrow$ $$\frac{T''}{T} = p^2 \quad \text{or} \quad \frac{d^2T}{d\theta^2} - p^2T = 0.$$

Auxiliary equation is $m^2 - p^2 = 0$

$$m = \pm p$$

$\therefore$ $$\text{C.F.} = c_7 e^{p\theta} + c_8 e^{-p\theta}$$

$$\text{P.I.} = 0.$$

$\therefore$ $$T = c_7 e^{p\theta} + c_8 e^{-p\theta}.$$

Hence, $u(r, \theta) = [c_5 \cos (p \log r) + c_6 \sin (p \log r)](c_7 e^{p\theta} + c_8 e^{-p\theta})$ ...(4)

Case III. When $\dfrac{r^2 R'' + rR'}{R} = -\dfrac{T''}{T} = 0$ (say)

(*i*) $r^2 R'' + rR' = 0.$

Put $r = e^z$ so that $z = \log r$ and let $D \equiv \dfrac{d}{dz}$, then above equation reduces to

$$[D(D-1) + D]R = 0$$

$$D^2 R = 0.$$

Auxiliary equation is $m^2 = 0$

$\Rightarrow$ $m = 0, 0.$

$\therefore$ $\text{C.F.} = (c_9 + c_{10} z)\, e^{0z} = c_9 + c_{10} \log r$

$\text{P.I.} = 0$

$\therefore$ $R = c_9 + c_{10} \log r.$

(*ii*) $-\dfrac{T''}{T} = 0$

$\Rightarrow$ $T'' = 0$

$\Rightarrow$ $T = c_{11} + c_{12}\theta.$

$\therefore$ $u(r, \theta) = (c_9 + c_{10} \log r)\, (c_{11} + c_{12}\theta)$ ...(5)

Of these three solutions (3), (4) and (5), we choose the solution consistent with the given boundary conditions.

Boundary conditions are

$u(r, 0) = 0$ ...(6)

$u(r, \pi) = 0$ ...(7)

$u(a, \theta) = T$ ...(8)

and $u \to 0$ as $r \to 0$ ...(9)

Solutions (4) and (5) do not satisfy boundary condition (9).

Hence, the consistent solution is

$u(r, \theta) = (c_1 r^p + c_2 r^{-p})\, (c_3 \cos p\theta + c_4 \sin p\theta)$ ...(10)

From (10), $u(r, 0) = 0 = (c_1 r^p + c_2 r^{-p})\, c_3$

$\Rightarrow$ $c_3 = 0.$

From (10),

$u(r, \theta) = (c_1 r^p + c_2 r^{-p})\, c_4 \sin p\theta$ ...(11)

$u(r, \pi) = 0 = (c_1 r^p + c_2 r^{-p})\, c_4 \sin p\pi$

$\Rightarrow$ $\sin p\pi = 0 = \sin n\pi \ (n \in I)$

$\therefore$ $p = n.$

$\therefore$ From (11), $u(r, \theta) = (c_1 r^n + c_1 r^{-n})\, c_4 \sin n\theta$ ...(12)

Condition $u \to 0$ as $r \to 0$ is satisfied only and only when $c_2 = 0$.

Hence from (12), $u(r, \theta) = c_1 c_4 r^n \sin n\theta = b_n r^n \sin n\theta.$

The most general solution is

$$u(r, \theta) = \sum_{n=1}^{\infty} b_n r^n \sin n\theta \qquad \text{...(13)}$$

$$u(a, \theta) = T = \sum_{n=1}^{\infty} b_n a^n \sin n\theta$$

where
$$b_n a^n = \frac{2}{\pi}\int_0^{\pi} \{T \sin n\theta \, d\theta\}$$

$$= \frac{2T}{\pi}\left(\frac{-\cos n\theta}{n}\right)_0^{\pi} = \frac{2T}{n\pi}(1 - \cos n\pi)$$

$$= \frac{2T}{n\pi}\{1 - (-1)^n\} = \begin{cases} \dfrac{4T}{n\pi}; & n \text{ is odd} \\ 0 \ ; & n \text{ is even} \end{cases}$$

∴
$$b_n = \begin{cases} \dfrac{4T}{n\pi a^n}; & n \text{ is odd} \\ 0 \ ; & n \text{ is even} \end{cases}$$

From (13),
$$u(r, \theta) = \frac{4T}{\pi} \sum_{n=1,3,5,...}^{\infty} \frac{1}{n} \cdot \frac{r^n}{a^n} \sin n\theta$$

$$u(r, \theta) = \frac{4T}{\pi} \sum_{n=1}^{\infty} \frac{1}{(2n-1)}\left(\frac{r}{a}\right)^{2n-1} \sin (2n-1)\theta$$

which is the required steady state temperature in the plate.

Example 2. *Solve :* $\dfrac{\partial^2 V}{\partial r^2} + \dfrac{1}{r}\dfrac{\partial V}{\partial r} + \dfrac{1}{r^2}\dfrac{\partial^2 V}{\partial \theta^2} = 0$ *with boundary conditions*

(i) V is finite when $r \to 0$ *(ii)* $V = \Sigma C_n \cos n\theta$ *on* $r = a$. (G.B.T.U. 2010)

Sol. Solution to given differential equation is

$$V = \Sigma (A_n r^n + B_n r^{-n}) \cos (n\theta + \alpha)$$

When $r = a$,
$$V = \Sigma C_n \cos n\theta$$

∴
$$\Sigma C_n \cos n\theta = \Sigma(A_n a^n + B_n a^{-n}) \cos (n\theta + \alpha)$$

∴
$$C_n = A_n a^n + B_n a^{-n}, \ \alpha = 0$$

When $r \to 0$, V is finite.

∴
$$B_n = 0 \qquad \text{(otherwise V becomes } \infty)$$

∴
$$A_n = \frac{C_n}{a^n}$$

∴
$$V = \Sigma C_n \left(\frac{r}{a}\right)^n \cos n\theta.$$

Example 3. *The edge r = a of a circular plate is kept at temperature f(θ). The plate is insulated so that there is no loss of heat from either surface. Find the temperature distribution in steady state.*

Sol. Here, we have to take the solution in polar coordinates.

The solution is

$$u = (c_1 \cos p\theta + c_2 \sin p\theta)(c_3 r^p + c_4 r^{-p}) \quad ...(1)$$

Since, the temperature remains finite at $r = 0$

$$\therefore \quad c_4 = 0 \quad ...(2)$$

Also, if we increase θ by 2π, we arrive at the same point. So the solution (1) should be periodic with period 2π.

Therefore $p = n$, an integer. Hence, we may write the general solution as

$$u = \sum_{n=0}^{\infty} (c_1 \cos n\theta + c_2 \sin n\theta) c_3 r^n$$

$$= \sum_{n=0}^{\infty} (A_n \cos n\theta + B_n \sin n\theta) r^n \quad | \; c_1c_3 = A_n \; c_2c_3 = B_n \text{ (say)}$$

Applying to this, the condition

$$u = f(\theta) \quad \text{for} \quad r = a, \text{ we get}$$

$$f(\theta) = \sum_{n=0}^{\infty} (A_n \cos n\theta + B_n \sin n\theta) a^n$$

where $$a^n A_n = \frac{1}{\pi} \int_0^{2\pi} f(\theta) \cos n\theta \, d\theta$$

and $$a^n B_n = \frac{1}{\pi} \int_0^{2\pi} f(\theta) \sin n\theta \, d\theta$$

Example 4. *Find a harmonic function ϕ in the semi-circle $r < a$, $0 < \theta < \pi$ which vanishes on $\theta = 0$ and takes the value c on $\theta = \pi$ and on the curved portion $r = a$.*

Sol. A harmonic function is a function satisfying Laplace's equation.

Solution to $r^2 \dfrac{\partial^2 \phi}{\partial r^2} + r \dfrac{\partial \phi}{\partial r} + \dfrac{\partial^2 \phi}{\partial \theta^2} = 0$ is

$$\phi = (A \cos p\theta + B \sin p\theta)(Cr^p + Dr^{-p}) \quad ...(1)$$

Since $\phi \to 0$ as $r \to 0 \quad \therefore \quad D = 0$

$$\therefore \quad \phi = (A \cos p\theta + B \sin p\theta) Cr^p \quad ...(2)$$

Imposing on (2), the zero boundary conditions

$$\phi(r, 0) = 0 \quad \text{and} \quad \phi(r, \pi) = 0, \text{ we get}$$

$$A = 0 \quad \text{and} \quad p = n \; (n \in I)$$

Putting in (2) and adding up various solutions for $n = 1, 2, 3, ...$, we get

$$\phi = \sum_{n=1}^{\infty} B_n r^n \sin n\theta \quad ...(3)$$

This solution will not satisfy both the given boundary conditions of the problem namely

$$\left.\begin{aligned} &(i)\ \phi = 0 \text{ when } \theta = 0 \\ \text{and} \quad &(ii)\ \phi = c \text{ when } \theta = \pi \end{aligned}\right\} \quad ...(4)$$

So we add to (3), the solution $\phi = A_0\theta + B_0$ which satisfies Laplace's equation. We choose A_0, B_0 so that (4) is satisfied.

Then, $\quad B_0 = 0 \quad \text{and} \quad c = A_0\pi$

Hence, $$\phi = \frac{c\theta}{\pi} + \sum_{n=1}^{\infty} B_n r^n \sin n\theta \qquad ...(5) \text{ satisfies (4)}$$

Applying to (5), the condition that $\phi = c$ when $r = a$, we get

$$c = \frac{c\theta}{\pi} + \sum_{n=1}^{\infty} B_n a^n \sin n\theta$$

$$\Rightarrow \quad c\left(1 - \frac{\theta}{\pi}\right) = \sum_{n=1}^{\infty} B_n a^n \sin n\theta$$

$$\therefore \quad B_n a^n = \frac{2}{\pi}\int_0^{\pi} c\left(1 - \frac{\theta}{\pi}\right) \sin n\theta \, d\theta$$

$$B_n a^n = \frac{2c}{n\pi} \quad \Rightarrow \quad B_n = \frac{2c}{n\pi a^n} \qquad ...(6)$$

$\therefore$ From (5) and (6),

$$\phi = \frac{c\theta}{\pi} + \frac{2c}{\pi}\sum_{n=1}^{\infty} \frac{1}{n}\left(\frac{r}{a}\right)^n \sin n\theta$$

TEST YOUR KNOWLEDGE

1. Show that the steady state temperature distribution in a semi-circular plate of radius a whose bounding diameter is kept at 0°C, while the circumference is kept at 60°C is given by

$$u(r, \theta) = \frac{240}{\pi}\sum_{n=1}^{\infty} \frac{1}{(2n-1)}\left(\frac{r}{a}\right)^{2n-1} . \sin(2n-1)\theta.$$

2. A semi-circular plate of radius a has its circumference kept at temperature $u(a, \theta) = k\theta(\pi - \theta)$ while the bounding diameter is kept at zero temperature. Assuming the surfaces of the plate to be insulated, show that the steady-state temperature distribution of the plate is given by

$$u(r, \theta) = \frac{8k}{\pi}\sum_{n=1}^{\infty} \left(\frac{r}{a}\right)^{2n-1} . \frac{\sin(2n-1)\theta}{(2n-1)^3}.$$

3. The bounding diameter of a semi-circular plate of radius a is kept at 0°C and the temperature along the semi-circular boundary is given by

$$u(a, \theta) = \begin{cases} 50\theta, & \text{when } 0 < \theta < \dfrac{\pi}{2} \\ 50(\pi - \theta), & \text{when } \dfrac{\pi}{2} < \theta < \pi \end{cases}.$$

Show that the steady-state temperature distribution given by

$$u(r, \theta) = \frac{200}{\pi}\sum_{n=1}^{\infty} \frac{(-1)^{n+1}}{(2n-1)^2}\left(\frac{r}{a}\right)^{2n-1} . \sin(2n-1)\theta.$$

5.14. TRANSMISSION LINE EQUATIONS

[U.P.T.U. (C.O.) 2009]

Consider the flow of electricity in an insulated cable. Let V be the potential and I the current at time t at a point P of the cable at a distance x from a given point O. Let $V + \delta V$ and $I + \delta I$ be the potential and the current at the point $Q(x + \delta x)$ at the same time.

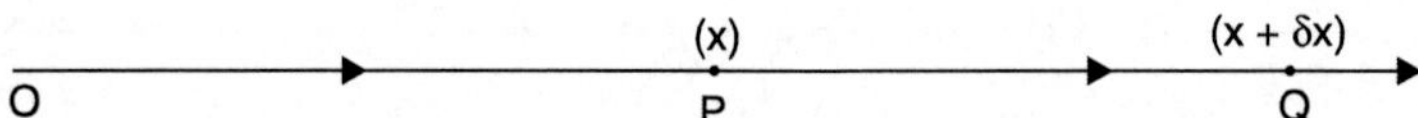

Let R, L, C, G be respectively the resistance, inductance, capacitance and leakance to the ground per unit length of the cable, each assumed to be constant.

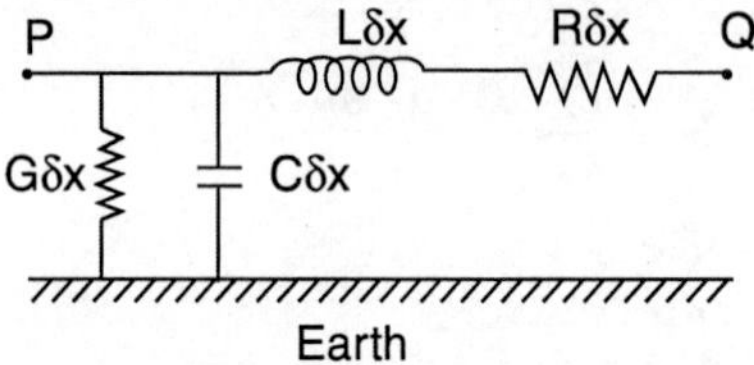

Since, the potential drop across the segment PQ = potential drop due to resistance + potential drop due to inductance

$$\therefore \qquad -\delta V = (R\delta x)I + (L\delta x)\frac{\partial I}{\partial t}$$

Dividing by δx and proceeding to the limits as $\delta x \to 0$, we have

$$-\frac{\partial V}{\partial x} = RI + L\frac{\partial I}{\partial t} \qquad ...(1)$$

Similarly, the decrease in current in crossing the segment PQ = decrease in current due to capacitance and leakance

$$\therefore \qquad -\delta I = (G\delta x)V + (C\delta x)\frac{\partial V}{\partial t}$$

Dividing by δx and proceeding to the limits as $\delta x \to 0$, we have

$$-\frac{\partial I}{\partial x} = GV + C\frac{\partial V}{\partial t} \qquad ...(2)$$

Differentiating (1) and (2) partially w.r.t. x and t respectively, we have

$$-\frac{\partial^2 V}{\partial x^2} = R\frac{\partial I}{\partial x} + L\frac{\partial^2 I}{\partial x \partial t} \qquad ...(3)$$

and
$$-\frac{\partial^2 I}{\partial x \partial t} = G\frac{\partial V}{\partial t} + C\frac{\partial^2 V}{\partial t^2} \qquad ...(4)$$

Eliminating I from (2), (3) and (4), we get

$$-\frac{\partial^2 V}{\partial x^2} = R\left(-GV - C\frac{\partial V}{\partial t}\right) + L\left(-G\frac{\partial V}{\partial t} - C\frac{\partial^2 V}{\partial t^2}\right)$$

or
$$\boxed{\frac{\partial^2 V}{\partial x^2} = LC\frac{\partial^2 V}{\partial t^2} + (RC + LG)\frac{\partial V}{\partial t} + RGV} \qquad ...(5)$$

Now, differentiating (1) and (2) w.r.t. t and x respectively, we have

$$-\frac{\partial^2 V}{\partial x \partial t} = R\frac{\partial I}{\partial t} + L\frac{\partial^2 I}{\partial t^2} \quad ...(6)$$

and
$$-\frac{\partial^2 I}{\partial x^2} = G\frac{\partial V}{\partial x} + C\frac{\partial^2 V}{\partial x \partial t} \quad ...(7)$$

Eliminating V from (1), (6), and (7), we get

$$-\frac{\partial^2 I}{\partial x^2} = G\left(-RI - L\frac{\partial I}{\partial t}\right) + C\left(-R\frac{\partial I}{\partial t} - L\frac{\partial^2 I}{\partial t^2}\right)$$

or
$$\boxed{\frac{\partial^2 I}{\partial x^2} = LC\frac{\partial^2 I}{\partial t^2} + (LG + RC)\frac{\partial I}{\partial t} + RGI} \quad ...(8)$$

The equations (5) and (8) are called the **telephone equations.**

5.14.1. If L = G = 0, the equations (5) and (8) become

$$\boxed{\frac{\partial^2 \mathbf{V}}{\partial x^2} = \mathbf{RC}\frac{\partial \mathbf{V}}{\partial t}} \quad \text{and} \quad \boxed{\frac{\partial^2 \mathbf{I}}{\partial x^2} = \mathbf{RC}\frac{\partial \mathbf{I}}{\partial t}}$$

which are known as the *telegraph equations.* They are similar to the equations in one dimensional heat flow. [*U.P.T.U. (C.O.) 2009*]

5.14.2. If R = G = 0, the equations (5) and (8) become

$$\boxed{\frac{\partial^2 \mathbf{V}}{\partial x^2} = \mathbf{LC}\frac{\partial^2 \mathbf{V}}{\partial t^2}} \quad \text{and} \quad \boxed{\frac{\partial^2 \mathbf{I}}{\partial x^2} = \mathbf{LC}\frac{\partial^2 \mathbf{I}}{\partial t^2}}$$

which are known as the *radio equations.* They are similar to the wave equation.

[*U.P.T.U. (C.O.) 2009*]

5.14.3. If R and G are negligible, the transmission lines become

$$\frac{\partial v}{\partial x} = -\mathbf{L}\frac{\partial i}{\partial t} \quad \text{and} \quad \frac{\partial i}{\partial x} = -\mathbf{C}\frac{\partial v}{\partial t}$$

5.14.4. If L = C = 0, the equations (5) and (8) become

$$\frac{\partial^2 \mathbf{V}}{\partial x^2} = \mathbf{RGV} \quad \text{and} \quad \frac{\partial^2 \mathbf{I}}{\partial x^2} = \mathbf{RGI}$$

which are *equations for submarine cable.*

Note. We have sofar considered the transient state solutions only. The **steady-state solutions** of transmission lines are however obtained by assuming $v = V e^{iwt}$ and $i = I e^{iwt}$, where V and I are complex functions of x only. Substituting these in (5) and (6), we get two ordinary linear diff. eqns. of II order which can be solved at once.

ILLUSTRATIVE EXAMPLES

Example 1. *Find the current i and voltage e in a line of length l, t seconds after the ends are suddenly grounded, given that*

$$i(x, 0) = i_0,\ e(x, 0) = e_0 \sin \frac{\pi x}{l}$$

Also R and G are negligible. (U.P.T.U. 2008)

Sol. Since R and G are negligible, transmission line equations become

$$\frac{\partial e}{\partial x} = -\mathrm{L}\frac{\partial i}{\partial t} \quad \text{...(1)}$$

and
$$\frac{\partial i}{\partial x} = -\mathrm{C}\frac{\partial e}{\partial t} \quad \text{...(2)}$$

For elimination of i, differentiating (1) partially w.r.t. x and (2) partially w.r.t. t, we have

$$\frac{\partial^2 e}{\partial x^2} = -\mathrm{L}\frac{\partial^2 i}{\partial x \partial t} \quad \text{and} \quad \frac{\partial^2 i}{\partial t \partial x} = -\mathrm{C}\frac{\partial^2 e}{\partial t^2}$$

whence
$$\frac{\partial^2 e}{\partial x^2} = \mathrm{LC}\frac{\partial^2 e}{\partial t^2} \quad \text{...(3)}$$

The initial conditions are $i(x, 0) = i_0,\ e(x, 0) = e_0 \sin \frac{\pi x}{l}$ ...(4)

Since, the ends are suddenly grounded, the boundary conditions are

$$e(0, t) = e(l, t) = 0 \quad \text{...(5)}$$

Also $i = i_0$ (constant) when $t = 0$

$$\therefore \quad \frac{\partial i}{\partial x} = 0 \text{ which gives } \frac{\partial e}{\partial t} = 0 \text{ when } t = 0 \quad \text{...(6)} \quad | \text{ Using (2)}$$

Now let $e = \mathrm{XT}$ be a solution of (3) where X is a function of x only and T is a function of t only.

$$\frac{\partial^2 e}{\partial x^2} = \mathrm{X''T} \text{ and } \frac{\partial^2 e}{\partial t^2} = \mathrm{XT''}$$

$\therefore$ From (3), $\mathrm{X''T} = \mathrm{LCXT''}$

Separating the variables $\frac{\mathrm{X''}}{\mathrm{X}} = \mathrm{LC}\frac{\mathrm{T''}}{\mathrm{T}} = -p^2$ (say)

This leads to the ordinary differential equations

$$\frac{d^2\mathrm{X}}{dx^2} + p^2\mathrm{X} = 0 \quad \text{and} \quad \frac{d^2\mathrm{T}}{dt^2} + \frac{p^2}{\mathrm{LC}}\mathrm{T} = 0$$

$$\therefore \quad \mathrm{X} = c_1 \cos px + c_2 \sin px$$

$$\mathrm{T} = c_3 \cos \frac{pt}{\sqrt{\mathrm{LC}}} + c_4 \sin \frac{pt}{\sqrt{\mathrm{LC}}}$$

$$\Rightarrow \quad e = \mathrm{XT} = (c_1 \cos px + c_2 \sin px)\left(c_3 \cos \frac{pt}{\sqrt{\mathrm{LC}}} + c_4 \sin \frac{pt}{\sqrt{\mathrm{LC}}}\right) \quad \text{...(7)}$$

Applying the boundary conditions (5), we have

$$c_1 = 0 \quad \text{and} \quad p = \frac{n\pi}{l}, \; n \text{ being an integer}$$

$\therefore$ Equation (7) becomes

$$e = c_2 \sin \frac{n\pi x}{l} \left(c_3 \cos \frac{n\pi t}{l\sqrt{LC}} + c_4 \sin \frac{n\pi t}{l\sqrt{LC}} \right)$$

or
$$e = \sin \frac{n\pi x}{l} \left(A \cos \frac{n\pi t}{l\sqrt{LC}} + B \sin \frac{n\pi t}{l\sqrt{LC}} \right) \quad ...(8) \mid \text{where } A = c_2 c_3 \text{ and } B = c_2 c_4$$

$$\frac{\partial e}{\partial t} = \sin \frac{n\pi x}{l} \left(-\frac{An\pi}{l\sqrt{LC}} \sin \frac{n\pi t}{l\sqrt{LC}} + \frac{Bn\pi}{l\sqrt{LC}} \cos \frac{n\pi t}{l\sqrt{LC}} \right)$$

Since $\frac{\partial e}{\partial t} = 0$ when $t = 0$, we get [From (6)]

$$B = 0$$

$\therefore$ From (8), $\quad e = A \sin \frac{n\pi x}{l} \cos \frac{n\pi t}{l\sqrt{LC}}$

By superposition, $e = \sum_{n=1}^{\infty} A_n \sin \frac{n\pi x}{l} \cos \frac{n\pi t}{l\sqrt{LC}}$ is also a solution.

But $\quad e = e_0 \sin \frac{\pi x}{l}$ when $t = 0$ [From (4)]

$$\therefore \quad e_0 \sin \frac{\pi x}{l} = \sum_{n=1}^{\infty} A_n \sin \frac{n\pi x}{l}$$

$$\Rightarrow \quad A_1 = e_0 \quad \text{and} \quad A_2 = A_3 = \ldots\ldots = 0$$

Hence, $\quad e = e_0 \sin \frac{\pi x}{l} \cos \frac{\pi t}{l\sqrt{LC}}$

Now, $\quad -L \frac{\partial i}{\partial t} = \frac{\partial e}{\partial x}$ [From (1)]

$$\therefore \quad \frac{\partial i}{\partial t} = -\frac{1}{L} \cdot \frac{e_0 \pi}{l} \cos \frac{\pi x}{l} \cos \frac{\pi t}{l\sqrt{LC}}$$

Integrating w.r.t. t, regarding x as constant

$$i = -\frac{e_0 \pi}{Ll} \cos \frac{\pi x}{l} \cdot \frac{l\sqrt{LC}}{\pi} \sin \frac{\pi t}{l\sqrt{LC}} + f(x) \quad ...(9)$$

where $f(x)$ is an arbitrary constant function.

Since $i = i_0$ when $t = 0$, we have $i_0 = 0 + f(x)$ or $f(x) = i_0$

$\therefore$ From (9), we have $\quad i = i_0 - e_0 \sqrt{\frac{C}{L}} \cos \frac{\pi x}{l} \sin \frac{\pi t}{l\sqrt{LC}}.$

Example 2. *A transmission line 1000 km long is initially under steady-state conditions with potential 1300 volts at the sending end (x = 0) and 1200 volts at the receiving end (x = 1000). The terminal end of the line is suddenly grounded, but the potential at the source is kept at 1300 volts. Assuming the inductance and leakance to be negligible, find the potential E(x, t).*

Sol. Since L and G are negligible, we use the telegraph equation

$$\frac{\partial^2 E}{\partial x^2} = RC\frac{\partial E}{\partial t} \quad \text{or} \quad \frac{\partial E}{\partial t} = \frac{1}{RC}\cdot\frac{\partial^2 E}{\partial x^2} \qquad ...(1)$$

Here, E_s = initial steady voltage satisfying $\frac{\partial^2 E}{\partial x^2} = 0$

$$= 1300 - \frac{1300 - 1200}{1000}x = 1300 - 0.1x = E(x, 0) \qquad ...(2)$$

E_s' = steady voltage (after grounding the terminal end) when steady conditions are ultimately reached

$$= 1300 - \frac{1300 - 0}{1000}\,x = 1300 - 1.3x$$

$\therefore$ $E(x, t) = E_s' + E_r(x, t)$, where $E_r(x, t)$ is the transient part

$$= 1300 - 1.3x + \sum_{n=1}^{\infty} b_n \sin\frac{n\pi x}{l}\, e^{-\frac{n^2\pi^2 t}{l^2 RC}} \quad ...(3) \text{ where } l = 1000 \text{ km}$$

Putting $t = 0$ in (3), we have

$$E(x, 0) = 1300 - 1.3x + \sum_{n=1}^{\infty} b_n \sin\frac{n\pi x}{l}$$

or

$$1300 - 0.1x = 1300 - 1.3x + \sum_{n=1}^{\infty} b_n \sin\frac{n\pi x}{l} \qquad \text{[Using (2)]}$$

or

$$1.2x = \sum_{n=1}^{\infty} b_n \sin\frac{n\pi x}{l}$$

where

$$b_n = \frac{2}{l}\int_0^l 1.2x \sin\frac{n\pi x}{l}\,dx$$

$$= \frac{2.4}{l}\left[x\left(-\frac{\cos\frac{n\pi x}{l}}{\frac{n\pi}{l}}\right) - (1)\left(-\frac{\sin\frac{n\pi x}{l}}{\left(\frac{n\pi}{l}\right)^2}\right)\right]_0^l = \frac{2.4}{l}\cdot\frac{l}{n\pi}\,[-\,l\cos n\pi]$$

$$= -\,\frac{2.4\times 1000}{n\pi}\times(-1)^n \qquad [\because\ l = 1000]$$

$$= \frac{2400}{\pi}\cdot\frac{(-1)^{n+1}}{n}$$

Hence, $$E(x, t) = 1300 - 1.3x + \frac{2400}{\pi}\sum_{n=1}^{\infty}\frac{(-1)^{n+1}}{n}\sin\frac{n\pi x}{l}\, e^{-\frac{n^2\pi^2 t}{l^2 RC}}.$$

Example 3. *Neglecting R and G, find the e.m.f. v(x, t) in a line of length l, t seconds after the ends were suddenly grounded, given that* $i(x, 0) = i_0$ *and* $v(x, 0) = e_1 \sin\frac{\pi x}{l} + e_5 \sin\frac{5\pi x}{l}$.

(M.T.U 2012)

Sol. Since R and G are negligible, we use the radio equation

$$\frac{\partial^2 v}{\partial x^2} = \text{LC}\frac{\partial^2 v}{\partial t^2} \quad \text{...(1)}$$

Since, the ends are suddenly grounded, we have the boundary conditions

$$v(0, t) = 0,\ v(l, t) = 0 \quad \text{...(2)}$$

Also, the initial conditions are

$$\left.\begin{aligned} i(x, 0) &= i_0 \\ \text{and} \quad v(x, 0) &= e_1 \sin\frac{\pi x}{l} + e_5 \sin\frac{5\pi x}{l} \end{aligned}\right\} \quad \text{...(3)}$$

$$\therefore \quad \frac{\partial i}{\partial x} = -\text{C}\frac{\partial v}{\partial t} \text{ gives}$$

$$\left(\frac{\partial v}{\partial t}\right)_{t=0} = 0 \quad \text{...(4)}$$

Let $v = \text{XT}$ be the solution of (1) where X is a function of x only and T is a function of t only.

$\therefore$ From (1), $\quad \text{TX}'' = \text{LCXT}''$

$$\Rightarrow \quad \frac{\text{X}''}{\text{X}} = \text{LC}\frac{\text{T}''}{\text{T}} = -p^2 \quad \text{(say)}$$

$$\therefore \quad \text{X}'' + p^2\text{X} = 0 \quad \Rightarrow \quad \text{X} = c_1 \cos px + c_2 \sin px$$

and

$$\text{T}'' + \left(\frac{p^2}{\text{LC}}\right)\text{T} = 0$$

$$\Rightarrow \quad \text{T} = c_3 \cos\frac{p}{\sqrt{\text{LC}}}t + c_4 \sin\frac{p}{\sqrt{\text{LC}}}t$$

$$\therefore \quad v = \text{XT} = (c_1 \cos px + c_2 \sin px)\left(c_3 \cos\frac{pt}{\sqrt{\text{LC}}} + c_4 \sin\frac{pt}{\sqrt{\text{LC}}}\right) \quad \text{...(5)}$$

Using the boundary conditions (2), we get

$$c_1 = 0 \text{ and } p = \frac{n\pi}{l},\ n \in \text{I}$$

$$\therefore \quad v = \sin\frac{n\pi x}{l}\left(a_n \cos\frac{n\pi t}{l\sqrt{\text{LC}}} + b_n \sin\frac{n\pi t}{l\sqrt{\text{LC}}}\right) \quad \text{...(6)}$$

Using initial condition (4), we get $b_n = 0$

$\therefore$ From (6), $\quad v = a_n \sin\dfrac{n\pi x}{l}\cos\dfrac{n\pi t}{l\sqrt{\text{LC}}}$

Thus the most general solution of (1) is

$$v = \sum_{n=1}^{\infty} a_n \sin\frac{n\pi x}{l}\cos\frac{n\pi t}{l\sqrt{\text{LC}}} \quad \text{...(7)}$$

Finally by the initial condition (3), we have

$$e_1 \sin \frac{\pi x}{l} + e_5 \sin \frac{5\pi x}{l} = \sum_{n=1}^{\infty} a_n \sin \frac{n\pi x}{l}$$

$\therefore$ $a_1 = e_1$ and $a_5 = e_5$ while all other a's are zero.

Hence, $$v = e_1 \sin \frac{\pi x}{l} \cos \frac{\pi t}{l\sqrt{\text{LC}}} + e_5 \sin \frac{5\pi x}{l} \cos \frac{5\pi t}{l\sqrt{\text{LC}}}$$

Example 4. *Solve* $\frac{\partial^2 V}{\partial x^2} = LC \frac{\partial^2 V}{\partial t^2}$ *assuming that the initial voltage is* $V_0 \sin \frac{\pi x}{l}$; $V_t(x_0) = 0$ *and* $V = 0$ *at the ends* $x = 0$ *and* $x = l$ *for all* t. [U.P.T.U. (SUM) 2007]

Sol. Let $$\text{V} = \text{XT} \quad \text{...(1)}$$

where X is a function of x only and T is a function of t only.

$$\frac{\partial^2 \text{V}}{\partial x^2} = \text{TX}'' \quad \text{and} \quad \frac{\partial^2 \text{V}}{\partial t^2} = \text{XT}''$$

Substituting in the given equations, we get

$$\text{TX}'' = \text{LCXT}''$$

$$\frac{\text{X}''}{\text{X}} = \text{LC}\frac{\text{T}''}{\text{T}} = -p^2 \text{ (say)}$$

(*i*) $$\frac{\text{X}''}{\text{X}} = -p^2 \Rightarrow \text{X}'' + p^2\text{X} = 0$$

$\therefore$ $$\text{X} = c_1 \cos px + c_2 \sin px$$

(*ii*) $$\text{LC}\frac{\text{T}''}{\text{T}} = -p^2 \Rightarrow \text{T}'' + \frac{p^2}{\text{LC}}\text{T} = 0$$

$\therefore$ $$\text{T} = c_3 \cos \frac{pt}{\sqrt{\text{LC}}} + c_4 \sin \frac{pt}{\sqrt{\text{LC}}}$$

Hence, $$\text{V} = \text{XT} = (c_1 \cos px + c_2 \sin px)\left(c_3 \cos \frac{pt}{\sqrt{\text{LC}}} + c_4 \sin \frac{pt}{\sqrt{\text{LC}}}\right) \quad \text{...(2)}$$

Boundary conditions are

$$\text{V}(0, t) = 0 = \text{V}(l, t) \quad \text{and} \quad \frac{\partial \text{V}}{\partial t} = 0 \quad \text{when } t = 0$$

Applying conditions on (2), we get

$$0 = c_1\left(c_3 \cos \frac{pt}{\sqrt{\text{LC}}} + c_4 \sin \frac{pt}{\sqrt{\text{LC}}}\right)$$

$\Rightarrow$ $$c_1 = 0$$

From (2), $$\text{V} = c_2 \sin px \left(c_3 \cos \frac{pt}{\sqrt{\text{LC}}} + c_4 \sin \frac{pt}{\sqrt{\text{LC}}}\right) \quad \text{...(3)}$$

$$V(l, t) = 0 = c_2 \sin pl \left(c_3 \cos \frac{pt}{\sqrt{LC}} + c_4 \sin \frac{pt}{\sqrt{LC}} \right)$$

$\Rightarrow$ $\sin pl = 0 = \sin n\pi \ (n \in I)$

$\therefore$ $p = \frac{n\pi}{l}$

Hence, from (3),

$$V = c_2 \sin \frac{n\pi x}{l} \left[c_3 \cos \frac{n\pi t}{l\sqrt{LC}} + c_4 \sin \frac{n\pi t}{l\sqrt{LC}} \right] \quad ...(4)$$

$$\frac{\partial V}{\partial t} = c_2 \frac{n\pi}{l\sqrt{LC}} \sin \frac{n\pi x}{l} \left[-c_3 \sin \frac{n\pi t}{l\sqrt{LC}} + c_4 \cos \frac{n\pi t}{l\sqrt{LC}} \right]$$

At $t = 0$,

$$0 = c_2 \frac{n\pi}{l\sqrt{LC}} \sin \frac{n\pi x}{l} \cdot c_4$$

$\Rightarrow$ $c_4 = 0$

Hence from (4),

$$V = c_2 c_3 \sin \frac{n\pi x}{l} \cos \frac{n\pi t}{l\sqrt{LC}} \quad ...(5)$$

Now, $V(x, 0) = V_0 \sin \frac{\pi x}{l} = c_2 c_3 \sin \frac{n\pi x}{l}$

Comparing, we get

$$c_2 c_3 = V_0 \quad \text{and} \quad n = 1$$

Hence, the required solution is

$$V(x, t) = V_0 \sin \frac{\pi x}{l} \cos \frac{\pi t}{l\sqrt{LC}}.$$

TEST YOUR KNOWLEDGE

1. A steady voltage distribution of 20 volts at the sending end and 12 volts at the receiving end is maintained in a telephone wire of length l. A time $t = 0$, the receiving end is grounded. Find the voltage and current t sec later. Neglect leakance and inductance.

   [*M.T.U. 2011 ; U.P.T.U. (SUM) 2008*]

2. A line of length l is initially uncharged so that $i(x, 0) = 0$, $v(x, 0) = 0$, $\frac{\partial v}{\partial t} = 0$ when $t = 0$. At $t = 0$, one end $x = l$ is suddenly connected with a constant potential E while the other end is grounded. Neglecting R and G, show that

$$v(x, t) = \frac{Ex}{l} + \frac{2E}{\pi} \sum_{n=1}^{\infty} \frac{(-1)^n}{n} \sin \frac{n\pi x}{l} \cos \left(\frac{n\pi t}{l\sqrt{LC}} \right).$$

3. Show that a transmission line with negligible resistance and leakage propagates waves of current and potential with velocity equal to $\dfrac{i}{\sqrt{LC}}$ where L is self-inductance and C is the capacitance.
4. Derive the partial differential equation for transmission line and also derive the telegraph and radio equations under suitable assumptions. *[U.P.T.U. (C.O.) 2009]*

Answer

1. $$v(x, t) = \frac{20(l - x)}{l} + \frac{24}{\pi}\sum_{n=1}^{\infty}\frac{(-1)^{n+1}}{n}\sin\frac{n\pi x}{l}\, e^{-n^2\pi^2 t/RCl^2}$$

$$i(x, t) = \frac{20}{lR} + \frac{24}{lR}\sum_{n=1}^{\infty}(-1)^n \cos\frac{n\pi x}{l}\, e^{-n^2\pi^2 t/RCl^2}.$$

ASSIGNMENT-V

(2 Marks Questions for Section–A)

1. Classify the differential equation: $\dfrac{\partial^2 z}{\partial x^2} + x^2\dfrac{\partial^2 z}{\partial y^2} = 0$.
2. Classify the partial differential equation: $\dfrac{\partial^2 u}{\partial x^2} + \dfrac{\partial^2 u}{\partial y^2} = \dfrac{1}{c^2}\dfrac{\partial u}{\partial t}$ *(M.T.U. 2011)*
3. Classify the partial differential equation: $\dfrac{\partial^2 u}{\partial x^2} + \dfrac{\partial^2 u}{\partial y^2} = 0$. *(G.B.T.U. 2010)*
4. Classify: $f_{xx} + 2 f_{xy} + 4 f_{yy} = 0$
5. Classify: $\dfrac{\partial^2 z}{\partial x^2} = \dfrac{\partial^2 z}{\partial y^2}$ *[G.B.T.U. (SUM) 2010]*
6. Classify the partial differential equation: $\dfrac{\partial^2 u}{\partial x^2} + 3\dfrac{\partial^2 u}{\partial x \partial y} + \dfrac{\partial^2 u}{\partial y^2} = 0$ *(M.T.U. 2012)*
7. Explain briefly the method of separation of variables in solving a given partial differential equation. *(M.T.U. 2012)*
8. Write down the two dimensional wave equation. *(M.T.U. 2012)*
9. Mention two applications of partial differential equations in engineering. *[G.B.T.U. (AG) 2012]*
10. Name the following equations: *[G.B.T.U. (AG) 2012]*

    (i) $\dfrac{\partial^2 u}{\partial t^2} = c\dfrac{\partial^2 u}{\partial x^2}$ (ii) $\dfrac{\partial u}{\partial t} = c^2\dfrac{\partial^2 u}{\partial x^2}$
11. Apply the method of separation of variables to find the most appropriate solution of $\dfrac{\partial^2 u}{\partial x^2} + \dfrac{\partial^2 u}{\partial y^2} = \dfrac{1}{c^2}\dfrac{\partial u}{\partial t}$. *[G.B.T.U. (A.G.) 2012]*

12. What does the two dimensional wave equation represent?
13. Write down the partial differential equation for one dimensional wave equation. (*G.B.T.U. 2010*)
14. Solve: $4u_x + u_y = 3u$; $u(0, y) = e^{-5y}$. [*U.P.T.U. (SUM) 2009*]
15. Solve: $\frac{\partial u}{\partial t} = c^2 \frac{\partial^2 u}{\partial x^2}$ in the steady state. [*G.B.T.U. (A.G.) 2011*]
16. Classify: $\frac{\partial u}{\partial t} = c^2 \frac{\partial^2 u}{\partial x^2}$
17. Name the equation $\frac{\partial^2 u}{\partial x^2} + \frac{\partial^2 u}{\partial y^2} = 0$ [*G.B.T.U. (SUM) 2010*]
18. Write down the equation of steady state heat conduction in the rectangular plate. (*G.B.T.U. 2011*)
19. Write down the two dimensional steady state heat flow equation in polar coordinates. [*G.B.T.U. (SUM) 2010*]
20. Solve: $3u_x + 2u_y = 0$ where $u_x = \frac{\partial u}{\partial x}$, $u_y = \frac{\partial u}{\partial y}$. [*U.P.T.U. 2009*]

Answers

1. Elliptic
2. Parabolic
3. Elliptic
4. Elliptic
5. Hyperbolic
6. Hyperbolic
8. $\frac{\partial^2 u}{\partial t^2} = c^2 \left(\frac{\partial^2 u}{\partial x^2} + \frac{\partial^2 u}{\partial y^2} \right)$
10. (*i*) One dimensional wave equation (*ii*) One dimensional heat equation
11. $u(x, y, t) = (c_1 \cos k_1 x + c_2 \sin k_1 x)(c_3 \cos k_2 y + c_4 \sin k_2 y)\, c_5 e^{-c^2 k^2 t}$
12. Vibrations of a tightly stretched membrane
13. $\frac{\partial y}{\partial t} = c^2 \frac{\partial^2 y}{\partial x^2}$
14. $u(x, y) = e^{2x - 5y}$
15. $u = c_1 x + c_2$
16. Parabolic
17. Laplace equation in two dimensions
18. $\frac{\partial^2 u}{\partial x^2} + \frac{\partial^2 u}{\partial y^2} = 0$
19. $r^2 \frac{\partial^2 u}{\partial r^2} + r \frac{\partial u}{\partial r} + \frac{\partial^2 u}{\partial \theta^2} = 0$
20. $u(x, y) = c\, e^{\frac{k}{6}(2x - 3y)}$

EXAMINATION PAPERS
(WITH ANSWERS)

M.T.U., NOIDA AS-201

B. TECH.

(SEM. II) EVEN SEMESTER THEORY EXAMINATION, 2012–2013

ENGINEERING MATHEMATICS–II

Time: 3 Hours *Total Marks: 100*

Note: *Attempt questions from each Section as indicated. The symbols have their usual meaning.*

SECTION - A

1. Attempt **all** parts of this question. Each part carries 2 marks. **(2 × 10 = 20)**

(*a*) Verify for exactness the differential equation:
$y \exp.(xy) \cdot dx + [x \exp.(xy) + 2y]dy = 0.$

(*b*) State the criterion for linearly independent solutions of the homogeneous linear nth order differential equation.

(*c*) Explain ordinary and singular points of a differential equation of the form:
$a_2(x)y'' + a_1(x)y' + a_0(x)y = 0$

(*d*) Prove that: $J'_0(x) = -J_1(x)$

(*e*) If Laplace transform of $f(t)$ is $F(s)$, then show that Laplace transform of $[e^{at}f(t)]$ is $F(s - a)$, where a is any real number.

(*f*) Find: $L^{-1}\left[\dfrac{1}{s^2 - 3s + 3}\right]$.

(*g*) Find the partial differential equation which is satisfied by the relation $z = c_1xy + c_2$, where c_1 and c_2 are constants.

(*h*) Give two examples of non-linear partial differential equation of the first order.

(*i*) Write telegraph equations.

(*j*) Characterize the following partial differential equation into elliptic, parabolic and hyperbolic equations:

$$a\frac{\partial^2 z}{\partial x^2} + 2h\frac{\partial^2 z}{\partial x \partial y} + b\frac{\partial^2 z}{\partial y^2} + 2f\frac{\partial z}{\partial x} + 2g\frac{\partial z}{\partial y} + cz = f(x, y),$$

where a, b, c, h, f, g are constants.

SECTION - B

Attempt any **three** parts of this question. Each part carries 10 marks. **(10 × 3 = 30)**

2. (*a*) A light elastic string of length l is hung by one end. To the other end are tied successively particles of masses m_1 and m_2 and they produced statical extensions l_1 and l_2. If T_1 and T_2 are the periods of small oscillations corresponding to the two masses, show that:

$$\frac{T_1^2 - T_2^2}{l_1 - l_2} = \frac{4\pi^2}{g}.$$

(*b*) Find the series solution of the differential equation $xy'' + y' + x^2y = 0$.

(*c*) Find the solution of the differential equation:

$$\frac{d^2y}{dt^2} - 2\frac{dy}{dt} + y = e^t$$

with the initial conditions $y(t) = 0$ and $\frac{dy}{dt} = 1$ when $t = 0$ using Laplace transform.

(*d*) Solve the partial differential equation $(p^2 + q^2)y = qz$.

(*e*) Solve the one-dimesional heat equation given that $u(0, t) = 0$, $u(l, t) = 0$ and $u(x, 0) = x$, $0 < x < l$, where l is the length of the bar.

SECTION - C

Attempt any ***two*** *parts from each question of this Section. Each question carries 10 marks.*

[(2 × 5) × 5 = 50]

3. (*a*) Solve the differential equation:

$$x^2\frac{d^2y}{dx^2} + 4x\frac{dy}{dx} + 2y = e^{-x}.$$

(*b*) Solve by changing the independent variable:

$$x\frac{d^2y}{dx^2} + (4x^2 - 1)\frac{dy}{dx} + 4x^3y = 2x^3.$$

(*c*) Solve the system: $\dot{x}(t) = y,\ \dot{y}(t) = -x,\ x(0) = 0,\ y(0) = 0.$

4. (*a*) Prove that: $J_{-n}(x) = (-1)^n J_n(x)$.

(*b*) Prove that: $P_n(x) = \frac{1}{2^n \cdot n} \cdot \frac{d^n}{dx^n}(x^2 - 1)^n$.

(*c*) Prove that: $\int_{-1}^{1} P_n^2(x)\,dx = \frac{2}{2n+1}$

5. (*a*) Using Laplace transform, evaluate $\int_0^\infty \frac{e^{-t}\sin t}{t}\,dt$.

(*b*) Find the inverse Laplace transform of $\cot^{-1}\left(\frac{s+3}{2}\right)$.

(*c*) State convolution theorem and hence evaluate $L^{-1}\left\{\frac{s}{(s^2+1)(s^2+4)}\right\}$

6. (*a*) Obtain Fourier series of the function: $f(x) = \begin{cases} x, & -\pi < x < 0 \\ -x, & 0 < x < \pi \end{cases}$

(*b*) Find the half range cosine series of the function $f(x) = x \sin x$, $0 < x < \pi$.

(*c*) Solve $(D^2 - 2DD' + D'^2)z = \sin x$.

7. (*a*) Solve by the method of separation of variables:

$$\frac{\partial^2 u}{\partial x^2} = \frac{\partial u}{\partial y} + 2u\,,$$

$u(0, y) = 0$ and $\frac{\partial u}{\partial x}(0, y) = 1 + e^{-3y}$.

(*b*) A string is stretched and fastened to two points distance l apart. Find the displacement $y(x, t)$ at any point at a distance x from one end at time t, given that:

$$y(x, 0) = \text{A} \sin\left(\frac{2\pi x}{l}\right).$$

(*c*) Using the transformations $u = x - ct$ and $v = x + ct$, transform the equation:

$$\frac{\partial^2 y}{\partial t^2} = c^2 \frac{\partial^2 y}{\partial x^2}$$

to the form $\frac{\partial^2 y}{\partial u \partial v} = 0$. Hence show that $y(x, t) = f_1(x - ct) + f_2(x + ct)$.

Answers

1. (*b*) $W(y_1, y_2, ..., y_n) \neq 0$

(*f*) $\frac{2}{\sqrt{3}} e^{\frac{3}{2}t} \sin \frac{\sqrt{3}}{2} t$

(*g*) $y\frac{\partial z}{\partial y} = x\frac{\partial z}{\partial x}$

(*i*) $\frac{\partial^2 V}{\partial x^2} = RC\frac{\partial V}{\partial t}$ and $\frac{\partial^2 I}{\partial x^2} = RC\frac{\partial I}{\partial t}$

(*j*) $h^2 < ab \rightarrow$ elliptic
$h^2 = ab \rightarrow$ parabolic
$h^2 > ab \rightarrow$ hyperbolic

2. (*b*) $y = A\left[1 - \frac{x^3}{3^2} + \frac{x^6}{3^4(\lfloor 2)^2} - \frac{x^9}{3^6(\lfloor 3)^2} + \ldots\right] + B\left[y_1 \log x + 2a_0\left(\frac{x^3}{3^3} - \frac{1}{3^5(\lfloor 2)^2}\left(1 + \frac{1}{2}\right)x^6 + \ldots\right)\right]$

(*c*) $y = \left(t + \frac{t^2}{2}\right)e^t$

(*d*) $z^2 = (ax + b)^2 + a^2y^2$

(*e*) $u(x, t) = -\frac{2l}{\pi}\sum_{n=1}^{\infty} \frac{\cos n\pi}{n} \sin\frac{n\pi x}{l}\, e^{-\left(\frac{c^2 n^2 \pi^2 t}{l^2}\right)}$

3. (*a*) $y = \frac{c_1}{x} + \frac{c_2}{x^2} + \frac{1}{x^2} e^x$ where c_1 and c_2 are arbitrary constants of integration.

(*b*) $y = (c_1 + c_2 x^2) e^{-x^2} + \frac{1}{2}$

(*c*) $x = 0, y = 0$

5. (*a*) $\frac{\pi}{4}$

(*b*) $f(t) = \frac{e^{-3t} \sin 2t}{t}$

(*c*) $\frac{1}{3}(\cot t - \cos 2t)$

6. (*a*) $f(x) = -\frac{\pi}{2} + \frac{\pi}{4}\left[\frac{\cos x}{1^2} + \frac{\cos 3x}{3^2} + \frac{\cos 5x}{5^2} + \ldots\right]$

(*b*) $x \sin x = 1 - \frac{1}{2}\cos x - 2\left[\frac{\cos 2x}{1.3} - \frac{\cos 3x}{2.4} + \frac{\cos 4x}{3.5} + \ldots\right]$

(*c*) $z = f_1(y + x) + x f_2(y + x) - \sin x$

7. (*a*) $u(x, y) = \frac{1}{\sqrt{2}} \sinh \sqrt{2}x + e^{-3y} \sin x$

(*b*) $y(x, t) = \text{A} \sin\left(\frac{2\pi x}{l}\right)\cos\left(\frac{2\pi ct}{l}\right)$

(*c*) $y = \frac{1}{2}\left[f(x + ct) + g(x - ct)\right]$

G.B.T.U., LUCKNOW EAS203

B. TECH.

(SEM. II) EVEN THEORY EXAMINATION, 2012–2013

MATHEMATICS–II

Time: 3 Hours *Total Marks: 100*

Note: *Attempt questions from each Section as indicated. The symbols have their usual meaning.*

SECTION - A

1. Attempt **all** parts of this question: **(2 × 10 = 20)**

(*a*) Solve $\frac{d^2y}{dt^2} - 3\frac{dy}{dt} + 4y = 0$.

(*b*) Find the particular integral of $\frac{d^2y}{dx^2} = x^2 + 2x - 1$.

(*c*) Find the value of α and β for which $3x^2 = \alpha P_2(x) + \beta P_0(x)$.

(*d*) Determine the expression for $J_{-1/2}(x)$.

(*e*) Find the Laplace transform of $f(t) = t \sin \sqrt{7}t$.

(*f*) Find the function whose Laplace transform is $F(s) = \frac{8}{(s^2 - s - 2)}$

(*g*) If $f(x) = 1$ is expanded in a Fourier sine series in $(0, \pi)$, then find the value of b_n.

(*h*) Classify the following differential equation in the first quadrant

$$y^2u_{xx} - x^2u_{yy} = 0$$

(*i*) Solve $\frac{\partial u}{\partial x} = 3\frac{\partial u}{\partial t}$ using method of separation of variables.

(*j*) Write the boundary conditions and initial conditions for the displacement of a finite string of length L that is fixed at both ends and is released from rest with an initial displacement $f(x)$.

SECTION - B

2. Attempt any **three** parts of the following: **(3 × 10 = 30)**

(*a*) Apply method of variation of parameters to find the general solution of

$$\frac{d^2x}{dt^2} - 4\frac{dx}{dt} + 3x = \frac{e^t}{1+e^t}$$

(*b*) Find the Frobenius series solution of the following differential equation about $x = 0$.

$$2x^2y'' + 7x(x + 1)y' - 3y = 0.$$

(*c*) Solve the following differential equation using Laplace Transform:

$$\frac{d^2y}{dx^2} + 4\frac{dy}{dx} + 8y = \sin x \text{ ; } y(0) = 1, y'(0) = 0$$

(*d*) Find the Fourier series expansion of the following function of period 2π, defined as

$$f(x) = \begin{cases} -1, & -\pi < x < 0 \\ 1, & 0 \le x < \pi \end{cases}$$

Hence evaluate $1 - \frac{1}{3} + \frac{1}{5} - \frac{1}{7} + \ldots$

(*e*) Find the deflection $u(x, t)$ of a tightly stretched vibrating string of unit length that is initially at rest and whose initial position is given by

$$\sin \pi x + \frac{1}{3}\sin(3\pi x) + \frac{1}{5}\sin(5\pi x), \ 0 \le x \le 1$$

SECTION - C

Note : *Attempt any **two** parts from each question of this section.* **(2 × 5) × 5 = 50**

3. (*a*) Solve $\frac{d^2y}{dx^2} + 4y = \sin^2 2x$ with conditions $y(0) = 0$, $y'(0) = 0$.

(*b*) Solve the following differential equation by reducing into normal form:

$$y'' + 2xy' + (x^2 - 8)y = x^2e^{-1/2x^2}.$$

(*c*) Solve $\frac{dx}{dt} + 2x + 4y = 1 + 4t$; $\frac{dy}{dt} + x - y = \frac{3}{2}t^2$.

4. (*a*) Prove that $\int_{-1}^{1} P_m(x)P_n(x)\,dx = 0, \ m \ne n.$

(*b*) Prove that $\frac{d}{dx}[xJ_n(x)J_{n+1}(x)] = x\{J_n^2(x) - J_{n+1}^2(x)\}$.

(*c*) Solve $4y'' + 9xy = 0$ in terms of Bessel function.

5. (*a*) Find the Laplace transform of $f(t) = \int_0^t \frac{1}{u}e^{-4u}\sin 3u\,du$.

(*b*) Find the inverse Laplace Transform of $\frac{1}{s^2(s+1)^2}$ using Convolution theorem.

(*c*) Find the Laplace transform of following function which is defined in one period as

$$f(t) = \begin{cases} t, & 0 \le t \le 1 \\ 1, & 1 \le t \le 2 \end{cases}$$

6. (*a*) Solve the following partial differential equation:

$$\frac{\partial^2 z}{\partial x^2} - \frac{\partial^2 z}{\partial x \partial y} - 2\frac{\partial^2 z}{\partial y^2} + 2\frac{\partial z}{\partial x} + 2\frac{\partial z}{\partial y} = \sin(2x + y)$$

(*b*) Solve $r + (a + b)s + abt = xy$.

(*c*) Find the half range cosine series expansion of $f(x) = x - x^2$ in $0 < x < 1$.

7. (*a*) Solve $\frac{\partial^2 z}{\partial x^2} - \frac{\partial z}{\partial y} = 0$ using method of separation of variables to obtain the solution that tends to zero as $y \to \infty$ for all x.

(*b*) Solve $\frac{\partial^2 u}{\partial x^2} = 2u + \frac{\partial u}{\partial y}$ using method of separation of variables subject to the conditions $u = 0$ and $\frac{\partial u}{\partial x} = e^{-3y}$ when $x = 0$ for all values of y.

(*c*) Solve $\frac{\partial^2 u}{\partial x^2} + \frac{\partial^2 u}{\partial y^2} = 0$ subject to the conditions $u(0, y) = 0$, $u(x, 0) = 0$, $u(1, y) = 0$ and $u(x, 1) = 100 \sin \pi x$.

Answers

1. (*a*) $y = e^{\frac{3}{2}t}\left(c_1 \cos \frac{\sqrt{7}}{2}t + c_2 \sin \frac{\sqrt{7}}{2}t\right)$ (*b*) $\frac{x^4}{12} + \frac{x^3}{3} - \frac{x^2}{2}$ (*c*) $\alpha = 2, \beta = 1$

(*d*) $J_{-1/2}(x) = \sqrt{\frac{2}{\pi x}} \cos x$ (*e*) $\frac{2\sqrt{7}p}{(p^2 + 7)^2}$

(*f*) $\frac{16}{3}e^{t/2} \sinh \frac{3}{2}t$ (*g*) $\frac{2}{n\pi}[1 - (-1)^n]$

(*h*) hyperbolic (*i*) $u(x, t) = c_1 c_2 e^{-p^2(3x + t)}$

(*j*) $y(0, t) = 0 = y(L, t)$} Boundary conditions

$$\left.\begin{aligned} \left(\frac{\partial y}{\partial t}\right)_{t=0} &= 0 \\ y(x, 0) &= f(x) \end{aligned}\right\} \text{Initial conditions}$$

2. (*a*) $x = \left[\frac{1}{2}\log(e^{-t} + 1) + c_1\right]e^t + \left[-\frac{1}{4}(e^{-t} + 1)^2 - \frac{1}{2}\log(e^{-t} + 1) + (e^{-t} + 1) + c_2\right]e^{3t}$

(*b*) $y = A\sqrt{x}\left(1 - \frac{7}{18}x + \frac{49}{264}x^2 - \ldots\right) + Bx^{-3}\left(1 - \frac{21}{5}x + \frac{49}{5}x^2 - \ldots\right)$

(c) $y = e^{-2x}\left(\frac{69}{65}\cos 2x + \frac{131}{130}\sin 2x\right) - \frac{1}{65}(4\cos x - 7\sin x)$

(d) $f(x) = \frac{4}{\pi}\left(\sin x + \frac{\sin 3x}{3} + \frac{\sin 5x}{5} + \ldots\right); \frac{\pi}{4}$

(e) $u(x, t) = \sin \pi x \cos \pi ct + \frac{1}{3}\sin 3\pi x \cos 3\pi ct + \frac{1}{5}\sin 5\pi x \cos 5\pi ct$

3. (a) $y = c_1 \cos 2x + c_2 \sin 2x + \frac{1}{8}\left(1 + \frac{1}{3}\cos 4x\right)$

(b) $y = e^{-x^2/2}\left[c_1 e^{3x} + c_2 e^{-3x} - \frac{1}{9}\left(x^2 + \frac{2}{9}\right)\right]$

(c) $x = c_1 e^{2t} + c_2 e^{-3t} + t + t^2;\ y = -c_1 e^{2t} + \frac{c_2}{4}e^{-3t} - \frac{t^2}{2}$

4. (c) $y = x^{1/2}[c_1 J_{1/3}(x^{3/2}) + c_2 J_{-1/3}(x^{3/2})]$

5. (a) $\frac{1}{p}\cot^{-1}\left(\frac{p+4}{3}\right)$ (b) $(t + 2)e^{-t} + t - 2$

(c) $\frac{1}{p^2(1 - e^{-2p})}[(1 - e^{-p})^2 - pe^{-p}]$

6. (a) $z = f_1(y - x) + e^{-2x} f_2(2x + y) - \frac{1}{6}\cos(2x + y)$

(b) $z = f_1(y - ax) + f_2(y - bx) + \frac{1}{6}x^3 y - \left(\frac{a + b}{24}\right)x^4$

(c) $f(x) = \frac{1}{6} - \frac{4}{\pi^2}\sum_{\substack{n=2 \\ (n \text{ is even})}}^{\infty} \frac{1}{n^2}\cos n\pi x$

7. (a) $z(x, y) = (c_1 \cos px + c_2 \sin px)\, c_3 e^{-c^2 p^2 y}$

(b) $u(x, y) = e^{-3y} \sin x$

(c) $u(x, y) = 100 \sin \pi x \left(\frac{\sinh \pi y}{\sinh \pi}\right)$

MAHAMAYA TECHNICAL UNIVERSITY, NOIDA EAS203/ASM201

B. TECH.

(SEM. II) THEORY EXAMINATION, 2011–2012

MATHEMATICS–II

Time : 3 Hours *Total Marks : 100*

Note : *Attempt questions from each Section as indicated. The symbols have their usual meaning.*

SECTION - A

1. Attempt **all** parts of this question. Each part carries **2** marks. **10 × 2 = 20**

(*a*) Prove that if M and N in $M(x, y)dx + N(x, y)dy = 0$. Satisfy the equation $\frac{\partial M}{\partial y} + \frac{3}{y} M = \frac{\partial N}{\partial x}$, then y^3 is an integrating factor.

(*b*) $y = (c_1 + c_2 x + c_3 x^2)\, e^x$ is the solution of the differential equation ...., c_1, c_2, c_3 are constants.

(*c*) Classify the singular points of the differential equation $x^2 \frac{d^2y}{dx^2} + ax\frac{dy}{dx} + by = 0$, a and b are constants.

(*d*) Show that $\sum_{n=0}^{\infty} P_n(x) = \frac{1}{\sqrt{2}} \frac{1}{\sqrt{1-x}}$.

(*e*) State the conditions for the existence of Laplace Transform.

(*f*) State Convolution Theorem.

(*g*) State Dirichlet conditions for the expansion of $f(x)$ in Fourier series.

(*h*) Classify the partial differential equation $\frac{\partial^2 u}{\partial x^2} + 3\frac{\partial^2 u}{\partial x \partial y} + \frac{\partial^2 u}{\partial y^2} = 0$.

(*i*) Explain briefly the method of separation of variables in solving a given partial differential equation.

(*j*) The two-dimensional wave equation is ....

SECTION - B

Note : *Attempt any* ***three*** *parts of this question. Each part carries equal marks :* **3 × 10 = 30**

2. (*a*) An R-L-C circuit connected in series has R = 90 Ohms, C = $\frac{1}{140}$ farad, L = 10 henries and an applied voltage E(*t*) = 10 cos *t*. Assuming no initial charge on the capacitor, but an initial current of 1 ampere at $t = 0$, when the voltage is first applied, find the subsequent charge on the capacitor and the amplitude of the steady-state charge.

(*b*) Find the series solution, about $x = 0$, of the equation $x\frac{d^2y}{dx^2} + \frac{dy}{dx} - xy = 0$, by the Frobenius method.

(*c*) Using convolution, solve the initial value problem $\frac{d^2y}{dt^2} + 9y = \sin 3t$ given $y = 0$, $\frac{dy}{dt} = 0$ at $t = 0$.

(*d*) Find the Fourier series representation upto second harmonics of $f(x)$ which is given in the following table:

x	0	1	2	3	4	5
$f(x)$	9	18	24	28	26	20

(*e*) Solve the boundary value problem $\frac{\partial z}{\partial x} + \frac{\partial^2 z}{\partial y^2} = 0$, satisfying the conditions $z(x, 0) = 0$ $z(x, \pi) = 0$, $z(0, y) = 4 \sin 3y$.

SECTION - C

Note : *Attempt any* ***two*** *parts from each question of this section. Each part carries equal marks.* **5 × 10 = 50**

3. (*a*) If $(x + y)^n$ is an integrating factor of $(4x^2 + 2xy + 6y)\,dx + (2x^2 + 9y + 3x)\,dy = 0$, find n and then solve the equation.

(*b*) Solve: $(D^2 - 3D + 2)\,y = \sin(e^{-x})$

(*c*) Solve: $\left(\frac{d}{dx} + \frac{1}{x}\right)^2 y = x^{-4}$.

4. (*a*) Prove that $(n + 1)\,P_{n+1}(x) = (2n + 1)\,x\,P_n(x) - nP_{n-1}(x)$.

(*b*) Show that $\int x J_0^2(x)\,dx = \frac{1}{2}x^2\left[J_0^2(x) + J_1^2(x)\right] + c$

(*c*) Show that $J_3(x) = \left(\frac{8}{x^2} - 1\right)J_1(x) - \frac{4}{x}J_0(x)$.

5. (*a*) State second shifting theorem for Laplace transform and hence find the Laplace transform of the following function:

$$f(t) = \begin{cases} e^{t-a}, & t > a \\ 0, & t < a \end{cases}$$

(*b*) Find the inverse Laplace transform of $\dfrac{s}{(s^2 + a^2)^3}$.

(*c*) Show that $\displaystyle\int_0^{\infty} \frac{\cos 6t - \cos 4t}{t}\, dt = \log \frac{2}{3}$

6. (*a*) Find the Fourier series of $f(x) = \dfrac{3x^2 - 6\pi x + 2\pi^2}{12}$ in the interval $(0, 2\pi)$. Hence, deduce that $\dfrac{\pi^2}{6} = 1 + \dfrac{1}{2^2} + \dfrac{1}{3^2} + \ldots$

(*b*) Find the half-range sine series of $f(x) = (lx - x^2)$ in the interval $(0, l)$. Hence, deduce that $\dfrac{\pi^3}{32} = 1 - \dfrac{1}{3^3} + \dfrac{1}{5^3} - \dfrac{1}{7^3} + \ldots.$

(*c*) Solve: $(D^2 + DD' - 6D'^2)\, z = y \sin x$

7. (*a*) Solve: $\dfrac{\partial u}{\partial t} = \alpha \dfrac{\partial^2 u}{\partial x^2}$, α constant, subject to the boundary conditions $u(0, t) = 0$, $u(\pi, t) = 0$ and the initial condition $u(x, 0) = \sin 2x$.

(*b*) Find the deflection of the vibrating string which is fixed at the ends $x = 0$ and $x = 2$ and the motion is started by displacing the string into the form $\sin^3\left(\dfrac{\pi x}{2}\right)$ and releasing it with zero initial velocity at $t = 0$.

(*c*) Determine the electromotive force $e(x, t)$ in a transmission line of length b, t seconds after the ends were suddenly grounded. Assume that R and G are negligible and the initial conditions are $i(x, 0) = i_0$ and $e(x, 0) = e_1 \sin \dfrac{\pi x}{b} + e_5 \sin \dfrac{5\pi x}{b}$. Here G and R denote the terms for the effect of leakage and resistance respectively.

G.B. TECHNICAL UNIVERSITY, LUCKNOW — EAS-203

B. TECH.

(SEM. II) THEORY EXAMINATION, 2011–2012

MATHEMATICS–II

Time : 3 Hours — *Total Marks : 100*

Note : *Attempt* ***all*** *questions.*

SECTION - A

1. Attempt **all** parts of this question. **(10 × 2 = 20)**

(*a*) Find the general solution of $(2D + 1)^2 y = 0$, where $D = \dfrac{d}{dt}$.

(*b*) Find the particular integral of $\dfrac{d^2y}{dx^2} - y = x^2$.

(*c*) Evaluate $\int_{-1}^{1} x^2 P_2(x)\,dx$.

(*d*) Evaluate $\int_0^{\pi/2} \sqrt{\pi x}\, J_{1/2}(2x)\,dx$.

(*e*) Find the Laplace transform of $f(t) = t^4 e^{2t}$.

(*f*) Find the function whose Laplace transform is $\dfrac{e^{-\pi s}}{s^2 + 2}$.

(*g*) Find the constant term if the function $f(x) = x + x^2$ is expanded in Fourier series defined in $(-1, 1)$.

(*h*) Find the particular integral of $(D^2 + DD')\,z = \sin(x + y)$ where $D = \dfrac{\partial}{\partial x}$, $D' = \dfrac{\partial}{\partial y}$.

(*i*) Find the steady state temperature distribution in a rod of length 20 cm whose ends are kept at 40°C and 60°C respectively.

(*j*) Find the general solution of $\dfrac{\partial u}{\partial x} = \dfrac{\partial u}{\partial y}$ using method of separation of variables.

SECTION - B

2. Attempt any **three** parts of the following: **(3 × 10 = 30)**

(*a*) Apply method of variation of parameter to solve $x^2 \dfrac{d^2y}{dx^2} + 4x\dfrac{dy}{dx} + 2y = e^x$.

(*b*) Use Frobenius series method to find the series solution of $(1 - x^2)\, y'' - xy' + 4y = 0$.

(*c*) Solve $y'' + 3y' + 2y = te^{-t}$, $y(0) = 1$, $y'(0) = 0$, using Laplace transform method.

(*d*) Find the Fourier series expansions of the function

$$f(x) = \begin{cases} -1, & \text{for } \; -\pi < x < -\pi/2 \\ 0, & \text{for } \; -\pi/2 < x < \pi/2 \\ 1, & \text{for } \; \pi/2 < x < \pi \end{cases}$$

Hence deduce that

$$\frac{\pi}{4} = 1 - \frac{1}{3} + \frac{1}{5} - \frac{1}{7} + \ldots$$

(*e*) Find the deflection of the vibrating string of unit length whose end points are fixed if the initial velocity is zero and the initial deflection is given by

$$u(x, 0) = \begin{cases} 1, & 0 \le x \le \dfrac{1}{2} \\ -1, & \dfrac{1}{2} < x \le 1 \end{cases}$$

SECTION - C

Note : *Attempt any **two** parts from each question of this section.* **[(2 × 5) × 5 = 50]**

3. (*a*) Solve the following differential equation

$$\frac{d^2y}{dx^2} + 2\frac{dy}{dx} + y = x^2 e^{-x} \cos x.$$

(*b*) Solve the following equation by reducing into normal form

$$\frac{d^2y}{dx^2} + 2x\frac{dy}{dx} + (x^2 - 8)\, y = x^2 e^{-x^2/2}$$

(*c*) An RL circuit has an e.m.f. given (in volts) by 4 sin *t*, a resistance of 100 Ohms, an inductance of 4 henries and no initial current. Find the current at any time *t*.

4. (*a*) Express $f(x) = x^4 + 3x^3 - x^2 + 5x - 2$ in terms of Legendre's polynomials.

(*b*) Solve the following differential equation in terms of Bessel's function

$$\frac{d^2y}{dx^2} + \frac{1}{x}\frac{dy}{dx} + \left(8 - \frac{1}{x^2}\right) y = 0.$$

(*c*) Prove that:

(*i*) $P_n(1) = 1$, (*ii*) $\dfrac{d}{dx}\{x^n J_n(x)\} = x^n J_{n-1}(x)$.

5. (*a*) Find the Laplace transform of $f(t) = \dfrac{e^{-t} \sin t}{t}$.

(*b*) Use convolution theorem to find the inverse Laplace transform of $\dfrac{1}{s^3 (s^2 + 1)}$.

(c) Apply Laplace transform technique to solve

$$\frac{dx}{dt} + y = \sin t, \quad \frac{dy}{dt} + x = \cos t; \; x(0) = 2, \; y(0) = 0.$$

6. (a) Find the half range cosine series expansion of $f(x) = x - x^2$ in $0 < x < 1$.

(b) Solve: $(x - y)\, y^2 p + (y - x)\, x^2 q = (x^2 + y^2) z$.

(c) Solve: $\dfrac{\partial^2 z}{\partial x^2} - 3\dfrac{\partial^2 z}{\partial x \partial y} + 2\dfrac{\partial^2 z}{\partial y^2} = e^{x+y} + \cos(x + 2y)$.

7. (a) Apply method of separation of variables to solve $\dfrac{\partial^2 z}{\partial x \partial y} = e^{-x} \cos y$, given that $z = 0$ when $x = 0$ and $\dfrac{\partial z}{\partial x} = 0$ when $y = 0$.

(b) Find the temperature distribution in a rod of length 2 m whose end points are fixed at temperature zero and the initial temperature distribution is $f(x) = 100\, x$.

(c) Solve: $\dfrac{\partial^2 u}{\partial x^2} + \dfrac{\partial^2 u}{\partial y^2} = 0$, subject to boundary conditions $u(0, y) = 0 = u(\pi, y)$, and $u(x, 0) = u_0$, $\lim\limits_{y \to \infty} u(x, y) = 0$, $0 < x < \pi$.

U.K.T.U., DEHRADUN

TMA-201

B. TECH.

(SEM. II) EXAMINATION, 2012

MATHEMATICS–II

Time : 3 Hours *Total Marks : 100*

Note : *Attempt all questions. All questions carry equal marks.*

1. Attempt any **four** parts of the following: **5 × 4 = 20**

(*a*) Solve: $(y^2 e^{xy^2} + 4x^3)\,dx + (2xye^{xy^2} - 3y^2)\,dy = 0$

(*b*) Solve: $(1 + y^2)\,dx = (\tan^{-1} y - x)\,dy$

(*c*) Solve: $(D^2 - 2D + 1)\,y = x \sin x$

(*d*) $\dfrac{dx}{dt} + 2x - 3y = t \quad \dfrac{dy}{dt} - 3x + 2y = e^{2t}$.

(*e*) Solve: $\dfrac{d^2y}{dx^2} + \cot x \dfrac{dy}{dx} + 4y \operatorname{cosec}^2 x = 0$ by changing the independent variable.

(*f*) Apply the method of variation of parameters to solve: $\dfrac{d^2y}{dx^2} + n^2 = \sec nx$.

2. Attempt any **two** parts of the following: **10 × 2 = 20**

(*a*) Find Laplace Transform of (*i*) $te^{at} \sin at$ (*ii*) $(\cos at - \cos bt)/t$

(*b*) (*i*) Find $L^{-1}\left[\log \dfrac{s+1}{s-1}\right]$ (*ii*) Find $L^{-1}\left[\dfrac{1}{s(s+a)^3}\right]$

(*c*) Using Laplace Transform solve the following equations: $\dfrac{d^2x}{dt^2} + x = t \cos 2t$.

Given $x(0) = x'(0) = 0$.

3. Attempt any **two** parts of the following: **10 × 2 = 20**

(*a*) (*i*) Test for convergence the series $\dfrac{1}{1.2.3} + \dfrac{3}{2.3.4} + \dfrac{5}{3.4.5} + \ldots\ldots\infty$

(*ii*) Test for convergence the series $\dfrac{1}{2\sqrt{1}} + \dfrac{x^2}{3\sqrt{2}} + \dfrac{x^4}{4\sqrt{3}} + \dfrac{x^6}{5\sqrt{4}} - \ldots\ldots\infty$

(*b*) Discuss the convergence of the series $\sum_{2}^{\infty} \frac{1}{n\,(\log n)^p}$; $p > 0$, by Integral test.

(*c*) Show that the Geometric series $\sum_{n=0}^{\infty} r^n$, $(r > 0)$ is convergent when $r < 1$ and divergent when $r \geq 1$.

4. Attempt any **two** parts of the following:

(*a*) Find the Fourier series expansions for $f(x)$, if

$$f(x) = \begin{cases} -\pi, & -\pi < x < 0 \\ x, & 0 < x < \pi \end{cases}, \text{ Deduce that } \frac{1}{1^2} + \frac{1}{3^2} + \frac{1}{5^2} + \ldots = \frac{\pi^2}{8}$$

(*b*) Expand $f(x) = \begin{cases} \frac{1}{4} - x, & 0 < x < 1/2 \\ x - 3/4, & 1/2 < x < 1 \end{cases}$ as the Fourier sine series.

(*c*) Solve: $(D^3 - 4D^2 D' + 4DD'^2)\, z = 6\sin(3x + 2y)$

5. Attempt any **two** parts of the following: **10 × 2 = 20**

(*a*) A tightly stretched string with fixed end points $x = 0$ and $x = l$ is initially in a position given by $y(x, 0) = y_0 \sin(\pi x/l)$. If it is released from rest from this position, find the displacement y at any distance x from one end at any time t.

(*b*) A homogeneous rod of conducting material of length '1' has its ends kept at zero temperature. The temperature at the centre is T and falls uniformly to zero at the two ends. Find the temperature distribution.

(*c*) Solve: $\frac{\partial u}{\partial x} + \frac{\partial u}{\partial y} = 3u$ given $u(0, y) = 4e^{-y} - e^{-5y}$, by the method of separation of variables.

U.K.T.U., DEHRADUN

TMA-201

B. TECH.

(SEM. II) EXAMINATION, 2011

MATHEMATICS–II

Time : 3 Hours *Total Marks : 100*

Note : *Attempt all questions.*

1. Attempt any **four** of following: **5 × 4 = 20**

(*i*) Solve: $x\,dx + y\,dy = \dfrac{a^2(x\,dy - y\,dx)}{x^2 + y^2}$.

(*ii*) Solve: $\dfrac{dz}{dx} + \dfrac{z}{x}\log z = \dfrac{z}{x^2}(\log z)^2$.

(*iii*) Solve: $(D^2 + a^2)\,y = \sec ax$.

(*iv*) Solve the following simultaneous equations

$$\frac{dx}{dy} + \frac{dy}{dt} - 2y = 2\cos t - 7\sin t$$

$$\frac{dx}{dt} - \frac{dy}{dt} + 2x = 4\cos t - 3\sin t$$

(*v*) Solve: $\dfrac{d^2y}{dx^2} + \dfrac{2}{x}\dfrac{dy}{dx} + \dfrac{a^2}{x^4}y = 0$.

(*vi*) Apply the method of variation of parameters to solve $\dfrac{d^2y}{dx^2} + y = \tan x$.

2. Attempt any **two** of the following: **10 × 2 = 20**

(*i*) (*a*) If $f(t)$ is continous and of exponential order a as $t \to \infty$, then prove that Laplace transform of $f(t)$ exists for $x > a$.

(*b*) Find the Laplace transform of the following periodic function:

$$f(t) = \frac{t}{T} \text{ for } 0 < t < T.$$

(*ii*) If $\bar{f}_1(s)$ and $\bar{f}_2(s)$ are the Laplace transforms of $f_1(t)$ and $f_2(t)$ respectively, then prove that $\bar{f}_1(s)\,.\,\bar{f}_2(s) = L\left\{\int_0^t f_1(u).f_2(t-u)\,du\right\}$.

Hence evaluate $L^{-1}\left\{\dfrac{s^2}{(s^2 + a^2)(s^2 + b^2)}\right\}$.

(*iii*) Solve the following simultaneous differential equations by using Laplace transformation: $Dx - y = e^t$, $Dy + x = \sin t$, $x_0 = 1$, $y_0 = 0$.

3. Attempt any **two** of the following: **10 × 2 = 20**

(*i*) Test the convergence or divergence of the following series:

(*a*) $\sum_{n=2}^{\infty} \frac{1}{n(\log n)^p} \ (p > 0)$ (*b*) $\sum_{n=1}^{\infty} \frac{1}{\sqrt{n} + \sqrt{(n+1)}}$

(*ii*) State and prove the Cauchy's root test. Hence test for convergence the following series $\sum_{n=1}^{\infty} \left(1 + \frac{1}{\sqrt{n}}\right)^{-n^{3/2}}$

(*iii*) (*a*) Show that the following series converges uniformly in any interval: $\sum_{n=1}^{\infty} \frac{\cos nx}{n^p}$

(*b*) Prove that $\int_0^1 \left(\sum_{n=1}^{\infty} \frac{x^n}{n^2}\right) dx = \sum \frac{1}{n^2(n+1)}$.

4. Attempt any **four** of the following: **5 × 4 = 20**

(*i*) Find the Fourier series for the function $f(x) = x + x^2$ in the interval $-\pi < x < \pi$. Hence show that $\frac{\pi^2}{6} = 1 + \frac{1}{2^2} + \frac{1}{3^2} + \dots$.

(*ii*) Obtain Fourier series for the function $f(x)$ given by

$$f(x) = 1 + 2x/\pi, \quad -\pi \le x \le 0$$
$$= 1 - 2x/\pi, \quad 0 \le x \le \pi$$

(*iii*) Express $f(x) = x$ as a half-range sine series in $0 < x < 2$.

(*iv*) Eliminate the arbitrary function f and g from the following equation:

$$v = f(x + iy) + g(x - iy), \text{ where } i = \sqrt{(-1)}$$

(*v*) Find the particular integral of $(D - D' - 1)(D - D' - 2)z = \sin(2x + 3y)$ where $D \equiv \frac{\partial}{\partial x}$, $D' \equiv \frac{\partial}{\partial y}$.

(*vi*) Show that the equation $\frac{\partial^2 z}{\partial x^2} + 2x \frac{\partial^2 z}{\partial x \partial y} + (1 - y^2) \frac{\partial^2 z}{\partial y^2} = 0$ is elliptic for all values of x and y in the region $x^2 + y^2 < 1$, parabolic on the boundary and hyperbolic out side the region.

5. Attempt any **two** of the following: **10 × 2 = 20**

(*i*) A tightly stretched string with fixed end points $x = 0$ and $x = l$ is initially in a position given by $y(x, 0) = y_0 \sin(\pi x/l)$. If it is released from rest from this position, find the displacement y at any distance x from one end at any time t.

(*ii*) Solve: $\dfrac{\partial^2 u}{\partial x^2} + \dfrac{\partial^2 u}{\partial y^2} = 0$, $0 < x < \pi$, $0 < y < \pi$, which satisfies the conditions:

$u(0, y) = u(\pi, y) = u(x, \pi) = 0$ and $u(x, 0) = \sin^2 x$.

(*iii*) A rod of length L has its ends A and B kept at 0°C and 100°C, respectively, until steady state conditions prevail. If the temperature of B is then reduce suddenly to 0°C and kept so, while that of A is maintained, find the temperature $u(x, t)$ at distance x from A at time t.

Index

O

P

R

S

T

U

V

W

Z